WOMEN, CULTURE AND SOCIETY
A Reader

Third Edition

Edited by
Barbara J. Balliet
Patricia McDaniel
for
The Women's Studies Program
Rutgers University—New Brunswick

President and Chief Executive Officer   Mark C. Falb
Vice President, Director of National Book Program   Alfred C. Grisanti
Editorial Development Supervisor   Georgia Botsford
Developmental Editor   Liz Recker
Vice President, Production Editorial   Ruth A. Burlage
Production Manager   Jo Wiegand
Production Editor   Charmayne McMurray
Permission Editor   Colleen Zelinsky
Design Manager   Jodi Splinter
Senior Vice President, College Division   Thomas W. Gantz
Vice President and National Field Manager   Brian Johnson
Managing Editor, College Field   Paul Gormley
Associate Editor, College Field   Gregory DeRosa

Cover art copyright © by Geraldine Gillmore. Reprinted by permission.

CONTENTS

INTRODUCTION

The book you have before you is intended to introduce you to some of the issues and debates in women's studies. It maps out the contours of the field of study that emerged from the second wave of the women's movement in the 1960s, moved into universities in women's studies courses and programs in the 1970s, and today encompasses over 680 programs in the United States. The Women's Studies Program at Rutgers University, New Brunswick, was one of the first programs organized in the U.S. Initiated by a small, energetic group of faculty from Douglass and Livingston colleges, the program grew from a single course, "The Educated Woman in Literature," taught by Elaine Showalter in 1969.

Today, the Women's Studies Program at Rutgers includes an undergraduate major and minor, a graduate certificate, and a master's degree program. Together with four research centers at Douglass, The Institute for Research on Women, the Center for Women's Global Leadership, the Center for the American Woman and Politics, and the Center for Women and Work, Women's Studies is a member of the Institute for Women's Leadership headed by Mary Hartman. These locations sustain a rich and lively scholarly dialogue around many of the key questions of women's activism, feminist theories, and interdisciplinary studies.

The subject of inquiry in Women's Studies is women, their lives and conditions, and the explanations for their inequality, both historically and currently. The method of study is interdisciplinary, meaning that Women's Studies draws upon the methodologies of history, economics, sociology, philosophy, psychology, and literary criticism to delve into the situation of women. It also draws upon many different kinds of writings to analyze women's lives and to develop new ways of thinking about the world. This collection includes poetry and personal essays as well as more traditional forms of academic writing.

This diverse array of analytic tools is necessary to explore the multiple and different ways women are situated socially, economically, and politically. The last two decades of activism and scholarship have raised questions about whether all women can be considered as a category or class united by their shared biological characteristics and a social status inferior to men. The authors in this collection question the utility of identifying women as a group on the basis of biology, either as a way to mark their differences from men, or their similarities to other women. They focus instead on how gender has been socially and historically constructed, and how race, class, nation, ethnicity, and sexuality intersect and overlap with one another and with gender to destabilize the category of "woman."

The history of feminism in the Western world has been told largely as a story of white, middle-class women seeking the same civic and political rights as their brothers. During the late sixties and early seventies, this understanding of feminism was effectively challenged by women of color, working-class women, lesbians, and women from regions beyond the West. Their demands for a re-definition of feminism forced a continuing reconceptualization of feminist thinking and practice. Women's different social locations shape their perspectives and needs, and just as there is no longer a unitary understanding of "woman," there is no single "feminism." Rather, many feminisms enrich the political and cultural landscape.

The book is organized around ten broad themes. The first section provides a small sampling of historical documents integral to the first and second waves of the women's movement in the United States. The second focuses on some of the categories by which we mark people as different—gender, race, class, and sexuality—and how these categories are socially and historically produced by individuals and institutions. The third section of the book examines some of the means by which codes of behavior for women and men are created and reinforced, while the fourth focuses on codes of behavior that govern women's bodies in particular.

The fifth portion of the book looks at some of the ways violence against women is institutionalized, both in the United States and internationally. It is followed by a section which examines reproductive rights and women's health, focusing on how women in different economic, racial, ethnic, and national circumstances are fashioned in terms of their health and reproductive capacities. The seventh section explores women's relationships to the family, to domestic labor, and to the economy, investigating how women's roles in the family affect the way they are viewed as workers outside the home and what kinds of work are considered appropriate for them. The next section looks at the varying locations of women in the global economy, documenting the growth of women's poverty worldwide and the assumptions that underlie state efforts to provide financial assistance to women and children. The ninth section focuses on the relationship between women today and popular culture.The book ends by addressing the history and current state of feminist politics and organizing.

Histories of Feminisms, First and Second Waves

The readings in this section locate some of the different historical paths of the development of feminist movements. Feminism has embraced a wide range of political ideas and strategies, associating its critique of gender oppression with the insights of other powerful political analyses such as liberalism, socialism and Marxism. This section is not an exhaustive survey of feminist social movements, but rather suggests some of the issues, conflicts and problems that feminists have encountered as they have attempted to build a movement to end sexism and to eradicate discrimination based on gender. The readings include manifestos and historical documents that outline different women's vision for political, economic and social change. Each document provides an analysis of the reasons behind women's inequality and suggests how to improve women's lives. Reading these documents will expose some of the rich variety of feminist definitions, analyses and goals.

The Declaration of Sentiments and Resolutions marks the formal beginning of an organized women's rights movement in the United States. At an 1848 meeting called to consider "the social, civil and religious condition and rights of women," Elizabeth Cady Stanton, Lucretia Mott and other organizers used the Declaration of Independence as a model for the Seneca Falls Declaration. Compare its goals with the views on women expressed in the next document written by Harriet Beecher Stowe, author of *Uncle Tom's Cabin*, and her older sister Catherine Beecher in 1869. How does each document position women in society?

These documents date from the first wave of organized womanhood in the United States. The second group of documents represent the reawakening of feminist activity in the period after World War II. How are their concerns similar to those of the first wave? How do they differ? What issues do they focus on? Several distinct strains of feminist activity are discernable in these documents. Middle-class women, beneficiaries of the greater access to education, business and the professions gained by the first wave of feminism, began to agitate for full equality with men in politics, education, employment and law. These women's goals were made manifest in the National Organization for Women's (NOW) Bill of Rights adopted at the organization's first national conference in 1967. A second root for the renewal of feminist activity grew from the activism of women in the civil rights, new left, student and black nationalist movements of the sixties. In this era of widespread social change, each of these movements presented a critique of American society: the civil rights movement sought to end segregation and discrimination against black Americans by securing political and legal change, making the country conscious of its failure to live up to its democratic promise; the new left argued that America's deepest problems stemmed from an uncritical embrace of capitalism, economic and military imperialism and vehemently opposed the Vietnam War and the expansion of the "military industrial complex"; and black nationalism opposed political and economic integration as a strategy to empower African-Americans taking more militant positions and tactics to end racial injustice. More radical politically than the women drawn to NOW, these women coined the term "women's liberation" and looked beyond equality within the political and economic system to remaking the society to ensure social and economic justice. Many of these women had experienced sexism within the new left, civil rights or black power movement. By 1965 women active in the largest new left organization, Students for a Democratic Society (SDS) had organized to condemn male chauvinism and to call for more meaningful roles within the organization. The Redstockings Manifesto (1969) demonstrates some of the most important insights of radical women, including the significance of connecting forms of oppression such as sexism and poverty, the conviction that the personal is political and the strategy of consciousness raising.

The Combahee River Collective Statement (1977), written by three members of the collective, Barbara Smith, Beverly Smith and Demita Frazier, is one of the most significant documents in the history of second wave feminism. Black women had been actively involved in shaping feminist activism throughout the sixties. Francis Beale, an African American civil rights activist and journalist, wrote an influential analysis of the connections between racism and sexism. "Double Jeopardy: To Be Black and Female" appeared in Robin Morgan's anthology of women's liberation writings, *Sisterhood is Powerful*. Beale was soon joined in print by other black women activists including Pauli Murray and Angela Davis. By 1970, Toni Cade Bambara edited a pathbreaking volume, *The Black Woman*, a collection of black feminist thought that encouraged the organization of black feminists and criticized sexism in the black community and the racism of both mainstream feminist organizations such as NOW and the women's liberation movement. The Statement outlines a history of contemporary black feminist thought, details the political evolution of the collective and suggests an agenda for a black feminist movement.

Suggestions for Further Reading

Allen, Paula Gunn. 1992. *The Sacred Hoop: Recovering the Feminine in American Indian Tradition*. Boston: Beacon Press.

Bambara, Toni Cade, ed. 1970. *The Black Woman: An Anthology*. New York: Mentor.

Cott, Nancy F. 1987. *The Grounding of Modern Feminism*. New Haven: Yale University Press.

Davis, Angela. 1981. *Women, Race and Class*. New York: Random House.

De Beauvoir, Simone. 1989 (1952). *The Second Sex*. Translated and edited by H.M. Parshley. New York: Vintage.

Friedan, Betty. 1976. *It Changed My Life: Writings on the Women's Movement*. New York: Random House.

Frye, Marilyn. 1983. *The Politics of Reality: Essays in Feminist Theory*. Freedom, CA: The Crossing Press.

Gilbert, Olive. 1991 (1850). *Narrative of Sojourner Truth, A Bondswoman of Olden Time: With A History of Her Labors and Correspondence Drawn from Her "Book of Life."* New York: Oxford University Press.

Moraga, Cherrie, and Gloria Anzaldua, eds. 1981. *This Bridge Called My Back: Writings by Radical Women of Color*. Watertown, MA: Persephone Press.

Morgan, Robin, ed. 1970. *Sisterhood Is Powerful: An Anthology of Writings from the Women's Liberation Movement*. New York: Vintage Books.

Schneir, Miriam, ed. 1972. *Feminism: The Essential Historical Writings*. New York: Random House.

Schneir, Miriam, ed. 1994. *Feminism in Our Time: The Essential Writings, World War Two to the Present*. New York: Vintage Books.

Smith, Barbara, ed. 1983. *Home Girls: A Black Feminist Anthology*. New York: Kitchen Table: Women of Color Press.

Walker, Alice. 1984. *In Search of Our Mother's Gardens: Womanist Prose*. San Diego, CA: Harcourt Brace.

Declaration of Sentiments and Resolutions, Seneca Falls

Elizabeth Cady Stanton
Susan B. Anthony
Matilda Joslyn Gage

When, in the course of human events, it becomes necessary for one portion of the family of man to assume among the people of the earth a position different from that which they have hitherto occupied, but one to which the laws of nature and of nature's God entitle them, a decent respect to the opinions of mankind requires that they should declare the causes that impel them to such a course.

We hold these truths to be self-evident: that all men and women are created equal; that they are endowed by their Creator with certain inalienable rights; that among these are life, liberty, and the pursuit of happiness; that to secure these rights governments are instituted, deriving their just powers from the consent of the governed. Whenever any form of government becomes destructive of these ends, it is the right of those who suffer from it to refuse allegiance to it and to insist upon the institution of a new government, laying its foundation on such principles, and organizing its powers in such form, as to them shall seem most likely to effect their safety and happiness. Prudence, indeed, will dictate that governments long established should not be changed for light and transient causes; and accordingly all experience hath shown that mankind are more disposed to suffer, while evils are sufferable, than to right themselves by abolishing the forms to which they were accustomed. But when a long train of abuses and usurpations, pursuing invariably the same object evinces a design to reduce them under absolute despotism, it is their duty to throw off such government, and to provide new guards for their future security. Such has been the patient sufferance of the women under this government, and such is now the necessity which constrains them to demand the equal station to which they are entitled.

From Elizabeth Cady Stanton, Susan B. Anthony, and Matilda Joslyn Gage, eds. *History of Woman Suffrage,* Vol. 1, 1881.

The history of mankind is a history of repeated injuries and usurpations on the part of man toward woman, having in direct object the establishment of an absolute tyranny over her. To prove this, let facts be submitted to a candid world.

He has never permitted her to exercise her inalienable right to the elective franchise.

He has compelled her to submit to laws, in the formation of which she had no voice.

He has withheld from her rights which are given to the most ignorant and degraded men—both natives and foreigners.

Having deprived her of this first right of a citizen, the elective franchise, thereby leaving her without representation in the halls of legislation, he has oppressed her on all sides.

He has made her, if married, in the eye of the law, civilly dead.

He has taken from her all right in property, even to the wages she earns.

He has made her, morally, an irresponsible being, as she can commit many crimes with impunity, provided they be done in the presence of her husband. In the covenant of marriage, she is compelled to promise obedience to her husband, he becoming, to all intents and purposes, her master—the law giving him power to deprive her of her liberty, and to administer chastisement.

He has so framed the laws of divorce, as to what shall be the proper causes, and in case of separation, to whom the guardianship of the children shall be given, as to be wholly regardless of the happiness of women—the law, in all cases, going upon a false supposition of the supremacy of man, and giving all power into his hands.

After depriving her of all rights as a married woman, if single, and the owner of property, he has taxed her to support a government which recognizes her only when her property can be made profitable to it.

He has monopolized nearly all the profitable employments, and from those she is permitted to follow, she receives but a scanty remuneration. He closes against her all the avenues to wealth and distinction which he considers most honorable to himself. As a teacher of theology, medicine, or law, she is not known.

He has denied her the facilities for obtaining a thorough education, all colleges being closed against her.

He allows her in Church, as well as State, but a subordinate position, claiming Apostolic authority for her exclusion from the ministry, and, with some exceptions, from any public participation in the affairs of the Church.

He has created a false public sentiment by giving to the world a different code of morals for men and women, by which moral delinquencies which exclude women from society, are not only tolerated, but deemed of little account in man.

He has usurped the prerogative of Jehovah himself, claiming it as his right to assign for her a sphere of action, when that belongs to her conscience and to her God.

He has endeavored, in every way that he could, to destroy her confidence in her own powers, to lessen her self-respect, and to make her willing to lead a dependent and abject life.

Now, in view of this entire disfranchisement of one-half the people of this country, their social and religious degradation—in view of the unjust laws above mentioned, and because women do feel themselves aggrieved, oppressed, and fraudulently deprived of their most sacred rights, we insist that they have immediate admission to all the rights and privileges which belong to them as citizens of the United States.

In entering upon the great work before us, we anticipate no small amount of misconception, misrepresentation, and ridicule; but we shall use every instrumentality within our power to effect our object. We shall employ agents, circulate tracts, petition the State and National legislatures, and endeavor to enlist the pulpit and the press in our behalf. We hope this Convention will be followed by a series of Conventions embracing every part of the country.

Resolutions

Whereas, the great precept of nature is conceded to be, that "man shall pursue his own true and substantial happiness." Blackstone in his Commentaries remarks, that this law of Nature being coeval with mankind, and dictated by God himself, is of course superior in obligation to any other. It is binding over all the globe, in all countries and at all times; no human laws are of any validity if contrary to this, and such of them as are valid, derive all their force, and all their validity, and all their authority, mediately and immediately, from this original; therefore,

Resolved, That such laws as conflict, in any way, with the true and substantial happiness of woman, are contrary to the great precept of nature and of no validity, for this is "superior in obligation to any other."

Resolved, That all laws which prevent woman from occupying such a station in society as her conscience shall dictate, or which place her in a position inferior to that of man, are contrary to the great precept of nature, and therefore of no force or authority.

Resolved, That woman is man's equal—was intended to be so by the Creator, and the highest good of the race demands that she should be recognized as such.

Resolved, That the women of this country ought to be enlightened in regard to the laws under which they live, that they may no longer publish their degradation by declaring themselves satisfied with their present position, nor their ignorance, by asserting that they have all the rights they want.

Resolved, That inasmuch as man, while claiming for himself intellectual superiority, does accord to woman moral superiority, it is pre-eminently his duty to encourage her to speak and teach, as she has an opportunity, in all religious assemblies.

Resolved, That the same amount of virtue, delicacy, and refinement of behavior that is required of woman in the social state, should also be required of man, and the same transgressions should be visited with equal severity on both man and woman.

Resolved, That the objection of indelicacy and impropriety, which is so often brought against woman when she addresses a public audience, comes with a very ill-grace from those who encourage, by their attendance, her appearance on the stage, in the concert, or in feats of the circus.

Resolved, That woman has too long rested satisfied in the circumscribed limits which corrupt customs and a perverted application of the Scriptures have marked out for her, and that it is time she should move in the enlarged sphere which her great Creator has assigned her.

Resolved, That it is the duty of the women of this country to secure to themselves their sacred right to the elective franchise.

Resolved, That the equality of human rights results necessarily from the fact of the identity of the race in capabilities and responsibilities.

Resolved, therefore, That, being invested by the Creator with the same capabilities, and the same consciousness of responsibility for their exercise, it is demonstrably the right and duty of woman, equally with man, to promote every righteous cause by every righteous means; and especially in regard to the great subjects of morals and religion, it is self-evidently her right to participate with her brother in teaching them, both in private and in public, by writing and by speaking, by any instrumentalities proper to be used, and in any assemblies proper to be held; and this being a self-evident truth growing out of the divinely implanted principles of hu-man nature, any custom or authority adverse to it, whether modern or wearing the hoary sanction of antiquity, is to be regarded as a self-evident falsehood, and at war with mankind.

[At the last session Lucretia Mott offered and spoke to the following resolution:]

Resolved, That the speedy success of our cause depends upon the zealous and untiring efforts of both men and women, for the overthrow of the monopoly of the pulpit, and for the securing to woman an equal participation with men in the various trades, professions, and commerce.

The American Woman's Home

Catherine E. Beecher
Harriet Beecher Stowe

Introduction

The authors of this volume, while they sympathize with every honest effort to relieve the disabilities and sufferings of their sex, are confident that the chief cause of these evils is the fact that the honor and duties of the family state are not duly appreciated, that women are not trained for these duties as men are trained for their trades and professions, and that, as the consequence, family labor is poorly done, poorly paid, and regarded as menial and disgraceful.

To be the nurse of young children, a cook, or a housemaid, is regarded as the lowest and last resort of poverty, and one which no woman of culture and position can assume without loss of caste and respectability.

It is the aim of this volume to elevate both the honor and the remuneration of all the employments that sustain the many difficult and sacred duties of the family state, and thus to render each department of woman's true profession as much desired and respected as are the most honored professions of men.

When the other sex are to be instructed in law, medicine, or divinity, they are favored with numerous institutions richly endowed, with teachers of the highest talents and acquirements, with extensive libraries, and abundant and costly apparatus. With such advantages they devote nearly ten of the best years of life to preparing themselves for their profession; and to secure the public from unqualified members of these professions, none can enter them until examined by a competent body, who certify to their due preparation for their duties.

Woman's profession embraces the care and nursing of the body in the critical periods of infancy and sickness, the training of

Catherine E. Beecher and Harriet Beecher Stowe (1869). Watkins Glen, NY: Library of Victoria Culture, American Life Foundation (1979).

the human mind in the most impressible period of childhood, the instruction and control of servants, and most of the government and economies of the family state. These duties of woman are as sacred and important as any ordained to man; and yet no such advantages for preparation have been accorded to her, nor is there any qualified body to certify the public that a woman is duly prepared to give proper instruction in her profession.

This unfortunate want, and also the questions frequently asked concerning the domestic qualifications of both the authors of this work, who have formerly written upon such topics, make it needful to give some account of the advantages they have enjoyed in preparation for the important office assumed as teachers of woman's domestic duties.

The sister whose name is subscribed is the eldest of nine children by her own mother, and of four by her step-mother; and having a natural love for children, she found it a pleasure as well as a duty to aid in the care of infancy and childhood. At sixteen, she was deprived of a mother, who was remarkable not only for intelligence and culture, but for a natural taste and skill in domestic handicraft. Her place was awhile filled by an aunt remarkable for her habits of neatness and order, and especially for her economy. She was, in the course of time, replaced by a step-mother, who had been accustomed to a superior style of housekeeping, and was an expert in all departments of domestic administration.

Under these successive housekeepers, the writer learned not only to perform in the most approved manner all the manual employments of domestic life, but to honor and enjoy these duties.

At twenty-three she commenced the institution which ever since has flourished as "The Hartford Female Seminary," where, at the age of twelve, the sister now united with her in the authorship of this work became her pupil, and, after a few years, her associate. The removal of the family to the West, and failure of health, ended a connection with the Hartford Seminary, and originated a similar one in Cincinnati, of which the younger authoress of this work was associate principal till her marriage.

At this time, the work on *Domestic Economy,* of which this volume may be called an enlarged edition, although a great portion of it is entirely new, embodying the latest results of science, was prepared by the writer as a part of the *Massachusetts School Library,* and has since been extensively introduced as a textbook into public schools and higher female seminaries. It was followed by its sequel, *The Domestic Receipt-Book,* widely circulated by the Harpers in every State of the Union.

These two works have been entirely remodeled, former topics rewritten, and many new ones introduced, so as to include all that is properly embraced in a complete Encyclopedia of Domestic Economy.

In addition to the opportunities mentioned, the elder sister, for many years, has been studying the causes and the remedies for the decay of constitution and loss of health so increasingly prevalent among American women, aiming to promote the establishment of *endowed* institutions, in which women shall be properly trained for their profession, as both housekeepers and health-keepers. What advantages have thus been received and the results thus obtained will appear in succeeding pages.

During the upward progress of the age, and the advance of a more enlightened Christianity, the writers of this volume have gained more elevated views of the true mission of woman—of the dignity and importance of her distinctive duties, and of the true happiness which will be the reward of a right appreciation of this mission, and a proper performance of these duties.

There is at the present time an increasing agitation of the public mind, evolving many theories and some crude speculations as to woman's rights and duties. That there is a great social and moral power in her keeping, which is now seeking expression by organization, is manifest, and that resulting plans and efforts will involve some mistakes, some collisions, and some failures, all must expect.

But to intelligent, reflecting, and benevolent women—whose faith rests on the character and teachings of Jesus Christ—there are great principles revealed by Him, which in the end will secure the grand result which He taught and suffered to achieve. It is hoped that in the following pages these principles will be so exhibited and illustrated as to aid in securing those rights and advantages which Christ's religion aims to provide for all, and especially for the most weak and defenseless of His children.

The Christian Family

It is the aim of this volume to elevate both the honor and the remuneration of all employments that sustain the many difficult and varied duties of the family state, and thus to render each department of woman's profession as much desired and respected as are the most honored professions of men.

What, then, is the end designed by the family state which Jesus Christ came into this world to secure?

It is to provide for the training of our race to the highest possible intelligence, virtue, and happiness, by means of the self-sacrificing labors of the wise and good, and this with chief reference to a future immortal existence.

The distinctive feature of the family is self-sacrificing labor of the stronger and wiser members to raise the weaker and more

ignorant to equal advantages. The father undergoes toil and self-denial to provide a home, and then the mother becomes a self-sacrificing laborer to train its inmates. The useless, troublesome infant is served in the humblest offices; while both parents unite in training it to an equality with themselves in every advantage. Soon the older children become helpers to raise the younger to a level with their own. When any are sick, those who are well become self-sacrificing ministers. When the parents are old and useless, the children become their self-sacrificing servants.

Thus the discipline of the family state is one of daily self-devotion of the stronger and wiser to elevate and support the weaker members. Nothing could be more contrary to its first principles than for the older and more capable children to combine to secure to themselves the highest advantages, enforcing the drudgeries on the younger, at the sacrifice of their equal culture.

Jesus Christ came to teach the fatherhood of God and consequent brotherhood of man. He came as the "first-born Son" of God and the Elder Brother of man, to teach by example the self-sacrifice by which the great family of man is to be raised to equality of advantages as children of God. For this end, he "humbled himself" from the highest to the lowest place. He chose for his birth place the most despised village; for his parents the lowest in rank; for his trade, to labor with his hands as a carpenter, being "subject to his parents" thirty years. And, what is very significant, his trade was that which prepares the family home, as if he would teach that the great duty of man is labor—to provide for and train weak and ignorant creatures. Jesus Christ worked with his hands nearly thirty years, and preached less than three. And he taught that his kingdom is exactly opposite to that of the world, where all are striving for the highest positions. "Whoso will be great shall be your minister, and whoso will be chiefest shall be servant of all."

The family state then, is the aptest earthly illustration of the heavenly kingdom, and in it woman is its chief minister. Her great mission is self-denial, in training its members to self-sacrificing labors for the ignorant and weak: if not her own children, then the neglected children of her Father in heaven. She is to rear all under her care to lay up treasures, not on earth, but in heaven. All the pleasures of this life end here; but those who train immortal minds are to reap the fruit of their labor through eternal ages.

To man is appointed the out-door labor— to till the earth, dig the mines, toil in the foundries, traverse the ocean, transport merchandise, labor in manufactories, construct houses, conduct civil, municipal, and state affairs, and all the heavy work, which, most of the day, excludes him from the comforts of a home. But the great stimulus to all these toils, implanted in the heart of every true man, is the desire for a home of his own, and the hopes of paternity. Every man who truly lives for immortality responds to the beatitude, "Children are a heritage from the Lord: blessed is the man that hath his quiver full of them!" The more a father and mother live under the influence of that "immortality which Christ hath brought to light," the more is the blessedness of rearing a family understood and appreciated. Every child trained aright is to dwell forever in exalted bliss with those that gave it life and trained it for heaven.

The blessed privileges of the family state are not confined to those who rear children of their own. Any woman who can earn a livelihood, as every woman should be trained to do, can take a properly qualified female associate, and institute a family of her own, receiving to its heavenly influences the orphan, the sick, the homeless, and the sinful, and by motherly devotion train them to follow the self-denying example of Christ, in educating his earthly children for true happiness in this life and for his eternal home.

And such is the blessedness of aiding to sustain a truly Christian home, that no one comes so near the pattern, the All-perfect One as those who might hold what men call a higher place, and yet humble themselves to the lowest in order to aid in training the young, "not as men-pleasers, but as servants to Christ, with good-will doing service as to the Lord, and not to men." Such are preparing for high places in the kingdom of heaven. "Whosoever will be chiefest among you, let him be your servant."

It is often the case that the true humility of Christ is not understood. It was not in having a low opinion of his own character and claims, but it was in taking a low place in order to raise others to a higher. The worldling seeks to raise himself and family to an equality with others, or, if possible, a superiority to them. The true follower of Christ comes down in order to elevate others.

The maxims and institutions of this world have ever been antagonistic to the teachings and example of Jesus Christ. Men toil for wealth, honor, and power, not as means for raising others to an equality with themselves but mainly for earthly, selfish advantages. Although the experience of this life shows that children brought up to labor have the fairest chance for a virtuous and prosperous life, and for hope of future eternal blessedness, yet it is the aim of most parents who can do so, to lay up wealth that their children need not labor with the hands as Christ did. And although exhorted by our Lord not to lay up treasure on earth, but rather the imperishable riches which are gained in toiling to train the ignorant and reform the sinful, as yet a large portion of the professed followers of Christ, like his first disciples, are "slow of heart to believe."

Not less have the sacred ministries of the family state been undervalued and warred upon in other directions; for example, the Romish Church has made celibacy a prime virtue, and given its highest honors to those who forsake the family state as ordained by God. Thus came great communities of monks and nuns, shut out from the love and labors of a Christian home; thus, also, came the monkish systems of education, collecting the young in great establishments away from the watch and care of parents, and the healthful and self-sacrificing labors of a home. Thus both religion and education have conspired to degrade the family state.

Still more have civil laws and social customs been opposed to the principles of Jesus Christ. It has ever been assumed that the learned, the rich, and the powerful are not to labor with the hands, as Christ did, and as Paul did when he would "not eat any man's bread for naught, but wrought with labor, not because we have not power" [to live without hand-work,] "but to make ourselves an example." (2 Thess. 3.)

Instead of this, manual labor has been made dishonorable and unrefined by being forced on the ignorant and poor. Especially has the most important of all hand-labor, that which sustains the family, been thus disgraced; so that to nurse young children,

and provide the food of a family by labor, is deemed the lowest of all positions in honor and profit, and the last resort of poverty. And so our Lord, who himself took the form of a servant, teaches, "How hardly shall they that have riches enter the kingdom of heaven!"—that kingdom in which all are toiling to raise the weak, ignorant, and sinful to such equality with themselves as the children of a loving family enjoy. One mode in which riches have led to antagonism with the true end of the family state is in the style of living, by which the hand-labor, most important to health, comfort, and beauty, is confined to the most ignorant and neglected members of society, without any effort being made to raise them to equal advantages with the wise and cultivated.

And, the higher civilization has advanced, the more have children been trained to feel that to labor, as did Christ and Paul, is disgraceful, and to be made the portion of a degraded class. Children of the rich grow up with the feeling that servants are to work for them, and they themselves are not to work. To the minds of most children and servants, "to be a lady," is almost synonymous with "to be waited on, and do no work." It is the earnest desire of the authors of this volume to make plain the falsity of this growing popular feeling, and to show how much happier and more efficient family life will become when it is strengthened, sustained, and adorned by family work.

Redstockings Manifesto

Redstockings

I. After centuries of individual and preliminary political struggle, women are uniting to achieve their final liberation from male supremacy. Redstockings is dedicated to building this unity and winning our freedom.

II. Women are an oppressed class. Our oppression is total, affecting every facet of our lives. We are exploited as sex objects, breeders, domestic servants, and cheap labor. We are considered inferior beings, whose only purpose is to enhance men's lives. Our humanity is denied. Our prescribed behavior is enforced by the threat of physical violence.

Because we have lived so intimately with our oppressors, in isolation from each other, we have been kept from seeing our personal suffering as a political condition. This creates the illusion that a woman's relationship with her man is a matter of interplay between two unique personalities, and can be worked out individually. In reality, every such relationship is a *class* relationship, and the conflicts between individual men and women are *political* conflicts that can only be solved collectively.

III. We identify the agents of our oppression as men. Male supremacy is the oldest, most basic form of domination. All other forms of exploitation and oppression (racism, capitalism, imperialism, etc.) are extensions of male supremacy; men dominate women, a few men dominate the rest. All power structures through history have been male-dominated and male-oriented. Men have controlled all political, economic, and cultural institutions and backed up this control with physical force. They have used their power to keep women in an inferior position. *All men* receive economic, sexual, and psychological benefits from male supremacy. *All men* have oppressed women.

IV. Attempts have been made to shift the burden of responsibility from men to institutions or to women themselves. We con-

From *Feminism in Our Time* by Miriam Schneir, ed. (Random House).

demn these arguments as evasions. Institutions alone do not oppress; they are merely tools of the oppressor. To blame institutions implies that men and women are equally victimized, obscures the fact that men benefit from the subordination of women, and gives men the excuse that they are forced to be oppressors. On the contrary, any man is free to renounce his superior position provided that he is willing to be treated like a woman by other men.

We also reject the idea that women consent to or are to blame for their own oppression. Women's submission is not the result of brainwashing, stupidity, or mental illness but of continual, daily pressure from men. We do not need to change ourselves, but to change men.

The most slanderous evasion of all is that women can oppress men. The basis for this illusion is the isolation of individual relationships from their political context and the tendency of men to see any legitimate challenge to their privileges as persecution.

V. We regard our personal experience, and our feelings about that experience, as the basis for an analysis of our common situation. We cannot rely on existing ideologies as they are all products of male supremacist culture. We question every generalization and accept none that are not confirmed by our experience.

Our chief task at present is to develop female class consciousness through sharing experience and publicly exposing the sexist foundation of all our institutions. Consciousness-raising is not "therapy" which implies the existence of individual solutions and falsely assumes that the male-female relationship is purely personal, but the only method by which we can ensure that our program for liberation is based on the concrete realities of our lives.

The first requirement for raising class consciousness is honesty, in private and in public, with ourselves and other women.

VI. We identify with all women. We define our best interest as that of the poorest, most brutally exploited woman.

We repudiate all economic, racial, educational, or status privileges that divide us from other women. We are determined to recognize and eliminate any prejudices we may hold against other women.

We are committed to achieving internal democracy. We will do whatever is necessary to ensure that every woman in our movement has an equal chance to participate, assume responsibility, and develop her political potential.

VII. We call on all our sisters to unite with us in struggle.

We call on all men to give up their male privileges and support women's liberation in the interest of our humanity and their own.

In fighting for our liberation, we will always take the side of women against their oppressors. We will not ask what is "revolutionary" or "reformist," only what is good for women.

The time for individual skirmishes has passed. This time we are going all the way.

The Combahee River Collective Statement[1]

Combahee River Collective

We are a collective of Black feminists who have been meeting together since 1974.[2] During that time we have been involved in the process of defining and clarifying our politics, while at the same time doing political work within our own group and in coalition with other progressive organizations and movements. The most general statement of our politics at the present time would be that we are actively committed to struggling against racial, sexual, heterosexual, and class oppression, and see as our particular task the development of integrated analysis and practice based upon the fact that the major systems of oppression are interlocking. The synthesis of these oppressions creates the conditions of our lives. As Black women we see Black feminism as the logical political movement to combat the manifold and simultaneous oppressions that all women of color face.

We will discuss four major topics in the paper that follows: (1) the genesis of contemporary Black feminism; (2) what we believe, i.e., the specific province of our politics; (3) the problems in organizing Black feminists, including a brief herstory of our collective; and (4) Black feminist issues and practice.

I. The Genesis of Contemporary Black Feminism

Before looking at the recent development of Black feminism we would like to affirm that we find our origins in the historical reality of Afro-American women's continuous life-and-death struggle for survival and liberation. Black women's extremely negative relationship to the American political system (a system of white male rule) has always been determined by our membership in two oppressed racial and sexual castes. As Angela Davis points out in "Reflections on the Black Woman's Role in the Community of Slaves," Black women have always embodied, if only in their physical manifestation, an adversary stance to white male rule and have actively resisted its inroads upon them and their communities in both dramatic and subtle ways. There have always been Black women activists—some known, like Sojourner Truth, Harriet Tubman, Frances E. W. Harper, Ida B. Wells Barnett, and Mary Church Terrell, and thousands upon thousands unknown—who have had a shared awareness of how their sexual identity combined with their racial identity to make their whole life situation and the focus of their political struggles unique. Contemporary Black feminism is the outgrowth of countless generations of personal sacrifice, militancy, and work by our mothers and sisters.

A Black feminist presence has evolved most obviously in connection with the second wave of the American women's movement beginning in the late 1960s. Black, other Third World, and working women have been involved in the feminist movement from its start, but both outside reactionary forces and racism and elitism within the movement itself have served to obscure our participation. In 1973, Black feminists, primarily located in New York, felt the necessity of forming a separate Black feminist group. This became the National Black Feminist Organization (NBFO).

Black feminist politics also have an obvious connection to movements for Black liberation, particularly those of the 1960s and 1970s. Many of us were active in those movements (Civil Rights, Black nationalism, the Black Panthers), and all of our lives were greatly affected and changed by their ideologies, their goals, and the tactics used to achieve their goals. It was our experience and disillusionment within these liberation movements, as well as experience on the periphery of the white male left, that led to the need to develop a politics that was anti-racist, unlike those of white women, and anti-sexist, unlike those of Black and white men.

There is also undeniably a personal genesis for Black feminism, that is, the political realization that comes from the seemingly personal experiences of individual Black women's lives. Black feminists and many more Black women who do not define themselves as feminists have all experienced sexual oppression as a constant factor in our day-to-day existence. As children we realized that we were different from boys and that we were treated differently. For example, we were told in the same breath to be quiet both for the sake of being "ladylike" and to make us less objectionable in the eyes of white people. As we grew older we became aware of the threat of physical and sexual abuse by men. However, we had no way of conceptualizing what was so apparent to us, what we knew was really happening.

Black feminists often talk about their feelings of craziness before becoming conscious of the concepts of sexual politics, patriarchal rule, and most importantly, feminism, the political analysis and practice that we women use to struggle against our oppression. The fact that racial politics and indeed racism are pervasive factors in our lives did not allow us, and still does not allow most Black women, to look more deeply into our own experiences and, from that sharing and growing consciousness, to build a politics that will change our lives and inevitably end our oppression. Our development must also be tied to the contemporary economic and political position of Black people. The post World War II generation of Black youth was the first to be able to minimally partake of certain educational and employment options, previously closed completely to Black people. Although our economic position is still at the very bottom of the American capitalistic economy, a handful of us have been able to gain certain tools as a result of tokenism in education and employment which potentially enable us to more effectively fight our oppression.

A combined anti-racist and anti-sexist position drew us together initially, and as we developed politically we addressed ourselves to heterosexism and economic oppression under capitalism.

II. What We Believe

Above all else, our politics initially sprang from the shared belief that Black women are inherently valuable, that our liberation is a necessity not as an adjunct to somebody else's but because of our need as human persons for autonomy. This may seem so obvious as to sound simplistic, but it is apparent that no other ostensibly progressive movement has ever considered our specific oppression as a priority or worked seriously for the ending of that oppression. Merely naming the pejorative stereotypes attributed to Black women (e.g. mammy, matriarch, Sapphire, whore, bulldagger), let alone cataloguing the cruel, often murderous, treatment we receive, indicates how little value has been placed upon our lives during four centuries of bondage in the Western hemisphere. We realize that the only people who care enough about us to work consistently for our liberation are us. Our politics evolve from a healthy love for ourselves, our sisters and our community which allows us to continue our struggle and work.

This focusing upon our own oppression is embodied in the concept of identity politics. We believe that the most profound and potentially most radical politics come directly out of our own identity, as opposed to working to end somebody else's oppression. In the case of Black women this is a particularly repugnant, dangerous, threatening, and therefore revolutionary concept because it is obvious from looking at all the political movements that have preceded us that anyone is more worthy of liberation than ourselves. We reject pedestals, queenhood, and walking ten paces behind. To be recognized as human, levelly human, is enough.

We believe that sexual politics under patriarchy is as pervasive in Black women's lives as are the politics of class and race. We also often find it difficult to separate race from class from sex oppression because in our lives they are most often experienced simultaneously. We know that there is such a thing as racial-sexual oppression which is neither solely racial nor solely sexual, e.g., the history of rape of Black women by white men as a weapon of political repression.

Although we are feminists and Lesbians, we feel solidarity with progressive Black men and do not advocate the fractionalization that white women who are separatists demand. Our situation as Black people necessitates that we have solidarity around the fact of race, which white women of course do not need to have with white men, unless it is their negative solidarity as racial oppressors. We struggle together with Black men against racism, while we also struggle with Black men about sexism.

We realize that the liberation of all oppressed peoples necessitates the destruction of the political-economic systems of capitalism and imperialism as well as patriarchy. We are socialists because we believe that work must be organized for the collective benefit of those who do the work and create the products, and not for the profit of the bosses. Material resources must be equally distributed among those who create these resources. We are not convinced, however, that a socialist revolution that is not also a feminist and anti-racist revolution will guarantee our liberation. We have arrived at the necessity for developing an understanding of class relationships that takes into account the specific class position of Black women who are generally marginal in the labor force, while at this particular time some of us are temporarily viewed as doubly desirable tokens at white-collar and professional levels. We need to articulate the real class situation of persons who are not merely raceless, sexless workers, but for whom racial and sexual oppression are significant determinants in their working/economic lives. Although we are in essential agreement with Marx's theory as it applied to the very specific economic relationships he analyzed, we know that his analysis must be extended further in order for us to understand our specific economic situation as Black women.

A political contribution which we feel we have already made is the expansion of the feminist principle that the personal is political. In our consciousness-raising sessions, for example, we have in many ways gone beyond white women's revelations because we are dealing with the implications of race and class as well as sex. Even our Black women's style of talking/testifying in Black language about what we have experienced has a resonance that is both cultural and political. We have spent a great deal of energy delving into the cultural and experiential nature of our oppression out of necessity because none of these matters has ever been looked at before. No one before has ever examined the multilayered texture of Black women's lives. An example of this kind of revelation/conceptualization occurred at a meeting as we discussed the ways in which our early intellectual interests had been attacked by our peers, particularly Black

males. We discovered that all of us, because we were "smart" had also been considered "ugly," i.e., "smart-ugly." "Smart-ugly" crystallized the way in which most of us had been forced to develop our intellects at great cost to our "social" lives. The sanctions in the Black and white communities against Black women thinkers is comparatively much higher than for white women, particularly ones from the educated middle and upper classes.

As we have already stated, we reject the stance of Lesbian separatism because it is not a viable political analysis or strategy for us. It leaves out far too much and far too many people, particularly Black men, women, and children. We have a great deal of criticism and loathing for what men have been socialized to be in this society: what they support, how they act, and how they oppress. But we do not have the misguided notion that it is their maleness, per se—i.e., their biological maleness—that makes them what they are. As Black women we find any type of biological determinism a particularly dangerous and reactionary basis upon which to build a politic. We must also question whether Lesbian separatism is an adequate and progressive political analysis and strategy, even for those who practice it, since it so completely denies any but the sexual sources of women's oppression, negating the facts of class and race.

III. Problems in Organizing Black Feminists

During our years together as a Black feminist collective we have experienced success and defeat, joy and pain, victory and failure. We have found that it is very difficult to organize around Black feminist issues, difficult even to announce in certain contexts that we are Black feminists. We have tried to think about the reasons for our difficulties, particularly since the white women's movement continues to be strong and to grow in many directions. In this section we will discuss some of the general reasons for the organizing problems we face and also talk specifically about the stages in organizing our own collective.

The major source of difficulty in our political work is that we are not just trying to fight oppression on one front or even two, but instead to address a whole range of oppressions. We do not have racial, sexual, heterosexual, or class privilege to rely upon, nor do we have even the minimal access to resources and power that groups who possess any one of these types of privilege have.

The psychological toll of being a Black woman and the difficulties this presents in reaching political consciousness and doing political work can never be underestimated. There is a very low value placed upon Black women's psyches in this society, which is both racist and sexist. As an early group member once said, "We are all damaged people merely by virtue of being Black women." We are dispossessed psychologically and on every other level, and yet we feel the necessity to struggle to change the condition of all Black women. In "A Black Feminist's Search for Sisterhood," Michele Wallace arrives at this conclusion:

> We exist as women who are Black who are feminists, each stranded for the moment, working independently because there is not yet an environment in this society remotely congenial to our struggle—because, being on the bottom, we would have to do what no one else has done: we would have to fight the world.[3]

Wallace is pessimistic but realistic in her assessment of Black feminists' position, particularly in her allusion to the nearly classic isolation most of us face. We might use our position at the bottom, however, to make a clear leap into revolutionary action.

If Black women were free, it would mean that everyone else would have to be free since our freedom would necessitate the destruction of all the systems of oppression.

Feminism is, nevertheless, very threatening to the majority of Black people because it calls into question some of the most basic assumptions about our existence, i.e., that sex should be a determinant of power relationships. Here is the way male and female roles were defined in a Black nationalist pamphlet from the early 1970s:

> We understand that it is and has been traditional that the man is the head of the house. He is the leader of the house/nation because his knowledge of the world is broader, his awareness is greater, his understanding is fuller and his application of this information is wiser. . After all, it is only reasonable that the man be the head of the house because he is able to defend and protect the development of his home. . . Women cannot do the same things as men—they are made by nature to function differently. Equality of men and women is something that cannot happen even in the abstract world. Men are not equal to other men, i.e. ability, experience or even understanding. The value of men and women can be seen as in the value of gold and silver— they are not equal but both have great value. We must realize that men and women are a complement to each other because there is no house/family without a man and his wife. Both are essential to the development of any life.[4]

The material conditions of most Black women would hardly lead them to upset both economic and sexual arrangements that seem to represent some stability in their lives. Many Black women have a good understanding of both sexism and racism, but because of the everyday constrictions of their lives, cannot risk struggling against them both.

The reaction of Black men to feminism has been notoriously negative. They are, of course, even more threatened than Black women by the possibility that Black feminists might organize around our own needs. They realize that they might not only lose valuable and hardworking allies in their struggles but that they might also be forced to change their habitually sexist ways of interacting with and oppressing Black women. Accusations that Black feminism divides the Black struggle are powerful deterrents to the growth of an autonomous Black women's movement.

Still, hundreds of women have been active at different times during the three-year existence of our group. And every Black woman who came, came out of a strongly-felt need for some level of possibility that did not previously exist in her life.

When we first started meeting early in 1974 after the NBFO first eastern regional conference, we did not have a strategy for organizing, or even a focus. We just wanted to see what we had. After a period of months of not meeting, we began to meet again late in the year and started doing an intense variety of consciousness-raising. The overwhelming feeling that we had is that after years and years we had finally found each other. Although we were not doing political work as a group, individuals continued their involvement in Lesbian politics, sterilization abuse and abortion rights work, Third World Women's International Women's Day activities, and support activity, for the trials of Dr. Kenneth Edelin, Joan Little, and Inéz García. During our first summer, when membership had dropped off considerably, those of us remaining devoted serious discussion to the possibility of opening a refuge for battered women in a Black community. (There was no refuge in Boston at that time.) We also decided around that time to become an independent collective since we had serious disagreements with

NBFO's bourgeois-feminist stance and their lack of a clear political focus.

We also were contacted at that time by socialist feminists, with whom we had worked on abortion rights activities, who wanted to encourage us to attend the National Socialist Feminist Conference in Yellow Springs. One of our members did attend and despite the narrowness of the ideology that was promoted at that particular conference, we became more aware of the need for us to understand our own economic situation and to make our own economic analysis.

In the fall, when some members returned, we experienced several months of comparative inactivity and internal disagreements which were first conceptualized as a Lesbian-straight split but which were also the result of class and political differences. During the summer those of us who were still meeting had determined the need to do political work and to move beyond consciousness-raising and serving exclusively as an emotional support group. At the beginning of 1976, when some of the women who had not wanted to do political work and who also had voiced disagreements stopped attending of their own accord, we again looked for a focus. We decided at that time, with the addition of new members, to become a study group. We had always shared our reading with each other, and some of us had written papers on Black feminism for group discussion a few months before this decision was made. We began functioning as a study group and also began discussing the possibility of starting a Black feminist publication. We had a retreat in the late spring which provided a time for both political discussion and working out interpersonal issues. Currently we are planning to gather together a collection of Black feminist writing. We feel that it is absolutely essential to demonstrate the reality of our politics to other Black women and believe that we can do this through writing and distributing our work. The fact that individual Black feminists are living in isolation all over the country, that our own numbers are small, and that we have some skills in writing, printing, and publishing makes us want to carry out these kinds of projects as a means of organizing Black feminists as we continue to do political work in coalition with other groups.

IV. Black Feminist Issues and Projects

During our time together we have identified and worked on many issues of particular relevance to Black women. The inclusiveness of our politics makes us concerned with any situation that impinges upon the lives of women, Third World and working people. We are of course particularly committed to working on those struggles in which race, sex and class are simultaneous factors in oppression. We might, for example, become involved in workplace organizing at a factory that employs Third World women or picket a hospital that is cutting back on already inadequate health care to a Third World community, or set up a rape crisis center in a Black neighborhood. Organizing around welfare and daycare concerns might also be a focus. The work to be done and the countless issues that this work represents merely reflect the pervasiveness of our oppression.

Issues and projects that collective members have actually worked on are sterilization abuse, abortion rights, battered women, rape and health care. We have also done many workshops and educationals on Black feminism on college campuses, at women's conferences, and most recently for high school women.

One issue that is of major concern to us and that we have begun to publicly address is racism in the white women's movement. As Black feminists we are made constantly and painfully aware of how little effort white women have made to understand and combat their racism, which requires among other things that they have a more than superficial comprehension of race, color, and Black history and culture. Eliminating racism in the white women's movement is by definition work for white women to do, but we will continue to speak to and demand accountability on this issue.

In the practice of our politics we do not believe that the end always justifies the means. Many reactionary and destructive acts have been done in the name of achieving "correct" political goals. As feminists we do not want to mess over people in the name of politics. We believe in collective process and a nonhierarchical distribution of power within our own group and in our vision of a revolutionary society. We are committed to a continual examination of our politics as they develop through criticism and self-criticism as an essential aspect of our practice. In her introduction to *Sisterhood is Powerful* Robin Morgan writes:

> I haven't the faintest notion what possible revolutionary role white heterosexual men could fulfill, since they are the very embodiment of reactionary-vested-interest-power.

As Black feminists and Lesbians we know that we have a very definite revolutionary task to perform and we are ready for the lifetime of work and struggle before us.

Notes

1. The Combahee River Collective was a Black feminist group in Boston whose name came from the guerrilla action conceptualized and led by Harriet Tubman on June 2, 1863, in the Port Royal

region of South Carolina. This action freed more than 750 slaves and is the only military campaign in American history planned and led by a woman.

2. This statement is dated April 1977.

3. Wallace, Michele. "A Black Feminist's Search for Sisterhood," *The Village Voice*, 28 July 1975, pp. 6-7.

4. Mumininas of Committee for Unified Newark, Mwanamke Mwananchi (The Nationalist Woman), Newark, N.J., ©1971, pp. 4-5.

Thinking about the Categories

PART II

The articles in this section focus on some of the categories by which we mark people as different—gender, race, class, and sexuality—and on how these categories arise not from natural, biological differences, but are socially and historically constructed. In addition, they show how membership in these overlapping, interdependent categories can become a basis for inequality. A theme that runs throughout many of the articles, but is most fully developed in the final set, is how these categories are produced not just by individuals, but also by institutions, such as schools. Rather than merely being an unintended outcome of institutional practices, assumptions about gender, race, class, and sexuality underlie the organization of institutions and serve to privilege some groups at the expense of others.

Audre Lorde challenges us to examine how all forms of difference, including age, race, class, and sex, have been the means for oppressing all but a small minority on the globe. But, she argues, rather than ignoring difference we should begin to value its richness and potential for re-imagining ourselves. As a reader, you will be asked to think about how your view of yourself is related to how you see others. What commonalities and differences shape your perceptions and values? How do societies' construction of differences manifest themselves in legal, political, and economic arenas? How are women's lives affected by the differences they encounter, embody, or defy? What strategies can be employed for accepting differences as valuable resources for enriching society, as Lorde suggests, rather than as divisive burdens, the building blocks for privilege, poverty, and inequity?

Suggestions for Further Reading

Afshar, Haleh and Mary Maynard, eds. 1994. *The Dynamics of Race and Gender: Some Feminist Interventions*. Bristol, PA: Taylor and Francis.

Allen, Paula Gunn. 1992. *The Sacred Hoop: Recovering the Feminine in American Indian Tradition*. Boston: Beacon Press.

Anderson, Margaret and Patricia Hill Collins, eds. 1995. *Race, Class, and Gender: An Anthology*. Belmont, CA: Wadsworth.

Bammer, Angelika, ed. 1994. *Displacements: Cultural Identities in Question*. Bloomington, IN: Indiana University Press.

Blackwood, Evelynn. 1984. "Sexuality in Certain Native American Tribes: The Case of Cross-Gender Females," *Signs*, 10, 27–42.

Davis, Angela. 1983. *Women, Race, and Class*. New York: Vintage.

Doan, Laura, ed. 1994. *The Lesbian Postmodern*. New York: Columbia University Press.

Eliason, Michele J. 1996. "Identity Formation for Lesbian, Bisexual, and Gay Persons: Beyond a 'Minoritizing' View," *Journal of Homosexuality*, 30, 3, 31–58.

Frankenburg, Ruth. 1993. *White Women, Race Matters: The Social Construction of Whiteness*. Minneapolis: University of Minnesota Press.

Helms, Janet, ed. 1990. *Black and White Racial Identity: Theory, Research, and Practice*. New York: Greenwood.

Hull, Gloria T., et. al., eds. 1982. *All The Women Are White, All The Blacks Are Men, But Some of Us Are Brave*. Old Westbury, NY: Feminist Press.

James, Stanlie M. and Abena P. A. Busia, eds. 1993. *Theorizing Black Feminisms: The Visionary Pragmatism of Black Women*. New York: Routledge.

Katz, Jonathan. 1990. "The Invention of Heterosexuality," *Socialist Review*, 20, 7–34.

King, Deborah. 1988. "Multiple Jeopardy, Multiple Consciousness: The Context of a Black Feminist Ideology," *Signs*, 14, 42–72.

Leong, Russell, ed. 1996. *Asian American Sexualities: Dimensions of the Gay and Lesbian Experience*. New York: Routledge.

Mohanty, Chandra Talpade, Ann Russo and Lourdes Torres, eds. 1991. *Third World Women and the Politics of Feminism*. Bloomington and Indianapolis: Indiana University Press.

Rothenberg, Paula, ed. 1992. *Race, Class and Gender in the United States: An Integrated Study*. New York: St. Martin's Press.

Spelman, Elizabeth. 1988. *Inessential Woman: Problems of Exclusion in Feminist Thought*. Boston: Beacon Press.

Tucker, Naomi, ed. 1995. *Bisexual Politics: Theories, Queries, and Visions*. New York: Haworth Press.

Young, Lola. 1996. *Fear of the Dark: Race, Gender and Sexuality in the Cinema*. London & New York: Routledge.

Fiction

Allison, Dorothy. 1993. *Bastard Out of Carolina*. New York: Plume.

Alvarez, Julia. 1992. *How The Garcia Girls Lost Their Accents*. New York: Plume.

Alvarez, Julia. 1997. *Yo!* New York: Plume

Brown, Rita Mae. 1973. *Rubyfruit Jungle*. New York: Bantam Books.

Butler, Octavia. 1979. *Kindred*. Garden City, NY: Doubleday.

Chopin, Kate. 1980. *The Awakening*. New York: Putnam.

Dog, Mary Crow. 1990. *Lakota Woman*. New York: G. Weidenfeld.

Donoghue, Emma. 1995. *Stir-fry*. London: Penguin.

Gilman, Charlotte Perkins. 1979. *Herland*. New York: Pantheon.

Jen, Gish. 1992. *Typical American*. New York: Penguin.

Kingston, Maxine Hong. 1976. *The Woman Warrior: Memories of a Girlhood Among Ghosts*. New York: Knopf.

Lorde, Audre. 1982. *Zami, A New Spelling of My Name*. Watertown, MA: Persephone Press.

Morrison, Toni. 1987. *Beloved*. New York: New American Library.

Naylor, Gloria. 1989. *Mama Day*. New York: Vintage.

Piercy, Marge. 1976. *Woman on the Edge of Time*. New York: Knopf.

Sinclair, April. 1994. *Coffee Will Make You Black*. New York: Hyperion.

Tan, Amy. 1989. *The Joy Luck Club*. New York: Putnam.

Olsen, Tillie. 1980. *Tell Me A Riddle*. London: Virago.

5

The Family

Frederic Engels

Reconstructing thus the past history of the family, Morgan, in agreement with most of his colleagues, arrives at a primitive stage when unrestricted sexual freedom prevailed within the tribe, every woman belonging equally to every man and every man to every woman.

According to Morgan, from this primitive state of promiscuous intercourse there developed, probably very early:

I. The Consanguine Family, The First Stage of the Family

Here the marriage groups are separated according to generations: all the grandfathers and grandmothers within the limits of the family are all husbands and wives of one another; so are also their children, the fathers and mothers; the latter's children will form a third circle of common husbands and wives; and their children, the great-grandchildren of the first group, will form a

fourth. In this form of marriage, therefore, only ancestors and progeny, and parents and children, are excluded from the rights and duties (as we should say) of marriage with one another. Brothers and sisters, male and female cousins of the first, second, and more remote degrees, are all brothers and sisters of one another, and *precisely for that reason* they are all husbands and wives of one another.

II. The Punaluan Family

If the first advance in organization consisted in the exclusion of parents and children from sexual intercourse with one another, the second was the exclusion of sister and brother. On account of the greater nearness in age, this second advance was infinitely more important, but also more difficult, than the first. It was effected gradually, beginning probably with the exclusion from sexual intercourse of one's own broth-

---

From *Origin of the Family, Private Property and the State* by Frederic Engels.

ers and sisters (children of the same mother) first in isolated cases and then by degrees as a general rule (even in this century exceptions were found in Hawaii), and ending with the prohibition of marriage even between collateral brothers and sisters, or, as we should say, between first, second, and third cousins. It affords, says Morgan, "a good illustration of the operation of the principle of natural selection." There can be no question that the tribes among whom inbreeding was restricted by this advance were bound to develop more quickly and more fully than those among whom marriage between brothers and sisters remained the rule and the law. How powerfully the influence of this advance made itself felt is seen in the institution which arose directly out of it and went far beyond it—the gens, which forms the basis of the social order of most, if not all, barbarian peoples of the earth and from which in Greece and Rome we step directly into civilization.

After a few generations at most, every original family was bound to split up. The practice of living together in a primitive communistic household which prevailed without exception till late in the middle stage of barbarism set a limit, varying with the conditions but fairly definite in each locality, to the maximum size of the family community. As soon as the conception arose that sexual intercourse between children of the same mother was wrong, it was bound to exert its influence when the old households split up and new ones were founded (though these did not necessarily coincide with the family group). One or more lines of sisters would form the nucleus of the one household and their own brothers the nucleus of the other. It must have been in some such manner as this that the form which Morgan calls the punaluan family originated out of the consanguine family. According to the Hawaiian custom, a number of sisters, natu-ral or collateral (first, second or more remote cousins) were the common wives of their common husbands, from among whom, however, their own brothers were excluded. These husbands now no longer called themselves brothers, for they were no longer necessarily brothers, but *punalua*—that is, intimate companion, or partner. Similarly, a line of natural or collateral brothers had a number of women, *not* their sisters, as common wives, and these wives called one another *punalua*. This was the classic form of family structure [*Familienformation*], in which later a number of variations was possible, but whose essential feature was the mutually common possession of husbands and wives within a definite family circle, from which, however, the brothers of the wives—first one's own and later also collateral—and conversely also the sisters of the husbands, were excluded.

In all forms of group family, it is uncertain who is the father of a child; but it is certain who its mother is. Though she calls *all* the children of the whole family her children and has a mother's duties toward them, she nevertheless knows her own children from the others. It is therefore clear that in so far as group marriage prevails, descent can only be proved on the *mother's* side and that therefore only the *female* line is recognized. And this is in fact the case among all peoples in the period of savagery or in the lower stage of barbarism. It is the second great merit of Bachofen that he was the first to make this discovery. To denote this exclusive recognition of descent through the mother and the relations of inheritance which in time resulted from it, he uses the term "mother right," which for the sake of brevity I retain. The term is, however, ill-chosen, since at this stage of society there cannot yet be any talk of "right" in the legal sense.

III. The Pairing Family

A certain amount of pairing, for a longer or shorter period, already occurred in group marriage or even earlier; the man had a chief wife among his many wives (one can hardly yet speak of a favorite wife), and for her he was the most important among her husbands. This fact has contributed considerably to the confusion of the missionaries, who have regarded group marriage sometimes as promiscuous community of wives, sometimes as unbridled adultery. But these customary pairings were bound to grow more stable as the gens developed and the classes of "brothers" and "sisters" between whom marriage was impossible became more numerous. The impulse given by the gens to the prevention of marriage between blood relatives extended still further. Thus among the Iroquois and most of the other Indians at the lower stage of barbarism, we find that marriage is prohibited between *all* relatives enumerated in their system—which includes several hundred degrees of kinship. The increasing complication of these prohibitions made group marriages more and more impossible; they were displaced by the *pairing family*. In this stage, one man lives with one woman, but the relationship is such that polygamy and occasional infidelity remain the right of the men, even though for economic reasons polygamy is rare, while from the woman the strictest fidelity is generally demanded throughout the time she lives with the man and adultery on her part is cruelly punished. The marriage tie can, however, be easily dissolved by either partner; after separation, the children still belong as before to the mother alone.

Thus the history of the family in primitive times consists in the progressive narrowing of the circle, originally embracing the whole tribe, within which the two sexes have a common conjugal relation. The continuous exclusion, first of nearer, then of more and more remote relatives, and at last even of relatives by marriage, ends by making any kind of group marriage practically impossible. Finally, there remains only the single, still loosely linked pair, the molecule with whose dissolution marriage itself ceases. This in itself shows what a small part individual sex love, in the modern sense of the word, played in the rise of monogamy. Yet stronger proof is afforded by the practice of all peoples at this stage of development. Whereas in the earlier forms of the family, men never lacked women but, on the contrary, had too many rather than too few, women had now become scarce and highly sought after. Hence it is with the pairing marriage that there begins the capture and purchase of women—widespread *symptoms*, but no more than symptoms, of the much deeper change that had occurred.

The pairing family, itself too weak and unstable to make an independent household necessary or even desirable, in no wise destroys the communistic household inherited from earlier times. Communistic housekeeping, however, means the supremacy of women in the house; just as the exclusive recognition of the female parent, owing to the impossibility of recognizing the male parent with certainty, means that the women—the mothers—are held in high respect. One of the most absurd notions taken over from 18th century enlightenment is that in the beginning of society woman was the slave of man. Among all savages and all barbarians of the lower and middle stages, and to a certain extent of the upper stage also, the position of women is not only free, but honorable. As to what it still is in the pairing marriage, let us hear the evidence of Ashur Wright, for many years missionary among the Iroquois Senecas:

As to their family system, when occupying the old long houses [communistic households comprising several families], it is probable that some one clan [gens] predominated, the women taking in husbands, however, from the other clans [gentes]. . . . Usually, the female portion ruled the house. . . . The stores were in common; but woe to the luckless husband or lover who was too shiftless to do his share of the providing. No matter how many children, or whatever goods he might have in the house, he might at any time be ordered to pick up his blanket and budge; and after such orders it would not be healthful for him to attempt to disobey. The house would be too hot for him; and . . . he must retreat to his own clan [gens]; or, as was often done, go and start a new matrimonial alliance in some other. The women were the great power among the clans [gentes], as everywhere else. They did not hesitate, when occasion required, "to knock off the horns," as it was technically called, from the head of a chief, and send him back to the ranks of the warriors [Morgan, 1963: 464 *fn*].

The communistic household, in which most or all of the women belong to one and the same gens, while the men come from various gentes, is the material foundation of that supremacy of the women which was general in primitive times, and which it is Bachofen's third great merit to have discovered. The reports of travelers and missionaries, I may add, to the effect that women among savages and barbarians are overburdened with work in no way contradict what has been said. The division of labor between the two sexes is determined by quite other causes than by the position of woman in society. Among peoples where the women have to work far harder than we think suitable, there is often much more real respect for women than among our Europeans. The lady of civilization, surrounded by false homage and estranged from all real work, has an infinitely lower social position than the hard-working woman of barbarism, who was regarded among her people as a real lady (lady, *frowa, Frau*—mistress) and who was also a lady in character.

The first beginnings of the pairing family appear on the dividing line between savagery and barbarism; they are generally to be found already at the upper stage of savagery, but occasionally not until the lower stage of barbarism. The pairing family is the form characteristic of barbarism, as group marriage is characteristic of savagery and monogamy of civilization. To develop it further, to strict monogamy, other causes were required than those we have found active hitherto. In the single pair the group was already reduced to its final unit, its two-atom molecule: one man and one woman. Natural selection, with its progressive exclusions from the marriage community, had accomplished its task; there was nothing more for it to do in this direction. Unless new, *social* forces came into play, there was no reason why a new form of family should arise from the single pair. But these new forces did come into play.

We now leave America, the classic soil of the pairing family. No sign allows us to conclude that a higher form of family developed here or that there was ever permanent monogamy anywhere in America prior to its discovery and conquest. But not so in the Old World.

Here the domestication of animals and the breeding of herds had developed a hitherto unsuspected source of wealth and created entirely new social relations. Up to the lower stage of barbarism, permanent wealth had consisted almost solely of house, clothing, crude ornaments and the tools for obtaining and preparing food—boat, weapons, and domestic utensils of the simplest kind. Food had to be won afresh day by day. Now, with their herds of horses, camels, asses, cattle, sheep, goats, and pigs, the advancing pastoral peoples—the Semites on the Euphrates and the Tigris, and the Aryans in the Indian country of the Five Streams (Punjab), in the Ganges region, and in the steppes then much more abundantly watered by the Oxus and the Jaxartes—had acquired property which only needed supervision and the rudest care to reproduce itself in steadily increasing quantities and to supply the most abundant food in the form of milk and meat. All former means of procuring food now receded into the background; hunting, formerly a necessity, now became a luxury.

But to whom did this new wealth belong? Originally to the gens, without a doubt. Private property in herds must have already started at an early period, however. Is it difficult to say whether the author of the so-called first book of Moses regarded the patriarch Abraham as the owner of his herds in his own right as head of a family community or by right of his position as actual hereditary head of a gens. What is certain is that we must not think of him as a property owner in the modern sense of the word. And it is also certain that at the threshold of authentic history we already find the herds everywhere separately owned by heads of families, as are the artistic products of barbarism (metal implements, luxury articles and, finally, the human cattle—the slaves).

For now slavery had also been invented. To the barbarian of the lower stage, a slave was valueless. Hence the treatment of defeated enemies by the American Indians was quite different from that at a higher stage. The men were killed or adopted as brothers into the tribe of the victors; the women were taken as wives or otherwise adopted with their surviving children. At this stage human labor power still does not produce any considerable surplus over and above its maintenance costs. That was no longer the case after the introduction of cattle breeding, metalworking, weaving and, lastly, agriculture. Just as the wives whom it had formerly been so easy to obtain had now

acquired an exchange value and were bought, so also with labor power, particularly since the herds had definitely become family possessions. The family did not multiply so rapidly as the cattle. More people were needed to look after them; for this purpose use could be made of the enemies captured in war, who could also be bred just as easily as the cattle themselves.

Once it had passed into the private possession of families and there rapidly begun to augment, this wealth dealt a severe blow to the society founded on pairing marriage and the matriarchal gens. Pairing marriage had brought a new element into the family. By the side of the natural mother of the child it placed its natural and attested father with a better warrant of paternity, probably, than that of many a "father" today. According to the division of labor within the family at that time, it was the man's part to obtain food and the instruments of labor necessary for the purpose. He therefore also owned the instruments of labor, and in the event of husband and wife separating, he took them with him, just as she retained her household goods. Therefore, according to the social custom of the time, the man was also the owner of the new source of subsistence, the cattle, and later of the new instruments of labor, the slaves. But according to the custom of the same society, his children could not inherit from him. For as regards inheritance, the position was as follows:

At first, according to mother right—so long, therefore, as descent was reckoned only in the female line—and according to the original custom of inheritance within the gens, the gentile relatives inherited from a deceased fellow member of their gens. His property had to remain within the gens. His effects being insignificant, they probably always passed in practice to his nearest gentile relations—that is, to his blood relations on the mother's side. The children of the dead man, however, did not belong to his gens, but to that of their mother; it was from her that they inherited, at first conjointly with her other blood-relations, later perhaps with rights of priority; they could not inherit from their father because they did not belong to his gens within which his property had to remain. When the owner of the herds died, therefore, his herds would go first to his brothers and sisters and to his sister's children, or to the issue of his mother's sisters. But his own children were disinherited.

Thus on the one hand, in proportion as wealth increased it made the man's position in the family more important than the woman's, and on the other hand created an impulse to exploit this strengthened position in order to overthrow, in favor of his children, the traditional order of inheritance. This, however, was impossible so long as descent was reckoned according to mother right. Mother right, therefore, had to be overthrown, and overthrown it was. This was by no means so difficult as it looks to us today. For this revolution—one of the most decisive ever experienced by humanity—could take place without disturbing a single one of the living members of a gens. All could remain as they were. A simple decree sufficed that in the future the offspring of the male members should remain within the gens, but that of the female should be excluded by being transferred to the gens of their father. The reckoning of descent in the female line and the matriarchal law of inheritance were thereby overthrown, and the male line of descent and the paternal law of inheritance were substituted for them. As to how and when this revolution took place among civilized peoples, we have no knowledge. It falls entirely within prehistoric times. But that it *did* take place is more than sufficiently proved by the abundant traces of mother right which have been collected.

The overthrow of mother right was the *world historical defeat of the female sex.* The man took command in the home also; the woman was degraded and reduced to servitude; she became the slave of his lust and a mere instrument for the production of children. This degraded position of the woman, especially conspicuous among the Greeks of the heroic and still more of the classical age, has gradually been palliated and glossed over, and sometimes clothed in a milder form; in no sense has it been abolished.

The establishment of the exclusive supremacy of the man shows its effects first in the patriarchal family, which now emerges as an intermediate form. Its essential characteristic is not polygyny, of which more later, but "the organization of a number of persons, bond and free, into a family under paternal power for the purpose of holding lands and for the care of flocks and herds. . . . (In the Semitic form) the chiefs, at least, lived in polygamy. . . . Those held to servitude and those employed as servants lived in the marriage relation" [Morgan, 1963: 474].

Its essential features are the incorporation of unfree persons and paternal power; hence the perfect type of this form of family is the Roman. The original meaning of the word "family" *(familia)* is not that compound of sentimentality and domestic strife which forms the ideal of the present-day philistine; among the Romans it did not at first even refer to the married pair and their children but only to the slaves. *Famulus* means domestic slave, and *familia* is the total number of slaves belonging to one man. As late as the time of Gaius, the *familia, id est patrimonium* (family, that is, the patrimony, the inheritance) was bequeathed by will. The term was invented by the Romans to denote a new social organism whose head ruled over wife and children and a number of slaves, and was invested under Roman paternal power with rights of life and death over them all.

> This term, therefore, is no older than the iron-clad family system of the Latin tribes, which came in after field agriculture and after legalized servitude, as well as after the separation of the Greeks and Latins [Morgan, 1963: 478].

Marx adds:

> The modern family contains in germ not only slavery (*servitus*) but also serfdom, since from the beginning it is related to agricultural services. It contains *in miniature* all the contradictions which later extend throughout society and its state.

Such a form of family shows the transition of the pairing family to monogamy. In order to make certain of the wife's fidelity and therefore of the paternity of the children, she is delivered over unconditionally into the power of the husband; if he kills her, he is only exercising his rights.

IV. The Monogamous Family

It develops out of the pairing family, as previously shown, in the transitional period between the upper and middle stages of barbarism; its decisive victory is one of the signs that civilization is beginning. It is based on the supremacy of the man, the express purpose being to produce children of undisputed paternity; such paternity is demanded because these children are later to come into their father's property as his natural heirs. It is distinguished from pairing marriage by the much greater strength of the marriage tie, which can no longer be dissolved at either partner's wish. As a rule, it is now only the man who can dissolve it and put away his wife. The right of conjugal infidelity also remains secured to him, at

any rate by custom (the *Code Napoléon* explicitly accords it to the husband as long as he does not bring his concubine into the house), and as social life develops he exercises his right more and more; should the wife recall the old form of sexual life and attempt to revive, it, she is punished more severely than ever.

It is the existence of slavery side by side with monogamy, the presence of young, beautiful slaves belonging unreservedly to the *man*, that stamps monogamy from the very beginning with its specific character of monogamy *for the woman only*, but not for the man. And that is the character it still has today.

This is the origin of monogamy as far as we can trace it back among the most civilized and highly developed people of antiquity. It was not in any way the fruit of individual sex love, with which it had nothing whatever to do; marriages remained as before marriages of convenience. It was the first form of the family to be based not on natural but on economic conditions—on the victory of private property over primitive, natural communal property. The Greeks themselves put the matter quite frankly: the sole exclusive aims of monogamous marriage were to make the man supreme in the family and to propagate, as the future heirs to his wealth, children indisputably his own. Otherwise, marriage was a burden, a duty which had to be performed whether one liked it or not to gods, state, and one's ancestors. In Athens the law exacted from the man not only marriage but also the performance of a minimum of so-called conjugal duties.

Thus when monogamous marriage first makes its appearance in history, it is not as the reconciliation of man and woman, still less as the highest form of such a reconciliation. Quite the contrary monogamous marriage comes on the scene as the subjugation of the one sex by the other; it announces a struggle between the sexes unknown throughout the whole previous prehistoric period. In an old unpublished manuscript written by Marx and myself in 1846,[1] I find the words: "The first division of labor is that between man and woman for the propagation of children." And today I can add: The first class opposition that appears in history coincides with the development of the antagonism between man and woman in monogamous marriage, and the first class oppression coincides with that of the female sex by the male. Monogamous marriage was a great historical step forward; nevertheless, together with slavery and private wealth, it opens the period that has lasted until today in which every step forward is also relatively a step backward, in which prosperity and development for some is won through the misery and frustration of others. It is the cellular form of civilized society in which the nature of the oppositions and contradictions fully active in that society can be already studied.

With the rise of the inequality of property—already at the upper gage of barbarism, therefore—wage labor appears sporadically side by side with slave labor, and at the same time, as its necessary correlate, the professional prostitution of free women side by side with the forced surrender of the slave. Thus the heritage which group marriage has bequeathed to civilization is double-edged, just as everything civilization brings forth is double-edged, double-tongued, divided against itself, contradictory: here monogamy, there hetaerism with its most extreme form, prostitution. For hetaerism is as much a social institution as any other; it continues the old sexual freedom—to the advantage of the men. Actually, not merely tolerated but gaily practiced by the ruling classes particularly, it is condemned in words. But in reality this condemnation never falls on the men concerned, but only on the women; they are despised and outcast in order that the unconditional supremacy of men over the female sex may be once more proclaimed as a fundamental law of society.

Thus, wherever the monogamous family remains true to its historical origin and clearly reveals the antagonism between the man and the woman expressed in the man's exclusive supremacy, it exhibits in miniature the same oppositions and contradictions as those in which society has been moving, without power to resolve or overcome them, ever since it split into classes at the beginning of civilization.

Our jurists, of course, find that progress in legislation is leaving women with no further ground of complaint. Modern civilized systems of law increasingly acknowledge first, that for a marriage to be legal it must be a contract freely entered into by both partners and secondly, that also in the married state both partners must stand on a common footing of equal rights and duties. If both these demands are consistently carried out, say the jurists, women have all they can ask.

This typically legalist method of argument is exactly the same as that which the radical republican bourgeois uses to put the proletarian in his place. The labor contract is to be freely entered into by both partners. But it is considered to have been freely entered into as soon as the law makes both parties equal on *paper*. The power conferred on the one party by the difference of class position, the pressure thereby brought to bear on the other party—the real economic position of both—that is not the law's business. Again, for the duration of the labor contract, both parties are to have equal rights in so far as one or the other does not expressly surrender them. That economic relations compel the worker to surrender even the last semblance of equal rights—here again, that is no concern of the law.

In regard to marriage, the law, even the most advanced, is fully satisfied as soon as the partners have formally recorded that they are entering into the marriage of their own free consent. What goes on in real life behind the juridical scenes, how this free consent comes about—that is not the business of the law and the jurist. And yet the most elementary comparative jurisprudence should show the jurist what this free consent really amounts to. In the countries where an obligatory share of the paternal inheritance is secured to the children by law and they cannot therefore be disinherited—in Germany, in the countries with French law and elsewhere—the children are obliged to obtain their parents' consent to their marriage. In the countries with English law, where parental consent to a marriage is not legally required, the parents on their side have full freedom in the testamentary disposal of their property and can disinherit their children at their pleasure. It is obvious that in spite and precisely because of this fact freedom of marriage among the classes with something to inherit is in reality not a whit greater in England and America than it is in France and Germany.

As regards the legal equality of husband and wife in marriage, the position is no better. The legal inequality of the two partners bequeathed to us from earlier social conditions is not the cause but the effect of the economic oppression of the woman. In the old communistic household, which comprised many couples and their children, the task entrusted to the women of managing the household was as much a public, a socially necessary industry as the procuring of food by the men. With the patriarchal family and still more with the single monogamous family, a change came. Household management lost its public character. It no longer

concerned society. It became a *private service*; the wife became the head servant, excluded from all participation in social production. Not until the coming of modern large-scale industry was the road to social production opened to her again—and then only to the proletarian wife. But it was opened in such a manner that, if she carries out her duties in the private service of her family, she remains excluded from public production and unable to earn; and if she wants to take part in public production and earn independently, she cannot carry out family duties. And the wife's position in the factory is the position of women in all branches of business, right up to medicine and the law. The modern individual family is founded on the open or concealed domestic slavery of the wife, and modern society is a mass composed of these individual families as its molecules.

In the great majority of cases today, at least in the possessing classes, the husband is obliged to earn a living and support his family, and that in itself gives him a position of supremacy without any need for special legal titles and privileges. Within the family he is the bourgeois, and the wife represents the proletariat. In the industrial world, the specific character of the economic oppression burdening the proletariat is visible in all its sharpness only when all special legal privileges of the capitalist class have been abolished and complete legal equality of both classes established. The democratic republic does not do away with the opposition of the two classes; on the contrary, it provides the clear field on which the fight can be fought out. And in the same way, the peculiar character of the supremacy of the husband over the wife in the modern family, the necessity of creating real social equality between them and the way to do it, will only be seen in the clear light of day when both possess legally complete equality of rights. Then it will be plain that the first condition for the liberation of the wife is to bring the whole female sex back into public industry, and that this in turn demands that the characteristic of the monogamous family as the economic unit of society be abolished.

We thus have three principal forms of marriage which correspond broadly to the three principal stages of human development: for the period of savagery, group marriage; for barbarism, pairing marriage; for civilization, monogamy supplemented by adultery and prostitution. Between pairing marriage and monogamy intervenes a period in the upper stage of barbarism when men have female slaves at their command and polygamy is practiced.

As our whole presentation has shown, the progress which manifests itself in these successive forms is connected with the peculiarity that women, but not men, are increasingly deprived of the sexual freedom of group marriage. In fact, for men group marriage actually still exists even to this day. What for the woman is a crime entailing grave legal and social consequences is considered honorable in a man or, at the worse, a slight moral blemish which he cheerfully bears.

We are now approaching a social revolution in which the economic foundations of monogamy as they have existed hitherto will disappear just as surely as those of its complement—prostitution. Monogamy arose from the concentration of considerable wealth in the hands of a single individual—a man—and from the need to bequeath this wealth to the children of that man and of no other. For this purpose, the monogamy of the woman was required, not that of the man, so this monogamy of the woman did not in any way interfere with open or concealed polygamy on the part of the man. But by transforming by far the greater portion,

at any rate, of permanent, heritable wealth—the means of production—into social property, the coming social revolution will reduce to a minimum all this anxiety about bequeathing and inheriting. Having arisen from economic causes, will monogamy then disappear when these causes disappear?

One might answer, not without reason: far from disappearing, it will on the contrary begin to be realized completely. For with the transformation of the means of production into social property there will disappear also wage labor, the proletariat, and therefore the necessity for a certain—statistically calculable—number of women to surrender themselves for money. Prostitution disappears; monogamy, instead of collapsing, at last becomes a reality—also, for men.

Full freedom of marriage can therefore only be generally established when the abolition of capitalist production and of the property relations created by it has removed all the accompanying economic considerations which still exert such a powerful influence on the choice of a marriage partner. For then there is no other motive left except mutual inclination.

If now the economic considerations also disappear which made women put up with the habitual infidelity of their husbands—concern for their own means of existence and still more for their children's future—then, according to all previous experience, the equality of woman thereby achieved will tend infinitely more to make men really monogamous than to make women polyandrous.

Note

1. The reference here is to *Deutsche Ideologie (German Ideology)*, written by Marx and Engels in Brussels in 1845–46 and first published in 1932 by the Marx-Engels-Lenin Institute in Moscow. *See* Marx-Engels, 1970:51.)

6

A Question of Class

Dorothy Allison

The first time I heard, "They're different than us, don't value human life the way we do," I was in high school in Central Florida. The man speaking was an army recruiter talking to a bunch of boys, telling them what the army was really like, what they could expect overseas. A cold angry feeling swept over me. I had heard the word *they* pronounced in that same callous tone before. *They*, those people over there, those people who are not us, they die so easily, kill each other so casually. They are different. *We,* I thought. *Me.*

When I was six or eight back in Greenville, South Carolina, I had heard that same matter-of-fact tone of dismissal applied to me. "Don't you play with her. I don't want you talking to them." Me and my family, we had always been *they*. Who am I? I wondered, listening to that recruiter. Who are my people? We die so easily, disappear so completely—we/they, the poor and the queer. I pressed my bony white trash fists to

my stubborn lesbian mouth. The rage was a good feeling, stronger and purer than the shame that followed it, the fear and the sudden urge to run and hide, to deny, to pretend I did not know who I was and what the world would do to me.

My people were not remarkable. We were ordinary, but even so we were mythical. We were the *they* everyone talks about—the ungrateful poor. I grew up trying to run away from the fate that destroyed so many of the people I loved, and having learned the habit of hiding, I found I had also learned to hide from myself. I did not know who I was, only that I did not want to be *they*, the ones who are destroyed or dismissed to make the "real" people, the important people, feel safer. By the time I understood that I was queer, that habit of hiding was deeply set in me, so deeply that it was not a choice but an instinct. Hide, hide to survive, I thought, knowing that if I told the truth about my life, my family, my sexual desire, my history, I would move over into that unknown territory, the land of they, would never have the chance to name my own life, to understand it or claim it.

Why are you so afraid? my lovers and friends have asked me the many times I have suddenly seemed a stranger, someone who would not speak to them, would not do the things they believed I should do, simple things like applying for a job, or a grant, or some award they were sure I could acquire easily. Entitlement, I have told them, is a matter of feeling like we rather than they. You think you have a right to things, a place in the world, and it is so intrinsically a part of you that you cannot imagine people like me, people who seem to live in your world, who don't have it. I have explained what I know over and over, in every way I can, but I have never been able to make clear the degree of my fear, the extent to which I feel myself denied: not only that I am queer in a world that hates queers, but that I was born poor into a world that despises the poor. The need to make my world believable to people who have never experienced it is part of why I write fiction. I know that some things must be felt to be understood, that despair, for example, can never be adequately analyzed; it must be lived. But if I can write a story that so draws the reader in that she imagines herself like my characters, feels their sense of fear and uncertainty, their hopes and terrors, then I have come closer to knowing myself as real, important as the very people I have always watched with awe.

I have known I was a lesbian since I was a teenager, and I have spent a good twenty years making peace with the effects of incest and physical abuse. But what may be the central fact of my life is that I was born in 1949 in Greenville, South Carolina, the bastard daughter of a white woman from a desperately poor family, a girl who had left the seventh grade the year before, worked as a waitress, and was just a month past fifteen when she had me. That fact, the inescapable impact of being born in a condition of poverty that this society finds shameful, contemptible, and somehow deserved, has had dominion over me to such an extent that I have spent my life trying to overcome or deny it. I have learned with great difficulty that the vast majority of people believe that poverty is a voluntary condition.

I have loved my family so stubbornly that every impulse to hold them in contempt has sparked in me a countersurge of pride—complicated and undercut by an urge to fit us into the acceptable myths and theories of both mainstream society and a lesbian-feminist reinterpretation. The choice becomes Steven Spielberg movies or Erskine Caldwell novels, the one valorizing and the other caricaturing, or the patriarchy as villain, trivializing the choices the men and women of my family have made. I have had to fight broad generalizations from every theoretical viewpoint.

Traditional feminist theory has had a limited understanding of class differences and of how sexuality and self are shaped by both desire and denial. The ideology implies that we are all sisters who should only turn our anger and suspicion on the world outside the lesbian community. It is easy to say that the patriarchy did it, that poverty and social contempt are products of the world of the fathers, and often I felt a need to collapse my sexual history into what I was willing to share of my class background, to pretend that my life both as a lesbian and as a working-class escapee was constructed by the patriarchy. Or conversely, to ignore how much my life was shaped by growing up poor and talk only about what incest did to my identity as a woman and as a lesbian. The difficulty is that I can't ascribe everything that has been problematic about my life simply and easily to the patriarchy, or to incest, or even to the invisible and much-denied class structure of our society.

In my lesbian-feminist collective we had long conversations about the mind/body split, the way we compartmentalize our lives to survive. For years I thought that that concept referred to the way I had separated my activist life from the passionate secret life in which I acted on my sexual desires. I was convinced that the fracture was fairly simple, that it would be healed when there was time and clarity to do so—at about the same point when I might begin to understand sex. I never imagined that it was not a split but a splintering, and I passed whole portions of my life—days, months, years—in pure directed progress, getting up every morning and setting to work, working so hard and so continually that I avoided examining in any way what I know about my life. Busywork became a trance state. I ignored who I really was and how I became that person, continued in that daily progress, became an automaton who was what she did.

I tried to become one with the lesbian-feminist community so as to feel real and valuable. I did not know that I was hiding, blending in for safety just as I had done in high school, in college. I did not recognize the impulse to forget. I believed that all those things I did not talk about, or even let myself think too much about, were not important, that none of them defined me. I had constructed a life, an identity in which I took pride, an alternative lesbian family in which I felt safe, and I did not realize that the fundamental me had almost disappeared.

It is surprising how easy it was to live that life. Everyone and everything cooperated with the process. Everything in our culture—books, television, movies, school, fashion—is presented as if it is being seen by one pair of eyes, shaped by one set of hands, heard by one pair of ears. Even if you know you are not part of that imaginary creature—if you like country music not symphonies, read books cynically, listen to the news unbelievingly, are lesbian not heterosexual, and surround yourself with your own small deviant community—you are still shaped by that hegemony, or your resistance to it. The only way I found to resist that homogenized view of the world was to make myself part of something larger than myself. As a feminist and a radical lesbian organizer, and later as a sex radical (which eventually became the term, tong with pro-sex feminist, for those who were not antipornography but anti-censorship, those of us arguing for sexual diversity), the need to belong, to feel safe, was just as important for me as for any heterosexual, nonpolitical citizen, and sometimes even more important because the rest of my life was so embattled.

The first time I read the Jewish lesbian Irena Klepfisz's poems,[1] I experienced a frisson of recognition. It was not that my people had been "burned off the map" or murdered as hers had. No, we had been encouraged to destroy ourselves, made invisible because we did not fit the myths of the noble poor generated by the middle class. Even now, past forty and stubbornly proud of my family, I feel the draw of that mythology, that romanticized, edited version of the poor. I find myself looking back and wondering what was real, what was true. Within my family, so much was lied about, joked about, denied, or told with deliberate indirection, an undercurrent of humiliation or a brief pursed grimace that belied everything that had been said. What was real? The poverty depicted in books and movies was romantic, a backdrop for the story of how it was escaped.

The poverty portrayed by left-wing intellectuals was just as romantic, a platform for assailing the upper and middle classes, and from their perspective, the working-class hero was invariably male, righteously indignant, and inhumanly noble. The reality of self-hatred and violence was either absent or caricatured. The poverty I knew was dreary, deadening, shameful, the women powerful in ways not generally seen as heroic by the world outside the family.

My family's lives were not on television, not in books, not even comic books. There was a myth of the poor in this country, but it did not include us, no matter how hard I tried to squeeze us in. There was an idea of the good poor—hard-working, ragged but clean, and intrinsically honorable. I understood that we were the bad poor: men who drank and couldn't keep a job; women, invariably pregnant before marriage, who quickly became worn, fat, and old from working too many hours and bearing too many children; and children with runny noses, watery eyes, and the wrong attitudes. My cousins quit school, stole cars, used drugs, and took dead-end jobs pumping gas or waiting tables. We were not noble, not grateful, not even hopeful. We knew ourselves despised. My family was ashamed of being poor, of feeling hopeless. What was there to work for, to save money for, to fight for or struggle against? We had generations before us to teach us that nothing ever changed, and that those who did try to escape failed.

My mama had eleven brothers and sisters, of whom I can name only six. No one is left alive to tell me the names of the others. It was my grandmother who told me about my real daddy, a shiftless pretty man who was supposed to have married, had six children, and sold cut-rate life insurance to poor Black people. My mama married when I was a year old, but her husband died just after my little sister was born a year later.

When I was five, Mama married the man she lived with until she died. Within the first year of their marriage Mama miscarried, and while we waited out in the hospital parking lot, my stepfather molested me for the first time, something he continued to do until I was past thirteen. When I was eight or so, Mama took us away to a motel after my stepfather beat me so badly it caused a family scandal, but we returned after two weeks. Mama told me that she really had no choice: she could not support us alone. When I was eleven I told one of my cousins that my stepfather was molesting me. Mama packed up my sisters and me and took us away for a few days, but again, my stepfather swore he would stop, and again we went back after a few weeks. I stopped talking for a while, and I have only vague memories of the next two years.

My stepfather worked as a route salesman, my mama as a waitress, laundry worker, cook, or fruit packer. I could never understand, since they both worked so hard and such long hours, how we never had enough money, but it was also true of my mama's brothers and sisters who worked hard in the mills or the furnace industry. In fact, my parents did better than anyone else in the family. But eventually my stepfather was fired and we hit bottom—nightmarish months of marshals at the door, repossessed furniture, and rubber checks. My parents worked out a scheme so that it appeared my stepfather had abandoned us, but instead he went down to Florida, got a new job, and rented us a house. He returned with a U-Haul trailer in the dead of night, packed us up, and moved us south.

The night we left South Carolina for Florida, my mama leaned over the backseat of her old Pontiac and promised us girls, "It'll be better there." I don't know if we believed her, but I remember crossing Georgia in the early morning, watching the red clay hills and swaying grey blankets of moss recede through the back window. I kept looking at the trailer behind us, ridiculously small to contain everything we owned. Mama had packed nothing that wasn't fully paid off, which meant she had only two things of worth: her washing and sewing machines, both of them tied securely to the trailer walls. Throughout the trip I fantasized an accident that would burst that trailer, scattering old clothes and cracked dishes on the tarmac.

I was only thirteen. I wanted us to start over completely, to begin again as new people with nothing of the past left over. I wanted to run away from who we had been seen to be, who we had been. That desire is one I have seen in other members of my family. It is the first thing I think of when trouble comes—the geographic solution. Change your name, leave town, disappear, make yourself over. What hides behind that impulse is the conviction that the life you have lived, the person you are, is valueless, better off abandoned, that running away is easier than trying to change things, that change itself is not possible. Sometimes I think it is this conviction—more seductive than alcohol or violence, more subtle than sexual hatred or gender injustice—that has dominated my life and made real change so painful and difficult.

Moving to Central Florida did not fix our lives. It did not stop my stepfather's violence, heal my shame, or make my mother happy. Once there, our lives became controlled by my mother's illness and medical bills. She had a hysterectomy when I was about eight and endured a series of hospitalizations for ulcers and a chronic back problem. Through most of my adolescence she superstitiously refused to allow anyone to mention the word *cancer*. When she was not sick, Mama and my stepfather went on working, struggling to pay off what seemed an insurmountable load of debts.

By the time I was fourteen, my sisters and I had found ways to discourage most of our stepfather's sexual advances. We were not close, but we united against him. Our efforts were helped along when he was referred to a psychotherapist after he lost his temper at work, and was prescribed drugs that made him sullen but less violent. We were growing up quickly, my sisters moving toward dropping out of school while I got good grades and took every scholarship exam I could find. I was the first person in my family to graduate from high school, and the fact that I went on to college was nothing short of astonishing.

We all imagine our lives are normal, and I did not know my life was not everyone's. It was in Central Florida that I began to realize just how different we were. The people we met there had not been shaped by the rigid class structure that dominated the South Carolina Piedmont. The first time I looked around my junior high classroom and realized I did not know who those people were—not only as individuals but as categories, who their people were and how they saw themselves—I also realized that they did not know me. In Greenville, everyone knew my family, knew we were trash, and that meant we were supposed to be poor, supposed to have grim low-paid jobs, have babies in our teens, and never finish school. But Central Florida in the 1960s was full of runaways and immigrants, and our mostly white working-class suburban school sorted us out not by income and family background but by intelligence and aptitude tests. Suddenly I was boosted into the college-bound track, and while there was plenty of contempt for my inept social skills, pitiful wardrobe, and slow drawling accent, there was also something I had never experienced before: a protective anonymity, and a kind of grudging respect and curiosity about who I might become. <u>Because they did not see poverty and hopelessness as a foregone conclusion for my life, I could begin to imagine other futures for myself.</u>

In that new country, we were unknown. The myth of the poor settled over us and glamorized us. I saw it in the eyes of my teachers, the Lion's Club representative who paid for my new glasses, and the lady from the Junior League who told me about the scholarship I had won. Better, far better, to be one of the mythical poor than to be part of the *they* I had known before. I also experienced a new level of fear, a fear of losing what had never before been imaginable. Don't let me lose this chance, I prayed, and lived in terror that I might suddenly be seen again as what I knew myself to be.

As an adolescent I thought that my family's escape from South Carolina played like a bad movie. We fled the way runaway serfs might have done, with the sheriff who would have arrested my stepfather the imagined border guard. I am certain that if we had remained in South Carolina, I would have been trapped by my family's heritage of poverty, jail, and illegitimate children—that even being smart, stubborn, and a lesbian would have made no difference.

My grandmother died when I was twenty, and after Mama went home for the funeral, I had a series of dreams in which we still lived up in Greenville, just down the road from where Granny died. In the dreams I had two children and only one eye, lived in a trailer, and worked at the textile mill. Most of my time was taken up with deciding when I would finally kill my children and myself. The dreams were so vivid, I became convinced they were about the life I was meant to have had, and I began to work even harder to put as much distance as I could between my family and me. I copied the dress, mannerisms, attitudes, and ambitions of the girls I met in college, changing or hiding my own tastes, interests, and desires. I kept my lesbianism a secret, forming a relationship with an effeminate male friend that served to shelter and disguise us both. I explained to friends do that I went home so rarely because my stepfather and I fought too much for me to be comfortable in his house. But that was only part of the reason I avoided home, the easiest reason. The truth was that I feared the person I might become in my mama's house, the woman of my dreams—hateful, violent, and hopeless.

It is hard to explain how deliberately and thoroughly I ran away from my own life. I did not forget where I came from, but I gritted my teeth and hid it. When I could not get enough scholarship money to pay for graduate school, I spent a year of rage working as a salad girl, substitute teacher, and maid. I finally managed to find a job by agreeing to take any city assignment where the Social Security Administration needed a clerk. Once I had a job and my own place far away from anyone in my family, I became sexually and politically active, joining the Women's Center support staff and falling in love with a series of middle-class women who thought my accent and stories thoroughly charming. The stories I told about my family, about South Carolina, about being poor itself, were all lies, carefully edited to seem droll or funny. I knew damn well that no one would want to hear the truth about poverty, the hopelessness and fear, the feeling that nothing I did would ever make any difference and the raging resentment that burned beneath my jokes. Even when my lovers and I formed an alternative lesbian family, sharing what we could of our resources, I kept the truth about my background and who I knew myself to be a carefully obscured mystery. I worked as hard as I could to make myself a new person, an emotionally healthy radical lesbian activist, and I believed completely that by remaking myself I was helping to remake the world.

For a decade, I did not go home for more than a few days at a time.

When in the 1980s I ran into the concept of feminist sexuality, I genuinely did not know what it meant. Though I was, and am, a feminist, and committed to claiming the right to act on my sexual desires without tailoring my lust to a sex-fearing society, demands that I explain or justify my sexual fantasies have left me at a loss. How does anyone explain sexual need?

The Sex Wars are over, I've been told, and it always makes me want to ask who won. But my sense of humor may be a little obscure to women who have never felt threatened by the way most lesbians use and mean the words *pervert* and *queer*. I use the word queer to mean more than lesbian. Since I first used it in 1980 I have always meant it to imply that I am not only a lesbian but a transgressive lesbian—femme, masochistic, as sexually aggressive as the women I seek out, and as pornographic in my imagination and sexual activities as the heterosexual hegemony has ever believed.

My aunt Dot used to joke, "There are two or three things I know for sure, but never the same things and I'm never as sure as I'd like." What I know for sure is that class, gender, sexual preference, and prejudice— racial, ethnic, and religious—form an intricate lattice that restricts and shapes our lives, and that resistance to hatred is not a simple act. Claiming your identity in the cauldron of hatred and resistance to hatred is infinitely complicated, and worse, almost unexplainable.

I know that I have been hated as a lesbian both by "society" and by the intimate world of my extended family, but I have also been hated or held in contempt (which is in some ways more debilitating and slippery than hatred) by lesbians for behavior and sexual

practices shaped in large part by class. My sexual identity is intimately constructed by my class and regional background, and much of the hatred directed at my sexual preferences is class hatred—however much people, feminists in particular, like to pretend this is not a factor. The kind of woman I am attracted to is invariably the kind of woman who embarrasses respectably middle-class, politically aware lesbian feminists. My sexual ideal is butch, exhibitionistic, physically aggressive, smarter than she wants you to know, and proud of being called a pervert. Most often she is working class, with an aura of danger and an ironic sense of humor. There is a lot of contemporary lip service paid to sexual tolerance, but the fact that my sexuality is constructed within, and by, a butch/femme and leather fetishism is widely viewed with distaste or outright hatred.

For most of my life I have been presumed to be misguided, damaged by incest and childhood physical abuse, or deliberately indulging in hateful and retrograde sexual practices out of a selfish concentration on my own sexual satisfaction. I have been expected to abandon my desires, to become the normalized woman who flirts with fetishization, who plays with gender roles and treats the historical categories of deviant desire with humor or gentle contempt but never takes any of it so seriously as to claim a sexual identity based on these categories. It was hard enough for me to shake off demands when they were made by straight society. It was appalling when I found the same demands made by other lesbians.

One of the strengths I derive from my class background is that I am accustomed to contempt. I know that I have no chance of becoming what my detractors expect of me, and I believe that even the attempt to please them will only further engage their contempt, and my own self-contempt as well. Nonetheless, the relationship between the life I have lived and the way that life is seen by strangers has constantly invited a kind of self-mythologizing fantasy. It has always been tempting for me to play off of the stereotypes and misconceptions of mainstream culture, rather than describe a difficult and sometimes painful reality.

I am trying to understand how we internalize the myths of our society even as we resist them. I have felt a powerful temptation to write about my family as a kind of morality tale, with us as the heroes and middle and upper classes as the villains. It would be within the romantic myth, for example, to pretend that we were the kind of noble Southern whites portrayed in the movies, mill workers for generations until driven out by alcoholism and a family propensity for rebellion and union talk. But that would be a lie. The truth is that no one in my family ever joined a union.

Taken to its limits, the myth of the poor would make my family over into union organizers or people broken by the failure of the unions. As far as my family was concerned union organizers, like preachers, were of a different class, suspect and hated however much they might be admired for what they were supposed to be trying to achieve. Nominally Southern Baptist, no one in my family actually paid much attention to preachers, and only little children went to Sunday school. Serious belief in anything—any political ideology, any religious system, or any theory of life's meaning and purpose—was seen as unrealistic. It was an attitude that bothered me a lot when I started reading the socially conscious novels I found in the paperback racks when I was eleven or so. I particularly loved Sinclair Lewis's novels and wanted to imagine my own family as part of the working man's struggle.

"We were not joiners," my aunt Dot told me with a grin when I asked her about the union. My cousin Butch laughed at that, told me the union charged dues, and said, "Hell, we can't even be persuaded to toss money in the collection plate. An't gonna give it to no union man." It shamed me that the only thing my family wholeheartedly believed in was luck and the waywardness of fate. They held the dogged conviction that the admirable and wise thing to do was keep a sense of humor, never whine or cower, and trust that luck might someday turn as good as it had been bad—and with just as much reason. Becoming a political activist with an almost religious fervor was the thing I did that most outraged my family and the Southern working-class community they were part of.

Similarly, it was not my sexuality, my lesbianism, that my family saw as most rebellious; for most of my life, no one but my mama took my sexual preference very seriously. It was the way I thought about work, ambition, and self-respect. They were waitresses, laundry workers, counter girls. I was the one who went to work as a maid, something I never told any of them. They would have been angry if they had known. Work was just work for them, necessary. You did what you had to do to survive. They did not so much believe in taking pride in doing your job as in stubbornly enduring hard work and hard times. At the same time, they held that there were some forms of work, including maid's work, that were only for Black people, not white, and while I did not share that belief, I knew how intrinsic it was to the way my family saw the world. Sometimes I felt as if I straddled cultures and belonged on neither side. I would grind my teeth at what I knew was my family's unquestioning racism while continuing to respect their pragmatic endurance. But more and more as I grew older, what I felt was a deep estrangement from their view of the world, and gradually a sense of shame that would have been completely incomprehensible to them.

"Long as there's lunch counters, you can always find work," I was told by my mother and my aunts. Then they'd add, "I can get me a little extra with a smile." It was obvious there was supposed to be nothing shameful about it, that needy smile across a lunch counter, that rueful grin when you didn't have rent, or the half-provocative, half-pleading way my mama could cajole the man at the store to give her a little credit. But I hated it, hated the need for it and the shame that would follow every time I did it myself. It was begging, as far as I was concerned, a quasi-prostitution that I despised even while I continued to rely on it. After all, I needed the money.

"Just use that smile," my girl cousins used to joke, and I hated what I knew they meant. After college, when I began to support myself and study feminist theory I became more contemptuous rather than more understanding of the women in my family. I told myself that prostitution is a skilled profession and my cousins were never more than amateurs. There was a certain truth in this, though like all cruel judgments rendered from the outside, it ignored the conditions that made it true. The women in my family, my mother included, had sugar daddies, not johns, men who slipped them money because they needed it so badly. From their point of view they were nice to those men because the men were nice to them, and it was never so direct or crass an arrangement that they would set a price on their favors. Nor would they have described what they did as prostitution. Nothing made them angrier than the suggestion that the men who helped them out did it just for their favors. They worked for a living, they swore, but this was different.

I always wondered if my mother hated her sugar daddy, or if not him then her need for what he offered her, but it did not seem to me in memory that she had. He was an old man, half-crippled, hesitant and needy, and he treated my mama with enormous consideration and, yes, respect. The relationship between them was painful, and since she and my stepfather could not earn enough to support the family, Mama could not refuse her sugar daddy's money. At the same time the man made no assumptions about that money buying anything Mama was not already offering. The truth was, I think, that she genuinely liked him, and only partly because he treated her so well.

Even now, I am not sure whether there was a sexual exchange between them. Mama was a pretty woman, and she was kind to him, a kindness he obviously did not get from anyone else in his life. Moreover, he took extreme care not to cause her any problems with my stepfather. As a teenager, with a teenager's contempt for moral failings and sexual complexity of any kind, I had been convinced that Mama's relationship with that old man was contemptible. Also, that I would never do such a thing. But the first time a lover of mine gave me money and I took it, everything in my head shifted. The amount was not much to her, but it was a lot to me and I needed it. While I could not refuse it, I hated myself for taking it and I hated her for giving it. Worse, she had much less grace about my need than my mama's sugar daddy had displayed toward her. All that bitter contempt I felt for my needy cousins and aunts raged through me and burned out the love. I ended the relationship quickly, unable to forgive myself for selling what I believed should only be offered freely—not sex but love itself.

When the women in my family talked about how hard they worked, the men would spit to the side and shake their heads. Men took real jobs—harsh, dangerous, physically daunting work. They went to jail, not just the cold-eyed, careless boys who scared me with their brutal hands, but their gentler, softer brothers. It was another family thing, what people expected of my mama's people, mine. "His daddy's that one was sent off to jail in Georgia, and his uncle's another. Like as not, he's just the same," you'd hear people say of boys so young they still had their milk teeth. We were always driving down to the county farm to see somebody, some uncle, cousin, or nameless male relation. Shaven-headed, sullen, and stunned, they wept on Mama's shoulder or begged my aunts to help. "I didn't do nothing, Mama," they'd say, and it might have been true, but if even we didn't believe them, who would? No one told the truth, not even about how their lives were destroyed.

One of my favorite cousins went to jail when I was eight years old, for breaking into pay phones with another boy. The other boy was returned to the custody of his parents. My cousin was sent to the boys' facility at the county farm. After three months, my mama took us down there to visit, carrying a big basket of fried chicken, cold cornbread, and potato salad. Along with a hundred others we sat out on the lawn with my cousin and watched him eat like he hadn't had a full meal in the whole three months. I stared at his near-bald head and his ears marked with fine blue scars from the carelessly handled razor. People were laughing, music was playing, and a tall, lazy, uniformed man walked past us chewing on toothpicks and watching us all closely. My cousin kept his head down, his face hard with hatred, only looking back at the guard when he turned away.

"Sons-a-bitches," he whispered, and my mama shushed him. We all sat still when the guard turned back to us. There was a long moment of quiet, and then that man let his face relax into a big wide grin.

"Uh-huh," he said. That was all he said. Then he turned and walked away. None of us spoke. None of us ate. He went back inside soon after, and we left. When we got back to the car, my mama sat there for a while crying quietly. The next week my cousin was reported for fighting and had his stay extended by six months.

My cousin was fifteen. He never went back to school, and after jail he couldn't join the army. When he finally did come home we never talked, never had to. I knew without asking that the guard had had his little revenge, knew too that my cousin would break into another phone booth as soon as he could, but do it sober and not get caught. I knew without asking the source of his rage, the way he felt about clean, well-dressed, contemptuous people who looked at him like his life wasn't as important as a dog's. I knew because I felt it too. That guard had looked at me and Mama with the same expression he used on my cousin. We were trash. We were the ones they built the county farm to house and break. The boy who was sent home was the son of a deacon in the church, the man who managed the hardware store.

As much as I hated that man, and his boy, there was a way in which I also hated my cousin. He should have known better, I told myself, should have known the risk he ran. He should have been more careful. As I grew older and started living on my own it was a litany I used against myself even more angrily than I used it against my cousin. I knew who I was, knew that the most important thing I had to do was protect myself and hide my despised identity, blend into the myth of both the good poor and the reasonable lesbian. When I became a feminist activist, that litany went on reverberating in my head, but by then it had become a groundnote, something so deep and omnipresent I no longer heard it, even when everything I did was set to its cadence.

By 1975 I was earning a meager living as a photographer's assistant in Tallahassee, Florida. But the real work of my life was my lesbian-feminist activism, the work I did with the local women's center and the committee to found a women's studies program at Florida State University. Part of my role, as I saw it, was to be a kind of evangelical lesbian feminist, and to help develop a political analysis of this woman-hating society. I did not talk about class, except to give lip service to how we all needed to think about it, the same way I thought we needed to think about racism. I was a determined person, living in a lesbian collective—all of us young and white and serious—studying each new book that purported to address feminist issues, driven by what I saw as a need to revolutionize the world.

Years later it's difficult to convey just how reasonable my life seemed to me at that time. I was not flippant, not consciously condescending, not casual about how tough a struggle remaking social relations would be, but like so many women of my generation, I believed absolutely that I could make a difference with my life, and I was willing to give my life for the chance to make that difference. I expected hard times, long slow periods of self-sacrifice and grinding work, expected to be hated and attacked in public, to have to set aside personal desire, lovers, and family in order to be part of something greater and more important than my individual concerns. At the same time, I was working ferociously to take my desires, my sexuality, my needs as a woman and a lesbian more seriously. I believed I was making the personal political revolution with my life every moment, whether I was scrubbing the floor of the childcare center, setting up a new budget for the women's

lecture series at the university, editing the local feminist magazine, or starting a women's bookstore. That I was constantly exhausted and had no health insurance, did hours of dreary unpaid work and still sneaked out of the collective to date butch women my housemates thought retrograde and sexist never interfered with my sense of total commitment to the feminist revolution. I was not living in a closet: I had compartmentalized my own mind to such an extent that I never questioned why I did what I did. And I never admitted what lay behind all my feminist convictions—a class-constructed distrust of change, a secret fear that someday I would be found out for who I really was, found out and thrown out. If I had not been raised to give my life away, would I have made such an effective, self-sacrificing revolutionary?

The narrowly focused concentration of a revolutionary shifted only when I began to write again. The idea of writing stories seemed frivolous when there was so much work to be done, but everything changed when I found myself confronting emotions and ideas that could not be explained away or postponed until after the revolution. The way it happened was simple and unexpected. One week I was asked to speak to two completely different groups: an Episcopalian Sunday school class and a juvenile detention center. The Episcopalians were all white, well-dressed, highly articulate, nominally polite, and obsessed with getting me to tell them (without their having to ask directly) just what it was that two women did together in bed. The delinquents were all women, 80 percent Black and Hispanic, wearing green uniform dresses or blue jeans and workshirts, profane, rude, fearless, witty, and just as determined to get me to talk about what it was that two women did together in bed.

I tried to have fun with the Episcopalians, teasing them about their fears and insecurities, and being as bluntly honest as I could about my sexual practices. The Sunday school teacher, a man who had assured me of his liberal inclinations, kept blushing and stammering as the questions about my growing up and coming out became more detailed. I stepped out into the sunshine when the meeting was over, angry at the contemptuous attitude implied by all their questioning, and though I did not know why, so deeply depressed I couldn't even cry.

The delinquents were another story. Shameless, they had me blushing within the first few minutes, yelling out questions that were part curiosity and partly a way of boasting about what they already knew. "You butch or femme?" "You ever fuck boys?" "You ever want to?" "You want to have children?" "What's your girlfriend like?" I finally broke up when one very tall, confident girl leaned way over and called out, "Hey, girlfriend! I'm getting out of here next weekend. What you doing that night?" I laughed so hard I almost choked. I laughed until we were all howling and giggling together. Even getting frisked as I left didn't ruin my mood. I was still grinning when I climbed into the waterbed with my lover that night, grinning right up to the moment when she wrapped her arms around me and I burst into tears.

That night I understood, suddenly, everything that had happened to my cousins and me, understood it from a wholly new and agonizing perspective, one that made clear how brutal I had been to both my family and myself. I grasped all over again how we had been robbed and dismissed, and why I had worked so hard not to think about it. I had learned as a child that what could not be changed had to go unspoken, and worse, that those who cannot change their own lives have every reason to be ashamed of that fact

and to hide it. I had accepted that shame and believed in it, but why? What had I or my cousins done to deserve the contempt directed at us? Why had I always believed us contemptible by nature? I wanted to talk to someone about all the things I was thinking that night, but I could not. Among the women I knew there was no one who would have understood what I was thinking, no other working-class woman in the women's collective where I was living. I began to suspect that we shared no common language to speak those bitter truths.

In the days that followed I found myself remembering that afternoon long ago at the county farm, that feeling of being the animal in the zoo, the thing looked at and laughed at and used by the real people who watched us. For all his liberal convictions, that Sunday school teacher had looked at me with the eyes of my cousin's long-ago guard. I felt thrown back into my childhood, into all the fears I had tried to escape. Once again I felt myself at the mercy of the important people who knew how to dress and talk, and would always be given the benefit of the doubt, while my family and I would not.

I experienced an outrage so old I could not have traced all the ways it shaped my life. I realized again that some are given no quarter, no chance, that all their courage, humor, and love for each other is just a joke to the ones who make the rules, and I hated the rule-makers. Finally, I recognized that part of my grief came from the fact that I no longer knew who I was or where I belonged. I had run away from my family, refused to go home to visit, and tried in every way to make myself a new person. How could I be working class with a college degree? As a lesbian activist? I thought about the guards at the detention center. They had not stared at me with the same picture-window emptiness they turned on the girls who came to hear me, girls who were closer to the life I had been meant to live than I could bear to examine. The contempt in their eyes was contempt for me as a lesbian, different and the same, but still contempt.

While I raged, my girlfriend held me and comforted me and tried to get me to explain what was hurting me so bad, but I could not. She had told me so often about her awkward relationship with her own family, the father who ran his own business and still sent her checks every other month. She knew almost nothing about my family, only the jokes and careful stories I had given her. I felt so alone and at risk lying in her arms that I could not have explained anything at all. I thought about those girls in the detention center and the stories they told in brutal shorthand about their sisters, brothers, cousins, and lovers. I thought about their one-note references to those they had lost, never mentioning the loss of their own hopes, their own futures, the bent and painful shape of their lives when they would finally get free. Cried-out and dry-eyed, I lay watching my sleeping girlfriend and thinking about what I had not been able to say to her. After a few hours I got up and made some notes for a poem I wanted to write, a bare, painful litany of loss shaped as a conversation between two women, one who cannot understand the other, and one who cannot tell all she knows.

It took me a long time to take that poem from a raw lyric of outrage and grief to a piece of fiction that explained to me something I had never let myself see up close before—the whole process of running away, of closing up inside yourself, of hiding. It has taken me most of my life to understand that, to see how and why those of us who are born poor and different are so driven to give ourselves away or lose ourselves, but most of all, simply to disappear as the people we really are. By the time that poem became the story "River of Names,"[2] I had made the decision to reverse that process: to claim my family, my true history, and to tell the truth not only about who I was but about the temptation to lie.

By the time I taught myself the basics of storytelling on the page, I knew there was only one story that would haunt me until I understood how to tell it—the complicated, painful story of how my mama had, and had not, saved me as a girl. Writing *Bastard Out of Carolina*[3] became, ultimately, the way to claim my family's pride and tragedy, and the embattled sexuality I had fashioned on a base of violence and abuse.

The compartmentalized life I had created burst open in the late 1970s after I began to write what I really thought about my family. I lost patience with my fear of what the women I worked with, mostly lesbians, thought of who I slept with and what we did together. When schisms developed within my community; when I was no longer able to hide within the regular dyke network; when I could not continue to justify my life by constant political activism or distract myself by sleeping around; when my sexual promiscuity, butch/femme orientation, and exploration of sadomasochistic sex became part of what was driving me out of my community of choice—I went home again. I went home to my mother and my sisters, to visit, talk, argue, and begin to understand.

Once home I saw that as far as my family was concerned, lesbians were lesbians whether they wore suitcoats or leather jackets. Moreover, in all that time when I had not made peace with myself, my family had managed to make a kind of peace with me. My girlfriends were treated like slightly odd versions of my sisters' husbands, while I was simply the daughter who had always been difficult but was still a part of their lives. The result was that I started trying to confront what had made me unable really to talk to my sisters for so many years. I discovered that they no longer knew who I was either, and it took time and lots of listening to each other to rediscover my sense of family, and my love for them.

It is only as the child of my class and my unique family background that I have been able to put together what is for me a meaningful politics, to regain a sense of why I believe in activism, why self-revelation is so important for lesbians. There is no all-purpose feminist analysis that explains the complicated ways our sexuality and core identity are shaped, the way we see ourselves as part of both our birth families and the extended family of friends and lovers we invariably create within the lesbian community. For me, the bottom line has simply become the need to resist that omnipresent fear, that urge to hide and disappear, to disguise my life, my desires, and the truth about how little any of us understand—even as we try to make the world a more just and human place. Most of all, I have tried to understand the politics of *they,* why human beings fear and stigmatize the different while secretly dreading that they might be one of the different themselves. Class, race, sexuality, gender—and all the other categories by which we categorize and dismiss each other—need to be excavated from the inside.

The horror of class stratification, racism, and prejudice is that some people begin to believe that the security of their families and communities depends on the oppression of others, that for some to have good lives there must be others whose lives are truncated and brutal. It is a belief that dominates this culture. It is what makes the poor whites of the South so determinedly racist and the middle class so contemptuous of the poor. It is a myth that allows some to imagine that they build their lives on the ruin of others, a secret core of shame for the middle class, a goad and a spur to the marginal working class, and cause enough for the homeless and poor to feel no constraints on hatred or violence. The power of the myth is made even more apparent when we examine how, within the lesbian and feminist communities where we have addressed considerable attention to the politics of marginalization, there is still so much exclusion and fear, so many of us who do not feel safe.

I grew up poor, hated, the victim of physical, emotional, and sexual violence, and I know that suffering does not ennoble. It destroys. To resist destruction, self-hatred, or lifelong hopelessness, we have to throw off the conditioning of being despised, the fear of becoming the *they* that is talked about so dismissively, to refuse lying myths and easy moralities, to see ourselves as human, flawed, and extraordinary. All of us—extraordinary.

Notes

1. *A Few Words in the Mother Tongue: Poems, Selected and New* (Eighth Mountain Press: Portland, Oregon, 1990)
2. *Trash* (Firebrand Books: Ithaca, New York, 1988)
3. Dutton: New York, 1992.

7

The Five Sexes:
Why Male and Female Are
Not Enough

Anne Fausto-Sterling

In 1843 Levi Suydam, a twenty-three-year-old resident of Salisbury, Connecticut, asked the town board of selectmen to validate his right to vote as a Whig in a hotly contested local election. The request raised a flurry of objections from the opposition party, for reasons that must be rare in the annals of American democracy: it was said that Suydam was more female than male and thus (some eighty years before suffrage was extended to women) could not be allowed to cast a ballot. To settle the dispute a physician, one William James Barry, was brought in to examine Suydam. And, presumably upon encountering a phallus, the good doctor declared the prospective voter male. With Suydam safely in their column the Whigs won the election by a majority of one.

Barry's diagnosis, however, turned out to be somewhat premature. Within a few days he discovered that, phallus notwithstanding, Suydam menstruated regularly and had a vaginal opening. Both his/her physique and his/her mental predispositions were more complex than was first suspected. S/he had narrow shoulders and broad hips and felt occasional sexual yearnings for women. Suydam's "feminine propensities, such as a fondness for gay colors, for pieces of calico, comparing and placing them together, and an aversion for bodily labor, and an inability to perform the same, were remarked by many," Barry later wrote. It is not clear whether Suydam lost or retained the vote, or whether the election results were reversed.

Western culture is deeply committed to the idea that there are only two sexes. Even language refuses other possibilities; thus to write about Levi Suydam I have had to invent conventions—*s/he* and *his/her*—to denote someone who is clearly neither male nor female or who is perhaps both sexes at once. Legally, too, every adult is either man

This article is reprinted by permission of *The Sciences* and is from the March/April 1993 issue. Individual subscriptions are $28 per year. Write to: *The Sciences*, 2 East 63rd Street, New York, NY 10021.

or woman, and the difference, of course, is not trivial. For Suydam it meant the franchise; today it means being available for, or exempt from, draft registration, as well as being subject, in various ways, to a number of laws governing marriage, the family and human intimacy. In many parts of the United States, for instance, two people legally registered as men cannot have sexual relations without violating anti-sodomy statues.

But if the state and the legal system have an interest in maintaining a two-party sexual system, they are in defiance of nature. For biologically speaking, there are many gradations running from female to male; and depending on how one calls the shots, one can argue that along that spectrum lie at least five sexes—and perhaps even more.

For some time medical investigators have recognized the concept of the intersexual body. But the standard medical literature uses the term *intersex* as a catch-all for three major subgroups with some mixture of male and female characteristics: the so-called true hermaphrodites, whom I call herms, who possess one testis and one ovary (the sperm- and egg-producing vessels, or gonads); the male pseudohermaphrodites (the "merms"), who have testes and some aspects of the female genitalia but no ovaries; and the female pseudohermaphrodites (the "ferms"), who have ovaries and some aspects of the male genitalia but lack testes. Each of those categories is in itself complex; the percentage of male and female characteristics, for instance, can vary enormously among members of the same subgroup. Moreover, the inner lives of the people in each subgroup—their special needs and their problems, attractions and repulsions—have gone unexplored by science. But on the basis of what is known about them I suggest that the three intersexes, herm, merm and ferm, deserve to

be considered additional sexes each in its own right. Indeed, I would argue further that sex is a vast, infinitely malleable continuum that defies the constraints of even five categories.

Not surprisingly, it is extremely difficult to estimate the frequency of intersexuality, much less the frequency of each of the three additional sexes: it is not the sort of information one volunteers on a job application. The psychologist John Money of Johns Hopkins University, a specialist in the study of congenital sexual-organ defects, suggests intersexuals may constitute as many as 4 percent of births. As I point out to my students at Brown University, in a student body of about 6,000 that fraction, if correct, implies there may be as many as 240 intersexuals on campus—surely enough to form a minority caucus of some kind.

In reality though, few such students would make it as far as Brown in sexually diverse form. Recent advances in physiology and surgical technology now enable physicians to catch most intersexuals at the moment of birth. Almost at once such infants are entered into a program of hormonal and surgical management so that they can slip quietly into society as "normal" heterosexual males or females. I emphasize that the motive is in no way conspiratorial. The aims of the policy are genuinely humanitarian, reflecting the wish that people be able to "fit in" both physically and psychologically. In the medical community, however, the assumptions behind that wish—that there be only two sexes, that heterosexuality alone is normal, that there is one true model of psychological health—have gone virtually unexamined.

The word *hermaphrodite* comes from the Greek names Hermes, variously known as the messenger of the gods, the patron of music, the controller of dreams or the protector of livestock, and Aphrodite, the goddess of sexual love and beauty. According to Greek mythology, those two gods parented Hermaphroditus, who at age fifteen became half male and half female when his body fused with the body of a nymph he fell in love with. In some true hermaphrodites the testis and the ovary grow separately but bilaterally; in others they grow together within the same organ, forming an ovo-testis. Not infrequently, at least one of the gonads functions quite well, producing either sperm cells or eggs, as well as functional levels of the sex hormones—androgens or estrogens. Although in theory it might be possible for a true hermaphrodite to become both father and mother to a child, in practice the appropriate ducts and tubes are not configured so that the egg and sperm can meet.

In contrast with the true hermaphrodites, the pseudohermaphrodites possess two gonads of the same kind along with the usual male (XY) or female (XX) chromosomal makeup. But their external genitalia and secondary sex characteristics do not match their chromosomes. Thus merms have testes and XY chromosomes, yet they also have a vagina and a clitoris, and at puberty they often develop breasts. They do not menstruate, however. Ferms have ovaries, two X chromosomes and sometimes a uterus, but they also have at least partly masculine external genitalia. Without medical intervention they can develop beards, deep voices and adult-size penises.

No classification scheme could more than suggest the variety of sexual anatomy encountered in clinical practice. In 1969, for example, two French investigators, Paul Guinet of the Endocrine Clinic in Lyons and Jacques Decourt of the Endocrine Clinic in Paris, described ninety-eight cases of true hermaphroditism—again, signifying people with both ovarian and testicular tissue—solely according to the appearance of the external genitalia and the accompanying ducts. In some cases the people exhibited strongly feminine development. They had separate openings for the vagina and the urethra, a cleft vulva defined by both the large and the small labia, or vaginal lips, and at puberty they developed breasts and usually began to menstruate. It was the oversize and sexually alert clitoris, which threatened sometimes at puberty to grow into a penis, that usually impelled them to seek medical attention. Members of another group also had breasts and a feminine body type, and they menstruated. But their labia were at least partly fused, forming an incomplete scrotum. The phallus (here an embryological term for a structure that during usual development goes on to form either a clitoris or a penis) was between 1.5 and 2.8 inches long; nevertheless, they urinated through a urethra that opened into or near the vagina.

By far the most frequent form of true hermaphrodite encountered by Guinet and Decourt—55 percent—appeared to have a more masculine physique. In such people the urethra runs either through or near the phallus, which looks more like a penis than a clitoris. Any menstrual blood exits periodically during urination. But in spite of the relatively male appearance of the genitalia, breasts appear at puberty. It is possible that a sample larger than ninety-eight so-called true hermaphrodites would yield even more contrasts and subtleties. Suffice it to say that the varieties are so diverse that it is possible to know which parts are present and what is attached to what only after exploratory surgery.

The embryological origins of human hermaphrodites clearly fit what is known about male and female sexual development. The embryonic gonad generally chooses early in development to follow either a male or a female sexual pathway; for the ovo-testis, however, that choice is fudged. Similarly, the embryonic phallus most often ends up as a clitoris or a penis, but the existence of intermediate states comes as no surprise to the embryologist. There are also uro-genital swellings in the embryo that usually either stay open and become the vaginal labia or fuse and become a scrotum. In some hermaphrodites, though, the choice of opening or closing is ambivalent. Finally, all mammalian embryos have structures that can become the female uterus and the fallopian tubes, as well as structures that can become part of the male sperm-transport system. Typically either the male or the female set of those primordial genital organs degenerates, and the remaining structures achieve their sex-appropriate future. In hermaphrodites both sets of organs develop to varying degrees.

Intersexuality itself is old news. Hermaphrodites, for instance, are often featured in stories about human origins. Early biblical scholars believed Adam began life as a hermaphrodite and later divided into two people—a male and a female—after falling from grace. According to Plato there once were three sexes—male, female and hermaphrodite—but the third sex was lost with time.

Both the Talmud and the Tosefta, the Jewish books of law, list extensive regulations for people of mixed sex. The Tosefta expressly forbids hermaphrodites to inherit their fathers' estates (like daughters), to seclude themselves with women (like sons) or to shave (like men). When hermaphrodites menstruate they must be isolated from men (like women); they are disqualified from serving as witnesses or as priests (like women), but the laws of pederasty apply to them.

In Europe a pattern emerged by the end of the Middle Ages that, in a sense, has lasted to the present day: hermaphrodites were compelled to choose an established gender role and stick with it. The penalty for transgression was often death. Thus in the 1600s a Scottish hermaphrodite living as a woman was buried alive after impregnating his/her master's daughter.

For questions of inheritance, legitimacy, paternity, succession to title and eligibility for certain professions to be determined, modern Anglo-Saxon legal systems require that newborns be registered as either male or female. In the U.S. today sex determination is governed by state laws. Illinois permits adults to change the sex recorded on their birth certificates should a physician attest to having performed the appropriate surgery. The New York Academy of Medicine, on the other hand, has taken an opposite view. In spite of surgical alterations of the external genitalia, the academy argued in 1966, the chromosomal sex remains the same. By that measure, a person's wish to conceal his or her original sex cannot outweigh the public interest in protection against fraud.

During this century the medical community has completed what the legal world began—the complete erasure of any form of embodied sex that does not conform to a male-female, heterosexual pattern. Ironically, a more sophisticated knowledge of the complexity of sexual systems has led to the repression of such intricacy.

In 1937 the urologist Hugh H. Young of Johns Hopkins University published a volume title *Genital Abnormalities, Hermaphroditism and Related Adrenal Diseases*. The book is remarkable for its erudition, scientific insight and open-mindedness. In it Young drew together a wealth of carefully documented case histories to demonstrate and study the medical treatment of such "accidents of birth." Young did not pass judgment on the people he studied, nor did he attempt to coerce into treatment those intersexuals who rejected that option. And he showed unusual even-handedness in referring to those people who had had sexual experiences as both men and women as "practicing hermaphrodites."

One of Young's more interesting cases was a hermaphrodite named Emma who had grown up as a female. Emma had both a penis-size clitoris and a vagina, which made it possible for him/her to have "normal" heterosexual sex with both men and women. As a teenager Emma had had sex with a number of girls to whom s/he was deeply attracted; but at the age of nineteen s/he had married a man. Unfortunately, he had given Emma little sexual pleasure (though *he* had had no complaints), and so throughout that marriage and subsequent ones Emma had kept girlfriends on the side. With some frequency s/he had pleasurable sex with them. Young describes his subject as appearing "to be quite content and even happy." In conversation Emma occasionally told him of his/her wish to be a man, a circumstance Young said would be relatively easy to bring about. But Emma's reply strikes a heroic blow for self-interest:

> Would you have to remove that vagina? I don't know about that because that's my meal ticket. If you did that, I would have to quit my husband and go to work, so I think I'll keep it and stay as I am. My husband supports me well, and even though I don't have any sexual pleasure with him, I do have lots with my girlfriends.

Yet even as Young was illuminating intersexuality with the light of scientific reason, he was beginning its suppression. For his book is also an extended treatise on the most modern surgical and hormonal methods of changing intersexuals into either males or females. Young may have differed from his successors in being less judgmental and controlling of the patients and their families, but he nonetheless supplied

the foundation on which current intervention practices were built.

By 1969, when the English physicians Christopher J. Dewhurst and Ronald R. Gordon wrote *The Intersexual Disorders*, medical and surgical approaches to intersexuality had neared a state of rigid uniformity. It is hardly surprising that such a hardening of opinion took place in the era of the feminine mystique—of the post-Second World War flight to the suburbs and the strict division of family roles according to sex. That the medical consensus was not quite universal (or perhaps that it seemed poised to break apart again) can be gleaned from the near-hysterical tone of Dewhurst and Gordon's book, which contracts markedly with the calm reason of Young's founding work. Consider their opening description of an intersexual newborn:

> One can only attempt to imagine the anguish of the parents. That a newborn should have a deformity . . . [affecting] so fundamental an issue as the very sex of the child . . . is a tragic event which immediately conjures up visions of a hopeless psychological misfit doomed to live always as a sexual freak in loneliness and frustration.

Dewhurst and Gordon warned that such a miserable fate would, indeed, be a baby's lot should the case be improperly managed; "but fortunately," they wrote, "with correct management the outlook is infinitely better than the poor parents—emotionally stunned by the event—or indeed anyone without special knowledge could ever imagine."

Scientific dogma has held fast to the assumption that without medical care hermaphrodites are doomed to a life of misery. Yet there are few empirical studies to back up that assumption, and some of the same research gathered to build a case for treatment contradicts it. Francies Benton, another of Young's practicing hermaphrodites, "had not worried over his condition, did not wish to be changed, and was enjoying life." The same could be said of Emma, the opportunistic hausfrau. Even Dewhurst and Gordon, adamant about the psychological importance of treating intersexuals at the infant stage, acknowledged great success in "changing the sex" of older patients. They reported on twenty cases of children reclassified into a different sex after the supposedly critical age of eighteen months. They asserted that all the reclassifications were "successful," and they wondered then whether reregistration could be "recommended more readily than [had] been suggested so far."

The treatment of intersexuality in this century provides a clear example of what the French historian Michel Foucault has called biopower. The knowledge developed in biochemistry, embryology, endocrinology, psychology and surgery has enabled physicians to control the very sex of the human body. The multiple contradictions in that kind of power call for some scrutiny. On the one hand, the medical "management" of intersexuality certainly developed as part of an attempt to free people from perceived psychological pain (though whether the pain was the patient's, the parents' or the physician's is unclear). And if one accepts the assumption that in a sex-divided culture people can realize their greatest potential for happiness and productivity only if they are sure they belong to one of only two acknowledged sexes, modern medicine has been extremely successful.

On the other hand, the same medical accomplishments can be read not as progress but as a mode of discipline. Hermaphrodites have unruly bodies. They do not fall naturally into a binary classification; only a surgical shoehorn can put them there. But why should we care if a "woman," defined as one who has breasts, a vagina, a uterus and ovaries and who menstruates, also has a clitoris

large enough to penetrate the vagina of another woman? Why should we care if there are people whose biological equipment enables them to have sex "naturally" with both men and women? The answers seem to lie in a cultural need to maintain clear distinctions between the sexes. Society mandates the control of intersexual bodies because they blur and bridge the great divide. Inasmuch as hermaphrodites literally embody both sexes, they challenge traditional beliefs about sexual difference: they possess the irritating ability to live sometimes as one sex and sometimes the other, and they raise the specter of homosexuality.

But what if things were altogether different? Imagine a world in which the same knowledge that has enabled medicine to intervene in the management of intersexual patients has been placed at the service of multiple sexualities. Imagine that the sexes have multiplied beyond currently imaginable limits. It would have to be a world of shared powers. Patient and physician, parent and child, male and female, heterosexual and homosexual—all those oppositions and others would have to be dissolved as sources of division. A new ethic of medical treatment would arise, one that would permit ambiguity in a culture that had overcome sexual division. The central mission of medical treatment would be to preserve life. Thus hermaphrodites would be concerned primarily not about whether they can conform to society but about whether they might develop potentially life-threatening conditions—hernias, gonadal tumors, salt imbalance caused by adrenal malfunction—that sometimes accompany hermaphroditic development. In my ideal world medical intervention for intersexuals would take place only rarely before the age of reason; subsequent treatment would be a cooperative venture between physician, patient and other advisers trained in issues of gender multiplicity.

I do not pretend that the transition to my utopia would be smooth. Sex, even the supposedly "normal," heterosexual kind, continues to cause untold anxieties in Western society. And certainly a culture that has yet to come to grips—religiously and, in some states, legally—with the ancient and relatively uncomplicated reality of homosexual love will not readily embrace intersexuality. No doubt the most troublesome arena by far would be the rearing of children. Parents, at least since the Victorian era, have fretted, sometimes to the point of outright denial, over the fact that their children are sexual beings.

All that and more amply explains why intersexual children are generally squeezed into one of the two prevailing sexual categories. But what would be the psychological consequences of taking the alternative road—raising children as unabashed intersexuals? On the surface that tack seems fraught with peril. What, for example, would happen to the intersexual child amid the unrelenting cruelty of the school yard? When the time came to shower in gym class, what horrors and humiliations would await the intersexual as his/her anatomy was displayed in all its nontraditional glory? In whose gym class would s/he register to begin with? What bathroom would s/he use?

And how on earth would Mom and Dad help shepherd him/her through the mine field of puberty?

In the past thirty years those questions have been ignored, as the scientific community has, with remarkable unanimity, avoided contemplating the alternative route of unimpeded intersexuality. But modern investigators tend to overlook a substantial body of case histories, most of them compiled between 1930 and 1960, before surgical intervention became rampant. Almost without exception, those reports describe children who grew up knowing they were intersexual (though they did not advertise it) and adjusted to their unusual status. Some of the studies are richly detailed—described at the level of gym-class showering (which most intersexuals avoided without incident); in any event, there is not a psychotic or a suicide in the lot.

Still, the nuances of socialization among intersexuals cry out for more sophisticated analysis. Clearly, before my vision of sexual multiplicity can be realized, the first openly intersexual children and their parents will have to be brave pioneers who will bear the brunt of society's growing pains. But in the long view—though it could take generations to achieve—the prize might be a society in which sexuality is something to be celebrated for its subtleties and not something to be feared or ridiculed.

Sexual Inversion in Women

Havelock Ellis
John Addington Symonds

Homosexuality has been observed in women from very early times, and in very widespread regions. Refraining from any attempt to trace its history, and coming down to Europe in the seventeenth century, we find a case of sexual inversion in a woman, which seems to be recorded in greater detail than any case in a man had yet been recorded.[1] Moreover, Westphal's first notable case, which may be said to inaugurate the scientific study of sexual inversion, was in a woman. This passion of women for women has, also, formed a favourite subject with the novelist, who has until lately been careful to avoid the same subject as presented in the male.[2] It seems probable that homosexuality is little, if at all, less common in woman than in man.[3]

Yet we know comparatively little of sexual inversion in women; of the total number of recorded cases of this abnormality, now very considerable, but a small proportion are in women, and the chief monographs on the subject devote but little space to women.

I think there are several reasons for this. Notwithstanding the severity with which homosexuality in women has been visited in a few cases, for the most part men seem to have been indifferent towards it; when it has been made a crime or a cause for divorce in men, it has usually been considered as no offence at all in women.[4] Another reason is that it is less easy to detect in women; we are accustomed to a much greater familiarity and intimacy between women than between men, and we are less apt to suspect the existence of any abnormal passion. And allied with this cause we have also to bear in mind the extreme ignorance and the extreme reticence of women regarding any abnormal or even normal manifestation of their sexual life. A woman may feel a high degree of sexual attraction for another woman without realising that her affection is sexual, and when she does realise it she is

From *Sexual Inversion* by Havelock Ellis and John Addington Symonds, 1897.

nearly always very unwilling to reveal the nature of her intimate experience, even with the adoption of precautions, and although the fact may be present to her that by helping to reveal the nature of her abnormality she may be helping to lighten the burden of it on other women. Among the numerous confessions voluntarily sent to Krafft-Ebing there is not one by a woman. There is, I think one other reason why sexual inversion is less obvious in a woman. We have some reason to believe that, while a slight degree of homosexuality is commoner in women than in men, and is favoured by the conditions under which women live, well marked and fully developed cases of inversion are rarer in women than in men. This result would be in harmony with what we know as to the greater affectibility of the feminine organism to slight stimuli, and its less liability to serious variation.[5]

The same kind of aberrations that are found among men in lower races are also seen in women, though they are less frequently recorded. In New Zealand it is stated on the authority of Moerenhout (though I have not been able to find the reference) that the women practised Lesbianism. In South America, where inversion is common among men, we find similar phenomena in women. Among Brazilian tribes Gandavo wrote:

> "There are certain women among these Indians who determine to be chaste and know no man. These leave every womanly occupation and imitate the men. They wear their hair the same way as the men, they go to war with them or hunting, bearing their bows; they continue always in the company of men, and each has a woman who serves her and with whom she lives."[6]

This has some analogy with the phenomena seen among South American men. Dr. Holder, however, who has carefully studied the *bote,* tells me that he has met no corresponding phenomena in women.

In Bali, according to Jacobs,[7] homosexuality is almost as common among women as among men, though it is more secretly exercised; the methods of gratification adopted are either digital or lingual, or else by bringing the parts together (tribadism).

Among Arab women, according to Kocher, homosexual practices are rare, though very common among Arab men. In Egypt, according to Godard, Kocher, and others, it is almost fashionable, and every woman in the harem has a "friend." Among the negroes and mulattoes of French Creole, homosexuality is very common. "I know a lady of great beauty," he remarks, "a stranger in Guadalupe and the mother of a family, who is obliged to stay away from the markets and certain shops because of the excessive admiration of mulatto women and negresses, and the impudent invitations which they dare to address to her."[8] He refers to several cases of more or less violent sexual attempts by women on young coloured girls of 12 or 14, and observes that such attempts by men on children of their own sex are much rarer. In India (as also in Cochin China, according to Lorion) inversion among women seems to be very rare, at all events in Bengal, even among female prisoners. Surgeon-Captain Buchanan, Superintendent of the Central Jail of Bengal, at Bhagalpur, tells me he has never come across a case, and that his head gaoler, a native with twenty-five years' experience, has never heard of such a thing, although among men it is extremely common. It may be added that feminine criminality in India is rare, and that in this prison there are only 50 women to 1,300 men, although the women are received from a district twice as large as the men. As with male homosexuality, there are geographical, or rather, perhaps, racial peculiarities in the distribution of female homosexuality. Thus, in the last century, Casanova remarked that the women of Provence are specially inclined to Lesbianism.

In prisons and lunatic asylums in Europe, homosexual practices flourish among the women fully as much, it may probably be said, as among the men. There is, indeed, some reason for supposing that these phenomena are here even more decisively marked than among men.[9] Such manifestations are often very morbid, and doubtless often very vicious; I have no light to throw upon them and I do not propose to consider them.

With girls, as with boys, it is in the school, at the evolution of puberty, that homosexuality first shows itself. It may originate either peripherally or centrally. In the first case two children, perhaps when close to each other in bed, more or less unintentionally generate in each other a certain amount of sexual irritation, which they foster by mutual touching and kissing. This is a spurious kind of homosexuality; it is merely the often precocious play of the normal instinct, and has no necessary relation to true sexual inversion. In the girl who is congenitally predisposed to homosexuality it will continue and develop; in the majority it will be forgotten as quickly as possible, not without shame, in the presence of the normal object of sexual love. It is specially fostered by those employments which keep women in constant association not only by day but often at night also, without the company of men. This is, for instance, the case with the female servants in large hotels, among whom homosexual practices have been found very common.[10] Laycock, many years ago, noted the prevalence of manifestations of this kind, which he regarded as hysterical, among seamstresses, lacemakers, etc., confined for long hours in close contact to one another in heated rooms. The

circumstances under which numbers of young women are employed during the day in large shops and factories, and sleep in the establishment, two in a room or even two in a bed, are favourable to the development of homosexual practices.[11]

In theatres this cause is associated with the general tendency for homosexuality to be connected with dramatic aptitude, a point to which I shall have to refer later on. I am indebted to a friend for the following note: "Passionate friendships among girls, from the most innocent to the most elaborate excursions in the direction of Lesbos, are extremely common in theatres, both among actresses and, even more, among chorus and ballet girls. Here the pell-mell of the dressing-rooms, the wait of perhaps two hours between the performances, during which all the girls are cooped up, in a state of inaction and of excitement, in a few crowded dressing rooms, affords every opportunity for the growth of this particular kind of sentiment. In most of the theatres there is a little circle of girls, somewhat avoided by the others, or themselves careless of further acquaintanceship, who profess the most unbounded devotion to one another. Most of these girls are equally ready to flirt with the opposite sex, but I know certain ones among them who will scarcely speak to a man, and who are never seen without their particular 'pal' or 'chum,' who, if she gets moved to another theatre, will come round and wait for her friend at the stage-door. But here again it is but seldom that the experience is carried very far. The fact is that the English girl, especially of the lower and middle classes, whether she has lost her virtue or not, is extremely fettered by conventional notions. Ignorance and habit are two restraining influences from the carrying out of this particular kind of perversion to its logical conclusions. It is, therefore, among the upper ranks, alike of society and of prostitution, that Lesbianism is most definitely to be met with, for here we have much greater liberty of action, and much greater freedom from prejudices."

The cases in which the source is central, rather than peripheral, nevertheless merge into the foregoing, with no clear line of demarcation. In such cases a school girl or young woman forms an ardent attachment for another girl, probably somewhat older than herself, often a school-fellow, sometimes her school-mistress, upon whom she will lavish an astonishing amount of affection and devotion. This affection may or may not be returned; usually the return consists of a gracious acceptance of the affectionate services. The girl who expends this wealth of devotion is surcharged with emotion, but she is often unconscious of or ignorant of the sexual impulse, and she seeks for no form of sexual satisfaction. Kissing and the privilege of sleeping with the friend are, however, sought, and at such time it often happens that even the comparatively unresponsive friend feels more or less definite sexual emotion (pudendal turgescence with secretion of mucus and involuntary twitching of the neighbouring muscles), though little or no attention may be paid to this phenomenon, and in the common ignorance of girls concerning sex matters it may not be understood. In some cases there is an attempt, either instinctive or intentional, to develop the sexual feeling by close embraces and kissing. This rudimentary kind of homosexual relationship is, I believe, more common among girls than among boys, and for this there are several reasons: (1) A boy more often has some acquaintance with sexual phenomena and would frequently regard such a relationship as unmanly; (2) the girl has a stronger need of affection and self-devotion to another person than a boy has; (3) she has not, under our existing social conditions which compel young women to hold the opposite sex at arm's length, the same opportunities of finding an outlet for her sexual emotions; while (4) conventional propriety recognises a considerable degree of physical intimacy between girls, thus at once encouraging and cloaking the manifestations of homosexuality.

These passionate friendships, of a more or less unconsciously sexual character, are certainly common. It frequently happens that a period during which a young woman falls in love at a distance with some young man of her acquaintance alternates with periods of intimate attachment to a friend of her own sex. No congenital inversion is usually involved. I may quote as fairly typical the following observation supplied by a lady who cannot be called inverted:—

"Like so many other children and girls, I was first taught self-indulgence by a girl at school, and I passed on my knowledge to one or two others, with one of whom I remember once, when we were just sixteen, spending the night sensually. We were horribly ashamed after, and that was the only time. When I was only eight there was a girl of thirteen who liked to play with my body, and taught me to play with hers, though I rather disliked doing so. We slept together, and this went on at intervals for six months. These things for the sake of getting enjoyment, and not with any passion, are not uncommon with children, but less common, I think, than people sometimes imagine. I believe I could recall without much difficulty the number of times such things happened with me. In the case I mentioned when I did for one night feel—or try to excite in myself and my girl companion of sixteen—sensual passion, we had as little children slept together a few times and done these things, and meeting after an absence, just at that age, recalled our childish memories, and were carried away by sensual impulse. But I never felt any peculiar affection or passion for her even at the time, nor she for me. We only felt that our sensual nature was strong at the time, and had betrayed us into something we were ashamed of, and, therefore, we avoided letting ourselves sleep too close after that day. I think we even disliked each other, and were revolted whenever we thought of that night, feeling that each had degraded the other and herself."

It generally happens in the end either that relationship with a man brings the normal impulse into permanent play, or the steadying of the emotions in the stress of practical life leads to a knowledge of the real nature of such feelings and a consequent distaste for them. In some cases, on the other hand, such relationships, especially when formed after school life, are fairly permanent. An energetic emotional woman, not usually beautiful, will perhaps be devoted to another who may have found some rather specialised life-work but who may be very unpractical, and who has probably a very feeble sexual instinct; she is grateful for her friend's devotion, but may not actively reciprocate it. The actual specific sexual phenomena generated in such cases vary very greatly. The emotion may be latent or unconscious; it may be all on one side; it is often more or less recognised and shared. Such cases are on the borderland of true sexual inversion, but they cannot be included within its region. Sex in these relationships is scarcely the essential and fundamental element; it is more or less subordinate and parasitic. There is often a semblance of a sex relationship from the marked divergence of the friends in physical and psychic qualities, and the nervous development of one or both the friends is often slightly abnormal. We have to regard such relationships as hypertrophied friendships, the hypertrophy being due to unemployed sexual instinct.

For many of the remarks which I have to make regarding true inversion in women I am not able to bring forward the justificatory individual instances. I posses a considerable amount of information, but, owing to the tendencies already mentioned, this information is for the most part more or less fragmentary, and I am not always free to use it.

A class of women to be first mentioned, a class in which homosexuality, while fairly distinct, is only slightly marked, is formed by the women to whom the actively inverted woman is most attracted. These women differ in the first place from the normal or average woman in that they are not repelled or disgusted by lover-like advances from persons of their own sex. They are not usually attractive to the average man, though to this rule there are many exceptions. Their faces may be plain or ill-made, but not seldom they possess good figures, a point which is apt to carry more weight with the inverted woman than beauty of face. Their sexual impulses are seldom well marked, but they are of strongly affectionate nature. On the whole, they are women who are not very robust and well-developed, physically or nervously, and who are not well adopted for childbearing, but who still possess many excellent qualities, and they are always womanly. One may perhaps say that they are the pick of the women whom the average man would pass by. No doubt this is often the reason why they are open to homosexual advances, but I do not think it is the sole reason. So far as they may be said to constitute a class, they seem to possess a genuine though not precisely sexual preference for women over men, and it is this coldness rather than lack of charm which often renders men rather indifferent to them.

The actively inverted woman differs from the woman of the class just mentioned in one fairly essential character: a more or less distinct trace of masculinity. She may not be, and frequently is not, what would be called a "mannish" woman, for the latter may imitate men on grounds of taste and habit unconnected with sexual perversion, while in the inverted woman the masculine traits are part of an organic instinct which she by no means always wished to accentuate. The inverted woman's masculine element may in the least degree consist only in the fact that she makes advances to the woman to whom she is attracted and treats all men in a cool, direct manner, which may not exclude comradeship, but which excludes every sexual relationship, whether of passion or merely of coquetry. As a rule the inverted woman feels absolute indifference towards men, and not seldom repulsion. And this feeling, as a rule, is instinctively reciprocated by men.

Case XXVIII.—Miss S., age 38, living in a city of the United States of America, a business woman of fine intelligence, prominent in professional and literary circles. Her general health is good, but she belongs to a family in which there is a marked neuropathic element. She is of rather phlegmatic temperament, well poised, always perfectly calm and self-possessed, rather retiring in disposition, with gentle, dignified bearing.

She says she cannot care for men, but that all her life has been "glorified and made beautiful by friendship with women," whom she loves as a man loves women. Her character is, however, well disciplined, and her friends are not aware of the nature of her affections. She tries not to give all her love to one person, and endeavours (as she herself expresses it) to use this "gift of loving" as a stepping-stone to high mental and spiritual attainments. She is described by one who has known her for several years as "having a high nature, and instincts unerringly toward high things." ◆

Case XXIX.—Miss M., aged 29, the daughter of English parents (both musicians), who were both of what is described as "intense" temperaments, and there is a neurotic element in the family; she is herself, however, free

from nervous disease, though very sensitive in nature. At birth she was very small (? born prematurely). In a portrait taken at the age of 4 the nose, mouth and ears are abnormally large, and she wears a little boy's hat. As a child she did not care for dolls or for pretty clothes, and often wondered why other children found so much pleasure in them. "As far back as my memory goes," she writes, "I cannot recall a time when I was not different from other children. I felt bored when other little girls came to play with me, though I was never rough or boisterous in my sports." Sewing was distasteful to her. Still she cared little more for the pastimes of boys, and found her favourite amusement in reading, especially adventures and fairy tales. She was quiet, timid and self-conscious. The instinct first made its appearance in the latter part of her eighth or the first part of her ninth year. She was strongly attracted by the face of a teacher who used to appear at a side window on the second floor of the school-building and ring a bell to summon the children to their classes. The teacher's face seemed very beautiful but sad, and she thought about her continually. A year later this teacher was married and left the school, and the impression gradually faded away. The next feelings were experienced when she was about eleven years of age. A young lady came to visit a next-door neighbour, and made so profound an impression on the child that she was ridiculed by her playmates for preferring to sit in a dark corner on the lawn—where she might watch this young lady—rather than to play games. Being a sensitive child, after this experience she was careful not to reveal her feelings to anyone. She felt instinctively that in this she was different from other children. So she did not speak to anyone of her feelings. Her sense of beauty developed early, but there was always an indefinable feeling of melancholy associated with it. The twilight—a dark night when the stars shone brightly—all of these had a very depressing effect upon her but possessed a strong attraction nevertheless, and pictures appealed to her. At the age of twelve, she fell in love with a schoolmate, and wept bitterly because they could not be confirmed at the same time. The face of this friend reminded her of one of Dolce's Madonnas which she loved. Later on she loved an invalid friend very dearly, and devoted herself to her care; and upon the death of this friend, eight years afterwards, she resolved never to let her heart go out to anyone again. She is reticent regarding the details of these relationships, but it is evident that specific physical gratification plays no part in them. "I love few people," she writes, "but in these instances when I have permitted my heart to go out to a friend I have always experienced most exalted feelings, and have been made better by them morally, mentally and spiritually. Love is with me a religion. The very nature of my affection for my friends precludes the possibility of any element entering into it which is not absolutely pure and sacred."

With regard to her attitude towards the other sex, she writes: "I have never felt a dislike for men, but have good comrades among them. During my childhood I associated with both girls and boys, enjoying them all, but wondering why the girls cared to flirt with boys. Later in life I have had other friendships with men, some of whom cared for me, much to my regret, for, naturally, I do not care to marry."

She is a musician, and herself attributes her nature in part to her artistic temperament. She is of good intelligence and always stood well in her classes, but the development of the intellectual faculties is somewhat uneven. While weak in mathematics, she shows remarkable talent for various branches of physical science, to which of late years she has devoted herself, but has always been hampered by this deficiency in mathematics. She is small, though her features are rather large. Medical examination shows a small vagina and orifice, though scarcely, perhaps, abnormally so in proportion to her size. A further more detailed examination has recently been made in connection with the present history (though not at my instance) by an obstetric physician of high standing, and I am indebted to his kindness for the following notes:—

"Anatomically Miss M. is very near being a normal woman. Her pelvic measurements are about normal, being—

Bis-ant. superior spines		9 1/2 in.
Bis-iliac crests		10 1/2 in.
Bi-greater trochanteric		12 in.
External conjugate		7 in.
Height		5 ft. 4 in.
Neck	Around its base	13 1/4 in.
Measure-	On level with cricoid cart.	11 1/2 in.
ments	About the larynx	11 1/2 in.

Sexual Organs—(a) Internal: Uterus and ovaries appear normal (b) External; Small clitoris, with this irregularity, that the lower folds of the labia minora, instead of uniting one with the other and forming the fraenum, are extended upward along the sides of the clitoris, while the upper folds are poorly developed, furnishing the clitoris with a very scant hood. The labia majora depart from normal conformation in being fuller in their posterior half than in their anterior part, so that when the subject is in the supine position they sag, as it were, presenting a slight resemblance to fleshy sacs, but in substance and structure they feel normal.

"The deviations mentioned are all I am able to note from the strictly normal form and shape of these organs.

"The general conformation of the body is feminine. But with arms, palms up, extended in front of her with inner sides of hands touching, she cannot bring the inner side of forearms together, as nearly every woman can, showing that the feminine angle of arm is lost. The breasts are of fair size, and the nipples readily respond to titillation. Titillation of the sexual organs receives no response at all. [This does not show that the sexual sense is lost, but proves the absence of any habits of excessive sexual excitement leading to sexual hyperaesthesia.] I am persuaded, however, that Miss M. possesses the sexual sense to a very marked degree."

She is left-handed and shows a better development throughout on the left side. She is quiet and dignified, but has many boyish tricks of manner and speech which seem to be instinctive; she tries to watch herself continually, however, in order to avoid them, affecting feminine ways and feminine interests, but always being conscious of an effort in so doing.

Miss M. can see nothing wrong in her feelings; and until, a year ago, she came across the translation of Krafft-Eding's book she had no idea "that feelings like mine were 'under the ban of society' as he puts it, or were considered unnatural and depraved." She would like to help to bring light on the subject and to lift the shadow from other lives. ◆

Case XXX.—Miss B., age 26. Among her brothers and sisters, one is of neurotic temperament, another is inverted. She is herself perfectly healthy.

She has no repugnance to men, and would even like to try marriage, if the union were not permanent, but, except in one instance, she has never felt any sexual attraction to a man. In this exceptional instance, she soon realized that she was not adapted for heterosexual relationships, and broke off the engagement she had formed.

She is attracted to women of various kinds, though she recognises that there are some women to whom only men are attracted. Some years since she had a friend to whom she was very strongly attached, but the physical manifestations do not appear to have become very pronounced. Since then her thoughts have been much occupied by several women to whom she has made advances, which have not been encouraged to pass beyond ordinary friendship. In one case, however, she has formed an intimate relationship with a girl somewhat younger than herself, and a very feminine personality, who accepts Miss B.'s ardent love with pleasure, but in a passive manner, and who does not consider that the relationship would stand in the way of her marrying, though she would on no account tell her husband.

The relationship has for the first time aroused Miss B.'s latent sexual emotions. She seems to find sexual satisfaction in kissing and embracing her friend's body, but there appears to be no orgasm. This relationship has made a considerable change in her, and rendered her radiant and happy.

In her behaviours towards men Miss B. reveals no sexual shyness. Men are not usually attracted to her.

There is nothing striking in her appearance; her person and manners, though careless, are not conspicuously man-like. She is fond of exercise, and smokes a good deal, has artistic tastes, is indifferent to dress. ◆

In the next case the inversion is more fully developed:

Case XXXI.—Miss H., aged 30. Among her paternal relatives there is a tendency to eccentricity and to nervous disease. Her grandfather drank; her father was eccentric and hypochondriacal; and suffered from obsessions. Her mother and mother's relatives are entirely healthy, and normal in disposition.

At the age of 4 she liked to see the nates of a little girl who lived near. When she was about six the nursemaid, sitting in the fields, used to play with her own parts, and told her to do likewise, saying it would make a baby come; she occasionally touched herself in consequence, but without producing any effect of any kind. When she was about 8 she used to see various nursemaids uncover their children's sexual parts and show them to each other. She used to think about this when alone, and also about whipping. She never cared to play with dolls, and in her games always took the part of a man. Her first rudimentary sex feelings appeared at the age of 8 or 9, and were associated with dreams of whipping and being whipped, which were most vivid between the ages of 11 and 14, when they died away on the appearance of affection for girls. She menstruated at 12.

Her earliest affection, at the age of 13, was for a schoolfellow, a graceful, coquettish girl with long golden hair and blue eyes. Her affection displayed itself in performing all sorts of small services for this girl, in constantly thinking about her, and in feeling deliciously grateful for the smallest return. At the age of 14 she had a similar passion for a cousin; she used to look forward with ecstasy to her visits, and especially to the rare occasions when the cousin slept with her; her excitement was then so great that she could not sleep, but there was no conscious sexual excitement. At the age of 15 or 16 she fell in love with another cousin; her experiences with this girl were full of delicious sensations; if the cousin only touched her neck, a thrill went through her body which she now regards as sexual. Again, at 17, she had an overwhelming, passionate fascination for a schoolfellow, a pretty, commonplace girl, whom she idealised and etherealised to an extravagant extent. This passion was so violent that her health was to some extent impaired, but it was purely unselfish, and there was nothing sexual in it. On leaving school at the age of 19 she met a girl of about the same age as herself, very womanly, but not much attracted to men. This girl became very much attached to her, and sought to gain her love. After some time Miss H. was attracted by this love, partly from the sense of power it gave her, and an intimate relation grew up. This relation became vaguely physical, Miss H. taking the initiative, but her friend desiring such relations and taking extreme pleasure in them; they used to touch and kiss each other tenderly (especially on the *mons veneris*), with equal ardour. They each experienced a strong pleasurable feeling in doing this, and sexual erethism, but no orgasm, and it does not appear that this ever occurs. Their general behaviour to each other was that of lovers, but they endeavoured as far as possible to hide this fact from the world. This relation lasted for several years, and would have continued, had not Miss H.'s friend, from religious and moral scruples, put an end to the physical relationship. Miss H. had been very well and happy during this relationship; this interference with it seems to have exerted a disturbing influence, and also to have aroused her sexual desires, though she was still scarcely conscious of their real nature. Soon afterwards another girl of voluptuous type made love to

Miss H., to which the latter yielded, giving way to her feelings as well as to her lover of domination. She was afterwards ashamed of this episode. Her remorse was so great that when her friend, repenting her scruples, implored her to let their relationship be on the same footing as of old, Miss H., in her turn, resisted every effort to restore the physical relation. She kept to this resolution for some years, and sought to divert her thoughts into intellectual channels. When she again formed an intimate relationship it was with a congenial friend, and lasted for several years.

She has never masturbated. Occasionally, but very rarely, she has had dreams of riding accompanied by pleasurable sexual emotion (she cannot recall any actual experience to suggest this, though fond of riding). She has never had any kind of sexual dreams about a male; of late years she has occasionally had erotic dreams about women.

Her feeling towards men is not in the slightest degree sexual, and she has never had the slightest attraction towards a man. She likes them as good comrades, as men like each other. She much enjoys the society of men but simply on account of their intellectual attraction. Her feeling towards marriage has always been one of absolute repugnance. She can, however, imagine a man whom she could love or marry.

She is attracted to womanly women—sincere, reserved, pure, but courageous in character. She is not attracted to intellectual women, but at the same time cannot endure silly women. The physical qualities that attract her most are not so much beauty of face as graceful, but not too slender a body with beautiful curves. The women she is drawn to are usually somewhat younger than herself. Women are much attracted to her, and without any effort on her part. She likes to take the active and protecting *rôle* with them. She is herself energetic in character, and with a somewhat neurotic temperament.

She finds sexual satisfaction in tenderly touching, caressing and kissing the loved one's body. (There is no *cunnilingus*, which she regards with abhorrence.) She feels more tenderness than passion. There is a high degree of sexual erethism when kissing, but orgasm is rare and is produced by lying on the friend or by the friend lying on her, without any special contact. She likes being herself kissed, but not so much as taking the active part.

She believes that homosexual love is morally right when it is really part of a person's nature, and provided that the nature of homosexual love is always made plain to the object of such affection. She does not approve of it as a mere makeshift, or expression of sensuality, in normal women. She has sometimes resisted the sexual expression of her feelings, once for years at a time, but always in vain. The effect on her of loving women is distinctly good, she asserts, both spiritually and physically, while repression leads to morbidity and hysteria. She has suffered much from neurasthenia at various periods, but under appropriate treatment it has slowly diminished. The inverted instinct is too deeply rooted to eradicate, but it is well under control.[12] ◆

The chief characteristic of the sexually inverted woman is a certain degree of masculinity. As I have already pointed out, a woman who is inclined to adopt the ways and garments of men is by no means necessarily inverted. In the volume of *Women Adventurers*, edited by Mrs. Normal for the Adventure Series, there is no trace of inversion; in most of these cases, indeed, love for a man was precisely the motive for adopting male garments and manners. Again, Colley Cibber's daughter, Charlotte Charke, a boyish and vivacious woman, who spent much of her life in men's clothes, and ultimately wrote a lively volume of memoirs, appears never to have been attracted to women, though women were often attracted to her, believing her to be a man; it is, indeed, noteworthy that women seem with special frequency to fall in love with disguised persons of their own sex.[13] There is, however,

a very pronounced tendency among sexually inverted women to adopt male attire when practicable. In such cases male garments are not usually regarded as desirable chiefly on account of practical convenience, nor even in order to make an impression on other women, but because the wearer feels more at home in them. Thus Moll mentions the case of a young governess of sixteen who, while still unconscious of her sexual perversion, used to find pleasure when everyone was out of the house in putting on the clothes of a youth belonging to the family.[14] And when they still retain female garments these usually show some traits of masculine simplicity, and there is nearly always a disdain for the petty feminine artifices of the toilet. Even when this is not obvious there are all sorts of instinctive gestures and habits which may suggest to female acquaintances the remark that such a person "ought to have been a man." The brusque, energetic movements, the attitude of the arms, the direct speech, the inflexions of the voices, the masculine straightforwardness and sense of honour, and especially the attitude towards men, free from any suggestion either of shyness or audacity, will often suggest the underlying psychic abnormality to a keen observer.[15] Although there is sometimes a certain general coarseness of physical texture, we do not find any trace of a beard or moustache.[16]

It is probable, however, that there are more genuine approximations to the masculine type. The muscles are everywhere firm with a comparative absence of soft connective tissue, so that an inverted woman may give an unfeminine impression to the sense of touch. Not only is the tone of the voice often different, but there is reason to suppose that this rests on a basis of anatomical modification. At Moll's suggestion, Flatau examined the larynx in twenty-three inverted women, and found in several a very decidedly masculine type of larynx, especially in cases of distinctly congenital origin. In the habits not only is there frequently a pronounced taste for smoking (sometimes found in quite feminine women), but there is also a dislike and sometimes incapacity for needlework and other domestic occupations, while there is often some capacity for athletics. No masculine character is usually to be found in the sexual organs, which are sometimes undeveloped. Notwithstanding these characters, however, sexual inversion in a woman is as a rule not more obvious than in a man. At the same time, the inverted woman is not usually attractive to men. She herself generally feels the greatest indifference to men, and often cannot understand why a woman should love a man, though she easily understands why a man should love a woman. She shows, therefore, nothing of that sexual shyness and engaging air of weakness and dependence which are an invitation to men. The man who is passionately attracted to an inverted woman is usually of rather a feminine type. For instance, in one case present to my mind, he was of somewhat neurotic heredity, of slight physique, not sexually attractive to women, and very domesticated in his manner of living—in short, a man who might easily have been passionately attracted to his own sex.

While the inverted woman is cold, or at most comradely, in her bearing towards men, she may become shy and confused in the presence of attractive persons of her own sex, even unable to undress in their presence, and full of tender ardour for the woman whom she loves.

The passion find expression in sleeping together, kissing and close embraces, with more or less sexual excitement, the orgasm sometimes occurring when one lies on the other's body; the extreme gratification is *cunnilingus (in lambendo lingua genitalia alterius)*, sometimes called sapphism. There is no connection, as was once supposed, between sexual inversion in women and an enlarged clitoris, which has very seldom been found in such cases, and never, so far as I am aware, to an extent that would permit of its use in coitus with another woman.

The inverted woman is an enthusiastic admirer of feminine beauty, especially of the statuesque beauty of the body, unlike in this the normal woman whose sexual emotion is but faintly tinged by aesthetic feeling. In her sexual habits we rarely find the degree of promiscuity which is not uncommon among inverted men. I am inclined to agree with Moll that homosexual women love more faithfully and lastingly than homosexual men.[17] Sexually inverted women are not rarely married; Moll, from various confidences which he has received, believes that inverted women have not the same horror of normal coitus as inverted men; this is probably due to the fact that the women under such circumstances can retain a certain passivity. In other cases there is some degree of psycho-sexual hermaphroditism, although, as among inverted men, the homosexual instinct seems usually to give the greater relief and gratification.

It has been stated by many observers who are able to speak with some authority—in America, in France, in Germany, in England—that homosexuality is increasing among women.[18] It seems probable that this is true. There are many influences in our civilisation to-day which encourage such manifestations. The modern movement of emancipation—the movement to obtain the same rights and duties, the same freedom and responsibility, the same education and the same work—must be regarded as, on the whole, a wholesome and inevitable movement. But it carries with it certain disadvantages. It has involved an increase in feminine criminality and in feminine insanity, which are being elevated towards the masculine standard. In connection with these we can scarcely be surprised to find an increase in homosexuality which has always been regarded as belonging to an allied, if not the same, group of phenomena. Women are, very justly, coming to look upon knowledge and experience generally as their right as much as their brother's right. But when this doctrine is applied to the sexual sphere it finds certain limitations. Intimacies of any kind between young men and young women are as much discouraged socially now as ever they were; as regards higher education, the mere association of the sexes in the lecture-room or the laboratory or the hospital is discouraged in England and in America. Marriage is decaying, and while men are allowed freedom, the sexual field of women is becoming restricted to trivial flirtation with the opposite sex, and to intimacy with their own sex; having been taught independence of men and disdain for the old theory which placed women in the moated grange of the home to sigh for a man who never comes, a tendency develops for women to carry this independence still further and to find love where they find work. I do not say that these unquestionable influences of modern movements can directly cause sexual inversion, though they may indirectly, in so far as they promote hereditary neurosis; but they develop the germs of it, and they probably cause a spurious imitation. This spurious imitation is due to the fact that the congenital anomaly occurs with special frequency in woman of high intelligence who, voluntarily or involuntarily, influence others.

The frequency of homosexual practices among prostitutes is a fact of some interest and calls for special explanation, for at the first glance it seems in opposition to all that we know concerning the exciting causes of homosexuality. Regarding the fact there can be no question.[19] It has been noted by all who are acquainted with the lives of prostitutes, though opinion may differ as to its frequency; at Berlin, Moll was told in well-informed quarters, the proportion of prostitutes with Lesbian tendencies is about 25 per cent. This was precisely the proportion at Paris many years ago, according to Parent-Duchatelet, who investigated the matter minutely; to-day, according to Chevalier, it is larger; and Bourneville believes that 75 per cent of the inmates of the Parisian venereal hospitals have practised homosexuality. In London, so far as my inquiries extend, homosexuality among prostitutes is very much less prevalent, and in a well-marked form is confined to a comparatively small section.

I am indebted to a friend for the following note: "From my experience of the Parisian prostitute, I gather that Lesbianism in Paris is extremely prevalent, indeed, one might almost say normal. In particular, most of the chahut-dancers of the Moulin-Rouge, Casino de Paris, and the other public balls, are notorious for going in couples, and, for the most part, they prefer not to be separated, even in their most professional moments with the other sex. In London, the thing is, naturally, much less obvious, and, I think, much less prevalent; but it is certainly not infrequent. A certain number of well-known prostitutes are known for their tendencies in this direction, which do not, however, interfere in any marked way with the ordinary details of their profession. I do not personally know of a single prostitute who is exclusively Lesbian; I have heard vaguely that there are one or two such anomalies. But I have heard a swell *cocotte* at the Corinthian announce to the whole room that she was going home with a girl; and no one doubted the statement. Her name, indeed, was generally coupled with that of a fifth-rate actress. Another woman of the same kind has a little clientele of women who buy her photographs in Burlington Arcade. In the lower ranks of the profession, all this is much less common. One often finds women who have simply never heard of such a thing; they know of it in regard to men, but not in regard to women. And they are for the most part quite horrified at the notion, which they consider part and parcel of 'French beastliness.' Of course, almost every girl has her friend, and, when not separately occupied, they often sleep together; but, while in separate, rare cases, this undoubtedly means all that it can mean, for the most part, so far as one can judge, it means no more than it would mean among ordinary girls."

It is evident that there must be some radical causes for the frequency of homosexuality among prostitutes. One such cause doubtless lies in the character of the prostitute's relations with men; these relations are of a professional character, and as the business element becomes emphasized, the possibility of sexual satisfaction diminishes; at the best, also, there lacks the sense of social equality, the feeling of possession, and scope for the exercise of feminine affection and devotion. These the prostitute must usually be forced to find either in a "bully" or in another woman. It is interesting in this connection to recall the comparative frequency with which, in men, a love-disappointment with a woman serves to develop a homosexual tendency. Apart from this it must be borne in mind that, in a very large number of cases, the prostitute shows in slight or more marked degree many of the signs of neurotic heredity, of physical and mental "degeneration," so that it is almost possible to look upon prostitutes as a special human variety analogous to instinctive criminals.[20] The irregular life of the prostitute, the undue amount of sexual irritation, and indulgence in alcohol still further emphasise this unbalancing influence; and so

we have an undue tendency to homosexuality, just as we have it among criminals, and, to a much less extent, among persons of genius and intellect.[21]

Notes

1. This is the case of Catherina Margaretha Lincken, who married another woman, somewhat after the manner of the Hungarian Countess V. in our own day, i.e., with the aid of an artificial male organ. She was condemned to death for sodomy, and executed in 1721, at the age of 27 (F. C. Müller, "Ein weiterer Fall von conträrer Sexualempfindang," *Friedrich's Blätter,* Heft iv., 1891). This was in Germany, and it is somewhat remarkable that even at a much earlier period such an instrument appears to have been used by German women, for in the twelfth century Bishop Burchardt of Worms speaks of its use as a thing "which some women are accustomed to do." I have found a notice of a similar case in France, during the sixteenth century, in Montaigne's *Journal du Voyage en Italie en 1580* (written by his secretary); it took place near Vitry le Français. Seven or eight girls belonging to Chaumont, we are told, resolved to dress and to work as men: one of these came to Vitry to work as a weaver, and was looked upon as a well-conditioned young man, and liked by everyone. At Vitry she became betrothed to a woman, but, a quarrel arising, no marriage took place. Afterwards "she fell in love with a woman whom she married, and with whom she lived for four or five months, to the wife's great contentment, it is said; but having been recognized by some one from Chaumont, and brought to justice, she was condemned to be hanged. She said she would even prefer this to living again as a girl, and was hanged for using illicit inventions to supply the defects of her sex" (*Journal,* ed. by D'Ancona, 1889, p. 11).

2. Diderot's famous novel, *La Religieuse,* which, when first published, was thought to have been actually written by a nun, deals with the torture to which a nun was put by the perverse lubricity of her abbess, for whom, it is said, Diderot found a model in the Abbess of Chelles, a daughter of the Regent, and thus a member of a family which for several generations showed a marked tendency to inversion. Balzac, who treated so many psychological aspects of love in a more or less veiled manner, has touched on this in *La Fille aux Yeux d'Or*, in a vague and extravagantly romantic fashion. Gautier (using some slight foundation in fact) made the adventures of a woman who was predisposed to homosexuality, and slowly realises the fact, the central motive of his wonderful romance, *Mademoiselle de Maupin.* He approached the subject purely as an artist and poet,

but his handling of it shows remarkable insight. Zola has described sexual inversion with characteristic frankness in *Nana* and elsewhere. Some fifteen years ago a popular novelist, A. Belot, published a novel called *Mademoiselle Giraud, ma Femme*, which was much read; the novelist took the attitude of a moralist who is bound to treat frankly but with all decorous propriety a subject of increasing social gravity. The story is that of a man whose bride will not allow his approach on account of her own *liaison* with a female friend continued after marriage. This book appears to have given origin to a large number of novels, which I have not read, and some of which are said to touch the question with considerably less affectation of propriety. Among other novelists of higher rank who have dealt with the matter may be mentioned Guy de Maupassant, Bourget, Daudet, and Catulle Mendès. Among poets who have used the motive of homosexuality in women with more or less boldness may be found Lamartine (*Regina*), Swinburne (first series of *Poems and Ballads*), and Verlaine (*Parallèlement*).

3. As regards Germany, see Moll, *Die Conträre Sexualempfindung*, 2nd ed., p. 315. It is noteworthy that a considerable proportion of the number of cases in which inversion has led to crimes of violence, or otherwise acquired medico-legal importance, has been among women. Perhaps the most widely known example is the Memphis case, which occurred in the United States, and has been studied by Dr. Arthur Macdonald ("Oberservation de Sexualité Pathologique Feminine," *Archives d'Anthropologie Criminelle*, May, 1895). In this case a congenital sexual invert, Alice Mitchell, planned a marriage with Freda Ward, taking a male name and costume. This scheme was frustrated by Freda's sister, and Alice Mitchell then cut Freda's throat. There is no reason to suppose that she was insane at the time of the murder. She was a typical invert of a very pronounced kind. Her mother had been insane and had homicidal impulses. She herself was considered unbalanced, and was masculine in her habits from her earliest years. Her face was obviously unsymmetrical and she had an appearance of youthfulness below her age. She was not vicious, and had little knowledge of sexual matters, but when she kissed Freda she was ashamed of being seen, while Freda could see no reason for being ashamed. Another American case (for some details concerning which I am indebted to Dr. J. G. Kiernan, of Chicago) is that of the "Tiller Sisters," two quinteroons, who for many years had acted together under that name in cheap theatres. One, who was an invert, with a horror of men dating from early girlhood, was sexually attached to the other, who was without inborn perversion, and was eventually induced by a man to leave the invert. The latter, overcome by jealousy, broke into the apartment of the couple, and shot the man dead. She was tried, and sent to prison for life. A defence of insanity was made, but for this there was no evidence.

4. This apparently widespread opinion is represented by the remark of a young man in the last century (concerning the Lesbian friend of the woman he wishes to marry), quoted in the Comte de Tilly's *Souvenirs:* "J'avoue que c'est un genre de rivalité qui ne me donne aucune humeur; au contraire, cela m'amuse et j'ai l'immoralité d'en rire."

5. See H. Ellis, *Man and Woman,* chs xiii and xv.

6. Gandavo, quoted by Lomacco, *Archivie par l'Antropologie*, 1889, fasc. 1.

7. As quoted by Bartels, *Das Weib,* 1895, Bd. 1., p. 390.

8. Corre, *Crime en Pays Creoles*, 1889.

9. In a Spanish prison, not many years ago, when a new governor endeavored to reform the homosexual manners of the women, the latter made his post so uncomfortable that he was compelled to resign. Salillas *Vida Penal en España*, asserts that all the evidence shows the extraordinary expansion of Lesbian love in prisons. The *mujeres hombrunas* receive masculine names—Pepe, Chulo, Bernardo, Valiente; new comers are surrounded in the courtyard by a crowd of lascivious women who overwhelm them with honeyed compliments and gallantries and promises of protection, the most robust virago having most successes; a single day and night complete the initiation. The frequency of sexual manifestations in insane women is well recognised. With reference to homosexual manifestations, I will merely quote the experience of Dr. Venturi in Italy: "In the asylums which I have directed I have found inverted tendencies even more common than have other observers; and the vice is not peculiar to any disease or age, for nearly all insane women, except in acute forms of insanity, are subject to it. Tribadism must thus be regarded as without doubt a real equivalent and substitute for coitus, as these persons frankly regard it, in this unlike paederasty which does not satisfy in insane men the normal sexual desires." (Venturi, *Le Degenerasions psichosessuale,* 1892, p. 148.

10. I quote the following from a private letter written on the Continent: "An English resident has told me that his wife has lately had to send away her parlourmaid (a pretty girl) because she was always taking in strange women to sleep with her. I asked if she had been taken from hotel service and found, as I expected, that she had. But neither my friend nor his wife suspected the real cause of these nocturnal visits."

11. At Wolverhampton, some years ago, the case was reported of a woman in a galvanising "store," who

after dinner indecently assaulted a girl who was a new hand. Two young women held the victim down and this seems to show that homosexual vice was here common and recognized.

12. The most completely recorded case of sexual inversion in a woman is that of the Hungarian Countess Sarolta V., whose false marriage with a young woman attracted much notice in the papers a few years ago. I regard this case as in most respects so typical (excepting only as regards the fraud which led to its publicity) that I have summarized it rather fully in Appendix F., basing my account chiefly on the very full medico-legal report of the case published a few years ago by Dr. C. Birnbacher in *Friedrichs Blätter f. gericht. Med.*

13. A very interesting example of a woman with an irresistible impulse to adopt men's clothing and lead a man's life, but who did not, so far as is known, possess any sexual impulses, is that of Mary Frith, commonly called Moll Cutpurse, who lived in London at the beginning of the seventeenth century. The *Life and Death of Mrs. Mary Frith* appeared in 1662; Middleton and Rowley also made her the heroine of their delightful comedy, *The Roaring Girl* (Mermaid Series, Middleton's Plays, vol. 2), somewhat idealising her, however. She seems to have belonged to a neurotic and eccentric stock; "each of the family," her biographer says, "had his particular freak." As a child she only cared for boy's games, and could never adapt herself to any women's avocations. "She had a natural abhorrence to the tending of children." Her disposition was altogether masculine: "she was not for mincing obscenity, but would talk freely, whatever came uppermost." She never had any children, and was not taxed with debauchery: "No man can say or affirm that ever she had a sweetheart or any such fond thing to dally with her"; a mastiff was the only thing she joyed in. Her life was not altogether honest, but not so much from any organic tendency to crime, it seems, as because her abnormal nature and restlessness made her an outcast. She was too fond of drink, and is said to have been the first woman who smoked tobacco. Nothing is said or suggested of any homosexual practices, but we see clearly here what may be termed the homosexual diathesis. Another and more distinguished instance was Sir James Barry.

14. A few cases have been recorded of inverted women who have spent the greater part of their lives in men's clothing and been generally regarded as men. I may cite the case of Lucy Ann Slater, *alias* the Rev. Joseph Lobdell, recorded by Dr. Wise (*Alienist and Neurologist*, 1883). She was masculine in character, features, and attire. In early life she married and had a child, but had no affection for her husband, who eventually left her. As usual in such cases, her masculine habits appeared in early childhood. She was expert with the rifle, lived the life of a trapper and hunter among the Indians, and was known as the "Female Hunter of Long Eddy." She published a book regarding those experiences. I have not been able to see it, but it is said to be quaint and well written. She regarded herself as practically a man, and became attached to a young woman of good education, who had also been deserted by her husband. The affection was strong and emotional, and of course without deception. It was interrupted by her recognition and imprisonment as a vagabond, but on the petition of her "wife" she was released. "I may be a woman in one sense," she said, "but I have peculiar organs which make me more a man than a woman." She alluded to an enlarged clitoris which she could erect, she said, as a turtle protrudes its head, but there was no question of its use in coitus. She was ultimately brought to the asylum with paroxymal attacks of exaltation and erotamania (without self-abuse apparently) and corresponding periods of depression, and she died with progressive dementia. I may also mention the case (briefly recorded in the *Lancet*, February 22nd, 1884) of a person called John Coulter, who was employed for twelve years as a labourer by the Belfast Harbour Commissioners. When death resulted from injuries caused in falling downstairs, it was found that this person was a woman. She was fifty years of age, and had apparently spent the greater part of her life as a man. When employed in early life as a man-servant on a farm, she had married her mistress's daughter. The pair were married for twenty-nine years, but during the last six years lived apart, owing to the "husband's" dissipated habits. No one ever suspected her sex. She was of masculine appearance and good muscular development. The "wife" took charge of the body and buried it.

15. I may quote a description by Prof. Zuccarelli, of Naples, of an unmarried middle-class woman of thirty-five, the subject of inversion, as being characteristic of this bearing in its most developed form. "While retaining feminine garments her bearing is as nearly as possible a man's. She wears her thin hair thrown carelessly back *alla Umberto*, and fastened in a simple knot at the back of her head. The breasts are little developed, and compressed beneath a high corset; her gown is narrow without the expansion demanded of fashion. Her straw hat with broad plaits is perhaps adorned by a feather or she wears a small hat like

a boy's. She does not carry an umbrella or sunshade, and walks out alone, refusing the company of men; or is accompanied by a woman, as she prefers, offering her arm and carrying the other hand at her waist, with the air of a fine gentleman. In a carriage her bearing is peculiar and unlike that habitual with women. Seated in the middle of the double seat, her knees being crossed or else the legs well separated, with a virile air and careless easy movement she turns her head in every direction, finding an acquaintance here and there with her eye, saluting men and women with a large gesture of the hand as a business man would. In conversation her pose is similar; she gesticulates much, is vivacious in speech, with much power of mimicry, and while talking she arches the inner angles of her eyebrow, making vertical wrinkles at the center of her forehead. Her laugh is open and explosive and uncovers her white rows of teeth. With men she is on terms of careless equality." ("Inversione congenita dell' istino sessuale in una donna" *L'Anomalo*, February, 1889.)

16. It is a mistake to suppose that bearded women approach the masculine type. See Max Bartel's elaborate study, "Ueber abnormal Behaarung heim Menschen," *Zeitschrift fur Ethnologic*, Bd. XIII, 1881, p. 219. And for the same condition in insanity, L. Harris Liston, "Cases of Bearded Women," *British Med. Journal*, June 2nd, 1894.

17. It is noteworthy how many inverted women have, with more or less fraud, been married to the woman of their choice, the couple living happily together for long periods. In one case, which is probably unique, the ceremony was gone through without any deception on any side. A congenitally inverted Englishwoman of distinguished intellectual ability, now dead, was attached to the wife of a clergyman, who, in full cognisance of all the facts of the case, privately married the two ladies in his own church.

18. There are few traces of homosexuality among women in English social history. In Charles II's court, the *Mémoires de Grammont* tell us (as Dr. Kiernan has reminded me), that Miss Hobart was credited with Lesbian tendencies: "Mademoiselle Hobart était d'un caractère aussi nouveau pour lors en Angleterre que sa figure paraissait singulierè dans un pays où, d'être jeune, et de n'être pas plus ou moins belle, est un reproche. Elle avait de la taille, quelque chose de fort délibéré dans l'air, beaucoup d'esprit, et cet esprit était fort orné sans être fort discret. Elle avait beaucoup de vivacité dans une imagination peu réglée, et beaucoup de feu dans des yeux peu touchants. . . . Blentôt le bruit véritable ou faux de cette singularité se répandit dans le cour. On y était assex grossier

pour n'avoir jamais entendu parler de ce raffinement de l'ancienne Grèce sur les goûts de la tendresse, et l'on se mit en tête que l'illustre Hobart, qui paraissait si tendre pour les belles, était quelque chose de plus de ce qu'elle paraissait." The passage is interesting because it shows us how rare was the exception.

19. Even among Arab prostitutes it is found, according to Kocher, though among Arab women generally it is rare.

20. This point of view has been specially emphasized by Lombroso and his followers; see Lombroso and Ferrero, *La Donna Delinquente*. Apart from this, these authors regard homosexuality among prostitutes as due to the following causes (p. 410, *et seq.*):—(a) excessive and often unnatural venery; (b) confinement in a prison, with separation from men; (c) close association with the same sex, such as is common in brothels; (d) maturity and old age, inverting the secondary sexual characters and predisposing to sexual inversion; (e) disgust of men produced by a prostitute's profession, combined with the longing for love.

21. As the three following chapters relate, for the most part, equally to men and to women, I have not in the present chapter discussed those aspects of inversion which are common to both sexes. But I have pleasure in recording here the opinions of Dr. K., a woman physician in the United States (to whom I have acknowledged my indebtedness in the Preface), more especially since they substantially accord with my own independent results. Referring to her special investigations of sexual inversion in women, she writes: "I have always maintained that this phenomenon, wherever found, indicates a psychic condition which can be properly governed, but cannot be eradicated. I believe that it is a condition due to pre-natal influences, possible to defective nutrition in intra-uterine life, if the cause is not still more remote. It is unmistakably a sign of degeneration in the race. Also it is my firm belief that the affections, nervous and other, to which this condition sometimes leads, come as a result of the condition, or of the vices which sometimes accompany it. But such effects are not an inevitable result. Of the eight cases which I have reported to you, seven are perfectly sound, physically, and four are remarkable for their intellectual qualities. . . . As to the value of suggestion, I must confess that the experiments along this line which I have witnessed were not of a nature to arouse any enthusiasm. In all such cases I would recommend that the moral sense be trained and fostered, and the persons allowed to keep their individuality, being taught to remember always that they are different from others, and that they

must not infringe upon the happiness or rights of others, rather sacrificing their own feelings or happiness when necessary. It is good discipline for them, and will serve in the long run to bring them more favour and affection than any other course. This quality or idiosyncrasy is not essentially evil, but, if rightly used, may prove a blessing to others and a power for good in the life of the individual, nor does it reflect any discredit upon its possessor." In a further more recent communication Dr. K. has been good enough to record the general impressions which her study of sexual inversion in women give rise to. (See Appendix G.)

Scientific Racism and the Emergence of the Homosexual Body

Siobhan Somerville

One of the most important insights developed in the fields of lesbian and gay history and the history of sexuality has been the notion that homosexuality and, by extension, heterosexuality are relatively recent inventions in Western culture, rather than transhistorical or "natural" categories of human beings. As Michel Foucault and other historians of sexuality have argued, although sexual acts between two people of the same sex had been punishable through legal and religious sanctions well before the late nineteenth century, they did not necessarily define individuals as homosexual per se.[1] Only recently, in the late nineteenth century, did a new understanding of sexuality emerge, in which sexual acts and desires became constitutive of identity. Homosexuality as the condition, and therefore identity, of particular bodies is thus a production of that historical moment.

Medical literature, broadly defined to include the writings of physicians, sexologists, and psychiatrists, has been integral to this historical argument. Although medical discourse was by no means the only—nor necessarily the most powerful—site of the emergence of new sexual identities, it does nevertheless offer rich sources for at least partially understanding the complex development of these categories in the late nineteenth and early twentieth centuries. Medical and sexological literature not only became one of the few sites of explicit engagement with questions of sexuality during this period but also held substantial definitional power within a culture that sanctioned science to discover and tell the truth about bodies.

As historians and theorists of sexuality have refined a notion of the late nineteenth-century "invention" of the homosexual, their discussions have drawn primarily upon

From the *Journal of the History of Sexuality*, 5:2, pages 243–266 by Siobhan Somerville. Published by University of Texas Press. Reprinted by permission of the author.

theories and histories of gender. George Chauncey, in particular, has provided an invaluable discussion of the ways in which paradigms of sexuality shifted according to changing ideologies of gender during this period.[2] He notes a gradual change in medical models of sexual deviance from a notion of sexual inversion, understood as a reversal of one's sex role, to a model of homosexuality, defined as deviant sexual object choice. These categories and their transformations, argues Chauncey, reflected concurrent shifts in the cultural organization of sex/gender roles within a context of white middle-class gender ideologies.

While gender insubordination offers a powerful explanatory model for the "invention" of homosexuality, ideologies of gender also, of course, shaped and were shaped by dominant constructions of race. Indeed, although it has received little acknowledgment, it is striking that the "invention" of the homosexual occurred at roughly the same time that racial questions were being reformulated, particularly in the United States. This was the moment, for instance, of *Plessy v. Ferguson*, the 1896 U.S. Supreme Court ruling that insisted that "black" and "white" races were "separate but equal." Both a product of and a stimulus to a nationwide and brutal era of racial segregation, this ruling had profound and lasting effects in legitimatizing an apartheid structure that remained legally sanctioned for over half of the twentieth century. The *Plessy* case distilled in legal form many widespread contemporary fears about race and racial difference at the time. A deluge of "Jim Crow" and antimiscegenation laws, combined with unprecedented levels of racial violence, most visibly manifested in widespread lynching, reflected an aggressive attempt to classify and separate bodies as either "black" or "white."

Is it merely a historical coincidence that the classification of bodies as either "homosexual" or "heterosexual" emerged at the same time that the United States was aggressively policing the imaginary boundary between "black" and "white" bodies? Although some historians of sexuality have included brief acknowledgment of nineteenth-century discourses of racial difference, the particular relationship and potentially mutual effects of discourses of homosexuality and race remain unexplored.[3] This silence around race may be due in part to the relative lack of explicit attention to race in medical and sexological literature of the period. These writers did not self-consciously interrogate race, nor were those whose gender insubordination and sexual transgression brought them under the medical gaze generally identified by race in these accounts.[4] Yet the lack of explicit attention to race in these texts does not mean that it was irrelevant to sexologists' endeavors. Given the upheavals surrounding racial definition during this period, it is reasonable to imagine that these texts were as embedded within the contemporary racial ideologies of gender.

Take, for instance, the words of Havelock Ellis, whose massive *Studies in the Psychology of Sex* was one of the most important texts of the late nineteenth-century medical and scientific discourse on sexuality. "I regard sex as the central problem of life," began the general preface to the first volume. Justifying such unprecedented boldness toward the study of sex, Ellis explained, "And now that the problem of religion has practically been settled, and that the problem of labour has at least been placed on a practical foundation, the question of sex—*with the racial questions that rest on it*—stands before the coming generations as the chief problem for solution."[5] Despite Ellis's oddly breezy dismissal of the problems of labor and religion, which were far from settled at the time, this passage points suggestively to a link between sexual and racial anxieties. Yet, what exactly did Ellis mean by "racial questions"? More significantly, what was his sense of the relationship between racial questions and the question of "sex"? Although Ellis himself left those issues unresolved, his elliptical declaration nevertheless suggested that a discourse of race—however elusively—somehow hovered around or within the study of sexuality.

In this article, I offer speculations on how late nineteenth- and early twentieth-century discourses of race and sexuality might not be merely juxtaposed, but brought together in ways that illuminate both. I suggest that the concurrent bifurcations of categories of race and sexuality were not only historically coincident but in fact structurally interdependent and perhaps mutually productive. My goal, however, is not to garner and display unequivocal evidence of the direct influence of racial categories on those who were developing scientific models of homosexuality. Nor am I interested in identifying individual writers and thinkers as racist or not. Rather, my focus here is on racial ideologies, the cultural assumptions and systems of representation about race through which individuals understood their relationships within the world.[6] My emphasis lies in understanding the relationships between the medical/scientific discourse around sexuality and the dominant scientific discourse around race during this period, that is, scientific racism.

My approach combines literary and historical methods of reading, particularly those that have been so crucial to lesbian and gay studies—the technique of reading to hear "the inexplicable presence of the thing not named,"[7] of being attuned to the queer presences and implications in texts that do not otherwise name them. Without this collective project to see, hear, and confirm queer inflections where others would deny their existence, it is arguable that gay and lesbian studies itself, and particularly our knowledge and understanding of the histories, writing, and cultures of lesbians and gay men, would be impoverished, if not impossible. In a similar way, I propose to use the techniques of queer reading, but to modulate my analysis from a focus on sexuality and gender to one alert to racial resonances as well.

My attention, then, is focused on the racial pressure points in exemplary texts from the late nineteenth-century discourse on sexuality, including those written by Ellis and other writers of the period who made explicit references to homosexuality. I suggest that the structures and methodologies that drove dominant ideologies of race also fueled the pursuit of scientific knowledge about the homosexual body: both sympathetic and hostile accounts of homosexuality were steeped in assumptions that had driven previous scientific studies of race.[8] My aim is not to replace a focus on gender and sexuality with that of race but, rather, to understand how discourses of race and gender buttressed one another, often competing, often overlapping, in shaping emerging models of homosexuality.

I suggest three broadly defined ways in which discourses of sexuality seem to have been particularly engaged, sometimes overtly, but largely implicitly, with the discourse of scientific racism. All of these models pathologized both the nonwhite body and the nonheterosexual body to greater or lesser extents. Although I discuss these models in separate sections here, they often coexisted, despite their contradictions. These models are speculative and are intended as a first step toward understanding the myriad and historically specific ways that racial and sexual discourses shaped each other at the moment that homosexuality entered scientific discourse.

Visible Differences: Sexology and Comparative Anatomy

Ellis's *Sexual Inversion*, the first volume of *Studies in the Psychology of Sex* to be published, became a definitive text in late nineteenth-century investigations of homosexuality.[9] Despite the series' titular focus on the psychology of sex, *Sexual Inversion* was a hybrid text, poised in methodology between the earlier field of comparative anatomy, with its procedures of bodily measurement, and the nascent techniques of psychology, with its focus on mental development.[10] In *Sexual Inversion* Ellis hoped to provide scientific authority for the position that homosexuality should be considered not a crime but, rather, a congenital (and thus involuntary) physiological abnormality. Writing *Sexual Inversion* in the wake of England's 1885 Labouchère Amendment, which prohibited "any act of gross indecency" between men, Ellis intended in large part to defend homosexuality from "law and public opinion" which, in his view, combined "to place a heavy penal burden and a severe social stigma on the manifestations of an instinct which to those persons who possess it frequently appears natural and normal."[11] In doing so, Ellis attempted to drape himself in the cultural authority of a naturalist, eager to exert his powers of observation in an attempt to classify and codify understandings of homosexuality.[12]

Like other sexologists, Ellis assumed that the "invert" might be visually distinguishable from the "normal" body through anatomical markers, just as the differences between the sexes had traditionally been mapped upon the body. Yet the study of sexual difference was not the only methodo-

logical precedent for the study of the homosexual body. In its assumptions about somatic differences, I suggest, *Sexual Inversion* also drew upon and participated in a history of the scientific investigation of race.

Race, in fact, became an explicit, though ambiguous, structural element in Ellis's *Sexual Inversion*. In chapter 5, titled "The Nature of Sexual Inversion," Ellis attempted to collate the evidence contained in his collection of case studies, dividing his general conclusions into various analytic categories. Significantly, "Race" was the first category he listed, under which he wrote, "All my cases, 80 in number, are British and American, 20 living in the United States and the rest being British. Ancestry, from the point of view of race, was not made a matter of special investigation" (p. 264). He then listed the ancestries of the individuals whose case studies he included, which he identified as "English . . . Scotch . . . Irish . . . German . . . French . . . Portuguese . . . [and more or less Jewish" (p. 264). He concluded that "except in the apparently frequent presence of the German element, there is nothing remarkable in this ancestry" (p. 264). Ellis used the term "race" in this passage interchangeably with national origin, with the possible exception of Jewish identity. These national identities were perceived to be at least partially biological and certainly hereditary in Ellis's account, though subordinate to the categories "British" and "American." Although he dismissed "ancestry, from the point of view of race" as a significant category, its place as the first topic within the chapter suggested its importance to the structure of Ellis's analysis.[13]

Ellis's ambiguous use of the term "race" was not unusual for scientific discourse during this period, in which it might refer to groupings based variously on geography, religion, class, or color.[14] The use of the term to mean a division of people based on physical (rather than genealogical or national) differences had originated in the late eighteenth century when Johann Friedrich Blumenbach first classified human beings into five distinct groups in *On the Natural Variety of Mankind*. This work in turn became a model for the nineteenth-century fascination with anthropometry, the measurement of the human body.[15] Behind these anatomical measurements lay the assumption that the body was a legible text, with various keys or languages available for reading its symbolic codes. In the logic of biological determinism, the surface and interior of the individual body rather than its social characteristics, such as language, behavior, or clothing, became the primary sites of its meaning. "Every peculiarity of the body has probably some corresponding significance in the mind, and the causes of the former are the remoter causes of the latter," wrote Edward Drinker Cope, a well-known American paleontologist, summarizing the assumptions that fueled the science of comparative anatomy.[16] Although scientists debated which particular anatomical features carried racial meanings—skin, facial angle, pelvis, skull, brain mass, genitalia—nevertheless the theory that anatomy predicted intelligence and behavior remained remarkably constant. As Nancy Stepan and Sander Gilman have noted, "The concepts within racial science were so congruent with social and political life (with power relations, that is) as to be virtually uncontested from inside the mainstream of science."[17]

Supported by the cultural authority of an ostensibly objective scientific method, these readings of the body became a powerful instrument for those seeking to justify the economic and political disenfranchisement of various racial groups within systems of slavery and colonialism. As Barbara Fields has noted, however, "Try as they would, the scientific racists of the past failed to discover any objective criterion upon which to classify people; to their chagrin, every criterion they tried varied more within so-called races than between them."[18] Although the methods of science were considered to be outside the political and economic realm, in fact, as we know, these anatomical investigations, however professedly innocent their intentions, were driven by racial ideologies already firmly in place.[19]

Ideologies of race, of course, shaped and reflected both popular and scientific understandings of gender. As Gilman has argued, "Any attempt to establish that the races were inherently different rested to no little extent on the sexual difference of the black."[20] Although popular racist mythology in the nineteenth-century United States focused on the supposed difference between the size of African-American and white men's genitalia, the male body was not necessarily the primary site of medical inquiry into racial difference.[21] Instead, as a number of medical journals from this period demonstrate, comparative anatomists repeatedly located racial difference through the sexual characteristics of the female body.[22]

In exploring the influence of scientific studies of race on the emerging discourse of sexuality, it is useful to look closely at a study from the genre of comparative anatomy. In 1867, W. H. Flower and James Murie published an "Account of the Dissection of a Bushwoman," which carefully cataloged the various "more perishable soft structures of the body" of a young Bushwoman.[23] They placed their study in a line of inquiry concerning the African woman's body that had begun at least a half-century earlier with French naturalist Georges Cuvier's description of the woman popularly known as the "Hottentot Venus" or Saartje Baartman, who was displayed to European audiences fascinated by her "steatopygia" (protruding buttocks).[24] Significantly, starting with Cuvier, this tradition of comparative anatomy located the boundaries of race through the sexual and reproductive anatomy of the African female body, ignoring altogether the problematic absence of male bodies from their study.

Flower and Murie's account lingered on two specific sites of difference: the "protuberance of the buttocks, so peculiar to the Bushman race" and "the remarkable development of the labia minora," which were "sufficiently well marked to distinguish these parts from those of any ordinary varieties of the human species" (p. 208). The racial difference of the African body, implied Flower and Murie, was located in its literal excess, a specifically sexual excess that placed her body outside the boundaries of the "normal" female. To support their conclusion, Flower and Murie included corroborating "evidence" in the final part of their account. They quoted a secondhand report, "received from a scientific friend residing at the Cape of Good Hope," describing the anatomy of "two pure bred Hottentots, mother and daughter" (p. 208). This account also focused on the women's genitalia, which they referred to as "appendages" (p. 208). Although their account ostensibly foregrounded boundaries of race, their portrayal of the sexual characteristics of the Bushwoman betrayed Flower and Murie's anxieties about gender boundaries. The characteristics singled out as "peculiar" to this race, the (double) "appendages," fluttered between genders, at one moment masculine, at the next moment exaggeratedly feminine. Flower and Murie constructed the site of *racial* difference by marking the sexual and reproductive anatomy of the African woman as "peculiar"; in their charac-

terization, sexual ambiguity delineated the boundaries of race.

The techniques and logic of late nineteenth-century sexologists, who also routinely included physical examinations in their accounts, reproduce the methodologies employed by comparative anatomists like Flower and Murie. Many of the case histories included in Krafft-Ebing's *Psychopathia Sexualis*, for instance, included a paragraph detailing any anatomical peculiarities of the body in question.[25] Although Krafft-Ebing could not draw any conclusions about somatic indicators of "abnormal" sexuality, physical examinations remained a staple of the genre. In Ellis's *Sexual Inversion*, case studies often focused more intensely on the bodies of female "inverts" than those of their male counterparts.[26] Although the specific sites of anatomical inspection (hymen, clitoris, labia, vagina) differed, the underlying theory remained constant: women's genitalia and reproductive anatomy held a valuable and presumably visual key to ranking bodies according to norms of sexuality.

Sexologists reproduced not only the methodologies of the comparative anatomy of races, but also its iconography. One of the most consistent medical characterizations of the anatomy of both African-American women and lesbians was the myth of an unusually large clitoris.[27] As late as 1921, medical journals contained articles declaring that "a physical examination of [female homosexuals] will in practically every instance disclose an abnormally prominent clitoris." Significantly, this author added, "This is particularly so in colored women."[28] In an earlier account of racial differences between white and African-American women, one gynecologist had also focused on the size and visibility of the clitoris; in his examinations, he had perceived a distinction between the "free" clitoris of "negresses" and the "imprisonment" of the clitoris of the "Aryan American woman."[29] In constructing these oppositions, these characterizations literalized the sexual and racial ideologies of the nineteenth-century "Cult of True Womanhood," which explicitly privileged white women's sexual "purity," while it implicitly suggested African-American women's sexual accessibility."[30]

The case histories in Ellis's *Sexual Inversion* differed markedly according to gender in the amount and degree of attention given to the examination of anatomical details. "As regards the sexual organs it seems possible," Ellis wrote, "so far as my observations go, to speak more definitely of inverted women than of inverted men" (p. 256). Ellis justified his greater scrutiny of women's bodies in part by invoking the ambiguity surrounding women's sexuality in general: "we are accustomed to a much greater familiarity and intimacy between women than between men, and we are less apt to suspect the existence of any abnormal passion" (p. 204). To Ellis, the seemingly imperceptible differences between normal and abnormal intimacies between women called for greater scrutiny into the subtleties of their anatomy. He included the following detailed account as potential evidence for understanding the fine line between the lesbian and the "normal" woman:

> *Sexual Organs.*—(a) Internal: Uterus and ovaries appear normal. (b) External: Small clitoris, with this irregularity, that the lower folds of the labia minora, instead of uniting one with the other and forming the frenum, are extended upward along the sides of the clitoris, while the upper folds are poorly developed, furnishing the clitoris with a scant hood. The labia majora depart from normal conformation in being fuller in their posterior half than in their anterior part, so that when the subject is in the supine position they sag, as it were, presenting a slight resemblance to fleshy sacs, but in substance and structure they feel normal. [I. 136]

This extraordinary taxonomy, performed for Ellis by an unnamed "obstetric physician of high standing," echoed earlier anatomical catalogs of African women. The exacting eye (and hand) of the investigating physician highlighted every possible detail as meaningful evidence. Through the triple repetition of "normal" and the use of evaluative language like "irregularity" and "poorly developed," the physician reinforced his position of judgment. Without providing criteria for what constituted "normal" anatomy, the physician simply knew irregularity by sight and touch. Moreover, his characterization of what he perceived as abnormal echoed the anxious account by Flower and Murie. Although the description of the clitoris in this account is a notable exception to the tendency to exaggerate its size, the account nevertheless scrutinized another site of genital excess. The "fleshy sacs" of this woman, like the "appendages" fetishized in the earlier account, invoked the anatomy of a phantom male body inhabiting the lesbian's anatomical features.[31]

Clearly, anxieties about gender shaped both Ellis's and Flower and Murie's taxonomies of the lesbian and the African woman. Yet their preoccupation with gender cannot be understood as separate from the larger context of scientific assumptions during this period, which one historian has characterized as "the full triumph of Darwinism in American thought."[32] Gender, in fact, was crucial to Darwinist ideas. One of the basic assumptions within the Darwinian model was the belief that, as organisms evolved through a process of natural selection, they also showed greater signs of differentiation between the (two) sexes. Following this logic, various writers used sexual characteristics as indicators of evolutionary progress toward civilization. In *Man and*

Woman, for instance, Ellis himself cautiously suggested that since the "beginnings of industrialism," "more marked sexual differences in physical development seem (we cannot speak definitely) to have developed than are usually to be found in savage societies."[33] In this passage, Ellis drew from theories developed by biologists like Patrick Geddes and J. Arthur Thomson. In their important work *The Evolution of Sex*, which traced the role of sexual difference in evolution, Geddes and Thomson stated that "hermaphroditism is primitive; the unisexual state is a subsequent differentiation. The present cases of normal hermaphroditism imply either persistence or reversion."[34] In characterizing either lesbians' or African-American women's bodies as less sexually differentiated than the norm (always posited as white heterosexual women's bodies), anatomists and sexologists drew upon notions of natural selection to dismiss these bodies as anomalous "throwbacks" within a scheme of cultural and anatomical progress.

The Mixed Body

The emergence of evolutionary theory in the late nineteenth century foregrounded a view of continuity between the "savage" and "civilized" races, in contrast to earlier scientific thinking about race, which had focused on debates about the origins of different racial groups. Proponents of monogeny, on the one hand, argued that all races derived from a single origin. Those who argued for polygeny, on the other hand, argued that different races descended from separate biological and geographical sources, a view, not coincidentally, that supported segregationist impulses.[35] With Darwin's publication of *Origin of the Species* in 1859, the debate between polygeny and monogeny was replaced by evolutionary theory, which was appropriated as a powerful scientific model for understanding race. Its controversial innovation was its emphasis on the continuity between animals and human beings. Evolutionary theory held out the possibility that the physical, mental, and moral characteristics of human beings had evolved gradually over time from ape-like ancestors.[36] Although the idea of continuity depended logically on the blurring of boundaries within hierarchies, it did not necessarily invalidate the methods or assumptions of comparative anatomy. On the contrary, the notion of visible differences and racial hierarchies were deployed to corroborate Darwinian theory.

The concept of continuity was harnessed to growing attention to miscegenation, or "amalgamation," in social science writing in the first decades of the twentieth century. Edward Byron Reuter's *The Mulatto in the United States*, for instance, pursued an exhaustive quantitative and comparative study of the mulatto population and its achievements in relation to those of "pure" white or African ancestry. Reuter traced the presence of a distinct group of mixed-race people back to early American history: "Their physical appearance, though markedly different from that of the pure blooded race, was sufficiently marked to set them off as a peculiar people."[37] Reuter, of course, was willing to admit the viability of "mulattoes" only within a framework that emphasized the separation of races. Far from using the notion of the biracial body to refute the belief in discrete markers of racial difference, Reuter perpetuated the notion by focusing on the distinctiveness of this "peculiar people."

Miscegenation was, of course, not only a question of race but also one of sex and sexuality. Ellis recognized this intersection implicitly, if not explicitly. His sense of the "racial questions" implicit in sex was surely informed by his involvement with eugenics, the movement in Britain, Europe, and the

United States that, to greater or lesser degrees, advocated selective reproduction and "race hygiene."[38] In the United States, eugenics was both a political and scientific response to the growth of a population beginning to challenge the dominance of white political interests. The widespread scientific and social interest in eugenics was fueled by anxieties expressed through the popularized notion of (white) "race suicide." This phrase, invoked most famously by Theodore Roosevelt, summed up nativist fears about a perceived decline in reproduction among white Americans. The new field of eugenics worked hand in hand with growing antimiscegenation sentiment and policy, provoked not only by attempts for political representation among African-Americans but also by the influx of large populations of immigrants.[39] As Mark Haller has pointed out, "Racists and [immigration] restrictionists . . . found in eugenics the scientific reassurances they needed that heredity shaped man's personality and that their assumptions rested on biological facts."[40] Ellis saw himself as an advocate for eugenics policies. As an active member of the British National Council for Public Morals, Ellis wrote several publications concerning eugenics, including *The Problem of Race Regeneration*, a pamphlet advocating "voluntary" sterilization of the unfit as a policy in the best interest of "the race."[41] In a letter to Francis Galton in 1907, Ellis wrote, "In the concluding volume of my Sex 'Studies' I shall do what I can to insinuate the eugenic attitude."[42]

The beginnings of sexology, then, were related to and perhaps even dependent on a pervasive climate of eugenicist and antimiscegenation sentiment and legislation. Even at the level of nomenclature, anxieties about miscegenation shaped sexologists' attempts to find an appropriate and scientific name for the newly visible object of their study.

Introduced in 1892 through the English translation of Krafft-Ebing's *Psychopathia Sexualis*, the term "homosexuality" itself stimulated a great deal of uneasiness. In 1915, Ellis reported that "most investigators have been much puzzled in coming to a conclusion as to the best, most exact, and at the same time most colorless names [for same-sex desire]."[43] Giving an account of the various names proposed, such as Ulrichs's "Uranian" and Westphal's "contrary sexual feeling" Ellis admitted that "homosexuality" was the most widespread term used. Far from the ideal "colorless" term, however, "homosexuality" evoked Ellis's distaste for its mixed origins: in a regretful aside, he noted that "it has, philologically, the awkward disadvantage of being a bastard term compounded of Greek and Latin elements" (p. 2). In the first edition of *Sexual Inversion*, Ellis had stated his alarm more directly: "'Homosexual' is a barbarously hybrid word."[44] A similar view was expressed by Edward Carpenter, an important socialist organizer in England and an outspoken advocate of homosexual and women's emancipation at this time. Like Ellis, Carpenter winced at the connotations of illegitimacy in the word: "'homosexual,' generally used in scientific works, is of course a bastard word. 'Homogenic' has been suggested, as being from two roots, both Greek, i.e., 'homos,' same, and 'genos,' sex."[45] Carpenter's suggestion, "homogenic," of course, resonated both against and within the vocabularies of eugenics and miscegenation. Performing these etymological gyrations with almost comic literalism, Ellis and Carpenter expressed pervasive cultural sensitivities around questions of racial origins and purity. Concerned above all with legitimacy, they attempted to remove and rewrite the mixed origins of "homosexuality." Ironically, despite their suggestions for alternatives, the "bastard" term took hold among sexologists, thus yoking together, at least rhetorically, two kinds of mixed bodies— the racial "hybrid" and the invert.

Although Ellis exhibited anxieties about biracial bodies, for others who sought to naturalize and recuperate homosexuality, the evolutionary emphasis on continuity offered potentially useful analogies. Xavier Mayne, for example, one of the earliest American advocates of homosexual rights, wrote, "Between whitest of men and the blackest negro stretches out a vast line of intermediary races as to their colours: brown, olive, red, tawny, yellow."[46] He then invoked this model of race to envision a continuous spectrum of gender and sexuality: "Nature abhors the absolute, delights in the fractional. . . . Intersexes express the half-steps, the between-beings."[47] In this analogy, Mayne reversed dominant cultural hierarchies that privileged purity over mixture. Drawing upon irrefutable evidence of the "natural" existence of biracial people, Mayne posited a direct analogy to a similarly mixed body, the intersex, which he positioned as a necessary presence within the natural order.

Despite Carpenter's complaint about "bastard" terminology, he, like Mayne, also occasionally appropriated the scientific language of racial mixing in order to resist the association between homosexuality and degeneration. In *The Intermediate Sex*, he attempted to theorize homosexuality outside of the discourse of pathology or abnormality; he too suggested a continuum of genders, with "intermediate types" occupying a place between the poles of exclusively heterosexual male and female. In an appendix to *The Intermediate Sex*, Carpenter offered a series of quotations supporting his ideas, some of which drew upon racial analogies: "Anatomically and mentally we find all shades existing from the pure genus man to

the pure genus woman. Thus there has been constituted what is well named by an illustrious exponent of the science 'The Third Sex.' . . . As we are continually meeting in cities women who are one-quarter, or one-eighth, or so on, *male* . . . so there are in the Inner Self similar half-breeds, all adapting themselves to circumstances with perfect ease."[48] Through notions of "shades" of gender and sexual "half-breeds," Carpenter appropriated dominant scientific models of race to construct and embody what he called the intermediate sex. These racial paradigms, in addition to models of gender, offered Carpenter a coherent vocabulary for understanding and expressing a new vision of sexual bodies.

Sexual "Perversion" and Racialized Desire

By the early twentieth century, medical models of sexuality had begun to shift in emphasis, moving away from a focus on the body and toward psychological theories of desire. It seems significant that this shift took place within a period that also saw a transformation of scientific notions about race. As historians have suggested, in the early twentieth century, scientific claims for exclusively biological models of racial difference were beginning to be undermined, although, of course, these models have persisted in popular understandings of race.[49]

In what ways were these shifts away from biologized notions of sexuality and race related in scientific literature? One area in which they overlapped and perhaps shaped one another was through models of interracial and homosexual desire. Specifically, two tabooed sexualities—miscegenation and homosexuality—became linked in sexological and psychological discourse through the model of "abnormal" sexual object choice.

The convergence of theories of "perverse" racial and sexual desire shaped the assumptions of psychologists like Margaret Otis, whose analysis of "A Perversion Not Commonly Noted" appeared in a medical journal of 1913. Otis noted that in all-girl institutions, including reform schools and boarding schools, she had observed widespread "love-making between the white and colored girls."[50] Both fascinated and alarmed, Otis remarked that this perversion was "well known in reform schools and institutions for delinquent girls," but that "this particular form of the homosexual relation has perhaps not been brought to the attention of scientists" (p. 113). Performing her ostensible duty to science, Otis carefully described these rituals of interracial romance and the girls' "peculiar moral code." In particular, she noted that the girls incorporated racial difference into courtship rituals self-consciously patterned on traditional gender roles: "One white girl . . . admitted that the colored girl she loved seemed the man, and thought it was so in the case of the others" (p. 114). In Otis's account, the actions of the girls clearly threatened the keepers of the institutions, who responded to the perceived danger with efforts to racially segregate their charges (who were, of course, already segregated by gender). Otis, however, left open the motivation for segregation: Did the girls' intimacy trouble the authorities because it was homosexual or because it was interracial? Otis avoided exploring this question and offered a succinct theory instead: "The difference in color, in this case, takes the place of difference in sex" (p. 113).

Otis's explicit discussion of racial difference and homosexuality was extremely rare amidst the burgeoning social science literature on sexuality in the early twentieth century.[51] Significantly, Otis characterized this phenomenon as a type of "the homosexual relation" and not as a particular form of interracial sexuality. Despite Otis's focus on desire rather than physiology, her characterization of the schoolgirls' "system" participated in stereotypes based on the earlier anatomical models. She used a simple analogy between race and gender in order to understand their desire: black was to white as masculine was to feminine.

Recent historical work on the lesbian subject in turn-of-the-century America offers useful ways of thinking about the implications of Otis's account, and perhaps in the culture at large. In a compelling analysis of the highly publicized 1892 murder of Freda Ward by her lover, Alice Mitchell, Lisa Duggan has argued that what initially pushed the women's relationship beyond what their peers accepted as normal was Mitchell's decision to pass as a man.[52] Passing, according to Duggan, was "a strategy so rare among bourgeois white women that their plan was perceived as so radically inappropriate as to be insane."[53] Duggan characterizes passing as a kind of red flag that visually marked Mitchell and Ward's relationship. Suddenly, with the prospect of Mitchell's visible transformation from "woman" to "man," the sexual nature of their relationship also came into view—abnormal and dangerous to the eyes of their surveyors.

Following Duggan's line of analysis, I suggest that racial difference performed a similar function in Otis's account. In turn-of-the-century American culture, where Jim Crow segregation erected a structure of taboos against any kind of public (non-work-related) interracial relationship, racial difference visually marked the alliances between the schoolgirls as already suspicious. In a culture in which Ellis could remark that he was accustomed to women being on intimate terms, race became a visible marker for the sexual nature of that liaison. In effect, the institution of racial segregation and its fiction of "black" and "white" produced the girls' interracial romances as "perverse."[54]

It is possible that the discourse of sexual pathology, in turn, began to inform scientific understandings of race. By 1903, a southern physician drew upon the language of sexology to legitimate a particularly racist fear: "A perversion from which most races are exempt, prompt the negro's inclinations towards the white woman, whereas other races incline toward the females of their own."[55] Using the medical language of perversion to naturalize and legitimate the dominant cultural myth of the black rapist, this account characterized interracial desire as a type of congenital abnormal sexual object choice. In the writer's terms, the desire of African-American men for white women (though not the desire of white men for African-American women) could be understood and pathologized by drawing upon emergent models of sexual orientation.[56]

Divergences in Racial and Sexual Science

The inextricability of the "invention" of homosexuality and heterosexuality from the extraordinary pressures attached to racial definition in the late nineteenth century obtained, of course, at a particular historical moment. Although sexologists' search for physical signs of sexual orientation mirrored the methods of comparative racial anatomists, the modern case study marked a significant departure from comparative anatomy by attaching a self-generated narrative to the body in question. As Jeffrey Weeks has written, Krafft-Ebing's *Psychopathia Sexualis* was a decisive moment in the "invention" of the homosexual because "it was the eruption into print of the speaking pervert, the individual marked, or marred, by his (or her) sexual impulses."[57]

The case study challenged the tendency of scientific writers to position the homosexual individual as a mute body whose surface was to be interpreted by those with professional authority. Whether to grant a voice, however limited, to the homosexual body was a heavily contested methodological question among sexologists. The increasingly central position of the case study in the literature on homosexuality elicited concern from contemporary professionals, who perceived an unbridgeable conflict between autobiography and scientific objectivity. Invested in maintaining authority in medical writing, Morton Prince, for example, a psychologist who advocated searching for a "cure" to homosexuality, described in exasperation his basic distrust of the case history as a source of medical evidence, especially in the case of "perverts": "Even in taking an ordinary medical history, we should hesitate to accept such testimony as final, and I think we should be even more cautious in our examination of autobiographies which attempt to give an analysis, founded on introspection, of the feelings, passions and tastes of degenerate individuals who attempt to explain their first beginnings in early childhood."[58] The "speaking pervert," for Prince, was a challenge to the "truth" of medical examination and threatened to contradict the traditional source of medical evidence, the patient's mute physical body as interpreted by the physician. In Prince's view, the case history also blurred the boundaries between the legal and medical spheres: "Very few of these autobiographies will stand analysis. Probably there is no class of people whose statements will less stand the test of a scorching cross-examination than the moral pervert. One cannot help feeling that if the pervert was thus examined by an independent observer, instead of being allowed to tell his own story without interruption, a different tale would be told, or great gaps would be found, which are now nicely bridged, or many asserted facts would be resolved into pure inferences."[59] A "different tale" indeed. Prince's focus on "testimony" and "cross-examination" illustrated the overlapping interest and methods of the medical and the legal spheres. His tableau of litigation placed the homosexual individual within an already guilty body, one that defied the assumption that it was a readable text; its anatomical markers did not necessarily correspond to predictable sexual behaviors. The sure duplicity of this body demanded investigation by the prosecutor/physician, whose professional expertise somehow guaranteed his access to the truth.

Ellis, who sought legitimacy both for himself as a scientist and for the nascent field of sexology, also worried about the association between autobiographical accounts and fraud. In *Sexual Inversion*, he stated that "it may be proper, at this point, to say a few words as to the reliability of the statements furnished by homosexual persons. This has sometimes been called in question" (p. 89). Although he also associated the homosexual voice with duplicity, Ellis differed from Prince by placing this unreliability within a larger social context. He located the causes of insincerity not in the homosexual individual, but in the legal system that barred homosexuality: "we cannot be surprised at this [potential insincerity] so long as inversion is counted a crime. The most normal persons, under similar conditions, would be similarly insincere" (p. 89).

With the movement toward the case study and less biologized psychoanalytic models of sexuality, sexologists relied less and less upon the methodologies of comparative anatomy and implicitly acknowledged that physical characteristics were inadequate evidence for the "truth" of the body in ques-

tion. Yet the assumptions of comparative anatomy did not completely disappear; although they seemed to contradict more psychological understandings of sexuality, notions of biological difference continued to shape cultural understandings of sexuality, particularly in popular representations of lesbians and gay men.

Troubling Science

My efforts here have focused on the various ways that late nineteenth- and early twentieth-century scientific discourses around race became available to sexologists and physicians as a way to articulate emerging models of homosexuality. Methodologies and iconographics of comparative anatomy attempted to locate discrete physiological markers of difference by which to classify and separate types of human beings. Sexologists drew upon these techniques to try to position the "homosexual" body as anatomically distinguishable from the "normal" body. Likewise, medical discourses around sexuality appear to have been steeped in pervasive cultural anxieties toward "mixed" bodies, particularly the mulatto, whose symbolic position as a mixture of black and white bodies was literalized in scientific accounts. Sexologists and others writing about homosexuality borrowed the model of the mixed body as a way to make sense of the "invert." Finally, racial and sexual discourses converged in psychological models that understood "unnatural" desire as a marker of perversion: in these cases, interracial and same-sex sexuality became analogous.

Although scientific and medical models of both race and sexuality held enormous definitional power at the turn of the century, they were variously and complexly incorporated, revised, resisted, or ignored both by the individuals they sought to categorize and within the larger cultural imagination.

My speculations are intended to raise questions and to point toward possibilities for further historical and theoretical work. How, for instance, were analogies between race and sexual orientation deployed or not within popular cultural discourses? In religious discourses? In legal discourses? What were the material effects of their convergence or divergence? How have these analogies been used to organize bodies in other historical moments, and, most urgently, in our own?

In the last few years alone, for example, there has been a proliferation of "speaking perverts"—in political demonstrations, television, magazines, courts, newspapers, and classrooms. Despite the unprecedented opportunities for lesbian, gay, bisexual, and queer speech, however, recent scientific research into sexuality has reflected a determination to discover a biological key to the origins of homosexuality. Highly publicized new studies have purported to locate indicators of sexual orientation in discrete niches of the human body, ranging from a particular gene on the X chromosome to the hypothalamus, a segment of the brain.[60] In an updated and more technologically sophisticated form, comparative anatomy is being granted a peculiar cultural authority in the study of sexuality.

These studies, of course, have not gone uncontested, arriving as they have within a moment characterized not only by the development of social constructionist theories of sexuality but also, in the face of AIDS, by a profound and aching skepticism toward prevailing scientific methods and institutions. At the same time, some see political efficacy in these new scientific studies, arguing that gay men and lesbians might gain access to greater rights if sexual orientation could be proven an immutable biological difference. Such arguments make an analogy, whether explicit or unspoken, to precedents

of understanding race as immutable difference. Reverberating through these arguments are echoes of late nineteenth- and early twentieth-century medical models of sexuality and race, whose earlier interdependence suggests a need to understand the complex relationships between constructions of race and sexuality during our own very different historical moment. How does the current effort to rebiologize sexual orientation and to invoke the vocabulary of immutable difference reflect or influence existing cultural anxieties and desires about racialized bodies? To what extent does the political deployment of these new scientific "facts" about sexuality depend upon reinscribing biologized racial categories? These questions, as I have tried to show for an earlier period, require a shift in the attention and practices of queer reading and lesbian and gay studies, one that locates questions of race as inextricable from the study of sexuality, rather than a part of our peripheral vision.

Notes

1. See, e.g., Michel Foucault, *The History of Sexuality*, vol. 1 (New York, 1980); George Chauncey, "From Sexual Inversion to Homosexuality: Medicine and the Changing Conceptualization of Female Deviance," *Salamagundi*, nos. 58–59 (Fall 1982–Winter 1983), pp. 114–46; Jeffrey Weeks, *Sex, Politics, and Society: The Regulation of Sexuality since 1800* (New York, 1981); David Halperin, "Is There a History of Sexuality?" in *The Lesbian and Gay Studies Reader*, ed. Henry Abelove, Michèle Aina Barale, and David M. Halperin (New York, 1993), pp. 416–31; and Robert Padgug, "Sexual Matters: Rethinking Sexuality in History," *Radical History Review* 20 (Spring/Summer 1979): 3–23. On the invention of the classification of heterosexuality, see Jonathan Katz, "The Invention of Heterosexuality," *Socialist Review* 20 (1990): 17–34. For a related and intriguing argument that locates the earlier emergence of hierarchies of reproductive over nonreproductive sexual activity, see Henry Abelove, "Some Speculations on the History of 'Sexual Intercourse' during the 'Long

Eighteenth Century' in England," *Genders* 6 (1989): 125–30.

2. Chauncey.

3. David Halperin has briefly and provocatively suggested that "all scientific inquiries into the aetiology of sexual orientation, after all, spring from a more or less implicit theory of sexual races, from the notion that there exist broad general divisions between types of human beings corresponding, respectively, to those who make a homosexual and those who make a heterosexual object-choice. When the sexual racism underlying such inquiries is more plainly exposed, their rationale will suffer proportionately—or so one may hope," in "Homosexuality: A Cultural Construct," in his *One Hundred Years of Homosexuality: And Other Essays on Greek Love* (New York, 1990), p. 50. In a recent article, Abdul R. JanMohammed offers a useful analysis and critique of Foucault's failure to examine the intersection of the discourse of sexuality and race. See his "Sexuality on/of the Racial Border: Foucault, Wright, and the Articulation of 'Racialized Sexuality,'" in *Discourses of Sexuality: From Aristotle to AIDS,* ed. Domna C. Stanton (Ann Arbor, MI, 1992), pp. 94–116. I explore a different (though related) set of questions in this article.

4. In *Disorders of Desire: Sex and Gender in Modern American Sexology* (Philadelphia, 1990), Janice Irvine notes that, e.g., "the invisibility of Black people in sexology as subjects or researchers has undermined our understanding of the sexuality of Black Americans and continues to be a major problem in modern sexology." She adds that Kinsey, the other major sexologist of the twentieth century, planned to include a significant proportion of African-American case histories in his *Sexual Behavior in the Human Male* (1948) and *Sexual Behavior in the Human Female* (1953) but failed to gather a sufficient number of them, and so "unwittingly colluded in the racial exclusion so pervasive in sex research" (p. 43).

5. Havelock Ellis, *Studies in the Psychology of Sex*, vol. 1, *Sexual Inversion* (1897; London, 1900), x; emphasis added.

6. My use of the concept of ideology draws upon Barbara Fields, "Slavery, Race, and Ideology in the United States of America," *New Left Review* 181 (1990): 95–118; Louis Althusser, "Ideology and Ideological State Apparatuses (Notes towards an Investigation)," in his *Lenin and Philosophy and Other Essays,* trans. Ben Brewster (New York, 1971), pp. 121–73; and Teresa de Lauretis, "The Technology of Gender," in her *Technologies of Gender: Essays on Theory, Film, and Fiction* (Bloomington, IN, 1987), pp. 1–30.

7. I borrow this phrase from Willa Cather's essay, "The Novel Démeublé," in her *Not under Forty* (New York, 1922), p. 50.

8. I am not implying, however, that racial anxieties caused the invention of the homosexual, nor that the invention of the homosexual caused increased racial anxieties. Both of these causal arguments seem simplistic and, further, depend upon separating the discourses of race and sexuality, whose convergence, in fact, I am eager to foreground.

9. Havelock Ellis, *Studies in the Psychology of Sex*, vol. 2, *Sexual Inversion*, 3d ed. (Philadelphia, 1915). Further references to this edition will be noted parenthetically unless otherwise stated. Although *Sexual Inversion* was published originally as vol. 1, Ellis changed its position to vol. 2 in the 2d and 3d eds., published in the United States in 1901 and 1915, respectively. In the later editions, vol. 1 became *The Evolution of Modesty*. Ellis originally coauthored *Sexual Inversion* with John Addington Symonds. For a discussion of their collaboration and the eventual erasure of Symonds from the text, see Wayne Koestenbaum, *Double Talk: The Erotics of Male Literary Collaboration* (New York, 1989), pp. 43–67.

10. In "Sex and the Emergence of Sexuality," *Critical Inquiry* 14 (Autumn 1987): 16–48, Arnold I. Davidson characterizes Ellis's method as "psychiatric" (as opposed to "anatomical") reasoning. Arguing that "sexuality itself is a product of the psychiatric style of reasoning" (p. 23), Davidson explains, "the iconographical representation of sex proceeds by depiction of the body, more specifically by depiction of the genitalia. The iconographical representation of sexuality is given by depiction of the personality, and it most usually takes the form of depiction of the face and its expressions" (p. 27). The case studies in *Sexual Inversion*, and especially those of women, however, tend to contradict this broad characterization. My understanding of Ellis differs from that of Davidson, who readily places Ellis in a psychiatric model; instead, Ellis might be characterized as a transitional figure, poised at the crossroads between the fields of comparative anatomy and psychiatry. To borrow Davidson's terms, anatomical reasoning does not disappear; it stays in place, supporting psychiatric reasoning.

11. Ellis, *Sexual Inversion* (1900), xi. Ironically, upon publication in 1897 *Sexual Inversion* was judged to be not a scientific work, but "a certain lewd, wicked, bawdy, scandalous libel"; effectively banned in England, subsequent copies were published only in the United States. See Jeffrey Weeks, "Havelock Ellis and the Politics of Sex Reform," in Sheila Rowbotham and Jeffrey Weeks, *Socialism and the New Life: The Personal and Sexual Politics of Edward Carpenter and*

Havelock Ellis (London, 1977), p. 154; and Phyllis Grosskurth, *Havelock Ellis: A Biography* (New York, 1980), pp. 191–204.

12. For further discussion of Ellis's similarity to Charles Darwin as a naturalist and their mutual interest in "natural" modesty, see Ruth Bernard Yeazell, "Nature's Courtship Plot in Darwin and Ellis," *Yale Journal of Criticism* 2 (1989): 33–53.

13. Elsewhere in *Sexual Inversion*, Ellis entertained the idea that certain races or nationalities had a "special proclivity" to homosexuality (p. 4), but he seemed to recognize the nationalistic impulse behind this argument and chided those who wielded it: "The people of every country have always been eager to associate sexual perversions with some other country than their own" (pp. 57–58).

14. Classic discussions of the term's history include Peter 1. Rose, *The Subject Is Race* (New York, 1968), pp. 30–43; and Thomas F. Gossett, *Race: The History of an Idea in America* (Dallas, 1963). For a history of various forms and theories of biological determinism, see Stephen Jay Gould, *The Mismeasure of Man* (New York, 1981).

15. John S. Haller, Jr., *Outcasts from Evolution: Scientific Attitudes of Racial Inferiority, 1859–1900* (Urbana, IL, 1971), p. 4.

16. Quoted in ibid., p. 196. On Cope, see also Gould, *The Mismeasure of Man*, pp. 115–18.

17. Nancy Leys Stepan and Sander Gilman, "Appropriating the Idioms of Science: The Rejection of Scientific Racism," in *The Bounds of Race: Perspectives on Hegemony and Resistance*, ed. Dominick LaCapra (Ithaca, NY, 1991), p. 74.

18. Fields (n. 6 above), p. 97, n. 3.

19. John Haller, p. 48.

20. Sander Gilman, *Difference and Pathology: Stereotypes of Sexuality, Race, and Madness* (Ithaca, NY, 1985), p. 112.

21. According to Gilman, "When one turns to autopsies of black males from [the late nineteenth century], what is striking is the absence of any discussion of the male genitalia" (p. 89). The specific absence of male physiology as a focus of nineteenth-century scientific texts, however, should not minimize the central location of the African-American male body in popular cultural notions of racial difference, esp. in the spectacle of lynching, which had far-reaching effects on both African-American and white attitudes toward the African-American male body. One might also consider the position of the racialized male body in one of the most popular forms of nineteenth-century entertainment, the minstrel show. See Eric Lott, *Love and Theft: Blackface Minstrelsy and the American Working Class* (New York, 1993).

22. The *American Journal of Obstetrics* (*AJO*) was a frequent forum for these debates. On the position of the hymen, e.g., see C. H. Fort, "Some Corroborative Facts in Regard to the Anatomical Difference between the Negro and White Races," *AJO* 10 (1877): 258–259; H. Otis Hyatt, "Note on the Normal Anatomy of the Vulvo-Vaginal Orifice," *AJO* 10 (1877): 253–58; A. G. Smythe, "The Position of the Hymen in the Negro Race," *AJO* 10 (1877): 638–39; Edward Turnipseed, "Some Facts in Regard to the Anatomical Differences between the Negro and White Races," *AJO* 10 (1877): 32–33. On the birth canal, see Joseph Tabor Johnson, "On Some of the Apparent Peculiarities of Parturition in the Negro Race, with Remarks on Race Pelves in General," *AJO* 8 (1875): 88–123. This focus on women's bodies apparently differed from earlier studies. In her recent work on gender and natural history, Londa Schiebinger discusses how eighteenth-century comparative anatomists and anthropologists developed their theories by examining male bodies. See *Nature's Body: Gender in the Making of Modern Science* (Boston, 1993), esp. pp. 143–83.

23. W. H. Flower and James Murie, "Account of the Dissection of a Bushwoman," *Journal of Anatomy and Physiology* 1 (1887): 208. Subsequent references will be noted parenthetically within the text. Flower was the conservator of the Museum of the Royal College of Surgeons of England; Murie was prosecutor to the Zoological Society of London. For brief discussions of this account, see Gilman, pp. 88–89; and Anita Levy, *Other Women: The Writing of Class, Race, and Gender, 1832–1898* (Princeton, NJ, 1991), pp. 70–72. Although she does not consider questions surrounding the lesbian body, Levy offers an astute reading of this case and its connection to scientific representations of the body of the prostitute.

24. Georges Cuvier, "Extraits d'observations faites sur le cadavre d'une femme connue à Paris et à Londres sous le nom de Vénus Hottentote," *Memoires du Musée d'histoire naturelle* 3 (1817): 259–74. After her death in 1815 at the age of 25, Baartman's genitalia were preserved and redisplayed within the scientific space of the Musée de l'Homme in Paris. On Baartman, see Schiebinger, *Nature's Body*, pp. 160–72; and Stephen Jay Gould, *The Flamingo's Smile* (New York, 1985), pp. 291–305.

25. Richard von Krafft-Ebing, *Psychopathia Sexualis*, 12th ed., trans. Franklin S. Klaf (1903; reprint, New York, 1965).

26. This practice continued well into the twentieth century. See, e.g., Jennifer Terry's discussion of the anatomical measurement of lesbians by the Committee for the Study of Sex Variants in the

1930s, in "Lesbians under the Medical Gaze: Scientists Search for Remarkable Differences," *Journal of Sex Research* 27 (August 1990): 317–39, and "Theorizing Deviant Historiography," *Differences 3* (Summer 1991): 55–74.

27. In the first edition of *Sexual Inversion*, Ellis, who did search the lesbian body for masculine characteristics, nevertheless refuted this claim about the clitoris: "there is no connection, as was once supposed, between sexual inversion and an enlarged clitoris" (p. 98).

28. Perry M. Lichtenstein, "The 'Fairy' and the Lady Lover," *Medical Review of Reviews* 27 (1921): 372. In "Lesbians under the Medical Gaze," Terry discusses sexologist's conjectures about the size of lesbians' genitalia in a report published in 1941. Researchers were somewhat uncertain whether perceived excesses were congenital or the result of particular sex practices. On the history of scientific claims about the sexual function of the clitoris, see Thomas Laqueur, *Making Sex: Body and Gender from the Greeks to Freud* (Cambridge, MA 1990), pp. 233–37.

29. Morris, "Is Evolution Trying to Do Away with the Clitoris?" (paper presented at the meeting of the American Association of Obstetricians and Gynecologists, St. Louis, September 21, 1892), Yale University Library, New Haven, CT.

30. See Hazel Carby, *Reconstructing Womanhood: The Emergence oft the Afro-American Woman Novelist* (New York, 1987), pp. 20–39; and Barbara Welter, "The Cult of True Womanhood, 1820–1860," in her *Dimity Convictions: The American Woman in the Nineteenth Century* (Columbus, OH, 1976), pp. 21–41.

31. Characterizing this passage as "punitively complete," Koestenbaum (n. 9 above) has suggested that Ellis also had personal motivations for focusing so intently on the lesbian body: "Ellis, by taking part in this over-description of a lesbian, studied and subjugated the preference of his own wife; marrying a lesbian, choosing to discontinue sexual relations with her, writing *Sexual Inversion* with a homosexual [Symonds], Ellis might well have felt his own heterosexuality questioned" (pp. 54, 55).

32. George Fredrickson, *The Black Image in the White Mind: The Debate on Afro-American Character and Destiny, 1817–1914* (New York, 1971), p. 246.

33. Havelock Ellis, *Man and Woman: A Study of Human Secondary Sexual Characters* (1894; New York, 1911), p. 13. Of course, the "beginnings of industrialism" coincided with the late eighteenth century, the period during which, as Schiebinger has shown, anatomists began looking for more subtle marks of differentiation. See Londa Schiebinger, *The Mind Has No Sex? Women in the Origins of Modern Science* (Cambridge, MA, 1989), pp. 189–212.

34. Patrick Geddes and J. Arthur Thomson, *The Evolution of Sex* (London, 1889; New York, 1890), p. 80. Ellis no doubt read this volume closely, for he had chosen it to inaugurate a series of popular scientific books (the Contemporary Science Series) that he edited for the Walter Scott company. For more on this series, see Grosskurth (n. above), pp. 114–17.

35. For a full account of the debates around monogeny and polygeny, see Gould, *The Mismeasure of Man* (n. 14 above), pp. 30–72. Polygeny was a predominantly American theoretical development and was widely referred to as the "American school' of anthropology.

36. See Nancy Stepan, *The Idea of Race in Science: Great Britain, 1800–1960* (Hamden, CT, 1982), p. 53.

37. Edward Byron Reuter, *The Mulatto in the United States: Including a Study of the Role of Mixed-Blood Races throughout the World* (Boston, 1918), p. 338. Interestingly, in a paper delivered to the Eugenics Society of Britain in 1911, Edith Ellis (who had at least one long-term lesbian relationship while she was married to Havelock Ellis) had also used the phrase "peculiar people" to describe homosexual men and women. See Grosskurth, pp. 237–38.

38. Francis Galton (a cousin of Charles Darwin) introduced and defined the term "eugenics" in his *Inquiries into Human Faculty and Its Development* as "the cultivation of the race" and "the science of improving stock, which . . . takes cognisance of all influences that tend in however remote a degree to give to the more suitable races or strains of blood a better chance of prevailing speedily over the less suitable than they otherwise would have had" (1883; reprint, New York, 1973).

39. For a discussion of Roosevelt's place within the racial ideology of the period, see Thomas G. Dyer, *Theodore Roosevelt and the Idea of Race* (Baton Rouge, LA, 1980). See also John Higham, *Strangers in the Land: Patterns of American Nativism, 1860–1925* (New York, 1955; reprint, 1963), pp. 146–57.

40. Mark H. Haller, *Eugenics: Hereditarian Attitudes in American Thought* (New Brunswick, NJ, 1963), p. 144.

41. Jeffrey Weeks, *Sexuality and Its Discontents: Meanings, Myths, and Modern Sexualities* (Boston, 1985), p. 76; Grosskruth, p. 410. See also Havelock Ellis, "The Sterilization of the Unfit," *Eugenics Review* (October 1909): 203–6.

42. Quoted by Grosskurth, p. 410.

43. Ellis, *Sexual Inversion* (1915), p. 2.

44. Ellis, *Sexual Inversion* (1900), p. 1n.

45. Edward Carpenter, "The Homogenic Attachment," in his *The Intermediate Sex: A Study of Some Transitional Types of Men and Women*, 5th ed. (London, 1918), p. 40n.

46. Xavier Mayne [Edward Irenaeus Prime Stevenson], *The Intersexes: A History of Similisexualism as A Problem in Social Life* [Naples?], ca. 1908; reprint, New York, 1975), p. 14.

47. Ibid., pp. 15, 17.

48. Quoted in Carpenter, *The Intermediate Sex*, pp. 133, 170. Carpenter gives the following citations for these quotations: Dr. James Burnet, *Medical Times and Hospital Gazette*, vol. 34, no. 1497 (London, November 10, 1906); and Charles G. Leland, "The Alternate Sex" (London, 1904), pp. 41, 57.

49. In *New People: Miscegenation and Mulattoes in the United States* (New York, 1980), Joel Williamson suggests that a similar psychologization of race was underway: "By about 1900 it was possible in the South for one who was biologically purely white to become behaviorally black. Blackness had become not a matter of visibility, not even, ironically, of the one-drop rule. It had passed on to become a matter of inner morality and outward behavior" (p. 108). See also Elazar Barkan, *The Retreat of Scientific Racism: Changing Concepts of Race in Britain and the United States between the World Wars* (New York, 1992). Legal scholars have begun to explore the analogies between sodomy law and antimiscegenation statutes. See, e.g., Andrew Koppelman, "The Miscegenation Analogy: Sodomy Law as Sex Discrimination," *Yale Law Journal* 98 (November 1988): 145–64. See also Janet Halley, "The Politics of the Closet: Towards Equal Protection for Gay, Lesbian, and Bisexual Identity," *UCLA Law Review* 36 (1989): 915–76. I am grateful to Julia Friedlander for bringing this legal scholarship to my attention.

50. Margaret Otis, "A Perversion Not Commonly Noted," *Journal of Abnormal Psychology* 8 (June–July 1913): 113–16. Subsequent references will be noted parenthetically within the text.

51. Chauncey (n. 1 above) notes that "by the early teens the number of articles of abstracts concerning homosexuality regularly available to the American medical profession had grown enormously" (p. 115, n. 3).

52. Lisa Duggan, "The Trials of Alice Mitchell: Sensationalism, Sexology, and the Lesbian Subject in Turn-of-the-Century America," *Signs: Journal of Women in Culture and Society* 18 (Summer 1993): 791–814.

53. Ibid., p. 798.

54. In a useful discussion of recent feminist analyses of identity, Lisa Walker suggests that a similar trope of visibility is prevalent in white critics' attempts to theorize race and sexuality. See her "How to Recognize a Lesbian: The Cultural Politics of Looking Like What You Are," *Signs: Journal of Women in Culture and Society* 18 (Summer 1993): 866–90.

55. W. T. English, "The Negro Problem from the Physician's Point of View," *Atlanta Journal-Record of Medicine* 5 (October 1903): 468.

56. On the other hand, antilynching campaigns could also invoke the language of sexology. Although the analogy invoked sadism, rather than homosexuality, in 1935 a psychologist characterized lynching as a kind of "Dixie sex perversion. . . . Much that is commonly stigmatized as cruelty is a perversion of the sex instinct." Quoted in Phyllis Klotman, "'Tearing a Hole in History': Lynching as Theme and Motif," *Black American Literature Forum* 19 (1985): 57. The original quote appeared in the *Baltimore Afro-American* (March 16, 1935).

57. Weeks, *Sexuality and Its Discontents* (n. 41 above), p. 67. Weeks points out that beginning with Krafft-Ebing's *Psychopathia Sexualis* (n. 25 above), the case study became the standard in sexological writing. The dynamic between the medical literature and a growing self-identified gay (male) subculture is exemplified by the growth of different editions of this single work. The first edition of *Psychopathia Sexualis*, published in 1886, contained forty-five case histories and 110 pages; by 1903, the twelfth edition contained 238 case histories and 437 pages. Many of the subsequent case histories were supplied by readers who responded to the book with letters detailing their own sexual histories. This information suggests that, to at least some extent, an emerging gay male subculture was able to appropriate the space of "professional" medicolegal writing for its own use, thus blurring the boundaries between professional medical and popular literature.

58. Morton Prince, "Sexual Perversion or Vice? A Pathological and Therapeutic Inquiry," *Journal of Nervous and Mental Disease* 25 (April 1898): 237–56, reprinted in his *Psychotherapy and Multiple Personality: Selected Essays*, ed. Nathan G. Hale (Cambridge, MA, 1975), p. 91.

59. Prince, *Psychotherapy and Multiple Personality*, p. 92.

60. See, e.g., Natalie Angier, "Report Suggests Homosexuality Is Linked to Genes," *New York Times* (July 16, 1993, pp. A1, A12 and "Zone of Brian Linked to Men's Sexual Orientation," *New York Times* (August 30, 1991), pp. A1, D8. See also Simon LeVay, *The Sexual Brain* (Cambridge, MA, 1993).

What It Means to Be Gendered Me:
Life on the Boundaries of a Dichotomous Gender System

Betsy Lucal

I understood the concept of "doing gender" (West and Zimmerman 1987) long
before I became a sociologist. I have been
living with the consequences of inappropriate "gender display" (Goffman 1976; West
and Zimmerman 1987) for as long as I can
remember.

My daily experiences are a testament to
the rigidity of gender in our society, to the
real implications of "two and only two"
when it comes to sex and gender categories
(Garfinkel 1967; Kessler and McKenna
1978). Each day, I experience the consequences that our gender system has for my
identity and interactions. I am a woman who
has been called "Sir" so many times that I
no longer even hesitate to assume that it is
being directed at me. I am a woman whose
use of public rest rooms regularly causes
reactions ranging from confused stares to
confrontations over what a man is doing in
the women's room. I regularly enact a variety of practices either to minimize the need
for others to know my gender or to deal with
their misattributions.

I am the embodiment of Lorber's (1994)
ostensibly paradoxical assertion that the
"gender bending" I engage in actually might
serve to preserve and perpetuate gender
categories. As a feminist who sees gender
rebellion as a significant part of her contribution to the dismantling of sexism, I find
this possibility disheartening.

In this article, I examine how my experiences both support and contradict Lorber's
(1994) argument using my own experiences
to illustrate and reflect on the social construction of gender. My analysis offers a
discussion of the consequences of gender
for people who do not follow the rules as
well as an examination of the possible implications of the existence of people like me
for the gender system itself. Ultimately, I
show how life on the boundaries of gender

Betsy Lucal, *Gender and Society*, December 1999, pages 781–797. Copyright 1999 Sage Publications. Reprinted
by permission of Sage Publications, Inc.

affects me and how my life, and the lives of others who make similar decisions about their participation in the gender system, has the potential to subvert gender.

Because this article analyzes my experiences as a woman who often is mistaken for a man, my focus is on the social construction of gender for women. My assumption is that, given the gendered nature of the gendering process itself, men's experiences of this phenomenon might well be different from women's.

The Social Construction of Gender

It is now widely accepted that gender is a social construction, that sex and gender are distinct, and that gender is something all of us "do." This conceptualization of gender can be traced to Garfinkel's (1967) ethnomethodological study of "Agnes."[1] In this analysis, Garfinkel examined the issues facing a male who wished to pass as, and eventually become, a woman. Unlike individuals who perform gender in culturally expected ways, Agnes could not take her gender for granted and always was in danger of failing to pass as a woman (Zimmerman 1992).

This approach was extended by Kessler and McKenna (1978) and codified in the classic "Doing Gender" by West and Zimmerman (1987). The social constructionist approach has been developed most notably by Lorber (1994, 1996). Similar theoretical strains have developed outside of sociology, such as work by Butler (1990) and Weston (1996). Taken as a whole, this work provides a number of insights into the social processes of gender, showing how gender(ing) is, in fact, a process.

We apply gender labels for a variety of reasons; for example, an individual's gender cues our interactions with her or him. Successful social relations require all participants to present, monitor, and interpret gender displays (Martin 1998; West and Zimmerman 1987). We have, according to Lorber, "no social place for a person who is neither woman nor man" (1994, 96); that is, we do not know how to interact with such a person. There is, for example, no way of addressing such a person that does not rely on making an assumption about the person's gender ("Sir" or "Ma'am"). In this context, gender is "omnirelevant" (West and Zimmerman 1987). Also, given the sometimes fractious nature of interactions between men and women, it might be particularly important for women to know the gender of the strangers they encounter; do the women need to be wary, or can they relax (Devor 1989)?

According to Kessler and McKenna (1978), each time we encounter a new person, we make a gender attribution. In most cases, this is not difficult. We learn how to read people's genders by learning which traits culturally signify each gender and by learning rules that enable us to classify individuals with a wide range of gender presentations into two and only two gender categories. As Weston observed, "Gendered traits are called attributes for a reason: People attribute traits to others. No one possesses them. Traits are the product of evaluation" (1996, 21). The fact that most people use the same traits and rules in presenting genders makes it easier for us to attribute genders to them.

We also assume that we can place each individual into one of two mutually exclusive categories in this binary system. As Bern (1993) notes, we have a polarized view of gender; there are two groups that are seen as polar opposites. Although there is "no rule for deciding 'male' or 'female' that will always work" and no attributes "that always and without exception are true of only one gender" (Kessler and McKenna 1978, 158,

1), we operate under the assumption that there are such rules and attributes.

Kessler and McKenna's analysis revealed that the fundamental schema for gender attribution is to "See someone as female only when you cannot see [the person] as male" (1978, 158). Individuals basically are assumed to be male/men until proven otherwise, that is, until some obvious marker of conventional femininity is noted. In other words, the default reading of a nonfeminine person is that she or he is male; people who do not deliberately mark themselves as feminine are taken to be men. Devor attributed this tendency to the operation of gender in a patriarchal context: "Women must mark themselves as 'other'," whereas on the other hand, "few cues [are required] to identify maleness" (1989, 152). As with language, masculine forms are taken as the generically human; femininity requires that something be added. Femininity "must constantly reassure its audience by a willing demonstration of difference" (Brownmiller 1984, 15).

Patriarchal constructs of gender also devalue the marked category. Devor (1989) found that the women she calls "gender blenders" assumed that femininity was less desirable than masculinity; their gender blending sometimes was a product of their shame about being women. This assumption affects not only our perceptions of other people but also individuals' senses of their own gendered selves.

Not only do we rely on our social skills in attributing genders to others, but we also use our skills to present our own genders to them. The roots of this understanding of how gender operates lie in Goffman's (1959) analysis of the "presentation of self in everyday life," elaborated later in his work on "gender display" (Goffman 1976). From this perspective, gender is a performance, "a stylized repetition of acts" (Butler 1990, 140, emphasis removed). Gender dis-

play refers to "conventionalized portrayals" of social correlates of gender (Goffman 1976). These displays are culturally established sets of behaviors, appearances, mannerisms, and other cues that we have learned to associate with members of a particular gender.

In determining the gender of each person we encounter and in presenting our genders to others, we rely extensively on these gender displays. Our bodies and their adornments provide us with "texts" for reading a person's gender (Bordo 1993). As Lorber noted, "Without the deliberate use of gendered clothing, hairstyles, jewelry, and cosmetics, women and men would look far more alike" (1994, 18–19). Myhre summarized the markers of femininity as "having longish hair; wearing makeup, skirts, jewelry, and high heels; walking with a wiggle; having little or no observable body hair; and being in general soft, rounded (but not too rounded), and sweet-smelling" (1995, 135). (Note that these descriptions comprise a Western conceptualization of gender.) Devor identified "mannerisms, language, facial expressions, dress, and a lack of feminine adornment" (1989, x) as factors that contribute to women being mistaken for men.

A person uses gender display to lead others to make attributions regarding her or his gender, regardless of whether the presented gender corresponds to the person's sex or gender self-identity. Because gender is a social construction, there may be differences among one's sex, gender self-identity (the gender the individual identifies as), presented identity (the gender the person is presenting), and perceived identity (the gender others attribute to the person).[2] For example, a person can be female without being socially identified as a woman, and a male person can appear socially as a woman. Using a feminine gender display, a man can present the identity of a woman and, if the display is successful, be perceived as a woman.

But these processes also mean that a person who fails to establish a gendered appearance that corresponds to the person's gender faces challenges to her or his identity and status. First, the gender nonconformist must find a way in which to construct an identity in a society that denies her or him any legitimacy (Bem 1993). A person is likely to want to define herself or himself as "normal" in the face of cultural evidence to the contrary. Second, the individual also must deal with other people's challenges to identity and status—deciding how to respond, what such reactions to their appearance mean, and so forth.

Because our appearances, mannerisms, and so forth constantly are being read as part of our gender display, we do gender whether we intend to or not. For example, a woman athlete, particularly one participating in a nonfeminine sport such as basketball, might deliberately keep her hair long to show that, despite actions that suggest otherwise, she is a "real" (i.e., feminine) woman. But we also do gender in less conscious ways such as when a man takes up more space when sitting than a woman does. In fact, in a society so clearly organized around gender, as ours is, there is no way in which to not do gender (Lorber 1994).

Given our cultural rules for identifying gender (i.e., that there are only two and that masculinity is assumed in the absence of evidence to the contrary), a person who does not do gender appropriately is placed not into a third category but rather into the one with which her or his gender display seems most closely to fit; that is, if a man appears to be a woman, then he will be categorized as "woman," not as something else. Even if a person does not want to do gender or would like to do a gender other than the two

recognized by our society, other people will, in effect, do gender for that person by placing her or him in one and only one of the two available categories We cannot escape doing gender or, more specifically, doing one of two genders. (There are exceptions in limited contexts such as people doing "drag" [Butler 1990, Lorber 1994].)

People who follow the norms of gender can take their genders for granted. Kessler and McKenna asserted, "Few people besides transsexuals think of their gender as anything other than 'naturally' obvious"; they believe that the risks of not being taken for the gender intended "are minimal for nontranssexuals" (1978, 126). However, such an assertion overlooks the experiences of people such as those women Devor (1989) calls "gender blenders" and those people Lorber (1994) refers to as "gender benders." As West and Zimmerman (1987) pointed out, we all are held accountable for, and might be called on to account for, our genders.

People who, for whatever reasons, do not adhere to the rules, risk gender misattribution and any interactional consequences that might result from this misidentification. What are the consequences of misattribution for social interaction? When must misattribution be minimized? What will one do to minimize such mistakes? In this article, I explore these and related questions using my biography.

For me, the social processes and structures of gender mean that, in the context of our culture, my appearance will be read as masculine. Given the common conflation of sex and gender, I will be assumed to be a male. Because of the two-and-only-two genders rule, I will be classified, perhaps more often than not, as a man—not as an atypical woman, not as a genderless person. I must be one gender or the other; I cannot be neither, nor can I be both. This norm has a variety of mundane and serious consequences for my everyday existence. Like Myhre (1995), I have found that the choice not to participate in femininity is not one made frivolously.

My experiences as a woman who does not do femininity illustrate a paradox of our two-and-only-two gender system. Lorber argued that "bending gender rules and passing between genders does not erode but rather preserves gender boundaries" (1994, 21). Although people who engage in these behaviors and appearances do "demonstrate the social constructedness of sex, sexuality, and gender" (Lorber 1994, 96), they do not actually disrupt gender. Devor made a similar point: "When gender blending females refused to mark themselves by publicly displaying sufficient femininity to be recognized as women, they were in no way challenging patriarchal gender assumptions" (1989, 142). As the following discussion shows, I have found that my own experiences both support and challenge this argument. Before detailing these experiences, I explain my use of my self as data.

My Self as Data

This analysis is based on my experiences as a person whose appearance and gender/sex are not, in the eyes of many people, congruent. How did my experiences become my data? I began my research "unwittingly" (Krieger 1991). This article is a product of "opportunistic research" in that I am using my "unique biography, life experiences, and/or situational familiarity to understand and explain social life" (Riemer 1988, 121; see also Riemer 1977). It is an analysis of "unplanned personal experience," that is, experiences that were not part of a research project but instead are part of my daily encounters (Reinharz 1992).

This work also is, at least to some extent, an example of Richardson's (1994) notion of writing as a method of inquiry. As a sociologist who specializes in gender, the more I learned, the more I realized that my life could serve as a case study. As I examined my experiences, I found out things— about my experiences and about theory—that I did not know when I started (Richardson 1994).

It also is useful, I think, to consider my analysis an application of Mills's (1959) "sociological imagination." Mills (1959) and Berger (1963) wrote about the importance of seeing the general in the particular. This means that general social patterns can be discerned in the behaviors of particular individuals. In this article, I am examining portions of my biography, situated in U.S. society during the 1990s, to understand the "personal troubles" my gender produces in the context of a two-and-only-two gender system. I am not attempting to generalize my experiences; rather, I am trying to use them to examine and reflect on the processes and structure of gender in our society.

Because my analysis is based on my memories and perceptions of events, it is limited by my ability to recall events and by my interpretation of those events. However, I am not claiming that my experiences provide the truth about gender and how it works. I am claiming that the biography of a person who lives on the margins of our gender system can provide theoretical insights into the processes and social structure of gender. Therefore, after describing my experiences, I examine how they illustrate and extend, as well as contradict, other work on the social construction of gender.

Gendered Me

Each day, I negotiate the boundaries of gender. Each day, I face the possibility that someone will attribute the "wrong" gender to me based on my physical appearance.

I am six feet tall and large-boned. I have had short hair for most of my life. For the past several years, I have worn a crew cut or flat top. I do not shave or otherwise remove hair from my body (e.g., no eyebrow plucking). I do not wear dresses, skirts, high heels, or makeup. My only jewelry is a class ring, a "men's" watch (my wrists are too large for a "women's" watch), two small earrings (gold hoops, both in my left ear), and (occasionally) a necklace. I wear jeans or shorts, T-shirts, sweaters, polo/golf shirts, button-down collar shirts, and tennis shoes or boots. The jeans are "women's" (I do have hips) but do not look particularly "feminine." The rest of the outer garments are from men's departments. I prefer baggy clothes, so the fact that I have "womanly" breasts often is not obvious (I do not wear a bra). Sometimes, I wear a baseball cap or some other type of hat. I also am white and relatively young (30 years old).[3]

My gender display—what others interpret as my presented identity—regularly leads to the misattribution of my gender. An incongruity exists between my gender self-identity and the gender that others perceive. In my encounters with people I do not know, I sometimes conclude, based on our interactions, that they think I am a man. This does not mean that other people do not think I am a man, just that I have no way of knowing what they think without interacting with them.

Living with It

I have no illusions or delusions about my appearance. I know that my appearance is likely to be read as "masculine" (and male) and that how I see myself is socially irrelevant. Given our two-and-only-two gender structure, I must live with the consequences of my appearance. These consequences fall into two categories: issues of identity and issues of interaction.

My most common experience is being called "Sir" or being referred to by some other masculine linguistic marker (e.g., "he," "man"). This has happened for years, for as long as I can remember, when having encounters with people I do not know.[4] Once, in fact, the same worker at a fast-food restaurant called me "Ma'am" when she took my order and "Sir" when she gave it to me.

Using my credit cards sometimes is a challenge. Some clerks subtly indicate their disbelief, looking from the card to me and back at the card and checking my signature carefully. Others challenge my use of the card, asking whose it is or demanding identification. One cashier asked to see my driver's license and then asked me whether I was the son of the cardholder. Another clerk told me that my signature on the receipt "had better match" the one on the card. Presumably, this was her way of letting me know that she was not convinced it was my credit card.

My identity as a woman also is called into question when I try to use women-only spaces. Encounters in public rest rooms are an adventure. I have been told countless times that "This is the ladies' room." Other women say nothing to me, but their stares and conversations with others let me know what they think. I will hear them say, for example, "There was a man in there." I also get stares when I enter a locker room. However, it seems that women are less concerned about my presence there, perhaps because, given that it is a space for changing clothes, showering, and so forth, they will be able to make sure that I am really a woman. Dressing rooms in department stores also are problematic spaces. I remember shopping with my sister once and being offered a chair outside the room when I began to accompany her into the dressing room.

Women who believe that I am a man do not want me in women-only spaces. For example, one woman would not enter the rest room until I came out, and others have told me that I am in the wrong place. They also might not want to encounter me while they are alone. For example, seeing me walking at night when they are alone might be scary.[5]

I, on the other hand, am not afraid to walk alone, day or night. I do not worry that I will be subjected to the public harassment that many women endure (Gardner 1995). I am not a clear target for a potential rapist. I rely on the fact that a potential attacker would not want to attack a big man by mistake. This is not to say that men never are attacked, just that they are not viewed, and often do not view themselves, as being vulnerable to attack.

Being perceived as a man has made me privy to male-male interactional styles of which most women are not aware. I found out, quite by accident, that many men greet, or acknowledge, people (mostly other men) who make eye contact with them with a single nod. For example, I found that when I walked down the halls of my brother's all-male dormitory making eye contact, men nodded their greetings at me. Oddly enough, these same men did not greet my brother; I had to tell him about making eye contact and nodding as a greeting ritual. Apparently, in this case I was doing masculinity better than he was!

I also believe that I am treated differently, for example, in auto parts stores (staffed almost exclusively by men in most cases) because of the assumption that I am a man. Workers there assume that I know what I need and that my questions are legitimate requests for information. I suspect that I am treated more fairly than a feminine-ap-pearing woman would be. I have not been able to test this proposition. However, Devor's participants did report "being treated more respectfully" (1989, 132) in such situations.

There is, however, a negative side to being assumed to be a man by other men. Once, a friend and I were driving in her car when a man failed to stop at an intersection and nearly crashed into us. As we drove away, I mouthed "stop sign" to him. When we both stopped our cars at the next intersection, he got out of his car and came up to the passenger side of the car, where I was sitting. He yelled obscenities at us and pounded and spit on the car window. Luckily, the windows were closed. I do not think he would have done that if he thought I was a woman. This was the first time I realized that one of the implications of being seen as a man was that I might be called on to defend myself from physical aggression from other men who felt challenged by me. This was a sobering and somewhat frightening thought.

Recently, I was verbally accosted by an older man who did not like where I had parked my car. As I walked down the street to work, he shouted that I should park at the university rather than on a side street nearby. I responded that it was a public street and that I could park there if I chose. He continued to yell, but the only thing I caught was the last part of what he said: "Your tires are going to get cut!" Based on my appearance that day—I was dressed casually and carrying a backpack, and I had my hat on backward—I believe he thought that I was a young male student rather than a female professor. I do not think he would have yelled at a person he thought to be a woman—and perhaps especially not a woman professor.

Given the presumption of heterosexuality that is part of our system of gender, my interactions with women who assume that I am a man also can be viewed from that perspective. For example, once my brother and I were shopping when we were "hit on" by two young women. The encounter ended before I realized what had happened. It was only when we walked away that I told him that I was pretty certain that they had thought both of us were men. A more common experience is realizing that when I am seen in public with one of my women friends, we are likely to be read as a heterosexual dyad. It is likely that if I were to walk through a shopping mall holding hands with a woman, no one would look twice, not because of their openmindedness toward lesbian couples but rather because of their assumption that I was the male half of a straight couple. Recently, when walking through a mall with a friend and her infant, my observations of others' responses to us led me to believe that many of them assumed that we were a family on an outing, that is, that I was her partner and the father of the child.

Dealing with It

Although I now accept that being mistaken for a man will be a part of my life so long as I choose not to participate in femininity, there have been times when I consciously have tried to appear more feminine. I did this for a while when I was an undergraduate and again recently when I was on the academic job market. The first time, I let my hair grow nearly down to my shoulders and had it permed. I also grew long fingernails and wore nail polish. Much to my chagrin, even then one of my professors, who did not know my name, insistently referred to me in his kinship examples as "the son." Perhaps my first act on the way to my current stance was to point out to this man, politely and after class, that I was a woman.

More recently, I again let my hair grow out for several months, although I did not alter other aspects of my appearance. Once my hair was about two and a half inches long (from its original quarter inch), I realized, based on my encounters with strangers, that I had more or less passed back into the category of "woman." Then, when I returned to wearing a flat top, people again responded to me as if I were a man.

Because of my appearance, much of my negotiation of interactions with strangers involves attempts to anticipate their reactions to me. I need to assess whether they will be likely to assume that I am a man and whether that actually matters in the context of our encounters. Many times, my gender really is irrelevant, and it is just annoying to be misidentified. Other times, particularly when my appearance is coupled with something that identifies me by name (e.g., a check or credit card) without a photo, I might need to do something to ensure that my identity is not questioned. As a result of my experiences, I have developed some techniques to deal with gender misattribution.

In general, in unfamiliar public places, I avoid using the rest room because I know that it is a place where there is a high likelihood of misattribution and where misattribution is socially important. If I must use a public rest room, I try to make myself look as nonthreatening as possible. I do not wear a hat, and I try to rearrange my clothing to make my breasts more obvious. Here, I am trying to use my secondary sex characteristics to make my gender more obvious rather than the usual use of gender to make sex obvious. While in the rest room, I never make eye contact, and I get in and out as quickly as possible. Going in with a woman friend also is helpful; her presence legitimizes my own. People are less likely to think I am entering a space where I do not belong when I am with someone who looks like she does belong.[6]

To those women who verbally challenge my presence in the rest room, I reply, "I know," usually in an annoyed tone. When they stare or talk about me to the women they are with, I simply get out as quickly as possible. In general, I do not wait for someone I am with because there is too much chance of an unpleasant encounter.

I stopped trying on clothes before purchasing them a few years ago because my presence in the changing areas was met with stares and whispers. Exceptions are stores where the dressing rooms are completely private, where there are individual stalls rather than a room with stalls separated by curtains, or where business is slow and no one else is trying on clothes. If I am trying on a garment clearly intended for a woman, then I usually can do so without hassle. I guess the attendants assume that I must be a woman if I have, for example, a women's bathing suit in my hand. But usually, I think it is easier for me to try the clothes on at home and return them, if necessary, rather than risk creating a scene. Similarly, when I am with another woman who is trying on clothes, I just wait outside.

My strategy with credit cards and checks is to anticipate wariness on a clerk's part. When I sense that there is some doubt or when they challenge me, I say, "It's my card." I generally respond courteously to requests for photo ID, realizing that these might be routine checks because of concerns about increasingly widespread fraud. But for the clerk who asked for ID and still did not think it was my card, I had a stronger reaction. When she said that she was sorry for embarrassing me, I told her that I was not embarrassed but that she should be. I also am particularly careful to make sure that my signature is consistent with the back of the card. Faced with such situations, I feel somewhat nervous about signing my name—which, of course, makes me worry that my signature will look different from how it should.

Another strategy I have been experimenting with is wearing nail polish in the dark bright colors currently fashionable. I try to do this when I travel by plane. Given more stringent travel regulations, one always must present a photo ID. But my experiences have shown that my driver's license is not necessarily convincing. Nail polish might be. I also flash my polished nails when I enter airport rest rooms, hoping that they will provide a clue that I am indeed in the right place.

There are other cases in which the issues are less those of identity than of all the norms of interaction that, in our society, are gendered. My most common response to misattribution actually is to appear to ignore it, that is, to go on with the interaction as if nothing out of the ordinary has happened. Unless I feel that there is a good reason to establish my correct gender, I assume the identity others impose on me for the sake of smooth interaction. For example, if someone is selling me a movie ticket, then there is no reason to make sure that the person has accurately discerned my gender. Similarly, if it is clear that the person using "Sir" is talking to me, then I simply respond as appropriate. I accept the designation because it is irrelevant to the situation. It takes enough effort to be alert for misattributions and to decide which of them matter; responding to each one would take more energy than it is worth.

Sometimes, if our interaction involves conversation, my first verbal response is enough to let the other person know that I am actually a woman and not a man. My voice apparently is "feminine" enough to shift people's attributions to the other category. I know when this has happened by the apologies that usually accompany the mistake. I usually respond to the apologies by saying something like "No problem" and/or "It happens all the time." Sometimes, a misattributor will offer an account for the mistake, for example, saying that it was my hair or that they were not being very observant.

These experiences with gender and misattribution provide some theoretical insights into contemporary Western understandings of gender and into the social structure of gender in contemporary society. Although there are a number of ways in which my experiences confirm the work of others, there also are some ways in which my experiences suggest other interpretations and conclusions.

What Does It Mean?

Gender is pervasive in our society. I cannot choose not to participate in it. Even if I try not to do gender, other people will do it for me. That is, given our two-and-only-two rule, they must attribute one of two genders to me. Still, although I cannot choose not to participate in gender, I can choose not to participate in femininity (as I have), at least with respect to physical appearance.

That is where the problems begin. Without the decorations of femininity, I do not look like a woman. That is, I do not look like what many people's commonsense understanding of gender tells them a woman looks like. How I see myself, even how I might wish others would see me, is socially irrelevant. It is the gender that I appear to be (my "perceived gender") that is most relevant to my social identity and interactions with others. The major consequence of this fact is that I must be continually aware of which gender I "give off" as well as which gender I "give" (Goffman 1959).

Because my gender self-identity is "not displayed obviously, immediately, and consistently" (Devor 1989, 58), I am somewhat

of a failure in social terms with respect to gender. Causing people to be uncertain or wrong about one's gender is a violation of taken-for-granted rules that leads to embarrassment and discomfort; it means that something has gone wrong with the interaction (Garfinkel 1967; Kessler and McKenna 1978). This means that my nonresponse to misattribution is the more socially appropriate response; I am allowing others to maintain face (Goffman 1959, 1967). By not calling attention to their mistakes, I uphold their images of themselves as competent social actors. I also maintain my own image as competent by letting them assume that I am the gender I appear to them to be.

But I still have discreditable status; I carry a stigma (Goffman 1963). Because I have failed to participate appropriately in the creation of meaning with respect to gender (Devor 1989). I can be called on to account for my appearance. If discredited, I show myself to be an incompetent social actor. I am the one not following the rules, and I will pay the price for not providing people with the appropriate cues for placing me in the gender category to which I really belong.

I do think that it is, in many cases, safer to be read as a man than as some sort of deviant woman. "Man" is an acceptable category; it fits properly into people's gender worldview. Passing as a man often is the "path of least resistance" (Devor 1989; Johnson 1997). For example, in situations where gender does not matter, letting people take me as a man is easier than correcting them.

Conversely, as Butler noted, "We regularly punish those who fail to do their gender right" (1990, 140). Feinberg maintained, "Masculine girls and women face terrible condemnation and brutality—including sexual violence—for crossing the boundary of what is 'acceptable' female expression" (1996, 114). People are more likely to harass me when they perceive me to be a woman who looks like a man. For example, when a group of teenagers realized that I was not a man because one of their mothers identified me correctly, they began to make derogatory comments when I passed them. One asked, for example, "Does she have a penis?"

Because of the assumption that a "masculine" woman is a lesbian, there is the risk of homophobic reactions (Gardner 1995; Lucal 1997). Perhaps surprisingly, I find that I am much more likely to be taken for a man than for a lesbian, at least based on my interactions with people and their reactions to me. This might be because people are less likely to reveal that they have taken me for a lesbian because it is less relevant to an encounter or because they believe this would be unacceptable. But I think it is more likely a product of the strength of our two-and-only-two system. I give enough masculine cues that I am seen not as a deviant woman but rather as a man, at least in most cases. The problem seems not to be that people are uncertain about my gender, which might lead them to conclude that I was a lesbian once they realized I was a woman. Rather, I seem to fit easily into a gender category—just not the one with which I identify.

In fact, because men represent the dominant gender in our society, being mistaken for a man can protect me from other types of gendered harassment. Because men can move around in public spaces safely (at least relative to women), a "masculine" woman also can enjoy this freedom (Devor 1989).

On the other hand, my use of particular spaces—those designated as for women only—may be challenged. Feinberg provided an intriguing analysis of the public rest room experience. She characterized women's reactions to a masculine person in a public rest room as "an example of gender-phobia" (1996, 117), viewing such women as policing gender boundaries rather than believing that there really is a man in the women's rest room. She argued that women who truly believed that there was a man in their midst would react differently. Although this is an interesting perspective on her experiences, my experiences do not lead to the same conclusion! Enough people have said to me that "This is the ladies' room" or have said to their companions that "There was a man in there" that I take their reactions at face value.

Still, if the two-and-only-two gender system is to be maintained, participants must be involved in policing the categories and their attendant identities and spaces. Even if policing boundaries is not explicitly intended, boundary maintenance is the effect of such responses to people's gender displays.

Boundaries and margins are an important component of both my experiences of gender and our theoretical understanding of gendering processes. I am, in effect, both woman and not-woman. As a woman who often is a social man but who also is a woman living in a patriarchal society, I am in a unique position to see and act. I sometimes receive privileges usually limited to men, and I sometimes am oppressed by my status as a deviant woman. I am, in a sense, an outsider-within (Collins 1991). Positioned on the boundaries of gender categories, I have developed a consciousness that I hope will prove transformative (Anzaldua 1987).

In fact, one of the reasons why I decided to continue my nonparticipation in femininity was that my sociological training suggested that this could be one of my contributions to the eventual dismantling of patriarchal gender constructs. It would be my way of making the personal political. I accepted being taken for a man as the price I would pay to help subvert patriarchy. I believed that all of the inconveniences I was enduring meant that I actually was doing something to bring down the gender structures that entangled all of us.

Then, I read Lorber's (1994) *Paradoxes of Gender* and found out, much to my dismay, that I might not actually be challenging gender after all. Because of the way in which doing gender works in our two-and-only-two system, gender displays are simply read as evidence of one of the two categories. Therefore, gender bending, blending, and passing between the categories do not question the categories themselves. If one's social gender and personal (true) gender do not correspond, then this is irrelevant unless someone notices the lack of congruence.

This reality brings me to a paradox of my experiences. First, not only do others assume that I am one gender or the other, but I also insist that I really am a member of one of the two gender categories. That is, I am female; I self-identify as a woman. I do not claim to be some other gender or to have no gender at all. I simply place myself in the wrong category according to stereotypes and cultural standards; the gender I present, or that some people perceive me to be presenting, is inconsistent with the gender with which I identify myself as well as with the gender I could be "proven" to be. Socially, I display the wrong gender; personally, I identify as the proper gender.

Second, although I ultimately would like to see the destruction of our current gender structure, I am not to the point of personally abandoning gender. Right now, I do not want people to see me as genderless as much as I want them to see me as a woman. That is, I would like to expand the category of "woman" to include people like me. I, too,

am deeply embedded in our gender system, even though I do not play by many of its rules. For me, as for most people in our society, gender is a substantial part of my personal identity (Howard and Hollander 1997). Socially, the problem is that I do not present a gender display that is consistently read as feminine. In fact, I consciously do not participate in the trappings of femininity. However, I do identify myself as a woman, not as a man or as someone outside of the two-and-only-two categories.

Yet, I do believe, as Lorber (1994) does, that the purpose of gender, as it currently is constructed, is to oppress women. Lorber analyzed gender as a "process of creating distinguishable social statuses for the assignment of rights and responsibilities" that ends up putting women in a devalued and oppressed position (1994, 32). As Martin put it, "Bodies that clearly delineate gender status facilitate the maintenance of the gender hierarchy" (1998, 495).

For society, gender means difference (Lorber 1994). The erosion of the boundaries would problematize that structure. Therefore, for gender to operate as it currently does, the category "woman" cannot be expanded to include people like me. The maintenance of the gender structure is dependent on the creation of a few categories that are mutually exclusive, the members of which are as different as possible (Lorber 1994). It is the clarity of the boundaries between the categories that allows gender to be used to assign rights and responsibilities as well as resources and rewards.

It is that part of gender—what it is used for—that is most problematic. Indeed, is it not patriarchal—or, even more specifically, heteropatriarchal—constructions of gender that are actually the problem? It is not the differences between men and women, or the categories themselves, so much as the meanings ascribed to the categories and, even more important, the hierarchical nature of gender under patriarchy that is the problem (Johnson 1997). Therefore, I am rebelling not against my femaleness or even my womanhood; instead, I am protesting contemporary constructions of femininity and, at least indirectly, masculinity under patriarchy. We do not, in fact, know what gender would look like if it were not constructed around heterosexuality in the context of patriarchy.

Although it is possible that the end of patriarchy would mean the end of gender, it is at least conceivable that something like what we now call gender could exist in a postpatriarchal future. The two-and-only-two categorization might well disappear, there being no hierarchy for it to justify. But I do not think that we should make the assumption that gender and patriarchy are synonymous.

Theoretically, this analysis points to some similarities and differences between the work of Lorber (1994) and the works of Butler (1990), Goffman (1976, 1977), and West and Zimmerman (1997). Lorber (1994) conceptualized gender as social structure, whereas the others focused more on the interactive and processual nature of gender. Butler (1990) and Goffman (1976, 1977) view gender as a performance, and West and Zimmerman (1987) examined it as something all of us do. One result of this difference in approach is that in Lorber's (1994) work, gender comes across as something that we are caught in—something that, despite any attempts to the contrary, we cannot break out of. This conclusion is particularly apparent in Lorber's argument that gender rebellion, in the context of our two-and-only-two system, ends up supporting what it purports to subvert. Yet, my own experiences suggest an alternative possibility that is more in line with the view of gender offered by West and Zimmerman (1987): If gender is a product of interaction,

and if it is produced in a particular context, then it can be changed if we change our performances. However, the effects of a performance linger, and gender ends up being institutionalized. It is institutionalized, in our society, in a way that perpetuates inequality, as Lorber's (1994) work shows. So, it seems that a combination of these two approaches is needed.

In fact, Lorber's (1994) work seems to suggest that effective gender rebellion requires a more blatant approach—bearded men in dresses, perhaps, or more active responses to misattribution. For example, if I corrected every person who called me "Sir," and if I insisted on my right to be addressed appropriately and granted access to women-only spaces, then perhaps I could start to break down gender norms. If I asserted my right to use public facilities without being harassed, and if I challenged each person who gave me "the look," then perhaps I would be contributing to the demise of gender as we know it. It seems that the key would be to provide visible evidence of the nonmutual exclusivity of the categories. Would this break down the patriarchal components of gender? Perhaps it would, but it also would be exhausting.

Perhaps there is another possibility. In a recent book, The Gender Knot, Johnson (1997) argued that when it comes to gender and patriarchy, most of us follow the paths of least resistance; we "go along to get along," allowing our actions to be shaped by the gender system. Collectively, our actions help patriarchy maintain and perpetuate a system of oppression and privilege. Thus, by withdrawing our support from this system by choosing paths of greater resistance, we can start to chip away at it. Many people participate in gender because they cannot imagine any alternatives. In my classroom, and in my interactions and encounters with strangers, my presence can make it difficult for people not to see that there are other paths. In other words, following from West and Zimmerman (1987), I can subvert gender by doing it differently.

For example, I think it is true that my existence does not have an effect on strangers who assume that I am a man and never learn otherwise. For them, I do uphold the two-and-only-two system. But there are other cases in which my existence can have an effect. For example, when people initially take me for a man but then find out that I actually am a woman, at least for that moment, the naturalness of gender may be called into question. In these cases, my presence can provoke a "category crisis" (Garber 1992, 16) because it challenges the sex/gender binary system.

The subversive potential of my gender might be strongest in my classrooms. When I teach about the sociology of gender, my students can see me as the embodiment of the social construction of gender. Not all of my students have transformative experiences as a result of taking a course with me; there is the chance that some of them see me as a "freak" or as an exception. Still, after listening to stories about my experiences with gender and reading literature on the subject, many students begin to see how and why gender is a social product. I can disentangle sex, gender, and sexuality in the contemporary United States for them. Students can begin to see the connection between biographical experiences and the structure of society. As one of my students noted, I clearly live the material I am teaching. If that helps me to get my point across, then perhaps I am subverting the binary gender system after all. Although my gendered presence and my way of doing gender might make others—and sometimes even me—uncomfortable, no one ever said that dismantling patriarchy was going to be easy.

Notes

1. Ethnomethodology has been described as "the study of commonsense practical reasoning" (Collins 1988, 274). It examines how people make sense of their everyday experiences. Ethnomethodology is particularly useful in studying gender because it helps to uncover the assumptions on which our understandings of sex and gender are based.

2. I thank an anonymous reviewer for suggesting that I use these distinctions among the parts of a person's gender.

3. I obviously have left much out by not examining my gendered experiences in the context of race, age, class, sexuality, region, and so forth. Such a project clearly is more complex. As Weston pointed out, gender presentations are complicated by other statuses of their presenters: "What it takes to kick a person over into another gendered category can differ with race, class, religion, and time" (1996, 168). Furthermore, I am well aware that my whiteness allows me to assume that my experiences are simply a product of gender (see, e.g., hooks 1981; Lucal 1996; Spelman 1988; West and Fenstermaker 1995). For now, suffice it to say that it is my privileged position on some of these axes and my more disadvantaged position on others that combine to delineate my overall experience.

4. In fact, such experiences are not always limited to encounters with strangers. My grandmother, who does not see me often, twice has mistaken me for either my brother-in-law or some unknown man.

5. My experiences in rest rooms and other public spaces might be very different if I were, say, African American rather than white. Given the stereotypes of African American men, I think that white women would react very differently to encountering me (see, e.g., Staples [1986] 1993).

6. I also have noticed that there are certain types of rest rooms in which I will not be verbally challenged, the higher the social status of the place, the less likely I will be harassed. For example, when I go to the theater, I might get stared at, but my presence never has been challenged.

7. An anonymous reviewer offered one possible explanation for this. Women see women's rest rooms as their space; they feel safe, and even empowered, there. Instead of fearing men in such space, they might instead pose a threat to any man who might intrude. Their invulnerability in this situation is, of course, not physically based but rather socially constructed. I thank the reviewer for this suggestion.

References

Anzaldua, G. 1987. Borderlands/La Frontera. San Francisco: Aunt Lute Books.

Bern, S. L. 1993. The lenses of gender. New Haven, CT. Yale University Press.

Berger, R. 1963. Invitation to sociology. New York: Anchor.

Bordo, S. 1993. Unbearable weight. Berkeley: University of California Press.

Brownmiller, C. 1984. Femininity. New York: Fawcett.

Butler, J. 1990. Gender trouble. New York: Routledge.

Collins, P. H. 1991. Black feminist thought. New York: Routledge.

Collins, R. 1988. Theoretical sociology. San Diego: Harcourt Brace Jovanovich.

Devor, H. 1989. Gender blending: Confronting the limits of duality. Bloomington: Indiana University Press.

Feinberg, L. 1996. Transgender warriors. Boston: Beacon.

Garber, M. 1992. Vested interests: Cross-dressing and cultural anxiety. New York: HarperPerennial.

Gardner, C. B. 1995. Passing by: Gender and public harassment. Berkeley: University of California.

Garfinkel, H. 1967. Studies in ethnomethodology. Englewood Cliffs, NJ: Prentice Hall.

Goffman, E. 1959. The presentation of self in everyday life. Garden City, NY: Doubleday.

___. 1963. Stigma. Englewood Cliffs, NJ: Prentice Hall.

___. 1967. Interaction ritual. New York: Anchor/Doubleday.

___. 1976. Gender display. Studies in the Anthropology of Visual Communication 3:69–77.

___. 1977. The arrangement between the sexes. Theory and Society 4:301–31.

hooks, b. 1981. Ain't I a woman: Black women and feminism. Boston: South End Press.

Howard, J. A., and J. Hollander. 1997. Gendered situations, gendered selves. Thousand Oaks, CA: Sage.

Kessler, S. J., and W. McKenna. 1978. Gender: An ethnomethodological approach. New York: John Wiley.

Krieger, S. 1991. Social science and the self. New Brunswick, NJ: Rutgers University Press.

Johnson, A. G. 1997. The gender knot: Unraveling our patriarchal legacy, Philadelphia: Temple University Press.

Lorber, J. 1994. Paradoxes of gender. New Haven, CM Yale University Press.

___. 1996. Beyond the binaries: Depolarizing the categories of sex, sexuality, and gender. Sociological Inquiry 66:143–59.

Local, B. 1996. Oppression and privilege: Toward a relational conceptualization of race. Teaching Sociology 24:245–55.

___. 1997. "Hey, this is the ladies' room!": Gender misattribution and public harassment. Perspectives on Social Problems 9:43–57.

Martin, K. A. 1998. Becoming a gendered body: Practices of preschools. American Sociological Review 63:494–511.

Mills, C. W. 1959. The sociological imagination. London: Oxford University Press.

Myhre, J. R. M. 1995. One bad hair day too many, or the hairstory of an androgynous young feminist. In Listen up: Voices from the next feminist generation, edited by B. Findlen. Seattle, WA: Seal Press.

Reinharz, S. 1992. Feminist methods in social research. New York: Oxford University Press.

Richardson, L. 1994. Writing: A method of inquiry. In Handbook of Qualitative Research, edited by N. K. Denzin and Y. S. Lincoln. Thousand Oaks, CA: Sage.

Riemer, J. W. 1977. Varieties of opportunistic research. Urban life 5:467–77.

___. 1988. Work and self. In Personal sociology, edited by P. C. Higgins and J. A. Johnson. New York: Praeger.

Spelman, E. V. 1988. Inessential woman: Problems of exclusion in feminist thought. Boston: Beacon.

Staples, B. 1993. Just walk on by. In Experiencing race, class, and gender in the United States, edited by V. Cyrus. Mountain View, CA: Mayfield. (Originally published 1986.)

West, C., and S. Fenstermaker. 1995. Doing difference. Gender & Society 9:8–37.

West, C., and D. H. Zimmerman. 1987. Doing gender. Gender & Society 1:125–51.

Weston, K. 1996. Render me, gender me. New York: Columbia University Press.

Zimmerman, D. H. 1992. They were all doing gender, but they weren't all passing: Comment on Rogers. Gender & Society 6:192–98.

Theorizing Difference from Multiracial Feminism

Maxine Baca Zinn
Bonnie Thornton Dill

Women of color have long challenged the hegemony of feminisms constructed primarily around the lives of white middle-class women. Since the late 1960s, U.S. women of color have taken issue with unitary theories of gender. Our critiques grew out of the widespread concern about the exclusion of women of color from feminist scholarship and the misinterpretation of our experiences,[1] and ultimately "out of the very discourses, denying, permitting, and producing difference."[2] Speaking simultaneously from "within and against" *both* women's liberation *and* antiracist movements, we have insisted on the need to challenge systems of domination,[3] not merely as gendered subjects but as women whose lives are affected by our location in multiple hierarchies.

Recently, and largely in response to these challenges, work that links gender to other forms of domination is increasing. In this article, we examine this connection further as well as the ways in which difference and diversity infuse contemporary feminist studies. Our analysis draws on a conceptual framework that we refer to as "multiracial feminism."[4] This perspective is an attempt to go beyond a mere recognition of diversity and difference among women to examine structures of domination, specifically the importance of race in understanding the social construction of gender. Despite the varied concerns and multiple intellectual stances which characterize the feminisms of women of color, they share an emphasis on race as a primary force situating genders differently. It is the centrality of race, of institutionalized racism, and of struggles against racial oppression that link the various feminist perspectives within this framework. Together, they demonstrate that racial meanings offer new theoretical directions for feminist thought.

From *Feminist Studies*, Volume 22, Number 2 (Summer 1996): 321-331. Reprinted by permission of the publisher, Feminist Studies, Inc., c/o Department of Women's Studies, University of Maryland, College Park, MD 20742.

Tensions in Contemporary Difference Feminism

Objections to the false universalism embedded in the concept "woman" emerged within other discourses as well as those of women of color.[5] Lesbian feminists and postmodern feminists put forth their own versions of what Susan Bordo has called "gender skepticism."[6]

Many thinkers within mainstream feminism have responded to these critiques with efforts to contextualize gender. The search for women's "universal" or "essential" characteristics is being abandoned. By examining gender in the context of other social divisions and perspectives, difference has gradually become important—even problematizing the universal categories of "women" and "men." Sandra Harding expresses the shift best in her claim that "there are no gender relations *per se*, but only gender relations as constructed by and between classes, races, and cultures."[7]

Many feminists now contend that difference occupies center stage as *the* project of women studies today.[8] According to one scholar, "difference has replaced equality as the central concern of feminist theory."[9] Many have welcomed the change, hailing it as a major revitalizing force in U.S. feminist theory.[10] But if *some* priorities within mainstream feminist thought have been refocused by attention to difference, there remains an "uneasy alliance"[11] between women of color and other feminists.

If difference has helped revitalize academic feminisms, it has also "upset the apple cart" and introduced new conflicts into feminist studies.[12] For example, in a recent and widely discussed essay, Jane Rowland Martin argues that the current preoccupation with difference is leading feminism into dangerous traps. She fears that in giving privileged status to a predetermined set of analytic categories (race, ethnicity, and class), "we affirm the existence of nothing but difference." She asks, "How do we know that for us, difference does not turn on being fat, or religious, or in an abusive relationship?"[13]

We, too, see pitfalls in some strands of the difference project. However, our perspectives take their bearings from social relations. Race and class differences are crucial, we argue, not as individual characteristics (such as being fat) but insofar as they are primary organizing principles of a society which locates and positions groups within that society's opportunity structures.

Despite the much-heralded diversity trend within feminist studies, difference is often reduced to mere pluralism: a "live and let live" approach where principles of relativism generate a long list of diversities which begin with gender, class, and race and continue through a range of social structural as well as personal characteristics.[14] Another disturbing pattern, which bell hooks refers to as "the commodification of difference," is the representation of diversity as a form of exotica, "a spice, seasoning that livens up the dull dish that is mainstream white culture."[15] The major limitation of these approaches is the failure to attend to the power relations that accompany difference. Moreover, these approaches ignore the inequalities that cause some characteristics to be seen as "normal" while others are seen as "different" and thus, deviant.

Maria C. Lugones expresses irritation at those feminists who see only the *problem* of difference without recognizing *difference*.[16] Increasingly, we find that difference is recognized. But this in no way means that difference occupies a "privileged" theoretical status. Instead of using difference to rethink the category of women, difference is often a euphemism for women who differ from the traditional norm. Even in purporting to accept difference, feminist pluralism often creates a social reality that reverts to universalizing women:

> So much feminist scholarship assumes that when we cut through all of the diversity among women created by differences of racial classification, ethnicity, social class, and sexual orientation, a "universal truth" concerning women and gender lies buried underneath. But if we can face the scary possibility that no such certainty exists and that persisting in such a search will always distort or omit someone's experiences, with what do we replace this old way of thinking? Gender differences and gender politics begin to look very different if there is no essential woman at the core.[17]

What Is Multiracial Feminism?

A new set of feminist theories have emerged from the challenges put forth by women of color. Multiracial feminism is an evolving body of theory and practice informed by wide-ranging intellectual traditions. This framework does not offer a singular or unified feminism but a body of knowledge situating women and men in multiple systems of domination. U.S. multiracial feminism encompasses several emergent perspectives developed primarily by women of color: African Americans, Latinas, Asian Americans, and Native Americans, women whose analyses are shaped by their unique perspectives as "outsiders within"—marginal intellectuals whose social locations provide them with a particular perspective on self and society.[18] Although U.S. women of color represent many races and ethnic backgrounds—with different histories and cultures—our feminisms cohere in their treatment of race as a basic social division, a structure of power, a focus of political struggle, and hence a fundamental force in shaping women's and men's lives.

This evolving intellectual and political perspective uses several controversial terms. While we adopt the label "multiracial," other terms have been used to describe this broad framework. For example, Chela Sandoval refers to "U.S. Third World feminisms,"[19] while other scholars refer to "indigenous feminisms." In their theory text-reader, Alison M. Jagger and Paula M. Rothenberg adopt the label "multicultural feminism."[20]

We use "multiracial" rather than "multicultural" as a way of underscoring race as a power system that interacts with other structured inequalities to shape genders. Within the U.S. context, race, and the system of meanings and ideologies which accompany it, is a fundamental organizing principle of social relationships.[21] Race affects all women and men, although in different ways. Even cultural and group differences among women are produced through interaction within a racially stratified social order. Therefore, although we do not discount the importance of culture, we caution that cultural analytic frameworks that ignore race tend to view women's differences as the product of group-specific values and practices that often result in the marginalization of cultural groups which are then perceived as exotic expressions of a normative center. Our focus on race stresses the social construction of differently situated social groups and their varying degrees of advantage and power. Additionally, this emphasis on race takes on increasing political importance in an era where discourse about race is governed by color-evasive language[22] and a preference for individual rather than group remedies for social inequalities. Our analyses insist upon the primary and pervasive nature of race in contemporary U.S. society while at the same time acknowledging how race both shapes and is shaped by a variety of other social relations.

In the social sciences, multiracial feminism grew out of socialist feminist thinking. Theories about how political economic forces shape women's lives were influential as we began to uncover the social causes of racial ethnic women's subordination. But socialist feminism's concept of capitalist patriarchy, with its focus on women's unpaid (reproductive) labor in the home failed to address racial differences in the organization of reproductive labor. As feminists of color have argued, "reproductive labor has divided along racial as well as gender lines, and the specific characteristics have varied regionally and changed over time as capitalism has reorganized."[23] Despite the limitations of socialist feminism, this body of literature has been especially useful in pursuing questions about the interconnections among systems of domination.[24]

Race and ethnic studies was the other major social scientific source of multiracial feminism. It provided a basis for comparative analyses of groups that are socially and legally subordinated and remain culturally distinct within U.S. society. This includes the systematic discrimination of socially constructed racial groups and their distinctive cultural arrangements. Historically, the categories of African American, Latino, Asian American, and Native American were constructed as both racially and culturally distinct. Each group has a distinctive culture, shares a common heritage, and has developed a common identity within a larger society that subordinates them.[25]

We recognize, of course, certain problems inherent in an uncritical use of the multiracial label. First, the perspective can be hampered by a biracial model in which only African Americans and whites are seen as racial categories and all other groups are viewed through the prism of cultural differences. Latinos and Asians have always occupied distinctive places within the racial hierarchy, and current shifts in the composition of the U.S. population are racializing these groups anew.[26]

A second problem lies in treating multiracial feminism as a single analytical framework, and its principle architects, women of color, as an undifferentiated category. The concepts "multiracial feminism," "racial ethnic women," and "women of color" "homogenize quite different experiences and can falsely universalize experiences across race, ethnicity, sexual orientation, and age."[27] The feminisms created by women of color exhibit a plurality of intellectual and political positions. We speak in many voices, with inconsistencies that are born of our different social locations. Multiracial feminism embodies this plurality and richness. Our intent is not to falsely universalize women of color. Nor do we wish to promote a new racial essentialism in place of the old gender essentialism. Instead, we use these concepts to examine the structures and experiences produced by intersecting forms of race and gender.

It is also essential to acknowledge that race is a shifting and contested category whose meanings construct definitions of all aspects of social life.[28] In the United States it helped define citizenship by excluding everyone who was not a white, male property owner. It defined labor as slave or free, coolie or contract, and family as available only to those men whose marriages were recognized or whose wives could immigrate with them. Additionally, racial meanings are contested both within groups and between them.[29]

Although definitions of race are at once historically and geographically specific, they are also transnational, encompassing diasporic groups and crossing traditional geographic boundaries. Thus, while U.S.

multiracial feminism calls attention to the fundamental importance of race, it must also locate the meaning of race within specific national traditions.

The Distinguishing Features of Multiracial Feminism

By attending to these problems, multiracial feminism offers a set of analytic premises for thinking about and theorizing gender. The following themes distinguish this branch of feminist inquiry.

First, multiracial feminism asserts that gender is constructed by a range of interlocking inequalities, what Patricia Hill Collins calls a "matrix of domination."[30] The idea of a matrix is that several fundamental systems work with and through each other. People experience race, class, gender, and sexuality differently depending upon their social location in the structures of race, class, gender, and sexuality. For example, people of the same race will experience race differently depending upon their location in the class structure as working class, professional managerial class, or unemployed; in the gender structure as female or male; and in structures of sexuality as heterosexual, homosexual, or bisexual.

Multiracial feminism also examines the simultaneity of systems in shaping women's experience and identity. Race, class, gender, and sexuality are not reducible to individual attributes to be measured and assessed for their separate contribution in explaining given social outcomes, an approach that Elizabeth Spelman calls "pop-bead metaphysics, "where a woman's identity consists of the sum of parts neatly divisible from one another.[31] The matrix of domination seeks to account for the multiple ways that women experience themselves as gendered, raced, classed, and sexualized.

Second, multiracial feminism emphasizes the intersectional nature of hierarchies at all levels of social life. Class, race, gender, and sexuality are components of both social structure and social interaction. Women and men are differently embedded in locations created by these cross-cutting hierarchies. As a result, women and men throughout the social order experience different forms of privilege and subordination, depending on their race, class, gender, and sexuality. In other words, intersecting forms of domination produce *both* oppression *and* opportunity. At the same time that structures of race, class, and gender create disadvantages for women of color, they provide unacknowledged benefits for those who are at the top of these hierarchies—whites, members of the upper classes, and males. Therefore, multiracial feminism applies not only to racial ethnic women but also to women and men of all races, classes, and genders.

Third, multiracial feminism highlights the relational nature of dominance and subordination. Power is the cornerstone of women's differences.[32] This means that women's differences are *connected* in systematic ways.[33] Race is a vital element in the pattern of relations among minority and white women. As Linda Gordon argues, the very meanings of being a white woman in the United States have been affected by the existence of subordinated women of color: "They intersect in conflict and in occasional cooperation, but always in mutual influence."[34]

Fourth, multiracial feminism explores the interplay of social structure and women's agency. Within the constraints of race, class, and gender oppression, women create viable lives for themselves, their families, and their communities. Women of color have resisted and often undermined the forces of power that control them. From acts of quiet dignity and steadfast determination to involvement in revolt and rebellion, women struggle to shape their own lives. Racial oppression has been a common focus of the "dynamic of oppositional agency" of women of color. As Chandra Talpade Mohanty points out, it is the nature and organization of women's opposition which mediates and differentiates the impact of structures of domination.[35]

Fifth, multiracial feminism encompasses wide-ranging methodological approaches, and like other branches of feminist thought, relies on varied theoretical tools as well. Ruth Frankenberg and Lata Mani identify three guiding principles of inclusive feminist inquiry: "building complex analyses, avoiding erasure, specifying location."[36] In the last decade, the opening up of academic feminism has focused attention on social location in the production of knowledge. Most basically, research by and about marginalized women has destabilized what used to be considered as universal categories of gender. Marginalized locations are well suited for grasping social relations that remained obscure from more privileged vantage points. Lived experience, in other words, creates alternative ways of understanding the social world and the experience of different groups of women within it. Racially informed standpoint epistemologies have provided new topics, fresh questions, and new understandings of women and men. Women of color have, as Norma Alarcón argues, asserted ourselves as subjects, using our voices to challenge dominant conceptions of truth.[37]

Sixth, multiracial feminism brings together understandings drawn from the lived experiences of diverse and continuously changing groups of women. Among Asian Americans, Native Americans, Latinas, and Blacks are many different national cultural and ethnic groups. Each one is engaged in the process of testing, refining, and reshaping these broader categories in its own image. Such internal differences heighten awareness of and sensitivity to both commonalities and differences, serving as a constant reminder of the importance of comparative study and maintaining a creative tension between diversity and universalization.

Difference and Transformation

Efforts to make women's studies less partial and less distorted have produced important changes in academic feminism. Inclusive thinking has provided a way to build multiplicity and difference into our analyses. This has led to the discovery that race matters for everyone. White women, too, must be reconceptualized as a category that is multiply defined by race, class, and other differences. As Ruth Frankenberg demonstrates in a study of whiteness among contemporary women, all kinds of social relations, even those that appear neutral, are, in fact, racialized. Frankenberg further complicates the very notion of a unified white identity by introducing issues of Jewish identity.[38] Therefore, the lives of women of color cannot be seen as a *variation* on a more general model of white American womanhood. The model of womanhood that feminist social science once held as "universal" is also a product of race and class.

When we analyze the power relations constituting all social arrangements and shaping women's lives in distinctive ways, we can begin to grapple with core feminist issues about how genders are socially constructed and constructed differently. Women's difference is built into our study of gender. Yet this perspective is quite far removed from the atheoretical pluralism implied in much contemporary thinking about gender.

Multiracial feminism, in our view, focuses not just on differences but also on the way in which differences and domination intersect and are historically and socially constituted. It challenges feminist scholars to go beyond the mere recognition and inclusion of difference to reshape the basic concepts and theories of our disciplines. By attending to women's social location based on race, class, and gender, multiracial feminism seeks to clarify the structural sources of diversity. Ultimately, multiracial feminism forces us to see privilege and subordination as interrelated and to pose such questions as: How do the existences and experiences of all people—women and men, different racial-ethnic groups, and different classes—shape the experiences of each other? How are those relationships defined and enforced through social institutions that are the primary sites for negotiating power within society? How do these differences contribute to the construction of both individual and group identity? Once we acknowledge that all women are affected by the racial order of society, then it becomes clear that the insights of multiracial feminism provide an analytical framework, not solely for understanding the experiences of women of color but for understanding *all* women, and men, as well.

Notes

1. Maxine Baca Zinn, Lynn Weber Cannon, Elizabeth Higginbotham, and Bonnie Thornton Dill, "The Costs of Exclusionary Practices in Women's Studies," *Signs* 11 (winter 1986): 290–303.
2. Chela Sandoval, "U.S. Third World Feminism: The Theory and Method of Oppositional Consciousness in the Postmodern World," *Genders* (spring 1991): 1–24.
3. Ruth Frankenberg and Lata Mani, "Cross Currents, Crosstalk: Race, 'Postcoloniality,' and the Politics of Location," *Cultural Studies* 7 (May 1993): 292–310.
4. We use the term "multiracial feminism" to convey the multiplicity of racial groups and feminist perspectives.
5. A growing body of work on difference in feminist thought now exists. Although we cannot cite all the current work, the following are representative: Michèle Barrett, "The Concept of Difference," *Feminist Review* 26 (July 1987): 29–42; Christina Crosby, "Dealing with Difference," in *Feminists Theorize the Political*, ed. Judith Butler and Joan W. Scott (New York: Routledge, 1992), 130–43; Elizabeth Fox-Genovese, "Difference, Diversity, and Divisions in an Agenda for the Women's Movement," in *Color, Class, and Country: Experiences of Gender*, ed. Gay Young and Bette J. Dickerson (London: Zed Books, 1994), 232–48; Nancy A. Hewitt, "Compounding Differences," *Feminist Studies* 18 (summer 1992): 313–26; Maria C. Lugones, "On the Logic of Feminist Pluralism," in *Feminist Ethics*, ed. Claudia Card (Lawrence: University of Kansas Press, 1991), 35–44; Rita S. Gallin and Anne Ferguson, "The Plurality of Feminism: Rethinking 'Difference,'" in *The Woman and International Development Annual* (Boulder: Westview Press, 1993), 3: 1–16; and Linda Gordon, "On Difference," *Genders* 10 (spring 1991): 91–111.
6. Susan Bordo, "Feminism, Postmodernism, and Gender Skepticism," in *Feminism/Postmodernism*, ed. Linda J. Nicholson (London: Routledge, 1990), 133–56.
7. Sandra G. Harding, *Whose Science? Whose Knowledge? Thinking from Women's Lives* (Ithaca: Cornell University Press, 1991), 179.
8. Crosby, 131.
9. Fox-Genovese, 232.
10. Faye Ginsberg and Anna Lowenhaupt Tsing, Introduction to *Uncertain Terms, Negotiating Gender in American Culture*, ed. Faye Ginsberg and Anna Lowenhaupt Tsing (Boston: Beacon Press, 1990), 3.
11. Sandoval, 2.
12. Sandra Morgan, "Making Connections: Socialist-Feminist Challenges to Marxist Scholarship," in *Women and a New Academy: Gender and Cultural Contexts*, ed. Jean F. O'Barr (Madison: University of Wisconsin Press, 1989), 149.
13. Jane Rowland Martin, "Methodological Essentialism, False Difference, and Other Dangerous Traps," *Signs* 19 (spring 1994): 647.
14. Barrett, 32.
15. bell hooks, *Black Looks: Race and Representation* (Boston: South End Press, 1992), 21.
16. Lugones, 35–44.
17. Patricia Hill Collins, Foreword to *Women of Color in U.S. Society*, ed. Maxine Baca Zinn and Bonnie Thornton Dill (Philadelphia: Temple University Press, 1994), xv.
18. Patricia Hill Collins, "Learning from the Outsider Within: The Sociological Significance of Black Feminist Thought," *Social Problems* 33 (December 1986): 514–32.

19. Sandoval, 1.

20. Alison M. Jagger and Paula S. Rothenberg, *Feminist Frameworks: Alternative Theoretical Accounts of the Relations between Women and Men*, 3d ed. (New York: McGraw-Hill, 1993).

21. Michael Omi and Howard Winant, *Racial Formation in the United States: From the 1960s to the 1980s*, 2d ed. (New York: Routledge, 1994).

22. Ruth Frankenberg, *The Social Construction of Whiteness: White Women, Race Matters* (Minneapolis: University of Minnesota Press, 1993).

23. Evelyn Nakano Glenn, "From Servitude to Service Work: Historical Continuities in the Racial Division of Paid Reproductive Labor," *Signs* 18 (autumn 1992): 3. See also Bonnie Thornton Dill, "Our Mothers' Grief: Racial-Ethnic Women and the Maintenance of Families," *Journal of Family History* 13, no. 4 (1988): 415–31.

24. Morgan, 146.

25. Maxine Baca Zinn and Bonnie Thornton Dill, "Difference and Domination," in *Women of Color in U.S. Society*, 11–12.

26. See Omi and Winant, 53–76, for a discussion of racial formation.

27. Margaret L. Andersen and Patricia Hill Collins, *Race, Class, and Gender: An Anthology* (Belmont, Calif.: Wadsworth, 1992), xvi.

28. Omi and Winant.

29. Nazli Kibria, "Migration and Vietnamese American Women: Remaking Ethnicity," in *Women of Color in U.S. Society*, 247–61.

30. Patricia Hill Collins, *Black Feminist Thought: Knowledge, Consciousness, and the Politics of Empowerment* (Boston: Unwin Hyman, 1990).

31. Elizabeth Spelman, *Inessential Women: Problems of Exclusion in Feminist Thought* (Boston: Beacon Press, 1988), 136.

32. Several discussions of difference make this point. See Baca Zinn and Dill, 10; Gordon, 106; and Lynn Weber, in the "Symposium on West and Fenstermaker's 'Doing Difference,'" *Gender & Society* 9 (August 1995): 515–19.

33. Glenn, 10.

34. Gordon, 106.

35. Chandra Talpade Mohanty, "Cartographies of Struggle: Third World Women and the Politics of Feminism," in *Third World Women and the Politics of Feminism*, ed. Chandra Talpade Mohanty, Ann Russo, and Lourdes Torres (Bloomington: Indiana University Press, 1991), 13.

36. Frankenberg and Mani, 306.

37. Norma Alarçon, "The Theoretical Subject(s) of *This Bridge Called My Back* and Anglo-American Feminism," in *Making Face, Making Soul, Haciendo Caras: Creative and Critical Perspectives by Women of Color*, ed. Gloria Anzaldúa (San Francisco: Aunt Lute, 1990), 356.

38. Frankenberg. See also Evelyn Torton Beck, "The Politics of Jewish Invisibility," *NWSA Journal* (fall 1988): 93–102.

Age, Race, Class, and Sex:
Women Redefining Difference

Audre Lorde

Much of Western European history conditions us to see human differences in simplistic opposition to each other: dominant/subordinate, good/bad, up/down, superior/inferior. In a society where the good is defined in terms of profit rather than in terms of human need, there must always be some group of people who, through systematized oppression, can be made to feel surplus, to occupy the place of the dehumanized inferior. Within this society, that group is made up of Black and Third World people, working-class people, older people, and women.

As a forty-nine-year-old Black lesbian feminist socialist mother of two, including one boy, and a member of an interracial couple, I usually find myself a part of some group defined as other, deviant, inferior, or just plain wrong. Traditionally, in american society, it is the members of oppressed, objectified groups who are expected to stretch out and bridge the gap between the actualities of our lives and the consciousness of our oppressor. For in order to survive, those of us for whom oppression is as american as apple pie have always had to be watchers, to become familiar with the language and manners of the oppressor, even sometimes adopting them for some illusion of protection. Whenever the need for some pretense of communication arises, those who profit from our oppression call upon us to share our knowledge with them. In other words, it is the responsibility of the oppressed to teach the oppressors their mistakes. I am responsible for educating teachers who dismiss my children's culture in school. Black and Third World people are expected to educate white people as to our humanity. Women are expected to educate men. Lesbians and gay men are expected to educate the heterosexual world. The oppressors maintain their position and evade responsibility for their own actions. There is a constant

From *Sister Outsider: Essays and Speeches by Audre Lorde* by Audre Lorde. Pp. 114–123. Copyright © 1984 by Audre Lorde. Reprinted by permission of The Crossing Press.

drain of energy which might be better used in redefining ourselves and devising realistic scenarios for altering the present and constructing the future.

Institutionalized rejection of difference is an absolute necessity in a profit economy which needs outsiders as surplus people. As members of such an economy, we have all been programmed to respond to the human differences between us with fear and loathing and to handle that difference in one of three ways: ignore it, and if that is not possible, copy it if we think it is dominant, or destroy it if we think it is subordinate. But we have no patterns for relating across our human differences as equals. As a result, those differences have been misnamed and misused in the service of separation and confusion.

Certainly there are very real differences between us of race, age, and sex. But it is not those differences between us that are separating us. It is rather our refusal to recognize those differences, and to examine the distortions which result from our misnaming them and their effects upon human behavior and expectation.

Racism, the belief in the inherent superiority of one race over all others and thereby the right to dominance. Sexism, the belief in the inherent superiority of one sex over the other and thereby the right to dominance. Ageism. Heterosexism. Elitism. Classism.

It is a lifetime pursuit for each one of us to extract these distortions from our living at the same time as we recognize, reclaim, and define those differences upon which they are imposed. For we have all been raised in a society where those distortions were endemic within our living. Too often, we pour the energy needed for recognizing and exploring difference into pretending those differences are insurmountable barriers, or that they do not exist at all. This results in a voluntary isolation, or false and treacherous connections. Either way, we do not develop tools for using human difference as a springboard for creative change within our lives. We speak not of human difference, but of human deviance.

Somewhere, on the edge of consciousness, there is what I call a mythical norm, which each one of us within our hearts knows "that is not me." In America, this norm is usually defined as white, thin, male, young, heterosexual, christian, and financially secure. It is with this mythical norm that the trappings of power reside within this society. Those of us who stand outside that power often identify one way in which we are different, and we assume that to be the primary cause of all oppression, forgetting other distortions around difference, some of which we ourselves may be practicing. By and large within the women's movement today, white women focus upon their oppression as women and ignore differences of race, sexual preference, class, and age. There is a pretense to a homogeneity of experience covered by the word *sisterhood* that does not in fact exist.

Unacknowledged class differences rob women of each others' energy and creative insight. Recently a women's magazine collective made the decision for one issue to print only prose, saying poetry was a less "rigorous" or "serious" art form. Yet even the form our creativity takes is often a class issue. Of all the art forms, poetry is the most economical. It is the one which is the most secret, which requires the least physical labor, the least material, and the one which can be done between shifts, in the hospital pantry, on the subway, and on scraps of surplus paper. Over the last few years, writing a novel on tight finances, I came to appreciate the enormous differences in the material demands between poetry and prose. As we reclaim our literature, poetry has been the major voice of poor, working class, and Colored women. A room of one's own may be a necessity for writing prose, but so are reams of paper, a typewriter, and plenty of time. The actual requirements to produce the visual arts also help determine, along class lines, whose art is whose. In this day of inflated prices for material, who are our sculptors, our painters, our photographers? When we speak of a broadly based women's culture, we need to be aware of the effect of class and economic differences on the supplies available for producing art.

As we move toward creating a society within which we can each flourish, ageism is another distortion of relationship which interferes without vision. By ignoring the past, we are encouraged to repeat its mistakes. The "generation gap" is an important social tool for any repressive society. If the younger members of a community view the older members as contemptible or suspect or excess, they will never be able to join hands and examine the living memories of the community, nor ask the all important question, "Why?" This gives rise to a historical amnesia that keeps us working to invent the wheel every time we have to go to the store for bread.

We find ourselves having to repeat and relearn the same old lessons over and over that our mothers did because we do not pass on what we have learned, or because we are unable to listen. For instance, how many times has this all been said before? For another, who would have believed that once again our daughters are allowing their bodies to be hampered and purgatoried by girdles and high heels and hobble skirts?

Ignoring the differences of race between women and the implications of those differences presents the most serious threat to the mobilization of women's joint power.

As white women ignore their built-in privilege of whiteness and define *woman* in terms of their own experience alone, then women of Color become "other," the outsider whose experience and tradition is too "alien" to comprehend. An example of this is the signal absence of the experience of women of Color as a resource for women's studies courses. The literature of women of Color is seldom included in women's literature courses and almost never in other literature courses, nor in women's studies as a whole. All too often, the excuse given is that the literatures of women of Color can only be taught by Colored women, or that they are too difficult to understand, or that classes cannot "get into" them because they come out of experiences that are "too different." I have heard this argument presented by white women of otherwise quite clear intelligence, women who seem to have no trouble at all teaching and reviewing work that comes out of the vastly different experiences of Shakespeare, Moliere, Dostoyefsky, and Aristophanes. Surely there must be some other explanation.

This is a very complex question, but I believe one of the reasons white women have such difficulty reading Black women's work is because of their reluctance to see Black women as women and different from themselves. To examine Black women's literature effectively requires that we be seen as whole people in our actual complexities—as individuals, as women, as human—rather than as one of those problematic but familiar stereotypes provided in this society in place of genuine images of Black women. And I believe this holds true for the literatures of other women of Color who are not Black.

The literatures of all women of Color recreate the textures of our lives, and many white women are heavily invested in ignoring the real differences. For as long as any difference between us means one of us must be inferior, then the recognition of any difference must be fraught with guilt. To allow women of Color to step out of stereotypes is too guilt provoking, for it threatens the complacency of those women who view oppression only in terms of sex.

Refusing to recognize difference makes it impossible to see the different problems and pitfalls facing us as women.

Thus, in a patriarchal power system where whiteskin privilege is a major prop, the entrapments used to neutralize Black women and white women are not the same. For example, it is easy for Black women to be used by the power structure against Black men, not because they are men, but because they are Black. Therefore, for Black women, it is necessary at all times to separate the needs of the oppressor from our own legitimate conflicts within our communities. This same problem does not exist for white women. Black women and men have shared racist oppression and still share it, although in different ways. Out of that shared oppression we have developed joint defenses and joint vulnerabilities to each other that are not duplicated in the white community, with the exception of the relationship between Jewish women and Jewish men.

On the other hand, white women face the pitfall of being seduced into joining the oppressor under the pretense of sharing power. This possibility does not exist in the same way for women of Color. The tokenism that is sometimes extended to us is not an invitation to join power; our racial "otherness" is a visible reality that makes that quite clear. For white women there is a wider range of pretended choices and rewards for identifying with patriarchal power and its tools.

Today, with the defeat of ERA, the tightening economy, and increased conservatism, it is easier once again for white women to believe the dangerous fantasy that if you are good enough, pretty enough, sweet enough, quiet enough, teach the children to behave, hate the right people, and marry the right men, then you will be allowed to coexist with patriarchy in relative peace, at least until a man needs your job or the neighborhood rapist happens along. And true, unless one lives and loves in the trenches it is difficult to remember that the war against dehumanization is ceaseless.

But Black women and our children know the fabric of our lives is stitched with violence and with hatred, that there is no rest. We do not deal with it only on the picket lines, or in dark midnight alleys, or in the places where we dare to verbalize our resistance. For us, increasingly, violence weaves through the daily tissues of our living—in the supermarket, in the classroom, in the elevator, in the clinic and the schoolyard, from the plumber, the baker, the saleswoman, the bus driver, the bank teller, the waitress who does not serve us.

Some problems we share as women, some we do not. You fear your children will grow up to join the patriarchy and testify against you, we fear our children will be dragged from a car and shot down in the street, and you will turn your backs upon the reasons they are dying.

The threat of difference has been no less blinding to people of Color. Those of us who are Black must see that the reality of our lives and our struggle does not make us immune to the errors of ignoring and misnaming difference. Within Black communities where racism is a living reality, differences among us often seem dangerous and suspect. The need for unity is often misnamed as a need for homogeneity, and a Black feminist vision mistaken for betrayal of our common interests as a people. Because of the continuous battle against racial erasure that Black women and Black men share, some Black women still refuse to recognize that we are also oppressed as women, and that sexual hostility against Black women is practiced not only by the white racist society, but implemented within our Black communities as well. It is a disease striking the heart of Black nationhood, and silence will not make it disappear. Exacerbated by racism and the pressures of powerlessness, violence against Black women and children often becomes a standard within our communities, one by which manliness can be measured. But these woman-hating acts are rarely discussed as crimes against Black women.

As a group, women of Color are the lowest paid wage earners in america. We are the primary targets of abortion and sterilization abuse, here and abroad. In certain parts of Africa, small girls are still being sewed shut between their legs to keep them docile and for men's pleasure. This is known as female circumcision, and it is not a cultural affair as the late Jomo Kenyatta insisted, it is a crime against Black women.

Black women's literature is full of the pain of frequent assault, not only by a racist patriarchy, but also by Black men. Yet the necessity for and history of shared battle have made us, Black women, particularly vulnerable to the false accusation that antisexist is anti-Black. Meanwhile, woman-hating as a recourse of the powerless is sapping strength from Black communities, and our very lives. Rape is on the increase, reported and unreported, and rape is not aggressive sexuality, it is sexualized aggression. As Kalamu ya Salaam, a Black male writer points out, "As long as male domination exists, rape will exist. Only women revolting and men made conscious of their responsibility to fight sexism can collectively stop rape."[1]

Differences between ourselves as Black women are also being misnamed and used to separate us from one another. As a Black lesbian feminist comfortable with the many different ingredients of my identity, and a woman committed to racial and sexual freedom from oppression, I find I am constantly being encouraged to pluck out some one aspect of myself and present this as the meaningful whole, eclipsing or denying the other parts of self. But this is a destructive and fragmenting way to live. My fullest concentration of energy is available to me only when I integrate all the parts of who I am, openly, allowing power from particular sources of my living to flow back and forth freely through all my different selves, without the restrictions of externally imposed definition. Only then can I bring myself and my energies as a whole to the service of those struggles which I embrace as part of my living.

A fear of lesbians, or of being accused of being a lesbian, has led many Black women into testifying against themselves. It has led some of us into destructive alliances, and others into despair and isolation. In the white women's communities, heterosexism is sometimes a result of identifying with the white patriarchy, a rejection of that interdependence between women-identified women which allows the self to be, rather than to be used in the service of men. Sometimes it reflects a die-hard belief in the protective coloration of heterosexual relationships, sometimes a self-hate which all women have to fight against, taught us from birth.

Although elements of these attitudes exist for all women, there are particular resonances of heterosexism and homophobia among Black women. Despite the fact that woman-bonding has a long and honorable history in the African and African-american communities, and despite the knowledge and accomplishments of many strong and creative women-identified Black women in the political, social and cultural fields, heterosexual Black women often tend to ignore or discount the existence and work of Black lesbians. Part of this attitude has come from an understandable terror of Black male attack within the close confines of Black society, where the punishment for any female self-assertion is still to be accused of being a lesbian and therefore unworthy of the attention or support of the scarce Black male. But part of this need to misname and ignore Black lesbians comes from a very real fear that openly women-identified Black women who are no longer dependent upon men for their self-definition may well reorder our whole concept of social relationships.

Black women who once insisted that lesbianism was a white woman's problem now insist that Black lesbians are a threat to Black nationhood, are consorting with the enemy, are basically un-Black. These accusations, coming from the very women to whom we look for deep and real understanding, have served to keep many Black lesbians in hiding, caught between the racism of white women and the homophobia of their sisters. Often, their work has been ignored, trivialized, or misnamed, as with the work of Angelina Grimke, Alice Dunbar-Nelson, Lorraine Hansberry. Yet women-bonded women have always been some part of the power of Black communities, from our unmarried aunts to the amazons of Dahomey.

And it is certainly not Black lesbians who are assaulting women and raping children and grandmothers on the streets of our communities.

Across this country, as in Boston during the spring of 1979 following the unsolved murders of twelve Black women, Black lesbians are spearheading movements against violence against Black women.

What are the particular details within each of our lives that can be scrutinized and altered to help bring about change? How do we redefine difference for all women? It is not our differences which separate women, but our reluctance to recognize those differences and to deal effectively with the distor-

tions which have resulted from the ignoring and misnaming of those differences.

As a tool of social control, women have been encouraged to recognize only one area of human difference as legitimate, those differences which exist between women and men. And we have learned to deal across those differences with the urgency of all oppressed subordinates. All of us have had to learn to live or work or coexist with men, from our fathers on. We have recognized and negotiated these differences, even when this recognition only continued the old dominant/subordinate mode of human relationship, where the oppressed must recognize the masters' difference in order to survive.

But our future survival is predicated upon our ability to relate within equality. As women, we must root out internalized patterns of oppression within ourselves if we are to move beyond the most superficial aspects of social change. Now we must recognize differences among women who are our equals, neither inferior nor superior, and devise ways to use each others' difference to enrich our visions and our joint struggles.

The future of our earth may depend upon the ability of all women to identify and develop new definitions of power and new patterns of relating across difference. The old definitions have not served us, nor the earth that supports us. The old patterns, no matter how cleverly rearranged to imitate progress, still condemn us to cosmetically altered repetitions of the same old exchanges, the same old guilt, hatred, recrimination, lamentation, and suspicion.

For we have, built into all of us, old blueprints of expectation and response, old structures of oppression, and these must be altered at the same time as we alter the living conditions which are a result of those structures. For the master's tools will never dismantle the master's house.

As Paulo Freire shows so well in *The Pedagogy of the Oppressed*,[2] the true focus of revolutionary change is never merely the oppressive situations which we seek to escape, but that piece of the oppressor which is planted deep within each of us, and which knows only the oppressors' tactics, the oppressors' relationships.

Change means growth, and growth can be painful. But we sharpen self-definition by exposing the self in work and struggle together with those whom we define as different from ourselves, although sharing the same goals. For Black and white, old and young, lesbian and heterosexual women alike, this can mean new paths to our survival.

We have chosen each other
and the edge of each others battles
the war is the same
if we lose
someday women's blood will congeal
upon a dead planet
if we win
there is no telling
we seek beyond history
for a new and more possible meeting.[3]

Notes

1. From "Rape: A Radical Analysis, An African-American Perspective" by Kalamu ya Salaam in *Black Books Bulletin*, vol. 6, no. 4 (1980).
2. Seabury Press, New York, 1970.
3. From "Outlines," unpublished poem.

Miscegenation Law, Court Cases, and Ideologies of "Race" in Twentieth-Century America

Peggy Pascoe

On March 21, 1921, Joe Kirby took his wife, Mayellen, to court. The Kirbys had been married for seven years, and Joe wanted out. Ignoring the usual option of divorce, he asked for an annulment, charging that his marriage had been invalid from its very beginning because Arizona law prohibited marriages between "persons of Caucasian blood, or their descendants" and "negroes, Mongolians or Indians, and their descendants." Joe Kirby claimed that while he was "a person of the Caucasian blood," his wife, Mayellen, was "a person of negro blood."[1]

Although Joe Kirby's charges were rooted in a well-established—and tragic—tradition of American miscegenation law, his court case quickly disintegrated into a definitional dispute that bordered on the ridiculous. The first witness in the case was Joe's mother, Tula Kirby, who gave her testimony in Spanish through an interpreter.

Joe's lawyer laid out the case by asking Tula Kirby a few seemingly simple questions:

> *Joe's lawyer:* To what race do you belong?
> *Tula Kirby:* Mexican.
> *Joe's lawyer:* Are you white or have you Indian blood?
> *Kirby:* I have no Indian blood.

. . . .

> *Joe's lawyer:* Do you know the defendant [Mayellen] Kirby?
> *Kirby:* Yes.
> *Joe's lawyer:* To what race does she belong?
> *Kirby:* Negro.

Then the cross-examination began.

> *Mayellen's lawyer:* Who was your father?
> *Kirby:* Jose Romero.
> *Mayellen's lawyer:* Was he a Spaniard?
> *Kirby:* Yes, a Mexican.
> *Mayellen's lawyer:* Was he born in Spain?

From *Journal of American History*, 83 (June 1996), 44-69. Reprinted by permission of the Journal of American History.

Kirby: No, he was born in Sonora.

Mayellen's lawyer: And who was your mother?

Kirby: Also in Sonora.

Mayellen's lawyer: Was she a Spaniard?

Kirby: She was on her father's side.

Mayellen's lawyer: And what on her mother's side?

Kirby: Mexican.

Mayellen's lawyer: What do you mean by Mexican, Indian, a native [?]

Kirby: I don't know what is meant by Mexican.

Mayellen's lawyer: A native of Mexico?

Kirby: Yes, Sonora, all of us.

Mayellen's lawyer: Who was your grandfather on your father's side?

Kirby: He was a Spaniard.

Mayellen's lawyer: Who was he?

Kirby: His name was Ignacio Quevas.

Mayellen's lawyer: Where was he born?

Kirby: That I don't know. He was my grandfather.

Mayellen's lawyer: How do you know he was a [S]paniard then?

Kirby: Because he told me ever since I had knowledge that he was a Spaniard.

Next the questioning turned to Tula's opinion about Mayellen Kirby's racial identity.

> *Mayellen's lawyer:* You said Mrs. [Mayellen] Kirby was a negress. What do you know about Mrs. Kirby's family?
>
> *Kirby:* I distinguish her by her color and the hair; that is all I do know.[2]

The second witness in the trial was Joe Kirby, and by the time he took the stand, the people in the courtroom knew they were in murky waters. When Joe's lawyer opened with the question "What race do *you* belong to?" Joe answered "Well, and paused, while Mayellen's lawyer objected to the question on the ground that it called for a conclusion by the witness, "Oh, no," said the judge, "it is a matter of pedigree." Eventually allowed to answer the question, Joe said, "I belong to the white race I suppose." Under cross-examination, he described his father as having been of the "Irish race," although he

admitted, "I never knew any one of his people."[3]

Stopping at the brink of this morass, Joe's lawyer rested his case. He told the judge he had established that Joe was "Caucasian." Mayellen's lawyer scoffed, claiming that Joe had "failed utterly to prove his case" and arguing that "[Joe's] mother has admitted that. She has [testified) that she only claims a quarter Spanish blood; the rest of it is native blood." At this point the court intervened. "I know," said the judge, "but that does not signify anything."[4]

From the Decline and Fall of Scientific Racism to an Understanding of Modernist Racial Ideology

The Kirbys' case offers a fine illustration of Evelyn Brooks Higginbotham's observation that, although most Americans are sure they know "race" when they see it, very few can offer a definition of the term. Partly for this reason, the questions of what "race" signifies and what signifies "race" are as important for scholars today as they were for the participants in *Kirby v. Kirby* seventy-five years ago.[5] Historians have a long—and recently a distinguished—record of exploring this question.[6] Beginning in the 1960s, one notable group charted the rise and fall of scientific racism among American intellectuals. Today, their successors, more likely to be schooled in social than intellectual history, trace the social construction of racial ideologies, including the idea of "whiteness," in a steadily expanding range of contexts.[7]

Their work has taught us a great deal about racial thinking in American history. We can trace the growth of racism among antebellum immigrant workers and free-soil northern Republicans; we can measure its breadth in late-nineteenth-century segregation and the immigration policies of the 1920s. We can follow the rise of Anglo-Saxonism from Manifest Destiny through the Spanish-American War and expose the appeals to white supremacy in woman suffrage speeches. We can relate all these developments (and more) to the growth and elaboration of scientific racist attempts to use biological characteristics to scout for racial hierarchies in social life, levels of civilization, even language.

Yet the range and richness of these studies all but end with the 1920s. In contrast to historians of the nineteenth- and early-twentieth-century United States, historians of the nation in the mid- to late-twentieth century seem to focus on racial ideologies only when they are advanced by the far Right (as in the Ku Klux Klan) or by racialized groups themselves (as in the Harlem Renaissance or black nationalist movements). To the extent that there is a framework for surveying mainstream twentieth-century American racial ideologies, it is inherited from the classic histories that tell of the post-1920s decline and fall of scientific racism. Their final pages link the demise of scientific racism to the rise of a vanguard of social scientists led by the cultural anthropologist Franz Boas: when modern social science emerges, racism runs out of intellectual steam. In the absence of any other narrative, this forms the basis for a commonly held but rarely examined intellectual trickle-down theory in which the attack on scientific racism emerges in universities in the 1920s and eventually, if belatedly, spreads to courts in the 1940s and 1950s and to government policy in the 1960s and 1970s.

A close look at such incidents as the *Kirby* case, however, suggests a rather different historical trajectory, one that recognizes that the legal system does more than just reflect social or scientific ideas about race; it also produces and reproduces them.[8] By following a trail marked by four miscegenation cases—the seemingly ordinary *Kirby v. Kirby* (1922) and *Estate of Monks* (1941) and the pathbreaking *Perez v. Lippold* (1948) and *Loving v. Virginia* (1967)—this article will examine the relation between modern social science, miscegenation law, and twentieth-century American racial ideologies, focusing less on the decline of scientific racism and more on the emergence of new racial ideologies.

In exploring these issues, it helps to understand that the range of nineteenth-century racial ideologies was much broader than scientific racism. Accordingly, I have chosen to use the term *racialism* to designate an ideological complex that other historians often describe with the terms "race" or "racist." I intend the term *racialism* to be broad enough to cover a wide range of nineteenth-century ideas, from the biologically marked categories scientific racists employed to the more amorphous ideas George M. Fredrickson has so aptly called "romantic racialism."[9] Used in this way, "racialism" helps counter the tendency of twentieth-century observers to perceive nineteenth-century ideas as biologically "determinist" in some simple sense. To racialists (including scientific racism), the important point was not that biology determined culture (indeed, the split between the two was only dimly perceived), but that race, understood as an indivisible essence that included not only biology but also culture, morality, and intelligence, was a compellingly significant factor in history and society.

My argument is this: During the 1920s, American racialism was challenged by several emerging ideologies, all of which depended on a modern split between biology and culture. Between the 1920s and the 1960s, those competing ideologies were winnowed down to the single, powerfully persuasive belief that the eradication of racism depends on the deliberate nonrecognition of race. I will call that belief *modernist racial ideology* to echo the self-conscious "modernism" of social scientists, writers, artists, and cultural rebels of the early twentieth century. When historians mention this phenomenon, they usually label it "antiracist" or "egalitarian" and describe it as in stark contrast to the "racism" of its predecessors. But in the new legal scholarship called critical race theory, this same ideology, usually referred to as "color blindness," is criticized by those who recognize that it, like other racial ideologies, can be turned to the service of oppression.[10]

Modernist racial ideology has been widely accepted; indeed, it compels nearly as much adherence in the late-twentieth-century United States as racialism did in the late nineteenth century. It is therefore important to see it not as what it claims to be-the nonideological end of racism—but as a racial ideology of its own, whose history shapes many of today's arguments about the meaning of race in American society.

The Legacy of Racialism and the *Kirby* Case

Although it is probably less familiar to historians than, say, school segregation law, miscegenation law is an ideal place to study both the legacy of nineteenth-century racialism and the emergence of modern racial ideologies.[11] Miscegenation laws, in force from the 1660s through the 1960s, were among the longest lasting of American racial restrictions. They both reflected and produced significant shifts in American racial thinking. Although the first miscegenation laws had been passed in the colonial period, it was not until after the demise of slavery that they began to function as the ultimate sanction of the American system of

white supremacy. They burgeoned along with the rise of segregation and the early-twentieth-century devotion to "white purity." At one time or another, 41 American colonies and states enacted them; they blanketed western as well as southern states.[12]

By the early twentieth century, miscegenation laws were so widespread that they formed a virtual road map to American legal conceptions of race. Laws that had originally prohibited marriages between whites and African Americans (and, very occasionally, American Indians) were extended to cover a much wider range of groups. Eventually, 12 states targeted American Indians, 14 Asian Americans (Chinese, Japanese, and Koreans), and 9 "Malays" (or Filipinos). In Arizona, the *Kirby* case was decided under categories first adopted in a 1901 law that prohibited whites from marrying "negroes, Mongolians or Indians"; in 1931, "Malays" and "Hindus" were added to this list.[13]

Although many historians assume that miscegenation laws enforced American taboos against interracial sex, marriage, more than sex, was the legal focus.[14] Some states did forbid both interracial sex and interracial marriage, but nearly twice as many targeted only marriage. Because marriage carried with it social respectability and economic benefits that were routinely denied to couples engaged in illicit sex, appeals courts adjudicated the legal issue of miscegenation at least as frequently in civil cases about marriage and divorce, inheritance, or child legitimacy as in criminal cases about sexual misconduct.[15]

By the time the *Kirby* case was heard, lawyers and judges approached miscegenation cases with working assumptions built on decades of experience. There had been a flurry of challenges to the laws during Reconstruction, but courts quickly fended off arguments that miscegenation laws violated the Fourteenth Amendment guarantee of "equal protection." Beginning in the late 1870s, judges declared that the laws were constitutional because they covered all racial groups "equally."[16] Judicial justifications reflected the momentum toward racial categorization built into the nineteenth-century legal system and buttressed by the racialist conviction that everything from culture, morality, and intelligence to heredity could be understood in terms of race.

From the 1880s until the 1920s, lawyers whose clients had been caught in the snare of miscegenation laws knew better than to challenge the constitutionality of the laws or to dispute the perceived necessity for racial categorization; these were all but guaranteed to be losing arguments. A defender's best bet was to do what Mayellen Kirby's lawyer tried to do: to persuade a judge (or jury) that one particular individual's racial classification was in error. Lawyers who defined their task in these limited terms occasionally succeeded, but even then the deck was stacked against them. Wielded by judges and juries who believed that setting racial boundaries was crucial to the maintenance of ordered society, the criteria used to determine who fit in which category were more notable for their malleability than for their logical consistency. Genealogy, appearance, claims to identity, or that mystical quality, "blood"—any of these would do.[17]

In Arizona, Judge Samuel L. Pattee demonstrated that malleability in deciding the *Kirby* case. Although Mayellen Kirby's lawyer maintained that Joe Kirby "appeared" to be an Indian, the judge insisted that parentage, not appearance, was the key to Joe's racial classification:

> Mexicans are classed as of the Caucasian Race. They are descendants, supposed to be, at least of the Spanish conquerors of that country, and unless it can be shown that they

are mixed up with some other races, why the presumption is that they are descendants of the Caucasian race.[18]

While the judge decided that ancestry determined that Joe Kirby was "Caucasian," he simply assumed that Mayellen Kirby was "Negro." Mayellen Kirby sat silent through the entire trial; she was spoken about and spoken for but never allowed to speak herself. There was no testimony about her ancestry; her race was assumed to rest in her visible physical characteristics. Neither of the lawyers bothered to argue over Mayellen's racial designation. As Joe's lawyer later explained,

> The learned and discriminating judge . . . had the opportunity to gaze upon the dusky countenance of the appellant [Mayellen Kirby) and could not and did not fail to observe the distinguishing characteristics of the African race and blood.[19]

In the end, the judge accepted the claim that Joe Kirby was "Caucasian" and Mayellen Kirby "Negro" and held that the marriage violated Arizona miscegenation law; he granted Joe Kirby his annulment. In so doing, the judge resolved the miscegenation drama by adding a patriarchal moral to the white supremacist plot. As long as miscegenation laws regulated marriage more than sex, it proved easy for white men involved with women of color to avoid the social and economic responsibilities they would have carried in legally sanctioned marriages with white women. By granting Joe Kirby an annulment, rather than a divorce, the judge not only denied the validity of the marriage while it had lasted but also in effect excused Joe Kirby from his obligation to provide economic support to a divorced wife.[20]

For her part, Mayellen Kirby had nothing left to lose. She and her lawyer appealed to the Arizona Supreme Court. This time they threw caution to the winds. Taking a first step toward the development of modern racial ideologies, they moved beyond their carefully limited argument about Joe's individual racial classification to challenge the entire racial logic of miscegenation law. The Arizona statute provided a tempting target for their attack, for under its "descendants" provision, a person of "mixed blood" could not legally marry anyone. Pointing this out, Mayellen Kirby's lawyer argued that the law must therefore be unconstitutional. He failed to convince the court. The appeals court judge brushed aside such objections. The argument that the law was unconstitutional, the judge held:

> is an attack . . . [Mayellen Kirby] is not entitled to make for the reason that there is no evidence that she is other than of the black race. . . . It will be time enough to pass on the question she raises. . . . when it is presented by some one whose rights are involved or affected.[21]

The Culturalist Challenge to Racialism

By the 1920s, refusals to recognize the rights of African American women had become conventional in American law. So had refusals to recognize obvious inconsistencies in legal racial classification schemes. Minions of racialism, judges, juries, and experts sometimes quarreled over specifics, but they agreed on the overriding importance of making and enforcing racial classifications.

Lawyers in miscegenation cases therefore neither needed nor received much courtroom assistance from experts. In another legal arena, citizenship and naturalization law, the use of experts, nearly all of whom advocated some version of scientific racism, was much more common. Ever since the 1870s, naturalization lawyers had relied on scientific racists to help them decide which racial and ethnic groups met the United States naturalization requirement of

being "white" persons. But in a series of cases heard in the first two decades of the twentieth century, this strategy backfired. When judges found themselves drawn into a heated scientific debate on the question of whether "Caucasian" was the same as "white," the United States Supreme Court settled the question by discarding the experts and reverting to what the justices called the opinion of the "common man."[22]

In both naturalization and miscegenation cases, judges relied on the basic agreement between popular and expert (scientific racist) versions of the racialism that permeated turn-of-the-century American society. But even as judges promulgated the common sense of racialism, the ground was shifting beneath their feet. By the 1920s, lawyers in miscegenation cases were beginning to glimpse the courtroom potential of arguments put forth by a pioneering group of self-consciously "modern" social scientists willing to challenge racialism head on.

Led by cultural anthropologist Franz Boas, these emerging experts have long stood as the heroes of histories of the decline of scientific racism (which is often taken to stand for racism as a whole). But for modern social scientists, the attack on racialism was not so much an end in itself as a function of the larger goal of establishing "culture" as a central social science paradigm. Intellectually and institutionally, Boas and his followers staked their claim to academic authority on their conviction that human difference and human history were best explained by culture. Because they interpreted character, morality, and social organization as cultural, rather than racial, phenomena and because they were determined to explore, name, and claim the field of cultural analysis for social scientists, particularly cultural anthropologists, sociologists, and social psychologists, they are perhaps best described as culturalists.[23]

To consolidate their power, culturalists had to challenge the scientific racist paradims they hoped to displace. Two of the arguments they made were of particular significance for the emergence of modern racial ideologies. The first was the argument that the key notion of racialism—race—made no biological sense. This argument allowed culturalists to take aim at a very vulnerable target. For most of the nineteenth century, scientific racists had solved disputes about who fit into which racial categories by subdividing the categories. As a result, the number of scientifically recognized races had increased so steadily that by 1911, when the anthropologist Daniel Folkmar compiled the intentionally definitive *Dictionary of Races and Peoples,* he recognized "45 races or peoples among immigrants coming to the United States." Folkmar's was only one of several competing schemes, and culturalists delighted in pointing out the discrepancies between them, showing that scientific racists could not agree on such seemingly simple matters as how many races there were or what criteria—blood, skin color, hair type—best indicated race.[24]

In their most dramatic mode, culturalists went so far as to insist that physical characteristics were completely unreliable indicators of race; in biological terms, they insisted, race must be considered indeterminable. Thus, in an influential encyclopedia article on "race" published in the early thirties, Boas insisted that "it is not possible to assign with certainty any one individual to a definite group." Perhaps the strongest statement of this kind came from Julian Huxley and A. C. Haddon, British scientists who maintained that "the term *race* as applied to human groups should be dropped from the vocabulary of science." Since Huxley was one of the first culturalists trained as a biologist, his credentials added luster to

his opinion. In this and other forms, the culturalist argument that race was biologically indeterminable captured the attention of both contemporaries and later historians.[25]

Historians have paid much less attention to a second and apparently incompatible argument put forth by culturalists. It started from the other end of the spectrum, maintaining, not that there was no such thing as biological race, but that race was nothing more than biology. Since culturalists considered biology of remarkably little importance, consigning race to the realm of biology pushed it out of the picture. Thus Boas ended his article on race by concluding that although it remained "likely" enough that scientific study of the "anatomical differences between the races" might reveal biological influences on the formation of personality, "the study of cultural forms shows that such differences are altogether irrelevant as compared with the powerful influence of the cultural environment in which the group lives."[26]

Following this logic, the contrast between important and wide-reaching culture and unimportant (but biological) race stood as the cornerstone of many culturalist arguments. Thus the cultural anthropologist Ruth Benedict began her influential 1940 book, *Race: Science and Politics,* with an analysis of "what race is *not,*" including language, customs, intelligence, character, and civilization. In a 1943 pamphlet coauthored with Gene Weltfish and addressed to the general public, she explained that real "racial differences" occurred only in "nonessentials such as texture of head hair, amount of body hair, shape of the nose or head, or color of the eyes and the skin." Drawing on these distinctions, Benedict argued that race was a scientific "fact," but that racism, which she defined as "the dogma that the hope of civilization depends upon eliminating some races and keeping others pure," was no more than a "modern superstition."[27]

Culturalists set these two seemingly contradictory depictions of race—the argument that biological race was nonsense and the argument that race was merely biology—right beside each other. The contradiction mattered little to them. Both arguments effectively contracted the range of racialist thinking, and both helped break conceptual links between race and character, morality, psychology, and language. By showing that one after another of these phenomena depended more on environment and training than on biology, culturalists moved each one out of the realm of race and into the province of culture, widening the modern split between culture and biology. Boas opened his article on race by staking out this position. "The term race is often used loosely to indicate groups of men differing in appearance, language, or culture," he wrote, but in his analysis, it would apply "solely to the biological grouping of human types."[28]

In adopting this position, culturalist intellectuals took a giant step away from popular common sense on the issue of race. Recognizing—even at times celebrating—this gap between themselves and the public, they devoted much of their work to dislodging popular racial assumptions. They saw the public as lamentably behind the times and sadly prone to race "prejudice," and they used their academic credentials to insist that racial categories not only did not rest on common sense, but made little sense at all.[29]

The *Monks* Case and the Making of Modern Racial Ideologies

This, of course, was just what lawyers challenging miscegenation laws wanted to hear. Because culturalist social scientists could offer their arguments with an air of scientific and academic authority that might persuade judges, attorneys began to invite them to appear as expert witnesses. But when culturalists appeared in court, they entered an arena where their argument for the biological indeterminacy of race was shaped in ways neither they nor the lawyers who recruited them could control.

Take, for example, the seemingly curious trial of Marie Antoinette Monks of San Diego, California, decided in the Superior Court of San Diego County in 1939. By all accounts, Marie Antoinette Monks was a woman with a clear eye for her main chance. In the early 1930s, she had entranced and married a man named Allan Monks, potential heir to a Boston fortune. Shortly after the marriage, which took place in Arizona, Allan Monks declined into insanity. Whether his mental condition resulted from injuries he had suffered in a motorcycle crash or from drugs administered under the undue influence of Marie Antoinette, the court would debate at great length. Allan Monks died. He left two wills: an old one in favor of a friend named Ida Lee and a newer one in favor of his wife, Marie Antoinette. Ida Lee submitted her version of the will for probate, Marie Antoinette challenged her claim, and Lee fought back. Lee's lawyers contended that the Monks marriage was illegal. They charged that Marie Antoinette Monks, who had told her husband she was a "French" countess, was actually "a Negro" and therefore prohibited by Arizona law from marrying Allan Monks, whom the court presumed to be Caucasian.[30]

Much of the ensuing six-week-long trial was devoted to determining the "race" of Marie Antoinette Monks. To prove that she was "a Negro," her opponents called five people to the witness stand: a disgruntled friend of her husband, a local labor commissioner, and three expert witnesses, all of whom offered arguments that emphasized biological indicators of race. The first so-called expert, Monks's hairdresser, claimed that she could tell that Monks was of mixed blood from looking at the size of the moons of her fingernails, the color of the "ring" around the palms of her hands, and the "kink" in her hair. The second, a physical anthropologist from the nearby San Diego Museum, claimed to be able to tell that Monks was "at least one-eighth negroid" from the shape of her face, the color of her hands, and her "protruding heels," all of which he had observed casually while a spectator in the courtroom. The third expert witness, a surgeon, had grown up and practiced medicine in the South and later served at a Southern Baptist mission in Africa. Having once walked alongside Monks when entering the courthouse (at which time he tried, he said, to make a close observation of her), he testified that he could tell that she was of "one-eighth negro blood" from the contour of her calves and heels, from the "peculiar pallor" on the back of her neck, from the shape of her face, and from the wave of her hair.[31]

To defend Monks, her lawyers called a friend, a relative, and two expert witnesses of their own, an anthropologist and a biologist. The experts both started out by testifying to the culturalist position that it was impossible to tell a person's race from physical characteristics, especially if that person was, as they put it, "of mixed blood." This was the argument culturalists used whenever they were cornered into talking about biology, a phenomenon they tended to

regard as so insignificant a factor in social life that they preferred to avoid talking about it at all.

But because this argument replaced certainty with uncertainty, it did not play very well in the *Monks* courtroom. Seeking to find the definitiveness they needed to offset the experts who had already testified, the lawyers for Monks paraded their own client in front of the witness stand, asking her to show the anthropologist her fingernails and to remove her shoes so that he could see her heels. They lingered over the biologist's testimony that Monks's physical features resembled those of the people of southern France. In the end, Monks's lawyers backed both experts into a corner; when pressed repeatedly for a definite answer, both reluctantly admitted that it was their opinion that Monks was a "white" woman.[32]

The experts' dilemma reveals the limitations of the argument for racial indeterminacy in the courtroom. Faced with a conflict between culturalist experts, who offered uncertainty and indeterminacy, and their opponents, who offered concrete biological answers to racial questions, judges were predisposed to favor the latter. To judges, culturalists appeared frustratingly vague and uncooperative (in other words, lousy witnesses), while their opponents seemed to be good witnesses willing to answer direct questions.

In the *Monks* case, the judge admitted that his own "inexpert" opinion—that Marie Antoinette "did have many characteristics that I would say . . . [showed] mixed negro and some other blood"—was not enough to justify a ruling. Turning to the experts before him, he dismissed the hairdresser (whose experience he was willing to grant, but whose scientific credentials he considered dubious); he passed over the biologist (whose testimony, he thought, could go either way); and he dismissed the two anthropologists, whose testimonies, he said, more or less canceled each other out. The only expert the judge was willing to rely on was the surgeon, because the surgeon "seemed . . . to hold a very unique and peculiar position as an expert on the question involved from his work in life."[33]

Relying on the surgeon's testimony, the judge declared that Marie Antoinette Monks was "the descendant of a negro" who had "one-eighth negro blood . . . and 7/8 caucasian blood"; he said that her "race" prohibited her from marrying Allan Monks and from inheriting his estate. The racial categorization served to invalidate the marriage in two overlapping ways. First, as a "negro," Marie Antoinette could not marry a white under Arizona miscegenation law; and second, by telling her husband-to-be that she was "French," Marie Antoinette had committed a "fraud" serious enough to render the marriage legally void. The court's decision that she had also exerted "undue influence" over Monks was hardly necessary to the outcome.[34]

As the *Monks* case suggests, we should be careful not to overestimate the influence culturalists had on the legal system. And, while in courtrooms culturalist experts were trying—and failing—to convince judges that biological racial questions were unanswerable, outside the courts their contention that biological racial answers were insignificant was faring little better. During the first three decades of the twentieth century, scientists on the "racial" side of the split between race and culture reconstituted themselves into a rough alliance of their own. Mirroring the modern dividing line between biology and culture, its ranks swelled with those who claimed special expertise on biological questions. There were biologists and physicians; leftover racialists such as physical anthropologists, increasingly shorn of their claims to expertise in

every arena *except* that of physical characteristics; and, finally, the newly emerging eugenicists.[35]

Eugenicists provided the glue that held this coalition together. Narrowing the sweep of nineteenth-century racialist thought to focus on biology, these modern biological experts then expanded their range by offering physical characteristics, heredity, and reproductive imperatives as variations on the biological theme. They were particularly drawn to arenas in which all these biological motifs came into play; accordingly, they placed special emphasis on reforming marriage laws. Perhaps the best-known American eugenicist, Charles B. Davenport of the Eugenics Record Office, financed by the Carnegie Institution, outlined their position in a 1913 pamphlet, *State Laws Limiting Marriage Selection Examined in the Light of Eugenics,* which proposed strengthening state control over the marriages of the physically and racially unfit. Davenport's plan was no mere pipe dream. According to the historian Michael Grossberg, by the 1930s, 41 states used eugenic categories to restrict the marriage of "lunatics," "imbeciles," "idiots," and the "feebleminded"; 26 states restricted the marriages of those infected with syphilis and gonorrhea; and 27 states passed sterilization laws. By midcentury, blood tests had become a standard legal prerequisite for marriage.[36]

Historians have rather quickly passed over the racial aspects of American eugenics, seeing its proponents as advocates of outmoded ideas soon to be beached by the culturalist sea change. Yet until at least World War II, eugenicists reproduced a modern racism that was biological in a particularly virulent sense. For them, unlike their racialist predecessors (who tended to regard biology as an indicator of a much more expansive racial phenomenon), biology really was the essence of race. And unlike nineteenth-century scientific racists (whose belief in discrete racial dividing lines was rarely shaken by evidence of racial intermixture), twentieth-century eugenicists and culturalists alike seemed obsessed with the subject of mixed-race individuals.[37]

In their determination to protect "white purity," eugenicists believed that even the tightest definitions of race by blood proportion were too loose. Setting their sights on Virginia, in 1924 they secured passage of the most draconian miscegenation law in American history. The act, entitled "an Act to preserve racial integrity," replaced the legal provision that a person must have one-sixteenth of "negro blood" to fall within the state's definition of "colored" with a provision that:

> It shall hereafter be unlawful for any white person in this State to marry any save a white person, or a person with no other admixture of blood than white and American Indian. For the purpose of this act, the term "white person" shall apply only to the person who has no trace whatsoever of any blood other than Caucasian; but persons who have one-sixteenth or less of the blood of the American Indian and have no other non-Caucasic blood shall be deemed to be white persons.

Another section of the Virginia law (which provided for the issuance of supposedly voluntary racial registration certificates for Virginia citizens) spelled out the "races" the legislature had in mind. The list, which specified "Caucasian, Negro, Mongolian, American Indian, Asiatic Indian, Malay, or any mixture thereof, or any other non-Caucasic strains," showed the lengths to which lawmakers would go to pin down racial categories. Within the decade, the Virginia law was copied by Georgia and echoed in Alabama. Thereafter, while supporters worked without much success to extend

such laws to other states, defenders of miscegenation statutes added eugenic arguments to their rhetorical arsenal.[38]

Having been pinned to the modern biological wall and labeled as "mixed race," Marie Antoinette Monks would seem to have been in the perfect position to challenge the constitutionality of the widely drawn Arizona miscegenation law. She took her case to the California Court of Appeals, Fourth District, where she made an argument that echoed that of Mayellen Kirby two decades earlier. Reminding the court of the wording of the Arizona statute, her lawyers pointed out that "on the set of facts found by the trial judge, [Marie Antoinette Monks] is concededly of Caucasian blood as well as negro blood, and therefore a descendant of a Caucasian." Spelling it out, they explained:

> As such, she is prohibited from marrying a negro or any descendant of a negro, a Mongolian or an Indian, a Malay or a Hindu, or any of the descendants of any of them. Likewise . . . as a descendant of a negro she is prohibited from marrying a Caucasian or descendant of a Caucasian, which of course would include any person who had any degree of Caucasian blood in them.

Because this meant that she was "absolutely prohibited from contracting valid marriages in Arizona," her lawyers argued that the Arizona law was an unconstitutional constraint on her liberty.[39]

The court, however, dismissed this argument as "interesting but in our opinion not tenable." In a choice that speaks volumes about the depth of attachment to racial categories, the court narrowed the force of the argument by asserting that "the constitutional problem would be squarely presented" only if one mixed-race person were seeking to marry another mixed-race person, then used this constructed hypothetical to dodge the issue:

While it is true that there was evidence that appellant [Marie Antoinette Monks] is a descendant of the Caucasian race, as well as of the Negro race, the other contracting party [Allan Monks] was of unmixed blood and therefore the hypothetical situation involving an attempted alliance between two persons of mixed blood is no more present in the instant case than in the Kirby case. . . . The situations conjured up by respondent are not here involved. . . . Under the facts presented the appellant does not have the benefit of assailing the validity of the statute.

This decision was taken as authoritative. Both the United States Supreme Court and the Supreme Judicial Court of Massachusetts (in which Monks had also filed suit) refused to reopen the issue.[40]

Perhaps the most interesting thing about the Monks case is that there is no reason to believe that the public found it either remarkable or objectionable. Local reporters who covered the trial in 1939 played up the themes of forgery, drugs, and insanity; their summaries of the racial categories of the Arizona law and the opinions of the expert witnesses were largely matter-of-fact.[41]

In this seeming acceptability to the public lies a clue to the development of modern racial ideologies. Even as judges narrowed their conception of race, transforming an all-encompassing phenomenon into a simple fact to be determined, they remained bound by the provisions of miscegenation law to determine who fit in which racial categories. For this purpose, the second culturalist argument, that race was merely biology, had far more to offer than the first, that race was biologically indeterminable. The conception of race as merely biological seemed consonant with the racial categories built into the laws, seemed supportable by clear and unequivocal expert testimony, and fit comfortably within popular notions of race.

The Distillation of Modernist Racial Ideology: From *Perez* to *Loving*

In the *Monks* case we can see several modern racial ideologies—ranging from the argument that race was biological nonsense to the reply that race was essentially biological to the possibility that race was merely biology—all grounded in the split between culture and biology. To distill these variants into a unified modernist racial ideology, another element had to be added to the mix, the remarkable (in American law, nearly unprecedented) proposal that the legal system abandon its traditional responsibility for determining and defining racial categories. In miscegenation law, this possibility emerged in a case that also, and not coincidentally, featured the culturalist argument for biological racial indeterminacy.

The case was *Perez v. Lippold*. It involved a young Los Angeles couple, Andrea Perez and Sylvester Davis, who sought a marriage license. Turned down by the Los Angeles County clerk, they challenged the constitutionality of the California miscegenation law directly to the California Supreme Court, which heard their case in October 1947.[42]

It was not immediately apparent that the *Perez* case would play a role in the development of modernist racial ideology. Perhaps because both sides agreed that Perez was "a white female" and Davis "a Negro male," the lawyer who defended the couple, Daniel Marshall, did not initially see the case as turning on race categorization. In 1947, Marshall had few civil rights decisions to build on, so he tried an end-run strategy: he based his challenge to miscegenation laws on the argument that because both Perez and Davis were Catholics and the Catholic Church did not prohibit interracial marriage, California miscegenation law was an arbitrary and unreasonable restraint on their freedom of religion.

The freedom-of-religion argument made some strategic sense, since several courts had held that states had to meet a high standard to justify restrictions on religious expression. Accordingly, Marshall laid out the religion argument in a lengthy petition to the California Supreme Court. In response, the state offered an even lengthier defense of miscegenation laws. The state's lawyers had at their fingertips a long list of precedents upholding such laws, including the *Kirby* and *Monks* cases. They added eugenic arguments about racial biology, including evidence of declining birth rates among "hybrids" and statistics that showed high mortality, short life expectancies, and particular diseases among African Americans. They polished off their case with the comments of a seemingly sympathetic Roman Catholic priest.[43]

Here the matter stood until the California Supreme Court heard oral arguments in the case. At that session, the court listened in silence to Marshall's opening sally that miscegenation laws were based on prejudice and to his argument that they violated constitutional guarantees of freedom of religion. But as soon as the state's lawyer began to challenge the religious freedom argument, one of the court's associate justices, Roger Traynor, impatiently interrupted the proceedings. "What," he asked, "about equal protection of the law?"

> *Mr. Justice Traynor:* . . . it might help to explain the statute, what it means. What is a negro?
> *Mr. Stanley:* We have not the benefit of any judicial interpretation. The statute states that a negro [Stanley evidently meant to say, as the law did, "a white"] cannot marry a negro, which can be construed to mean a full-blooded negro,

since the statute also says mulatto, Mongolian, or Malay.

> *Mr. Justice Traynor:* What is a mulatto? One-sixteenth blood?
> *Mr. Stanley:* Certainly certain states have seen fit to state what a mulatto is.
> *Mr. Justice Traynor:* If there is 1/8 blood, can they marry? If you can marry with 1/8, why not with 1/16, 1/32, 1/64? And then don't you get in the ridiculous position where a negro cannot marry anybody? If he is white, he cannot marry black, or if he is black, he cannot marry white.
> *Mr. Stanley:* I agree that it would be better for the Legislature to lay down an exact amount of blood, but I do not think that the statute should be declared unconstitutional as indefinite on this ground.
> *Mr. Justice Traynor:* That is something anthropologists have not been able to furnish, although they say generally that there is no such thing as race.
> *Mr. Stanley:* I would not say that anthropologists have said that generally, except such statements for sensational purposes.
> *Mr. Justice Traynor:* Would you say that Professor Wooten of Harvard was a sensationalist? The crucial question is how can a county clerk determine who are negroes and who are whites.[44]

Although he addressed his questions to the lawyers for the state, Justice Traynor had given Marshall a gift no lawyer had ever before received in a miscegenation case: judicial willingness to believe in the biological indeterminacy of race. It was no accident that this argument came from Roger Traynor. A former professor at Boalt Hall, the law school of the University of California, Berkeley, Traynor had been appointed to the court for his academic expertise rather than his legal experience; unlike his more pragmatic colleagues, he kept up with developments in modern social science.[45]

Marshall responded to the opening Traynor had provided by making sure that his next brief included the culturalist argument that race was biological nonsense. In it, he asserted that experts had determined that "race, as popularly understood, is a myth"; he played on the gap between expert opinion and laws based on irrational "prejudice" rooted in "myth, folk belief, and superstition"; and he dismissed his opponents' reliance on the "grotesque reasoning of eugenicists" by comparing their statements to excerpts from Adolf Hitler's *Mein Kampf.*[46]

Marshall won his case. The 1948 decision in the *Perez* case was remarkable for many reasons. It marked the first time since Reconstruction that a state court had declared a state miscegenation law unconstitutional. It went far beyond existing appeals cases in that the California Supreme Court had taken the very step the judges in the *Kirby* and *Monks* cases had avoided—going beyond the issue of the race of an individual to consider the issue of racial classification in general. Even more remarkable, the court did so in a case in which neither side had challenged the racial classification of the parties. But despite these accomplishments, the *Perez* case was no victory for the culturalist argument about the biological indeterminacy of race. Only the outcome of the case—that California's miscegenation law was unconstitutional—was clear. The rationale for this outcome was a matter of considerable dispute.

Four justices condemned the law and three supported it; altogether, they issued four separate opinions. A four-justice majority agreed that the law should be declared unconstitutional but disagreed about why. Two justices, led by Traynor, issued a lengthy opinion that pointed out the irrationality of racial categories, citing as authorities a virtual who's who of culturalist social scientists, from Boas, Huxley, and Haddon to Gunnar Myrdal. A third justice issued a concurring opinion that pointedly ignored the rationality or irrationality of

race classifications to criticize miscegenation laws on equality grounds, contending that laws based on "race, color, or creed" were—and always had been—contrary to the Declaration of Independence, the Constitution, and the Fourteenth Amendment; as this justice saw it, the Constitution was color-blind. A fourth justice, who reported that he wanted his decision to "rest upon a broader ground than that the challenged statutes are discriminatory and irrational," based his decision solely on the religious freedom issue that had been the basis of Marshall's original argument.[47]

In contrast, a three-justice minority argued that the law should be upheld. They cited legal precedent, offered biological arguments about racial categories, and mentioned a handful of social policy considerations. Although the decision went against them, their agreement with each other ironically formed the closest thing to a majority in the case. In sum, although the *Perez* decision foreshadowed the day when American courts would abandon their defense of racial categories, its variety of judicial rationales tells us more about the range of modern racial ideologies than it does about the power of any one of them.[48]

Between the *Perez* case in 1948 and the next milestone miscegenation case, *Loving v. Virginia,* decided in 1967, judges would search for a common denominator among this contentious variety, trying to find a position of principled decisiveness persuasive enough to mold both public and expert opinion. One way to do this was to back away from the culturalist argument that race made no biological sense, adopting the other culturalist argument that race was biological fact and thus shifting the debate to the question of how much biological race should matter in determining social and legal policy.

In such a debate, white supremacists tried to extend the reach of biological race as far as possible. Thus one scientist bolstered his devotion to white supremacy by calling Boas "that appalling disaster to American social anthropology whose influence in the end has divorced the social studies of man from their scientific base in physical biology."[49] Following the lead of eugenicists, he and his sympathizers tried to place every social and legal superstructure on a biological racial base.

In contrast, their egalitarian opponents set limits. In their minds, biological race (or "skin color," as they often called it), was significant only because its visibility made it easy for racists to identify those they subjected to racial oppression. As Myrdal, the best-known of the mid-twentieth-century culturalist social scientists, noted in 1944 in his monumental work, *An American Dilemma:*

> In spite of all heterogeneity, the average white man's unmistakable observation is that *most Negroes in America have dark skin and woolly hair,* and he is, of course, right. . . . [the African American's] African ancestry and physical characteristics are fixed to his person much more ineffaceably than the yellow star is fixed to the Jew during the Nazi regime in Germany.[50]

To Myrdal's generation of egalitarians, the translation of visible physical characteristics into social hierarchies formed the tragic foundation of American racism.

The egalitarians won this debate, and their victory paved the way for the emergence of a modernist racial ideology persuasive enough to command the kind of widespread adherence once commanded by late-nineteenth-century racialism. Such a position was formulated by the United States Supreme Court in 1967 in *Loving v. Virginia,* the most important miscegenation case ever heard and the only one now widely remembered.

The *Loving* case involved what was, even for miscegenation law, an extreme example. Richard Perry Loving and Mildred Delores Jeter were residents of the small town of Central Point, Virginia, and family friends who had dated each other since he was seventeen and she was eleven. When they learned that their plans to marry were illegal in Virginia, they traveled to Washington, D.C., which did not have a miscegenation law, for the ceremony, returning in June 1958 with a marriage license, which they framed and placed proudly on their wall. In July 1958, they were awakened in the middle of the night by the county sheriff and two deputies, who had walked through their unlocked front door and right into their bedroom to arrest them for violating Virginia's miscegenation law. Under that law, an amalgam of criminal provisions enacted in 1878 and Virginia's 1924 "Act to preserve racial integrity," the Lovings, who were identified in court records as a "white" man and a "colored" woman, pleaded guilty and were promptly convicted and sentenced to a year in jail. The judge suspended their sentence on the condition that "both accused leave . . . the state of Virginia at once and do not return together or at the same time to said county and state for a period of twenty-five years."[51]

In 1963, the Lovings, then the parents of three children, grew tired of living with relatives in Washington, D.C., and decided to appeal this judgment. Their first attempts ended in defeat. In 1965, the judge who heard their original case not only refused to reconsider his decision but raised the rhetorical stakes by opining:

> Almighty God created the races white, black, yellow, malay and red, and he placed them on separate continents. And but for the interference with his arrangement there would be no

cause for such marriages. The fact that he separated the races shows that he did not intend for the races to mix.

But by the time their argument had been processed by the Supreme Court of Appeals of Virginia (which invalidated the original sentence but upheld the miscegenation law), the case had attracted enough attention that the United States Supreme Court, which had previously avoided taking miscegenation cases, agreed to hear an appeal.[52]

On the side of the Lovings stood not only their own attorneys, but also the National Association for the Advancement of Colored People (NAACP), the NAACP Legal Defense and Education Fund, the Japanese American Citizens League (JACL), and a coalition of Catholic bishops. The briefs they submitted offered the whole arsenal of arguments developed in previous miscegenation cases. The bishops offered the religious freedom argument that had been the original basis of the *Perez* case. The NAACP and the JACL stood on the opinions of culturalist experts, whose numbers now reached beyond social scientists well into the ranks of biologists. Offering both versions of the culturalist line on race, NAACP lawyers argued on one page, "The idea of 'pure' racial groups, either past or present, has long been abandoned by modern biological and social sciences," and on another, "Race, in its scientific dimension, refers only to the biogenetic and physical attributes manifest by a specified population. It does not, under any circumstances, refer to culture (learned behavior), language, nationality, or religion." The Lovings' lawyers emphasized two central points: Miscegenation laws violated both the constitutional guarantee of equal protection under the laws and the constitutional protection of the fundamental right to marry.[53]

In response, the lawyers for the state of Virginia tried hard to find some ground on which to stand. Their string of court precedents upholding miscegenation laws had been broken by the *Perez* decision. Their argument that Congress never intended the Fourteenth Amendment to apply to interracial marriage was offset by the Supreme Court's stated position that congressional intentions were inconclusive. In an attempt to distance the state from the "white purity" aspects of Virginia's 1924 law, Virginia's lawyers argued that since the Lovings admitted that they were a "white" person and a "colored" person and had been tried under a section of the law that mentioned only those categories, the elaborate definition of "white" offered in other sections of Virginia law was irrelevant.[54]

On only one point did the lawyers for both parties and the Court seem to agree: None of them wanted to let expert opinion determine the outcome. The lawyers for Virginia knew only too well that during the twentieth century, the scientific foundations of the eugenic biological argument in favor of miscegenation laws had crumbled, so they tried to warn the Court away by predicting that experts would mire the Court in "a veritable Serbonian bog of conflicting scientific opinion." Yet the Lovings' lawyers, who seemed to have the experts on their side, agreed that "the Court should not go into the morass of sociological evidence that is available on both sides of the question." "We strongly urge," they told the justices, "that it is not necessary." And the Court, still reeling from widespread criticism that its decision in the famous 1954 case *Brown v. Board of Education* was illegitimate "sociological jurisprudence," was not about to offer its opponents any more of such ammunition.[55]

The decision the Court issued was, in fact, carefully shorn of all reference to expert opinion; it spoke in language that both reflected and contributed to a new popular common sense on the issue of race. Recycling earlier pronouncements that "distinctions between citizens solely because of their ancestry" were "odious to a free people whose institutions are founded upon the doctrine of equality" and that the Court "cannot conceive of a valid legislative purpose . . . which makes the color of a person's skin the test of whether his conduct is a criminal offense," the justices reached a new and broader conclusion. Claiming (quite inaccurately) that "We have consistently denied the constitutionality of measures which restrict the rights of citizens on account of race," the Court concluded that the racial classifications embedded in Virginia miscegenation laws were "so directly subversive of the principle of equality at the heart of the Fourteenth Amendment" that they were "unsupportable." Proclaiming that it violated both the equal protection and the due process clauses of the Fourteenth Amendment, the Court declared the Virginia miscegenation law unconstitutional.[56]

Legacies of Modernist Racial Ideology

The decision in the *Loving* case shows the distance twentieth-century American courts had traveled. The accumulated effect of several decades of culturalist attacks on racialism certainly shaped their thinking. The justices were no longer willing to accept the notion that race was the all-encompassing phenomenon nineteenth-century racialist thinkers had assumed it to be; they accepted the divisions between culture and biology and culture and race established by modern social scientists. But neither were they willing to declare popular identification of race with physical characteristics (like "the color of a person's skin") a figment of the imagination. In their minds, the scope of the term

"race" had shrunk to a point where biology was all that was left; "race" referred to visible physical characteristics significant only because racists used them to erect spurious racial hierarchies. The Virginia miscegenation law was a case in point; the Court recognized and condemned it as a statute clearly "designed to maintain White Supremacy."[57]

Given the dependence of miscegenation laws on legal categories of race, the Court concluded that ending white supremacy required abandoning the categories. In de-emphasizing racial categories, they joined mainstream mid-twentieth-century social scientists, who argued that because culture, rather than race, shaped meaningful human difference, race was nothing more than a subdivision of the broader phenomenon of ethnicity. In a society newly determined to be "color-blind," granting public recognition to racial categories seemed to be synonymous with racism itself.[58]

And so the Supreme Court promulgated a modernist racial ideology that maintained that the best way to eradicate racism was the deliberate nonrecognition of race. Its effects reached well beyond miscegenation law. Elements of modernist racial ideology marked many of the major mid-twentieth-century Supreme Court decisions, including *Brown v. Board of Education*. Its effects on state law codes were equally substantial; during the 1960s and 1970s, most American states repealed statutes that had defined "race" (usually by blood proportion) and set out to erase racial terminology from their laws.[59]

Perhaps the best indication of the pervasiveness of modernist racial ideology is how quickly late-twentieth-century conservatives learned to shape their arguments to fit its contours. Attaching themselves to the modernist narrowing of the definition of race to biology and biology alone, conservative thinkers began to contend that, unless their ideas rested solely and explicitly on a belief in biological inferiority, they should not be considered racist. They began to advance "cultural" arguments of their very own, insisting that their proposals were based on factors such as social analysis, business practicality, or merit—on anything, in other words, except biological race. In their hands, modernist racial ideology supports an Alice-in-Wonderland interpretation of racism in which even those who argue for racially oppressive policies can adamantly deny being racists.

This conservative turnabout is perhaps the most striking, but not the only, indication of the contradictions inherent in modernist racial ideology. Others run the gamut from administrative law to popular culture. So while the United States Supreme Court tries to hold to its twentieth-century legacy of limiting, when it cannot eradicate, racial categories, United States government policies remain deeply dependent on them. In the absence of statutory definitions of race, racial categories are now set by the United States Office of Management and Budget, which in 1977 issued a "Statistical Directive" that divided Americans into five major groups—American Indian or Alaskan Native, Asian or Pacific Islander, Black, White, and Hispanic. The statistics derived from these categories help determine everything from census counts to eligibility for inclusion in affirmative action programs to the drawing of voting districts.[60] Meanwhile, in one popular culture flash-point after another—from the Anita Hill/Clarence Thomas hearings to the *O. J. Simpson* case, mainstream commentators insist that "race" should not be a consideration even as they explore detail after detail that reveals its social pervasiveness.[61]

These gaps between the (very narrow) modernist conception of race and the (very wide) range of racial identities and racial oppressions bedevil today's egalitarians. In the political arena, some radicals have begun to argue that the legal system's deliberate nonrecognition of race erodes the ability to recognize and name racism and to argue for such policies as affirmative action, which rely on racial categories to overturn rather than to enforce oppression. Meanwhile, in the universities, a growing chorus of scholars is revitalizing the argument for the biological indeterminacy of race and using that argument to explore the myriad of ways in which socially constructed notions of race remain powerfully salient. Both groups hope to do better than their culturalist predecessors at eradicating racism.[62]

Attaining that goal may depend on how well we understand the tortured history of mid-twentieth-century American ideologies of race.

Notes

1. Ariz. Rev. Stat. Ann. sec. 3837 (1913); "Appellant's Abstract of Record," Aug. 8, 1921, pp, 1–2, *Kirby v. Kirby,* docket 1970 (microfilm: file 36.1.134), Arizona Supreme Court Civil Cases (Arizona State Law Library, Phoenix).

2. "Appellant's Abstract of Record," 12–13, 13–15, 15, *Kirby v. Kirby.*

3. *Ibid.,* 16–18.

4. *Ibid.,* 19.

5. Evelyn Brooks Higginbotham, "African-American Women's History and the Metalanguage of Race," *Signs,* 17 (Winter 1992), 253. See Michael Omi and Howard Winant, *Racial Formation in the United States: From the 1960s to the 1990s* (New York, 1994); David Theo Goldberg, ed., *Anatomy of Racism* (Minneapolis, 1990); Henry Louis Gates Jr., ed., *"Race," Writing, and Difference* (Chicago, 1986); Dominick LaCapra, ed., *The Bounds of Race: Perspectives on Hegemony and Resistance* (Ithaca, 1991); F. James Davis, *Who Is Black? One Nation's Definition* (University Park, 1991); Sandra Harding, ed., *The "Racial" Economy of Science: Toward a Democratic Future* (Bloomington, 1993); Maria P. P. Root, ed., *Racially Mixed People in America* (Newbury Park, 1992); and Ruth Frankenberg, *White Women, Race Matters: The Social Construction of Whiteness* (Minneapolis, 1993).

6. Among the most provocative recent works are Higginbotham, "African-American Women's History"; Barbara J. Fields, "Ideology and Race in American History," in *Region, Race, and Reconstruction: Essays in Honor of C. Vann Woodward,* ed. J. Morgan Kousser and James M. McPherson (New York, 1982), 143–78; Thomas C. Holt, "Marking: Race, Race-Making, and the Writing of History," *American Historical Review,* 100 (Feb. 1995), 1–20 and David R. Roediger, *Towards the Abolition of Whiteness: Essays on Race, Politics, and Working Class History* (London, 1994).

7. On scientific racism, see Thomas F. Gossett, *Race: The History of an Idea in America* (Dallas, 1963); George W. Stocking Jr., *Race, Culture, and Evolution: Essays in the History of Anthropology* (1968; Chicago, 1982); 1968; John S. Haller Jr., *Outcasts from Evolution: Scientific Attitudes to Racial Inferiority, 1859–1900* (Urbana, 1971); George M. Fredrickson, *The Black Image in the White Mind: The Debate on Afro-American Character and Destiny, 1817–1914* (New York, 1971); Thomas G. Dyer, *Theodore Roosevelt and the Idea of Race* (Baton Rouge, 1980); Carl N. Degler, *In Search of Human Nature: The Decline and Revival of Darwinism in American Social Thought* (New York, 1991); and Elazar Barkan, *Retreat of Scientific Racism: Changing Concepts of Race in Britain and the United States between the World Wars* (Cambridge, Eng., 1992). On the social construction of racial ideologies, see the works cited in footnote 6, above, and Ronald T. Takaki, *Iron Cages: Race and Culture in Nineteenth-Century America* (New York, 1979); Reginald Horsman, *Race and Manifest Destiny: The Origins of American Racial Anglo-Saxonism* (Cambridge, Mass., 1981); Alexander Saxton, *The Rise and Fall of the White Republic: Class Politics and Mass Culture in Nineteenth-Century America* (London, 1990); David R. Roediger, *The Wages of Whiteness: Race and the Making of the American Working Class* (London, 1991); Audrey Smedley, *Race in North America: Origin and Evolution of a Worldview* (Boulder, 1993); and Tomas Almaguer, *Racial Fault Lines: The Historical Origins of White Supremacy in California* (Berkeley, 1994).

8. On law as a producer of racial ideologies, see Barbara J. Fields, "Slavery, Race, and Ideology in the United States of America," *New Left Review,* 181 (May–June 1990), 7; Eva Saks, "Representing Miscegenation Law," *Raritan,* 8 (Fall 1988), 56–60; and Collette Guillaumin, "Race and Nature: The System of Marks," *Feminist Issues,* 8 (Fall 1988), 25–44.

9. See especially Fredrickson, *Black Image in the White Mind.*

10. For intriguing attempts to define American modernism, see Daniel J. Singal, ed., *Modernist Culture in America* (Belmont, 1991); and Dorothy Ross, ed., *Modernist Impulses in the Human Sciences, 1870–1930* (Baltimore, 1994). For the view from critical race theory, see Brian K. Fair, "Foreword: Rethinking the Colorblindness Model," *National Black Law Journal,* 13 (Spring 1993), 1–82; Neil Gotanda, "A Critique of Our Constitution Is Color-Blind," *Stanford Law Review,* 44 (Nov. 1991), 1–68; Gary Peller, "Race Consciousness," *Duke Law Journal* (Sept. 1990), 758–847; and Peter Fitzpatrick, "Racism and the Innocence of Law," in *Anatomy of Racism,* ed. Goldberg, 247–62.

11. Many scholars avoid using the word *miscegenation,* which dates to the 1860s, means race mixing, and has, to twentieth-century minds, embarrassingly biological connotations; they speak of laws against "interracial" or "cross-cultural" relationships. Contemporaries usually referred to "anti-miscegenation" laws. Neither alternative seems satisfactory, since the first avoids naming the ugliness that was so much a part of the laws and the second implies that "miscegenation" was a distinct racial phenomenon rather than a categorization imposed on certain relationships. I retain the term *miscegenation* when speaking of the laws and court cases that relied on the concept, but not when speaking of people or particular relationships. On the emergence of the term, see Sidney Kaplan, "The Miscegenation Issue in the Election of 1864," *Journal of Negro History,* 24 (July 1949), 274–343.

12. Most histories of interracial sex and marriage in America focus on demographic patterns, rather than legal constraints. See, for example, Joel Williamson, *New People: Miscegenation and Mulattoes in the United States* (New York, 1980); Paul R. Spickard, *Mixed Blood: Intermarriage and Ethnic Identity in Twentieth-Century America* (Madison, 1989); and Deborah Lynn Kitchen, "Interracial Marriage in the United States, 1900–1980" (Ph.D. diss., University of Minnesota, 1993). The only historical overview is Byron Curti Martyn, "Racism in the United States: A History of the Anti-Miscegenation Legislation and Litigation" (Ph.D. diss., University of Southern California, 1979). On the colonial period, see A. Leon Higginbotham Jr. and Barbara K. Kopytoff, "Racial Purity and Interracial Sex in the Law of Colonial and Antebellum Virginia," *Georgetown Law Journal,* 77 (Aug. 1989), 1967–2029; George M. Fredrickson, *White Supremacy: A Comparative Study in American and South African History* (New York, 1981), 99–108; and James Hugo

Johnston, *Race Relations in Virginia & Miscegenation in the South, 1776–1860* (Amherst, 1970), 165–90. For later periods, see Peter Bardaglio, "Families, Sex, and the Law: The Legal Transformation of the Nineteenth-Century Southern Household" (Ph.D. diss., Stanford University, 1987), 37–106, 345–49; Peter Wallenstein, "Race, Marriage, and the Law of Freedom: Alabama and Virginia, 1860s-1960s," *Chicago-Kent Law Review*, 70 (no. 2, 1994), 371–437; David H. Fowler, *Northern Attitudes towards Interracial Marriage: Legislation and Public Opinion in the Middle Atlantic and the States of the Old Northwest, 1780–1930* (New York, 1987); Megumi Dick Osumi, "Asians and California's Anti-Miscegenation Laws," in *Asian and Pacific American Experiences: Women's Perspectives*, ed. Nobuya Tsuchida (Minneapolis, 1982), 2–8; and Peggy Pascoe, "Race, Gender, and Intercultural Relations: The Case of Interracial Marriage," *Frontiers*, 12 (no. 1, 1991), 5–18. The count of states is from the most complete list in Fowler, *Northern Attitudes*, 336–439.

13. Ariz. Rev. Stat. Ann. sec. 3092 (1901); 1931 Ariz. Sess. Laws ch. 17. Arizona, Idaho, Maine, Massachusetts, Nevada, North Carolina, Oregon, Rhode Island, South Carolina, Tennessee, Virginia, and Washington passed laws that mentioned American Indians. Arizona, California, Georgia, Idaho, Mississippi, Missouri, Montana, Nebraska, Nevada, Oregon, South Dakota, Utah, Virginia, and Wyoming passed laws that mentioned Asian Americans. Arizona, California, Georgia, Maryland, Nevada, South Dakota, Utah, Virginia, and Wyoming passed laws that mentioned "Malays." In addition, Oregon law targeted "Kanakas" (native Hawaiians), Virginia "Asiatic Indians," and Georgia both "Asiatic Indians" and "West Indians." See Fowler, *Northern Attitudes*, 336–439; 1924 Va. Acts ch. 371; 1927 Ga. Laws no. 317; 1931 Ariz. Sess. Laws ch. 17; 1933 Cal. Stat. ch. 104; 1935 Md. Laws ch. 60; and 1939 Utah Laws ch. 50.

14. The most insightful social and legal histories have focused on sexual relations rather than marriage. See, for example, Higginbotham and Kopytoff, "Racial Purity and Interracial Sex"; Karen Getman, "Sexual Control in the Slaveholding South: The Implementation and Maintenance of a Racial Caste System," *Harvard Women's Law Journal*, 7 (Spring 1984), 125–34; Martha Hodes, "Sex across the Color Line: White Women and Black Men in the Nineteenth-Century American South" (Ph.D. diss., Princeton University, 1991); and Martha Hodes, "The Sexualization of Reconstruction Politics: White Women and Black Men in the South after the Civil War," in *American*

Sexual Politics: Sex, Gender, and Race since the Civil War, ed. John C. Fout and Maura Shaw Tantillo (Chicago, 1993), 59–74; Robyn Weigman, "The Anatomy of Lynching," *ibid.*, 223–45; Jacquelyn Dowd Hall, "'The Mind That Burns in Each Body': Women, Rape, and Racial Violence," in *Powers of Desire: The Politics of Sexuality*, ed. Ann Snitow, Christine Stansell, and Sharon Thompson (New York, 1983), 328–49; Kenneth James Lay, "Sexual Racism: A Legacy of Slavery," *National Black Law Journal*, 13 (Spring 1993), 165–83; and Kevin J. Mumford, "From Vice to Vogue: Black/White Sexuality and the 1920s" (Ph.D. diss., Stanford University, 1993). One of the first works to note the predominance of marriage in miscegenation laws was Mary Frances Berry, "Judging Morality: Sexual Behavior and Legal Consequences in the Late Nineteenth-Century South," *Journal of American History*, 78 (Dec. 1991), 838–39. On the historical connections among race, marriage, property, and the state, see Saks, "Representing Miscegenation Law," 39–69; Nancy F. Cott, "Giving Character to Our Whole Civil Polity: Marriage and the Public Order in the Late Nineteenth Century," in *U.S. History as Women's History: New Feminist Essays*, ed. Linda K. Kerber, Alice Kessler-Harris, and Kathryn Kish Sklar (Chapel Hill, 1995), 107–21; Ramon A. Gutierrez, *When Jesus Came, the Corn Mothers Went Away: Marriage, Sexuality, and Power in New Mexico, 1500–1846* (Stanford, 1991); Verena Martinez-Alier, *Marriage, Class, and Colour in Nineteenth-Century Cuba: A Study of Racial Attitudes and Sexual Values in a Slave Society* (Ann Arbor, 1989); Patricia J. Williams, "Fetal Fictions: An Exploration of Property Archetypes in Racial and Gendered Contexts," in *Race in America: The Struggle for Equality*, ed. Herbert Hill and James E. Jones Jr. (Madison, 1993), 425–37; and Virginia R. Dominguez, *White by Definition: Social Classification in Creole Louisiana* (New Brunswick, 1986).

15. Of the 41 colonies and states that prohibited interracial marriage, 22 also prohibited some form of interracial sex. One additional jurisdiction (New York) prohibited interracial sex but not interracial marriage; it is not clear how long this 1638 statute was in effect. See Fowler, *Northern Attitudes*, 336–439. My database consists of every appeals court case I could identify in which miscegenation law played a role: 227 cases heard between 1850 and 1970, 132 civil and 95 criminal. Although cases that reach appeals courts are by definition atypical, they are significant because the decisions reached in them set policies later followed in more routine cases and because the

texts of the decisions hint at how judges conceptualized particular legal problems. I have relied on them because of these interpretive advantages and for two more practical reasons. First, because appeals court decisions are published and indexed, it is possible to compile a comprehensive list of them. Second, because making an appeal requires the preservation of documents that might otherwise be discarded (such as legal briefs and court reporters' trial notes), they permit the historian to go beyond the judge's decision.

16. Decisions striking down the laws include *Burns v. State*, 48 Ala. 195 (1872); *Bonds v. Foster*, 36 Tex. 68 (1871–1872); *Honey v. Clark*, 37 Tex. 686 (1873); *Hart v. Hoss*, 26 La. Ann. 90 (1874); *State v. Webb*, 4 Cent. L. J. 588 (1877); and *Ex parte Brown*, 5 Cent. L. J. 149 (1877). Decisions upholding the laws include *Scott v. State*, 39 Ga. 321 (1869); *State v. Hairston*, 63 N.C. 451 (1869); *State v. Reinhardt*, 63 N.C. 547 (1869); *In re Hobbs*, 12 F. Cas. 262 (1871) (No. 6550); *Lonas v. State*, 50 Tenn. 287 (1871); *State v. Gibson*, 36 Ind. 389 (1871); *Ford v. State*, 53 Ala. 150 (1875); *Green v. State*, 58 Ala. 190 (1877); *Frasher v. State*, 3 Tex. Ct. App. R. 263 (1877); *Ex Parte Kinney*, 14 F. Cas. 602 (1879) (No. 7825); *Ex parte Francois*, 9 F. Cas. 699 (1879) (No. 5047); *Francois v. State*, 9 Tex. Ct. App. R. 144 (1880); *Pace v. State*, 69 Ala. 231 (1881); *Pace v. Alabama*, 106 U.S. 583 (1882); *State v. Jackson*, 80 Mo. 175 (1883); *State v. Tutty*, 41 F. 753 (1890); *Dodson v. State*, 31 S.W. 977 (1895); *Strauss v. State*, 173 S.W. 663 (1915); *State v. Daniel*, 75 So. 836 (1917); *Succession of Mingo*, 78 So. 565 (1917–18); and *In re Paquet's Estate*, 200 P. 911 (1921).

17. Individual racial classifications were successfully challenged in *Moore v. State*, 7 Tex. Ct. App. R. 608 (1880); *Jones v. Commonwealth*, 80 Va. 213 (1884); *Jones v. Commonwealth*, 80 Va. 538 (1885); *State v. Treadaway*, 52 So. 500 (1910); *Flores v. State*, 129 S.W. 1111 (1910); *Ferrall v. Ferrall*, 69 S.E. 60 (1910); *Marre v. Marre*, 168 S.W. 636 (1914); *Neuberger v. Gueldner*, 72 So. 220 (1916); and *Reed v. State*, 92 So. 511 (1922).

18. "Appellant's Abstract of Record," 19, *Kirby v. Kirby.*

19. "Appellee's Brief," Oct. 3, 1921, p. 6, *ibid.*

20. On the theoretical problems involved in exploring how miscegenation laws were gendered, see Pascoe, "Race, Gender, and Intercultural Relations"; and Peggy Pascoe, "Race, Gender, and the Privileges of Property: On the Significance of Miscegenation Law in United States History," in *New Viewpoints in Women's History: Working Papers from the Schlesinger Library 50th*

Anniversary Conference, March 4–5, 1994, ed. Susan Ware (Cambridge, Mass., 1994), 99–122. For an excellent account of the gendering of early miscegenation laws, see Kathleen M. Brown, *Good Wives and Nasty Wenches: Gender, Race, and Power in Colonial Virginia* (Chapel Hill, 1996).

21. "Appellant's Brief," Sept. 8, 1921, *Kirby v. Kirby; Kirby v. Kirby*, 206 P. 405, 406 (1922). On *Kirby* see Roger Hardaway, "Unlawful Love: A History of Arizona's Miscegenation Law," *Journal of Arizona History*, 27 (Winter 1986), 377–90.

22. For examples of reliance on experts, see *In re Ah Yup*, 1 F. Cas. 223 (1878) (No. 104); *In re Kanaka Nian*, 21 P. 993 (1889); *In re Saito*, 62 F. 126 (1894). On these cases, see Ian F. Haney Lopez, *White by Law: The Legal Construction of Race* (New York, forthcoming). For reliance on the "common man," see *U.S. v. Bhagat Singh Thind*, 261 U.S. 204 (1923). On *Thind*, see Sucheta Mazumdar, "Racist Responses to Racism: The Aryan Myth and South Asians in the United States," *South Asia Bulletin*, 9 (no. 1, 1989), 47–55; Joan M. Jensen, *Passage from India: Asian Indian Immigrants in North America* (New Haven, 1988), 247–69; and Roediger, *Towards the Abolition of Whiteness*, 181–84.

23. The rise of Boasian anthropology has attracted much attention among intellectual historians, most of whom seem to agree with the 1963 comment that "it is possible that Boas did more to combat race prejudice than any other person in history"; see Gossett, *Race*, 418. In addition to the works cited in footnote 7, see I. A. Newby, *Jim Crow's Defense: Anti-Negro Thought in America, 1900–1930* (Baton Rouge, 1965), 21; and John S. Gilkeson Jr., "The Domestication of 'Culture' in Interwar America, 1919–1941," in *The Estate of Social Knowledge*, ed. JoAnne Brown and David K. van Keuren (Baltimore, 1991), 153–74. For more critical appraisals, see Robert Proctor, "Eugenics among the Social Sciences: Hereditarian Thought in Germany and the United States," *ibid.*, 175–208; Hamilton Cravens, *The Triumph of Evolution: The Heredity-Environment Controversy, 1900–1941* (Baltimore, 1988); and Donna Haraway, *Primate Visions: Gender, Race, and Nature in the World of Modern Science* (New York, 1989), 127–203. The classic—and still the best—account of the rise of cultural anthropology is Stocking, *Race, Culture, and Evolution*. See also George W. Stocking Jr., *Victorian Anthropology* (New York, 1987), 284–329.

24. U.S. Immigration Commission, *Dictionary of Races or Peoples* (Washington, 1911), 2. For other scientific racist classification schemes, see *Encyclopaedia Britannica*, 11th ed., s.v.

"Anthropology"; and *Encyclopedia Americana: A Library of Universal Knowledge* (New York, 1923), s.v. "Ethnography" and "Ethnology."

25. Franz Boas, "Race," in *Encyclopaedia of the Social Sciences,* ed. Edwin R. A. Seligman (15 vols., New York, 1930–1935), XIII, 27; Julian S. Huxley and A. C. Haddon, *We Europeans: A Survey of "Racial" Problems* (London, 1935), 107.

26. Boas, "Race," 34. For one of the few instances when a historian has noted this argument, see Smedley, *Race in North America,* 275–82.

27. Ruth Benedict, *Race: Science and Politics* (New York, 1940), 12; Ruth Benedict and Gene Weltfish, *The Races of Mankind* (Washington, 1943), 5; Benedict, *Race,* 12.

28. Boas, "Race," 25–26.

29. See, for example, Huxley and Haddon, *We Europeans,* 107, 269–73; Benedict and Weltfish, *Races of Mankind,* Benedict, *Race;* and Gunnar Myrdal, *An American Dilemma: The Negro Problem and Modern Democracy* (New York, 1944), 91–115.

30. The Monks trial can be followed in *Estate of Monks,* 4 Civ. 2835, Records of California Court of Appeals, Fourth District (California State Archives, Roseville); and *Gunn P. Giraudo,* 4 Civ. 2832, *ibid.* (Gunn represented another claimant to the estate.) The two cases were tried together. For the 7-volume "Reporter's Transcript," see *Estate of Monks,* 4 Civ. 2835, *ibid.*

31. "Reporter's Transcript," vol. 2, pp. 660–67, vol. 3, pp. 965–76, 976–98, *Estate of Monks.*

32. *Ibid.,* vol. 5, pp. 1501–49, vol. 6, pp. 1889–1923.

33. *Ibid.,* vol. 7, pp. 2543, 2548.

34. "Findings of Fact and Conclusions of Law," in "Clerk's Transcript," Dec. 2, 1940, *Gunn v. Giraudo,* 4 Civ. 2832, p. 81. One intriguing aspect of the *Monks* case is that the seeming exactness was unnecessary. The status of the marriage hinged on the Arizona miscegenation law, which would have denied validity to the marriage whether the proportion of "blood" in question was "one-eighth" or "one drop."

35. For descriptions of those interested in biological aspects of race, see Stocking, *Race, Culture, and Evolution,* 271–307; I. A. Newby, *Challenge to the Court: Social Scientists and the Defense of Segregation, 1954–1966* (Baton Rouge, 1969); and Cravens, *Triumph of Evolution,* 15–55. On eugenics, see Proctor, "Eugenics among the Social Sciences," 175–208; Daniel J. Kevles, *In the Name of Eugenics: Genetics and the Uses of Human Heredity* (New York, 1985); Mark H. Haller, *Eugenics: Hereditarian Attitudes in American Thought* (New Brunswick, 1963); and William H.

Tucker, *The Science and Politics of Racial Research* (Urbana, 1994), 54–137.

36. Charles B. Davenport, *Eugenics Record Office Bulletin No. 9: State Laws Limiting Marriage Selection Examined in the Light of Eugenics* (Cold Spring Harbor, 1913); Michael Grossberg, "Guarding the Altar: Physiological Restrictions and the Rise of State Intervention in Matrimony," *American Journal of Legal History,* 26 (July 1982), 221–24.

37. See, for example, C[harles] B[enedict] Davenport and Morris Steggerda, *Race Crossing in Jamaica* (1929; Westport, 1970); Edward Byron Reuter, *Race Mixture: Studies in Intermarriage and Miscegenation* (New York, 1931); and Emory S. Bogardus, "What Race Are Filipinos?" *Sociology and Social Research,* 16 (1931–1932), 274–79.

38. 1924 Va. Acts ch. 371; 1927 Ga. Laws no. 317; 1927 Ala. Acts no. 626. The 1924 Virginia act replaced 1910 Va. Acts ch. 357, which classified as "colored" persons with 1/16 or more "negro blood." The retention of an allowance for American Indian "blood" in persons classed as white was forced on the bill's sponsors by Virginia aristocrats who traced their ancestry to Pocahontas and John Rolfe. See Paul A. Lombardo, "Miscegenation, Eugenics, and Racism: Historical Footnotes to *Loving v. Virginia,"* *U. C. Davis Law Review,* 21 (Winter 1988), 431–52; and Richard B. Sherman, "'The Last Stand': The Fight for Racial Integrity in Virginia in the 1920s," *Journal of Southern History,* 54 (Feb. 1988), 69–92.

39. "Appellant's Opening Brief," *Gunn v. Giraudo,* 12–13. This brief appears to have been prepared for the California Supreme Court but used in the California Court of Appeals, Fourth District. On February 14, 1942, the California Supreme Court refused to review the Court of Appeals decision. See *Estate of Monks,* 48 C.A. 2d 603, 621 (1941).

40. *Estate of Monks,* 48 C.A. 2d 603, 612–15 (1941); *Monks v. Lee,* 317 U.S. 590 (*appeal dismissed,* 1942), 711 (*reh'g denied,* 1942); *Lee v. Monks,* 62 N.E. 2d 657 (1945); *Lee v. Monks,* 326 U.S. 696 (*cert. denied,* 1946).

41. On the case, see *San Diego Union,* July 21, 1939–Jan. 6, 1940. On the testimony of expert witnesses on race, see *ibid.,* Sept. 21, 1939, p. 4A; *ibid.,* Sept. 29, 1939, p. 10A; and *ibid.,* Oct. 5, 1939, p. 8A.

42. *Perez v. Lippold,* L.A. 20305, Supreme Court Case Files (California State Archives). The case was also known as *Perez v. Moroney* and *Perez v. Sharp* (the names reflect changes of personnel in the Los Angeles County clerk's office). I have used the title given in the *Pacific Law Reporter,* the most easily available version of the final decision: *Perez v. Lippold,* 198 P. 2d 17 (1948).

43. "Petition for Writ of Mandamus, Memorandum of Points and Authorities and Proof of Service," Aug. 8, 1947, *Perez v. Lippold;* "Points and Authorities in Opposition to Issuance of Alternative Writ of Mandate," Aug. 13, 1947, *ibid.;* "Return by Way of Demurrer," Oct. 6, 1947, *ibid.;* "Return by Way of Answer," Oct. 6, 1947, *ibid.;* "Respondent's Brief in Opposition to Writ of Mandate," Oct. 6, 1947, *ibid.*

44. "[Oral Argument] On Behalf of Respondent," Oct. 6, 1947, pp. 3–4, *ibid.*

45. Stanley Mosk, "A Retrospective," *California Law Review,* 71 (July 1983), 1045; Peter Anderson, "A Remembrance," *ibid.,* 1066–71.

46. "Petitioners' Reply Brief," Nov. 8, 1947, pp. 4, 44, 23–24, *Perez v. Lippold.*

47. *Perez v. Lippold,* 198 P. 2d at 17–35, esp. 29, 34.

48. *Ibid.,* 35–47.

49. For the characterization of Franz Boas, by Robert Gayres, editor of the Scottish journal *Mankind Quarterly,* see Newby, *Challenge to the Court,* 323. On *Mankind Quarterly* and on mid-twentieth-century white supremacist scientists, see Tucker, *Science and Politics of Racial Research.*

50. Myrdal, *American Dilemma,* 116–17.

51. *Loving v. Commonwealth,* 147 S.E. 2d 78, 79 (1966). For the *Loving* briefs and oral arguments, see Philip B. Kurland and Gerhard Casper, eds., *Landmark Briefs and Arguments of the Supreme Court of the United States: Constitutional Law,* vol. LXIV (Arlington, 1975), 687–1007. Edited cassette tapes of the oral argument are included with Peter Irons and Stephanie Guitton, ed., *May It Please the Court: The Most Significant Oral Arguments Made before the Supreme Court since 1955* (New York, 1993). For scholarly assessments, see Wallenstein, "Race, Marriage, and the Law of Freedom"; Walter Wadlington, "The Loving Case: Virginia's Antimiscegenation Statute in Historical Perspective," in *Race Relations and the Law in American History: Major Historical Interpretations,* ed. Kermit L. Hall (New York, 1987), 600–634; and Robert J. Sickels, *Race, Marriage, and the Law* (Albuquerque, 1972).

52. *Loving V. Virginia,* 388 U.S. 1, 3 (1967); Wallenstein, "Race, Marriage, and the Law of Freedom," 423–25, esp. 424; *New York Times,* June 12, 1992, p. B7. By the mid-1960s some legal scholars had questioned the constitutionality of miscegenation laws, including C. D. Shokes, "The Serbonian Bog of Miscegenation," *Rocky Mountain Law Review,* 21(1948–1949), 425–33: Wayne A. Melton, "Constitutionality of State Anti-Miscegenation Statutes," *Southwestern Law Journal,* 5 (1951), 451–61; Andrew D.

Weinberger, "A Reappraisal of the Constitutionality of Miscegenation Statutes," *Cornell Law Quarterly,* 42 (Winter 1957), 208–22; Jerold D. Cummins and John L. Kane Jr., "Miscegenation, the Constitution, and Science," *Dicta,* 38 (Jan.–Feb. 1961), 24–54; William D. Zabel, "Interracial Marriage and the Law," *Atlantic Monthly,* 216 (Oct. 1965), 75–79; and Cyrus E. Phillips IV, "Miscegenation: The Courts and the Constitution," *William and Mary Law Review,* 8 (Fall 1966), 133–42.

53. Kurland and Casper, eds., *Landmark Briefs,* 741–88, 847–950, 960–72, esp. 898–99, 901.

54. *Ibid.,* 789–845, 976–1003.

55. *Ibid,* 834, 1007.

56. *Loving v. Virginia,* 388 U.S. at 12.

57. *Ibid.,* 11.

58. The notion that American courts should be "color-blind" is usually traced to Supreme Court Justice John Harlan. Dissenting from the Court's endorsement of the principle of "separate but equal" in *Plessy v. Ferguson,* Harlan insisted that "Our Constitution is color-blind, and neither knows nor tolerates classes among citizens." *Plessy v. Ferguson,* 163 U.S. 537, 559 (1896). But only after *Brown v. Board of Education,* widely interpreted as a belated endorsement of Harlan's position, did courts begin to adopt color blindness as a goal. *Brown v. Board of Education,* 347 U.S. 483 (1954). On the history of the color-blindness ideal, see Andrew Kull, *The Color-Blind Constitution* (Cambridge, Mass., 1992). On developments in social science, see Omi and Winant, *Racial Formation in the United States,* 14–23.

59. *Brown v. Board of Education,* 347 U.S. 483 (1954). The Court declared distinctions based "solely on ancestry" "odious" even while upholding curfews imposed on Japanese Americans during World War II; see *Hirabayashi v. United States,* 320 U.S. 81 (1943). It declared race a "suspect" legal category while upholding the internment of Japanese Americans; see *Korematsu v. United States,* 323 U.S. 214 (1944). By 1983, no American state had a formal race-definition statute still on its books. See Chris Ballentine, "'Who Is a Negro?' Revisited: Determining Individual Racial Status for Purposes of Affirmative Action," *University of Florida Law Review,* 35 (Fall 1983), 692. The repeal of state race-definition statutes often accompanied repeal of miscegenation laws. See, for example, 1953 Mont. Laws ch. 4; 1959 Or. Laws ch. 531; 1965 Ind. Acts ch. 15; 1969 Fla. Laws 69–195; and 1979 Ga. Laws no. 543.

60. The fifth of these categories, "Hispanic," is sometimes described as "ethnic," rather than "racial." For very different views of the current

debates, see Lawrence Wright, "One Drop of Blood," *New Yorker,* July 25, 1994, pp. 46–55; and Michael Lind, *The Next American Nation: The New Nationalism and the Fourth American Revolution* (New York, 1995), 97–137.

61. *People v. O. J. Simpson,* Case no. BA 097211, California Superior Court, L.A. County (1994).

62. See, for example, Kimberle Williams Crenshaw, "Race, Reform, and Retrenchment: Transformation and Legitimation in Antidiscrimination Law," *Harvard Law Review,* 101 (May 1988), 1331–87; Dana Y. Takagi, *The Retreat from Race: Asian-American Admissions and Racial Politics* (New Brunswick, 1992), 181–94; and Girardeau A. Spann, *Race against the Court: The Supreme Court and Minorities in Contemporary America* (New York, 1993), 119–49. See footnote 5, above. On recent work in the humanities, see Tessie Liu, "Race," in *A Companion to American Thought,* ed. Richard Wightman Fox and James T. Kloppenberg (Cambridge, Mass., 1995), 564–67. On legal studies, see Richard Delgado and Jean Stefancic, "Critical Race Theory: An Annotated Bibliography," *Virginia Law Review,* 79 (March 1993), 461–516.

Identities

PART III

The articles in this section explore some of the sites where ways of thinking about gender and codes of behavior for women and men are constructed and enforced. John Berger locates one of these sites in the visual arts, where the ideal woman has historically been represented as a passive object of visual pleasure for male spectators. Gloria Steinem provides contemporary examples of this form of representation in her discussion of advertising. Both authors highlight the ways in which visual portrayals of women and their bodies both reflect and influence the way we think about women—as passive, silent nonactors valued primarily for their appearance.

Visual representations of women in popular culture are frequently limited to white women, a fact which both reflects and establishes white standards of beauty and proper feminine behavior as the ideal. The influence of these standards is evident in Judy Tzu-Chun Wu's exploration of the role of beauty pageants in a Chinese American community. She shows us the perceived power and real limitations of embracing white standards of femininity in an effort to promote racial equality, highlighting the political and cultural significance of the beauty pageant.

The second set of readings focuses on male gender identity and codes of behavior. Michael Kimmel and Yen Le Espiritu show that masculinity depends for its existence not only upon femininity (as its opposite), but also upon a hierarchy among men. This hierarchy varies by race, class, age, ethnicity, and sexual orientation, so that some men are considered more masculine than others. Those that fall on the bottom rungs of the hierarchy can claim few of the privileges of masculinity, and are instead subject to discrimination, ostracism, and violence.

As you read, consider contemporary representations of women and men that you see in advertisements, on television, at the movies. What standards of appearance and of conduct do they promote? Do they reinforce or challenge gender, racial, and class differences among and between women and men? How could they be altered for liberatory ends?

Suggestions for Further Reading

Carson, Diane, Linda Dittmar and Janice R. Welsch, eds. 1994. *Multiple Voices in Feminist Film Criticism*. Minneapolis: University of Minnesota Press.

Cook, Pam and Philip Dodd, eds. 1993. *Women and Film: A Sight and Sound Reader*. Philadelphia: Temple University Press.

Connell, R. W. 1995. *Masculinities*. Berkeley: University of California Press.

Credon, Pamela J., ed. 1994. *Women, Media and Sport: Challenging Gender Values*. Thousand Oaks, CA: Sage Publications.

Ducille, Ann. 1994. "Dyes and Dolls: Multicultural Barbie and the Merchandising of Difference," *Differences: A Journal of Feminist Cultural Criticism*, *6*, 48–68.

Faludi, Susan. September 5, 1994. "The Naked Citadel," *The New Yorker*, 62–81.

Gaunt, Kyra D. 1995. "African American Women between Hopscotch and Hip-Hop: Must be the Music (That's Turnin Me On)." Pp. 277–308 in Angharard N. Valdivia, ed. *Feminism, Multiculturalism, and the Media: Global Diversities*. Thousand Oaks, CA: Sage Publications.

Heide, Margaret J. 1995. *Television Culture and Women's Lives: Thirtysomething and the Contradictions of Gender*. Philadelphia: University of Pennsylvania Press.

hooks, bell. 1992. *Black Looks: Race and Representation*. Boston: South End Press.

Kimmel, Michael. 1996. *Manhood in America: A Cultural History*. New York: Free Press.

Kimmel, Michael, ed. 1987. *Changing Men: New Directions in Research on Men and Masculinity*. Newbury Park, CA: Sage Publications.

Koskoff, Ellen, ed. 1987. *Women and Music in Cross-Cultural Perspective*. Westport, CT: Greenwood Press.

Messner, Michael A. & Donald F. Sabo. 1994. *Sex, Violence and Power in Sports: Rethinking Masculinity*. Freedom, CA: Crossing Press.

Mullings, Leith. 1994. "Images, Ideology, and Women of Color." Pp. 265–289 in Maxine Baca Zinn and Bonnie Thornton Dill, eds. *Women of Color in U.S. Society*. Philadelphia: Temple University Press.

Pollock, Griselda, ed. 1988. *Vision and Difference: Femininity, Feminism, and Histories of Art*. London & New York: Routledge.

Rajan, Rajeswari Sunder. 1993. *Real and Imagined Women: Gender, Culture, and Postcolonialism*. London & New York: Routledge.

Rhode, Deborah L. 1997. "Media Images." Pp. 66–94 in *Speaking of Sex: The Denial of Gender Inequality*. Cambridge, MA: Harvard University Press.

Shohat, Ella and Robert Stam. 1994. *Unthinking Eurocentrism: Multiculturalism and the Media*. London & New York: Routledge.

Spender, Dale. 1991. *Man Made Language*. London: Pandora Press.

Stearns, Peter N. 1990. *Be a Man! Males in Modern Society*. New York: Holmes and Meier.

Tajima, R. 1989. "Lotus Blossoms Don't Bleed: Images of Asian Women." Pp. 308–317 in Asian Women United of California, eds. *Making Waves: An Anthology of Writings By and About Asian American Women*. Boston: Beacon Press.

14

Ways of Seeing

John Berger

According to usage and conventions which are at last being questioned but have by no means been overcome, the social presence of a woman is different in kind from that of a man. A man's presence is dependent upon the promise of power which he embodies. If the promise is large and credible his presence is striking. If it is small or incredible, he is found to have little presence. The promised power may be moral, physical, temperamental, economic, social, sexual—but its object is always exterior to the man. A man's presence suggests what he is capable of doing to you or for you. His presence may be fabricated, in the sense that he pretends to be capable of what he is not. But the pretence is always towards a power which he exercises on others.

By contrast, a woman's presence expresses her own attitude to herself, and defines what can and cannot be done to her. Her presence is manifest in her gestures, voice, opinions, expressions, clothes, chosen surroundings, taste—indeed there is nothing she can do which does not contribute to her presence. Presence for a woman is so intrinsic to her person that men tend to think of it as an almost physical emanation, a kind of heat or smell or aura.

To be born a woman has been to be born, within an allotted and confined space, into the keeping of men. The social presence of women has developed as a result of their ingenuity in living under such tutelage within such a limited space. But this has been at the cost of a woman's self being split into two. A woman must continually watch herself. She is almost continually accompanied by her own image of herself. Whilst she is walking across a room or whilst she is weeping at the death of her father, she can scarcely avoid envisaging herself walking or weeping. From earliest childhood she has been taught and persuaded to survey herself continually.

And so she comes to consider the *surveyor* and the *surveyed* within her as the two constituent yet always distinct elements of her identity as a woman.

She has to survey everything she is and everything she does because how she appears to others, and ultimately how she appears to men, is of crucial importance for what is normally thought of as the success of her life. Her own sense of being in herself is supplanted by a sense of being appreciated as herself by another.

Men survey women before treating them. Consequently how a woman appears to a man can determine how she will be treated. To acquire some control over this process, women must contain it and interiorize it. That part of a woman's self which is the surveyor treats the part which is the surveyed so as to demonstrate to others how her whole self would like to be treated. And this exemplary treatment of herself by herself constitutes her presence. Every woman's presence regulates what is and is not "permissible" within her presence. Every one of her actions—whatever its direct purpose or motivation—is also read as an indication of how she would like to be treated. If a woman throws a glass on the floor, this is an example of how she treats her own emotion of anger and so of how she would wish it to be treated by others. If a man does the same, his action is only read as an expression of his anger. If a woman makes a good joke this is an example of how she treats the joker in herself and accordingly of how she as a joker-woman would like to be treated by others. Only a man can make a good joke for its own sake.

One might simplify this by saying: *men act* and *women appear*. Men look at women. Women watch themselves being looked at. This determines not only most relations be-

tween men and women but also the relation of women to themselves. The surveyor of woman in herself is male: the surveyed female. Thus she turns herself into an object—and most particularly an object of vision: a sight.

In one category of European oil painting women were the principal, ever-recurring subject. That category is the nude. In the nudes of European painting we can discover some of the criteria and conventions by which women have been seen and judged as sights.

The first nudes in the tradition depicted Adam and Eve. It is worth referring to the story as told in Genesis:

> And when the woman saw that the tree was good for food, and that it was a delight to the eyes, and that the tree was to be desired to make one wise, she took of the fruit thereof and did eat; and she gave also unto her husband with her, and he did eat.

> And the eyes of them both were opened, and they knew that they were naked; and they sewed fig-leaves together and made themselves aprons. . . . And the Lord God called unto the man and said unto him, "Where are thou?" And he said, "I heard thy voice in the garden, and I was afraid, because I was naked; and I hid myself. . . ."

> Unto the woman God said, "I will greatly multiply thy sorrow and thy conception; in sorrow thou shalt bring forth children; and thy desire shall be to thy husband and he shall rule over thee."

What is striking about this story? They became aware of being naked because, as a result of eating the apple, each saw the other differently. Nakedness was created in the mind of the beholder.

The second striking fact is that the woman is blamed and is punished by being made subservient to the man. In relation to the woman, the man becomes the agent of God.

In the medieval tradition the story was often illustrated, scene following scene, as in a strip cartoon.

During the Renaissance the narrative sequence disappeared, and the single moment depicted became the moment of shame. The couple wear fig-leaves or make a modest gesture with their hands. But now their shame is not so much in relation to one another as to the spectator.

Later the shame becomes a kind of display.

When the tradition of painting became more secular, other themes also offered the opportunity of painting nudes. But in them all there remains the implication that the subject (a woman) is aware of being seen by a spectator.

She is not naked as she is.

She is naked as the spectator sees her.

Often—as with the favourite subject of Susannah and the Elders—this is the actual theme of the picture. We join the Elders to spy on Susannah taking her bath. She looks back at us looking at her.

In another version of the subject by Tintoretto, Susannah is looking at herself in a mirror. Thus she joins the spectators of herself.

The mirror was often used as a symbol of the vanity of woman. The moralizing, however, was mostly hypocritical.

You painted a naked woman because you enjoyed looking at her, you put a mirror in her hand and you called the painting *Vanity,* thus morally condemning the woman whose nakedness you had depicted for your own pleasure.

The real function of the mirror was otherwise. It was to make the woman connive in treating herself as, first and foremost, a sight.

The Judgement of Paris was another theme with the same inwritten idea of a man or men looking at naked women.

But a further element is now added. The element of judgement. Paris awards the apple to the woman he finds most beautiful. Thus Beauty becomes competitive. (Today The Judgement of Paris has become the Beauty Contest.) Those who are not judged beautiful are *not beautiful*. Those who are, are given the prize.

The prize is to be owned by a judge—that is to say to be available for him. Charles the Second commissioned a secret painting from Lely. It is a highly typical image of the tradition. Nominally it might be a *Venus and Cupid*. In fact it is a portrait of one of the King's mistresses, Nell Gwynne. It shows her passively looking at the spectator staring at her naked.

This nakedness is not, however, an expression of her own feelings; it is a sign of her submission to the owner's feelings or demands. (The owner of both woman and painting.) The painting, when the King showed it to others, demonstrated this submission and his guests envied him.

It is worth noticing that in other non-European traditions—in Indian art, Persian art, African art, Pre-Columbian art—nakedness is never supine in this way. And if, in these traditions, the theme of a work is sexual attraction, it is likely to show active sexual love as between two people, the woman as active as the man, the actions of each absorbing the other.

We can now begin to see the difference between nakedness and nudity in the European tradition. In his book on *The Nude* Kenneth Clark maintains that to be naked is simply to be without clothes, whereas the nude is a form of art. According to him, a nude is not the starting point of a painting, but a way of seeing which the painting achieves. To some degree, this is true—although the way of seeing "nude" is not necessarily confined to art: there are also nude photographs, nude poses, nude gestures.

What is true is that the nude is always conventionalized—and the authority for its conventions derives from a certain tradition of art.

What do these conventions mean? What does a nude signify? It is not sufficient to answer these questions merely in terms of the art-form, for it is quite clear that the nude also relates to lived sexuality.

To be naked is to be oneself.

To be nude is to be seen naked by others and yet not recognized for oneself. A naked body has to be seen as an object in order to become a nude. (The sight of it as an object stimulates the use of it as an object.) Nakedness reveals itself. Nudity is placed on display.

To be naked is to be without disguise.

To be on display is to have the surface of one's own skin, the hairs of one's own body, turned into a disguise which, in that situation, can never be discarded. The nude is condemned to never being naked. Nudity is a form of dress.

In the average European oil painting of the nude the principal protagonist is never painted. He is the spectator in front of the picture and he is presumed to be a man. Everything is addressed to him. Everything must appear to be the result of his being there. It is for him that the figures have assumed their nudity. But he, by definition, is a stranger—with his clothes still on.

Consider the *Allegory of Time and Love* by Bronzino.

The complicated symbolism which lies behind this painting need not concern us now because it does not affect its sexual appeal—at the first degree. Before it is anything else, this is a painting of sexual provocation.

The painting was sent as a present from the Grand Duke of Florence to the King of France. The boy kneeling on the cushion and kissing the woman is Cupid. She is Venus. But the way her body is arranged has nothing to do with their kissing. Her body is arranged in the way it is, to display it to the man looking at the picture. This picture is made to appeal to *his* sexuality. It has nothing to do with her sexuality. (Here and in the European tradition generally, the convention of not painting the hair on a woman's body helps towards the same end. Hair is associated with sexual power, with passion. The woman's sexual passion needs to be minimized so that the spectator may feel that he has the monopoly of such passion.) Women are there to feed an appetite, not to have any of their own.

It is true that sometimes a painting includes a male lover.

But the woman's attention is very rarely directed towards him. Often she looks away from him or she looks out of the picture towards the one who considers himself her true lover—the spectator-owner.

Venus, Cupid, Time, and Love
by Bronzino 1503–1572.
Courtesy of Alinari/Art Resource, NY.

There was a special category of private pornographic paintings (especially in the eighteenth century) in which couples making love make an appearance. But even in front of these it is clear that the spectator-owner will in fantasy oust the other man, or else identify with him. By contrast the image of the couple

Les Oréades by Bougureau 1825–1905
Courtesy of Giraudon/Art Resource, NY.

in non-European traditions provokes the notion of many couples making love. "We all have a thousand hands, a thousand feet and will never go alone."

Almost all post-Renaissance European sexual imagery is frontal—either literally or metaphorically—because the sexual protagonist is the spectator-owner looking at it.

The absurdity of this male flattery reached its peak in the public academic art of the nineteenth century.

Men of state, of business, discussed under paintings like this. When one of them felt he had been outwitted, he looked up for consolation. What he saw reminded him that he was a man.

There are a few exceptional nudes in the European tradition of oil painting to which very little of what has been said above applies. Indeed they are no longer nudes—they break the norms of the art-form; they are paintings of loved women, more or less naked. Among the hundreds of thousands of nudes which make up the tradition there are perhaps a hundred of these exceptions. In each case the painter's personal vision of the particular women he is painting is so strong that it makes no allowance for the spectator. The painter's vision binds the woman to him so that they become as inseparable as couples in stone. The spectator can witness their relationship—but he can do no more: he is forced to recognize himself as the outsider he is. He cannot deceive himself into believing that she is naked for him. He cannot turn her into a nude. The way the painter has painted her includes her will and her intentions in the very structure

Danäe by Rembrandt 1606–1669
Courtesy of Scala/Art Resource, NY.

of the image, in the very expression of her body and her face.

The typical and the exceptional in the tradition can be defined by the simple naked/nude antinomy, but the problem of painting nakedness is not as simple as it might at first appear.

What is the sexual function of nakedness in reality? Clothes encumber contact and movement. But it would seem that nakedness has a positive visual value in its own right: we want to *see* the other naked: the other delivers the sight of themselves and we seize upon it—sometimes quite regardless of whether it is for the first time or the hundredth. What does this sight of the other mean to us, how does it, at that instant of total disclosure, affect our desire?

Their nakedness acts as a confirmation and provokes a very strong sense of relief. She is a woman like any other: or he is a man like any other: we are overwhelmed by the marvellous simplicity of the familiar sexual mechanism.

We did not, of course, consciously expect this to be otherwise: unconscious homosexual desires (or unconscious heterosexual desires if the couple concerned are homosexual) may have led each to half expect something different. But the "relief" can be explained without recourse to the unconscious.

We did not expect them to be otherwise, but the urgency and complexity of our feelings bred a sense of uniqueness which the sight of the other, as she is or as he is, now dispels. They are more like the rest of their sex than they are different. In this revelation lies the warm and friendly—as opposed to cold and impersonal—anonymity of nakedness.

One could express this differently: at the moment of nakedness first perceived, an element of banality enters: an element that exists only because we need it.

Up to that instant the other was more or less mysterious. Etiquettes of modesty are not merely puritan or sentimental: it is reasonable to recognize a loss of mystery. And the explanation of this loss of mystery may be largely visual. The focus of perception shifts from eyes, mouth, shoulders, hands—all of which are capable of such subtleties of expression that the personality expressed by them is manifold—it shifts from these to the sexual parts, whose formation suggests an utterly compelling but single process. The other is reduced or elevated—whichever you prefer—to their primary sexual category: male or female. Our relief is the relief of finding an unquestionable reality to whose direct demands our earlier highly complex awareness must now yield.

We need the banality which we find in the first instant of disclosure because it grounds us in reality. But it does more than that. This reality, by promising the familiar, proverbial mechanism of sex, offers, at the same time, the possibility of the shared subjectivity of sex.

The loss of mystery occurs simultaneously with the offering of the means for creating a shared mystery. The sequence is: subjective—objective—subjective to the power of two.

We can now understand the difficulty of creating a static image of sexual nakedness. In lived sexual experience nakedness is a process rather than a state. If one moment of that process is isolated, its image will seem banal and its banality, instead of serving as a bridge between two intense imaginative states, will be chilling. This is one reason why expressive photographs of the naked are even rarer than paintings. The easy solution for the photographer is to turn the figure into a nude which, by generalizing both sight and viewer and making sexuality unspecific, turns desire into fantasy.

Let us examine an exceptional painted image of nakedness. It is a painting by Rubens of his young second wife whom he married when he himself was relatively old.

Helene Fourment in a Fur Coat
by Rubens 1577–1640
Courtesy of Foto Marburg/Art Resource, NY.

We see her in the act of turning, her fur about to slip off her shoulders. Clearly she will not remain as she is for more than a second. In a superficial sense her image is as instantaneous as a photograph's. But, in a more profound sense, the painting "contains" time and its experience. It is easy to imagine that a moment ago before she pulled the fur round her shoulders, she was entirely naked. The consecutive stages up to

and away from the moment of total disclosure have been transcended. She can belong to any or all of them simultaneously.

Her body confronts us, not as an immediate sight, but as experience—the painter's experience. Why? There are superficial anecdotal reasons: her dishevelled hair, the expression of her eyes directed towards him, the tenderness with which the exaggerated susceptibility of her skin has been painted. But the profound reason is a formal one. Her appearance has been literally recast by the painter's subjectivity. Beneath the fur that she holds across herself, the upper part of her body and her legs can never meet. There is a displacement sideways of about nine inches: her thighs, in order to join on to her hips, are at least nine inches too far to the left.

Rubens probably did not plan this: the spectator may not consciously notice it. In itself it is unimportant. What matters is what it permits. It permits the body to become impossibly dynamic. Its coherence is no longer within itself but within the experience of the painter. More precisely, it permits the upper and lower halves of the body to rotate separately, and in opposite directions, round the sexual centre which is hidden: the torso turning to the right, the legs to the left. At the same time this hidden sexual centre is connected by means of the dark fur coat to all the surrounding darkness in the picture, so that she is turning both around and within the dark which has been made a metaphor for her sex.

Apart from the necessity of transcending the single instant and of admitting subjectivity, there is, as we have seen, one further element which is essential for any great sexual image of the naked. This is the element of banality which must be undisguised but not chilling. It is this which distinguishes between voyeur and lover. Here such banality is to be found in Rubens's compulsive painting of the fat softness of Hélène Four-ment's flesh which continually breaks every ideal convention of form and (to him) continually offers the promise of her extraordinary particularity.

The nude in European oil painting is usually presented as an admirable expression of the European humanist spirit. This spirit was inseparable from individualism. And without the development of a highly conscious individualism the exceptions to the tradition (extremely personal images of the naked), would never have been painted. Yet the tradition contained a contradiction which it could not itself resolve. A few individual artists intuitively recognized this and resolved the contradiction in their own terms, but their solutions could never enter the tradition's *cultural terms.*

The contradiction can be stated simply. On the one hand the individualism of the artist, the thinker, the patron, the owner: on the other hand, the person who is the object of their activities—the woman—treated as a thing or an abstraction.

Dürer believed that the ideal nude ought to be constructed by taking the face of one body, the breasts of another, the legs of a third, the shoulders of a fourth, the hands of a fifth—and so on.

The result would glorify Man. But the exercise presumed a remarkable indifference to who any one person really was.

In the art-form of the European nude the painters and spectator-owners were usually men and the persons treated as objects, usually women. This unequal relationship is so deeply embedded in our culture that it still structures the consciousness of many women. They do to themselves what men do to them. They survey, like men, their own femininity.

In modern art the category of the nude has become less important. Artists themselves began to question it. In this, as in many other respects, Manet represented a turning point. If one compares his *Olympia* with Titian's original, one sees a woman, cast in the traditional role, beginning to question that role, somewhat defiantly.

The Venus of Urbino by Titian 1487–1576
Courtesy of Alinari/Art Resource, NY.

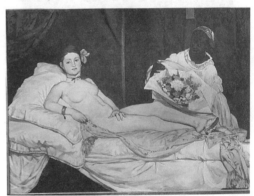

Olympia by Manet 1832–1883
Courtesy of Giraudon/Art Resource, NY.

The ideal was broken. But there was little to replace it except the "realism" of the prostitute—who became the quintessential woman of early avant-garde twentieth-century painting. (Toulouse-Lautrec, Picasso, Rouault, German Expressionism, etc.) In academic painting the tradition continued.

Today the attitudes and values which informed that tradition are expressed through other more widely diffused media—advertising, journalism, television.

But the essential way of seeing women, the essential use to which their images are put, has not changed. Women are depicted in a quite different way from men—not because the feminine is different from the masculine—but because the "ideal" spectator is always assumed to be male and the image of the woman is designed to flatter him. If you have any doubt that this is so, make the following experiment. Choose from this book an image of a traditional nude. Transform the woman into a man. Either in your mind's eye or by drawing on the reproduction. Then notice the violence which that transformation does. Not to the image, but to the assumptions of a likely viewer.

"Loveliest Daughter of Our Ancient Cathay!": Representations of Ethnic and Gender Identity in the Miss Chinatown U.S.A. Beauty Pageant

Judy Tzu-Chun Wu

In February 1958, seventeen young women came from throughout the country to compete in the first Miss Chinatown U.S.A. Beauty Pageant. Sponsored by the San Francisco Chinese Chamber of Commerce (CCC) as part of the Chinese New Year celebration, the competition sought to find "the most beautiful Chinese girl with the right proportion of beauty, personality and talent." The organizers promised that "honor, fame and awards . . . is (sic) ahead for her majesty in this, the most Cinderella-like moment of her young life." June Gong, a 21 year-old senior majoring in Home Economics at the University of New Hampshire, captured the title of the first Miss Chinatown U.S.A. Although she expressed surprise at winning, Gong had a history of competing successfully in beauty contests. She had won the titles of freshman queen and football queen at college. In 1957, she placed second in the Miss New Hampshire

beauty pageant, a preliminary for the Miss America competition. She also won the 1957 Miss New York Chinatown title, which provided her with the opportunity to compete in the national pageant. Years later, she explained that the Miss Chinatown U.S.A. pageant was not "a beauty contest"; it was "more like a matter of ethnic representation." Having grown up in Miami, Florida, with only a few Chinese families, Gong's participation in the San Francisco event provided her with the opportunity to come into contact with the largest community of Chinese people outside of China and to learn about her ancestral culture.[1]

The popularity of the first Miss Chinatown U.S.A. beauty pageant made the event one of the highlights of the Chinese New Year celebration, which it continues to be today. Without it, one organizer explained, there would be no focus to the celebration: no pageant, no coronation ball, no Miss Chi-

From *Journal of Social History*, 31, pp. 5-31. Copyright © 1997 by Journal of Social History. Reprinted by permission.

natown float for the annual parade, and no fashion show. These Chinese New Year events draw hundreds of thousands of tourists into San Francisco's Chinatown, serving the dual purposes of educating the public about Chinese American culture and attracting business for Chinatown merchants.

The Miss Chinatown U.S.A. Beauty Pageant has served as a beauty competition, a promotional event to attract tourism, and a means for exploring and celebrating ethnic identity. Because of its multiple purposes, an analysis of the pageant provides insights into Chinese American efforts to construct both gender and ethnic identity during the post-World-War-II era. In defining the ideal woman to represent Chinatown, pageant organizers responded to developing cultural, economic, and political tensions within the Chinese American community and the broader American society. In turn, these efforts to represent Chinese American womanhood generated a variety of responses, which reflected community conflicts surrounding not only gender roles and ethnic identity but also class divisions and international politics.[2]

Using pageant publications, oral histories, and Bay Area and Chinese American community newspapers, this paper analyzes the Miss Chinatown U.S.A. beauty pageant from its origins and popularization in the late 1950s and the 1960s, through the growing controversy that surrounded it in the late 1960s and 1970s. During the height of the Cold War and the era of racial integration, pageant supporters successfully balanced tensions within the Chinese American community and with the broader society by depicting their ethnic identity as a non-threatening blend of Eastern Confucian and modern Western cultures. However, with the rise of social movements during the late 1960s and 1970s, this conception of

ethnic identity came under attack for presenting an outdated and exotic image of Chinese Americans in general and women in particular. Critics argued that Miss Chinatown did not represent the "real" Chinatown women who tended to be working class or the revolutionary Asian women in the Third World. Pageant supporters responded by emphasizing the importance of beautiful and articulate Chinese American women as role models for promoting respect for the community.[3]

Ethnic beauty pageants, a subject rarely explored by scholars, provide an opportunity to examine how idealized versions of womanhood reflect broader concerns about power and culture. In a recently published collection of essays devoted to the study of beauty pageants, *Beauty Queens on the Global Stage*, the editors, Colleen Ballerino Cohen, Richard Wilk, and Beverly Stoeltje, argue that pageants:

> showcase values, concepts, and behavior that exist at the center of a group's sense of itself and exhibit values of morality, gender, and place. . . . The beauty contest stage is where these identities and cultures can be—and frequently are—made public and visible.

In studying the formation and evolution of a community ceremony, I had the opportunity to not only examine how the pageant publicly and visibly reflects the community's identity and culture, but also how the event shaped and developed community values. In other words, the history of the pageant and the community dialogue that the event generated provide insight into evolving conflicts concerning ethnic and gender identity as well as class divisions and international politics.[4]

Furthermore, the study of the Miss Chinatown U.S.A. beauty pageant suggests the need to reevaluate dichotomous models of gender and ethnic systems. Beauty pageants do not simply victimize women through male domination; both women and men supported, as well as criticized, the pageant. Similarly, the cultural content of the pageant cannot be evaluated in terms of ethnic assimilation versus retention. Rather, both pageant supporters and critics defined ethnic identity by synthesizing elements of both Chinese and American traditions. While contending groups questioned their opponents' cultural authenticity and commitment to women's advancement, their conflicts often arose because they advocated different strategies to advance similar goals of gender and racial equality.

A Melting Pot of the East and the West

From the very beginning of the pageant, organizers had an ideal image of Miss Chinatown contestants as the perfect blend of Chinese and American cultures. Businessman and community leader H. K. Wong, who is credited with coming up with the idea of the pageant, explained that contenders for the crown must have the "looks that made China's beauties so fascinating" as well as the language skills to answer "key questions" in their own native dialect during the quiz portion of the competition. In addition to these Chinese attributes, contestants had to display modern American qualities. They needed "adequate education, training and the versatility to meet the challenge of the modern world." The Cheongsam (long gown) dresses that contestants wore symbolized this theme of "East-meets-West." First introduced by Manchu women of the Qing Dynasty, the Cheong-sam, "the figure-delineating sheath dress with high-necked collar and slit skirt," became "the national costume of Chinese women." For the purposes of the pageant, modern dressmakers modified the design of the Cheong-sam to emphasize the cleavage area, creating "the 'poured-in' look so highly de-

sired." Furthermore, the slit up the side of the dress was increased "to endow the basically simple Cheong-sam with a touch of intrigue . . . [,] a tantalizing suggestion about the beauty of its wearer." This conception of Chinese American identity as a blend of East and West allowed pageant supporters to negotiate cultural, economic, and political tensions within the Chinese American community and with the broader community during the late 1950s and 1960s.[5]

Organizers argued that the beauty pageant demonstrated both the assimilation of the Chinese American community and their need to preserve Chinese culture. CCC leaders explained that they wanted to organize "something western" to attract the interest of the American-born generations as they became more assimilated. After nearly a century of racial exclusion and segregation, Chinese Americans became increasingly integrated into American society during the post-World-War-II era. Because of the alliance between China and the U.S. during the war, Chinese Americans for the first time gained the right to become naturalized citizens. With changes in segregationist residential restrictions after the War, middle-class Chinese Americans began moving out of Chinatown. They also gained access to white-collar jobs as occupational racial barriers decreased. These opportunities encouraged college-educated Chinese American women to join the labor force. The pageant provided a means for Chinese Americans to demonstrate their assimilation by inviting young, educated women to participate in an event which was becoming popular in American society during the post-War era, the beauty pageant.[6]

At the same time, the pageant also sought to preserve Chinese culture among those who were merging into the mainstream. For contestants like June Gong, San Francisco

Chinatown represented their first contact with a large population of Chinese Americans. She exclaimed upon her arrival in San Francisco, "I had never seen so many Chinese people." Her unfamiliarity with Chinese culture made the event exciting and educational. She recalled that "it was even fun discovering Chinese food." Other contestants expressed similar sentiments about the pageant. One contestant from Glendale, Arizona explained that she came to San Francisco to catch "her first glimpse of Chinese life." She told a reporter, "When you're born and raised in Glendale, China doesn't mean too much to you. . . . To me, San Francisco's Chinatown is China."[7]

In addition to promoting awareness of Chinese culture among contestants, organizers pointed out that the beauty pageant fostered a more cohesive sense of identity among Chinese Americans across generations and throughout the country. Because the pageant successfully attracted young Chinese American women and encouraged their interest in Chinese culture, the event helped bring together generations that might have been separated by cultural differences. One organizer explained that H. K. Wong thought of the pageant as "a joyful event to get the families and the parents involved in the New Year show." In addition, the pageant fostered cooperation among Chinese Americans nationwide. In order to attract contestants from diverse geographical regions, pageant organizers sought the assistance of Chinese Chambers of Commerce, merchant organizations, and families' associations in other cities. Some areas that already had community beauty pageants began sending their representatives to San Francisco. Others initiated contests in order to participate in the Miss Chinatown U.S.A. beauty pageant. The solidification of these networks helped foster

a sense of a national Chinese American identity.[8]

The pageant and the New Year festival not only promoted an awareness of ethnic identity among Chinese Americans, but the events also educated the general public about the value of Chinese culture. As the embodiment of the positive aspects of ethnic identity, Miss Chinatown U.S.A. held symbolic importance in promoting greater acceptance of Chinese Americans. Historically, the white community viewed Chinatown as a disease-ridden society populated by unattached men. The stereotypes of Chinese American women as exotic slave girls or sequestered women with bound feet symbolized the moral corruption of the community. The pageant offered an alternative view of Chinese American women, which in turn emphasized the progress of the community. First, the pageant demonstrated the demographic changes of the community from a "bachelor society" to a "family society." By presenting beautiful, charming, and intelligent Chinese American women, the competition also paid tribute to the families of these contestants, as implied by the lyric from the official pageant song, "loveliest daughter of our Ancient Cathay." Second, the pageant also demonstrated the modernization of Chinese American gender roles. One pageant booklet charted the advances of women "from dim memories of wee bound-feet to present day stiletto heels." In this statement, the accessory of high heels is supposed to symbolize the advancement and independence of Chinese American women. While bound feet suggests the enforced debilitation of women by outdated cultural practices, the ability to wear high heels suggests women's economic power to purchase modern commodities. Chinese American women, like their American counterparts, were becoming part of a commercialized world.[9]

These images of Chinese American women and the conception of ethnic identity as a blend of the East and the West not only served to educate the broader American public but also helped draw tourists to Chinatown. While the pageant was usually attended by Chinese Americans, the proceeds from the event helped fund the annual New Year Parade, which attracted hundreds of thousands of non-Chinese people. In addition, pageant contestants served as models for advertisements for the festival, and their presence at various New Year events helped attract tourists, who shopped in Chinatown stores and ate in Chinese restaurants.

The developing commercial viability of Chinatown coincided with broader social interest in Asian culture following World War II. The military presence in the Pacific theater during the War and the political, commercial, and military interest in Asian countries during the Cold War led to increased contact between Western and Asian peoples. American popular culture reflected this fascination with the "Orient," which also included "Orientals" in the U.S.; San Francisco officials and business leaders actively supported the Chinese New Year festival and the Miss Chinatown U.S.A. Beauty Pageant for commercial purposes. As early as 1957, political and civic leaders expressed interest in promoting the festival as a distinctively San Franciscan cultural event that would draw tourists into the city. They wanted a festival "to rival Mardi Gras." The presence of ethnic beauty queens constituted an important component of the plan to encourage tourism. One non-Chinese festival organizer envisioned that "we'll have floats from Siam, Japan and Korea and we'll have pretty Chinese girls from all over the world . . . [and] I really think we will have an attraction to equal the Mardi Gras in five years."[10]

The joint interests of the CCC and city officials in promoting the commercial benefits of Chinatown fostered tensions as well as cooperation. Ironically, while Chinatown organizers sought to promote the compatibility of East and West through their events, white organizers cautioned Chinese Americans against over-assimilation. In a speech to the Chinese Historical Society of America, journalist Donald Canter, who regularly covered the Chinese New Year festival and Miss Chinatown U.S.A. beauty pageant, explained that the annual parade had become so Americanized that, "I wasn't quite sure whether I was viewing the Rose Parade in Pasadena or a New Year's parade of the largest Chinatown outside the Orient." To promote more tourism for the community, he encouraged organizers to highlight Chinese cultural practices. Instead of having the Miss Chinatown queen and princesses ride in floats for the parade, he suggested the "possibility of having the Queen, and possibly her court, carried in sedan chairs with the carriers performing their chore in relays." He argued that this practice would be "much more Chinese" and would appeal:

> much more to the imagination of the hundreds of thousands viewing this annual spectacle. . . . Wouldn't they write their folks and friends across the country about that eerie spectacle of a Chinese Queen and Chinese princesses being carried in Chinese sedan chairs? . . . And consequently, with a proper Chinese sense for reality, wouldn't [that] lure more tourists and their dollars into San Francisco and Chinatown?

To attract white tourists interested in seeing the "bizarre," Canter encouraged CCC leaders to emphasize an "Orientalist" image of Chinatown by creating cultural practices that were not relevant to Chinese Americans.[11]

CCC leaders did not entirely disagree with this approach of portraying Chinatown as something "exotic" and "foreign" in order to maintain its commercial viability. Pageant publications regularly invited tourists to visit San Francisco Chinatown because of its resemblance to "the Orient." The souvenir booklet explained that "if you have not been to the Orient, your trip to Chinatown will be as if you were visiting Formosa or Hong Kong." At the same time that pageant organizers promoted a positive conception of Chinese American identity to encourage self-pride and cultural awareness, they also consciously promoted an exotic image to fulfill the expectations of white tourists.[12]

The CCC efforts to balance their agenda of ethnic representation and commercial viability were further complicated by the international political context of the Cold War, which ignited immense hostility towards Communist China. The *San Francisco Chronicle* regularly placed its coverage of the New Year events next to articles on the People's Republic of China (PRC). To distance themselves from the negative images of "Red China," pageant and festival organizers emphasized a non-aggressive conception of Chinese culture. One CCC publication explained that the Chinese:

> seldom express their passion, particularly in public. This, combined with the Confucian doctrine of the dignity of man, makes them a calm and pacific race. Fatalism plays an important role in the Chinese mind. Generally they are quite content with their station in life. For this reason, the western sense of the word "revolution" has no appeal to the Chinese mind.

This portrayal of Chinese American identity as orderly and content with the existing order also encompassed Cold War conceptions of gender identity. Pageant founder H. K. Wong explained that the pageant represented a quest by "Chinatown Elders . . . for

[a] Queen with Ancient Virtues of Chinese Womanhood." He defined the ideal Chinese woman as obeying the patriarchal figures of the Chinese family. She must respect "first your father, then your brother, then your husband." This emphasis on female submissiveness was part of a more general portrayal of Chinese people as culturally passive. Both conceptions of ethnic and gender identity were consciously promoted to counter the notion that all Chinese were potentially red subversives. Furthermore, pageant supporters also implied that their version of Chinese culture was more authentic than the changes taking place in the PRC, because they traced their cultural origins to "Confucian" doctrines.[13]

CCC organizers simultaneously claimed Chinese cultural authenticity and emphasized their loyalty to America. They argued that the ability to celebrate their culture in the U.S. demonstrated the superiority of American society. According to James H. Loo, president of the CCC in 1962,

> In the turmoil of the world situation, we citizens of Chinese ancestry want to take this opportunity to demonstrate to the peoples of the world, particularly those who are living behind the iron and bamboo curtains, how American democracy really works. . . . We, like many Europeans, who came to settle in this free land, are also proud of our ancient culture and endeavor to retain the best of our heritage. The New Year celebration exemplifies the expression of such a love of freedom and liberty.

The close affiliation of the Taiwanese government (ROC) with the pageant and the festival reinforced CCC antagonism towards communism. Members of the ROC Consulate participated regularly in the festival and the pageant. Officials were presented as dignitaries during the beauty pageant and the New Year parade. The wife of the consul also served several times as a judge for the Miss Chinatown U.S.A. contest. Chow Shu-Kai, ROC Ambassador to the U.S., explained that his country supported the pageant and the festival as a reminder to "our compatriots on the mainland of China, who do not have the means to celebrate nor the freedom to commemorate occasions significant and meaningful according to the traditions of the old country." The ambassador as well as CCC officials emphasized the freedom of Chinese Americans to celebrate their culture and the authenticity of their version of Chinese culture compared to communist China.[14]

To support their argument that the beauty pageant represented an expression of authentic Chinese culture, organizers pointed to a Chinese tradition of appreciating female beauty. Although the more conservative Chinese philosophers emphasized female modesty and advocated the seclusion of women to the inner quarters of the home, poets, playwrights, as well as folk storytellers celebrated the beauty of famous women. H. K. Wong drew on these literary traditions to describe the standard of beauty used to select Miss Chinatown. He suggested that

> the elusive memory of ancient China's greatest beauties might lurk in the judges' minds as they ponder their decision. Their thoughts might linger on the centuries-old Chinese concept of beauty such as melon-seed face, new moon eyebrows, phoenix eyes, peachlike cheek, shapely nose, cherry lips, medium height, willowy figure, radiant smile and jet black hair.

Interestingly, the modern beauty pageant did resemble certain Chinese cultural practices. During the Northern Sung, Ming and Qing dynasties, the imperial court instituted a female draft to select palace maids, consorts, and wives. Choices were based on both the girl's personal appearance and on her family status. Pageant organizers used these Chinese traditions of appreciating

feminine beauty to justify the Miss Chinatown U.S.A. competition as an expression of Chinese, as well as American, culture.[15]

The conception of ethnic and gender identity promoted by the Miss Chinatown U.S.A. and Chinese New Year Festival during the 1950s and 1960s emphasized the blend of the exotic, passive Confucian East and the modern, democratic West. This interpretation of Chinese American culture allowed pageant supporters to negotiate tensions within the community and with the broader society during the post-World-War-II era. Reacting to the integrationist impulse among Chinese Americans, Chinatown organizers used an "American" event to attract the interest of the younger generation and to encourage the maintenance of Chinese culture. The pageant's emphasis on modern Chinese American women also served to educate the broader public about the "progress" of the community, even as the exotic foreignness of the events attracted tourists for Chinatown. The community's ability to celebrate their ancestral culture demonstrated the freedom that existed within democratic societies, while the pageant's emphasis on a non-revolutionary, Confucian notion of Chinese culture allowed Chinese Americans to claim cultural authenticity while also distancing themselves from the negative images of Communist Chinese.

The formulation of gender and ethnic identity presented by the Miss Chinatown beauty pageant suggests the vulnerability of the Chinese American community during the 1950s. While the aftermath of World War II brought increased economic and social opportunities, Chinese Americans also sensed the possibilities of community dispersion and political persecution. In this context, the pageant represented a means to promote a sense of community among Chinese Americans and between Chinese

Americans and the broader American population.

The ability of the Miss Chinatown U.S.A. beauty pageant to reconcile tensions within the Chinese American community and with the broader society helped the event achieve widespread popularity. Throughout the 1960s, spectators annually filled the Masonic Auditorium which seated over 3,000. One organizer for the New Year parade recalled that the pageant was the premier event for Chinatown, attracting the "who's who" of the community. Because of the popularity of the pageant, people often complained of the difficulties of obtaining tickets for the event. Those who could not get tickets either watched the pageant as it was televised to another auditorium or else listened to the program on radio. By the 1960s, then, the pageant had become a recognized tradition in the community.[16]

"China Dolls" and "Iron Girls": Contending Images of Chinese American Women

During the late 1960s and 1970s, a generation of Chinese Americans who became involved with grass-roots social movements increasingly criticized the popular Miss Chinatown U.S.A. beauty pageant. Influenced by the civil rights, Black liberation, anti-war, and women's movements, college-educated and community youth began organizing to address social problems within Chinatown. While some advocated social reform, others questioned the fundamental assumptions of American capitalism and sought inspiration from Third World and socialist movements. Their criticisms of the Miss Chinatown U.S.A. beauty pageant and the Chinese New Year Festival demonstrated their attempts to redefine the ethnic and gender identities of Chinese Americans.

The rise in political consciousness among a young generation of Chinese Americans coincided with changing demographic trends in the Chinatown community. In 1965, the U.S. Congress abolished discriminatory national-origins quotas, allowing immigrants from Asian countries to come to the U.S. in the same proportions as Europeans. The new Chinese immigrants followed preexisting demographic patterns. Educated professionals and technicians settled in areas outside of Chinatown, while unskilled workers and those with limited English facility became part of the older community. The heavy influx of working-class immigrants into San Francisco's Chinatown, estimated at "two to four thousand new residents" annually, both revitalized the community and exacerbated its social problems. With this rise in population, Chinatown's poverty level increased, its housing conditions deteriorated, and health and social services became inadequate. Both parents in Chinese immigrant families were likely to work long hours in service and light manufacturing jobs for low wages. Immigrant women also worked a "second shift," which included taking care of children and doing housework. Because of the crowded conditions in Chinatown and the poor quality of housing available, immigrant families were likely to live in small tenement rooms with inadequate plumbing facilities, no central heating, communal kitchens and bathrooms. These poor and overcrowded living conditions increased the health risks among community residents.[17]

Like other ghetto communities, however, Chinatown lacked the resources to respond to the needs of its residents. Government programs like the San Francisco Equal Employment Opportunity Commission were reluctant to allocate funds to assist immigrants or to address systemic problems within the community. Chinese Americans also lacked the political clout to combat the widespread belief that Asian Americans constituted model minorities who could succeed solely through hard work and perseverance.

In reaction to the ghettoization of Chinatown, young activists advocated new solutions to address these problems. They sought to educate themselves and the broader public about the needs of the community, and they demanded the reallocation of government and community resources for social services. During the 1960s and 1970s, liberal and radical activists formed agencies to serve the economic, educational, cultural, and social concerns of Chinatown residents. They also initiated grass-roots campaigns to mobilize Chinese Americans to demand better living and working conditions. As part of their broader agenda to fundamentally change the existing social structure, they began criticizing the popular Miss Chinatown U.S.A. beauty pageant. The new generation of activists questioned the role of tourism in the community, the images of Chinese American women promoted by the pageant, and the appropriateness of Confucian values and the ROC in representing Chinese culture. For them, Miss Chinatown represented a symbol of a commercialized, anti-revolutionary, middle-class Chinese American identity, exactly what reformers, radicals, and feminists sought to change in the community.

During the 1960s and 1970s, critics of the pageant and New Year festival increasingly questioned the use of community resources to promote tourism and the educational benefits provided by tourism. *East West*, a liberal Chinese American newspaper, noted that Chinese New Year

> is the time when people near and far come to visit the Chinatown. . . . But would the visitors be able to see the real Chinatown? Would

they have a chance to meet our residents? Would they begin to understand our many community problems? At the moment, what we are showing the visitors are the rides in the carnival, beauty contestants, an occasional cherry bomb, and busy restaurants where service could best be described as chaotic.

Because of the enormous crowds that the Chinese New Year attracted, keeping peace and order proved difficult. While the city's fire chief annually threatened to ban firecrackers to lessen chances of injury and fire, the police chief increased security during Chinese New Year to prevent fights and public disturbances. In 1969, a full-fledged riot broke out, resulting in thirty-five arrests and eighty-nine injuries. An observer's account suggests that Chinese New Year did not necessarily inspire greater appreciation of Chinese culture. George Chu, who described himself as "a square middle-class Chinese," explained that Chinese New Year was a particularly volatile time in the community. Because of racial tensions, fights between Chinese and whites had the potential to escalate. These tensions were exacerbated by the behavior of white tourists, who indiscriminately threw firecrackers without watching for people around them. Others strolled through the community, "tearing posters and paper lanterns from the booths for souvenirs, [acting] as if Chinatown was theirs for the picking." Police security for the festival did not help the situation since officers tended to ignore these incidents. When they did intervene, they tended to assume the Chinese were at fault. Even Chinatown residents who volunteered to help patrol the streets were warned that "when the cops come, stay out of it; they can't tell the Chinese apart." Some Chinese Americans, angry about the racist treatment by the police and the disrespect of tourists, criticized the CCC for promoting the festival.[18]

The tensions between business leaders and activists came into focus when the Holiday Inn decided to build a hotel to provide luxury accommodations for tourists in Chinatown. As part of the hotel's promotional campaign, they sponsored a contestant, Celeste Wong (alias), for the Miss Chinatown U.S.A. beauty pageant. As a publicity stunt for the gala grand opening of the Holiday Inn, Wong jumped out of a giant fortune cookie. Across the street, members of the Red Guard Party, a radical organization of Chinatown youth, and other Asian Americans staged a rally protesting the "invasion of Chinatown's territory" by the Holiday Inn. Citing the crowded conditions of San Francisco's Chinatown, protesters asked "how many of our people have had to move out of their shops and homes to make way for the growing financial district?" Questioning the displacement of Chinatown people for commercial enterprises like the Holiday Inn, the protesters demanded "low cost housing for our people!" During the New Year Parade, some protesters went so far as to throw eggs at Celeste Wong for representing the Holiday Inn. In the end, she had to be removed from the float because of public hostility. Activists criticized the Miss Chinatown U.S.A. beauty pageant for helping to promote a false commercial image of Chinatown in order to attract tourism. One community activist highlighted the contradictions between the tourist image of Chinatown and the actual experiences of its residents.

> In Holiday Inn . . . there is a swimming pool on the roof and a grand view of the city . . . there is the plush of soft carpets, bright lights, and spacious quarters . . . there are bell boys in smart uniforms . . . there are hostesses in mini skirts and cheong sams . . . there is . . . Miss Holiday Inn, and now Miss San Francisco Chinatown . . . there are tourists and business men with their briefcases . . . it's all there, across from Portsmouth Square, where

the poor, the old, and the very young while their time away before the sun goes down.[19]

The growing awareness about racial and class oppression also fostered critiques of the Miss Chinatown U.S.A. beauty pageant for objectifying Chinese American women. Beginning in the late 1960s and escalating throughout the decade, Chinese Americans criticized the pageant for judging women based on physical standards and portraying them as "China dolls." Their criticisms were partly inspired by the broader movement for women's equality. In 1968, women involved with the budding feminist movement conducted a widely-publicized protest of the Miss America pageant in Atlantic City. They crowned "a live sheep to symbolize the beauty pageant's objectification of female bodies, and filled a 'freedom trashcan' with objects of female torture—girdles, bras, curlers, issues of *Ladies' Home Journal*." Although no bras were actually burned, the media referred to protesters as "bra-burners," which then became a simplistic derogatory term to refer to feminists.[20]

Chinese Americans concerned about women's issues echoed white feminist criticisms of beauty pageants. Although Miss Chinatown contestants were supposedly judged according to their intelligence, "talent, beauty, charm and knowledge of Chinese culture," critics argued that physical appearance tended to be the main criterion. Pageant observers pointed out that many "would-be queens" displayed a "sad lack of 'talent.'" Others commented that the interview session of the contest did not really demonstrate the contestants' knowledge of Chinese culture or their intelligence. After attending her first Miss Chinatown U.S.A. beauty pageant, Judy Yung criticized the candidates for obviously memorizing their responses to the Chinese portion of the interview session: "But even with preparation, their answers don't always make sense, since they speak Chinese with a heavy American accent." Because of these problems, the Chinese portion of the interview eventually became optional in 1980. Yung further complained that the English portion of the interview did not challenge the intelligence of the contestants, for judges asked questions such as

> (1) If you saw your best friend cheating, what would you do? or (2) If you dressed informally to a formal party, what would you do? or (3) If you found your hem falling during a public appearance, what would you do? Evidently, the judges are more interested in finding out how you can get out of difficult situations than what your knowledge and opinions are on current events and social problems.

Other critics of the pageant pointed out that the main purpose of the event was to display a "parade of flesh." One documentary film maker portrayed the 1973 Miss Chinatown beauty pageant, which took place during the year of the Ox, as a "Livestock Show."[21]"

Chinese American feminists expanded beyond mainstream criticisms that beauty pageants objectified women by pointing out the racial implications of certain female images. Critics argued that despite the flowery language used to describe Chinese standards of beauty, the Miss Chinatown U.S.A. beauty pageant actually used white standards to judge Chinese American women. One community member stated her belief that the contest "shows that the closer you look like the Whites, the prettier you are." Another critic agreed that Asian Americans internalized "white standards" of beauty promoted by mass media. These images emphasized that "a beautiful woman has a high-bridged, narrow nose, a large bosom, and long legs." She pointed out that while "these and many other physical traits are not inherent in most Asian women," beauty pag-

eants like the Miss Chinatown U.S.A. contest encouraged women to achieve that ideal. Asian women "can compensate by setting our hair, curling our eyelashes, or wearing false ones, applying gobs of eye make-up, and going to great lengths to be the most 'feminine' women in the world." In attempting to achieve this feminine image, Chinese American women perpetuated the stereotype of Asian women as the "exotic-erotic-Susie Wong-Geisha girl dream of white American males." As white women became active in demanding social equality, Asian women became associated with the sexuality and the submissiveness of the "ideal" woman.[22]

Contestant statements and articles on the beauty pageant support this notion that white standards of physical beauty were used to judge the competition. Some candidates, organizers, and observers believed that judges preferred taller contestants. One entrant, who was 5 foot 2, complained that "it was obvious those girls with height had it." Other evidence suggests that "Caucasian" eyes represented a standard of beauty for Chinese American contestants. When one 1973 entrant was asked if she had any special attributes that might make her stand out, she said that her eyes might be an advantage, because they were "larger than [those of] some of the girls." Larger eyes with double eyelids and longer eye lashes have traditionally been associated with a "western look," as opposed to smaller eyes with single eyelids. During the late 1960s, the double eyelid look gained increasing popularity among Asians in Asia and the U.S. To achieve that look, women resorted to various methods. While teenagers "place[d] scotch tape or a gluey substance over their eyelids overnight," those with more resources paid for "plastic surgery to westernize Oriental eyes." One pageant souvenir book even carried an advertisement for cosmetic surgery to convert "'oriental eyes' with single eyelids into 'Caucasian eyes' (with double eyelids)."[23]

This emphasis on physical appearance placed psychological and emotional burdens on the contestants. In preparing for the competition, entrants experienced subtle and overt pressures to alter their physical appearance through cosmetics, dieting, and even plastic surgery. This emphasis on viewing women as sexual objects may have led to more abusive forms of behavior, such as sexual harassment. Celeste Wong remembered that "a lot of the people who directed the activities in Chinatown were older men who took advantage of the situation. . . . You'd be in a taxi or car with somebody and all of a sudden you'd feel a hand slipping under your dress." Her sponsor, the Holiday Inn hotel, provided her with a white male escort and required her to attend various functions to promote their business projects. Once, when the Holiday Inn flew her to Memphis for the opening of a hotel, her escort reserved only one room for both of them. Only sixteen years old at the time, Wong responded to these advances by ignoring them or escaping from the situations. However, she did not have the words or confidence to expose the treatment she received. Wong later interpreted these incidents as a result of the beauty pageant, which encouraged young women to present themselves as physically desirable. The sexual harassment "had to do with the contest and had to do with being a young woman who's supposed [to] just win based on what you looked like." The men who harassed her translated the accessibility of her body image for commercial and cultural purposes as an accessibility of her body for their sexual purposes.[24]

In addition to exposing the personal and psychological effects of beauty pageants, community activists also criticized the pageant for promoting an elite image of Chinese American women. Because the competition sought to highlight educated, accomplished, poised, and beautiful Chinese American women, critics considered the image of contestants "bourgeois." They argued that "most of the contestants come from wealthy and influential backgrounds and know very little about Chinatown, the ghetto." Because the competition sought to present "the most 'beautiful' Chinese women in their fine clothes and just perfect make-up, pranc[ing] around the stage," critics did not consider this image as representative of Chinese American women. They pointed out that "the majority of Chinese women are hardworking, either with jobs or full-time family responsibilities, and in most cases it's both. They are not women of leisure and their 'beauty' is not in their 'made-up, worked on for hours' physical outward appearance." Instead of promoting exceptional women as representative of Chinese American womanhood, critics sought further recognition of the problems facing women as workers and family members.[25]

Activists preferred to promote an image of Chinese American women as protesters of injustice. Challenging the CCC's portrayal of Chinese culture as passive and non-revolutionary, the critics pointed to the growing militancy of women in Chinatown and throughout the Third World. Just as some Chinatown publications regularly featured women from beauty contests, papers with more liberal and radical agendas emphasized women's activism in movements for social justice. For example, articles in the latter papers frequently covered the struggles of garment workers, striking for better working conditions and wages. The photographs of middle-aged women holding picket signs represented a dramatic departure from the images of young women in cheong-sams and make-up. Community members concerned about working women's issues also began celebrating International Women's Day in Chinatown during this time period. Occurring in early March, this annual event could be interpreted as a symbolic alternative to the Miss Chinatown U.S.A. beauty pageant, which usually took place in late January or February.

These images of women as protesters rather than beauty queens were directly inspired by Third World female revolutionaries. Radicals criticized the CCC's emphasis on Confucian values as representative of Chinese culture. Instead, they sought inspiration from the new socialist societies forming throughout Asia. *Getting Together*, the newspaper for an Asian American Marxist-Leninist organization, regularly featured images of female cadre and revolutionaries transforming patriarchal family structures and building new societies in the People's Republic of China (PRC), Vietnam, the Philippines, and North Korea. Community radicals sought inspiration from the image of China's "Iron Girls," a group of women "who took on the most difficult and demanding tasks at work" and who developed legendary reputations for exerting superhuman energy. Community activists who promoted the Third World revolutionary women as role models for Chinese American women criticized the involvement of the ROC in the Chinese New Year Festival. As an alternative, pro-PRC supporters organized a noncommercial celebration of Chinese New Year. Rather than emphasizing China's Confucian tradition, their Spring Festival highlighted "the creative and innovative aspects of Chinese culture," as represented by developments in the PRC.[26]

The criticisms leveled against the Chinese New Year Festival and the Miss Chinatown U.S.A. pageant during the late 1960s and 1970s represented a contest over the definition of ethnic and gender identity. Influenced by radical social movements, a new generation of Chinese Americans began advocating new forms of inter-racial, gender, and class relationships. Instead of promoting a commercial image of Chinatown to attract tourists, the activists demanded support from city officials and community leaders to address social issues. Instead of encouraging women to achieve certain standards of beauty or personal advancement, they advocated community responsibility and political activism. Instead of seeking cultural inspiration from a Confucian past and political legitimation from nationalist Taiwan, they turned to Communist China. The vociferousness of community debates regarding gender and ethnic identity reflected the high degree of conflict within San Francisco Chinatown during the late 1960s and 1970s.

The Reform Tradition of Radicalism

The responses of pageant supporters to their critics demonstrate the diverse and often contradictory strategies available to advance racial and gender equality. On the one hand, pageant organizers and contestants expressed fundamental disagreement with the agenda of community reformers, radicals, and feminists. They questioned the cultural authenticity of their critics and disagreed with their views on tourism, the class bias of the pageant, and the gender roles portrayed through the image of Miss Chinatown. At the same time, pageant and New Year festival supporters also proclaimed their commitment to community service, accurate portrayals of Chinese culture, and women's achievements. While their critics sought to expose the contradictions involved in the Miss Chinatown U.S.A. beauty contest, pageant supporters revealed the contradictions embedded within the social movements that advocated racial and gender equality.

Reacting to criticisms of the pageant and the Chinese New Year festival, supporters questioned the ability of their critics to speak on behalf of Chinatown. One observer of the Holiday Inn rally suggested that the young radicals protesting for the good of the "community" did not necessarily understand the community. He pointed out that when one journalist asked the protesters what some older female residents were talking about in Chinese, "all the youths could respond was, 'I don't understand Chinese.'"Just as pageant critics questioned the ability of the CCC and other establishment leaders to represent the community, the ability of the liberals and radicals to speak on behalf of Chinatown also came into question.[27]

Claiming that they had the interest of the community at heart, pageant and festival supporters argued for the benefits of tourism. They suggested that "there's nothing wrong in bringing in large crowds" to Chinatown. Tourism provided an economic lifeline by supporting the restaurants and stores which in turn employed Chinatown residents. Furthermore, the public exposure gained through the Miss Chinatown U.S.A. beauty pageant and Chinese New Year festival helped Chinese Americans gain national and international attention. Some community members agreed that "in spite of the commercialization of Chinese New Year, it does help remind us that we belong to a unique culture." New Year festival supporters further suggested that those who wanted a less commercial version of Chinese New Year should turn to private celebrations. One organizer explained that "you have to understand the private and public celebrations are two very different things. . . . People will go on having the traditional New Year family reunions, feasts and gift-

giving regardless of the parade." Pageant supporters thus downplayed their power to define ethnic identity by emphasizing the community's ability to celebrate cultural events in diverse ways.[28]

Pageant supporters also argued that the beauty competition transcended class divisions and helped promote upward mobility. They pointed to the enormous popularity of the pageant among the working class in Chinatown and the opportunities that the contest provided for women. Cynthia Chin-Lee, a 1977 contestant from Harvard University, agreed with this argument. She remembered that the pageant was more of a casual, fun experience for her, because "I was going to Harvard and I knew I had a different type of career ahead of me." However, other contestants who "didn't have real high power careers" approached the competition more seriously, because it offered an opportunity for social recognition and career advancement. The experiences of Rose Chung, Miss Chinatown 1981, illustrate the argument that beauty pageants provided opportunities for working-class women. Growing up in a single-parent household, Chung remembered that she stayed home to take care of her four siblings while her mother worked as a seamstress. The pageant offered an opportunity to gain public exposure and participate in a glamorous event. After winning the Miss Chinatown title, she received a $2000 scholarship and free trips to locations in the U.S., Canada, and Asia. Chung also became an instant celebrity, receiving recognition from the Chinatown community. She recalled that because of her sheltered childhood, she "always wanted to participate in community activities." After she won the Miss Chinatown title, Chung served as the president of the women's auxiliary group of her family association, as president of the San Francisco General Hospital Chinese Employee Association, and as a member of the Republican County Central Committee. She traces these accomplishments to her victory in the Miss Chinatown U.S.A. pageant.[29]

Pageant defenders also countered their critics by challenging the goals and methods of the women's movement. They disagreed with feminist critics on issues concerning the importance of beauty, marriage, and radical protest. Although supporters acknowledged that beauty pageants objectified women and fostered their feelings of insecurity, they believed that the competition provided overriding benefits. Because of the racial discrimination against minorities in mainstream pageants such as the Miss America contest, the Miss Chinatown U.S.A. and other ethnic pageants gave women of those backgrounds the opportunity to achieve recognition. The experiences of Sandra Wong, Miss 1973 Chinatown U.S.A., demonstrated this function of ethnic beauty pageants. Prior to entering the Miss Chinatown pageant, Wong competed twice in the local Miss San Leandro contest. Had she won, she would have been the first Asian American to be represented in the Miss California contest, a preliminary for the Miss America pageant. Although Wong won both the talent and swimsuit contests during her first attempt, she did not win the competition. During both years, she placed as first runner-up. She did not publicly protest these results as racially motivated, but others did. Journalist John Lum's exposé of Wong's experiences concluded that "discrimination doesn't only extend to housing, education, and jobs, it extends to beauty 'contests,' too." Because of racial discrimination in mainstream beauty pageants, as well as in careers involving modeling, acting and performance, pageant defenders argued that the Miss Chinatown U.S.A. competition was important for promoting positive images of Chinese Americans.

These supporters disagreed with feminist critics who argued that emphasis on external appearances necessarily degraded women.[30]

Pageant backers also explained their disregard for feminist criticisms by proclaiming their support for more traditional female roles. When questioned about their thoughts on "women's lib" and on their future plans, many contestants discussed their dual commitments to career and marriage. Contestants during the late 1960s tended to view the two goals in conflict and prioritized marriage over careers. For example, 1967 contestant Irene Ung acknowledged gender discrimination against women in her field of international marketing when she remarked that "being a woman can be a handicap when you're looking for a man's job in a man's world." However, Ung did not necessarily aspire to "a career of working." "Like any other girl," Ung explained, "someday I'll want to get married and have children," goals which presumably set her apart from the feminist movement. Other contestants also voiced their preference for more "gentlemen-like" behavior from their male companions. One contestant explained that she "still enjoys having her cigarette lit and having somebody hold the door for her." She interpreted these desires as antagonistic to the feminist agenda. Still other contestants expressed their dissatisfaction with critiques of beauty pageants by emphasizing the radical image of feminists. Sandra Wong explained that she did not believe the women's liberation movement's members "protesting and burning their bras." By explaining that feminists and beauty contestants operated in separate worlds and held different values, pageant supporters could partly explain their disregard of feminist criticisms.[31]

Even as they questioned their critics' authority and disagreed with the radical agenda, pageant defenders also professed similar goals of racial and gender equality. In response to criticisms raised during the 1960s and 1970s, organizers and participants altered the pageant and the New Year festival to assist community service projects and to project a less "plastic" version of Chinese culture. They also argued that the pageant promoted the goal of gender equality by emphasizing the importance of female bonding, women's achievements in the public realm, and sexual liberation. Pageant defenders argued that they, like their critics, shared the goals of advancing the Chinese American community and Chinese American women.

These reform efforts were often initiated by a new generation of pageant supporters who had activist credentials. Gordon Yaw provides one example. Yaw's family moved out of San Francisco when he was a young boy, but he returned to attend Chinese school. Because he grew up in an Oakland neighborhood where the Black Panthers had a positive influence, Yaw became involved with the Berkeley Third World Strike during the late 1960s. Through his protest activities, he met many Asian American students who criticized the CCC and other Chinatown establishment leaders for ignoring the needs of the community. They also condemned the Miss Chinatown U.S.A. beauty pageant as a symbol of the status quo. Rather than just criticize the event, however, Yaw became involved and encouraged others to volunteer in order to change the pageant and the Chinese New Year festival. *East West* editors applauded these efforts, pointing out that "as presently arranged, most of the New Year activities are organized by and for only a small segment of the community. Changes are needed to involve the young and those in the middle years, as well as the elderly, with meaningful activities."[32]

The involvement of younger people altered some of the content of the New Year festival. Through the lobbying efforts of Chinatown youth organizations, the CCC consented to include a community-sponsored Street Fair as part of the celebration in 1969. Rather than having a "traditional carnival organized by professional concessionaires," members of thirty youth organizations came together to create a street fair to raise funds for community services. The events, which included a run through Chinatown, ping-pong tournaments, cooking and shadow boxing demonstrations, were intended to "inform the public about Chinese culture, history and tradition" as well as to involve community members in recreational social activities. The organizers of the Street Fair wanted to use Chinese New Year to benefit the community directly. Beauty pageant contestants also demonstrated a growing consciousness about the need for social service. While pageant queens previously helped to raise funds and generate publicity about community projects, such as playgrounds for children, contestants in the 1970s also expressed career ambitions to serve the community. As one 1974 entrant explained, her life goal was "to be a social worker."[33]

In addition to emphasizing community service in the New Year festivities, the new generation of organizers and participants also sought to alter the cultural content of the events. Sensitive to charges that the festival projected an artificial tourist-oriented version of Chinese culture, organizers sought to revitalize the image of the celebration. For example, David Lei, one of the younger generation of organizers, traveled to Taiwan to research Chinese culture and purchase artifacts. To encourage tourists to look beyond "the old 'chop suey image' where people have a very superficial idea of what's Chinese culture," he "included a block-long bridal procession of the Han period" in the 1977 parade. Organizers of the beauty pageant also sought to incorporate Chinese culture into the event. One year, pageant organizer Louella Leon scripted the pageant in the form of a Chinese opera. The demographic changes in the Chinese American population also helped revitalize cultural aspects of the pageant. As immigrants from Hong Kong and Taiwan entered the pageant, contestants demonstrated greater knowledge and familiarity with Chinese language and culture.[34]

In addition to promoting community service and cultural education, younger pageant supporters also expressed their commitment to women's accomplishments. Like contemporary women's rights activists, they emphasized the importance of "sisterhood," women's achievements in the public realm, and sexual liberation. Almost all the contestants explained that their desire to meet other Chinese women constituted an important motivation for their decisions to enter the pageant. Jennifer Chung, a 1967 contestant, expressed her hope for "everlasting friends[hip]" with the other contestants. In their parting statements, Miss Chinatowns frequently invoked the rhetoric of female friendships. These expressions of "sisterhood" may not have reflected real experiences. When asked if she had developed any close friendships with other contestants, Chung admitted that her busy schedule preparing for the pageant did not allow her time to do so. Competition among contestants and the unequal treatment of winners and losers after the pageant presented obstacles as well. Despite the unevenness of women's relationships with one another, the use of rhetoric emphasizing female bonding suggests that pageant supporters viewed sisterhood as an important value that helped to justify the competition.[35]

Whatever the obstacles to female friendships, the beauty competition promoted female achievements according to organizers. Participating in the Miss Chinatown U.S.A. beauty pageant provided contestants with an opportunity to acquire poise, grace, confidence, and public-speaking experience. These skills provided an important foundation for activities in the public realm. As one community member remarked, the pageant "gives Chinese girls an opportunity to meet people and get into things. Too many of them sit at home and don't do anything." In fact, many contestants viewed the pageant as a steppingstone to other challenges. In contrast to late 1960s' contestants, who prioritized marriage over their careers, the 1970s' contestants mainly discussed their future work plans or else emphasized the compatibility of marriage with careers. Jeannie Fung, Miss Chinatown U.S.A. 1975, expressed her desire to "be a medical technician and eventually to teach in junior college." Arleen Chow, a 1972 contestant, discussed the complementary roles of worker and mother. She believed that "a girl can do a man's job, mentally and physically, if trained properly. . . . The wife should be both a parent and a supporter." For these contestants, participation in the pageant did not conflict with goals for women's social equality. Many contestants explained that they supported women's liberation to the extent that they believed in equal access to jobs and in "equal pay for equal jobs." In fact, the description of pageant contestants as "intelligent, ambitious, and mature women" matched the image of "modern" career women.[36]

Perhaps in response to feminist criticisms, the Chinese Chamber of Commerce also began to promote female leadership among pageant organizers. Although women had always participated in organizing the pageant, the leadership positions had previously been male-dominated. In 1974, the CCC selected Carolyn Gan as the first female editor-in-chief for the annual souvenir book. In 1979, a woman was elected to the CCC board of directors. The all female fashion show committee also made some adjustments in 1976 that appeared to respond to feminist critiques. In the midst of community debates about the exploitation of women, the fashion committee decided to include male models and men's fashions in the traditionally all female fashion show. While these changes could be interpreted as responses to the growing criticisms of the pageant, their limited nature also demonstrate the difficulty of fundamentally changing the pageant or the CCC. The numbers of women in recognized leadership roles remained small, while the inclusion of male models and fashions occurred for only one year.

In addition to these attempts to integrate the leadership and content of the pageant, some proponents further claimed that their support for sexual liberation demonstrated their commitment to women's equality. In 1974, the fashion show committee included a "feminist fashion" selection that emphasized revealing clothing. One of the "Women's Lib" outfits was described as "a black full-length evening gown with neckline in back swooping to the waist." Others associated female activists with wearing mini-skirts. These interpretations of "feminism" emphasized women's willingness to express their sexual desirability in shocking ways. Ironically, this emphasis on physical exposure reinforced the objectification of female bodies that feminists criticized. For example, 1972 contestant Patricia Moy decided to give a speech on free love as her talent presentation. She argued that:

a. No one objects to free love, love meaning everything excluding the physical act of sex, which can be considered love. . . .

b. Virginity shouldn't be a prerequisite for marriage.

c. Homosexuality is not necessarily "bad" as society has always labeled it.

The main points of her speech coincided with developing feminist critiques of socially constructed heterosexual ideals and represented a radical departure from more conservative Chinese notions of sexuality. However, the manner of her presentation during the pageant suggests that she may have reinforced traditional sexual roles for women rather than transcended them. She began her act "by stripping off the top half of her pantsuit to reveal a bikini top, and then proceeded to deliver her original speech on free love, virginity, and homosexuality." Moy's decision to expose her body expressed her sexual freedom but also encouraged audience "gawkers" to view her as a sexual object.[37]

This relationship between increased sexual freedom and sexual exposure offers one explanation for the introduction of the swimsuit component to the Miss Chinatown U.S.A. beauty pageant. When the competition first began in 1958, organizers prided themselves for not having their contestants parade around in bathing suits. However, organizers introduced a "playsuit" portion in 1962, in which contestants displayed themselves in short-skirt outfits. In 1967, the bathing suit replaced the playsuit. One organizer claimed that the new requirement responded to the contestants' interest in displaying their beauty through wearing swimsuits. Although this explanation is not confirmed by other sources, his comment suggests that arguments for sexual liberation may have been used to justify sexual exploitation.[38]

During the 1960s and 1970s, pageant participants and supporters responded to critics both by disagreeing with them and by expressing their own commitments to gender and racial equality. The ability of pageant organizers to use the same concepts to refer to different strategies demonstrates the tensions within movements promoting social equality. By emphasizing the importance of individual role models to inspire Chinese Americans, women, and members of the working class, pageant supporters negated arguments calling for systemic structural changes. By stressing the importance of promoting beautiful images for Chinese Americans because of racial discrimination, pageant defenders downplayed the danger of encouraging women to use their physical appearance to gain social acceptance. Their arguments reveal the multiple and often contradictory strategies that could be used to advance racial and gender equality.

The Modern Chinese and Chinese American Woman

The debates surrounding the Miss Chinatown U.S.A. and Chinese New Year festival demonstrate the complex struggles to define Chinese American identity through gender images. The intensity of criticisms against the pageant coincided with the degree of community conflict surrounding issues of ethnic representation and gender roles, as well as class divisions and international allegiances. During the Cold War, organizers of the Miss Chinatown U.S.A. beauty pageant successfully balanced tensions within the Chinese American community. By representing the Chinese community as a blend of the East and West, sponsors were able to address growing generational and cultural conflicts at a time when Chinese Americans sought to integrate into the broader community while also maintaining their cultural values. This conception of Chinese American identity as embodied by Miss Chinatown also served cultural, economic, and political purposes in the community's relationship with the broader society. However,

as social movements of the 1960s raised fundamental critiques of the existing racial, sexual, and economic hierarchies, the Miss Chinatown pageant also came under attack. Pageant and festival supporters disagreed fundamentally with their critics on the importance of tourism, the evaluation of women based on physical standards, and the role of the ROC in the pageant. However, a new generation of organizers did reform certain aspects of the pageant in response to the criticisms. By emphasizing the importance of individual role models, pageant organizers justified the pageant as a means to promote gender and ethnic equality.

While the overt conflict surrounding the pageant decreased in the 1980s with the decline of radical social movements, the process of negotiating gender and ethnic identity continues both internationally and domestically. Both the PRC's changing attitudes towards commercial images of women and the motivations of Miss Chinatown U.S.A. contestants in the 1980s demonstrate the ambiguous benefits of beauty pageants.

With the normalization of relations between Communist China and the U.S. in 1979, political pressure was placed on CCC leaders to lessen its pro-Taiwan stance and extend a hand of welcome to the PRC. Pageant and festival supporters did so reluctantly. In the 1979 Chinese New Year Parade, Chinese school marching bands and an airline sponsor of the Miss Chinatown U.S.A. beauty pageant displayed the Nationalist flag, even after Mayor Dianne Feinstein asked for assurances from organizers that this would not occur. In 1980, after Feinstein applied political pressure, the CCC reluctantly issued a last-minute invitation to the envoy of the PRC and then quickly withdrew the invitation to both the communist and the nationalist representatives. Pageant organizers chose to distance themselves from both countries rather than be forced to extend friendship to Communist China.

Despite the reluctance of the CCC to establish relations with the PRC, China was shifting its public image to accommodate the political, economic, and social changes that occurred following the Cultural Revolution. Ironically, even as Chinatown radicals promoted Third World socialist role models of working and revolutionary women, the PRC was commercializing the image of women to promote economic development and trade with the West. According to historians Emily Honig and Gail Hershatter, "adornment and sexuality, topics that had been off-limits to the generation of the Cultural Revolution, dominated publications for young women in the 1980s. Attention to beauty and fashion was part of a growing concern with the quality of personal life, and clearly captured the public fancy." Some state-owned businesses in China began instituting beauty requirements to hire women for service jobs. Beauty pageants reportedly have become very popular throughout China. Ironically, the living Chinese culture that community radicals promoted was evolving to adopt Western practices of commodifying women's beauty.[39]

Just as Communist China recognized the commercial uses of women's bodies in promoting their national economy, Chinese American women in the 1980s and 1990s continued to use the pageant as a means for personal and community advancement. According to film-maker Valerie Soe, Miss Chinatown 1984 Cynthia Gouw first entered the Los Angeles pageant as part of an undercover reporting assignment for a school newspaper. Gouw was supposed to "expose the contest from a feminist, leftist, socialist point of view . . . [and uncover] the oppression of Asian American women." However, after Gouw won the Miss L.A. and then the

Miss Chinatown U.S.A. titles, she decided not to criticize the event. Gouw argued that there was no contradiction between the pageant and her feminist and political beliefs:

> I didn't feel exploited at all. . . . I want to show people that I can be very articulate and assertive as opposed to a stereotypical beauty pageant winner. . . . What I want to represent to the Asian population is that I am very concerned about the community.

Gouw suggests that her personal advancement reflected upon the entire community, because groups who have traditionally been disadvantaged, women as well as racial minorities, need role models and spokespersons. After she won Miss Chinatown U.S.A., Gouw entered and won the Spokesmodel competition for Star Search. Since then, she has appeared in films and TV commercials and worked as a news reporter. For her, the pageant opened up numerous opportunities, allowing her to achieve, in the words of Valerie Soe, the "American Dream." The question of whether Gouw in fact transcended stereotypes of Chinese American women, or merely benefited from perpetuating them, remains unanswered.[40]

The history of the Miss Chinatown U.S.A. pageant, from the early years of success through the years of controversy, demonstrates how idealized roles of womanhood represent broader concerns about power. Activists of the late 1960s and 1970s, like commercial leaders of the late 1950s, recognized the significance of gender roles in defining the identity of a community. The intensity of their debates about the pageant reflected a contest over ethnic and gender identity as well as international politics and class relations. The persistent success of the Miss Chinatown U.S.A. beauty pageant into the 1980s and 1990s suggests its unique ability to reconcile conflicting impulses within the Chinese American community. The competition continues to provide a means for exceptional Chinese American women to use their physical appearance and personality skills to achieve recognition within the existing commercialized society. The cultural event promotes recognition of disadvantaged groups without threatening the fundamental American values of individualism and meritocracy. The continued popularity of the pageant combined with the decrease in vocal opposition suggests the decline of alternative strategies that advocate structural change and group-based solutions to achieve gender and racial equality.

Department of History
Stanford, CA 94305-2024

Notes

1. *Miss Chinatown U.S.A. Pageant Program*, 21–22–23 February 1958; "June Chin," *California Living Magazine*, 17 February 1985, p. 9. The overall Chinese American population in 1960 was 237,292. Of the 29,000 Chinese living in San Francisco in 1960, 18,000 lived in Chinatown.

2. Although the pageant held symbolic value for Chinese American communities throughout the country, I focus on San Francisco and Bay Area responses to the competition as a part of the annual Chinese New Year celebration. On the one hand, San Francisco's Chinatown could be considered unique because of its large Chinese population, its historical relationship with the Nationalist Republic of China, and its exposure to local social movements. On the other hand, the tensions in San Francisco's community, the unofficial capital of American Chinatowns, were often representative of the conflicts in other Chinese American communities.

3. The main newspapers used for research include: *East West, San Francisco Journal*, and *Getting Together*, all bilingual Chinese American publications based in San Francisco's Chinatown; *Chinatown News*, a Chinese Canadian publication based in Vancouver, B.C.; *Asian Week*, an Asian American publication based in San Francisco; and the *San Francisco Chronicle*. Because of my limited Chinese reading skills, I was not able to access systematically Chinese language materials. Consequently, the experiences and perspectives of Chinese Americans who felt more comfortable expressing themselves in Chinese will not be represented as well as those who wrote in English.

The perspectives of the former are not less valuable, but are nevertheless not accessible to me at this point. Fortunately, the staff of the bilingual newspapers did publish translations of some Chinese articles on the Miss Chinatown U.S.A. beauty pageant.

4. Colleen Ballerino Cohen, Richard Wilk, Beverly Stoeltje, eds., *Beauty Queens on the Global Stage: Gender, Contests, and Power* (New York, 1996), p. 2. This collection examines a variety of beauty contests throughout the world for their significance concerning not only gender roles but also ethnic, class and national identity formation. Prior to the publication of this collection, most scholars of beauty contests tended to focus on the Miss America pageant, which involves predominantly white contestants. See Frank Deford, *There She Is* (New York, 1971), A. R. Riverol, *Live From Atlantic City* (Bowling Green, OH, 1992), and Lois W. Banner, *American Beauty* (New York, 1983). A few scholars have analyzed state or local beauty pageants and their significance in terms of community representation. See Frank Deford, "Beauty and Everlasting Faith at the Local Level," *Audience 1971* 1:5, p. 56–72; Geoffrey Dunn and Mark Schwartz, directors, *Miss . . . or Myth?* (Distributors: Cinema Guild, 1986), film; Robert Lavenda, "Minnesota Queen Pageants: Play, Fun, and Dead Seriousness in a Festive Mood," *Journal of American Folklore* 101:400 (1988): 68–175.

For the most part, scholars of Chinese American women have not analyzed the Miss Chinatown U.S.A. beauty pageant. Their studies tend to focus on the emergence of women from the private realm of family concerns to the public realm of political organizing and work. See Huping Ling, "Surviving on the Gold Mountain: Chinese American Women and Their Lives," (Ph.D. dissertation, Miami University, 1991); Stacey G. H. Yap, *Gather Your Strength, Sisters: The Emerging Role of Chinese Women Community Workers* (New York, 1989); and Judy Yung, *Unbound Feet: A Social History of Chinese Women in San Francisco* (Berkeley, 1995). One exception is Judy Yung's paper entitled, "Miss Chinatown USA and the Representation of Beauty." She presented it at the 1992 Association for Asian American Studies National Conference in San Jose, but it is not available to the public at this time.

5. The title for this section is quoted from James H. Loo, "Who are the Chinese?" *San Francisco Chinatown On Parade* (San Francisco, 1961), pp. 6–7.

Beginning in the 1910s, San Francisco's Chinatown organizations sporadically sponsored community pageants as fundraisers for social services, such as the Chinese Hospital. In 1948, various merchant, family, and civic organizations initiated an annual Miss Chinatown pageant. Inspired by the earlier tradition of fundraising, the winners were determined by the contestants' ability to sell raffle tickets to benefit a social cause. H. K. Wong is credited with proposing the joint sponsorship of the beauty contest and the public celebration of the Chinese New Year festival in 1953. In the late 1950s, the CCC altered the format of the pageant so that a panel of judges selected winners based on such criteria as beauty, personality, and poise. Lim P. Lee, "The Chinese New Year Festival," *Asian Week*, 5 February 1981, p. 4, and "The Chinese New Year Festival II," *Asian Week*, 12 February 1981, [p. 2]; H. K. Wong, "Miss Chinatown USA Pageant," *San Francisco Chinese New Year Festival*, Souvenir Program, 4–7 February 1960; Alice Lowe, "Concealing—Yet Revealing," *San Francisco Chinatown On Parade*, pp. 26–27.

6. Julie Smith, "A Little Tiff At the Chinese New Year," *San Francisco Chronicle*, 18 February 1977, p. 2; the proportions of Chinese Americans in the labor force exceeded those for white women during the decade of the 1940s. Whereas 39.5 percent of white women worked for pay compared to 22.3 percent of Chinese women in 1940, 30.8 percent of Chinese women compared to 28.1 percent of white women worked in 1950. In 1960, 44.2 percent of Chinese women worked in the labor force compared to only 36.0 percent of white women. The gap in labor participation between the two groups continued to increase. Huping Ling, "Surviving on the Gold Mountain: Chinese American Women and Their Lives," pp. 134–135.

Following the War, the Miss America pageant increasingly gained popularity, culminating in its first national televised broadcast in 1954. Whereas previous pageants held significance mainly for the local audience of Atlantic City, television made the event a truly national one so that by 1959, every state was finally represented at the "Miss America" pageant. A. R. Riverol, *Live From Atlantic City*, p. 56.

7. "June Chin," *California Living Magazine*; Donald Canter, "In New Year of the Boar: Chinatown 'Moves West,'" 9 February 1959, clipping from Chinese Historical Society, San Francisco, Box 3, folder 16. The collection is located at the Asian American Studies Library of the University of California, Berkeley. Hereafter cited as CHS-SF.

8. Lim P. Lee, "The Chinese New Year Festival," *Asian Week*, 5 February 1981, p. 4.

9. Pageant souvenir booklets regularly included informational pieces explaining Chinese culture to audiences unfamiliar with the community.

Victor and Brett de Bary Nee use the terms "bachelor society" and "family society" to characterize the evolution of the San Francisco's Chinatown community; see *Longtime Californ': A Documentary Study of an American Chinatown* (Stanford, 1972). The development of the beauty pageant coincided with the balancing of sex ratios among Chinese Americans. In 1890, when the Chinese population reached a 19th-century peak of 107,488 in the U.S., men outnumbered women 26.8 to 1. Due to the combined influence of natural birth rates and immigration, the sex ratio became 1.3 to 1 by 1960. (Huping Ling, "Surviving on the Gold Mountain," p. 127.) For further discussions of Chinese American family and community life in the late 19th and early 20th centuries, see Peggy Pascoe, "Gender Systems in Conflict: The Marriages of Mission-Educated Chinese American Women, 1874–1939," in *Unequal Sisters: A Multicultural Reader in U.S. Women's History*, ed. by Ellen Carol DuBois and Vicki L. Ruiz (New York, 1990) and Sucheng Chan, "The Exclusion of Chinese Women, 1870–1943," in *Entry Denied: Exclusion and the Chinese Community in America, 1882–1943* (Philadelphia, 1991).

Lyrics to "Miss Chinatown" by Charles L. Leong and Kenneth Lee, 1964, published in *Miss Chinatown U.S.A.: Chinese New Year Festival Souvenir Program*, 1975. Robert H. Lavenda makes a similar argument that contestants of community pageants tend to represent "the community's daughters." Lavenda, "Minnesota Queen Pageants: Play, Fun, and Dead Seriousness in a Festive Mode," *Journal of American Folklore* 101 (1988), p. 169. Daisy Chinn, "Women of Initiative," *San Francisco Chinatown on Parade*, p. 64.

10. For an examination of how international relations influence portrayals of Asian Americans in popular culture, see *Slaying the Dragon*, directed by Deborah Gee (San Francisco: NAATA/Cross Current Media, 1987). In the late 1950s, C. Y. Lee's *Flower Drum Song* (New York, 1957) a love story about intergenerational and cultural tensions set in San Francisco's Chinatown, became a best-seller. Rodgers and Hammerstein subsequently turned the book first into a Broadway musical hit and then into a motion picture, leading Hollywood and Broadway to declare 1959 the "year of the Oriental." Chinatown organizers cashed in on the publicity by honoring and promoting the author of the book during the New Year festivals in the late 1950s and early 1960s.

As part of the city's efforts to promote the Miss Chinatown U.S.A. beauty pageant and the Chinese New Year Festival, mayors, police commissioners, and supervisors regularly appeared in the annual parade. Politicians and their wives served as judges for the pageant, and in 1963 the San Francisco Convention and Visitors Bureau became a co-sponsor of the festival. "To Rival Mardi Gras? Mayor Urges Big Chinatown Festival," 24 January 1957, CHS-SF, Box 3, folder 16; Arthur Hoppe, "Festival Overture, Opus I: Montgomery St. Hails Chinese New Year," clipping from CHS-SF, Box 3, folder 15.

11. Donald Canter, "Speech," Chinese Historical Society of America, 1965, CHS-SF, Box 3, folder 27.

12. T. Kong Lee, President, Chinese Chamber of Commerce, "Welcome to Chinatown," *San Francisco Chinatown on Parade*, p. 2.

13. James H. Loo, "Who are the Chinese?" *San Francisco Chinatown on Parade*, pp. 6–7; W. K. Wong, "Interview," *Longtime Californ'*, pp. 244–245.

14. *San Francisco Chinatown Souvenir Annual*, 1962.

15. H. K. Wong, "Concept of Beauty," *San Francisco Chinatown on Parade*, p. 79; Evelyn S. Rawski, "Ch'ing imperial Marriage and Problems of Rulership," in *Marriage and Inequality in Chinese Society*, ed. by Ruble S. Watson and Patricia Buckley Ebrey (Berkeley, 1991), p. 180; Although pageant organizers argued that the beauty pageant drew inspiration from Chinese as well as American cultural practice, scholars attribute the growing popularity of beauty pageants in Asian countries following World War II to the commercialization and Westernization of those countries. Corporations in Taiwan, Hong Kong, Japan, the Philippines, and Southeast Asia increasingly sponsored pageants as a way to help advertise their products and to promote tourism. Some scholars further suggest that businesses "actively promote[d] Western-style sexual objectification as a means of insuring employee loyalty" by channeling the energy of female workers towards self-beautification through purchasing commodities. Barbara Ehrenreich and Annette Fuentes, "Life on the Global Assembly Line," *Feminist Frameworks*, ed. by Alison M. Jaggar and Paula S. Rothenberg (New York, 1984), p. 285.

16. David Lei, Telephone Interview, San Francisco, 23 November 1993; Shirley Sun, "Jumbo Banana Split Proves Too Much for Beautiful May Chiang," *East West*, 21 February 1967, p. 5.

17. In 1971, 41 percent of Chinatown's population fell below the federally defined poverty level partly because of the low wages paid to immigrant workers. Immigrant men commonly found service jobs, such as waiters, and tended to work "ten hours a day, six days a week, for wages that average from $350 to an occasional high of $700 a month." Immigrant women usually worked as garment workers, receiving pay not by the hour but by the piece. These low wages as well as the lack of cultural familiarity made it unlikely that immigrant families would move out of Chinatown, despite the fact that 77 percent of the housing was considered substandard by city codes. In 1970, the population density of the community was the second highest in the country with 120 to 180 persons per acre. These crowded conditions created enormous health risks as demonstrated by the fact that Chinatown had the highest tuberculosis and suicide rates in the nation. To service its population of over forty thousand people, Chinatown had only one hospital with sixty beds. Nee, *Longtime Californ'*, pp. xxi–xxv.

18. "The Most Visible Event," *East West*, 14 February 1973, p. 2; George Chu, "A Wild Night in Old Chinatown," *San Francisco Chronicle*, 9 March 1969, pp. 18, 21. The racial tensions between Chinatown residents and white tourists and police officers were not necessarily new. However, the growing numbers of Chinese American youth as a result of immigration and the increased awareness of racial injustice during the 1960s raised the volatility of inter-group contact.

19. "Liberate Holiday Inn," *Getting Together*, February 1971, p. 2; Jade Fong, "The CHI-am Corner," *East West*, 3 February 1971, p. 3.

20. Sara Evans, *Personal Politics: The Roots of Women's Liberation in the Civil Rights Movement and the New Left* (New York, 1979), p. 214, and "No More Miss America! August 1968," in *Sisterhood Is Powerful*, ed. by Robin Morgan (New York, 1970), pp. 521–524.

21. "A Queen for the Year of the Canine," *East West*, 10 December 1969, p. 1; Ben Wong-Torres, "Miss Chinatown—a Few Immodest Proposals," *East West*, 11 March 1967, p. 3; Judy Yung wrote under the pen name Jade Fong, "The CHI-am Corner," *East West*, 1 March 1972, p. 3; Mabel Ng, "The Chinatown Pageant . . . A Miscarriage of Grace," *East West*, 30 January 1974, p. 10; Wei Chih, "Queen Contestants," translated from the *Chinese Pacific Weekly*, 16 January 1975, printed in *East West*, 22 January 1975, p. 2; Curtis Choy, *The Year of the Ox: The 1973 Livestock Show* (Oakland, 1985).

22. Lisa Fangonilo, quoted in "What Do You Think about the Miss Chinatown USA Beauty Contest?" *East West*, 27 January 1971, p. 9; Pam Lee, "Letter to the Editor," *East West*, 15 April 1970, p. 2.

23. Louella Leon, conversation with author. As of 1987, "the average height of Miss Chinatown U.S.A. winners is 5 feet 5.3 inches." *Miss Chinatown U.S.A. Pageant Souvenir Program*, 1987; Paul Hui, "Alice Kong Also Ran . . . "*East West*, 20 February 1974, p. 5; Curtis Choy, *The*

Year of the Ox; "Oriental Eyes Get Western Look," *Chinatown News*, 3 December 1969, p. 4.

The 1970 Miss Chinatown U.S.A. beauty pageant souvenir book carried an advertisement for cosmetic surgery by a Dr. David Wang, who invented a special technique for converting "'oriental eyes' with single eyelids into 'Caucasian eyes' (with double eyelids)." Wang developed this technique through experiments done on volunteers who tended to be female "movie actresses, singing stars and participants in beauty contests." "Dr. David Wang—Face-Lifting Surgeon," *Chinatown News*, 18 December 1969, pp. 10–15.

24. The experiences of Nathele Sue Dong, reported in a promotion piece for the pageant, demonstrate the importance of cosmetics for helping contestants compete successfully. When Dong decided to run for the Miss Chinatown U.S.A. pageant in 1961, one of her supporters encouraged her to seek the advice of Helen Lew, the director of the Patricia Stevens modeling agency. Lew taught Dong the importance of cosmetics, clothing, jewelry, and hair-styling for creating the image of a beauty pageant contestant:

Helen told the girl the only reason her face was shiny was because she'd never worn make-up, corrected it with a color that blends with Nathele's skin. Two pencil strokes and Nathele's eyebrows were intriguingly accentuated and slightly higher; a green Chinese dress (because green is very becoming with the Oriental skin) brought out the red pigment in her face. Nathele's first pair of earrings (rhinestone drops), a visit to the hairdresser (her hair shaped in closer), and you can see for yourself how Nathele has acquired the poise, personality and good looks required of a candidate for Miss Chinatown USA. ("They Look Twice Now," *San Francisco News-Call Bulletin*, 17 February 1961 CHS-SF, Box 3, folder 20.)

One Miss Chinatown contestant reportedly had a face lift operation prior to the pageant. (Manchester Fu, "Manny and the Celestial 5," *East West*, 21 January 1970, p. 3); Many observers noted the disappointment of candidates who did not win a title in the pageant. Ronda Wei Jeyn-Ching, Miss Chinatown 1980, commented that "many young girls develop a poor self-image after failing to win a pageant title." ("A Parting Queen's Reflections," *Asian Week*, 26 February 1981). This feeling of inferiority partly arose from their failure to fulfill the expectations of parents and sponsors. Pageant organizer Louella "Lulu" Leon recalled that one contestant who did not win a title began crying backstage. She became even more traumatized when her mother yelled at her for making mistakes and not presenting herself in the best light during the competition. Because of what occurred, organizers decided to ban family members from backstage areas of the pageant. (Louella Leon communicated this incident regarding the contestant who lost in a conversation with me.)

Celeste Wong (pseudonym), Interview, San Francisco, 8 December 1993; Wong had lied about her age to enter the Miss Chinatown U.S.A. beauty pageant, which required contestants to be between the ages of 17 and 26.

25. Pamela Tau, *East West*, 3 February 1971, p. 5; Pam Lee, "Letter to the Editor," *East West*, 15 April 1970, p. 2; "Reflections on Chinese New Year—2 Views," *Getting Together*, 3–16 February 1973, p. 3.

26. Emily Honig and Gail Hershatter, *Personal Voices: Chinese Women in the 1980s*, (Stanford, 1988), p. 24; "Public Invited to Spring Festival Celebration," *San Francisco Journal*, 9 February 1977.

27. Stan Yee, "Notes of a Chinese Bum on Holiday Inn," *East West*, 20 January 1971, p. 2.

28. Ann F. Nakao, "A Hard Look: The Fires behind Chinatown's Parade," *San Francisco Examiner*, 15 February 1977, p. 8; Carole Jan Lee, "Carole's Barrel," *East West*, 18 February 1970.

29. Cynthia Denise Chin-Lee, Telephone Interview, Palo Alto, 20 February 1994; Rose Chung, Telephone Interview, San Francisco, 2 December 1993.

30. John Lum, "The Miss San Leandro Contest: There's No Point to It," *East West*, 17 May 1972, p. 6; Y. C. Hong, a judge for the 1965 competition, explained that if he had a daughter, he would not wish her to enter the contest because he sympathized "with the heartaches of many beautiful girls who failed to get within the 'magic circle' and the disappointments of their parents and sponsors." Despite these reservations, he applauded the contestants for entering the competition and demonstrating the positive aspects of Chinese American culture. He believed that "it is a good thing for our Chinese in showing the peoples of the world that we do have many beautiful and talented Chinese girls from all parts of the country." Y. C. Hong, "Letter to the Editor," *East West*, 21 March 1967, p. 2.

31. Irene Ung, "Irene Ung Satisfied with Simple Things in Life," *East West*, 21 February 1967, p. 7; "Interviews with Two Bay Area Beauty Pageant Contestants," *East West*, 4 February 1976, p. 11; Doris G. Worsham, "There is a 'There' for Her," *Oakland Tribune*, 17 February 1973; clipping found in "Beauty Contests—CA" folder at UC Berkely's Asian American Studies Library.

32. Gordon Yaw, Telephone Interview, Oakland, 7 February 1994; "Consider the Alternatives," *East West*, 30 January 1974, p. 2.

33. "Only a 'Fair' Fair," *East West*, 19 March 1969, p. 2; Katie Choy, "E-W interviews 'Miss Chinatown' Contestants," *East West*, 23 January 1974, p. 6.

34. Nakao, "A Hard Look," pp. 1, 6.

35. Shirley Sun, "Tall & Lissome Jennifer Chung Fulfills Her Childhood Dream," *East West*, 21 February 1967, p. 6. Thanking the other contestants, Miss Chinatown U.S.A. 1976 Linda Chun wrote that we "are all dear friends and I shall cherish our moments together always." Linda Sue Kwai En Chun, "Reflections," *Chinatown San Francisco*, Souvenir Program, 1977, p. 42; Celeste Wong recalled that after she won the title of Miss San Francisco Chinatown, her fellow contestants were not as friendly towards her. Celeste Wong, Interview.

36. Melanie Feng, "What Do You Think about the Miss Chinatown USA Beauty Contest?" *East West*, 27 January 1971, p. 4; Katie Choy and Paul K. Hui, "3 Beauties Interviewed," *East West*, 22 January 1975, p. 5; Judy Quan, "Three Queen Contestants: the Person Behind the Face," *East West*, 16 February 1972, p. 7; Worsham, "There is a 'There' for Her"; Fang Wei Lyan, "Under Those Plastic Smiles," *East West*, 21 January 1967, pp. 1–2.

   In some cases, the pageant provided more opportunities for women to gain exposure to certain public sectors. Women interested in modeling, movie, or public relations careers viewed the pageant as a good way to gain recognition. After winning the Miss Chinatown U.S.A. title, Sandra Wong auditioned for a movie role opposite Clint Eastwood. Contestants who won trips to Asia gained some exposure to international politics by meeting such dignitaries as ROC President Chiang Kai-shek. Contestants might also learn about international finance, for the Chinese Chamber of Commerce used these "goodwill tours" to build trade relations with Taiwan, Hong Kong, and other Asian countries. The participation of recognizable national and state politicians, such as Anne Chennault and March K. Wong, as pageant judges also provided models of successful Chinese American women who transcended traditional female roles. In other words, pageant supporters argued that they, like their feminist critics, sought to promote female achievements in the public realm.

37. Mary Jew, "Fantastic Turnout at Fashion Show," *East West*, 13 February 1974, p. 5; "Come Alive," Editorial, *East West* 28 August 1968, p. 2; Judy Quan, "Three Queen Contestants: The Person Behind the Face," *East West*, 16 February 1972, p. 7. Moy did not win the pageant; Wally Lee, "Wahine Stewardess Miss Chinatown USA," *East West*, 23 February 1972, pp. 1–10.

38. Hing C. Tse, Interview, San Francisco, 12 November 1993.

39. Honig and Hershatter, *Personal Voices: Chinese Women in the 1980s*, p. 335; "China Wants Good-Looking Stewardesses," *Chinatown News*, 18 January 1980, reprint from *New York Times*.

40. Cynsin: *An American Princess*, video by Valerie Soe, 1991; Lorena Tong, "Miss Chinatown Cynthia Gouw Insists She Is Not the 'Beauty Pageant' Type," *East West*, 5 December 1984, p. 8.

16

Sex, Lies, and Advertising

Gloria Steinem

Suppose archaeologists of the future dug up women's magazines and used them to judge American women. What would they think of us–and what can we do about it?

About three years ago, as *glasnost* was beginning and *Ms.* seemed to be ending, I was invited to a press lunch for a Soviet official. He entertained us with anecdotes about new problems of democracy in his country. Local Communist leaders were being criticized in their media for the first time, he explained, and they were angry.

"So I'll have to ask my American friends," he finished pointedly, "how more *subtly* to control the press." In the silence that followed, I said, "Advertising."

The reporters laughed, but later, one of them took me aside: How dare I suggest that freedom of the press was limited? How dare I imply that his newsweekly could be influenced by ads?

I explained that I was thinking of advertising's media-wide influence on most of what we read. Even newsmagazines use "soft" cover stories to sell ads, confuse readers with "advertorials," and occasionally self-censor subjects known to be a problem with big advertisers.

But, I also explained, I was thinking especially of women's magazines. There, it isn't just a little content that's devoted to attracting ads, it's almost all of it. That's why advertisers—not readers—have always been the problem for *Ms.* As the only women's magazine that didn't supply what the ad world euphemistically describes as "supportive editorial atmosphere" or "complementary copy" (for instance, articles that praise food/fashion/beauty subjects to "support" and "complement" food/fashion/beauty ads), *Ms.* could never attract enough advertising to break even.

"Oh, *women's* magazines," the journalist said with contempt. "Everybody knows they're catalogs—but who cares? They have nothing to do with journalism."

I can't tell you how many times I've had this argument in 25 years of working for many kinds of publications. Except as moneymaking machines—"cash cows" as they are so elegantly called in the trade—women's magazines are rarely taken seriously. Though changes being made by women have been called more far-reaching than the industrial revolution—and though many editors try hard to reflect some of them in the few pages left to them after all the ad-related subjects have been covered—the magazines serving the female half of this country are still far below the journalistic and ethical standards of news and general interest publications. Most depressing of all, this doesn't even rate an expose.

If *Time* and *Newsweek* had to lavish praise on cars in general and credit General Motors in particular to get GM ads, there would be a scandal—maybe a criminal investigation. When women's magazines from *Seventeen* to *Lear's* praise beauty products in general and credit Revlon in particular to get ads, it's just business as usual.

I. When *Ms.* began, we didn't consider *not* taking ads. The most important reason was keeping the price of a feminist magazine low enough for most women to afford. But the second and almost equal reason was providing a forum where women and advertisers could talk to each other and improve advertising itself. After all, it was (and still is) as potent a source of information in this country as news or TV and movie dramas.

We decided to proceed in two stages. First, we would convince makers of "people products" used by both men and women but advertised mostly to men—cars, credit cards, insurance, sound equipment, finan-

cial services, and the like—that their ads should be placed in a women's magazine. Since they were accustomed to the division between editorial and advertising in news and general interest magazines, this would allow our editorial content to be free and diverse. Second, we would add the best ads for whatever traditional "women's products" (clothes, shampoo, fragrance, food, and so on) that surveys showed *Ms.* readers used. But we would ask them to come in *without* the usual quid pro quo of "complementary copy."

We knew the second step might be harder. Food advertisers have always demanded that women's magazines publish recipes and articles on entertaining (preferably ones that name their products) in return for their ads; clothing advertisers expect to be surrounded by fashion spreads (especially ones that credit their designers); and shampoo, fragrance, and beauty products in general usually insist on positive editorial coverage of beauty subjects, plus photo credits besides. That's why women's magazines look the way they do. But if we could break this link between ads and editorial content, then we wanted good ads for "women's products," too.

By playing their part in this unprecedented mix of *all* the things our readers need and use, advertisers also would be rewarded: ads for products like cars and mutual funds would find a new growth market; the best ads for women's products would no longer be lost in oceans of ads for the same category; and both would have access to a laboratory of smart and caring readers whose response would help create effective ads for other media is well.

I thought then that our main problem would be the imagery in ads themselves. Carmakers were still draping blondes in evening gowns over the hoods like ornaments. Authority figures were almost always male, even in ads for products that only women used. Sadistic, he-man campaigns even won industry praise. (For instance, *Advertising Age* had hailed the infamous Silva Thin cigarette theme, "How to Get a Woman's Attention: Ignore her," as "brilliant.") Even in medical journals, tranquilizer ads showed depressed housewives standing beside piles of dirty dishes and promised to get them back to work.

Obviously, *Ms.* would have to avoid such ads and seek out the best ones—but this didn't seem impossible. *The New Yorker* had been selecting ads for aesthetic reasons for years, a practice that only seemed to make advertisers more eager to be in its pages. *Ebony* and *Essence* were asking for ads with positive black images, and though their struggle was hard, they weren't being called unreasonable.

Clearly, what *Ms.* needed was a very special publisher and ad sales staff. I could think of only one woman with experience on the business side of magazines—Patricia Carbine, who recently had become a vice president of *McCall's* as well as its editor in chief—and the reason I knew her name was a good omen. She had been the managing editor at *Look* (really *the* editor, but its owner reused to put a female name at the top of his masthead) when I was writing a column there. After I did an early interview with Cesar Chavez, then just emerging as a leader of migrant labor, and the publisher turned it down because he was worried about ads from Sunkist, Pat was the one who intervened. As I learned later, she had told the publisher she would resign if the interview wasn't published. Mainly because *Look* couldn't afford to lose Pat, it *was* published (and the ads from Sunkist never arrived).

Though I barely knew this woman, she had done two things I always remembered: put her job on the line in a way that editors often talk about but rarely do, and been so loyal to her colleagues that she never told me or anyone outside *Look* that she had done so.

Fortunately, Pat did agree to leave *McCall's* and take a huge cut in salary to become publisher of *Ms.* She became responsible for training and inspiring generations of young women who joined the *Ms.* ad sales force, many of whom went on to become "firsts" at the top of publishing. When *Ms.* first started, however, there were so few women with experience selling space that Pat and I made the rounds of ad agencies ourselves. Later, the fact that *Ms.* was asking companies to do business in a different way meant our saleswomen had to make many times the usual number of calls—first to convince agencies and then client companies besides—and to present endless amounts of research. I was often asked to do a final ad presentation, or see some higher decision-maker, or speak to women employees so executives could see the interest of women they worked with. That's why I spent more time persuading advertisers than editing or writing for *Ms.* and why I ended up with an unsentimental education in the seamy underside of publishing that few writers see (and even fewer magazines can publish).

Let me take you with us through some experiences, just as they happened:

• Cheered on by early support from Volkswagen and one or two other car companies, we scrape together time and money to put on a major reception in Detroit. We know U.S. carmakers firmly believe that women choose the upholstery, not the car, but we are armed with statistics and reader mail to prove the contrary: a car is an important purchase for women, one that symbolizes mobility and freedom.

But almost nobody comes. We are left with many pounds of shrimp on the table, and quite a lot of egg on our face. We blame ourselves for not guessing that there would be a baseball pennant play-off on the same day, but executives go out of their way to explain they wouldn't have come anyway. Thus begins ten years of knocking on hostile doors, presenting endless documentation, and hiring a full-time saleswoman in Detroit; all necessary before *Ms.* gets any real results.

This long saga has a semihappy ending: foreign and, later, domestic carmakers eventually provided *Ms.* with enough advertising to make cars one of our top sources of ad revenue. Slowly, Detroit began to take the women's market seriously enough to put car ads in other women's magazines, too, thus freeing a few pages from the hothouse of fashion-beauty-food ads.

But long after figures showed a third, even a half, of many car models being bought by women, U.S. makers continued to be uncomfortable addressing women. Unlike foreign carmakers, Detroit never quite learned the secret of creating intelligent ads that exclude no one, and then placing them in women's magazines to overcome past exclusion. (*Ms.* readers were so grateful for a routine Honda ad featuring rack and pinion steering, for instance, that they sent fan mail.) Even now, Detroit continues to ask, "Should we make special ads for women?" Perhaps that's why some foreign cars still have a disproportionate share of the U.S. women's market.

• In the *Ms.* Gazette, we do a brief report on a congressional hearing into chemicals used in hair dyes that are absorbed through the skin and may be carcinogenic. Newspapers report this too, but Clairol, a Bristol-Myers subsidiary that makes dozens of products— a few of which have just begun to advertise in *Ms.*—is outraged. Not at newspapers or newsmagazines, just at us. It's bad enough that *Ms.* is the only women's magazine re-

fusing to provide the usual "complementary" articles and beauty photos, but to criticize one of their categories—that is going too far.

We offer to publish a letter from Clairol telling its side of the story. In an excess of solicitousness, we even put this letter in the Gazette, not in Letters to the Editors where it belongs. Nonetheless—and in spite of surveys that show *Ms.* readers are active women who use more of almost everything Clairol makes than do the readers of any other women's magazine—*Ms.* gets almost none of these ads for the rest of its natural life.

Meanwhile, Clairol changes its hair coloring formula, apparently in response to the hearings we reported.

• Our saleswomen set out early to attract ads for consumer electronics: sound equipment, calculators, computers, VCRs, and the like. We know that our readers are determined to be included in the technological revolution. We know from reader surveys that *Ms.* readers are buying this stuff in numbers as high as those of magazines like *Playboy;* or "men 18 to 34," the prime targets of the consumer electronics industry. Moreover, unlike traditional women's products that our readers buy but don't need to read articles about, these are subjects they want covered in our pages. There actually is a supportive editorial atmosphere.

"But women don't understand technology," say executives at the end of ad presentations. "Maybe not," we respond, "but neither do men—and we all buy it."

"If women do buy it," say the decision-makers, "they're asking their husbands and boyfriends what to buy first." We produce letters from *Ms.* readers saying how turned off they are when salesmen say things like "let me know when your husband can come in."

After several years of this, we get a few ads for compact sound systems. Some of them come from JVC, whose vice president, Harry Elias, is trying to convince his Japanese bosses that there is something called a women's market. At his invitation, I find myself speaking at huge trade shows in Chicago and Las Vegas, trying to persuade JVC dealers that showrooms don't have to be locker rooms where women are made to feel unwelcome. But as it turns out, the shows themselves are part of the problem. In Las Vegas, the only women around the technology displays are seminude models serving champagne. In Chicago, the big attraction is Marilyn Chambers, who followed Linda Lovelace of *Deep Throat* fame as Chuck Traynor's captive and/or employee. VCRs are being demonstrated with her porn videos.

In the end, we get ads for a car stereo now and then, but no VCRs; some IBM personal computers, but no Apple or Japanese ones. We notice that office magazines like *Working Woman* and *Savvy* don't benefit as much as they should from office equipment ads either. In the electronics world, women and technology seem mutually exclusive. It remains a decade behind even Detroit.

• Because we get letters from little girls who love toy trains, and who ask our help in changing ads and box-top photos that feature little boys only, we try to get toy-train ads from Lionel. It turns out that Lionel executives have been concerned about little girls. They made a pink train, and were surprised when it didn't sell.

Lionel bows to consumer pressure with a photograph of a boy and a girl—but only on some of their boxes. They fear that, if trains are associated with girls, they will be devalued in the minds of boys. Needless to say, *Ms.* gets no train ads, and little girls remain a mostly unexplored market. By 1986, Lionel is put up for sale.

But for different reasons, we haven't had much luck with other kinds of toys either. In spite of many articles on child-rearing; an annual listing of nonsexist, multi-racial toys by Letty Cottin Pogrebin; Stories for Free Children, a regular feature also edited by Letty; and other prizewinning features for or about children, we get virtually no toy ads. Generations of *Ms.* saleswomen explain to toy manufacturers that a larger proportion of *Ms.* readers have preschool children than do the readers of other women's magazines, but this industry can't believe feminists have or care about children.

• When *Ms.* begins, the staff decides not to accept ads for feminine hygiene sprays or cigarettes: they are damaging and carry no appropriate health warnings. Though we don't think we should tell our readers what to do, we do think we should provide facts so they can decide for themselves. Since the antismoking lobby has been pressing for health warnings on cigarette ads, we decide to take them only as they comply.

Philip Morris is among the first to do so. One of its brands, Virginia Slims, is also sponsoring women's tennis and the first national polls of women's opinions. On the other hand, the Virginia Slims theme, "You've come a long way, baby," has more than a "baby" problem. It makes smoking a symbol of progress for women.

We explain to Philip Morris that this slogan won't do well in our pages, but they are convinced its success with some women means it will work with all women. Finally, we agree to publish an ad for a Virginia Slims calendar as a test. The letters from readers are critical—and smart. For instance: Would you show a black man picking cotton, the same man in a Cardin suit, and symbolize the antislavery and civil rights movements by smoking? Of course not. But instead of honoring the test results, the Philip Morris people seem angry to be proven wrong. They take away ads for all their many brands.

This costs *Ms.* about $250,000 the first year. After five years, we can no longer keep track. Occasionally, a new set of executives listens to *Ms.* saleswomen, but because we won't take Virginia Slims, not one Philip Morris product returns to our pages for the next 16 years.

Gradually, we also realize our naiveté in thinking we could decide against taking cigarette ads. They became a disproportionate support of magazines the moment they were banned on television, and few magazines could compete and survive without them; certainly not *Ms.*, which lacks so many other categories. By the time statistics in the 1980s showed that women's rate of lung cancer was approaching men's, the necessity of taking cigarette ads has become a kind of prison.

• General Mills, Pillsbury, Carnation, Del-Monte, Dole, Kraft, Stauffer, Hormel, Nabisco: you name the food giant, we try it. But no matter how desirable the *Ms.* readership, our lack of recipes is lethal.

We explain to them that placing food ads only next to recipes associates food with work. For many women, it is a negative that works *against* the ads. Why not place food ads in diverse media without recipes (thus reaching more men, who are now a third of the shoppers in supermarkets anyway), and leave the recipes to specialty magazines like *Gourmet* (a third of whose readers are also men)?

These arguments elicit interest, but except for an occasional ad for a convenience food, instant coffee, diet drinks, yogurt, or such extras as avocados and almonds, this mainstay of the publishing industry stays closed to us. Period.

• Traditionally, wines and liquors didn't advertise to women: men were thought to make the brand decisions, even if women did the buying. But after endless presentations, we begin to make a dent in this category. Thanks to the unconventional Michel Roux of Carillon Importers (distributors of Grand Marnier, Absolut Vodka, and others), who assumes that food and drink have no gender, some ads are leaving their men's club.

Beermakers are still selling masculinity. It takes *Ms.* fully eight years to get its first beer ad (Michelob). In general, however, liquor ads are less stereotyped in their imagery—and far less controlling of the editorial content around them—than are women's products. But given the under-representation of other categories, these very facts tend to create a disproportionate number of alcohol ads in the pages of *Ms.* This in turn dismays readers worried about women and alcoholism.

• We hear in 1980 that women in the Soviet Union have been producing feminist *samizdat* (underground, self-published books) and circulating them throughout the country. As punishment, four of the leaders have been exiled. Though we are operating on our usual shoestring, we solicit individual contributions to send Robin Morgan to interview these women in Vienna.

The result is an exclusive cover story that includes the first news of a populist peace movement against the Afghanistan occupation, a prediction of *glasnost* to come, and a grass-roots, intimate view of Soviet women's lives. From the popular press to women's studies courses, the response is great. The story wins a Front Page award.

Nonetheless, this journalistic coup undoes years of efforts to get an ad schedule from Revlon. Why? Because the Soviet women on our cover are not wearing makeup.

• Four years of research and presentations go into convincing airlines that women now make travel choices and business trips.

United, the first airline to advertise in *Ms.*, is so impressed with the response from our readers that one of its executives appears in a film for our ad presentations. As usual, good ads get great results.

But we have problems unrelated to such results. For instance: because American Airlines flight attendants include among their labor demands the stipulation that they could choose to have their last names preceded by "Ms." on their name tags—in a long-delayed revolt against the standard, "I am your pilot, Captain Rothgart, and this is your flight attendant, Cindy Sue" —American officials seem to hold the magazine responsible. We get no ads.

There is still a different problem at Eastern. A vice president cancels subscriptions for thousands of copies on Eastern flights. Why? Because he is offended by ads for lesbian poetry journals in the *Ms.* Classified. A "family airline," as he explains to me coldly on the phone, has to "draw the line somewhere."

It's obvious that *Ms.* can't exclude lesbians and serve women. We've been trying to make that point ever since our first issue included an article by and about lesbians, and both Suzanne Levine, our managing editor, and I were lectured by such heavy hitters as Ed Kosner, then editor of *Newsweek* (and now of *New York Magazine*), who insisted that *Ms.* should "position" itself against lesbians. But our advertisers have paid to reach a guaranteed number of readers, and soliciting new subscriptions to compensate for Eastern would cost $150,000, plus rebating money in the meantime.

Like almost everything ad-related, this presents an elaborate organizing problem. After days of searching for sympathetic members of the Eastern board, Frank Thomas, president of the Ford Foundation, kindly offers to call Roswell Gilpatrick, a director of Eastern. I talk with Mr. Gilpatrick, who calls Frank Borman, then the president of Eastern. Frank Borman calls me to say that his airline is not in the business of censoring magazines: *Ms.* will be returned to Eastern flights.

• Women's access to insurance and credit is vital, but with the exception of Equitable and a few other ad pioneers, such financial services address men. For almost a decade after the Equal Credit Opportunity Act passes in 1974, we try to convince American Express that women are a growth market— but nothing works.

Finally, a former professor of Russian named Jerry Welsh becomes head of marketing. He assumes that women should be cardholders, and persuades his colleagues to feature women in a campaign. Thanks to this 1980s series, the growth rate for female cardholders surpasses that for men.

For this article, I asked Jerry Welsh if he would explain why American Express waited so long. "Sure," he said, "they were afraid of having a 'pink' card."

Women of color read *Ms.* in disproportionate numbers. This is a source of pride to *Ms.* staffers, who are also more racially representative than the editors of other women's magazines. But this reality is obscured by ads filled with enough white women to make a reader snowblind.

Pat Carbine remembers mostly "astonishment" when she requested African American, Hispanic, Asian, and other diverse images. Marcia Ann Gillespie, a *Ms.* editor who was previously the editor in chief of *Essence,* witnesses ad bias a second time: having tried for *Essence* to get white advertisers to use black images (Revlon did so eventually, but L'Oréal, Lauder, Chanel, and other companies never did), she sees similar problems getting integrated ads for an integrated magazine. Indeed, the ad world often creates black and Hispanic ads only for black and Hispanic media. In an exact parallel of the fear that marketing a product to women will endanger its appeal to men, the response is usually, "But your [white] readers won't identify."

In fact, those we are able to get—for instance, a Max Factor ad made for *Essence* that Linda Wachner gives us after she becomes president—are praised by white readers, too. But there are pathetically few such images.

• By the end of 1986, production and mailing costs have risen astronomically, ad income is flat, and competition for ads is stiffer than ever. The 60/40 preponderance of edit over ads that we promised to readers becomes 50/50; children's stories, most poetry, and some fiction are casualties of less space; in order to get variety into limited pages, the length (and sometimes the depth) of articles suffers; and, though we do refuse most of the ads that would look like a parody in our pages, we get so worn down that some slip through. Still, readers perform miracles. Though we haven't been able to afford a subscription mailing in two years, they maintain our guaranteed circulation of 450,000.

Nonetheless, media reports on *Ms.* often insist that our unprofitability must be due to reader disinterest. The myth that advertisers simply follow readers is very strong. Not one reporter notes that other comparable magazines our size (say, *Vanity Fair* or *The Atlantic*) have been losing more money in one year than *Ms.* has lost in 16 years. No matter how much never-to-be-recovered cash is poured into starting a magazine or keeping one going, appearances seem to be all that matter. (Which is why we haven't been able to explain our fragile state in public. Nothing causes ad-flight like the smell of nonsuccess.)

My healthy response is anger. My not-so-healthy response is constant worry. Also an obsession with finding one more rescue. There is hardly a night when I don't wake up with sweaty palms and pounding heart, scared that we won't be able to pay the printer or the post office; scared most of all that closing our doors will hurt the women's movement.

Out of chutzpah and desperation, I arrange a lunch with Leonard Lauder, president of Estée Lauder. With the exception of Clinique (the brainchild of Carol Phillips), none of Lauder's hundreds of products has been advertised in *Ms.* A year's schedule of ads for just three or four of them could save us. Indeed, as the scion of a family-owned company whose ad practices are followed by the beauty industry, he is one of the few men who could liberate many pages in all women's magazines just by changing his mind about "complementary copy."

Over a lunch that costs more than we can pay for some articles, I explain the need for his leadership. I also lay out the record of *Ms.:* more literary and journalistic prizes won, more new issues introduced into the mainstream, new writers discovered, and impact on society than any other magazine; more articles that became books, stories that became movies, ideas that became television series, and newly advertised products that became profitable; and, most important for him, a place for his ads to reach women who aren't reachable through any other women's magazine. Indeed, if there is one constant characteristic of the ever-changing *Ms.* readership, it is their impact as leaders. Whether it's waiting until later to have first babies, or pioneering PABA as sun protection in cosmetics, *whatever* they are doing today, a third to a half of American women will be doing three to five years from now. It's never failed.

But, he says, *Ms.* readers are not our women. They're not interested in things like fragrance and blush-on. If they were, *Ms.* would write articles about them.

On the contrary, I explain, surveys show they are more likely to buy such things than the readers of, say, *Cosmopolitan* or *Vogue.* They're good customers because they're out in the world enough to need several sets of everything: home, work, purse, travel, gym, and so on. They just don't need to read articles about these things. Would he ask a men's magazine to publish monthly columns on how to shave before he advertised Aramis products (his line for men)?

He concedes that beauty features are often concocted more for advertisers than readers. But *Ms.* isn't appropriate for his ads anyway, he explains. Why? Because Estée Lauder is selling "a kept-woman mentality."

I can't quite believe this. Sixty percent of the users of his products are salaried, and generally resemble *Ms.* readers. Besides, his company has the appeal of having been started by a creative and hardworking woman, his mother, Estée Lauder.

That doesn't matter, he says. He knows his customers, and they would like to be kept women. That's why he will never advertise in *Ms.*

In November 1987, by vote of the *Ms.* Foundation for Education and Communication (*Ms.*'s owner and publisher, the media subsidiary of the *Ms.* Foundation for Women), *Ms.* was sold to a company whose officers, Australian feminists Sandra Yates and Anne Summers, raised the investment money in their country that *Ms.* couldn't find in its own. They also started *Sassy* for teenage women.

In their two-year tenure, circulation was raised to 550,000 by investment in circulation mailings, and, to the dismay of some readers, editorial features on clothes and new products made a more traditional bid for ads. Nonetheless, ad pages fell below previous levels. In addition, *Sassy*, whose fresh voice and sexual frankness were an unprecedented success with young readers, was targeted by two mothers from Indiana who began, as one of them put it, "calling every Christian organization I could think of." In response to this controversy, several crucial advertisers pulled out.

Such links between ads and editorial content were a problem in Australia, too, but to a lesser degree. "Our readers pay two times more for their magazines," Anne explained, "so advertisers have less power to threaten a magazine's viability."

"I was shocked," said Sandra Yates with characteristic directness. "In Australia, we think you have freedom of the press—but you don't."

Since Anne and Sandra had not met their budget's projections for ad revenue, their investors forced a sale. In October 1989, *Ms.* and *Sassy* were bought by Dale Lang, owner of *Working Mother, Working Woman*, and one of the few independent publishing companies left among the conglomerates. In response to a request from the original *Ms.* staff—as well as to reader letters urging that *Ms.* continue, plus his own belief that *Ms.* would benefit his other magazines by blazing a trail—he agreed to try the ad-free, reader—supported *Ms.* you hold now and to give us complete editorial control.

II. Do you think, as I once did, that advertisers make decisions based on solid research? Well, think again. "Broadly speaking," says Joseph Smith of Oxtoby-Smith, Inc., a consumer research firm, "there is no persuasive evidence that the editorial context of an ad matters."

Advertisers who demand such "complementary copy," even in the absence of respectable studies, clearly are operating under a double standard. The same food companies place ads in *People* with no recipes. Cosmetics companies support *The New*

Yorker with no regular beauty columns. So where does this habit of controlling the content of women's magazines come from?

Tradition. Ever since *Ladies Magazine* debuted in Boston in 1828, editorial copy directed to women has been informed by something other than its readers' wishes. There were no ads then, but in an age when married women were legal minors with no right to their own money, there was another revenue source to be kept in mind: husbands. "Husbands may rest assured," wrote editor Sarah Josepha Hale, "that nothing found in these pages shall cause her [his wife] to be less assiduous in preparing for his reception or encourage her to 'usurp station' or encroach upon prerogatives of men."

Hale went on to become the editor of *Godey's Lady's Book,* a magazine featuring "fashion plates": engravings of dresses for readers to take to their seamstresses or copy themselves. Hale added "how to" articles, which set the tone for women's service magazines for years to come: how to write politely, avoid sunburn, and—in no fewer than 1,200 words—how to maintain a goose quill pen. She advocated education for women but avoided controversy. Just as most women's magazines now avoid politics, poll their readers on issues like abortion but rarely take a stand, and praise socially approved lifestyles, Hale saw to it that *Godey's* avoided the hot topics of its day: slavery, abolition, and women's suffrage.

What definitively turned women's magazines into catalogs, however, were two events: Ellen Butterick's invention of the clothing pattern in 1863 and the mass manufacture of patent medicines containing everything from colored water to cocaine. For the first time, readers could purchase what magazines encouraged them to want. As such magazines became more profitable,

they also began to attract men as editors. (Most women's magazines continued to have men as top editors until the feminist 1970s.) Edward Bok, who became editor of *The Ladies' Home Journal* in 1889, discovered the power of advertisers when he rejected ads for patent medicines and found that other advertisers canceled in retribution. In the early 20th century, *Good Housekeeping* started its Institute to "test and approve" products. Its Seal of Approval became the grandfather of current "value added" programs that offer advertisers such bonuses as product sampling and department store promotions.

By the time suffragists finally won the vote in 1920, women's magazines had become too entrenched as catalogs to help women learn how to use it. The main function was to create a desire for products, teach how to use products, and make products a crucial part of gaining social approval, pleasing a husband, and performing as a homemaker. Some unrelated articles and short stories were included to persuade women to pay for these catalogs. But articles were neither consumerist nor rebellious. Even fiction was usually subject to formula: if a woman had any sexual life outside marriage, she was supposed to come to a bad end.

In 1965, Helen Gurley Brown began to change part of that formula by bringing "the sexual revolution" to women's magazines— but in an ad-oriented way. Attracting multiple men required even more consumerism, as the Cosmo Girl made clear, than finding one husband.

In response to the workplace revolution of the 1970s, traditional women's magazines—that is, "trade books" for women working at home—were joined by *Savvy, Working Woman,* and other trade books for women working in offices. But by keeping the fashion/beauty/ entertaining articles necessary to get traditional ads and then adding career articles besides, they inadvertently produced the antifeminist stereotype of Super Woman. The male-imitative, dress-for-success woman carrying a briefcase became the media image of a woman worker, even though a blue-collar woman's salary was often higher than her glorified secretarial sister's, and though women at a real briefcase level are statistically rare. Needless to say, these dress-for-success women were also thin, white, and beautiful.

In recent years, advertisers' control over the editorial content of women's magazines has become so institutionalized that it is written into "insertion orders" or dictated to ad salespeople as official policy. The following are recent typical orders to women's magazines:

• Dow's Cleaning Products stipulates that ads for its Vivid and Spray 'n Wash products should be adjacent to "children or fashion editorial"; ads for Bathroom Cleaner should be next to "home furnishing/family" features; and so on for other brands. "If a magazine fails for 1/2 the brands or more," the Dow order warns, "it will be omitted from further consideration."

• Bristol-Myers, the parent of Clairol, Windex, Drano, Bufferin, and much more, stipulates that ads be placed next to "a full page of compatible editorial."

• S.C. Johnson & Son, makers of Johnson Wax, lawn and laundry products, insect sprays, hair sprays, and so on, orders that its ads *"should not be opposite extremely controversial features or material antithetical to the nature of the advertised product."* (Italics theirs.)

• Maidenform, manufacturer of bras and other apparel, leaves a blank for the particular product and states: "The creative concept of the ____ campaign, and the very nature of the product itself appeal to the positive emotions of the reader/consumer.

Therefore, it is imperative that all editorial adjacencies reflect that same positive tone. The editorial must not be negative in content or lend itself contrary to the ____ product imagery/message (e.g. *editorial relating to illness, disillusionment, large size fashion, etc.)*." (Italics mine.)

• The De Beers diamond company, a big seller of engagement rings, prohibits magazines from placing its ads with "adjacencies to hard news or anti/love-romance themed editorial."

• Procter & Gamble, one of this country's most powerful and diversified advertisers, stands out in the memory of Anne Summers and Sandra Yates (no mean feat in this context): its products were not to be placed in any issue that included any material on gun control, abortion, the occult, cults, or the disparagement of religion. Caution was also demanded in any issue covering sex or drugs, even for educational purposes.

Those are the most obvious chains around women's magazines. There are also rules so clear they needn't be written down: for instance, an overall "look" compatible with beauty and fashion ads. Even "real" nonmodel women photographed for a woman's magazine are usually made up, dressed in credited clothes, and retouched out of all reality. When editors do include articles on less-than-cheerful subjects (for instance, domestic violence), they tend to keep them short and unillustrated. The point is to be "upbeat." Just as women in the street are asked, "Why don't you smile, honey?" women's magazines acquire an institutional smile.

Within the text itself, praise for advertisers' products has become so ritualized that fields like "beauty writing" have been invented. One of its frequent practitioners explained seriously that "It's a difficult art. How many new adjectives can you find? How much greater can you make a lipstick sound? The FDA restricts what companies can say on labels, but we create illusion. And ad agencies are on the phone all the time pushing you to get their product in. A lot of them keep the business based on how many editorial clippings they produce every month. The worst are products," like Lauder's as the writer confirmed, "with their own name involved. It's all ego."

Often, editorial becomes one giant ad. Last November, for instance, Lear's featured an elegant woman executive on the cover. On the contents page, we learned she was wearing Guerlain makeup and Samsara, a new fragrance by Guerlain. Inside were full-page ads for Samsara and Guerlain antiwrinkle cream. In the cover profile, we learned that this executive was responsible for launching Samsara and is Guerlain's director of public relations. When the *Columbia Journalism Review* did one of the few articles to include women's magazines in coverage of the influence of ads, editor Frances Lear was quoted as defending her magazine because "this kind of thing is done all the time."

Often, advertisers also plunge odd-shaped ads into the text, no matter what the cost to the readers. At *Woman's Day,* a magazine originally founded by a supermarket chain, editor in chief Ellen Levine said, "The day the copy had to rag around a chicken leg was not a happy one."

Advertisers are also adamant about where in a magazine their ads appear. When Revlon was not placed as the first beauty ad in one Hearst magazine, for instance, Revlon pulled its ads from all Hearst magazines. Ruth Whitney, editor in chief of Glamour, attributes some of these demands to "ad agencies wanting to prove to a client that they've squeezed the last drop of blood out of a magazine." She also is, she says, "sick and tired of hearing that women's magazines are controlled by cigarette ads."

Relatively speaking, she's right. To be as censoring as are many advertisers for women's products, tobacco companies would have to demand articles in praise of smoking and expect glamorous photos of beautiful women smoking their brands.

I don't mean to imply that the editors I quote here share my objections to ads: most assume that women's magazines have to be the way they are. But it's also true that only former editors can be completely honest. "Most of the pressure came in the form of direct product mentions," explains Sey Chassler, who was editor in chief of *Redbook* from the sixties to the eighties. "We got threats from the big guys, the Revlons, blackmail threats. They wouldn't run ads unless we credited them."

"But it's not fair to single out the beauty advertisers because these pressures came from everybody. Advertisers want to know two things: What are you going to charge me? What *else* are you going to do for me? It's a holdup. For instance, management felt that fiction took up too much space. They couldn't put any advertising in that. For the last ten years, the number of fiction entries into the National Magazine Awards has declined."

"And pressures are getting worse. More magazines are more bottom-line oriented because they have been taken over by companies with no interest in publishing."

"I also think advertisers do this to women's magazines especially," he concluded, "because of the general disrespect they have for women."

Even media experts who don't give a damn about women's magazines are alarmed by the spread of this ad-edit linkage. In a climate *The Wall Street Journal* describes as an unacknowledged Depression for media, women's products are increasingly able to take their low standards wherever they go. For instance: newsweeklies publish uncritical stories on fashion and fitness. *The New York Times Magazine* recently ran an article on "firming creams," complete with mentions of advertisers. Vanity Fair published a profile of one major advertiser, Ralph Lauren, illustrated by the same photographer who does his ads, and turned the lifestyle of another, Calvin Klein, into a cover story. Even the outrageous *Spy* has toned down since it began to go after fashion ads.

And just to make us really worry, films and books, the last media that go directly to the public without having to attract ads first, are in danger, too. Producers are beginning to depend on payments for displaying products in movies, and books are now being commissioned by companies like Federal Express.

But the truth is that women's products—like women's magazines—have never been the subjects of much serious reporting anyway. News and general interest publications, including the "style" or "living" sections of newspapers, write about food and clothing as cooking and fashion, and almost never evaluate such products by brand name. Though chemical additives, pesticides, and animal fats are major health risks in the United States, and clothes, shoddy or not, absorb more consumer dollars than cars, this lack of information is serious. So is ignoring the contents of beauty products that are absorbed into our bodies through our skins, and that have profit margins so big they would make a loan shark blush.

III. What could women's magazines be like if they were as free as books? as realistic as newspapers? as creative as films? as diverse as women's lives? We don't know.

But we'll only find out if we take women's magazines seriously. If readers were to act in a concerted way to change traditional practices of all women's maga-

zines and the marketing of all women's products, we could do it. After all, they are operating on our consumer dollars; money that we now control. You and I could:

• write to editors and publishers (with copies to advertisers) that we're willing to pay *more* for magazines with editorial independence, but will *not* continue to pay for those that are just editorial extensions of ads;

• write to advertisers (with copies to editors and publishers) that we want fiction, political reporting, consumer reporting—whatever is, or is not, supported by their ads;

• put as much energy into breaking advertising's control over content as into changing the images in ads, or protesting ads for harmful products like cigarettes;

• support only those women's magazines and products that take us seriously as readers and consumers.

Those of us in the magazine world can also use the carrot-and-stick technique. For instance: pointing out that, if magazines were a regulated medium like television, the demands of advertisers would be against FCC rules. Payola and extortion could be punished. As it is, there are probably illegalities. A magazine's postal rates are determined by the ratio of ad to edit pages, and the former costs more than the latter. So much for the stick.

The carrot means appealing to enlightened self-interest. For instance: there are many studies showing that the greatest factor in determining an ad's effectiveness is the credibility of its surroundings. The "higher the rating of editorial believability," concluded a 1987 survey by the *Journal of Advertising Research,* "the higher the rating of the advertising." Thus, an impenetrable wall between edit and ads would also be in the best interest of advertisers.

Unfortunately, few agencies or clients hear such arguments. Editors often maintain the false purity of refusing to talk to them at all. Instead, they see ad salespeople who know little about editorial, are trained in business as usual, and are usually paid by commission. Editors might also band together to take on controversy. That happened once when all the major women's magazines did articles in the same month on the Equal Rights Amendment. It could happen again.

It's almost three years away from life between the grindstones of advertising pressures and readers' needs. I'm just beginning to realize how edges got smoothed down—in spite of all our resistance.

I remember feeling put upon when I changed "Porsche" to "car" in a piece about Nazi imagery in German pornography by Andrea Dworkin—feeling sure Andrea

would understand that Volkswagen, the distributor of Porsche and one of our few supportive advertisers, asked only to be far away from Nazi subjects. It's taken me all this time to realize that Andrea was the one with a right to feel put upon.

Even as I write this, I get a call from a writer for *Elle*, who is doing a whole article on where women part their hair. Why, she wants to know, do I part mine in the middle?

It's all so familiar. A writer trying to make something of a nothing assignment; an editor laboring to think of new ways to attract ads; readers assuming that other women must want this ridiculous stuff; more women suffering for lack of information, insight, creativity, and laughter that could be on these same pages.

I ask you: Can't we do better than this?

Basketball Is Feminism

Danya Reich

I know that when a woman walks onto the court, she's not expected to be as good as the rest of the men. I experience this time and again as our co-ed team plays in its all-male league. Before each game, our opponents look at us with incredulity, sometimes asking four times if we're absolutely sure we're on the right court. Yes, I tell them, they are scheduled to play us (and, yes, some of us are women—Shhh). They then assume they will clobber us. And, for the most part, they do.

I grew up with Ms. magazines lying around the house and the pervasive feminist mantra that I could do anything, despite being host to two X chromosomes. While women were becoming doctors, lawyers, and architects, if a courageous ten-year old girl wanted to play Little League, she still had to sue the town to do so. The traditionally male world of competitive sports was still, well, a tradition. Blame genetics, blame environment—I was a timid little girl. And timid little girls didn't play basketball.

After I graduated from four square and hop scotch, I took ballet. I did gymnastics. I was even a cheerleader for a while. Not only do these traditionally "female" activities lack the camaraderie of a team sport but they certainly do not provide for a practical athletic future. At a certain age, I no longer had the ability nor the desire to do a backbend anymore and my pleated cheerleading skirt hung limply in my closet above the obligatory saddle shoes. I found myself to be a woman without a sport. And a resentful woman, at that.

Two years ago, I watched some co-workers play pick-up basketball games at lunch. They were having so much fun. The teamwork, the skill, the intelligence, the stamina, the sheer athleticism—I could see that basketball embodied everything that my prior athletic history hadn't. It also terrified me—I didn't know how to play and I didn't want to admit that to the men I knew I'd have to play with. When did these people learn to play and where was I (turning pirouettes, no doubt)? I pouted on the sidelines—always a cheerleader, never a "cheer-ee."

One day, I was really pissed off about life and work, and I just wanted to shoot some baskets, goddammit. I skipped lunch to get on the court before the real players came out. Within a few minutes, they showed up and assuming I was there for the same reasons they assigned me to a team. Before I could explain this embarrassing situation, the game was in full swing. Ball-handling was out of the question, so I played my own personal version of defense. I looked like a fool, but I'd never been happier. At the age of 28, my basketball career had begun.

The reality is that, even in 1996, basketball is still predominantly a male sport. It's the odd girl who has learned to play and the odd boy who hasn't. There are a few women that I play with—but essentially I'm forced to publicly display my ineptitude to men. My reputation as a strong and competent woman is at stake.

My first basketball-playing environments, though co-ed, were actually very nurturing and supportive. In these situations, I was never self-conscious about my gender—just my subpar skill level. However, when I started playing on the Exterminating Angels (in the New York Urban League), and my co-ed team came face-to-face with a fresh crop of male opponents on a weekly basis, all that changed. They would take one look at me and expect me to suck.

One week, after the predictable sideways glances, our opposing team realized they'd be playing some "girls." One of their large, uniformed players said to me, "Hey, go easy on me. No hand checks in this game," and

then winked. I smiled outwardly but I seethed inside. (The insult was clear, though I had to later ask a teammate what a "hand check" was.) A nearby twelve-year old girl caught the exchange and piped in, "You're playing the boys team? I've gotta see this!"

The moment when sexism steps into your path is stunning, especially when you're not expecting it. It makes you question your faith in yourself and your place in the world. Basketball took on a much larger meaning. It was no longer just a game. It was a threat to my female pride.

At pre-game warm-up, I hated picking up the ball for the first time. Until that moment, as I stretched or taped my fingers, I maintained the illusion—or fantasy—that I was a ringer. After all, they really couldn't be sure. I could endure the snickers, comments and winks with my dignity still intact. But, once I picked up that ball, I knew the jig was up. I exposed myself as the novice that I am. And, each time, I dreaded that soul-bearing moment.

All I wanted was to walk on that court and show them that I was just as good, could dribble as quickly and shoot as accurately. Just because I'm not a man doesn't mean I can't play basketball. But I can't show them that. Because I can't do it yet. I've only been playing for two years, and they've been playing most of their lives, I keep telling myself that—but it doesn't make up for anything. After all, that's part of the stereotype. Suddenly I find myself attributing my lack of skill to my gender (as do most of my opponents in this league) and not my inexperience. On the basketball court I do not roar, I whimper.

Not only was I playing right into their stereotype, I was reinforcing it. Being treated as an individual seemed an obvious right of birth to me. Why then—at one glance—am I not taken as seriously as any boy? I dreaded the Urban League games, yet nothing in the world would keep me from going back. Maybe I wasn't good enough, but I'd be damned if I would let that stop me. I had discovered a very cool world and I was not about to give it up. Someone suggested that I play on a women's team, that maybe I'd have a better experience. Excuse me?

When I was asked to be part of the Exterminating Angel team, never once did I think to ask who we'd be playing. And when I realized that it was an all-male league, that, too, didn't phase me. I've earned my right to go where I want to go. I didn't choose this battle, but now that I've encountered it, I can only fight it. I just wasn't sure how.

If I don't want to continue to give these guys fuel for their fire, then I can't keep stepping out on that court and proving them right. On the other hand, if I don't want to give up this new-found passion for basket-

ball, I have to perpetuate a stereotype that I have been raised to fight against. In my search to reconcile the sport I love and my allegiance to my sex, I thought of my brother. His no-nonsense remedy is a simple one, "Quit your yapping and just play ball." In the end, that is the only option.

Gender roles are crystal clear on the court, whereas they've been thankfully muddied in most other aspects of my life. For me, basketball may be one of the last remaining bastions of male dominance to overcome. It's my new frontier. So I will continue to play and, therefore, continue to prove "them" right, because practice is the only path to eventually being able to prove "them" wrong. Through feminism, I have the courage and desire to forge on in basketball. Through basketball, I've discovered feminism. Much to my surprise, I have become a feminist basketball player.

18

Masculinity as Homophobia:
Fear, Shame, and Silence in the Construction of Gender Identity

Michael S. Kimmel

"Funny thing," [Curley's wife] said. "If I catch any one man, and he's alone, I get along fine with him. But just let two of the guys get together an' you won't talk. Jus' nothin' but mad." She dropped her fingers and put her hands on her hips. "You're all scared of each other, that's what. Ever' one of you's scared the rest is goin' to get something on you."

John Steinbeck, Of Mice and Men (1937)

We think of manhood as eternal, a timeless essence that resides deep in the heart of every man. We think of manhood as a thing, a quality that one either has or doesn't have. We think of manhood as innate, residing in the particular biological composition of the human male, the result of androgens or the possession of a penis. We think of manhood as a transcendent tangible property that each man must manifest in the world, the reward presented with great ceremony to a young novice by his elders for having successfully completed an arduous initiation ritual. In the words of poet Robert Bly (1990), "the structure at the bottom of the male psyche is still as firm as it was twenty thousand years ago" (p. 230).

In this chapter, I view masculinity as a constantly changing collection of meanings that we construct through our relationships with ourselves, with each other, and with our world. Manhood is neither static nor timeless; it is historical. Manhood is not the manifestation of an inner essence; it is socially constructed. Manhood does not bubble up to consciousness from our biological makeup; it is created in culture. Manhood means different things at different times to

From Harry Brod and Michel Kaufman, eds., *Theorizing Masculinities*, copyright 1994 by Sage Publications, Inc. Reprinted by permission of Sage Publications, Inc.

different people. We come to know what it means to be a man in our culture by setting our definitions in opposition to a set of "others"—racial minorities, sexual minorities, and, above all, women.

Our definitions of manhood are constantly changing, being played out on the political and social terrain on which the relationships between women and men are played out. In fact, the search for a transcendent, timeless definition of manhood is itself a sociological phenomenon—we tend to search for the timeless and eternal during moments of crisis, those points of transition when old definitions no longer work and new definitions are yet to be firmly established.

This idea that manhood is socially constructed and historically shifting should not be understood as a loss, that something is being taken away from men. In fact, it gives us something extraordinarily valuable—agency, the capacity to act. It gives us a sense of historical possibilities to replace the despondent resignation that invariably attends timeless, ahistorical essentialisms. Our behaviors are not simply "just human nature," because "boys will be boys." From the materials we find around us in our culture—other people, ideas, objects—we actively create our worlds, our identities. Men, both individually and collectively, can change.

In this chapter, I explore this social and historical construction of both hegemonic masculinity and alternate masculinities, with an eye toward offering a new theoretical model of American manhood.[1] To accomplish this I first uncover some of the hidden gender meanings in classical statements of social and political philosophy, so that I can anchor the emergence of contemporary manhood in specific historical and social contexts. I then spell out the ways in which this version of masculinity emerged

in the United States, by tracing both psychoanalytic developmental sequences and a historical trajectory in the development of marketplace relationships.

Classical Social Theory as a Hidden Meditation of Manhood

Begin this inquiry by looking at four passages from that set of texts commonly called classical social and political theory. You will, no doubt, recognize them, but I invite you to recall the way they were discussed in your undergraduate or graduate courses in theory:

> The bourgeoisie cannot exist without constantly revolutionizing the instruments of production, and thereby the relations of production, and with them the whole relations of society. Conservation of the old modes of production in unaltered form, was, on the contrary, the first condition of existence for all earlier industrial classes. Constant revolutionizing of production, uninterrupted disturbance of all social conditions, everlasting uncertainty and agitation distinguish the bourgeois epoch from all earlier ones. All fixed, fast-frozen relations, with their train of ancient and venerable prejudices and opinions are swept away, all new-formed ones become antiquated before they can ossify. All that is solid melts into air, all that is holy is profaned, and man is at last compelled to face with sober senses, his real conditions of life, and his relation with his kind. (Marx & Engels, 1848/1964)

> An American will build a house in which to pass his old age and sell it before the roof is on; he will plant a garden and rent it just as the trees are coming into bearing; he will clear a field and leave others to reap the harvest; he will take up a profession and leave it, settle in one place and soon go off elsewhere with his changing desires. . . . At first sight there is something astonishing in this spectacle of so many lucky men restless in the midst of abun-

dance. But it is a spectacle as old as the world; all that is new is to see a whole people performing in it. (Tocqueville, 1835/1967)

Where the fulfillment of the calling cannot directly be related to the highest spiritual and cultural values, or when, on the other hand, it need not be felt simply as economic compulsion, the individual generally abandons the attempt to justify it at all. In the field of its highest development, in the United States, the pursuit of wealth, stripped of its religious and ethical meaning, tends to become associated with purely mundane passions, which often actually give it the character of sport. (Weber, 1905/1966)

We are warned by a proverb against serving two masters at the same time. The poor ego has things even worse: it serves three severe masters and does what it can to bring their claims and demands into harmony with one another. These claims are always divergent and often seem incompatible. No wonder that the ego so often fails in its task. Its three tyrannical masters are the external world, the super ego and the id. . . . It feels hemmed in on three sides, threatened by three kinds of danger, to which, if it is hard pressed it reacts by generating anxiety. . . . Thus, the ego, driven by the id, confined by the super ego, repulsed by reality, struggles to master its economic task of bringing about harmony among the forces and influences working in and upon it; and we can understand how it is that so often we cannot suppress a cry: "Life is not easy!" (Freud, "The Dissection of the Psychical Personality," 1933/1966)

If your social science training was anything like mine, these were offered as descriptions of the bourgeoisie under capitalism, of individuals in democratic societies, of the fate of the Protestant work ethic under the ever rationalizing spirit of capitalism, or of the arduous task of the autonomous ego in psychological development. Did anyone ever mention that in all four cases the theorists were describing men? Not just "man" as in generic mankind,

but a particular type of masculinity, a definition of manhood that derives its identity from participation in the marketplace, from interaction with other men in that marketplace—in short, a model of masculinity for whom identity is based on homosocial competition? Three years before Tocqueville found Americans "restless in the midst of abundance," Senator Henry Clay had called the United States "a nation of self-made men."

What does it mean to be "self-made"? What are the consequences of self-making for the individual man, for other men, for women? It is this notion of manhood—rooted in the sphere of production, the public arena, a masculinity grounded not in landownership or in artisanal republican virtue but in successful participation in marketplace competition—this has been the defining notion of American manhood. Masculinity must be proved, and no sooner is it proved than it is again questioned and must be proved again—constant, relentless, unachievable, and ultimately the quest for proof becomes so meaningless that it takes on the characteristics, as Weber said, of a sport. He who has the most toys when he dies wins.

Where does this version of masculinity come from? How does it work? What are the consequences of this version of masculinity for women, for other men, and for individual men themselves? These are the questions I address in this chapter.

Masculinity as History and the History of Masculinity

The idea of masculinity expressed in the previous extracts is the product of historical shifts in the grounds on which men rooted their sense of themselves as men. To argue that cultural definitions of gender identity are historically specific goes only so far; we have to specify exactly what those models were. In my historical inquiry into the development of these models of manhood[2] I chart the fate of two models for manhood at the turn of the 19th century and the emergence of a third in the first few decades of that century.

In the late 18th and early 19th centuries, two models of manhood prevailed. The *Genteel Patriarch* derived his identity from landownership. Supervising his estate, he was refined, elegant, and given to casual sensuousness. He was a doting and devoted father, who spent much of his time supervising the estate and with his family. Think of George Washington or Thomas Jefferson as examples. By contrast, the *Heroic Artisan* embodied the physical strength and republican virtue that Jefferson observed in the yeoman farmer, independent urban craftsman, or shopkeeper. Also a devoted father, the Heroic Artisan taught his son his craft, bringing him through ritual apprenticeship to status as master craftsman. Economically autonomous, the Heroic Artisan also cherished his democratic community, delighting in the participatory democracy of the town meeting. Think of Paul Revere at his pewter shop, shirtsleeves rolled up, a leather apron—a man who took pride in his work.

Heroic Artisans and Genteel Patriarchs lived in casual accord, in part because their gender ideals were complementary (both supported participatory democracy and individual autonomy, although patriarchs tended to support more powerful state machineries and also supported slavery) and because they rarely saw one another: Artisans were decidedly urban and Genteel Patriarchs ruled their rural estates. By the 1830s, though, this casual symbiosis was shattered by the emergence of a new vision of masculinity, *Marketplace Manhood.*

Marketplace Man derived his identity entirely from his success in the capitalist marketplace, as he accumulated wealth, power, status. He was the urban entrepreneur, the businessman. Restless, agitated, and anxious, Marketplace Man was an absentee landlord at home and an absent father with his children, devoting himself to his work in an increasingly homosocial environment—a male-only world in which he pits himself against other men. His efforts at self-making transform the political and economic spheres, casting aside the Genteel Patriarch as an anachronistic feminized dandy—sweet, but ineffective and outmoded, and transforming the Heroic Artisan into a dispossessed proletarian, a wage slave.

As Tocqueville would have seen it, the coexistence of the Genteel Patriarch and the Heroic Artisan embodied the fusion of liberty and equality. Genteel Patriarchy was the manhood of the traditional aristocracy, the class that embodied the virtue of liberty. The Heroic Artisan embodied democratic community, the solidarity of the urban shopkeeper or craftsman. Liberty and democracy, the patriarch and the artisan, could, and did, coexist. But Marketplace Man is capitalist man, and he makes both freedom and equality problematic, eliminating the freedom of the aristocracy and proletarianizing the equality of the artisan. In one sense, American history has been an effort to restore, retrieve, or reconstitute the virtues of Genteel Patriarchy and Heroic Artisanate as they were being transformed in the capitalist marketplace.

Marketplace Manhood was a manhood that required proof, and that required the acquisition of tangible goods as evidence of success. It reconstituted itself by the exclusion of "others"—women, nonwhite men, nonnative-born men, homosexual men—and by terrified flight into a pristine mythic homosocial Eden where men could, at last, be real men among other men. The story of the ways in which Marketplace Man becomes American Everyman is a tragic tale, a tale of striving to live up to impossible ideals of success leading to chronic terrors of emasculation, emotional emptiness, and a gendered rage that leaves a wide swath of destruction in its wake.

Masculinities as Power Relations

Marketplace Masculinity describes the normative definition of American masculinity. It describes his characteristics—aggression, competition, anxiety—and the arena in which those characteristics are deployed—the public sphere, the marketplace. If the marketplace is the arena in which manhood is tested and proved, it is a gendered arena, in which tensions between women and men and tensions among different groups of men are weighted with meaning. These tensions suggest that cultural definitions of gender are played out in a contested terrain and are themselves power relations.

All masculinities are not created equal; or rather, we are all *created* equal, but any hypothetical equality evaporates quickly because our definitions of masculinity are not equally valued in our society. One definition of manhood continues to remain the standard against which other forms of manhood are measured and evaluated. Within the dominant culture, the masculinity that defines white, middle class, early middle-aged, heterosexual men is the masculinity that sets the standards for other men, against which other men are measure and, more often than not, found wanting. Sociologist Erving Goffman (1963) wrote that in America, there is only "one complete, unblushing male":

> a young, married, white, urban, northern heterosexual, Protestant father of college education, fully employed, of good complexion, weight and height, and a recent record in sports. Every American male tends to look out upon the world from this perspective.. ... Any

male who fails to qualify in any one of these ways is likely to view himself . . . as unworthy, incomplete, and inferior. (p. 128)

This is the definition that we will call "hegemonic" masculinity, the image of masculinity of those men who hold power, which has become the standard in psychological evaluations, sociological research, and self-help and advice literature for teaching young men to become "real men" (Connell, 1987). The hegemonic definition of manhood is a man *in* power, a man *with* power, and a man *of* power. We equate manhood with being strong, successful, capable, reliable, in control. The very definitions of manhood we have developed in our culture maintain the power that some men have over other men and that men have over women.

Our culture's definition of masculinity is thus several stories at once. It is about the individual man's quest to accumulate those cultural symbols that denote manhood, signs that he has in fact achieved it. It is about those standards being used against women to prevent their inclusion in public life and their consignment to a devalued private sphere. It is about the differential access that different types of men have to those cultural resources that confer manhood and about how each of these groups then develop their own modifications to preserve and claim their manhood. It is about the power of these definitions themselves to serve to maintain the real-life power that men have over women and that some men have over other men.

This definition of manhood has been summarized cleverly by psychologist Robert Brannon (1976) into four succinct phrases:

1. "No Sissy Stuff!" One may never do anything that even remotely suggests femininity. Masculinity is the relentless repudiation of the feminine.

2. "Be a Big Wheel." Masculinity is measured by power, success, wealth, and status. As the current saying goes, "He who has the most toys when he dies wins."

3. "Be a Sturdy Oak." Masculinity depends on remaining calm and reliable in a crisis, holding emotions in check. In fact, proving you're a man depends on never showing your emotions at all. Boys don't cry.

4. "Give 'em Hell." Exude an aura of manly daring and aggression. Go for it. Take risks.

These rules contain the elements of the definition against which virtually all American men are measured. Failure to embody these rules, to affirm the power of the rules and one's achievement of them is a source of men's confusion and pain. Such a model is, or course, unrealizable for any man. But we keep trying, valiantly and vainly, to measure up. American masculinity is a relentless test.[3] The chief test is contained in the first rule. Whatever the variation by race, class, age, ethnicity, or sexual orientation, being a man means "not being like women." This notion of antifeminity lies at the heart of contemporary and historical conceptions of manhood, so that masculinity is defined more by what one is not rather than who one is.

Masculinity as the Flight from the Feminine

Historically and developmentally, masculinity has been defined as the flight from women, the repudiation of femininity. Since Freud, we have come to understand that developmentally the central task that every little boy must confront is to develop a secure identity for himself as a man. As Freud had it, the oedipal project is a process of the boy's renouncing his identification with and deep emotional attachment to his mother and then replacing her with the father as the object of identification. Notice that he reidentifies but never reattaches. This entire process, Freud argued, is set in motion by the boy's sexual desire for his mother. But the father stands in the son's path and will not yield his sexual property to his puny son. The boy's first emotional experience, then, the one that inevitably follows his experience of desire, is fear—fear of the bigger, stronger, more sexually powerful father. It is this fear, experienced symbolically as the fear of castration, Freud argues, that forces the young boy to renounce his identification with mother and seek to identify with the being who is the actual source of his fear, his father. In so doing, the boy is now symbolically capable of sexual union with a motherlike substitute, that is, a woman. The boy becomes gendered (masculine) and heterosexual at the same time.

Masculinity, in this model, is irrevocably tied to sexuality. The boy's sexuality will now come to resemble the sexuality of his father (or at least the way he imagines his father)—menacing, predatory, possessive, and possibly punitive. The boy has come to identify with his oppressor; now he can become the oppressor himself. But a terror remains, the terror that the young man will be unmasked as a fraud, as a man who has not completely and irrevocably separated from mother. It well be other men who will do the unmasking. Failure will de-sex the man, make him appear as not fully a man. He will be seen as a wimp, a Mama's boy, a sissy.

After pulling away from his mother, the boy comes to see her not as a source of nurturance and love, but as an insatiably infantalizing creature, capable of humiliating him in front of his peers. She makes him dress up in uncomfortable and itchy clothing, her kisses smear his cheeks with lipstick, staining his boyish innocence with the mark of feminine dependency. No wonder so many boys cringe from their mothers' embraces with groans of "Aw, Mom! Quit it!" Mothers represent the humiliation of infancy, helplessness, dependency. "Men act as though they were being guided by (or rebelling against) rules and prohibitions enunciated by a moral mother," writes psychohistorian Geoffrey Gorer (1964). As a result, "all the niceties of masculine behavior—modesty, politeness, neatness, cleanliness—come to be regarded as concessions to feminine demands, and not good in themselves as part of the behavior of a proper man" (pp. 56, 57).

The flight from femininity is angry and frightened, because mother can so easily emasculate the young boy by her power to render him dependent, or at least to remind him of dependency. It is relentless; manhood becomes a lifelong quest to demonstrate its achievement, as if to prove the unprovable to others, because we feel so unsure of it ourselves. Women don't often feel compelled to "prove their womanhood"—the phrase itself sounds ridiculous. Women have different kinds of gender identity crises; their anger and frustration, and their own symptoms of depression, come more from being excluded than from questioning whether they are feminine enough.[4]

The drive to repudiate the mother as the indication of the acquisition of masculine gender identity has three consequences for the young boy. First, he pushes away his real mother, and with her the traits of nurturance, compassion, and tenderness she may have embodied. Second, he suppresses those traits in himself, because they will reveal his incomplete separation from mother. His life becomes a lifelong project to demonstrate that he possesses none of his mother's traits. Masculine identity is born in the renunciation of the feminine, not in

the direct affirmation of the masculine, which leaves masculine gender identity tenuous and fragile.

Third, as if to demonstrate the accomplishment of these first two tasks, the boy also learns to devalue all women in his society, as the living embodiments of those traits in himself he has learned to despise. Whether or not he was aware of it, Freud also described the origins or sexism—the systematic devaluation of women—in the desperate efforts of the boy to separate from mother. We may *want* "a girl just like the girl that married dear old Dad," as the popular song had it, but we certainly don't want to *be like* her.

This chronic uncertainty about gender identity helps us understand several obsessive behaviors. Take, for example, the continuing problem of the school-yard bully. Parents remind us that the bully is the *least* secure about his manhood, and so he is constantly trying to prove it. But he "proves" it by choosing opponents he is absolutely certain he can defeat; thus the standard taunt to a bully is to "pick on someone your own size." He can't, though, and after defeating a smaller and weaker opponent, which he was sure would prove his manhood, he is left with the empty gnawing feeling that he has not proved it after all, and he must find another opponent, again one smaller and weaker, that he can again defeat to prove it to himself.[5]

One of the more graphic illustrations of this lifelong quest to prove one's manhood occurred at the Academy Awards presentation in 1992. As aging, tough guy actor Jack Palance accepted the award for Best Supporting Actor for this role in the cowboy comedy *City Slickers,* he commented that people, especially film producers, think that because he is 71 years old, he's all washed up, that he's no longer competent. "Can we take a risk on this guy?" he quoted them as saying, before he dropped to the floor to do a set of one-armed push-ups. It was pathetic to see such an accomplished actor still having to prove that he is virile enough to work and, as he also commented at the podium, to have sex.

When does it end? Never. To admit weakness, to admit frailty or fragility, is to be seen as a wimp, a sissy, not a real man. But seen by whom?

Masculinity as a Homosocial Enactment

Other men: We are under the constant careful scrutiny of other men. Other men watch us, rank us, grant our acceptance into the realm of manhood. Manhood is demonstrated for other men's approval. It is other men who evaluate the performance. Literary critic David Leverenz (1991) argues that "ideologies of manhood have functioned primarily in relation to the gaze of male peers and male authority" (p. 769). Think of how men boast to one another of their accomplishments—from their latest sexual conquest to the size of the fish they caught—and how we constantly parade the markers of manhood—wealth, power, status, sexy women—in front of other men, desperate for their approval.

That men prove their manhood in the eyes of other men is both a consequence of sexism and one of its chief props. "Women have, in men's minds, such a low place on the social ladder of this country that it's useless to define yourself in terms of a woman," noted playwright David Mamet. "What men need is men's approval." Women become a kind of currency that men use to improve their ranking on the masculine social scale. (Even those moments of heroic conquest of women carry, I believe, a current of homosocial evaluation.) Masculinity is a *homosocial* enactment. We test ourselves, perform heroic feats, take enor-

mous risks, all because we want other men to grant us our manhood.

Masculinity as a homosocial enactment is fraught with danger, with the risk of failure, and with intense relentless competition. "Every man you meet has a rating or an estimate of himself which he never loses or forgets," wrote Kenneth Wayne (1912) in his popular turn-of-the-century advice book. "A man has his own rating, and instantly he lays it alongside of the other man" (p. 18). Almost a century later, another man remarked to psychologist Sam Osherson (1992) that "[b]y the time you're an adult, it's easy to think you're always in competition with men, for the attention of women, in sports, at work" (p. 291).

Masculinity as Homophobia

If masculinity is a homosocial enactment, its overriding emotion is fear. In the Freudian model, the fear of the father's power terrifies the young boy to renounce his desire for his mother and identify with his father. This model links gender identity with sexual orientation: The little boy's identification with father (becoming masculine) allows him to now engage in sexual relations with women (he becomes heterosexual). This is the origin of how we can "read" one's sexual orientation through the successful performance of gender identity. Second, the fear that the little boy feels does not send him scurrying into the arms of his mother to protect him from his father. Rather, he believes he will overcome his fear by identifying with its source. We become masculine by identifying with our oppressor.

But there is a piece of the puzzle missing, a piece that Freud, himself, implied but did not follow up.[6] If the pre-oedipal boy identifies with mother, he *sees the world through mother's eyes.* Thus, when he confronts father during his great oedipal crisis, he experiences a split vision: He sees his father as his mother sees his father, with a combination of awe, wonder, terror, *and desire*. He simultaneously sees the father as he, the boy, would like to see him—as the object not of desire but of emulation. Repudiating mother and identifying with father only partially answers his dilemma. What is he to do with that homoerotic desire, the desire he felt because he saw father the way that his mother saw father?

He must suppress it. Homoerotic desire is cast as feminine desire, desire for other men. Homophobia is the effort to suppress that desire, to purify all relationships with other men, with women, with children of its taint, and to ensure that no one could possibly ever mistake one for a homosexual. Homophobic flight from intimacy with other men is the repudiation of the homosexual within—never completely successful and hence constantly reenacted in every homosocial relationship. "The lives of most American men are bounded, and their interests daily curtailed by the constant necessity to prove to their fellows, and to themselves, that they are not sissies, not homosexuals," writes psychoanalytic historian Geoffrey Gorer (1964). "Any interest or pursuit which is identified as a feminine interest or pursuit becomes deeply suspect for men" (p. 129).

Even if we do not subscribe to Freudian psychoanalytic ideas, we can still observe how, in less sexualized terms, the father is the first man who evaluates the boy's masculine performance, the first pair of male eyes before whom he tries to prove himself. Those eyes will follow him for the rest of his life. Other men's eyes will join them—the eyes of role models such as teachers, coaches, bosses, or media heroes; the eyes of his peers, his friends, his workmates; and the eyes of millions of other men, living and dead, from whose constant scrutiny of his performance he will never be free. "The tradition of all the dead generations weighs like a nightmare on the brain of the living," was how Karl Marx put it over a century ago (1848/1964, p. 11). "The birthright of every American male is a chronic sense of personal inadequacy," is how two psychologists describe it today (Woolfold & Richardson, 1978, p. 57).

That nightmare from which we never seem to awaken is that those other men will see that sense of inadequacy, they well see that in our own eyes we are not who we are pretending to be. What we call masculinity is often a hedge against being revealed as a fraud, an exaggerated set of activities that keep others from seeing though us, and a frenzied effort to keep at bay those fears within ourselves. Our real fear "is not fear of women but of being ashamed or humiliated in front of other men, or being dominated by stronger men" (Leverenz, 1986, p. 451).

This, then, is the great secret of American manhood: *We are afraid of other men.* Homophobia is a central organizing principle of our cultural definition of manhood. Homophobia is more than the irrational fear of gay men, more than the fear that we might be perceived as gay. "The word 'faggot' has nothing to do with homosexual experience or even with fears of homosexuals," writes David Leverenz (1986). "It comes out of the depths of manhood: a label of ultimate contempt for anyone who seems sissy, untough, uncool" (p. 455). Homophobia is the fear that other men will unmask us, emasculate us, reveal to us and the world that we do not measure up, that we are not real men. We are afraid to let other men see that fear. Fear makes us ashamed, because the recognition of fear in ourselves is proof to ourselves that we are not as manly as we pretend, that we are, like the young man in a poem by Yeats, "one that ruffles in a manly pose for all his timid heart." Our fear is the fear of humiliation. We are ashamed to be afraid.

Shame leads to silence—the silences that keep other people believing that we actually approve of the things that are done to women, to minorities, to gays and lesbians in our culture. The frightened silence as we scurry past a woman being hassled by men on the street. That furtive silence when men make sexist or racist jokes in a bar. That clammy-handed silence when guys in the office make gay-bashing jokes. Our fears are the sources of our silences, and men's silence is what keeps the system running. This might help to explain why women often complain that their male friends or partners are often so understanding when they are alone and yet laugh at sexist jokes or even make those jokes themselves when they are out with a group.

The fear of being seen as a sissy dominates the cultural definitions of manhood. It starts so early. "Boys among boys are ashamed to be unmanly," wrote one educator in 1871 (cited in Rotundo, 1993, p. 254). I have a standing bet with a friend that I can walk onto any playground in America where 6-year-old boys are happily playing and by asking one question, I can provoke a fight. That question is simply: "Who's a sissy around here?" Once posed, the challenge is made. One of two things is likely to happen. One boy will accuse another of being a sissy, to which that boy will respond that he is not a sissy, that the first boy is. They may have to fight it out to see who's lying. Or a whole group of boys will surround one boy and all shout "He is! He is!" That boy will either burst into tears and run home crying, disgraced, or he will have to take on several boys at once, to prove that he's not a sissy. (And what will his father or older brothers tell him if he chooses to run home crying?) It will be some time before he regains any sense of self-respect.

Violence is often the single most evident marker of manhood. Rather it is the willingness to fight, the desire to fight. The origin of our expression that one has a chip on one's shoulder lies in the practice of an adolescent boy in the country or small town at the turn of the century, who would literally walk around with a chip of wood balanced on his shoulder—a signal of his readiness to fight with anyone who would take the initiative of knocking the chip off (See Gorer, 1964, p. 38; Mead, 1965).

As adolescents, we learn that our peers are a kind of gender police, constantly threatening to unmask us as feminine, as sissies. One of the favorite tricks when I was an adolescent was to ask a boy to look at his fingernails. If he held his palm toward his face and curled his fingers back to see them, he passed the test. He'd looked at his nails "like a man." But if he held the back of his hand away from his face, and looked at this fingernails with arm outstretched, he was immediately ridiculed as a sissy.

As young men we are constantly riding those gender boundaries, checking the fences we have constructed on the perimeter, making sure that nothing even remotely feminine might show through. The possibilities of being unmasked are everywhere. Even the most seemingly insignificant thing can pose a threat or activate that haunting terror. On the day the students in my course "Sociology of Men and Masculinities" were scheduled to discuss homophobia and male-male friendships, one student provided a touching illustration. Noting that it was a beautiful day, the first day of spring after a brutal northeast winter, he decided to wear shorts to class. "I had this really nice pair of new Madras shorts," he commented. "But then I thought to myself, these shorts have lavender and pink in them. Today's class topic is homophobia. Maybe today is not the best day to wear these shorts."

Our efforts to maintain a manly front cover everything we do. What we wear. How we talk. How we walk. What we eat. Every mannerism, every movement contains a coded gender language. Think, for example, of how you would answer the question: How do you "know" if a man is homosexual? When I ask this question in classes or workshops, respondents invariably provide a pretty standard list of stereotypically effeminate behaviors. He walks a certain way, talks a certain way, acts a certain way. He's very emotional; he shows his feelings. One woman commented that she "knows" a man is gay if he really cares about her; another said she knows he's gay if he shows no interest in her, if he leaves her alone.

Now alter the question and imagine what heterosexual men do to make sure no one could possibly get the "wrong idea" about them. Responses typically refer to the original stereotypes, this time as a set of negative rules about behavior. Never dress that way. Never talk or walk that way. Never show your feelings or get emotional. Always be prepared to demonstrate sexual interest in women that you meet, so it is impossible for any woman to get the wrong idea about you. In this sense, Homophobia, the fear of being perceived as gay, as not a real man, keeps men exaggerating all the traditional rules of masculinity, including sexual predation with women. Homophobia and sexism go hand in hand.

The stakes of perceived sissydom are enormous—sometimes matters of life and death. We take enormous risks to prove our manhood, exposing ourselves disproportionately to health risks, workplace hazards, and stress-related illnesses. We commit suicide three times as often as women. Psychiatrist Willard Gaylin (1992) explains that it is "invariably because of perceived social humiliation," most often tied to failure in business:

> Men become depressed because of loss of status and power in the world of men. It is not the loss of money, or the material advantages that money could buy, which produces the despair that leads to self-destruction. It is the "shame," the "humiliation," the sense of personal "failure." . . . A man despairs when he has ceased being a man among men. (p. 32)

In one survey, women and men were asked what they were most afraid of. Women responded that they were most afraid of being raped and murdered. Men responded that they were most afraid of being laughed at (Noble, 1992, pp. 105–106).

Homophobia as a Cause of Sexism, Heterosexism, and Racism

Homophobia is intimately interwoven with both sexism and racism. The fear—sometimes conscious, sometimes not—that others might perceive us as homosexual propels men to enact all manner of exaggerated masculine behaviors and attitudes to make sure that no one could possibly get the wrong idea about us. One of the centerpieces of that exaggerated masculinity is putting women down, both by excluding them from the public sphere and by the quotidian put-downs in speech and behaviors that organize the daily life of the American man. Women and gay men become the "other" against which heterosexual men project their identities, against whom they stack the decks so as to compete in a situation in which they will always win, so that by suppressing them, men can stake a claim for their own manhood. Women threaten emasculation by representing the home, workplace, and familial responsibility, the negation of fun. Gay men have historically played the role of the consummate sissy in the American popular mind because homosexuality is seen as an inversion of normal gender development. There have been other "others." Through American history, various groups have represented the sissy, the non-men against whom American men played out their definitions of manhood, often with vicious results. In fact, these changing groups provide an interesting lesson in American historical development.

At the turn of the 19th century, it was Europeans and children who provided the contrast for American men. The "true American was vigorous, manly, and direct, not effete and corrupt like the supposed European," writes Rupert Wilkinson (1986). "He was plain rather than ornamented, rugged rather than luxury seeking, a liberty loving common man or natural gentleman rather than an aristocratic oppressor or servile minion" (p. 96). The "real man" of the early 19th century was neither noble nor serf. By the middle of the century, black slaves had replaced the effete nobleman. Slaves were seen as dependent, helpless men, incapable of defending their women and children, and therefore less than manly. Native Americans were cast as foolish and naive children, so they could be infantalized as the "Red Children of the Great White Father" and therefore excluded from full manhood.

By the end of the century, new European immigrants were also added to the list of the unreal men, especially the Irish and Italians, who were seen as too passionate and emotionally volatile to remain controlled sturdy oaks, and Jews, who were too bookishly effete and too physically puny to truly measure up. In the mid-20th century, it was also Asians—first the Japanese during the Second World War, and more recently, the Vietnamese during the Vietnam War—who have served as unmanly templates against which American men have hurled their gendered rage. Asian men were seen as small, soft, and effeminate—hardly men at all.

Such a list of "hyphenated" Americans—Italian-, Jewish-, Irish-, African-, Native-, Asian-, gay—composes the majority of American men. So manhood is only possible for a distinct minority, and the definition has been constructed to prevent the others from achieving it. Interestingly, this emasculation of one's enemies has a flip side—and one that is equally gendered. These very groups that have historically been cast as less than manly were also, often simultaneously, cast as hypermasculine, as sexually aggressive, violent rapacious beasts, against whom "civilized" men must take a decisive stand and thereby rescue civilization. Thus black men were depicted as rampaging sexual beasts, women as carnivorously carnal, gay men as sexually insatiable, southern European men as sexually predatory and voracious, and Asian men as vicious and cruel torturers who were immorally disinterested in life itself, willing to sacrifice their entire people for their whims. But whether one saw these groups as effeminate sissies or as brutal uncivilized savages, the terms with which they were perceived were gendered. These groups become the "others," the screens against which traditional conceptions of manhood were developed.

Being seen as unmanly is a fear that propels American men to deny manhood to others, as a way of proving the unprovable—that one is fully manly. Masculinity becomes a defense against the perceived threat of humiliation in the eyes of other men, enacted through a "sequence of postures"—things we might say, or do, or even think, that, if we thought carefully about them, would make us ashamed of ourselves (Savran, 1992, p. 16). After all, how many of us have made homophobic or sexist remarks, or told racist jokes, or made lewd comments to women on the street? How many of us have translated those ideas and those words into actions, by physically attacking gay men, or forcing or cajoling a woman to have sex even though she didn't really want to because it was important to score?

Power and Powerlessness in the Lives of Men

I have argued that homophobia, men's fear of other men, is the animating condition of the dominant definition of masculinity in America, that the reigning definition of masculinity is a defensive effort to prevent being emasculated. In our efforts to suppress or overcome those fears, the dominant culture exacts a tremendous price from those deemed less than fully manly: women, gay men, nonnative-born men, men of color. This perspective may help clarify a paradox in men's lives, a paradox in which men have virtually all the power and yet do not feel powerful (see Kaufman, 1993).

Manhood is equated with power—over women, over other men. Everywhere we look, we see the institutional expression of that power—in state and national legislatures, on the boards of directors of every major U.S. corporation or law firm, and in every school and hospital administration. Women have long understood this, and feminist women have spent the past three decades challenging both the public and the private expressions of men's power and acknowledging their fear of men. Feminism as a set of theories both explains women's fear of men and empowers women to confront it both publicly and privately. Feminist women have theorized that masculinity is about the drive for domination, the drive for power, for conquest.

This feminist definition of masculinity as the drive for power is theorized from women's point of view. It is how women experience masculinity. But it assumes a symmetry between the public and the private that does not conform to men's experiences. Feminists observe that women, as a group, do not hold power in our society. They also observe that individually, they, as women, do not feel powerful. They feel afraid, vulnerable. Their observation of the social reality and their individual experiences are therefore symmetrical. Feminism also observes that men, as a group, *are* in power. Thus, with the same symmetry, feminism has tended to assume that individually men must feel powerful.

This is why the feminist critique of masculinity often falls on deaf ears with men. When confronted with the analysis that men have all the power, many men react incredulously. "What do you mean, men have all the power?" they ask. "What are you talking about? My wife bosses me around. My kids boss me around. My boss bosses me around. I have no power at all! I'm completely powerless!"

Men's feelings are not the feelings of the powerful, but of those who see themselves as powerless. These are the feelings that come inevitably from the discontinuity between the social and the psychological, between the aggregate analysis that reveals how men are in power as a group and the psychological fact that they do not feel powerful as individuals. They are the feelings of men who were raised to believe themselves entitled to feel that power, but do not feel it. No wonder many men are frustrated and angry.

This may explain the recent popularity of those workshops and retreats designed to help men to claim their "inner" power, their "deep manhood," or their "warrior within." Authors such as Bly (1990), Moore and Gillette (1991, 1992, 1993a, 1993b), Farrell (1986, 1993), and Keen (1991) honor and respect men's feelings of powerlessness and acknowledge those feelings to be both true and real. "They gave white men the semblance of power," notes John Lee, one of the leaders of these retreats (Quoted in *Newsweek*, p. 41). "We'll let you run the country, but in the meantime, stop feeling, stop talking, and continue swallowing your pain and your hurt." (We are not told who "they" are.)

Often the purveyors of the mythopoetic men's movement, that broad umbrella that encompasses all the groups helping men to retrieve this mythic deep manhood, use the image of the chauffeur to describe modern man's position. The chauffeur looks as though he is in command. But to the chauffeur himself, they note, he is merely taking orders. He is not at all in charge.[7]

Despite the reality that everyone knows chauffeurs do not have the power, this image remains appealing to the men who hear it at these weekend workshops. But there is a missing piece to the image, a piece concealed by the framing of the image in terms of the individual man's experience. That missing piece is that the person who is giving the orders is also a man. Now we have a relationship *between* men—between men giving orders and other men taking those orders. The man who identifies with the chauffeur is entitled to be the man giving the orders, but he is not. ("They," it turns out, are other men.)

The dimension of power is now reinserted into men's experience not only as the product of individual experience but also as the product of relations with other men. In this sense, men's experience of powerlessness is *real*—the men actually feel it and certainly act on it—but it is not *true*, that is, it does not accurately describe their condition. In contrast to women's lives, men's lives are structured around relationships of power and men's differential access to power, as well as the differential access to that power of men as a group. Our imperfect analysis of our own situation leads us to believe that we men need *more* power, rather than leading us to support feminists' efforts to rearrange power relationships along more equitable lines.

Philosopher Hanna Arendt (1970) fully understood this contradictory experience of social and individual power:

> Power corresponds to the human ability not just to act but to act in concert. Power is never the property of an individual; it belongs to a group and remains in existence only so long as the group keeps together. When we say of somebody that he is "in power" we actually refer to his being empowered by a certain number of people to act in their name. The moment the group, from which the power originated to begin with . . . disappears, "his power" also vanishes. (p. 44)

Why, then, do American men feel so powerless? Part of the answer is because we've constructed the rules of manhood so that only the tiniest faction of men come to believe that they are the biggest of wheels, the sturdies of oaks, the most virulent repudiators of femininity, the most daring and aggressive. We've managed to disempower the overwhelming majority of American men by other means—such as discriminating on the basis of race, class, ethnicity, age, or sexual preference.

Masculinist retreats to retrieve deep, wounded, masculinity are but one of the ways in which American men currently struggle with their fears and their shame. Unfortunately, at the very moment that they work to break down the isolation that governs men's lives, as they enable men to express those fears and that shame, they ignore the social power that men continue to exert over women and the privileges from which they (as the middle-aged, middle-class white men who largely make up these retreats) continue to benefit—regardless of their experiences as wounded victims of oppressive male socialization.[8]

Others still rehearse the politics of exclusion, as if by clearing away the playing field of secure gender identity of any that we deem less than manly—women, gay men, nonnative-born men, men of color—middle-class, straight, white men can reground their sense of themselves without those haunting fears and that deep shame that they are unmanly and will be exposed by other men. This is the manhood of racism, of sexism, of homophobia. It is the manhood that is so chronically insecure that it trembles at the idea of lifting the ban on gays in the military, that is so threatened by women in the workplace that women become the targets of sexual harassment, that is so deeply frightened of equality that it must ensure that the playing field of male competition remains stacked against all newcomers to the game.

Exclusion and escape have been the dominant methods American men have used to keep their fears of humiliation at bay. The fear of emasculation by other men, of being humiliated, of being seen as a sissy, is the leitmotif in my reading of the history of American manhood. Masculinity has become a relentless test by which we prove to other men, to women, and ultimately to ourselves, that we have successfully mastered the part. The restlessness that men feel today is nothing new in American history; we have been anxious and restless for almost two centuries. Neither exclusion nor escape has ever brought us the relief we've sought, and there is no reason to think that either will solve our problems now. Peace of mind, relief from gender struggle, will come only from a politics of inclusion, not exclusion, from standing up for equality and justice, and not by running away.

Notes

1. Of course, the phrase "American manhood" contains several simultaneous fictions. There is no single manhood that defines all American men; "America" is meant to refer to the United States proper, and there are significant ways in which this "American manhood" is the outcome of forces that transcend both gender and nation, that is, the global economic development of industrial capitalism. I use it, therefore, to describe the specific hegemonic version of masculinity in the United States, that normative constellation of attitudes, traits, and behaviors that became the standard against which all other masculinities are measured and against which individual men measure the success of their gender accomplishments.

2. Much of this work is elaborated in *Manhood: The American Quest* (in press).

3. Although I am here discussing only American masculinity, I am aware that others have located this chronic instability and efforts to prove manhood in the particular cultural and economic arrangements of Western society. Calvin, after all, inveighed against the disgrace "for men to become effeminate," and countless other theorists have described the mechanics of manly proof. (See, for example, Siedler, 1994.)

4. I do not mean to argue that women do not have anxieties about whether they are feminine enough. Ask any woman how she feels about being called aggressive; it sends a chill into her heart because her femininity is suspect. (I believe that the reason for the enormous recent popularity of sexy lingerie among women is that it enables women to remember they are still feminine underneath their corporate business suit—a suit that apes masculine styles.) But I think the stakes are not as great for women and that women have greater latitude in defining their identities around these questions than men do. Such are the ironies of sexisms: The powerful have a narrower range of options than the powerless, because the powerless can *also* imitate the powerful and get away with it. It may even enhance status, if done with charm and grace—that is, is not threatening. For the powerful, any hint of behaving like the powerless is a fall from grace.

5. Such observations also led journalist Heywood Broun to argue that most of the attacks against feminism came from men who were shorter than 5 ft. 7 in. "The man who, whatever his physical size, feels secure in his own masculinity and in his own relation to life is rarely resentful of the opposite sex" (cited in Symes, 1930, p. 139).

6. Some of Freud's followers, such as Anna Freud and Alfred Adler, did follow up on these

suggestions. (See especially, Adler, 1980.) I am grateful to Terry Kupers for his help in thinking through Adler's ideas.

7. The image is from Warren Farrell, who spoke at a workshop I attended at the First International Man's Conference, Austin, Texas, October 1991.

8. For a critique of these mythopoetic retreats, see Kimmel and Kaufman, Chapter 14, this volume.

References

Adler, A. (1980). *Cooperation between the sexes: Writing on women, love and marriage, sexuality and its disorders* (H. Ansbacher & R. Ansbacher, Eds. & Trans.). New York: Jason Aronson.

Arendt, H. (1970). *On revolution.* New York: Viking.

Bly, R. (1990). *Iron John: A book about men.* Reading, MA: Addison-Wesley.

Brannon, R. (1976). The male sex role—and what it's done for us lately. In R. Brannon & D. David (Eds.), *The forty-nine percent majority* (pp. 1–40). Reading, MA: Addison-Wesley.

Connell, R. W. (1987) *Gender and power.* Stanford, CA: Stanford University Press.

Farrell, W. (1986). *Why men are the way they are.* New York: McGraw-Hill.

Farrell, W. (1993). *The myth of male power: Why men are the disposable sex.* New York: Simon & Schuster.

Freud, S. (1933/1966). *New introductory lectures on psychoanalysis.* (L. Strachey, Ed.). New York: Norton.

Gaylin, W. (1992) *The male ego.* New York: Viking.

Goffman, E. (1963). *Stigma.* Englewood Cliffs, NJ: Prentice Hall.

Gorer, G. (1964). *The American people: A study in national character.* New York: Norton.

Kaufman, M. (1993). *Cracking the armour: Power and pain in the lives of men.* Toronto: Viking Canada.

Keen, S. (1991). *Fire in the belly.* New York: Bantam.

Kimmel, M. S. (in press). *Manhood: The American quest.* New York: HarperCollins.

Leverenz, D. (1986). Manhood, humiliation and public life: Some stories. *Southwest Review, 71.* Fall.

Leverenz, D. (1991). The last real man in America: From Natty Bumppo to Batman. *American Literary Review, 3.*

Marx, K. and F. Engels. (1848/1964). The communist manifesto. In R. Tucker (Ed.). *The Marx-Engels reader.* New York: Norton.

Mead, M. (1965). *And keep your powder dry.* New York: William Morrow.

Moore, R. & Gillette, D. (1991). *King, warrior, magician lover.* New York: HarperCollins.

Moore, R. & Gillette, D. (1992). *The king within: Accessing the king in the male psyche.* New York: William Morrow.

Moore, R. & Gillette, D. (1993a). *The warrior within: Accessing the warrior in the male psyche.* New York: Willaim Morrow.

Moore, R. & Gillette, D. (1993b). *The magician within: Accessing the magician in the male psyche.* New York: William Morrow.

Noble, V. (1992). A helping hand from the guys. In K. L. Hagan (Ed.), *Women respond to the men's movement.* San Francisco: HarperCollins.

Osherson, S. (1992). *Wrestling with love: How men struggle with intimacy, with women, children, parents, and each other.* New York: Fawcett.

Rotundo, E. A. (1993). *American manhood: Transformations in masculinity from the revolution to the modern era.* New York: Basic Books.

Savran, D. (1992). *Communists, cowboys, and queers: The politics of masculinity in the works of Arthur Miller and Tennessee Williams.* Minneapolis: University of Minnesota Press.

Seidler, V. J. (1994). *Unreasonable men: Masculinity and social theory.* New York: Routledge.

Symes, L. (1930). The new masculinism. *Harper's Monthly, 161.* January.

Tocqueville, A. de. (1835/1967). *Democracy in America.* New York: Anchor.

Wayne, K. (1912). *Building the young man.* Chicago: A. C. McClurg.

Weber, M. (1905/1966). *The Protestant ethic and the spirit of capitalism.* New York: Charles Scribner's.

What men need is men's approval. (1993, January 3). *The New York Times,* p. C-11.

Wilkinson, R. (1986). *American tough: The tough-guy tradition and American character.* New York: Harper & Row.

Woolfolk, R. L. & Richardson, F. (1978). *Sanity, stress and survival.* New York: Signet.

All Men Are Not Created Equal:
Asian Men in U.S. History

Yen Le Espiritu

Today, virtually every major metropolitan market across the United States has at least one Asian American female newscaster. In contrast, there is a nearly total absence of Asian American men in anchor positions (Hamamoto, 1994, p. 245; Fong-Torres, 1995). This gender imbalance in television news broadcasting exemplifies the racialization of Asian American manhood: Historically, they have been depicted as either asexual or hypersexual; today, they are constructed to be less successful, assimilated, attractive, and desirable than their female counterparts (Espiritu, 1996, pp. 95–98). The exclusion of Asian men from Eurocentric notions of the masculine reminds us that not all men benefit—or benefit equally—from a patriarchal system designed to maintain the unequal relationship that exists between men and women. The feminist mandate for gender solidarity tends to ignore power differentials among men, among women, and between white women and men of color. This exclusive focus on gender bars traditional feminists from recognizing the oppression of men of color: the fact that there are men, and not only women, who have been "feminized" and the fact that some white middle-class women hold cultural power and class power over certain men of color (Cheung, 1990, pp. 245–246; Wiegman, 1991, p. 311). Presenting race and gender as relationally constructed, King-Kok Cheung (1990) exhorted white scholars to acknowledge that, like female voices, "the voices of many men of color have been historically silenced or dismissed" (p. 246). Along the same line, black feminists have referred to "racial patriarchy"—a concept that calls attention to the white/patriarch master in U.S. history and his dominance over the black male as well as the black female (Gaines, 1990, p. 202).

Throughout their history in the United States, Asian American men, as immigrants and citizens of color, have faced a variety of economic, political, and ideological racism that have assaulted their manhood. During the pre-World War II period, racialized and gendered immigration policies and labor conditions emasculated Asian men, forcing them into womanless communities and into "feminized" jobs that had gone unfilled due to the absence of women. During World War II, the internment of Japanese Americans stripped Issei (first generation) men of their role as the family breadwinner, transferred some of their power and status to the U.S.-born children, and decreased male dominance over women. In the contemporary period, the patriarchal authority of Asian immigrant men, particularly those of the working class, has also been challenged due to the social and economic losses that they suffered in their transition to life in the United States. As detailed below, these three historically specific cases establish that the material existences of Asian American men have historically contradicted the Eurocentric, middle-class constructions of manhood.

Asian Men in Domestic Service

Feminist scholars have argued accurately that domestic service involves a three-way relationship between privileged white men, privileged white women, and poor women of color (Romero, 1992). But women have not been the only domestic workers. During the pre-World War II period, racialized and gendered immigration policies and labor conditions forced Asian men into "feminized" jobs such as domestic service, laundry work, and food preparation.[1] Due to their noncitizen status, the closed labor market, and the shortage of women, Asian immigrant men, first Chinese and later migrant men, first Chinese and later

Japanese, substituted to some extent for female labor in the American West. David Katzman (1978) noted the peculiarities of the domestic labor situation in the West in this period: "In 1880, California and Washington were the only states in which a majority of domestic servants were men" (p. 55).

At the turn of the twentieth century, lacking other job alternatives, many Chinese men entered into domestic service in private homes, hotels, and rooming houses (Daniels, 1988, p. 74). Whites rarely objected to Chinese in domestic service. In fact, through the 1900s, the Chinese houseboy was the symbol of upper-class status in San Francisco (Glenn, 1986, p. 106). As late as 1920, close to 50 percent of the Chinese in the United States were still occupied as domestic servants (Light, 1972, p. 7). Large numbers of Chinese also became laundrymen, not because laundering was a traditional male occupation in China, but because there were very few women of any ethnic origin—and thus few washerwomen—in gold-rush California (Chan, 1991, pp. 33–34). Chinese laundrymen thus provided commercial services that replaced women's unpaid labor in the home. White consumers were prepared to patronize a Chinese laundryman because as such he "occupied a status which was in accordance with the social definition of the place in the economic hierarchy suitable for a member of an 'inferior race'" (cited in Siu, 1987, p. 21). In her autobiographical fiction *China Men,* Maxine Hong Kingston presents her father and his partners as engaged in their laundry business for long periods each day—a business considered so low and debased that, in their songs, they associate it with the washing of menstrual blood (Goelnicht, 1992, p. 198). The existence of the Chinese houseboy and launderer—and their forced "bachelor" status—further bolstered the stereotype of the feminized and asexual or homosexual Asian man. Their feminization, in turn, confirmed their assignment to the state's labor force which performed "women's work."

Japanese men followed Chinese men into domestic service. By the end of the first decade of the twentieth century, the U.S. Immigration Commission estimated that 12,000 to 15,000 Japanese in the western United States earned a living in domestic service (Chan, 1991, pp. 39–40). Many Japanese men considered housework beneath them because in Japan only lower-class women worked as domestic servants (Ichioka, 1988, p. 24). Studies of Issei occupational histories indicate that a domestic job was the first occupation for many of the new arrivals; but unlike Chinese domestic workers, most Issei eventually moved on to agricultural or city trades (Glenn, 1986. p. 108). Filipino and Korean boys and men likewise relied on domestic service for their livelihood (Chan, 1991, p. 40). In his autobiography *East Goes West*, Korean immigrant writer Younghill Kang (1937) related that he worked as a domestic servant for a white family who treated him "like a cat or a dog" (p. 66).

Filipinos, as stewards in the U.S. Navy, also performed domestic duties for white U.S. naval officers during the ninety-four years of U.S. military presence in the Philippines. U.S. bases served as recruiting stations for the U.S. armed forces, particularly the navy. Soon after the United States acquired the Philippines from Spain in 1898, its navy began actively recruiting Filipinos—but only as stewards and mess attendants. Barred from admissions to other ratings, Filipino enlistees performed the work of domestics, preparing and serving the officers' meals, and caring for the officers' galley, wardroom, and living spaces. Ashore, their duties ranged from ordinary housework to food services at the U.S. Naval Academy hall. Unofficially, Filipino stewards also have been ordered to perform menial chores such as walking the officers' dogs and acting as personal servants for the officers' wives (Espiritu, 1995, p. 16).

As domestic servants, Asian men became subordinates of not only privileged white men but also privileged white women. The following testimony from a Japanese house servant captures this unequal relationship:

> Immediately the ma'am demanded me to scrub the floor. I took one hour to finish. Then I had to wash windows. That was very difficult job for me. Three windows for another hour! . . . The ma'am taught me how to cook. . . . I was sitting on the kitchen chair and thinking what a change of life it was. The ma'am came into the kitchen and was so furious! It was such a hard work for me to wash up all dishes, pans, glasses, etc., after dinner. When I went into the dining room to put all silvers on sideboard, I saw the reflection of myself on the looking glass. In a white coat and apron! I could not control my feelings. The tears so freely flowed out from my eyes, and I buried my face with my both arms (quoted in Ichioka, 1988, pp. 25–26).

The experiences of Asian male domestic service workers demonstrate that not all men benefit equally from patriarchy. Depending on their race and class, men experience gender differently. While male domination of women may tie all men together, men share unequally in the fruits of this domination. For Asian American male domestic workers, economic and social discriminations locked them into an unequal relationship with not only privileged white men but also privileged white women (Kim, 1990, p. 74).

The racist and classist devaluation of Asian men had gender implications. The available evidence indicates that immigrant men reasserted their lost patriarchal power in denigrating a weaker group: Asian women. In *China Men,* Kingston's immigrant father, having been forced into "feminine" subject positions, lapses into silence, breaking the silence only to titter curses against women (Goellnicht, 1992, pp. 200–201). Kingston (1980) traces her father's abuse of Chinese women back to his feeling of emasculation in America: "We knew that it was to feed us you had to endure demons and physical labor" (p. 13). On the other hand, some men brought home the domestic skills they learned on the jobs. Anamaria Labao Cabato relates that her Filipino-born father, who spent twenty-eight years in the navy as a steward, is "one of the best cooks around" (Espiritu, 1995, p. 143). Leo Sicat, a retired U.S. Navy man, similarly reports that "we learned how to cook in the Navy, and we brought it home. The Filipino women are very fortunate because the husband does the cooking. In our household, I do the cooking, and my wife does the washing" (Espiritu, 1995, p. 108). Along the same line, in some instances, the domestic skills which men were forced to learn in their wives' absence were put to use when husbands and wives reunited in the United States. The history of Asian male domestic workers suggests that the denigration of women is only one response to the stripping of male privilege. The other is to institute a revised domestic division of labor and gender relations in the families.

Changing Gender Relations: The Wartime Internment of Japanese Americans

Immediately after the bombing of Pearl Harbor, the incarceration of Japanese Americans began. On the night of 7 December 1941, working on the principle of guilt by association, the Federal Bureau of Investigation (FBI) began taking into custody persons of Japanese ancestry who had connections to the Japanese government. On 19 February 1942, President Franklin Delano Roosevelt signed Executive Order 9066, arbitrarily suspending civil rights of U.S. citizens by authorizing the "evacuation" of 120,000 persons of Japanese ancestry into concentration camps, of whom approximately fifty percent were women and sixty percent were U.S.-born citizens (Matsumoto, 1989, p. 116).

The camp environment—with its lack of privacy, regimented routines, and new power hierarchy—inflicted serious and lasting wounds on Japanese American family life. In the crammed twenty-by-twenty-five-foot "apartment" units, tensions were high as men, women, and children struggled to recreate family life under very trying conditions. The internment also transformed the balance of power in families: husbands lost some of their power over wives, as did parents over children. Until the internment, the Issei man had been the undisputed authority over his wife and children: he was both the breadwinner and the decision-maker for the entire family. Now "he had no rights, no home, no control over his own life" (Houston and Houston, 1973, p. 62). Most important, the internment inverted the economic roles—and thus the status and authority—of family members. With their means of livelihood cut off indefinitely, Issei men lost their role as breadwinners. Despondent over the loss of almost everything they had worked so hard to acquire, many Issei men felt useless and frustrated, particularly as their wives and children became less dependent on them. Daisuke Kitagawa (1967) reports that in the Tule Lake relocation center, "the [Issei] men looked as if they had suddenly aged ten years. They lost the capacity to plan for their own futures, let alone those of their sons and daughters" (p. 91).

Issei men responded to this emasculation in various ways. By the end of three years' internment, formerly enterprising, energetic Issei men had become immobilized with feelings of despair, hopelessness, and insecurity. Charles Kikuchi remembers his father—who "used to be a perfect terror and dictator"—spending all day lying on his cot: "He probably realizes that he no longer controls the family group and rarely exerts himself so that there is little family conflict as far as he is concerned" (Modell, 1973, p. 62). But others, like Jeanne Wakatsuki Houston's father, reasserted their patriarchal power by abusing their wives and children. Stripped of his roles as the protector and provider for his family, Houston's father "kept pursuing oblivion through drink, he kept abusing Mama, and there seemed to be no way out of it for anyone. You couldn't even run" (Houston and Houston, 1973, p. 61). The experiences of the Issei men underscore the intersections of racism and sexism—the fact that men of color live in a society that creates sex-based norms and expectations (i.e., man as breadwinner) which racism operates simultaneously to deny (Crenshaw, 1989, p. 155).

Camp life also widened the distance and deepened the conflict between the Issei and their U.S.-born children. At the root of these tensions were growing cultural rifts between the generations as well as a decline in the power and authority of the Issei fathers. The cultural rifts reflected not only a general process of acculturation, but were accelerated by the degradation of everything Japanese and the simultaneous promotion of Americanization in the camps (Chan, 1991, p. 128; see also Okihiro, 1991, pp. 229–232). The younger Nisei also spent much more time away from their parents' supervision. As a consequence, Issei parents gradually lost their ability to discipline their children, whom they seldom saw during the day. Much to the chagrin of the conservative parents, young men and women began to spend more time with each other unchaperoned—at the sports events, the dances, and other school functions. Freed from some of the parental constraints, the Nisei women socialized more with their peers and also expected to choose their own husbands and to marry for "love"—a departure from the old customs of arranged marriage (Matsumoto, 1989, p. 117). Once this occurred, the prominent role that the father played in marriage arrangements—and by extension in their children's lives—declined (Okihiro, 1991, p. 231).

Privileging U.S. citizenship and U.S. education, War Relocation Authority (WRA) policies regarding camp life further inverted the power hierarchy between the Japan-born Issei and their U.S.-born children. In the camps, only Nisei were eligible to vote and to hold office in the Community Council; Issei were excluded because of their alien status. Daisuke Kitagawa (1967) records the impact of this policy on parental authority: "In the eyes of young children, their parents were definitely inferior to their grown-up brothers and sisters, who as U.S. citizens could elect and be elected members of the Community Council. For all these reasons many youngsters lost confidence in, and respect for, their parents" (p. 88). Similarly, the WRA salary scales were based on English-speaking ability and on citizenship status. As a result, the Nisei youths and young adults could earn relatively higher wages than their fathers. This shift in earning abilities eroded the economic basis for parental authority (Matsumoto, 1989, p. 116).

At war's end in August 1945, Japanese Americans had lost much of the economic ground that they had gained in more than a generation. The majority of Issei women and men no longer had their firms, businesses, and financial savings; those who still owned property found their homes dilapidated and vandalized and their personal belongings stolen or destroyed (Broom and Riemier, 1949). The internment also ended Japanese American concentration in agriculture and small businesses. In their absence, other groups had taken over these ethnic niches. This loss further eroded the economic basis of parental authority since Issei men no longer had businesses to hand down to their Nisei sons (Broom and Riemer, 1949, p. 31). Historian Roger Daniels (1988) declared that by the end of World War II, "the generational struggle was over: the day of the Issei had passed" (286). Issei men, now in their sixties, no longer had the vigor to start over from scratch. Forced to find employment quickly after the war, many Issei couples who had owned small businesses before the war returned to the forms of manual labor in which they began a generation ago. Most men found work as janitors, gardeners, kitchen helpers, and handymen; their wives toiled as domestic servants, garment workers, and cannery workers (Yanagisako, 1987, p. 92).

Contemporary Asian America: The Disadvantaged

Relative to earlier historical periods, the economic pattern of contemporary Asian America is considerably more varied, a result of both the postwar restructured economy and the 1965 Immigration Act.[2] The dual goals of the 1965 Immigration Act—to facilitate family reunification and to admit educated workers needed by the U.S. economy—have produced two distinct chains of emigration from Asia: one comprising the relatives of working-class Asians who had immigrated to the United States prior to 1965; the other of highly trained immigrants who entered during the late 1960s and early 1970s (Liu, Ong, and Rosenstein, 1991).

Given their dissimilar backgrounds, Asian Americans "can be found throughout the income spectrum of this nation" (Ong, 1994, p. 4). In other words, today's Asian American men both join whites in the well-paid, educated, white collar sector of the workforce *and* join Latino immigrants in lower-paying secondary sector jobs (Ong and Hee, 1994). This economic diversity contradicts the model minority stereotype—the common belief that most Asian American men are college educated and in high-paying professional or technical jobs.

The contemporary Asian American community includes a sizable population with limited education, skills, and English-speaking ability. In 1990, 18 percent of Asian men and 26 percent of Asian women in the United States, age 25 and over, had less than a high school degree. Also, of the 4.1 million Asians 5 years and over, 56 percent did not speak English "very well" and 35 percent were linguistically isolated (U.S. Bureau of the Census, 1993, Table 2). The median income for those with limited English was $20,000 for males and $15,600 for females; for those with less than a high school degree, the figures were $18,000 and $15,000, respectively. Asian American men and women with both limited English-speaking ability and low levels of education fared the worst. For a large portion of this disadvantaged population, even working full-time, full-year brought in less than $10,000 in earnings (Ong and Hee, 1994, p. 45).

The disadvantaged population is largely a product of immigration: Nine tenths are immigrants (Ong and Hee, 1994). The majority enter as relatives of the pre-1956 working-class Asian immigrants. Because immigrants tend to have socioeconomic backgrounds similar to those of their sponsors, most family reunification immigrants represent a continuation of the unskilled and semiskilled Asian labor that emigrated before 1956 (Liu, Ong, and Rosenstein, 1991). Southeast Asian refugees, particularly the second-wave refugees who arrived after 1978, represent another largely disadvantaged group. This is partly so because refugees are less likely to have acquired readily transferable skills and are more likely to have made investments (in training and education) specific to the country of origin (Chiswick, 1979; Monero, 1980). For example, there are significant numbers of southeast Asian military men with skills for which there is no longer a market in the United States. In 1990, the overall economic status of the Southeast Asian population was characterized by unstable, minimum-wage employment, welfare dependency and participation in the informal economy (Gold and Kibria, 1993). These economic facts underscore the danger of lumping all Asian Americans together because many Asian men do not share in the relatively favorable socioeconomic outcomes attributed to the "average" Asian American.

Lacking the skills and education to catapult them into the primary sector of the economy, disadvantaged Asian American men and women work in the secondary labor market—the labor-intensive, low-capital service, and small manufacturing sectors. In this labor market, disadvantaged men generally have fewer employment options than women. This is due in part to the decline of male-occupied manufacturing jobs and the concurrent growth of female-intensive industries in the United States, particularly in service, microelectronics, and apparel manufacturing. The garment industry, microelectronics, and canning industries are top employers of immigrant women (Takaki, 1989, p. 427; Mazumdar, 1989, p. 19; Villones, 1989, p. 176; Hossfeld, 1994, pp. 71–72). In a study of Silicon Valley (California's famed high-tech industrial region), Karen Hossfeld (1994) reported that the employers interviewed preferred to hire immigrant women over immigrant men for entry-level, operative jobs (p. 74). The employers' "gender logic" was informed by the patriarchal and racist beliefs that women can afford to work for less, do not mind dead-end jobs, and are more suited physiologically to certain kinds of detailed and routine work. As Linda Lim (1983) observes, it is the "*comparative disadvantage* of women in the wage-labor market that gives them a comparative advantage vis-à-vis men in the occupations and industries where they are concentrated—so-called female ghettoes of employment" (p. 78). A white male production manager and hiring supervisor in a California Silicon Valley assembly shop discusses his formula for hiring:

> Just three things I look for in hiring [entry-level, high-tech manufacturing operatives]: small, foreign, and female. You find those three things and you're pretty much automatically guaranteed the right kind of work force. These little foreign gals are grateful to be hired—very, very grateful—no matter what (Hossfeld, 1994, p. 65).

Refugee women have also been found to be more in demand than men in secretarial, clerical, and interpreter jobs in social service work. In a study of Cambodian refugees in Stockton, California, Shiori Ui (1991) found that social service agency executives preferred to hire Cambodian women over men when both had the same qualifications. One executive explained his preference, "It seems that some ethnic populations relate better to women than men. . . . Another thing is that the pay is so bad" (cited in Ui, 1991, p. 169). As a result, in the Cambodian communities in Stockton, it is often women—and not men—who have greater economic opportunities and who are the primary breadwinners in their families (Ui, 1991, p. 171).

Due to the significant decline in the economic contributions of Asian immigrant men, women's earnings comprise an equal or greater share of the family income. Because the wage each earns is low, only by pooling incomes can a husband and wife earn enough to support a family (Glenn, 1983, p. 42). These shifts in resources have challenged the patriarchal authority of Asian men. Men's loss of status and power—not only in the public but also in the domestic arena—places severe pressure on their sense of well-being. Responding to this pressure, some men accepted the new division of labor in the family (Ui, 1991, pp. 170–173); but many others resorted to spousal abuse and divorce (Luu, 1989, p. 68). A Korean immigrant man describes his frustrations over changing gender roles and expectations:

> In Korea [my wife] used to have breakfast ready for me. . . . She didn't do it any more because she said she was too busy getting ready to go to work. If I complained she talked back at me, telling me to fix my own breakfast. . . . I was very frustrated about her, started fighting and hit her (Yim, 1978, quoted in Mazumdar, 1989, p. 18).

Loss of status and power has similarly led to depression and anxieties in Hmong males. In particular, the women's ability—and the men's inability—to earn money for households "has undermined severely male omnipotence" (Irby and Pon, 1988, p. 112). Male unhappiness and helplessness can be detected in the following joke told at a family picnic, "When we get on the plane to go back to Laos, the first thing we will do is beat up the women!" The joke—which generated laughter by both men and women—drew upon a combination of "the men's unemployability, the sudden economic value placed on women's work, and men's

fear of losing power in their families" (Donnelly, 1994, pp. 74–75). As such, it highlights the interconnections of race, class, and gender—the fact that in a racist and classist society, working-class men of color have limited access to economic opportunities and thus limited claim to patriarchal authority.

Conclusion

A central task in feminist scholarship is to expose and dismantle the stereotypes that traditionally have provided ideological justifications for women's subordination. But to conceptualize oppression only in terms of male dominance and female subordination is to obscure the centrality of classism, racism, and other forms of inequality in U.S. society (Stacey and Thorne, 1985, p. 311). The multiplicities of Asian men's lives indicate that ideologies of manhood and womanhood have as much to do with class and race as they have to do with sex. The intersections of race, gender, and class mean that there are also hierarchies among women and among men and that some women hold power over certain groups of men. The task for feminist scholars, then, is to develop paradigms that articulate the complicity among these categories of oppression, that strengthen the alliance between gender and ethnic studies, and that reach out not only to women, but also to men, of color.

Notes

1. One of the most noticeable characteristics of pre-World War II Asian America was a pronounced shortage of women. During this period, U.S. immigration policies barred the entry of most Asian women. America's capitalist economy also wanted Asian male workers but not their families. In most instances, families were seen as a threat to the efficiency and exploitability of the workforce and were actively prohibited.

2. The 1965 Immigration Act ended Asian exclusion and equalized immigration rights for all nationalities. No longer constrained by exclusion

laws, Asian immigrants began arriving in much larger numbers than every before. In the 1980s, Asia was the largest source of U.S. legal immigrants, accounting for 40 percent to 47 percent of the total influx (Min, 1995, p. 12).

References

Broom, Leonard and Ruth Riemer. 1949. *Removal and Return: The Socio-Economic Effects of the War on Japanese Americans*. Berkeley: University of California Press.

Chan, Sucheng. 1991. *Asian Americans: An Interpretive History*. Boston: Twayne.

Cheung, King-Kok. 1990. "The Woman Warrior Versus the Chinaman Pacific: Must a Chinese American Critic Choose Between Feminism and Heroism?" Pp. 23–251 in *Conflicts in Feminism*, edited by Marianne Hirsch and Evelyn Fox Keller. New York and London: Routledge.

Cheswick, Barry. 1979. "The Economic Progress of Immigrants: some apparently universal patterns." In W. Fellner (ED.), *Contemporary Economic Problems*. pp. 357–399. Washington, DC: American Enterprise Institute.

Crenshaw, Kimberlee. 1989. "Demarginalizing the Intersection of Race and Sex: A Black Feminist Critique of Antidiscrimination Doctrine, Feminist Theory and Antiracist Politics." In *University of Chicago Legal Forum: Feminism in the Law: Theory, Practice, and Criticism* (pp. 139–167). Chicago: University of Chicago Press.

Daniels, Roger. 1988. *Asian America: Chinese and Japanese in the United States Since 1850*. Seattle: Washington University Press.

Donnelly, Nancy D. 1994. *Changing Lives of Refugee Hmong Women*. Seattle: Washington University Press.

Espiritu, Yen Le. 1995. *Filipino American Lives*. Philadelphia: Temple University Press.

Espiritu, Yen Le. 1996. *Asian American Women and Men: Labor, Laws, and Love*. Thousand Oaks, CA: Sage.

Fong-Torres, Ben. 1995. "Why Are There No Male Asian Anchormen on TV?" Pp. 208–211 in *Men's Lives*, 3rd ed., edited by Michael S. Kimmel and Michael A. Messner. Boston: Allyn and Bacon.

Gaines, Jane. 1990. "White Privilege and Looking Relations: Race and Gender in Feminist Film Theory." Pp. 197–214 in *Issues in Feminist Film Criticism*, edited by Patricia Erens. Bloomington: Indiana University Press.

Glenn, Evelyn Nakano. 1983. "Split Household, Small Producer and Dual Wage Earner: An Analysis of Chinese-American Family Strategies." *Journal of Marriage and the Family*. February 35–46.

Glenn, Evelyn Nakano. 1986. *Issei, Nisei, War Bride: Three Generations of Japanese American Women at Domestic Service*. Philadelphia: Temple University Press.

Goellnicht, Donald C. 1992. "Tang Ao in America: Male Subject Positions in *China Men*." Pp. 191–212 in *Reading the Literatures of Asian America*, edited by Shirley Geok-lin-Lim and Amy Ling. Philadelphia: Temple University Press.

Gold, Steve and Nazli Kibria. 1993. "Vietnamese Refugees and Blocked Mobility." *Asian and Pacific Migration Review* 2:27–56.

Hamamoto, Darrell. 1994. *Monitored Peril: Asian Americans and the Politics of Representation*. Minneapolis: University of Minnesota Press.

Hossfeld, Karen J. 1994. "Hiring Immigrant Women: Silicon Valley's 'Simple Formula.'" Pp. 65–93 in *Women of Color in U.S. Society*, edited by Maxine Baca Zinn and Bonnie Thornton Dill. Philadelphia: Temple University Press.

Houston, Jeanne Wakatsuki and James D. Houston. 1973. *Farewell to Manzanar*. San Francisco: Houghton Mifflin.

Ichioka, Yuji. 1988. *The Issei: The World of the First Generation Japanese Immigrants, 1885–1924*. New York: The Free Press.

Irby, Charles and Ernest M. Pon. 1988. "Confronting New Mountains: Mental Health Problems Among Male Hmong and Mien Refugees. *Amerasia Journal* 14: 109–118.

Kang, Younghill. 1937. *East Goes West*. New York: C. Scribner's Sons.

Katzman, David. 1978. "Domestic Service: Women's Work." Pp. 377–391 in *Women Working: Theories and Facts in Perspective*, edited by Ann Stromberg and Shirley Harkess. Palo Alto: Mayfield.

Kim, Elaine. 1990. "'Such Opposite Creatures': Men and Women in Asian American Literature." *Michigan Quarterly Review*, 68–93.

Kingston, Maxine Hong. 1980. *China Men*. New York: Knopf.

Kitagawa, Daisuke. 1967. *Issei and Nisei: The Internment Years*. New York: Seabury Press.

Kitano, Harry H. L. 1991. "The Effects of the Evacuation on the Japanese Americans." Pp. 151–162 in *Japanese Americans: From Relocation to Redress*, edited by Roger Daniels, Sandra C. Taylor, and Harry Kitano. Seattle: University of Washington Press.

Light, Ivan. 1972. *Ethnic Enterprise in America: Business and Welfare Among Chinese, Japanese, and Blacks*. Berkeley and Los Angeles: University of California Press.

Lim, Linda Y. C. 1983. "Capitalism, Imperialism, and Patriarchy: The Dilemma of Third-World Women Workers in Multinational Factories." Pp. 70–91 in *Women, Men, and the International Division of Labor*, edited by June Nash and Maria Patricia Fernandez-Kelly. Albany: State University of New York.

Liu, John, Paul Ong, and Carolyn Rosenstein. 1991. "Dual Chain Migration: Post-1965 Filipino Immigration to the United States." *International Migration Review* 25 (3):487–513.

Luu, Van. 1989. "The Hardships of Escape for Vietnamese Women." Pp. 60–72 in *Making Waves: An Anthology of Writings by and about Asian American Women*, edited by Asian Women United of California. Boston: Beacon Press.

Matsumoto, Valerie. 1989. "Nisei Women and Resettlement During World War II." Pp. 115–126 in *Making Waves: An Anthology of Writings by and about Asian American Women*, edited by Asian Women United of California. Boston: Beacon Press.

Mazumdar, Sucheta. 1989. "General Introduction: A Woman-Centered Perspective on Asian American History." Pp. 1–22 in *Making Waves: An Anthology of Writings by and about Asian American Women*, edited by Asian Women United of California. Boston: Beacon Press.

Min, Pyong Gap. 1995. "Korean Americans." Pp. 199–231 in *Asian Americans: Contemporary Trends and Issues*, edited by Pyong Gap Min. Thousand Oaks, CA: Sage.

Modell, John, ed. 1973. *The Kikuchi Diary: Chronicle from an American Concentration Camp*. Urbana: University of Illinois Press.

Montero, Darrell. 1980. *Vietnamese Americans: Patterns of Settlement and Socioeconomic Adaptation in the United States*. Boulder, CO: Westview.

Okihiro, Gary Y. 1991. *Cane Fires: The Anti-Japanese Movement in Hawaii, 1865–1945*. Philadelphia: Temple University Press.

Ong, Paul. 1994. "Asian Pacific Americans and Public Policy."

Ong, Paul and Suzanne Hee. 1994. "Economic Diversity." Pp. 31–56 in the *The State of Asian Pacific America: Economic Diversity, Issues, & Policies*, edited by Paul Ong. Los Angeles: LEAP Asian Pacific American Public Policy Institute and UCLA Asian American Studies Center.

Romero, Mary. 1992. *Maid in the U.S.A.* New York: Routledge.

Siu, Paul. 1987. *The Chinese Laundryman: A Study in Social Isolation*. New York: New York University Press.

Stacey, Judith and Barrie Thorne. 1985. "The Missing Feminist Revolution in Sociology." *Social Problems* 32:301–316.

Takaki, Ronald. 1989. *Strangers from a Different Shore: A History of Asian Americans*. Boston: Little, Brown.

Ui, Shiori. 1991. "'Unlikely Heroes': The Evolution of Female Leadership in a Cambodian Ethnic Enclave." Pp. 161–177 in *Ethnography Unbound: Power and Resistance in the Modern Metropolis*, edited by Michael Burawoy et al. Berkeley: University of California Press.

U.S. Bureau of the Census. 1993. *We the American Asians*. Washington, DC: U.S. Government Printing Office.

Villones, Rebecca. 1989. "Women in the Silicon Valley." Pp. 172–176 in *Making Waves: An Anthology of Writings by and about Asian American Women*, edited by Asian Women United of California. Boston: Beacon Press.

Wiegman, Robyn. 1991. "Black Bodies/American Commodities: Gender, Race, and the Bourgeois Ideal in Contemporary Film." Pp. 308–328 in *Unspeakable Images: Ethnicity and the American Cinema*, edited by Lester Friedman. Urbana and Chicago: University of Illinois Press.

Yanagisako, Sylvia Junko. 1987. "Mixed Metaphors: Native and Anthropological Models of Gender and Kinship Domains." Pp. 86–118 in *Gender and Kinship: Essays Toward a Unified Analysis*, edited by Jane Fishburne Collier and Sylvia Junko Yanagisako. Stanford: Stanford University Press.

20

Teaching the Boys:
New Research on Masculinity and Gender Strategies for Schools

R. W. Connell

I. What about the Boys?

Educational Questions

In recent years, controversies about boys, men, and education have boiled up in a number of countries. In the United States, a proposal to establish boys-only public schools in Detroit was halted at the last minute in 1991 by legal action that declared them discriminatory. In Australia, after media controversy about boys' academic "failure" relative to girls, a parliamentary inquiry into boys' education was launched in 1994. In Germany, educational programs on gender issues have multiplied outside the schools, both for youth and for men. In Japan, debate has begun about the prospects for a new "men's studies."[1]

This is not the first time such issues have been aired. At the end of the 1960s, for instance, there was a minor panic in the United States about schools' destroying "boy culture" and denying boys their "reading rights" because of the prevalence of women teachers and the "feminine, frilly content" of elementary education.[2]

The context, however, has changed. Second-wave feminism has now influenced public thinking for more than two decades, and one of its long-term consequences has been to unsettle traditional ideas about men and masculinity. A surprisingly popular therapeutic men's movement, whose best-known figure is Robert Bly, has made an issue of men's emotional troubles and boys' difficulties in acquiring a secure masculinity. In the United States, the "Promise Keepers" and the "Million Man March" show the resonance of such issues for religious conservatives and the black community. Some pop psychologists work up statistics of men's troubles (such as earlier death and

From *Teachers College Record*, 98, pp. 206-235. Reprinted by permission of Teachers College Record and the author.

higher rates of injury) into claims that men, not women, are the truly disadvantaged sex.[3]

Similar claims are increasingly heard in education. Discrimination against girls has ended, the argument runs. Indeed, thanks to feminism, girls have special treatment and special programs. Now, what about the boys? It is boys who are slower to learn to read, more likely to drop out of school, more likely to be disciplined, more likely to be in programs for children with special needs. In school it is girls who are doing better, boys who are in trouble—and special programs for boys that are needed.[4]

More heat than light has been generated by these claims. Counter-claims are made: that for girls, success in schooling does not translate into postschool equality; that boys get more attention in school than girls at present; that programs for boys would entrench privilege, not contest it.[5] The media love to turn the issue into a pro-girl versus pro-boy (or pro-feminist versus antifeminist) shootout.

But the educational issues are far more complex. How real is the formal equality provided by coeducation? Are girls benefited in some ways, boys in others? How far can we make generalizations about "boys" as a bloc? If boys are having trouble in school, which boys, and what are the sources of their trouble? How far can schools affect masculinity and its enactment? If they can affect masculinity at all, through what kind of programs, and what kind of pedagogy, should they try?

It is clear from responses to current debates about boys that many teachers and parents see these issues as urgent. Schools are launching "programs for boys" whether researchers and policymakers give them guidance or not. Some of the resulting efforts are, unfortunately, little informed by accurate knowledge or careful thinking

about masculinity. Equally unfortunately, researchers have not done a great deal to help the schools. It is time for this situation to change. It can change, because a new generation of social-scientific research on masculinity allows a fresh understanding of the issues in education.

The purpose of this article is to provide a framework for thinking about gender issues in the education of boys, focusing on the industrialized countries. The rest of Part I summarizes the main conclusions of the new masculinity research, and considers the place of the school in the broader process of masculinity formation. In the light of these results, Parts II and III examine educational research, especially ethnographies, for evidence on the making of masculinities in schools—looking first at schools as agents, then at pupils. Part IV uses the results of this analysis to explore the logic of educational work with boys. Part V returns to the public controversies about boys' education and considers the groups and interests in play, and the prospects of changing gender relations.

The New Research on Masculinity

In the last ten years, international social-science research on masculinity has expanded dramatically and moved in new directions. A picture is emerging that differs significantly from older ideas of the "male sex role," and even more from conceptions of "natural" masculinity.[6] Major conclusions of this research are:

1. Multiple Masculinities. Historians and anthropologists have shown that there is no one pattern of masculinity that is found everywhere. Different cultures, and different periods of history, construct masculinity differently. Some cultures make heroes of soldiers, and regard violence as the ultimate test of masculinity; others look at soldiering with disdain and regard violence as contemptible. Some cultures regard homosexual sex as incompatible with true masculinity; others think no one can be a real man without having had homosexual relationships.[7]

It follows that in multicultural societies such as the contemporary United States there are likely to be multiple definitions of masculinity. Sociological research shows this to be true. There are, for instance, differences in the expression of masculinity between Latino and Anglo men in the United States, and between Greek and Anglo boys in Australia. The meaning of masculinity in working-class life is different from the meaning in middle-class life, not to mention among the very rich and the very poor.[8]

Equally important, more than one kind of masculinity can be found within a given cultural setting. Within any workplace, neighborhood, or peer group, there are likely to be different understandings of masculinity and different ways of "doing" masculinity. In the urban middle class, for instance, there is a version of masculinity organized around dominance (e.g., emphasizing "leadership" in management) and another version organized around expertise (e.g., emphasizing "professionalism" and technical knowledge).[9]

2. Hierarchy and Hegemony. Different masculinities do not sit side-by-side like dishes in a smorgasbord; there are definite relations between them. Typically, some masculinities are more honored than others. Some may be actively dishonored, for example, homosexual masculinities in modern Western culture. Some are socially marginalized, for example, the masculinities of disempowered ethnic minorities. Some are exemplary, taken as symbolizing admired traits, for example, the masculinities of sporting heroes.[10]

The form of masculinity that is culturally dominant in a given setting is called *hegemonic masculinity.* "Hegemonic" signifies a position of cultural authority and leadership, not total dominance; other forms of masculinity persist alongside. The hegemonic form need not be the most common form of masculinity. (This is familiar in school peer groups, for instance, where a small number of highly influential boys are admired by many others who cannot reproduce their performance.) Hegemonic masculinity is, however, highly visible. It is likely to be what casual commentators have noticed when they speak of "the male role."[11]

Hegemonic masculinity is hegemonic not just in relation to other masculinities, but in relation to the gender order as a whole. It is an expression of the privilege men *collectively* have over women. The hierarchy of masculinities is an expression of the unequal shares in that privilege held by different groups of men.[12]

3. Collective Masculinities. The gender structures of a society define particular patterns of conduct as "masculine" and others as "feminine." At one level, these patterns characterize individuals. Thus we say that a particular man (or woman) is masculine, or behaves in a masculine way. But these patterns also exist at the collective level. Masculinities are defined and sustained in institutions, such as corporations, armies, governments—or schools. Masculinities are defined collectively in the workplace, as shown in industrial research; and in informal groups like street gangs, as shown in criminological research.[13]

Masculinity also exists impersonally in culture. Video games such as Mortal Kombat, for instance, not only circulate stereotyped images of violent masculinity; they require the player to enact this masculinity (symbolically) in order to play the game at all. Sociological research on sport has shown how an aggressive masculinity is created organizationally by the structure of organized sport, by its pattern of competition, its system of training, and its steep hierarchy of levels and rewards. Images of this masculinity are circulated on an enormous scale by sports media, though most individuals fit very imperfectly into the slots thus created.[14]

4. Active Construction. Masculinities do not exist prior to social behavior, either as bodily states or as fixed personalities. Rather, masculinities come into existence as people act. They are accomplished in everyday conduct or organizational life, as configurations of social practice.

Ethnomethodological research has shown how we "do gender" in everyday life, for instance, in the way we conduct conversations. A similar insight has thrown new light on the link between masculinity and crime. This is not a product of a fixed masculine character being expressed through crime; rather, it results from a variety of people—from impoverished youth gangs on the street to white-collar criminals at the computer—using crime as a resource to construct particular masculinities. Masculinities, it appears, are far from settled. From bodybuilders in the gym, to managers in the boardroom, to boys in the elementary school playground, a whole lot of people are working very hard to produce what they believe to be appropriate masculinities.[15]

5. Layering. One of the key reasons why masculinities are not settled is that they are not simple, homogeneous patterns. Close-focus research on gender, in both psychoanalysis and ethnography, often reveals contradictory desires and logics. A man's active heterosexuality may exist as a thin emotional layer concealing a deeper homosexual desire; a boy's identification with men may coexist or struggle with identification with women; the public enactment of an exemplary masculinity may covertly require actions that undermine it.[16]

The layering of desires, emotions, or logics may not be obvious at first glance, but the issue is important to investigate because such contradictions are sources of tension and change in gender patterns.

6. Dynamics. From the fact that different masculinities exist in different cultures and historical epochs, we can deduce that masculinities are amenable to change. In the layering of masculinities we see one of the sources of change, and in the hierarchy of masculinities we see one of the motives. Historians have traced changes in masculinity as struggles for hegemony—for instance, redefining patterns of managerial masculinity in British manufacturing industry, or capturing old forms of masculine practice (such as the duel in nineteenth-century France) for rising social groups.[17]

To speak of the "dynamics" of masculinity is to acknowledge that particular masculinities are composed, historically, and may also be decomposed, contested, and replaced. There is an active politics of gender in everyday life. Sometimes it finds spectacular public expression, as in the Million Man March; more often it is local and limited. But however muted, the dynamics of masculinity is an important issue for educators, since educational agendas flow from the possibilities of change in gender relations.

The Place and Limits of School Processes

Since schools are routinely blamed for social problems of every description, from unemployment to godlessness, it is not surprising that they should also be blamed for problems about boys. It is, therefore, important to register the fact that the school is not the only institution shaping masculinities, and may not be the most important. Psycho-analysis has made us familiar with the emotional dynamics of the family as an influence on gender, an argument recently renewed—and carefully located in the history of gender relations—in Nielsen and Rudberg's developmental model of gender formation.[18] The sociology of culture makes us aware of the importance of mass communications in the contemporary gender order. Media research documents what we know intuitively, that mass media are crammed with representations of masculinities—from rock music, beer commercials, sit-coms, action movies, and war films to news programs—that circulate on a vast scale.[19]

Given these forces, why pay attention to the school? Teachers discussing problems about boys often suggest that they are confronting intractable patterns fixed outside the school. Certainly children bring conceptions of masculinity into the school with them. Jordan has wittily documented the "Warrior Narratives" brought into an Australian kindergarten, where some of the boys disrupted a carefully nonsexist regime by playing games involving guns, fighting, and fast cars. This is hardly an isolated experience; witness the Ninja Turtles and X-Men of the American second-grade classroom studied by Dyson.[20]

Such a feeling among teachers is reinforced by the two most popular explanations of masculinity in recent decades. The first is the "sociobiological" view that masculine behavior springs from the biological nature of men and boys: that it is coded in the genes, a result of testosterone, and so forth. Bodily difference is, of course, important in gender, which broadly can be understood as the structure through which reproductive relationships and differences are drawn into the historical process of human society. To say this is *not*, however, to agree that there is a "biological basis" for masculinity. The

historical and ethnographic research mentioned above demonstrates that there is no standard pattern of masculinity that biology could have produced. Careful examination of the arguments about testosterone shows there is no one-way determination of behavior by hormones; indeed, there is evidence that social structure influences the production of hormones! Masculinity is not a biological entity that exists prior to society; rather, masculinities are ways that societies interpret and employ male bodies.[21]

The second popular interpretation of masculinity sees it as the internalization of a "male sex role," following broad cultural expectations for men. Sex-role theory was the intellectual framework of the liberal feminism that launched affirmative action programs for girls in the 1970s. Role theory attributes more importance to education than sociobiology does, but treats schools essentially as conduits for society-wide norms, and children as passive recipients of socialization. The approach gives little understanding of the detail of school life, such as girls using conventions of femininity to *resist* control, or boys producing multiple masculinities. Role theory is notoriously unable to grasp issues of power, or to grasp the diversity of race and class. Though "sex-role" language remains the most common way of talking about gender in schools, it is fundamentally inadequate as a conceptual framework.[22]

That the school is an important player in the shaping of modern masculinities can be suggested, but not demonstrated, by research within schools. It is more strongly demonstrated from outside, for instance, by life-history studies of masculinity such as Messner's work on American athletes, or my research with groups of Australian men.[23] Schools figure significantly in these narratives, for instance, in the preparation and choice of an athletic career. The practical judgment of parents, reflected in the demand for "boys' programs," is also not to be ignored. Though we will never have a simple way of measuring the relative influence of different institutions, there seems to be good warrant for considering schools one of the major sites of masculinity formation.

A "site" can be understood in two ways. It can be examined as an institutional *agent* of the process. To understand this, we must explore the structures and practices by which the school forms masculinities among its pupils. Alternatively, we can examine the school as the *setting* in which other agencies are in play, especially the agency of the pupils themselves. Parts II and III of this article explore these two aspects of the school in turn.

Since almost all the discussion of gender focuses on gender difference, we should from the start be alert to gender *similarity*. Public controversies over gender differences in educational outcomes ("The girls are beating the boys!") persistently ignore the extent of overlap, focusing on small differences between means and ignoring measures of dispersion.

Many educational practices iron out gender differences. Common curriculum, shared timetable, and the experience of living daily in the same architecture and the same classroom routines are not trivial parts of boys' and girls' school experience. Teachers may deliberately set out to de-emphasize gender difference, laying their emphasis on individual growth, as King noted about British infant schools in the heyday of 1970s progressivism.[24] The whole history of feminism shows that education systems can be a force for gender equity as well as inequality. This issue can lead to serious problems in the interpretation of quantitative research, of the very common kind that goes looking for statistical differences between groups of boys and girls. Schools may be having a gender *effect* without producing gender *difference*. The school is having a gender effect, for instance, when it changes gender relations so as to produce more similarity.

II. Schools as Agents in the Making of Masculinities

Schools' Gender Regimes

A key step in understanding gender in schools is to "think institutionally," as Hansot and Tyack argue. While their research concerned the large-scale history of segregated schooling, the point also applies to the individual school. As with corporations, workplaces, and the state, gender is embedded in the institutional arrangements through which a school functions: divisions of labor, authority patterns, and so on. The totality of these arrangements is a school's *gender regime*. Gender regimes differ between schools, though within limits set by the broader culture and the constraints of the local education system.[25]

Theoretical work on gender allows us to sort out the different components of a school's gender regime. Four types of relationships are involved:

1. Power Relations. These include supervision and authority among teachers and patterns of dominance, harassment, and control over resources among pupils. A familiar and important pattern is the association of masculinity with authority, and the concentration of men in supervisory positions in school systems. Among pupils, power relations may be equally visible. Prendergast's ethnography in a British working-class high school shows, for instance, how control over playground space for informal football games was crucial in maintaining the hegemony of an aggressive, physical masculinity in this school's peer group life.[26]

2. Division of Labor. This includes work specializations among teachers, such as concentrations of women in domestic science, language, and literature teaching, and men in science, mathematics, and industrial arts. It also includes the informal specializations among pupils, from the elementary classroom where a teacher asks for a "big strong boy" to help move a piece of furniture, to the gendered choice of electives in vocational education at secondary and post-secondary levels.

3. Patterns of Emotion. What the sociologist Hochschild has called the "feeling rules" for occupations can be found in teaching, often associated with specific roles in a school: the tough deputy principal, the drama teacher, and so forth. Among the most important feeling rules in schools are those concerned with sexuality. As research in both Britain and Canada suggests, the prohibition on homosexuality may be particularly important in definitions of masculinity.[27]

4. Symbolization. Schools import much of the symbolization of gender from the wider culture, but they have their own symbol systems too: uniforms and dress codes, formal and informal language codes, and so forth. A particularly important symbolic structure in education is the gendering of knowledge, the defining of certain areas of the curriculum as masculine and others as feminine.

Through these intersecting structures of relationships, schools create institutional definitions of masculinity. Such definitions are impersonal; they exist as social facts. Pupils participate in these masculinities simply by entering the school and living in its structures. The terms on which they participate, however, are negotiable—whether adjusting to the patterns, rebelling against them, or trying to modify them.

Gender regimes need not be internally coherent, and they are certainly subject to change. This is vividly shown in Draper's recent account of the "re-establishment of gender relations following a school merger" in Britain, an unusual study that catches gender arrangements in the midst of change. It shows how different groups of pupils and teachers involved in the merger had conflicting agendas and interests, with sometimes startling results—from boys wearing eyeshadow to girls subverting school uniform.[28]

Teachers' autobiographies, especially those of feminist teachers, contain many narratives of encounters with oppressive gender regimes in schools and of attempts—sometimes successful—to change them.[29] Children as well as teachers work on the gender regime. In the American elementary schools studied by Thorne, the meanings of gender were constantly being debated and revised by the children, the gender boundaries both enforced and challenged on the playground and in classrooms.[30]

Masculinizing Practices

There is no mystery about why some schools made masculinities: They were intended to. Dr. Arnold, the famous reforming headmaster of Rugby, saw the private schools of nineteenth-century Britain as moral machinery for molding Christian gentlemen. A fascinating historical study, Heward's *Making a Man of Him*, traces the effects some generations after Dr. Arnold. Using letters to and from the headmaster, Heward reconstructs the interplay between Ellesmere College, a minor private school, and the class and gender strategies of its boys' families. The school defined and enforced a suitable masculinity among its boys through rigidly enforced conventional dress, discipline (prefects having the authority to beat younger boys), academic competition and hierarchy (emphasized by constant testing), team games, and gender segregation among the staff. In the wake of the Great Depression, Ellesmere modified its formula, increasing its academic and vocational emphasis and decreasing its emphasis on sport.[31]

The discipline, dress code, and so forth can be considered a set of *masculinizing practices* governed by the gender regime of the school. Different circumstances produce different formulas. In another illuminating historical study, Morrell traces the production of a rugged, rather than cerebral, masculinity on the colonial frontier. The white boarding schools of Natal, South Africa, in the half-century to 1930, also used the prefect system and gender segregation. But these schools laid more emphasis on toughness and physical hierarchy among the boys, through masculinizing practices such as initiation, "fagging," physical punishment, and spartan living conditions. This agenda was obviously connected with the context of colonial conquest, and the goal of maintaining racial power over colonized peoples.[32]

These vehement gender regimes show the potential of the school as a masculinity-making device, but such cases are hardly the norm in contemporary public education. Coeducation has muted the masculinizing agenda—but has it been eliminated?

In some ways, coeducational settings make it easier to mark difference, that is, to establish symbolic oppositions between girls and boys. School uniforms or conventions of dress, separate toilets, forms of address, practices such as lining boys and girls up separately, or creating classroom competitions of "the boys" against "the girls" all do this job. Formal texts may reinforce the lesson from popular culture that masculinity is defined by difference from femininity. As

Sleeter and Grant have shown in a study of textbooks used in American schools up to grade eight, gender patterns have persisted despite a recent shift by writers and publishers to nonsexist language. Representations of men have remained more stereotyped than those of women.[33]

Broad features of coeducational schools' gender regimes thus sustain particular definitions of masculinity. Does this turn into a positive masculinizing practice? Studies of particular areas of schools' work indicate that it does. A case in point is the schools' treatment of sexuality. Sex education classes generally teach an unreflective heterosexual interpretation of students' desires, in which masculine sexuality is defined by a future of marriage and fatherhood. This can be seen in Trudell's remarkably detailed ethnography of sex education in an American high school.[34]

Since formal sex education is mostly ineffective, such classes will probably not be a major source of gender meanings for the pupils. But, as Mac an Ghaill's important British study of school sexuality and masculinity demonstrates, these ideas are backed by a much wider range of practices. A heterosexual construction of masculine and feminine as opposites (as in "the opposite sex," "opposites attract") runs through a great deal of the school's informal culture and curriculum content. Homosexual experience is generally blanked out from the official curriculum. Gay youth are liable to experience hostility from school officials and straight youth, while teachers experience heavy constraint in dealing with sexual diversity.[35]

Coeducational schools, then, typically operate with an informal but powerful ideology of gender difference, and do put pressure on boys to conform to it. In certain areas of the school's gender regime the pressure approaches that of the vehement regimes discussed above, and a regular vortex of masculinity formation can be seen.

Masculinity Vortices

Boys' Subjects

The first vortex arises in the gender division of labor and symbolization. Most of the academic curriculum is common to girls and boys, and while certainly conveying gender messages, does so diffusely.

But in certain areas of study, pathways diverge and gender messages become more concentrated. Grant and Sleeter's study of "Five Bridges" junior high school in the United States found that while the school made an equal formal offer of learning to boys and girls, it allowed virtual segregation in some subject areas. These were especially practical subjects such as shop and child development. Indeed, the school cued this segregation by its own gender division of labor among teachers.[36]

This is a widespread pattern. Systemwide data on subject enrollments in New South Wales (Australia) secondary schools show a minority of subjects with marked gender differences in enrollment. They include physics and chemistry, engineering, and industrial technology, where boys predominate; and home science, textiles, and design, where girls do.[37]

This segregation does not arise by chance; these curriculum areas are culturally gendered. Industrial arts (shop) teaching, for instance, is historically connected with manual trades where there was a strong culture of workplace masculinity and where women used to be excluded. As Mealyea's case study of new industrial arts teachers demonstrates, it can be difficult for men with backgrounds in such trades to accept the new policies of gender equity and inclusiveness.[38]

Academic subjects may also have strong gender meanings. It has long been recognized that physical sciences are culturally defined as masculine and have a concentration of men teachers. Martino's sophisticated analysis of secondary classes in Western Australia shows how subject English, by contrast, is feminized. In the eyes of many of the boys, English classes are distanced by their focus on the expression of emotions, their apparent irrelevance to men's work, the lack of set rules and unique answers, and the contrast with activities defined as properly masculine, such as sport.[39]

Discipline

The second vortex is linked to power relations. Adult control in schools is enforced by a disciplinary system that often becomes a focus of masculinity formation.

Teachers from infants to secondary level may use gender as a means of control, for instance, shaming boys by saying they are "acting like a girl." Punishment too is liable to be gendered. When corporal punishment was legal, boys were much more often beaten than girls. Nonviolent punishments still bear down more heavily on boys. For instance, a recent study of suspensions in a working-class area of Sydney found that 84 percent of the pupils suspended were boys, as were 87 percent of the pupils with repeat suspensions.[40]

Where the hegemony of the school is secure, boys may learn to wield disciplinary power themselves as part of their learning of masculine hierarchy. This was the basis of the old prefect system. Where hegemony is lacking, a "protest masculinity" may be constructed through defiance of authority, all too familiar in working-class schools.[41] With corporal punishment, defiance requires bravery in the face of pain, a masculinity test of the crudest kind. Even with nonviolent discipline, such as the "punishing room" in the African-American school studied by Ferguson, the contest with authority can become a focus of excitement, labeling, and the formation of masculine identities.[42]

Sport

The third vortex blends power, symbolization, and emotion in a particularly potent combination. Here the schools are using consumer society's key device for defining hegemonic masculinity.[43]

Foley's ethnography of a high school in a south Texas town gives a vivid description of "the great American football ritual." He shows that not only the football team but the school population as a whole use the game for celebration and reproduction of the dominant codes of gender. The game directly defines a pattern of aggressive and dominating performance as the most admired form of masculinity, and indirectly marginalizes others. The cheerleaders become models of desirability among the girls, and their desirability further defines the hierarchy of masculinities among the boys, since only the most securely positioned boys will risk ridicule by asking them for a date.[44]

The only thing wrong with Foley's account is the suggestion that this is peculiarly American. Ice hockey in Canada, rugby in South Africa and New South Wales, soccer in Britain, are heavily masculinized contact sports that play a similar cultural role.[45]

Girls too participate in school sport, though not with the same frequency as boys. Typically the high-profile boys' sports are markedly more important in the cultural life of schools. The coaches of boys' representative teams can be important figures in a high school. Physical education teachers have an occupational culture that, on Skelton's autobiographical account, centers on a conventional masculinity that is "not only dominant, but neutralized as natural and good, part of the expected and unquestioned nature of things."[46]

Selection and Differentiation

The masculinizing practices of boys' subjects, discipline, and sport tend to produce, directly, a specific kind of masculinity. But this is not the only way that masculinities are produced in schools. Some aspects of the school's functioning shape masculinities indirectly, and may have the effect not of producing one masculinity but of emphasizing differences between masculinities. The most important case is, undoubtedly, educational selection.

The competitive academic curriculum, combined with tracking, streaming, or selective entry, is a powerful social mechanism that defines some pupils as successes and others as failures, broadly along social-class lines. There are strong reactions among the pupils to this compulsory sorting-and-sifting, whose gender dimension has been visible (though not always noticed) since the early days of school ethnographies.

The most clear-cut examples are from studies of boys' schools. The famous cases of the "lads" and the "ear'oles" in the British working-class school studied by Willis show a difference not only in conformity to school but in styles of masculinity. The "ear'oles," defined by the other group as effeminate, are using the school as a pathway to careers, while the "lads" are headed for the factory floor. A structurally similar pattern, in a very different class context, is the hostility between the sporting "Bloods" and the academic "Cyrils" in the Australian ruling-class school studied by Kessler et al.[47]

The pattern can also be traced in coeducational schools. Mac an Ghaill, for instance, distinguishes the "Academic Achievers" from the "Macho Lads," the "New Enterprisers," and the "Real Englishmen" as subcultures of masculinity in the school he studied.[48] As Garvey puts it, streaming itself becomes a masculinizing practice. But it is a practice that produces plural masculinities, in a structured gender order among boys, not a single pattern of masculinity.[49]

III. Pupils as Agents, School as Setting

Peer Culture

One of the most important features of school as a social setting is its informal peer group life. The peer milieu has its own gender order, distinct though not fixed. There is turbulence and uncertainty as young people try to define their own sexualities and identities. With the approach of adolescence, interactions between boys and girls are liable to be sexualized, by flirting, innuendo, and teasing. The heterosexual "romance" pattern of gender relations persists through high school into college, where it can still dominate student life, as Holland and Eisenhart's intensive study shows.[50]

The romance pattern defines masculinity in general through the masculine/feminine dichotomy, but also feeds into the hierarchy of masculinities, since heterosexual success is a formidable source of peer group prestige. Foley's study of a Texas high school gives an extended account of the parties and other social events at which masculinity is displayed and hierarchies reinforced. In this milieu the interplay of gender and ethnicity constructs several versions of masculinity: Anglo jocks, Mexican-American antiauthoritarian "vatos," and the "silent majority."[51]

Peer culture is now closely linked with mass communication. Mass culture generates images and interpretations of masculinity that flow chaotically into school life and are reworked by the pupils through everyday conversation, ethnic tensions on the playground, sexual adventures, and so on. Some are racially based, such as the image of uncontrollable, violent black masculinity that is familiar in white racism—and has now been seized by young black men (for instance in rap music) as a source of power. Some of these representations are at odds with school agendas. Others (such as interest in sports) are likely to mesh; we should not assume a constant tension between peer culture and school.

Adolescent boys' peer talk constantly uses sexuality to establish hierarchies: "fag," "slag," and so forth. Research in secondary schools in several countries has found widespread verbal harassment of girls by boys. Yet at this age sex is still being learned. Wood's study of boys' sex talk in a London secondary school annex emphasizes the element of fantasy, uncertainty, and boasting. The boys' pretensions can be punctured when a tough girl, or group of girls, pushes back. Wood notes the different registers of boys' sex talk, for instance the greater hesitancy in a mixed group.[52]

In these observations the collective dimension of masculinity is clear. The peer groups, not individuals, are the bearers of gender definitions. This is presumably the explanation for a familiar observation by parents and teachers, that boys who create trouble in a group by aggression, disruption, and harassment, that is, an exaggerated performance of hegemonic masculinity, can be cooperative and peaceable on their own.

Taking Up the Offer

As noted in Part I of this article, masculinities and femininities are actively constructed, not simply received. Society, school, and peer milieu make boys an offer of a place in the gender order; boys determine how they take it up.

Protest masculinity is a case in point. The majority of boys learn to negotiate school discipline with only a little friction. A certain number, however, take the discipline system as a challenge, especially in peer networks that make a heavy investment in ideas of toughness and confrontation. One such, in my life-history research, was Jack Harley, a young man who grew up in poverty in an Anglo family in Sydney. Jack clashed early and often with teachers: "They bring me down, I'll bring them down." Eventually he assaulted a teacher and landed in a juvenile detention center, from which he graduated to burglary, car theft, and adult prison. Expulsion from school and disrupted learning were consequences not of a passively suffered fate but of Jack's vigorous response to his situation.[53]

"Taking up the offer" is a key to understanding disciplinary problems in schools and boys' involvement in violence and sexual harassment. Groups of boys engage in these practices, not because they are driven to it by raging hormones, but in order to acquire or defend prestige, to mark difference, and to gain pleasure. As indicated by the criminological research mentioned in Part I, rule-breaking becomes central to the making of masculinity when boys lack other resources for gaining these ends.

However, the active construction of masculinity need not lead to conflict with the school. There are forms of masculinity much more compatible with the school's educational program and disciplinary needs. This is especially true of middle-class masculinities organized around careers, which emphasize competition through expertise rather than physical confrontation. It seems likely that the construction of masculinities that emphasize responsibility and group cohesion, rather than aggression and individuality, has helped in the educational success of youth from Chinese and Japanese ethnic backgrounds in North America. Boys who

launch themselves on such trajectories are likely to have a much smoother educational passage. The schools as currently organized are a resource for them, and they are an asset for their schools.[54]

The active responses are collective as well as individual. Thorne's documentation of the gender "boundary work" done in elementary schools shows purposive group activity.[55] So does the rejection by certain boys of a key part of hegemonic masculinity, heterosexual desire. For those boys who begin to think of themselves as gay, a vital step is finding a social network in which homosexual desire seems something other than a ghastly mistake.[56]

The making of masculinities in schools, then, is far from the simple learning of norms suggested by "sex-role socialization." It is a process with multiple pathways, shaped by class and ethnicity, producing diverse outcomes. The process involves complex encounters between growing children, in groups as well as individually, and a powerful but divided and changing institution. In some areas of school life, masculinizing practices are conspicuous, even obtrusive; in other areas they are hardly visible at all. Some masculinizing effects are intended by the school, some are unintended, and some are not wanted at all—but still occur. Two implications are very clear: There is a need for educational thinking about this situation, and there are many possibilities for educational work. Let us now consider the shape this work might take.

IV. Educational Strategies in Work with Boys

Goals

Reviewing recent German programs for boys, Kindler identifies three main goals:

self-knowledge, developing the boys' capacity for relationships, and learning antisexist behavior.[57] Generalized a little, these are broadly applicable.

1. The Goal of Knowledge. This is very much underemphasized in current discussions, though "cognitive objectives" are the traditional center of educational discussion. In two senses, knowledge is a goal in work with boys.

First, current patterns of masculinity formation push many boys away from areas of knowledge with which they ought to be in contact. Subject English, discussed earlier, is a case in point; more broadly, languages and communication skills.

Second, acquiring knowledge of gender, in one's own society and others, is a goal of some importance. Learning the facts of the situation, participating in the experiences of other groups, and making a critical examination of existing culture and knowledge are general educational goals that are quite applicable to this subject matter.

This was accepted by the Australian parliamentary inquiry on boys' education mentioned above, which proposed that gender relations be included in the "core" subject matter of the public schools.[58] This is now a principle in Australian gender equity policy. A movement in the same direction can be detected in the universities, where curricula in fields from literature to law now grapple with issues of gender. One must acknowledge that the movement is uneven.

2. The Goal of Good Human Relationships. If school education is a preparation for later life, part of its business is developing capacities for human relationships. But in contemporary Western societies, this capacity is gender-specialized: It is widely regarded as an aspect of femininity. Some elements of masculinity formation in schools—such as the cult of competitive sport—work against the development of this capacity in boys.

Some contemporary programs for boys address this issue head-on, and make relationship capacities their center. An example is the "Personal Development Program for Boys" created by a group of teachers in Australia. ("Personal Development" is a local rubric under which health, sex education, relationships, and emotions are combined.) The program consists of a set of structured sessions on these topics: developing communication skills; domestic violence; conflict resolution; gender awareness; valuing girls and "feminine" qualities; health, fitness, and sexuality; life relationship goals. The program is intended to promote both gender equity and emotional support for boys, with an emphasis on being positive.[59]

3. The Goal of Justice. This involves somewhat more complicated issues, and requires a longer discussion. Gender first came onto educational agendas as an equity issue, where change was sought to redress injustice. The usual response to equity issues by governments is to set up programs for disadvantaged groups. So far, the main educational response to gender issues has been setting up programs for girls.

Some advocates now cast educational issues about boys in that mold, defining boys as a disadvantaged group. This is not a credible argument. On almost any measure of resources—whether wealth and income, cultural authority, levels of education, political influence, control of organizations—and in all parts of the world, men are the *advantaged* group in gender relations.[60] It would require an unbelievable reversal, in an unbelievably short time, for boys to have lost this advantage and become a disadvantaged group.

These advantages come with certain costs, and if one focuses only on the costs, an appearance of disadvantage can be produced. Men's social power, for instance, is partly exercised through institutions of violence, and men thus become the major targets of violence as well as the main perpetrators. In some situations these costs are concentrated on particular groups of men; the appalling levels of imprisonment among African-American men in the United States and Aboriginal men in Australia are notable examples. This is an issue of justice, and the educational implications will be discussed shortly.

The material advantages that men in general have, and that boys in general can expect, mean they have a broad interest in the status quo in gender relations. This interest is easily mobilized in education, as in other arenas. Kenworthy recounts a lesson in an Australian high school, based on a poem about a woman stockman (equivalent, in American terms, to a woman cowboy). The lesson worked well for a class of girls, and for a mixed class. But in an all-male class it was disrupted, under the leadership of some dominant boys who introduced a misogynist discourse and resisted opening up the gender issues. The boys in the class who could or would adopt a feminine reader position were scorned by the dominant group, in a classic display of the micro-politics of hegemony.[61]

Boys are not, as boys, a disadvantaged group, and the goal of educational work is therefore not to redress a gender disadvantage from which they suffer. We should not misread the statistics of sex differences. For instance, sufficient elementary-school boys have difficulty learning to read to produce lower average scores for boys as a common outcome of "sex difference" studies on language skills. Literacy practitioners suggest that the restricted cultural interests associated with hegemonic masculinity—fathers pushing their boys to concentrate on sports,

for instance—are a major reason.[62] To the extent that this is true, the gender difference in reading scores is not a measure of boys' "disadvantage," but an index of the short-term cost of maintaining a long-term privilege.

Yet the goal of justice is relevant to the education of boys, in three ways. First, some of the processes of masculinity construction explored earlier in this article do hamper or disrupt the education of *particular groups of boys*, who are disadvantaged in class or ethnic terms. For instance, the pattern of "protest masculinity," and the high levels of conflict and dropout connected with it, is a major problem in secondary schools serving communities in poverty. The attempt to achieve justice in education in relation to poverty must therefore address issues of masculinity.

The second way concerns the extent to which schools as institutions are just or unjust. In an important recent examination of the concept of justice, Young identifies two broad types of social relationships that are unjust: oppression, which restricts the capacity for self-expression; and domination, which restricts participation in social decision-making.[63] Both types of relationship can be found in schools. The gender practices of boys may perpetuate them, and some boys are victims of them. Harassment of girls, homophobic abuse, the hierarchy of masculinities, bullying, and racial vilification are examples. Pursuing justice in schools requires addressing the gender patterns that support these practices.

The third way concerns the quality of education. Education is a moral trade, and a good education must embody social justice. If we are not pursuing gender justice in the schools, then we are offering boys a degraded education—even though society may be offering them long-term privilege.

Forms

German workers have made a useful distinction between "gender-specific" and "gender-relevant" programs. The main form of educational work on gender, throughout the industrialized world, has been gender-specific programs for girls. As issues about masculinity have been raised, the commonest response has been to develop gender-specific programs for boys. The "Personal Development Program for Boys" outlined above is an example, and there is now considerable practical experience with such programs in the United States, Britain, Germany, and Australia.

Gender-specific programs on masculinity are commonly small-scale, and based on discussion in intimate groups. They may, however, operate on a larger scale. Chiarolli describes a whole-school program that started when principal and staff at a Catholic boys' secondary school became concerned about sexism. They launched a range of actions addressing gender stereotypes and attitudes: library displays, a parent evening, guest speakers, student projects in the community, home economics classes for the boys, scrutiny of the division of labor among adults in the school, and a broad examination of the existing curriculum.[64]

Gender-relevant programs involve both boys and girls, and attempt to thematize, that is, bring to light for examination and discussion, the gender dimension in social life and education. The lesson on the "woman stockman" discussed above is a small-scale example; a whole-school antiviolence program (assuming it grapples with issues of masculinity) is a larger-scale one.

Though gender-specific programs are more familiar, some aspects of the construction of masculinity point to the need for gender-relevant programs. The symbolic gendering of knowledge, the distinction of "boys' subjects" from "girls' subjects" and the unbalancing of curriculum that follows, requires a gender-relevant not gender-specific response—redesign of curriculum, timetable, division of labor among teachers, and so forth. The definition of masculinities in peer group life, and the creation of hierarchies of masculinity, is a process that involves girls as well as boys. It can hardly be addressed with one of these groups in isolation from the other.

The gender-relevant logic is not the same as gender-neutrality, that is, simply attempting to avoid gender distinction. Quite the contrary: Gender-relevant programs name and address gender. A much more interesting, gender-inclusive, pedagogy becomes possible, as pupils have the opportunity to see the world from standpoints they normally regard as Other. Sapon-Shevin and Goodman suggest that this process is critical in sex education, and call it "learning to be the opposite sex." Given the multiplicity of masculinities, a gender-inclusive curriculum means taking the standpoint of other masculinities, as well as femininities.[65]

Methods

Educational work with boys "must *start* with the boys' own interests, experiences and opinions," Askew and Ross argued some time ago.[66] We cannot read off a strategy for boys by trigonometry from the needs of girls. Practitioners are unanimous about the importance of developing, as Denborough puts it, "respectful ways of working with young men" even on an issue like male violence.[67]

Accordingly, practical accounts of gender-specific programs for boys and men typically emphasize student-centered methods. Gould recommends a "tactics of engagement" for university courses. Reay describes an experiential program with boys in a British elementary school. Browne, arguing that "we all learn best from what we face in our own lives," develops a model for experimental programs in Australian secondary schools.[68]

There is, however, a general problem with this approach. The tactics of engagement presuppose willing students. This cannot be presupposed in mass education, where classes for boys are vulnerable to the tactics of disruption—as Kenworthy found.[69] Reay's perceptive account of a teaching experience at upper elementary level shows constant compromises between teacher and taught. For instance, she found herself accommodating rather than challenging peer-group hierarchies. Reay wryly concludes that at the end of the program, whatever they had learned about gender, the boys had certainly learned how to please the teacher.[70]

Experiential approaches, then, need to be supplemented with methods that allow more distancing. Nilan, for instance, uses script development both to bring out assumptions about masculinity and to allow students to debate them. Denborough, dealing with the very difficult issue of masculinity and violence, emphasizes getting boys to look for the counter-narrative to the conventional one—an approach that draws on the research analysis of subordinated and marginalized masculinities. Davies, a post-structuralist in the classroom, has children performing astonishing feats of textual deconstruction and discursive analysis about gender. (Even Davies, however, cannot prevent the boys in her groups resisting their removal from textual authority.)[71]

There is nothing against combining experiential with text-based methods, or indeed other methods. Dealing with gender across the curriculum clearly requires a mixture of teaching methods.

Whatever methods are used, work on gender with boys and men will be successful only if it opens possibilities, if it finds ways for them to move forward. The masculinity-therapists are right about the damaging effect of a certain kind of feminist criticism, which lumps all males together and relentlessly blames them. In teaching university courses about gender, I have repeatedly seen men students discouraged by the endless facts of sexism, experiencing feminist ideas mainly through guilt, and turning away because the alternative was to be overwhelmed. A sense of agency, of goals being achievable, is vital. The more sophisticated feminist approaches to masculinity, such as Segal's *Slow Motion*, discriminate between groups of men and offer support to this process of change.[72]

Institutional Change

Reflecting on the encounter between women teachers and the heavily patriarchal culture of a Christian Brothers school, Angus acutely observes that change in the cultural handling of masculinity requires organizational change as well.[73] Educational work on gender with boys, if it is to be more than a flash in the pan, requires institutional change in schools and systems.

Some of these changes are technical. Gender-specific classroom programs, for instance, require timetable changes in a coeducational school. Others are more substantial. Given the institutional definition of masculinity, the whole gender regime of a school is at issue. Grappling with the production of masculinity in the "vortices" discussed above means replacing confrontational disciplinary systems, restructuring physical education to emphasize participation rather than competitive selection, and restructuring the gender-divided curriculum.

The curriculum issue, of course, goes well beyond an individual school. Curricula are partly controlled by system authorities, examination and testing boards, textbook publishers, employers' certification demands, and entry requirements of colleges. It is possible to move this aggregate, as feminist work in natural science and technology has shown, but it is not easy. Similarly, changing pedagogy and changing the gender division of labor among teachers require action at system level, and in teacher training institutions.

System-level change is more likely to happen if cued by changes already building up within schools. The current approach of developing school-level programs is, in that sense, justified. But it is important to move on from the school level. A useful way of doing so is to set up systemic standards. Organizational change is more likely to happen when the people who hold organizational power have clear criteria to meet. It would be useful, and relatively cheap, to monitor school systems' performance on such issues as gender segregation in the curriculum, levels of violence and sexual harassment, the presence of men in early childhood education and women in administration, and the presence of curriculum units focused on gender relations.

V. The Process of Change

In 1991 the Toronto School Board sponsored an innovative "retreat" in which forty high school boys and forty high school girls, together with their teachers, worked on issues of sexism and change in masculinity. They used group discussion, drama, and separate and joint meetings, then took the results back to their schools.[74]

After the Year of the Angry White Male, as the 1994 Republican election victory was called, one may doubt that many school systems in the United States would care to follow this example. Debates in Australia, where gender issues have attracted more attention at the policymaking level than in

most other countries, have similarly run into an impasse with the "competing victims syndrome," as Cox aptly calls it.[75] Does the discussion of masculinity and schooling have much chance of producing major change?

The discussion has certainly raised major issues. Recent public debates have addressed three important questions: violence and harassment in schools, gender differences in academic outcomes, and the alienation of boys from schooling. The research surveyed in this article identifies two further issues of comparable importance: gender-divided curriculum pathways, and the organizational patterns that construct masculinities in schools.

These are long-standing issues, which do not come and go with a change in political climate. Whether they are turned into a reform program, however, depends a great deal on the interests and consciousness of the groups concerned. We must, therefore, appraise the groups and interests involved.

The Boys

The broad gender privilege of men gives boys an interest in the current gender order. What might lead them to participate in educational work that must call that interest into question, and may require them to decline the offer of gender privilege?

Actual programs for boys, as Kindler reports, have found a range of motives. They include curiosity, personal crisis, a sense of lack, a sense of justice, a desire for sharing and personal growth, and a desire for space for nontraditional conduct.[76]

There are three underlying interests that might support these motives. First is the emotional and physical costs of patriarchy for boys and men. As Kaufman's discussion of violence emphasizes, these costs are far from trivial.[77] Second is the interest boys and men have in personal relationships with women and girls. Boys have relationships, often close, with mothers, sisters, classmates, lovers, neighbors. They have relational interests, we might say, that cut across gender boundaries. Third are the general interests boys share with the women and girls in their lives because they are collective human interests. The shared interest in a healthy environment, for instance, can support study of the role of dominant masculinities in environmental destruction.

Parents and Communities

The role of parents in relation to school programs about masculinity has yet to come into focus. There is a long-standing discussion about the new masculinity and fathering, but this is usually understood to concern the family, not the school. Parents and parent groups have recently expressed public concern about boys' education, and there are indications that this is not a shallow interest. I know of schools that have been surprised by the extent of parent involvement when they announced an initiative on the subject.

Parents are easily represented as a force for conservatism in such matters. There is some basis for this view. For instance, religious Right mobilizations, using parent representation, have severely limited the capacity of American schools to deliver realistic sex education—a major problem in AIDS prevention.[78]

Yet many parents are aware of changes in gender relations, and are deeply concerned about issues like AIDS and sexual violence. Many parents want the schools to address these issues for boys in a realistic and timely way. Parents of boys are often also parents of girls, and have an interest in a better future for their daughters. There are parent organizations that have committed themselves to deal with boys' issues in a gender

equity framework.[79] Parent involvement is not a synonym for gender conservatism.

Social Movements

The feminist movement was the first to place gender issues on educational agendas. For a long time its main practical concern in education has been programs for girls. To some extent, therefore, feminists have been outflanked by the recent upsurge of interest in programs for boys. A key response has been to develop comprehensive "gender-equity" policies, which are gender-relevant rather than gender-specific. Feminists face a continuing dilemma about resources. In an era of cuts to public-sector budgets, any expansion of gender programs for boys—even those intended to produce less patriarchal masculinities—is likely to compete for funds with programs for girls.

The contemporary "men's movement" is deeply divided. There is a gender-justice current (e.g., the National Organization for Men Against Sexism), a masculinity-therapy current (e.g., the "mythopoetic" men's retreats), a restore-patriarchy current (e.g., the "Promise Keepers"), and others. No unified educational program will come out of this. However, the arguments between these currents will certainly affect the balance between gender equity and boys' troubles as themes of programs for boys.

Teachers

Teachers are the work force of educational reform; if anything large is to happen in schools, teachers must be engaged in making it happen. As Angus observes in the study cited above, to the extent that conventional masculinity "works" in the current educational environment, a lot of male teachers have little motive to change.[80] Yet some men do become involved in counter-sexist work with boys. The teaching profession too contains a diversity of masculinities.

Further, teachers and administrators experience the occupational stress caused by violence and resistance among boys. Teachers have an interest in meeting challenges in their work: teaching well, reducing disruptions to learning, and achieving educational justice in the face of difficulties. There are, then, industrial and professional reasons for educators to concern themselves with issues about masculinity.

I think it virtually certain that, in the industrialized countries, the inter-play of these groups and interests will drive an expansion of current educational work on masculinity and programs for boys. This is unlikely to grow to the scale of programs for girls, because different locations in the gender order produce a different dynamic of social mobilization. But a need has been articulated and a response is developing around it. What form the expansion will take is still an open question.

It is clear that schools have a considerable capacity to make and remake gender. They are not the engine of gender revolution that liberal feminism, focused on the task of changing attitudes and norms, once believed. Nevertheless, the school system is a weighty institution, a major employer, a key means of transmitting culture between generations. It has direct control over its own gender regimes, which have a considerable impact on the experience of children growing up; and it can set standards, pose questions, and supply knowledge for other spheres of life.

For the most part, these capacities impact on the making of masculinities in an unreflective, inchoate way. The planned masculinizing regimes of the old boarding schools have been replaced, in mass public education, with a hodgepodge of practices impacting on the lives of boys, which are rarely thought through in gender terms. Such practices as school sport, discipline, and curriculum division may have strong masculinizing effects—but may be at odds with each other, or in conflict with other purposes of the school. The tendency of masculinity formation, in certain situations, to undermine or completely disrupt the teaching function of the school is particularly worrying.

A key task at present, then, is simply bringing these issues to light, asking educators to reflect on what the schools are currently doing. As this article has indicated, there is a good deal of research available that can help with this thinking. The research forcibly shows—in contrast to much popular thinking—that "boys" are not a homogeneous bloc, that masculinities vary and change, and that in gender, institutions (as well as bodies) matter. All these are important conditions for educational work.

Another condition is awareness of the possibility of change. This awareness is being forced on the schools by developments in the world around them. The Anglo-Saxon world generally regards Japan as a bastion of patriarchy, and in some areas (e.g., politics and corporate management) this is true. Nevertheless, a recent book by Ito describes changes in Japanese media images of men, the emergence of companionate marriages and shared child care, renegotiations of sexuality, and explicit critiques (by men as well as women) of traditional Japanese ideals of masculinity.[81] With such challenges emerging all over the industrialized world, no contemporary education system is going to escape these issues. Addressing them thoughtfully, schools can make a real contribution to a future of more civilized, and more just, gender relations.

Notes

1. *Wall Street Journal*, August 11, 1991; S. O'Doherty (chair), *Challenges and Opportunities: A Discussion Paper. Report on the Inquiry into Boys' Education* (Sydney: New South Wales Government Advisory Committee on Education, Training and Tourism, 1994); Heinz Kindler, *Maske(r)ade: Jungen- und männerarbeit für die praxis* (Schwäbisch Gmünd und Tübingen: Neuling, 1993); and Nakamura, Akira, *Watashi-no Danseigaku* [My Men's Studies] (Tokyo: Kindaibugei-sha, 1994).

2. Patricia Sexton, *The Feminized Male: Classrooms, White Collars, and the Decline of Manliness* (New York: Random House, 1969); and David E. Austin, Velma B. Clark, and Gladys W. Fitchett, *Reading Rights for Boys: Sex Role in Language Experience* (New York: Appleton-Century-Crofts, 1971).

3. An excellent account of the often mystifying "men's movement" is Michael Schwalbe, *Unlocking the Iron Cage: The Men's Movement, Gender Politics, and the American Culture* (New York: Oxford University Press, 1996); a rousing rendition of the idea of men as victims is Warren Farrell, *The Myth of Male Power: Why Men Are the Disposable Sex* (New York: Simon & Schuster, 1993).

4. Samples of these ideas, alongside others, can be found in *Boys in Schools: Addressing the Real Issues—Behaviour, Values and Relationships*, ed. Rollo Browne and Richard Fletcher (Sydney: Finch, 1995).

5. Wellesley College Center for Research on Women, *How Schools Shortchange Girls*. (Washington, D.C.: American Association of University Women Educational Foundation and National Education Association, 1992); and "But the Girls Are Doing Brilliantly!" *The Gen* (Newsletter of the Gender Equity Network, Department of Employment Education and Training, Australia), August 1993, entire issue.

6. This research is surveyed in R. W. Connell, *Masculinities* (Berkeley: University of California Press, 1995); Harry Brod and Michael Kaufman, eds., *Theorizing Masculinities* (Thousand Oaks, Calif.: Sage, 1994); and Lynne Segal, *Slow Motion: Changing Masculinities, Changing Men* (London: Virago, 1990). A major forum for current work is the U.S. journal *Masculinities*.

7. An example of disdain for soldiering in Confucian culture is Hui-Chen Wang Liu, *The Traditional Chinese Clan Rules* (New York: Association for Asian Studies and J. J. Augustin, 1959). The classic documentation of ritualized homosexuality is Gilbert H. Herdt, *Guardians of the Flutes: Idioms of Masculinity* (New York: McGraw-Hill, 1981).

8. Pierrette Hondagneu-Sotelo and Michael A. Messner, "Gender Displays and Men's Power: The 'New Man' and the Mexican Immigrant Man," in *Theorizing Masculinities*, ed. Brod and Kaufman, pp. 200–18; James C. Walker, *Louts and Legends: Male Youth Culture in an Inner-City School* (Sydney: Allen & Unwin, 1988); and Mike Donaldson, *Time of Our Lives: Labour and Love in the Working Class* (Sydney: Allen & Unwin, 1991).

9. Jeff Hearn and David L. Collinson, "Theorizing Unities and Differences between Men and between Masculinities," in *Theorizing Masculinities*, ed. Brod and Kaufman, pp. 97–118; and Connell, *Masculinities*, chap. 7.

10. Michael S. Kimmel, "Masculinity as Homophobia: Fear, Shame and Silence in the Construction of Gender Identity," in *Theorizing Masculinities*, ed. Brod and Kaufman, pp. 119–41; and Ken Plummer, ed., *Modern Homosexualities: Fragments of Lesbian and Gay Experience* (London: Routledge, 1992).

11. Connell, "The Social Organization of Masculinity," ch. 3 in his *Masculinities*, pp. 67–92.

12. For thoughtful discussion of this privilege, and its consequences for men, see William J. Goode, "Why Men Resist," in *Rethinking the Family: Some Feminist Questions*, ed. Barrie Thorne and Marilyn Yalom (New York: Longman, 1982), pp. 131–50.

13. Cynthia Cockburn, *In the Way of Women: Men's Resistance to Sex Equality in Organizations* (London: Macmillan, 1991); Cynthia Enloe, *Bananas, Beaches and Bases: Making Feminist Sense of International Politics* (Berkeley: University of California Press, 1990); and James W. Messerschmidt, *Masculinities and Crime: Critique and Reconceptualization of Theory* (Lanham, MD: Rowman & Littlefield, 1993).

14. Michael A. Messner and Donald F. Sabo, *Sex, Violence & Power in Sports: Rethinking Masculinity* (Freedom, Calif.: Crossing Press, 1994); and Jim McKay and Debbie Huber, "Anchoring Media Images of Technology and Sport," *Women's Studies International Forum* 15 (1992): 205–18.

15. Candace West and Sarah Fenstemaker, "Power, Inequality and the Accomplishment of Gender: An Ethnomethodological View," in *Theory on Gender/Feminism on Theory*, ed. Paula England (New York: Aldine de Gruyter, 1993), pp. 151–74; Messerschmidt, *Masculinities and Crime*; and Barrie Thorne, *Gender Play: Girls and Boys at*

School (New Brunswick, NJ: Rutgers University Press, 1993).

16. R.W. Connell, "Psychoanalysis on Masculinity," in *Theorizing Masculinities*, ed. Brod and Kaufman, pp. 11–38; and Alan M. Klein, *Little Big Men: Bodybuilding Subculture and Gender Construction* (Albany: State University of New York Press, 1993).

17. Michael Roper, "Yesterday's Model: Product Fetishism and the British Company Man, 1945–85," in *Manful Assertions: Masculinities in Britain Since 1800*, ed. Michael Roper and John Tosh (London: Routledge, 1991), pp. 190–211; and Robert A. Nye, *Masculinity and Male Codes of Honor in Modern France* (New York: Oxford University Press, 1993). For a recent analysis of broad changes in masculinity see Michael Kimmel, *Manhood in America: A Cultural History* (New York: Free Press, 1996).

18. Harriet Bjerrum Nielsen and Monica Rudberg, *Psychological Gender and Modernity* (Oslo: Scandinavian University Press, 1994).

19. Steve Craig, ed., *Men, Masculinity and the Media* (Newbury Park, Calif.: Sage, 1992).

20. Ellen Jordan, "Fighting Boys and Fantasy Play: The Construction of Masculinity in the Early Years of School," *Gender and Education* 7 (1995): 69–86; and Anne Haas Dyson, "The Ninjas, the X-Men, and the Ladies: Playing with Power and Identity in an Urban Primary School," *Teachers College Record* 96 (1994): 219–39.

21. Theodore D. Kemper, *Social Structure and Testosterone* (New Brunswick, NJ: Rutgers University Press, 1990). To make the final sentence precise, I should add that "masculinity" can also be an interpretation placed on a female body, through analogy with the interpretation of male bodies.

22. An excellent survey of this literature is Sara Delamont, *Sex Roles and the School*, 2nd ed. (London: Routledge, 1990). Jean Anyon, "Intersections of Gender and Class: Accommodation and Resistance in Gender and Gender Development," in *Gender, Class and Education*, ed. Steven Walker and Len Barton (Barcombe, Lewes: Falmer, 1983), pp. 19–37, gives the classic account of the use of femininity as resistance. R. W. Connell, *Gender and Power* (Stanford: Stanford University Press, 1987) provides a systematic critique of sex role theory.

23. Michael A. Messner, *Power at Play: Sports and the Problem of Masculinity* (Boston: Beacon Press, 1992); and Connell, *Masculinities*, chapter 4–7, pp. 89–181.

24. Ronald King, *All Things Bright and Beautiful? A Sociological Study of Infants' Classrooms* (Chichester: Wiley, 1978).

25. Elisabeth Hansot and David Tyack, "Gender in Public Schools: Thinking Institutionally," *Signs* 13 (1988): 741–60. The concept of "gender regimes" is proposed in Sandra Kessler et al., "Gender Relations in Secondary Schooling," *Sociology of Education* 58 (1985): 34–48.

26. Shirley Prendergast, "Boys, Bodies and Pedagogy: Constructing Emotions in School" (Paper delivered at Gender, Body and Love Seminar, Centre for Women's Research, University of Oslo, May 1996).

27. Máirtín Mac an Ghaill, *The Making of Men: Masculinities, Sexualities and Schooling* (Buckingham: Open University Press, 1994); and Blye Frank, "Straight/strait Jackets for Masculinity: Educating for 'Real' Men," *Atlantis* 18 (1993): 47–59.

28. Joan Draper, "We're Back with Gobbo: The Re-establishment of Gender Relations Following a School Merger," in *Gender and Ethnicity in Schools: Ethnographic Accounts*, ed. Peter Woods and Martyn Hammersley (London: Routledge/Open University, 1993), pp. 49–74.

29. R.W. Connell, *Teachers' Work* (Sydney: Allen & Unwin, 1985).

30. Thorne, *Gender Play*. Compare the incoherence of gender ideology in the junior high school studied by Carl A. Grant and Christine E. Sleeter, *After the School Bell Rings* (Philadelphia: Falmer, 1986).

31. Christine Heward, *Making a Man of Him: Parents and their Sons' Education at an English Public School 1929–50* (London: Routledge, 1988).

32. Robert Morrell, "Masculinity and the White Boys' Boarding Schools of Natal, 1880–1930," *Perspectives in Education* 15 (1993/1994): 27–52.

33. C. E. Sleeter and C. A. Grant, "Race, Class, Gender and Disability in Current Textbooks," in *The Politics of the Textbook*, ed. M. W. Apple and L. K. Christian-Smith (New York: Routledge, 1991), pp. 78–110.

34. Bonnie N. Trudell, *Doing Sex Education: Gender Politics and Schooling* (New York: Routledge, 1993).

35. Mac an Ghaill, *Making of Men*.

36. Grant and Sleeter, *After the School Bell Rings*.

37. R. W. Connell, *Boys and Schools: A Guide to Issues, Concepts and Facts* (Sydney: Equity Programs Unit, Department of School Education, New South Wales, 1995).

38. Robert Mealyea, "Reproducing Vocatonalism in Secondary Schools: Marginalization in Practical Workshops," in *Education, Inequality and Social Identity*, ed. L. Angas (London: Falmer, 1993), pp. 160–95.

39. Wayne Martino, "Masculinity and Learning: Exploring Boys' Underachievement and

Under-Representation in Subject English," *Interpretations* 27 (1994): 22–57.

40. D. White, *A Summary of Suspensions in Four High Schools in the Hoxton Park Cluster* (Sydney: Author, 1993).

41. R. W. Connell, "Cool Guys, Swots and Wimps: The Interplay of Masculinity and Education," *Oxford Review of Education* 15 (1989): 291–303.

42. Ann Ferguson, *Boys Will Be Boys: Defiant Acts and the Social Construction of Black Masculinity* (Draft Ph.D. diss., University of California at Berkeley, 1994).

43. For an introduction to this work see Messner and Sabo, *Sex, Violence & Power in Sports.*

44. Douglas E. Foley, *Learning Capitalist Culture: Deep in the Heart of Tejas* (Philadelphia: University of Pennsylvania Press, 1990).

45. Richard Gruneau and David Whitson, *Hockey Night in Canada: Sport, Identities and Cultural Politics* (Toronto: Garamond, 1993); James C. Walker, *Louts and Legends: Male Youth Culture in an Inner-City School* (Sydney: Allen & Unwin, 1988); and David Robins and Philip Cohen, *Knuckle Sandwich: Growing Up in the Working-class City* (Harmondsworth: Penguin, 1978).

46. In New South Wales in 1993, for instance, elementary school boys made up 61 percent of participants in representative sport competitions, girls 39 percent; see Connell, *Boys and Schools.* A. Skelton, "On Becoming a Male Physical Education Teacher: The Informal Culture of Students and the Construction of Hegemonic Masculinity," *Gender and Education* 5 (1993): 289–303.

47. Paul Willis, *Learning to Labour: How Working Class Kids Get Working Class Jobs* (Farnborough: Saxon House, 1977); and Kessler et al., "Gender Relations in Secondary Schooling."

48. Mac an Ghaill, *Making of Men.*

49. Terry Garvey, "Streaming as a Masculinizing Practice in the 1950s and 1960s" (Paper presented to the Annual Conference of the Australian and New Zealand History of Education Society, Perth, Western Australia, 1994).

50. Dorothy C. Holland and Margaret A. Eisenhart, *Educated in Romance: Women, Achievement, and College Culture* (Chicago: University of Chicago Press, 1990).

51. Foley, *Learning Capitalist Culture.*

52. Sandra Milligan and Karen Thomson, *Listening to Girls* (Australia: Ashenden and Associates, 1992); Sue Lees, *Losing Out: Sexuality and Adolescent Girls* (London: Hutchinson, 1986); Robert B. Everhart, *Reading, Writing and Resistance: Adolescence and Labor in a Junior High School* (Boston: Routledge & Kegan Paul, 1983); and Julian Wood, "Groping Towards Sexism: Boys'

Sex Talk," in *Gender and Generation*, ed. Angela McRobbie and Mica Nava (London: Macmillan, 1984), pp. 54–84.

53. Connell, *Masculinities*, chap. 4, "Live Fast and Die Young," pp. 93–119.

54. See the cases from ruling-class schools in R. W. Connell, D. J. Ashenden, S. Kessler, and G. W. Dowsett, *Making the Difference: Schools, Families and Social Division* (Sydney: Allen & Unwin, 1982). For the educational success of "Asian" students, see Dana Y. Takagi, *The Retreat from Race: Asian-American Admissions and Racial Politics* (New Brunswick: Rutgers University Press, 1992); and for "Asian" masculinities in North America, Cliff Cheng, ed., *Masculinities in Organizations* (Thousand Oaks, Calif.: Sage, forthcoming).

55. Thorne, *Gender Play.*

56. Mac an Ghaill, *Making of Men*; and R. W. Connell, M. Davis, and G. W. Dowsett, "A Bastard of a Life: Homosexual Desire and Practice among Men in Working-Class Milieux," *Australian and New Zealand Journal of Sociology* 29 (1993): 112–35.

57. Kindler, *Maske(r)ade.*

58. O'Doherty, *Challenges and Opportunities.*

59. John Dunn et al., *Personal Development Program for Boys* (Canberra: ACT Government, n.d. [c. 1992]).

60. Since this basic fact about gender relations is persistently denied by some in the "men's movement," I quote the most recent survey of global human development: "One of the most significant differences within the overall HDI [Human Development Index] score for any country is between males and females. Men generally fare better than women on almost every socio-economic indicator (except life expectancy since, for biological reasons, women tend to live longer than men). . . . All countries treat women worse than men" (United Nations Development Programme, *Human Development Report 1994* [New York: Oxford University Press, 1994], pp. 96–97).

61. Colin Kenworthy, "'We Want to Resist Your Resistant Readings': Masculinity and Discourse in the English Classroom," *Interpretations* 27 (1994): 74–95.

62. E.g., Gwenda Sanderson, "Being 'Cool' *and* a Reader," in *Boys in Schools*, ed. Browne and Fletcher, pp. 152–67.

63. Iris M. Young, *Justice and the Politics of Difference* (Princeton: Princeton University Press, 1990).

64. Maria Chiarolli, "Gender Issues and the Education of Boys," *Catholic Ethos* 7 (1992): 2–3.

65. For the idea of a gender-inclusive curriculum, see Lyn Yates, *The Education of Girls: Policy,*

Research and the Question of Gender (Hawthorn: Australian Council for Educational Research, 1993). On sex education, see Mara Sapon-Shevin and Jesse Goodman, "Learning to Be the Opposite Sex: Sexuality Education and Sexual Scripting in Early Adolescence," in *Sexuality and the Curriculum,* ed. James T. Sears (New York: Teachers College Press, 1992), pp. 89–105.

66. Sue Askew and Carol Ross, *Boys Don't Cry* (Philadelphia: Open University Press, 1988), p. 91.

67. David Denborough, *Step by step: Developing Respectful Ways of Working with Young Men to Reduce Violence* (Sydney: Men Against Sexual Assault, 1994), entire issue.

68. Meredith Gould, "Teaching about Men and Masculinity," *Teaching Sociology* 12 (1985): 285–98; Diane Reay, "Working with Boys," *Gender and Education* 2 (1990): 269–82; and Rollo Browne, "Working with Boys and Masculinity," in *Boys in Schools*, ed. Browne and Fletcher, p. 88.

69. Kenworthy, "We Want to Resist Your Resistant Readings."

70. Reay, "Working with Boys."

71. Pam Nilan, "Making Up Men," *Gender Education* 7 (1995): 175–87; Denborough, *Step by Step*, and Bronwyn Davies, *Shards of Glass: Children Reading and Writing Beyond Gendered Identitites* (Sydney: Allen & Unwin, 1993).

72. Segal, *Slow Motion.*

73. Lawrence, Angus, "Women in a Male Domain: Gender and Organizational Culture in a Christian Brothers College," in *Education, Inequality and Social Identity*, ed. Lawrence Angus (London: Falmer, 1993), pp. 57–90.

74. Myra Novogrodsky, Michael Kaufman, Dick Holland, and Margart Wells, "Retreat for the Future: An Anti-sexist Workshop for High Schoolers," *Our Schools/Ourselves* 3, 4 (1992): 67–87.

75. Eva Cox, "Boys and Girls and the Costs of Gendered Behaviour," *Proceedings of the Promoting Gender Equity Conference* (Canberra: Ministerial Council for Education, Employment, Training and Youth Affairs, 1995), p. 304.

76. Kindler, *Maske(r)ade*, pp. 114–17.

77. Michael Kaufman, *Cracking the Armour: Power, Pain, and the Lives of Men* (Toronto: Viking, 1993).

78. William Sabella, "Introducing AIDS Education in Connecticut Schools," *New England Journal of Public Policy* 4 (1988): 335–41.

79. New South Wales Federation of Parents and Citizens Associations, *Submission to the Parliamentary Enquiry on Boys' Education* (Sydney: Federation of PArents and Citizens Associations, 1994).

80. Angus, "Women in a Male Domain."

81. Ito Kimo, *Otokorashisa-no-yukue* [Directions for Masculinities] (Tokyo: Shinyo-sha, 1993).

The Body

PART IV

This section focuses on the politics of women's appearance. It asks you to consider some of the implications of representing women not just as "objects of vision," as John Berger suggested in the last section, but as visions of beauty. They show us that while it may be tempting to regard some women's responses to the demands of the beauty industry (to be thin, or to have straight hair, for example) as individual pathologies, we need to consider what it is about the social world we live in that compels so many women and girls to engage in behaviors ranging from the painful to the deadly. Catrina Brown argues that many of these behaviors are normalized by treating only their extreme forms, such as starvation, as deviant, while their more moderate forms, such as dieting, are considered acceptable. This process of normalization, in turn, masks the use of appearance and body size as a form of social control of women. The final reading, by Kathy Peiss, reminds us to temper our critique of the beauty industry by considering some of the ways women have appropriated it for empowerment. She focuses on how African American women at the turn of the century used beauty products as a way to counter racist stereotypes of black people.

Suggestions for Further Reading

Akan, Gloria E. and Carlos M. Grilo. 1995. "Sociocultural Influences on Eating Attitudes and Behaviors, Body Image, and Psychological Functioning: A Comparison of African-American, Asian-American and Caucasian College Women," *International Journal of Eating Disorders*, 18, 181–187.

Bordo, Susan. *Unbearable Weight: Feminism, Western Culture, and the Body*. Berkeley: University of California Press.

Carter, Pam. 1996. "Breast Feeding and the Social Construction of Heterosexuality, or 'What Breasts are Really For.'" Pp. 99–119 in Janet Holland and Lisa Adkins, eds. *Sex, Sensibility and the Gendered Body*. New York: St. Martin's Press.

Chapkis, Wendy. 1986. *Beauty Secrets: Women and the Politics of Appearance.* Boston, MA: South End Press.

Cohen, Colleen Ballerino, Richard Wilk and Beverly Stoeltje. 1995. *Beauty Queens on the Global Stage: Gender, Contests, and Power.* New York: Routledge.

Fine, Michelle and Pat MacPherson. 1993. "Over Dinner: Feminism and Adolescent Female Bodies." In Sari Knopp Biklen and Diane Pollard, eds. *Gender and Education.* Chicago: University of Chicago Press.

Holland, Janet, Caroline Ramazanoglu and Rachel Thomson. 1996. "In the Same Boat? The Gendered (In)Experience of First Heterosex." Pp. 143–160 in Diane Richardson, ed. *Theorising Heterosexuality: Telling It Straight.* Buckingham, U.K.: Open University Press.

hooks, bell. 1995. "Black Beauty and Black Power: Internalized Racism." Pp. 119–132 in *Killing Rage: Ending Racism.* New York: Henry Holt and Co.

Kanafani, Aida S. 1983. *Aesthetics and Ritual in the United Arab Emirates: The Anthropology of Food and Personal Adornment Among Arab Women.* Beirut: American University of Beirut.

Lee, Janet. 1990. "Menarche and the (Hetero)Sexualization of the Female Body," *Gender and Society,* 8, 343–362

Matushka. 1996. "Barbie Gets Breast Cancer." Pp. 247–264 in Nan Bauer Maglin and Donna Perry, eds. *Bad Girls, Good Girls: Women, Sex, and Power in the Nineties.* New Brunswick, NJ: Rutgers University Press.

Najmabadi, Afsaneh. 1993. "Veiled Discourse—Unveiled Bodies," *Feminist Studies,* 19, 487–519.

Ong, Aihwa, and Michael G. Peletz, eds. 1995. *Bewitching Women, Pious Men: Gender and Body Politics in Southeast Asia.* Berkeley: University of California Press.

Rhode, Deborah L. 1997. "Media Images." Pp. 66–94 in *Speaking of Sex: The Denial of Gender Inequality.* Cambridge, MA: Harvard University Press.

Sault, Nicole, ed. 1994. *Many Mirrors: Body Image and Social Relations.* New Brunswick, NJ: Rutgers University Press.

Sittenfeld, Curtis. 1995. "Your Life as a Girl." Pp. 36–44 in Barbara Findlen, ed., *Listen Up: Voices From the Next Feminist Generation.* Seattle, WA: Seal.

Toubia, Nahid. 1994. *Female Genital Mutilation: A Call for Global Action.* New York: Women, Inc.

Fiction

Grant, Stephanie. 1995. *The Passion of Alice.* Boston: Houghton Mifflin Co.

Kaysen, Susanna. 1993. *Girl, Interrupted.* New York: Turtle Bay Books.

Lamb, Wally. 1993. *She's Come Undone.* New York: Pocket Books.

Mantel, Hilary. 1995. *An Experiment in Love.* New York: Viking.

Walker, Alice. 1992. *Possessing the Secret of Joy.* New York: Harcourt, Brace, Jovanovich.

Hair:
A Narrative

Cheryl Clarke

it is passing strange to be in the company
of black women
and be the only one who does not worry
about
not being with a man
and even more passing strange
is to be among black women
and be the only one wearing her hair natural
or be the only one who has used a straightening
iron

An early childhood memory:

me: sitting in the kitchen
holding down onto my chair
shoulders hunching
toes curling in my sneakers.

my mother: standing behind me
bracing herself against the stove
greasing the edges of my scalp

and the roots of my hair violently
heating the straightening comb alternately
and asking between jerking and pulling:

 'why couldn't you have *good* hair?'

by the time mother finished pressing my
virgin wool
to patent leather,
I was asking why I had to have hair at all.

(the first time I heard a straightening iron
crackle
through my greased kitchen, I thought a
rattlesnake
had got loose.)

so much pain to be black, heterosexual, and
female
to be trained for some *Ebony* magazine mail
order man

---

wanting a woman with long hair, big legs, and able
to bear him five sons.
hardly any man came to be worth the risk of nappy edges.

the straightening iron: sado-masochistic ar-
tifact
salvaged from some chamber of the Inquisi-
tion
and given new purpose in the new world.
what was there
about straight hair
that made me want to suffer
the mythical anguish of hell
to have it?
made me a recluse
on any rainy, snowy, windy, hot, or humid day,
away from any activity that produced the least
moisture to the scalp.
most of all sex.
(keeping the moisture from my scalp
always meant more to me
than fucking some dude.)
there was not
a bergamot
or a plastic cap
that could stop
water
from undoing
in a matter of minutes
what it had taken hours of torture
to *almost* perfect.
I learned to hate water.

I am virgo and pragmatic
at fifteen I made up my mind
if I had to sweat my hair back with anyone
it would be my beautician.
she made the pretense bearable.

once a month I would wait several hours
in that realm of intimacy

for my turn in her magical chair
for my four vigorous shampoos
for her nimble fingers to massage
my hair follicles to arousal
for her full bosom to embrace
my willing head
against the war of tangles
against the burning metamorphosis
she touched me naked
taught me art
gave me good advice
gave me language
made me love something bout myself
Willie Mays' wife thought integration
meant she could get a permanent in a
white woman's beauty salon.
and my beautician telling me to love myself
applying the chemical
careful of the time
soothing me with endearments
and cool water to stop the burning
then the bristle rollers
to let me dry forever
under stacks of *Jet, Tan*, and *Sepia*
and then the magnificence of the comb-out.

'au naturel' and the promise of
black revolutionary cock a la fanon
made our relationship suspect.
I asked for tight curls.
my beautician gave me a pick
and told me no cock was worth so drastic a change.
I struggled to be liberated from the supremacy
of straight hair,
stopped hating water
gave up the desire for the convertible sports coup
and applied the lessons of my beautician
who never agreed with my choice
and who nevertheless still gives me language, art,
intimacy, good advice,
and four vigorous shampoos per visit.

The Continuum:
Anorexia, Bulimia, and Weight Preoccupation

Catrina Brown

Preoccupation with weight among women is not restricted to a few women, nor does it include only women who are bulimic or anorexic. Dieting and weight control have become an accepted and rewarded way of life. Today, women who are not concerned about their weight are the social anomaly. Anorexia (self-starvation) and bulimia (binging and purging) are the extremes on a continuum of weight preoccupation among women in affluent Western societies.

The statistics are alarming: almost 95 percent of anorexics and bulimics are women (Bemis 1987; Striegel-Moore, Silberstein, and Rodin 1986); up to 20 percent of female college students are bulimic (Garfinkel and Garner 1982) and 79 percent experience bulimic episodes (Halmi, Falk, and Schwartz 1980). The statistics for dieting and weight preoccupation in our society are no less alarming: by age 18, 80 percent of

women have dieted to lose weight (Sternhell 1985), and by age 13, 60 percent have already begun to diet (Friedman and Maranda 1984).

The weight-preoccupation continuum often includes fear of fatness, denial of appetite, exaggeration of body size, depression, emotional eating, and rigid dieting. Only a matter of degree separates those women who diet, work out, and obsess about their body shape and calorie intake from the more extreme behaviours of anorexia and bulimia. We cannot stigmatize anorexia and bulimia as individual pathologies or diseases, at the same time that we approve, even praise, the behaviour of those women who exercise and diet to attain the culturally prescribed body ideal. The tendency to separate the social obsession with thinness from anorexia and bulimia allows the latter to be treated as individual problems and isolated diseases, disconnected from popular culture in patriarchal society.

Many women diet throughout their lives, repeatedly gaining and losing weight (Orbach 1978). While most women report feeling better about themselves when they lose weight, this sense of well-being is precarious: dieting has a very high "failure" rate, and 90 to 95 percent gain back even more weight than they lost, which likely contributes to the continuous dieting among women (Chernin 1981; Dyrenforth, Wooley, and Wooley 1980; Robinson 1985). Many women come to believe that losing weight is the key to solving the major problems in their lives (Millman 1980; Orbach 1978). Through weight loss they expect to feel more confident, to like themselves better, to be more outgoing, and to be happier.

When the body doesn't measure up, most women feel they themselves don't either. For many women, having the wrong body overshadows their talents, positive attributes, and accomplishments. Several years ago talk-show host Oprah Winfrey had a very public weight loss of 67 pounds, and proudly pronounced that nothing she had ever accomplished had meant as much to her, nothing had made her feel more in control of herself, nothing had made her feel better about herself. Nothing else, it seems, counted.

One survey of 33,000 women found that 75 percent felt they were too fat (Sternhell 1985), and, of these, 45 percent were actually "underweight" according to height/weight charts. If the more liberal revised 1983 height/weight charts advocating higher acceptable body weights had been used instead of the 1959 Metropolitan Life Insurance figures, even more of those women would have been considered "underweight." Clearly, not only anorexic women over-estimate body size and think they are

fat when they are thin. Most women have difficulty accepting their bodies, and the problems of anorexic and bulimic women are just more extreme forms of a common experience. Women tend to appraise their bodies in relation to an "ideal," and against this measure they find that their bodies are never good enough. Thus, the "distorted" perception of body image typically associated with anorexia is not unlike that of the average woman (Lawrence and Lowenstein 1979, p. 42).

A feminist approach to eating disorders and weight preoccupation recognizes how the conditions of women's lives shape their experience with weight and eating. Although Western women today have made inroads in attaining gender equality, the sense of control women feel they have over their lives and themselves is very precarious. Weight preoccupation among women is not simply a manifestation of widespread acceptance of an ideal presented by the media. The ambiguous halfway point between the demands of liberation and of traditional femininity in which women find themselves is such that controlling the body and eating behaviour is one of a few meaningful and promising ways to establish an acceptable sense of self. By focusing dissatisfaction on the body, women often displace the real sources of their unhappiness. Women's collective preoccupation with weight is testimony that we have a long way to go, yet it is evidence that we are struggling, both conforming to and resisting the conditions of our lives.

Those who have adopted the continuum concept of women's eating and body-image problems tend to stress the differences rather than similarities between women who are labeled anorexic or bulimic, and women who are weight preoccupied (Garner, Olmstead, and Garfinkel 1983; Garner, Olmstead, Polivy, and Garfinkel 1984). The starting-point for understanding eating problems, then, is one that focuses on the differences in women's experiences. Such a framework obscures the fact that anorexia and bulimia are widespread problems among women, and that these problems must be situated in relation to the weight preoccupation typical of most women in Western society. A framework which emphasizes the similarities between women on a continuum of troubled eating and weight preoccupation allows for a feminist understanding and approach to working with women.

A continuum framework which recognizes that there are more similarities than differences among anorexic and bulimic women and those who diet and exercise to control their weight allows us to question traditional understandings of eating disorders. The continuum approach challenges the idea that anorexic women are substantially more disturbed, or that their behaviour provides a form of psychological organization which is radically different from that of women preoccupied with weight. Indeed, it is both characteristic and acceptable within contemporary Western society for women to displace feelings, needs, and dissatisfactions onto their relationship with their eating and their bodies.

The relationship women have with their bodies and eating is shaped and given meaning within the larger context of women's lives in patriarchal society. How women deal with their bodies and their psychological distress is mediated by socially acceptable strategies. It is therefore objectionable to label those who adopt more extreme measures as psychopathological, disordered, or diseased while simultaneously encouraging and rewarding dieting and weight preoccupation as healthy and normal when much of this more common behaviour is, itself, very extreme.

We can distinguish differences in degree of behaviour and the subsequent results of this behaviour without adopting a framework or starting-point that emphasizes difference and separates anorexic and bulimic women's experience from that of those who are less preoccupied with or have less invested in controlling their bodies. It is possible to be committed to a feminist approach which opposes the disease- or medical-model view of "eating disorders," and yet recognize that phenomena that can be described as "anorexia," "bulimia," or "weight preoccupation" exist.

Imagine the following situation:

> Cathy has decided that today she will not eat because she "pigged out" yesterday. She rides her bike to work determined that if she makes herself exercise she will lose weight. All day she feels hungry, but is pleased that she hasn't eaten anything. She feels very in control; however, as evening progresses she can't stop thinking about the food she is craving to eat. If she can make herself not eat for a few more days then maybe she can eat whatever she wants. After pumping out 60 sit ups she goes to bed hungry feeling a little thinner. (Brown and Forgay 1987, p. 12)

Is Cathy anorexic or bulimic, or is she just like many women who are desperate to be thin? It is impossible to tell, but what is clear is these experiences differ only in degree. If we examine the American Psychiatric Association's criteria for anorexia and bulimia, we find that, at least in part, these descriptions fit behaviours exhibited by most women. How is it possible that such behaviours are routinely framed as psychiatric disorders when most women share them?

Many women who would not be considered anorexic or bulimic by the medical and psychiatric establishment adopt lifestyles that revolve around weight control and cycles of starving and binging. Dieting often precedes bulimia, as food deprivation is frequently followed by binge eating if food is available. The desire to eat is a natural response to starvation whether it is self-induced or the result of famine. This inability to stop eating when food is available is a common reaction among all people who are denied essential food intake (Bruch 1973; Keys et al. 1950). People who are starved have been found to become preoccupied with eating and to talk incessantly about food, and among some anorexic women the need to eat when starving themselves of food precipitates binge eating.

Many women who become weight preoccupied find themselves at different places on the continuum over their lives. Some women exchange anorexia and emaciation for bulimic binging and purging. Bulimic women may, at some points, vomit to purge, and at others use laxatives, diuretics, or exercise. Bulimic women may stop purging but continue to binge and find themselves gaining weight. These shifts, in themselves, are not uncommon and suggest that the psychological underpinnings remain quite similar, regardless of what form the weight preoccupation takes.

According to the American Psychiatric Association's *Diagnostic and Statistical Manual of Mental Disorders (DSM-III-R)*, the diagnostic criteria for anorexia include an intense fear of becoming fat, a disturbed body image that involves feeling fat even when thin, loss of at least 15 percent of one's original body weight, refusal to maintain a normal body weight for one's age and height, and no known physical cause for the weight loss (American Psychiatric Association 1987). Yet most women are afraid of becoming fat, and most overestimate their body size. Many women try to keep their weights at levels lower than those considered "normal" for them. The psychiatric criteria provoke a number of questions. What happens when a fat woman loses 15 percent

of her body weight, refuses to eat, becomes preoccupied with losing weight, and ceases to menstruate? Is she anorexic, even though she is fat? At what point does she become "anorexic"; that is, is she "normal" one day and "anorexic" the next? Although her feelings about her self, her life, and her behaviours may have remained consistent over time, not until she has actually become emaciated do people consider her to have a problem. Prior to the emaciation, her behaviours and psychological stance are likely to be encouraged and rewarded.

Presumably, anorexia develops over time, as emaciation and amenorrhea do not occur spontaneously. The psychiatric criteria reflect a poor understanding of the degree of desperation and anxiety the average woman in our society experiences around eating and her body shape and size. Not only are the psychiatric descriptions of anorexia nervosa and bulimia removed from the overall social context that precipitates weight obsession, they are static and fixed rather than fluid and temporal. Within such mainstream approaches, one simply is anorexic or has "recovered." This either/or evaluation perpetuates the understanding and treatment of these problems as diseases. Conversely, when anorexia and bulimia are framed as part of a continuum of weight preoccupation among women, an alternative evaluation is possible, one that reflects a different understanding of women's psychological distress in society.

The psychiatric criteria themselves change over time, suggesting that the characteristics associated with anorexia and bulimia are not immutable, but socially defined. For instance, in 1980 the *DSM-III*, required women to have lost 25 percent of their body weight, revised down to 15 percent in 1987. As the criteria for anorexia have become less stringent, more women are able to fit the diagnostic label. Since the

1980 delineation of eating disorders in the *DSM-III*, a new code called "Eating Disorder Not Otherwise Specified" has been added to the *DSM-III-R*. While the 1980 criteria for eating disorders could already be criticized for being so broad as to describe most women, the 1987 addition now includes: "a person of average weight who does not have binge eating episodes, but frequently engages in self-induced vomiting for fear of gaining weight"; "all of the features of Anorexia Nervosa in a female except absence of menses"; and "all of the features of Bulimia Nervosa except the frequency of binge eating episodes" (1987, p. 65).

These labels and criteria are not sacrosanct; rather, they reflect the powerful and dominant medical paradigm. This paradigm represents a particular way of understanding the social world and human problems. For example, "drapetomia" was a label once used to describe Black Americans who had attempted to escape slavery and human bondage. Homosexuality was, until recently, considered a psychiatric problem, and its psychiatric criteria were outlined in the *DSM-III*. The proposed diagnostic category "Masochistic Personality Disorder" was critiqued by feminists, but replaced by another sexist diagnostic label, "Self-defeating Personality Disorder" in the *DSM-III-R*. Another proposed diagnostic category is "Late Luteal Phase Dysphoric Disorder," which defines Premenstrual Syndrome as a psychiatric disorder. These labels and diagnoses reflect a particular understanding of social relations. They define and often reinforce socially hegemonic ideologies concerning race, sexual orientation, and gender. While women's suffering has often been born out of the confinement, limitations, and expectations of patriarchal society, individual women have been institutionalized, drugged, and labeled as disordered. This approach to women's pain and suffering depoliticizes the social origins of the problems; invalidates and delegitimizes women's experiences; and negates women's expression of pain, dissatisfaction, and resistance.

By splitting women's fear of being or of becoming fat away from the context of their feelings and experiences, the medical model is unable to understand the meaning of these fears. When contextualized, women's fear of fat makes perfect sense. However, we must take a closer look at what this experience is really like for women. Anorexic women's lives, like those of most women preoccupied with weight, are dominated by fixations on food, thinness, and weight control, and by a personal sense of inadequacy and lack of control. A lifestyle evolves out of these feelings of inadequacy and ineffectiveness that centres on attempts to reduce these feelings through control of the body. Hyperactivity and exercise are further ways anorexic women and many weight-obsessed women seek to control the body. An anorexic woman's physical activities are often rigidly and ritualistically structured, like her other behaviours, in an attempt to gain a feeling of personal control, and with it a sense of personal adequacy. She will deny her skeletal appearance and impending death, desperately holding on to the only control she feels she has over her life: control over her body. While anorexic women usually know they are not fat, they feel fat, and like most women preoccupied with weight, they experience this feeling as untenable.

When an anorexic woman describes herself as "feeling out of control," she is often expressing that inner feelings of inadequacy make her feel very helpless. If she is already feeling inadequate, the conflicting needs to eat and to be thin exacerbate that inadequacy. She feels overwhelmed in the face of the demands she places on herself to achieve and do well. Anorexic women have often been described pejoratively as "perfectionistic," yet this tendency is, in part, often an expression of the need to please and receive approval from others. This need to please others is not uncommon among women socialized in a male-dominant culture where women learn to take care of others' needs at their own emotional expense. Despite anorexic women's achievements and successes in life, they usually feel they are failing, regardless of how they appear to others. For most women, the need to receive approval from others and to achieve in the world is a way to feel better about oneself.

Anorexia is something women do for themselves—it is an uncertain attempt to achieve self-empowerment and well-being. The result is what Marilyn Lawrence calls a "control paradox": the more anorexic women feel the need to exert control over their bodies, the more out of control they often are (Lawrence 1979; Brown 1990a, 1990b). An anorexic woman is communicating to others, and herself, that something is gravely wrong—that she is very unhappy. Her behaviours and her body serve as a statement of her frustration, and she may perceive them as the only way she can express feelings so they do not impinge upon or upset others. She has learned in her life that she cannot risk the direct communication of her feelings. She is frustrated with her inability to develop a sense of self she can accept and that she feels others will accept as well. Some have suggested that anorexic women are struggling to develop a self (Chernin 1985; Friedman 1985; Orbach 1986).

Initial success with weight loss often brings praise from others and encouragement to continue to lose weight. The control established over the basic human urge to eat, especially when starving, is compelling as it makes the anorexic woman feel stronger. The anorexic woman feels she should be able to control her urge to eat. She experiences a personal sense of failure if she succumbs and eats, a reaction that is also common among bulimic women and most dieters. Conversely, women often feel a sense of power and personal satisfaction when they can contain and curb their appetites, even when they are emaciated and near death. The accomplishment of self-control, not weight or food intake in themselves, becomes the central issue. For anorexic and bulimic women as well as dieters, controlling the body becomes one viable way to feel more in control of one's self and one's life. It is a control such women are usually unwilling to let go of unless an alternative means of gaining control over their lives is established.

Anorexic women struggle to meet their own emotional needs. Their bodies communicate their deep emotional fragility and the need for emotional nourishment. Most dieters exert significant control over themselves and their eating, often denying and depriving themselves of food and the comfort it offers. But this pales in comparison with the degree of denial and deprivation anorexic women achieve, which parallels the degree of emotional deprivation many of them have experienced in their lives. Paradoxically, the sense of achievement or accomplishment this denial and deprivation produces makes anorexic women feel powerful.

Bulimia is perhaps more widespread among women than is anorexia. Bulimic women may be of any weight, from very thin to fat by social standards, depending on their "set-point" or physiologically programmed body weight, and the extent and nature of the binging and purging. Both anorexic and bulimic women live lives dichotomized around feeling in control and feeling out of control, and both states they associate with eating and not eating. Bulimic women often feel they have found the perfect private solution to the pressure to be thin since they can eat as they like, control their weight, and please others simultaneously. In this sense, bulimia conforms more to social expectations of women, as bulimic women's behaviour remains hidden and secret, and their emotional turmoil is obscured from others' vision. Such is not the case with anorexic women whose unwillingness to eat is often displeasing to others, and whose emaciation is mute testimony to their emotional suffering.

The *DSM-III-R* criteria for bulimia include recurrent episodes of binge eating of high-calorie food over a short period of time when one is alone (American Psychiatric Association 1987). Binge eating stops because of fullness, sleep, or vomiting, and is followed by depression and a self-deprecating mood. Bulimia is characterized by repeated attempts to lose weight by following very prescriptive diets, by self-induced vomiting, or by overuse of laxatives or diuretics, and by frequent weight fluctuations of at least ten pounds. Diagnostic criteria also include an awareness there is a problem with the eating behaviour, and that, like anorexia, it is not caused by a physical disorder.

Bulimic women's binge/purge cycles often convey the ambivalence they feel towards feeding and nourishing themselves. While eating is always connected to how we feel and what we need, for some it becomes the central way of fulfilling emotional needs. Many "compulsive" or "emotional" eaters use food in an attempt to fill up the "emptiness" they feel inside, or as a distraction from dissatisfaction or unhappiness.

Many similarities exist between dieters who binge and bulimic women who binge and purge. While binge eating is frequently

a response to dieting, many women report emotional reasons for binging. Dieting is often especially difficult for those who depend on food to meet their emotional needs. It will not provide weight loss for these women for, as soon as the diet is over, eating will be resumed as the way to meet emotional needs. For many, binge eating is a way to give comfort and nurturance to oneself. Dieting is then experienced as both physiological and emotional deprivation. Binging can be called "comfort eating" as it often provides a distraction from uncomfortable feelings and produces the desired effect of numbing emotional pain. Conversely, some women feel they punish themselves by eating until they are in physical pain. Purging is equally as important as binging; most women purge through vomiting or laxative use, and even exercise, as a way to provide a release of emotional tension, especially anger. The binging and purging of bulimic women plays out an internal emotional drama involving uncertainty, vulnerability, emotional neediness, and rage. Binging and purging behaviour is not unlike the "slashing" or "cutting" some women do to express and release their pain.

We live in a culture which encourages women to nurture others but to expect emotional denial and deprivation for themselves. It is, then, not surprising that women have difficulty getting their needs met, or that they often feel some ambivalence about having their own emotional needs nurtured. These experiences are reflected in anorexic and bulimic women's treatment of their bodies, eating, and selves.

Histories of sexual abuse or physical battery are common among women with anorexia and bulimia.[1] Such women often have difficulty expressing anger at the abuser and blame themselves, taking out their anger on their own bodies (Wooley and Wooley 1986). Abuse of the body also sets women up to have difficulty with their own physical and emotional boundaries. Abusive histories often produce a poor sense of self, a lack of control or safety in life, and difficulty establishing positive relationships. Many of these issues are reflected in women's struggle with weight and eating.

The "psychiatrization" of relatively normative behaviour in the *DSM-III-R* criteria for anorexia and bulimia suggests that the psychiatric profession tends to be very distanced from women's experiences in our society. Most women acknowledge they binge eat, or eat for emotional reasons. When they "binge" eat they tend to eat high-calorie sweet food, or "junk" food, and this binging is almost always done when they are alone. Women admonish themselves for this behaviour and promise themselves they will diet or exercise in compensation. They tend to feel guilty, ashamed, and out of control. Paradoxically, women tend to feel very bad about themselves after comfort eating. The fact that this phenomena has become a subject in popular culture, such as the "Cathy" comicstrip, illustrates the normativity of this experience.

In 1987 compulsive exercise was added to the use of laxatives, diuretics, and vomiting in the *DSM-III-R* criteria for bulimia.[2] Many women who exercise compulsively share the same attitude as women who purge, that is: "I can have my cake and eat it too." Bulimic exercisers attain a tremendous sense of control over their lives through the control they achieve over their bodies. Compulsive exercising, like dieting, is often admired and encouraged, although it is as much a part of the problem as self-starvation, vomiting, and laxative use among many women. While these behaviours are all part of the continuum of weight preoccupation, and may express women's psychological distress, they need not be considered psychiatric disorders.

Adopting a continuum model of weight preoccupation encourages a greater sense of identification with the experiences of women who become anorexic or bulimic. Too often a we/they dichotomy is perpetuated even among those feminists who are knowledgeable about weight and shape issues. When we place the entire continuum of obsession with weight within a social framework, we can see the similarities between the dynamics propelling the development of eating disorders and those of most women's obsession with weight and shape in our society.

The degree of psychological conflict women experience about weight, shape, and eating is an important indicator of position along the continuum of weight preoccupation. Clearly, most women in Western societies would like to be thin. Feeling thin or achieving thinness is an accomplishment, and often produces a corresponding increase in self-esteem and a feeling of having control over one's life. For anorexic and bulimic women, the self-esteem enacted through controlling their bodies is pivotal. The "extremeness" of the anorexic woman's starvation or the bulimic woman's binging and purging is often an indication of there being more at stake.

Yet anorexia and bulimia are not centrally about weight or eating. Rather, those behaviours represent an attempt to deal with psychological distress in women's lives. Viewing these behaviours as "dieting gone crazy" frames these problems in terms of weight and eating and can obscure larger and often more substantial issues. To address the real issues or problems in women's lives, helpers must assist women in discovering why they focus on weight and eating.

A feminist approach to eating disorders differs from the medical model analysis and treatment of these problems. Where the medical model tends to offer an asocial, decontextualized, and highly individualized explanation of eating disorders, a feminist model seeks to understand the connection between women's relationship to our bodies and the conditions of our lives. Traditional approaches to working with eating disorders tend to focus on weight and eating, the chief objective being behavioural change. The emotional rollercoaster women often ride in relation to how they are feeling about their bodies and eating is much larger than simple concern about weight and shape, although arguably there is no such thing as simple concern about weight and shape for women. For each woman who diets, who thinks about the size of her thighs, who starves herself during the week so she can "pig out" or "binge" on the weekend, thinness offers many rewards.

For many women, thinness represents feelings of being in control, successful, attractive, valued, worthy, lovable, sexually attractive, and powerful. However, some women feel too vulnerable and powerless when they feel thin and are more comfortable at a higher body weight. Fatness for most women, though, means feeling out of control, powerless, unattractive, unworthy, devalued, ashamed, and like a failure. Women's investment in attaining thinness is a completely rational phenomenon, given the degree of fat prejudice and hatred that exists in our society. We believe we will be better off if we are thin and we know with a certainty we will be punished for being fat.

It is not just anorexic or bulimic women who refer to "feeling fat" or "feeling thin." What does it mean to feel thin or to feel fat? The feeling has very little to do with actual body size. Most women who say "I feel fat" mean "I feel bad"; when they feel thin, they feel good. Ultimately, by focusing our dissatisfaction on the body rather than on the condition of our lives, nothing significant changes.

Traditional psychiatric accounts describe anorexic and bulimic behaviour in such a way that such behaviour appears bizarre and irrational. These accounts do not address the way women's behaviours are connected to how they feel. Women's own stories of their experiences are almost never included in the institutionalized accounts. By presenting a disembodied, detached, and pathologizing view of women's experiences, traditional frameworks silence women.

How can we pathologize women's fear of being fat, or their investment in controlling their bodies when these are among the few legitimate mechanisms women have for developing a sense of control over their lives? We need to hear the voices of individual women as they struggle through their relationships with weight and eating. The body and eating are embedded with meaning in all cultures. Both eating behaviour and how the body is presented and adorned express meaning about individuals and society. The woman who starves herself to sixty pounds is making a meaningful statement; she is not crazy. Indeed, she desperately needs to be heard and will not be ready emotionally to relinquish self-starvation until she is. Bulimic women who spend the better part of their waking day binging and purging are desperately communicating and expressing the chaos they feel about their lives. Other women who exercise for hours every day often do so not only for the sake of fitness, but to feel a greater sense of self control. Hence, weight-obsessed women will continue their behaviour until they no longer need it as a way to be heard.

Western culture continues to invest a woman's appearance with extraordinary significance in judging her overall value. In Western societies, appearance is inseparable from identity, social value, and hence self-esteem. Women learn they should not feel good about themselves unless they look a particular way. We are told by family, friends, lovers, doctors, journalists, and the media that we cannot feel good about ourselves if we are fat. What women value about themselves commonly reflects the values of society. Some, however, have begun to question the validity of these beliefs, as is evident from the numbers of women who have been active in challenging the social values of thinness and hatred of fatness.

Each time we diet, each time we judge our personal value on the basis of appearance, each time we criticize others or feel better than them based on how they look, each time we positively reinforce weight loss, or even each time we sit around in groups and complain in a comradely way about our bodies, we contribute to the perpetuation of the pressure to be thin. As women, we are not simply victimized by social values and pressure, but take an active role in keeping the phenomenon of weight preoccupation alive. Overcoming weight preoccupation, giving up dieting, or accepting one's body as it is, is by no means easy, but the only way off the treadmill is for women themselves to reject the value of thinness and rebel against its tyranny. We need to recognize the strength and courage it takes to rebel against predominant social values. Most importantly, we must recognize the necessity of our doing so.

Notes

1. Research on and documentation of the relationship between sexual abuse and eating disorders have become more widespread. The following writers have observed a connection between sexual abuse and eating disorders through either clinical work or research: Abraham and Beaumont 1982; Bass and Davis 1988; Beckman and Burns 1990; Brown 1990a, 1990b; Beaumont, Abraham, and Simpson 1981; Brown and Forgay 1987; Buchok 1990; Calam and Slade 1989; Goldfarb 1987; Hall et al. 1989; Hambridge 1988; Kearney-Cooke 1988; Miller 1990; Oppenheimer et al. 1985; Palmer et al. 1990; Root 1988; Root and Fallon 1988, 1989; Runtz and Briere 1986; Schecter, Scharwtz, and Greenfield 1987; Sloan and Leichner 1985; Smolak, Levine, and Sullins 1990; Waller 1991; Wooley and Wooley 1986.

2. Some women avoid sleep in an effort to burn calories, and others chew food but do not swallow it. Diet pills can be used by women to compensate for periods of unrestrained eating. Strong prescription diet pills used to curb appetite are often stimulants and thus interrupt sleeping and eating patterns. The behaviour of women using these pills can resemble that of anorexia.

Making Up, Making Over:
Cosmetics, Consumer Culture, and Women's Identity

Kathy Peiss

A painted face is a false face, a true falshood [sic], not a true face.

Thomas Tuke, Discourse Against Painting and Tincturing, 1616

By changing the way you look . . . you can create a new you!

Cosmopolitan, 1991

In 1938 *Mademoiselle* magazine reported that the cosmetics firm Volupté had produced two new lipsticks for the market. These were "lipstick for types": one for "girls who lean toward pale-lacquered nails, quiet smart clothes and tiny strands of pearls"; the other "for the girl who loves exciting clothes, pins a strass pin big as a saucer to her dress, and likes to be just a leetle bit shocking" One had a "soft mat finish" while the other covered the lips "with a gleaming lustre." The names given to these lipsticks were, respectively, *Lady* and *Hussy*. As *Mademoiselle* put it, "Each of these two categories being as much a matter of mood as a matter of fact, we leave you to decide which you prefer to be."[1]

These products may not have fared well on the market, but the assumptions behind their promotion are remarkable. Social identities that had once been fundamental to women's consciousness, fixed in parentage, class position, conventions of respectability, and sexual codes, were now released from small swiveling cylinders. Not only could women choose these categories of identity, but for two dollars, they could enjoy both. "Lady" and "hussy" were no longer the moral poles of womanhood but rather "types" and "moods" defined largely

From *The Sex of Things: Gender and Consumption in Historical Perspective* by Victoria de Grazia, ed. Copyright © 1996 The Regents of the University of California.

by external signs. Products of a consumer culture, these lipsticks, trivial in themselves, underscore new relationships between cosmetics, appearance, and female identity in the twentieth century. For nineteenth-century Americans, being a lady meant forswearing visible cosmetics: the painted woman was a figure of deception and alterity, an inauthentic self and a debased social "other." By the 1930s, as this lipstick example makes clear, makeup had become integral to self-expression and the belief that identity was a purchasable style.

This essay focuses on changing cultural perceptions of the relationship between women's identity and appearance—the gendered self and self-presentation—and the effects of a commodity/consumer culture upon those perceptions. It explores the cultural and ideological construction of cosmetic practices, how commercially sold makeup problematized and signified women's identity.

In recent years, historians have debated the implications of twentieth-century American consumer culture for notions of personal and social identity. In Warren Susman's classic formulation, consumer culture transformed the self defined by "character" into one typified by "personality." By the early 1900s, the new apparatus of commerce—advertising agencies, mass communications, large-scale retailing, consumer credit, commercial leisure—fostered both a quantitative and qualitative change in Americans' relationship to goods. These changes reached deeply into the psyche. Where mid-nineteenth-century Americans had believed in the fixity of identity, a fundamental self rooted in a moral economy of hard work and thrift, by the 1920s, self had become largely a matter of merchandising and performance and was built around commodities, style, and personal magnetism. Historians since Susman have quarreled with the periodization of this formulation,

finding "cultures of consumption" to exist in North America and Europe long before the early twentieth century. They argue with the distinction between character and personality, observing that definitions of the self through external markers—which purportedly characterize personality in the early twentieth century—were widespread in the Victorian era as well.[2]

Given several decades of feminist and postmodernist analysis, it is now apparent how much gender, and difference more generally, have shaped the conceptualization of identity in consumer culture. "Character" and "personality" contrast constellations of traits and values that have been deeply gendered: work/leisure, production/consumption, internal/external, natural/artificial, fixed/mutable, serious/superficial. Character appears less a matter of cultural consensus and more a cultural problem of the Victorian era, tied to the achievement, inscription, and essentializing of the social differences of gender, class, and race. If this is the case, what then does it mean that, in the early twentieth century, the traits and values associated with the second halves of these opposite pairs—all coded feminine—became so dominant in American cultural discourses?[3]

Among the central issues for us to explore, then, is the constitution of the gendered consumer in relation to other socially determined identities. Unfortunately, much of the foundational work on consumer culture naturalizes or overgeneralizes this question. To explain consumer behavior, scholars often rely on overarching psychological theories that simply assume a feminine actor. Feminist analyses that foreground gender frequently reduce the question to a debate over consumption's oppressive versus liberatory effects on women. Given the incipient state of the field, generalizations are not yet warranted. Buying a lipstick and buying a car, for instance, are different consumer acts occurring in distinct discursive and social contexts, although both involve, among other things, consumption, appearance, and identity. Historians will need to explore the distinctions among different forms of consumption and place consumption fully in context, before we can generally assess the effects of a consumer society on gender constitution and on women's lives.

This essay examines one specific consumer commodity, cosmetics, and the cultural meanings applied to powder and paint. Across time and cultures, cosmetics have been important means of expressing social status, commonality, and difference. In the twentieth century, a period of highly unstable and contested gender definitions, cosmetics—as mass-produced and mass-distributed commodities—became especially salient markers of normative female identity. This essay suggests some of the cultural processes through which that occurred.

Cosmetics as a Cultural, Problem in Nineteenth-Century America

In Western culture, the face, of all parts of the human body, has been marked as particularly meaningful, a unique site of expression, beauty, and character. The privileged position of the face as a sign of individual being was a commonplace of American thought in the nineteenth century. Believing in the commensurability of external appearance and the internal self, Americans held to a physiognomic paradigm, despite anxious perceptions that appearances might be deceiving. Physiognomic principles were closely wedded to a Romanticist moral aesthetic directed especially at female identity and beauty. In this view, physical beauty had "a representative and correspondent" relationship to spiritual beauty and moral goodness. Beauty thus originated less in visual sensation and formal aesthetics than in internal character. Writers specifically marked expressive eyes and transparent complexion as the critical media linking surface beauty to inner spirit.[4]

If beauty signified goodness, achieving beauty became a moral dilemma. Should a woman try to increase her beauty, and if so, how should she do it? The consensus in fiction and prescriptive literature in the pre-Civil War period was that beauty could be achieved only through moral improvement, a process that involved the spiritual and the physical body. By the 1830s, as Karen Halttunen has shown, a cult of sentimentality and sincerity advocated "moral cosmetics"—soap, exercise, and temperance—for the development of virtue, health, and beauty.[5]

The idealization of the "natural" face occurred, it should be noted, in a country that was already, in some sense, a consumer society. The middle classes were busily engaged in purchasing consumer goods, reading magazines and novels, taking in advertisements. Other places in which "private" and "public" met—the clothed body, the well-furnished parlor—were accepted, indeed celebrated, as sites of commodity culture. For nineteenth-century women, the clean, natural face was part of a consciously composed presentation of the self, in which artifice shaped the body to a fashionable silhouette and clothing was exuberantly ornamental.[6] The face, however, was understood to be outside fashion and consumption. It conveyed the fixity and essence of identity in contrast to the mutability, conformism, and social nature of dress. Still, women improved their faces (outside the realm of purchasable goods) through "complexion management"—pinching cheeks and biting lips, or wearing colored bonnet linings to enhance facial tints.[7] The "natural" thus must be seen as a culturally constructed category orienting standards of beauty, taste, and respectability.

Visible cosmetics entered into middle-class discourse as "corporeal hypocrisy." Symbolic of artifice, deception, and masking, they raised the value of "facial truth" required by the physiognomic paradigm. Americans contrasted skin-improving cosmetics, typically creams and lotions, with skin-masking paints, including powders and rouge. As one writer put it, "Paints must not be confounded with Cosmetics, which often really do impart whiteness, freshness, suppleness, and brilliancy to the skin . . . these consequently assist Nature, and make amends for her defects." Paints, another said, masked nature's handiwork, hiding expression and truth behind an "encrusted mould," a "mummy surface."[8]

This typology—cosmetic and paint, nature and artifice—extended to the arena of manufacture and distribution. From at least the seventeenth century, skin-improving cosmetics were part of "kitchen-physic," the household manufacture of medicines and therapeutic substances long viewed as women's domain. These cosmetics were made in the Galenic tradition, using herbs and organic substances considered harmless. Handwritten recipe books, printed household manuals, and guides to beauty—all containing cosmetic recipes—were commonplace in the nineteenth century.[9]

Paints, in contrast, represented to many the entire class of proprietary cosmetics sold on the market by manufacturing chemists, patent medicine firms, and pharmacists. These frequently contained dangerous chemical compounds, including compounds of mercury, lead, and arsenic. The toxicity and commercialization of paints occasioned public concern and provoked anxiety over deceptive appearances and bodily dangers. Even when paints were made of relatively safe organic substances, people worried over such cosmetics' commodity form: paints, enamels, and powders represented quite literally larger fears about the corrosive effects of the market—the false colors of sellers, the superficial brilliance of advertisers, the masking of true value.[10]

In the postrevolutionary United States, paints also signified a discredited aristocratic culture of "high-style" gentility. In the eighteenth century, cosmetics use had been more a matter of class than of gender. Upper-class colonists of both sexes imitated the fashions of the English aristocracy by applying rouge, powder, and even beauty patches.[11] During and after the American Revolution, however, luxurious dry goods, decorative fashions, and imported cosmetics were attacked as patrician styles to be shunned in a republican society of manly citizens and virtuous domestic women. The transformation in attitudes toward self-presentation was most pronounced in men, for whom older styles of authority were newly defined as effeminate. By the 1830s, the democratization of politics had heightened the association between citizenship and rugged manliness. In such a climate, cosmetic practices among men became, at most, covert and unacknowledged.[12]

Women, too, were instructed to shun paints and artifice, but in the service of new notions of femininity. In early-nineteenth-century discourse, the feminine was identified with spiritual equality, domestic sovereignty, and a transcendent purity rooted in, but not limited to, sexual chastity. These views reinforced, and in turn were deepened by, the growing cultural authority of a middle class whose identity was structured, in large part, around essential gender/sexual difference.[13] This fixed, pre-existing feminine self was to be transparently represented, and indeed stabilized, through "natural beauty."

Cosmetics continued to represent profound anxieties about women's nature and authenticity. Paint marked vices that for centuries had been associated with women—corrupt and uncontrolled sexuality, vanity, and deceit. "Oriental" Jezebel continued to be a point of reference for unacceptable female behavior in nineteenth-century Biblical commentary: painting the face with kohl and rouge triggered sermons on women's love of finery, their idolatry, and their objectionable sexuality.[14] Cosmetics were associated as well with illicit commerce, the merchandising of women's bodies in prostitution. In popular speech and song the stereotypical painted woman remained the prostitute, who brazenly advertised her immoral profession through rouge and eye paint. Newspapers, tracts, and other sources frequently mentioned, in a formulaic way, the "painted, diseased, drunken women, bargaining themselves away" in theaters, in public carriages, or in the streets.[15]

Still, the painted woman was in the nineteenth century a figure of accretions, a layering of earlier meanings with newer inflections. The earlier rhetoric of cosmetic practices frequently served to make cultural distinctions based on contemporary consumption styles and gender behavior *within* the middle and upper classes. By the Civil War, this language was increasingly directed against fast young ladies on the marriage market and middle-aged women seemingly more attentive to youth and fashion then maternity. A number of virulent attacks on fashionable women's appearance occurred in the 1860s and 1870s. Expressing anxiety over women's transgressive behavior, these articulated popular distaste for the rising "shoddy aristocracy" and *nouveau riche* (figure 1). The ultrafashionable woman, called by one author "a compound . . . of false hair, false teeth, padding of various kinds, paint, powder, and enamel," betrayed feminine nature by visiting the enameler's studio.[16] Such criticisms underscored and potentially enforced intra-class

standards of genteel appearance, taste, and morality as they proscribed "selfish" female consumption.

Cosmetics not only marked symbolic distinctions between and within social classes but also reinforced racial typologies and hierarchies. The advocacy of the natural face masked the most widespread face-altering cosmetic practice in the nineteenth century, whitening the skin. Age-old anxiety over cosmetic deceit dovetailed with racial fears, particularly in the postemancipation advice literature. One cautionary tale about cosmetic washes containing lead or bismuth appeared repeatedly. The product was intended to whiten the skin but had the reverse effect when it came in contact with sulfur in the air. The setting for this story varied—a public lecture, a laboratory, a summer resort—but in each case the cosmetic-using woman was humiliated because her "lily white" complexion had been muddied and darkened.[17]

By the late nineteenth century, the linkage between cosmetics and racial identity, articulated increasingly in the languages of Darwinism and anthropology, served to mark boundaries of civilization and savagery. Face paint, which falsified beauty, hindered the progress of civilization by distorting the evolutionary process of sexual selection. One writer called visible cosmetics a "lingering taint of the savage and barbarous"; others ridiculed ultrafashionable American women, juxtaposing them with Pygmies, Hottentots, and other African peoples.[18] Such social classifications received reinforcement through common representational strategies. Smithsonian anthropologist Robert Shufeldt, for example, used photographs in his 1891 account of "Indian types of beauty"; the most beautiful posed in the guise of Victorian ladies, while those considered ugly appeared ethnographically, their seminaked bodies, frontal pose, and

Figure 1. *Every One Recognizes Your Ability to Paint (Yourself)*. Trade card, ca. 1870.

Figure 2. Robert W. Shufeldt, *A Belle of Laguna,* 1891.
Courtesy of Division of Rare and Manuscript Collections, Cornell University Library.

Figure 3. Robert W. Shufeldt, *Mohave Women,* 1891.
Courtesy of Division of Rare and Manuscript Collections,
Cornell University Library.

cosmetic paint conveying their "alien" and savage nature (figures 2 and 3).[19]

The dominant discourse on cosmetics, then, placed paint outside the truthful representation of personal and social identity, identifying cosmetics with disrepute and deceit, a debased female and non-European "other." This discourse was an effort to re-inscribe the fixity and naturalness of social hierarchies by ensuring that external manifestations corresponded to inner being. The longstanding association of visible cosmetics with illicit sexuality and commerce, newly applied to nineteenth-century society, contributed to the bourgeois definition of the feminine. Even so, artifice and artfulness threatened to undermine this paradigm.

Making up for the Show

In the post-Civil War decades, cultural tensions over female appearance and identity seem to have deepened substantially. Evidence of such anxiety abounds: warnings about prostitutes disguised as shoppers and saleswomen appearing to be "ladies"; advice to marriageable men on how to tell authentic beauties from fakes; stories of light-skinned octoroons passing into white society. Whether women's social status was quantitatively more fluid and unstable at this time would be difficult to establish, but certainly this perception was widespread.[20]

Scattered evidence in diaries and letters suggests that some nineteenth-century women embraced visible cosmetics and the potential for transgression and illusion they offered. During and after the Civil War, fashionable women, young and old, played with and subverted notions of natural beauty and appropriate female behavior. Ellen Ruggles Strong, a member of New York's social elite and wife of civic leader George Templeton Strong, provides one example. At various parties, philanthropic events, and hospital relief sites, Ellen could

be seen, in diarist Mary Lydig Daly's words, "painted like a wanton." Her husband, however, clothed Ellen in the garb of true womanhood: "poor, little Ellen in her ignorance and simplicity," "a noble little girl." Although her own voice is missing, Ellen's skillful performance is not. Artfully, she portrayed the dutiful wife who appeared at hospitals and charity events, who gave up waltzing when her husband disapproved, and who shunned Tiffany's vanities as he watched. Out of his presence, she dabbled in the world of fashion, seductive young men, parties, and pleasures.[21] Her beauty secrets, unseen by men yet visible to women, were integral to her rendering of both parts.

This performance of identity—constituting the self through appearance and gesture—was fundamentally at odds with notions of fixed personal and social identity. While such performances may inherently constitute identity,[22] they became more visible and apparent *as performances* in the late nineteenth and early twentieth centuries. Increasingly incorporated into Americans' understanding of the self, notions of performance reconfigured the ways in which cosmetic practices were understood as well. What had been perceived as a falsifying, deceptive practice might instead be understood as dramatic enactment in a culture increasingly oriented to "looks," display, spectatorship, and consumptions.[23]

The legitimation of visible cosmetics occurred first in contexts where women were consciously representing themselves to others, performing a role, or creating themselves as spectacles to be viewed. In the photographer's studio and the theater, we can see particular ways in which the physiognomic paradigm was undermined.

Photographic portrait taking became an occasion, as Alan Trachtenberg has put it, for "the making of oneself over into a social image," with the urban photographer's gallery a "new kind of city place devoted to performance." Patrons appeared dressed in their fanciest clothing, laden with jewelry, and they struck unnatural poses. Photographers began to teach their clients the art of self-portrayal. H. J. Rodgers' manual, for example, advised sitters on understanding their physiognomy, choosing appropriate fashions, and using cosmetics to enhance the face; the book included pages of cosmetic recipes.[24]

Although photographers praised the facticity of the photograph over the painted portrait, from the sitter's perspective the surface image of the photograph pulled in another direction, toward a critical assessment of appearance itself. The truth of the photograph could be quite painful, "too natural, to please any other than very beautiful sitters."[25] Given the disparity between self-image and photographic "truth," American women who might not wear cosmetics in their daily lives demanded to have their faces made up at the portrait studios. As the photograph became a popular commodity, it may have made manifest the tensions latent in the physiognomic paradigm by making beauty a more problematic category. What had once been a matter mainly for the imagination and the mirror was now externalized and fixed on the photographic plate. As "factual" representations of appearance, photographs measured the distance between ideal beauty and reality.

In the post-Civil War years, these measurements of appearance became even more palpable as actresses and professional "beauties" rose from women of questionable morality to celebrities and "stars." Although the United States had been enchanted by such female performers as Jenny Lind and Fanny Kemble in the antebellum period, women achieved a new prominence on the stage after 1860. While many of these were players in serious drama, the most visible and controversial were those who performed in burlesques and shows that combined sexual display with comic dialogue. Such figures as Adah Mencken and the British Blondes brought to the American stage a new kind of actress, who blurred the line between the performance of a theatrical role and the performance of her "real self." These women brought a new theatricality into everyday life, fostering a contentious debate over artifice and cosmetic effects. Their use of blonde hair dye and visible makeup became the popular rage, at least in New York.[26]

Female actresses were not only much talked about, they seem to have been incorporated into the private lives of Americans in new ways. By the 1860s, celebrity *carte de visite* photographs circulated widely. These images of retouched and idealized actresses were traded and placed in photograph albums, often on the same pages as pictures of family and friends. Significantly, stage actresses were the first group to offer advertising testimonials for cosmetics. The new conceptual separation of prostitutes and actresses opened a space for the promotion of the use of makeup as a legitimate female cultural practice.[27]

The close relationship between makeup and performance began to justify the use of cosmetics more generally in the nineteenth century. Women wore makeup on occasions involving public or semipublic display, such as amateur theatricals, tableaux vivants, coming-out parties, and balls. The advice literature of the late nineteenth century distinguished between daytime and evening activities, permitting face powder and rouge in settings that involved a play-world of artificial light, spectacle, and pleasures. Artifice was allowable, beauty manuals now conceded, if used in the service of representing a woman's "true" identity. An old woman who used rouge to deceive a man into marriage was a "painted Jezebel," observed one advice book, but reddening the cheeks was a "fair stratagem" of the young woman if its use originated in "an innocent desire to please."[28] Here the older view of cosmetics was acknowledged but displaced by a new understanding of artifice based on the intentions and desires of the cosmetics consumer.

Connotations of women as tarnished merchandise continued to mark cosmetics: the prostitute remained the touchstone of condemnatory views of these commodities. But a critical new element was advanced in the late nineteenth century: that making up was preparation for women's legitimate public performances. This view implied a degree of agency, self-creation, and pleasure in self-representation. For the nascent beauty industry, this became the new paradigm of female appearance.

The Cosmetics Industry and the Makeover

In the late nineteenth century, a growing trade in cosmetics and beauty products, reinforced by the proliferation of magazines, advice literature, and advertising, began to intervene in the cultural discourse over the authenticity of the female face. Before that time, the cosmetics trade was small-scale and locally based. Typically a pharmacist or hairdresser would compound creams and lotions for sale to a familiar clientele. Some "patent cosmetics" were stocked by pharmacists and general stores, but there was little national distribution or advertising of cosmetic products.[29] By 1880 a spider's web of establishments—pharmaceutical houses, perfumers, beauty salons, drugstores, wholesale suppliers, the incipient mail order trade, and department stores—provided the infrastructure for beauty culture. This commercial nexus reached into every level of the social scale; by the early 1900s, beauty products were available to urban immigrants, African-Americans, and rural women.[30]

Commercial beauty culture converted complexion management from a largely private act to a public and visible ritual. Middle- and upper-class beauty parlors, like department stores, assiduously catered to their female clientele in the quality of their fixtures and the personal services provided by beauty operators. Even the cheaper salons created the experience of self-indulgence and sensuous pleasure, offering not only hairdressing but facial treatments and massage. Commercial Beauty culture popularized the democratic and anxiety-inducing idea that beauty could be achieved by all women—if only they used the correct products and treatments. Initially beauty culturists were reticent about visible cosmetics, favoring "natural" methods of achieving beauty over paints. Until World War I, advertisements rarely promoted rouge or eyebrow pencils, even though drugstores and salons carried them.

Nevertheless, beauty culturists and cosmetics manufacturers evolved a language of metamorphosis for their services and products that spoke directly to the troubled relationship between appearance and identity. Before-and-after advertisements, instructions for makeup applications, and cosmetology manuals spoke of transformation, what women's magazines today call the makeover. Cosmetics not only remade external appearance, they became a crucial aspect of self-realization.

The notion of makeover resonated throughout the emergent cosmetics industry. A number of its leading female entrepreneurs had made *themselves* over as they pursued business success. Helena Rubinstein, for example, claimed for herself an aristocratic heritage and extensive scientific training. She in fact came from a petit bourgeois family in Austria; her training consisted of a year or two in medical school; the face cream formula that launched her business came from a pharmacist uncle. Elizabeth Arden, Rubinstein's greatest competitor, promoted an image of wealthy Anglo-Saxon gentility and hauteur for herself and her company. She began life, however, as Florence Nightingale Graham, born into a Canadian lower-middle-class family. Like many young women, she migrated to New York to find work and support herself. Starting out as a receptionist and beauty operator, she eventually became an independent salon owner and successful entrepreneur.[31]

In the 1910s and 1920s, the makeover promised both personal and social transformation, although its precise meaning varied within a market divided along the lines of class, race, and age. Arden and Rubinstein, for example, quietly urged their wealthy clientele to make up in the French style to become fashion leaders, to distinguish themselves from the less modern bourgeois women who scorned makeup or hid their makeup practices. Mass-market manufacturers, in contrast, depicted the makeover as the first step toward achieving upward mobility and personal popularity. They conceived of public arenas, from the workplace to the boardwalk, as performance sites where young women could succeed through manufactured beauty.

In promising transformation, the cosmetics industry blurred the distinction between the made-up face as *revealing* a woman's inner self and the made-up face *constituting* that self. The Armand complexion powder campaign exemplified the mixed message. This mass-market firm ran a series of advertisements in 1929 appealing to popular interest in psychology and beauty. Armand's advertising directed each woman to "find yourself," offering a free question-and-answer booklet written by a "famous psychologist and a noted beauty expert." However, individuality was readily submerged into a typology that coded personality in terms of facial appearance. Except for hairstyle and color, the faces of these women were hardly distinguishable, yet their personalities were classed with names—Sheba, Cleopatra, Cherie—that appear to be ethnic euphemisms. By the mid-1920s companies packaged products on the basis of personality types defined largely by skin tone, eye color, or hair color.[32]

Cosmetic promotions found new ways to dislodge the sense of fixity and naturalism in the feminine. The early advertising for Pompeian face cream stressed conventional mother-daughter relationships, using the language of Victorian sentimentality and images that showed distinct differences in age and social role. By 1923, Pompeian was depicting the youthful modern mother. "You're getting younger every day!" observed the daughter, and indeed she was literally correct: mother had exactly the same face as her child. Maybelline advertisements broke the age-old association between eye makeup and "painted Jezebels" by promoting images of popular film actresses that were eroticized, yet within the realm of public acceptability. Advertising especially in confession and movie magazines, they urged young white working-class women to identify with these glamorous stars.[33]

By the early twentieth century, a mass cosmetics trade, supported by the coordinated efforts of advertising agencies, women's magazines, and professional beauty "experts," had validated a female identity signified by, and to some extent formed in, the marking and coloring of the face. Through this claim, which simultaneously prescribed feminine appearance and played upon the consumer's belief in her individuality, the cosmetics industry attempted to make its products necessary to American women's appearance and sense of self.

The Beauty Culture of the "Other"

From the perspective of the late twentieth century, it may be hard not to view the aims and methods of commercial beauty culture in any but cynical terms. Decades of advertising and advice have touted the centrality of external beauty in women's successful negotiation of life and the role of cosmetics in enhancing self-esteem. For many feminists, these promises are simply manipulative and victimizing tactics to sell products.[34] The historical evidence suggests, however, that the cosmetics industry exploited already existing tensions in the relationship between appearance and female identity. Moreover, the specific rhetoric of cosmetic transformation, and the general promotion of beauty culture in the early twentieth century, spoke to genuine concerns and desires whose terms were bound up in the changing experiences of women. The proliferation of cosmetics in the consumer market coincided with women's new relationship to the public sphere: their expanding but contested participation in economic, political, and social activities formerly understood in cultural terms as masculine. Women's growing presence in the labor force generated anxiety that was frequently represented in bodily and sexual imagery. Indeed, a number of the new jobs open to women required particular attention to appearance and interpersonal behavior. Saleswomen, waitresses, secretaries, entertainers and others working in the clerical and service sectors transformed themselves into the "types" expected in these jobs. Even factory workers found themselves sorted

into different kinds of labor based on the appearance of respectability, good grooming, and ethnic identity. Guidance counselors in high schools and colleges, orienting young people to the job market, offered vocational advice to women in part on the basis of attractiveness and other physical attributes. At the same time, working women brought cosmetic practices into their work cultures as a source of on-the-job pleasure and assertions: saleswomen, for example, exasperated department store managers with their excessive use of face powder.[35]

The social organization of sexuality and marriage similarly reinforced the importance of appearance in the early twentieth century. Dating and courtship increasingly occurred in a market context, in commercialized leisure and consumption activities where women could trade on their looks. The popular ideology of romantic love, articulated not only in mass-circulation magazines but in peer group cultures in schools and workplaces, promulgated notions of personal magnetism and fascination that, for women, merged with physical beauty.[36]

A closer look at the relationship of the cosmetics trade to specific communities of women should lead us to consider seriously the claims and concerns expressed by both producers and consumers of cosmetics. This is particularly the case for immigrant women, working-class women, and African-American women—the very groups against whom ideals of beauty had been defined in the nineteenth century. For women culturally defined as other, commercial beauty culture could become an arena in which issues not only of appearance but of personal, social, and even political identity might be staged and discussed.

In the early twentieth century, young immigrant and second-generation women, for example, signaled their new "American" status by adopting the conventions of external beauty promoted not only in cosmetics advertisements and beauty salons but in their interactions with peers. Cosmetics were often the grounds for intergenerational conflict, seen by young women as necessary for participation in social life but perceived by parents as sexually provocative. While many women used "respectable" amounts of powder and rouge, others embraced the theatricality of cosmetics. Some delighted in *showing* the artifice—making up their faces in restaurants or pulling powder puffs out of stocking tops at dance halls. Significantly, the most extreme cosmetics users in the early 1920s appear to have been working-class truants and delinquents, who wore thick layers of face powder and rouge, painted bow lips, and beaded eyelashes. Adopting an "artificial" facial appearance, they rejected the stigmatizing labels others placed on them, such as "problem girls" or "whores," and, imitating their movie idols, transformed themselves into romantic heroines.[37]

An even more telling example is the development of an African-American hair-care and cosmetics industry in the early 1900s, marketing to consumers who had been culturally denied the possibility of beauty in the nineteenth century.[38] Although white-owned patent medicine firms began to cultivate a Black consumer market in the 1880s and 1890s, such African-American entrepreneurs as Anthony Overton, Madame C. J. Walker, and Annie Turnbo Malone revolutionized the trade. The timing of their industry's development is notable: the industry took off in the period of disfranchisement and entrenched segregation in the South, worsening economic conditions, an expanding Black population in southern cities, and the beginnings of the great migration to the North.

The period was also significant for Black women's individual and collective response to decades of abuse, poverty, and discrimination. An important part of this response was the public denunciation of stereotypes of Black womanhood and the search for new, empowering identities. Although it is middle-class, educated African-American women who offer the fullest evidence of this response, women outside this group sought new modes of self-definition as well. An important dimension of this effort lay in the making over of appearance. As Azalia Hackley, author of a beauty manual for "colored girls," wrote: "The time has come to fight, not only for rights, but for looks as well."[39]

Debates over hair staighteners and skin bleaches—the most controversial of many beauty products used by African-American women—exemplify both the empowering and constraining meanings expressed through self-presentation. Many Black women reformers, political leaders, and journalists drew the conclusion that the use of these products was evidence of white aesthetic and psychological domination.[40] Yet white emulation, in a literal sense, seems an insufficient explanation for their popularity. Although some African-Americans indeed "passed" into white society, bleaches and straighteners held little possibility of effecting such a transformation.[41] More to the point, European aesthetic domination shaped status distinctions *among* African-Americans. Lighter skin, straight hair, and European features were believed advantageous for gaining job opportunities and good marriage partners. Still, careful observers noted a more complex valuation of color than a simple hierarchy of whiteness. St. Clair Drake and Horace Cayton, in their study of Black Chicago in the 1940s, remarked: "When Negroes disapprove of 'blackness' they often mean a whole com-

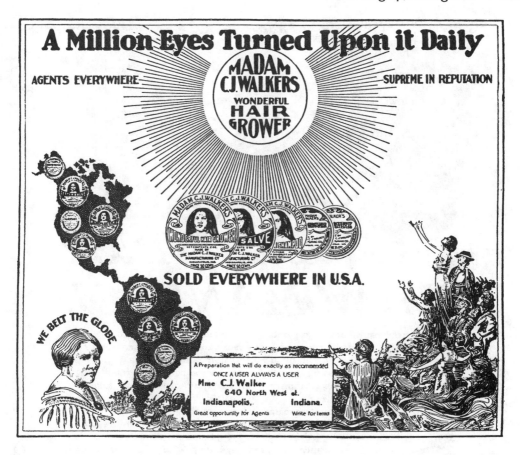

Figure 4. Madame C.J. Walker advertisement, 1919.

plex: dark-skin color, pronounced Negroid features and kinky hair."[42] It is this aesthetic complex, integral to white ideologies buttressing discrimination, and not an explicit desire to "look white" that African-American beauty culturists directly addressed. Gaining respect and dignity were the terms by which appearance became a basis of African-American commercial enterprise and consumption.

African-American beauty culturists made cosmetics central to the ideal of the "New Negro Woman." As consumers of beauty products, they argued, Black women could change the stereotyped representations that socially and sexually de-

based them. At the same time, evoking the Washingtonian emphasis on race pride and self-help, they called for public support of commercial beauty culture because these ventures empowered women as producers. Trained to be salon owners, beauty operatives, and sales agents, African-American women would gain opportunities for economic advancement unavailable to female domestic or agricultural workers.

Madam C. J. Walker, perhaps the best-known African-American woman entrepreneur, tirelessly promoted this understanding of beauty culture (figures 4 and 5). Her own efforts to provide as a single mother, which had prompted her entry into the hair-care

Figure 5. Madame C.J. Walker advertisement, 1925.

business, expanded into a larger "struggle . . . to build up Negro womanhood." She especially identified with poor Black women who toiled in the kitchen or the fields: "Don't think because you have to go down in the wash-tub that you are any less a lady." Beauty culture, Walker argued, offered economic emancipation for Black women subjected to a rigidly sex- and race-segregated labor market. Indeed, thousands of women, rural and urban, made a living or supplemented their income selling the "Walker System."[43]

Asserting that an attractive and well-groomed appearance would "glorify our womanhood," Walker studiously avoided the language of white emulation. Company advertising in the 1920s, after Walker's death, even further emphasized the central role of appearance in creating and expressing identity. A 1928 ad stated: "Radiate an air of prosperity and who is to know if your purse is lined with gold or not? Personal cleanliness, neatness, whitened teeth, luxurious hair, a flawless complexion and dainty hands—these are the things that impress others and pave the way for your success by building confidence." Individual success, however, could not be divorced from racial advancement. Amidst images of black businessmen, prosperous farms, and churches, it proclaimed, "Amazing Progress of Colored Race—Improved Appearance Responsible."[44]

Walker and other African-American entrepreneurs asserted that beauty products would effect personal and social transformation by lifting Black women from the cultural debasement represented in racist stereotypes of kinky hair and unkempt appearance. That is, cosmetics "performed" respectability and modernity. This position had limitations entrepreneurs and consumers of beauty culture never fully addressed in these years: they did not develop an ex-plicit critique of white-defined beauty standards, nor did they come to terms with the effects of that aesthetic on the products and images promoted and consumed. At the same time, it is clear that African-American beauty culture signified a modern identity to many Black women and was integrated into their claims for the dignity and self-definition that had historically been denied them in American life.[45]

Conclusion

In this case study, the early-twentieth-century discourse on cosmetics, as articulated by producers and consumers of these commodities, shifted the burden of female identity from an essential, interior self to one formed in the marking and coloring of the face. Makeup contributed to the constitution of women's identity, no longer to its falsification. In the period for 1900 to 1930, making up became one of the tangible ways women in their everyday lives confirmed their identities as women: they *became* women in the application of blusher, mascara, and lipstick. These applications carried various and contested meanings for women. If one effect of the cosmetics industry was to represent "woman" as a kind of merchandise or objectified spectacle, another was to destabilize nineteenth-century cultural hierarchies among women, open economic opportunities, and represent, however inadequately, new claims for cultural legitimacy. These commodities offered women a language through which they could articulate new demands, concerns, and desires: this in a period when women's relationships to the civic, economic, and social "public" realms were under renegotiation, a period when social differences of gender, race, ethnicity, and class were being challenged and redefined. In this context, external appearances could be manipulated to represent and mediate new notions of identity. Significantly, this possibility was seized not only be white middle-class women, the subjects of most studies of consumer culture, but also by immigrant, white working-class and African-American women as well.

Notes

1. *Mademoiselle* 7, no. 1 (June 1938): 13.
2. Warren I. Susman, "'Personality' and the Making of Twentieth-Century Culture," in *Culture as History* (New York, 1984), 271–86. See also T. J. Jackson Lears, "From Salvation to Self-Realization: Advertising and the Therapeutic Roots of the Consumer Culture, 1880–1930," in *The Culture of Consumption*, ed. Richard Wightman Fox and T. J. Jackson Lears (New York, 1983), 1–38; Simon J. Bronner, ed. *Consuming Visions: Accumulation and Display of Goods in America, 1880–1920* (New York, 1989); William Leach, "Transformations in a Culture of Consumption: Women and Department Stores, 1890–1925," *Journal of American History* 71 (September 1984): 319–42; William Leach, *Land of Desire: Merchants, Power, and the Rise of a New American Culture* (New York, 1993); Larry May, *Screening Out the Past: The Birth of Mass Culture and the Motion Picture Industry* (New York, 1980). T. J. Jackson Lear's recent work takes issue with Susman's framework: see "Beyond Veblen: Rethinking Consumer Culture in America," in *Consuming Visions*, ed. Simon J. Bronner, 73–98.
3. Important theoretical contributions include: Joan Wallach Scott, *Gender and the Politics of History* (New York, 1988); Judith Butler, *Gender Trouble: Feminism and the Subversion of Identity* (New York, 1990). See also Andreas Huyssen, "Mass Culture as Woman: Modernism's Other," in *Studies in Entertainment: Critical Approaches to Mass Culture,* ed. Tania Modleski (Bloomington, Ind., 1986) 188–207.
4. The "physiognomic paradigm" is brilliantly explicated in Allan Sekula, "The Body and the Archive," *October*, no. 39 (winter 1986): 3–64. See also Joanne Finkelstein, *The Fashioned Self* (Philadelphia, 1991), 15–77. Primary sources include: Alexander Walker, *Beauty* (New York, 1844), xix; Wilson Flagg, *An Analysis of Female Beauty* (Boston, 1833); Sir James Clark, *The Ladies' Guide to Beauty* (New York, 1858); *Etiquette for Ladies* (Philadelphia, 1841), 116, 126.
5. Karen Halttunen, *Confidence Men and Painted Women* (New Haven, 1982), esp. 56–91. For primary documentation, see *Godey's Ladies Book* 29 (July 1844): 32; Caroline Lee Hentz, "The Beauty Transformed," *Godey's Ladies Book* 21 (November 1840): 194–202; idem, "The Fatal Cosmetic," *Godey's Ladies Book* 18 (June 1839): 265–74; [Hannah Murray and Mary Murray], *The American Toilet* (New York, 1827).
6. On fashion in the "consumer revolution" of the eighteenth century, see Neil McKendrick, John Brewer, and J. H. Plumb, *The Birth of a Consumer Society: The Commercialization of Eighteenth-Century England* (Bloomington, Ind., 1982), 34–99; Jennifer Jones, "The Taste for Fashion and Frivolity" (Ph.D. diss., Princeton University, 1991). On nineteenth-century clothing fashion, see Lois W. Banner, *American Beauty* (Chicago, 1983); Claudia B. Kidwell and Margaret C. Christman, *Suiting Everyone: The Democratization of Clothing in America* (Washington, D.C., 1974). The commodification of the nineteenth-century home is treated in Clifford E. Clark Jr., *The American Family Home, 1800–1960* (Chapel Hill, 1986), 103–130; Kenneth L. Ames, "Meaning in Artifacts: Hall Furnishings in Victorian American" *Journal of Interdisciplinary History* 9 (summer 1978): 19–46; Karen Halttunen, "From Parlor to Living Room: Domestic Space, Interior Decoration, and the Culture of Personality," in *Consuming Visions: Accumulation and Display of Goods in America, 1880–1920*. ed. Simon J. Bronner (New York, 1989), 157–89. See also David Jaffee, "Peddlers of Progress and the Transformation of the Urban North, 1760–1860," *Journal of American History* 78 (September 1991): 511–35.
7. Mrs. S A. Walker, *Female Beauty* (New York, 1846), 286–300, and color plates.
8. *The Book of Health and Beauty* (London, 1837), xviii, xvii; *Etiquette for Ladies*, 126.
9. Virginia Smith, "The Popularisation of Medical Knowledge: The Case of Cosmetics," *Society for the Social History of Medicine Bulletin*, no. 39 (1986): 12–15; Londa Schiebinger, *The Mind Has No Sex? Women in the Origins of Modern Science* (Cambridge, 1989), 112–16. For unpublished recipe books, see those of Mrs. Lowell and Mrs. Charles Smith, Garrison Family Papers, MS Group 60, Sophia Smith Collection, Smith College, Northampton, Massachusetts. Published household manuals and beauty guides are numerous; see the sources given in nn. 4, 8, and 17 and the extensive collection at the American Antiquarian Society, Worcester, Massachusetts. Bibliographic information on cookbooks may be found in Eleanor Lowenstein, *Bibliography of*

American Cookery Books, 1742–1860 (Worcester, Mass., 1972).

10. Lydia Maria Child, *Letters from New York,* 2d ser., 5th ed. (New York, 1848), 248–50; *Humbug: A Look at Some Popular Impositions* (New York, 1859), 37–42, 92. Cosmetic makers took their cue from the patent medicine trade, discussed in James Harvey Young, *The Toadstool Millionaires* (Princeton, 1961).

11. Gilbert Vail, *A History of Cosmetics in America* (New York, 1947), 34–38, 49–53, 74–78. The constellation of practices denoting gentility is discussed in Richard L. Bushman, "High Style and Vernacular Culture," *Colonial British America,* ed. Jack P. Greene and J. R. Pole (Baltimore, 1984), 345–83.

12. Vail, *A History of Cosmetics,* 95. For a general discussion, see also Kathy Peiss, "Of Men and Makeup: The Gendering of Cosmetics in Twentieth-Century America" (paper presented at the Material Culture of Gender/The Gender of Material Culture conference, Winterthur Museum, 11 November 1989). The history of American men's appearance remains to be written. For an important study of the European case, see David Kuchta, "Inconspicuous Consumption: Masculinity, Political Economy, and Fashion in England, 1550–1776 (Ph.D. diss., University of California, Berkeley, 1991).

13. On middle-class formation and gender, see especially Mary Ryan, *The Cradle of the Middle Class* (Cambridge, Mass., 1981); Christine Stansell, *City of Women* (New York, 1986), 68–75, 156–168; Nancy Cott, *Bonds of Womanhood* (New Haven, 1977). The emergence of a scientific discourse on sexual difference is discussed in Thomas Laqueur, *Making Sex: Body and Gender from the Greeks to Freud* (Cambridge, Mass., 1990); and Cynthia Eagle Russett, *Sexual Science: The Victorian Construction of Womanhood* (Cambridge, Mass., 1989).

14. 2 Kings 9:30–37; also Ezekiel 23:40–49. Religious criticism of cosmetics was most pronounced in Puritanism, which linked cosmetics use to adultery and witchcraft. See Annette Drew-Bear, "Cosmetics and Attitudes toward Women in the Seventeenth Century," *Journal of Popular Culture* 9 (summer 1975): 31–37. For an example of nineteenth-century "scientific" Biblical criticism on Jezebel, see John Peter Lange, *Commentary on the Holy Scriptures; Volume VI of the Old Testament* (New York, 1887), 99–108.

15. George G. Foster, *New York by Gaslight and Other Urban Sketches,* ed. Stuart M. Blumin (Berkely, 1990), 154; Mary Ryan, *Women in Public* (Baltimore, 1990), 29; Marion S. Goldman, *Gold Diggers and Silver Miners: Prostitution and Social Life on the Comstock Lode* (Ann Arbor, 1981), 100. See also Stansell, *City of Women,* 187–88; Mariana Valverde, "The Love of Finery: Fashion and the Fallen Woman in Nineteenth-Century Social Discourse," *Victorian Studies* 32 (winter 1989): 169–88.

16. James D. McCabe, *Lights and Shadows of New York Life* (Philadelphia, 1872), 154; see also George Ellington, *The Women of New York* (1869; reprint, New York, 1972), 42–51, 82–90.

17. *Beauty: Its Attainment and Preservation* (New York, 1890), 232–33; Clark, *Ladies' Guide to Beauty,* iv–v; E. G. Storke, ed., *The Family and Householder's Guide* (Auburn, N.Y., 1859), 179.

18. Harry T. Finck, *Romantic Love and Personal Beauty* (New York, 1887), 327–29, 426, 452–59 (quote 458); Joseph Simms, *Physiognomy Illustrated or, Nature's Revelation of Character* (New York, 1891), 262–69, 505–31; Captain Mayne Reid, *Odd People* (Boston, 1864).

19. Robert W. Shufeldt, *Indian Types of Beauty,* pamphlet reprinted from *The American Field,* 1891, in the Department of Rare Books and Manuscripts, Kroch Library, Cornell University. See also Melissa Banta and Curtis M. Hinsley, *From Site to Sight: Anthropology, Photography, and the Power of Imagery* (Cambridge, Mass., 1986), 38–47.

20. For a brilliant discussion of this point in the context of legal history, see Amy Dru Stanley, "Conjugal Bonds and Wage Labor," *Journal of American History* 75 (1988): 471–500.

21. Cf. Harold Earl Hammond, ed., *Diary of a Union Lady, 1861–1865* (New York, 1962), 123, 321–22, 331–32; and Allan Nevins and Milton Halsey Thomas, eds., *The Diary of George Templeton Strong* (New York, 1952), 1:320, 317.

22. On this point, see Judith Butler, "Performative Acts and Gender Constitution: An Essay in Phenomenology and Feminist Theory," *Theatre Journal* 40 (December 1988): 519–31.

23. On this large cultural development, see Leach, "Transformations in a Culture of Consumption"; idem, *Land of Desire;* Rachel Bowlby, *Just Looking: Consumer Culture in Dreiser, Gissing, and Zola* (New York, 1985); Rosalind H. Williams, *Dream Worlds: Mass Consumption in Late-Nineteenth-Century France* (Berkeley, 1982); Robert C. Allen, *Horrible Prettiness: Burlesque and American Culture* (Chapel Hill, 1991).

24. Alan Trachtenberg, *Reading American Photographs* (New York, 1989), 14–70 (quote p. 40); see also William Welling, *Photography in America* (New York, 1978). H. J. Rodgers, *Twenty-Three Years under a Sky-Light* (Hartford,

1872); see also "Chip," *How to Sit for Your Photograph* (Philadelphia, [1872]).

25. Trachtenberg, *Reading American Photographs,* 24. See also *Photographic Art-Journal* 1(August 1851): 212; Beaumont Newhall, *The Daguerreotype in America* (New York, 1968), 69, 77; Mrs. A. M. Richards, *Memories of a Grandmother* (Boston, 1854), 13–14.

26. On actresses' cultural influence, see Allen, *Horrible Prettiness;* Banner, *American Beauty,* 106–54; Tracy C. Davis, *Actresses as Working Women* (London, 1991). On the hair dye controversy, see also the *New York Times,* 22 November 1868, 3; 28 March 1869, 4. For contemporary commentary, see Olive Logan, *Apropos of Women and Theaters* (New York, 1869).

27. On the *carte de visite* craze, see *Humphrey's Journal* 13 (1 March 1862): 326–30; 14 (1 October 1862): 123–24; 16 (15 July 1864): 84; *Photographic News* 6 (9 May 1862): 225–26. My discussion of the personal use and idealization of actresses' images is based on an examination of photograph albums, Visual Arts Workshop, Rochester, New York, and the *cartes de visite* and stereograph collections, International Museum of Photography, George Eastman House, Rochester, New York. See also Elizabeth Anne McCauley, *A. A. E. Disderi and the Carte de Visite Portrait Photograph* (New Haven, 1985); Dan Younger, "Cartes-de-Visite: Precedents and Social Influences," *California Museum of Photography Bulletin* 6, no. 4 (1987): 4–5. Abigail Solomon-Godeau (in "The Legs of the Countess," *October* 39 [winter 1986]: 65–69, 77–78, 94) and Faye Dudden (personal communication) have suggested that actresses learned how to heighten their beauty in photographs through conventionalized pose, gesture, and makeup.

28. I. A. Mathews and Co., *Hints on Various Subjects Connected with Our Business* (Buffalo, 1856), 72–73. On makeup and performance, see Richard Hudnut, *Twentieth-Century Toilet Hints* (New York, 1899), 28, 50; *Personal Beauty* (New York, 1875), 47; "Laird's Bloom of Youth," leaflet in Cosmetics files, Warshaw Collection of Business Americana, National Museum of American History, Smithsonian Institution. See also Edith Wharton, *The House of Mirth* (New York, 1905); and Theodore Dreiser, *Sister Carrie* (New York, 1991), for descriptions of tableaux vivants and amateur theatricals.

29. There is little quantitative evidence on cosmetics manufacturing in the nineteenth century, since it tended to be subsumed in manufacturing censuses under such categories as perfumes and soaps. Wholesale drug catalogues from 1800 to 1900 show a significant expansion in cosmetics stock after 1865, and again in the 1890s. Cf. T. W. Dyott, *Approved Patent and Family Medicines* (Philadelphia, 1814); H. B. Foster's *Prices Current* (Concord, N.H., 1860); McKesson and Robbins, *Prices Current of Drugs and Druggists' Articles* (New York, 1872); Peter Van Schaack and Sons, *Annual Price Current* (Chicago, 1899). One can infer from the daybooks and formularies of several New York and New Jersey drugists circa 1850–1880 that they ordered some commercially prepared cosmetics and continued to compound their own. See Bryan Hough, Daybook, 1856–1861; George E. Putney, Druggist's Invoice Book, 1857–1882; George H. White, Pharmacist's Book of Recipes, ca. 1857–1872, all in New Jersey Room, Alexander Library, Rutgers University, New Brunswick, N.J.

30. On the growth and organization of this industry, see Kathy Peiss, "Making Faces: The Cosmetics Industry and the Cultural Construction of Gender, 1890–1930," *Genders* 7 (spring 1990): 143–69; Banner, *American Beauty;* Margaret Allen, *Selling Dreams: Inside the Beauty Business* (New York, 1981).

31. Maxene Fabe, *Beauty Millionaire: The Life of Helena Rubinstein* (New York, 1972); Patrick O'Higgins, *Madame: An Intimate Biography of Helena Rubinstein* (New York, 1971); Alfred Allan Lewis and Constance Woodworth, *Miss Elizabeth Arden* (New York, 1972); Allen, *Selling Dreams,* 22–32.

32. Armand advertising proofs, Ayer Book 382, especially advt. no. 10039, 1929, N. W. Ayer Collection, National Museum of American History, Smithsonian Institution.

33. Cf. Pompeian advertisement in *Woman's Home Companion,* November 1909; and *Pictorial Review,* October 1923, 104; my thanks to Ellen Todd for her observations on the latter image. Maybelline advertising appeared in *Photoplay* and *True Story* in the 1920s.

34. For the most recent statement of this position, see Naomi Wolf, *The Beauty Myth* (New York, 1991).

35. See, for example, Lisa Fine, *The Souls of the Skyscraper* (Philadelphia, 1990), 62, 142, 175; Susan Porter Benson, *Counter Cultures: Saleswomen, Managers, and Customers in American Department Stores, 1890–1940* (Urbana, 1986), 139–40, 236–38; Alice Kessler-Harris, *Out to Work* (New York, 1982), 135–40; Dorothy Sue Cobble, *Dishing It Out* (Urbana, 1992), 122–31.

36. Kathy Peiss, *Cheap Amusements: Working Women and Leisure in Turn of the Century New York* (Philadelphia, 1986); Beth Bailey, *From Front Porch to Back Seat: Courtship in*

Twentieth-Century America (Baltimore, 1989); Pamela Haag, "In Search of 'The Real Thing': Ideologies of Love, Modern Romance, and Women's Sexual Subjectivity in the U.S., 1920–1940," *Journal of the History of Sexuality* 2 (April 1992): 547–77.

37. On working-class women's use of cosmetics, see Peiss, *Cheap Amusements;* Marlou Belyea, "The Joy Ride and the Silver Screen: Commercial Leisure, Delinquency, and Play Reform in Los Angeles, 1990–1980" (Ph.D. diss., Boston University, 1983), 309–10; Mary Odem, "Single Mothers, Delinquent Daughters, and the Juvenile Court in Early-Twentieth-Century Los Angeles," *Journal of Social History* 25 (September 1991): 27–44. On immigrants and American style, see Andrew Heinze, *Adapting to Abundance: Jewish Immigrants, Mass Consumption, and the Search for American Identity* (New York, 1990); Elizabeth Ewen, *Immigrant Women in the Land of Dollars* (New York, 1985). For the influence of the motion pictures on popular style and appearance, see Herbert Blumer, *Movies and Conduct* (New York, 1933), 30–44.

38. The following discussion derives from my chapters on the African-American beauty industry in *Making Faces: Cosmetics and American Culture* (forthcoming). See also Gwendolyn Robinson, "Class, Race, and Gender: A transcultural Theoretical and Sociohistorical Analysis of Cosmetic Institutions and Practices to 1920" (Ph.D. diss., University of Illinois, Chicago, 1984).

39. E. Azalia Hackley, *The Colored Girl Beautiful* (Kansas City, Mo., 1916), 36. For a discussion of the new discourses on Black womanhood, see Hazel V. Carby, *Reconstructing Womanhood: The Emergence of the Afro-American Novelist* (New York, 1987), 95–120.

40. These criticisms appear in the radical press of the post-World War I period, including the *Messenger, Crusader,* and *Negro World,* as well as such "race papers" as the *New York Age.* The most nuanced analyses, however, came from the earlier black-female reform tradition. See, for example, Nanie Burroughs, "Not Color But Character," *Voice of the Negro* 1 (July 1904): 277–78; Fannie Barrier Williams, "The Colored Girl," *Voice of the Negro* 2 (June 1905): 400–403; Anna Julia Cooper, *A Voice from the South* (1892; reprint, New York, 1969), 75.

41. The cosmetic effects of bleach creams, for example, varied with the active ingredients. Some lightened blemishes and discolorations; others peeled the top layer of the skin, revealing the lighter layer below. However, the effect was a temporary one because exposure to the sun returned the skin to its original state. See Gerald A Spencer, *Cosmetology in the Negro* (New York, 1944).

42. Horace Cayton and St. Clair Drake, *Black Metropolis* (New York, 1945), 503. On the continuing salience of color hierarchies in distributing opportunity and resources, see Verna Keith and Cedric Herring, "Skin Tone and Stratification in the Black Community," *American Journal of Sociology* 97 (November 1991): 760–779. See also Lawrence Levine's important discussion of color and the blues in *Black Culture and Black Consciousness* (New York, 1977) 284–93.

43. National Negro Business League, *Report of the Fifteenth Annual Convention* (Muskogee, Okla., 1914), 152; *Report of the Thirteenth Annual Convention* (Chicago, 1912), 154–55; *Report of the Fourteenth Annual Convention* (Philadelphia, 1913), 211–212. On Madam C. J. Walker's remarkable life, see A'Lelia Perry Bundles, *Madame C. J. Walker* (New York, 1991); Robinson, "Class, Race, and Gender" (video documentary, 1988). For contemporary commentaries, see F. B. Ransom, "Manufacturing Toilet Articles: A Big Negro Business," *Messenger* 5 (December 1923): 937; George S. Schuyler, "Madam C. J. Walker," *Messenger* 6 (August 1924): 251–58 passim.

44. "Amazing Progress of Colored Race," two-page Madam C. J. Walker advertisement, *Oklahoma Eagle,* 3 March 1928, clipping in box 262, f4, Barnett Collection, Chicago Historical Society, Chicago, Illinois.

45. See letters written to Madam C. J. Walker accompanying product orders in 1918, boxes 34–36, Madam C. J. Walker Collection (1910–1980), Indiana Historical Society, Indianapolis, Indiana. I am grateful to A'Lelia Bundles for granting me permission to see these records and to archivist Wilma Gibbs for her assistance.

24

If Men Could Menstruate

Gloria Steinem

Living in India made me understand that a white minority of the world has spent centuries conning us into thinking a white skin makes people superior, even though the only thing it really does is make them more subject to ultraviolet rays and wrinkles.

Reading Freud made me just as skeptical about penis envy. The power of giving birth makes "womb envy" more logical, and an organ as external and unprotected as the penis makes men very vulnerable indeed.

But listening recently to a woman describe the unexpected arrival of her menstrual period (a red stain had spread on her dress as she argued heatedly on the public stage) still made me cringe with embarrassment. That is, until she explained that, when finally informed in whispers of the obvious event, she had said to the all-male audience, "and you should be *proud* to have a menstruating woman on your stage. It's probably the first real thing that's happened to this group in years!"

Laughter. Relief. She had turned a negative into a positive. Somehow her story merged with India and Freud to make me finally understand the power of positive thinking. Whatever a "superior" group has will be used to justify its superiority, and whatever an "inferior" group has will be used to justify its plight. Black men were given poorly paid jobs because they were said to be "stronger" than white men, while all women were relegated to poorly paid jobs because they were said to be "weaker." As the little boy said when asked if he wanted to be a lawyer like his mother, "Oh no, that's women's work." Logic has nothing to do with oppression.

So what would happen if suddenly, magically, men could menstruate and women could not?

Clearly, menstruation would become an enviable, boast-worthy, masculine event:

Men would brag about how long and how much.

Young boys would talk about it as the envied beginning of manhood. Gifts, religious ceremonies, family dinners, and stag parties would mark the day.

To prevent monthly work loss among the powerful, Congress would fund a National Institute of Dysmenorrhea. Doctors would research little about heart attacks, from which men were hormonally protected, but everything about cramps.

Sanitary supplies would be federally funded and free. Of course, some men would still pay for the prestige of such commercial brands as Paul Newman Tampons, Muhammad Ali's Rope-a-Dope Pads, John Wayne Maxi Pads, and Joe Namath Jock Shields— "For Those Light Bachelor Days."

Statistical surveys would show that men did better in sports and won more Olympic medals during their periods.

Generals, right-wing politicians, and religious fundamentalists would cite menstruation ("*men*-struation") as proof that only men could serve God and country in combat ("You have to give blood to take blood"), occupy high political office ("Can women be properly fierce without a monthly cycle governed by the planet Mars?"), be priests, ministers, God Himself ("He gave this blood for our sins"), or rabbis ("Without a monthly purge of impurities, women are unclean").

Male liberals or radicals, however, would insist that women are equal, just different; and that any woman could join their ranks if only she were willing to recognize the primacy of menstrual rights ("Everything else is a single issue") or self-inflict a major wound every month ("You *must* give blood for the revolution").

Street guys would invent slang ("He's a three-pad man") and "give fives" on the corner with some exchange like, "Man, you lookin' *good!*"

"Yeah, man, I'm on the rag!"

TV shows would treat the subject openly. *(Happy Days:* Richie and Potsie try to convince Fonzie that he is still "The Fonz," though he has missed two periods in a row. *Hill Street Blues:* The whole precinct hits the same cycle.) So would newspapers. (SUMMER SHARK SCARE THREATENS MENSTRUATING MEN. JUDGE CITES MONTHLIES IN PARDONING RAPISTS.) And so would movies. (Newman and Redford in *Blood Brothers!)*

Men would convince women that sex was more pleasurable at "that time of the month." Lesbians would be said to fear blood and therefore life itself, though all they needed was a good menstruating man.

Medical schools would limit women's entry ("they might faint at the sight of blood").

Of course, intellectuals would offer the most moral and logical arguments. Without that biological gift for measuring the cycles of the moon and planets, how could a woman master any discipline that demanded a sense of time, space, mathematics—or the ability to measure anything at all? In philosophy and religion, how could women compensate for being disconnected from the rhythm of the universe? Or for their lack of symbolic death and resurrection every month?

Menopause would be celebrated as a positive event, the symbol that men had accumulated enough years of cyclical wisdom to need no more.

Liberal males in every field would try to be kind. The fact that "these people" have no gift for measuring life, the liberals would explain, should be punishment enough.

And how would women be trained to react? One can imagine right-wing women agreeing to all these arguments with a staunch and smiling masochism. ("The ERA would force housewives to wound themselves every month": Phyllis Schlafly.

"Your husband's blood is as sacred as that of Jesus—and so sexy, too?": Marabel Morgan.) Reformers and Queen Bees would adjust their lives to the cycles of the men around them. Feminists would explain endlessly that men, too, needed to be liberated from the false idea of Martian aggressiveness, just as women needed to escape the bonds of "menses-envy." Radical feminists would add that the oppression of the nonmenstrual was the pattern for all other oppressions. ("Vampires were our first freedom fighters!") Cultural feminists would exalt a female bloodless imagery in art and literature. Socialist feminists would insist that, once capitalism and imperialism were overthrown, women would menstruate, too. ("If women aren't yet menstruating in Russia," they would explain, "it's only because true socialism can't exist within capitalist encirclement.")

In short, we would discover, as we should already guess, that logic is in the eye of the logician. (For instance, here's an idea for theorists and logicians: If women are supposed to be less rational and more emotional at the beginning of our menstrual cycle when the female hormone is at its lowest level, then why isn't it logical to say that, in those few days, women behave the most like the way men behave all month long? I leave further improvisations up to you.)

The truth is that, if men could menstruate, the power justifications would go on and on.

If we let them.

Violence

PART V

The articles in this section focus on some of the ways that, as Ntozake Shange puts it, "we pay for being born a girl": sexual harassment, female genital mutilation, battery, rape, and murder. The authors illustrate that violence against women cannot be treated as a problem of individual men, but must be analyzed as a system akin to terrorism by which males control and dominate women. Central to this system is the way in which violence and victimhood are intertwined with traditional notions of masculinity and femininity—a phenomenon some feminists have labeled a "rape culture." Two of the articles explore this rape culture in more detail, highlighting the characteristics of social environments that promote or inhibit rape. A. Ayres Boswell and Joan Z. Spade focus on male-female interactions at fraternity parties, while Julie Mostov examines how women's link to the nation and to national identity puts them at risk of rape in contests over national borders. They suggest that efforts to alter the culture of rape need to incorporate changes at ground level—that is, in everyday interactions between women and men—as well as changes in the ways women are represented in public discourse— moving away from women as symbols of the life and health of the nation to women as symbols of political and economic action.

Suggestions for Further Reading

Barry, Kathleen, Charlotte Bunch and Shirley Castley. 1984. *International Feminism: Networking Against Female Sexual Slavery.* New York: The International Women's Tribune Center.

Bunch, Charlotte and Roxanne Carillo. 1991. *Gender Violence: A Development and Human Rights Issue.* New Brunswick, NJ: Center for Women's Global Leadership.

Burbank, Victoria K. "Cross-Cultural Perspectives on Aggression in Women and Girls: An Introduction," *Sex Roles,* 30, 169–176.

Chan, C. S. 1987. "Asian-American Women: Psychological Responses to Sexual Exploitation and Cultural Stereotypes," *Asian-American Psychological Association Journal*, 12, 11–15.

Choi, Alfred and Jeffrey L. Edelson. 1996. "Social Disapproval of Wife Assaults: A National Survey of Singapore," *Journal of Comparative Family Studies*, 27, 73–88.

Cooper-White, Pamela. 1995. *The Cry of Tamar: Violence Against Women and the Church's Response*. Minneapolis, MN: Fortress Press.

Copelon, Rhonda. 1995. "Gendered War Crimes: Conceptualizing Rape in Time of War." In Julie Stone Peters and Andrea Wolper, eds. *Women's Rights, Human Rights: International Feminist Perspectives*. New York: Routledge.

Davies, Miranda. 1994. *Women and Violence*. Atlantic Highlands, NJ: Zed Books.

Dorkenoo, Efua. 1994. *Cutting the Rose: Female Genital Mutilation: The Practice and Its Prevention*. London: Minority Rights Group.

Fischman, Yael. 1996. "Sexual Torture as an Instrument of War," *American Journal of Orthopsychiatry*, 66, 161–162.

Heise, Lori L., Alanagh Raikes, Charlotte H. Watts, and Anthony B. Zwi. 1994. "Violence Against Women: A Neglected Public Health Issue in Less Developed Countries," *Social Science and Medicine*, 39, 1165–1179.

Kim, Elaine. 1987. "Sex Tourism in Asia: A Reflection of Political and Economic Inequality." In Eui-Young Yu and E. Phillips, eds. *Korean Women in Transition*. Los Angeles: Center for Korean American and Korean Studies.

Levinson, D. 1989. *Family Violence in Cross-Cultural Perspective*. Newbury Park, CA: Sage Publications.

Mills, Linda. 1996. "Empowering Battered Women Transnationally: The Case for Postmodern Interventions," *Social Work*, 41, 261–268.

Omvedt, G. 1990. *Violence Against Women: New Movements and New Theories in India*. New Delhi: Kali for Women.

Rich, B. Ruby. 1993. "Never a Victim: Jodie Foster, A New Kind of Female Hero." In Pam Cook and Philip Dodd, eds. *Women and Film: A Sight and Sound Reader*. Philadelphia: Temple University Press.

Schuler, Margaret, ed. 1992. *Freedom from Violence: Women's Strategies from Around the World*. New York: UNIFEM.

Stiglmayer, Alexandra, ed. 1994. *Mass Rape: The War Against Women in Bosnia-Herzegovina*. Lincoln: University of Nebraska Press.

Thomas, Dorothy Q. and Michele E. Beasley. 1993. "Domestic Violence as a Human Rights Issue," *Human Rights Quarterly*, 15, 36–62.

White, Evelyn C. 1994. *Chain Chain Change: For Black Women in Abusive Relationships*. Seattle, WA: Seal Press.

25

is not so gd to be born a girl

Ntozake Shange

Is not so gd to be born a girl/ some times. that's why societies usedta throw us away/ or sell us/ or play with our vaginas/ cuz that's all girls were gd for/ at least women cd carry things & cook/ but to be born a girl is not good sometimes/ some places/ such abominable things cd happen to us. i wish it waz gd to be born a girl everywhere/ then i wd know for sure that no one wd be infibulated/ that's a word no one wants us to know/ "infibulation" is sewing our vaginas up with cat gut or weeds or nylon thread to insure our virginity/ virginity insurance=infibulation/ that can also make it impossible for us to live thru labor/ make it impossible for the baby to live thru labor/ infibulation lets us get infections that we cant mention cuz disease in the ovaries is a sign that we're dirty anyway/ so wash yrself cuz once infibulated we have to be cut open to have you know what/ the joy of the phallus/ that we may know nothing abt/

ever/ especially if something else not good that happens to little girls happens/ if we've been excised/ had our labia removed with glass or scissors/ if we've lost our clitoris because our pleasure is profane & the presence of our naturally evolved clitoris wd disrupt the very unnatural dynamic of polygamy/ so with no clitoris, no labia, & infibulation/ we're sewn-up, cut-up, pared down & sore if not dead/ & oozing puss, if not terrified that so much of our body waz wrong & did not belong on earth/ such thoughts lead to a silence/ that hangs behind veils & straight jackets/ it really is not so good to be born a girl when we have to be infibulated, excised, clitorectomized & still be afraid to walk the streets or stay home at night.

i'm so saddened that being born a girl makes it dangerous to attend midnight mass unescorted. some places if we're born girls & some one else who's very sick & weak &

cruel/ attacks us & breaks our hymen/ we have to be killed/ sent away from our families/ forbidden to touch our children. these strange people who wound little girls are known as attackers, molesters, & rapists. they are known all over the world & are proliferating at a rapid rate. to be born a girl who will always have to worry not only abt the molesters, the attackers & the rapists/ but also abt their peculiarities/ does he stab too/ or shoot/ does he carry an ax/ does he spit on you/ does he know if he doesn't drop sperm we cant prove we've been violated/ those subtlties make being a girl too complex/ for some of us & we go crazy/ or never go anyplace.

some of us have never had an open window or a walk alone/ but sometimes our homes are not safe for us either/ rapists & attackers & molesters are not strangers to everyone/ they are related to somebody/ & some of them like raping & molesting their family members better than a girl-child they don't know yet/ this is called incest & girl children are discouraged from revealing attacks from uncle or daddy/ cuz what wd mommy do/ after all daddy may have seen to it that abortions were outlawed in his state/ so that mommy might have too many children/ to care abt some "fun" daddy might have been having with the 2 year old/ she's a girl after all/ we have to get used to it/ but infibulation, excision, clitorectomies, rape, & incest/ are irrevocable life-deniers/ life-stranglers & disrespectful of natural elements/ i wish these things wdnt happen anywhere anymore/ then i cd say it waz gd to be born a girl everywhere/ even though gender is not destiny/ right now being born a girl is to be born threatened/ i dont respond well to threats/ i want being born a girl to be a cause for celebration/ cause for protection & nourishment of our birthright/ to live freely with passion, knowing no fear/ that our species waz somehow incorrect.

& we are now plagued with rapists & clitorectomies. we pay for being born girls/ but we owe no one anything/ not our labia, not our clitoris, not our lives. we are born girls & live to be women who live our own lives/ to live our lives/
to have/
our lives/
to live.

26

Sexual Terrorism

Carole J. Sheffield

No two of us think alike about it, and yet it is clear to me, that question underlies the whole movement, and our little skirmishing for better laws, and the right to vote, will yet be swallowed up in the real question, viz: Has a woman a right to herself? It is very little to me to have the right to vote, to own property, etc., if I may not keep my body, and its uses, in my absolute right. Not one wife in a thousand can do that now.

–Lucy Stone, in a letter to Antoinette Brown, July 11, 1855

The right of men to control the female body is a cornerstone of patriarchy. It is expressed by their efforts to control pregnancy and childbirth and to define female health care in general. Male opposition to abortion is rooted in opposition to female autonomy. Violence and the threat of violence against females represent the need of patriarchy to deny that a woman's body is her own property and that no one should have access to it without her consent. Violence and its corollary, fear, serve to terrorize females and to maintain the patriarchal definition of woman's place.

The word *terrorism* invokes images of furtive organizations of the far right or left, whose members blow up buildings and cars, hijack airplanes, and murder innocent people in some country other than ours. But there is a different kind of terrorism, one that so pervades our culture that we have learned to live with it as though it were the natural order of things. Its target is females—of all ages, races, and classes. It is the common characteristic of rape, wife battery, incest, pornography, harassment, and all forms of sexual violence. I call it *sexual terrorism* because it is a system by which males frighten and, by frightening, control and dominate females.

The concept of terrorism captured my attention in an "ordinary" event. One afternoon I collected my laundry and went to a nearby laundromat. The place is located in a small shopping center on a very busy highway. After I had loaded and started the machines, I became acutely aware of my environment. It was just after 6:00 P.M. and dark, the other stores were closed, the laundromat was brightly lit, and my car was the only one in the lot. Anyone passing by could readily see that I was alone and isolated. Knowing that rape is often a crime of opportunity, I became terrified. I wanted to leave and find a laundromat that was busier, but my clothes were well into the wash cycle, and, besides, I felt I was being "silly," "paranoid." The feeling of terror persisted, so I sat in my car, windows up and doors locked. When the wash was completed, I dashed in, threw the clothes into the dryer, and ran back out to my car. When the clothes were dry, I tossed them recklessly into the basket and hurriedly drove away to fold them in the security of my home.

Although I was not victimized in a direct, physical way or by objective or measurable standards, I felt victimized. It was, for me, a terrifying experience. I felt controlled by an invisible force. I was angry that something as commonplace as doing laundry after a day's work jeopardized my well-being. Mostly I was angry at being unfree: a hostage of a culture that, for the most part, encourages violence against females, instructs men in the methodology of sexual violence, and provides them with ready justification for their violence. I was angry that I could be victimized by being "in the wrong place at the wrong time." The essence of terrorism is that one never knows when is the wrong time and where is the wrong place.

Following my experience at the laundromat, I talked with my students about terrorization. Women students began to open up and reveal terrors that they had kept secret because of embarrassment: fears of jogging alone, shopping alone, going to the movies alone. One woman recalled feelings of terror in her adolescence when she did child care for extra money. Nothing had ever happened, and she had not been afraid of anyone in particular, but she had felt a vague terror when being driven home late at night by the man of the house.

The male students listened incredulously and then demanded equal time. The harder they tried, the more they realized how very different—qualitatively, quantitatively, and contextually—their fears were. All agreed that, while they experienced fear in a violent society, they did not experience terror, nor did they experience fear of rape or sexual mutilation. They felt more in control, either from a psychophysical sense of security that they could defend themselves or from a confidence in being able to determine wrong places and times. All the women admitted feeling fear and anxiety when walking to their cars on the campus, especially after an evening class or activity. None of the men experienced fear on campus at any time. The men could be rather specific in describing where they were afraid: in Harlem, for example, or in certain parts of downtown Newark, New Jersey—places that have a reputation for violence. But either they could avoid these places or they felt capable of self-protective action. Above all, male students said that they *never* feared being attacked simply because they were male. They *never* feared going to a movie or to a mall alone. Their daily activities were not characterized by a concern for their physical integrity.

The differences between men's and women's experiences of fear underscore the meaning of sexual terrorism: that women's lives are bounded by both the reality of pervasive sexual danger and the fear that reality engenders. In her study of rape, Susan Brownmiller argues that rape is "nothing more or less than a conscious process of intimidation by which all men keep all women in a state of fear."[1] In their study *The Female Fear,* Margaret T. Gordon and Stephanie Riger found that one-third of women said they worry at least once a month about being raped. Many said they worry daily about the possibility of being raped. When they think about rape, they feel terrified and somewhat paralyzed. A third of women indicated that the fear of rape is "part of the background" of their lives and "one of those things that's always there." Another third claimed they never worried about rape but reported taking precautions, "sometimes elaborate ones," to try to avoid being raped.[2] Indeed, women's attempts to avoid sexual intrusion take many forms. To varying degrees, women change and restrict their behavior, life-styles, and physical appearances. They will pay higher costs for housing and transportation and even make educational and career choices to attempt to minimize sexual victimization.

Sexual terrorism includes nonviolent sexual intimidation and the threat of violence as well as overt sexual violence. For example, although an act of rape, an unnecessary hysterectomy, and the publishing of *Playboy* magazine appear to be quite different, they are in fact more similar than dissimilar. Each is based on fear, hostility, and a need to dominate women. Rape is an act of aggression and possession. Unnecessary hysterectomies are extraordinary abuses of power rooted in men's concept of women as primarily reproductive beings and in their need to assert power over that reproduction. *Playboy,* like all forms of pornography, attempts to control women through the power

of definition. Male pornographers define women's sexuality for their male customers. The basis of pornography is men's fantasies about women's sexuality.

Components of Sexual Terrorism

The literature on terrorism does not provide a precise definition.[3] Mine is taken from Hacker, who says that "terrorism aims to frighten, and by frightening, to dominate and control."[4] Writers agree more readily on the characteristics and functions of terrorism than on a definition. This analysis will focus on five components to illuminate the similarities and distinctions between sexual terrorism and political terrorism. The five components are ideology, propaganda, indiscriminate and amoral violence, voluntary compliance, and society's perception of the terrorist and the terrorized.

An *ideology* is an integrated set of beliefs about the world that explains the way things are and provides a vision of how they ought to be. Patriarchy, meaning the "rule of the fathers," is the ideological foundation of sexism in our society. It asserts the superiority of males and the inferiority of females. It also provides the rationale for sexual terrorism. The taproot of patriarchy is the masculine/warrior ideal. Masculinity must include not only a proclivity for violence but also all those characteristics claimed by warriors: aggression, control, emotional reserve, rationality, sexual potency, etc. Marc Feigen Fasteau, in *The Male Machine,* argues that "men are brought up with the idea that there ought to be some part of them, under control until released by necessity, that thrives on violence. This capacity, even affinity, for violence, lurking beneath the surface of every real man, is supposed to represent the primal untamed base of masculinity"[5]

Propaganda is the methodical dissemination of information for the purpose of promoting a particular ideology. Propaganda, by definition, is biased or even false information. Its purpose is to present one point of view on a subject and to discredit opposing points of view. Propaganda is essential to the conduct of terrorism. According to Francis Watson, in *Political Terrorism: The Threat and the Response,* "Terrorism must not be defined only in terms of violence, but also in terms of propaganda. The two are in operation together. Violence of terrorism is a coercive means for attempting to influence the thinking and actions of people. Propaganda is a persuasive means for doing the same thing."[6] The propaganda of sexual terrorism is found in all expressions of the popular culture: films, television, music, literature, advertising, pornography. The propaganda of sexual terrorism is also found in the ideas of patriarchy expressed in science, medicine, and psychology.

The third component, which is common to all forms of political terrorism, consists of "indiscriminateness, unpredictability, arbitrariness, ruthless destructiveness and amorality."[7] Indiscriminate violence and amorality are also at the heart of sexual terrorism. Every female is a potential target of violence—at any age, at any time, in any place. Further, as we shall see, amorality pervades sexual violence. Child molesters, incestuous fathers, wife beaters, and rapists often do not understand that they have done anything wrong. Their views are routinely shared by police officers, lawyers, and judges, and crimes of sexual violence are rarely punished in American society.

The fourth component of the theory of terrorism is voluntary compliance. The institutionalization of a system of terror requires the development of mechanisms other than sustained violence to achieve its goals. Violence must be employed to maintain terrorism, but sustained violence can be costly and debilitating. Therefore, strategies for ensuring a significant degree of voluntary compliance must be developed. Sexual terrorism is maintained to a great extent by an elaborate system of sex-role socialization that in effect instructs men to be terrorists in the name of masculinity and women to be victims in the name of femininity.

Sexual and political terrorism differ in the final component, perceptions of the terrorist and the victim. In political terrorism we know who is the terrorist and who is the victim. We may condemn or condone the terrorist, depending on our political views, but we sympathize with the victim. In sexual terrorism, however, we blame the victim and excuse the offender. We believe that the offender either is "sick" and therefore in need of our compassion or is acting out normal male impulses.

Types of Sexual Terrorism

While the discussion that follows focuses on four types of sexual terrorism—rape, wife abuse, sexual abuse of children, and sexual harassment—recent feminist research has documented other forms of sexual terrorism, including threats of violence, flashing, street hassling, obscene phone calls, stalking, coercive sex, pornography, prostitution, sexual slavery, and femicide. What women experience as sexually intrusive and violent is not necessarily reflected in our legal codes, and those acts that are recognized as criminal are often not understood specifically as crimes against women—as acts of sexual violence.

Acts of sexual terrorism include many forms of intrusion that society accepts as common and are therefore trivialized. For example, a recent study of women's experiences of obscene phone calls found that women respondents overwhelmingly found these calls to be a form of sexual intimidation and harassment.[8] While obscene phone calls are illegal, only in rare cases do women report them and the police take them seriously. In contrast, some forms of sexual terrorism are so extraordinary that they are regarded not only as aberrant but also as incomprehensible. The execution of fourteen women students at the University of Montreal on December 6, 1989, is one example of this. Separating the men from the women in a classroom and shouting, "You're all fucking feminists," twenty-five-year-old Marc Lepine systematically murdered fourteen women. In his suicide letter, claiming that "the feminists have always enraged me," Lepine recognized his crime as a political act.[9] For many women, this one act of sexual terrorism galvanized attention to the phenomenon of the murder of women because they are women. "Femicide," according to Jane Caputi and Diana E. H. Russell, describes "the murders of women by men motivated by hatred, contempt, pleasure, or a sense of ownership of women."[10] Most femicide, unlike the Montreal massacre, is committed by a male acquaintance, friend, or relative. In *Surviving Sexual Violence,* Liz Kelly argues that sexual violence must be understood as a continuum—that is, "a continuous series of events that pass into one another" united by a "basic common character."[11] Viewing sexual violence in this way furthers an understanding of both the "ordinary" and "extraordinary" forms of sexual terrorism and the range of abuse that women experience in their lifetimes.

Many types of sexual terrorism are crimes, yet when we look at the history of these acts, we see that they came to be considered criminal not so much to protect women as to adjust power relationships among men. Rape was originally a violation of a father's or husband's property rights;

consequently, a husband by definition could not rape his wife. Wife beating was condoned by the law and still is condemned in name only. Although proscriptions against incest exist, society assumes a more serious posture toward men who sexually abuse other men's daughters. Sexual harassment is not a crime, and only recently has it been declared an actionable civil offense. Crimes of sexual violence are characterized by ambiguity and diversity in definition and interpretation. Because each state and territory has a separate system of law in addition to the federal system, crimes and punishments are assessed differently throughout the country.

Rape

Rape statutes have been reformed in the past decade, largely to remove the exemption for wife rape and to use gender-neutral language. The essence of the definition of rape, however, remains the same: sexual penetration (typically defined as penile-vaginal, but may include oral and anal sodomy or penetration by fingers or other objects) of a female by force or threat of force, against her will and without her consent.[12]

Traditional views of rape are shaped by male views of sexuality and by men's fear of being unjustly accused. Deborah Rhode argues, in *Justice and Gender,* that this reflects a "sexual schizophrenia." That is, forced sexual intercourse by a stranger against a chaste woman is unquestionably regarded as a heinous crime, whereas coercive sex that does not fit this model is largely denied.[13] Since most women are raped by men they know, this construction excludes many forms of rape.

Because rape is considered a sexual act, evidence of force and resistance is often necessary to establish the nonconsent needed to convict rapists. Such proof is not demanded of a victim of any other crime. If females do not resist rape as much as possible, "consent" is assumed.

By 1990, forty-two states had adopted laws criminalizing rape in marriage: sixteen states recognize that wife rape is a crime and provide no exemptions; twenty-six states penalize wife rape but allow for some exemptions under which husbands cannot be prosecuted for raping their wives. Eight states do not recognize wife rape as a crime.[14] In spite of statutory reform, wife rape remains a greatly misunderstood phenomenon, and the magnitude of sexual abuse by husbands is not known. In Diana E. H. Russell's pioneering study on rape in marriage, 14 percent of the female respondents reported having been raped by their husbands.[15] The prevalence of wife rape, however, is believed to be much higher; approximately 40 percent of women in battered women's shelters also report having been raped by their husbands.[16] Victims of wife rape, according to one study, are at a greater risk of being murdered by their husbands, or of murdering them, than women who are physically but not sexually assaulted. [17]

Wife Abuse

For centuries it has been assumed that a husband had the right to punish or discipline his wife with physical force. The popular expression "rule of thumb" originated from English common law, which allowed a husband to beat his wife with a whip or stick no bigger in diameter than his thumb. The husband's prerogative was incorporated into American law. Several states once had statutes that essentially allowed a man to beat his wife without interference from the courts.[18]

In 1871, in the landmark case of *Fulgham v. State,* an Alabama court ruled that "the privilege, ancient though it be, to beat her

with a stick, to pull her hair, choke her, spit in her face or kick her about the floor or to inflict upon her other like indignities, is not now acknowledged by our law."[19] The law, however, has been ambiguous and often contradictory on the issue of wife abuse. While the courts established that a man had no right to beat his wife, it also held that a woman could not press charges against her abusive husband. In 1910, the U.S. Supreme Court ruled that a wife could not charge her husband with assault and battery because it "would open the doors of the court to accusations of all sorts of one spouse against the other and bring into public notice complaints for assaults, slander and libel."[20] The courts virtually condoned violence for the purpose of maintaining peace.

Laws and public attitudes about the illegality of wife abuse and the rights of the victim have been slowly evolving. During the 1980s, there was a proliferation of new laws designed to address the needs of victims of domestic violence and to reform police and judicial responses to wife abuse. These measures include temporary or permanent protection orders, state-funded or state-assisted shelters, state-mandated data collection, and proarrest or mandatory arrest policies.[21] Most states, however, continue to define domestic violence as a misdemeanor crime, carrying jail sentences of less than one year. Felony crimes are punishable by more than one year in jail, and police officers tend to arrest more often for felony offenses. The distinction between misdemeanor and felony crimes is also based on the use of weapons and the infliction of serious injuries.[22] While wife abuse is still considered a misdemeanor crime, a National Crime Survey revealed that at least 50 percent of the domestic "simple assaults" involved bodily injury as serious as or more serious than 90 percent of all rapes, robberies, and aggravated assaults.[23]

Sexual Abuse of Children

Defining sexual abuse of children is very difficult. The laws are complex and often contradictory. Generally, sexual abuse of children includes statutory rape, molestation, carnal knowledge, indecent liberties, impairing the morals of a minor, child abuse, child neglect, and incest. Each of these is defined, interpreted, and punished differently in each state.

The philosophy underlying statutory-rape laws is that a child below a certain age—arbitrarily fixed by law—is not able to give meaningful consent. Therefore, sexual intercourse with a female below a certain age, even with consent, is rape. Punishment for statutory rape, although rarely imposed, can be as high as life imprisonment. Coexistent with laws on statutory rape are laws on criminal incest. Incest is generally interpreted as sexual activity, most often intercourse, with a blood relative. The difference, then, between statutory rape and incest is the relation of the offender to the child. Statutory rape is committed by someone outside the family; incest, by a member of the family. The penalty for incest, also rarely imposed, is usually no more than ten years in prison. This contrast suggests that sexual abuse of children is tolerated when it occurs within the family and that unqualified protection of children from sexual assault is not the intent of the law.

Sexual Harassment

Sexual harassment is a new term for an old phenomenon. The research on sexual harassment, as well as the legal interpretation, centers on acts of sexual coercion or intimidation on the job and at school. Lin Farley, in *Sexual Shakedown: The Sexual Harassment of Women on the Job,* describes sexual harassment as "unsolicited nonreciprocal male behavior that asserts a woman's sex role over her function as a worker. It can be any or all of the following: staring at, commenting upon, or touching a woman's body; requests for acquiescence in sexual behavior; repeated nonreciprocated propositions for dates; demands for sexual intercourse; and rape."[24]

In 1980 the Equal Employment Opportunity Commission issued federal guidelines that defined sexual harassment as any behavior that "has the purpose or effect of unreasonably interfering with an individual's work performance or creating an intimidating or hostile or offensive environment." Such behavior can include "unwelcome sexual advances, requests for sexual favors, and other verbal or physical conduct of a sexual nature."[25] It was not until six years later, however, that the Supreme Court, in *Meritor Savings Bank FSB v. Vinson,* ruled that sexual harassment was a form of sex discrimination under Title VII of the Civil Rights Act of 1964.[26]

In October 1991 national attention was focused on the issue of sexual harassment as a result of allegations made against Supreme Court justice nominee Clarence Thomas by Professor Anita Hill. (Thomas was subsequently confirmed as a Supreme Court justice by a vote of fifty-two to forty-eight.) While there was a blizzard of media attention about sexual harassment, what emerged most clearly from the confirmation hearings was that the chasm between women's experiences of sexual harassment and an understanding of the phenomenon by society in general had not been bridged. Perhaps most misunderstood was the fact that Professor Hill's experience and her reaction to it were typical of sexually harassed women.[27]

Characteristics of Sexual Terrorism

Those forms of sexual terrorism that are crimes share several common characteristics. Each will be addressed separately, but in the real world these characteristics are linked together and form a vicious circle, which functions to mask the reality of sexual terrorism and thus to perpetuate the system of oppression of females. Crimes of violence against females (1) cut across socioeconomic lines; (2) are the crimes least likely to be reported; (3) when reported, are the crimes least likely to be brought to trial or to result in conviction; (4) are often blamed on the victim; (5) are generally not taken seriously; and (6) fuse dominance and sexuality.

Violence Against Females Cuts Across Socioeconomic Lines

The question "Who is the typical rapist, wife beater, incest offender, etc.?" is raised constantly. The answer is simple: men. Female sexual offenders are exceedingly rare. The men who commit acts of sexual terrorism are of all ages, races, and religions; they come from all communities, income levels, and educational levels; they are married, single, separated, and divorced. The "typical" sexually abusive male does not exist.

One of the most common assumptions about sexual violence is that it occurs primarily among the poor, uneducated, and predominantly non-white populations. Actually, violence committed by the poor and nonwhite is simply more visible because of their lack of resources to secure the privacy that the middle and upper classes can purchase. Most rapes, indeed, most incidents of sexual assault, are not reported, and therefore the picture drawn from police records must be viewed as very sketchy.

The data on sexual harassment in work situations indicates that it occurs among all job categories and pay ranges. Sexual harassment is committed by academic men, who are among the most highly educated members of society. In a 1991 *New York Times* poll, five out of ten men said they had said or done something that "could have been construed by a female colleague as harassment."[28]

All the studies on wife abuse testify to the fact that wife beating crosses socioeconomic lines. Wife beaters include high government officials, members of the armed forces, businessmen, policemen, physicians, lawyers, clergy, blue-collar workers, and the unemployed.[29] According to Maria Roy, founder and director of New York's Abused Women's Aid in Crisis, "We see abuse of women on all levels of income, age, occupation, and social standing. I've had four women come in recently whose husbands are Ph.D.s—two of them professors at top universities. Another abused woman is married to a very prominent attorney. We counseled battered wives whose husbands are doctors, psychiatrists, even clergymen."[30]

Similarly, in Vincent De Francis's classic study of 250 cases of sexual crimes committed against children, a major finding was that incidents of sexual assault against children cut across class lines.[31] Since sexual violence is not "nice," we prefer to believe that nice men do not commit these acts and that nice girls and women are not victims. Our refusal to accept the fact that violence against females is widespread throughout society strongly inhibits our ability to develop meaningful strategies to eliminate it. Moreover, because of underreporting, it is difficult to ascertain exactly how widespread it is.

Crimes of Sexual Violence Are the Least Likely to Be Reported

Underreporting is common for all crimes against females. There are two national sources for data on crime in the United States: the annual Uniform Crime Reports (UCR) of the Federal Bureau of Investigation, which collects information from police departments, and the National Crime Survey (NCS), conducted by the U.S. Department of justice, which collects data on personal and household criminal victimizations from a nationally representative sample of households.

The FBI recognizes that rape is seriously underreported by as much as 80 to 90 percent. According to FBI data for 1990, 102,555 rapes were reported.[32] The FBI Uniform Crime Report for 1990 estimates that a forcible rape occurs every five minutes.[33] This estimate is based on reported rapes; accounting for the high rate of underreporting, the FBI estimates that a rape occurs every two minutes. The number of forcible rapes reported to the police has been increasing every year. Since 1986, the rape rate has risen 10 percent.[34]

The National Crime Survey (renamed in 1991 as the National Crime Victimization Survey) data for 1990 reports 130,260 rapes.[35] This data is only slightly higher than FBI data; researchers argue that NCS data has serious drawbacks as well.[36] Just as victims are reluctant to report a rape to the police, many are also reluctant to reveal their victimization to an NCS interviewer. In fact, the NCS does not ask directly about rape (although it will in the future). A respondent may volunteer the information when asked questions about bodily harm. The NCS also excludes children under twelve, thus providing no data on childhood sexual assault.

In April 1992 the National Victim Center and the Crime Victims Research and Treat-

ment Center released a report entitled "Rape in America," which summarized two nationwide studies: the National Women's Study, a three-year longitudinal survey of a national probability sample of 4,008 adult women, and the State of Services for Victims of Rape, which surveyed 370 agencies that provide rape crisis assistance.[37] The National Women's Study sought information about the incidence of rape and information about a number of health issues related to rape, including depression, posttraumatic stress disorder, suicide attempts, and alcohol- and drug-related problems.

The results of the National Women's Study confirm a belief held by many experts that the UCR and NCS data seriously underrepresents the occurrence of rape. According to the National Women's Study, 683,000 adult women were raped during a twelve-month period from the fall of 1989 to the fall of 1990.[38] This data is significantly higher than UCR and NCS data for approximately the same period. Moreover, once rapes of female children and adolescents under the age of eighteen and rapes of boys or men were not included in the study, the 683,000 rapes of adult women do not reflect an accurate picture of all rapes that occurred during that period. The data in this study also confirms the claim that acquaintance rape is far more pervasive than stranger rape. While 22 percent of victims were raped by someone unknown to them, 36 percent were raped by family members: 9 percent by husbands or ex-husbands, 11 percent by fathers or stepfathers, 16 percent by other relatives. Ten percent were raped by a boyfriend or ex-boyfriend and 29 percent by nonrelatives such as friends or neighbors (3 percent were not sure or refused to answer).[39]

Perhaps the most significant finding of the National Women's Study is that rape in the United States is "a tragedy of youth."[40]

The study found that 29 percent of rapes occurred to female victims under the age of eleven, 32 percent occurred to females between the ages of eleven and seventeen, and 22 percent occurred to females between the ages of eighteen and twenty-four.[41] Other research suggests that one in four women will be the victim of rape or an attempted rape by the time they are in their midtwenties, and at least three-quarters of those assaults will be committed by men known to the victims.[42] Lifetime probability for rape victimization is as high as 50 percent; that is, one out of two women will be sexually assaulted at least once in her lifetime.[43]

The FBI's Uniform Crime Report indexes 10 million reported crimes a year but does not collect statistics on wife abuse. Since statutes in most states do not identify wife beating as a distinct crime, incidents of wife abuse are usually classified under "assault and battery" and "disputes." Estimates that 50 percent of American wives are battered every year are not uncommon in the literature.[44] Recent evidence shows that violence against wives becomes greatest at and after separation.[45] Divorced and separated women account for 75 percent of all battered women and report being battered fourteen times as often as women still living with their partners.[46] These women are also at the highest risk of being murdered by their former husbands. Thirty-three percent of all women murdered in the United States between 1976 and 1987 were murdered by their husbands.[47]

"The problem of sexual abuse of children is of unknown national dimensions," according to Vincent De Francis, "but findings strongly point to the probability of an enormous national incidence many times larger than the reported incidence of the physical abuse of children."[48] He discussed the existence of a wide gap between the reported incidence and the actual occurrence of sexual assaults against children and suggested that "the reported incidence represents the top edge of the moon as it rises over the mountain."[49] Research definitions as to what constitutes sexual abuse and research methodologies vary widely, resulting in reported rates ranging from 6 percent to 62 percent for female children and 3 percent to 31 percent for male children.[50] David Finkelhor suggests that the lowest figures support the claim that child sexual abuse is far from a rare occurrence and that the higher reported rates suggest a "problem of epidemic proportions."[51]

In a study of 126 African-American women and 122 white women in Los Angeles County, 62 percent reported at least one experience of sexual abuse before the age of eighteen.[52] The same men who beat their wives often abuse their children. Researchers have found that "the worse the wife-beating, the worse the child abuse."[53] It is estimated that fathers may sexually abuse children in 25 percent to 33 percent of all domestic abuse cases. There is also a strong correlation between child abuse and the frequency of marital rape, particularly where weapons are involved.[54]

Incest, according to author and researcher Florence Rush, is the *Best Kept Secret*.[55] The estimates, however speculative, are frightening. In a representative sample of 930 women in San Francisco, Diana E. H. Russell found that 16 percent of the women had been sexually abused by a relative before the age of eighteen and 4.5 percent had been sexually abused by their fathers (also before the age of eighteen).[56] Extrapolating to the general population, this research suggests that 160,000 women per million may have been sexually abused before the age of eighteen, and 45,000 women per million may have been sexually abused by their fathers.[57]

Accurate data on the incidence of sexual harassment is impossible to obtain. Women have traditionally accepted sexual innuendo as a fact of life and only recently have begun to report and analyze the dimensions of sexual coercion in the workplace. Research indicates that sexual harassment is pervasive. In 1978 Lin Farley found that accounts of sexual harassment within the federal government, the country's largest single employer, were extensive.[58] In 1988 the U.S. Merit Systems Protection Board released an updated study that showed that 85 percent of working women experience harassing behavior at some point in their lives.[59]

In 1976 over nine thousand women responded to a survey on sexual harassment conducted by *Redbook* magazine. More than 92 percent reported sexual harassment as a problem, a majority of the respondents described it as serious, and nine out of ten reported that they had personally experienced one or more forms of unwanted sexual attentions on the job.[60] The Ad Hoc Group on Equal Rights for Women attempted to gather data on sexual harassment at the United Nations. Their questionnaire was confiscated by U.N. officials, but 875 staff members had already responded; 73 percent were women, and more than half of them said that they had personally experienced or were aware of incidents of sexual harassment at the U.N.[61] In May 1975, the Women's Section of the Human Affairs Program at Cornell University in Ithaca, New York, distributed the first questionnaire on sexual harassment. Of the 155 respondents, 92 percent identified sexual harassment as a serious problem, 70 percent had personally experienced some form of sexual harassment, and 56 percent reported incidents of physical harassment.[62] A 1991 *New York Times/CBS* poll found that four out of ten women experienced sexual harassment at work, yet only 4 percent reported it.[63]

In *The Lecherous Professor,* Billie Wright Dziech and Linda Weiner note that the low reportage of sexual harassment in higher education is due to the victims' deliberate avoidance of institutional processes and remedies.[64] A pilot study conducted by the National Advisory Council on Women's Educational Programs on Sexual Harassment in Academia concluded:

> The sexual harassment of postsecondary students is an increasingly visible problem of great, but as yet unascertained, dimensions. Once regarded as an isolated, purely personal problem, it has gained civil rights credibility as its scale and consequences have become known, and is correctly viewed as a form of illegal sex-based discrimination.[65]

Crimes of Violence Against Females Have the Lowest Conviction Rates

The common denominator in the underreporting of all sexual assaults is fear. Females have been well trained in silence and passivity. Early and sustained sex-role socialization teaches that women are responsible for the sexual behavior of men and that women cannot be trusted. These beliefs operate together. They function to keep women silent about their victimization and to keep other people from believing women when they do come forward. The victim's fear that she will not be believed and, as a consequence, that the offender will not be punished is not unrealistic. Sex offenders are rarely punished in our society.

Rape has the lowest conviction rate of all violent crimes. The likelihood of a rape complaint ending in conviction is 2 to 5 percent.[66] While the intent of rape reform legislation was to shift the emphasis from the victim's experiences to the perpetrator's acts,[67] prosecutions are less likely to be pursued if the victim and perpetrator are acquainted, and juries are less likely to return a conviction in cases where the victim's behavior or *alleged behavior* (emphasis mine) departed from traditional sex-role expectations.[68]

Data on prosecution and conviction of wife beaters is practically nonexistent. This is despite the fact that battery is, according to the U.S. Surgeon General, the "single largest cause of injury to women in the U.S." and accounts for one-fifth of all emergency room visits by women.[69] Police departments have generally tried to conciliate rather than arrest. Guided by the "stitch rule," arrests were made only when the victim's injuries required stitches. Police routinely instructed the parties to "break it up" or "talk it out" or asked the abuser to "take a walk and cool off." Male police officers, often identifying with the male abuser, routinely failed to advise women of their rights to file a complaint.[70]

As a result of sustained political activism on behalf of abused women, many states have revised their police training and have instituted pro- or even mandatory arrest policies. In 1984 the Attorney General's Task Force on Family Violence argued that the legal response to such violence be predicated on the abusive act and not on the relationship between the victim and the abuser.[71] A key issue, however, is the implementation of such reform. The record shows that the criminal justice system has responded inconsistently.[72]

Studies in the late 1970s and 1980s showed that batterers receive minimal fines and suspended sentences. In one study of 350 abused wives, none of the husbands served time in jail.[73] And while the result of pro- and mandatory arrest policies is a larger number of domestic violence cases entering the judicial system,[74] "there is considerable evidence that judges have yet to abandon the historical view of wife abuse."[75] In 1981 a Kansas judge suspended the fine of a convicted assailant on the con-

dition that he buy his wife a box of candy.[76] In 1984 a Colorado judge sentenced a man to two years on work release for fatally shooting his wife five times in the face. Although the sentence was less than the minimum required by law, the judge found that the wife had "provoked" her husband by leaving him.[77] Recent task force reports on gender bias in the courts reveal a pattern of nonenforcement of protective orders, trivialization of complaints, and disbelief of females when there is no visible evidence of severe injuries.[78] In 1987 a Massachusetts trial judge scolded a battered woman for wasting his time with her request for a protective order. If she and her husband wanted to "gnaw" on each other, "fine," but they "shouldn't do it at taxpayers' expense." The husband later killed his wife, and taxpayers paid for a murder trial.[79]

The lack of support and protection from the criminal justice system intensifies the double bind of battered women. Leaving the batterer significantly increases the risk of serious injury or death, while staying significantly increases the psychological terrorism and frequency of abuse. According to former Detroit Police Commander James Bannon, "You can readily understand why the women ultimately take the law into their own hands or despair of finding relief at all. *Or why the male feels protected by the system in his use of violence"* (emphasis mine).[80]

In his study of child sexual abuse, Vincent De Francis found that plea bargaining and dismissal of cases were the norm. The study sample consisted of 173 cases brought to prosecution. Of these, 44 percent (seventy-six cases) were dismissed, 22 percent (thirty-eight cases) voluntarily accepted a lesser plea, 11 percent (six cases) were found guilty of a lesser charge, and 2 percent (four cases) were found guilty as charged. Of the remaining thirty-five cases, either they were pending (fifteen) or terminated because the offender was committed to a mental institution (five) or because the offender absconded (seven), or no information was available (eight). Of the fifty-three offenders who were convicted or pleaded guilty, thirty offenders escaped a jail sentence. Twenty-one received suspended sentences and were placed on probation, seven received suspended sentences without probation, and two were fined a sum of money. The other 45 percent (twenty-three offenders) received prison terms from under six months to three years; five were given indeterminate sentences—that is, a minimum term of one year and a maximum term subject to the discretion of the state board of parole.[81]

In Diana E. H. Russell's study of 930 women, 648 cases of child sexual abuse were disclosed. Thirty cases—5 percent—were reported to the police; four were cases of incestuous abuse, and twenty-six were extrafamilial child sexual abuse. Only seven cases resulted in conviction.[82]

Most of the victims of sexual harassment in the Cornell University study were unwilling to use available procedures, such as grievances, to remedy their complaints, because they believed that nothing would be done. Their perception is based on reality; of the 12 percent who did complain, over half found that nothing was done in their cases.[83] The low adjudication and punishment rates of sexual-harassment cases are particularly revealing in light of the fact that the offender is known and identifiable and that there is no fear of "mistaken identity," as there is in rape cases. While offenders accused of familial violence—incest and wife abuse—are also known, concern with keeping the family intact affects prosecution rates.

Blaming the Victim of Sexual Violence Is Pervasive

The data on conviction rates of men who have committed acts of violence against females must be understood in the context of attitudes about women. Our male-dominated society evokes powerful myths to justify male violence against females and to ensure that these acts will rarely be punished. Victims of sexual violence are almost always suspect. We have developed an intricate network of beliefs and attitudes that perpetuate the idea that "victims of sex crimes have a hidden psychological need to be victimized."[84] We tend to believe either that the female willingly participated in her victimization or that she outright lied about it. Either way, we blame the victim and excuse or condone the offender.

Consider, for example, the operative myths about rape, wife battery, incest, and sexual harassment.

Rape

All women want to be raped.
No woman can be raped if she doesn't want it (you-can't-thread-a-moving-needle argument.)
She asked for it.
She changed her mind afterward.
When she says no, she means yes.
If you are going to be raped, you might as well relax and enjoy it.

Wife Abuse

Some women need to be beaten.
A good kick in the ass will straighten her out.
She needs a punch in the mouth every so often to keep her in line.
She must have done something to provoke him.

Incest

The child was the seducer.
The child imagined it.

Sexual Harassment

> She was seductive.
> She misunderstood. I was just being
>   friendly.

Underlying all the myths about victims of sexual violence is the belief that the victim causes and is responsible for her own victimization. In the National Women's Study, 69 percent of the rape victims were afraid that they would be blamed for their rape, 71 percent did not want their family to know they had been sexually abused, and 68 percent did not want people outside of their family knowing of their victimization.[85] Diana Scully studied convicted rapists and found that these men both believed in the rape myths and used them to justify their own behavior.[86] Underlying the attitudes about the male offender is the belief that he could not help himself: that is, he was ruled by his biology and/or he was seduced. The victim becomes the offender, and the offender becomes the victim. These two processes, blaming the victim and absolving the offender, protect the patriarchal view of the world by rationalizing sexual violence. Sexual violence by a normal male against an innocent female is unthinkable; therefore, she must have done something wrong or it would not have happened. This view was expressed by a Wisconsin judge who sentenced a twenty-four-year-old man to ninety days' work release for sexually assaulting a five-year-old girl. The judge, claiming that the child was an "unusually promiscuous young lady," stated that "no way do I believe that [the defendant] initiated sexual contact."[87] Making a victim believe she is at fault erases not only the individual offender's culpability but also the responsibility of the society as a whole. Sexual violence remains an individual problem, not a sociopolitical one.

One need only read the testimony of victims of sexual violence to see the powerful effects of blaming the victim. From the National Advisory Council on Women's Educational Programs Report on Sexual Harassment of Students:

> I was ashamed, thought it was my fault, and was worried that the school would take action against me (for "unearned" grades) if they found out about it

> This happened seventeen years ago, and you are the first person I've been able to discuss it with in all that time. He's still at _____, and probably still doing it.

> I'm afraid to tell anyone here about it, and I'm just hoping to get through the year so I can leave.[88]

From *Wife-Beating: The Silent Crisis,* Judge Stewart Oneglia comments,

> Many women find it shameful to admit they don't have a good marriage. The battered wife wraps her bloody head in a towel, goes to the hospital, and explains to the doctor she fell down the stairs. After a few years of the husband telling her he beats her because she is ugly, stupid, or incompetent, she is so psychologically destroyed that she believes it.

A battered woman from Boston relates,

> I actually thought if I only learned to cook better or keep a cleaner house, everything would be okay. I put up with the beatings for five years before I got desperate enough to get help.[89]

Another battered woman said,

> When I came to, I wanted to die, the guilt and depression were so bad. Your whole sense of worth is tied up with being a successful wife and having a happy marriage. If your husband beats you, then your marriage is a failure, and you're a failure. It's so horribly the opposite of how it is supposed to be.[90]

Katherine Brady shared her experience as an incest survivor in *Father's Days: A True*

Story of Incest. She concluded her story with the following:

> I've learned a great deal by telling my story. I hope other incest victims may experience a similar journey of discovery by reading it. If nothing else, I would wish them to hear in this tale the two things I needed most, but had to wait years to hear: "You are not alone and you are not to blame."[91]

Sexual Violence Is Not Taken Seriously

Another characteristic of sexual violence is that these crimes are not taken seriously. Society manifests this attitude by simply denying the existence of sexual violence, denying the gravity of these acts, joking about them, and attempting to legitimate them.

Many offenders echo the societal norm by expressing genuine surprise when they are confronted by authorities. This seems to be particularly true in cases of sexual abuse of children, wife beating, and sexual harassment. In her study of incest, Florence Rush found that child molesters very often do not understand that they have done anything wrong. Many men still believe that they have an inalienable right to rule "their women." Batterers, for example, often cite their right to discipline their wives; incestuous fathers cite their right to instruct their daughters in sexuality. These men are acting on the belief that women are the property of men.

The concept of females as the property of men extends beyond the family unit, as the evidence on sexual harassment indicates. "Are you telling me that this kind of horsing around may constitute an actionable offense?" queried a character on a television special on sexual harassment.[92] This represents the typical response of a man accused of sexual harassment. Men have been taught that they are the hunters, and women—all women—are fair game. The mythology about the workaday world abounds with sexual innuendo. Concepts of "sleazy" (i.e., sexually accessible) nurses and dumb, big-breasted, blond secretaries are standard fare for comedy routines. When the existence of sexual violence can no longer be denied, a common response is to joke about it in order to belittle it. "If you are going to be raped, you might as well enjoy it" clearly belittles the violence of rape. The public still laughs when Ralph threatens Alice with "One of these days, POW—right in the kisser." Recently, a television talk-show host remarked that "incest is a game the whole family can play." The audience laughed uproariously.

Sexual Violence Is about Violence, Power, and Sex

The final characteristic common to all forms of violence against females is perhaps the most difficult to comprehend. During the past decade, many researchers argued (as I did in earlier versions of this article) that sexual violence is not about sex but about violence. I now believe, however, that the "either-or" dichotomy—either sexual violence is about sex or it's about violence—is false and misleading. Male supremacy identifies females as having a basic "flaw"—a trait that distinguishes males and females and legitimates women's inferior status. This "flaw" is female sexuality: it is tempting and seductive and therefore disruptive, capable of reproducing life itself and therefore powerful.[93] Through sexual terrorism men seek to bring this force under control. The site of the struggle is the female body and female sexuality.

Timothy Beneke, in *Men on Rape*, argues that "not every man is a rapist but every man who grows up in America and learns American English learns all too much to think like a rapist" and that "for a man, rape has plenty to do with sex."[94] Twenty years of research and activism have documented that women largely experience rape, battery, incest, and sexual harassment as violence. That women and men often have vastly different experiences is not surprising. Under patriarchy men are entitled to sex; it is a primary vehicle by which they establish and signal their masculinity. From the male perspective, female sexuality is a commodity, something they must take, dominate, or own. Our popular culture routinely celebrates this particular notion of masculinity. Women are permitted to have sex, but only in marriage (the patriarchal ideal), or at least in love relationships. Women earn their femininity by managing their sexuality and keeping it in trust for a potential husband. The double standard of sexuality leads inevitably to coercion and sexual violence.

Many believe that re-visioning rape as violence not only accurately reflects many women's experiences but also is a more productive strategy for reforming legislation and transforming public attitudes. While arguing that "theoretically and strategically" the "rape as violence" position is the better one, attorney and author Susan Estrich points out that such an approach obscures the reality that the majority of rapes are coerced or forced but unaccompanied by conventional violence.[95] In fact, one consequence of this approach is that it precludes protest from women who experience sexual intrusions in ways not typically seen as violent.

It is argued that in sexual harassment the motive is power, not sex. There is a wide consensus that sexual harassment is intended to "keep women in their place." Yet, the means by which this is attempted or accomplished are sexual: rude comments about sex or about a woman's body, pornographic gestures or posters, demands for sexual favors, rape, etc. Clearly, to the harassers, a woman's place is a largely sex-

ual one; her very presence in the workplace sexualizes it. In the accounts of women's experiences with sexual harassment in *Sexual Harassment: Women Speak Out*,[96] themes of sexual power and sexual humiliation resonate in each essay.

In wife battery the acts of violence are intended to inflict harm on the woman and ultimately to control her, but the message of the violence is explicitly sexual. For example, the most common parts of a woman's body attacked during battering are her face and her breasts—both symbols of her sexuality and her attractiveness to men. During pregnancy, the focus of the attack often shifts to the abdomen—a symbol of her reproductive power. In addressing the "either-or" debate in the sexual abuse of children, David Finkelhor points out "sex is always in the service of other needs. Just because it is infused with nonsexual motives does not make child sexual abuse different from other kinds of behavior that we readily call 'sexual'."[97]

Conclusion

The dynamic that underscores all manifestations of sexual terrorism is misogyny—the hatred of women. Violence against women is power expressed sexually. It is violence eroticized. Diana E. H. Russell argues that "we are socialized to sexualize power, intimacy, and affection, and sometimes hatred and contempt as well."[98] For women in the United States, sexual violence and its threat are central issues in their daily lives. Both violence and fear are functional. Without the power to intimidate and punish women sexually, the domination of women in all spheres of society—political, social, and economic—could not exist.

Notes

1. Susan Brownmiller, *Against Our Will: Men, Women and Rape* (New York: Simon and Schuster, 1975), 5.
2. Gordon and Riger, 22.
3. Yonah Alexander, "Terrorism and the Mass: Some Considerations," in Yonah Alexander, David Carlton, and Paul Wilkinson (eds.), *Terrorism: Theory and Practice* (Boulder, CO: Westview Press, 1979), 159; Ernest Evans, *Calling a Truce to Terrorism: The American Response to International Terrorism* (Westport, CT: Greenwood Press, 1979), 3; Charmers Johnson, "Perspectives on Terrorism," in Walter Laquer (ed.), *The Terrorism Reader* (Philadelphia: Temple University Press, 1978), 273; Thomas P. Thornton, "Terror as a Weapon of Political Agitation," in Harry Eckstein (ed.), *The Internal War* (New York: Free Press, 1964), 73; Eugene Walter, *Terror and Resistance* (New York: Oxford University Press, 1969), 6; Francis M. Watson, *Political Terrorism: The Threat and the Response* (Washington, DC: R. B. Luce Co., 1976), 15; Paul Wilkinson, *Political Terrorism* (New York: John Wiley and Sons, 1974), 11.
4. Frederick F. Hacker, *Crusaders, Criminals and Crazies: Terrorism in Our Time* (New York: W. W. Norton and Co., 1976), xi.
5. Marc Feigen Fasteau, *The Male Machine* (New York: McGraw-Hill Book Co., 1974), 144.
6. Watson, 15.
7. Wilkinson, 17.
8. Sheffield, "Obscene Phone Calls," 487.
9. Malette and Chalouh, 100.
10. Caputi and Russell, 34.
11. Kelly, 76.
12. Estrich, 8; UCR, 43; Koss and Harvey, 4.
13. Rhode, 245.
14. Russell, *Rape in Marriage*, 21–22.
15. Ibid., xxii.
16. Ibid., xxvi.
17. Campbell, 340.
18. *Bradley v. State*, 1 Miss. (7 Walker) 150 (1824); *State v. Black*, 60 N.C. (Win.) 266 (1864).
19. *Fulgham v. State*, 46 Ala. 143 (1871).
20. *Thompson v. Thompson*, 218 U.S. 611 (1910).
21. SchWeber and Feinman, 30.
22. *Arrest in Domestic Violence Cases: A State by State Summary* (New York: National Center on Women and Family Law, Inc., 1987), 1.
23. Langan and Innes, 1.
24. Lin Farley, *Sexual Shakedown: The Sexual Harassment of Women on the Job* (New York: McGraw-Hill Book Co., 1978), 14–15.
25. U.S. House of Representatives, 1980: 8.
26. *Meritor Savings Bank FSB v. Vinson*, 477 U.S. 57 (1986).
27. Lewin, A22; *Sexual Harassment: Research and Resources. A Report in Progress* (New York: The National Council for Research on Women, 1991), 10–13.
28. Kolbert, 1.
29. Roger Langley and Richard C. Levy, *Wife-Beating: The Silent Crisis* (New York: E. P. Dutton, 1977), 43.
30. Ibid., 44.
31. Vincent De Francis, *Protecting the Child Victim of Sex Crimes Committed by Adults* (Denver: American Humane Society, 1969), vii.
32. UCR, 1991, 16.
33. Ibid., 7.
34. Ibid., 16.
35. *Criminal Victimization in the United States,* 1990, 5.
36. Koss and Harvey, 11–17.
37. *Rape in America*, 1.
38. Ibid., 2.
39. Ibid., 4.
40. Ibid., 3.
41. Ibid.
42. Parrot and Bechofer, ix.
43. Crites, 36.
44. Langley and Levy, 3.
45. Zorn, 423.
46. Harlow, 5.
47. Caputi and Russell, 35.
48. De Francis, vii.
49. Ibid.
50. Finkelhor, *Sourcebook*, 19.
51. Ibid.
52. Russell, *Secret Trauma*, 69.
53. Bowker et al., 164.
54. Ibid.
55. Florence Rush, *The Best Kept Secret* (Englewood Cliffs, NJ: Prentice-Hall, 1980), 5.
56. Russell, *Secret Trauma*, 10.
57. Ibid.
58. Farlen, 31.
59. Rhode, 232.
60. Ibid, 20.
61. Ibid, 21.
62. Ibid, 20.
63. Kolbert, A17.
64. Dziech and Weiner, xxi.
65. Frank J. Till, *Sexual Harassment: A Report on the Sexual Harassment of Students* (Washington, DC: National Advisory Council on Women's Educational Programs, 1980), 3.
66. Rhode, 246.
67. Koss and Harvey, 5.
68. LaFree, 240.
69. Zorza, 243.

70. Rhode, 239.
71. *Attorney General's Task Force*, 4.
72. Ibid.
73. Rhode, 241.
74. Goolkasian, 3.
75. Crites, 41.
76. Ibid., 45.
77. Ibid.
78. Schafran, 280, 283–84.
79. Goodman, 13.
80. James Bannon, as quoted in Del Martin, *Battered Wives* (New York: Pocket Books, 1977), 115.
81. De Francis, 190–91.
82. Russell, *Secret Trauma*, 85.
83. Farley, 22.
84. Georgia Dullea, "Child Prostitution: Causes Are Sought" (*New York Times*, Sept. 4, 1979), p. C11.
85. *Rape in America*, 4.
86. Scully, 58.
87. Stanko, 95.
88. Till, 28,
89. Ibid., 115.
90. Ibid., 116.
91. Katherine Brady, *Father's Days: A True Story of Incest* (New York: Dell Publishing Co., 1981), 253.
92. Till, 4.
93. Sheffield, "Social Control," 172.
94. Timothy Beneke, *Men on Rape: What They Have to Say About Sexual Violence* (New York: St. Martin's Press, 1982), 16.
95. Estrich, 83.
96. Sumrall and Taylor
97. Finkelhor, *New Theory*, 34.
98. Russell, *Secret Trauma*, 393.

Resources

Attorney General's Task Force on Family Violence, Final Report. Washington, DC, 1984.

Lee H. Bowker, Michelle Arbitell, and J. Richard McFerron. "On the Relationship Between Wife Beating and Child Abuse," in Kersti Yllo and Michele Bograd (eds.), *Feminist Perspectives on Wife Abuse.* Newbury Park, CA: Sage Publications, Inc., 1988.

Jacquelyn C. Campbell. "Women's Responses to Sexual Abuse in Intimate Relationships." *Health Care for Women International* 8 (1989).

Jane Caputi and Diana E. H. Russell. "Femicide: Speaking the Unspeakable," in "Everyday Violence Against Women, Special Report." *Ms.* 1, no. 2 (1990).

Crime in the United States: Uniform Crime Reports, 1990. Washington, DC: U.S. Department of Justice, 1991.

Criminal Victimization in the United States, 1990. Washington, DC: U.S. Department of Justice, 1992.

Laura L. Crites. "Wife Abuse: The Judicial Record," in Laura L. Crites and Winifred L. Hepperle, *Women, the Courts and Equality.* Beverly Hills, CA: Sage Publications, Inc., 1987.

Billie Wright Dziech and Linda Weiner. *The Lecherous Professor: Sexual Harassment on Campus* (2nd ed.). Chicago: University of Illinois Press, 1990.

Susan Estrich. *Real Rape.* Cambridge, MA: Harvard University Press, 1987.

David Finkelhor. *A Sourcebook on Child Sexual Abuse.* Beverly Hills, CA: Sage Publications, Inc., 1986.

David Finkelhor (ed.). *Child Sexual Abuse: New Theory and Research.* New York: The Free Press, 1984.

David Finkelhor and Kersti Yllo. *License to Rape: Sexual Abuse of Wives.* New York: The Free Press, 1985.

Ellen Goodman. "My Equal Rights Winners." *Boston Globe,* Aug. 25, 1987, p. 13.

Gail A. Goolkasian. "Confronting Domestic Violence: The Role of the Criminal Court Judges." Washington, DC: U.S. Department of Justice, National Institute of justice, 1986.

Margaret T. Gordon and Stephanie Riger. *The Female Fear.* New York: The Free Press, 1989.

Caroline Wolf Harlow. "Female Victims of Violent Crime." Washington, DC: U.S. Department of Justice, 1991.

Liz Kelly. *Surviving Sexual Violence.* Minneapolis: University of Minnesota Press, 1988.

Elizabeth Kolbert. "Sexual Harassment at Work Is Pervasive, Survey Suggests." *New York Times,* Oct. 11, 1991, pp. 1, A17.

Mary P. Koss and Mary R. Harvey. *The Rape Victim: Clinical and Community Interventions* (2nd ed.). Newbury Park, CA: Sage Publications, Inc., 1991.

Gary D. LaFree. *Rape and Criminal Justice: The Social Construction of Sexual Assault.* Belmont, CA: Wadsworth Publishing Co., 1989.

Patrick A. Langan and Christopher Innes. "Preventing Domestic Violence Against Women." Washington, DC: U.S. Department of Justice, Bureau of Justice Statistics, 1986.

Tamar Lewin. "Law on Sex Harassment Is Recent and Evolving." *New York Times.* Oct. 8, 1991, p. A22.

Louise Malette and Marie Chalouh. *The Montreal Massacre.* Translated by Marlene Wildeman. Charlottetown, Prince Edward Island: Gynergy Books, 1991.

Andrea Parrot and Laurie Bechofer. *Acquaintance Rape: The Hidden Crime.* New York: John Wiley and Sons, Inc., 1991.

Rape in America: A Report to the Nation. Prepared by the National Victim Center and the Crime Victims Research and Treatment Center, New York, Apr. 23, 1992.

Deborah L. Rhode. *Justice and Gender: Sex Discrimination and the Law*. Cambridge, MA: Harvard University Press, 1989.

Diana E. H. Russell. *Rape in Marriage* (2nd ed.). Indianapolis: Indiana University Press, 1990.

Diana E. H. Russell. *The Secret Trauma: Incest in the Lives of Girls and Women*. New York: Basic Books, Inc. 1986.

Lynn Hecht Schafran. "Documenting Gender Bias in the Courts: The Task Force Approach." *Judicature* 70 (1987): 280, 283–84.

Claudine SchWeber and Clarice Feinman, eds. *Criminal Justice Politics and Women: The Aftermath of Legally Mandated Change*. New York: The Haworth Press, 1985.

Diana Scully. *Understanding Sexual Violence: A Study of Convicted Rapists*. Boston: Unwin Hyman, Inc., 1990.

Carole Sheffield. "The Invisible Intruder: Women's Experiences of Obscene Phone Calls." *Gender and Society* 3, no. 4 (1989): 483–88.

Carole Sheffield. "Sexual Terrorism: The Social Control of Women," in Beth B. Hess and Myra Marx Feree (eds.), *Analyzing Gender: A Handbook of Social Science Research*. Beverly Hills, CA: Sage Publications, Inc., 1987.

Elizabeth A. Stanko. *Intimate Intrusions: Women's Experiences of Male Violence*. London: Routledge and Kegan Paul, 1985.

Amber Coverdale Sumrall and Dena Taylor. *Sexual Harassment: Women Speak Out*. Freedom, CA: The Crossing Press, 1992.

U.S. House of Representatives. Hearings on Sexual Harassment in the Federal Government, Committee on the Post Office and Civil Service, Subcommittee on Investigations. Washington, DC: U.S. Government Printing Office, 1980.

Joan Zorza. "Woman Battering: A Major Cause of Homelessness." *Clearinghouse Review* (Special Issue) 24, no. 4 (1991): 421–29.

Fraternities and Collegiate Rape Culture: Why Are Some Fraternities More Dangerous Places for Women?

A. Ayres Boswell
Joan Z. Spade

Date rape and acquaintance rape on college campuses are topics of concern to both researchers and college administrators. Some estimate that 60 to 80 percent of rapes are date or acquaintance rape (Koss, Dinero, Seibel, and Cox 1988). Further, 1 out of 4 college women say they were raped or experienced an attempted rape, and 1 out of 12 college men say they forced a woman to have sexual intercourse against her will (Koss, Gidycz, and Wisniewski 1985).

Although considerable attention focuses on the incidence of rape, we know relatively little about the context or the *rape culture* surrounding date and acquaintance rape. Rape culture is a set of values and beliefs that provide an environment conducive to rape (Buchwald, Fletcher, & Roth 1993; Herman 1984). The term applies to a generic culture surrounding and promoting rape, not the specific settings in which rape is likely to occur. We believe that the specific settings also are important in defining relationships between men and women.

Some have argued that fraternities are places where rape is likely to occur on college campuses (Martin and Hummer 1989; O'Sullivan 1993; Sanday 1990) and that the students most likely to accept rape myths and be more sexually aggressive are more likely to live in fraternities and sororities, consume higher doses of alcohol and drugs, and place a higher value on social life at college (Gwartney-Gibbs and Stockard 1989; Kalof and Cargill 1991). Others suggest that sexual aggression is learned in settings such as fraternities and is not part of predispositions or preexisting attitudes (Boeringer, Shehah, and Akers 1991). To prevent further incidences of rape on college campuses, we need to understand what it is about fraternities in particular and college life in general that may contribute to the maintenance of a rape culture on college campuses.

Our approach is to identify the social contexts that link fraternities to campus rape and promote a rape culture. Instead of assuming that all fraternities provide an environment conducive to rape, we compare the interactions of men and women at fraternities identified on campus as being especially *dangerous* places for women, where the likelihood of rape is high, to those seen as *safer* places, where the perceived probability of rape occurring is lower. Prior to collecting data for our study, we found that most women students identified some fraternities as having more sexually aggressive members and a higher probability of rape. These women also considered other fraternities as relatively safe houses, where a woman could go and get drunk if she wanted to and feel secure that the fraternity men would not take advantage of her. We compared parties at houses identified as high-risk and low-risk houses as well as at two local bars frequented by college students. Our analysis provides an opportunity to examine situations and contexts that hinder or facilitate positive social relations between undergraduate men and women.

The abusive attitudes toward women that some fraternities perpetuate exist within a general culture where rape is intertwined in traditional gender scripts. Men are viewed as initiators of sex and women as either passive partners or active resisters, preventing men from touching their bodies (LaPlante, McCormick, and Brannigan 1980). Rape culture is based on the assumptions that men are aggressive and dominant whereas women are passive and acquiescent (Buchwald et al. 1993; Herman 1984). What occurs on college campuses is an extension of the portrayal of domination and aggression of men over women that exemplifies

the double standard of sexual behavior in U.S. society (Barthel 1988; Kimmel 1993).

Sexually active men are positively reinforced by being referred to as "studs," whereas women who are sexually active or report enjoying sex are derogatorily labeled as "sluts" (Herman 1984; O'Sullivan 1993). These gender scripts are embodied in rape myths and stereotypes such as "She really wanted it; she just said no because she didn't want me to think she was a bad girl" (Burke, Stets, and Pirog-Good 1989; Jenkins and Dambrot 1987; Lisak and Roth 1988; Malamuth 1986; Muehlenhard and Linton 1987; Peterson and Franzese 1987). Because men's sexuality is seen as more natural, acceptable, and uncontrollable than women's sexuality, many men and women excuse acquaintance rape by affirming that men cannot control their natural urges (Miller and Marshall 1987).

Whereas some researchers explain these attitudes toward sexuality and rape using an individual or a psychological interpretation, we argue that rape has a social basis, one in which both men and women create and recreate masculine and feminine identities and relations. Based on the assumption that rape is part of the social construction of gender, we examine how men and women "do gender" on a college campus (West and Zimmerman 1987). We focus on fraternities because they have been identified as settings that encourage rape (Sanday 1990). By comparing fraternities that are viewed by women as places where there is a high risk of rape to those where women believe there is a low risk of rape as well as two local commercial bars, we seek to identify characteristics that make some social settings more likely places for the occurrence of rape.

Method

We observed social interactions between men and women at a private coeducational school in which a high percentage (49.4 percent) of students affiliate with Greek organizations. The university has an undergraduate population of approximately 4,500 students, just more than one third of whom are women; the students are primarily from upper-middle-class families. The school, which admitted only men until 1971, is highly competitive academically.

We used a variety of data collection approaches: observations of interactions between men and women at fraternity parties and bars, formal interviews, and informal conversations. The first author, a former undergraduate at this school and a graduate student at the time of the study, collected the data. She knew about the social life at the school and had established rapport and trust between herself and undergraduate students as a teaching assistant in a human sexuality course.

The process of identifying high- and low-risk fraternity houses followed Hunter's (1953) reputational approach. In our study, 40 women students identified fraternities that they considered to be high risk, or to have more sexually aggressive members and higher incidence of rape, as well as fraternities that they considered to be safe houses. The women represented all four years of undergraduate college and different living groups (sororities, residence halls, and off-campus housing). Observations focused on the four fraternities named most often by these women as high-risk houses and the four identified as low-risk houses.

Throughout the spring semester, the first author observed at two fraternity parties each weekend at two different houses (fraternities could have parties only on weekends at this campus). She also observed students' interactions in two popular uni-versity bars on weeknights to provide a comparison of students' behavior in non-Greek settings. The first local bar at which she observed was popular with seniors and older students; the second bar was popular with first-, second-, and third-year undergraduates because the management did not strictly enforce drinking age laws in this bar.

The observer focused on the social context as well as interaction among participants at each setting. In terms of social context, she observed the following: ratio of men to women, physical setting such as the party decor and theme, use and control of alcohol and level of intoxication, and explicit and implicit norms. She noted interactions between men and women (i.e., physical contact, conversational style, use of jokes) and the relations among men (i.e., their treatment of pledges and other men at fraternity parties). Other than the observer, no one knew the identity of the high- or low-risk fraternities. Although this may have introduced bias into the data collection, students on this campus who read this article before it was submitted for publication commented on how accurately the social scene is described.

In addition, 50 individuals were interviewed, including men from the selected fraternities, women who attended those parties, men not affiliated with fraternities, and self-identified rape victims known to the first author. The first author approached men and women by telephone or on campus and asked them to participate in interviews. The interviews included open-ended questions about gender relations on campus, attitudes about date rape, and their own experiences on campus.

To assess whether self-selection was a factor in determining the classification of the fraternity, we compared high-risk houses to low-risk houses on several characteristics. In terms of status on campus, the high- and low-risk houses we studied attracted about the same number of pledges; however, many of the high-risk houses had more members. There was no difference in grade point averages for the two types of houses. In fact, the highest and lowest grade point averages were found in the high-risk category. Although both high- and low-risk fraternities participated in sports, brothers in the low-risk houses tended to play intramural sports whereas brothers in the high-risk houses were more likely to be varsity athletes. The high-risk houses may be more aggressive, as they had a slightly larger number of disciplinary incidents and their reports were more severe, often with physical harm to others and damage to property. Further, in year-end reports, there was more property damage in the high-risk houses. Last, more of the low- risk houses participated in a campus rape-prevention program. In summary, both high- and low-risk fraternities seem to be equally attractive to freshmen men on this campus, and differences between the eight fraternities we studied were not great; however, the high-risk houses had a slightly larger number of reports of aggression and physical destruction in the houses and the low-risk houses were more likely to participate in a rape prevention program.

Results

The Settings

Fraternity Parties

We observed several differences in the quality of the interaction of men and women at parties at high-risk fraternities compared to those at low-risk houses. A typical party at a low-risk house included an equal number of women and men. The social atmosphere was friendly, with considerable interaction between women and men. Men and women danced in groups and in couples, with many of the couples kissing and displaying affection toward each other. Brothers explained that, because many of the men in these houses had girlfriends, it was normal to see couples kissing on the dance floor. Coed groups engaged in conversations at many of these houses, with women and men engaging in friendly exchanges, giving the impression that they knew each other well. Almost no cursing and yelling was observed at parties in low-risk houses; when pushing occurred, the participants apologized. Respect for women extended to the women's bathrooms, which were clean and well supplied.

At high-risk houses, parties typically had skewed gender ratios, sometimes involving more men and other times involving more women. Gender segregation also was evident at these parties, with the men on one side of a room or in the bar drinking while women gathered in another area. Men treated women differently in the high-risk houses. The women's bathrooms in the high-risk houses were filthy, including clogged toilets and vomit in the sinks. When a brother was told of the mess in the bathroom at a high-risk house, he replied, "Good, maybe some of these beer wenches will leave so there will be more beer for us."

Men attending parties at high-risk houses treated women less respectfully, engaging in jokes, conversations, and behaviors that degraded women. Men made a display of assessing women's bodies and rated them with thumbs up or thumbs down for the other men in the sight of the women. One man attending a party at a high-risk fraternity said to another, "Did you know that this week is Women's Awareness Week? I guess that means we get to abuse them more this week." Men behaved more crudely at parties at high-risk houses. At one party, a brother dropped his pants, including his underwear, while dancing in front of several women. Another brother slid across the dance floor completely naked.

The atmosphere at parties in high-risk fraternities was less friendly overall. With the exception of greetings, men and women rarely smiled or laughed and spoke to each other less often than was the case at parties in low-risk houses. The few one-on-one conversations between women and men appeared to be strictly flirtatious (lots of eye contact, touching, and very close talking). It was rare to see a group of men and women together talking. Men were openly hostile, which made the high-risk parties seem almost threatening at times. For example, there was a lot of touching, pushing, profanity, and name calling, some done by women.

Students at parties at the high-risk houses seemed self-conscious and aware of the presence of members of the opposite sex, an awareness that was sexually charged. Dancing early in the evening was usually between women. Close to midnight, the sex ratio began to balance out with the arrival of more men or more women. Couples began to dance together but in a sexual way (close dancing with lots of pelvic thrusts). Men tried to pick up women using lines such as "Want to see my fish tank?" and "Let's go upstairs so that we can talk; I can't hear what you're saying in here."

Although many of the same people who attended high-risk parties also attended low-risk parties, their behavior changed as they moved from setting to setting. Group norms differed across contexts as well. At a party that was held jointly at a low-risk house with a high-risk fraternity, the ambience was that of a party at a high-risk fraternity with heavier drinking, less dancing, and fewer conversations between women and men. The men from both high- and low-risk fraternities were very aggressive; a

fight broke out, and there was pushing and shoving on the dance floor and in general.

As others have found, fraternity brothers at high-risk houses on this campus told about routinely discussing their sexual exploits at breakfast the morning after parties and sometimes at house meetings (cf. Martin and Hummer 1989; O'Sullivan 1993; Sanday 1990). During these sessions, the brothers we interviewed said that men bragged about what they did the night before with stories of sexual conquests often told by the same men, usually sophomores. The women involved in these exploits were women they did not know or knew but did not respect, or *faceless victims*. Men usually treated girlfriends with respect and did not talk about them in these storytelling sessions. Men from low-risk houses, however, did not describe similar sessions in their houses.

The Bar Scene

The bar atmosphere and social context differed from those of fraternity parties. The music was not as loud, and both bars had places to sit and have conversations. At all fraternity parties, it was difficult to maintain conversations with loud music playing and no place to sit. The volume of music at parties at high-risk fraternities was even louder than it was at low-risk houses, making it virtually impossible to have conversations. In general, students in the local bars behaved in the same way that students did at parties in low-risk houses with conversations typical, most occurring between men and women.

The first bar, frequented by older students, had live entertainment every night of the week. Some nights were more crowded than others, and the atmosphere was friendly, relaxed, and conducive to conversation. People laughed and smiled and behaved politely toward each other. The ratio of men to women was fairly equal, with students congregating in mostly coed groups. Conversation flowed freely and people listened to each other.

Although the women and men at the first bar also were at parties at low- and high-risk fraternities, their behavior at the bar included none of the blatant sexual or intoxicated behaviors observed at some of these parties. As the evenings wore on, the number of one-on-one conversations between men and women increased and conversations shifted from small talk to topics such as war and AIDS. Conversations did not revolve around picking up another person, and most people left the bar with same-sex friends or in coed groups.

The second bar was less popular with older students. Younger students, often under the legal drinking age, went there to drink, sometimes after leaving campus parties. This bar was much smaller and usually not as crowded as the first bar. The atmosphere was more mellow and relaxed than it was at the fraternity parties. People went there to hang out and talk to each other.

On a couple of occasions, however, the atmosphere at the second bar became similar to that of a party at a high-risk fraternity. As the number of people in the bar increased, they removed chairs and tables, leaving no place to sit and talk. The music also was turned up louder, drowning out conversation. With no place to dance or sit, most people stood around but could not maintain conversations because of the noise and crowds. Interactions between women and men consisted mostly of flirting. Alcohol consumption also was greater than it was on the less crowded nights, and the number of visibly drunk people increased. The more people drank, the more conversation and socializing broke down. The only differences between this setting and that of a party at a high-risk house were that broth-

ers no longer controlled the territory and bedrooms were not available upstairs.

Gender Relations

Relations between women and men are shaped by the contexts in which they meet and interact. As is the case on other college campuses, *hooking up* has replaced dating on this campus, and fraternities are places where many students hook up. Hooking up is a loosely applied term on college campuses that had different meanings for men and women on this campus.

Most men defined hooking up similarly. One man said it was something that happens

> when you are really drunk and meet up with a woman you sort of know, or possibly don't know at all and don't care about. You go home with her with the intention of getting as much sexual, physical pleasure as she'll give you, which can range anywhere from kissing to intercourse, without any strings attached.

The exception to this rule is when men hook up with women they admire. Men said they are less likely to press for sexual activity with someone they know and like because they want the relationship to continue and be based on respect.

Women's version of hooking up differed. Women said they hook up only with men they cared about and described hooking up as kissing and petting but not sexual intercourse. Many women said that hooking up was disappointing because they wanted longer-term relationships. First-year women students realized quickly that hookups were usually one-night stands with no strings attached, but many continued to hook up because they had few opportunities to develop relationships with men on campus. One first-year woman said that "70 percent of hook-ups never talk again and try to avoid one another; 26 percent may actually hear from them or talk to them again, and 4 percent may actually go on a date, which can lead to a relationship." Another first-year woman said, "It was fun in the beginning. You get a lot of attention and kiss a lot of boys and think this is what college is about, but it gets tiresome fast."

Whereas first-year women get tired of the hook-up scene early on, many men do not become bored with it until their junior or senior year. As one upperclassman said, "The whole game of hooking up became really meaningless and tiresome for me during my second semester of my sophomore year, but most of my friends didn't get bored with it until the following year."

In contrast to hooking up, students also described monogamous relationships with steady partners. Some type of commitment was expected, but most people did not anticipate marriage. The term *seeing each other* was applied when people were sexually involved but free to date other people. This type of relationship involved less commitment than did one of boyfriend/girlfriend but was not considered to be a hook-up.

The general consensus of women and men interviewed on this campus was that the Greek system, called "the hill," set the scene for gender relations. The predominance of Greek membership and subsequent living arrangements segregated men and women. During the week, little interaction occurred between women and men after their first year in college because students in fraternities or sororities live and dine in separate quarters. In addition, many non-Greek upper-class students move off campus into apartments. Therefore, students see each other in classes or in the library, but there is no place where students can just hang out together.

Both men and women said that fraternities dominate campus social life, a situation that everyone felt limited opportunities for meaningful interactions. One senior Greek man said,

> This environment is horrible and so unhealthy for good male and female relationships and interactions to occur. It is so segregated and male dominated. . . . It is our party, with our rules and our beer. We are allowing these women and other men to come to our party. Men can feel superior in their domain.

Comments from a senior woman reinforced his views: "Men are dominant; they are the kings of the campus. It is their environment that they allow us to enter; therefore, we have to abide by their rules." A junior woman described fraternity parities as

> good for meeting acquaintances but almost impossible to really get to know anyone. The environment is so superficial, probably because there are so many social cliques due to the Greek system. Also, the music is too loud and the people are too drunk to attempt to have a real conversation, anyway.

Some students claim that fraternities even control the dating relationships of their members. One senior woman said, "Guys dictate how dating occurs on this campus, whether it's cool, who it's with, how much time can be spent with the girlfriend and with the brothers." Couples either left campus for an evening or hung out separately with their own same-gender friends at fraternity parties, finally getting together with each other at about 2 a.m. Couples rarely went together to fraternity parties. Some men felt that a girlfriend was just a replacement for a hook-up. According to one junior man, "Basically a girlfriend is someone you go to at 2 a.m. after you've hung out with the guys. She is the sexual outlet that the guys can't provide you with."

Some fraternity brothers pressure each other to limit their time with and commitment to their girlfriends. One senior man said, "The hill [fraternities] and girlfriends don't mix." A brother described a constant battle between girl friends and brothers over who the guy is going out with for the night, with the brothers usually winning. Brothers teased men with girlfriends with remarks such as "whipped" or "where's the ball and chain?" A brother from a high-risk house said that few brothers at his house had girlfriends; some did, but it was uncommon. One man said that from the minute he was a pledge he knew he would probably never have a girlfriend on this campus because "it was just not the norm in my house. No one has girlfriends; the guys have too much fun with [each other]."

The pressure on men to limit their commitment to girlfriends, however, was not true of all fraternities or of all men on campus. Couples attended low-risk fraternity parties together, and men in the low-risk houses went out on dates more often. A man in one low-risk house said that about 70 percent of the members of his house were involved in relationships with women, including the pledges (who were sophomores).

Treatment of Women

Not all men held negative attitudes toward women that are typical of a rape culture, and not all social contexts promoted the negative treatment of women. When men were asked whether they treated the women on campus with respect, the most common response was "On an individual basis, yes, but when you have a group of men together, no." Men said that, when together in groups with other men, they sensed a pressure to be disrespectful toward women. A first-year man's perception of the treatment of women was that "they are treated with more respect to their faces, but behind closed doors, with a group of men present, respect for women is not an issue." One senior man stated, "In general, college-aged men don't treat women their age with

respect because 90 percent of them think of women as merely a means to sex." Women reinforced this perception. A first-year woman stated, "Men here are more interested in hooking up and drinking beer than they are in getting to know women as real people." Another woman said, "Men here use and abuse women."

Characteristic of rape culture, a double standard of sexual behavior for men versus women was prevalent on this campus. As one Greek senior man stated, "Women who sleep around are sluts and get bad reputations; men who do are champions and get a pat on the back from their brothers." Women also supported a double standard for sexual behavior by criticizing sexually active women. A first-year woman spoke out against women who are sexually active: "I think some girls here make it difficult for the men to respect women as a whole."

One concrete example of demeaning sexually active women on this campus is the "walk of shame." Fraternity brothers come out on the porches of their houses the night after parties and heckle women walking by. It is assumed that these women spent the night at fraternity houses and that the men they were with did not care enough about them to drive them home. Although sororities now reside in former fraternity houses, this practice continues and sometimes the victims of hecklings are sorority women on their way to study in the library.

A junior man in a high-risk fraternity described another ritual of disrespect toward women called "chatter." When an unknown woman sleeps over at the house, the brothers yell degrading remarks out the window at her as she leaves the next morning such as "Fuck that bitch" and "Who is that slut?" He said that sometimes brothers harass the brothers whose girlfriends stay over instead of heckling those women.

Fraternity men most often mistreated women they did not know personally. Men and women alike reported incidents in which brothers observed other brothers having sex with unknown women or women they knew only casually. A sophomore woman's experience exemplifies this anonymous state: "I don't mind if 10 guys were watching or it was videotaped. That's expected on this campus. It's the fact that he didn't apologize or even offer to drive me home that really upset me." Descriptions of sexual encounters involved the satisfaction of men by nameless women. A brother in a high-risk fraternity described a similar occurrence:

A brother of mine was hooking up upstairs with an unattractive woman who had been pursuing him all night. He told some brothers to go outside the window and watch. Well, one thing led to another and they were almost completely naked when the woman noticed the brothers outside. She was then unwilling to go any further, so the brother went outside and yelled at the other brothers and then closed the shades. I don't know if he scored or not, because the woman was pretty upset. But he did win the award for hooking up with the ugliest chick that weekend.

Attitudes Toward Rape

The sexually charged environment of college campuses raises many questions about cultures that facilitate the rape of women. How women and men define their sexual behavior is important legally as well as interpersonally. We asked students how they defined rape and had them compare it to the following legal definition: the perpetration of an act of sexual intercourse with a female against her will and consent, whether her will is overcome by force or fear resulting from the threat of force, or by drugs or intoxicants; or when, because of mental deficiency, she is incapable of exercising rational judgment. (Brownmiller 1975, 368)

When presented with this legal definition, most women interviewed recognized it as well as the complexities involved in applying it. A first-year woman said, "If a girl is drunk and the guy knows it and the girl says, 'Yes, I want to have sex,' and they do, that is still rape because the girl can't make a conscious, rational decision under the influence of alcohol." Some women disagreed. Another first-year woman stated, "I don't think it is fair that the guy gets blamed when both people involved are drunk."

The typical definition men gave for rape was "when a guy jumps out of the bushes and forces himself sexually onto a girl." When asked what date rape was, the most common answer was "when one person has sex with another person who did not consent." Many men said, however, that "date rape is when a woman wakes up the next morning and regrets having sex." Some men said that date rape was too gray an area to define. "Consent is a fine line," said a Greek senior man student. For the most part, the men we spoke with argued that rape did not occur on this campus. One Greek sophomore man said, "I think it is ridiculous that someone here would rape someone." A first-year man stated, "I have a problem with the word rape. It sounds so criminal, and we are not criminals; we are sane people."

Whether aware of the legal definitions of rape, most men resisted the idea that a woman who is intoxicated is unable to consent to sex. A Greek junior man said, "Men should not be responsible for women's drunkenness." One first-year man said, "If that is the legal definition of rape, then it happens all the time on this campus." A senior man said, "I don't care whether alcohol is involved or not; that is not rape. Rapists are people that have something seriously wrong with them." A first-year man even claimed that when women get drunk, they invite sex. He said, "Girls get so drunk here and then come on to us. What are we supposed to do? We are only human."

Discussion and Conclusion

These findings describe the physical and normative aspects of one college campus as they relate to attitudes about and relations between men and women. Our findings suggest that an explanation emphasizing rape culture also must focus on those characteristics of the social setting that play a role in defining heterosexual relationships on college campuses (Kalof and Cargill 1991). The degradation of women as portrayed in rape culture was not found in all fraternities on this campus. Both group norms and individual behavior changed as students went from one place to another. Although individual men are the ones who rape, we found that some settings are more likely places for rape than are others. Our findings suggest that rape cannot be seen only as an isolated act and blamed on individual behavior and proclivities, whether it be alcohol consumption or attitudes. We also must consider characteristics of the settings that promote the behaviors that reinforce a rape culture.

Relations between women and men at parties in low-risk fraternities varied considerably from those in high-risk houses. Peer pressure and situational norms influenced women as well as men. Although many men in high- and low-risk houses shared similar views and attitudes about the Greek system, women on this campus, and date rape, their behaviors at fraternity parties were quite different.

Women who are at highest risk of rape are women whom fraternity brothers did not know. These women are faceless victims, nameless acquaintances—not friends. Men said their responsibility to such persons and the level of guilt they feel later if the hook-ups end in sexual intercourse are much lower if they hook up with women they do not know. In high-risk houses, brothers treated women as subordinates and kept them at a distance. Men in high-risk houses actively discouraged ongoing heterosexual relationships, routinely degraded women, and participated more fully in the hook-up scene; thus, the probability that women would become faceless victims was higher in these houses. The flirtatious nature of the parties indicated that women go to these parties looking for available men, but finding boyfriends or relationships was difficult at parties in high-risk houses. However, in the low-risk houses, where more men had long-term relationships, the women were not strangers and were less likely to become faceless victims.

The social scene on this campus, and on most others, offers women and men few other options to socialize. Although there may be no such thing as a completely safe fraternity party for women, parties at low-risk houses and commercial bars encouraged men and women to get know each other better and decreased the probability that women would become faceless victims. Although both men and women found the social scene on this campus demeaning, neither demanded different settings for socializing, and attendance at fraternity parties is a common form of entertainment.

These findings suggest that a more conducive environment for conversation can promote more positive interactions between men and women. Simple changes would provide the opportunity for men and women to interact in meaningful ways such as adding places to sit and lowering the volume of music at fraternity parties or having parties in neutral locations, where men are not in control. The typical party room in fraternity houses includes a place to dance but not to sit and talk. The music often is loud, making it difficult, if not impossible, to carry on conversations; however, there were more conversations at the low-risk parties, where there also was more respect shown toward women. Although the number of brothers who had steady girlfriends in the low-risk houses as compared to those in the high-risk houses may explain the differences, we found that commercial bars also provided a context for interaction between men and women. At the bars, students sat and talked and conversations between men and women flowed freely, resulting in deep discussions and fewer hook-ups.

Alcohol consumption was a major focus of social events here and intensified attitudes and orientations of a rape culture. Although pressure to drink was evident at all fraternity parties and at both bars, drinking dominated high-risk fraternity parties, at which nonalcoholic beverages usually were not available and people chugged beers and became visibly drunk. A rape culture is strengthened by rules that permit alcohol only at fraternity parties. Under this system, men control the parties and dominate the men as well as the women who attend. As college administrators crack down on fraternities and alcohol on campus, however, the same behaviors and norms may transfer to other places such as parties in apartments or private homes where administrators have much less control. At commercial bars, interaction and socialization with others were as important as drinking, with the exception of the nights when the bar frequented by under-class students became crowded. Although one solution is to offer nonalcoholic social activities, such events receive little support on this campus. Either these alternative events lacked the prestige of the fraternity parties or the alcohol was seen as necessary to unwind, or both.

In many ways, the fraternities on this campus determined the settings in which men and women interacted. As others before us have found, pressures for conformity to the norms and values exist at both high-risk and low-risk houses (Kalof and Cargill 1991; Martin and Hummer 1989; Sanday 1990). The desire to be accepted is not unique to this campus or the Greek system (Holland and Eisenhart 1990; Horowitz 1988; Moffat 1989). The degree of conformity required by Greeks may be greater than that required in most social groups, with considerable pressure to adopt and maintain the image of their houses. The fraternity system intensifies the "group think syndrome" (Janis 1972) by solidifying the identity of the in-group and creating an us/them atmosphere. Within the fraternity culture, brothers are highly regarded and women are viewed as outsiders. For men in high-risk fraternities, women threatened their brotherhood; therefore, brothers discouraged relationships and harassed those who treated women as equals or with respect. The pressure to be one of the guys and hang out with the guys strengthens a rape culture on college campus by demeaning women and encouraging the segregation of men and women.

Students on this campus were aware of the contexts in which they operated and the choices available to them. They recognized that, in their interactions, they created differences between men and women that are not natural, essential, or biological (West and Zimmerman 1987). Not all men and women accepted the demeaning treatment of women, but they continued to participate in behaviors that supported aspects of a rape culture. Many women participated in the hook-up scene even after they had been humiliated and hurt because they had few other means of initiating contact with men on campus. Men and women alike played out this scene, recognizing its injustices in many cases but being unable to change the course of their behaviors.

Although this research provides some clues to gender relations on college campuses, it raises many questions. Why do men and women participate in activities that support a rape culture when they see its injustices? What would happen if alcohol were not controlled by groups of men who admit that they disrespect women when they get together? What can be done to give men and women on college campuses more opportunities to interact responsibly and get to know each other better? These questions should be studied on other campuses with a focus on the social settings in which the incidence of rape and the attitudes that support a rape culture exist. Fraternities are social contexts that may or may not foster a rape culture.

Our findings indicate that a rape culture exists in some fraternities, especially those we identified as high-risk houses. College administrators are responding to this situation by providing counseling and educational programs that increase awareness of date rape including campaigns such as "No means no." These strategies are important in changing attitudes, values, and behaviors; however, changing individuals is not enough. The structure of campus life and the impact of that structure on gender relations on campus are highly determinative. To eliminate campus rape culture, student leaders and administrators must examine the situations in which women and men meet and restructure these settings to provide opportunities for respectful interaction. Change may not require abolishing fraternities; rather, it may require promoting settings that facilitate positive gender relations.

References

Barthel, D. 1988. *Putting on appearances: Gender and advertising.* Philadelphia: Temple University Press.

Boeringer, S. B., C. L. Sheban, and R. L. Akers. 1991. Social contexts and social learning in sexual coercion and aggression: Assessing the contribution of fraternity membership. *Family Relations* 40:58–64.

Brownmiller, S. 1975. *Against our will: Men, women and rape.* New York: Simon & Schuster.

Buchwald, E., P. R. Fletcher, and M. Roth, eds. 1993. *Transforming a rape culture.* Minneapolis, MN: Milkweed Editions.

Burke, P., J. E. Stets, and M. A. Pirog-Good. 1989. Gender identity, self-esteem, physical abuse and sexual abuse in dating relationships. In *Violence in dating relationships: Emerging social issues,* edited by M. A. Pirog-Good and J. E. Stets. New York: Praeger.

Gwartney-Gibbs, P., and J. Stockard. 1989. Courtship aggression and mixed-sex peer groups. In *Violence in dating relationships: Emerging social issues,* edited by M. A. Pirog-Good and J. E. Stets. New York: Praeger.

Herman, D. 1984. The rape culture. In *Women: A feminist perspective,* edited by J. Freeman. Mountain View, CA: Mayfield.

Holland, D.C., and M. A. Eisenhart. 1990. *Educated in romance: Women, achievement, and college culture.* Chicago: University of Chicago Press.

Horowitz, H. L. 1988. *Campus life: Undergraduate cultures from the end of the 18th century to the present.* Chicago: University of Chicago Press.

Hunter, F. 1953. *Community power structure.* Chapel Hill: University of North Carolina Press.

Jenkins, M. J., and F. H. Dambrot. 1987. The attribution of date rape: Observer's attitudes and sexual experiences and the dating situation. *Journal of Applied Social Psychology* 17:875–95.

Janis, I. L. 1972. *Victims of group think.* Boston: Houghton Mifflin.

Kalof, L, and T. Cargill. 1991. Fraternity and sorority membership and gender dominance attitudes. *Sex Roles* 25:417–23.

Kimmel, M. S. 1993. Clarence, William, Iron Mike, Tailhook, Senator Packwood, Spur Posse, Magic . . . and us. In *Transforming a rape culture,* edited by E. Buchwald, P. R. Fletcher, and M. Roth. Minneapolis, MN: Milkweed Editions.

Koss, M. P, T. E. Dinero, C. A. Seibel, and S. L. Cox. 1988. Stranger and acquaintance rape: Are there differences in the victim's experience? *Psychology of Women Quarterly* 12:1–24.

Koss, M.P., C. A. Gidycz, and N. Wisniewski. 1985. The scope of rape: Incidence and prevalence of sexual aggression and victimization in a national sample of higher education students. *Journal of Consulting and Clinical Psychology* 55:162–70.

LaPlante, M. N., N. McCormick; and G. G. Brannigan, 1980. Living the sexual script: College students' views of influence in sexual encounters. *Journal of Sex Research* 16:338–55.

Lisak, D., and S. Roth. 1988. Motivational factors in nonincarcerated sexually aggressive men. *Journal of Personality and Social Psychology* 55:795–802.

Malamuth, N. 1986. Predictors of naturalistic sexual aggression. *Journal of Personality and Social Psychology* 50:953–62.

Martin; P. Y., and R. Hummer:. 1989. Fraternities and rape on campus. *Gender & Society* 3:457–73.

Miller, B., and J. C. Marshall. 1987. Coercive sex on the university campus. *Journal of College Student Personnel* 28:38–47.

Moffat, M. 1989. *Coming of age in New Jersey: College life in American culture.* New Brunswick, NJ: Rutgers University Press.

Muehlenhard; C. L., and M. A. Linton. 1987. Date rape and sexual aggression in dating situations: Incidence and risk factors. *Journal of Counseling Psychology* 34:186–96.

O'Sullivan, C. 1993. Fraternities and the rape culture. In *Transforming a rape culture,* edited by E. Buchwald, P. R. Fletcher, and M. Roth. Minneapolis, MN: Milkweed Editions.

Peterson, S. A., and B. Franzese. 1987. Correlates of college men's sexual abuse of women. *Journal of College Student Personnel* 28:223–28.

Sanday, P. R. 1990. *Fraternity gang rape: Sex, brotherhood, and privilege on campus.* New York: New York University Press.

West, C., and D. Zimmerman. 1987. Doing gender. *Gender & Society* 1:125–51.

"Our Women"/"Their Women":
Symbolic Boundaries, Territorial Markers, and Violence in the Balkans

Julie Mostov

Boundaries form indispensable protections against violation and violence; but the divisions they sustain in doing so also carry cruelty and violence. . . . Boundaries both foster and inhibit freedom, they both protect and violate life.[1]

In the Balkans and, particularly, in the former Yugoslavia, activities aimed at securing, contesting, or expanding existing territorial boundaries comprise an important part of ethnonational programs. Competing for political power, would-be national leaders embellish the wrongs and bemoan the hardships suffered by "their" people against a historical backdrop of disputed borders and conflicting claims to territories "won or lost" in past wars. They redraw contested borders and promise to secure proper ones, by force if necessary. Or they point to the plight of co-nationals living outside of the existing borders. They warn of possible losses of territory or tantalize with possible gains.

The redrawing of territorial boundaries to realize the congruence of nation and state,[2] particularly when the presumed boundaries of the nation are the myths and memories of the dominant ethnic group,[3] involves what Katherine Verdery calls a "homogenizing, differentiating, or classifying discourse."[4] It involves a kind of map-making that draws boundaries among people, either separating them from one another or pulling them together under one roof. It corrals people into newly constructed and constricting boundaries, inevitably stripping them of attachments and identities and imposing new ones.[5]

Thus boundaries designed to protect can, at the same time, be barriers to peace and security. They can be tools of violent exclusion and aggression. This essay explores the ways in which traditional gender roles and patriarchal culture play a part in the construction of such barriers and the violent map-making of ethnonationalisms. References are primarily to the former Yugoslavia, but the arguments apply to other countries in the region as well.

Symbolically, religion, language, gender, and in particular proper gender roles become boundaries in the national iconography. Women's bodies themselves become boundaries of the nation. Not only are women's bodies symbols of the fecundity of the nation and the vessels for its reproduction, but they are also territorial markers. Mothers, wives, and daughters designate the space of the nation and are, at the same time, the property of the nation. As markers and as property, mothers, daughters, and wives require the defense and protection of patriotic sons.

Myth-Making at Borders

The desire to make boundaries irreversible and to reiterate their "naturalness," which is part of the double process of state- and nation-building, makes recourse to the storehouse of national mythologies particularly appealing. Images drawn from epic tales and folklore, popularized in newly composed songs and in political speeches, trace the primordial, eternal nature of the nation and its battle against enemies. These images transfer the conflicts with "others" from the sphere of mere politics, economics, and history to the other-worldly sphere of myth. For example, Serbian warriors are portrayed as epic heroes fighting for sacred national values. But there is more to it. They are also waging a war for humanity against the "infidel." They are of epic proportion, and their adversaries are less than human, even monsters.[6]

The role of boundaries in national mythology (in songs, poetry, and literature) has often served to demarcate differences and to extend them to the symbolic realm as well as to erase geographic borders separating members of the nation.[7] The mythology

of border areas in which members of the nation are constantly faced with the threat of physical or moral (cultural) attacks by outsiders has figured significantly in the inflammatory politics of nationalist leaders in the borderlands (Krajina), populated by Serbs in Croatia and Bosnia.[8] According to one of the leading politicians among Bosnian Serb nationalists, Biljana Plavsic, the inhabitants of these borderlands have "developed and sharpened a highly sensitized ability to perceive threats to the nation and to develop protective mechanisms." Noting that it has always been said in her family that Serbs in Bosnia were better Serbs than were those in Serbia, she added that, as with all living organisms, those species that live near and are threatened by others are best able to adapt and survive.[9]

Tales and songs about border spaces are filled with warnings of external threats, bravery and bravado, and illicit crossings or transgressions. Popular among these tales are those that tell of the abduction of young girls—whisked away, seduced, or violently torn from their homelands. Such stories reveal the vulnerability or porousness of national boundaries. These stories highlight danger and opportunities for heroism and appeal to fantasies about the enemy. The erotic image of the enemy is tied to the transgression of borders: physical boundaries and cultural boundaries. Crossing the border, the "alien" bandit attempts to take something away or to invade the "national" space.[10] At the same time, each side fantasizes about invading the space of the other, stealing the identity of the alien society and installing its own culture.

Border fantasies develop with the gendering of boundaries[11] and spaces (landscapes, farmlands, and battlefields)[12] and with the collectivizing of "our women" and "their women." Feminine spaces are invaded (or filled) by masculine actors. The nation is adored and adorned, made strong and bountiful or raped and defiled, its limbs torn apart, its womb invaded. The vulnerability and seductiveness of women/borders require the vigilance of border guards; they also entice combatants into battle. It is significant that much of the armed conflict in the Yugoslav wars has taken place in borderlands.

Reproducing the Nation: Preserving Its Numbers

Women are biological reproducers of group members, of the ethnonation. They bear sons to fight and daughters to care for the motherland. Women who resist this role are deemed selfish, unwomanly, and unpatriotic; women who have abortions are, above all, traitors. Given the importance of demographic renewal in the struggles among contending ethnonational groups in the region, abortion is presented as a serious threat to the nation. Warnings of the symbolic and demographic consequences of such action abound in the rhetoric of national spokespersons (and are rarely publicly contested by male members of civic opposition groups).[13] According to the Croatian ruling party, for example, "A fetus is also Croat"—an innocent member of Mother Croatia.[14]

Croatian President Franjo Tudjman blamed the tragedy of the Croatian nation on "women, pornography, and abortion." Women who have abortions are "mortal enemies of the nation," and their gynecologists are "traitors." Their acts are appalling as they act to hinder "the birth of little Croats, that sacred thing which God has given society and the homeland." Women who have not given birth to at least four children are scolded as "female exhibitionists" who have not fulfilled their "unique sacred duty."[15]

The Serbian Orthodox Patriarch Pavle, in his widely broadcast Christmas message of 1995, warned that the low birthrate among Serbs was a "plague" visited on the nation. He also declared that women were too interested in enjoying themselves and not willing to bear and raise children because it might threaten their comfortable lives. He went on to say that "many mothers who had not wanted to have more than one child were now pulling out their hair and bitterly weeping over the loss of their only children in the war, often cursing God and others for that but forgetting to blame themselves for not bearing more children who could remain to comfort them. When they come before the final judgment, those mothers who didn't allow their children to be born will meet these children up above and they will then ask them: Why did you kill us, why didn't you give birth to us?"[16] He added that if the birthrate did not increase significantly in 10 years, Serbs would be a national minority in their own country and then would have nothing to say about their own fate.

Hungarian nationalists have also tied abortion to the "death of the nation." Abortion is described as a "national catastrophe." According to one article, "Four million Hungarians . . . had been killed by abortion in the thirty-five years of the liberal abortion policies of the Communists," more than had been killed at the famous battle of Mohacs against the Turks in 1526. Susan Gal, who cites this article, notes the choice of words: "not fetuses or even people, but Hungarians."[17]

Women as mothers are reproducers of the nation, but they are also potential enemies of and traitors to their nation, collaborators in its death. The other's women are enemies as reproducers, multiplying the number of outsiders, conspiring to dilute and destroy the nation with their numerous offspring. (Both Croats and Serbs warn of the rapid increase in birthrates of local Muslims and Albanians.)[18] Thus, while "our" women are to be revered as mothers, all women's bodies must be controlled. Because the ethnonational concept of nation defines the community as a family, motherhood and reproduction must be supervised by the guardians of the nation. Women's bodies as incubators are instrumental to the maintenance of the external and internal boundaries of the nation.

Nurturing the Nation: Preserving Its Distinctiveness

Women serve as custodians of national values, as signifiers of the boundaries of group identity, marking its difference from alien others.[19] Women preserve traditions in the home, observe dietary and other rituals, and, through their chastity and modesty, reflect the virtue of the nation. Proper roles for women are dictated by the situation: wife, mother, long-suffering victim; nurse and comforter; woman-warrior. Women are to be warm, tender, sensitive, sympathetic, and caring; yet, in the absence of males, they must be ready to protect the nation. A women's battalion that fought at the front in Krajina is said to have been formed by women ashamed that able-bodied men were resisting mobilization, dodging the war like traitors (much like the legendary traitor of Serbian folklore, Vuk Brankovic, who is said to have fled the battlefield and left Serbian King Lazar to fight alone against the Turks in the battle of Kosovo, 1389).[20]

Paired with epic heroes are brave mothers who sacrifice their sons and husbands for the nation and tend the wounds of the fallen warriors and faithful wives who keep the hearth burning and who bear the future generation of heroes. Women in mourning, peasant women forced out of their homes, women refugees packed into trucks with crying children, on the other hand, are symbols of the national tragedy and reasons for national revenge. Women professionals and other modern urban residents are left out of the national imagery of womanhood. The healthy outdoor girls, portrayed as the admiring girlfriends of the patriotic soldiers or paramilitary forces, are not "feminists," or weak city girls, but rather are physically and morally strong symbols of the purity and vitality of the nation.[21]

The "healthy" girls sitting in Pale (once a resort village on the outskirts of Sarajevo, now Bosnian Serb headquarters), or peasant mothers tied to the hearth—rather than those women who once sat in the offices, libraries, cafes, and clubs in Sarajevo—represent the primordial roots and natural character of the nation.[22] City life holds too many temptations and too many opportunities for boundary crossings.

Women who fail to observe the borders, who transgress them through mixed marriages and other personal relationships or who engage in activities that otherwise push them to the margins of the community, are castigated. Women critical of ethnonational leaders or active in the peace movements in the former Yugoslavia and feminist organizations are good examples. They are dehumanized in public discourse because they lack a national identity, which is the essence of one's being. For example, an article in the Zagreb daily, *Globus,* labeled as "witches" five women who dared to be critical of the policies of the ruling party in Croatia and publicly questioned its censorship policies. The headline stated, "Croatian Feminists Rape Croatia!" The author of the article was careful to point out their "failures" to marry Croatians, to remain married, or to have children. Clearly, they were women with identity problems.[23]

On the other hand, women become national heroines through suicide or martyrdom. A Belgrade magazine reported the story of Dragana, a mother of two who "acted like a real hero at a torture chamber in Bosanski Brod—she shot herself in the mouth."[24]

Women as Battleground

Since 1989, a common complaint of ethnonational leaders in Eastern Europe has been that communism imposed an artificial identity on members of the nation, degrading or denying the particular genius of their respective nations and encouraging a kind of ethnic blending. In the former Yugoslavia, many have played on this theme, arguing that an artificial "Yugoslav" identity robbed many of them of their real identifies. Serbs and Croats need to recover their links to their own cultures and revive the unique qualifies of their respective peoples. New Serbs or Croats or Bosnians would have to learn to imagine themselves not as Yugoslavs but as members of a recovered nation.

This process of national recovery and "self-determination" is understood in such a way that it appears inevitably linked to armed conflict. Claims to territory and sovereignty tied to redefined national identities are successfully asserted only by joining in the ancient battles of one's ancestors. Through warfare, members of the nation reconstitute their identity by brutally drawing the boundaries between themselves and others. Blood defines the boundaries of each community and seals the borders.

Confirming the naturalness of these new-old divisions and the continuity of the national struggle, contemporary warriors are said to fight alongside their noble "ancestors." Thus today's soldiers are described as "links" in a genetic chain, inheritors of battlegrounds and enemies. Serbian mythology, for example, stresses this notion of the intimate link between the living and the dead. This relationship is tied to the idea of sacred places where the blood of ancestors has been spilled and their bodies have been laid to rest. Ancestral soil—earth mixed with the bones of previous warriors—or the graves and the remains of fallen heroes become symbolic as well as territorial markers.

The ethnonational leader draws from this mythology and the ritual reuniting of soil and bones. Thus, in 1989, the bones of King Lazar, a famous Serbian hero who died in the fourteenth-century battle of Kosovo against the Turks, were carried around to the Orthodox monasteries and finally brought to rest in Kosovo, retracing the territory of the Serbian national community and asserting the "'fact' that Kosovo has always been the cradle of 'that which is Serbian.'"[25]

The "being" or essence of the nation is carried by male warriors, planted in the soil through their bones, and is passed to new generations through their semen. (Under the inspiration of a patriotic program at a refugee camp, one author went so far as to say that a feeling for the traditional metric verse of epic poems is "inborn" in the Serbian genetic code.[26])

Nationalist ideology thus assigns active roles, "subject positions," to men who will wage war, protecting and expanding their territory and possessions. It is over and through the feminine body that they pursue these goals. They forge their identities as males, as agents of the nation, over the symbolic and physical territory of the feminine "homeland." The latter must be secured and protected from transgression, for it holds the seeds and blood of past and future warriors. Over and through the actual bodies of women who reproduce the nation, men define its physical limits and preserve its sanctity. Over the battleground of women's bodies, borders are transgressed and redrawn.

The genetic material of the nation is supplied by men while women provide the vessel in which the nation and its treasure grow. This idea of women as containers and nurturers is linked with the spatial imagery of women as landscape over which soldiers march, as fields to harvest, as a natural resource, as territory to protect, as land that could be seized or invaded. The use of women in "symbolically marking the boundary of the group makes them particularly susceptible" to control strategies organized from within to maintain and defend the boundaries and vulnerable to violence from without designed to invade and violate these lines of demarcation.[27] The combination of roles assigned to women and patriarchal perceptions of women as susceptible to seduction heightens the sense of women's vulnerability and thus the vulnerability of "our" land, our possessions, our culture, and our values. At the same time, the positioning of women as objects—containers, transmitters, and symbols of nationhood—enhances the temptation to contest and degrade the other by violating "his" woman.

Rape of the Nation

The personification of nature as female translates easily to that of nation as woman, that is, as a woman's body that is always in danger of violation by foreign males.[28] According to V. Spike Peterson, "Nation-as-woman expresses a spatial, embodied femaleness: the land's fecundity, upon which the people depend, must be protected by defending the body/nation's boundaries against invasion and violation. But nation-as-woman is also a temporal metaphor: The rape of the body/nation not only violates frontiers but disrupts—by planting alien seed or destroying reproductive viability—the maintenance of the community through time." She adds that in this "patriarchal metaphor is the tacit agreement that men who cannot defend their woman/nation against rape have lost their 'claim' to that body, that land."[29]

Actual women's bodies are important here as part of a collective body. The nationalist discourse denies the specificity of female experience by giving larger symbolic meanings to the signifier of rape; that is, Bosnia (Croatia, Serbia) is being violated by the Serbian (Muslim, Albanian) rapist.[30] Because the nation itself is at stake, the crime of rape does not acquire meaning until it is committed by a foreign intruder.

Thus women are perceived as victims of oppression and brutality, but only at the hands of other nationalities.[31] Within the nation, women are seen as the property of fathers, husbands, or brothers and as national resources or, in Meredith Tax's words, as "fields to be sown."[32] A woman who has been raped is devalued property, and she signals defeat for the man who fails in his role as protector.

So, raping the other's women is a violation of territorial integrity, an act of war, a means of establishing jurisdiction and conquest. The territory/property of the "enemy males" is occupied through the "colonization" of female bodies. Rape is an invasion of the other's territory and a sign of his impotency. Men who cannot prevent the rape of "their" women are defeated as on the battlefield. They have failed to protect their borders.

The humiliation of men, whose women have been raped, is an important motivating factor. For the ethnonational leaders bound on changing the territory of their nation, rape becomes an instrument for permanently changing the ethnic makeup of the land. Under the much-abused notion of national self-determination, the brutality in "ethnic cleansing" is aimed at ensuring the irreversibility of any population changes necessary to majority control.[33] Accepting the "tacit agreement" of the patriarchal metaphor, men would not return to the place where "their" women were raped and humiliated.

Another way of putting this is that the terrain of women's bodies is seen as a battlefield over which the identities of the other can be destroyed. Rape at once pollutes and occupies the territory of the nation, transgresses its boundaries, defeats its protectors. Degrading the nation's symbol of fertility and purity, it physically blocks its continuity and threatens its existence. Such rape thus promises to "cleanse" the territory of the other and make it ours. In a war in which major goals are articulated in terms of map-making, it follows a frighteningly logical strategy.

The female body as a spoil of war becomes a territory whose borders spread through the "birth of an enemy son." Given the traditional notions expressed in warrior mythology of the male as the bearer of the genetic "stuff" of the nation and the female as property and a vessel in which sons and daughters of the nation grow, men become owners of the territory/womb as well as owners of the children women carry. This is expressed in the words of a rapist, reported by survivors in Bosnia: "You have an enemy child in your womb. One day my child will kill you."[34]

In one act, a rapist can defeat the male enemy, invade and conquer the other's territory/nation, and advance his own nation. This does not suggest that the thousands of rapes committed in the recent wars in the former Yugoslavia were directly motivated by such elaborate analysis, but it places them in a context of images familiar to people in the region. The words of perpetrators reported by witnesses and survivors and the public responses of leaders to these accounts lead us to believe that these acts were, to a large extent, undertaken, encouraged, and understood in such terms.[35]

National Romance with the Plight of "Our" Women

As symbols of national tragedy and reasons for national revenge, women who were brutally raped in the Bosnian war have continued to suffer more abuse in the service of nationhood. These women, whose suffering was so well documented by the press, became pawns in the power struggles of national politicians and strategists. Collectivized as raped Croatian, Muslim, or Serbian women, their individual stories were merely offered as examples of damage to the nation. Yet, the Croatian press publicized rapes of Muslim women much more than it did those of Croatian women, perhaps to keep the image of "their" women chaste or uncontaminated. It was necessary to portray Muslim women as violated to draw attention to the horror of Serbia's actions.[36] After the individual women's tragedies were displayed and counted as part of the nation's, they were publicly ignored. During 1992 and 1993, local political activists and journalists went looking for raped women who would tell their stories. Foreign journalists joined in as well. One of the jokes circulating among residents and volunteers in refugee camps in Croatia and Serbia was as follows. "What does a journalist ask when he comes to a camp?" Answer: "Is there anyone here who was raped and speaks English?"[37] The everyday emotional and existential struggles of the individual women survivors, while commented on intermittently by government officials, have been primarily the concern of feminist and other independent human rights groups.

Women Breaking the Boundaries

The feminization of territorial and symbolic space in the national-patriarchal metaphors discussed here also suggests a subversive role for women in redefining the notion of boundaries and nation. As creators of alternative "identities and spaces," women activists in peace movements and women's groups in the region are resisting the imposed boundaries of ethnonationalisms. (Examples of such groups include Women in Black in Belgrade and the Center for Women Victims of War in Zagreb.[38]) Through their activities and efforts, they hope to affirm their agency as women, as political actors, and as participants in the economic life of their communities. At the same time, they hope to prevent the instrumentalization of women's bodies in the service of the nation and stop the violence committed in their defense. They question the definition of nationhood produced by ethnonational leaders, the roles assigned them in sustaining and promoting the nation, and the criteria for membership in it. Moreover, they demonstrate that while recognizing the "reality" of international borders, they can reject the "hardness" of these lines. They can find ways to cross them, "soften" them, weaken their seductive enticement to war, and erase their significance as barriers between people. As symbols, actors, and objects, women fill important roles: in constructing borders, solidifying and sundering attachments, perpetuating identities and denying identities, and finally in breaking down boundaries and borders. It is this last role that holds the prospect for peace in the former Yugoslavia.

Notes

1. William Connolly, "Tocqueville, Territory, and Violence," *Theory, Culture, and Society* 11 (1994): 23.
2. Ernest Gellner, *Nations and Nationalism* (Oxford, UK: Basil Blackwell, 1983).
3. Anthony D. Smith, *National Identity* (London: Penguin Books, 1991), 9–13. According to Smith, this "genealogical model" of national identity defines the national community in terms of common culture, history, religion, myth, *and* presumed descent. The nation is understood as a kind of "super family."
4. Katherine Verdery, "Whither 'Nation' and 'Nationalism'?" *Daedalus* 122 (Summer 1993): 38.
5. Testimonies collected from Serbian refugees from Croatia, by the Fund for Humanitarian Law, for example, indicate that in some cases villagers were encouraged for strategic reasons to leave their homes by their own national militias, who did so by spreading the word of atrocities in neighboring towns. See, for example, J. Dulovic, "Papuk, 1991" *Vreme,* February 14, 1994, 27.
6. Ivan Colovic, "The Propaganda of War: Its Strategies," in *Yugoslavia: Collapse, War, Crimes,* ed. Sonja Biserko (Belgrade: Centre for Anti-War Action/Belgrade Circle, 1993), 115–19.
7. Ivan Colovic, "Teme Granice u Politickoj Mitologiji," manuscript in Serbo-Croatian, Belgrade, 1994, copy in author's possession.
8. The Krajina region of Croatia was an autonomous part of Hungary created as a military frontier region for the Austro-Hungarian armies. Predominantly Serbian, it supplied these armies, as well as later Yugoslav Partisan ones, with a disproportionately large number of officers and soldiers. See Bogdan Denitch, *Ethnic Nationalism: The Tragic Death of Yugoslavia* (Minneapolis: University of Minnesota Press, 1994).
9. Translated from Biljana Plavsic, *Borba,* July 28, 1993; Ivan Colovic, "Politicki mitovi-vreme i prostor," in *Pucanje od Zdravlja* (Belgrade: Biblioteka Krug, 1994), 117. (All translations from Serbo-Croatian texts are mine.)
10. For a variation of this, see Renata Salecl, "Nationalism, Anti-Semitism, and Anti-Feminism in Eastern Europe," *New German Critique* 57 (Fall 1992): 52.
11. Verdery writes that this "makes boundaries like the skin of the female body, fixed yet violable, in need of armed defense by inevitably masculine militaries"; see Katherine Verdery, "From Parent-State to Family Patriarchs: Gender and Nation in Contemporary Eastern Europe," *East*

European Politics and Societies 8 (Spring 1994): 249.

12. I return to this theme later. For an excellent treatment of it with respect to Romania, see ibid., 225–55.

13. For an example in another country, see Ann Snitow, "The Church Wins, Women Lose: Poland's Abortion Law," *Nation,* April 26, 1993, 556–557.

14. Salecl, "Nationalism, Anti-Semitism, and Anti-Feminism," 59.

15. Ibid.

16. *Vreme,* January 16, 1995, 11.

17. Susan Gal, "Gender in the Post-Socialist Transition: The Abortion Debate in Hungary," *East European Politics and Societies* 8 (Spring 1994) : 271. Verdery cites this example and others, such as "Abortion Is Genocide" and references to "seventeen million fetal Polish citizens"; see Verdery, "From Parent-State to Family Patriarchs," 250. See also Snitow, "The Church Wins, Women Lose."

18. Andjelka Milic, "Women and Nationalism in the Former Yugoslavia," in *Gender Politics and Post Communism: Reflections from Eastern Europe and the former Soviet Union,* ed. Nanette Funk and Magda Mueller (New York: Routledge, 1993), 112–13.

19. Women are nurturers of cultural values, "custodians of cultural particularisms," and the "symbolic repository of group identity"; see Deniz Kandiyoti, "Identity and Its Discontents: Women and the Nation," *Millennium* 20 (1991): 434.

20. *Pogledi,* April 16–30, 1993, 21–25.

21. The comic strip adventures of Captain Dragan, leader of a Serbia elite paramilitary unit, and his ninja-like warriors were extremely popular during the summer leading up to the war in Croatia. Captain Dragan was a contemporary "hero" fighting for Serbian values and recovering Serbian warrior or heroic traditions going back to the middle ages. He was virile and worshipped by his brave and loyal Serbian girlfriend, also prepared to fight to the death for her nation. See Ivan Colovic, *Bordel Ratnika,* 2nd ed. (Belgrade: Biblioteka XX Vek, 1994), 61–70, and idem, "The Propaganda of War."

22. In the eyes of some Serbian nationalists, Belgrade is an unfortunate example of the unhealthy, contaminated city, dangerous to the continued vitality of the nation. According to one, "Belgrade is an anti-Serbian [trash] bin" see "Pucanje od zdravlja," p. 39. See Colovic, "Politicki mitovi-vreme i prostor," 33–39.

23. *Globs,* December 11, 1992, 33–34. See Meredith Tax, "Five Women Who Won't Be Silenced," *The Nation,* May 10, 1993, 634–25.

24. *DUGA*, translated by Julie Mostov, August 16–29, 1992. Indeed, women have participated in the war in a number of roles, including that of soldier; but those roles celebrated in the press are of victim, martyr, patriot, and mother. See Mili, "Women and Nationalism," 115, and Julie Mertus, "'Woman' in the Service of National Identity," *Hastings Women's Law Journal* 5 (Winter 1994): 16–17.

25. Salecl, "Nationalism, Anti-Semitism, and Anti-Feminism," 55.

26. Colovic, "Politicki mitovi-vreme i prostor," 112.

27. Jan Jindy Pettman, "Women, Nationalism and the State: Towards an International Feminist Perspective" (Occasional Paper 4 in Gender and Development Studies, Asian Institute of Technology, Bangkok), cited in V. Spike Peterson, "Gendered Nationalism: Reproducing 'Us' versus 'Them,'" *Peace Review* 6 (March 1994): 5.

28. Jean Bethke Elshtain, "Sovereignty, Identity, Sacrifice," in *Gendered States,* ed. V. Spike Peterson (Boulder, CO: Lynne Rienner, 1992)

29. Peterson, "Gendered Nationalism," 4.

30. Linda Liu, "The Female Body and Nationalist Discourse: The Field of Life and Death Revisited," in *Scattered Hegemonies: Postmodernity and Transnational Feminist Practices,* ed. Inderpal Grewal and Caren Kaplan (Minneapolis: University of Minnesota Press, 1994), 44.

31. Cornelia Sorabji looks at this practice of recognizing rape as a serious crime only when it is committed against the nation in recent Yugoslav history. "[T]he rapes in Bosnia have at least some roots in Kosovo in 1986 when the press began to carry allegations of Albanians raping Serbs and vice versa. . . . At the same time penalties for rape and other forms of physical assault between members of different nationalities were increased. Rape was presented not as an abuse of an individual woman but as one nation's abuse of another, and international abuse as more grievous a crime than interpersonal violence. Contemporary Bosnia lives against this backdrop." See Cornelia Sorabji, "Crimes against Gender or Nation?" *War Report* 18 (February/March 1993): 16. Stasa Zajovic of Women in Black in Belgrade notes that violence against women as individuals by co-nationals becomes invisible and inconsequential as it is not an attack on the nation and is even understandable given the pressures of warfare; see Stasa Zajovic, "About 'Cleansing,'" in *Women for Peace*, ed. Stasa Zajovic (Belgrade: Women in Black, 1994), 64–67.

32. Meridith Tax, "Notes for a Letter to the State Department" (paper presented at the Network of East-West Women's conference on "Gender Nationalism and Democratization," Washington, DC, October 26–27, 1993).

33. In what I call a misappropriation of the notion of self-determination, the right to political and economic control of a territory has gone to the majority ethnonational group living there; that is, the right to define the nature of political institutions, interests, and way of life belongs to the majority ethnonational group as such. The way to secure this right is to make sure that its numerical superiority is not contested. See Julie Mostov, "Democracy and the Politics of National Identity," *Studies in East European Thought* 46 (June 1994): 9–31.

34. Zajovic, "About 'Cleansing,'" 67.

35. See Mertus "'Woman' in the Service," 19–20.

36. Ibid.

37. Stasa Zajovic, "The Abuse of Victims," in *Women for Peace*, 176; see also ibid.

38. The names and addresses of the growing number of women's centers and feminist organizations throughout the former Yugoslavia can be obtained through the Network for East-West Women, 395 Riverside Drive, Suite 2F, New York, NY 10025, e-mail: neww@igc.apc.org, or through the STAR Project, 1090 Vermont Avenue, N.W., 7th Floor, Washington, DC e-mail: ccc@delphi-int.org.

Health and Reproduction

PART VI

In this section, reproductive rights and women's health are linked as connected feminist concerns. Although the feminist demand for reproductive rights has often been interpreted solely as a demand for access to safe and legal abortions, these readings define reproductive rights more broadly. Demands for reproductive rights include not only the right to safe and legal abortions, but also the freedom from sterilization abuse and from economic and often racist public policies that interfere with one's choice to be a parent or not.

Nancy Krieger and Elizabeth Fee discuss how two major categories related to health, race and sex, came to be viewed as strictly biological variables, while the social dimensions of gender, ethnicity, and class were ignored by medical practioners and policy makers. They ask: "Is there any alternative way of understanding these population patterns of health and disease?" Their article turns our attention to how the categories used in biomedical thought and practice have shaped the information we have about the health, disease, and treatment of women and men.

On the global stage, several articles consider how the introduction of new reproductive technologies furthers or limits existing discrimination against women. The Forum Against Sex Determination and Sex Pre-Selection, an activist group from India, argues that sex determination tests can not be examined apart from the wider forms of discrimination faced by women in India. Jacqueline Pitanguy's article examines the re-emergence of a feminist movement in Brazil and its efficacy in transforming women's demands, particularly those regarding reproductive health, into public policy. In "Norplant in the Nineties" Sonia Correa considers debates over the introduction, marketing and use of a new form of reproductive technology worldwide. Considering the history of abuses in the introduction and testing of contraceptives, what factors should feminists weigh in evaluating the efficacy and safety of these technologies?

Closer to home, Cynthia Daniels reveals how assumptions about the profound connection between the mother and fetus operate to exclude the father from discussions about fetal health. This exclusion has the effect of locating all blame for fetal harm on mothers, particularly

333

women's behavior during gestation. This directs attention away from men's actions in shaping fetal health both before conception and throughout pregnancy.

The articles in this section oblige us to consider how women in different economic, racial, ethnic and national circumstances are fashioned in terms of their health and reproductive capacities. They also critique some of the assumptions made by feminists in the West in light of very different circumstances and problems faced by women in other areas of the world.

Suggestions for Further Reading

Bollinia, Paola and Harald Siem. 1995. "No Real Progress Towards Equity: Health of Migrants and Ethnic Minorities on the Eve of the Year 2000," *Social Science and Medicine*, 41, 819–828.

Burbank, Victoria K. 1995. "Gender Hierarchy and Adolescent Sexuality: The Control of Female Sexuality in an Australian Aboriginal Community," *Ethos*, 23, 33–46.

Chen, Lincoln C., Arthur Kleinman, and Norma C. Ware, eds. 1994. *Health and Social Change in International Perspective*. Boston, MA: Harvard University Press.

Coliver, Sandra, ed. 1995. *The Right to Know: Human Rights and Access to Reproductive Health Information*. Philadelphia: University of Pennsylvania Press.

Dangizer, Renee. 1994. "The Social Impact of HIV/AIDS in Developing Countries," *Social Science and Medicine*, 39, 905–917.

Dixon-Mueller, Ruth. 1993. *Population Policy and Women's Rights: Transforming Reproductive Choice*. Westport, CT: Praeger.

Doyal, Lesley. 1995. *What Makes Women Sick: Gender and the Political Economy of Health*. New Brunswick, NJ: Rutgers University Press.

Ginsburg, Faye D. and Rayna Rapp, eds. 1995. *Conceiving the New World Order: The Global Politics of Reproduction*. Berkeley: University of California Press.

Gottshalk, Janet, and Leeann Teymour. 1993. "Third World Women Call for a Balanced Perspective on Women's Health," *Health Care for Women International*, 14, 111–116.

Hartmann, Betsy. 1995. *Reproductive Rights and Wrongs: The Global Politics of Population Control*. Boston: South End Press.

Henderson, Jodi C. 1994. "Abortion and the Global Crisis in Women's Health." In Laurie Ann Mazur, ed. *Beyond the Numbers: A Reader on Population, Consumption, and the Environment*. Washington, DC: Island Press.

Koss, Mary P., Lori Heise and Nancy F. Russo. 1994. "The Global Health Burden of Rape," *Psychology of Women Quarterly*, 18, 509–537.

Land, Helen. 1994. "AIDS and Women of Color," *Families in Society*, 75, 355–361.

McFarlane, Judith, Kelly, Elizabeth, Rodriguez, Rachel and John Fehir. 1994. "De Madres a Madres: Women Building Community Coalition for Health," *Health Care for Women International*, 15, 465–476.

Obermeyer, Carla Makhlouf. 1993. "Culture, Maternal Health Care, and Women's Status: A Comparison of Morocco and Tunisia," *Studies in Family Planning*, 24, 354–365.

Ping, Tu, and Herbert L. Smith. 1995. "Determinants of Induced Abortion and Their Policy Implications in Four Counties in North China," *Studies in Family Planning*, 26, 278–286.

Sargent, Carolyn F., and Caroline B. Brettell, eds. 1996. *Gender and Health: An International Perspective*. Upper Saddle River, NJ: Prentice Hall.

Serbanescu, Florina, Leo Morris, Paul Stupp, and Alin Stanescu. 1995. "The Impact of Recent Policy Changes on Fertility, Abortion, and Contraceptive Use in Romania," *Studies in Family Planning*, 26, 76–88.

Torkington, Ntombenhle Protasia Khoti. 1995. "Black Migrant Women and Health," *Women's Studies International Forum*, 18, 153–158.

Man-Made Medicine and Women's Health:
The Biopolitics of Sex/Gender and Race/Ethnicity

Nancy Krieger
Elizabeth Fee

Glance at any collection of national health data for the United States, whether pertaining to health, disease, or the health care system, and several obvious features stand out (1–5). First, we notice that most reports present data in terms of race, sex, and age. Some races are clearly of more interest than others. National reports most frequently use racial groups called "white" and "black," and increasingly, they use a group called "Hispanic." Occasionally, we find data on Native Americans, and on Asians and Pacific Islanders. Whatever the specific categories chosen, the reports agree that white men and women, for the most part, have the best health, at all ages. They also show that men and women, across all racial groups, have different patterns of disease: obviously, men and women differ for conditions related to reproduction (women, for example, do not get testicular cancer),

but they differ for many other conditions as well (for example, men on average have higher blood pressure and develop cardiovascular disease at an earlier age). And, in the health care sector, occupations, just like diseases, are differentially distributed by race and sex.

All this seems obvious. But it isn't. We know about race and sex divisions because this is what our society considers important. This is how we classify people and collect data. This is how we organize our social life as a nation. This is therefore how we structure our knowledge about health and disease. And this is what we find important as a subject of research (6–9).

It seems so routine, so normal, to view the health of women and men as fundamentally different, to consider the root of this difference to be biological sex, and to think about race as an inherent, inherited characteristic that also affects health (10). The work of looking after sick people follows the same categories. Simply walk into a hospital and observe that most of the doctors are white men, most of the registered nurses are white women, most of the kitchen and laundry workers are black and Hispanic women, and most of the janitorial staff are black and Hispanic men. Among the patients, notice who has appointments with private clinicians and who is getting care in the emergency room; the color line is obvious. Notice who provides health care at home: wives, mothers, and daughters. The gender line at home and in medical institutions is equally obvious (11–15).

These contrasting patterns, by race and sex, are longstanding. How do we explain them? What kinds of explanations satisfy us? Some are comfortable with explanations that accept these patterns as natural, as the result of natural law, as part of the natural order of things. Of course, if patterns are that way by nature, they cannot be changed. Others aim to understand these patterns precisely in order to change them. They look for explanations suggesting that these patterns are structured by convention, by discrimination, by the politics of power, and by unreasonable law. These patterns, in other words, reflect the social order of people.

In this chapter, we discuss how race and sex became such all-important, self-evident categories in 19th and 20th century biomedical thought and practice. We examine the consequences of these categories for our knowledge about health and for the provision of health care. We then consider alternative approaches to studying race/ethnicity, gender, and health. And we address these issues with reference to a typically suppressed and repressed category: that of social class.

The Social Construction of "Race" and "Sex" as Key Biomedical Terms and Their Effect on Knowledge about Health

In the 19th century, the construction of "race" and "sex" as key biomedical categories was driven by social struggles over human inequality. Before the Civil War, the dominant understanding of race was as a natural/theological category—black-white differences were innate and reflected God's will (16–19). These differences were believed to be manifest in every aspect of the body, in sickness and in health. But when abolitionists began to get the upper hand in moral and theological arguments, proponents of slavery appealed to science as the new arbiter of racial distinction.

In this period, medical men were beginning to claim the mantle of scientific knowledge and assert their right to decide controversial social issues (20–22). Recognizing the need for scientific authority, the state of Louisiana, for example, commissioned one prolific proponent of slavery, Dr. Samuel Cartwright, to prove the natural inferiority of blacks, a task that led him to detail every racial difference imaginable—in texture of hair, length of bones, vulnerability to disease, and even color of the internal organs (23–25). As the Civil War changed the status of blacks from legal chattel to bona fide citizens, however, medical journals began to question old verities about racial differences and, as importantly, to publish new views of racial similarities (26, 27). Some authors even attributed black-white differences in health to differences in socioeconomic position. But by the 1870s, with the destruction of reconstruction, the doctrine of innate racial distinction again triumphed. The scientific community once again deemed "race" a fundamental biological category (28–32).

Theories of women's inequality followed a similar pattern (33–36). In the early 19th century, traditionalists cited scripture to prove women's inferiority. These authorities agreed that Eve had been formed out of Adam's rib and that all women had to pay the price of her sin—disobeying God's order, seeking illicit knowledge from the serpent, and tempting man with the forbidden apple. Women's pain in childbirth was clear proof of God's displeasure.

When these views were challenged in the mid-19th century by advocates of women's rights and proponents of liberal political theory, conservatives likewise turned to the new arbiters of knowledge and sought to buttress their position with scientific facts and medical authority (37, 38). Biologists busied themselves with measuring the size of women's skulls, the length of their bones, the rate of their breathing, and the number of their blood cells. And considering all the evidence, the biologists concluded that women were indeed the weaker sex (39–41).

Agreeing with this stance, medical men energetically took up the issue of women's health and equality (42–45). They were convinced that the true woman was by nature sickly, her physiological systems at the mercy of her ovaries and uterus. Because all bodily organs were interconnected, they argued, a woman's monthly cycle irritated her delicate nervous system and her sensitive, small, weak brain. Physicians considered women especially vulnerable to nervous ailments such as neurasthenia and hysteria. This talk of women's delicate constitutions did not, of course, apply to slave women or to working-class women—but it was handy to refute the demands of middle-class women whenever they sought to vote or gain access to education and professional careers. At such moments, many medical men declared the doctrine of separate spheres to be the ineluctable consequence of biology.

At the same time, 19th century medical authorities began to conceptualize class as a natural, biological distinction. Traditional, pre-scientific views held class hierarchies to be divinely ordained; according to the more scientific view that emerged in the early 19th century, class position was determined by innate, inherited ability. In both cases, class was perceived as an essentially stable, hierarchical ranking. These discussions of class usually assumed white or Western European populations and often applied only to males within those populations.

With the impact of the industrial revolution, classes took on a clearly dynamic character. As landowners invested in canals and railroads, as merchants became capitalist entrepreneurs, and as agricultural workers were transformed into an industrial proletariat, the turbulent transformation of the social order provoked new understandings of class relationships (46). The most developed of these theories was that of Karl Marx, who emphasized the system of classes as a social and economic formation and stressed the contradictions between different class interests (47). From this point onward, the very idea of social class in many people's minds implied a revolutionary threat to the social order.

In opposition to Marxist analyses of class, the theory of Social Darwinism was formulated to suggest that the new social inequalities of industrial society reflected natural law (48–51). This theory was developed in the midst of the economic depression of the 1870s, at a time when labor struggles, trade union organizing, and early socialist movements were challenging the political and economic order. Many scientists and medical men drew upon Darwin's idea of "the struggle for survival," first expressed in the *Origin of the Species* in 1859 (52), to justify social inequality. They argued that those on top, the social elite, must by definition be the "most fit" because they had survived so well. Social hierarchies were therefore built on and reflected real biological differences. Poor health status simultaneously was sign and proof of biological inferiority.

By the late 19th century, theories of race, gender, and class inequality were linked together by the theory of Social Darwinism, which promised to provide a scientific basis for social policy (48–51). In the realm of race, for example, proponents of Social Darwinism blithely predicted that the "Negro question" would soon resolve itself—the "Negro" would naturally become extinct, eliminated by the inevitable workings of "natural selection" (29, 53). Many public health officers—particularly in the southern states—agreed that "Negroes" were an inherently degenerate, syphilitic, and tubercular race, for whom public health interventions could do little (54–57). Social Darwinists also argued that natural and sexual selection would lead to increasing differentiation between the sexes (34, 48, 58). With further evolution, men would become ever more masculine and women ever more feminine. As proof, they looked to the upper classes, whose masculine and feminine behavior represented the forefront of evolutionary progress.

Over time, the Social Darwinist view of class gradually merged into general American ideals of progress, meritocracy, and success through individual effort. According to the dominant American ideology, individuals were so mobile that fixed measures of social class were irrelevant. Such measures were also un-American. Since the Paris Commune, and especially since the Bolshevik revolution, discussions of social class in the United States were perceived as politically threatening. Although fierce debates about inequality continued to revolve around the axis of nature versus nurture, the notion of class as a social relationship was effectively banished from respectable discourse and policy debate (48, 59). Social position was once again equated only with rank, now understood as socioeconomic status.

In the early 20th century, Social Darwinists had considerable influence in shaping public views and public policy (48, 59–64). They perceived two new threats to American superiority: the massive tide of immigration from eastern and southern Europe, and the declining birth rate—or "race suicide"—among American white women of Anglo-Saxon and Germanic descent. Looking to the fast-developing field of genetics, now bolstered by the rediscovery of Gregor Mendel's laws and T. H. Morgan's fruit fly experiments (65–68), biological determinists regrouped under the banner of eugenics. Invoking morbidity and mortality data that showed a high rate of tuberculosis and infectious disease among the immigrant poor (69–71), they declared "ethnic" Europeans a naturally inferior and sickly stock and thus helped win passage of the Immigration Restriction Act in 1924 (72–74). This legislation required the national mix of immigrants to match that entering the United States in the early 1870s, thereby severely curtailing immigration of racial and ethnic groups deemed inferior. "Race/ethnicity," construed as a biological reality, became ever more entrenched as the *explanation* of racial/ethnic differences in disease; social explanations were seen as the province of scientifically illiterate and naive liberals, or worse, socialist and Bolshevik provocateurs.

Other developments in the early 20th century encouraged biological explanations of sex differences in disease and in social roles. The discovery of the sex chromosomes in 1905 (75–77) reinforced the idea that gender was a fundamental biological trait, built into the genetic constitution of the body. That same year, Ernest Starling coined the term "hormone" (78) to denote the newly characterized chemical messengers that permitted one organ to control—at a distance—the activities of another. By the mid-1920s, researchers had isolated several hormones integral to reproductive physiology and popularized the notion of "sex hormones" (79–83). The combination of sex chromosomes and sex hormones was imbued with almost magical powers to shape human behavior in gendered terms; women were now at the mercy of their genetic limitations and a changing brew of hormonal imperatives (84, 85). In the realm of medicine, researchers turned to sex chromosomes and hormones to understand cancers of the uterus and breast and a host of other sex-linked diseases (86-90); they no longer saw the need to worry about environmental influences. In the workplace, of course, employers said that sex chromosomes and hormones dictated which jobs women could—and could not—perform (45, 91, 92). This in turn determined the occupational hazards to which women would be exposed—once again, women's health and ill-health were really a matter of their biology.

Within the first few decades of the 20th century, these views were institutionalized within scientific medicine and the new public health. At this time, the training of physicians and public health practitioners was being recast in modern, scientific terms (93–95). Not surprisingly, biological determinist views of racial/ethnic and sex/gender differences became a natural and integral part of the curriculum, the research agenda, and medical and public health practice.

Over time, ethnic differences in disease among white European groups were downplayed and instead, the differences between whites and blacks, whites and Mexicans, and whites and Asians were emphasized. Color was now believed to define distinct biological groups.

Similarly, the sex divide marked a gulf between two completely disparate groups. Within medicine, women's health was relegated to obstetrics and gynecology; within public health, women's health needs were seen as being met by maternal and child health programs (8, 45, 96). Women were perceived as wives and mothers; they were important for childbirth, childcare, and domestic nutrition. Although no one denied that some women worked, women's occupational health was essentially ignored because women were, after all, only temporary workers. Outside the specialized realm of reproduction, all other health research concerned men's bodies and men's diseases. Reproduction was so central to women's biological existence that women's non-reproductive health was rendered virtually invisible.

Currently, it is popular to argue that the lack of research on white women and on men and women in nonwhite racial/ethnic groups resulted from a perception of white men as the norm (97–99). This interpretation, however, is inaccurate. In fact, by the time that researchers began to standardize methods for clinical and epidemiologic research, notions of difference were so firmly embedded that whites and nonwhites, women and men, were rarely studied together. Moreover, most researchers and physicians were interested only in the health status of whites and, in the case of women, only in their reproductive health. They therefore used white men as the research subjects of choice for all health conditions other than women's reproductive health and paid attention to the health status of nonwhites only to measure degrees of racial difference. For the most part, the health of women and men of color and the nonreproductive health of white women were simply ignored. It is critical to read these omissions as evidence of a logic of difference rather than as an assumption of similarity.

This framework has shaped knowledge and practice to the present. In the United States, vital statistics present health information in terms of race and sex and age, conceptualized only as biological variables—ignoring the social dimensions of gender and ethnicity. Data on social class are not collected. At the same time, public health professionals are unable adequately to explain or to change inequalities in health between men and women and between diverse racial/ethnic groups. We now face the question: Is there any alternative way of understanding these population patterns of health and disease?

Alternative Ways of Studying Race, Gender, and Health: Social Measures for Social Categories

The first step in creating an alternative understanding is to recognize that the categories we traditionally treat as simply biological are in fact largely social. The second step is to realize we need social concepts to understand these social categories. The third step is to develop social measures and appropriate strategies for a new kind of health research (10).

With regard to race/ethnicity, we need to be clear that "race" is a spurious biological concept (100–102). Although historical patterns of geographic isolation and migration account for differences in the distribution of certain genes, genetic variation within so-

called racial groups far exceeds that across groups. All humans share approximately 95 percent of their genetic makeup (100, p. 155). Racial/ethnic differences in disease thus require something other than a genetic explanation.

Recognizing this problem, some people have tried to substitute the term "ethnicity" for "race" (103, 104). In the public health literature, however, "ethnicity" is rarely defined. For some, it apparently serves as a polite way of referring to what are still conceptualized as "racial"/biological differences. For others, it expresses a new form of "cultural" determinism, in which ethnic differences in ways of living are seen as autonomous "givens" unrelated to the social status of particular ethnic groups within our society (105, 106). This cultural determinism makes discrimination invisible and can feed into explanations of health status as reductionist and individualistic as those of biological determinism.

For a different starting point, consider the diverse ways in which racism operates, at both an institutional and interpersonal level (107–109). Racism is a matter of economics, and it is also more than economics. It structures living and working conditions, affects daily interactions, and takes its toll on people's dignity and pride. All of this must be considered when we examine the connection between race/ethnicity and health.

To address the economic aspects of racism, we need to include economic data in all studies of health status (110, 111). Currently, our national health data do not include economic information—instead, racial differences are often used as indicators of economic differences. To the extent that economics are taken into account, the standard approach assumes that differences are either economic or "genetic." So, for those conditions where racial/ethnic differences persist even within economic strata—hypertension and preterm delivery, for example—the assumption is that something biological, something genetic, is at play. Researchers rarely consider the noneconomic aspects of racism or the ways in which racism continues to work within economic levels.

Some investigators, however, are beginning to consider how racism shapes people's environments. Several studies, for example, document the fact that toxic dumps are most likely to be located in poor neighborhoods and are disproportionately located in poor neighborhoods of color (112–114). Other researchers are starting to ask how people's experience of and response to discrimination may influence their health (115–118). A recent study of hypertension, for example, found that black women who responded actively to unfair treatment were less likely to report high blood pressure than women who internalized their responses (115). Interestingly, the black women at highest risk were those who reported *no* experiences of racial discrimination.

Countering the traditional practice of always taking whites as the standard of comparison, some researchers are beginning to focus on other racial/ethnic groups to better understand why, within each of the groups, some are at higher risk than others for particular disease outcomes (119–121). They are considering whether people of color may be exposed to specific conditions that whites are not. In addition to living and working conditions, these include cultural practices that may be positive as well as negative in their effects on health. Some studies, for example, point to the importance of black churches in providing social support (122–124). These new approaches break with monolithic assumptions about what it means to belong to a given ra-

cial/ethnic group and consider diversity *within* each group. To know the color of a person's skin is to know very little.

It is equally true that to know a person's sex is to know very little. Women are often discussed as a single group defined chiefly by biological sex, members of an abstract, universal (and implicitly white) category. In reality, we are a mixed lot, our gender roles and options shaped by history, culture, and deep divisions across class and color lines. Of course, it is true that women, in general, have the capacity to become pregnant, at least at some stages of our lives. Traditionally, women as a group are defined by this reproductive potential. Usually ignored are the many ways that gender as a social reality gets into the body and transforms our biology—differences in childhood expectations about exercise, for example, affect our subsequent body build (38, 125).

From a health point of view, women's reproductive potential does carry the possibility of specific reproductive ills ranging from infertility to preterm delivery to cervical and breast cancer. These reproductive ills are not simply associated with the biological category "female," but are differentially experienced according to social class and race/ethnicity. Poor women, for example, are much more likely to suffer from cervical cancer (119, 126). By contrast, at least among older women, breast cancer is more common among the affluent (126, 127). These patterns, which at times can become quite complex, illustrate the general point that, even in the case of reproductive health, more than biological sex is at issue. Explanations of women's reproductive health that ignore the social patterning of disease and focus only on endogenous factors are thus inadequate.

If we turn to those conditions that afflict both men and women—the majority of all diseases and health problems—we must keep two things simultaneously in mind. First are the differences and similarities among diverse groups of women; second are the differences and similarities between women and men.

For a glimpse at the complexity of disease patterns, consider the example of hypertension (128, 129). As we mentioned, working-class and poor women are at greater risk than affluent women; black women, within each income level, are more likely to be hypertensive than white women (5). The risks of Hispanic women vary by national origin: Mexican women are at lowest risk, Central American women at higher risk, and Puerto Rican and Cuban women at the highest risk (130, 131). In what is called the "Hispanic paradox," Mexican-American women have a higher risk profile than Anglo-American women, yet experience lower rates of hypertension (132). To further complicate the picture, the handful of studies of Japanese and Chinese women in the United States show them to have low rates, while Filipina women have high rates, almost equal to those of African Americans (130, 133, 134). Rates vary across different groups of Native American women; those who live in the Northern plains have higher rates than those in the Southwest (130, 135). From all this, we can conclude that there is enormous variation in hypertension rates among women.

If we look at the differences between women and men, we find that men in each racial/ethnic group have higher rates of hypertension than women (129). Even so, the variation among women is sufficiently great that women in some racial/ethnic groups have higher rates than men in other groups. Filipina women, for example, have higher rates of hypertension than white men (5, 133). Obviously, the standard biomedical categories of race and sex cannot explain these patterns. If we want to understand hypertension, we will have to understand the complex distribution of disease among real women and men; these patterns are not merely distracting details but the proper test of the plausibility of our hypotheses.

As a second example, consider the well-known phenomenon of women's longer life expectancy. This difference is common to all industrialized countries, and amounts to about seven years in the United States (136, 137). The higher mortality of men at younger ages is largely due to higher accident rates, and at older ages, to heart disease.

The higher accident rates of younger men are not accidental. They are due to more hazardous occupations, higher rates of illicit drug and alcohol use, firearms injuries, and motor vehicle crashes—hazards related to gender roles and expectations (136, 137). The fact that men die earlier of heart disease—the single most common cause of death in both sexes—may also be related to gender roles. Men have higher rates of cigarette smoking and fewer sources of social support, suggesting that the masculine ideal of the Marlboro man is not a healthy one. Some contend that women's cardiovascular advantage is mainly biological, due to the protective effect of their hormone levels (138). Interestingly, however, a study carried out in a kibbutz in Israel, where men and women were engaged in comparable activities, found that the life expectancy gap was only four and a half years—just over half the national average (139). While biological differences between men and women now receive much of the research attention, it is important to remember that men are gendered beings too.

Clearly, our patterns of health and disease have everything to do with how we live in the world. Nowhere is this more evident than in the strong social class gradients apparent in almost every form of morbidity and mortality (110, 140–143). Yet here the lack of information and the conceptual confusion about the relationship between social class and women's health is a major obstacle. As previously noted, in this country, we have no regular method of collecting data on socioeconomic position and health. Even if we had such data, measures of social class generally assume male heads of households and male patterns of employment (111, 144). This, indeed, is one of the failures of class analyses—that they do not deal adequately with women (144–147).

Perhaps the easiest way to understand the problems of class measurements and women's health is briefly to mention the current debates in Britain, a country that has long collected social class data (148, 149). Men and unmarried women are assigned a social class position according to their employment; married women, however, are assigned a class position according to the employment of their husbands. As British feminist researchers have argued, this traditional approach obscures the magnitude of class differences in women's health (149). Instead, they are proposing measures of household class that take into account the occupations of both women and their husbands, and their ownership of household assets.

Here in the United States, we have hardly any research on the diverse measures of social class in relation to women's health. Preliminary studies suggest we also would do well to distinguish between individual and household class (150, 151). Other research shows that we can partly overcome the absence of social class information in U.S. medical records by using census data (126, 152). This method allows us to describe people in terms of the socioeconomic profile of their immediate neighborhood. When coupled with individual measures of social class, this approach reveals, for example, that working-class women who live in working-class neighborhoods are somewhat more likely to have high blood pressure than working-class women who live in more affluent neighborhoods (152). We thus need conceptually to separate three distinct levels at which class operates: individual, household, and neighborhood.

As a final example of why women's health cannot be understood without reference to issues of sex/gender, race/ethnicity, and social class, consider the case of AIDS (153–155). The definition of disease, the understanding of risk, and the approach to prevention are shaped by our failure fully to grasp the social context of disease. For the first decade, women's unique experiences of AIDS were rendered essentially invisible. The first definition of AIDS was linked to men, because it was perceived to be a disease of gay men and those with a male sex-linked disorder, hemophilia. The very listing of HIV-related diseases taken to characterize AIDS was a listing based on the male experience of infection. Only much later, after considerable protest by women activists, were female disorders—such as invasive cervical cancer—made part of the definition of the disease (156, 157).

Our understanding of risk is still constrained by the standard approaches. AIDS data are still reported only in terms of race, sex, and mode of transmission; there are no data on social class (158). We know, however, that the women who have AIDS are overwhelmingly women of color. As of July 1993, of the nearly 37,000 women diagnosed with AIDS, over one half were African American, another 20 percent were Hispanic, 25 percent were white, and about 1 percent were Asian, Pacific Islander, or Native American (158). What puts these women at risk? It seems clear that one determinant is the missing variable, social class. Notably, the women at highest risk are injection drug users, the sexual partners of injection drug users, and sex workers (154). The usual listing of behavioral and demographic risk factors, however, fails to capture the social context in which the AIDS epidemic has unfolded. Most of the epidemiological accounts are silent about the blight of inner cities, the decay of urban infrastructure under the Reagan-Bush administrations, unemployment, the drug trade, prostitution, and the harsh realities of everyday racism (159, 160). We cannot gain an adequate understanding of risk absent a real understanding of people's lives.

Knowledge of what puts women at risk is of course critical for prevention. Yet, just as the initial definitions of AIDS reflected a male-gendered perspective, so did initial approaches to prevention (161). The emphasis on condoms assumed that the central issue was knowledge, not male-female power relations. For women to use condoms in heterosexual sex, however, they need more than bits of latex; they need male assent. The initial educational materials were created without addressing issues of power; they were male-oriented and obviously white—in both the mode and language of presentation. AIDS programs and services, for the most part, still do not address women's needs, whether heterosexual, bisexual, or lesbian. Pregnant women and women with children continue to be excluded from most drug treatment programs. And when women become sick and die, we have no remotely adequate social policies for taking care of the families left behind.

In short, our society's approach to AIDS reflects the larger refusal to deal with the ways in which sex/gender, race/ethnicity, and class are inescapably intertwined with health. This refusal affects not only what we know and what we do about AIDS, but also the other issues we have mentioned—hyper-tension, cancer, life expectancy—and many we have not (162). As we have tried to argue, the issues of women's health cannot be understood only in biological terms, as simply the ills of the female of the species. Women and men are different, but we are also similar—and we both are divided by the social relations of class and race/ethnicity. To begin to understand how our social constitution affects our health, we must ask, repeatedly, what is different and what is similar across the social divides of gender, color, and class. We cannot assume that biology alone will provide the answers we need; instead, we must reframe the issues in the context of the social shaping of our human lives—as both biological creatures and historical actors. Otherwise, we will continue to mistake—as many before us have done—what is for what must be, and leave unchallenged the social forces that continue to create vast inequalities in health.

References

1. National Center for Health Statistics. *Health, United States, 1991.* DHHS Pub. No. (PHS) 92-1232. U.S. Public Health Service, Hyattsville, Md., 1992.
2. National Center for Health Statistics. *Vital Statistics of the United States—1988. Vol. I, Natality.* DHHS Pub. No. (PHS) 90-1100. U.S. Government Printing Office, Washington, D.C., 1990.
3. National Center for Health Statistics. *Vital Statistics of the United States—1987. Vol. II, Mortality, Part A.* DHHS Pub. No. (PHS) 90-1101. U.S. Government Printing Office, Washington, D.C., 1990.
4. National Center for Health Statistics. *Vital Statistics of the United States—1988. Vol. II, Mortality, Part B.* DHHS Pub. No. (PHS) 90–1102. U.S. Government Printing Office, Washington, D.C., 1990.
5. U.S. Department of Health and Human Services. *Health Status of Minorities and Low-Income Groups,* Ed. 3. U.S. Government Printing Office, Washington, D.C., 1991.
6. Krieger, N. The making of public health data: Paradigms, politics, and policy. *J. Public Health Policy* 13: 412–427, 1992.

7. Navarro, V. Work, ideology, and science: The case of medicine. In *Crisis, Health, and Medicine: A Social Critique,* edited by V. Navarro, pp. 142–182. Tavistock, New York, 1986.

8. Fee, E. (ed.). *Women and Health: The Politics of Sex in Medicine.* Baywood, Amityville, N.Y., 1983.

9. Tesh, S. *Hidden Arguments: Political Ideology and Disease Prevention Policy.* Rutgers University Press, New Brunswick, N.J., 1988.

10. Krieger, N., et al. Racism, sexism, and social class: Implications for studies of health, disease, and well-being. *Am. J. Prev. Med,* 9 (suppl 2): 82–122, 1993.

11. Butler, I., et al. *Sex and Status: Hierarchies in the Health Workforce.* American Public health Association, Washington, D.C., 1985.

12. Sexton, P. C. *The New Nightingales: Hospital Workers, Unions, New Women's Issues.* Enquiry Press, New York, 1982.

13. Melosh, B. *The Physician's Hand: Work Culture and Conflict in American Nursing.* Temple University Press, Philadelphia, 1982.

14. Wolfe, S. (ed.). *Organization of Health Workers and Labor Conflict.* Baywood, Amityville, N.Y., 1978.

15. Feldman, P. H., Sapienza, A. M., and Kane, N. M. *Who Cares for Them? Workers in the Home Care Industry.* Greenwood Press, New York, 1990.

16. Krieger, N. Shades of difference: Theoretical underpinnings of the medical controversy on black/white differences in the United States, 1830–1870. *Int. J. Health Serv.* 17:256–278, 1987.

17. Stanton, W. *The Leopard's Spots: Scientific Attitudes Towards Race in America, 1815–59.* University of Chicago Press, Chicago, 1960.

18. Stepan, N. *The Idea of Race in Science, Great Britain, 1800–1860.* Archon Books, Hamden, Conn., 1982.

19. Jordan, W. D. *White Over Black: American Attitudes toward the Negro, 1550–1812.* University of North Carolina Press, Chapel Hill, 1968.

20. Rosenberg, C. E. *No Other Gods: On Science and American Social Thought.* Johns Hopkins University Press, Baltimore, Md., 1976.

21. Daniels, G. H. The process of professionalization in American science: The emergent period, 1820–1860. *Isis* 58: 151–166, 1967.

22. Rothstein, W. G. *American Physicians in the 19th Century: From Sects to Science.* Johns Hopkins University Press, Baltimore, Md., 1972.

23. Cartwright, S. A. Report on the diseases and physical peculiarities of the Negro race. *New Orleans Med. Surg. J.* 7: 691–715, 1850.

24. Cartwright, S. A. Alcohol and the Ethiopian: Or, the moral and physical effects of ardent spirits on the Negro race, and some accounts of the peculiarities of that people. *New Orleans Med. Surg. J.* 15: 149–163, 1858.

25. Cartwright, S. A. Ethnology of the Negro or prognathous race—A lecture delivered November 30,1857, before the New Orleans Academy of Science. *New Orleans Med. Surg. J.* 15: 149–163, 1858.

26. Reyburn, R. Remarks concerning some of the diseases prevailing among the Freed-people in the District of Columbia (Bureau of Refugees, Freedmen and Abandoned Lands). *Am. J. Med. Sci.* (n.s.) 51: 364–369, 1806.

27. Byron, J. Negro regiments—Department of Tennessee. *Boston Med Surg. J.* 69: 43–44, 1863.

28. Foner, E. *Reconstruction: America's Unfinished Revolution, 1863–1877.* Harper & Row, New York City, 1988.

29. Haller, J. S. Jr. *Outcasts from Evolution: Scientific Attitudes of Racial Inferiority, 1859–1900.* University of Illinois Press, Urbana, 1971.

30. Stocking, G. W. *Race, Culture, and Evolution: Essays in the History of Anthropology.* Free Press, New York, 1968.

31. Lorimer, D. *Colour, Class and the Victorians.* Holmes & Meier, New York, 1978.

32. Gamble, V. N. (ed.). *Germs Have No Color Line: Blacks and American Medicine, 1900–1940.* Garland, New York, 1989.

33. Barker-Benfield, G. J. *The Horrors of the Half-Known Life. Male Attitudes toward Women and Sexuality in Nineteenth-Century America.* Harper & Row, New York, 1976.

34. Fee, E. Science and the woman problem: Historical perspectives. In *Sex Differences: Social and Biological Perspectives,* edited by M. S. Teitelbaum, pp. 175–223. Anchor/Doubleday, New York, 1976.

35. Jordanova, L. *Sexual Visions: Images of Gender in Science and Medicine between the Eighteenth and Twentieth Centuries.* University of Wisconsin Press, Madison, 1989.

36. Ehrenreich, B., and English, D. *Complaints and Disorders: The Sexual Politics of Sickness.* The Feminist Press, Old Westbury, N.Y., 1973.

37. Russett, C. E. *Sexual Science: The Victorian Construction of Womanhood.* Harvard University Press, Cambridge, Mass., 1989.

38. Hubbard, R. *The Politics of Women's Biology.* Rutgers University Press, New Brunswick, N.J., 1990.

39. Fee, E. Nineteenth-century craniology: The study of the female skull. *Bull. Hist. Med* 53:415–433, 1979.

40. Smith-Rosenberg, C., and Rosenberg, C. E. The female animal: Medical and biological views of

woman and her role in 19th century America. *J. Am. Hist.* 60: 332–356, 1979.

41. Gould, S. J. *The Mismeasure of Man.* W. W. Norton, New York, 1981.

42. Smith-Rosenberg, C. Puberty to menopause: The cycle of femininity in nineteenth-century America. *Feminist Stud.* 1: 58–72, 1973.

43. Smith-Rosenberg, C. *Disorderly Conduct: Visions of Gender in Victorian America.* Knopf, New York, 1985.

44. Haller, J. S., and Haller, R. M. *The Physician and Sexuality in Victorian America.* University of Illinois Press, Urbana, 1974.

45. Apple, R. D. (ed.). *Women, Health, and Medicine in America: A Historical Handbook.* Rutgers University Press, New Brunswick, N.J., 1990.

46. Williams, R. *Culture & Society: 1780–1950,* revised edition. Columbia University Press, New York, 1983 [1958].

47. Marx, K. *Capital,* vol. I. International Publishers, New York, 1967 [1867].

48. Hofstadter, R. *Social Darwinism in American Thought.* Beacon Press, Boston, 1955.

49. Young, R. M. *Darwin's Metaphor: Nature's Place in Victorian Culture.* Cambridge University Press, Cambridge, U.K., 1985.

50. Kevles, D. J. *In the Name of Eugenics: Genetics and the Uses of Human Heredity.* Knopf, New York, 1985.

51. Chase, A. *The Legacy of Malthus: The Social Costs of the New Scientific Racism.* Knopf, New York, 1977.

52. Darwin, C. *On the Origin of Species by Means of Natural Selection or the Preservation of Favoured Races in the Struggle for Life.* Murray, London, 1859.

53. Anderson, M. J. *The American Census: A Social History.* Yale University Press, New Haven, Conn., 1988.

54. Hoffman, F. L. *Race Traits and Tendencies of the American Negro.* American Economic Association, New York, 1896.

55. Harris, D. Tuberculosis in the Negro. *JAMA* 41: 827, 1903.

56. Allen, L. C. The Negro health problem. *Am. J. Public Health* 5: 194, 1915.

57. Beardsley, E. H. *A History of Neglect: Health Care for Blacks and Mill Workers in the Twentieth-Century South.* University of Tennessee Press, Knoxville, 1987.

58. Geddes, P., and Thompson, J. A. *The Evolution of Sex.* Walter Scott, London, 1889.

59. Ludmerer, K. M. *Genetics and American Society: A Historical Appraisal.* Johns Hopkins University Press, Baltimore, Md., 1972.

60. Higham, J. *Strangers in the Land: Patterns of American Nativism, 1860–1925.* Rutgers University Press, New Brunswick, N.J., 1955.

61. Haller, M. H. *Eugenics: Hereditary Attitudes in American Thought.* Rutgers University Press, New Brunswick, N.J., 1963.

62. Pickens, D. K. *Eugenics and the Progressives.* Vanderbilt University Press, Nashville, Tenn., 1968.

63. King, M., and Ruggles, S. American immigration, fertility, and race suicide at the turn of the century. *J. Interdisciplinary Hist.* 20: 347–369, 1990.

64. Degler, C. N. *In Search of Human Nature: The Decline and Revival of Darwinism in American Social Thought.* Oxford University Press, Oxford, 1991.

65. Allen, G. E. *Life Science in the Twentieth Century.* Cambridge University Press, Cambridge, U.K., 1978.

66. Castle, W. E. The beginnings of Mendelism in America. In *Genetics in the Twentieth Century,* edited by L. C. Dunn, pp. 59–76. Macmillan, New York, 1951.

67. Wilkie, J. S. Some reasons for the rediscovery and appreciation of Mendel's work in the first years of the present century. *Br. J. Hist. Sci.* 1: 5–18, 1962.

68. Morgan, T. H. *The Theory of the Gene.* Yale University Press, New Haven, 1926.

69. Kraut, A. M. *The Huddled Masses: The Immigrant in American Society, 1800–1921,* Harlan Davison, Arlington Heights, Ill., 1982.

70. Stoner, G. W. Insane and mentally defective aliens arriving at the Port of New York. *N.Y. Med. J.* 97: 957–960, 1913.

71. Solis-Cohen, S. T. The exclusion of aliens from the United States for physical defects. *Bull. Hist. Med.* 21: 33–50, 1947.

72. Ludmerer, K. Genetics, eugenics, and the Immigration Restriction Act of 1924. *Bull. Hist. Med.* 46: 59–81, 1972.

73. Barkan, E. Reevaluating progressive eugenics: Herbert Spencer Jennings and the 1924 immigration legislation. *J. Hist. Biol.* 24: 91–112, 1991.

74. Kraut, A. M. Silent travelers: Germs, genes, and American efficiency, 1890–1924. *Soc. Sci. Hist.* 12: 377–393, 1988.

75. Farley, J. *Gametes & Spores: Ideas About Sexual Reproduction, 1750–1914.* Johns Hopkins University Press, Baltimore, Md., 1982.

76. Allen, G. Thomas Hunt Morgan and the problem of sex determination. *Proc. Am. Philos. Soc.* 110: 48–57, 1966.

77. Brush, S. Nettie M. Stevens and the discovery of sex determination by chromosomes. *Isis* 69: 163–172, 1978.

78. Starling, E. The Croonian lectures on the chemical correlation of the functions of the body. *Lancet* 2:339–341, 423–425, 501–503, 579–583, 1905.

79. Lane-Claypon, J. E. and Starling, E. H. An experimental enquiry into the factors which determine the growth and activity of the mammary glands. *Proc. R. Soc London [Biol.]* 77: 505–522, 1906.

80. Marshall, F. A. *The Physiology of Reproduction.* Longmans, Green and Co,, New York, 1910.

81. Oudshoorn, N. Endocrinologists and the conceptualization of sex. *J. Hist. Biol. 23:* 163–187, 1990.

82. Oudshoorn, N. On measuring sex hormones: The role of biological assays in sexualizing chemical substances. *Bull. Hist. Med.* 64: 243–261, 1990.

83. Borrell, M. Organotherapy and the emergence of reproductive endocrinology. *J. Hist. Biol.* 18: 1–30, 1985.

84. Long, D. L. Biology, sex hormones and sexism in the 1920s. *Philos. Forum* 5: 81–96, 1974.

85. Cobb, I. G. *The Glands of Destiny (A Study of the Personality).* Macmillan, New York, 1928.

86. Allen, E. (ed.). *Sex and Internal Secretions: A Survey of Recent Research.* Williams & Wilkins, Baltimore, Md., 1939.

87. Frank, R. *The Female Sex Hormone.* Charles C. Thomas, Springfield, Ill., 1929.

88. Lathrop, A. E. C., and Loeb, L. Further investigations of the origin of tumors in mice. III. On the part played by internal secretions in the spontaneous development of tumors. *J. Cancer Res.* 1: 1–19, 1916.

89. Lane-Claypon, J. E. *A Further Report on Cancer of the Breast, With Special Reference to its Associated Antecedent Conditions,* Reports on Public Health and Medical Subjects, No. 32. Her Majesty's Stationery Office, London, 1926.

90. Wainwright, J. M. A comparison of conditions associated with breast cancer in Great Britain and America. *Am. J. Cancer* 15: 2610–2645, 1931.

91. Chavkin, W. (ed.). *Double Exposure: Women's Health Hazards on the Job and at Home.* Monthly Review Press, New York, 1984.

92. Ehrenreich, B. and English, D. *For Her Own Good: 150 Years of the Experts Advice to Women.* Anchor Books, Garden City, N.Y., 1979.

93. Starr, P. *The Social Transformation of American Medicine.* Basic Books, New York, 1982.

94. Fee, E. *Disease and Discovery: A History of the Johns Hopkins School Hygiene and Public Health, 1916–1939.* Johns Hopkins University Press, Baltimore, Md., 1987.

95. Fee, E., and Acheson, R. M. (eds.). *A History of Education in Public Health: Health that Mocks the Doctors' Rules.* Oxford University Press, Oxford, 1991.

96. Meckel, R. *Save the Babies: American Public Health Reform and the Prevention of Infant Mortality, 1850–1920.* Johns Hopkins University Press, Baltimore, Md., 1990.

97. Rodin, J., and Ickovics, J. R. Women's health: Review and research agenda as we approach the 21st century. *Am. Psychol.* 45: 1018–1034, 1990.

98. Healy, B. Women's health, public welfare. *JAMA* 266: 566–568, 1991.

99. Kirchstein, R. L. Research on women's health. *Am. J. Public Health* 81: 291–293, 1991.

100. Lewontin, R. *Human Diversity.* Scientific American Books, New York, 1982.

101. King, J. C. *The Biology of Race.* University of California Press, Berkeley, 1981.

102. Cooper, R., and David, R. The biological concept of race and its application to epidemiology. *J. Health Polit. Policy Law* 11: 97–116, 1986.

103. Cooper, R. Celebrate diversity—or should we? *Ethnicity Dis.* 1: 3–7, 1991.

104. Crews, D. E., and Bindon, J. R. Ethnicity as a taxonomic tool in biomedical and biosocial research. *Ethnicity Dis.* 1: 42–49, 1991.

105. Mullings, L. Ethnicity and stratification in the urban United States. *Ann. N. Y. Acad. Sci.* 318: 10–22, 1978.

106. Feagin, J. R. *Racial and Ethnic Relations,* Ed. 3. Prentice-Hall, Englewood Cliffs, N.J., 1989.

107. Feagin, J. R. The continuing significance of race: Anti-black discrimination in public places. *Am. Sociol. Rev.* 56: 101–116, 1991.

108. Essed, P. *Understanding Everyday Racism: An Interdisciplinary Theory.* Sage Publications, Newbury Park, Calif., 1991.

109. Krieger, N., and Bassett, M. The health of black folk: Disease, class and ideology in science. *Monthly Rev.* 38: 74–85, 1986.

110. Navarro, V. Race or class versus race and class: Mortality differentials in the United States. *Lancet* 2: 1238–1240, 1990.

111. Krieger, N., and Fee, E. What's class got to do with it? The state of health data in the United States today. *Socialist Rev.* 23: 59–82, 1993.

112. Polack, S., and Grozuczak, J. *Reagan, Toxics and Minorities: A Policy Report.* Urban Environment Conference, Washington, D.C., 1984.

113. Commission for Racial Justice, United Church of Christ. *Toxic Wastes and Race in the United States: A National Report on the Racial and Socioeconomic Characteristics of Communities with Hazardous Waste Sites.* United Church of Christ, New York, 1987.

114. Mann, E. *L.A.'s Lethal Air: New Strategies for Policy, Organizing, and Action.* Labor/Community Center, Los Angeles, 1991. Los Angeles, 1991.

115. Krieger, N. Racial and gender discrimination: Risk factors for high blood pressure? *Soc. Sci. Med.* 30: 1273–1281, 1990.

116. Armstead. C. A., et al. Relationship of racial stressors to high blood pressure and anger expression in black college students. *Health Psychol.* 8: 541–556, 1989.

117. James, S. E., et al. John Henryism and blood pressure differences among black men. II. The role of occupational stressors. *J. Behav. Med.* 7: 259–275, 1984.

118. Dressler, W. W. Social class, skin color, and arterial blood pressure in two societies. *Ethnicity Dis.* 1: 60–77, 1991.

119. Fruchier, R. G., et al. Cervix and breast cancer incidence in immigrant Caribbean women. *Am. J. Public Health* 80: 722–724, 1990.

120. Kleinman, J. C. Fingerhut. L. A., and Prager, K. Differences in infant mortality by race, nativity, and other maternal characteristics. *Am. J. Dis. Child.* 145: 194–199, 1991.

121. Cabral, H., et al. Foreign-born and U.S.-born black women: Differences in health behaviors and birth outcomes. *Am. J. Public Health* 80: 70–72, 1990.

122. Taylor, R. J., and Chatters, L. M. Religious life. In *Life in Black America,* edited by J. S. Jackson, pp. 105–123. Sage, Newbury Park, Calif., 1991.

123. Livingston, I. L., Levine, D. M., and Moore, R. D. Social integration and black interracial variation in blood pressure. *Ethnicity Dis.* 1: 135–149, 1991.

124. Eng, E., Hatch, J., and Callan, A. Institutionalizing social support through the church and into the community. *Health Ed. Q.* 12: 81–92, 1985.

125. Lowe, M. Social bodies: The interaction of culture and women's biology. In *Biological Woman—The Convenient Myth,* edited by R. Hubbard, M. S. Henefin, and B. Fried, pp. 91–116. Schenkman, Cambridge, Mass., 1982.

126. Devesa, S. S., and Diamond, E. L. Association of breast cancer and cervical cancer incidence with income and education among whites and blacks. *J. Natl. Cancer Inst.* 65: 515–528,1980.

127. Krieger, N. Social class and the black/white crossover in the age-specific incidence of breast cancer: A study linking census-derived data to population-based registry records. *Am. J. Epidemiol.* 131: 804–814, 1990.

128. Krieger, N. The influence of social class, race and gender on the etiology of hypertension among women in the United States. In *Women, Behavior, and Cardiovascular Disease,* proceedings of a conference sponsored by the National Heart, Lung, and Blood Institute, Chevy Chase, Md., September 25–27, 1991. U.S. Government Printing Office, Washington, D.C., 1994, in press.

129. U.S. Department of Health and Human Services. *Report of the Secretary's Task Force on Black &*

Minority Health, Volume IV: Cardiovascular Disease, Part 2. Washington, D.C., 1986.

130. Martinez-Maldonado, M. Hypertension in Hispanics, Asians and Pacific Islanders, and Native Americans. *Circulation* 83: 1467–1469, 1991.

131. Caralis, P. U. Hypertension in the Hispanic-American population. *Am. J. Med.* 88 (Suppl. 3b): 9s–16s, 1990.

132. Haffner, S. M., et al. Decreased prevalence of hypertension in Mexican-Americans. *Hypertension* 16: 255–232, 1990.

133. Stavig, G. R., Igra, A., and Leonard, A. R. Hypertension and related health issues among Asians and Pacific Islanders in California. *Public Health Rep.* 103: 28–37, 1998.

134. Angel, A., Armstrong, M. A., and Klatsky, A. L. Blood pressure among Asian Americans living in Northern California. *Am. J. Cardiol.* 54: 237–240, 1987.

135. Alpert, J. S., et al. Heart disease in Native Americans. *Cardiology* 78: 3–12, 1991.

136. Waldron, I. Sex differences in illness, incidence, prognosis and mortality: Issues and evidence. *Soc. Sci. Med.* 17: 1107–1123, 1983.

137. Wingard, D. L. The sex differential in morbidity, mortality, and lifestyle. *Annu. Rev. Public Health.* 5: 433–458, 1984.

138. Gold, E. (ed.). *Changing Risk of Disease in Women: An Epidemiological Approach.* Colbamore Press, Lexington, Mass., 1984.

139. Leviatan, V., and Cohen, J. Gender differences in life expectancy among kibbutz members. *Soc. Sci. Med.* 21: 545–551, 1985.

140. Syme, S. L., and Berkman, L. Social class: Susceptibility and sickness. *Am. J. Epidemiol.* 104: 1–8, 1976.

141. Antonovsky, A. Social class, life expectancy and overall mortality. *Milbank Mem. Fund Q.* 45: 31–73, 1967.

142. Townsend, P., Davidson, N., and Whitehead, M. *Inequalities in Health: The Black Report and The Health Divide.* Penguin, Harmondsworth, U.K., 1988.

143. Marmot, M. G., Kogevinas, M., and Elston, M. A. Social/economic status and disease. *Annu. Rev. Public Health* 8: 111–135, 1987.

144. Roberts, H. (ed.). *Women's Health Counts.* Routledge, London, 1990.

145. Dale, A., Gilbert, G. N., and Arber, S. Integrating women into class theory. *Sociology* 19: 384–409, 1985.

146. Duke, V., and Edgell, S., The operationalisation of class in British sociology: Theoretical and empirical considerations. *Br. J. Sociol.* 8: 445–463, 1987.

147. Charles, N. Women and class—A problematic relationship. *Sociol. Rev.* 38: 43–89, 1990.

148. Morgan, M. Measuring social inequality: Occupational classifications and their alternatives. *Community Med.* 5: 116–124, 1983.

149. Moser, K. A., Pugh, H., and Goldblatt, P. Mortality and the social classification of women. In *Longitudinal Study: Mortality and Social Organization, Series LS, No. 6,* edited by P. Goldblatt, pp. 146–162. Her Majesty's Stationery Office, London, 1990.

150. Krieger, N. Women and social class: A methodological study comparing individual, household, and census measures as predictors of black/white differences in reproductive history. *J. Epidemiol. Community Health* 45: 35–42, 1991.

151. Ries, P. Health characteristics according to family and personal income, United States. *Vital Health Stat.* 10 (147). DHHS Pub. No. (PHS) 85-1575. National Center for Health Statistics. U.S. Government Printing Office, Washington, D.C., 1985.

152. Krieger, N. Overcoming the absence of socioeconomic data in medical records: Validation and application of a census-based methodology. *Am. J. Public Health* 82: 703–710, 1992.

153. Carovano, K. More than mothers and whores: Redefining the AIDS prevention needs of women. *Int. J. Health Serv.* 21: 131–142, 1991.

154. PANOS Institute. *Triple Jeopardy: Women & AIDS.* Panos Publications, London, 1990.

155. Anastos, K., and Marte, C. Women—The missing persons in the AIDS epidemic. *HealthPAC,* Winter 1989, pp. 6–13.

156. Centers for Disease Control. 1993 Revised classification system for HIV infection and expanded surveillance case definition for AIDS among adolescents and adults. *MMWR* 41: 961–962, 1992.

157. Kanigel, R. U.S. broadens AIDS definition: Activists spur change by Centers for Disease Control. *Oakland Tribune,* January 1, 1993, p. A1.

158. Centers for Disease Control and Prevention. *HIV/AIDS Surveillance Rep.* 5: 1–19, July 1993.

159. Drucker, E. Epidemic in the war zone: AIDS and community survival in New York City. *Int. J. Health Serv.* 20: 601–616, 1990.

160. Freudenberg, N. AIDS Prevention in the United States: Lessons from the first decade. *Int. J. Health Serv.* 20: 589–600, 1990.

161. Fee, E. and Krieger, N. Thinking and rethinking AIDS: Implications for health policy. *Int. J. Health Serv.* 23: 323–346, 1993.

162. Fee, E., and Krieger, N. Understanding AIDS: Historical interpretations and the limits of biomedical individualism. *Am. J. Public Health* 83: 1477–1486, 1993.

30

Feminist Politics and Reproductive Rights:
The Case of Brazil

Jacqueline Pitanguy

I n this text I discuss the role that feminism, as a new actor in Brazilian politics, has played in the enhancement of women's rights as citizens and, more specifically, in the assertion of their reproductive rights. My purpose is to point out the limits and possibilities that the feminist movement has faced as it attempted to reshape the political arena by raising new questions, positioning them as relevant issues, including them in the discourse of those to whom society ascribes legitimacy as speakers, and transmuting women's demands, especially those related to reproductive health, into public policies. Although actors, including the Catholic Church, have contributed nationally and internationally to advances and backlashes in the configuration of women's reproductive rights, I will focus mainly on the interaction between feminism and the state.

From a methodological point of view, the text combines both description and political analysis. It is neither neutral nor objective. It is a story told by someone whose search for the underlying logic of the events is deeply marked by having been a protagonist in this struggle. This perspective naturally influences my understanding of Brazil's women's movement both as an autonomous political actor and in its interaction with the state.

This chapter is organized in three sections. The first deals with the appearance of feminism as a social force in Brazil, the second discusses the relationship between feminists and other actors, and the third focuses more specifically on reproductive health and rights. The text does not consider the feminist struggles which took place in the first decades of this century because at that time women's movements prioritized the conquest of "formal" political rights such as the right to vote (1932). Health was not a central issue, and reproductive rights had not emerged as part of the struggle for women's citizenship.

Although Brazilian women as a group have been historically excluded from power and social justice, race and poverty color the experience of this exclusion. In multiracial societies with significant income disparities, social movements do not "speak for" homogeneous constituencies. Nonetheless, in this text, I will present my perception of the main trends in feminist political action which have united women in spite of differences in class or color.

Feminism as a Political Actor

The Emergence of Feminist Agenda

In considering the rise of the feminist movement in Brazil, some background on Brazilian politics and economics is essential.[1] The history of twentieth century Brazil is marked by two long periods of authoritarian rule. The first, installed in 1930 by a populist civilian leader, lasted until 1946. The second, installed by the military in 1964, lasted for 21 years, with fluctuations over time in the degree of state violence and repression of democratic institutions. Today, Brazil has a multi-party, presidential system and civil society includes a number of associations, non-governmental organizations (NGOs) and social movements. Each state has its own legislative, executive and judiciary body and national decisions are taken at the federal level.

According to the International Monetary Fund's (IMF) figures for 1991, Brazil is the ninth-largest economy in the world in terms of Gross Domestic Product (GDP), but the growth of GDP has never implied greater social justice. Income is highly concentrated; 53 percent of the GDP goes to the richest 10 percent of the population. The

social consequences of this situation were aggravated in the 1980s, when the crisis of the external debt interrupted investments, and rigid programs for structural adjustment were adopted. The adjustment policies led to a decrease in the well-being of the population as a result of high inflation rates, increases in the public deficit and decreases in salaries and social investments. Brazil has also seen a rise in urbanization since the 1970s; more than 70 percent of the population now lies in urban areas due to an acceleration in internal migration.

As of the late 1980s, Brazilian women have one of the highest levels of labor force participation in Latin America (40 percent), but median income for women is only 54 percent of men's, and women are highly concentrated in the tertiary sector and in less prestigious occupations. Despite the general context of a deficient and exclusionary educational system, there has been significant improvement in women's access to education over the last decades. Women's participation rates in education are similar to or even higher than men's at all levels of education.

Politically, few women have attained formal power in the legislature, executive and judiciary, although women participate heavily in social movements and civic associations. In 1991, the National Congress had a predominantly male profile; women represented only 5.4 percent of members of the chamber of deputies and 2.5 percent of members of the Senate. Women's movements are, however, considered a strong political force in Brazil and more than 2500 organized groups and associations are estimated to be operating throughout the country. In the last decade, important advances have been made in improving women's legal status and in creating institutional spaces inside the executive body to attend to women's demands.

In Brazil, as in most Latin American countries, women have not been part of the political arena until recently. Exclusion—whether based on sex, class, race, ethnicity or other variables—has characterized the structural arrangements of most Latin American societies, even the so-called democratic ones. In fact, in our societies, the question of exclusion is inherent to analysis of social and political participation and leads immediately to the following question: who are the citizens? And, consequently, what issues and themes are part of the public debate?

Although repressive governments prevalent in Latin America during the last decades have provided a difficult context for women's struggle for full citizenship, the recent history of this continent also shows that social movements, along with other democratic forces, can overthrow dictatorships and reshape the political sphere. Latin America is still a continent of social injustice and exclusion but new actors, including women's organizations, now play a role in shaping the political debate. How women have resisted political exclusion in Latin America has varied with cultural and historical characteristics as well as with the general political context of each country, but it is possible to identify some trends. Generally, feminism emerged in Latin America's public arena in times of authoritarianism and military dictatorship. With the re-democratization process, which in some countries started in the late 1970s, feminism faced the challenge of expanding the concept of democracy to include gender equity. Beyond this general framework, however, each country varies considerably. In Brazil, it is generally agreed that feminism has been visible and strong, one of the first women's movements to gain access to government power. The success of its collective action is related to the capability of these new protagonists to gain space, visibility and weight in the balance of power.

In 1964 a military regime took power in Brazil, and the late 1960s and 1970s were marked by the consolidation of that regime through the militarization of political power and the diversification and modernization of the State's repressive apparatus. The most repressive phase of the authoritarian rule between 1969 and 1973 paralleled the so-called economic miracle, when the growth rate of the Gross Domestic Product reached as high as 13.6% per year and industrialization and urbanization accelerated. However, most Brazilians, as is now widely recognized, benefitted little from this growth.

From 1964 to 1974, the institutions of civil society organized to resist the military regime, to struggle against it and to survive that struggle. There was little room for the individuation of political actors; "the people united against dictatorship" was the slogan used by the opposition. These people, in political terms, had no sex and no race. Political mobilization took the form of mobilizing and strengthening opposition to the government. Civic rights, political freedom, and criticism of the economic model were the predominant and "legitimate" questions of public debate.

In 1974 the military allowed parliamentary elections, confident their candidates would win. Trusting in the substantial economic growth, they expected that an electoral victory would bring legitimacy to the authoritarian system. However, the elections—a clear referendum on the government—resulted in a significant defeat for ARENA, the government party. After 1974, the government began a gradual transition to democracy, relying on a strong ARENA and the maintenance of coercive methods to control the speed and intensity of the transition. During this time, Gross Domestic

Product growth rates declined, becoming negative in 1981 and 1983.

In 1978, when the government was defeated in the main urban centers, the process of legislative renewal and transition to democracy speeded up. The opposition party was able to pass a law that ended the two-party system imposed by the military. Other parties, formerly clandestine or recently-founded, emerged. Although the military was not fully displaced until 1985, it is generally agreed that from 1978 forward, the government lost its hegemony (Guilherme dos Santos 1982; Reis and O'Donnel 1988; Diniz 1985).

In 1982 there were elections for state governors, in which the opposition won in most important states and the government party obtained only 36 percent of parliamentary votes. Central power remained, however, in the hands of the military and during 1983–1984, Brazilian society mobilized its largest mass movement, DIRETAS JA, calling for presidential elections. This mass movement had the support of the various political parties, civic and professional associations, unions, and social movements, expressing the diversity of the opposition and the emergence of a new political culture in the country.

The political transition took place, as mentioned earlier, against a backdrop of economic difficulty; there occurred as well significant differentiation among the protagonists previously united in the struggle for democracy. In the late 1970s, the country experienced intense political mobilization with the resurgence of labor unions, which had until then been persecuted and placed under the control of the government, and the appearance of other forms of political activism. The strengthening of social movements such as the black movement, the women's movement, and movements for demarcation of Indian lands and protection of the environment marked the end of a homogeneous concept of "the people." Issues of class, sex and race began to enter the political arena to qualify the opposition and to reshape the concept of democracy.[2]

These new voices joined in with the claims from many different groups and organizations that, acting outside the political parties, already represented a strong voice in the opposition. Movements for amnesty, press associations, human rights groups, and ecclesiastic communities based on Liberation Theology highlighted the violence of the state, individual freedom and political rights. Among the social movements that built collective action on the basis of projecting their individuality politically, women's movements, where feminism was the ideological base, became some of the most expressive.

Although feminist ideas were known to a few women in the 1960s, feminism was largely perceived at the time as a movement more suited to affluent societies. Only in 1975 did feminism appear as an organized social movement, following a seminar organized by a group of women under the auspices of the United Nations. The seminar was held after the government defeat in the parliamentary elections, when the rhetoric of transition was combined with a recrudescence of political violence. The seminar provided the catalyst that brought forward and organized a number of issues that were already percolating in the minds of individuals and small groups.

To many Brazilian feminists, that seminar is a watershed in the sense that it introduced and gave visibility to a number of issues, bringing new controversies and more complexity to the public debate. Women's demands—for control of their bodies, the right to regulate their fertility, sexuality not necessarily attached to procreation, efforts to combat domestic violence and non-discriminatory legislation—had until then been perceived by many progressive forces dedicated to the "major" question of political freedom as irrelevant and divisive, even ridiculous.

The period from 1975 to 1979 can be characterized as the period in which the feminist agenda was established in the country. The feminist agenda included, basically, two connected proposals: first, to bring women's issues into other large organizations like labor unions, political parties, neighbors' associations, and professional associations; and second, to expand throughout the country the number of groups that explicitly assumed a feminist identity.

It is important to note, however, that the feminist identity itself is not a given, essentialist or a historical concept, but the result of a process of alliances, disputes and networking whose configuration developed from the internal dynamics of the feminist movement and from its relations with the other actors in the political arena. Nor did feminists act as a monolithic group. There were differences among the various feminist groups, which were reflected in the issues raised and in the strategic alliances established with other social forces. This trait is not peculiar to feminism, but a general characteristic of social movements; they build solidarity based on the political definition of a common identity. Most of them incorporate, in their dynamics, the discussion of the elements which would define such identity and the ways in which this identity should be projected in the public space (Boschi 1987; Calderon and Santos 1987).

Democratization: Feminists Face Other Actors

During the 1970s, there was no dialogue with the state or federal executive power, which was still dominated by the military and their civilian representatives. The executive branch expressed toward the women's movement the same general attitude expressed toward civil society in general: a deep mistrust and perception as a menace to order. After the government's electoral defeat of 1974 and the strengthening of the opposition party, feminists tried to interact with the legislative branch by proposing changes to the family code, under which men were considered heads of households. Although communication channels with the Congress were more open than those with the executive, they were still frail and no lasting relationships resulted from that attempt.

From 1975 to 1979, feminists engaged in debates and alliances with the political left, although resistance to issues seen as taboo or problematic was present in large sections of the opposition which did not want to break their alliances with the progressive Church. Marxist parties and organizations, which considered class struggle the key motor of historical change, tended to perceive certain issues raised by feminists, especially in relation to sexuality, as superfluous or as secondary "superstructural" contradictions. Since many feminists also defined themselves as leftists, and were involved in various forms of opposition to dictatorship and struggles for social justice, the accusation that they were dividing and weakening the opposition was particularly painful and hard to resolve.

For some feminists, especially those with a Marxist background, the inclusion of questions not "directly" related to socioeconomic conditions represented therefore a difficult challenge. The need to define the movement's agenda, establishing priorities in the face of scarce resources, regional disparities, and unfair distribution of wealth, social benefits and education, led many activists to ask if there was any sense in talking about ownership of the body, about pleasure and sexuality, when women needed food and sanitation. These questions point to the challenge of combining universals and specifics, of drafting agendas that match significant variations in the concrete socioeconomic conditions under which gender relations are experienced, and of building collective identities out of diversity.

Differences among feminists on these questions tended to be not so much a matter of principle as of priorities, alliances and timing for political actions; it was generally agreed that issues concerning sexuality and reproduction were core organizing principles for the movement. The divergence rested on the pertinence of raising such issues at particular political conjunctures. In the end, the double identity of many feminists as leftists and as members of the growing women's movement was responsible for the fact that, by the end of the decade, the "left" was more receptive to the feminist agenda and had begun incorporating some women's issues into its own agenda.

This process was catalyzed by the fact that in 1979, Congress enacted a law that gave amnesty to political refugees. Thousands of Brazilians who fled the country in the 1960s and 1970s returned, including a significant number of women who had participated in the struggle against dictatorship. These men and women brought back to the country new ideas about gender and power. Many had gone to Europe, where they were exposed to feminist ideas, as well as to environmentalist and "green" platforms. On their return to Brazil, they became important activists in social movements. The rebirth of the labor unions also brought a very important new interlocutor for feminists in the early 1980s. Many meetings and conferences were organized jointly by feminist organizations and union leaders, and special attention was given to the social rights of the female worker.

From 1979 to 1982, feminists in many urban centers decided to work inside the more progressive political parties, trying to bring feminist issues to party platforms and discourses. Although in general the parties have a strong male profile, a bureaucratic structure and a traditional perception of power and politics, they could not ignore the new questions raised by women. Many of them began to include some feminist demands in their programs, especially those related to labor and education.

The most progressive sector of the Catholic Church—which had been important allies in the denunciation of the state's violence—was also an important point of reference for feminists, who tried to network with civic Church organizations (*comunidades eclesiasticas de base*) which had an outspoken female membership. From the beginning, the interaction with the Church proved difficult, bringing out important divisions among feminists as to the tactics and strategies that the movement should follow. While the Church accepted the struggle against sexual and domestic violence and incorporated demands for daycare centers and protection of maternity rights, it strongly rejected any discussion of sexuality, contraception, or abortion, thus excluding key elements of reproductive rights from the dialogue. For some feminist groups, the importance of networking with the Church was so significant that they preferred to postpone the discussion of issues that would bring conflict, and to emphasize the questions perceived as legitimate by the

Church. For others, it was more important to build a clear feminist identity, in which sexuality and reproduction were central, than to expand alliances at such a cost.

In the 1980s, with the strengthening of political parties, labor unions and other social movements, the Church lost its relevance as a strategic ally and the feminist movement, as a whole, no longer accepted the exclusion of sexuality and reproductive rights from the national debate. In fact, in cities like Rio de Janeiro and Sao Paulo, the decriminalization of abortion became a major issue, bringing public attention to the consequences of illegal abortion in a country where approximately 1.7 million abortions are performed yearly.

This period also brought an expansion in centers for women's studies in the universities, as well as an increase in gender-oriented theses and research. Although still in a ghetto—where, even today, it largely remains —the feminist discourse gained academic legitimacy, expanding the voices that make it visible, and indirectly increasing its weight in the balance of power. Even during the 1970s the universities had been an important site for the development of feminist ideas. During the military period, students and some faculty represented an important force in the opposition to the military and, even though they were heavily controlled by police and most of their forums and organizations were outlawed, the universities provided an important space for conferences, seminars, debates, and activities in which feminist issues were raised with little restraint, and sexuality was not considered an illegitimate theme.

Feminism reached the general public though the visibility given to feminist issues in the media, even if media attention was still permeated by stereotypes and false premises. A feminist alternative press emerged and played an important role in facilitating communication among the various groups and in raising issues not dealt with by the media.

It is generally agreed that, by the end of the 1970s, feminism had gained space in Brazilian society as a political movement, even if not all women's issues had the same visibility or weight in the political debate. Using an analogy from the Christian faith, I would say that some women's issues, like sexual and domestic violence and social rights concerning maternity and labor leave, had gained sufficient legitimacy and were on their way to "heaven." Most others, including those concerning sexuality and contraception, were still in political "limbo," where society places the issues that are kept waiting until a change in the balance of power brings them forward. Others, like abortion, remained in political "hell," where questions which are seen as too dangerous or controversial are kept. By the early 1980s, although women's citizenship rights were still neither a central issue nor one supported by consensus among the dominant political forces, the feminist debate had opened important doors to bring women's issues into public discourse. With the movement for decriminalization, even abortion moved from "hell" to "limbo," where it remains until today.

The road that leads from the critique of power to the exercise of power is a very difficult one. Its contours are framed by the general political processes of the Country and involve reshaping of the crucial relationship between state and civil society, between social movements and institutional power.

In 1982, during the first direct elections for state governments and parliaments, women from different groups and political affiliations wrote a common agenda, called the Feminist Alert for the Elections, and presented it to the various parties. This agenda contained their main demands, including a state program to ensure access to contraception, and to safe abortion in circumstances (rape and risk of life) already guaranteed by the law, as well as a proposal to decriminalize abortion. Although abortion still remained taboo, some parties included issues concerning reproductive health in their programs.

Some of the less controversial feminist demands were included in the campaigns of the opposition parties. Even though they were not key elements, the presence of these issues on party platforms indicated an important advance into the institutional channels of power, which had been hitherto indifferent to women's demands. The victory of the opposition in states where the women's movement was quite strong, like Rio de Janeiro, Sao Paulo and Minas Gerais, the presence of feminists in the winning parties, the support that the opposition candidates had received from women's movements, and the visibility and weight of women's demands were all advantages for women in negotiations with the newly-elected state-level executive powers.

This new political juncture challenged feminists to step inside government. There was fear of being co-opted and a lack of consensus among the various women's groups as to the strategies to adopt. Part of the movement considered that it was necessary to participate in the democratization of the country, using state power to bring a gender perspective to public policies and struggling for the creation of state-level councils to improve women's legal and social condition. Another element of the movement approved of the idea of opening such spaces but was not willing to step into them. They offered to work from the outside with those who took government positions. A smaller part of the movement decided to remain autonomous and free to criticize. All

three positions proved to be beneficial for the expansion of women's citizenship rights in Brazil. During the 1980s, most feminist groups had some kind of interaction with the government and the relationships were not antagonistic, but respectful and supportive.

The creation of the State Council for Women's Rights (*Conselho Estadual da Condicao Feminina*) in Sao Paulo in 1983 marked the beginning of the transformation of feminist discourses and demands into public policy. Almost a decade had elapsed since feminism emerged as a political actor. By 1985, when the democratization process reached the federal executive level and the first civilian was elected president, there were already two such state councils for women's rights in operation, and the first Special Police Station to Attend Women Victims of Sexual or Domestic Violence (DEAM) had been inaugurated.

Although the dominant forces in government at the time involved an alliance between a conservative and a liberal party, the change of power was welcomed by all progressive sectors. The prospect of democratizing the state and building bridges with civil society marked a moment of hope and belief in government. The idea of creating an organization, operating at the highest national level, that would be responsible for drawing up and implementing public policies with a gender perspective mobilized many feminists who considered Sao Paulo's experience with the State Council for Women's Rights (*Conselho Estadual da Condicao Feminina*) a positive one, in terms of implementing gender sensitive public policies.

The networking, alliances, and disputes involved in creating this body took approximately six months. In this period, the country's elected president died and his vice president, a more conservative man, assumed the presidency. The National Council for Women's Rights (CNDM) was installed by Congressional Law No. 7,353 in August 1985. At that time, the new government needed to expand its base of support to increase its legitimacy and, therefore, the executive branch did not have a very clear ideological profile. It was a government of compromises and alliances. The state's machinery, however, was still heavy and corporate, as it had been adapted to serve the previous military regime. Despite this CNDM could act speedily in its early phase.

Although CNDM was administratively under the jurisdiction of the Ministry of Justice, the President of the Council reported directly to the President of the Republic, and the board had the autonomy to make decisions about the lines of action and allocation of resources. In five years, CNDM developed programs addressing reproductive health, violence, labor and rural women, black women, education, culture and legislation. It also compiled information and documentation and set up a communications department, since the media was widely used in national campaigns.

From 1985 to 1990, the number of state offices dedicated to improving women's situation multiplied. By 1989 there were 34 Councils of Women's Rights operating at the state and municipal level and over 100 DEAM police stations. Operating within a federal system, these organizations were linked to local authorities, but also maintained a direct relationship with CNDM. The latter coordinated a forum of Councils of Women and networked with the DEAMs in order to maintain the national focus so necessary in a country as large as Brazil.

From 1986 to 1988, CNDM devoted special attention to the new Constitution which was being prepared by a newly elected Congress. In 1986 it organized a meeting in the National Congress, attended by more than 2,000 women from very different backgrounds (in terms of class, occupation, color) from all regions of the country. The major result of this meeting was the approval of the "Letter of Brazilian Women to the Constituents," which has largely influenced the work that developed, in partnership with other women's organizations, to ensure women constitutional rights. Approximately 80 percent of their demands were included, partially or totally, in the Constitution.

Public Policies and Reproductive Rights

The story of feminism in Brazil is deeply connected with the struggle against population control programs oriented toward demographic goals, and for the implementation of a comprehensive women's public health program. Feminists have always placed contraception in the framework of a woman's life cycle and have fought for integrated delivery of information, contraception, and reproductive and sexual health services. This philosophy has guided the participation of women's health advocates in ministerial commissions and in campaigns against abuses of women's integrity, whether they come from family planning services or from the doctors and scientists responsible for new contraceptive technologies.

Feminist commitment to reproductive rights has grown even as a dramatic demographic transition is underway in the country, with a large drop in fertility rates, despite a tripling of population size between 1940 and 1991. Demographers recognize two trends operating in this period. A general decrease in mortality rates led to population growth rates of over 3 percent annually in the 1950s and 1960s. The second trend combines the decrease in mortality rates with a sharp fall in fertility rates.

As a result, the rate of population growth has fallen from 2.9 percent in the 1960s to 1.8 percent in 1985–1990, even without an explicit governmental anti-natalist policy.

Until the 1960s, overpopulation was not an issue in Brazil; population growth was perceived as a positive factor both for economic development and geopolitical security. The power of the Catholic Church, which is influential in government and institutional hierarchies though exerting less influence on people's daily life decisions, also contributed to a passive pro-natalist policy. Despite this policy, and the existence of legislation outlawing all contraceptive devices and abortifacient, family planning was introduced "unofficially" in Brazil on a large scale by private international organizations in the 1960s. By the 1980s, 71 percent of women between the ages of 15 and 54 who were married or with a partner used contraception, a percentage similar to that of European countries or the United States. In certain states, especially in the northeast, the sterilization rate is as high as 70 percent, and in certain socioeconomic groups—where the proportion of black women is highest—50 percent of the women sterilized are under 29 years old. Sterilization is generally performed during the birth process, and Brazil has one of the highest—60 percent—rates for Caesarian sections in the world.[3]

Until the 1970s the state did little to control population, and the shift from pro-natalist policy to the "official" acceptance of family planning was quite slow. In fact, the government's first two programs in this area, the Prevention Plan for High Risk Pregnancy (PPGAR, 1977) and Prev-Saude (1980), were scrapped for budgetary and political reasons. In 1979, however, the government changed the legislation which prevented the promotion of contraceptive methods. In the late 1970s and early 1980s,

the neo-Malthusian perspective, predominant in the countries of the North, gained credence among civil and military "elites" as the preoccupation with territorial occupation lost ground to urban poverty and violence. Family planning also met the needs of increasing numbers of women working and living in urban areas, who had to guarantee family survival in the slum-like conditions of the cities without the support of an extended family network. The 1970s also correspond to the expansion of the media, especially television, which started to operate on a national basis and bring to remote areas, by means of soap operas, the values of the "modern" urban middle class, among them the idea of small nuclear families.

In 1983, an important program resulted from dialogue among the Ministry of Health, a group of feminist women's health advocates and the university. Federal power was still in the hands of the military but the democratic transition was on course and inside the state's machinery there were public officers willing to work with members of civil society. This program was called Program of Integral Assistance to Women's Health (PAISM). Its introduction made official the involvement of the state in reproductive health and framed this involvement within the feminist perspective of respect for women's integrity. Today, PAISM's philosophy and proposed actions are considered by many as an example of a feminist approach to public policy. Its main goals were to increase the coverage and quality of prenatal assistance and of childbirth assistance, to implement and expand activities for the control of breast and cervical cancer, to prevent and treat STD's, to develop fertility regulation activities through the implementation of family planning methods and techniques, and to diagnose and treat infertility. Although PAISM does not mention abortion, not even to regulate its delivery in circumstances of rape or risk of life, it represented a step forward.[4]

In 1986, health professionals inaugurated the National Health Conference, the first under democracy. At their initial meeting, they set up the principles of public health and the norms to decentralize the delivery of services. For the first time in these annual reunions, women's representatives were given a space to bring the issue of reproductive health to that forum.

The Letter of Brazilian Women to the Constituents which, as stated earlier, was initiated by CNDM, was delivered to the National Congress in March of 1987. This letter had two basic premises: that health is a right of all and a duty of the state, and that women have the right to health care delivered under a comprehensive and integral perspective, independent of her role as child-bearer. These principles clearly indicate the shaping of a new concept of reproductive rights, claiming simultaneously a woman's authority over her body, and a redefinition of the state's duty to the body. Under these general principles, the letter also asked for the prohibition of any coercive measure, from the state or from national or international organizations, to impose or deny contraception. Special attention was given to the issue of contraceptive testing and its effects on women's health. The supervision of the production of chemicals and hormonal methods of contraception and the prohibition of commercialization of drugs still in the stage of testing were also demanded.

The issue of contraceptive testing had mobilized feminists in Brazil since 1984 when doctors at the University of Campinas began to test Norplant under the aegis of the Population Council. Women questioned the testing of subjects without their full knowledge and acceptance, and denounced unethical experimental practices, largely contributing to the fact that in April 1986 the Ministry of Health cancelled the authorization for the tests. While the Norplant episode demonstrated the power of feminists in winning a battle against a very powerful section of physicians, it also indicated the need to look for some common ground with such groups, an effort that was initiated in the late 1980s and early 1990s (Barroso and Correa 1991; Dacach and Israel 1993).

By the time the National Council for Women's Rights (CNDM) was founded in 1985, much had already been done by women's movements to introduce the question of reproductive health and rights into the public debate and government discourse. However, the new government had not taken any further initiative in this matter. One of the first initiatives by CNDM on this issue was to offer to collaborate with the Ministry of Health to produce educational booklets, slides and videotapes, and to ask that large numbers of a booklet planned under PAISM be produced. After negotiations with the Ministry of Social Security, the health minister agreed to print five million copies and distribute them through the public health network, as well as to mothers who took their children to public day-care centers. This agreement was given high visibility in the press.

The booklet talked about women's rights to information and contraception, and asserted that it was important for women to join organized movements to preserve and exercise these rights. The booklet also described various contraceptive methods, including the IUD. The reaction of the Catholic Church to the booklet was immediate. The President of the National Confederation of Bishops pressed the Minister of Social Security not to print the booklet, claiming that the IUD was an abortive method and could not be supported by the government. The Church's campaign against the IUD led the Ministry of Health to withdraw this contraceptive device from the range of methods offered by PAISM until it could be evaluated by a body internal to the ministry. CNDM confronted the Church, arguing separation of church and state, and claiming that the IUD should be evaluated for possible side effects rather than on the question of whether it was abortive. The minister came to a compromise, agreeing to alter only 200,000 copies of the booklet.[5]

This episode is important because, for the first time, women, speaking from inside the government, were part of the negotiations. They could not beat the Church, but neither could they be ignored. They were an uncomfortable new actor in a scenario where, traditionally, decisions concerning a woman's body have been made without consulting her. While this episode once again made clear the impossibility of aligning with the Church in matters concerning sexual behavior and contraception, it must also be remembered that this same Confederation of Bishops had asked for CNDM's advice in a national campaign to improve the status of women.

In 1987 CNDM organized, along with the Ministry of Health, the National Women's Conference on Health and Rights, where general principles of the Letter of Brazilian Women to the Constituents and of PAISM were reaffirmed and abortion was declared to be a matter of public health. The more than 3,000 women who attended the meeting were mostly health professionals and women's health advocates. They called for the legalization of abortion and focused attention on abuses of private family planning programs, which were distributing oral contraceptives without considering a woman's physical health, and performing sterilizations on a large scale.

Women's lobbying and strategies were partially successful. Article 226, paragraph 7 of the country's new Constitution defines the protection of reproductive rights as a duty of the state and a right of all citizens.

> . . . based on principles of human dignity and responsible paternity, family planning is considered the free choice of the couple. The state is responsible for providing educational and scientific resources necessary for the exercise of this right. Any coercive action on the part of public or private institutions is strictly forbidden. (Brazilian Constitution, 1988)

When the text was originally presented to the Congress by CNDM, it did not include the words "responsible paternity" or "couple." These words were introduced as part of the political bargain with conservative sectors. But, in general, women agreed that an important step had been taken in the redefinition of citizenship rights and the reconfiguration of the relationship between the individual and the state.

Another initiative of CNDM was to address the ministers of health and social security, asking them to "obey the law" by providing abortion services in public hospitals in the circumstance of rape or life-threatening illness. Although, as expected, this initiative received no support, it brought public attention to the discrepancy between laws and actions, the resulting damage to women's health, and to the government's refusal to face the question of abortion, in a country where, in 1991, abortion was the fifth leading cause for hospitalization in the country (DATASUS, Ministry of Health). It is well known that often a woman will induce an abortion and come bleeding to the hospital, complaining that she had a spontaneous "loss."

The struggle over abortion against the Catholics and Evangelists, allied with national and international groups to protect the fetus was one of most difficult battles

CNDM has fought. CNDM understood from the beginning that they were up against the strength and commitment of the religious groups and the general indifference of the Congress, who, with very few exceptions, regarded abortion as taboo. Along with women's groups, a common strategy was developed in order to neutralize the arguments of the Church and pro-life groups. Since petitions could be considered by Congress provided they included 30,000 signatures, CNDM argued that abortion was not a constitutional matter and women's groups presented a petition to legalize abortion in order to counteract the pro-life petitions. The strategy was to impede a backlash, and on those terms, the strategy was successful. Both positions were argued on the floor of the Congress, and Congress decided that abortion was not a constitutional issue. Given the strength of the opposition forces in this issue, this result was considered a victory.

A new president was elected in November 1989 and assumed office in March 1990. During the election, the conservative forces in the government gained power. The Board of Directors of CNDM understood that the opposition's power was mounting and that they had only a brief window of opportunity to shape the political dialogue and influence the candidates' platforms on the abortion issue. In July 1989, CNDM organized an unprecedented nationally televised debate where the candidates answered questions related only to women's issues. The questions were compiled by women's groups and state councils, and telephoned to each candidate. All candidates were asked to clarify their position regarding abortion. Only one candidate declared ideological support for abortion, and only one declared that abortion violated his principles; all other candidates gave waffling answers based on political expediency. Their answers re-flected the fact that women were too strong to be ignored completely on this issue, but that the Church continued to have a strong and powerful voice. The candidates compromised by saying that they were personally against abortion, but would entertain a plebiscite on the issue. Feminists, as a political force, had succeeded in putting "women's issues" on the political agenda,

In 1989, CNDM organized another meeting where the Letter of Women in Defense of Their Health was prepared and approved. Based on the same principles as the 1986 letter, this document asked for immediate state action in the implementation of PAISM and denounced the high rates of maternal mortality (150 per 100,000), lack of attention to birth delivery and the need for a reduction in caesareans (one of the highest rates in the world, closely associated with sterilization), decriminalization of voluntary abortion, emphasis on reversible contraceptive methods to decrease the use of sterilization, and the reaffirmation that family planning should aim at improving women's health, not demographic goals. This was the last important event organized by CNDM.

After the promulgation of the Constitution, CNDM started to suffer from pressure and criticism from various conservative sectors. Industrialists and owners of commercial enterprises protested against the cost of extended labor rights and social benefits, including four months of paid maternity leave and five days of paternal leave (for birth or adoption), a policy which was ridiculed. Rural proprietors protested against the extension of labor rights to rural women. Changes in the family code such as the abolition of the male prerogatives as head of the family and requiring a marriage certificate in order to be recognized as a family, the affirmation of the state's duty to impede domestic violence and to provide family planning, among others—were considered too advanced by some conservative sectors. The Church was deeply dissatisfied with women's advances on the reproductive front, and was still smarting from the success of the feminist movement and CNDM in impeding the inclusion of a provision to protect the life of the unborn in the Constitution.

By that time, the government, facing one of the largest external debts in the world, extremely high rates of inflation and acute public deficits, was searching for support among the most conservative parties and sectors of society. The years of ideological flexibility were over. The Ministry of Land Reform, which represented excluded and exploited rural workers, was dismantled. Although the government was not a monolithic block, and certain sectors supported CNDM's initiatives, women as a political category were not strong enough to withstand all these pressures, and simultaneously to struggle against a new and conservative Minister of justice.

The last large event promoted by CNDM was the launching, in the National Congress, of the campaign, "Women's Health, a Right to be Conquered," in 1989. Soon afterward, the board and the president of CNDM resigned. They realized that their weight in the balance of governmental power was not enough to allow them to pursue critical lines of policy action, and that to remain would have meant being co-opted. As of today, the feminist movement has no direct representation in the federal executive. In spite of the fact that CNDM was not abolished, it lost its political and budgetary autonomy, and is currently occupied by women with no ties to feminism. National articulation of women's issues is now done by the forum of state-level councils, in difficult circumstances.

Conclusion

Given the general picture of women's health in Brazil, and the fact that PAISM is not still fully implemented, that abortion is still illegal, and that sterilization is still the most widely used contraceptive method, one might argue that feminists have had very little impact. That is not, however, my understanding. In some states, largely influenced by the Women's Councils, there are initiatives for the implementation of PAISM and of the responsibility of the state for this program. Feminists constantly challenge Health Ministers and state authorities. Sterilization abuses have been widely discussed throughout the country, the Senate has installed an Investigatory Commission and a new law project is being discussed, with the participation of feminists, so as to impede abuses. Abortion, which was in political limbo for almost a decade, is emerging as a visible and important issue. As a consequence of this political development, civil organizations have grown stronger, and women's groups are a large constituent of the recently formed NGO's. Currently there are two measures, proposed by feminists before both houses of Congress, which would decriminalize abortion. Women are also organizing themselves to influence the government positions for the 1994 World Conference on Population and Development in Cairo.

A feminist health network was created in 1991, which incorporates more than 50 regional groups. The network is called the National Feminist Network on Health and Reproductive Rights, and was recently invited to send a representative to the National Health Council, a board advising the President.

And yet, this is just the beginning of progress after centuries of gender exclusion and discrimination. Much remains to be done in this particular field where political strategies and alliances are allied to sex and sexuality, to values and emotions, and to the taboos and dangers that impregnate the field of reproductive health. In a country with a long history of political authoritarianism, the road to women's reproductive health is constantly being interrupted and rebuilt.

Notes

1. For more detailed information on Brazilian women's social, demographic, political and economic situation see "Latin American Women in Data: Brazil." The study was done by CEPIA, under the general coordination of J. Pitanguy and edited and published by T. Valdez. FIASCO, Santiago, Chile.

2. This political mobilization raises questions that cut vertically and, thus, challenge the horizontal class divisions among groups acting to create a new political culture (Boschi 1984).

3. For more information on contraception and fertility rate decline in Brazil, see Berquo 1989.

4. Abortion is still a taboo for government. PAISM was enacted only in 1987, and today it is not really implemented throughout the country. This distance between discourse and practice characterizes the difficulty of exercising reproductive rights already guaranteed by laws and programs.

5. There is no written account of this episode, of which I give testimony as a protagonist.

References

Alvarez, S. 1990. *Engendering democracy in Brazil.* Princeton, NJ.: Princeton University Press.

Alvez, B., and J. Pitanguy. 1981. *O que e feminismo.* Sao Paulo: Brasiliense.

Alvez, M. H. 1988. Grassroots organizations, trade unions and the church: A challenge to controlled *abertura* in Brazil. *Latin American Perspectives* 11(1): 73–102.

Barroso, C., et al. 1987. *Homem-mulher: Crises e conquistas.* Sao Paulo: Melhoramentos.

Barroso, C., and S. Correa. 1991. Servidores publicos versus profesionales laborales, la política de investigacion sobre anticonceptivos. *Estúdios Sociológicos* 9(25): 7–104.

Berquo, E. 1989. A esterilização feminina no Brasil hoje. In *Quando a paciente e mulher.* See CNDM 1989.

Blay, E. 1979. The political participation of women in Brazil: Female mayors. *Signs: A Journal of Women in Culture and Society* 1: 42–59.

Boschi, R. P. 1983. *Movimentos coletivos no Brasil urbano.* Rio de Janeiro: Zahar Editores.

___. 1984. *The art of association: Social movements, the middle class and grass roots politics in Brasil.* Post-doctoral report. Stanford University.

___. 1987. *A arte de associação: Política de base e democracia no Brasil,* Rio de Janeiro: Vertice.

Brazil. 1988. Federal Constitution.

Brazil, Ministry of Health. 1990. DATASUS, a database of the Ministry of Health.

Brito, A. 1986. Brazilian women in exile: The quest for identity. *Latin American Perspectives* 13(2): 58–80.

Bruschini, M. C. A., and F. Rosemberg, eds. 1982. *Trabalhadoras do Brasil.* Sao Paulo: Brasiliense.

Calderon, F., and M. Santos. 1987. Movimentos sociales y gestacion de cultura political. In *Cultura politica y democratizacion,* comp. N. Lechner, et al. Buenos Aires: CLACSO/FLASCO and ICI.

Conselho Nacional dos Direitos da Mulher (CNDM). 1986. *Carta das mulheres aos constituintes.* Brasilia.

___. 1987. *Para viver o amor.* Brasilia.

___. 1989a. *Carta das mulheres pelos seus direitos reprodutivos.* Brasilia.

___. 1989b. *Quando a paciente e mulher.* Brasilia.

Costa, A. 1992. *O Paism, uma politica de assistência integral a saúde da mulher a ser resgatada.* Sao Paulo: Comisao cidadania e reprodução.

Dacach, S., and G. Israel. 1993. *As rotas do Norplant®.* Rio de Janeiro: CBAG.

Diniz, E. 1985. A transição politica no Brasil. *Dados* 28(3): 329–46.

FLASCO and CEPIA. 1993. *Mulheres Latino-Americanas em Dados: o Brasil.* Santiago, Chile.

Goldberg, A. 1982. Feminism in authoritarian regime. Paper presented at the 22d International Political Science Association (IPSA) World Congress, in Rio de Janeiro.

Pitanguy, J. 1985. The women's movement and political parties in Brazil: A discussion on power and representivity. Paper presented at the 23d IPSA World Congress, in Paris.

___. 1990, Políticas publicas y ciudadania. *Transiciones* 13: 13–23.

Reis, F. W., and G. O'Donnel, eds. 1988. *A democracia no Brasil: Dilemas e perspectivas.* Sao Paulo: Vertice.

Santos, W. G. 1982. Autoritarismo e Após: Convergências e Divergências entre Brasil e Chile. *Dados* 25(2): 151–163.

Sen, G., and C. Grown. 1987. *Development, crises and alternative visions: Third world women's perspectives.* New York: Monthly Review Press.

Beyond "A Woman's Right to Choose": Feminist Ideas about Reproductive Rights

31

Rosalind Petchesky

. . . that all the while the Foetus is forming . . . even to the Moment that the Soul is infused, so long it is absolutely not in her Power only, but in her right, to kill or keep alive, save or destroy, the Thing she goes with, she won't call it Child; and that therefore till then she resolves to use all manner of Art, to the help of Drugs and Physicians, whether Astringents, Diuretics, Emeticks, or of whatever kind, nay even to Purgations, Potions, Poisons, or any thing that Apothecaries or Druggists can supply. . . .

–Daniel Defoe

Behind Defoe's scathing condemnation of female malice in the act of abortion lies the presence of not only "right-to-life" antecedents in seventeenth-century England but the idea among women that abortion is a "woman's right." Linda Gordon lays the groundwork for a feminist theory of reproductive freedom, observing that, throughout history, women have practiced forms of birth control and abortion; recurrent moral or legal prohibitions against such practices merely "forced women underground in their search for reproductive control."[1] Similarly, George Devereux, surveying 350 primitive, ancient, and preindustrial societies, asserts "that there is every indication that abortion is an absolutely universal phenomenon, and that it is impossible even to construct an imaginary social system in which no woman would ever feel at least impelled to abort."[2] The universality in birth control practices helps us to understand that reproductive freedom for women is not simply a matter of developing more sophisticated techniques. While the ascent from "purgations, potions, and poisons" to vacuum aspiration doubtless represents a gain for women, abortion and reproductive freedom remain political, not technological, agendas—which feminists find necessary to mobilize over and over again. Because we are in the thick of that mobilization at present, it is important to examine the political ideas that have informed movements for reproductive freedom historically and today.

Two essential ideas underlie a feminist view of reproductive freedom. The first is derived from the biological connection between women's bodies, sexuality, and reproduction. It is an extension of the general principle of "bodily integrity," or "bodily self-determination," to the notion that women must be able to control their bodies and procreative capacities. The second is a "historical and moral argument" based on the social position of women and the needs that such a position generates. It states that, insofar as women, under the existing division of labor between the sexes, are the ones most affected by pregnancy, since they are the ones responsible for the care and rearing of children, it is women who must decide about contraception, abortion, and child-bearing.

These two ideas grow out of different philosophical traditions and have different, sometimes contradictory, reference points and political priorities. The first emphasizes the *individual* dimensions of reproduction, the second the *social* dimensions. The first appeals to a "fixed" level of the biological person, while the other implies a set of social arrangements, a sexual division of labor, developed historically, that may be changed under new conditions. Finally, one is rooted in the conceptual framework of "natural rights," while the other invokes the legitimating principle of "socially determined needs."

In what follows I analyze the origins and theoretical implications of these two ideas; I take account of the radical and conservative elements in each and highlight tensions between them that may never be totally resolved. My argument is that reproductive freedom—indeed, the very nature of reproduction—is social and individual at the same time; it operates "at the core of social life" as well as within and upon women's individual bodies.[3]

Thus, a coherent analysis of reproductive freedom requires a perspective that is both Marxist and feminist. This dual perspective is also necessary on the level of political practice. For even if it were true, as some "right-to-lifers" have charged, that the women's movement is self-contradictory in demanding both control by women over reproductive matters and greater sharing of responsibility for such matters between women and men, both these goals are indispensable to a feminist program for reproductive freedom. We have to struggle for a society in which responsibility for contraception, procreation, and childrearing is no longer relegated to women primarily; and, at the same time, we have to defend the principle of control over our bodies and our reproductive capacities. In the long run, we have to ask whether women's control over reproduction is what we want, whether it is consistent with equality; in the short run, we have never experienced the concrete historical conditions under which we could afford to give it up.

Controlling Our Bodies

The principle that grounds women's reproductive freedom in a "right to bodily self-determination," or "control over one's body," has three distinct but related bases: liberalism, neo-Marxism, and biological contingency. Its liberal roots may be traced to the Puritan revolution in seventeenth-century England. In that period, the Leveller idea of a "property in one's own person" was linked explicitly to nature and paralleled the idea of a "natural right" to property in goods: "To every individual in nature is given an individual property by nature, not to be invaded or usurped by any: for every one as he is himselfe, so he hath a selfe propriety, else could he not be himselfe, and on this no second may presume to deprive any of without manifest violation and affront to the very principles of nature, and of the Rules of equity and justice between man and man. . . ."[4] A person, to be a person, must have control over himself or herself, in body as well as in mind. This Leveller notion of individual selfhood, although phrased in masculine terms, had specific applications to the conditions of women in the seventeenth century: the enactment of the Puritan idea of marriage as a contract, restrictions against wife beating, and the liberalization of divorce.[5] It had other applications that affected men and women: the introduction of habeas corpus in 1628 (bodies cannot be detained without cause); and, above all, a resistance to the idea of selling, or alienating, one's body to another through wage labor. Thus, the original notion of "property in one's person" was not only an assertion of individualism in an abstract sense but had a particular radical edge that rejected the commoditization of bodies through an emergent labor market. The Levellers were saying: My body is not property; it is not transferable; it belongs only to me.

While the liberal origins of the "bodily integrity" principle are clear, its radical implications should not be forgotten. In its more recent juridical expressions, for example the so-called right to privacy, the principle has been applied to defend prisoners from physical abuse, undocumented aliens from bodily searches, and patients from involuntary treatment or medical experimen-

tation, as well as in the well-known "reproductive rights" cases.[6] While privacy, like property, has a distinctly negative connotation that is exclusionary and asocial, when applied to persons as persons—in their concrete, physical being—it also has a positive sense that roughly coincides with the notion of "individual self-determination." Control over one's body is an essential part of being an individual with needs and rights, a concept that is the most powerful legacy of the liberal political tradition.

This principle clearly applies to persons as persons and not only to women. Nevertheless, it was the soil that nourished the growth of feminism in the eighteenth and nineteenth centuries, and many of the gains sought by women under the rubrics of "liberty" and "equality" still have not been won.[7] A certain idea of individuality is also not antithetical to a Marxist tradition, which distinguishes between the idea of individual human beings as historically determined, concrete, and particular in their needs and the ideology of "individualism" (i.e., "the individual" conceived as isolated, atomized, exclusive in *his* possessions, disconnected from larger social fabrics). As Agnes Heller puts it, the former idea recognizes that the end of socialist transformation is ultimately the satisfaction of individual needs, which are always concrete and specific (unlike rights, which belong to "citizens" or "persons" in the abstract). Thus, "Marx recognizes no needs other than those of individual people"; while understanding needs as generally social or "socially produced," such needs "are the needs of individual human beings." "When the domination of things over human beings ceases, when relations between human beings no longer appear as relations between things, then *every* need governs 'the need for the development of the individual,' the need for the self-realization of the human personality."[8]

Similarly, Marcuse argues in favor of restoring a sense of individual "happiness" to a revolutionary ethic ("general happiness apart from the happiness of individuals is a meaningless phrase"). Through his analysis of contemporary forms of domination and repression that alienate individuals from a sense of connectedness with their own bodies and thus with the physical and social world, Marcuse arrives at a hedonism containing a liberatory element. That element is a sense of "complete immediacy," of "sensuality," which is a necessary precondition for the "development of personality" and the participation of individuals in social life. The link between eroticism and politics is a "receptivity that is open and that opens itself [to experience]."[9] Control over one's body is a fundamental aspect of this immediacy, this "receptivity," a requirement of being a person and engaging in conscious activity. Understood thus, it is a principle of radical ethics that should never be abandoned.

The direct connection between "control over one's body" and feminist claims regarding women's control over reproduction seemed obvious to early birth control advocates. Ezra Heywood, an anarchist birth controller in the 1870s, asserted "Woman's Natural Right to ownership of and control over her own body-self—a right inseparable from Women's intelligent existence."[10] This connection is as real today. Because pregnancies occur in women's bodies, the continued possibility of an "unwanted" pregnancy affects women in a very specific sense, not only as potential bearers of fetuses, but also in their capacity to enjoy sexuality and maintain their health. A woman's right to decide on abortion when her health and her sexual self-determination

are at stake is "nearly allied to her right to be."[11]

Reproduction affects women as women; it transcends class divisions and penetrates everything—work, political and community involvements, sexuality, creativity, dreams. Gordon illustrates this point with reference to the conditions that generated the nineteenth-century birth control movement:

> The desire for and the problems in securing abortion and contraception made up a *shared female experience.* Abortion technique was apparently not much safer among upper-class doctors than among working-class midwives. The most commonly used contraceptives—douches, withdrawal—were accessible to women of every class. And what evidence there is of the subjective experience of women in their birth-control attempts also suggests that the desire for spaced motherhood and smaller families existed in every class, and that the desire was so passionate that women would take severe risks to win a little space and control in their lives. *The individual theory and practice of birth control stems from a biological female condition that is more basic even than class.*[12]

It is surprising to find Gordon reverting to a "biological female condition" in the midst of an analysis of the social construction of women's reproductive experience. Yet it reminds us that the "bodily integrity" principle has an undeniable biological component. As long as women's bodies remain the medium for pregnancies, the connection between women's reproductive freedom and control over their bodies represents not only a moral and political claim but also, on some level, a material necessity. This acknowledgment of biological reality should not be mistaken for biological determinist thinking about women; my point is simply that biology is a *capacity* as well as a limit.[13] That it is women who get pregnant has been the source of our confinement (in all senses) and our (limited) power. An abundance of feminist anthropological literature reminds us that pollution rituals, fertility cults, prohibitions against abortion, and chastity rules imposed on wives and daughters are signs of men's envy and fear of women's reproductive capacity. Indeed, the current attack on abortion in the United States and elsewhere in the West has been interpreted by some feminists as a massive recurrence of male "womb envy."

I would be the last to romanticize the control that comes from our biological connection to childbearing, or to underestimate its repressive social aspects. On the other hand, women's control over their bodies is not like preindustrial workers' control over their tools; it cannot be wrested away through changes in technology or legal prohibitions and repression—which is why no modern society has succeeded for long in outlawing abortion or birth control, only in driving it "underground."

It is important, however, to keep in mind that woman's reproductive situation is never the result of biology alone, but of biology mediated by social and cultural organization. That is, it is not inevitable that women, and not men, should bear the main consequences of unintended pregnancy and thus that their sexual expression be inhibited by it. Rather, it is the result of the socially ascribed primacy of motherhood in women's lives. Yet biology as it is socially mediated by male-dominant institutions affects all women. Today there is prolific evidence of this "shared female experience." The cutbacks in abortion funding, whose hardest impact has been on low-income women, have spearheaded a right-wing movement to curtail abortion services and reimbursements for working-class and middle-class women dependent on health insurance plans as well. While sterilization abuse has mainly been directed at poor, Third World, and mentally disabled women, the ultimatum to well-paid women chemical workers that they get sterilized or lose their jobs has widened our perspective on this issue.[14] Indeed, the fact that female sterilization, an irreversible procedure, has become the most widely used, medically encouraged, and economically reimbursable method of contraception among all but the very young in the United States,[15] as evidence grows of the pill's dangers to health and abortions are restricted, raises questions about reproductive "choices" for *most* women. That the two major birth control methods in current use are, on the one hand, irreversible, and, on the other hand, dangerous to health, affects women of all classes. It is a condition set, not by reproductive technology, but by a reproductive politics that seeks to curtail the efforts of women "to win a little space and control in their lives" and freely to express their sexuality.

The principle of "control over our bodies," then, has a material as well as a moral and a political basis. The "liberal," the "radical" or "neo-Marxist," and the "biological" elements of this principle should not be seen as alternatives to one another but as different levels of meaning that give the principle its force and complexity. Sorting out these levels should make it easier for us to distinguish between situations when we are describing "control over our bodies" as a *material fact*, when we are asserting it as a *right,* and when we are defining it as part of a larger set of socially determined *human needs*.

Yet the idea of "a woman's right to choose" as the main principle of reproductive freedom is insufficient and problematic at the same time as it is politically compelling. For one thing, this principle evades moral questions about when, under what conditions, and for what purposes reproductive decisions should be made. Feminists writing on abortion usually have not claimed that a pregnant woman "owns" the fetus or that it is part of her body. On the contrary, feminists have generally characterized an unwanted pregnancy as a kind of bodily "invasion."[16] Recognizing a real conflict between the survival of the fetus and the needs of the woman and those dependent on her, the feminist position says merely that women must decide because it is their bodies that are involved, and because they have primary responsibility for the care and development of any children born.

But determining who should decide—the political question—does not tell us anything about the moral and social values women ought to bring to this decision.[17] Should women get an abortion on the grounds that they prefer a different gender, which amniocentesis can now determine? Such a decision would be blatantly sexist, and nobody's claim to "control over her body" could make it right or compatible with feminist principles. That is, "a woman's right to control her body" is not absolute, but we have not developed a socialist-feminist morality that would tell us what the exceptions should be.

Admitting that we have not fully articulated a feminist morality of abortion does not imply that all or most women who get abortions do so thoughtlessly or irresponsibly. On the contrary, women who seek abortions know and experience better than anyone else the difficulty of that decision. Much more serious is the potential danger in the assertion of women's right to control over reproduction as absolute or exclusive, for it can be turned back on us to reinforce the view of all reproductive activity as the special, biologically destined province of women. This danger grows out of the concept of "rights" in general, a concept that is inherently static and abstracted from social conditions. Rights are by definition claims staked within a given order of things. They are demands for access for oneself, or for

"no admittance" to others; but they do not challenge the social structure, the social relations of production and reproduction.[18] The claim for "abortion rights" seeks access to a necessary service, but by itself it fails to address the social relations and sexual divisions around which responsibility for pregnancy and children is assigned. In real-life struggles, this limitation exacts a price, for it lets men and society neatly off the hook.

The notion of rights has tremendous polemical power, but rights tend to be seen as isolated, rather than as part of a total revolutionary program. This is different from Marx and Engels's view of "bourgeois rights" as necessary preconditions and as means to building a class-conscious movement but not as ends in themselves (as feminists often think of them). It is also different from the more radical concept of control over one's body as a social and individual need, implicit in the requirements of personality and sensual "receptivity." Needs, unlike rights, exist only in connection with individuals and within concrete historical circumstances. For a Native American woman on welfare, who every time she appears in the clinic for prenatal care is asked whether she would like an abortion, "the right to choose an abortion" may appear dubious if not offensive.[19]

Finally, the idea of a "woman's right to choose" is vulnerable to political manipulation, as demonstrated in recent legislative and judicial debates. Thus "right-to-lifers" exploit the liberal concept of "informed consent" by promoting legislation that would require abortion patients to be "informed" in graphic detail of a fetus' physiological characteristics at each stage of development. Physicians opposing the federal, California, and New York City regulations to curb involuntary sterilization, particularly the requirement of a thirty-day waiting period, have claimed that such regulation is "paternalistic" and inhibits women's "right to choose" sterilization.[20] During hearings before the House Select Committee on Population in 1978, a spokesman for the Upjohn Company, manufacturer of Depo-Provera (an injectible contraceptive drug currently banned from U.S. distribution because of evidence it is carcinogenic), opposed FDA regulation of contraceptives on the ground that it "deprives the public of free choice": ". . . safety cannot be absolute—it can be defined *only in relative and personal terms*. The individual with advice from his or her physician—not a governmental regulatory agency—should decide which risks are 'reasonable' under these circumstances."[21]

That judgments about contraceptive safety can be made only "in relative and personal terms" assails the commitment to establishing and enforcing generalizable standards of health and safety that transcend individual judgments. Moreover, when the risks include thromboembolisms, myocardial infarction, breast cancer, and cervical cancer, the need for social standards and their vigorous enforcement is a matter of life and death. Recent applications of laissez-faire ideology to reproductive policy are clearly part of a larger right-wing push that seeks "deregulation" in many spheres; seen within this general political context, they are to be expected. But the ease with which the principle of individuality and control over one's own body may be perverted into bourgeois individualism—and capitalist greed—should make us pause, clear our heads, and think through more rigorously the social conditions of individual control.

The Social Relations of Reproduction

The idea that biological reproduction is a social activity, distinct from the activity of childrearing and determined by changing material conditions and social relations, is essentially Marxist. In *The German Ideology*, Marx defines "three aspects of social activity": along with "the production of material life" and "the production of new needs," human procreation—reproduction within the family—is also a "social relationship." That is, it involves not only "natural," or biological, relations but social, cooperative relations among men and women through sexual and procreative practices. That activity is social insofar as it is cooperative, purposive, and above all conscious.[22] We can extend this view to human sexuality in general, which, whether heterosexual, homosexual, or bisexual, is fundamentally social, involving reciprocity, the conscious articulation and re-creation of desire; not merely satisfying a need but doing so in an interactive context that people create together. Moreover, sexual meanings and practices, like the meanings and practices of motherhood, vary enormously through history, across cultures, and within the same culture indicating that these "natural" realms of human experience are incessantly mediated by social praxis and design.[23]

If this variability characterizes sexual and maternal experience, how much more is it true of contraception, abortion, and childrearing practices—all domains that, throughout civilization, have been transformed by conscious human interventions.[24] A woman does not simply "get pregnant" and "give birth" like the flowing of tides and seasons. She does so under the constraint of *material conditions* that set limits on "natural" reproductive processes—for example, existing birth control methods and technology and access to them; class divisions and the distribution/financing of health care; nutrition; employment, particularly of women; and the state of the economy generally. And she does so within a specific network of *social relations* and social arrangements involving herself, her sexual partner(s), her children and kin, neighbors, doctors, family planners, birth control providers and manufacturers, employers, the church, and the state.

Georg Lukács takes up the idea of a "metabolism," or necessary interaction, between the natural and social aspects of human life. He suggests that the progressive socialization of "natural being" through "social practice" is the essence of history.[25] To dichotomize "nature" and "society" is false; and, by inference, it is also false to assume a split between women's "biological" functions and her "social" ones. Hilda Scott similarly reflects this view in paraphrasing the Czech demographer Helena Svarcova: "Marx's observation . . . suggests looking for the dialectical relationship between the natural and social sides of reproduction, instead of regarding them as two parallel but independent processes. In this view, human population is seen as the unity of biological and social aspects which condition each other, the social aspects being the chief but not the only factor."[26]

The attempt to develop a social conception of reproduction is, of course, not limited to Marxists. Demographers, for example, conventionally acknowledge the importance of social conditions in determining population, but within a set of completely mechanistic assumptions. A social phenomenon such as changing birthrates is thus viewed solely in terms of statistically measurable demographic events (numbers of women in a given childbearing cohort, numbers entering the labor force, availability and use of contraceptives, and so on) as though it were a natural, unintended occurrence.[27] Population-oriented anthropologists emphasize not only the tremendous variability but the rational, deliberate character of methods for controlling population and fertility among all societies, including the most primitive.[28] However, they view such activity from a functionalist perspective, as "adaptive mechanisms" adopted by the culture as a whole, undifferentiated by sexual divisions or divisions of power. Utterly lacking is any sense that the methods and goals of reproduction, and control over them, may themselves be a contested area within the culture—particularly between women and men.

In contrast, an analysis of reproductive activity in terms of the "social relations of reproduction" would emphasize the historical dynamism of consciousness and social conflict and the historical agency of social groups. Social divisions, based on differing relationships to power and resources, mediate the institutional and cultural arrangements through which biology, sexuality, and reproduction among human beings are expressed, and such relations are essentially antagonistic and complex. At the most basic level they involve gender divisions, or the sexual division of labor (itself a predominantly cultural product); but in class-divided societies, they are also entangled with divisions based on class. Gordon's book is laced with examples of the ways in which, in nineteenth- and twentieth-century America, women's birth control possibilities were directly affected by their class position, which determined their relationship to medical and family planning distribution systems. Thus the diaphragm— "the most effective available contraceptive in the 1930s" —was virtually inaccessible to working-class and poor women, due to material conditions such as the lack of privacy, running water, and access to private clinics and medical instruction through which diaphragms were dispensed.[29] Today, class and race divisions in reproductive health care determine not only women's access to decent gynecological services, counseling, and the like, but their risk of exposure to involuntary sterilization, dangerous contraceptive drugs, or unnecessary hysterectomy.

The social relations of reproduction are also complicated by the forms of consciousness and struggle through which they are expressed in different historical periods. Sometimes antagonisms remain implicit or repressed; sometimes, under conditions that need to be understood more precisely, birth control and abortion become areas of open sexual and class conflict. Anthropological and historical studies, while scant, record the particularity of reproductive relations to class and culture and the ways those relations are recurrently ones of social division. Devereux, for example, describes societies in which abortion, or retaliation against involuntarily-induced abortion, represented a clear act of female defiance.[30] Flandrin, in his analysis of late medieval church views toward contraception and sexual relations, points out that the evidence of widespread contraceptive practice indicates that conscious, even unrepentant resistance to the dominant ecclesiastical morality must have been common in Europe from the fifteenth to the eighteenth centuries.[31] These examples suggest that the critical issue for feminists is not so much the content of women's choices, or even the "right to choose," as it is the social and material conditions under which choices are made. The "right to choose" means little when women are powerless. In cultures where "illegitimacy" is stigmatized or where female infants are devalued, women may resort to abortion or infanticide with impunity; but that option

clearly grows out of female subordination. Similarly, women may have autonomy over reproduction and childbirth, as in New Guinea, while being totally excluded from everything else.[32] Or, like the women employees at the American Cyanamid plant in West Virginia, they may "choose" sterilization as the alternative to losing their jobs. To paraphrase Marx, women make their own reproductive choices, but they do not make them just as they please; they do not make them under conditions they create but under conditions and constraints they, as mere individuals, are powerless to change.[33] That individuals do not determine the social framework in which they act does not nullify their choices nor their moral capacity to make them. It only suggests that we have to focus less on "choice" and more on how to transform the social conditions of choosing, working, and reproducing.

At present, the organized forces that shape the class-specific socially constructed character of women's reproductive experience in the United States are powerful and diverse. The intervention of doctors, particularly obstetrician-gynecologists, in women's control over their reproductive lives has been pervasive; yet medical control over reproduction is far from monolithic. Private and public population control agencies have cooperated with the medical profession, as "medical indications" and "medical effectiveness" became euphemisms for technical efficiency in population control. But these agencies maintain a financial and institutional power base independent of doctors. Further, the large-scale commercialization of birth control products and services has meant that other interests, such as pharmaceutical and insurance companies, have become important influences on the methods available to women, their safety or risk, and whether they will be reimbursed.

This conjuncture of medical, corporate, and state interests in the "management" of reproduction has defined the choices of all women, but in a way that is crucially different depending on one's class and race. Still the major providers of birth control and abortion information and services to women, physicians are widely known to vary the information and the quality of services they provide based on the class and race of their patients. For example, private doctors in Maryland were found to provide abortions with much greater regularity to their middle-class than to their lower-class patients.[34] Similarly, cases of sterilization abuse by physicians in the public health services have occurred almost entirely among black, Native American, and Mexican-American welfare recipients, as well as women who are prisoners or mentally retarded.[35] Low-income and non-English-speaking women are regularly denied information about safer, "nonmedical" methods of birth control because of racist and class-biased assumptions that they are not "competent" to "manage" such methods. Moreover, it is poor and Third World women who are likely to be used as experimental subjects in international population control programs for testing or "dumping" contraceptive chemicals or implants whose safety has been questioned by the FDA.[36] Finally, in a capitalist society, class is the mightiest determinant of the material resources that help make having and raising children joyful rather than burdensome.

It would be wrong, however, to picture women of any class as the passive victims of medical, commercial, and state policies of reproductive control. In hearings before the House Select Committee on Population and in lawsuits, women of all classes have successfully challenged drug companies and doctors regarding the severe health hazards of the pill, Depo-Provera, and other synthetic hormones.[37] Groups of Mexican American, Native American, black, and other women have joined with women's health and reproductive rights groups to fight against involuntary sterilization in the courts and through extensive federal and state regulations. An active, vocal movement to defend women's reproductive freedom and "abortion rights" is growing in the United States and Western Europe and is currently a major force in the feminist movement.

What is "reproductive freedom" from the standpoint of historical materialism? On what principle is women's struggle to secure control over the terms and conditions of reproduction based? A materialist view of reproductive freedom would justify this struggle in terms of the principle of socially determined need. The moral imperative grows out of the historically and culturally defined position that women find themselves in through motherhood. Because it is primarily women who bear the consequences of pregnancy and the responsibility for children, the conditions of reproduction and contraception affect them directly and in every aspect of their lives. Therefore, it is women primarily who should have control over whether, when, and under what conditions to have children. Moreover, an emphasis on the social rather than biological basis of reproductive activity implies that such activity is once and for all removed from any "privatized" or "personal sphere" and may legitimately be claimed for political and social intervention. That intervention may take the form of measures to protect or regulate reproductive health—for example, to assure the safety and voluntariness of contraceptive methods—or to transform the material conditions that currently divide women's reproductive options according to class and race.

On the other hand, a materialist view of reproductive freedom recognizes the historical contingency of the conditions in which women seek reproductive control. For most of history, women's "choices" over reproduction have been exercised in a framework in which reproduction and motherhood have determined their relationship to society. A materialist (and feminist) view looks forward to an eventual transcendence of the existing social relations of reproduction so that gender is not ultimately the determinant of responsibility. This implies that society be transformed so that men, or society itself, bear an equal responsibility for nurturance and child care. Then the basis of the need would have changed and control over reproduction might not belong primarily to women.[38] It is here, however, that a contrary feminist sensibility begins to rankle and the limitations of a historical materialist, or traditional Marxist, framework for defining reproductive freedom become apparent. These limitations are disturbingly suggested in Alison Jaggar's "Marxist feminist" defense of abortion, which argues that the "right" of women to an abortion is "contingent" upon "women's situation in our society": ". . . if the whole community assumes the responsibility for the welfare of mothers and children, [then] the community as a whole should now have a share in judging whether or not a particular abortion should be performed. . . ."[39]

Can we really imagine the social conditions in which we would be ready to renounce control over our bodies and reproductive lives—to give over the decision as to whether, when, and with whom we will bear children to the "community as a whole"? The reality behind this nagging question is that control over reproductive decisions, particularly abortion, has to do not only with "the welfare of mothers and children" but very fundamentally with sexuality and with women's bodies as such. The analysis emphasizing the social relations of

reproduction tends to ignore, or deny, the level of reality most immediate for individual women: that it is their bodies in which pregnancies occur. Indeed, that analysis becomes false insofar as it disregards the immediate, sensual reality of individuals altogether. In order to make this connection, a theory of reproductive freedom has to have recourse to other conceptual frameworks, particularly one that is more commonly associated with a feminist tradition and asserts women's right to and need for bodily self-determination.

Reproductive Politics, Past and Future

> Even if contraception were perfected to infallibility, so that no woman need ever again bear an unwanted child; even if laws and customs change—as long as women and women only are the nurturers of children, our sons will grow up looking only to women for compassion, resenting strength in women as 'control,' clinging to women when we try to move into a new mode of relationship.[40]

How do we break out of the apparent contradiction between "women's right to control" over reproduction and their need not to be defined by reproduction? How do we transform the social relations of reproduction to bring men, as potential fathers, into those relations on an equal basis? How would such a transformation affect the principle of "control over our bodies"? The two ideas of reproductive freedom discussed here must be incorporated into a revolutionary feminist and socialist politics. Despite the real tensions between these ideas—stressing changes in the social relations of reproduction and stressing women's control over their bodies—neither is dispensable for feminists. Yet no political movement for "reproductive rights" or women's emancipation, including our own, has yet sustained this double agenda in a systematic and consistent way.

The failure to integrate these two ideas in practice in a political movement is illustrated dramatically by Atina Grossman's account of the abortion struggle that united feminists, socialists, and communists in Weimar Germany.[41] "The Communist left and its women's movement" saw abortion as primarily "a class issue": the proposed law making abortion a criminal act would affect working-class women most severely, since middle-class women could both afford and get access to illegal abortion and contraception. Feminists emphasized "women's right to sexual pleasure and control of their bodies," suggesting that maternity is a special female realm of experience that cuts across class divisions.

Grossman correctly stresses the positive aspects of this political campaign: It brought together in a single coalition the women's movement and the working-class movement; it appealed to women of all classes on the basis of their oppression as women in reproduction; it moved even the German Communist party (KPD), for mainly tactical reasons, to put forward a feminist slogan: "Your body belongs to you." Yet the different ideological bases on which groups supported the abortion struggle implied differing senses of why that campaign was important and must have had an impact on the cohesiveness of the movement and its ability to make its ideas felt, for "the politics of reproduction were never . . . adequately integrated into Communist ideology."[42] Thus a theory that related the need of individual women for control over their bodies to the needs of the working class as a whole was not—nor has it yet been—articulated.

Reproductive politics in the context of socialist revolutions have been still less cohesive or consciously feminist. In general, where liberalized abortion and divorce reforms have been introduced as a fundamen-tal aspect of socialist revolutions—for example, in the Soviet Union and Eastern Europe the purpose has been mainly to facilitate women's participation in industry and the breakup of feudal and patriarchal forms. Such measures have not been inspired by either of the ideas I have been examining, nor by a feminist movement self-consciously struggling to put those ideas into practice. Accounts of the Soviet Union in the 1920s and 1930s[43] and of Czechoslovakia in the 1950s and 1960s[44] richly and poignantly illustrate the limits of "reproductive reforms" when they are neither accompanied by material changes that would augment women's real power in society nor brought into effect through a mass independent women's movement. Foreshadowing experience in the United States since *Roe* v. *Wade*, such reforms were used in a later, reactionary period as a pretext for sexual and reproductive repression. The tendency these cases point to is a reactive chain of developments in which measures such as liberalized abortion and abolishing illegitimacy unleash a rise in sexual activity, abortions, and divorce followed by a period of backlash in which there is an outcry against the "breakup of the family," women are blamed and accused of "selfishness," and the society is chided by population experts about its declining birthrate. In the absence of either adequate material support (incomes, child care, health care, housing) or shared male responsibility for contraception and childrearing, women are left, after these reforms, in some ways more vulnerable than before.[45]

Scott's assessment of the situation in Czechoslovakia, while critical of the repressiveness for women of the later, backward shifts in abortion policy, tends nevertheless to focus the blame on abortion. She intimates that abortion is intrinsically a method of birth control that puts women at a disadvantage and "encourages irresponsibility on the part of men." "Abortion as a birth control method puts all the responsibility for the future of the unborn child [sic] on the woman. She makes the application, she agrees to the operation, she pays the fee. If, as in Czechoslovakia, she must go before an interruption commission, she is the one who receives the lecture, is subjected to pressure to have the child, is reproached for getting herself 'into trouble.' "[46] What is most striking in this account is the absence (as in Russia) of any women's organization, movement, or tradition that made reproductive freedom a value in its own right. Clearly, there is nothing inevitable, nothing written into "nature," about the presumed relationship between abortion and male "irresponsibility." One could perfectly well imagine a system of abortion decision making that involved potential fathers to the same degree as potential mothers, although whether women would or should give up their control over this decision is another question. What reinforces male irresponsibility is the reliance on abortion *in a social context in which the sex-gender division remains unchanged and in a political context in which that division remains unchallenged.*

That a socialist revolution is a necessary but far from sufficient basis for reproductive freedom is illustrated in a different way by the current antinatalist drive in China. The effort of the Chinese government to limit births to two per couple, through a massive campaign of propaganda and education as well as economic incentives,[47] raises numerous questions. While the political decision that the Chinese economy and educational system cannot support an increasingly young population may be rational on some level, one wonders, first, whether the economic sanctions on households are accompanied by as vigorous ef-

forts to equalize the position of women in work, economic, and political life; or to develop birth control education and methods for men. Moreover, do the measures fall more heavily on some groups so that poorer families feel a greater pressure to comply? Finally, how and by whom were the decisions made? Were those most affected by them (parents) involved in the process? One disturbing aspect of the Chinese policy is its emphasis on chemical contraceptives and IUDs, with all the known risks and side effects.[48] Once again it is women whose bodies are subjected to reproductive and contraceptive risk.

Strategies for establishing reproductive freedom must distinguish between different historical and political contexts. Under the conditions of advanced capitalism existing in the United States today—particularly as the right wing seeks to restore patriarchal control over whether, how, and with whom women have children—reproductive politics necessarily become a struggle for control. Moreover, that struggle is greatly complicated by persistent class and race divisions. For most women in capitalist society, the idea of reproductive control (or "choice") is unthinkable short of a vast array of social changes that are themselves predicated upon a socialist revolution. In the meantime, "control" in a more limited sense may mean different things to different women (birth control information is one thing, possession of your reproductive organs and custody of your children is another). In a class- and race-divided society, "pronatalist" and "antinatalist" policies coincide (e.g., restrictions on abortion *and* involuntary sterilization), making it necessary for "reproductive rights" proponents to articulate continually that "reproductive freedom means the freedom to have as well as not to have children."[49] Because women are subordinate economically, politically, and legally, a policy emphasizing male sharing of childrearing responsibility could well operate to divest women of control over their children in a situation where they have little else. (We are currently getting a foretaste of this danger, with increasing losses of custody fights by women, particularly lesbian mothers.) The "collective" principle could play into the suggestions of "right-to-lifers" that the responsibility for childbearing is too important to be left to women.

On the other hand, because the sexual division of labor around childrearing prevails and defines women's position, a policy emphasizing improved benefits and services to encourage childbearing may ease the material burdens of motherhood; but it may also operate to perpetuate the existing sexual division of labor and women's social subordination. This has been the case in Eastern and Western Europe. And in the United States it is easy to imagine an accretion of reforms such as pregnancy disability benefits, child-care centers, and maternity leave provisions, which, if unaccompanied by demands for transforming the total position of women, can be used to rationalize that position.[50] The point is not that present attempts to secure funded abortion, pregnancy and maternity benefits, child-care services, and other reforms should be abandoned but that those attempts must be moved beyond the framework of "a woman's right to choose" and connected to a broader revolutionary movement that addresses all the conditions for women's liberation.

A feminist and socialist transformation of the existing conditions of reproduction would seek to unleash the possibilities for material (economic and technological) improvements in reproduction from traditional family and sexual forms, to place those positive changes in a new set of social rela-

tions. Foremost among these new relations is that concerned with the care of children. Men must be "ready to share the responsibilities of full-time, universal child care as a social priority" —that is, the responsibility for children must be dissociated from gender, which necessarily means that it becomes dissociated from heterosexuality. The writings of feminist theorists[51] reveal deeply rooted cultural and psychic bases of traditional childrearing arrangements; they help explain why it is this aspect of presocialist patriarchy that seems most intractable in postrevolutionary societies. The changes we require are total; ". . . no decisive changes can be brought about by measures aimed at women alone, but, rather, the division of functions between the sexes must be changed in such a way that men and women have the same opportunities to be active parents and to be gainfully employed. This makes of women's emancipation not a 'woman question' but a function of the general drive for greater equality which affects everyone. . . . The care of children becomes a fact which society has to take into consideration."[52] Under different conditions from any that now exist, it may become possible to transcend some of the individualist elements of feminist thinking about reproductive freedom and move toward a concept of reproduction as an activity that concerns all of society. At the same time, a basis could be created for the genuine reproductive freedom of individuals, ending systems of domination that inhibit their control over their bodies. We need to envision what those conditions would be, even though they seem far from present reality. Charting the development of reproductive politics in the past, especially abortion, and rigorously analyzing their conditions in the present, ought to help us transform those politics in the future.

Notes

1. Linda Gordon, *Woman's Body, Woman's Right: A Social History of Birth Control in America* (Harmondsworth, England, and Baltimore: Penguin, 1977), p. 47.

2. George Devereux, "A Typological Study of Abortion in 350 Primitive, Ancient, and Pre-Industrial Societies," in *Abortion in America*, ed. Harold Rosen (Boston: Beacon, 1967), p. 98.

3. I am indebted to Zillah Eisenstein for this important clarification.

4. Quoted in C. B. MacPherson, *The Political Theory of Possessive Individualism* (London: Oxford University Press, 1962), p. 140.

5. See Keith Thomas, "Women and the Civil War Sects," *Past and Present* 13 (1958): 332–52. For accounts of Leveller doctrine as well as the ideas of more radical sects about women and individualism in this period, see Christopher Hill, *The World Turned Upside Down* (New York: Viking, 1972); idem, *The Century of Revolution, 1603-1714* (New York: Norton, 1961), Chaps. 4, 7, and 8; and MacPherson, Chap. 3.

6. *Griswold* v. *Connecticut*, 381 U.S. 479 (1965); *Eisenstadt* v. *Baird*, 405 U.S. 438 (1972); *Roe* v. *Wade*, 410 U.S. 113 (1973); and *Doe* v. *Bolton*, 410 U.S. 179 (1973). See also the fine summary and analysis of these cases as well as the June 1977 Supreme Court decisions on abortion in Kristin Booth Glen, "Abortion in the Courts: A Laywoman's Historical Guide to the New Disaster Area," *Feminist Studies* 4 (February 1978): 1–26.

7. Juliet Mitchell, "Women and Equality," in *The Rights and Wrongs of Women*, ed. Juliet Mitchell and Ann Oakley (Harmondsworth, England: Penguin, 1976).

8. Agnes Heller, *The Theory of Need in Marx* (New York: St. Martin's, 1976), pp. 67, 73.

9. Herbert Marcuse, *Negations: Essays in Critical Theory* (Boston: Beacon, 1968), pp. 166–71.

10. Gordon, p. 66.

11. Judge Dooling in *McRae* v. *Califano*, 491 F. Supp. 630 (1980), p. 742.

12. Gordon, p. 70; emphasis added.

13. Cf. Sara Ruddick: "Neither our own ambivalence toward our women's bodies nor the bigoted, repressive uses men, colonizers and racists have made of biology, should blind us to biology's possibilities. On the other hand, our belief in the biological body's psychosocial efficacy may be an illusion created by the fact that the people who engage in maternal practices almost always have female bodies." "Maternal Thinking," *Feminist Studies* (Summer 1980), p. 346.

14. "Four Women Assert Jobs Were Linked to Sterilization," *New York Times*, 5 January 1979; Rosalind Petchesky, "Workers, Reproductive Hazards and the Politics of Protection: An Introduction," *Feminist Studies* 5 (Summer 1979): 233–45; Michael J. Wright, "Reproductive Hazards and 'Protective' Discrimination," ibid., pp. 302–9; Wendy Chavkin, "Occupational Hazards to Reproduction—a Review of the Literature," ibid., pp. 310–25.

15. Committee for Abortion Rights and against Sterilization Abuse [CARASA], *Women Under Attack: Abortion, Sterilization Abuse, and Reproductive Freedom* [New York: CARASA, 1979); Rosalind Petchesky, "Reproduction, Ethics and Public Policy: The Federal Sterilization Regulations," *Hastings Center Report* 9 (October 1979): 29–42; Charles F. Westoff and James McCarthy, "Sterilization in the United States," *Family Planning Perspectives* 11 (May/June 1979): 147–52; and Charlotte F. Muller, "Insurance Coverage of Abortion, Contraception and Sterilization," *Family Planning Perspectives* 10 (March–April 1978): 71–77.

16. "There is no way a pregnant woman can passively let the fetus live; she must create and nurture it with her own body, a symbiosis that is often difficult, sometimes dangerous, uniquely intimate. However gratifying pregnancy may be to a woman who desires it, for the unwilling it is literally an invasion—the closest analogy is to the difference between lovemaking and rape. . . . Clearly, abortion is by normal standards an act of self-defense." Ellen Willis, *Beginning to See the Light* (New York: Alfred A. Knopf, 1981), p. 208. Cf. Judith Jarvis Thomson's classic essay, "A Defense of Abortion," in *The Rights and Wrongs of Abortion*, ed. M. Cohen et al. (Princeton: Princeton University Press, 1974), pp. 10, 12. Thomson uses philosophical sleight of hand to arrive at the same conclusion.

17. This point is made persuasively by Daniel Callahan, *Abortion: Law, Choice and Morality* (New York: Macmillan, 1970), p. 494; cf. Alison Jaggar, "Abortion and a Woman's Right to Decide," in *Women and Philosophy*, ed. Carol C. Gould and Marx W. Wartofsky (New York: Capricorn, 1976), p. 347.

18. Cf. Mitchell, pp. 384–85.

19. Meredith Tax, citing a remark by Pat Bellanger, representative of WARN (Women of All Red Nations), St. Paul, Minnesota.

20. Patricia Donovan, "Sterilizing the Poor and Incompetent," *Hastings Center Report* 6 (October 1976): 5; and Petchesky, "Reproduction. Ethics and Public Policy," p. 35.

21. U.S. Congress, House, Select Committee on Population, *Fertility and Contraception in the*

United States, 95th Cong., 2d sess., December 1978, p. 110.

22. Karl Marx, *The German Ideology*, in *Writings of the Young Marx on Philosophy and Society*, ed. Lloyd D. Easton and Kurt H. Guddat (Garden City, N.Y.: Anchor, 1967), pp. 419–22.

23. Rayna Rapp and Ellen Ross, "Sex and Society: A Research Note from Social History and Anthropology," *Comparative Studies in Society and History* 23 (January 1981): 51–72; Jeffrey Weeks, *Sex, Politics and Society: The Regulation of Sexuality since 1800* (London: Longman, 1981); *Radical History Review* 20 (Spring/Summer 1979): special issue on "Sexuality in History," esp. articles by Robert A. Padgug ("Sexual Matters: On Conceptualizing Sexuality in History," pp. 3–23) and Jeffrey Weeks ("Movements of Affirmation: Sexual Meanings and Homosexual Identities," pp. 164–79); Jean-Louis Flandrin, "Contraception, Marriage, and Sexual Relations in the Christian West," in *Biology of Man in History*, ed. Robert Forster and Orest Ranum (Baltimore: Johns Hopkins University Press, 1975); Michel Foucault, *The History of Sexuality*, vol. 1, *An Introduction* (New York: Pantheon, 1978); Gayle Rubin, "The Traffic in Women," in *Toward an Anthropology of Women*, ed. Rayna (Rapp) Reiter (New York: Monthly Review, 1975), pp. 157–210.

24. See, e.g., Gordon, Chaps. 1 and 2; Norman E. Himes, *Medical History of Contraception* (New York: Gamut, 1963); John T. Noonan, Jr., *Contraception* (Cambridge, Mass.: Harvard University Press, 1966); Devereux; Steven Polgar, "Population History and Population Policies from an Anthropological Perspective," *Current Anthropology* 13 (April 1972): 203–11.

25. Georg Lukács, *The Ontology of Social Being—2. Marx* (London: Merlin, 1978), pp. 5–7, 38–39.

26. Hilda Scott, *Does Socialism Liberate Women?* (Boston: Beacon, 1974), p. 159.

27. Thanks to Ellen Ross and Hal Benenson for reminding me of this point.

28. See Polgar; and Alexander Alland, *Adaptation in Human Evolution: An Approach to Medical Anthropology* (New York: Columbia University Press, 1970).

29. Gordon, pp. 309–12.

30. Devereux, pp. 113, 117.

31. Flandrin, pp. 25–28.

32. Sherry B. Ortner, "The Virgin and the State," *Feminist Studies* 4 (October 1978): 25; and Gordon, who cites similar examples from anthropological evidence and concludes: "These are women's choices, but hardly choices coming from positions of power" (p. 34).

33. Karl Marx, *The Eighteenth Brumaire of Louis Bonaparte* (New York: International Publishers, 1963), p. 15.

34. Constance A. Nathanson and Marshall H. Becker, "The Influence of Physicians' Attitudes on Abortion Performance, Patient Management and Professional Fees," *Family Planning Perspectives* 9 (July/August 1977): 158–63.

35. Ad Hoc Women's Studies Committee against Sterilization Abuse, *Workbook on Sterilization and Sterilization Abuse* (Bronxville, N.Y.: Women's Studies, Sarah Lawrence College, 1978); and CARASA, pp. 49–53.

36. See Barbara Ehrenreich, Mark Dowie, and Stephen Minkin, "The Charge, Gynocide; the Accused, the U.S. Government," reprinted in *CARASA News* 4 (January 1980): 13; Deborah Maine, "Depo: The Debate Continues," *Family Planning Perspectives* 10 (November/December 1978): 392.

37. U.S. Congress, House, Select Committee on Population, pp. 109–10.

38. The position presented here is obviously different from the technological determinism of Shulamith Firestone in *The Dialectic of Sex* (New York: Bantam, 1970). Firestone's simplistic view that women's position could be "revolutionized" by the introduction of *in vitro* fertilization, artificial uteruses, and other "advanced" features of reproductive technology ignores the social aspects of reproduction and the political question of who controls that technology, how control is organized socially and institutionally, and for what ends.

39. Jaggar, pp. 351, 356, 358.

40. Adrienne Rich, *Of Woman Born* (New York: Norton, 1976), p. 211.

41. Attina Grossman, "Abortion and the Economic Crisis: The 1931 Campaign against §218 in Germany," *New German Critique* 14 (Spring 1978): 119–37.

42. Ibid., p. 134.

43. Richard Stites shows how the revolutionary Russian Family Code, which abolished illegitimacy, eased divorce, and recognized de facto marriages, worked to women's disadvantage in the absence of either adequate means of material support for women and children or a feminist politics emphasizing men's role in reproduction. Similarly, the liberalized abortion law of 1920 became a pretext not only for abandonment and nonrecognition of paternity but for the lax and exploitative sexual relations that characterized this period. In these conditions of insecurity, the return to a traditional sanctification of marriage and motherhood in the 1930s, with heavy restrictions on abortion and divorce, was actually welcomed by many women, insofar as the new (1936) provisions reinforced men's responsibility

for providing protection to wife and children. Richard Stites, *The Women's Liberation Movement in Russia* (Princeton: Princeton University Press, 1978), pp. 367–69, 374, 386–87.

44. Scott documents the introduction of liberal abortion laws during the 1950s in Czechoslovakia, Hungary, and Rumania and its repressive aftermath. Following a major birthrate decline, as well as an apparently significant increase in the abortion rate, in the 1960s policy makers and population "experts" in these countries not only blamed abortion for social and demographic problems but accused women of "selfishness" and irresponsibility for seeking abortion and getting pregnant in the first place. A series of "maternal incentive" policies was introduced, including extended paid maternity leave, housewives' allowances, bonuses for additional children, etc., and "abortions for other than medical reasons in the case of childless married women and those with one child" were restricted. Scott, pp. 141, 132–33, 153.

45. A very moving and amusing expression of this pattern, and of people's confusion and personal conflict over heterosexual relations, marriage, and abortion in the 1920s in Russia, is the fine Soviet film *Bed and Sofa (Tretya Meshchanskaya)*, produced by V. Shklovsky and A. Room (1927).

46. Scott, p. 144. Cf. Kristin Luker's similar argument that abortion reform in the United States in the early 1970s encouraged "male disengagement from responsibility," in *Taking Chances: Abortion and the Decision Not to Contracept* (Berkeley: University of California Press, 1975), pp. 134–35.

47. James P. Sterba, "Chinese Will Try to Halt Growth of Population by End of Century," New York Times, 13 August 1979, p. A4; Walter Sullivan, "A Tough New Drive on Births in China," *New York Times*, 10 October 1979, pp. C1, C11.

48. Sullivan reports that "while various contraceptive preparations are taken by millions of Chinese women, only 10,000 men are taking the birth control substance gossypol experimentally." On the commune he visited, 95 percent of the sterilizations performed had been done on women. Sullivan, pp. C1, C11.

49. CARASA, p. 9.

50. To offset the birthrate decline in the United States, Princeton demographer Charles Westoff suggests a variation on a pronatalist incentives policy that would divide all American women into one-third who would "never have any children" and another two-thirds who "would have to reproduce at an average rate of three births per woman to maintain a replacement." While the former group would presumably be channeled into full-time employment, the latter would be drawn into their role of "breeders" through "a serious investment in childcare institutions" and other government-sponsored reproductive subsidies. "Some Speculations on the Future of Marriage and Fertility," *Family Planning Perspectives* 10 (March/April 1978): 79-82.

51. Nancy Chodorow, *The Reproduction of Mothering* (Berkeley: University of California Press, 1975); Dorothy Dinnerstein, *The Mermaid and the Minotaur* (New York: Harper & Row, 1976); Rich, *Of Woman Born*.

52. Scott, p. 190.

32

An Open Letter to a Diocesan Priest

Mary Jean Wolch

Two years ago, Mary Jean Wolch wrote a letter to her friends, including a prolife priest, about the pain of having given up her daughter for adoption years earlier. The priest's reply–welcoming her openness and reflecting his prolife beliefs–prompted her to write back and explain her feelings in greater depth. Here, Wolch makes her second letter public.

Dear Father,

Thank you for your reply to my letter. I must admit to some trepidation in sending it to you; we have known each other eight years, but I had never before shared with you that I am a birth mother.

More than a decade after the birth of my child, the pain of this experience erupted as the central event of the past year. I realized it was time to share with those who knew, and those who did not, what it has been like to live with the loss of a child through adoption, and how this event has profoundly impacted my life. That is why I wrote a letter this year describing this journey and sent it to the peo-ple in my life. It was not the typical letter one finds tucked among the Christmas cards.

I had not shared this experience with you before because I know you are strongly "prolife." Prolife people are the hardest ones to talk to about the birth mother's experience. Their perception of the experience is so disparate from its reality that discussion is difficult if not impossible. That is why I am writing today, to answer your questions and respond to your comments.

You asked if I had considered an abortion and who or what got me to change my mind. I was a single, 23-year-old college student and an active Catholic. I attended Mass,

From *Conscience, A Newsjournal of Prochoice Catholic Opinion,* published by Catholics for Free Choice. Vol. xiii, no. 3, May/June 1991. Copyright © 1991 by Mary Jean Wolch. Reprinted by permission of the author.

participated in campus ministry social justice actions, helped plan liturgies and retreats, and participated in Scripture study groups. I wanted with all my heart to be a "good" Catholic. I was taught to believe life began at conception. I was adamant that adoption was a better alternative than abortion. I believed this because the church said so, and the church had all truth, told all truth, and was all truth.

Then the "good Catholic girl" was pregnant. Suddenly a whole new awareness opened up for me as I realized what this experience meant for a woman going through it. Now I was experiencing what I had not heard discussed from the pulpit. It was a time of tremendous fear and despair. I prayed desperately, "God, get me through this." Having a baby is a very big deal. Prolife people who use the word "convenience" to describe a decision made about whether or not to have a baby are discounting a major life event. I had to take stock of my life. I had to weigh the limitations against the hopes and the dreams. I had to look at my finances, my marital state, the impact on employment and educational pursuits, the effect on my health, my emotional readiness for parenting, the support or lack of it from my family, and the social ostracism from my community. I had to make a decision based on these conditions and my future options as I rightly or wrongly perceived them at that moment.

This assessment is the reason women lose their children through adoption. The prolife voices hail this decision as courageous, unselfish, and loving. The same assessment is then condemned as "excuses" for women who choose abortion. The forced nature of the decision in both situations—in all its fear, despair, and powerlessness—is rarely acknowledged.

I chose against abortion because I believed it would be hypocritical to have an abortion after my adamant stand against that option for other women. I have always believed that Christ hates hypocrisy far more than sin. I might have given someone else permission to change their mind, but I could not give myself the same. As immature a love as it was, I loved this child's father. And I bonded early on with my child. I knew I could not be kicked out of school for being pregnant. I struggled to do "the right thing," as I had always heard it: have the baby and give it up for adoption. Thus I chose to go through the pregnancy.

In the course of this pregnancy, I moved from a strongly antiabortion position to the realization I could never tell another woman what her choice should be. The change in my belief was not a simple move from one position to another. It was the painful expansion of my horizons as I moved through this experience. My context was changing. I remember thinking over and over, "So this is what it's like to go through this." I was living on campus in the dorm, and as my "condition" became obvious, other women came to me and we talked. Three women told me of abortions they had had; one of them had starved and exercised herself into a miscarriage. None of these women had ever told anyone before. I had chosen a course different from theirs, yet we understood each other. We understood what goes into making this decision. This understanding allowed us to be supportive of each other.

My daughter's birth was the most powerful and joyous event of my life. Within me a war now raged around the adoption decision. I stalled on signing my relinquishment papers and made visits to the Catholic "foundling" home to hold her and feed her. In the end, the struggle to keep my daughter was defeated by my tremendous feelings of shame and powerlessness, by my frozen belief that it was not all right to come home with a baby to my parent's house, and by my religious programming, which said adoption is "the right thing to do."

It could be argued that this view of adoption—as the only choice for a woman shamed by pregnancy outside of marriage—is not the teaching of the church. Still, it was the perception I had formed from reading Catholic publications and writings and sitting in Sunday Mass year after year listening to sermons. In discussing theology with those who have had the opportunity for in-depth study, I have learned that the common understanding of the church's position on adoption is actually tangential to the essence of church teachings on family life and abortion. While the church teaches that unborn life is of the utmost importance, people in the pews often hear an added message that upholds the "traditional" two-parent family as morally superior and attaches shame to single motherhood as well as abortion. It is the responsibility of those in positions of teaching and preaching to address this issue.

Giving up your child for adoption satisfies the church's injunction against abortion, answers the prayer of the adoptive couple, and, we hope, provides for the child. In the push to do what is "best" for the child, agencies and persons working with birth mothers never address the sexuality and self-esteem issues that got most of these women into this situation in the first place. These groups, despite their intent, are primarily advocates for adoptive parents and babies. The assistance they offer birth mothers is limited to gestational support. Birth mothers leave this experience and these "resources" more damaged than when they arrived—more shame-filled, more devastated, and more needy. They have incurred a life-long and terrible wound to the psyche, the loss of their child. It is a loss most cannot even speak about. It is at this point that

adoption resources, adoptive parents, and the community abandon the birth mother. When one lives in a state of pain, isolation, and abandonment, it is not especially unusual to wind up pregnant again. This was my experience.

Six months after I had lost my baby forever, I was pregnant again. My life after losing my daughter was an emotional and spiritual devastation no one prepared me for. I had heard about the emotional and spiritual trauma of abortion for years. Not once in all that time had anyone, including those who "counseled" me, said this happened to birth mothers as well. Somehow, the decision to choose life was supposed to eliminate this consequence. Facing this decision again, I still believed there was no support for my child and me *together*. Just six months into the devastating aftermath of adoption, I knew I could never choose adoption again. I chose to have an abortion at eight weeks.

It was to be one of the most profound spiritual experiences of my life. Three days before my appointment, I found myself pacing around my apartment in anguish. I sat down and began to pray. I asked God to sit before me to my left, and the spirit of this child to sit to the right. Before these two, I poured out my pain and my grief. I acknowledged my mistake in having had sex with someone who did not care about me nor I about him. I told them about my daughter and the terrible pain of losing her. I told the child spirit I could not go through this right now, and I told her my sorrow about it. I promised when I got out of nursing school to take responsibility for a child who was already here. I accepted the responsibility for the abortion decision. I asked both, of them for forgiveness. And a miraculous thing occurred: I knew in that moment I was forgiven. The angel of death from the days of Moses passed over my house and did not strike me down. I experienced the unconditional love and mercy of my Creator in a way I never had before. The peace of that experience carried me through my appointment and ever since. It is a peace I have never known with the adoption experience.

The abortion forced me finally to get honest about my behavior. I had to accept that I was not a celibate person and that "pretend" celibacy is not a contraceptive. I had serious problems to work on in order to understand why I was in relationships with men who would not or could not love me. I had to understand the terrible needs and emptiness inside that drove me to use sex in ways that were harmful to myself and others. I had to give up the image of myself as a "good Catholic." I had to learn to accept myself as I was.

After these experiences, I quit going to Mass on Human Life Sundays. It was hard for me to understand the prayers and the grief of the church for the aborted unborn when there was nothing for the fetus who miscarried at two, three or four months, and sometimes later. No funeral, no death certificate, no mention in the bulletin. If a woman miscarries in the early stages of pregnancy and doesn't have a profound loss experience, no one finds this particularly aberrant. Who recognizes the loss of the woman grieving an early, spontaneous abortion? As a birth mother, I know how it feels to sit in the pew and have the loss of a child completely ignored. The church grieves the aborted unborn and abandons the silently weeping women in its midst. Innocence is held in greater esteem than life. The experiences of miscarriage, abortion and adoption are ignored. And the decisions and feelings of women are condemned.

When prolife people say to birth mothers, "Be glad you didn't have an abortion, because that's really hell," most never speak from actual experience. Pain is pain. I'm not

"glad" I had an abortion; yet for me the pain of an abortion did not touch the pain of adoption. This will not be every woman's truth. However, the women I know who have had devastating loss experiences around an abortion are few compared with the birth mothers. The vast majority of women who have chosen abortion speak of it as a sad and difficult part of their history. They have not experienced the trauma I struggle with around my adoption. Both adoption and abortion are forced choices. Both are unnatural separations of a mother and a child. Both are experiences of loss. Adoption, however, is never finished.

You spoke of your work with Project Rachel and asked if I had heard of it. I have. I wonder why they minister only to women who have traumatic loss experiences around abortion. The group I am part of—Catholic birth mothers—has been completely ignored. Is the ministry truly for healing, or is healing secondary to the political and social agenda of the church? I believe the church creates part of the trauma around abortion for Catholic women by making the experience such a capital crime it cannot even be spoken about—unless one has had a conversion to the prolife point of view.

I attend a birth parent support group, one of a handful in existence. At any given meeting, 50 to 75 percent of the women and men present are Catholics and former Catholics. Some are new birth parents; some have been living with this loss for 30 years or longer. Where is the church for us? The message I would give you is this: there are many devastating loss experiences around childbearing; abortion is only one. Adoption, stillbirth, miscarriage, infertility are others. Project Rachel needs to expand its focus to have any credibility with the larger group of women. If the church is to be there for all of us, the leadership and the community will have to recognize our issues and become sensitized to our experiences and our pain. There must be more listening, more compassion, and less condemnation. I have pondered these things in my heart, and I now find myself outside the Catholic circle of "perfect truth." My seamless garment is torn. I fail the prolife litmus test of a "true" and "good" Catholic. I feel as though I have lost my tribe, and my tribe has lost me. Healing for me has come only when I have owned my truth and not denied it. Why have this healing and the truth of my experience separated me from my church?

You and I are on opposite sides of the abortion issue because of our different life paths and experiences. Yet I attempt this dialogue because I feel it is important to do so. I believe God trusts women to make good decisions about their lives and, even when we do not, still loves us unconditionally. This is the truth we need the church's help to find. Women in crisis and pain will come to you, in your role as priest.

You must affirm God's unconditional love for them no matter what decision they make. As a priest who advocates adoption, you must recognize the need for long-term grief counseling of birth parents, for support groups, for changes in adoption practices. You can acknowledge birth parents from the pulpit on Mother's Day and Father's Day. You can acknowledge our loss and our existence to the community. You can strive to make your community a place of compassion for all the women in the pews, as well as a place of welcome for mothers and children who are together.

At the 1982 Jesuit Volunteer Corps orientation in San Antonio, I cut an article out of the paper. A 17-year-old woman named Cathy Petri was banned from speaking at the commencement ceremony at Incarnate Word High School, though she was valedictorian with a 4.0 grade point average. The reason? She had a 16-month-old daughter

and was unmarried. Cathy Petri chose life and was made an outcast. She does not stand alone. She joined a group far larger than she could ever imagine—the women who have faced the choice of adoption, abortion, or single parenthood. The church has failed to address the needs of these people. We are banned even from speaking, and thus we are made outcasts of our community.

What Price Abortion Counseling?

Family planning programs serving poor women are threatened with the loss of funds or the loss of their integrity under the U.S. Supreme Court's 5-4 decision May 23 upholding the Reagan-Bush "gag rule" on abortion. The regulations, adopted in 1988 but suspended pending court challenges, prohibit projects funded by the "Title X" program from counseling women about abortion. Clinics must refer pregnant women to prenatal care providers that promote the life and health of "mother and unborn child." Armed with the Court's new ruling in *Rust v. Sullivan,* the Bush administration is expected to begin enforcing the regulations by the end of July unless Congress passes legislation that would bar them.

A coalition of prochoice, health care and free speech groups have united in an emergency lobbying effort for the Title X Pregnancy Counseling Act, which would require Title X projects to offer counseling related to abortion as well as the other options. Catholics for a Free Choice, which had signed an amicus brief against the regulations, is among several Catholic women's groups in the coalition. The coalition is urging opponents of the regulations to meet with their representatives and senators during the July 1-7 recess.

What is at stake, they say, is the entire family planning program. If the gag rule is enforced, 4,000 clinics must decide whether to forgo federal funds—totaling $141 million in fiscal year 1991—or keep mum when clients ask for information about abortion. The clinics serve five million women, including 1.5 million teens. A number of clinics have said they will refuse the federal money.

Both houses of Congress may well approve the bill undoing the ruling, but not necessarily by the two-thirds majority needed to survive President Bush's veto.

The ruling is the first hint of the leanings of the Court's newest member, Justice David Souter, on abortion. A centrist so far, Souter joined the majority opinion in *Rust.* While his Rust vote is not a certain omen of his position on overturning Roe—it may reflect mere deference to executive branch authority—it does not hearten the prochoice movement. Lawsuits challenging the Utah and Guam abortion bans, suspended pending litigation, soon may give Souter an opportunity to vote on abortion.

Another case before the high court confirmed on a global basis the same policy upheld in *Rust.* In *Planned Parenthood Federation v. Agency for International Development,* the justices let stand without comment a lower court ruling upholding the ban imposed by the Reagan administration on financing for health care organizations abroad unless they promise not to use funds from any source to perform or discuss abortion.

Just When You Thought It Was Safe

Lest anyone thought the public relations experts at Hill and Knowlton had tamed every bishop's impulse to punish prochoice Catholic politicians, recent events put that idea to rest.

✦ Massachusetts Lt. Governor Paul Cellucci was banned from delivering the commencement address at Hudson Catholic High School, his alma mater, because of his prochoice views. Cellucci, who did not intend to discuss abortion, was invited by the school's senior class, of which his goddaughter was a member. But the invitation quickly was rescinded by Bishop Roberto Gonzalez, of western Boston, in an action approved by Cardinal Bernard Law. Not surprising, given Law's menacing comment on a Boston College speech by Planned Parenthood President Faye Wattleton. Wattleton was invited by a minority student group at the Catholic college to speak as a successful professional, without touching on abortion. Law expressed disappointment at seeing "a noble academic institution wrap itself in the shroud of death."

✦ In Montana, State Rep. Vivian Brooke saw a letter sent by Bishop Elden Curtiss of Helena to her parish priest which says Brooke should not take part in church activities until she is "reconciled" with church teachings on abortion. Brooke testified recently in favor of state legislation that would have codified *Roe v. Wade.* She also organized Montana Catholics for a Free Choice a year and a half ago and has received statewide press coverage for her efforts.

✦ Politicians are not the only targets. Georgetown University's February decision approving G.U. Choice as a student group drew a protest from Cardinal James Hickey, Archbishop of Washington. G.U. Choice is an educational organization dedicated to creating opportunities for students to learn about issues in the debate over choice. The university's approval, a watershed for Catholic colleges, affords G.U. Choice a mailbox and access to vans, facilities' space and funds. Although Georgetown reaffirmed its opposition to abortion at the same time that it approved the group, Hickey protested this academic freedom in his backyard. To no avail, he called on Georgetown to disown the group and declared the decision "inconsistent with the aims of an institution of higher learning that has a Catholic identity." A group of antichoice Georgetown students, faculty, and alumni plans to initiate a suit under canon law to fight the G.U Choice approval.

Contraceptive Boom

Birthrates are declining in every major region of the world as more and more couples in developing nations use contraceptives, the United Nations has reported.

The rate of contraceptive use in developing countries has risen from less than 10 percent of couples in the 1960s to 45 percent during the 1980s and 51 percent today, the UN said. Women in developing countries, who once had an average of six children, now have four. The East Asian birthrate dropped most sharply. During the first half of the 1960s, the rate was 6.1 births over each woman's lifetime; the rate dropped to 2.7 births during the latter half of the 1980s. In Africa, where contraceptive use is lowest, birth rates are highest—currently 6.2 births per woman, down slightly since the early 1960s.

In the United States, the good news is that the abortion rate is down 6 percent, the Alan Guttmacher Institute (AGI) reports in a study comparing 1980 and 1987 data. The bad news is that pregnancy and abortion rates have risen among teenagers younger than 15 and older minority teenagers.

In addition, the decline in the overall abortion rate may reflect a decrease in availability, not demand. For one thing, AGI noted, the ebbing abortion rate is not matched by any drop in the rate of unwanted pregnancies; either more women want to carry pregnancies to term, or more are forced to. In South Dakota, which had two abortion providers in 1985 and only one in 1987, the abortion rate dropped 14 percent, AGI said.

From 29.3 abortions per 1,000 American women in 1980, the rate dropped to 26.9 abortions in 1987. (AGI reports this as a 6 percent drop after controlling for changes in age, race and marital status within the population.) For teens younger than 15, the rate increased by nearly 18 percent, rising to 9.9 per 1,000 young women.

About-Face on Abortions for Military Women

Challenging a Pentagon policy in effect for the past three years, the House has voted to allow military women and dependents overseas to obtain abortions at their own expense at military health facilities. The Senate, which endorsed such legislation last year, is expected to follow suit. But the provision cleared the House by a narrow margin, 220-208, and would need a miracle to survive President Bush's promised veto. For now, it seems, many military women seeking to exercise their rights under the Constitution they defend will continue to face a choice between illegal abortions and travel expenses that can exceed $2,000.

Long Gestation for Pastoral on Women, Encyclical on Life

Several U.S. bishops at a Vatican meeting in late May heard an earful about the pastoral on women that American bishops have been drafting for years. Providing the critique were bishops from other continents. The American bishops said in a news conference that their colleagues abroad fear that the use of public consultation in developing pastorals might weaken church authority. Some bishops also felt their American colleagues were overemphasizing the equality of the sexes, and they countered the American request that the Vatican consider ordaining women as deacons. The pastoral seems destined to please no one, already having disappointed many American Catholic women. The first draft, issued in 1988, suggested new consideration of the church's teaching against contraception and refusal to ordain women priests. The second retreated on the birth control issue but urged women's admission to leadership positions not requiring ordination. Last year, the American bishops indefinitely postponed a final vote on the third version.

Pope John Paul II's encyclical on human life, whose release was expected last year, also remains on the drawing board. At a consistory in April, several bishops challenged the theological basis of the document in progress. The bottom line is not at issue, however. As the consistory came to a close, the cardinals urged the Pope to produce an encyclical affirming the "sacred inviolability of human life . . . which today is directly threatened from its very beginnings because of the spread of abortion." At the same meeting, Cardinal Joseph Ratzinger, head of the Congregation for the Doctrine of Faith, reiterated the church's opposition to contraception as a means to end abortion.

Between Fathers and Fetuses:
The Social Construction of Male Reproduction and the Politics of Fetal Harm

Cynthia R. Daniels

In contemporary American political discourse, "crack babies" have been treated as *filius nullius*—as if they had no biological fathers. With no link between fathers and fetuses, no inheritance of harm could be attributed to the father's use of drugs. The absence of fathers in debates over drug addiction and fetal harm has had profound consequences for women, for it has dictated that women alone bear the burden and blame for the production of "crack babies."

Since at least the late 1980s, and in some cases far earlier, studies have shown a clear link between paternal exposures to drugs, alcohol, smoking, environmental and occupational toxins, and fetal health problems. Yet men have been spared the retribution aimed at women. In fact, while women are targeted as the primary source of fetal health problems, reports of male reproductive harm often place sperm at the center of discourse as the "littlest ones" victimized by reproductive toxins, somehow without involving their male makers as responsible agents.

Scientific research linking reproductive toxins to fetal health problems reflects deeply embedded assumptions about men's and women's relation to reproductive biology. Critical analysis of the nature of fetal risks thus requires not only that the biology of risk be examined but that the "collective consciousness" that shapes scientific inquiry on gender difference be assessed. As Evelyn Fox Keller states, this consciousness is constituted by "a set of beliefs given existence by language rather than by bodies" (1992, 25). Debates over fetal risk are not so much about the prevention of fetal harm as they are about the *social production of truth* about the nature of men's and women's relation to reproduction.

Challenging the science and politics of fetal harm requires deconstructing the three symbols that constitute debate over fetal health risks: the "crack baby," "pregnant addict," and "absent father." These symbols "frame" political debate about addiction and fetal health, providing the lens through which science is developed and policy is made. As Kathy Ferguson has said of this process of framing, "The questions we can ask about the world are enabled, and other questions disabled, by the frame that orders the questioning. When we are busy arguing about the questions that appear within a certain frame, the frame itself becomes invisible; we become *enframed* within it" (Ferguson 1993, 7; emphasis in original; also see Fraser 1989).

In debates over fetal harm, this process of framing takes place in many social locations: in science labs, where the priorities of research are defined; in editorial rooms, where reporters decide which news warrants coverage and what slant to take on stories; and in courts and legislatures, where decisions are made regarding the definition of and culpability for social problems. As Paula Treichler has argued, contests over meaning—over the terms of political debate—have significance not just because they help to determine the distribution of material resources but because they legitimate the disproportionate power of actors to define (or contest) social reality (1990, 123).

My purpose in this article, therefore, is not simply to question the causality of fetal harm but to make visible the frame that has constructed understandings of causality. Science informed by gender myth is not just empirically suspect, but is politically loaded. That is, it helps to produce public health policies that target women and absolve men from culpability for fetal harm. This process is deeply racialized as well as gendered. As Mary Poovey has argued, ideological formulations of gender are "uneven" in the sense that they hold different implications for those positioned differently within the social formation (1988, 3). In similar context, the science and politics of fetal risks have held far different consequences for Anglo-American than for African-American women in the United States. So, too, as fathers are drawn into the circle of fetal causality, it may well be low income African-American men who become the target of social and political retribution.[1]

In this article, I examine the cultural characterizations of sperm and male reproduction in science, news stories, and public policy that have shielded men from culpability for fetal health problems.[2] After a brief discussion of the social construction of maternity and paternity, I analyze the symbols of the "crack baby," "pregnant addict," and "absent father" as central to public discourse on fetal harm. Finally, I explore the range of complex questions about biological gender difference generated by the politics of fetal risks and the problematic nature of the idea of individual causality in discussions of fetal harm.

Questions about the nature of fetal hazards enrich and complicate discussions of gender difference and biological reproduction. To what extent is it possible or desirable to collapse all gender distinctions in procreation as socially and historically constructed? How are the critical links between fathers and fetuses to be recognized without undermining women's exclusive claims to their bodies? While the father-fetal connection is essential to discussions of fetal risk, it may complicate women's claim to reproductive choice in other contexts.

Social Constructions of Maternity and Paternity

Feminist scholars have well documented the ways in which motherhood, female reproduction, and pregnancy have been socially and historically constructed.[3] Particular attention has been paid to the maternal-fetal relationship by scholars such as Barbara Duden, Barbara Katz Rothman, Rosalind Petchesky, Sarah Franklin, and Valorie Hartouni. Yet historical and theoretical scholarship on the social construction of fatherhood and masculinity has only recently emerged.[4]

On one level, it is not surprising that scientists exploring the sources of fetal health problems would look first to women. The maternal-fetal relationship seems certain, clear, and direct. It is publicly visible, and it appears to be exclusive. Unlike paternity, maternity is unquestionable. By contrast, the link between fathers and fetuses is both less certain and less visible. Questions of causality for men appear more complicated because the link between fathers and fetuses must always pass through the female body.

Yet the connection between fathers and fetuses is obscured less by biology than by the social construction of procreation. Despite appearances, questions of causality are as complex for women as they are for men. The maternal-fetal body is socially and biologically permeable. Maternal and fetal health are deeply affected by a woman's access to social resources such as health care and food, by her exposure to environmental toxins, and by her relationships with her sexual partner, her family, and her community. While men's physical distance from gestation creates the illusion that men's relation to fetal health is tangential, in reality, a man's use of drugs or alcohol or his exposures to toxins long before conception can profoundly affect the health of the children he fathers.

In Western industrial cultures, notions of masculinity have been historically associated with the denial of men's physical vulnerabilities and needs and the projection of these characteristics onto the maternal body. Men's denial (or dismissal) of bodily risks has been a hallmark of masculine status in both politics (where the sacrifice of the body in war is seen as the highest form of political honor) and the workplace (where men ignore risks or sacrifice their bodies in the interest of supporting their families).[5] Acknowledging bodily risks undermines one essential element of Western masculinity and requires a recognition by men that they are indeed both vulnerable and, in some instances, impotent in the face of the natural, social, or political forces that place them at risk.

Debates over fetal harm have been constituted by the analytically distinct and antithetical categories of male virility and vulnerability. Men were assumed either to be invulnerable to harm from the toxicity of drugs, alcohol, and environmental and occupational hazards or to be rendered completely infertile by any vulnerability to risk. In particular, sperm that crossed the line from virile to vulnerable by being damaged by reproductive toxins were assumed to be incapable of fertilization. And the converse operated as well: men not rendered infertile by their toxic exposures were assumed to be immune from any other form of reproductive risk (such as genetic damage).

Social constructions of maternity, by contrast, have been firmly aligned with assumptions of women's vulnerability. The science of reproductive risks historically developed in response to women's occupational exposures, where it was assumed that the physical stress and toxic exposures of the workplace would result in the degeneration of women's reproductive systems. Protective labor law selectively exaggerated the vulnerabilities of white women to occupational hazards and virtually ignored risks to working women of color.[6] Until well into the twentieth century, science, policy, and law deeply reflected the association of maternity with vulnerability.

Feminists have successfully challenged this association in the fields of occupational and environmental health. Yet since the 1980s, assumptions of maternal vulnerability have been reconstructed around risks to the fetus mediated through the maternal body. The idea of women's "hypersusceptibility" to risk thus shifted from assumptions of women as victims to women as vectors of fetal risk (Kenney 1992; Blank 1993; Daniels 1993).

Accompanying this shift from maternal to fetal vulnerability has been the development of the metaphor of the "pregnant addict" as "antimother" in public discourse. The image of the pregnant addict has become a racialized and gendered "condensation symbol"—one that evokes a whole range of unspoken associations about women, motherhood, race, and sexuality.[7] As Wahneema Lubiano argues, "Categories like 'black woman,' 'black women,' or particular subsets of those categories, like 'welfare mother/queen,' are not simply social taxonomies, they are also recognized by the national public as stories that describe the world in particular and politically loaded ways—and that is exactly why they are constructed, reconstructed, manipulated, and contested. . . . They provide simple, uncomplicated, and often wildly (and politically damaging) inaccurate information about what is 'wrong' with some people" (1992, 330–31). Condensation symbols operate as a kind of public shorthand, suggesting related narratives that remain latent—reminders of associations that work best when not fully or explicitly articulated.

The category of the "pregnant addict" is thus saturated with social meaning. Drug-addicted women have become magnets for social anxieties produced by a whole range of social and political transformations. For those distressed by women's drift from "selfless motherhood," pregnant addicts represent women's refusal to postpone their momentary "pleasure" (addiction) for the interests of the fetus. For those concerned with racial order and welfare dependency, pregnant addicts represent female desire and reproduction out of control, with women of color producing "damaged" babies at the state's expense.[8] Contests over meaning—over the very existence, for instance, of a category of women who can be called "pregnant addicts" or of infants we can call "crack babies"—have powerful political significance for defining the nature and causes of fetal health problems.

The cultural associations of paternity with virility and maternity with vulnerability formed the context within which the symbols of the crack baby, pregnant addict, and absent father emerged at the center of debate over fetal hazards.[9]

"Crack Babies" and "Pregnant Addicts"

It is October 1996 and in South Carolina Cornelia Whitner is about to enter prison for an eight-year term for criminal child neglect for having a baby born with cocaine metabolites in its system. In Racine, Wisconsin, Deborah Zimmerman is the first woman in the United States charged with the attempted murder of her fetus for drinking alcohol during her pregnancy. She faces up to forty years in prison. And in Chesterfield, New Hampshire, Rosemarie Tourigny, who is twelve weeks pregnant, is charged with endangering the welfare of a child after police find that her blood alcohol level is two times the limit for drunken driving. Lester Fairbanks, the town's acting police chief, reported that he arrested Tourigny because, "She can pickle herself all she wants, but that child doesn't have the opportunity to decide whether it's going to be retarded or not. . . . Somebody has to have responsibility for her unborn child." Tourigny, the local paper reports, plans to have an abortion.[10]

The prosecution of pregnant women for fetal neglect and abuse first emerged during the 1980s and continues today. Media attention began to focus on babies affected by maternal drug use with the release of a study in 1988 by Ira Chasnoff, director of the National Association for Perinatal Addiction Research and Education (NAPARE), which reported that 375,000 babies were born every year "exposed to illicit drugs in the womb" (Chasnoff 1989, 208–10). The study was fundamentally flawed in a number of ways. Chasnoff's sample was biased by the fact that thirty-four of the thirty-six hospitals surveyed were public inner-city hospitals. The study made no distinction between a single use of illegal drugs and chronic drug addiction during pregnancy, and it did not document the actual effects of drug use on newborn infants.

The limitations of Chasnoff's study were never reported. Instead, the press picked up and exaggerated the study's findings, often reporting that 375,000 babies were born every year "addicted to cocaine" (Brody 1988a, 1; 1988b, C1; Stone 1989, 3). As the distinctions between drug use and abuse collapsed, the reported numbers of crack babies exploded. By 1990, news stories reported that one out of every ten children was born "addicted to crack cocaine" or damaged by women's use of drugs (Daniels 1993). By 1993, nine influential national daily newspapers had run more than 197 stories on pregnancy and cocaine addiction alone.[11]

The mind-set created by this public discourse encouraged physicians, nurses, and social workers to attribute many serious problems experienced by infants at birth to the use of drugs or alcohol by the child's mother, particularly in low-income inner-city neighborhoods.

Symptoms associated with "crack babies" ranged from very specific conditions that could, in fact, be tied to maternal drug use (such as drug withdrawal) to low birth weight, small head circumference, irritability, respiratory problems, gastrointestinal problems, and diarrhea—conditions that could easily be caused by poor nutrition or a host of environmental factors.[12] More highly controlled studies estimated that approximately 41,000 babies were born nationally with clear symptoms of drug-related health problems (such as drug withdrawal symptoms), a far cry from the 375,000 presented by NAPARE as having been exposed to drugs in the womb (Dicker and Leighton 1990). The results of these studies were never reported by the national press, just as the press rarely reports research showing little or no association between moderate drug and alcohol use and fetal health problems (Koren and Klein 1991).[13]

The sense of social distress created by images of addicted babies wired to tubes in hospital incubators fed a profound need to blame. Public concern over crack babies contains all of the characteristics of a response to plague—fueling the impulse of privileged populations to locate, target and contain one group as the primary source of contamination and risk (Mack 1991). As Linda Singer has observed in relation to the spread of AIDS, the epidemic "provides an occasion and rationale for multiplying points of intervention into the lives and bodies of populations" (1993, 117). The policy response to the plague narrative was to find a target population to blame, and poor inner-city women were the most obvious targets. Newspaper stories contributed to this impulse by presenting images of African-American women as virtual monsters, snorting cocaine on the way to the delivery room and abandoning horribly damaged babies in hospitals. In some instances, drug use was characterized as a form of child abuse in utero, where cocaine "literally batters the developing child" (see Brody 1988a, 1; Stone 1989, 3).

Criminal prosecutors responded to the sense of crisis by targeting pregnant women for prosecution. By 1993 at least two hundred, and some estimate up to four hundred, women had been charged with fetal drug delivery, fetal abuse, or manslaughter (in cases where pregnancy had ended in a stillbirth). Despite the fact that almost every case challenged in the courts has resulted in the dismissal or acquittal of charges against women, prosecutors continue to bring criminal charges against women they suspect of drug or alcohol use during pregnancy. To date, almost all of these cases have been brought against African-American women.[14]

What has been the response of state and federal public health agencies to women and fetal health? Public health departments have produced warning labels on wine, beer, and liquor bottles and cans and on cigarette packages and an avalanche of public notices about pregnancy and alcohol consumption for display in restaurants and bars. Such labels stigmatize women by perpetuating assumptions that only women are vulnerable to risk and that women, therefore, are the primary source of fetal harm. Men are left entirely out of the frame as social attention focuses exclusively on the maternal-fetal nexus.

By implying women's ignorance or ill intentions, public health warnings aimed at pregnant women legitimate an atmosphere that encourages public retribution against women by focusing exclusively on individual behavior and not on the social and political causes of low birth weight, fetal birth defects, or other health problems. Retribution is invited by the fact that public health

warnings aimed at men (e.g., for heart disease, high blood pressure cigarette smoking, and steroid use) focus on behaviors that cause harm to *self*, whereas messages aimed at women focus exclusively on women's harm to *others* (the fetus).

One New Jersey public health ad displays an image of a pregnant woman holding a drink and warns, "A pregnant woman never drinks alone."[15] Yet a pregnant woman also never drinks without the effects of her home, her job, and her physical, social, and political environment. Even symptoms specific to drug or alcohol abuse, such as drug withdrawal or fetal alcohol syndrome, are complicated by simple factors such as poor nutrition. For instance, one study of pregnancy and alcohol use (that controlled for age, smoking, drug abuse, reproductive history, medical problems, socioeconomic status, and race) found that women who consumed at least three drinks a day but ate balanced diets experienced a rate of Fetal Alcohol Syndrome (FAS) of only 4.5 percent, while women who drank the same amount and were malnourished had an FAS rate of 71 percent (Bingol et al. 1987). The study showed that poor nutrition is tied directly to wealth. It also demonstrated that FAS is a measure not only of maternal alcoholism but also of economic class. There has been no press coverage of this study.

Public campaigns to "stem the tide of crack babies" are clearly racialized, primarily targeting women of color in low-income communities. Scientific research has supported the racialized nature of debate by focusing studies heavily on drugs used most commonly in poor inner cities (such as crack) and not on substances most often abused by higher-income women (such as prescription drugs). Public health warnings typically silhouette African-American or Latina women and are often produced in Spanish and directed at inner-city neighborhoods. One giant billboard of a baby tied to tubes in an incubator literally hangs over the heads of women in an African-American Los Angeles neighborhood, with the message: "He couldn't take the hit. If you're pregnant, don't take drugs" (Mitchell 1991, B1).

While African-American women are most often subject to prosecution, the symbol of the pregnant addict acts as a metaphor for all women's drift from "selfless motherhood." Metaphors organize human understanding by linking the unfamiliar to the familiar, helping to place that which is inexplicable in some known context. A metaphor "says that something much more concrete and graspable . . . is equivalent to the essential elements in another situation we have difficulty in grasping" (Fernandez 1986, 8). As failed mothers, "pregnant addicts" stand at the extreme of a spectrum of bad motherhood. Whether it is in debates over abortion or over mothers who work too much, or over pregnancy and addiction, this spectrum is constituted by women's failure to subordinate their selfish interests to the needs of "born" and "unborn" children. This broader cultural context makes certain kinds of causal explanations seem more believable than others in the science and politics of fetal risks.

Counteracting the symbol of the pregnant addict/antimother requires breaking the exclusive connection between pregnant women and "crack babies." The circle of causality has widened since feminist advocates began influencing media coverage of the issue and news stories began suggesting the links between fetal health and the combined effects of poverty, addiction, and exposures to workplace and environmental toxins.[16]

But drawing fathers into the circle of causality, essential to deconstruction of the symbol of the pregnant addict, has proven more difficult. Both metaphorically and literally, fathers were absent from virtually all of the news stories on fetal health and addiction. The absence of fathers in news reports of crack babies was made easier to believe by the racial subtext of the story: African-American women are often characterized as abandoned, single mothers—women dangerously unconstrained by nuclear family relations.

The "absent father" came to represent not only men's physical distance from the out-of-wedlock child but also men's distance from fetal harm. Embedded in scientific research and newspaper and magazine stories were also assumptions about male reproduction that posed serious barriers to the father-fetal connection.

Virile Fathers and the "All or Nothing" Sperm Theory

Scientific literature on reproductive toxicity has traditionally dismissed the links between paternal use of drugs and alcohol (or exposure to occupational or environmental toxins) and harm to fetal health because it was assumed that damaged sperm were incapable of fertilizing eggs. Indeed, male reproductive success was defined as the ability to penetrate an egg. Because penetration was the measure of normalcy, those sperm that succeeded were assumed to be healthy. By defining male reproductive health along the principles of this "all or nothing" theory, most scientific studies until the late 1980s dismissed the possibility that defective sperm could contribute to fetal health problems. The "all or nothing" theory was based on certain culturally imbued assumptions about the reproductive process. As Emily Martin has so well documented, scientists characterized the egg as the passive recipient and the sperm as conqueror in the process of fertilization (1991).

Scientists also proposed the idea that there were two distinct kinds of sperm: abnormal "kamikaze" sperm, incapable of fertilization, and "egg-getters" (Parker 1970; Baker and Bellis 1988). In the kamikaze sperm model, British scientists Robin Baker and Mark Bellis claim that in studies of rats "some sperm sacrifice themselves on a kamikaze mission to further the success of their brothers" (as quoted by Small 1991, 50). As Baker explains, "Abnormal sperm put their misshapen heads together and entwine their deformed tails to form a barrier that keeps out sperm from other males." This "sperm plug," located at the entrance to the cervix, presumably forms after their normal comrades, or what Baker and Bellis call the "egg-getters" have entered, allowing them to pursue fertilization upstream undeterred by "rival sperm" (Small 1991, 50).[17] The kamikaze sperm theory helped to distance men from fetal harm by reinforcing the presumption that abnormal sperm are functionally incapable of fertilizing an egg.

The kamikaze thesis also reinforced the idea that sperm competition was an essential element of procreation. Proponents of sperm competition suggested that the sperm of one male engaged in "search and destroy" missions of the sperm of enemy males by using enzymes "loaded" on sperm heads in acts of "tactical chemical warfare" (Small 1991, 50). Sperm competition implied that weakened, abnormal sperm would be destroyed in this process and that only the most virile would survive.

The theory of sperm competition is also predicated on the idea that female infidelity is biologically founded and that only the healthiest sperm survive the competition initiated by the female: "Females mate with several males because this allows them to pit the sperm of different males against each other in their reproductive tracts. In this way, they ensure that they are fertilized by

the best-quality sperm" (Mason 1991, 29; Bellis and Baker 1990).[18]

Articles on male infertility in popular science magazines, such as *Discover*, have also characterized the process of fertilization as a heroic achievement for the sperm and an act of passivity for the egg. Sperm require a distinct kind of virility to make it on the trip: "During the final moment of ejaculation, when catapulted forward at speeds up to 200 inches per second, sperm undergo intense shearing forces that could rip them apart," reports a 1991 story titled "Sperm Wars" (Small 1991, 51).

Carol Cohn has documented the extensive use of sexual metaphors in military planning for nuclear war (1990). The converse is also true: war metaphors abound in descriptions of sexual reproduction. Sperm "navigate" toward the cervix and "speed through the fallopian tubes" to pursue the "waiting egg." They then "fire their penetrating enzymes" into the outer layers of the egg in preparation for fertilization. The sperm then "bores in," and the egg "slams shut to all further intruders." As a caption exclaims under one photo of a sperm at the moment of penetration, "After an exhausting journey, this could be the winner" (Small 1991, 53). This is surely not a mission for the weak, misshapen, damaged, or otherwise feeble sperm. Abnormal sperm are simply "inadequate for conception" (49).[19]

The assumption that men harmed by toxic exposures would be rendered infertile deflected research away from the connections between fathers and fetal harm. As a result of the "virile sperm" theory of conception, scientific studies, until the late 1980s, focused almost exclusively on infertility as the primary outcome of hazardous exposures and the main source of reproductive problems for men. Male reproductive health was defined by "total sperm ejaculate" and healthy reproductive function was measured by "ejaculatory performance"—measures of volume, sperm concentration and number, sperm velocity and motility, sperm swimming characteristic, and sperm morphology, shape, and size (Burger et al. 1989).

Scientists who did try to pursue the father-fetal connection, such as Gladys Friedler at Boston University, who was the first to document a link in mice between paternal exposure to morphine and birth defects in their offspring in the 1970s, had difficulty funding their research or publishing their work. The significance of Friedler's work is that she found mutagenic effects from paternal exposures not only in the progeny of male mice exposed to morphine and alcohol but also in the second generation, or "grandchildren," of exposed mice. In all cases, she controlled for maternal exposures so that causality could be more clearly linked to paternal exposures.[20] Cultural constructions of male reproduction made Friedler's work simply unbelievable.

The Big Drop

A number of social and political events generated the first studies linking environmental exposures to male reproductive harm. The cultural construction of male reproduction was particularly evident in these early studies.

In 1979, scientific concern was raised by a study in Florida that documented a 40 percent overall drop in sperm count for men over the past fifty years. Scientists responded with "a flurry of sperm-count studies" about "the big drop" (Castleman 1993). By 1990, researchers at the University of Copenhagen had examined sixty-one sperm-count studies and determined that there had been, in fact, a 42 percent decline in sperm count over the past fifty years (Carlsen et at. 1992).[21]

Remarkably, in searching for a cause, scientists first focused on the fashion shift from boxer shorts to jockey shorts. Heat kills sperm, and because jockey shorts hold the testicles close to the body, they might decrease sperm production. They also suspected increased sexual activity. Men who engage in frequent sex have lower sperm counts than men who wait a number of days between sexual encounters. After controlling for both promiscuity levels and discounting the "jockey shorts" thesis, the Copenhagen researchers found an association between the increase in testicular cancer in key countries and substantial sperm-count declines. They speculated that the etiology of both could be found in exposures to environmental toxins (Carlsen et al. 1992).

In 1994 and 1995, public attention again focused on male susceptibility to harm after a number of studies suggested that male exposure to synthetic pesticides that "mimic" estrogens in the environment could be the cause of declining sperm counts. One report in particular documented a twenty-year drop in semen quality for men in Paris (Auger et al. 1995; Jensen et al 1995; Safe 1995). While controversy persists in the scientific community over the validity of such research, the popular press has given substantial coverage to the declining sperm-count story.[22]

Although still concentrating on male fertility, rather than on potential links between paternal exposure and fetal harm, sperm-count studies nevertheless suggested that male reproduction might be more vulnerable to hazards than previously assumed and that more research was needed on the potential links between toxic exposures and male health problems. But the links between paternal exposures and fetal health problems would not fully emerge until the assumption that damaged sperm were incapable of fertilization was thrown into question by a larger shift in the dominant paradigm of fertility and reproduction, a shift generated by the development of the "seductive egg" thesis.

The "Seductive Egg" Theory

The "seductive egg" theory originated from research on sea urchins. Unlike mammalian reproduction, sea urchins engage in "external fertilization"—sperm is released into the ocean where it must locate free-floating eggs in the sea. Scientists explained sperm's ability to find eggs of the same species by postulating that eggs release a substance or "chemical signal" that attracts sperm (Shapiro 1987). This process of sperm "chemotaxis" was then extended to research on human reproduction.

In 1991, research confirmed that when isolated in test tubes sperm swam toward the fluid surrounding the egg (Ezzell 1991). Major science magazines, such as *Nature, Science News, Science,* and *New Scientist*, reported the news in articles with titles such as "Does Egg Beckon Sperm When Time Is Right?" "Eggs Urge Sperm to Swim Up and See Them," and "Do Sperm Find Eggs Attractive?"[23] As *Science News* recharacterized the process of fertilization, "A human egg cell does not idle languidly in the female reproductive tract, like some Sleeping Beauty waiting for a sperm Prince Charming to come along and awaken it for fertilization. Instead new research indicates that most eggs actively beckon to would-be partners, releasing an as-yet-unidentified chemical to lure sperm cells" (Ezzell 1991, 214).

Newspapers such as the *New York Times* carried this characterization further, reporting that "fertile eggs secrete a compound that in test-tube experiments proved irresistible to sperm" (Angier 1992a, A19). These so-called seductive molecules send

"alluring chemical cues" to sperm. In addition, research suggested that "tiny hairs in the female reproductive tract move sperm along whether they are healthy or defective" (Blakeslee 1991, A1).

Emily Martin has noted that scientists confronted with this new evidence in the late 1980s vacillated between a model that emphasized the egg as seductress and the more mutual paradigm of sperm-egg fusion (1991). In either case, the sperm takes on a less aggressive role in the process of fertilization. The fusion model is devoid of (most of) the human agency imparted to eggs and sperm in traditional descriptions, calling instead for a characterization that relies on a simple chemical process.

In 1992, the *Los Angeles Times* reported the sperm-egg fusion model in this way: "Fertilization is a delicate process that requires several distinct steps, many of them involving the zona pellucida, a protective coating that surrounds the egg. The sperm first binds to a protein on that coating, then a thin sac on the head of the sperm—called the acrosome—breaks open, releasing enzymes that dissolve the coating. The sperm wiggles through the coating to come into contact with the egg membrane. There, PH-30 causes the sperm membrane to fuse with the egg membrane and, in the key step in fertilization, the sperm's contents are inserted into the egg" (Maugh 1992, A3).

This is a far cry from the perception of sperm at war and one that had implications for more general arguments about the links between "weak" or "damaged" sperm and fetal health. While only virile sperm can "bore in," even weak sperm can "wiggle" enough to fertilize an egg. Sperm damaged by reproductive toxins might thus be capable of fertilization.

Changing characterizations of the process of fertilization thus created a new context (valid or not) for research supporting the link between paternal exposures and fetal harm. Yet a mutual picture of procreation did not necessarily lessen women's culpability for fetal harm. In the "aggressive egg" model, women were once again at fault for seducing if not "bad men." then at least "bad sperm." While potentially drawing men into the circle of causality with women, cultural constructions embedded in scientific magazines and newspaper stories continued to lay the blame at women's door. Yet by 1991, growing evidence clearly implicated men in fetal health problems.

The Evidence of Male-Mediated Developmental Toxicology

Male reproductive exposures are now proven or strongly suspected of causing not only fertility problems but also miscarriage, low birth weight, congenital abnormalities, cancer, neurological problems, and other childhood health problems (Davis et al. 1992, 289).

Because adult males continuously produce sperm throughout their lives, the germ cells from which sperm originate are continuously dividing and developing. Sperm take approximately seventy-two days to develop to maturity and then move for another twelve days through the duct called the epididymis, where they acquire the ability to fertilize an egg (Moore 1989).[24] During this developmental process, sperm may be particularly susceptible to damage from toxins since cells that are dividing are more vulnerable to toxicity than cells that are fully developed and at rest, as are eggs in the female reproductive system.

Studies of male reproductive health and toxicity have concentrated primarily on the effects of occupational and environmental exposures of men and less on the effects of what scientists refer to as men's "lifestyle factors" such as drinking, smoking, or drug use.[25]

A number of events triggered studies of male reproduction during the 1970s and 1980s.[26] In 1977, men working at an Occidental Chemical plant in Lathrop, California, noticed a pattern of sterility among their coworkers. In the 1950s, the company had actually funded research on the carcinogenicity and reproductive effects of the pesticide produced there, DBCP (dibromochloropropane), but had quietly shelved the research after findings demonstrated associations between DBCP exposures and reproductive effects in lab animals (Robinson 1991, xiii–xv). Later studies confirmed that the men's sterility was linked to their DBCP exposure, and the chemical was banned from further use in the United States. By 1980, researchers had documented not only sterility but also increases in spontaneous abortion resulting from paternal exposure to DBCP (Kharrazi, Patashnik, and Goldsmith 1980). Seventeen studies have now evaluated the impact of pesticides and herbicides on male reproduction and paternal-fetal health (Olshan and Faustman 1993, 195).

Other studies have analyzed the effects of occupational exposures on paternal-fetal health, many of which have found significant associations between paternal exposures and fetal health problems. Paints, solvents, metals, dyes, and hydrocarbons have been associated with childhood leukemia and childhood brain tumors (Olshan and Faustman 1993, 196). Thirty-nine studies have examined the relationship between occupational exposures and spontaneous abortion. Toluene, xylene, benzene, TCE (trichloroethylene), vinyl chloride, lead, and mercury have all been associated with increased risks of spontaneous abortion (Lindbohm et al. 1991; Savitz, Sonnenfeld, and Olshan 1994).[27]

In analyses by occupation, janitors, mechanics, farmworkers, and metalworkers have been reported to have an excess of children with Down's syndrome (Olshan and Faustman 1993, 196). One study of 727 children born with anencephaly found correlations for paternal employment as painters (Colie 1993, 7). Painters and workers exposed to hydrocarbons have also been shown to have higher rates of children with childhood leukemia and brain cancer (Savitz and Chen 1990). More than thirty studies have examined the relationship between paternal occupation and childhood cancer (Holly et al. 1992; Olshan and Faustman 1993, 197).

By far, the greatest public concern over male reproductive toxicity has centered around men's wartime exposure to toxic chemicals. Vietnam veterans concerned about the effects of the herbicide Agent Orange called for studies on links between male exposures during the war and childhood diseases of their offspring. A 1980 study of more than five hundred men indicated that men who showed signs of toxic exposure to dioxin (TCDD) in Agent Orange had twice the incidence of children with congenital anomalies than men without symptoms (Stellman and Stellman 1980, 444).[28] Although the U.S. Congress commissioned a study of Agent Orange effects in 1991, the study was not released until 1996. While heated controversy persists in the scientific community over the legitimacy of associations between Vietnam War exposures and reproductive health problems (see Colie 1993, 6), the 1996 report sponsored by Congress does affirm the strong possibility of associations between dioxin exposures and birth defects for Vietnam veterans (Friend 1996, A1; Nesmith 1996, A14. *Wall Street Journal* 1996, B5).

In the mid-1990s, chemical exposures in the Persian Gulf War again fueled controversy over the possibility of male-mediated birth defects (Serrano 1994; Moehringer

1995, A3). To date, no systematic studies of paternal-fetal effects from Gulf War exposures have been completed. Despite growing public concern over the issue, government officials have argued that "the studies performed to date are unfinished, cannot be generalized, or are too weak methodologically to demonstrate convincingly that there are or are not abnormally high reproductive dysfunction rates among Persian Gulf veterans and their families" (as quoted by Serrano 1994, A12). Nevertheless, news stories have specifically covered the association between Gulf War exposures and childhood diseases in the offspring of veterans (Serrano 1994; Moehringer 1995, A3) and often mention the possibility of birth defects and reproductive problems in the context of reporting more general health problems experienced by veterans in stories on "Gulf War Syndrome" (Reynolds 1994, A11; Ritter 1994, A1).

Whether addressing occupational, environmental, or "lifestyle" exposures, there are problems with many of the studies on male-mediated teratogenicity. It is difficult, for instance, to specify the nature of men's exposures to toxic substances at work or in war. It is also difficult to get a sample size large enough to provide conclusive results, especially for conditions that are typically rare in children. And, as in all epidemiological studies, it is difficult to control for confounding factors, such as the effects of multiple chemical exposures and alcohol or drug use.

While the problem of confounding variables is common to all epidemiological studies of reproductive toxicity, for cultural reasons scientists are more acutely aware of these when studying men. For instance, studies of paternal effects are routinely criticized for not controlling for maternal exposures, while studies of women virtually never control for the exposures of fathers.

Studies on men's occupational and environmental exposures rarely control for men's use of drugs or alcohol. Studies that do focus on the effects of lifestyle factors on men's reproduction are criticized for not controlling for men's workplace exposures, while studies of women and drug use do not control for women's occupational exposures.

Still, even given the limitations of scientific knowledge, it is clear that men can pass on genetic defects to children. Down's syndrome and Prader Willi syndrome have been passed to children through the paternal germ cell. The question is whether similar processes can occur when environmental exposures cause genetic mutations in sperm (Colie 1993).

The biological processes of male-mediated teratogenicity have also been examined through clinical studies on animals and studies of the effect of toxic exposures directly on sperm. All of the problems of confounding variables associated with epidemiological research can be avoided by conducting animal studies. The earliest studies of the effects of illicit drugs, for instance, were conducted on mice.

What is the evidence of paternal-fetal effects of drugs, alcohol, and cigarette smoking?

Smoking

In a study of more than fourteen thousand birth records in San Francisco, researchers found associations between paternal smoking and various birth defects, including cleft lip, cleft palate, and hydrocephalus (Savitz, Schwingle, and Keels 1991). Significant associations also have been found between paternal smoking and brain cancer in children and between paternal smoking and low birth weight.[29] In addition, cotinine, a metabolite of nicotine, has been found in seminal fluid, although researchers are unsure what effect this might have on fetal health (Davis 1991a, 123; Davis et al. 1992, 290).

Bruce Ames of the University of California, Berkeley, has suggested that the link between smoking and birth defects could be due to smokers' low levels of vitamin C. Vitamin C helps to protect sperm from the genetic damage caused by oxidants in the body, yet the vitamin is depleted in the body of cigarette smokers. Ames found that men with low levels of the vitamin experienced double the oxidation damage to the DNA in their sperm (Schmidt 1992, 92).

Alcohol Use

Paternal alcohol use has been found to cause low birth weight and an increased risk of birth defects. In animal studies, paternal exposure to ethanol produced behavioral abnormalities in offspring. Alcoholism in men is known to produce testicular atrophy. Case reports suggest an association between paternal drinking and "malformations and cognitive deficiencies" in children of alcoholic men.[30]

Cocaine and Other Illicit Drugs

A 1990 study found that cocaine increased the number of abnormal sperm and decreased sperm motility in men. In a 1991 clinical study, Ricardo Yazigi, Randall Odem, and Kenneth Polakoski found that cocaine could bind to sperm and thereby be transmitted to the egg during fertilization. Reports of cocaine "piggybacking" on sperm have led to controversy in the scientific community over whether this could contribute to birth defects (Brachen et al. 1990; Yazigi, Odem, and Polakoski 1991). In animal studies, opiates (such as morphine and methadone) administered to father, but not mothers, have produced birth defects and behavioral abnormalities in the first *and* second generations of the fathers offspring

(Friedler and Wheeling 1979; Friedler 1985). Drug addiction in men using hashish, opium, and heroin has been shown to cause structural defects in sperm (El-Gothamy and El-Samahy 1992). Despite the limitations of scientific research on male reproduction, few scientists question that biological mechanisms exist for establishing links between paternal and fetal health.

The following sections analyze the coverage of research on male-mediated fetal risks by three different kinds of print media: popular scientific magazines, magazines for general readership, and nine influential U.S. daily newspapers.[31]

Male Reproduction in Popular Discourse–The Generation of Sperm Personhood

As scientific research began to explore the possibility that sperm could be damaged by toxic exposures, sperm began to take on distinctive personality traits in stories in popular magazines and newspapers reporting scientific research on male reproductive hazards.[32] Despite newspapers' claims to a higher level of "objectivity" in reporting, many stories in newspapers share a language and imagery common in popular magazine articles on male reproductive toxicity. Sympathy for sperm damaged by reproductive toxicity was specifically generated by the personification of sperm.

Sperm were characterized as the "little ones" produced by men. One magazine article tells the story of "Harry" as he tries to overcome an infertility problem by improving his diet and exercising regularly: "Harry's attitude was that . . . the condition of his whole body *ought* to affect the condition of the little ones it produced" (Poppy 1989, 69). Sperm development here becomes a distinctive form of male gestation:

"For seventy-four days or so, these cells lie passive in their tubules, growing quietly. Then the young sperm move along to the epididymis, a comma-shaped coil of tubing behind the testicle that would stretch for twenty feet if straightened out. For twelve days they finish maturing and gain the ability to swim" (69). In this story of gestation, the physiology of the male body is reconstructed as well: "The two testicles at the heart of a man's hopes each contain about seven hundred feet of tightly coiled seminiferous tubes" (69).[33]

Sperm also have distinctive personal traits. They have heads (sometimes more than one) and tails (sometimes misshapen). Some are "vigorous, well-aimed swimmers," while others "swim in dizzy circles and never head in the right direction" (Small 1991, 49). Sperm voyage, travel, and navigate. One scientific study reported that sperm even have a sense of smell and that "swimming sperm navigate toward a fertile egg by detecting its scent" (Angier 1992a, A19; also see Friend 1992, A1).

Publications as diverse as *Cell, Esquire,* and the *New York Times* share accounts that impart a consciousness to sperm. The "kamikaze" and "sperm competition" theories of Bellis and Baker suggest that sperm collaborate and compete as fraternity "brothers" or "enemies." One article in the *New York Times* reporting Bellis and Baker's research suggested that kamikaze sperm are "self-sacrificing" as they "commit suicide" for the good of the group (Browne 1988, C6).[34] In part, this characterization was generated directly from reports in scientific journals. For instance, in an article in *Cell,* Bennett Shapiro suggests that sperm face three existential dilemmas in reproduction—whether to swim, whether to pursue an egg, and whether to fertilize an egg, all of which shorten the "life span" of the sperm (1987). Popularized accounts of

Shapiro's theory capitalized on his imagery, suggesting that human sperm were faced with the ultimate question, "Do I give up my autonomy and individuality for the chance to fertilize an egg, or do I spurn responsibility and lead an independent and happy-go-lucky—but meaningless—existence?" (*Discover* 1987, 10–11).

With sperm personified as such, toxins that could damage male reproductive health are cast not as an assault on fetal health but as an assault against man's sperm. It turns out, one story reports, that "sperm is more fragile and potentially more dangerous than previously thought" (Merewood 1991, 54). In fact, it is the fragility of sperm—the literal and metaphorical blurring of the distinction between the vulnerable and the virile—that precisely makes sperm "more dangerous."

The visual images accompanying popular magazine stories reinforce sympathy for the sperm (and men) as victims. In 1991, *Health* magazine ran a story titled "Sperm under Siege" with visuals of bottles of chemicals and alcohol pointed threateningly at a group of sperm circling around a center target (Merewood 1991). A story in *Parenting* magazine presented an image of a man and his sperm huddled under an umbrella as chemical bottles, beer cans, and martini glasses rained down on them (Black and Moore 1992). One might expect men and their sperm to be characterized as victims in cases where men were involuntarily exposed to toxins at work, but both of these stories focused on men's (presumably voluntary) use of drugs and alcohol.

Although eggs have been characterized as "aggressors," stories of reproductive toxicity do not portray eggs as the victims of toxicity. While a *New York Times* story on women and drugs describes cocaine "repeatedly battering the child in utero," a *U.S. News and World Report* story on men and toxins describes sperm as "battered by chemicals" (Brody 1988b, C1; Schmidt 1992, 96). Of the stories in popular magazines on the effects of drugs or alcohol on male reproduction, only one contained images of men and babies, and this was of a father and healthy child with the subtitle, "The importance of the father in making healthy babies has been under appreciated" (Schmidt 1992, 96).[35] Only once the frame shifts to stories of soldiers affected by wartime exposures do images of sick children (and their mothers) begin to emerge in news coverage.

Newspaper Coverage of Male Reproductive Hazards

What kind of newspaper coverage has been generated by research on men and fetal health? Of the nine national daily newspapers I surveyed—those that often define the "news agenda" for local media coverage—only seventeen stories since 1985 have reported possible connections between all paternal exposures and fetal health effects (five on chemical wartime exposures in Vietnam and the Persian Gulf, five on cocaine, four on smoking, two on workplace exposures, and one article covering all causes).[36] By contrast, since 1985 these papers have run more than two hundred stories on pregnant women and cocaine addiction alone.

Since 1985, the *New York Times* has run a total of three stories and one op-ed piece on the links between paternal exposures and fetal health effects: one focused on the impact of cocaine, one on paternal smoking, and two on men's occupational exposures.[37] There has been no *New York Times* coverage of the links between paternal alcohol consumption and fetal health. By contrast, the *New York Times* alone has run at least twenty-seven stories on pregnant women and crack.[38]

Even in newspaper stories that address the connection between paternal exposures and fetal health, certain patterns of reporting emerge that function to reduce male culpability for fetal harm.

First, while men are absent from stories on maternal-fetal harm, *women are always present* in news stories on paternally mediated risks. In none of the stories are fathers solely responsible for fetal harm. In all of the stories that draw connections between paternal exposure to drugs, alcohol, or smoking and fetal harm, maternal exposure was also mentioned as a possible source of harm. In this way, male responsibility is always shared with women. One *New York Times* article modifies masculine responsibility in the following way: "If the effect is proven true, cocaine-using fathers may have to share more of the responsibility with cocaine-using mothers for birth defects in children" (1991b, C5). The same article further implicates women by suggesting that "sperm could pick up the drug in the reproductive tract of a cocaine-using woman after intercourse, opening the way for damage to the fetus by that route." A *Chicago Tribune* article reviewing a range of paternally mediated risks concludes that "women no longer have to carry the full responsibility for bearing a healthy infant" and that these "new data suggest that both may be responsible" (Merewood 1992, sec. 6, 8). Like child care and dishwashing, the man of the nineties now shares responsibility for reproductive risks with women. Particularly in discussions of drug-related risks, the presence of the pregnant woman means that the father is never cast as the primary source of harm. No article suggests or implies that "drug-clean" women may produce harmed babies as a result of their partners' drug use.

As a result of the nature of the exposures, culpability is treated somewhat differently in stories regarding men's wartime exposures. In the context of both the Vietnam War and the Persian Gulf War, stories specifically addressing male-mediated harm always include images of mothers with their ailing children.[39] The fathers/soldiers and mothers/wives thus become joint victims of military irresponsibility.

Second, maternally mediated fetal risks are assumed to be certain and known. Evidence of male-mediated risks are often prefaced with statements such as: "While doctors are well aware of the effects that maternal smoking, drinking and exposure to certain drugs can have on the fetus, far less is known about the father's role in producing healthy offspring" (Merewood 1992, sec. 6, 8). *U.S. News and World Report* begins its article on paternal fetal harm, "It is common wisdom that mothers-to-be should steer clear of toxic chemicals that could cause birth-defects. . . . Now similar precautions are being urged on fathers-to-be" (Schmidt 1992, 92).

Third, research on men is always *qualified and limited.* A *Chicago Tribune* story on men's role in producing healthy babies, for instance, states, "Research like this may sound convincing, but Dr. David Savitz . . . warns that it's far too early to panic. 'We have no documented evidence that certain exposures cause certain birth defects,' he says" (Merewood 1992, sec. 8). An article in the *Atlanta Constitution* reports that "cocaine use in fathers is unlikely to cause the same problems in babies as cocaine use by their mothers, which include premature birth, an elevated risk of death, growth retardation and nerve and behavior problems." Still, the same article later states that "research on rodents indicates males exposed to cocaine are more likely to have offspring with nervous, hormonal or behavioral problems" (Perl 1991, F3). A *New York Times* story repeats the reservations of one researcher: "But epidemiological studies cannot prove cause and effect, said Dr. John Peters. . . . In real life, people are exposed sporadically to combinations of substances that might interact. . . . To show more dramatic associations, he said, scientists would need to study *hundreds of thousands of people over many years*" (Blakeslee 1991, A1; emphasis added). Yet there are no such studies of women. Similar reservations are common in stories regarding wartime exposures, suggesting that "infant deaths and birth abnormalities are in line with expected percentages in the general population" (Serrano 1994, A12).

Fourth, male culpability is further reduced by the fact that news articles on paternal exposures to illegal drugs are *always contextualized by reference to "involuntary" environmental and workplace exposures.* As in many of the stories in popular magazine articles, newspaper stories often refer to drug use, alcohol consumption, and smoking as "lifestyle factors" (Merewood 1992) and place these with a string of possible exposures including "pesticides and workplace chemicals" (see Blakeslee 1991; Merewood 1991). Even the newspaper stories reporting the "piggybacking" of cocaine on sperm suggest that workplace chemicals may "latch onto sperm" in the same way (Perl 1991, F3). All of this suggests the uncertainty of linking men's drug abuse to fetal harm and the difficulty of narrowing causality to illegal drug use. These are precisely the kinds of qualifications and complications absent from reporting on maternal drug use. Perhaps not surprising, while newspaper coverage of wartime exposures mentions confounding problems associated with men's multiple chemical or occupational exposures, rarely do such stories suggest that the etiology of birth defects might be traced to soldiers' drug use.

Fifth, in stories on paternally mediated harm from drugs, alcohol, or cigarette smoking, *the language and images of harmed children and "crack babies" are absent from stories on men.* A sterile scientific terminology is used to describe studies on paternal "lifestyle" exposures, with the language of "suffering crack babies" replaced by "damaged DNA," "abnormal offspring," and "genetic anomalies." One *New York Times* story linking vitamin deficiencies (produced by male cigarette smoking) with fetal damage reported: "The study demonstrated a direct relationship between a diet low in vitamin C and increased DNA damage in sperm cells. . . . Any damage to this genetic structure may predispose a man to having children with genetic anomalies" (1992, C12). After reporting that children of fathers who smoke have been found to be at increased risk for leukemia and lymphoma, the article ends with the recommendation of a physician that men who smoke "either modify their diets to include fruits and vegetables or take a vitamin C supplement each day." While sperm "delivers," "transports," or "carries" the drug to the egg in such stories, it never "assaults" the fetus as stories on drug use and women imply. In stories on drug addiction, smoking, and alcohol consumption, when the sperm is not presented as itself a victim, sperm acts as a shield for men—deflecting or capturing the blame that might otherwise be placed on the father.

Indeed, in newspaper stories on drugs, alcohol, and smoking, the only images to accompany these stories were photographs or cartoon images of sperm. Yet of the 853 column inches dedicated to pregnancy, alcohol, and drug abuse by the *New York Times* in one two-year period, almost two hundred column inches were taken up by images of crack babies and their drug-addicted mothers (Schroedel mid Peretz 1993).

This pattern of images changes in stories regarding men's wartime exposures. Here, images of mothers, fathers, and their children often accompany the text. Particularly in stories on "Gulf War babies" news stories often focus on the pain suffered by both mothers and fathers in facing childhood cancers or heart defects (Moehringer 1995). Yet such images, unlike those accompanying many stories on maternally mediated exposures, serve to focus blame not on fathers but on the irresponsibility of either foreign threats (e.g., Saddam Hussein) or U.S. government authorities.

Clearly, reporters play an important role in framing and interpreting stories and imparting meaning to scientific research. Science reporters often pick up stories from professional journals such as the *Journal of the American Medical Association* or the *New England Journal of Medicine*. But what is the source of the slant on the story?[40] The complex process of "framing" takes place at multiple levels. Clearly, science is skewed in terms of the kinds of questions and answers legitimated for research. The absence of research on men and fetal health, of course, precludes public knowledge of paternal-fetal risks, even in cases where the experience of men and women may suggest relations of causality, such as in the California DBCP case (see Robinson 1991).

Second, once research is initiated, embedded assumptions about gender may skew or color scientific methodology and the interpretation of findings, diminishing the importance of paternal-fetal associations. As Koren et al. have found, editors of science journals often play an important role in screening out reports that violate standards of scientific "believability" (1989). After scientific research makes it into print in professional science journals, newspaper reporters screen findings through the complex lens of social meanings they bring to

the research (see Tuchman 1978, 1983, 1993). In the phrasing of a question, in what is "taken for granted," the framing of a story takes place not at the level of individual "bias" or conscious intention but through what Stuart Hall calls the "logic of social processes." As Hall argues in relation to television broadcasting, "The ideology has 'worked' in such a case because the discourse has spoken itself through him/her [the broadcaster]. Unwittingly, unconsciously, the broadcaster has served as a support for the reproduction of a dominant ideological discursive field" (1982, 88).

In the case of fetal harm, that discursive field is constituted by language and imagery that exculpates men by making invisible the biological mechanisms of paternal-fetal harm. One *New York Times* story reports that early animal and human studies on male reproductive risks had been ignored "because scientists could not identify any possible biological mechanism to explain its findings" (Blakeslee 1991, A1). Yet it is not biology but the lens of male virility that has rendered the biological mechanisms of paternal-fetal risk invisible. A shift in scientific research—and in its wake, scientific reporting—thus requires not just the progress of science but also the transformation of the gendered lens through which evidence is perceived. For even when research implicates men, this lens continues to operate to limit and qualify the implications of damaging research.

As Evelyn Fox Keller has observed of this process, unarticulated gender assumptions affect not only the questions and methodologies of scientific research but also "what counts as an acceptable answer or a satisfying explanation" (1992, 31). As such, scientists who venture into delegitimated territory are met with skepticism and caution by colleagues, editors, and newspaper reporters alike.

Paternal Effects and "Political Correctness"

Evidence of paternal-fetal harm has generated virtual silence from public health authorities and the courts. In an editorial in *Reproductive Toxicology*, Anthology Scialli argues that the impulse to link paternal exposures with fetal effects is a result not of science but of "political correctness." "There has been no quarrel that testicular toxicants can produce fertility impairment, but paternally mediated effects on conceived pregnancies is a different matter altogether." He concedes that "several" studies on paternally mediated effects have been "nicely performed and reported," but taken as a "whole they are "difficult to interpret" (1993, 189). Of those who defend the evidence of paternal-fetal links, he concludes: "The people who make these accusations appear to believe that paternally-mediated effects *must* occur in humans, for the sake of fairness. . . . It is argued that because father and mother make equal genetic contributions to the conceptus, they must have equal opportunity to transmit toxic effects. Students of developmental biology understand that there is nothing equal about male and female contributions to development. . . . There are several million unequivocal examples of children damaged by intrauterine exposure to toxicants encountered by the mother during gestation. There are no unequivocal examples for paternal exposures" (189).

Yet except for those rare and tragic cases where women are exposed to substances, such as thalidomide, that cause severe, visible deformities, the question of causality remains as complicated for women as it is for men. The fact that even the chronic abuse of drugs and alcohol by men has been dismissed, while so much attention has focused on even the occasional use of drugs and alcohol by pregnant women, points to the clear ways in which gendered constructions shape both the science and policy of risk. Research that suggests any acceptance of moderate maternal drug or alcohol use comes dangerously close to threatening cultural investment in maternal self-abnegation.

Even researchers who accept the validity of evidence on male-mediated fetal risks are led to quite different social and political conclusions. The most direct recommendation comes from Bruce Ames of the University of California, Berkeley, who, rather than advocate altering male behavior or printing warning signs on cigarette packages, recommends that the U.S. government raise the standard for minimum daily requirements for vitamin C for all Americans to account for the reproductive effects of paternal smoking (Wright 1993, 10).

Even in cases where men are exposed to known reproductive hazards, scientists have been remarkably reluctant to recommend the most simple restrictions on men. Controversy still exists, for instance, over whether men who are undergoing chemotherapy should abstain from procreation during treatment. Cyclophosphamide, used during chemotherapeutic treatment, is a known female reproductive hazard, and rodent studies indicate it might cause miscarriage, birth defects, and childhood tumors in the children conceived by men during treatment. Yet at the first major medical meeting on male-mediated developmental toxins at the University of Pittsburgh in 1992, men were given "conflicting advice" about whether to postpone procreation during cancer treatment or "bank" sperm before treatment).

In addition, in 1992 the journal *Human Reproduction* published a recommendation stating that sperm saved in the early stages of chemotherapy was safe "based on the belief that since the drugs did not kill sperm . . . the sperm were healthy (Miller 1992, 5).

Yet others argued that sperm that survive therapy may be more likely to carry genetic defects. One researcher simply recommended that men use condoms to protect their partners during treatment. But other scientists at the conference were wary of "confusing the public with the results of animal studies that may not apply directly to humans." "Speculation tends to get us into trouble" stated Jan Friedman, a clinical geneticist and specialist in birth defects (Miller 1992, 5).

Clearly, it is not the nature of the risk as much as the symbolic construction of the population targeted that has determined the public response to fetal harm.

Blame and Absolution: Public Policy and the Targeting of Women

When science fails to produce clear explanations for a risk to human health, the public response often results in an impulse to blame a target group in order to reestablish a sense of order and social control. But it must be remembered that who is absolved in this process is as important as who is blamed. Absolution is a privilege of those who have successfully distanced themselves from fetal risks. But this distance may be determined more by the social and political power of those who can place themselves outside the frame of causality than by true evidence of risk.

Public policies convey powerful messages about men and women. The pregnant addict has come to symbolize one of the newest political enemies on the American political frontier. Murray Edelman has described the idea of "political enemies" as those "characterized by an inherent trait or set of traits that marks them as evil, immoral, warped, or pathological and therefore a continuing threat regardless of what course of action they pursue, regardless of whether they win or lose in any particular

encounter, and even if they take no political action at all" (1988, 67).

The symbols used to frame understandings of addiction and fetal risk are important not only because they misdirect science, policy, and law but because, as they are currently constructed, they make it possible—and even incite the public—to target women and exculpate men for fetal harm. Anne Schneider and Helen Ingram have noted that in this process, state officials are likely to provide beneficial policy to powerful, positively constructed groups and to devise punitive punishments for those who are negatively constructed (1993). What are the specific conditions that have made the punitive targeting of women possible?

Targetability requires, first, the ability to *isolate* the target population—to draw sharp distinctions between those who are "clean" and those who are "corrupt." Research that focuses so heavily on the impact of crack cocaine on pregnancy makes it easier to distinguish between the clean and the corrupt for women.[41] By contrast, the scientific research on men focuses primarily on workplace and environmental toxins and only secondarily on smoking, alcohol consumption, and drug use. Links between fathers and fetuses therefore potentially implicate not a narrow category of men but men as a class for fetal health problems. Indeed, it seems likely that if and when men do become the targets of blame for fetal health problems, the focus may well be first on inner-city men of color who use crack cocaine.

Second, the symbolic frame used to shape science and policy makes it easier to target women as it casts them as violating dominant norms of acceptable social behavior and thus as acceptable objects of coercive state regulation. Since smoking and drinking have been culturally associated with masculinity, this hardly seems like a violation of acceptable behavior for men. Moreover, men as workers or as soldiers (in the case of Agent Orange or Gulf War exposures) are at risk as a result of fulfilling, not neglecting, their obligations as "good fathers" and citizens. Men are put at risk not by their own misbehavior but by the irresponsibility of others. The discourse of victimization thus pushes women to the center and men to the periphery as the cause of fetal harm.

Conclusion

The social meaning imparted to female gestation of the fetus has created the illusion that the connection between the mother and fetus is not only direct but exclusive. After the "fleeting" contribution of the father, women are assumed to be the primary sources of both fetal health and fetal harm. But this is clearly a social and political, as well as a biological, construction. Deconstructing the myths of maternity and paternity that have so far informed debates over fetal risk requires drawing men into reproduction. Yet there is an irony embedded in the politics of fetal harm. Male power in reproduction has often centered around men's claim of ownership over the fetus. In questions of fetal harm, just the opposite is true, for in this case, men's power is enhanced by their distance from the fetus. Ironically, there are similarities in the arguments made by those who defend women's right to reproductive choice and those who argue that men are more distant from fetal health problems. Both stress the significance of the fact that the fetus is a part of the pregnant woman's body. Both stress that only women mix their "body-labor" with the fetus in reproduction. From the pro-choice point of view, because gestation imposes a unique set of burdens on women, women alone must be granted the immutable right to consent to (or reject) pregnancy (McDonagh 1993).

But from the point of view of debates over fetal harm, gestation also means that there is an additional avenue for fetal harm not shared in the same way with men. It is clearly true that men's actions can have a profound effect on fetal health—both before conception and throughout pregnancy. But while the comparability of paternal and maternal sources of fetal harm is recognized, the distinction between men's and women's roles in procreation must not be collapsed. The recognition of this difference is essential both to women's right to choice and to the true protection of maternal and fetal health.

Science and media representations driven by assumptions of maternal-fetal vulnerability, on the one hand, and male virility, on the other, have led to both the negative targeting of women and the systematic neglect of men's health needs. Recognition of male vulnerability is thus essential to the science and politics of fetal harm. Yet it is important that, in the process of responding to political risks, the discussion not retreat into a position that denies the significance of gender difference and, in doing so, reinstitutes the essentialized invulnerable male body as referent for public policy and law.

Ultimately, talk about comparability of male and female risks perpetuates the misguided focus on individual causality and directs attention away from the more profound social determinants of parental and fetal health—good nutrition, good health care, and a clean and safe environment. Until the symbols of the crack baby, pregnant addict, and absent father are deconstructed in the public mind, pregnant women—and not poverty, poor health, violence, the disease of addiction, or irresponsibility on the part of men—will continue to be seen as the greatest threat to fetal health.

Notes

1. Challenging the methodological individualism of scientific research on fetal health problems, which focuses so heavily on "aberrant" individual behavior and too easily dismisses the social causes of fetal health problems, is thus equally essential to challenging the racial and gender politics of fetal harm.

2. A more detailed discussion of the rise of the concept of fetal rights and fetal protectionism can be found in Daniels 1993.

3. See, e.g., Petchesky 1987; Eisenstein 1988; Rothman 1989; Laqueur 1990; Franklin 1991; Martin 1991; Hartouni 1992; and Duden 1993.

4. For instance, see Brown 1988; Laqueur 1990; Ruddick 1990; Ferguson 1993; Lerman and Ooms 1993; and Shanley 1993.

5. For an interesting discussion of manhood and politics, see Brown 1988.

6. Baer 1978; Kessler-Harris 1982; Lehrer 1987; Daniels 1991, 1993.

7. The term *condensation symbol* is adopted from Edelman 1988, 73. For elaborations of the racialized construction of womanhood and maternity, see Lubiano 1992; and Crenshaw 1993.

8. The ideological construction of maternity/femininity and the pattern of public debates over fetal harm also reflect the history of medical discourse on women and public health risks. Particularly in relation to sexually transmitted diseases, and now in relation to women and AIDS, women are cast not as the victims of harm but as the vectors of risk for innocent children and men (Women and AIDS Book Group 1990; Corea 1992).

9. A more detailed analysis of the social and political construction of these concepts can be found in my longer treatment of this issue in Daniels 1993, where I analyze the scientific media, policy, and legal discourses surrounding the emergence of the idea of fetal protectionism and fetal rights.

10. Information on these cases is derived from Cornelia Whitner v. State of South Carolina, On Writ of Certiorari, Appeal from Pickens County, South Carolina Supreme Court Opinion No. 24468, July 15, 1996; State of Wisconsin v. Deborah J. Zimmerman, State of Circuit Court Branch 5, Racine County, File No. 96-CF-525, September 18, 1996; and Vigue 1996. For coverage of the Zimmerman case, also see O'Neill, Eskin, and Satter 1996.

11. These calculations are based on a review of the on-line ProQuest newspaper index. The nine newspapers on which my research is based are the *New York Times, Wall Street Journal, Washington Post, Christian Science Monitor, Los Angeles Times, Chicago Tribune, Boston Globe, Atlanta Constitution/Atlanta Journal,* and *USA Today.*

12. For a complete discussion of the symptoms associated with fetal cocaine exposure, see Zuckerman 1991, 26–35.

13. There are two stages to the "screening" process by which research makes it into the press. First, science journals review, accept, or reject reports of findings. Koren et al. have found a predisposition by professional scientific journals against reporting negative (or "null") associations between drug use and fetal risks (1989). Once scientific reports began to appear in journals, Koren and Klein 1991 found a similar predisposition by the press against reporting negative findings. Null associations are thus doubly burdened by the editorial processes of review in both journals and newspapers.

14. Personal interview with Lynn Paltrow, August 6, 1993, at the Center for Reproductive Law and Policy, New York City. Total numbers are now difficult to calculate since so many women are charged by local prosecutors who do not report their cases to any central, national source. For documentation of the first 167 cases, see Paltrow 1992.

15. Public health ad by the N.J. Perinatal Cooperative, 1993.

16. The precise causes of fetal health problems are immensely complicated. A woman living in the inner city is likely to have had little health care before she became pregnant and poor prenatal care as well. If she is employed in a hospital, she might be exposed to radiation, chemotherapeutic drugs, viruses, or sterilants, such as ethylene oxide. If she works in a laundromat or dry cleaners, she might be exposed to solvents, cleaners, or excessive heat. If she works in a factory, she might be required to do heavy lifting, or she might be exposed to toxic chemicals or the dust of heavy metals. If she lives in a low-income neighborhood, she is likely to be exposed to lead in her water or in the dust from old paint. She is also more likely to be the victim of violent crime. For information on reproductive toxicity at work, see Massachusetts Coalition for Occupational Safety and Health 1992.

17. Bellis and Baker 1990 suggest that abnormal sperm thus play a useful role in reproduction, explaining why approximately 40 percent of all sperm produced by the average man is abnormal.

18. Multiple mating, Bellis and Baker argue, is most useful when a female is "unable to judge ejaculate quality from a male's appearance" (1990, 379).

19. In fact, when fertility researchers began to develop a method of piercing the outer layer, or zona pellucida, of a fertile egg to assist the sperm in penetration, some scientists feared this might

increase the chance of birth defects in offspring because "immobile or feeble sperm—which normally don't stand much chance of penetrating the egg's inner sanctum—might be more likely to harbor serious DNA mutations than their more vigorous counterparts" (Richard D. Amelar of New York University, quoted in Fackelmann 1990, 379).

20. Personal interview with Gladys Friedler, April 1990, Bunting Institute, Radcliffe College, Boston. For the earliest published studies of Friedler's work, see Friedler and Wheeling 1979; Friedler 1985, 1987–88.

21. Sperm counts dropped from 113 million to 66 million per milliliter of semen. While this was far from the 20 million generally assumed to be the minimum for male fertility, it raised concern that the downward trend could continue.

22. See Berlau 1995; Cone 1995, A1; McKenna 1995, A1; Kolata 1996, B10; and Saltus 1996, 45–46.

23. Titles taken, respectively, from Roberts 1991; Vines 1991; and Aitken 1991.

24. This is the earliest article I have found that suggests abnormal sperm may be capable of fertilization because, as researchers postulate, speed may be more important than size or shape to the ability of a sperm to fertilize an egg.

25. For comprehensive reviews of the literature on male-mediated reproductive toxicology, see Davis et al. 1992; Colie 1993; Friedler 1993; and Olshan and Faustman 1993.

26. Some of the earliest epidemiological research studied the effects of radiation exposures on children born to men who survived the atomic bombs at Nagasaki and Hiroshima. But few associations were found between paternal exposures and childhood health problems, possibly due to the fact that so few men conceived children in the immediate aftermath of the bombing (in the six months after exposure, when effects of radiation are strongest). See Yoshimoto 1990; and Olshan and Faustman 1993, 198.

27. For useful tables summarizing these epidemiological associations and for good discussions of the strengths and limitations of these studies, see Olshan and Faustman 1993; Savitz, Sonnenfeld, and Olshan 1994; and Wright 1996.

28. Studies also showed increased rates of spinal malformations, spina bifida, congenital heart defects, and facial clefting in the children of veterans.

29. Studies of paternal smoking have also shown a strong link to lower birth weight for babies, in one study 8.4 ounces below average (if a father smoked two packs a day). See Davis 1991a, 123; Savitz and

Sandler 1991, 123–32; Merewood 1992, 8; Zhang and Ratcliffe 1993; and Martinez et al. 1994.

30. See Little and Sing 1987; Colie 1993, 3–9; Friedler 1993; Olshan and Faustman 1993, 197; Cicero et al. 1994.

31. Index searches were done on Uncover and ProQuest up to 1993 under all appropriate terms for male reproductive risks and fetal harm, including but not limited to various combinations of the terms *sperm, fetal risks, male reproduction, men and occupational/environmental hazards, addiction, birth defects, male fertility,* etc.

32. The personification of sperm is not a new phenomenon, but one that has been resurrected in new form in the 1990s. In the seventeenth century, scientists theorized that sperm actually contained miniature versions of man. The tiny sperm homunculus entered the uterus and attached itself to the womb, where it was simply nurtured by the woman. In fact, it was not until the nineteenth century that science confirmed the existence and importance of the female egg to the reproductive process. See Davis et al. 1992, 290.

33. Emily Martin has noted, and this is certainly confirmed by my research, that descriptions of male reproduction are clearly obsessed with measurements of tubule length (Martin 1991).

34. On the question of male self-sacrifice, one *New York Times* article reported a study that suggested that the energy required to produce sperm significantly shortened the lives of earthworms and that the same might be true of men. Worms whose sperm production was suspended lived significantly longer than worms that produced sperm throughout their life cycle (Angier 1992b, A18).

35. Few popular articles present negative images of men and the effects of toxicity, and those that do have been almost exclusively in British journals. One story in the *Economist* linking paternal drinking to fetal harm (titled "Sins of the Fathers") contained an image of a father sleeping on a couch with a baby playing on the floor next to him, the caption reading "Daddy's Boy" (*Economist* 1991, 87). Another story in the British journal *New Scientist* contained a photo of a man smoking while holding an infant on his lap, with the caption, "Smoking fathers leave a legacy of damage" (Wright 1993, 10). In the American context, the only reference I have found to paternal-fetal conflict appeared in a 1992 *Hastings Center Report.*

36. In addition to the *New York Times* articles cited previously, these stories are *Atlanta Constitution* 1990, B2; Friend 1991, A1; 1996, A1; *New York Times* 1991a, B8; Perl 1991, F3; Scott 1991, *Wall Street Journal* 1991, A1; 1996, B5; *Washington*

Post 1991, A8; Merewood 1992; Schmidt 1992; Serrano 1994, A1; Moehringer 1995, A3; and Nesmith 1996, A14. One *New York Times* story reported that "Vitamin C Deficiency in a Man's Diet Might Cause Problems for Offspring, but mentioned cigarette smoking as a potential cause of the problem in only one line *(New York Times* 1992, C12).

37. Blakeslee 1991, 1; Davis 1991b, A27; *New York Times* 1991a, B8, 1991b, C5.

38. Calculated from indexes in file on-line catalog ProQuest.

39. Serrano 1994; Moehringer 1995, A1; Friend 1996, A3; Nesmith 1996, A1; *Wall Street Journal* 1996, B5.

40. I recognize that this is only suggestive of the sources of framing. A more thorough investigation of this process would require a systematic study of the process by which reporters select scientific stories, the screening that takes place when reporters interview researchers and then select (and sometimes misrepresent) the statements of scientists, etc.

41. While all pregnant women who smoke and drink are suspect, it is simply not possible to subject these women—of all races and classes—to prosecution. This is not to say that women have not been prosecuted for alcohol addiction. Such cases are detailed in my interview with Paltrow (n. 14 above).

References

Aitken, John. 1991. "Do Sperm Find Eggs Attractive?" *Nature* 352 (May): 5321.

Angier, Natalie. 1992a. "Odor Receptors Discovered in Sperm Cells." *New York Times*, January 30.

___. 1992b. "In Worm, at Least, Making Sperm Is Found to Shorten a Male's Life." *New York Times*, December 3.

Atlanta Constitution. 1990. "Use of Cocaine May Reduce Male Fertility, Study Indicates." *Atlanta Constitution*, February 14.

Auger, Jacques, Jean Marie Kuntsmann, Francoise Czyglik, and Pierre Jouannet. 1995. "Decline in Semen Quality among Fertile Men in Paris during the Past Twenty Years." *New England Journal of Medicine* 332:281–85.

Baer, Judith A. 1978. *The Chains of Protection: The Judicial Response to Women's Labor Legislation.* Westport, Conn.: Greenwood.

Baker, Robin, and Mark A. Bellis. 1988. "'Kamikaze' Sperm in Mammals?" *Animal Behavior* 36(3):936–39.

Bellis, Mark, and Robin Baker. 1990. "Do Females Promote Sperm Competition? Data for Humans." *Animal Behaviour* 40(5):997–99.

Berlau, John. 1995. "Case of the Failing Sperm Counts:" *National Review*, June 26, 45–48.

Bingol, N., et al. 1987. "The Influence of Socioeconomic Factors on the Occurrence of Fetal Alcohol Syndrome." *Advances in Alcohol and Substance Abuse* 6(4):105–18.

Black, Rosemary, and Peter Moore. 1992. "The Myth of the Macho Sperm." *Parenting* 6(7):29–31.

Blakeslee, Sandra. 1991. "Research on Birth Defects Shifts to Flaws in Sperm." *New York Times*, January 1.

Blank, Robert. 1993. *Fetal Protection in the Workplace: Women's Rights, Business Interests and the Unborn.* New York: Columbia University Press.

Brachen, M. B., B. Eshenazi, K. Sachse, J. E. McSharry, et al. 1990. "Association of Cocaine Use with Sperm Concentration, Motility and Morphology." *Fertility and Sterility* 53: 315–22.

Brody, Jane E. 1988a. "Widespread Abuse of Drugs by Pregnant Women Is Found." *New York Times*, August 30.

___. 1988b. "Cocaine: Litany of Fetal Risks Grows." *New York Times*, September 6.

Brown, Wendy. 1988. *Manhood and Politics: A Feminist Reading in Political Theory.* Totowa, N.J.: Rowman & Littlefield.

Browne, Malcolm W. 1988. "Some Thoughts on Self Sacrifice." *New York Times*. July 5.

Burger, Edward J., Jr., Robert G. Tardiff, Anthony R. Scialli, and Harold Zenick, eds. 1989. *Sperm Measures and Reproductive Success.* New York: Liss.

Carlsen, Elisabeth, Aleksander Giwercman, Miels Keiding, and Miels E. Skakkebaek. 1992. "Evidence for Decreasing Quality of Semen during Past Fifty Years." *British Medical Journal* 305:609–12.

Castleman, Michael. 1993. "The Big Drop." *Sierra*, March/April, 36–38.

Chasnoff, Ira. 1989. "Drug Use and Women: Establishing a Standard of Care." *Annals of the New York Academy of Science* 562:208–10.

Cicero, Theodore J., Bruce Nock, Lynn H. O'Connor, Bryan N. Sewing, Michael L. Adams, and E. Robert Meyer. 1994. "Acute Paternal Alcohol Exposure Impairs Fertility and Fetal Outcome." *Life Sciences* 55:33–36.

Cohn, Carol. 1990. "'Clean Bombs' and Clean Language." In *Women, Militarism and War,* ed. Jean Bethke Elshtain and Sheila Tobias, 35–56. Savage, Md.: Rowman & Littlefield.

Colie, Christine F. 1993. "Male Mediated Teratogenesis." *Reproductive Toxicology* 7:3–9.

Cone, Marla. 1995. "Study Supports Finding of Male Fertility Decline." *Los Angeles Times*, February 2.

Corea, Gena. 1992. *The Invisible Epidemic.* New York: Basic.

Crenshaw, Kimberle. 1993, "Whose Story Is It, Anyway? Feminist and Antiracist Appropriations of Anita Hill." In *Race-ing Justice, Engendering Power*, ed. Toni Morrison, 402–40. London: Chatto & Windus.

Daniels, Cynthia R. 1991. "Competing Gender Paradigms: Gender Difference, Fetal Rights and the Case of Johnson Controls." *Policy Studies Review* 10(4): 51–68.

———. 1993. *At Women's Expense: State Power and the Politics of Fetal Rights*. Cambridge, Mass.: Harvard University Press.

Davis, Devra Lee. 1991a. "Paternal Smoking and Fetal Health." *Lancet* 337 (January 12): 123.

———. 1991b. "Fathers and Fetuses." *New York Times*, March 1.

Davis, Devra Lee, Gladys Friedler, Donald Mattison, and Robert Morris. 1992. "Male-Mediated Teratogenesis and Other Reproductive Effects: Biological and Epidemiologic Findings and a Plea for Clinical Research." *Reproductive Toxicology* 6:289–92.

Dicker, Marvin, and Eldin Leighton. 1990. "Trends in Diagnosed Drug Problems among Newborns: United States, 1979–1987." Paper presented at the annual meeting of the American Public Health Association, New York City, November.

Discover. 1987. "The Existential Decision of a Sperm." *Discover*, August, 10–11.

Duden, Barbara. 1993. *Disembodying Women*. Cambridge, Mass.: Harvard University Press.

Economist. 1991. "Sins of the Fathers." *Economist*, February 23, 87.

Edelman, Murray. 1988. *Constructing the Political Spectacle*. Chicago: University of Chicago Press.

Eisenstein, Zillah. 1988. The Female Body and the Law. Berkeley: University of California Press.

El-Gothamy, Zenab, and May El-Samahy. 1992. "Ultrastructure Sperm Defects in Addicts." *Fertility and Sterility* 57(3):699–702.

Ezzell, C. 1991. "Eggs Not Silent Partners in Conception." *Science News* 252 (April 6): 214.

Fackelmann, Kathy A. 1990. "Zona Blasters: There's More than One Way to Crack an Egg." *Science News* 138 (December 15): 376–79.

Ferguson, Kathy. 1993. *The Man Question: Visions of Subjectivity in Feminist Theory*. Berkely and Los Angeles: University of California Press.

Fernandez, James W. 1986. *Persuasions and Performances: The Play of Tropes in Cultures*. Bloomington: Indiana University Press.

Franklin, Sarah. 1991. "Fetal Fascinations: New Dimensions to the Medical-Scientific Construction of Fetal Personhood." In *Off-Centre: Feminism and Cutural Studies*, ed. Sarah Franklin, Celia Lury, and Jackie Stacey, 190–205. London: HarperCollins.

Fraser, Nancy. 1989. *Unruly Practices: Power, Discourse, and Gender in Contemporary Social Theory*. Minneapolis: University of Minnesota Press.

Friedler, Gladys. 1985. "Effects of Limited Paternal Exposure to Xenobiotic Agents on the Development of Progeny." *Neurobehavioral Toxicology and Teratology* 7:739–43.

———. 1987–88. "Effects on Future Generations of Paternal Exposure to Alcohol and Other Drugs." *Alcohol Health and Research World*, Winter, 126–29.

———. 1993. "Developmental Toxicology: Male-Mediated Effects." In *Occupational and Environmental Reproductive Hazards*, ed. Maureen Paul, 52–59. Baltimore: Williams & Wilkins.

Friedler, Gladys, and Howard S. Wheeling. 1979. "Behavioral Effects in Offspring of Male Mice Injected with Opioids Prior to Mating." In *Protracted Effects of Perinatal Drug Dependence*, vol. 2, *Pharmacology, Biochemistry and Behavior*, S23–S28. Fayetteville, N.Y.: ANKHO International.

Friend, Tim. 1991. "Sperm May Carry Cocaine to Egg." *USA Today*, October 9.

———. 1992. "Sperm Follow Their Noses." *USA Today*, January 30.

———. 1996. "Agent Orange May Be Linked to Birth Defects." *USA Today*, March 15.

Hall, Stuart. 1982. "The Rediscovery of 'Ideology': Return of the Repressed in Media Studies." In *Culture, Society and the Media*, ed. Michael Gurevitch, Tony Bennett, James Curran, and Janet Woollacott, 56–90. New York: Methuen.

Hartouni, Valorie. 1992. "Fetal Exposures: Abortion Politics and the Optics of Allusion." *Camera Obscura* 29:131–50.

Hastings Center Report. 1992. "Paternal-Fetal Conflict." *Hastings Center Report* March/April, 3.

Holly, Elizabeth, Diana Aston, David Ahn, and Jennifer Kristiansen. 1992. "Ewin's Bone Sarcoma, Paternal Occupational Exposure, and Other Factors. *American Journal of Epidemiology* 135:122–29.

Jensen, Tina Kold, Jorma Toppari, Niels Keiding, and Niels Erik Skakkeback. 1995. "Do Environmental Estrogens Contribute to the Decline in Male Reproductive Health?" *Clinical Chemistry* 41:1896–1901.

Keller, Evelyn Fox. 1992. *Secrets of Life, Secrets of Death*. New York: Routledge.

Kenney, Sally. 1992. *For Whose Protection? Reproductive Hazards and Exclusionary Policies in the United States and Britain*. Ann Arbor: University of Michigan Press.

Kessler-Harris, Alice. 1982. *Out to Work*. New York: Oxford University Press.

Kharrazi, M., G. Patashnik, and J. R. Goldsmith. 1980. "Reproductive Effects of Dibromochloropropane." *Israel Journal of Medical Science* 16:403–6.

Kolata, Gina. 1996. "Some Experts See a Fall, Others Poor Data." *New York Times*, March 19.

Koren, Gideon, K. Graham, H. Shear, and T. Einarson. 1989. "Bias against the Null Hypothesis." *Lancet* 2(8677):1440–42.

Koren, G., and N. Klein. 1991. "Bias against Negative Studies in Newspaper Reports of Medical Research." Journal of the American Medical Association 266(13):1824–26.

Laqueur, Thomas. 1990. "The Facts of Fatherhood." In *Conflicts in Feminism,* ed. Marianne Hirsch and Evelyn Fox Keller, 205–21. New York: Routledge.

Lehrer, Susan. 1987. *Origins of Protective Labor Legislation.* Albany, N.Y.: SUNY Press.

Lerman, Robert, and Theodora Ooms, eds. 1993. *Young Unwed Fathers: Changing Roles and Emerging Policies.* Philadelphia: Temple University Press.

Lindbohm, Marja-Lusa, Kari Hemminki, Michele G. Bonhomme, Ahti Anttila, Kaarina Rantala, Pirjo Heikkila, and Michael J. Rosenberg. 1991. "Effects of Paternal Occupational Exposure on Spontaneous Abortions." *American Journal of Public Health* 81: 1029–33.

Little, R. E., and C. F. Sing. 1987. "Father's Drinking and Infant Birth Weight: Report of an Association." *Teratology* 36:59–65.

Lubiano, Wahneema. 1992. "Black Ladies, Welfare Queens, and State Minstrels: Ideological War by Narrative Means." In *Race-ing Justice, Engendering Power,* ed. Toni Morrison, 323–63. London: Chatto & Windus.

Mack, Arien, ed. 1991. *In Time of Plague.* New York: New York University Press.

Martin, Emily. 1991. "The Egg and the Sperm: How Science Has Constructed a Romance Based on Stereotypical Male-Female Roles." *Signs: Journal of Women in Culture and Society* 16(3):485–501.

Martinez, Fernando, Anne Wright, Lynn Taussig, and the Group Health Medical Associates. 1994. "The Effect of Paternal Smoking on the Birthweight of Newborns Whose Mothers Did Not Smoke." *American Journal of Public Health* 84:1489–91.

Mason, George. 1991. "Female Infidelity—May the Best Sperm Win." *New Scientist*, January, 29.

Massachusetts Coalition for Occupational Safety and Health (MassCosh). 1992. *Confronting Reproductive Hazards on the Job.* Boston: MassCosh.

Maugh, Thomas H., II. 1992. "Sperm's Key Conception Protein Found." *Los Angeles Times*, March 19.

McDonagh, Eileen. 1993. "Good, Bad and Captive Samaritans: Adding in Pregnancy and Consent to the Abortion Debate." *Women and Politics* 13(3/4):31–49.

McKenna, M. A. J. 1995. "Declining Sperm Pose a Mystery." *Atlanta Costitution,* February 2.

Merewood, Anne. 1991. "Sperm under Siege." *Health*, April, 53–76.

___. 1992. "Studies Reveal Men's Role in Producing Healthy Babies." *Chicago Tribune,* January 12.

Miller, Susan Katz. 1992. "Can Children Be Damaged by Fathers' Cancer Therapy?" *New Scientist* 135:5.

Mitchell, John L. 1991. "Billboard's Message Is Graphically Anti-Drug." *Los Angeles Times*, March 30.

Moehringer, J. R. 1995. "Legagy of Worry." *Los Angeles Times*, October 22.

Moore, Harry. 1989. "Sperm You Can Count On." *New Scientist*, June 10, 38–91.

Nesmith, Jeff. 1996. "Studies Link Agent Orange to Birth Defects in Children of Vietnam Vets. *Atlanta Constitution*, March 15.

New York Times. 1991a. "Study Links Cancer in Young to Father's Smoking." *New York Times*, January 24.

___. 1991b. "Cocaine-Using Fathers Linked to Birth Defects." *New York Times*, October 15.

___. 1992. "Vitamin C Deficiency in a Man's Diet Might Cause Problems for Offspring." *New York Times*, February 12.

Olshan, Andrew F., and Elaine M. Faustman. 1993. "Male-Mediated Developmental Toxicity." *Reproductive Toxicology* 7:191–202.

O'Neill, Anne Marie, Leah Eskin, and Linda Satter. 1996. "Under the Influence." *People,* September 9, 53–55.

Paltrow, Lynn. 1992. "Criminal Prosecutions against Pregnant Women: National Update and Overview." Center for Reproductive Law and Policy, New York City.

Parker, G. A. 1970. "Sperm Competition and Its Evolutionary Consequences in the Insects." *Biological Review*, 45:525–67.

Perl, Rebecca. 1991. "Cocaine May Travel to Egg through Sperm, Study Says." *Atlanta Constitution*, October 9.

Petchesky, Rosalind. 1987. "Fetal Images: The Power of Visual Culture in the Politics of Reproduction." In *Reproductive Technologies: Gender, Motherhood and Medicine*, ed. Michelle Stanworth, 57–80. Minneapolis: University of Minnesota Press.

Poovey, Mary. 1988. *Uneven Developments*. Chicago: University of Chicago Press.

Poppy, John. 1989. "Upwardly Motile: A Man's Guide to Raising Healthier, Heartier, Happier Sperm." *Esquire*, June, 67–70.

Reynolds, Barbara. 1994. "How Soon the Cheering Stops When Veterans Become Ill." *USA Today*, November 11.

Ritter, John. 1994. "Gulf Troops Lacked Protection." *USA Today,* August 5.

Roberts, Leslie. 1991. "Does Egg Beckon Sperm When Time Is Right?" *Science* 252 (April): 214.

Robinson, James C. 1991. *Toil and Toxics: Workplace Struggles and Political Strategies for Occupational Health*. Berkeley and Los Angeles: University of California Press.

Rothman, Barbara Katz. 1989. *Recreating Motherhood*. New York: Norton.

Ruddick, Sara. 1990. "Thinking about Fathers." In *Conflicts in Feminism*, ed. Marianne Hirsch and Evelyn Fox Keller, 222–33. New York: Routledge.

Safe, Stephen H. 1995. "Environmental and Dietary Estrogens and Human Health: Is There a Problem?" *Environmental Health Perspectives* 103:346–51.

Saltus, Richard. 1996. "Sperm Count Drop: Is It Just Bad Data?" *Boston Globe*, May 20.

Savitz, D., and J. Chen. 1990. "Parental Occupation and Childhood Cancer." *American Journal of Epidemiology* 133:123–32.

Savitz, D., P. J. Schwingle, and M. A. Keels. 1991. "Influence of Paternal Age, Smoking and Alcohol Consumption on Congenital Anomalies." *Teratology* 44:429–40.

Savitz, D., Nancy Sonnenfeld, and Andrew Olshan. 1994. "Review of Epidemiologic Studies of Paternal Occupational Exposure and Spontaneous Abortion." *American Journal of Industrial Medicine* 25:361–83.

Schmidt, Karen F. 1992. "The Dark Legacy of Fatherhood." *U.S. News and World Report*, December 14, 92–96.

Schneider, Anne, and Helen Ingram. 1993. "Social Construction of Target Populations: Implications for Politics and Policy." *American Political Science Review* 87(2):334–47.

Schroedel, Jean Reith, and Paul Peretz. 1993. "A Gender Analysis of Policy Formation: The Case of Fetal Abuse." Paper presented at the Western Political Science Association meeting, Pasadena, Calif., March 18–20.

Scialli, Anthony. 1993. "Paternally Mediated Effects and Political Correctness." *Reproductive Toxicology* 7:189–90.

Scott, Janny. 1991. "Study Finds Cocaine Can Bind to Sperm." *Los Angeles Times*, October 9.

Serrano, Richard. 1994. "Birth Defects in Gulf Vets' Babies Stir Fear, Debate." *Los Angeles Times*, November 14.

Shanley, Mary. 1993. "Fathers' Rights, Mothers' Wrongs? Reflections on Unwed Fathers' Rights and Sex Equality." Paper presented at the American Political Science Association meeting, Washington, D.C., September 4–6.

Shapiro, Bennett M. 1987. "The Existential Decision of a Sperm." *Cell* 49:293–94.

Singer, Linda. 1993. *Erotic Welfare*. New York: Routledge.

Small, Meredith. 1991. "Sperm Wars." *Discover*, July, 48–53.

Stellman, S., and J. Stellman. 1980. "Health Problems among 535 Vietnam Veterans Potentially Exposed to Herbicides." *American Journal of Epidemiology* 112:444.

Stone, Andrea. 1989. "It's 'Tip of the Iceberg' in Protecting Infants." *USA Today*, August 25.

Treichler, Paula A. 1990. "Feminism, Medicine and the Meaning of Childbirth." In *Body Politics: Women and the Discourses of Science,* ed. Mary Jacobus, Evelyn Fox Keller, and Sally Shuttleworth, 113–38. New York: Routledge.

Tuchman, Gaye. 1978. *Making the News*. New York: Free Press.

———. 1983. "Consciousness Industries and the Production of Culture." *Journal of Communications* 33(3):330–41.

———. 1993. "Realism and Romance: The Study of Media Effects." *Journal of Communications* 43(4):36–41.

Vigue, Doreen Iudica. 1996. "Pregnant Woman Booked for Drinking." *Boston Globe*, August 15.

Vines, Gail. 1991. "Eggs Urge Sperm to Swim Up and See Them." *New Scientist* 13 (April): 21.

Wall Street Journal. 1991. "World-wide: Fathers Who Smoke." *Wall Street Journal*. January 24.

———. 1996. "Birth Defects May Relate to Agent Orange Herbicide." *Wall Street Journal*, March 15.

Washington Post. 1991. "Fathers' Smoking May Damage Sperm." *Washington Post*. January 25.

Women and AIDS Book Group. 1990. *Women, AIDS and Activism*. Boston: South End.

Wright, Brett. 1993. "Smokers' Sperm Spell Trouble for Future Generations." *New Scientist*, March 6, 10.

Wright, Lawrence. 1996. "Silent Sperm." *New Yorker*, January 15, 42–55.

Yazigi, Ricardo A., Randall R. Odem, and Kenneth L. Polakoski. 1991. "Demonstration of Specific Binding of Cocaine to Human Spermatozoa." *Journal of the American Medical Association* 266:1956–59.

Yoshimoto, Y. 1990. "Cancer Risk among Children of Atomic Bomb Survivors: A Review of RERF Epidemiologic Studies." *Journal of the American Medical Association* 264:596–600.

Zhang, Jun, and Jennifer Ratcliffe. 1993. "Paternal Smoking and Birthweight in Shanghai." *American Journal of Public Health* 83:207–10.

Zuckerman, Barry. 1991. "Drug-Exposed Infants: Understanding the Medical Risk." *Future of Children* 1 (Spring): 26–35.

Using Technology, Choosing Sex:
The Campaign Against Sex Determination and the Question of Choice
Forum Against Sex Determination and Sex Pre-Selection

In a world dominated by the scientific mode, Newtonian models for understanding natural and physical phenomena have displaced earlier worldviews, in which religion and the supernatural figured to a greater or lesser extent. Instead of placating such forces, we now endeavour to control them; scientific "knowledge" is being used to determine and achieve the desired ends.

One dramatic illustration of this is the use of a highly developed technology, amniocentesis, for detecting genetic abnormalities in foetuses and also as a means to determine their sex. Society has hitherto looked to gods and supernatural powers to realise its desire for male progeny; it has now turned to the practitioners of modern medicine.

This is not to say that the shift has been sudden. Traditional systems of medicine and healing have also contributed their share: Ayurveda lists a number of practices for determining the sex of the foetus after conception, and for selection at or after conception. Ayurvedic texts state that the sex of the foetus is determined only six weeks after conception, and therefore may be "manipulated" prior to this. Pre-selection exists in prescribed copulation postures, times and days; in diet, eating and consumption habits, especially after conception; certain rituals to be performed before and after conception, and so on.

What then do we find so different or shocking about modern allopathic medicine providing fail-safe techniques for sex determination and pre-selection? For one, the fact that they are precisely that: accurate and irreversible Then, in the security of its modernism and "neutrality" science reinforces or legitimises conservative, orthodox prejudices. Again, its philosophy has become the dominant mode of thinking in society today, and the belief is that it invests men with more or less full control over lives and bodies. For all these reasons we feel that its "achievements" need to be examined more closely.

Over the last ten years, efforts have been made to campaign against the practice of sex determination and sex pre-selection. In the following pages, we as members of the Forum Against Sex Determination and Sex Pre-selection (FASDSP) present our perception of this campaign in which we have been active participants as a group for the last seven years. We offer a detailed account of our efforts, a critique of our actions and strategies, an appraisal of our understanding and a formulation of the issues as they emerged in the course of the campaign.

Obviously, our journey has not been altogether smooth. We have consciously and unconsciously shifted lanes according to our understanding or as demanded by the prevailing situation. We wish to share our progress in order to help arrive at an understanding of the commonalities as well as the specificities of all the issues in which we are involved in one way or another.

The Government of India brought about a partial ban on sex determination tests in 1976. This followed a protest launched by women's groups against survey results which indicated that an overwhelming majority of couples (90 percent), who had volunteered for clinical trials at the All India Institute of Medical Sciences in Delhi, were desirous of aborting female foetuses once their sex was known. When the Government banned the tests in public hospitals, the issue was forgotten.

The existence of private clinics offering this test remained more or less unknown, until some national dailies published news and advertisements about a particular clinic in Chandigarh, in 1982. Immediately women's groups from Bombay, Delhi and other places issued a statement against the test. People's science and health groups such as the Lok Vidnyan Sangathana and the Medico Friends Circle, as well as research organisations such as the Centre for Women's Development Studies, Research Unit on Women's Studies, SNDT, Bombay, and the Voluntary Health Association of India joined in the protest, questioning the role of scientists and doctors who helped to propagate the tests.

During this period the emphasis of the campaign was mainly on writing articles in the media, and creating a pressure group by highlighting the issue. The focus of concern was the dangerous effects that these techniques could have, either of permanent damage to the foetus or injury to the woman's uterus. Further, the efficiency of the test was also questioned; indeed, the very information regarding the availability of such testing in private clinics came as a result of a newspaper report of a "wrong" detection in one, Dr. Bhandari's clinic in Amritsar, where a "male" foetus had been aborted. But when it started to look as if improving the test would eliminate all the problems associated with it, the campaign petered out.

In November 1985, a group of activists from women's groups and people's science groups in Bombay agreed on the need for more consistent action in banning the sex determination tests, seeing the extent to which they had spread. After a series of discussions, we came together as a joint action group, the Forum Against Sex Determination and Sex Pre-selection. Keeping in mind that one of the primary weaknesses of the earlier attempts at building up coordinated action was lack of a broader perspective, it was decided that the campaign must consider the issue at multiple levels. The question of sex determination and pre-selection was then primarily seen as: (i) an integral part of women's oppression and discrimination; (ii) a misuse of science and technology against people in general and women in particular; (iii) a human rights issue. Due to the multi-dimensional character of the issue, activists from various social action, people's science, health, human rights and legal action groups, as well as concerned individuals joined in the campaign, along with women's groups.

To handle the technical aspect of the issue, a two-pronged approach was used. All of us, including those with an aversion to science, medicine or any kind of "technical" stuff, went through the process of understanding the basic techniques. The focus of the campaign, however, was not on their "goodness" or "badness," but on the issue of discrimination between boys and girls in all sections of society. Linked to this was an attempt to show that sex determination was yet another form of violence against women, part of the chain made up of female infanticide, wife-burning, *sati*,[1] etc. The threat to the survival of women was itself evident from their declining sex ratio: from 972 females per 1,000 mates in 1901, to 929 females per 1,000 males in 1991, a rather shocking statistic.

After long discussions and an initial workshop to equip ourselves with the technicalities (medical, social and legal) of the matter, we set out. An immediate regulation of pre-natal diagnostic techniques was sought, for which, naturally, we had to turn to the legal and state machinery. Simultaneousiy, we wanted to conduct the campaign so that public pressure could be mounted, and our basic message *Ladki na ladke se kum* (A girl is no less than a boy) could reach the people.

The first problem with regard to framing any regulation was of proving that an abortion was consequent upon a sex determination test; next, one would need to modify the Medical Termination of Pregnancy Act. Not wanting to curtail women's right to abort, we did not pursue this idea for long. The alternative was a new law—the first law of its kind, regulating diagnostic techniques. We had decided not to ask for a total ban because we did feel that the detection of genetic abnormalities was essential in situations like ours, where mothers have to pay such a heavy price for bringing up children with birth defects. But strategically too, we felt that a demand for a total ban might be squashed altogether.

We formulated the Act as we would have liked it to be and tried to push the idea through with the state bureaucracy. A sympathetic health secretary and a few contacts in the Legislative Assembly helped the process. Signatures were collected from all over the country and from "eminent" persons from all walks of life. Lobbying was done with members of the Assembly and others who mattered. Articles were written in the media and events held to highlight the issue, mainly for press coverage, at crucial junctures in this legal campaign. We managed to be represented in the expert committee to formulate such a law. We also had a pilot study done in Bombay on the prevalence of sex determination tests, which revealed the following:

About 84 percent of the gynecologists interviewed for the study were performing amniocentesis for sex determination; on an average they together performed 270 amniocenteses per month.

Some doctors had been doing such tests for 10–12 years, but the majority (over 85 percent) had been doing so only for the past five. About 74 percent of the doctors said that over half the women who came for the tests were middle class, and more than 85 percent of the doctors said that they had tested no lower class women, although the areas selected for the study had a substantial lower class representation.

A majority of the women already had two or three daughters, while the percentage of those seeking a sex determination test after the birth of four or more daughters was relatively low. Significantly enough, about 24 percent of the doctors said that in 20 percent of the cases, women had only one daughter when they came in for the sex determination test, and 29 percent of the doctors said that up to 10 percent of the women already had one or more sons. A majority of the doctors thought the sex determination tests were a humane service for women who did not want any more daughters, and some even felt that they could be an important family planning device for our country.

Lobbying to get the Act passed remained our primary objective at this stage. It helped give us a direction; it helped to raise the issue on various platforms, and it focused attention on the point that we were trying to make.

In June, 1988, the Act came into being in the State of Maharashtra. Although it demonstrated the state's response to the campaign, the Act itself has certain provisions which are clearly counterproductive.

1. *Punishment for the woman*: According to the Act, a woman undergoing a sex determination test is presumed to be innocent, but is still fined Rs 50; if proved otherwise, she is subjected to imprisonment for three months and/or a fine of Rs 1,000.

In practice, a woman under severe pressure from her in-laws will tend to internalise blame and accept the punishment, thus making for further victimization. Meanwhile, the husband or parents-in-law are not held liable. An exceptional woman, who musters up courage to lodge a complaint under this Act, would not dare to do so if she were afraid of being punished by it.

2. *Granting licences to private labs/clinics/centres:* In Maharashtra, as anywhere else, the granting of licences to private institutions would only legitimise unethical practice carried out by them earlier. Government institutions all over India have been following the ban on the misuse of amniocentesis for the past several years, but not one case of violation of this ban has come to light so far. In Maharashtra, a reputed geneticist was found to be performing this test illegally after the ban and although the news was flashed in leading city newspapers, the government chose to ignore it. As far as the genetic testing for foetal abnormalities is concerned, looking at the number of people who have availed themselves of the facility in Maharashtra, we feel that the infrastructure and expertise available in government hospitals and those attached to medical colleges is sufficient to cater to their needs.

3. *Prohibiting access to the judiciary:* According to section 21(l) of the Maharashtra Act, no person other than the authorities laid down by the Act can seek the help of the judiciary against any alleged violation of it. The person has to give notice of not less than 60 days to the State Appropriate Authority or State Vigilance Committee in the prescribed format, which is not given in the rules governing the Act. If the committee itself is not formed in time, this clause delays all probability of any action.

4. *Non-answerability of government machinery:* The various bodies appointed under this Act are not accountable to the public. No punishment is given out to them for failing in their duty; this leaves people with no recourse in the face of repeated negligence on the part of the state.

Despite all its loopholes, however, the Act served to bring the issue into the limelight and it also gave us legal sanction to confront sex determination clinics. We were aware even then that it would not stop clinics from offering the "facility" altogether; what we hoped for was some restraint because of the illegality that was attached to it.

We were also aware that even a nominal implementation of the Act could take place only if people did not want to avail themselves of these facilities. In the initial stages of the campaign itself, however, we came to the painful realisation that the vast majority of people was not likely to spontaneously support the campaign. We tried our own very general ways of reaching out, of establishing connections between different issues and of emphasising the slogan that we had evolved specifically for the campaign: *Lladki na ladke se kum.* Films were made, songs written, meetings held at various places, and with all kinds of people. Skits were enacted with children, and positive action taken by holding parent-daughter marches and children's day programmes.

Along with this, in April–May 1988, eight organisations jointly organised a fortnight-long programme *Nari jeevan sangharsh yatra* (A quest to liberate women's lives). The focus of the programme was on all the issues related to women's survival. An exhibition, accompanied by a booklet, was set up, linking the issues of female foeticide and infanticide, wife-murder, rape, *sati*. Programmes comprising of videofilms, slide-shows, poster exhibitions, plays, skits, debates, etc., were organised at twelve different places in the city of Bombay.

Up until then, we had been so preoccupied with getting the law passed that we had little time to pause. Not that there were no doubts; having worked on other legal campaigns, we were quite aware of the limitations therein. However, the momentum set by the state administration and the prospect of an Act soon kept us going, forced us into taking some kind of action. The unanimous passing of the Act by the state government made for a sudden slowing down in pace. Central legislation was nowhere in sight and

the state bureaucracy was taking its own time to constitute committees, register private genetic clinics and laboratories and so on. We paused too.

We realised that there had been a growing restlessness within all of us about doing the kind of work required for getting legislation passed. That apart, we were most uncomfortable about really not being aware of what people in general felt about such legislation. Coupled with this was the fact that we were asking for more state control over women's lives. On the one hand, we have always been wary of state control, and on the other, the thrust of our campaign had been just this. In fact, in a society where the bias in favour of a male child is so predominant, our unyielding stand against sex determination certainly did not reflect majority opinion. So we had the unpleasant option of going against what the majority of people seems to believe in, and collaborating with the state which, most of the time, is anti-people.

In this situation, where we were forced to work with the state, we had tried to ensure some system of checks and balances. Access to information was one of these. The Act had provided for the mandatory publishing of periodic reports giving details of the number of tests carried out in registered centres, indications that required such tests, and their diagnoses. We tried to pursue this by demanding full access to all documents for members of the vigilance committees and the public. We also tried to get voluntary organisations represented on the former.

The experience of the State of Maharashtra, however, demonstrated the limitations of these suggestions in the face of an unwilling state machinery. No reports have been published to date. Committees took a long time to be formed and voluntary organisations were inadequately represented on them. Almost all the non-government appointees, including representatives from voluntary organisations working with women, are medical professionals. How and in whose favour these committees would work is anybody's guess.

In June 1989, local level committees were formed for all districts except Bombay, and in June 1992, registrations were given to 24 labs and clinics all over the state, 17 of them in Bombay! No case has been registered under the law so far, and the test is still available in Bombay.

In a sense, state legislation was effective only in marginally reducing the number of clinics and increasing the charges for the tests. In another sense, however, since the Maharashtra Act was passed, interest in the issue has been aroused in the entire country, something that had not happened earlier. Today, joint action forums have been formed in Bangalore, Delhi and several cities of Gujarat. Concerned groups in Chandigarh, Calcutta and Pune are also actively campaigning for an all-India ban on sex determination tests. As a result, three other state governments—Goa, Gujarat and Orissa—announced their intention to introduce similar legislation.

Having waited for a long time the Central Government has also finally introduced a bill in this regard. It has the same major loopholes as the Maharashtra Act, but this time, public opinion has been sought on the bill. A Joint Parliamentary Committee was constituted which has held discussions and dialogues with organisations and people active in the campaign in various cities.

Based on our experiences with the Maharashtra Act, there have been some changes in our stand. We feel today that only those who actually provide the facility should be penalised. We are therefore against any punishment being given to persons seeking the test, whether it is the woman herself or the family who might have persuaded her. In our opinion, the law is meant to regulate the *tests* and to prevent their misuse; thus only doctors or providers of the technique are responsible for their violation. Moreover, the burden of changing the social evil of discrimination against daughters is not the law's alone.

The Central Bill does not envisage any role for voluntary organisations in the vigilance committees; based on our experiences we feel that representation through voluntary organisations is not sufficient—*it is essential that the general public have direct access to information and judicial action.*

The proposed central legislation is in a sense an achievement of the nationwide campaign. The way in which this "achievement" has been credited to us, and the whole question of democratic principles and values, troubles us. In a way we see a parallel in our use of the law and in the establishment's promotion of technological solutions. Society tries to find solutions to social problems in technological innovations: are we, too, seeking such solutions through the agency of the law? Whenever we ask for reforms in existing laws or the formulation of new ones, are we expecting the government to be on the side of women?

This is the dilemma which confronts all women's groups. Whether it is the Dowry Prohibition Act or Section 498 A of the Indian Penal Code, or the Family Courts Act or the present Act under discussion we do believe that we really cannot rely on these alone or on government to get justice for women. But through the process of campaigning for them, through the protest and pressure generated, more and more women are exposed to diverse views, and a social atmosphere is created which can strengthen women in their struggle. Various groups can forge links and strengthen the movement by reaching out to more women and mobilising public awareness.

At the same time we feel that the demand for, and enactment of, such legislation is one way of making a statement opposing discrimination against women in society. It is necessary that the government be forced to take note of such practices in society, and register the fact that society, represented in parliament, takes serious objection to their continuance. It is also necessary to strip the garb of respectability from such brutal practices through their legitimation by modern medical technology. By making them illegal the tacit, social sanction that they enjoy can be removed.

Our other dilemmas are related to much wider issues. In the campaign we had taken the stand that these pre-natal diagnostic tests needed to be regulated, that they be allowed for the detection of genetic abnormalities, taking into account women's burden as the principal child rearers in our society. Although we have some questions on this point, we still feel, that until society takes collective responsibility for child care we would have to abide by our present stand.

While campaigning against sex determination and trying to think of how to launch a campaign against sex pre-selection, we were faced with a totally new dimension of the technologies themselves. A series of issues, such as in vitro fertilisation (IVF), gamete intra-fallopian tube (GIFT), and the whole domain of genetic engineering needed discussion. Not all of them could be explained away only as discrimination against women or the misuse of science and technology. We needed to undertake a critique of modern science and technology as well as society's views on all forms of reproduction.

At the conference of the Feminist International Network of Resistance to Repro-

ductive and Genetic Engineering (FINRRAGE) in March 1989 in Bangladesh, the debates left us baffled and bewildered at times. Intervention in nature's biological processes began as early as agriculture. How does one distinguish that intervention from the one made by genetic engineering? Artificial insemination (AI), IVF, hybridisation and so on are techniques that have long been used in farming and cattle breeding. Why is it that we begin to question and protest only when such engineering is proposed for human beings? Is our view genuinely holistic or are we still being propelled by an androcentric urge, the loss of this earth and its environment which is crucial for "us" human beings?

What does one mean by "eastern" and "western" science in today's context? While evolving or trying to evolve a new philosophy of science, how does one accept and understand the knowledge acquired so far? How does one work towards a non-reductionist methodology of science? We surely do not believe in saying a categorical "No" to technology. Is there a qualitative difference between the various technologies? If so, how does one identify it and, if not, how does one evolve the criteria by which a distinction can be made to help us determine those that are desirable and appropriate and those which are not.

The list of questions is unending and answers are not simple. We also know that they need much more collective thinking. What we fear, however, is that these and similar debates are getting further and further away from the people who are directly affected when technological innovations backfire—witness the gas leak at Bhopal, the control over women's reproduction whether in treating fertility or infertility, and so on. We realise that those of us who have access to information and can afford the luxury of theorising have the responsibility to make this a broad-based debate, to initiate and maintain communication to bridge the chasm. As of now our efforts are far from sufficient.

Finally there is the question of translating these debates into action. The campaign against sex determination and sex pre-selection is one limited example of these efforts. There are many more scattered all over the country—that question development, that force one to rethink modern science and technology, that identify whose interests are taken care of by what. In all of these a common feature has been that while, in the long term, the effects of environmental disasters are for "life on earth" itself, in the short term they appear to be a clash of interest between two sections of people.

On the Narmada dam issue, for example, the apparent gain of water for irrigation and power generated, especially for the state of Gujarat, seems to be posited against the loss of people's homes, communities and lifestyles. Cost-benefit figures differ because people's notions of costs and benefits differ. But due to the presence of a large number of people who are immediately affected, will suffer loss and do not benefit in any way from a project like the Narmada dam, there exists a broad people's base to the struggle against it.

The case of reproductive technologies, however, is slightly different. Here, typically, women are often compelled into accepting a harmful, dehumanising technology in a no-choice situation, where it seems to offer a viable solution, at least to their immediate problems. To a woman who is not allowed to use contraception and who is unwilling to shoulder the burden of repeated pregnancies, deliveries, miscarriages and abortions, an invisible injection/implant can be a solution; to a woman who has been branded barren, IVF can be a solution; to a woman whose only recognition is as a producer of sons, sex determination and sex pre-selection become solutions. All of these are important also because they give the illusion of bringing about a change in one's situation.

At the Forum Against Sex Determination and Sex Pre-selection, while continuing with our single issue campaign, we are broadening out to include specific action against other reproductive technology. In a sense, this is an attempt to evolve other methods of campaigning which may be more effective than the one chosen earlier. Today, we are at the stage when we are aware of the achievements and limitations of the earlier part of our campaign, yet unsure of where to turn next. What keeps us going is the commitment to persevere and move on, and to do so individually and collectively.

Note

1. The ritual immolation of a widow on her husband's funeral pyre.

Norplant® in the Nineties:
Realities, Dilemmas, Missing Pieces

Sônia Correa

Norplant® is a long-acting female contraceptive consisting of six silicone rods containing 30 mg of synthetic progestin.[1] The rods are implanted under the skin in the upper arm. Special equipment and technical proficiency are required to insert and remove the device. The implants protect against pregnancy for five years, by continuously releasing a sustained, low hormonal dose, which simultaneously suppresses ovulation and thickens the cervical mucus. Norplant® is considered by its creators to be an advance over previous methods of steroid contraception (pills and injectables) because it provides for a sustained, relatively constant blood concentration of the delivered steroid; this represents a significant improvement over the diurnal or tri-monthly variability inherent in other delivery systems.

Reproductive rights activists throughout the world have raised critical concerns about Norplant® since the first multi-center clinical trials began in the early 1980s. Through a review of literature, I will explore the feminist concerns and dilemmas within the present "Norplant® realities." I assess the validity of feminist concerns regarding the gap between written protocols and field operations, the efficacy and safety of the method and its potential for abuse. I also examine the limits of prevailing analytical and political frameworks as they inform the positions taken in the debate. As such, I point out the importance of context-specific mechanisms that mediate women's experiences of contraceptive technology.

Fifty-five countries have Norplant® implant experience[2] and 26 countries have regulatory approval for distribution. The number of users worldwide is estimated to be between 1.5 and 2 million women. These figures indicate that Norplant® has become a global "reality" in fertility regulation. In addition to its widespread, and growing, use Norplant® is an excellent case to examine several critical dimensions of the new reproductive technologies. Multiple funding sectors (public, private and commercial) brought the method into development, and the composition of the investment affects distribution patterns. In developing countries the dissemination is almost exclusively achieved through the so-called public sector, which includes governmental and nongovernmental programs. In the United States, a combined model prevails, in which Norplant® is sold at market price to those who can afford it while remaining cheap or free for poor women. This mixed format may emerge in other settings, wherever Norplant® becomes acceptable among high-income women.

Worldwide, the delivery of implants to less privileged, less educated and less informed women is, therefore, dependent on public or "made public" investment. When delivery is cloaked as being in the "public interest," in less-than-democratic situations, women's ability to insist upon adequate services and defend themselves against abuse is necessarily weaker; in such applications, ethical considerations about the method may be raised. Such considerations must necessarily address both the potential for abuse, as well as the ideological priorities in government subsidy.

Norplant® is a subject of controversy among feminists, researchers, and providers, as well as a matter of debate within the international reproductive rights movement itself.[3] In the feminist community, the critique of Norplant® developed within the framework of demographically-oriented population policies. The critique raised questions about the increasing control it was possible to wield over women's lives and bodies with the new technologies. On the opposite side of the fence, others advocated wide dissemination of Norplant® as part of a program of draconian fertility-control measures. Some voices, while recognizing the potential risks, have welcomed the implants as a new contraceptive option that may respond to the increasing preference for long-term methods in various contexts.

The Norplant® debate should not, therefore, be misinterpreted as a mere and occasional disagreement between factions of the feminist community and those involved in contraceptive technological development. The controversy is a manifestation of a deeper tension arising from the conflict ingrained in the *social production of technology*. Consequently, if a democratic perspective is to prevail, we cannot avoid or deny the uncomfortable confrontations and interrogations Norplant® demands. In fact, three volumes on Norplant® have been published recently,[4] each of which provides up-to-date information as a basis to evaluate the dilemmas posed by Norplant®.

Norplant® Geography

The development of a hormonal contraceptive implant has been global since its initiation in the early 1970s.[5] In the early 1980s, the Population Council began a global program of multi-center clinical trials and acceptability studies, involving 44 developing and developed countries, including the United States, Finland and Sweden. National programs frequently encompassed more than one research center, as was the case in Brazil, where 20 units were involved. The method is presently registered in more than 50 percent of the countries where trials have been performed. The most widely publicized exceptions are Brazil and India, following feminist action against early research efforts. The Food and Drug Administration (FDA) approved Norplant® for use in the United States in December 1990, which may have legitimated the method worldwide.

Norplant® has received regulatory approval for distribution in 26 countries.[6] A brief evaluation of the present "Norplant® map" demonstrates an enormous heterogeneity of cultural, political and economic conditions. Particularly striking are the discrepancies inherent in the structure and functioning of the existing health-care systems and the capacity of societies to monitor the dissemination of the method. We may consider, for instance, the difference between Sweden and Finland, on one hand, and Haiti or Rwanda on the other.

As global as Norplant® is, it is estimated that approximately 80 percent of users are concentrated in Indonesia and the United States. In 1992, 1.3 million Indonesian women were using the implant, while the Allan Guttmacher Institute (1992) has estimated the number of American women using Norplant® to be between 300,000 and 350,000. After a general review of the characteristics of Norplant®, I will focus mainly on the social context in which Norplant® has been approved and delivered to the public in Indonesia and the United States. The differences between these two countries in relation to dominant political and cultural values as well as social mediation mechanisms will be highlighted. They provide a provocative framework in which to scrutinize the social risks and benefits of Norplant®.

The Norplant® Debates: Agreements

In the ongoing and unresolved Norplant® debate, feminists, on the one side, and researchers and providers, on the other, agree on some major points. The first concerns the large amount of information available about Norplant®. Unlike conditions prevailing during the development and dissemination of earlier modern contraceptive technologies, research has been performed throughout the Norplant® process and the results are easily accessible. This vast literature includes pharmacological and acceptability studies, user's perception surveys and evaluations of insertion and removal procedures. Currently, a joint program of the World Health Organization (WHO), the Population Council (PC) and Family Health International Action (FHIA) is to conduct post-marketing surveillance studies in seven countries, involving an estimated sample of 8,000 subjects. Multi-level reports concerning the operational aspects of Indonesia's program have also recently been published.

Moreover, Norplant®'s characteristics were widely debated in the media, although the quality and content of the information circulated is the subject of disagreement. Feminists stress, for instance, that the press tended to praise Norplant®'s merits, while downplaying its risks and side effects. All agree, however, that Norplant®'s negative aspects, as well as the divergent opinions regarding the benefits and usefulness of the method, have been canvassed in the media and that the general public, in various countries, has been exposed to the controversy.

Common ground also exists regarding the characteristics of the method, common implant side effects and contraindications. Norplant® is highly effective in averting births; it is also systemic and long-acting. Its delivery requires previous and comprehensive health screening; technical expertise to insert and remove the device; and adequate follow-up including effective procedures to locate users by the end of the five-year period.[7] Because it is "a method potentially subject to involutarism because of the difficulty of self removal after insertion" (Petitti 1992), all parties agree that ensuring Norplant® removal on demand is probably the most critical dimension of an ethical delivery process.

The Norplant® Debates: Disagreements

Disagreements run through different and overlapping levels of analysis, but the primary area of controversy is in the area of research protocols and program guidelines. Policy makers tend to consider documents—presented and agreed upon by governments and providers—to be consistent with the realities of delivery system. Feminists, while valuing protocols and norms, identify and address the wide gap existing between written reports and field operations. The feminist critique originally addressed the limits of informed consent in early trials, where women frequently signed the consent form without being entirely aware of its meaning (Barroso and Correa 1990; Dacach and Israel 1993). Later on, the feminist critique expanded to include the drawbacks in screening and follow-up procedures, and most importantly, access to removal on demand in the context of existing delivery programs.

Finally, feminists were, and still are, deeply concerned with the ethical problems that may occur in the context of Norplant® delivery. Since the clinical trials, feminists have identified the potential for abuse, whether from the technical or non-technical characteristics of the method. They have often examined the macro- and micro-level constraints that may restrict women's autonomy in relation to reproductive decisions. As authors such as Freedman and Isaacs (1993) indicate, under the influence of these overlapping constraints, the borders between voluntary choice and coercion may become blurred.

Economic conditions, public sector bureaucracy, and the existence or absence of demographically-driven population policies are particularly relevant in the analysis of programs through which Norplant® is delivered. These factors also determine social pressure on women to regulate their fertility, whether exerted by government officers, village heads, religious leaders, or health providers. At the micro-level, gender, class and race inequalities pervade the circumstances surrounding women's reproductive experiences. In a clinical setting, poor and black women might easily submit to the determinations of doctors and other powerful personalities. In some contexts, women will "accept" a provider-dependent method in order to circumvent difficult sexual negotiations with husbands and partners, and/or cultural resistance to fertility regulation.

The Indonesian Context

Indonesia is a nation composed of some thousand islands in South East Asia; the largest islands are Java, Sumatra, Sulawesi and Kalimantan. Against a background of Javanese dominance, the Indonesian culture is as diverse as the geography. Islamic hegemony differs from other countries in the region, because of a complex integration with pre-existing practices and beliefs.

Since the 1960s, the country has been ruled by a bureaucratic authoritarian regime which has been accused of numerous human rights abuses. The high economic growth rates of the 1970s were followed by adjustment policies in the last decade, the effects of which were income contraction, unemployment, and reduced levels of public expenditures. Despite the economic slowdown, the government has managed to maintain its social development infrastructure. But infant mortality rates remain high in some areas: 77 per 1,000 in urban areas, 123 per 1,000 in rural areas and 141 per 1,000 in West Java (World Bank 1990). As Smith (1990) indicates, maternal mortality rates are much worse than those found in neighbouring South East Asian countries: The lowest estimate for maternal mortality rates in Indonesia is 450 per 100,000 live births (UNICEF 1988), while for young women between the age of fifteen and nineteen, it is as high as 1,100 per 100,000 live births, only lower than that of Ethiopia (Smith 1990).

The Indonesian population, estimated at 174 million, is the fifth largest in the world. The country has pursued strong population policies since the late 1960s, encompassing a central family planning structure with ministerial status, the National Family Planning Coordinating Board (BKKBN) and a transmigration program aimed at the spatial redistribution of the population. In an extremely heterogeneous society the fertility control policies are strongly centralized and rather homogenous in design and goals.

Mass campaigns—known as "safaris"— have been used extensively to promote contraceptive use in rural areas. BKKBN has promoted the involvement of village authorities in its activities and considers the program to be a "national family planning movement" (BKKBN 1992). Through dialogue with Islamic leaders, BKKBN has achieved its desired acceptance levels for contraceptive methods, excluding sterilization and abortion. Indonesian fertility control policies have managed to combine clear, target-oriented models, with flexibility to adapt to prevailing cultural circumstances (Warwick 1988).

The total fertility rate (TFR) declined from 5.4 in 1950 to 3.41 in 1988, and contraceptive prevalence rose from 10 percent of eligible couples in 1960 to 46 percent in 1988. In 1987, contraceptive prevalence rates among married women were as follows: Pill, 31.4 percent; IUD, 30.5 percent; injectables, 21 percent; female sterilization, 6.9 percent; male sterilization, 0.4 percent;

Norplant®, 0.8 percent; and other methods, 5.5 percent. Norplant® clinical trials have been performed since 1982 and its use was approved in 1985. A Norplant® Regional Training Center functions at the Raden Saleh Clinic in Jakarta, providing technical assistance to other programs in South and South East Asia.

Both Indonesian family planning and transmigration programs have been subject to long-standing and severe criticism. In November 1990, when the Sixth International Meeting on Women's Health was held in Manila, activists from all over the world drafted and signed a letter to the United States Agency for International Development (USAID) harshly questioning the conditions under which the Indonesians were disseminating Norplant®. Environmentalists have also criticized the effects of the transmigration program and human rights organizations have denounced circumstances of abuse in the relocation of persons to East Timor and Irian Jaya (formerly West Papua).

Despite these critiques, the World Bank (1990) advocates public subsidies for the Indonesian family planning program, as these expenditures will help to compensate for the necessary increase in economic and social investments. The Bank has expressed concerns about a *potential* stall in the fertility decline and advocates the rapid expansion of programs to the urban poor and to outlying islands, strongly emphasizing the need to increase the prevalence of long-acting methods and to overcome resistance to sterilization.

The American Context

In 1991 the American population was estimated at 252,688 million people and the fertility rate (TFR) established for 1988 was 1.9. The contraceptive prevalence rates are as follows: 29.7 percent of couples of reproductive age were sterilized, and 36.7 percent used non-surgical contraception.[8] A large proportion of internationally-oriented population organizations are based in the United States and the majority of scientific analysis and political discourse concerning global demographic growth originate in the United States. Nonetheless, the United States has no government fertility control policy of the kind implemented in developing countries. However, controversies surrounding reproductive politics have been consistent and intense in the last century. This peculiar history combines conservative reactions to family planning and abortion, as well as furor over eugenic measures aimed at the control of population growth among groups perceived as "inferior." Ferringa, Iden and Rosenfield (1992) point out the paradox: compulsory sterilization laws were common in the majority of states; as many as 45,000 people in the United States were sterilized between 1907 and 1945 and many of them were poor; compulsory sterilization was commonly practiced throughout the first half of this century; however, for all intents and purposes, sterilization as a voluntary contraceptive option did not exist for many women.

Coercion has certainly not disappeared in the recent process of fertility decline in the United States; analysis of it requires that other variables be taken into account. Petchesky (1990) demonstrates that the recent fertility decrease started before the surge in Pill and IUD use in the sixties, and that the decrease is linked to women's access to higher education and employment, as well as to structural changes in female occupational distribution. Marriages were postponed and, even given the rapid increase in the use of modern contraceptive methods, abortion remained a primary form of fertility regulation. As Petchesky notes, the Supreme Court decision legalizing abortion in 1973 must be seen as an "accommodation" of the state and the legal system to a *de facto* social practice.

The struggle for reproductive choice, which has been a recurrent organizing principle for the American women's movement, became a major political issue mobilizing the most diverse actors in American society in the 1980s. Norplant® introduction in 1990 provoked mixed reactions from feminists, but given the prevailing anti-choice atmosphere the method was welcomed because they did not want to fuel conservative positions on contraception. The method was also welcomed by those sectors advocating an increase in contraceptive use to reduce pregnancy and abortion rates, especially among black and low-income teen-agers.[9] On one hand, in a context of aggravated social inequality, access to new technology may be constrained for under-privileged groups. On the other hand, numerous initiatives aimed at disseminating Norplant® to low-income women have been proposed since 1990 and will be analyzed in a subsequent section.

Norplant® Realities

I will analyze the data collected concerning the present picture of Norplant® to realities in a framework paralleling the feminist critique of Norplant®. These criticisms emerged during the early Norplant® trials, and it is interesting to note that recent published literature in some cases reiterates these early suspicions.[10] More important than confirming early problems, however, the new material indicates that the drawbacks and ethical questions remain or have been intensified in the context of Norplant® program delivery.

Written Protocols and Field Operations: The Gap

This section focuses on Indonesia, since the data concerning Norplant® dissemination in the United States applies principally to the other aspects under discussion. Data presented was collected from the following sources: BKKBN (1992), Kasidi and Miller (1992), the Hanhart (1993) Lombok case study, Lubis (1989), Noerprama (1991), Prihastono (1990), The World Bank (1990) and Zimmerman (1990). The information on the United States was drawn from Samuels and Smith (1992).

Reading this material leads one to conclude that, in Indonesia, Norplant® insertions do not adequately follow existing guidelines; in particular, comprehensive health status evaluations of potential users are lacking. The absence of screening is directly related to the delivery system, particularly in the context of "safaris," though screening is not routine in clinical settings either. Providers explain that screening guidelines are not followed because women prefer not to have pelvic examinations (Noerprama 1991). This approach could be interpreted as a commitment to "user's perspective," but for the fact that health and gynecological problems that would contraindicate Norplant® use are not detected and, quite often, pregnant women have had implants inserted.[11]

In addition, health providers are not adequately trained and clinical settings lack written information on Norplant's® side effects. Women themselves are not consistently informed about side effects, removal on request, and the five-year term. Zimmerman's (1990) summary of focal group discussions in the Dominican Republic, Egypt and Indonesia confirms the information gap and asserts that health professionals themselves may feel insecure about the method.

Ward (1990) describes a conversation with an Indonesian Norplant® user who was entirely unaware of basic information on the method. Consequently, several reports emphasize the need to overcome the absence or inadequacy of counseling services for users.

Observing that clinical records on users were incomplete in some settings, Kasidi and Miller (1992) and Ward (1990) estimate that clinics lose track of an average of 10 percent of acceptors within the five-year period. Thus, an estimated 130,000 women could be using Norplant® after the expiration date. Users may also be difficult to trace because of migration. No analysis of the nexus between Norplant's® drawbacks and the transmigration program in Indonesia is currently available, but BKKBN data indicates a rapid increase in the numbers of Norplant® acceptors in Irian Jaya and Timor between 1990 and 1991.[12]

Concerning insertion and removal proficiency, Ward (1990) documented inadequate technical preparation of providers, shortage of equipment and hurried delivery. Kasidi and Miller's (1992) conclusions, although not explicit, emphasize the need to ensure aseptic techniques. Concerning removal on request, both Ward and Hanhart (1993) confirm that women requesting the procedure because they resented the side effects have been refused removal, or at least had the procedure delayed. Paradoxically, some women had the implant removed when, instead of referring to side effects, they told the providers they wanted to get pregnant. This calls into question the validity of much discontinuation research.

Despite the low public costs of Norplant®, the method is considered expensive by BKKBN and acceptors are expected, and persuaded, to use the implants until expiration. Lubis (1989) also reported "cost" as a drawback to removal after expiration; 37 percent of women using Norplant® after five years "stated that they did not have enough money to pay for removal fees."[13]

The various critical evaluations of Norplant® delivery in Indonesia have provoked a response from BKKBN. In a comprehensive official document circulated in 1992, BKKBN's program board acknowledged the drawbacks and distortions of its delivery system and the Indonesian government stated its determination to implement measures to correct them. Decisions taken in the top of the highly hierarchical Indonesian state machineries, in general, reach the bottom of the system. Therefore, such provisory comments by BKKBN may lead donor agencies to expect that "quality of care" and "choice" will be implemented in the near future. Most reproductive rights activists disagree. As their framework of analysis is neither instrumental or strictly operational, they consider the idea of enhancing "choice" to be highly debatable, if the broader context of authoritarian government and gender inequalities is not challenged. Observers of Indonesia also state that the changes, if they ever occur, may take longer than expected, and they point out the long-standing incongruence between BKKBN policy guidelines and field operations.

As if to confirm these concerns, the official literature contains no clear indication that BKKBN plans to reduce the rate of Norplant® distribution. BKKBN projects an increase of 17 percent in the number of acceptors for the 1993–1994 period (from 16 to 17 percent of all contraceptive users). Most importantly, World Bank (1990) recommendations indicate that prevailing trends in Indonesia may tend to the opposite direction: new target groups, rapid increases in the number of acceptors, and emphasis on long-term contraceptive use. Under such circumstances, if "quality of care" and "choice" are to become serious

parameters for program evaluation, sharp contradictions will necessarily arise among the diverse agents operating the Indonesia Norplant® program.

Efficacy vs. Safety

In her overview of eight Norplant® acceptability studies, Hardon (1993) raises a series of concerns deserving special attention. She contends that the clinical settings where the studies took place might have influenced the responses of subjects. She also underlines the lack of anthropological insights in the methodologies used to investigate user's experiences, particularly regarding women's perceptions of side effects.[14] Hardon also questions the criteria of acceptability, suggesting that continuation and discontinuation rates have prevailed as the guiding references in most studies.

The literature on Indonesia supports her argument. The findings concerning Norplant® acceptability could be better interpreted as an expression of dissatisfaction with previously-used methods, rather than as a sign of clear and definite preference for the implants. In Aripurani (1991), the dropout rate for contraceptive use because of health concerns is 29 percent for the Pill, 26 percent for IUDs, and 37 percent for injections. Lubis (1989) found that 43 percent of subjects shifted to implants because they did not like (or could not tolerate) side effects from the Pill, IUDs or injectables. The Noerprama final report on a five-year clinical trial (1982–1987) found that, in a sample of 338 subjects, 128 (37.9 percent) decided to insert a second set of rods after the five-year expiration term, but 96 (28.4 percent) opted to use condoms.

The efficacy vs. safety dilemma can also be explored from the standpoint of the relative danger of side effects. Scientists in general assess contraceptive hazards on a strict physiological basis and tend to minimize the importance of biological disturbances that are not life-threatening. In contexts where the maternal mortality rate is high—as it is in Indonesia—contraceptive risks may be downplayed because avoiding births is often simplistically equated with reducing the risks associated with pregnancy and childbirth, including septic abortion. The feminist approach, on the other hand, weighs the side effects from contraceptive use as they affect women's subjective and social experience. Heavy bleeding may imply exclusion from social and religious activities (Hanhart 1993). Amenorrhea may also be experienced as a sign of pregnancy, a circumstance often producing anxiety in users who have opted for a long-acting method. Feminists also consider physiological effects to be detrimental to women's well-being and economic abilities in many circumstances, such as the case of heavy tasks performed by female workers in agriculture and factories, or in the very special case of sex workers.

It must be acknowledged, however, that a significant proportion of post-marketing surveillance studies concentrate their attention on bleeding patterns and evaluate women's perception in regard to these disturbances. Zimmerman (1990) best illustrates this new trend, which is certainly welcomed by reproductive rights activists. But the imbalance between pharmacological studies dedicated to verifying efficacy and studies aiming for a better understanding of the physiology of contraceptive side effects has not been overcome. Feminists as well as other authors believe that more bio-medical research is needed to reach a better understanding of short- and long-term Norplant® effects.[15] In the literature, one preliminary report on a post-marketing surveillance survey on user's perspectives of side effects (Sivin 1990) documents a striking differ-

ence in the percentage of complaints related to bleeding patterns in Sri Lankan and Thai women. The authors themselves suggest it could be attributed to differences in body weight between the two populations, but the hypothesis is not fully explored on a strict biomedical basis.[16]

Given the rising incidence of sexually transmitted diseases (STDs), reproductive tract infections (RTIs), HIV and AIDS, contraceptive safety parameters must necessarily address contamination risks implied in related medical procedures, and reflect the urgent need to combine disease protection and fertility regulation. This conceptual revision applies to all existing methods (see Norsigian 1993).

Concerning Norplant®, the risk of contamination is present in several situations: insertion and removal procedures, since the data demonstrates that aseptic conditions are not the norm; and the questionable promotion of Norplant® in settings presenting a high incidence of STDs, HIV and AIDS. HIV is epidemic in many of the settings in which Norplant® use is being promoted, including Thailand, Haiti, Rwanda, Mexico and Kenya, as well as in poor, urban sectors of the United States.

Potential for Abuse

It is not only in Indonesia, or other non-democratic societies, where there is potential for abuse. In two court actions in the United States, judges sought to require the use of Norplant® as a condition for probation. The Alan Guttmacher Institute (1992) reports during the 1991–1992 period, approximately twenty bills, amendments and welfare reform proposals involving Norplant® use were proposed in 13 legislatures. Analyses of press materials (Gladwele 1991, Kantrowitz 1993) suggest that, while varying in emphases, all of them advanced measures aimed at the promotion of Norplant® use among black teenagers, poor and welfare women, or subjects prosecuted for child abuse.

To date none of these legislative propositions have been enacted. The American Medical Association's Board of Trustees, in April 1992, expressed its opposition to these types of proposals. The Blacks Women's Health Project (Scott 1992), while welcoming Norplant® as a "broadening of choice," listed concerns regarding the risks of coercion among black, poor and welfare women. The concerns of these and other organizations are substantiated by historical evidence of abuse, particularly concerning sterilization. It is also interesting to observe that, even before the FDA approval, the Population Council expressed its concern for abuse potential. In October 1990, George Zeidenstein, then the president of the organization, said that any abusive use of Norplant® would be an "awful perversion of the method" (Zeidenstein 1990). In December, Wayne Bardin, Director of Biomedical Research at the Population Council, asserted that coercion should not be attributed to the technology itself but would be related to social values (USA Today 1990).

This intense debate indicates that, despite increasing numbers of acceptors, Norplant® remains controversial in light of its potential for abuse. The Indonesian case demonstrates that the potential abuse of Norplant® is not a peculiarly American phenomenon. Hardon, Harnhart and Mintzes (1993) document numerous cases of coercion in diverse political and cultural settings. The Thai National Family Planning Program have phased down Norplant® delivery in urban areas, concentrating its effort to expand its use "among the hill tribes populations." (Kiatboonsri et al. 1993) The Finnish case quotes health providers who state that they do not consider Norplant® a method of first choice, but would recommend it to "asocial women" (Hemminki et al. 1993).

Lubis (1989), Hanhart (1993), and Ward (1990) describe subtle mechanisms of coercion at the microlevel in Indonesia. Relative to the American culture, individual views and decisions are less significant than those of important reference groups and authorities. As this is particularly true in the case of women, concepts of "choice," "autonomy," and "entitlement" can be void of substance. In Lombok some women have shifted from IUDs, with which they were satisfied, as a result of pressure from village authorities. Data collected in urban setting showed 10 percent of subjects have changed method after the explicit recommendation of family planning officers (Lubis 1989). The limits between "persuasion and coercion" in the attitudes of field workers may be very thin in some circumstances (Ward 1990).

The history of contraceptive use in the last century tells us that potential for abuse is not solely the attribute of specific methods. Sterilization certainly remains the primary illustration, but circumstances of abuse have also occurred in clinical trials for the Pill, injectables and IUDs and in introductory processes. There may be more abuse potential for Norplant® relative to the IUD because of the possibility of divorcing the method from the genitals, and hence from a bodily link to reproduction and sexuality. If technologies in general distance people from their bodies, not all of them manage to complete this disconnection: IUDs convey a clear link to sexual and reproductive function, since they must be inserted through the vagina into the uterus.[17] We can hypothesize that technologies which most effectively disconnect the body from the reproductive experience are those most prone to abuse.

Mechanism of Social Mediation

The published literature on Norplant® is striking in its absence of context; the lack of comprehensive information concerning social and political structures, particularly regarding gender equity, is suspicious. The Indonesian materials provide the best illustration of this gap. The collection of data is predominantly confined to the relation between technology and users, or else between users and providers. As the discussion of "delivery systems" is separated from its social and political context, gaps occur. Zimmerman (1990) found that women complain that not all health professionals—in the areas they live—have adequate information about Norplant® insertion and removal procedures or side effects; this is a typical example of the manner in which the delivery system is evaluated, wherein the social factors leading to adequate information or health-care have not been taken into account.

Most reports fail to capture the relationship between the social context of gender equity and the identified limitations of method delivery. Ward (1990), for example, fails to explore the gender implications that may explain the "avoidance of pelvic examination" in the Indonesian context. From Hanhart's (1993) description, where such aspects are examined, BKKBN's target-oriented models are described as perversely interwoven with a whole set of cultural perceptions concerning body, sexuality and women's role. Furthermore, the social power dimensions wherein women, instead of complaining of side effects, say they want to get pregnant to have the implant removed begs further analysis; the underlying motives that may have informed these attitudes on the part of providers and clients are not thoroughly investigated. Much of

the feminist literature emphasizes the implications of international fertility control policies and severely criticizes the role played by the so-called population establishment. But other political determinants and social mediating mechanisms—for example, state-society relations, economic trends and gender systems—are often absent or minimized in such analyses.

A clearer understanding of context is critical to the evaluation of Norplant® risks and benefits. Scientists and providers frequently react to the feminist critique by stating that Norplant's technical characteristics must be isolated from the contextual constraints leading to poor applications. It is extremely difficult to disentangle technical dimensions from delivery drawbacks and, most importantly, from structural class and gender inequalities which impregnate societies and the systems through which the technology is being disseminated. The attitudes of Norplant® providers in Indonesia may have resulted from poor training programs and lack of information, but they may also be related to the authoritarian political system, to BKKBN's "target model" approach, and to women's subordination. In the entirely different conditions of the United States, despite careful training and intense public debate, Norplant® has mobilized an intense appeal to coercion.

A better focus on context may as well illuminate the conceptual underpinnings of the Norplant® controversies. The major divergences defining the debate can be described as the opposition between those advocating "choice" as the privileged approach to fertility regulation, and those asserting that the powers of technology largely prevail over the ability of women to preserve freedom and autonomy of decision. The first approach suggests the individual woman is a consumer, facing the product without any social mediation. Power is attributed to the individual as if she can overcome social constraints and technological pitfalls. The existing "safety net" of mediating mechanisms which permits a first decision, occasional changes of mind and complaint against risk or abuse remains subsumed within the *fetishism of choice*.[18]

Anti-technology perspectives, in turn, fall into a similar trap. The conceptual matrix informing this position is anchored in the antagonism between male constructed science and female identity and body, a rather simplified dichotomy. As a result the production, introduction and use of technology is frequently void of its connections with concrete historical and existing social contexts. As the discourse is somehow construed as being "spoken from nowhere" (Harding 1993), what prevails is the *fetishism of systems*. Techniques and devices are depicted as forces far beyond the reach of human beings and consequently impossible to control.

However, the structure and content of mediating processes are fundamental reference points for the examination of all technology versus individual interactions, being particularly critical in the case of contraceptive technologies. Social and political mediating mechanisms always exist, but they may or may not favor women's empowerment and reproductive autonomy. Whenever the second set of circumstances prevail, technologies become powerful tools of political and social control.

Indonesia is a disheartening illustration of the first case and conveys a convincing argument for the anti-technology position. The cancellation of the Norplant® trial in Brazil may fall into an intermediate category, as it cannot be adequately understood without clear reference to the specific political conditions of the period, with particular attention to the emergence of a vocal and active reproductive rights movement (Barroso and Correa 1990). The United States, where multiple mechanisms *do* exist to back up individual choice for some women and provide for "coercion monitoring," remains at the other extreme.

Norplant® is certainly not the best contraceptive method for American women, but the rapid increase in its use since December 1990 was made possible and relatively "safe" because of a strong safety net of political and social mediation mechanisms. The first mechanism is the stability of democratic procedures, and within it operates an articulate and vocal reproductive rights movement, along with other concerned political actors. The second is the market system and the network of consumer advocacy and protection organizations. As history demonstrates, a Norplant® "accident" in the American context would cost millions of dollars to Wyeth.[19] The intense public debates and the media also play a role in the continuing monitoring of Norplant® use and abuse.

These structures do not exist everywhere, and they are particularly weak in most developing countries. Even in the very special circumstances of the United States, the analyses advanced by black women's organizations assert that existing safety nets may not extend to or be effective in those settings most directly affected by racial, ethnic and class inequality.

Looking Forward

The review of recent literature on Norplant® makes clear that many of the concerns raised ten years ago in reference to abuse potential have not lost their pungency. Collected field information illustrates what George Zeidenstein (1992)—confirming early feminist analyses—has recently pointed out as one of the sharpest dilemmas of the contraceptive research field: What we are faced with for present purposes, what creates our dilemma, is that the most effective reversible contraceptive methods—TCU 380 and Norplant®—are both dependable and very long acting. In that sense they can be seen, as the Norplant® system has already been seen by some officials in the United States, as short cuts to solutions of larger social problems.

Given these circumstances, the global monitoring of Norplant® worldwide constitutes a mammoth task, requiring substantial human and financial resources. Considering the comprehensive and often overburdened agenda of national reproductive rights movements, it is debatable whether Norplant® monitoring should become a priority in developing countries where the method is being disseminated.

An important lesson to be learned from the Norplant® debate is that feminist critical perspectives must be effectively heard and taken into account in the earliest stages of contraceptive research and development.[20] This is of special interest in the changing political environment leading up to the Third International Conference on Population and Development (ICPD) in 1994, as the new climate may favor the reframing of scientific premises in the field of reproductive technologies.[21]

Finally, if democratic principles and women's self determination are to be preserved and enhanced, the Norplant® trajectory also demonstrates that substantial changes must occur beyond the scientific and technological domain. Profound reforms are also needed throughout the multiple mediating mechanisms which may constrain the daily experience of human subjects making fertility decisions in concrete social contexts.

Notes

1. A different version, labeled Norplant® II, containing just two rods, is currently under trial in various countries.

2. The Population Council lists in this category countries that have clinical trials, preintroduction studies, small-scale service delivery, or through private sector training.

3. Members of the International Reproductive Rights Movement take a broad spectrum of positions on Norplant® Some groups—such as the Feminist International Network of Resistance Against Reproductive and Genetic Engineering (FINRRAGE), Rede em Defesa da Espécie Humana (Brazil), and Ubinig (Bangladesh)—propose a ban on the method. The National Organization of Women (NOW, United States) has welcomed it as a contraceptive breakthrough. The National Women's Health Network, the Boston Women's Health Book Collective, and the National Black Women's Health Project (all United States) accepts its approval while remaining concerned with potential for abuse and long-term health effects.

4. The first volume, *Norplant®: Under Her Skin*, published by Wemos and the Women's Health Action Foundation in the Netherlands, contains a general overview of Norplant® characteristics and acceptability research findings. It also presents five country case studies: Brazil, Egypt, Finland, Indonesia and Thailand. The second volume, *As Rotas do Norplant—Desvios da Contracepcao*, reviews the conditions leading to the cancellation of the Brazilian clinical trials in 1986, and provides up-to-date information on remaining subjects. The Kaiser volume, *Norplant® and Poor Women*, addresses a range of interrelated aspects in the United States context: clinical trials, side effects contraindications, potential for abuse, class and race dimensions, and future perspectives on contraceptive technology.

5. The development of a contraceptive hormonal implant was under the direction of Sheldon Segall, senior biomedical researcher at the Population Council. The first clinical trials started in Brazil and Chile in the early 1970s to determine the most effective combination of rods and hormones. The involvement of a Brazilian researcher, Dr. Elsimar Coutinho, in early implant research remains the object of intense criticism from the Brazilian feminist community, as a result of Coutinho's outspoken misogyny and racism.

6. Bangladesh (1990), Chile (1988), China (1989), Colombia (1986), Czechoslovakia (1989), Ecuador (1985), Finland (1983), Indonesia (1985), Jamaica (1992), Kenya (1989), Malaysia (1990),

Mali (1993) Mauritius (1991), Mexico (1991), Peru (1987), Palau (1992), Rwanda (1992), Singapore (1990), Soviet Union (1991), Sri Lanka (1987), Sweden (1985), Thailand (1986), United States (1990), United Kingdom (1993), Venezuela (1987). In addition, family planning programs in three countries—Haiti, Nepal and Tunisia—have been authorized to provide implants. Several other countries have also approved Norplant® for distribution, but they are not included on this list because they accept FDA approval in lieu of their own regulatory organizations. This list is from the Population Council's research department.

7. A comprehensive list of criteria to guide Norplant® delivery is provided by the Sample Norplant® Protocol formulated by the Planned Parenthood of America and published in Samuels and Smith (1992).

8. Statistical Abstract of the United States. 1992 US Department of Commerce. Bureau of Census.

9. See Arline Geronimus, chapter 5, in this volume for a discussion of the social fixation regarding low-income, black teenage fertility during the last decade.

10. For example, see Dacach and Israel (1993) for an analysis of the Brazilian trials. They state that the clinic has moved from its original location without informing the involved subjects, and refer to one case of infertility and one death. The Population Council's representative, in Brazil, Dr. Anibal Faundes, has circulated a letter contesting the first two accusations.

11. Noerprama (1991) found that "5.96 percent of acceptors were pregnant at the time of insertion because of misdiagnosis." For the 1.3 million Norplant® users in Indonesia, this percentage converts to an estimated 77,000 undetected pregnancies. The desire to avoid a pelvic examination was also detected by Zimmerman (1990) in other country settings.

12. Indonesia is a particularly controversial regarding the link between Norplant® use and population mobility, but migrations are frequent and intense in most of the developing countries where Norplant® is being disseminated.

13. Cost-effectiveness arguments are also used by providers to persuade women not to remove implants in Bangladesh and Thailand as Ubinig (1990) and Zimmerman (1990) indicate.

14. In fact, the literature demonstrates that anthropological approaches have been quite frequently used in Norplant® acceptability studies and remain critical in post-marketing surveillance surveys. They have been, however, mostly used to identify and circumvent cultural resistance to the method, instead of problematizing its characteristics and exploring women's experiences of the method.

15. See Rachel Snow's article in this volume, and consult Petitti's (1992) review of 130 Medline titles on Norplant® for the 1990-1991 period.

16. See forthcoming volume edited by Snow and Hall entitled *Steroid Contraceptives and Women's Response* for an up-to-date discussion on the plausible role of body fat in explaining contraceptive side effects.

17. An analysis of the "disconnecting" effects of technology appears in Judith Wajcman's article in this volume. The idea that "body dimensions" could explain Norplant's® appeal to coercion was an important contribution gathered from discussion at the authors' workshop in May 1993.

18. This term is borrowed from Marx's analysis of the ideological mechanism (le fetichisme de la marchandise) through which all the chains of natural and human exploitation implied in the process of production remain invisible in the final product.

19. International norms providing for precise information sheets in drug advertising has been fully respected in American Norplant® advertising. The risk of litigation also explains the enormous investment Wyeth has made to ensure the careful training of providers, as well as the caution providers themselves express with regard to the method. As one piece of anecdotal evidence supporting this contention, an informer told me that she was persuaded not to choose Norplant® by a Planned Parenthood doctor. Similar behavior was detected in Finland by Hemminki, Kajesalo and Ollila.

20. This is particularly critical in regards to the contraceptive vaccine research currently underway. See chapters in this volume by Judith Richter and Faye Schrater, for more discussion of these new contraceptive methods. See also Rachel Snow and Elizabeth Bartholet for feminist analyses of research priorities and development for reproductive technologies.

21. In May 1993, the Second Preparatory Committee for the ICPD met in New York. The forward-looking agenda which is emerging for Cairo may reframe the conceptual base of the population field. The principles emphasized in New York were the close linkage between population, environment and development; a strong commitment to human rights; an emphasis on women's empowerment and gender equity; and an acceptance of a reproductive health and rights framework to guide future "fertility management" programs.

References

Alan Guttmacher Institute. 1992. *Norplant®: Opportunities and perils for low-income women.* Washington, D.C.

Aripurnani, S., W. Hajidz, and A. Taslim. 1991. Family planning program in Indonesia: A plight for policy reorientation. Paper presented at the INGI Conference, in Washington, D.C.

Barroso, C., and S. Correa. 1990. Public servants v. liberal professionals: The politics of contraceptive research. Presented at the Symposium of Induced Fertility Change, Bellagio.

Dacach, S., and G. Israel. 1993. *As rotas do Norplant®: Desvios da contracepca.* Rio de Janeiro, Brazil: REDEH.

Ferringa, B., S. Iden, and A. Rosenfield. 1992. Norplant®: Potential for coercion. In *Norplant® and poor women: Dimensions of new contraceptives,* ed. S. Samuels and M. Smith. Menlo Park, Calif.: The Kaiser Forums.

Freedman, L., and S. Isaacs. 1993. Reproductive health, reproductive rights: Legal, policy and ethical issues. Prepared for the Ford Foundation Reproductive Health Program Officers Meeting.

Gladwele, M. 1991. Science confronts ethics in contraceptive implant: Long term birth control nears approval. *Washington Post,* April 28.

Hanhart, J. 1993. Women's views on Norplant®—A study from Lombok, Indonesia. In *Norplant®: Under her skin,* ed. B. Mintzes, A. Hardon, and J. Hanhart. Amsterdam: Wemos and Women's Health Action Foundation.

Harding, S. 1993. Reinventing ourselves as other: More new agents of history and knowledge. In *American feminist thought at century's end: A reader,* ed. L. S. Kauffman. Cambridge, Mass.: Blackwell Publishers.

Hardon, A. 1993. Norplant®: Conflicting views on safety and acceptability. In *Norplant: Under her skin,* ed. B. Mintzes, A. Hardon, and J. Hanhart. Amsterdam: Wemos and Women's Health Action Foundation.

Hemminki, E., K. Kajesalo, and E. Ollila. 1993. Experience of Norplant® by Finnish family planning practitioners. In *Norplant®: Under her skin,* ed. B. Mintzes, A. Hardon, and J. Hanhart. Amsterdam: Wemos and Women's Health Action Foundation.

Kantrowitz, B., and P. Wingert. 1993. The Norplant® debate. *Newsweek* (February):36–39.

Kasidi, H., and P. Miller. 1992. *Norplant® use dynamics diagnostics, 1991. Final Report.* BKKBN and The Population Council.

Keeler, W. 1990. Speaking of gender in Java. *Power and difference,* ed. J. Atkinson and S. Errington. Stanford, Calif.: Stanford University Press.

Kiatboonsri, P., P. Panut-Ampon, and J. Richter. 1993. Inserting Norplant® at all cost? A case study of a Norplant® training session in Thailand. In *Norplant: Under her skin,* ed. B. Mintzes, A. Hardon, and J. Hanhart. Amsterdam: Wemos and Women's Health Action Foundation.

Lubis, F., I. Sigit Sidi, B. Affandi, et al. 1989. User's attitude about Norplant® contraceptive subdermal implant. Yasasan Kusuma Buana Foundation, Jakarta. Mimeo.

Mintzes, B., A. Hardon, and J. Hanhart, eds. 1993. *Norplant®: Under her skin.* Women and Pharmaceuticals Project. Amsterdam: Wemos and Women's Health Action Foundation.

Noerprama, N.P. 1991. The Norplant® removal training and services at Dr. Kariadi Hospital, Semarang, Indonesia. *Advances in contraception* 7:389–401.

Norsigian, J. 1993. Feminist perspective on barrier use. Paper presented at conference sponsored by CONRAD and WHO, March 22, in Santo Domingo.

Petchesky, R. 1990. *Abortion and woman's choice: The state, sexuality and reproductive freedom,* rev. ed. Boston: Northeastern University Press.

Pettiti, D. 1992. Issues in Evaluating Norplant®. In *Norplant® and poor women,* ed. S. Samuels and M. Smith. 1992. The Kaiser Forums.

Population Council Research Division. 1993. Direct communication from Elizabeth Westley, September 14.

Prihastono, J. 1990. *Norplant® removal study: Factors associated with due and overdue 5 years removal.* Yasasan Kusuma Buana Foundation, Jakarta. Mimeo.

Samuels, S., and M. Smith, eds. 1992. Executive summary. *Norplant® and poor women,* ed. S. Samuels and M. Smith. The Kaiser Forums.

Scott, J. 1992. Norplant® and women of color. In *Norplant® and poor women,* ed. S. Samuels and M. Smith. The Kaiser Forums.

Sivin, I., et al. 1990. Contraceptives and women's complaints: Preliminary results from the post-marketing surveillance of Norplant®. Population Council. Mimeo.

Smith, I. 1990. The Indonesian family planning programme: A success story for women? Boston Women's Health Book Collective Documentation Center Mimeo.

Snow, R., and P. Hall, eds. In press. *Steroid contraceptives and women's response: Regional variability in side-effects and pharmacokinetics.* New York: Plenum Press.

Statistical Abstract of the United States. 1992. U.S. Department of Commerce, Bureau of the Census.

UBINIG. The price of Norplant® is tk 2,000. You cannot remove it. The clients are refused removal in Norplant® trial in Bangladesh. Boston Women's Health Book Collective Documentation Center. Mimeo.

Ward, S., I. Sigit Sidi, R. Simmons, and G. Simmons. 1990. Service delivery systems and quality of care in implantation of Norplant®. Report prepared for the Population Council.

Warwick, D. 1988. Culture and the management of family planning programs. *Studies in family planning* 19(1):1–18.

World Bank. 1990. Indonesia: Family planning perspectives in the 1990's. World Bank Country Study. Washington, D.C.

Zeidenstein, G. 1990. Unreleased press statement. Population Council, October 31.

—. 1992. Dilemmas of public sector contraceptive development. *International Symposium on Recent Advances in Female Reproductive Health Care: Proceedings*. Helsinki: Finnish Population and Family Welfare Federation.

—. 1993. Conversations with the author, April-May.

Zimmerman, M., J. Haffey, E. Crane, et al. 1990. Assessing the acceptability of Norplant® implants in four countries: Findings from focus group research. *Studies in Family Planning* 21(2):92–103.

Households
and Families

Part VII

The readings in this chapter grapple with the vexing issues of women and their relationships to the family, to domestic labor and to the economy. In the first selection, "Is There a Family?" Jane Collier, Michelle Z. Rosaldo, and Sylvia Yanagisako examine what social scientists, present and past mean by "The Family." They revisit the work of Bronislaw Malinowski, whose 1913 book on Australian aborigines convinced social scientists that a single, universal kind of family exists in all cultures. They suggest that his vision of the family is not universal, but is tied to Victorian debates about what the family should be, as well as to notions of progress that privilege European concepts of family over other possibilities for organizing human relationships. They argue that "The Family" Malinowski described is primarily a moral or ideological unit, "a way of organizing and thinking about human relationships in a world in which the domestic is perceived to be in opposition to a politics shaped outside the home, and in which individuals find themselves dependent on a set of relatively noncontingent ties in order to survive the dictates of an impersonal market and external political order." What is at stake in this debate? If we agree that the family is an ideological unit rather than a functional one, what new questions arise?

Paula Ettelbrick and Thomas Stoddard's article "Legalizing Lesbian and Gay Marriage: A Conversation for Many Voices" presents the debate over whether marriage for lesbians and gays should become a central component of a gay and lesbian civil rights agenda. Their essay returns us to some of the questions raised by the previous article. Marriage is both a relationship between individuals and a relationship recognized by the state and sanctioned by law which confers material benefits not available to the unmarried. It is a social institution. The authors ask us to consider what does the ability to marry mean? Since most states do not permit marriages between same sex individuals, what impact does the inability to marry have? What would change if gay and lesbian people could marry? What would remain the same?

"Is There a Family?" is primarily concerned with exploring the creation and development of the dominant concepts of family and women in the family in Western cultures; other selections in this section consider how these dominant cultural ideals function differently for

443

women depending on how closely they conform to the white, middle-class, western woman who is used as the ideal. Evelyn Nakano Glenn, a historical sociologist, turns her attention to how race, equally with gender, has shaped the organization of social reproduction. Rejecting a model that views race and gender as discrete systems of hierarchy, Glenn considers the interconnections between race and gender as she examines women's reproductive labor, which she defines as "the array of activities and relationships involved in maintaining people on a daily basis and intergenerationally." She traces the reproductive labor of racial, ethnic women in the twentieth century—from their employment in the first part of the century as servants relieving white women of domestic work, to their current, disproportionate employment as service workers in the health care institutions that increasingly replace or supplement caregiving in the home. Glenn's article makes clear that white women's support for the racial division of labor enhances their support for the gender division of labor—if one can hire a woman of color cheaply to do the housework, why struggle with a partner about more equitable sharing of household responsibilities?

Pat Mainardi's essay "The Politics of Housework" describes the many levels of resistance she encountered when she tried to reorganize the housework in her home. Her essay describes her male partner's ingenious efforts to deny and evade the reality and responsibilities of the dirty jobs of the home. Mainardi, a white woman, explores her complicity in supporting the "natural" order of things and the attractions of a vantage point "divorced from the reality of maintaining life." Her piece, written at the beginnings of women's liberation, reminds us of the need to reflect continually on the connections between how we act in our daily life and the ideals we express. Why does it matter who does the housework?

Suggestions for Further Reading

Baca Zinn, Maxine. 1989. "Family, Race and Poverty in the Eighties," *Signs*, 14, 856–874.

Bordrova, Valentina. 1994. "Glasnost and the 'Woman Question' in the Mirror of Public Opinion: Attitudes Towards Women, Work and the Family." In Valentine M. Moghadam, ed. *Democratic Reform and the Position of Women in Transitional Economies*. New York: Oxford University Press.

Borooah, Romy, et al. 1994. *Capturing Complexity: An Interdisciplinary Look at Women, Households, and Development*. Thousand Oaks, CA: Sage Publications.

Chin, Ko-Lin. 1994. "Out-of-Town Brides: International Marriage and Wife Abuse Among Chinese Immigrants," *Journal of Comparative Family Studies*, 25, 53–69.

Gelfand, Donald E., and John McCallum. 1994. "Immigration, the Family and Female Caregivers in Australia," *Journal of Gerontological Social Work*, 22, 41–59.

Heredia, Ruldolf C. and Edward Mathias. 1995. *The Family in a Changing World: Women, Children, and Strategies of Intervention*. New Delhi: Indian Social Institute.

Hochschild, Arlie. 1989. *The Second Shift: Working Parents and the Revolution at Home*. New York: Viking.

Ingoldsby, Bron B. and Suzanna Smith, eds. 1995. *Families in Multicultural Perspective*. New York: Guilford Press.

Jacoby, Hanan G. 1995. "The Economics of Polygamy in Sub-Saharan Africa: Female Productivity and the Demand for Wives in Cote D'Ivoire," *Journal of Political Economy*, 103, 938–971.

Kamo, Yoshinori. 1994. "Division of Household Work in the United States and Japan," *Journal of Family Issues*, 15, 348–378.

Levine, Robert A. 1994. *Child Care and Culture: Lessons from Africa*. New York: Cambridge University Press.

Lewellyn, Hendrik and Willy Pearson Jr. 1995. "Spousal Independence, Female Power, and Divorce: A Cross-Cultural Examination," *Journal of Comparative Family Studies*, 26, 217–232.

Luke, Carmen. 1994. "White Women in Interracial Families: Reflections on Hybridization, Feminine Identities, and Racialized Othering," *Feminist Issues*, 14, 49–72.

Makhlouf-Obermeyer, Carla. 1995. *Family, Gender, and Population in the Middle East: Policies in Context*. Cairo: American University in Cairo Press.

McClintock, Anne. 1993. "Family Feuds: Gender, Nationalism, and the Family," *Feminist Review*, 44, 61–80.

O'Connell, Helen. 1994. *Women and the Family*. Atlantic Highlands, NJ: Zed Press.

Reddy, Maureen T. 1994. *Crossing the Color Line: Race, Parenting, and Culture*. New Brunswick, NJ: Rutgers University Press.

Salaff, Janet W. 1995. *Working Daughters of Hong Kong: Filial Piety or Power in the Family?* New York: Columbia University Press.

Stacey, Judith. 1990. *Brave New Families: Stories of Domestic Upheaval in Late Twentieth Century America*. New York: Basic Books.

Stichter, Sharon and Jane L. Parpart, eds. 1990. *Women, Employment, and the Family in the International Division of Labor*. Philadelphia: Temple University Press.

Young, Gay. 1993. "Gender Inequality and Industrial Development: The Household Connection." *Journal of Comparative Family Studies*, 24, 1–20.

Is There a Family?
New Anthropological Views

Jane Collier
Michelle Z. Rosaldo
Sylvia Yanagisako

This essay poses a rhetorical question in order to argue that most of our talk about families is clouded by unexplored notions of what families "really" are like. It is probably the case, universally, that people expect to have special connections with their genealogically closest relations. But a knowledge of genealogy does not in itself promote understanding of what these special ties are about. The real importance of The Family in contemporary social life and belief has blinded us to its dynamics. Confusing ideal with reality, we fail to appreciate the deep significance of what are, cross-culturally, various ideologies of intimate relationship, and at the same time we fail to reckon with the complex human bonds and experiences all too comfortably sheltered by a faith in the "natural" source of a "nurture" we think is found in the home.

This essay is divided into three parts. The first examines what social scientists mean by The Family. It focuses on the work of Bronislaw Malinowski, the anthropologist who first convinced social scientists that The Family was a universal human institution. The second part also has social scientists as its focus, but it examines works by the nineteenth-century thinkers Malinowski refuted, for if—as we shall argue—Malinowski was wrong in viewing The Family as a universal human institution, it becomes important to explore the work of theorists who did not make Malinowski's mistakes. The final section then draws on the correct insights of nineteenth-century theorists to sketch some implications of viewing The Family, not as a concrete institution designed to fulfill universal human needs, but as an ideological construct associated with the modern state.

Malinowski's Concept of the Family

In 1913 Bronislaw Malinowski published a book called *The Family among the Australian Aborigines*,[1] in which he laid to rest earlier debates about whether all human societies had families. During the nineteenth century, proponents of social evolution argued that primitives were sexually promiscuous and therefore incapable of having families because children would not recognize their fathers.[2] Malinowski refuted this notion by showing that Australian aborigines, who were widely believed to practice "primitive promiscuity," not only had rules regulating who might have intercourse with whom during sexual orgies but also differentiated between legal marriages and casual unions. Malinowski thus "proved" that Australian aborigines had marriage, and so proved that aboriginal children had fathers, because each child's mother had but a single recognized husband.

Malinowski's book did not simply add data to one side of an ongoing debate. It ended the debate altogether, for by distinguishing coitus from conjugal relationships, Malinowski separated questions of sexual behavior from questions of the family's universal existence. Evidence of sexual promiscuity was henceforth irrelevant for deciding whether families existed. Moreover, Malinowski argued that the conjugal relationship, and therefore The Family, had to be universal because it fulfilled a universal human need. As he wrote in a posthumously published book:

> The human infant needs parental protection for a much longer period than does the young of even the highest anthropoid apes. Hence, no culture could endure in which the act of reproduction, that is, mating, pregnancy, and childbirth, was not linked up with the fact of legally-founded parenthood, that is, a rela-

tionship in which the father and mother have to look after the children for a long period, and, in turn, derive certain benefits from the care and trouble taken.[3]

In proving the existence of families among Australian aborigines, Malinowski described three features of families that he believed flowed from The Family's universal function of nurturing children. First, he argued that families had to have clear boundaries, for if families were to perform the vital function of nurturing young children, insiders had to be distinguishable from outsiders so that everyone could know which adults were responsible for the care of which children. Malinowski thus argued that families formed bounded social units, and to prove that Australian families formed such units, he demonstrated that aboriginal parents and children recognized one another. Each aboriginal woman had a single husband, even if some husbands had more than one wife and even if husbands occasionally allowed wives to sleep with other men during tribal ceremonies. Malinowski thus proved that each aboriginal child had a recognized mother and father, even if both parents occasionally engaged in sexual relations with outsiders.

Second, Malinowski argued that families had to have a place where family members could be together and where the daily tasks associated with child rearing could be performed. He demonstrated, for example, that aboriginal parents and their immature children shared a single fire—a home and hearth where children were fed and nurtured—even though, among nomadic aborigines, the fire might be kindled in a different location each night.

Finally, Malinowski argued that family members felt affection for one another—that parents who invested long years in caring for children were rewarded by their own and their children's affections for one another. Malinowski felt that long and intimate association among family members fostered close emotional ties, particularly between parents and children, but also between spouses. Aboriginal parents and their children, for example, could be expected to feel the same emotions for one another as did English parents and children, and as proof of this point, Malinowski recounted touching stories of the efforts made by aboriginal parents to recover children lost during conflicts with other aborigines or with white settlers and efforts made by the stolen aboriginal children to find their lost parents.

Malinowski's book on Australian aborigines thus gave social scientists a concept of The Family that consisted of a universal function, the nurturance of young children, mapped onto (1) a bounded set of people who recognized one another and who were distinguishable from other like groups; (2) a definite physical space, a hearth and home; and (3) a particular set of emotions, family love. This concept of The Family as an institution for nurturing young children has been enduring, probably because nurturing children is thought to be the primary function of families in modern industrial societies. The flaw in Malinowski's argument is the flaw common to all functionalist arguments: because a social institution is observed to perform a necessary function does not mean either that the function would not be performed if the institution did not exist or that the function is responsible for the existence of the institution.

Later anthropologists have challenged Malinowski's idea that families always include fathers, but, ironically, they have kept all the other aspects of his definition. For example, later anthropologists have argued that the basic social unit is not the nuclear family including father but the unit composed of a mother and her children: "Whether or not a mate becomes attached to

the mother on some more or less permanent basis is a variable matter."[4] In removing father from the family, however, later anthropologists have nevertheless retained Malinowski's concept of The Family as a functional unit, and so have retained all the features Malinowski took such pains to demonstrate. In the writings of modern anthropologists, the mother-child unit is described as performing the universally necessary function of nurturing young children. A mother and her children form a bounded group, distinguishable from other units of mothers and their children. A mother and her children share a place, a home and hearth. And, finally, a mother and her children share deep emotional bonds based on their prolonged and intimate contact.

Modern anthropologists may have removed father from The Family, but they did not modify the basic social science concept of The Family in which the function of child rearing is mapped onto a bounded set of people who share a place and who "love" one another. Yet it is exactly this concept of The Family that we, as feminist anthropologists, have found so difficult to apply. Although the biological facts of reproduction, when combined with a sufficiently elastic definition of marriage, make it possible for us, as social scientists, to find both mother-child units and Malinowski's conjugal-pairs-plus-children units in every human society, it is not at all clear that such Families necessarily exhibit the associated features Malinowski "proved" and modern anthropologists echo.

An outside observer, for example, may be able to delimit family boundaries in any and all societies by identifying the children of one woman and that woman's associated mate, but natives may not be interested in making such distinctions. In other words, natives may not be concerned to distinguish family members from outsiders, as Malinowski imagined natives should be when he argued that units of parents and children have to have clear boundaries in order for childrearing responsibilities to be assigned efficiently. Many languages, for example, have no word to identify the unit of parents and children that English speakers call a "family." Among the Zinacantecos of southern Mexico, the basic social unit is identified as a "house," which may include from one to twenty people.[5] Zinacantecos have no difficulty talking about an individual's parents, children, or spouse, but Zinacantecos do not have a single word that identifies the unit of parents and children in such a way as to cut it off from other like units. In Zinacanteco society, the boundary between "houses" is linguistically marked, while the boundary between "family" units is not.

Just as some languages lack words for identifying units of parents and children, so some "families" lack places. Immature children in every society have to be fed and cared for, but parents and children do not necessarily eat and sleep together as a family in one place. Among the Mundurucu of tropical South America, for example, the men of a village traditionally lived in a men's house together with all the village boys over the age of thirteen; women lived with other women and young children in two or three houses grouped around the men's house.[6] In Mundurucu society, men and women ate and slept apart. Men ate in the men's house, sharing food the women had cooked and delivered to them; women ate with other women and children in their own houses. Married couples also slept apart, meeting only for sexual intercourse.

Finally, people around the world do not necessarily expect family members to "love" one another. People may expect husbands, wives, parents, and children to have strong feelings about one another, but they do not necessarily expect prolonged and intimate contact to breed the loving sentiments Malinowski imagined as universally rewarding parents for the care they invested in children. The mother-daughter relationship, for example, is not always pictured as warm and loving. In modern Zambia, girls are not expected to discuss personal problems with, or seek advice from, their mothers. Rather, Zambian girls are expected to seek out some older female relative to serve as confidante.[7] Similarly, among the Cheyenne Indians who lived on the American Great Plains during the last century, a mother was expected to have strained relations with her daughters.[8] Mothers are described as continually admonishing their daughters, leading the latter to seek affection from their fathers' sisters.

Of course, anthropologists have recognized that people everywhere do not share our deep faith in the loving, self-sacrificing mother, but in matters of family and motherhood, anthropologists, like all social scientists, have relied more on faith than evidence in constructing theoretical accounts. Because we *believe* mothers to be loving, anthropologists have proposed, for example, that a general explanation of the fact that men marry mother's brothers' daughters more frequently than they marry father's sisters' daughters is that men naturally seek affection (i.e., wives) where they have found affection in the past (i.e., from mothers and their kin).[9]

Looking Backward

The Malinowskian view of The Family as a universal institution—which maps the "function" of "nurturance" onto a collectivity of specific persons (presumably "nuclear" relations) associated with specific spaces ("the home") and specific affective bonds ("love")—corresponds, as we have seen, to that assumed by most contemporary writers on the subject. But a consideration of available ethnographic evidence suggests that the received view is a good deal more problematic than a naive observer might think. If Families in Malinowski's sense are *not* universal, then we must begin to ask about the biases that, in the past, have led us to misconstrue the ethnographic record. The issues here are too complex for thorough explication in this essay, but if we are to better understand the nature of "the family" in the present, it seems worthwhile to explore the question, first, of why so many social thinkers continue to believe in Capital-Letter Families as universal institutions, and second, whether anthropological tradition offers any alternatives to a "necessary and natural" view of what our families are. Only then will we be in a position to suggest "new anthropological views" on the family today.

Our positive critique begins by moving backward. In the next few pages, we suggest that tentative answers to both questions posed above lie in the nineteenth-century intellectual trends that thinkers like Malinowski were at pains to reject. During the second half of the nineteenth century, a number of social and intellectual developments—among them, the evolutionary researches of Charles Darwin, the rise of "urban problems" in fast-growing cities, and the accumulation of data on non-Western peoples by missionaries and agents of the colonial states—contributed to what most of us would now recognize as the beginnings of modern social science. Alternately excited and perplexed by changes in a rapidly industrializing world, thinkers as diverse as socialist Frederick Engels[10] and bourgeois apologist Herbert Spencer[11]—to say nothing of a host of mythographers, historians of religion, and even feminists—attempted to identify the distinctive problems and potentials of their contemporary society

by constructing *evolutionary* accounts of "how it all began." At base, a sense of "progress" gave direction to their thought, whether, like Spencer, they believed "man" had advanced from the love of violence to a more civilized love of peace or, like Engels, that humanity had moved from primitive promiscuity and incest toward monogamy and "individual sex love." Proud of their position in the modern world, some of these writers claimed that rules of force had been transcended by new rules of law,[12] while others thought that feminine "mysticism" in the past had been supplanted by a higher male "morality."[13]

At the same time, and whatever else they thought of capitalist social life (some of them criticized, but none wholly abhorred it), these writers also shared a sense of moral emptiness and a fear of instability and loss. Experience argued forcefully to them that moral order in their time did not rest on the unshakable hierarchy—from God to King to Father in the home—enjoyed by Europeans in the past.[14] Thus, whereas Malinowski's functionalism led him to stress the underlying continuities in all human social forms, his nineteenth-century predecessors were concerned to understand the facts and forces that set their experiential world apart. They were interested in comparative and, more narrowly, evolutionary accounts because their lives were torn between celebration and fear of change. For them, the family was important not because it had at all times been the same but because it was at once the moral precondition for, the triumph of, and the victim of developing capitalist society. Without the family and female spheres, thinkers like John Ruskin feared we would fall victim to a market that destroys real human bonds.[15] Then again, while men like Engels could decry the impact of the market on familial life and love, he joined with more conservative counterparts to insist that our contemporary familial forms benefitted from the individualist morality of modern life and reached to moral and romantic heights unknown before.

Given this purpose and the limited data with which they had to work, it is hardly surprising that the vast majority of what these nineteenth-century writers said is easily dismissed today. They argued that in simpler days such things as incest were the norm; they thought that women ruled in "matriarchal" and peace-loving states or, alternatively, that brute force determined the primitive right and wrong. None of these visions of a more natural, more feminine, more sexy, or more violent primitive world squares with contemporary evidence about what, in technological and organizational terms, might be reckoned relatively "primitive" or "simple" social forms. We would suggest, however, that whatever their mistakes, these nineteenth-century thinkers *can* help us rethink the family today, at least in part because we are (unfortunately) their heirs, in the area of prejudice, and partly because their concern to characterize difference and change gave rise to insights much more promising than their functionalist critics may have thought.

To begin, although nineteenth-century evolutionary theorists did not believe The Family to be universal, the roots of modern assumptions can be seen in their belief that women are, and have at all times been, defined by nurturant, connective, and reproductive roles that *do not change* through time. Most nineteenth-century thinkers imaged social development as a process of differentiation from a relatively confused (and thus incestuous) and indiscriminate female-oriented state to one in which men fight, destroy their "natural" social bonds, and then forge public and political ties to create a human "order." For some, it seemed

reasonable to assume that women dominated as matriarchs in the undifferentiated early state, but even those theorists believed that women everywhere were "mothers" first, defined by "nurturant" concerns and thus excluded from the business of competition, cooperation, social ordering, and social change propelled and dominated by their male counterparts. And so, while nineteenth-century writers differed in their evaluations of such things as "women's status," they all believed that female reproductive roles made women different from and complementary to men and guaranteed both the relative passivity of women in human history and the relative continuity of "feminine" domains and functions in human societies. Social change consisted in the acts of men, who left their mothers behind in shrinking homes. And women's nurturant sphere was recognized as a complementary and necessary corrective to the more competitive pursuits of men, not because those thinkers recognized women as political actors who influence the world, but because they feared the unchecked and morally questionable growth of a male-dominated capitalist market.

For nineteenth-century evolutionists, women were associated, in short, with an unchanging biological role and a romanticized community of the past, while men were imaged as the agents of all social process. And though contemporary thinkers have been ready to dismiss manifold aspects of their now-dated school of thought, on this point we remain, perhaps unwittingly, their heirs. Victorian assumptions about gender and the relationship between competitive male markets and peace-loving female homes were not abandoned in later functionalist schools of thought at least in part because pervasive sexist biases make it easy to forget that women, like men, are important actors in *all* social worlds. Even more, the functionalists, themselves concerned to understand all human social forms in terms of biological "needs," turned out to strengthen earlier beliefs associating action, change, and interest with the deeds of men because they thought of kinship in terms of biologically given ties, of "families" as units geared to reproductive needs, and finally, of women as mere "reproducers" whose contribution to society was essentially defined by the requirements of their homes.

If most modern social scientists have inherited Victorian biases that tend ultimately to support a view uniting women and The Family to an apparently unchanging set of biologically given needs, we have at the same time failed to reckon with the one small area in which Victorian evolutionists were right. They understood, as we do not today, that families—like religions, economies, governments, or courts of law—are *not* unchanging but the product of various social forms, that the relationships of spouses and parents to their young are apt to be different things in different social orders. More particularly, although nineteenth-century writers had primitive society all wrong, they were correct in insisting that *family* in the modern sense—a unit bounded, biologically as well as legally defined, associated with property, self-sufficiency, with affect and a space "inside" the home—is something that emerges not in Stone Age caves but in complex state-governed social forms. Tribal peoples may speak readily of lineages, households, and clans, but—as we have seen—they rarely have a word denoting Family as a particular and limited group of kin; they rarely worry about differences between legitimate and illegitimate heirs or find themselves concerned (as we so often are today) that what children or parents do reflects on their family's public image and self-esteem. Political influence in tribal groups in fact consists in adding children to

one's home and, far from distinguishing Smith from Jones, encouraging one's neighbors to join one's household as if kin. By contrast, modern bounded Families try to keep their neighbors out. Clearly their character, ideology, and functions are not given for all times. Instead, to borrow the Victorian phrase, The Family is a "moral" unit, a way of organizing and thinking about human relationships in a world in which the domestic is perceived to be in opposition to a politics shaped outside the home, and in which individuals find themselves dependent on a set of relatively noncontingent ties in order to survive the dictates of an impersonal market and external political order.

In short, what the Victorians recognized and we have tended to forget is, first, that human social life has varied in its "moral"— we might say its "cultural" or "ideological"—forms, and so it takes more than making babies to make Families. And having seen The Family as something more than a response to omnipresent, biologically given needs, they realized too that Families do not everywhere exist; rather, the Family (thought to be universal by most social scientists today) is a moral and ideological unit that appears, not universally, but in particular social orders. The Family as we know it is not a "natural" group created by the claims of "blood" but a sphere of human relationships shaped by a state that recognizes Families as units that hold property, provide for care and welfare, and attend particularly to the young—a sphere conceptualized as a realm of love and intimacy *in opposition* to the more "impersonal" norms that dominate modern economies and politics. One can, in nonstate social forms, find groups of genealogically related people who interact daily and share material resources, but the contents of their daily ties, the ways they think about their bonds and their conception of the relationship between immediate "familial" links and other kinds of sociality, are apt to be different from the ideas and feelings we think rightfully belong to families we know. Stated otherwise, because our notions of The Family are rooted in a contrast between "public" and "private" spheres, we will not find that Families like ours exist in a society where public and political life is radically different from our own.

Victorian thinkers rightly understood the link between the bounded modern Family and the modern state, although they thought the two related by a necessary teleology of moral progress. Our point resembles theirs not in the *explanations* we would seek but in our feeling that if we, today, are interested in change, we must begin to probe and understand change in the families of the past. Here the Victorians, not the functionalists, are our rightful guides, because the former recognized that *all* human social ties have "cultural" or "moral" shapes and, more specifically, that the particular "morality" of contemporary familial forms is rooted in a set of processes that link our intimate experiences and bonds to public politics.

Toward a Rethinking

Our perspective on families therefore compels us to listen carefully to what the natives in other societies say about their relationships with genealogically close kin. The same is true of the natives in our own society. Our understanding of families in contemporary American society can be only as rich as our understanding of what The Family represents symbolically to Americans. A complete cultural analysis of The Family as an American ideological construct, of course, is beyond the scope of this essay. But we can indicate some of the directions such an analysis would take and how it would deepen our knowledge of American families.

One of the central notions in the modern American construct of The Family is that of nurturance. When antifeminists attack the Equal Rights Amendment, for example, much of their rhetoric plays on the anticipated loss of the nurturant, intimate bonds we associate with The Family. Likewise, when prolife forces decry abortion, they cast it as the ultimate denial of nurturance. In a sense, these arguments are variations of a functionalist view that weds families to specific functions. The logic of the argument is that because people need nurturance, and people get nurtured in The Family, then people need The Family. Yet if we adopt the perspective that The Family is an ideological unit rather than merely a functional unit, we are encouraged to subject this syllogism to closer scrutiny. We can ask, first, What do people mean by nurturance? Obviously, they mean more than mere nourishment—that is, the provision of food, clothing, and shelter required for biological survival. What is evoked by the word *nurturance* is a certain kind of relationship: a relationship that entails affection and love, that is based on cooperation as opposed to competition, that is enduring rather than temporary, that is noncontingent rather than contingent upon performance, and that is governed by feeling and morality instead of law and contract.

The reason we have stated these attributes of The Family in terms of oppositions is because in a symbolic system the meanings of concepts are often best illuminated by explicating their opposites. Hence, to understand our American construct of The Family, we first have to map the larger system of constructs of which it is only a part. When we undertake such an analysis of The Family in our society, we discover that what gives shape to much of our conception of The Family is its symbolic opposition to work and business, in other words, to the market relations of capitalism. For it is in the market, where we sell our labor and negotiate contract relations of business, that we associate with competitive, temporary, contingent relations that must be buttressed by law and legal sanctions.

The symbolic opposition between The Family and market relations renders our strong attachment to The Family understandable, but it also discloses the particularity of our construct of The Family. We can hardly be speaking of a universal notion of The Family shared by people everywhere and for all time, because people everywhere and for all time have not participated in market relations out of which they have constructed a contrastive notion of the family.

The realization that our idea of The Family is part of a set of symbolic oppositions through which we interpret our experience in a particular society compels us to ask to what extent this set of oppositions reflects real relations between people and to what extent it also shapes them. We do not adhere to a model of culture in which ideology is isolated from people's experience. On the other hand, neither do we construe the connection between people's constructs and people's experience to be a simple one of epiphenomenal reflection. Rather, we are interested in understanding how people come to summarize their experience in folk constructs that gloss over the diversity, complexity, and contradictions in their relationships. If, for example, we consider the second premise of the aforementioned syllogism—the idea that people get "nurtured" in families—we can ask how people reconcile this premise with the fact that relationships in families are not always this simple or altruistic. We need not resort to the evidence offered by social historians (e.g., Philippe Ariès[16] and Lawrence Stone[17]) of the harsh treatment and neglect of children

and spouses in the history of the Western family, for we need only read our local newspaper to learn of similar abuses among contemporary families. And we can point to other studies, such as Michael Young and Peter Willmott's *Family and Kinship in East London*,[18] that reveal how people often find more intimacy and emotional support in relationships with individuals and groups outside The Family than they do in their relationships with family members.

The point is not that our ancestors—or our contemporaries have been uniformly mean and nonnurturant to family members but that we have all been both nice and mean, both generous and ungenerous, to them. In like manner, our actions toward family members are not always motivated by selfless altruism but are also motivated by instrumental self-interest. What is significant is that, despite the fact that our complex relationships are the result of complex motivations, we ideologize relations within The Family as nurturant while casting relationships outside The Family—particularly in the sphere of work and business—as just the opposite.

We must be wary of oversimplifying matters by explaining away those disparities between our notion of the nurturant Family and our real actions toward family members as the predictable failing of imperfect beings. For there is more here than the mere disjunction of the ideal and the real. The American construct of The Family, after all, is complex enough to comprise some key contradictions. The Family is seen as representing not only the antithesis of the market relations of capitalism; it is also sacralized in our minds as the last stronghold against The State, as the symbolic refuge from the intrusions of a public domain that constantly threatens our sense of privacy and self-determination. Consequently, we can hardly be surprised to find that the punishments imposed on people who commit physical violence are lighter when their victims are their own family members.[19] Indeed, the American sense of the privacy of the things that go on inside families is so strong that a smaller percentage of homicides involving family members are prosecuted than those involving strangers.[20] We are faced with the irony that in our society the place where nurturance and noncontingent affection are supposed to be located is simultaneously the place where violence is most tolerated.

There are other dilemmas about The Family that an examination of its ideological nature can help us better understand. For example, the hypothesis that in England and the United States marriages among lower-income ("working-class") groups are characterized by a greater degree of "conjugal role segregation" than are marriages among middle-income groups has generated considerable confusion. Since Elizabeth Bott observed that working-class couples in her study of London families exhibited more "segregated" conjugal roles than "middle-class" couples, who tended toward more "joint" conjugal roles,[21] researchers have come forth with a range of diverse and confusing findings. On the one hand, some researchers have found that working-class couples indeed report more segregated conjugal role relationships—in other words, clearly differentiated male and female tasks, as well as interests and activities—than do middle-class couples.[22] Other researchers, however, have raised critical methodological questions about how one goes about defining a joint activity and hence measuring the degree of "jointness" in a conjugal relationship.[23] Platt's finding that couples who reported "jointness" in one activity were not particularly likely to report "jointness" in another activity is significant because it demonstrates that

"jointness" is not a general characteristic of a relationship that manifests itself uniformly over a range of domains. Couples carry out some activities and tasks together or do them separately but equally; they also have other activities in which they do not both participate. The measurement of the "jointness" of conjugal relationships becomes even more problematic when we recognize that what one individual or couple may label a "joint activity," another individual or couple may consider a "separate activity." In Bott's study, for example, some couples felt that all activities carried out by husband and wife in each other's presence were

> similar in kind regardless of whether the activities were complementary (e.g. sexual intercourse, though no one talked about this directly in the home interview), independent (e.g. husband repairing book while the wife read or knitted), or shared (e.g. washing up together, entertaining friends, going to the pictures together). It was not even necessary that husband and wife should actually be together. As long as they were both at home it was felt that their activities partook of some special, shared, family quality.[24]

In other words, the distinction Bott drew among "joint," "differentiated," and "autonomic" (independent) relationships summarized the way people thought and felt about their activities rather than what they were observed to actually do. Again, it is not simply that there is a disjunction between what people say they do and what they in fact do. The more cogent point is that the meaning people attach to action, whether they view it as coordinated and therefore shared or in some other way, is an integral component of that action and cannot be divorced from it in our analysis. When we compare the conjugal relationships of middle-income and low-income people, or any of the family relationships among different class, age, ethnic, and regional sectors of American society, we must recognize that our comparisons rest on differences and similarities in ideological and moral meanings as well as on differences and similarities in action.

Finally, the awareness that The Family is not a concrete "thing" that fulfills concrete "needs" but an ideological construct with moral implications can lead to a more refined analysis of historical change in the American or Western family than has devolved upon us from our functionalist ancestors. The functionalist view of industrialization, urbanization, and family change depicts The Family as responding to alterations in economic and social conditions in rather mechanistic ways. As production gets removed from the family's domain, there is less need for strict rules and clear authority structures in the family to accomplish productive work. At the same time, individuals who now must work for wages in impersonal settings need a haven where they can obtain emotional support and gratification. Hence, The Family becomes more concerned with "expressive" functions, and what emerges is the modern "companionate family." In short, in the functionalist narrative The Family and its constituent members "adapt" to fulfill functional requirements created for it by the industrialization of production. Once we begin to view The Family as an ideological unit and pay due respect to it as a moral statement, however, we can begin to unravel the more complex, dialectical process through which family relationships and The Family as a construct were mutually transformed. We can examine, for one, the ways in which people and state institutions acted, rather than merely reacted, to assign certain functions to groupings of kin by making them legally responsible for these functions. We can investigate the manner in which the increasing limitations placed on agents of the community and the state with regard to negotiating the relationships between family members enhanced the independence of The Family. We can begin to understand the consequences of social reforms and wage policies for the age and sex inequalities in families. And we can elucidate the interplay between these social changes and the cultural transformations that assigned new meanings and modified old ones to make The Family what we think it to be today.

Ultimately, this sort of rethinking will lead to a questioning of the somewhat contradictory modern views that families are things we need (the more "impersonal" the public world, the more we need them) and at the same time that loving families are disappearing. In a variety of ways, individuals today *do* look to families for a "love" that money cannot buy and find; our contemporary world makes "love" more fragile than most of us hope and "nurturance" more self-interested than we believe.[25] But what we fail to recognize is that familial nurturance and the social forces that turn our ideal families into mere fleeting dreams are *equally* creations of the world we know *today*. Rather than think of the ideal family as a world we lost (or, like the Victorians, as a world just recently achieved), it is important for us to recognize that while families symbolize deep and salient modern themes, contemporary families are unlikely to fulfill our equally modern nurturant needs.

We probably have no cause to fear (or hope) that The Family will dissolve. What we can begin to ask is what we *want* our families to do. Then, distinguishing our hopes from what we have, we can begin to analyze the social forces that enhance or undermine the realization of the kinds of human bonds we need.

Notes

1. Bronislaw Malinowski, *The Family among the Australian Aborigines* (London: University of London Press, 1913).

2. Lewis Henry Morgan, *Ancient Society* (New York: Holt, 1877).

3. Bronislaw Malinowski, A *Scientific Theory of Culture* (Chapel Hill: University of North Carolina Press, 1944), 99.

4. Robin Fox, *Kinship and Marriage* (London: Penguin Books, 1967), 39.

5. Evon Z. Vogt, *Zinacantan: A Maya Community in the Highlands of Chiapas* (Cambridge, Mass.: Harvard University Press, 1969).

6. Yolanda Murphy and Robert Murphy, *Women of the Forest* (New York: Columbia University Press, 1974).

7. Ilsa Schuster, *New Women of Lusaka* (Palo Alto, Calif.: Mayfield, 1979).

8. E. Adamson Hoebel, *The Cheyennes: Indians of the Great Plains* (New York: Holt, Rinehart & Winston, 1978).

9. George C. Homans and David M. Schneider, *Marriage, Authority, and Final Causes* (Glencoe, Ill.: Free Press, 1955).

10. Frederick Engels, *The Origin of the Family, Private Property and the State*, in *Karl Marx and Frederick Engels: Selected Works*, vol. 2 (Moscow: Foreign Language Publishing House, 1955).

11. Herbert Spencer, *The Principles of Sociology*, vol. 1, Domestic Institutions (New York: Appleton, 1973).

12. John Stuart Mill, *The Subjection of Women* (London: Longmans, Green, Reader & Dyer, 1869).

13. J. J. Bachofen, *Das Mutterrecht* (Stuttgart, 1861).

14. Elizabeth Fee, "The Sexual Politics of Victorian Social Anthropology," in *Clio's Banner Raised*, ed. M. Hartman and L. Banner (New York: Harper & Row, 1974).

15. John Ruskin, "Of Queen's Gardens," in *Sesame and Lilies* (London: J. M. Dent, 1907).

16. Philippe Ariès, *Centuries of Childhood*, trans. Robert Baldick (New York: Vintage Books, 1962).

17. Lawrence Stone, *The Family, Sex, and Marriage in England, 1500–1800* (London: Weidenfeld & Nicholson, 1977).

18. Michael Young and Peter Willmott, *Family and Kinship in East London* (London: Routledge & Kegan Paul, 1957).

19. Henry P. Lundsgaarde, *Murder in Space City: A Cultural Analysis of Houston Homicide Patterns* (New York: Oxford University Press, 1977).

20. Ibid.

21. Elizabeth Bott, *Family and Social Network: Roles, Norms, and External Relationships in Ordinary Urban Families* (London: Tavistock, 1957).

22. Herbert J. Gans, *The Urban Villagers* (New York: Free Press, 1962.); C. Rosser and C.Harris, *The Family and Social Change* (London: Routledge & Kegan Paul, 1965).

23. John Platt, "Some Problems in Measuring the Jointness of Conjugal Role-Relationships," *Sociology* 3 (1969): 287–97; Christopher Turner, "Conjugal Roles and Social Networks: A Re-examination of an Hypothesis," *Human Relations* 20 (1967): 121-30; and Morris Zelditch, Jr., "Family, Marriage and Kinship," in *A Handbook of Modern Sociology*, ed. R. E. L. Faris (Chicago: Rand McNally, 1964), 680–707.

24. Bott, Family and Social Network, p. 240.

25. See the following essay in this volume, Rayna Rapp's "Family and Class in Contemporary America: Notes toward an Understanding of Ideology."

Legalizing Lesbian & Gay Marriage:
A Conversation for Many Voices

Paula Ettelbrick
Thomas B. Stoddard

Most of us have probably shouted, "But gay people can't get married!" while explaining why we were less than thrilled to have to attend a cousin's wedding. Lesbians and gay men can't get married: 57 percent of straight people in the US disapprove of two people of the same sex living together as a married couple (according to a recent poll conducted by the *San Francisco Examiner*); and until recently, the odds of winning the right to marry have seemed impossible.

But slowly, the prospect of legal lesbian and gay marriage has become less of a fairytale. This year, Denmark changed its laws to allow them. And in the US, the Board of Directors of the Bar Association in San Francisco called for a change in the California laws that make marriage the sole province of heterosexuals. Legislation that extends minimal benefits to unmarried "domestic partners" recently was enacted in San Francisco and West Hollywood, which now join the ranks of Berkeley and Santa Cruz, California and Madison, Wisconsin where domestic partners have been granted even more partial benefits.

If the popularity of "The Wedding" (the event at the 1987 March on Washington for Lesbian and Gay Rights at which thousands of men and women "married" their partners of the same sex) is any indication of popular sentiment in our communities, many lesbians and gay men across the country would get hitched in a second, if we actually could.

But how big of a priority should the lesbian and gay movement place on seeking that right? While few would begrudge any couple the right to publicly celebrate their relationship, there is less consensus about how much energy we should expend to get the government to sanction those same relationships.

Lesbian and gay civil rights organizations across the country, including the New York-based Lambda Legal Defense and Education Fund have been debating this question. In the pages that follow, two Lambda staffmembers share some of the arguments that have surfaced as their organization has evaluated what kinds of precedent-setting cases it should take on.

Why Gay People Should Seek the Right to Marry

Thomas B. Stoddard

Even these days, when few lesbians and gay men enter into marriages recognized by law, absolutely every gay person has an opinion on marriage as an "institution." (The word "institution" brings to mind, perhaps appropriately, museums). After all, we all know quite a bit about the subject. Most of us grew up in marital households. Virtually all of us, regardless of race, creed, gender, and culture, have received lectures on the propriety, if not the sanctity, of marriage—which usually suggests that those who choose not to marry are both unhappy and unhealthy. We all have been witnesses, willing or not, to a lifelong parade of other people's marriages, from Uncle Harry and Aunt Bernice to the Prince and Princess of Wales. And at one point or another, some nosy relative has inevitably inquired of every gay person when he or she will finally "tie the knot" (an intriguing and probably apt cliche.)

I must confess at the outset that I am no fan of the "institution" of marriage as currently constructed and practiced. I may simply be unlucky, but I have seen preciously few marriages over the course of my forty years that invite admiration and emulation. All too often, marriage appears to petrify rather than satisfy and enrich, even for couples in their twenties and thirties who have had a chance to learn the lessons of feminism. Almost inevitably, the partners seem to fall into a "husband" role and a "wife"

role, with such latter-day modifications as the wife who works in addition to raising the children and managing the household.

Let me be blunt: in its traditional form, marriage has been oppressive, especially (although not entirely) to women. Indeed, until the middle of the last century, marriage was, at its legal and social essence, an extension of the husband and his paternal family. Under the English common law, wives were among the husband's "chattel" —personal property—and could not, among other things, hold property in their own names. The common law crime of adultery demonstrates the unequal treatment accorded to husbands and wives: while a woman who slept with a man who wasn't her husband committed adultery, a man who slept with a woman not his wife committed fornication. A man was legally incapable of committing adultery, except as an accomplice to an errant wife. The underlying offense of adultery was not the sexual betrayal of one partner by the other, but the wife's engaging in conduct capable of tainting the husband's bloodlines. (I swear on my Black's Law Dictionary that I have not made this up!)

Nevertheless, despite the oppressive nature of marriage historically, and in spite of the general absence of edifying examples of modern heterosexual marriage, I believe very strongly that every lesbian and gay man should have the right to marry the same-sex partner of his or her choice, and that the gay rights movement should aggressively seek full legal recognition for same-sex marriages. To those who might not agree, I respectfully offer three explanations, one practical, one political and one philosophical.

The Practical Explanation

The legal status of marriage rewards the two individuals who travel to the altar (or its secular equivalent) with substantial economic and practical advantages. Married couples may reduce their tax liability by filing a joint return. They are entitled to special government benefits, such as those given surviving spouses and dependents through the Social Security program. They can inherit from one another even when there is no will. They are immune from subpoenas requiring testimony against the other spouse. And marriage to an American citizen gives a foreigner a right to residency in the United States.

Other advantages have arisen not by law but by custom. Most employers offer health insurance to their employees, and many will include an employee's spouse in the benefits package, usually at the employer's expense. Virtually no employer will include a partner who is not married to an employee, whether of the same sex or not. Indeed, very few insurance companies even offer the possibility of a group health plan covering "domestic partners" who are not married to one another. Two years ago, I tried to find such a policy for Lambda, and discovered that not one insurance company authorized to do business in New York—the second-largest state in the country with more than 17 million residents—would accommodate us. (Lambda has tried to make do by paying for individual insurance policies for the same-sex partners of its employees who otherwise would go uninsured but these individual policies are usually narrower in scope than group policies, often require applicants to furnish individual medical information not required under most group plans, and are typically much more expensive per person.)

In short, the law generally presumes in favor of every marital relationship, and acts to preserve and foster it, and to enhance the rights of the individuals who enter into it. It is usually possible, with enough money and the right advice, to replicate some of the benefits conferred by the legal status of marriage through the use of documents like wills and power of attorney forms, but that protection will inevitably, under current circumstances, be incomplete.

The law (as I suspect will come as no surprise to the readers of this journal) still looks upon lesbians and gay men with suspicion, and this suspicion casts a shadow over the documents they execute in recognition of a same-sex relationship. If a lesbian leaves property to her lover, her will may be invalidated on the grounds that it was executed under the "undue influence" of the would-be beneficiary. A property agreement may be denied validity because the underlying relationship is "meretricious"—akin to prostitution. (Astonishingly, until the mid-seventies, the law throughout the United States deemed "meretricious" virtually any formal economic arrangement between two people not married to one another, on the theory that an exchange of property between them was probably payment for sexual services; the Supreme Court of California helped unravel the quaint legal fantasy in its 1976 ruling in the first famous "palimony" case, Marvin v. Marvin.) The law has progressed considerably beyond the uniformly oppressive state of affairs before 1969 but it is still far from enthusiastic about gay people and their relationships—to put it mildly.

Moreover, there are some barriers one simply cannot transcend outside of a formal marriage. When the Internal Revenue Code or the Immigration and Naturalization Act say "married," they mean "married" by definition of state statute. When the employer's group health plan says "spouse," it means "spouse" in the eyes of the law, not the eyes of the loving couple.

But there is another drawback. Couples seeking to protect their relationship through wills and other documents need knowledge, determination and—most importantly—money. No money, no lawyer. And no lawyer, no protection. Those who lack the sophistication or the wherewithal to retain a lawyer are simply stuck in most circumstances. Extending the right to marry to gay couples would assure that those at the bottom of the economic ladder have a chance to secure their relationship rights, too.

The Political Explanation

The claim that gay couples ought to be able to marry is not a new one. In the seventies, same-sex couples in three states—Minnesota, Kentucky and Washington—brought constitutional challenges to the marriage statutes, and in all three instances they failed. In each of the three, the court offered two basic justifications for fulfilling marriage to male-female couples: history and procreation. Witness this passage from the Supreme Court of Minnesota's 1971 opinion in Baker v. Nelson: "The institution of marriage as a union of man and woman, uniquely involving the procreation and rearing of children within a family, is as old as the book of Genesis. This historic institution manifestly is more deeply founded than the asserted contemporary concept of marriage and societal interests for which petitioners contend."

Today no American jurisdiction recognizes the right of two women or two men to marry one another, although several nations in northern Europe do. Even more telling, until earlier this year, there was little discussion within the gay rights movement about whether such a right should exist. As far as I can tell, no gay organization of any size, local or national has yet declared the right to marry as one of its goals.

With all due respect to my colleagues and friends who take a different view, I believe it is time to renew the efforts to overturn the existing marriage laws, and to do so in earnest, with a commitment of money and energy, through both the courts and the state legislatures. I am not naive about the likelihood of imminent victory. There is none. Nonetheless—and here I will not mince words—I would like to see the issue rise to the top of the agenda of every gay organization, including my own (although that judgment is hardly mine alone).

Why give it such prominence? Why devote resources to such a distant goal? Because marriage is, I believe, the political issue that most fully tests the dedication of people who are not gay to full equality for gay people, and also the issue most likely to lead ultimately to a world free from discrimination against lesbians and gay men.

Marriage is much more than a relationship sanctioned by law. It is the centerpiece of our entire social structure, the core of the traditional notion of "family." Even in its present tarnished state, the marital relationship inspires sentiments suggesting that it is something almost superhuman. The Supreme Court, in striking down an anti-contraception statute in 1965, called marriage "noble" and "intimate to the degree of being sacred." The Roman Catholic Church and the Moral Majority would go—and have gone—considerably further.

Lesbians and gay men are now denied entry to this "noble" and "sacred" institution. The implicit message is this: two men or two women are incapable of achieving such an exalted domestic state. Gay relationships are somehow less significant, less valuable. Such relationships may, from time to time and from couple to couple, give the appearance of a marriage, but they can never be of the same quality or importance.

I resent—indeed, I loathe—that conception of same-sex relationships. And I am convinced that ultimately the only way to overturn it is to remove the barrier to marriage that now limits the freedom of every gay man and lesbian.

That is not to deny the value of "domestic partnership" ordinances, statutes that prohibit discrimination based on "marital status," and other legal advances that can enhance the rights (as well as the dignity) of gay couples. Without question, such advances move us further along the path to equality. But their value can only be partial. (The recently enacted San Francisco "domestic partnership" ordinance, for example, will have practical value only for gay people who happen to be employed by the City of San Francisco and want to include their non-marital spouses in part of the city's fringe benefit package; the vast majority of gay San Franciscans—those employed by someone other than the city—have only a symbolic victory to savor.) Measures of this kind can never assure full equality. Gay relationships will continue to be accorded a subsidiary status until the day that gay couples have exactly the same rights as their heterosexual counterparts. To my mind, that means either that the right to marry be extended to us, or that marriage be abolished in its present form for all couples, presumably to be replaced by some new legal entity—an unlikely alternative.

The Philosophical Explanation

I confessed at the outset that I personally found marriage in its present avatar rather, well, unattractive. Nonetheless, even from a philosophical perspective, I believe the right to marry should become a stated goal of the gay rights movement.

First, and most basically, the issue is not the desirability of marriage, but rather the desirability of the right to marry. That I think two lesbians or two gay men should be entitled to a marriage license does not mean that I think all gay people should find appro-

priate partners and exercise the right, should it eventually exist. I actually rather doubt that I, myself would want to marry, even though I share a household with another man who is exceedingly dear to me. There are others who feel differently, for economic, symbolic or romantic reasons. They should, to my mind, unquestionably have the opportunity to marry if they wish and otherwise meet the requirements of the state (like being old enough).

Furthermore, marriage may be unattractive and even oppressive as it is currently structured and practiced, but enlarging the concept to embrace same-sex couples would necessarily transform it into something new. If two women can marry, or two men, marriage—even for heterosexuals—need not be a union of a "husband" and a "wife." Extending the right to marry to gay people—that is, abolishing the traditional gender requirements of marriage—can be one of the means, perhaps the principal one, through which the institution divests itself of the sexist trappings of the past.

Some of my colleagues disagree with me. I welcome their thoughts and the debates and discussions our different perspectives will trigger. The movement for equality for lesbians and gay men can only be enriched through this collective exploration of the question of marriage. But I do believe many thousands of gay people want the right to marry. And I think, too, they will earn that right for themselves sooner than most of us imagine.

Since When Is Marriage a Path to Liberation?

Paula L. Ettelbrick

"Marriage is an institution if you like living in institutions," according to a bit of T-shirt philosophy I saw recently. Certainly, marriage is an institution. It is one of the most venerable, impenetrable institutions in modern society. Marriage provides the ultimate form of acceptance for personal intimate relationships in our society, and gives those who marry an insider status of the most powerful kind.

Steeped in a patriarchal system that looks to ownership, property, and dominance of men over women as its basis, the institution of marriage long has been the focus of radical feminist revulsion. Marriage defines certain relationships as more valid than all others. Lesbian and gay relationships, being neither legally sanctioned or commingled by blood, are always at the bottom of the heap of social acceptance and importance.

Given the imprimatur of social and personal approval which marriage provides, it is not surprising that some lesbians and gay men among us would look to legal marriage for self-affirmation. After all, those who marry can be instantaneously transformed from "outsiders" to "insiders," and we have a desperate need to become insiders.

It could make us feel OK about ourselves, perhaps even relieve some of the internalized homophobia that we all know so well. Society will then celebrate the birth of our children and mourn the death of our spouses. It would be easier to get health insurance for our spouses, family memberships to the local museum, and a right to inherit our spouse's cherished collection of lesbian mystery novels even if she failed to draft a will. Never again would we have to go to a family reunion and debate about the correct term for introducing our lover/partner/significant other to Aunt Flora. Everything would be quite easy and very nice.

So why does this unlikely event so deeply disturb me? For two major reasons. First, marriage will not liberate us as lesbians and gay men. In fact, it will constrain us, make us more invisible, force our assimilation into the mainstream, and undermine the goals of gay liberation. Second, attaining the right to marry will not transform our society from one that makes narrow, but dramatic, distinctions between those who are married and those who are not married to one that respects and encourages choice of relationships and family diversity. Marriage runs contrary to two of the primary goals of the lesbian and gay movement: the affirmation of gay identity and culture; and the validation of many forms of relationships.

When analyzed from the standpoint of civil rights, certainly lesbians and gay men should have a right to marry. But obtaining a right does not always result in justice. White male firefighters in Birmingham, Alabama have been fighting for the "rights" to retain their jobs by overturning the city's affirmative action guidelines. If their "rights" prevail, the courts will have failed in rendering justice. The "right" fought for by the white male firefighters, as well as those who advocate strongly for the "rights" to legal marriage for gay people, will result, at best, in limited or narrowed "justice" for those closest to power at the expense of those who have been historically marginalized.

The fight for justice has as its goal the realignment of power imbalances among individuals and classes of people in society. A pure "rights" analysis often fails to incorporate a broader understanding of the underlying inequities that operate to deny justice to a fuller range of people and groups. In setting our priorities as a community, we must combine the concept of both rights and justice. At this point in time, making legal marriage for lesbian and gay couples a priority would set an agenda of gaining rights for a few, but would do nothing to correct the power imbalances between those who are married (whether gay or straight) and those who are not. Thus, justice would not be gained.

Justice for gay men and lesbians will be achieved only when we are accepted and supported in this society despite our differences from the dominant culture and the choices we make regarding our relationships. Being queer is more than setting up house, sleeping with a person of the same gender, and seeking state approval for doing so. It is an identity, a culture with many variations. It is a way of dealing with the world by diminishing the constraints of gender roles which have for so long kept women and gay people oppressed and invisible. Being queer means pushing the parameters of sex, sexuality, and family, and in the process transforming the very fabric of society. Gay liberation is inexorably linked to women's liberation. Each is essential to the other.

The moment we argue, as some among us insist on doing, that we should be treated as equals because we are really just like married couples and hold the same values to be true, we undermine the very purpose of our movement and begin the dangerous process of silencing our different voices. As a lesbian, I am fundamentally different from non-lesbian women. That's the point. Marriage, as it exists today, is antithetical to my liberation as a lesbian and as a woman because it mainstreams my life and voice. I do not want to be known as "Mrs. Attached-To-Somebody-Else." Nor do I want to give the state the power to regulate my primary relationship.

Yet the concept of equality in our legal system does not support differences, it only supports sameness. The very standard for equal protection is that people who are similarly situated must be treated equally. To make an argument for equal protection, we will be required to claim that gay and lesbian relationships are the same as straight relationships. To gain the right, we must compare ourselves to married couples. The law looks to the insiders as the norm, regardless of how flawed or unjust their institutions, and requires that those seeking the law's equal protection situate themselves in a similar posture to those who are already protected. In arguing for the right to legal marriage, lesbians and gay men would be forced to claim that we are just like heterosexual couples, have the same goals and purposes, and vow to structure our lives similarly. The law provides no room to argue that we are different, but are nonetheless entitled to equal protection.

The thought of emphasizing our sameness to married heterosexuals in order to obtain this "right" terrifies me. It rips away the very heart and soul of what I believe it is to be a lesbian in this world. It robs me of the opportunity to make a difference. We end up mimicking all that is bad about the institution of marriage in our efforts to appear to be the same as straight couples.

By looking to our sameness and deemphasizing our differences, we don't even place ourselves in a position of power that would allow us to transform marriage from an institution that emphasizes property and state regulation of relationships to an institution which recognizes one of the many types of valid and respected relationships. Until the constitution is interpreted to respect and encourage differences, pursuing the legalization of same-sex marriage would be leading our movement into a trap; we would be demanding access to the very institution which, in its current form, would undermine our movement to recognize many different kinds of relationships. We would be perpetuating the elevation of married relationships and of "couples" in general, and further eclipsing other relationships of choice.

Ironically, gay marriage, instead of liberating gay sex and sexuality, would further outlaw any gay and lesbian sex which is not performed in a marital context. Just as sexually active non-married women face stigma and double standards around sex and sexual activity, so too would non-married gay people. The only legitimate gay sex would be that which is cloaked in and regulated by marriage. Its legitimacy would stem not from an acceptance of gay sexuality, but because the Supreme Court and society in general fiercely protect the privacy of marital relationships. Lesbians and gay men who do not seek the state's stamp of approval would clearly face increased sexual oppression.

Undoubtedly, whether we admit it or not, we all need to be accepted by the broader society. That motivation fuels our work to eliminate discrimination in the workplace and elsewhere, fight for custody of our children, create our own families, and so on. The growing discussion about the right to marry may be explained in part by this need for acceptance. Those closer to the norm or to power in this country are more likely to see marriage as a principle of freedom and equality. Those who are more acceptable to the mainstream because of race, gender, and economic status are more likely to want the right to marry. It is the final acceptance, the ultimate affirmation of identity.

On the other hand, more marginal members of the lesbian and gay community (women, people of color, working class and poor) are less likely to see marriage as having relevance to our struggles for survival. After all, what good is the affirmation of our relationships (that is, marital relationships) if we are rejected as women, black, or working class.

The path to acceptance is much more complicated for many of us. For instance, if we choose legal marriage, we may enjoy the right to add our spouse to our health insurance policy at work, since most employment policies are defined by one's marital status, not family relationship. However, that choice assumes that we have a job and that our employer provides us with health benefits. For women, particularly women of color who tend to occupy the low-paying jobs that do not provide health care benefits at all, it will not matter one bit if they are able to marry their woman partners. The opportunity to marry will neither get them the health benefits nor transform them from outsider to insider.

Of course, a white man who marries another white man who has a full-time job with benefits will certainly be able to share in those benefits and overcome the only obstacle left to full societal assimilation—the goal of many in his class. In other words, gay marriage will not topple the system that allows only the privileged few to obtain decent health care. Nor will it close the privilege gap between those who are married and those who are not.

Marriage creates a two-tier system that allows the state to regulate relationships. It has become a facile mechanism for employers to dole out benefits, for businesses to provide special deals and incentives, and for the law to make distinctions in distributing meager public funds. None of these entities bothers to consider the relationship among people; the love, respect, and need to protect that exists among all kinds of family members. Rather, a simple certificate of the state, regardless of whether the spouses love, respect, or even see each other on a regular basis, dominates and is supported. None of this dynamic will change if gay men and lesbians are given the option of marriage.

Gay marriage will not help us address the systematic abuses inherent in a society that does not provide decent health care to all of its citizens, a right that should not depend on whether the individual 1) has sufficient resources to afford health care or health insurance, 2) is working and receives health insurance as part of compensation, or 3) is married to a partner who is working and has health coverage which is extended to spouses. It will not address the underlying unfairness that allows businesses to provide discounted services or goods to families and couples—who are defined to include straight, married people and their children, but not domestic partners.

Nor will it address the pain and anguish of the unmarried lesbian who receives word of her partner's accident, rushes to the hospital and is prohibited from entering the intensive care unit or obtaining information about her condition solely because she is not a spouse or family member. Likewise, marriage will not help the gay victim of domestic violence who, because he chose not to marry, finds no protection under the law to keep his violent lover away.

If the laws change tomorrow and lesbians and gay men were allowed to marry, where would we find the incentive to continue the progressive movement we have started that is pushing for societal and legal recognition, of all kinds of family relationships? To create other options and alternatives? To find a place in the law for the elderly couple who, for companionship and economic reasons, live together but do not marry? To recognize the right of a long-time, but unmarried gay partner to stay in his rent-controlled apartment after the death of his lover, the only named tenant on the lease? To recognize the family relationship of the lesbian couple and the two gay men who are jointly sharing child-raising responsibilities? To get the law to acknowledge that we may have more than one relationship worthy of legal protection?

Marriage for lesbians and gay men still will not provide a real choice unless we continue the work our community has begun to spread the privilege around to other relationships.

We must first break the tradition of piling benefits and privileges on to those who are married, while ignoring the real life needs of those who are not. Only when we de-institutionalize marriage and bridge the economic and privilege gap between the married and the unmarried will each of us have a true choice. Otherwise, our choice not to marry will continue to lack legal protection and societal respect.

The lesbian and gay community has laid the groundwork for revolutionizing society's views of family. The domestic partnership movement has been an important part of this progress insofar as it validates non-marital relationships. Because it is not limited to sexual or romantic relationships, domestic partnership provides an important opportunity for many who are not related by blood or marriage to claim certain minimal protections. It is crucial, though, that we avoid the pitfall of framing the push for legal recognition of domestic partners (those who share a primary residence and financial responsibilities for each other) as a stepping stone to marriage. We must keep our eyes on the goals of providing true alternatives to marriage and of radically reordering society's view of family.

The goals of lesbian and gay liberation must simply be broader than the right to marry. Gay and lesbian marriages may minimally transform the institution of marriage by diluting its traditional patriarchal dynamic, but they will not transform society. They will not demolish the two-tier system of the "haves" and the "have nots." We must not fool ourselves into believing that marriage will make it acceptable to be gay or lesbian. We will be liberated only when we are respected and accepted for our differences and the diversity we provide to this society. Marriage is not a path to that liberation.

The Politics of Housework

Pat Mainardi

Though women do not complain of the power of husbands, each complains of her own husband, or of the husbands of her friends. It is the same in all other cases of servitude; at least in the commencement of the emacipatory movement. The serfs did not at first complain of the power of their lords, but only of their tyranny.

John Stuart Mill, On the Subjugation of Women

Liberated women—very different from Women's Liberation! The first signals all kinds of goodies, to warm the hearts (not to mention other parts) of the most radical men. The other signals—*housework*. The first brings sex without marriage, sex before marriage, cosy housekeeping arrangements ("You see, I'm living with this chick") and the self-content of knowing that you're not the kind of man who wants a doormat instead of a woman. That will come later.

On the other hand is Women's Liberation—and housework. What? You say this is all trivial? Wonderful! That's what I thought. It seems perfectly reasonable. We both had careers, both had to work a couple of days a week to earn enough to live on. So why shouldn't we share the housework? So I suggested it to my mate and he agreed—most men are too hip to turn you down flat. You're right, he said. It's only fair.

Then an interesting thing happened. I can only explain it by stating that we women have been brainwashed more than even we can imagine. Probably too many years of seeing media-women coming over their shiny waxed floors or breaking down over their dirty shirt collars. Men have no such conditioning. They recognise the essential fact of housework right from the very beginning. Which is that it stinks.

Here's my list of dirty chores: buying groceries, carting them home and putting them away; cooking meals and washing dishes and pots; doing the laundry; digging out the place when things get out of control; washing floors. The list could go on but the sheer necessities are bad enough. All of us have to do these jobs, or get someone else to do them for us. The longer my husband contemplated these chores, the more repulsed he became, and so proceeded the change from the normally sweet considerate Dr. Jekyll into the crafty Mr. Hyde who would stop at nothing to avoid the horrors of—housework. As he felt himself backed into a corner laden with dirty dishes, brooms, mops, and reeking garbage, his front teeth grew longer and pointier, his fingernails haggled and his eyes grew wild. Housework trivial? Not on your life! Just try to share the burden.

So ensued a dialogue that's been going on for several years. Here are some of the high points:

"I don't mind sharing the housework, but I don't do it very well. We should each do the things we're best at."
Meaning: Unfortunately I'm no good at things like washing dishes or cooking. What I do best is a little light carpentry, changing light bulbs, moving furniture. (How often do you move furniture?)
Also meaning: Historically the lower classes (Blacks and women) have had hundreds of years doing menial jobs. It would be a waste of manpower to train someone else to do them now.
Also meaning: I don't like the dull stupid boring jobs, so you should do them.

"I don't mind sharing the work, but you'll have to show me how to do it."
Meaning: I ask a lot of questions and you'll have to show me everything, every time I do it because I don't remember so good. Also, don't try to sit down and read while I'm doing

my jobs because I'm going to annoy the hell out of you until it's easier to do them yourself.

"We used to be so happy! (Said whenever it was his turn to do something.)
Meaning: I used to be so happy.
Meaning: Life without housework is bliss. No quarrel here. Perfect agreement.

"We have different standards, and why should I have to work to your standards. That's unfair."
Meaning: If I begin to get bugged by the dirt and crap, I will say, "This place sure is a sty," or "How can anyone live like this?" and wait for your reactions. I know that all women have a sore called *guilt over a messy house*, or housework is ultimately my responsibility. If I rub this sore long and hard enough it'll bleed and you'll do the work. I can outwait you.
Also meaning: I can provoke innumerable scenes over the housework issue. Eventually, doing all the housework yourself will be less painful to you than trying to get me to do half.

"I've got nothing against sharing the housework, but you can't make me do it on your schedule."
Meaning: Passive resistance. I'll do it when I damn well please, if at all. If my job is doing dishes, it's easier to do them once a week. If taking out laundry, once a month. If washing the floors, once a year. If you don't like it, do it yourself oftener, and then I won't do it at all.

"I hate it more than you. You don't mind it so much."
Meaning: Housework is shitwork. It's the worst crap I've ever done. It's degrading and humiliating for someone of my intelligence to do it. But for someone of your intelligence . . .

"Housework is too trivial to even talk about."
Meaning: It's even more trivial to do. Housework is beneath my status. My purpose in life is to deal with matters of significance. Yours is to deal with matters of insignificance. You should do the housework.

"In animal societies, wolves, for example, the top animal is usually a male even where he is not chosen for brute strength but on the basis of cunning and intelligence. Isn't that interesting?"

Meaning: I have historical psychological anthropological and biological justification for keeping you down. How can you ask the top wolf to be equal?

"Women's Liberation isn't really a political movement."

Meaning: The Revolution is coming too close to home.

Also meaning: I am only interested in how I am oppressed, not how I oppress others. Therefore the war, the draft and the university are political. Women's Liberation is not.

"Man's accomplishments have always depended on getting help from other people, mostly women. What great man would have accomplished what he did if he had to do his own housework?"

Meaning: Oppression is built into the system and I as the white American male receive the benfits of this system. I don't want to give them up.

Postscript

Participatory democracy begins at home. If you are planning to implement your politics there are certain things to remember.

1. He is feeling it more than you. He's losing some leisure and you're gaining it. The measure of your oppression is his resistance.

2. Most men are not accustomed to doing monotonous, repetitive work which never issues in any lasting let alone important achievement. This is why they would rather repair a cabinet than wash dishes. If human endeavours are like a pyramid with man's highest achievements at the top, then keeping oneself alive is at the bottom. Men have always had servants (you) to take care of this bottom stratum of life while he has confined his efforts to the rarefied upper regions. It is thus ironic when they ask of women: "Where are your great painters, statesmen, etc." Mrs. Matisse ran a millinery shop so he could paint. Mrs. Martin Luther King kept his house and raised his babies.

3. It is a traumatising experience for someone who has always thought of himself as being against any oppression or exploitation of one human being by another to realise that in his daily life he has been accepting and implementing (and benefiting from) this exploitation: that his rationalisation is little different from that of the racist who says "Niggers don't feel pain" (women don't mind doing the shitwork), and that the oldest form of oppression in history has been the oppression of 50 percent of the population by the other 50 percent.

4. Arm yourself with some knowledge of the psychology of oppressed peoples everywhere and a few facts about the animal kingdom. I admit playing top wolf or who runs the gorillas is silly but as a last resort men bring it up all the time. Talk about bees. If you feel really hostile, bring up the sex life of spiders. After sex, she bites off his head. The psychology of oppressed peoples is not silly. Blacks, women, and immigrants have all employed the same psychological mechanisms to survive. Admiring the oppressor, glorifying the oppressor, wanting to be like the oppressor, wanting the oppressor to like them.

5. In a sense all men everywhere are slightly schizoid—divorced from the reality of maintaining life. This makes it easier for them to play games with it. It is almost a cliché that women feel greater grief at sending a son off to war or losing him to that war because they

bore him, suckled him, and raised him. The men who foment those wars did none of those things and have a more superficial estimate of the worth of human life. One hour a day is a low estimate of the amount of time one has to spend "keeping" oneself. By foisting this off on others, man has seven hours a week—one working day—more to play with his mind and not his human needs. Over the course of generations it is easy to see whence evolved the horrifying abstractions of modern life.

6. With the death of each form of oppression, life changes and new forms evolve. English aristocrats at the turn of the century were horrified at the idea of enfranchising working men, were sure that it signalled the death of civilisation and a return to barbarism. Some working men even fell for this line. Similarly with the minimm wage, abolition of slavery, and female suffrage. Life changes but it goes on. Don't fall for any crap about the death of everything if men take a turn at the dishes. They will imply that you are holding back the Revolution (their Revolution). But you are advancing it.

7. Keep checking up. Periodically consider who's actually doing the jobs. These things have a way of backsliding so that a year later once again the woman is doing everything. Use timesheets if necessary. Also bear in mind what the worst jobs are, namely the ones that have to be done every day or several times a day. Also the ones that are dirty—it's more pleasant to pick up books, newspapers, etc., than to wash dishes. Alternate the bad jobs. It's the daily grind that gets you down. Also make sure that you don't have the responsibility for the housework with occasional help from him. "I'll cook dinner for you tonight" implies that it's really your job and isn't he a nice guy to do some of it for you.

8. Most men had a bachelor life during which they did not starve or become encrusted with crud or buried under the litter. There is a taboo that says that women mustn't strain themselves in the presence of men—we haul around fifty pounds of groceries if we have to but aren't allowed to open a jar if there is someone around to do it for us. The reverse side of the coin is that men aren't supposed to be able to take care of themselves without a woman. Both are excuses for making women do the housework.

9. Beware of the double whammy. He won't do the little things he always did because you're now a "Liberated Woman," right? Of course, he won't do anything else either . . . I was just finishing this when my husband came in and asked what I was doing. Writing a paper on housework. *Housework?* he said. Housework? Oh, my God, how trivial can you get. A paper on housework.

Racial Ethnic Women's Labor:
The Intersection of Race, Gender, and Class Oppression

Evelyn Nakano Glenn

T he failure of the feminist movement to address the concerns of black, Hispanic, and Asian-American women is currently engendering widespread discussion in white women's organizations. Paralleling this discussion is a growing interest among racial ethnic women[1] in articulating aspects of their experiences that have been ignored in feminist analyses of women's oppression (e.g., oral histories by Sterling, 1979; Elessar, MacKenzie, and Tixier y Vigil, 1980; Kim, 1983, and social and historical studies by Dill, 1979; Mirande and Enriquez, 1979 Davis, 1981; hooks, 1981; Jones, 1984).[2]

As an initial corrective, racial ethnic scholars have begun research on racial ethnic women in relation to employment, the family and the ethnic community, both historically and contemporarily (e.g., Acosta-Belen, 1979; Mora and Del Castillo, 1980; Melville, 1980; Rodgers-Rose, 1980; Tsuchida, 1982). The most interesting of these studies describe the social world and day-to-day struggles of racial ethnic women, making visible what has up to now been invisible in the social sciences and humanities. These concrete data constitute the first step toward understanding the effects of race and gender oppression in the lives of racial ethnic women.

A necessary next step is the development of theoretical and conceptual frameworks for analyzing the interaction of race and gender stratification. Separate models exist for analyzing race, ethnic, or gender stratification. Although the "double" (race, gender) and "triple" (race, gender, class) oppression of racial ethnic women are widely acknowledged, no satisfactory theory has been developed to analyze what happens when these systems of oppression intersect. A starting point for developing such a theory would appear to lie in those models which view race and gender stratification as part of a larger systems of institutionalized inequality. During the 1970s two models which view race and gender divisions as embedded in and helping to maintain an overall system of class exploitation came to the fore: the *patriarchy* model developed by Marxist-feminists to explain the subordination of women (e.g., Weinbaum and Bridges, 1979; Sokoloff, 1980; Brown, 1981; and Hartmann, 1981a) and the *internal colonialism* model developed by activists and scholars to explain the historic subordination of blacks, Hispanics, Asian-Americans, and other people of color in the United States (e.g., Clark, 1965; Carmichael and Hamilton, 1967; Moore, 1970; Barrera Muñoz, and Ornelas, 1972; and Blauner, 1972).

At the center of the Marxist-feminist analysis is the concept of patriarchy, which may be defined as a hierarchical system of power which enables men as a class to have authority and power over women (Hartmann, 1976; Sokoloff, 1980). In this model the main mechanism by which control is achieved and maintained by men is the *sexual division of labor,* which places men in positions of authority over women and permits them to reap disproportionate benefits. Similarly, at the center of the internal colonialism model is a system of power relations by which subordinate minorities are kept politically and economically weak so they can be more easily exploited as workers. The main mechanism by which economic dependency is maintained is a *colonial labor system,* characterized by a segmented labor market, discriminatory barriers, and separate wage scales. This system ensures that people of color are relegated to the worst jobs (i.e., insecure, low-paying, dangerous, dirty, and dead-end).

Neither model explicitly recognizes the specific situation of racial ethnic women. The patriarchy model ignores differences among women based on race. When race is discussed, it is treated as a parallel system of stratification: an analogy is often made between "women" and "minorities," an analogy that involves comparison of the subordinate status of white women and minority men. Minority women are left in limbo. Similarly, the internal colonialism model ignores gender by treating members of colonized minorities as undifferentiated with respect to gender. Analyses of racial ethnic labor have generally focused only on male workers. Yet, these studies also assume that the detrimental impacts of the labor system on men is synonymous with the impacts on the group as a whole, men and women alike.

Despite the focus on only one axis of stratification, the patriarchy and internal colonialism models have some important commonalities. Each focuses on explaining the persistence of inequality and sees gender/race stratification as dynamically related to the organization of the economy. Thus, each implies a historical perspective, one that traces changes in the relations between dominant and subordinate groups in relation to the development of capitalism. Each emphasizes institutional arrangements that ensure control by the dominant group over the labor of the subordinate group. There thus seems to be some common ground for developing a more integrated framework by combining insights from the two perspectives.

This paper is a preliminary effort to identify aspects of the two models that might contribute to an integrated framework. I will start by briefly reviewing the Marxist-feminist analysis of women's subordination. I will then review racial ethnic women's experience as members of colonized minorities in the United States. In light of this experience, I will examine the paid and unpaid work of Chinese, Mexican-

American, and black women from the mid-nineteenth century to the present, showing how they diverge from those presumed to be typical of white women. In the concluding section, suggestions are made for revision of Marxist-feminist theory to be more inclusive of the race-gender interaction.

Marxist-Feminist Analysis

The Marxist-feminist perspective views women's subordination as a product of two interacting systems: patriarchy and capitalism. While generally adhering to the Marxist analysis of class exploitation, Marxist-feminists diverge by giving equal importance to patriarchy, which, they argue, existed prior to capitalism, though interacting with it as capitalism developed. According to this analysis, the main mechanism by which patriarchy was established and is maintained today is the sexual division of labor. The assignment of certain tasks (usually the more onerous and/or less valued) to women, and others (usually the more highly valued) to men, is considered more or less universal.

Under capitalism the sexual division of labor takes a particular form due to the separation of production of goods, and then services, from the household. As production was industrialized the household became increasingly privatized, and its functions reduced to consumption, which includes shopping and negotiating for services (Weinbaum and Bridges, 1979), and biological and social reproduction, including child care, cleaning, preparing food, and providing emotional support for the breadwinner. As capital took over production, households became increasingly dependent on the market for goods and therefore, on wages to purchase goods and services needed for survival. During the nineteenth century—in part because men could be more intensively exploited as wage laborers, while women could benefit capital as full-time consumers and reproducers—a specialization developed, whereby women were assigned almost exclusive responsibility for household consumption and reproduction and men were allocated responsibility for publicly organized production. This division became prescribed in the mid-nineteenth century with the development of the cult domesticity, which idealized the woman as the center of home and hearth (Welter, 1966). This division of labor contributed to the subordination of women by making them economically dependent on a male wage earner. Simultaneously, the domestic code controlled women's behavior by threatening those who deviated from it with the loss of their feminine identity.

The ideal of separate spheres was, of course, unattainable for many women whose fathers or husbands were unable to earn a family wage and who therefore had to engage in income producing activities to support themselves and their families (Lerner, 1969; Easton, 1976). Yet the conception of women as consumers and reproducers affected them too, depressing their position in the labor market. Women were defined as secondary workers, a status maintained by a sexual division in the labor market (i.e., occupational segregation). Jobs allocated to women were typically at the bottom of the authority hierarchy, low in wages, dead-end and frequently insecure. The secondary position of women in the labor force meant that women had little leverage to shift the burden of household work onto husbands, so they continued to be responsible for the domestic sphere. Moreover, because of low wages and insecure jobs, even when employed, women remained dependent on the additional wages of the male earner (Hartmann, 1976; Kessler-Harris, 1982).

This analysis has much to offer: it permits us to view women's subordination as part of a larger framework of economic exploitation. It also draws connections between women's domestic work and their work in the labor force, and shows how subordination in one sphere reinforces subordination in the other. It is intended as a general analysis that encompasses all women. Yet, it is built on class-and race-bounded experiences. To what extent do the concepts developed in the Marxist-feminist model apply to the experience of racial ethnic women? To what extent does the private-public split and women's association with the domestic sphere exist for racial ethnic women? To what extent has economic dependence on men been an important basis for racial ethnic women's subordination? To what extent do struggles over allocation of household labor create gender conflict in racial ethnic households?

In order to begin addressing these questions we need to examine the impacts of race stratification on racial ethnic women's work, both paid and unpaid. For this, I draw on both earlier and more recent research on the labor histories of "colonized minorities." Because histories of the various peoples in different regions of the country vary and because of the limited size and scope of this paper, I will limit my examination to three case studies for which there is comparable information from the mid-nineteenth century to the present: Mexican-Americans in the Southwest, Chinese in California, and blacks in the South.

Colonized Minorities in Industrializing America

The United States started out as a colonial economy which offered raw resources and land to European and American capitalists. In order to develop the economic infrastructure and extra resources, capitalists

needed labor, which was always in short supply. The presence of racial ethnic groups in this country is tied to this demand for labor. Most were brought to this country for the express purpose of providing cheap and malleable labor (Cheng and Bonacich, 1984).

Although European immigrants were also welcomed as a source of low-wage labor, they were incorporated into the urban economics of the north. Racial ethnics were recruited primarily to fill labor needs in economically backward regions: the West, Southwest, and South (Blauner, 1972). In the late nineteenth and early twentieth century, Chinese men constituted from a quarter to a third of the work force (reclaiming agricultural lands, building railroads, and working in mines), and 90 percent of the domestic and laundry workers in California (Saxton, 1971). During this same period, native Chicanos and Mexican immigrants (Mexicanos) were employed as miners, railroad hands, and agricultural laborers in the western states (Barrera, 1979). In the years following emancipation blacks were concentrated in agriculture, as well as in heavy labor in construction and domestic service in the South (Cheng and Bonacich, 1984). All three groups helped build the agricultural and industrial base on which subsequent industrial development rested, but were excluded from the industrial jobs that resulted.

Racial ethnic labor was cheaper for infrastructure building in two senses: racial ethnics were paid less (including lower benefits) and provided a reserve army to be drawn in when the economy expanded or labor was needed for a short-term project, and pushed out when the economy contracted or the particular project ended. Their cheapness was ensured by institutional barriers that undercut their ability to compete in the labor market. The labor market itself was stratified into separate tiers for whites and racial ethnics. The better paying, more skilled, cleaner, and secure jobs in highly capitalized industries were reserved for white workers, leaving the low paying, insecure, dangerous, seasonal, and dead-end jobs in competitive industries for people of color. A dual wage system was also characteristic of the colonial labor system; wages for racial ethnics were always lower than for whites in comparable jobs (Barrera, 1979). White workers benefited because better jobs were reserved for them. The dual labor system also buffered them from the effects of periodic depressions, since racial ethnics took the brunt of layoffs and unemployment.

Further, racial ethnics were prevented from competing for better work and improved conditions by legal and administrative restrictions. Restrictions on their rights and freedoms began right at the time of entry or incorporation into the United States. While the exact form of entry for the three groups differed, in all cases an element of subordination was involved. The most striking instance of forced entry was that of blacks, who were captured, torn from their homelands, transported against their will, and sold into slavery. This institution so structured their lives that even after emancipation former slaves were held in debt bondage by the southern sharecropping system (Painter, 1976). Equally involuntary was the incorporation of Mexicans residing in territories taken over by United States military conquest. Anglo settlers invaded what is now California, Texas, Arizona, New Mexico, and Colorado. When the United States seized the land, native Mexicans living in those areas were reduced to agricultural peons or wage laborers (Barrera, 1979). An intermediate case between forced and free entry was that of the Chinese. Their immigration was the result of

the economic and political chaos engendered, at least in part, by western colonial intrusion into China (Lyman, 1974). Many Chinese men entered the United States as contract laborers so they could support destitute kin in their villages. Under the credit ticket system they signed away seven years of labor in exchange for their passage (Ling, 1912).

These unfree conditions of entry imposed special liabilities on racial ethnics. Blacks were not citizens and counted in the census as only three-fifths of a person, Mexicans were defined as second-class citizens, and Chinese were aliens, ineligible for citizenship. All three groups were placed in separate legal categories, denied basic rights and protections, and barred from political participation. Thus, they could be coerced, intimidated, and restricted to the least desirable jobs, where they were especially vulnerable to exploitation.

The process of incorporation and entry into the labor system in turn had profound effects on the culture and family systems of racial ethnics. Native languages, religion, and other ways of life were constrained, destroyed, or transformed and kin ties and family authority undermined. As Blauner (1972, p. 66) notes:

> The labor system through which people of color became Americans tended to destroy or weaken their cultures and communal ties. Regrouping and new institutional forms developed, but in situations with extremely limited possibilities.

We are most familiar with assaults on family ties of blacks under slavery due to sale of individuals regardless of kin ties, slave master control over marriage and reproduction, and the brutal conditions of life. Scholars and policy analysts in the past argued that slavery permanently weakened kin ties and undermined the conjugal household, thereby creating a legacy of family pathology (Frazier, 1939; Moynihan, 1965). More recently, revisionist historians have argued that slaves resisted assaults on family integrity and managed to maintain conjugal and kin ties to a greater extent than previously believed (Blassingame, 1972; Fogel and Engerman, 1974; and Gutman, 1976). Gutman (1975) found that a large proportion of slave marriages were of long standing and many couples legalized their marriages when given the opportunity to do so after emancipation. Black families showed great strength in the face of assaults on kin networks, though their survival required great struggle and exacted great costs.

Less well known are the assaults on the culture and family lives of Chicanos and Chinese-Americans. In both groups households were broken apart by the demand for male labor. Many Mexican-American men were employed in the mining camps and on railroad gangs which required them to live apart from wives and children (Barrera, 1979). This was also true for male migrant agricultural workers until the 1880s when the family labor system became the preferred mode (Camarillo, 1979). In the case of the Chinese, only prime age males were recruited as workers, and wives and children had to be left behind (Coolidge, 1909). The Chinese Exclusion Act of 1882 not only prohibited further entry of Chinese laborers from bringing in wives and children (Wu, 1972; Lyman, 1974). This policy was aimed at preventing the Chinese from settling permanently, once their labor was no longer needed.

Given these conditions, what was the work of racial ethnic women in the nineteenth and early twentieth centuries?

Racial Ethnic Women's Work in Industrializing America

The specific conditions of life experienced by the three groups of women differed. However, the women shared some common circumstances due to their similar positions in the colonial labor system and the similar difficulties the system created for their families. All three groups of women had to engage in constant struggle for both immediate survival and the long-term continuation of the family and community. Because men of their groups were generally unable to earn a family wage, women had to engage in subsistence and income producing activities both in and out of the household. In addition they had to work hard to keep their families together in the face of outside forces that threatened their integrity.

Chinese-American Women

Perhaps the least is known about Chinese-American women in the nineteenth and early twentieth centuries. This may be due to the fact that very few working class Chinese women actually resided in the United States then. For most of the period from 1860 to 1920 the ratio of men to women ranged from 13 to 20 males for every female. As late as 1930 there were only 9,742 females aged 10 or over in a population that included 53,650 males of the same age (Glenn, 1983). It is estimated that over half of the men had left wives behind in China (Coolidge, 1909). Although most of these wives never came to the United States, their lives must be considered as part of the experience of analytic racial ethnics, for they raised subsequent generations of sojourners who went to America, often with false papers. Little research has been done on what women did in their home villages or how they survived.

The available evidence, based partly on some family history interviews I conducted and partly on other sources (Kingston, 1977; Hirata, 1979), suggests the following: the wife often resided with the husband's parents or other kin, who received remittances from the husband, acted on his behalf and oversaw the household. Wives took care of children, performed household work under the direction of the mother-in-law, and helped in subsistence farming. Her sexual chastity was carefully guarded, as was her overall behavior. She might never see her husband again or, if lucky, see him once or twice over the course of 20 or 30 years during his rare visits home.

In the late nineteenth century, aside from wives of merchants who were still allowed entry into the United States, the only notable group of Chinese women were prostitutes (Hirata, 1979; Goldman, 1981). The imbalanced sex ratio created a demand for sexual services. Except for a few years when women were able to immigrate on their own as free entrepreneurs, Chinese prostitutes were either indentured servants or outright slaves controlled by Chinese tongs or business associates. They had been sold by their parents or kidnapped and involuntarily transported. The controllers of the trade reaped huge profits from buying and selling women and hiring out their services. Women who ran away were hunted down and returned to their captors, usually with the collusion of the police and courts. Unable to speak English and without allies, the women could not defend themselves.

Initially the Chinese were dispersed throughout the West in mining towns, railroad camps, and agricultural fields. They were subjected to special penalties, such as a foreign miner's tax in California that rendered it difficult for them to make a living. Finally, during the economic depression of the 1870s, the Chinese were forcibly driven out of many areas (Nee and Nee, 1972). They congregated in urban Chinatowns, so that by the 1880s the Chinese were a largely urban population. In place of households, the men formed clan and regional associations for mutual welfare and protection (Lyman, 1977). By the early 1900s some Chinese men were able, with minimal capital, to establish laundries, restaurants, and stores, thereby qualifying as merchants eligible to bring over wives (Lyman, 1968). These small businesses were a form of self-exploitation; they were profitable only because all members of the family contributed their labor and worked long hours. Living quarters were often in back of the shop or adjacent to it, so that work and family life were completely integrated. Work in the family enterprise went on simultaneously with household maintenance and child care. First up and last to bed, women had even less leisure than the rest of the family. Long work hours in crowded and rundown conditions took its toll on the whole family. Chinatowns had abnormally high rates of tuberculosis and other diseases (Lee, Lim, and Wong, 1969).

It is unclear what proportion of women laboring in family laundries and shops were counted as gainfully employed in the census. They were undoubtedly severely undercounted. In any case some sizable proportion of women were employed as independent wage workers. As employees, Chinese women were concentrated in ethnic enterprises because of color bars in white-owned businesses. Nearly half of all gainfully employed women in 1930 worked in jobs that were typical of Chinese enterprise. Out of a work force of 1559, garment operatives and seamstresses accounted for 11.7 percent, sales and trade for 10.6 percent, laundry operatives for 7.3 percent, waitresses for 8.2 percent, and clerical workers for 11.2 percent. The only major form of employment outside the ethnic community was private household service, which accounted for 11.7 percent of Chinese women (U.S. Census 1933; for broad occupational distributions, see Table 1).

Mexican-American Women

The information on the work of Chicanas in the late nineteenth century is also sparse. Barrera (1979) suggests that prior to the 1870s Chicano families followed the traditional division of labor, with women responsible for household work and child care. Thus, Mexican-American women worked largely in the home. Under the conditions of life among working class and agricultural families this work was extensive and arduous (Jensen, 1981). In rural areas the household work included tending gardens and caring for domesticated animals.

Many Chicano men were employed in extracting industries which required them to live in work camps and company towns in unsettled territories. If a wife remained behind with the children in the home village, she had to engage in subsistence farming and raise children on her own. If she joined her husband in camp, she had to carry on domestic chores and child rearing under frontier conditions, forced to buy necessities in company stores that quickly used up meager wages. Even in the city the barrios often had no running water, and unsanitary conditions added to women's burdens of nursing the sick (Garcia, 1980).

By the 1880s Mexican-American women were increasingly being brought into the labor force. In cities such as Los Angeles, Santa Barbara, and El Paso, Chicanas were employed as servants, cooks, and laun-

Table 1. Occupational Distribution of Employed Black, Chinese-American, Mexican-American, and White women, 10 Years of Age and Over, 1930

Occupation	Percentage Black	Percentage Chinese	Percentage Mexican	Percentage White
Professional	3.4	11.3	3.0	16.5
Trade	0.8	15.3	9.0	10.7
Public Service	0.1	0.0	0.1	0.2
Clerical	0.6	11.2	2.6	22.4
Manufacturing	5.5	20.4	19.3	20.0
Transportation	0.1	1.1	0.5	3.1
Agriculture	26.9	1.5	21.2	4.5
Service (excluding servants and laundresses)	35.4	27.6	13.5	20.1
Servants/Laundresses	27.2	11.7	30.8	2.5
TOTAL	100.0	100.1	100.0	100.0

Source: U.S. Bureau of the Census, *Fifteenth Census of the Unites States. 1930, Population, Volume 5, General Report on Occupations, Chapter 3, Color and Nativity of Gainful Workers. (Washington, DC: Government Printing Office, 1933),* Tables 2, 4, and 6.

dresses (Camarillo, 1979; Garcia, 1980). An economic depression in the 1880s forced more women to seek outside wage work, not only in private households, but also as washer-women in commercial laundries, and as cooks, dishwashers, maids, and waitresses in hotels and other public establishments. In this same period women entered the agricultural labor market. Prior to that time prime-age male workers were preferred for seasonal and migratory field work. In the 1880s whole families began to be used, a pattern that accelerated during World War I (Camarillo, 1979, p. 91). By the 1920s family labor was common throughout the Southwest. Describing the situation in Colorado, Taylor (1929) noted that landowners felt that families, despite their lower productivity per unit, were preferable because they were a more stable work force that could be counted on to return year after year.

These trends are reflected in occupational patterns of Chicana women. Between 1880 and 1930, they tended to be employed in two main types of situations. A large part of the Chicana work force, 20 percent officially, were employed as farm laborers (Barrera, 1979). Many of these were employed as part of the piece rate system in which entire families worked and moved with the crops (Taylor, 1937; Fisher, 1953; McWilliams, 1971). Under this system women had to bear and raise children, cook and keep house, while also working long hours in the field or packing house. Infants accompanied their parents to the fields, and children started working from an early age. Living conditions in migrant camps were extremely harsh. Adults rarely lived past 55 and infant and child mortality was high. Children had no regular schooling because of constant movement and the need for their labor. Schools were geared to fit agricultural schedules and provided minimal train-

ing (Taylor, 1929). Once into the migrant pattern it was almost impossible for families or individuals to break out.

The second type of employment for Chicanas, primarily those in cities and towns, was in unskilled and semi-skilled "female" jobs. The distribution of jobs varied in different areas of the Southwest, but the most common occupations in all areas were service positions (household servants, waitresses, maids, cooks, and laundry operatives), which accounted for 44.3 percent of all employed Chicanas in 1930, and operatives in garment factories and food processing plants, which together employed 19.3 percent in 1930 (Table 1). The latter industries also employed Anglo women, but Chicanas were given the worst jobs and the lowest pay. They were victims of both occupational stratification and a dual wage system. Their plight was revealed in testimony by employers before the Texas Industrial Welfare System in El Paso in 1919. For example, F. B. Fletcher, a laundry owner representing the owners of the four largest laundries in El Paso testified that almost all the unskilled labor was performed by Mexican women, while the skilled positions as markers, sorters, checkers, supervisors, and office assistants went to Anglo women. Further, Mexican women were paid an average of $6.00 a week while Anglo women received $16.55. Fletcher argued that:

> This difference indicates that in this industry, the minimum wage can be fairly fixed for Mexican female help and for the American entirely different and distinct. (Garcia, 1981, p. 91)

Only by combining their wages with those of husbands and older children could Mexican-American women survive.

Whether engaged in subsistence farming, seasonal migratory labor, agricultural packing, laundry work, domestic service, or garment manufacturing, Chicanas had to raise their children under colonized conditions. As part of the continued legal and illegal takeover of land by Anglos in Texas and Colorado from 1848 to 1900, the Chicanos became a conquered people (McLemore, 1973, 1980). Defined and treated as inferior, their language and culture became badges of second-class status. Through their daily reproductive activities and work women played a critical role not only maintaining the family, but also in sustaining Mexican-American ways of life.

Black Women

Perhaps more than any other group of women, black women were from the start exempted from the myth of female disability. To be sure, they were exploited on the basis of their gender as breeders and raisers of slaves for plantation owners (Genovese, 1974). Their gender also made them liable to a special form of oppression, sexual assault. Nevertheless, their gender did not spare them from hard physical labor in the field (Jones, 1984). hooks (1981) claims plantation owners often preferred women for the hardest field work because they were the more reliable workers. In addition black women did the heavy housework and child care for white women; in that role they were subject to abuse and even physical beatings at the hands of their mistresses. As Angela Davis (1971) notes, under conditions of plantation slavery, staying alive, raising children, and maintaining some semblance of community were forms of resistance.

After emancipation, life for rural blacks remained harsh under the sharecropping system; blacks found themselves held in debt bondage. hooks (1981) suggests that landowners preferred sharecropping to hiring labor because black women were unwilling to be employed in the fields once slavery was abolished. With sharecropping women's labor could be exploited inten-

sively, since women had to work hard alongside the men in order to pay off the ever mounting debt to the owner. One observer of black farmers noted that these women:

> do double duty, a man's share in the field, and a woman's part at home. They do any kind of field work, even ploughing, and at home the cooking, washing, milling and gardening. (Lerner, 1973)

Although there were some independent black farmers, it became increasingly difficult for them to make a living. Jim Crow laws deprived blacks of legal rights and protections, while national farm policies favored large landowners. Independent black farmers were increasingly impoverished and finally driven off the land (Painter, 1976).

Aside from farming, the next largest group of black women were employed as laundresses and domestic servants. Black women constituted an exclusive servant caste in the South, since whites refused to enter a field associated with blacks from slave times (Katzman, 1978). As servants, black women often worked a 14- to 16-hour day and were on-call around the clock (Brown, 1938). They were allowed little time off to carry out their own domestic responsibilities, despite the fact that the majority of black domestics had children of their own. A married domestic might see her children once every two weeks, while devoting night and day to the care of her mistress's children. Her own children were left in the care of husband or older siblings (Katzman, 1978). Low wages were endemic. They had to be supplemented by children taking in laundry or doing odd jobs. Many black women testified that they could only survive through the tradition of the service pan—the term for leftover food that was left at the disposal of the colored cook (Lerner, 1973, p. 18).

Manufacturing and white-collar jobs were closed to black women, though some of the dirtiest jobs in industry were offered to them. They were particularly conspicuous in southern tobacco factories and to some extent in cotton mills and flour manufacturing. In the cotton mills black women were employed as common laborers in the yards, as waste gatherers and as scrubbers of machinery. The actual manufacturing jobs were reserved for white women (Foner and Lewis, 1981). Regarding black women in the tobacco industry, Emma Shields noted in a pamphlet she prepared for the Women's Bureau in 1922:

> Conditions of employment throughout the tobacco industry are deplorably wretched, and yet conditions for Negro women workers are very much worse than those for white women workers. . . . Negro women are employed exclusively in the rehandling of tobacco, preparatory to its actual manufacture. Operations in the manufacture of cigars and cigarettes are performed exclusively by white women workers. Negro women workers are absolutely barred from any opportunity for employment in the manufacturing operations. . . . It is not unusual to find the white women workers occupying the new modern sanitary parts of the factory, and the Negro women workers in the old sections which management has decided to be beyond any hope of improvement. (Quoted in Lerner, 1969)

World War I saw increasing migration of blacks to the urban North and, simultaneously, the entrance of blacks into factory employment there. As late as 1910, 90.5 percent of all black women were farm laborers and servants, but between 1910 and 1920, 48,000 black women entered factory work (Lerner, 1969). Most were employed in steam laundries, the rest in unmechanized jobs in industry as sweepers, cleaners, and ragpickers (Foner and Lewis, 1981).

During the entire period from 1870 to 1930 black women, regardless of rural or urban residence, were notable for their high rates of labor force participation, particularly among married women. In 1900, 26.0 percent of married black women were in the labor force compared to 3.8 percent of married white women (Pleck, 1980). They thus had to contend with the double day long before this became an issue for a majority of white women. Moreover, although their wages were consistently lower than those of white women, their earnings constituted a larger share of total family income, due to the marginal and low wage employment of black men (Byington, 1974). Finally, they had to perform their double duty in the face of poor and crowded living conditions, an educational system that provided inferior schooling for their children, uncertain income, and other trials.

Racial Ethnic Women's Work in the Contemporary Period

All three groups are predominately urban today, a process that began in the late nineteenth century for the Chinese, during World War I for blacks and after World War II for Chicanos. All also have experienced dramatic changes in occupational distributions since 1930.

Chinese Women Since World War II

The main change in circumstances for Chinese women is that they were allowed entry to the United States in large numbers for the first time after World War II. Many separated wives were able to join their spouses under the provisions of the Walter-McCarran Act of 1953, and whole family units were able to enter after passage of the liberalized 1965 immigration law (Li, 1977; U.S. Department of Justice, 1977). Since World War II female immigrants outnumbered males, and the sex ratio of the Chinese population now approaches equality, with the remaining imbalance existing only in the older age categories (U.S. Bureau of the Census, 1973). Women who have rejoined spouses or arrived with husbands are adapting to the post-war urban economy by entering the paid labor force. Handicapped by language, by family responsibilities, and gender and race discrimination in the skilled trades, both husbands and wives are employed in the secondary labor market—in low-wage service and competitive manufacturing sectors. The most typical constellation among immigrant families is a husband employed as a restaurant worker, store helper, or janitor and a wife employed as an operative in a small garment shop. The shops are located in, or close to, Chinatowns and typically are subcontracting firms run by Chinese. They often evade minimum wage laws by using an unofficial piece rate system (Nee and Nee, 1972).

An examination of the occupational distribution of Chinese-American women reveals a bimodal pattern. In 1970 (Table 2) Chinese women were concentrated in clerical (31.8 percent) and professional white collar work (19.4 percent), and in the operative category (22.5 percent). While the high proportion in white-collar fields indicates considerable success by second, third, and fourth generation women, generational mobility may be less than these figures suggest, since many professionals are actually recent immigrants of gentry origin rather than working-class Chinese-Americans who have moved up. Working-class Chinese women continue to be relegated to operative jobs in the garment trade. What Chinese women of all classes share is a higher than average rate of labor force participation (U.S. Bureau of the Census, 1973).

Post-war economic changes have undercut family enterprises such as laundries and small stores, so that working-class families today typically engage in dual wage earn-ing. They encounter difficulties due to the long work hours of parents and crowded and run-down housing. Working mothers are responsible for not only the lion's share of domestic chores, but often raise their children almost single-handedly. Husbands are frequently employed in the restaurant trade, which requires them to be at work from 11 in the morning until 10 in the evening or even midnight. Thus they are rarely around while their children are awake. The women's own work hours are often prolonged because they leave work during the day to cook meals or pick up children. They make up the time by returning to the shop for evening work or by taking materials home to sew at night (Ikels and Shang, 1979). Their energy is entirely absorbed by paid employment and domestic responsibilities. The one ray of light is their hope for their children's future.

Mexican-American Women

The Chicano population is still characterized by continued migration back and forth between Mexico and the United States. In 1970, 16 percent of the resident population in the United States was foreign-born (Massey, 1982, p. 10). Not surprisingly, Chicanos remain concentrated in the Southwest, with 78 percent residing in California and Texas in 1979 (Pachon and Moore, 1981). Contrary to their image as rural people, four out of five (79 percent) resided in metropolitan areas. In line with the urban shift has been a sharp reduction in the percentage of men and women engaged in agriculture. The proportion of women employed as farm workers fell from 21.2 percent in 1930 to 2.4 percent by 1979 (Tables 7.1 and 7.3). Due to the mechanization of agriculture which caused a sharp decline in the total number of farm workers, however, Chicana women constituted a higher *proportion* of women in agricultural labor

Table 2. Occupational Distribution of Black, Chinese-American, Mexican-American, and White Women in the United States, 1970

Occupation	Percentage Black	Percentage Chinese-American	Percentage Mexican-American	Percentage White[a]
Professional	11.3	19.4	6.4	16.6
Managerial	1.4	3.8	1.9	4.0
Sales	2.6	5.1	5.7	8.1
Clerical	20.7	31.8	25.9	37.0
Craft	1.4	1.2	2.3	1.8
Operative	16.5	22.5	25.8	13.7
Laborers (excluding farm)	1.5	0.9	1.8	0.9
Farming (including farm labor)	1.2	0.5	4.0	0.7
Service	25.5	12.8	20.6	15.3
Private household workers	17.8	2.0	5.5	1.9
TOTAL	99.9	100.0	99.9	100.0

Sources: U.S. Bureau of Census, *Subject Reports of the 1970 Census* PC(2)-1B, *Negro Population, Table 7; PC(2)-1C, Persons of Spanish Origin,* Table 8; PC(2)-1F, *Japanese, Chinese, and Filipinos in the United States.* Table 22 (Washington, DC: Government Printing Office, 1973) and U.S. Bureau of the Census, Census of the Population: 1970, *Detailed Characteristics of the Population,* Final Report, PC(1)-D1, *U.S. Summary,* Table 226, (Washington, DC: Government Printing Office, 1973).

Note: a. Category comprised of all women minus black and Spanish origin.

in 1979 than they did in 1930. For those still involved in migrant labor, conditions remain harsh, with extensive exploitation of children, despite child labor laws (Taylor, 1976).

The period from 1930 to the present saw a steady rise in the occupational status of Mexican-Americans. As with other racial ethnic groups the occupational dispersion of Chicanos is related to labor shortages during wars, especially World War II. In the post-war period, rising numbers of Chicanas found employment in clerical and sales jobs, though they still lagged behind white women, especially in sales. The lower rates in white-collar jobs were matched by over-representation in blue-collar and service occupations. Mexican-American women were concentrated in operative jobs, principally in garment factories, laundries, and food processing plants, which together accounted for 25.0 percent of their employment in 1979 (Table 3). These enterprises tended to be small competitive firms that paid minimum wages and were often seasonal. Another 23.4 percent of all employed Chicanas were in service jobs, including private household work.

Mexican-American women have traditionally had among the lowest rates of labor force participation among racial ethnic women (Almquist and Weherle-Einhorn, 1978). However, in the 1970s Chicanas rapidly entered the labor market, so that by 1980 their rates were similar to that of whites, though lower than those for black

Table 3. Occupational Distribution of Employed Black, Mexican-American, and White Women, 16-Years Old and Over, 1979

Occupation	Percentage Black[a]	Percentage Mexican-American	Percentage White
Professional	14.2	6.4	16.4
Managerial	3.4	3.5	6.8
Sales	3.1	5.1	7.4
Clerical	29.0	31.1	35.9
Crafts	1.2	1.8	1.9
Operatives	15.3	25.0	11.0
Laborer (excluding farm)	1.6	1.3	1.3
Farming (including farm labor)	0.8	2.4	1.3
Service (including private household)	31.5	23.4	18.1
TOTAL	100.1	100.0	100.1

Source: U.S. Bureau of the Census, *Current Population Reports*, Series P-20, No. 354, *Persons of Spanish Origin in the United States: March 1979* (Washington, DC: Government Printing Office, 1980), Table 10. U.S. Bureau of Labor Statistics, *Employment and Earnings*, 27, No. 1 (1980), Table 22.

Note: a. Category consists of "black and other."

and Asian-American women (Massey, 1982). The lower rates may be related to two other circumstances which usually depress employment: education and family size. Chicanas have the lowest education levels of the three groups and also have the largest number of children. These factors in turn mean that when Chicanas are in the labor force, they are at a great disadvantage. In 1976 nearly one-third (31.5 percent) of all employed Chicanas had eight years of education or less: comparable figures for blacks were 14.1 percent and for whites 7.6 percent (U.S. Department of Labor, 1977).

In short, though Mexican-American women have achieved greater employment parity with Anglo women, they continue to have lower educational levels and heavier family burdens. In addition, they encounter racial barriers to white-collar employment.

Black Women

Black women have also experienced shifts in employment since World War II. The postwar period saw a great decline in domestic service as a major category of women's work. Because black women were so concentrated in it they have shown the most dramatic decline. Whereas in 1940, three out of five (59.5 percent) employed black females were in domestic service, by 1960 that proportion had dropped to a little over a third (36.2 percent), and by 1980 to one out of fourteen (7.4 percent) (U.S. Census, 1993, 1973; Westcott, 1982). Partially replacing service in private households has been service employment in public establishments, particularly in food service and health care, where the number of low-level jobs has proliferated. These jobs accounted for 25.4 percent of black female employment in 1980, compared to 16.0 percent of white women (Westcott, 1982).

U.S. Census data (Table 3) show that black women are over-represented in the operatives category, where 15.3 percent were employed in 1979, in contrast to 11.0 percent of whites. As in the past, there is a stratified labor market and a dual wage system. Baker and Levenson (1975a) examined the careers of black, Hispanic, and white graduates of a New York City vocational high school, and found that black and Hispanic women were disproportionately tracked into lower paying operative jobs in the garment industry, while better paying jobs outside the garment industry were reserved for white graduates. Years later the difference in pay and mobility was even greater as black and Hispanic women were progressively disadvantaged (Baker and Levenson, 1975b).

The last barrier to fall was white-collar employment. A dramatic increase in professional-technical, clerical, and sales employment took place after 1950. By 1979, the former accounted for 14.2 percent of black female employment, the latter two together for 32.1 percent. Differences remained, however, in that white-collar employment accounted for over two-thirds of white women's jobs, but less than half of black women's employment. In addition, within white-collar jobs, black women were concentrated in lower level jobs. For example, in 1980 black women constituted 10.8 percent of all clerical workers, but they made up over 15 percent of such lower level positions as file clerks, mail handlers, key punchers, and office machine operators, and less than 6 percent of more skilled positions as secretaries, bank tellers and bookkeepers (Glenn and Tolbert, 1985). In effect, though black women have experienced desegregation at the level of broad occupations, they have been resegregated at the finer level of detailed job categories.

Other measures also show continued disadvantage for black women. They have a 50 percent higher unemployment rate and somewhat lower earnings (U.S. Department of Labor, 1977). The largest gap is in terms of median family income, due to discrimination against black men. Even with the mother in the labor force, the median family income for black families with children under 18 years old was $14,461 in 1975 compared to $17,588 for similar white families (U.S. Department of Labor, 1977). Even though they could not raise family income to white levels by being employed, black women's wages made a bigger difference to overall family income. The gap between blacks and whites was even greater if the mother was not employed: the median for black families without mothers in the labor force was $8,912 compared to $14,796 for whites (U.S. Department of Labor, 1977). Regardless of income level, the economic fate of the black conjugal family rested on an economic partnership between men and women. Moreover, even among relatively affluent black families, the need to combat racism was a theme that infused daily life and absorbed the energy of parents in socializing their children (Willie, 1981). Women's role as nurturers required them to combat the daily assaults on their children's self-esteem and to be vigilant in protecting them from psychic injury.

Implications for Feminist Analysis

The history of racial ethnic women's work in the United States reveals their oppression not just as women, but also as members of colonized minorities. As members of colonized minorities, their experiences differed fundamentally from those used to construct Marxist-feminist theory.

Thus, concepts within that framework require reformulation if it is to generate analyses that are inclusive of racial ethnic women. I will briefly examine three concepts in Marxist-feminist theory that need to be redefined to take into account the interaction of race and gender. These are the separation between private and public spheres, the primacy of gender conflict as a feature of the family, and the gender-based assignment of reproductive labor.

The growing separation of public and private spheres with industrialization was central to early Marxist-feminist analyses of women's oppression under capitalism. However, recent historical comparative research has called into question the extent to which private and public constituted separate and bounded spheres for all classes and groups. Scholars note that in industrializing societies working class women engage in many income-earning activities, such as doing piecework at home, taking in boarders, or trading on the informal market, which cannot be easily categorized as private or public (Jensen, 1980). Moreover, industrial wage work and family life have been found to interact in complex ways, so that, for example, women's family roles may include and overlap with their roles as workers (Harevan, 1977). The examination of racial ethnic women's work adds to the critiques growing out of this research.

The nature of the split, and the extent to which women are identified with the public sphere, seems to vary by class and ethnicity, and differences among groups in women's relationship to public and private spheres needs to be examined. Like many other working-class women, racial ethnic women were never out of public production. They were integrated into production in varying ways. Black women were involved in agriculture and waged domestic service from the time of slavery. Chinese-American women frequently engaged in unpaid labor in family enterprises, where there was little separation between public and private life. Mexican-American women were initially more confined to household-based labor than the other groups, but this labor included a great deal of actual production, since men's wages were insufficient to purchase the necessities of life. Thus, a definition of womanhood exclusively in terms of domesticity never applied to racial ethnic women, as it did not to many working-class white women.

Where racial ethnic women diverge from other working-class women is that, as members of colonized minorities, their definition as laborers in production took precedence over their domestic roles. Whereas the wife-mother roles of white working-class women were recognized and accorded respect by the larger society, the maternal and reproductive roles of racial ethnic women were ignored in favor of their roles as workers. The lack of consideration for their domestic functions is poignantly revealed in the testimony of black domestics cited earlier, who were expected to leave their children and home cares behind while devoting full time to the care of the white employer's home and children. Similarly, Chinese- and Mexican-American women and children were treated as units of labor, capable of toiling long hours without regard to their need for private life. This is not to say that racial ethnic women themselves did not see themselves in terms of their family identities, but that they were not so defined by the larger society, which was interested in them only as workers.

Another area of divergence is in the scope of what is included in the so-called private sphere. For racial ethnic women the domestic encompasses a broad range of kin and community relations beyond the nuclear family. Under conditions of economic insecurity, scarce resources, and cultural assault, the conjugal household was not self-sufficient. Racial and ethnic peoples have historically relied on a larger network of extended kin, including fictive relatives and clan associations, for goods and services. This means that women's reproductive work in the "private" sphere included contributions to this larger circle, within which women took care of each others' children, loaned each other goods, and helped nurse the sick. Beyond the kin network women's work extended to the ethnic community, with much effort being expended in support of the church, political organizing, and other activities on behalf of "the race" (*la raza*). Women often are the core of community organizations, and their involvement often is spurred by a desire to defend their children, their families, and their ways of life (Ellesar, MacKenzie, and Tixier y Vigil, 1980; Gilkes, 1982; Yap, 1983). In short, race, as organized within a colonial labor system, interacted with gender (patriarchy) and class (capitalism) to determine the structure of private and public spheres and women's relationship to these spheres.

A second aspect of Marxist-feminist theory that requires reformulation in light of race is the concept of the family as a locus of gender conflict. The Marxist-feminist analysis of the family is a response to traditional approaches that treat the family as an entity with unitary interest; in particular, it challenges the functionalist view of the division of labor as complementary rather than exploitative. By focusing on inequality—the economic dependence of women and the inequitable division of labor—some Marxist-feminists see members of the family as divided in their interests, with conflict manifested in a struggle over resources and housework (e.g., Hartmann, 1981b; Thorne, 1982; for a contrasting view, see Humphries, 1977). In this view the conjugal family oppresses women; the liberation of women requires freeing them from familial authority and prescribed roles.

Examination of racial ethnic women's experiences draws attention to the other side of the coin—the family as a source of resistance to oppression from outside institutions.[3] The colonial labor system made it impossible for men of color to support their families with their labor alone and therefore ruled out economic dependence for women. The issue for racial ethnic women was not so much economic equality with husbands, but rather the adequacy of overall family income. Because racial ethnic men earned less, women's wages comprised a larger share of total family income in dual wage-earner families. In the case of family enterprises, common among Asian-Americans, family income depended on the labor of men and women equally. Thus, in both dual wage-earner and small business families, men and women were mutually dependent; dependence rarely ran in one direction.

As for the division of household labor, Marxist-feminist analysis sees it as benefiting men, who receive a greater share of services while contributing less labor. In the racial ethnic family, conflict over the division of labor is muted by the fact that institutions outside the family are hostile to it. The family is a bulwark against the atomizing effects of poverty and legal and political constraints. By transmitting folkways and language, socializing children into an alternative value system, and providing a base for self-identity and esteem, the family helps to maintain racial ethnic culture. Women do a great deal of the work of keeping the family together and teaching children survival skills. This work is experienced as a form of resistance to oppression rather than as a form of exploitation by men. In the colonial situation the common interest of family members in survival, the maintenance of family authority, and the continuation of cultural traditions are emphasized. This is not to say that there are no conflicts over the division of labor but struggles against outside forces take precedence over struggles within the family. Thus, the racial stratification system shapes the forms of intrafamilial and extra-familial conflict, and determines the arenas in which struggle occurs.

A third concept in Marxist-feminist theory that would benefit from consideration of race oppression is the very useful notion of reproductive labor. Following an early brief formulation by Marx, Marxist-feminists identified two distinct forms of labor, production and reproduction (Sokoloff, 1980). Reproduction refers to activities that recreate the labor force: the physical and emotional maintenance of current workers, and the nurturing and socializing of future workers. In other words, people as well as things have to be produced. Although both men and women engage in production, women are still the ones who carry out most of the reproduction. In large part this is because much reproductive work remains at the household level, which is women's domain. In considering the situation of racial ethnic women, it is useful to recognize the existence of a racial as well as a sexual division of reproductive labor. Historically, racial ethnic women have been assigned distinct responsibilities for reproductive labor.

In the early industrial period racial ethnic and immigrant women were employed as household servants, thereby performing reproductive labor for white native families. The labor of black and immigrant servants made possible the woman "belle" ideal for white middle-class women. Even where white immigrant domestics were employed, the dirtiest and most arduous tasks—laundering and heavy cleaning—were often assigned to black servants. There was a three-way division of labor in the home, with white middle-class women at the top of the hierarchy, followed by white immigrants, with racial ethnics at the bottom. In the late industrial period, as capital took over more areas of life, reproductive activities also were increasingly taken out of the household and turned into paid services which yielded profits (Braverman, 1974). Today, such activities as caring for the elderly (old age homes), preparing food (restaurants and fast-food stands), and providing emotional support (counselling services) have been brought into the cash nexus. As this has happened, women have been incorporated into the labor force to perform these tasks for wages. Within this female-typed public reproduction work, however, there is further stratification by race. Racial ethnic women perform the more menial, less desirable tasks. They prepare and serve food, clean rooms and change bed pans, while white women, employed as semiprofessionals and white-collar workers, perform the more skilled and administrative tasks. The stratification is visible in hospitals, where whites predominate among registered nurses, while the majority of health care aides and housekeeping staff are blacks and latinas. Just as white women in tobacco manufacturing benefited by getting cleaner and more mechanized jobs by dint of the dirty preparation work done by black women, so white women professionals enjoy more desirable working conditions because racial ethnic women perform the less desirable service tasks. The better pay white women receive also allows them to purchase services and goods that ease their reproductive labor at home.

This point leads to a final consideration. It may be tempting to conclude that racial ethnic women differ from white women simply by the addition of a second axis of oppression, namely race. It would be a mistake, though, not to recognize the dialectical relation between white and racial ethnic women. Race, gender, and class interact in such a way that the histories of white and racial ethnic women are intertwined. Whether one considers the split between public and private spheres, conflict within the family, between the family and outside institutions, or productive and reproductive labor, the situation of white women has depended on the situation of women of color. White women have gained advantages from the exploitation of racial ethnic women, and the definition of white womanhood has to a large extent been cast in opposition to the definition of racial ethnic women (Palmer, 1983). Marxist-feminist theory and the internal colonialism model both recognize white men as the dominant exploiting group; however it is equally important to emphasize the involvement of white women in the exploitation of racial ethnic people and the ways in which racial ethnic men have benefited from the even greater exploitation of racial ethnic women.

Notes

1. The term racial ethnic designates groups that are simultaneously racial and ethnic minorities. It is used here to refer collectively to blacks, latinos, and Asian-Americans groups that share a legacy of labor exploitation and special forms of oppression described in the body of this paper. It is offered as an alternative to more commonly used designations, namely, minority groups, people of color, and Third World minorities, each of which is problematic at some level.

2. Sokoloff (1980) points out that whereas earlier Marxist-feminists viewed gender oppression as a by-product of capitalism, what she calls "later" Marxist-feminists developed the concept of patriarchy as a separate system that predated capitalism and that interacts with class exploitation under capitalism.

3. This general line of argument may also apply to white working-class families. However, I would assert that there were crucial differences in the historical experiences of white working-class and racial ethnic families. The family system of the white working class was not subject to institutional attacks (such as forced separation) directed against black, Chicano, and Chinese families. Moreover, white working-class women were accorded some respect for their domestic roles.

References

Acosta-Belen, Edna. ed. 1979. *The Puerto Rican Woman.* New York: Praeger.

Almquist, Elizabeth M. 1979. *Minorities, Gender and Work.* Lexington, MA: D.C. Heath.

Almquist, Elizabeth M. and Juanita L. Weherle-Einhorm. 1978. "The Doubly Disadvantaged: Minority Women in the Labor Force." Pp. 63–88 in *Women Working,* edited by Ann H. Stromberg and Shirley Harkess. Palo Alto, CA: Mayfield.

Baca-Zinn, Maxine. 1982. Review Essay: Mexican American Women in the Social Sciences. *Signs* 8:259–272.

Baker, Sally Hillsman and Bernard Levenson. 1975a. Job Opportunities of Black and White Working-Class Women. *Social Problems* 22:510–532.

___. 1975b. *Earnings Prospects of Black and White Working Class Women.* Unpublished Paper.

Barrera, Mario. 1979. *Race and Class in the Southwest.* Notre Dame, IN: University of Notre Dame Press.

Barrera, Mario., Carlos Muñoz and Charles Onelas. 1972. "The Barrio as an Internal Colony" In *Urban Affairs Annual Review* 6, edited by Harlan Hahn.

Blassingame, John. 1972. *The Slave Community.* New York: Oxford University Press.

Blauner, Robert. 1972. *Racial Oppression in America.* New York: Harper & Row.

Braverman, Harry. 1974. *Labor and Monopoly Capital.* New York: Monthly Review Press.

Brown, Carol. 1981. "Mothers, Fathers and Children: From Private to Public Patriarchy." Pp. 239–269 in *Women and Revolution: A Discussion of the Unhappy Marriage of Marxism and Feminism,* edited by Lydia Sargent. Boston: South End.

Brown, Jean Collier. 1938. *The Negro Woman Worker.* Women's Bureau Bulletin 165. U.S. Department of Labor. Washington, DC: Government Printing Office.

Byington, Margaret. 1974. *Homestead: The Households of a Milltown.* Pittsburgh, PA: University of Pittsburgh Press.

Camarillo, Albert. 1979. *Chicanos in a Changing Society.* Cambridge, MA: Harvard University Press.

Carmichael, Stokely and Charles V. Hamilton. 1967. *Black Power: The Politics of Liberation in America.* New York: Vintage.

Cheng, Lucie and Edna Bonacich. 1984. *Labor Immigration Under Capitalism: Asian Immigrant Workers in the United States Before World War II.* Berkeley, CA: University of California Press.

Clark, Kenneth. 1965. *Dark Ghetto.* New York: Harper & Row.

Coolidge, Mary. 1909. *Chinese Immigration.* New York: Henry Holt.

Davis, Angela Y. 1971. "Reflections on the Black Woman's Place in the Community of Slaves." *The Black Scholar* 2:3–15.

___. 1981. *Women, Race and Class.* New York: Random House.

Dill, Bonnie Thornton. 1979. "The Dialectics of Black Womanhood." *Signs* 4:543–555.

Easton, Barbara. 1976. Industrialization and Femininity: A Case Study of Nineteenth-Century New England. *Social Problems* 23:389–401.

Elesser, Nan, Kyle MacKenzie, and Yvonne Tixier y Vigil. 1980 *Las Mujeres: Conversations from a Hispanic Community.* Old Westbury, NY: The Feminist Press.

Fisher, Lloyd, 1953. *The Harvest Labor Market in California.* Cambridge, MA: Harvard University Press.

Fogel, William and Stanley Engerman. 1974. *Time on the Cross.* Boston: Little, Brown.

Foner, Philip S. and Ronald L. Lewis. 1981. *The Black Worker: A Documentary History From Colonial Times to the Present*, Vol. VI, *The Era of Post-War Prosperity and the Great Depression, 1920–1936.* Philadelphia: Temple University Press.

Frazier, E. Franklin. 1939. *The Negro Family in the United States.* Chicago: University of Chicago Press.

Garcia, Mario T. 1980. "The Chicana in American History: The Mexican Women of El Paso, 1880–1920—A Case Study." *Pacific Historical Review* 49: 315–337.

___. 1981. *Desert Immigrants: The Mexicans of El Paso, 1880–1920.* New Haven: Yale University Press.

Genovese, Eugene. 1974. *Roll, Jordan, Roll.* New York: Pantheon.

Gilkes, Cheryl. 1982. "Successful Rebellious Professionals: The Black Woman's Professional Identity and Community Commitment." *Psychology of Women Quarterly* 6:289–311.

Glenn, Evelyn Nakano. 1983. "Split Household, Small Producer and Dual Wage Earner: An Analysis of Chinese American Family Strategies." *Journal of Marriage and the Family* 45:35–46.

Glenn, Evelyn Nakano and Charles M. Tolbert II. 1985. "Technology and Emerging Patterns of Stratification for Women of Color: Race and Gender Segregation of Computer Occupations." Revised version of a paper presented at the Women, Work and Technology Conference, University of Connecticut.

Goldman, Marion. 1981. *Goldiggers and Silverminers.* Ann Arbor: University of Michigan Press.

Gutman, Herbert G. 1975. "Persistent Myths About the Afro-American Family." *Journal of Interdisciplinary History* 6:181–210.

___. 1976. *The Black Family in Slavery and Freedom.* New York: Pantheon.

Harevan, Tamara. 1977. "Family Time and Industrial Time: Family and Work in a Planned Corporation Town, 1900–1924." In *Family and Kin in Urban Communities: 1900–1930.* New York: New Viewpoints.

Hartmann, Heidi. 1976. "Capitalism, Patriarchy and Job Segregation by Sex." *Signs* 1:137–169.

___. 1981a. The Unhappy Marriage of Marxism and Feminism: Towards a More Progressive Union. Pp. 1–41 in *Women and Revolution: A Discussion of the Unhappy Marriage of Marxism and Feminism,* edited by Lydia Sargent. Boston: South End.

___. 1981b. "The Family as a Locus for Gender, Class and Political Struggle: The Example of Housework." *Signs* 6(5):366–394.

Hirata, Lucie Cheng. 1979. "Free, Indentured and Enslaved: Chinese Prostitutes in Nineteenth Century America." *Signs* 5:3–29.

hooks, bell. 1981 *Ain't I a Woman: Black Women and Feminism.* Boston: South End.

Humphries, Jane. 1977. "Class Struggle and the Persistence of the Working Class Family." *Cambridge Journal of Economics* 1:241–258.

Ikels, Charlotte and Julia Shang. 1979. The Chinese in Greater Boston. Interim Report to the National Institute of Aging.

Jensen, Joan M. 1980. "Cloth, Butter and Boarders: Women's Household Production for the Market." *Review of Radical Political Economics* 12(2):14-24.

___. 1981. *With These Hands: Women Working on the Land.* Old Westbury, NY: Feminist Press.

Jones, Jacqueline. 1984. *Labor of Love, Labor of Sorrow: Black Women, Work and the Family from Slavery to the Present.* New York: Basic Books.

Katzman, David. 1978. *Seven Days a Week: Women and Domestic Service in Industrializing America.* New York: Oxford University Press.

Kessler-Harris, Alice. 1982. *Out to Work.* New York: Oxford University Press.

Kim, Elaine. 1983. *With Silk Wings: Asian American Women at Work.* San Francisco: Asian Women United of California.

Kingston, Maxine Hong. 1977. *The Woman Warrior.* New York: Vintage.

Lee, L. P., A. Lim, and H. K. Wong. 1969. *Report of the San Francisco Chinese Community Citizens' Survey and Fact Finding Committee* (Abridged Edition). San Francisco: Chinese Community Citizens' Survey and Fact Finding Committee.

Lerner, Gerda. 1969. "The Lady and the Mill Girl: Changes in the Status of a Woman in the Age of Jackson." *American Studies* 10:5–14.

___. 1973. *Black Women in White America: A Documentary History*. New York: Vintage.

Li, Peter S. 1977. "Fictive Kinship, Conjugal Ties and Kinship Claim Among Chinese Immigrants in the United States." *Journal of Comparative Family Studies* 8(1):47–64.

Ling, Pyan. 1912. "The Causes of Chinese Immigration." *Annals of the American Academy of Political and Social Sciences* 39:74–82.

Lyman, Stanford. 1968. "Marriage and Family Among Chinese Immigrants to America, 1850–1960." *Phylon* 29(4):321–330.

___. 1974. *Chinese Americans*. New York: Random House.

___. 1977. "Strangers in the City: The Chinese in the Urban Frontier." In *The Asian in North America*. Santa Barbara, CA: ABC Clio.

Massey, Douglas S. 1982. *The Demographic and Economic Position of Hispanics in the United States: 1980*. Report to the National Commission for Employment Policy. Philadelphia: Population Studies Center, University of Pennsylvania.

McLemore, Dale. 1973. "The Origins of Mexican American Subordination in Texas." *Social Science Quarterly* 53:656–670.

___. 1980. *Racial and Ethnic Relations in America*. Boston: Allyn & Bacon.

McWilliams, Carey. 1971. *Factories in the Field*. Santa Barbara, CA: Peregrine.

Melville, Margarita B., ed. 1980. *Twice a Minority: Mexican American Women*. St. Louis: C. V. Mosby.

Mirande, Alfredo and Evangelina Enriquez. 1979. *La Chicana: The Mexican American Woman*. Chicago: University of Chicago Press.

Mora, Magdelina and Adelaida R. Del Castillo, eds. 1980. *Mexican Women in the United States: Struggles Past and Present*. Los Angeles: Chicano Studies Publications.

Moore, Joan W. 1970. "Colonialism: The Case of Mexican Americans." *Social Problems* 17:463–472.

Moynihan, Daniel Patrick. 1965. "The Negro Family: The Case for National Action." Washington, DC: Government Printing Office. Prepared for the Office of Policy Planning and Research.

Nee, Victor and Brett deBary Nee. 1972. *Long Time Californ'*. New York: Pantheon Books.

Pachon, Harry P. and Joan W. Moore. 1981. "Mexican Americans." *Annals of the American Academy of Political and Social Sciences* 454:111–124.

Painter, Nell Irvin. 1976. *Exodusters: Black Migration to Kansas After the Reconstruction*. New York: W. W. Norton.

Palmer, Phyllis Marynick, 1983. "White Women/Black Women: The Dualism of Female Identity and Experience in the United States." *Feminist Studies* 9:151–170.

Pleck, Elizabeth H. 1979. "A Mother's Wages: Income Earning Among Married Italian and Black Women, 1896–1911." Pp. 367–392 in *A Heritage of Her Own*, edited by Nancy F. Cott and Elizabeth H. Pleck. New York: Touchstone Books.

Rodgers-Rose, La Frances. ed. 1989. *The Black Women*. Beverly Hills, CA: Sage.

Saxton, Alexander. 1971. *The Indispensable Enemy: Labor and the Anti-Chinese Movement in California*. Berkeley: University of California Press.

Sokoloff, Natalie. 1980. *Between Money and Love*. New York: Praeger.

Sterling, Dorothy. 1979. *Black Foremothers: Three Lives*. Old Westbury, NY: The Feminist Press.

Taylor, Paul S. 1929. "Mexican Labor in the United States: Valley of the South Platte." *University of California Publications in Economics* 6(2):95–235.

___. 1937. "Migratory Farm Labor in the United States." *Monthly Labor Review* (March):537–549.

Taylor, Ronald. 1976. *Sweatshops in the Sun*. Boston: Beacon.

Thorne, Barrie. 1982. "Feminist Rethinking of the Family: An Overview." Pp. 1–24 in *Rethinking the Family: Some Feminist Questions*, edited by Barrie Thorne and Marilyn Yalom. New York: Longman.

Tsuchida, Nobuya (ed.). 1982. *Asian and Pacific American Experiences: Women's Perspectives*. Minneapolis: Asian/Pacific American Learning Resource Center.

U.S. Bureau of the Census. 1933. *Fifteenth Census of the United States: 1930. Population, Volume V: General Report on Occupations* (Chapter 3, Color and Nativity of Gainful Workers). Washington, DC: Government Printing Office.

___. 1933. *Fifteenth Census of the United States: 1980. Population, Volume II: General Report, Statistics by Subject*. Washington, DC: Government Printing Office.

___. 1973. *Census of the Population: 1970*. Subject Reports, Final Report PC(2)1G. *Japanese, Chinese, and Filipinos in the United States*. Washington, DC: Government Printing Office.

U.S. Department of Justice 1977. *Immigration and Naturalization Service Annual Report*. Washington, DC: U.S. Department of Justice.

U.S. Department of Labor. 1977. *U.S. Working Women: A Databook*. Bureau of Labor Statistics, Bulletin 1977. Washington, DC: Government Printing Office.

Weinbaum, Batya and Amy Bridges. 1979. "The Other Side of the Paycheck: Monopoly Capital and the Structure of Consumption." In *Capitalist Patriarchy and the Cause for Social Feminism*, edited by Zillah R. Eisenstein. New York: Monthly Review Press.

Welter, Barbara. 1966. "The Cult of True Womanhood: 1820–1860." *American Quarterly* (Summer):151–174.

Westcott, Diane Nilsen. 1982. "Blacks in the 1970's: Did They Scale the Job Ladder?" *Monthly Labor Review* (June): 29–32.

Willie, Charles. 1981. *A New Look at Black Families*. Bayview, NY: General Hall.

Wu, C. 1972. *"Chink": A Documentary History of Anti-Chinese Prejudice in America*. New York: Meridian.

Yap, Stacey G. Y. 1983. *Gather Your Strength Sisters: The Careers of Chinese American Women Community Workers*. Unpublished doctoral dissertation, Boston University.

The Demise of Domesticity in America

Alice Kessler-Harris
Karen Brodkin Sacks

Incremental changes in our economy may seem to be of little consequence for ordinary people, and, yet, added together, they may produce unforeseen and radical results. In this paper, we want to take a historical view of deindustrialization and the current structural transformations in America's political economy to see how they are altering women's traditional roles. We believe that changes now in process will ultimately restructure family forms and gender relations, and open the possibility of transforming some of our social institutions. The changes described by several authors in this volume alter the way women and men think about themselves and about each other in relation to both the home and work. These emerging self concepts will tend to challenge nuclear family relationships as we know them. Specifically, we seek to explore the consequences for all of us when women act on new perceptions.

Our approach is grounded in recent data from the social sciences. It now seems apparent that the current structural transformation has increased female employment and male unemployment. The visible and immediate impact of this change is to alter the balance of power within families as they come to depend more heavily on women's wages. The most remarked-upon consequences of this changed power balance have been a sharp rise in divorce rates, in single-parent households, and in the pauperization of women. While family breakdowns constitute the most striking short-term trend, a longer-term qualitative analysis reveals a history that shows such breakdowns as parts of larger restructuring processes. Here women have been the main actors in creating new rules for family relationships, new forms of household organization, and, perhaps, even new relations between families and wage work, and families and the state.

We are witnessing a new stage in that process today, as we see a ripening of the contradiction between the realities of family life and the ideology by which these realities have been interpreted and channeled. That ideology, the domestic code, is being directly confronted, not only by self-styled feminists, but by large numbers of women who seek the rewards of the marketplace while denying any connection with feminism.

Before exploring these issues we want to stress that we use the terms "deindustrialization" and "structural transformation" in their traditional sense, meaning the movement to a service economy from our specific vantage point in time and culture. We are guilty, therefore, of a certain amount of ethnocentrism. For clearly the international capitalist economy is not becoming deindustrialized; rather the United States has lost its hegemony in basic industries, and many American corporations are locating an increasing portion of their production in the third world. From a third world perspective, industrialization is the norm. Our perspective comes from that part of the metropolis that consists of native-born women whose kin and immediate families are resident in the United States. Similarly, structural transformation has different possible meanings in different parts of the world. In some places, the dominant shift is from subsistence to capitalist or commercial agriculture; in others, from primary production or extraction to heavy manufacturing. In still others, notably the old industrial nations, the term refers to a shift in the kinds of jobs in which the waged workforce engages—from the production of goods to the production of "services." We use structural transformation in this latter sense.

The current transformation in what is produced, where it is produced, and by whom, is part of a continuing process by which the spread of capitalism has reshaped the world's political economy. In the United States, this penetration is now converting formerly unwaged and informal economic activities, such as meal preparation, child care, and the care of the aged, into profit-making enterprises. The result is to place women, whose lives are most immediately touched by these activities, at the forefront of change, and to pose questions for their families that may challenge the structure of capitalism itself.

Shifts in the Balance of Family Power

For most of the American working class for most of its history, the wage of even the principal (male) earner was inadequate to raise a family. As interpreted by labor unions and social reformers in the past, the demand for a "living wage" often meant that a man's wage be adequate to sustain a whole family. The current feminist movement has pointed out the double-edged nature of that demand, however (Hartmann, 1976; Humphries, 1977; Sen, 1980). On the one hand, such a wage provided married women with some economic security and limited the number of family members required to engage in alienating labor. On the other, the sexist assumption that men were the only legitimate wage earners increased wives' dependency on husbands and provided a basis for the intrafamily oppression of women. It also denied women without husbands access to a living wage. As Wandersee notes, "One of the basic facts of family economics during the early twentieth century was that most working-class males, and many of those in the middle class, were not paid enough to support their families according to the American standard of living." (1981:1). Even with the success of unions in heavy industry, it is debatable whether a single wage ever covered the costs of rearing a family in more than a minority of cases. But for most of the past, women were able to make up the differential between the male wage and the cost of survival through their own and community resources in ways that did not alter family relationships. The structural transformation of the last twenty-five years has made that no longer possible.

A variety of family strategies contributed to household well-being prior to World War II. Daughters and sons as well as husbands were typically wage-earners. Indeed, the vast majority of poor and working class parents found themselves dependent on their children's wages to keep their households afloat and expected their children to contribute to the collective endeavor. In addition, mothers, wives, and other non-wage-earning adults in the family participated in what has come to be called an informal economy, where they provided significant amounts of cash for family needs and stretched family income with their un-waged labor. These earning efforts, as the new scholarship in feminist and working-class history has demonstrated, were often hidden and unrecognized in terms of informal and casual enterprises—generally a mixture of petty entrepreneurial sales and service activities, such as taking in piece-work or laundry at home, baking goods for sale, peddling, or running a small store.

Large proportions of working-class wives and mothers took in lodgers. They thus provided to the unmarried of the working-class community some of the domestic services they performed directly for their own families, and made a cash contribution to the household budget as well (Jensen, 1980; Pleck, 1979; Smith, 1979). In the steel and coal regions of the midwest, as in the mushrooming cities of the East, boarders could contribute a significant share of a family's income. For example, some 40 percent of all families of immigrant steel work-

ers in Homestead, Pennsylvania, in the early twentieth century took in boarders. With one to four lodgers in a four-room house, a family could add about 25 percent to its income (Byington, 1911). In New England communities of Polish silk and cotton mill workers, four out of five people lived in houses with boarders (Lamphere, et al., 1980). Taking in boarders created larger households, and sometimes, when the boarders were women, increased the availability of domestic labor. In addition, boarding gave single members of the community a set of social places and links they might not otherwise have had. Significantly, this effort to bring cash into the household provided women with key roles in building working-class communities at the same time as it reinforced their home-centered roles.

The same might be said for most jobs in the informal economy: they were not only consistent with women's conventional roles at home, they reinforced them. Far from altering the balance of family relations, they perpetuated the notion that women could extend family income by being good wives and loyal family members. Moreover, they tied women into networks of kin and neighborhood activities that in turn tied the family into the social and economic life of the community, reinforcing the family's position within it and providing a larger context for women's hard work. We see such networks in studies of Italian and Jewish immigrant communities and more recently in analysis of urban black families, Appalachian families, and third world families (Kessler-Harris, 1982; Caulfield, 1974; Cohn, 1977; Stack, 1974; Yans-McLaughlin, 1977).

The transition in the economy since World War II has made wage work more available to women and reduced the incentive to continue informal earning activities. Produce and poultry, as well as clothing, can be bought more cheaply than produced at home. Large franchised chains reduce the possibility of women starting their own little grocery stores. At the same time, the commoditization of services has made such goods more easily bought by those to whom wives and mothers formerly provided them. Many fewer working-class mothers earn cash by boarding, cooking, washing, or sewing for others. The trade-off for women who need to supplement family incomes is the part-time job, where they earn wages to provide services their mothers or grandmothers would have offered from their own homes.

But what seems like a simple trade-off—women using their own wages to purchase the ready-to-eat or ready-to-wear commodities they no longer produce at home—in fact erodes men's domestic power and authority over them. By commoditizing new areas of domestic life, from cooking to child care and nursing the aged, capitalism simultaneously reduces the scope of private housework and undermines husbands' control over wives' labor power. At one level, increased reliance on commodities releases women from the excessive isolation of the home and thus has a feminist aspect. It may also represent women's decisions about how they wish to use their wages, offering the possibility of some autonomy and the potential for ameliorating their ever-increasing burdens (Spalter-Roth, 1983).[1] At another level, by placing women in positions parallel to husbands who earn wages, it deprives husbands of the unwaged labor from which they have historically benefitted, and thus of the self-esteem and privileges that have historically accompanied "supporting" a family (Rubin, 1976).

In addition, in the process of undermining male domestic privileges, women's actions are raising equally subversive questions about wages themselves: for what labor are wages paid and are they re-ally the "private property" of those to whom they are paid? These are not entirely new questions. Historically, struggle between husbands and wives occurred over whether the husband had use of "his" wages, or whether the wife had first claim on them because of her responsibility for buying food and children's clothing and paying the rent. The nineteenth-century women's rights movement engaged itself with this issue, and the conflict infused the temperance movement with much of its vitality among the North American and English proletariat (Bordin, 1981; Paulson, 1973; Blocker, 1985). For women especially, liquor embodied the evils of a philosophy that gave wage-earners ownership of their wages as private property. In contrast, a family-ownership philosophy underlay the practice of "tipping," where all earners of the household put their wages in a family pot to be allocated, usually by the mother, or by whomever played the role of household administrator (Humphries, 1977; Tilly and Scott, 1978).

Contemporary feminist analysis focusing on white families stresses the extent to which the wage has traditionally covered the cost of reproduction of the whole family and class of wage earners as well as the maintenance of those who actually earn the wages. Black families have depended more heavily on the wages of women as well as of men. With more wives and mothers of small children heavily involved in the wage labor force, the gender dimensions of the wage conflict have become more visible, such that women increasingly see wages as their private property and use them to assert their rights to autonomy and to resist subordination to husbands, as did wage-earning daughters in the nineteenth century. Yet mothers and wives lack the mobility of fathers and daughters, because mothers still tend to bear responsibility for dependent children. In this context, two contradictory aspects of wages-as-private-property become apparent. On the one hand, wages represent a basis for resisting gender and generational subordination within the family (a longer tradition for black families); on the other hand, they provide women with the opportunity to avoid family situations altogether. Today's wage-earning women seem to be resisting subordination more than rejecting a give and take that is part of family life. Men are less able to demand obedience from wives.

These conflicts are sustained and exacerbated by rising levels of white as well as black male unemployment in the face of more available (although poorly paid) jobs in sectors normally defined as female. For many families this implies increasing reliance on the female wage and increasing difficulty in defining it as merely supplemental. Intermittent campaigns to take women out of the workforce and to construct a nuclear family under the rule of a male breadwinner, such as have been undertaken by the Reagan administration, seem to have fallen prey to the need for two wage earners in the family. Also, as jobs in traditionally male areas decrease, conventional notions of masculinity are less effective in frightening men away from paid jobs in traditionally female occupations. Intrafamilial negotiations over power have emerged as the norm. What is to be decided first in family after family and finally in the sphere of social policy is whether the increasing discordance between the wages women actually earn and their traditionally subordinate roles in relations to husband and family can any longer be contained. This raises the question of what it means to be a wage earner and what wage-earning implies about "woman's place."

What Is Happening to "Woman's Place?"—Or Challenges to the Domestic Code

Families have been said to be based on the complementarity of opposites in everything from economics to temperament. The conventional dichotomy of society into a home or family sphere of love and emotion as women's place and responsibility, and a public sphere of power and work as men's, is often called the domestic code (Welter, 1966). The edges of both spheres are unravelling as current economic shifts influence the ways people behave.

The domestic ideology, or domestic code, is an interpretation about what work is and what it is not, about who works and who does not; about what a man is and does, and what a woman is and does. These ideas have become a part of our way of talking and thinking about our lives to each other and ourselves. They have ordered the family and defined social possibilities for men and women. And they have now become the basis of structural conflicts that have divided the genders and generations in both the family and factory (Ryan, 1981).

The domestic code provided a rationale for the reciprocally confirming notion that women who belonged at home lacked the impetus and ambition to make their way in the workforce, and therefore behaved in ways that justified their disadvantaged places in comparison with men. Women, who earned about 60 percent of male pay, were given the argument that their wages need not be large enough to support a family. And if poor pay and discrimination discouraged them from seeking jobs at all, rational observers suggested that this only proved that women were in fact better suited to the home.

Such circular reasoning provided easy justifications for employers to exploit women, for public policymakers to ignore those who asked for benefits and higher wages and for organized labor to refuse to take such demands seriously (Kessler-Harris, 1975:164). A favorite example comes from the American Association for Labor legislation, which in 1916 proposed a national health insurance scheme that would have, among other things, paid hospital expenses of pregnant women who withdrew from the workforce in the weeks immediately before and after childbirth. Critics protested that such generosity would give potential mothers an incentive to seek jobs, and the proposal was immediately withdrawn.

Despite the steadily growing dependence on wages of adult women for family survival in the working class and in much of the middle class, the domestic code has insisted that women's most essential role is that of wife-and-mother. The rise of post-World War II domesticity was based on a widely shared consensus that the health of the American economy depended heavily on women returning to the home and leaving their relatively well-paid wartime jobs to men. In return, these men were supposed to support their wives and children in a higher, middle-class lifestyle in the new suburbs that psychologists and financiers alike were promoting as integral to a solid peacetime economy. An especially virulent version of the domestic ideology emerged in this milieu: it insisted that women no longer "needed" to work, and thereupon denied them even the minimal privileges of work (advancement, health benefits, equal pensions, and so forth). They were admitted to jobs in which they were needed but in which career possibilities were blocked or nonexistent.

Like the attempt to negate the existence of a working class, which occurred in the same period and which assigned to those who lived in the suburbs middle-class attitudes and aspirations, these 1950s attitudes hid women who desired careers and salaries instead of wages. Women whose lifestyles did not conform to these expectations were viewed as deviants to be cured of their ills lest they set bad examples to others (Ehrenreich and English, 1979; Farnham and Lundberg, 1947; Ryan, 1979; Weisstein, 1970). They were depicted in the media as social problems, the causes of a variety of social sins from homosexuality and juvenile delinquency to the deterioration of American values and the Great Depression.

We now know that the imposed domesticity of the fifties masked the reality of what women were actually doing. Most of the Rosie the Riveters of World War II did not leave the workforce when they were forced out of their wartime jobs (Anderson, 1981; Gabin, 1982; Trey, 1972). Instead, they found other jobs in offices, hospitals, and banks, in nonunionized small factories, and in a variety of personal services. To be sure, these jobs did not pay as well as those the women lost and they preserved the traditional segmentation of the labor force. Yet the permanent expansion of women's workforce participation and the shift in government policy to encourage training women for certain kinds of jobs began in the wake of cold war needs for what Women's Bureau head Frieda Miller described as maintaining "the skills acquired by two and a half million women in wartime." (Kessler-Harris, 1982:304).

Behind the image of working-class prosperity lay the reality that working-class families needed more than one paycheck to participate in the more expensive suburban lifestyle. Part-time work, "mothers' shifts," seasonal jobs that allowed "vacations" when the kids were out of school all helped these "deviant" women disguise themselves as proper homemakers. During the 1950s the proportion of wives and mothers in the wage labor force grew by one third.

As more women went out to work, those women who had been earning wages all along appeared less deviant. Wage work became acceptable if it was presented as an extension of women's family responsibilities and as lacking any element of personal ambition. As any fan of Doris Day movies well knew, every smart woman who made it to the top gave up her career as soon as Mr. Right came along. As the media portraits altered and the paradigms of social science shifted to encompass the new realities, black women, married and single, who had always worked in higher proportions than white women, moved to the forefront. In the context of a new affirmation supported by an emerging civil rights movement, they asserted their real economic roles, demanded government policies that acknowledged labor force discrimination, and insisted on educational opportunities for their children. In some ways they were the vanguards of the then-still-incipient women's movement.

These contradictions matured throughout the 1950s until, by the early sixties, the domestic code that had confined women's increasing workforce participation to narrow spheres and had limited their aspirations to "helping out at home" began to break down. Helped by the meritocratic and egalitarian consciousness that emerged from the struggle for civil rights and against the Vietnam War, women began to demand the rewards of hard work. Those who left their homes out of financial need wanted the promotions and high wages that were the nominal rewards of hard work. By the mid-1970s, these women began to organize themselves into groups like Women Office Workers, Union Wage, and the Coalition of Labor Union Women to fight for equal pay for equal work, clearer job definitions, and access to promotions. Women who left home out of the search for satisfaction wanted the personal fulfillment that jobs promised. They hoped to teach or do social work in "helping" settings. Instead, they entered a tightening job market where social services were being cut back to the point where workers could not help clients; they could only police them. In both cases, women ran up against the barriers of the occupational ghetto rooted in notions that women belonged at home. The search for fair treatment in the workplace demanded that America come to terms with whether women's family roles needed to be so rigidly prescribed. The ever-increasing numbers of wage-earning women who confronted work roles governed by outdated notions of domesticity that limited and defined their relationships to the concept of family and their families added their voices to those of the young people and minorities of the 1960s who demanded that the society live up to its rhetoric.

Given the persistence of women's continuing relationships to paid work and given the structural sources out of which women's complaints arose, the domestic code is increasingly anachronistic. It contradicts the experience that families require prodigious amounts of unpaid work as well as increasing amounts of paid labor from women. And it sustains male attempts to hang on to patterns of behavior that emerged in families where women's unwaged labor predominated. To eliminate distinctions between the sexes seems particularly threatening in a society where other elements are in such flux. What is at stake is nothing less than the issue of whether woman's place is in the home.

What Is a Good Woman?—Or Women's Self-Definition Apart from Family Roles

To examine the material realities that push women into the workforce and that undermine the family's ability to keep them at home is to urge a re-vision of women's economic responsibilities and jobs. As wage work becomes the life labor of women as well as of men, and as women begin to insist on its rewards, their behavior and expectations of waged and unwaged work change. The result is to alter the way the "family" functions.

Women workers now make up almost half of the American labor force, and as some of the other papers in this volume indicate, they are the large majority of workers in some of the fastest-growing and lowest-paying industries, such as electronics manufacturing, hospitals and nursing homes, fast foods, data and word processing. More women head families and are the sole supports of children than ever before. The threat of consistently high unemployment makes women's earnings central even in families where a man is also working. The typical woman today is a wage worker in a job that pays poorly, gives her little possibility for advancement, and little control over her work or decision-making power in her work. The typical hourly wage-worker today is a woman. One recent analysis of the American class structure using such criteria concludes that women now make up the majority of the working class, and that together with minority men, women and minorities comprise a large majority of the American working class (Wright, Costello, et al., 1982).

As women are forced more intensively into wage labor, they develop a consciousness of themselves as doubly exploited at home and in the factory or office. While in the past women who entered wage work could protect themselves with the assumption that this role was temporary and that their identities resided in their home roles, the recognition of work as a permanent part of their lives no longer permits such self-deception. If honor and dignity now reside for women, as for men, at least to some extent in their paid work, then struggles for recognition on the job and for some element of control will become an increasing part of women's lives. The unity of home and work—of the social and economic spheres—will be established.

The result then is a series of struggles around both home and work. Women's collective action and overwhelming support for pay equity and active efforts against sexual harassment are affirmations of women's developing sense of self. Yet the rewards of success are seen to come at the expense of men, raising the level of competition between the sexes. While women workers are increasingly concerned about the impact of their double days on children, they still try to carry both wage labor and the unpaid labor of raising children and other dependents. Women's activism in joining trade unions (women are half of all new union members since the 1960s), and in litigating and agitating for workplace justice on a wide variety of fronts suggests that there is at least a potential for their transforming traditional notions about family and work and about men's and women's relationships. The steps needed for this transformation include demands for employer payments for family-oriented benefits— health insurance for pregnancy and birth, paid parenting leaves, paid time off for dependent care, paid child care, and shorter and more flexible working days.[2] These kinds of demands imply that women are using their roles as workers not to free themselves from family roles, but to sustain the social responsibilities formerly undertaken by families and defined as private affairs or nonwork. They are beginning to transform women's family tasks into responsibilities to be shared.

Women who insist on the freedom to perform successfully at work demand the same freedom in their personal behavior. To do well on the job while maintaining households with children requires a new subjective sense of self as well as new shared social definitions of women's objective needs. Thus behavior earlier seen as natural and described as dependent and gentle or—feminine—no longer appears natural at all to women who see such a stance as inhibiting their performance at work. The positive responses to such new self-perceptions appear in more expressive sexualities, in openness toward lesbianism and rejection of heterosexual relationships, in rising divorce rates, in increasing numbers of women who choose motherhood without marriage, and in a more tangible sense of independence on the part of young girls. The image of a "good" woman changes. And some of these changes meet no opposition from among men relieved of the need to be "good" men—or to provide entirely for their families (Ehrenreich, 1983). Yet insofar as notions of femininity provided the substructure on which the framework of domesticity (and therefore gender segmentation in the workforce and male dominance in the family) was built, its wholesome abandonment threatens to reveal the ideological nature of the current insistence on divisions into private and public spheres. It threatens in short, to open to the public eye the daily reality of a unified labor. This is because successful engagement with wage work for women and men who wish also to maintain satisfying family lives requires the cooperative work of both sexes, and perhaps

of several generations organized in households and families of various kinds. The cultural language and behavior that denies this unity must inevitably be called into question.

The Family and Society

These new perceptions, however, raise fundamental questions about the nature of the family in relation to the community and to kin, and about its function in maintaining social order. From the perspective of traditionalists, such questions are enormously threatening, suggesting not only the demise of the family but the end of respect for the values that the family had sustained. In the last few years we have seen the emergence of powerful groups like "Stop ERA," the "Committee for the Survival of a Free Congress," and the "Moral Majority" dedicated to making divorce less accessible, prohibiting abortions, and creating "pro-family" coalitions. In the end, such goals must involve removing women from all but the most menial jobs. As we have seen, this process runs counter to current economic and occupational trends. The result is a struggle around emerging values, which, we suggest, traditionalists will inevitably lose—at least in the long run.

In families these struggles grow out of women's new relationships to income and the way they influence community life. As we have seen, from a working-class woman's perspective, her ability to provide services and cash for household needs by her entrepreneurial activities has been slowly eroded since World War II. Working-class women have been pressed and encouraged to give up their autonomous income-generating activities for wage labor—at minimum wage as often as not—for the very corporations that undermined their unpaid labor at home. The suburbanization of their communities together with the growth of a service sector that provides women with both jobs and consumer services reduces the strength of informal kin and neighborhood support networks. Unlike earlier income-generating activities and jobs, new jobs for women conflict in time and space with family and community life. As wage-earning women pass into these jobs, community-based, informal economic activities can be expected to break down.

There are two sides to this process. On one side is a loss of kin-based and community activities built around women's entrepreneurial activities, and a simultaneous atomization into small household political economies. The decline—in number and real wages—of many working-class men's jobs has placed families under heightened economic pressure. Attempts to survive economically have led fathers to leave home in search of work and mothers to contribute a relatively larger share of the family's cash needs through their waged labor.

On the other side, women's decreased economic dependence on husbands has occurred simultaneously with an increase in the number of adult wage-earning sons and daughters who remain in the parental household. The same pressures that lead husbands to abandon family responsibilities may encourage young adults to share them. Economic pressures, most notably the cost of housing, seem to be at the root of a variety of domestic arrangements including group houses of unrelated adults with or without children, adult sons and daughters remaining in the parental house, adult children returning to the parental house as single parents on the breakup of their marriages, and couples with children living with the parents of one of them. All of these combinations involve adults of both genders and different generations in a single unit of economic cooperation, creating models of extended family survival that sustain larger kin networks.

A growing body of post-World War II studies of working-class family and kinship stresses the importance of economically based kin relations in attempts to cope with and surmount the divisive and disintegrative pressures that come from the intensification of a wage economy (Rapp, 1978, reviews much of this literature; see also Caulfield, 1974; Stack, 1974; Tilly and Scott, 1978). They emphasize the variety and importance of extended kinship and friendship networks for coping with poverty and economic insecurity whose source is primarily capitalist wage labor relations. Black families have faced these atomizing pressures for a long time because they have had the lowest-paid and least secure jobs, and they have historically had less access than whites to land or other forms of productive property. The extended kin networks that join many small households together, often over great distances, and that form the basis of non-nuclear family households, have been well-documented in black working-class communities. As some analysts are pointing out, they are becoming increasingly common among whites, as they respond in similar ways to similar pressures.

In the past, local kin and community links provided a significant basis of support for sustained workplace resistance among wage-earning daughters and other kin. For example, Kessler-Harris (1981:91) credits family support networks with helping women garment workers in New York City hold a key and turbulent strike for three months in 1909. This "Uprising of 20,000" was the victory that established a union in a garment industry made up of many scattered, small-scale shops—an amazing feat of organizing and unity. And Nancy MacLean (1982) extends this analysis to the importance of women's networks both in the strike and in the subsequent building of the International Ladies Garment Workers' Union (ILGWU). Organizing this scattered and diverse workforce clearly demanded significant, though largely unstudied, family and community organization. In the absence of women's informal economic activities, networks of class-based communities decrease and the kin group remains relatively isolated and less able to defend women's and men's class interests.

Isolation of the broader kin group is encouraged by some of the same forces that lead to new forms of family as well as by federal and state policies. The diminished economic power of some men relative to women under current economic circumstances has led to increased divorce rates, an increase in single-parent households, and to the related feminization of poverty that further atomizes family and household ties (Pearce and McAdoo, 1981). To shore up the nuclear family, policymakers urge state intervention—and the state in fact provides support, but in ways that discourage extended kin support systems (Boris and Bardaglio, 1983). Reciprocity and community self-provision still survive in many working-class neighborhoods, but since World War II those neighborhoods have been undermined by suburbanization, urban renewal, and increased penetration of capitalist economic relations.

In the past women were able to exert a certain amount of pressure vis-à-vis the state in their family roles because households were parts of locally based kin networks in more or less tightly integrated working-class communities. While women-centered networks sustained community support for strikes, they also reinforced the separation of work and family, even as they reinforced women's association with the latter. When women challenged employers

and the state in this way, they could still maintain a self-image of themselves as domestic beings. Today, working-class communities have been dispersed and considerably weakened vis-à-vis the state. Women have taken many of the family-related concerns they once dealt with through community self-help to the workplace with them. These issues, from pay equity with its implied demands for adulthood, to dependent health and child care, are now being transformed from private responsibilities of individuals to demands for social responsibility from corporations and the state in bearing the economic costs of social reproduction, or family life.

As women come to perceive "family" issues as social and public ones, they move beyond the community to the national arena. These perceptions are shared—and acted upon—across the political spectrum, even among those to whom they are anathema. Thus right-wing and right-to-life women join with the left and with feminists in demanding that the state deal with reproductive issues and with child and dependent care. The irony is that the right-wing paradoxically demands state intervention against a whole range of issues they assert ought to be private decisions. What we witness then is a manifestation of the shift from kin responsibility to shared adult social responsibility, and a corresponding shift in locus from community struggle to workplace and state-centered arenas. But since the core of the struggle revolves around who will have social power and how it will be used, the shifts in class and gender relations produced by recent economic trends are likely to produce particularly virulent battles. These struggles are being waged at a time when families have to confront the state directly and individually, as the larger community structures that women maintained and that have previously acted as buffers and brokers give way under the pressures of maintaining households in the context of the amount of time devoted to wage work.

Conclusion

The sum of these effects is to undermine the shared values, or "meaning system" (Parkin, 1971) by which men and women have defined their roles. The current turmoil creates a new kind of consciousness among women, which, minimally, appears to defuse the notion that women work for the sake of the family, and at its extreme can introduce for some women an autonomous and aggressive independence. Still other women will attempt to bring the familial ideals of cooperation and nurturance to bear upon what they hope will be a newly rearranged workforce.

But as we have seen, the new relations of women to family and production also move the locus of struggle from community to the workplace and alter the perception of issues from familial to social change. Around the political implications of these issues working people polarize, some defending the traditional family, others legitimizing various family forms. Both groups seek to encourage the state to act on their behalf. In response, the state intervenes to reinforce traditional roles while it simultaneously insists on formal equality for women. This contradiction cannot long persist. But action in either the direction of traditional roles or in that of a more than formal equality will create its own, perhaps shattering response. We believe the result will be new family relations, new relations between men and women, and a radical transformation of the relationship of family (in all its diversity) to political economy and the state.

Notes

1. In contrast to Vanek's earlier studies, Spalter-Roth's study of time spent in housework and wage work between 1970 and 1980 indicates that women decreased their housework hours with increased wagework, while men increased theirs slightly.
2. This comes at a moment in time when the prospect of continuing high unemployment and low wages reduce the capacity of all workers to influence their working lives.

References

Anderson, K. *Wartime Women*. Westport, CT: Greenwood Press, 1981.

Blocker, J. S. "Separate Paths: Suffragists and the Women's Temperance Crusade." *Signs* 10 (Spring, 1985): 460–476.

Bordin, R. *Woman and Temperance: The Quest for Power and Liberty 1873–1900*. Philadelphia: Temple University Press, 1985.

Boris, E. and Bardaglio, P. "The Transformation of Patriarchy: The Historic Role of the State." In I. Diamond (ed.), *Families, Politics and Public Policy: A Feminist Dialogue on Women and the State*. New York: Longman, 1983, pp. 70-93.

Byington, M. *Homestead: The Households of a Mill Town*. Pittsburgh: University of Pittsburgh Press, [1910] 1974.

Caulfield, M. "Imperialism, Family and Cultures of Resistance." *Socialist Revolution* 29 (1974): 67–85.

Cohn, M. "Italian-American Women in New York City: 1900–1950, Work and School," *Class, Sex and the Woman Worker*, M. Cantor & B. Laurie, (eds.) Westport: Greenwood Press, 1977, pp. 120-143.

Ehrenreich, B. *Hearts of Men: The American Dream and the Flight from Commitment*. New York: Doubleday, 1983.

Farnham, M. and Lundberg, F. *Modern Women: The Lost Sex*. New York: Harper and Bros, 1947.

Gabin, N. "They Have Placed a Penalty on Womanhood: The Protest Actions of Women Auto Workers in Detroit-area UAW Locals, 1945–1947." *Feminist Studies* 8, 2 (1982): 373–398.

Humphries, J. "Class Struggle and the Persistence of the Working Class Family." *Cambridge Journal of Economics* 1 (1977): 241–258.

Jensen, J. "Cloth, Butter and Boarders: Women's Household Production for the Market." *Review of Radical Political Economics* 12,2 (1980): 14–24.

Kessler-Harris, A. "Where are the Organized Women Workers?" *Feminist Studies* 3,1–2 (1975): 92–110.

Kessler-Harris, A. *Women Have Always Worked*. Old Westbury: Feminist Press, 1975.

Kessler-Harris, A. *Out to Work: A History of Wage-earning Women in the United States.* New York: Oxford University Press, 1981.

Lamphere, L., Hauser, E., Rubin, D., Michel, S. and Simmons, C. "The Economic Struggles of Female Factory Workers: A Comparison between Early and Recent French, Polish and Portuguese Immigrants." Proceedings of a conference on Educational and Occupational Needs of White Ethnic Women. Washington, D.C.: National Institute of Education, 1980.

MacLean, N. *The Culture of Resistance: Female Institution-building in the Ladies Garment Workers' Union 1905–1925.* Occasional Papers in Women's Studies, University of Michigan, 1982.

Parkin, F. *Class, Inequality and the Political Order.* New York: Praeger, 1971.

Paulson, R. *Women's Suffrage and Prohibition: A Comparative Study of Equality and Social Control.* Glenview, IL: Scott Foresman and Company, 1973.

Pearce, D., and McAdoo, H. P. *Women and Children: Alone and in Poverty.* Washington, D.C.: National Advisory Council on Equal Opportunity, 1981.

Pleck, E. "A Mother's Wages: Income Earning among Married Italian and Black Workers." In N. F. Cott & E. Pleck (eds.), *A Heritage of her Own.* New York: Simon and Schuster, 1979, pp. 367-392.

Rapp, R. "Family and Class in Contemporary America: Notes toward Understanding of Ideology." *Science and Society* 42,3 (1978): 278–300.

Rubin, L. *Worlds of Pain: Life in the Working-class Family.* New York: Basic Books, 1976.

Ryan, M. *Womanhood in America.* New York: Franklin Watts, 1979.

Ryan, M. *Cradle of the Middle Class: The Family in Oneida County, New York 1790–1865.* Cambridge: Cambridge University Press, 1981.

Smith, J. "Our Own Kind: Family and Community Networks in Providence" In N. F. Cott & E. Pleck (eds.), *A Heritage of our Own.* New York: Simon and Schuster, 1979, pp. 393-411.

Spalter-Roth, R. "Differentiating between the Living Standards of Husbands and Wives in Two-Wage-Earner Families, 1968 and 1979." *Journal of Economic History* 43, 1 (1983): 231–240.

Stack, C. *All Our Kin: Strategies for Survival in a Black Community.* New York: Harper Colophon, 1974.

Tilly, L. and Scott, J. *Women, Work and Family.* New York: Holt, Rinehart and Winston, 1978.

Trey, J. E. "Women and the War Economy—World War II." *Review of Radical Political Economics* 4,3 (1972): 1–17.

Vanek, J. "Time Spent in Housework." *Scientific American*, (November, 1974): 116–121.

Wandersee, W. *Women's Work and Family Values 1920–1940.* Cambridge: Harvard University Press, 1981.

Weisstein, N. "Kinde, Küche, Kirche as Scientific Law: Psychology Constructs the Female." In R. Morgan (ed.), *Sisterhood is Powerful.* New York: Vintage Books, 1970. pp. 205-219.

Welter, B. "The Cult of True Womanhood 1820–1860." *American Quarterly* 18,2 pt. 1 (1966): 151–174.

Wright, E., Costello, C., Hachen, D., and Sprague, J. "The American Class Structure." *American Sociological Review* 47,6 (1982): 709–726.

Yans-McLaughlin, V. *Family and Community: Italian Immigrants in Buffalo, 1880–1930.* Ithaca: Cornell University Press, 1977.

The Rise and Fall of "Mommy Politics": Feminism and Unification in (East) Germany

Myra Marx Ferree

The peaceful revolutions that swept Eastern Europe in 1989 ushered in a new era of capitalist development, most radically and rapidly in East Germany. Unlike other countries' struggles to find a new path, the reform of the German Democratic Republic (GDR) was rapidly converted into the drama of unification. In less than a year after the collapse of the government, on October 3, 1990, unification was completed, with the absorption of the GDR as five new states for the Federal Republic of Germany. More completely than elsewhere in Eastern Europe, women are now faced with life conditions drastically different from those in which they were raised and on which they oriented their lives. Although this will certainly open new opportunities for some women, it also represents a crisis of tremendous proportions for most.

Although women were not completely invisible in this period of social transforma-tion, only a few individuals (e.g., Bärbel Bohley, of the Initiative for Peace and Human Rights) and issues (e.g., the legal regulation of abortion in the unification treaty) emerged even briefly into the international spotlight. Nonetheless, women were active participants in the nonviolent revolution that overthrew the state. Moreover, unlike all other Eastern European nations, the GDR saw a veritable explosion of autonomous feminist activity.[1] Women not only fought alongside men for a new social order, but they also developed a distinctive gender analysis and organizations of their own. These feminist organizations and perspectives, newly freed from domination by the GDR's political agenda, are now struggling to survive in dramatically changed circumstances: absorption into the West German political system, a staggering rise in unemployment, and the abolition of many social and economic supports for mothers.

From *Feminist Studies*, Volume 19, Number 1 (Spring 1993): 89-115, by permission of the publisher, Feminist Studies, Inc., c/o Department of Women's Studies, University of Maryland, College Park, MD 20742.

The intent of this essay is to provide a brief overview of the emerging concerns and organizations of women in the former GDR and to offer a tentative analysis of some of the opportunities and obstacles they face. Because these are developments that are still very much in process, the picture that can be drawn is necessarily incomplete. As an outsider, my perception of the situation is also limited. Nonetheless, the significance of current changes for women in the East and West suggests that even a preliminary and tentative analysis may be helpful.

This essay is organized into three main sections. I begin with a necessarily abbreviated account of the status of women in the GDR and their ambiguous relationship to the state, as both beneficiaries of the state's generous social support for motherhood and as targets of sex discrimination. I argue that this situation, combined with the presence of certain facilitating social networks, contributed to the distinctive mobilization of women in the GDR. In the second section, I outline briefly the rapid and vigorous emergence of feminist organizations in East Germany and their current, marginalized position in a unified nation. In the final section, I look at some of the contradictions facing formerly-East German women in their new political and economic circumstances, following the collapse of the GDR's "mommy politics" and the imposition of a less generous but no less gendered set of policies in the expanded Federal Republic of Germany (FRG).

Methods and Sources. The description and analysis offered here rest on both published material and on observations and interviews conducted in East and West Germany immediately before and after unification (September to November 1990) and the following summer (May to August 1991). The published material includes newspaper articles, pamphlets, personal statements, letters and articles in alternative media, program statements by feminist groups, and research papers and commentaries by feminist scholars. In addition, I conducted thirty interviews in East and West Germany in the fall, visited feminist projects in Berlin and Leipzig, and conducted twenty-five additional interviews in the spring.

My interpersonal contacts in the East centered in two areas. One was a 1990 conference in East Berlin on gender equality policy attended by a few West German feminists and more than 100 feminists from all over the GDR. In addition to innumerable informal conversations at the conference, I was able to conduct additional formal interviews with four participants. I also sought out feminist activists, scholars, and women in politics in East Berlin, particularly those involved in setting up equality offices in state and local government, conducted formal interviews with nine equality officers, five academics, and seven other feminist activists there, and sat in on a number of feminist meetings. The second was through the newly emerging women's studies program at the (formerly Karl Marx) University in Leipzig. I conducted seven extensive individual interviews with a range of active and inactive feminists in the fall, participated in several group discussions and uncounted shorter conversations, and carried out four additional interviews in the summer.

State Policy and Gender Mobilization

One root of the particular mobilization potential of GDR women lay in the state's particular version of women's emancipation. Compared to other Eastern European countries, the GDR was both relatively affluent and more committed to direct action on behalf of women. Indeed, for decades, the Communist party (SED) in East Germany proclaimed the successful emancipation of women by virtue of its specific policies for equal rights. Unlike other East-bloc countries, its leaders did not claim that gender inequality would simply wither away by itself.[2] However, their sharp shift in the early 1970s from conventional socialist equality politics to "stage-two" policies[3] that actively facilitated the combination of employment and motherhood generated a contradiction that some women turned to feminism to resolve.

Stage-One Equality Politics. The GDR could rightfully claim not only to have encouraged women to enter the paid labor force but also to have increased women's occupational qualifications; by 1989, 91 percent of East German women of working age were employed,[4] and 87 percent had completed formal occupational training and thus were officially "skilled workers" or professionals. Not only were one-half of all university students women, but also there was no gap in formal job qualifications between women and men under age forty.[5]

These accomplishments can be attributed both to the GDR's continuing labor shortage (due to low levels of capital investment and relatively unproductive use of labor) and to the ideological commitment to women's equality, understood in classic socialist terms as bringing women out of the home and into "productive" work. However, the definition of productive work remained centered on the ideal of the male worker employed full-time in an industrial job.[6] As many socialist feminist theorists have pointed out, the conceptualization of "worker" in classical Marxist theory implicitly assumed a man freed of responsibility for reproductive labor.[7]

Over the period from 1949 to 1972, East Germany gradually implemented a set of policies that were designed to encourage women to approximate this ideal in their own lives: first, a legal right to employment and pressure to take a full-time job; then, specific affirmative action programs for obtaining higher level qualifications and for placing women in nontraditional occupations; finally, an effort to expand the availability of kindergartens and other child-care to facilitate the pattern of lifetime, full-time paid employment that was the male norm.[8]

Thus, by 1972 both a formal ideological anchoring and a specific set of concrete policies were in place which defined the meaning of equality as the equal treatment of women and men in an employment-centered way of life. Although such equality was certainly never fully achieved, its significance as a social norm should not be underestimated. The high rates of women's labor force participation and their educational qualifications and the widespread availability of public childcare were often accepted in the West as evidence that East German women were relatively "more emancipated" than their Western counterparts.[9] In the East, such evidence of formal equality was used to repress any discussion of gender inequality and to persuade women that the problems they continued to experience were their personal shortcomings.[10]

In fact, East Germany continued to have a strongly gender-segregated labor market. Women were 77 percent of all workers in education and 86 percent of those in health and social services; virtually all the secretaries, nurses, and preschool teachers were women. Women workers were also concentrated in gender-segregated industrial jobs, such as textiles and electronics assembly (68 percent) rather than machine shops (30 percent). Although East Germany formally barred women from only 30 of 289 officially recognized skilled trades, in practice women could not enter more than one-half of these occupations. In 1987 more than 60 percent of all girls entering apprenticeships went into only 16 of these trades.[11] Despite their formally equal qualifications, women in the East with full-time jobs also earned less than men—averaging DM 762 versus DM 1009 per month—and were concentrated at the bottom of the hierarchy, even in fields numerically dominated by women. Nonetheless, on average, GDR women's earnings constituted a considerably higher proportion of family income than women contributed in the West [40 vs 18 percent).[12]

The traditional socialist stress on increasing women's employment and skills represented only the first stage of the GDR's "emancipation" of women. The differences in labor force position observed in the 1980s were in part a result of the "second-stage" policies adopted after 1972 explicitly to facilitate women's ability to combine paid employment and motherhood, policies that led to *increasing* gender segregation in occupational training and employment.[13] These policies produced contradictions which East German women experienced as increasingly problematic prior to the revolution.[14]

Stage-Two "Mommy Politics." Beginning in the early 1970s, the GDR introduced specific, targeted policies to facilitate women's combining paid employment with motherhood. These policies were explicitly intended to stop the decline in rates of childbearing without resorting to coercive measures.[15] Reflecting this, the government made first-trimester abortion available on demand and offered free birth control (oral contraceptives). Instead of repression, the GDR chose a policy of actively encouraging motherhood with a variety of gender-specific incentives. These policies, commonly referred to in East Germany as *Muttipolitik* or "mommy politics," are at the heart of the contradictory experience of GDR women,

both those young enough to have personal experience of their double-edged effects and older women concerned about the retreat from equality these measures represented.[16]

Among the supportive measures introduced in the 1970s and gradually increased throughout the 1980s were paid time off for housework (a reduction of the "normal" work week from 43.5 to 40 hours for mothers of two children or more); a "baby year" of paid leave for the birth of the first child, increased to eighteen months of support for second and later births; four to eight weeks of paid leave for the care of sick children. Provision of childcare was also expanded and strengthened, so that as of 1988, 81 percent of preschool children were in heavily subsidized public facilities, costing about sixty-five cents per day per child. In addition to the "baby year," infant care was available in day nurseries in the community and at the mother's workplace. If childcare was not available, mothers' paid "baby year" could be extended to a total of up to three years.[17]

The theme of all these policies was the "compatibility of *motherhood* and paid employment," so only in the most exceptional circumstances were fathers allowed to claim benefits. Fathers were placed in roughly the same legal position as grandmothers. Should the mother's circumstances (illness, etc.) require substitute care, the father could petition to be allowed to play that role and receive the leave. The gendered language of the law reflected a gendered mode of thinking that not only defined women as mothers but also absolved men of any formal responsibilities as fathers.[18]

These gender-specific policies successfully established East German birth rates at 13.7 per thousand in 1985, while West German rates, equal to GDR rates in 1970, continued to drop to 9.6.[19] The extensive provisions for childcare for mothers obtaining education or occupational training encouraged women to have children young: 91 percent of all children were born to mothers under thirty, the majority to mothers under twenty-five. Early childbearing did not imply early (or any) marriage: in 1988, 32 percent of eighteen-to-thirty-year-olds were still single, and 30 percent of all births and 70 percent of first births were to unmarried mothers.[20] This became the normative pattern: for example, entire floors of dormitory housing at Leipzig University were set aside for single mothers and their children. Special preference in obtaining housing was given across the board to unmarried mothers, which was a further incentive to bear children early and without a husband. About one-third of all unmarried mothers were in cohabiting relations, which is approximately the same as the proportion of all unmarried women who were living with a male partner.[21] Having a child did not push a woman toward social or economic dependence on an individual man.

However, the gender-specific nature of the "baby year" and other benefits also established the gender division of labor in the household as official state policy. It was women, and women only, who were expected to care for sick children or manage the "second shift" of housework, because they were the ones who were "given" the time to do so. Men were not seen as having any role in child-rearing.[22] The turn to "mommy politics" that began in the early 1970s was also associated with noticeable increases in gender segregation on the job.[23] Men resentfully described the benefits given to mothers as "unearned privileges" inconsistent with an "achievement society," and women were encouraged to be grateful for the "privilege of being able to have a family and a job."[24] Media images shifted in this period to emphasize the dual responsi-

bilities of women *(Vereinbarkeit von Beruf und Familie)* and downplay themes of equality.[25] Because women were defined as "unreliable" workers, who were frequently absent, they were also seen (and saw themselves) as unsuited for the more demanding or responsible positions.[26]

Women who wanted to be taken seriously as scientists or managers had to struggle against the common perception that mothers were both privileged and irresponsible. Because the workplace was the most emphasized seat of identity in the GDR and the respect and esteem of colleagues psychologically central, this meant an increasing attack on the self-esteem of able and ambitious women. The low level of consciousness about gender stratification meant that the state's role in affirmative action was perceived as unjust ("why not have affirmative action for men?"), but there was no opportunity to raise consciousness or formulate an alternative in the workplace.[27]

"Mommy Politics" and Gender Mobilization. Because the male norm of long hours of paid employment was never challenged (or even discussed), "mommy politics" merely "allowed women to fall short" of this standard, being "deficient" as workers.[28] Discrimination in employment and promotion was increasingly widespread and rationalized as the legitimate cost women had to pay for their "special benefits." Thus, the women who entered the labor market between 1975 and 1985 experienced a steady decline in the range of occupational choices they were offered and in the opportunities they experienced on the job.[29] Moreover, women who found the "baby year" a period of painful social isolation tended to resent the automatic assumption that as women they were "naturally" responsible for childcare.[30] Because women had internalized their responsibility for paid work as part of their self-concept, it was

increasingly perceived as unfair that men did less than 25 percent of all housework, and that, in effect, the state had "officially" released them from all responsibilities at home.[31]

As the benefits of "mommy politics" came to be questioned, the absence of political channels through which women could express their interests and formulate alternatives became increasingly frustrating. It became particularly evident that the SED's version of a "women's movement organization," the Demokratischer Frauenbund Deutschlands (DFD), was not an access point *for* women but rather a party-controlled voice *to* women. The prevailing model of men making politics on women's behalf became a significant grievance in its own right.[32]

Thus, the "mommy politics" of the 1970s and 1980s were successful in making the combination of paid work and motherhood easier for women, but they were at the expense of the state's commitment to equality, inscribing the gender division of labor more firmly into both the family and the labor market. The contradiction between the state's energetic proclamations of "women's emancipation" and the experience of being treated first and foremost as mothers has been particularly pronounced for younger (under forty) and university-educated women.[33] The emergence of an autonomous feminist movement in East Germany is a response to this marginalized position.

Resources for Mobilization. Although the mixed messages of "mommy politics" laid the groundwork for a feminist critique, social movements also require a structural opportunity for individuals to come together, recognize the collective nature of their problems, and develop a collective response.[34] There were clear obstacles to doing so in East Germany. On the one hand,

public discussion of gender segregation and its costs to women was prohibited (any meetings of more than seven people needed official permission). Women's literature raised consciousness about women's double day, but this was not (and could not be) presented as anchored in official policies; instead "mommy politics" appeared to be a well-meaning but inadequate response to a "natural" problem.[35] On the other hand, the state also carried on an active campaign against "bourgeois feminism" that sought to discredit the language of feminism and the example of Western feminists as self-centered and antimale.[36]

However, there were also two facilitating conditions, both relatively unique to East Germany among the socialist states, that help account for the unparalleled explosion of feminist activity in the GDR. In the first place, the common German language made possible a certain degree of direct transmission of feminist thinking from the West, despite the state's efforts to hinder it. Particularly within the universities, but also through contacts with visiting family and friends, feminist arguments had a chance to be heard directly. Some academics could proudly point to extensive collections of feminist literature, and unofficial efforts to do women's studies were growing. Participation in certain research projects (e.g., studies on the position of women in science and technology) was frequently cited as consciousness-raising, and a few exchange visits with feminist researchers in West Germany were permitted.[37]

Second, the dominant religion in East Germany is liberal Protestant (Lutheran) rather than Roman Catholic or Orthodox and was more open than churches in other Eastern European countries to feminist theology and discussions on issues of gender and sexuality. Consequently, church groups, exempted from the GDR's draconian rules against meetings, could and did support a variety of feminist consciousness-raising groups, including the relatively extensive lesbian network that developed after 1985.[38] In the shelter of the church, women of all sorts (the majority of whom did not identify as Christian) held discussions that developed their critical perspective on the status of women, the relations between women and men, and the role of the state.

Thus, in addition to facing a particularly contradictory set of social policies, East German women had important social networks in the academy and in the churches in which women could come together to begin to formulate a collective response. These "submerged networks"[39] were critical in formulating an oppositional consciousness, which was then able to emerge into autonomous feminist activity. As the various lesbian, peace, and women's studies groups became aware of each other's existence (e.g., at a women's forum in Erfurt in 1988), the common issues of women's status and right to self-definition became increasingly central.[40]

By November 1, 1989, feminist academics issued a joint statement with the editors of the Communist party's conventional women's magazine (*Für Dich*), entitled "Is the Revolution Passing Women By?" In it, they explicitly pointed to the exclusion of women from influence in the ongoing transformation in Poland and Hungary and urged women not to lose the opportunity to have a voice in the reform of the GDR.[41] This widely disseminated document served as a critical mobilizing spark.

Feminist Organization and the Critique of "Mommy Politics"

By May 1989 (that is, several months before the massive outmigration and demonstrations that triggered the national crisis), 200 women from diverse local groups met in Jena to share feminist ideas. Among the points raised most prominently was the continued responsibility of women alone for housework and child-care, that is, the gap between the state's promised emancipation of women and the reality of the double day.[42] This "illegal women's movement" met again in October and began to consider creating more formal organizational structures.[43]

From this point on, local groups of feminists began to call *open* meetings all over the country; turnout consistently surpassed the organizers' expectations. As the unrest grew, and women found their concerns pushed to the margins, women's groups split off from general (male-dominated) human rights groups.[44] When New Forum pushed the slogan "the country needs new men," feminists around the country challenged this sexist language and the thinking behind it with the slogan "no new state without women" (*Ohne Frauen ist kein Staat zu machen*). Less than a month after the fall of the Berlin Wall, on December 3, 1989, approximately 1,200 women from women's groups all over the country gathered at a theater in Berlin to found a national umbrella organization, the Independent Women's Association (UFV).

The optimism and sense of vitality of this new movement were enormous. The UFV was organized to be both a coordinating council for the various autonomous local groups and projects (such as the Women's Caucus in Leipzig or EWA, First Female Uprising, in Berlin) and the political repre sentative for feminist interests at the national level.[45] Feminist groups at all levels worked quickly and effectively to establish themselves. The UFV played a significant role in formulating a "charter of social rights" endorsed by the national Round Table, as well as securing government commitment to an active equal rights policy for women.[46]

At this point, feminists shared several beliefs that guided their strategy. *First,* they expected the outcome of *die Wende,* the overthrow of the government, to be a reformed but still independent GDR. Thus, they sought political representation within the state and its institutions. Loosening Communist party control over such significant means of communication as the women's magazine *Für Dich* were early victories that were seen as important. At this time the UFV also believed it could claim the block of seats in the GDR parliament (12 percent) that had historically been allocated to the Communist party's tame organization of women (DFD).[47] A national level equality commission was formed, and Tatjana Böhm, a member of the UFV, became a member without portfolio of the "reform" cabinet under Prime Minister Hans Modrow.

Second, feminists assumed the continuation of the basic principles of the socialist state (such as the right to employment) and focused within this framework on limited changes that would better serve women's interests. Because women's employment and the provision of childcare were seen as self-evident, the movement directed its attention to specific reforms that would end the automatic assignment of women to the "second shift" (e.g., a gender-neutral or mandatory sharing of the "baby year," a reduction in work hours for everyone rather than a "housework day"). Dozens of different women's groups put forth their individual platforms for what a reformed GDR should do to achieve gender equality.[48]

Third, feminists believed that most of the political and economic structures within the GDR would continue to operate and required an active feminist presence to become more inclusive and representative of women. Thus, attention was directed to lobbying for positions within these organizations. Women's studies programs emerged in many universities; received space, budgets, and positions; and developed plans of study and research. The national government was successfully lobbied to mandate the establishment of "gender equality offices" in all cities with populations of more than 100,000. Beginning in February 1990, in Erfurt, women's centers were set up in a number of cities, often in a building or apartment formerly occupied by the security police (Stasi).[49]

In this early, heady period, the UFV was not only successful in putting a change in women's status on the political agenda but also in getting significant funding and recognition of their legitimate right to represent women in shaping the agenda as a whole.[50] From this perspective, they were highly critical of the GDR's past "mommy politics" and advocated abolition of gender-specific benefits, equal treatment in the labor force, and measures to actively encourage men to take their roles as fathers and husbands seriously. However, in March 1990, the situation took a new and dangerous turn.

From Reform to Unification. The women's movement was not alone in expecting that it would be able to move into positions of influence in the reformed GDR, as Solidarity had done in Poland. All the social movements expected at first to lead this reform and resisted the idea of unification, viewing the West German state as also in need of significant reform. The GDR's last independent election, March 1990, ended that dream. It was dominated by the affiliates of the well-organized West German parties, particularly the conservative CDU, which campaigned on a platform of rapid unification. The UFV entered into an alliance with the East German Greens which together won only two percent of the vote, or eight seats; because of intra-alliance politics, none of these were allocated to the feminists.

This two percent figure understates feminist strength, because not all feminists, even activists, voted for the UFV. Both the reformed communist party (PDS) and other social movements such as New Forum by now had feminist-led equality task forces and seemed to some a more effective route to political power. However, the shock of realizing that even a very large number of demonstrators can translate into a small number of votes was extremely demoralizing. The rewards of electoral politics were not proportional to their organizational costs, and confidence in future electoral alliances was shaken. In addition, political efforts to put feminist issues on the national agenda were increasingly unsuccessful, now that women were no longer defined as an effective voting bloc.[51]

In May, the newly elected transitional government under CDU party chief Lotbar deMazière established a five-person Department for the Equality of Women and Men, subordinated to the Ministry for Family and Women. The first unification treaty mentioned women only once—with the handicapped, as groups whose special needs had to be respected.[52] In the local elections, held May 6, 1990, UFV candidates won representation in a number of cities but in very small numbers. UFV members were also appointed to the local-level gender equality offices which began to operate that summer.

As early as February 1990, the unification process had been depicted as "three steps back" for women,[53] but it was only after the inevitability of unification began to sink in that the focus of the movement as a whole shifted from trying to create a feminist utopia to defending women's existing rights.[54] By summer of 1990, it was not only clear that the die was cast for annexation to the Federal Republic but also that the movement had to struggle to protect rights that women had taken for granted. Local feminist groups, with the support of gender equality officers and city representatives, fought (usually successfully) to keep childcare centers open. At that point, local funding for women's projects was still relatively easy to obtain. The equal rights offices offered legal advice and encouragement to women losing their jobs, and women's cultural and counseling centers and shelters for battered women opened in many cities.[55] Neither could do much to alleviate the now-rising tide of unemployment and growing feelings of resignation and helplessness.[56] The commitment to a "charter of social rights" to be guaranteed in unification did not disappear, but it became increasingly clear that the GDR had no leverage to insist on such provisions nationally.

The most prominent new struggle was over abortion, because adoption of West German law would limit abortion to situations in which two physicians had to certify that there was an approved medical or social reason for termination. Ever since 1975, when their constitutional court had overturned a law permitting abortion on demand in the first trimester, the issue of abortion has been a litmus test for West German feminists.[57] With widespread mobilization in the West as well as sporadic demonstrations in the East, the West German (conservative) government backed down from insisting that West German law on this matter would be immediately extended to the former GDR. A two-year transitional period was introduced in which separate laws would apply in each region, and a compromise that respects GDR women's experience seems likely.[58]

The electoral arena proved to be a difficult one for feminists. In the first postunification election in December 1990, votes from the East and West were tallied separately. The East's multimovement electoral coalition, Bündnis '90, of which the UFV was now a part, was expected to ally with the West's Greens, and perhaps the Social Democrats, and thus influence the levels and nature of social benefits. Surprisingly, however, the Greens in the West failed to obtain the 5 percent of the vote required for representation in the legislature. Their forty-four seats were completely gone and with them many West German feminist aspirations. The SPD (Social Democrats) were weakened, and the tiny Eastern parties, Bundnis '90 and the PDS, with eight and seventeen seats, respectively, had no effective allies in parliament. On the one hand, this demonstrated that West German feminists were no stronger in national electoral terms than their Eastern counterparts had been.[59] On the other hand, it suggested that the feminist consciousness of East German women should not be measured in terms of their voting strength either.

The difficulty is that the resources of social movements (intensity of commitment, risk taking) are not directly convertible into the resources on which an electoral strategy relies (party allegiance, large numbers of weakly committed voters). Like the U.S. suffrage movement, which was defined as ineffective in the 1920s when women did not immediately appear to be a coherent voting bloc, the East German movement lost credibility when it did not appear to represent the sentiments of large numbers of

women voters. In both instances this is at best a partial truth.

However, the perceived failure of the UFV to arouse greater resonance among women in East Germany, its inability to create an effective electoral presence, and the defeat of reform efforts such as the "charter of social rights" demoralized activists.[60] The first major meeting of the UFV after unification, in Leipzig in March 1991, was characterized by intensive debate over the value of parliamentary politics, with the sharpest division in the movement being that between those who would prefer to work on autonomous projects and ignore party politics and those who continued to see value in electoral activities.[61]

The assumption of institutional continuity also proved chimerical. All academic positions, including the newly formed women's studies programs, were "reviewed" by panels of West German professors (mostly male; only 5 percent of the West German professoriate is female) with the avowed purpose of eliminating those that are "political rather than academic." In this process, women academics as well as feminist programs are disproportionately being cut.[62] Newly established women's projects, such as shelters, must compete for funding in a situation of overwhelming cutbacks. Childcare centers are competing for the same local funds. Unemployment continues to rise and is disproportionately concentrated among women. A certain level of demoralization and defeatism seems justified by the circumstances. It appears that the adversity facing East German women will continue to increase, and there are few points of leverage open to feminist organizers.

In sum, the experiences of East German feminists in mobilizing a social movement have been mixed. On the one hand, existing networks among women provided an opportunity to develop an oppositional consciousness and rapidly create a formal organization that gave shape to feminism in East Germany as nowhere else in Eastern Europe. UFV's demands for proactive reform of the GDR focused on women's access to political power and the reform of "mommy politics" to provide gender-neutral social benefits, greater involvement of men in housework, and less definition of women's interests in terms of motherhood. On the other hand, the irresistible momentum toward unification halted these early steps toward reform. Feminists were blocked from having a significant political voice of their own and consigned to the margins of West German party politics. In addition, their effort to find an alternative to "mommy politics" was superseded by a defensive struggle to maintain the employment and reproductive rights they had taken for granted.

Women's Status and Politics in the "Transition to Capitalism"

The most dramatic change in women's lives after unification is in the conditions for women's combining paid employment with unpaid labor in the home. Along with the collapse of the economy in the East, there is also the difficulty of finding an appropriate strategy for challenging the gender division of labor. A second, and no less significant, transformation is the emergence of a distinctive sphere of civic action. The opportunity to act collectively and autonomously as women has increased dramatically, but the space thus created also allows the differences among women to become more politically salient.

The Unemployment Crisis. The first casualty of unification was the East German economy. Women are particularly hard hit,

in part because they were concentrated in some of the less capital-intensive, least modernized, and least productive sectors of the economy.[63] Official unemployment rates understate the extent of the problem, in part because those who have not formally been terminated but whose actual work hours have been cut back to zero are counted only as having reduced employment, partly because women who have lost their childcare are not officially "available to work" and are not counted as unemployed.[64] Despite these biases, even the official statistics show that women are disproportionately likely to lose their jobs and even more disproportionately likely to be given no new job offer. For example, in Berlin as of July 1990, women were 53 percent of the unemployed but only 29 percent of those receiving job referrals.[65] The official unemployment rate (excluding those in make-work jobs, retraining programs, or pensioned off at age fifty-five) in July 1991 was 14 percent for women and 10 percent for men, and the gap was widening monthly.[66] By October 1991, women were already 61 percent of all unemployed.[67]

Germany does not have antidiscrimination laws with significant sanctions attached, so even state employment offices take employers' gender preferences into account when making job referrals.[68] This is likely to have devastating consequences, as employers are openly resisting hiring women with young children or women over forty-five.[69] Because age discrimination is not illegal, women over forty-five find themselves even being excluded from government retraining programs on the grounds that they are "too old" to be employable. By 1991, 15 percent of all working-age women had withdrawn from the labor market (80 percent of whom were fifty-five to sixty years old).[70] West German protective legislation that excludes women from construction trades and some other branches of industry forces ex-GDR women trained as electricians and engineers out of these occupations; the older women are offered no alternatives, and younger women are expected to retrain as clerical workers. Women are also being disproportionately pushed out of management positions. In 1990, women were approximately one-third of all white-collar workers with supervisory responsibilities; just one year later, their share of these jobs had fallen to less than one-fifth.[71]

The conservative federal government opposes making the provision of childcare a basic social right and thus ended federal subsidies for childcare in July 1991.[72] Although state and local funding for childcare centers in the East was continued, mothers of young children were caught in a vicious circle: women who lost their jobs could no longer afford to pay the now-higher fees and withdrew their children, the center closed because the demand was insufficient, and all the mothers were then defined as "unavailable to work" because they did not have childcare.[73] Gender equality offices throughout the country mounted a campaign to inform women of these anticipated consequences with the result that by summer 1991 demand for childcare had stabilized even though unemployment figures continued to rise. Because the state and local governments are essentially bankrupt, the supply of childcare will continue to shrink unless the federal government changes its policy of nonsupport.

Despite the clear message that women should stay home and leave the jobs to men, women in the former GDR continue to see paid employment as a central life interest. In fact, the proportion of women who can imagine themselves in a career of full-time housework remains at 3 percent, and 51 percent of all women rate paid employment as a very important part of their lives.[74] The ideal marriage remains "one where both partners are employed and both are equally involved with the family and household," which 89 percent endorse.[75] Although acutely rising unemployment forces feminists to defend women's jobs from male competition in the short term, East German feminists also continue to affirm the desirability of affirmatively bringing men into jobs in childcare and nursing.[76]

The disappearance of benefits on which most GDR women have come to rely is a tremendous shock, but a retreat to full-time domesticity is not a feasible alternative—wages are notably low, consumption expectations are rising, men's jobs are uncertain, and the dominance of the male breadwinner model is declining in the West as well. The unemployment benefits women are now enjoying provide some with the unaccustomed "luxury" of being full-time homemakers, but this is a temporary respite. Particularly for the thirty-five-to-forty-nine-year-old women who have already managed the hardest years of juggling young children and jobs, the prospect of withdrawal from the labor market now that their children are older seems absurd. The response of many East German women is as much ambivalence to the new system as to the old. As one East German woman mused, "If I had to choose between a baby or a career, how would I have chosen, and how would I have ever lived with that choice?"[77] For many young (sixteen to thirty-five years) women, it is childbearing rather than employment that is being sacrificed. Birth rates have dropped radically (37 percent fewer live births in 1991 than in 1990), and abortion and sterilization rates are up.[78]

For East German feminists critical of the consequences of GDR policy, the problem is breaking the political equation between "woman" and "mother." But what is the practical alternative to "running after the poor overburdened working mother waving offers of new benefits?"[79] West Germany certainly provides no model for how to break down the gender segregation of the workplace nor evidence of successful strategies for involving men in reproductive labor. Instead, the FRG's conservative government elected in December 1990 is "encouraging" women to define themselves out of the labor market.

It is becoming increasingly clear that such moral suasion alone is insufficient. Along with the personal commitment to lifetime paid employment that women raised in the GDR take for granted, the traditional expectation that women contribute to their families' financial survival in times of need pulls East German women into the work force, even if they feel even more guilty and overburdened than before. Given the lack of any effective antidiscrimination law in Germany, one outcome is the proliferation of various forms of *de facto* or *de jure* exclusions of women from the better-paying portions of the labor market, as happened in the United States after World War II.[80] Feminist efforts to achieve a better position in the labor force are now superseded by a discouraging struggle to minimize these processes of exclusion and marginalization.[81]

The Civic Sphere. The development of an active women's movement in East Germany at least provides one point of resistance to these trends. Although it would be foolish to expect the small and currently demoralized groups of committed feminists to produce dramatic changes in the short run, the new political circumstances ushered in by the revolution of 1989 present long-term opportunities as well as costs. The most obvious change is in the emergence of a "third sphere" of social action, which can neither be subsumed into the "public" actions of the state nor defined as "private" or

merely personal relationships. This civic "sphere" is the locus of interpersonal relationships that have an explicitly public character and yet do not fall under the direct control of the state. It is the domain for the formation of collective identity and action.[82]

Although feminist theory tends not to question the dichotomy of public/private as much as its equation with male/female, the emergence of autonomous women's movements and their efforts to formulate a collective definition of women's interests suggests the significance of collective action, as a third, too-often invisible, sphere of political life. This does not imply a rejection of either the state or the family as arenas in which women's equal power would be significant and worth struggling for. But the GDR experience of having any efforts to form an autonomous women's movement repressed and the discussion of gender segregation and stereotyping forbidden highlights the significance of creating the *ongoing* conditions under which women can come together to formulate their own interests. Having the state take over and attempt to represent women's needs is unquestionably problematic; sustaining a female-centered sphere of collective action is therefore critical.

One of the highest priorities and thus far most successful efforts of feminists in the GDR has been simply to establish meeting places and means of communication. Feminist newspapers and magazines, information centers, libraries, support groups (with breakfast and childcare provided), and women's studies collectives and programs proliferated throughout the country. Although the outcome of individual groups' struggle to survive remains uncertain, the extensive infrastructure GDR women built in a very short period remains a resource for future mobilization efforts.[83] The organizational network that blossomed in the civic sphere has the potential to challenge state-directed policies "for women" by speaking out "as women."

For some feminists, the multiplicity of women's voices thus unleashed has been disconcerting. Given the contradictions of "mommy politics" in the past, the diversity of responses might seem predictable: some women argue for retaining as much as possible of the former policies, some for an end to all gender-related benefits as well as all gender discrimination, some for attempting to realize the West German one-earner model. Which claims does feminism stand for? For many women, feminism may not be distinguishable from the "freedom to choose" that the conservative government advocates, meaning thereby a legitimation of full-time housework as an alternative to paid employment for women, or from the "right to work" of the socialist state, which meant in practice the necessity of a double shift for women alone. Although the failure of the UFV to attract a large enough number of voters to be an effective political party produced an unwarranted dismay about the "absence of feminist consciousness," the debate on the meaning and political program of feminism has just begun.[84]

The gender equality offices established in the first flush of reform may play an important role in this process. These offices continue to operate in virtually every city of any magnitude. A book-length directory of women's organizations and groups in the former GDR in 1991 listed 272 active gender equality offices.[85] The women in these offices often define their mandate as bringing the widest possible range of women's groups into coalitions to support women's rights. They have been influential in the abortion rights mobilization and have played a critical role in supporting the establishment of shelters for battered women.

These women serve also as a linking mechanism between diverse interest groups of women (e.g., the older women in the successor organization to the DFD, the feminists in the UFV, the women's caucuses of the Unemployed Workers Association and of the various political parties) and a "halfway house" for the movement in its currently weakened state.[86] However, it is significant that they do not adopt the terminology of the somewhat comparable offices in the West and call themselves "women's affairs offices." In the East, these offices typically are much more critical of special treatment for women and insist that gender equality, not benefits for women, is the appropriate goal.[87]

In sum, feminists began by defining the former GDR as a limited but reformable stage in the accomplishment of women's liberation. Although the state represented itself as already fully responsive to women's needs, women themselves struggled successfully to challenge that definition and to articulate their own interests.[88] The political mobilization and expression of such interests continues, but unification and the imposition of a new set of gender-stereotypic policies have created new problems that consciousness raising under the old system never considered. The democratization of politics, in particular the emergence of an actively mobilized civil sphere, allowed the proliferation of local groups where new political demands are being formulated as well as development of grassroots political strategies for defending existing rights.

Conclusion: Beyond "Mommy Politics"?

To a much greater extent than other states, the GDR formally pursued a policy that could well be called institutionalizing a "mommy track" or what Betty Friedan called "second-stage" feminist politics,[89] that is, a set of wide-ranging incentives to encourage women to combine paid employment with motherhood and to provide practical support for those who were doing so. As a result, virtually all women in the relevant age group were employed and virtually all had at least one child. The shift to this "second stage," however, was also associated with formally recognizing a gender division of labor as normative and limiting women's actual opportunities in the labor force.

This is a dilemma familiar to those who have looked at the history of protective legislation in the United States and elsewhere. Policies that have positive effects in reducing the hazards and stress of combining paid work and reproductive labor for many women also have significant costs in encouraging both formal and covert gender discrimination. Once the state recognizes women's motherhood, the state's inability to see women as anything but mothers makes "mommy politics" problematic. An "equal rights" perspective also has drawbacks that are increasingly evident in the United States.[90] However, the increase in gender segregation and discrimination produced by East Germany's "mommy politics" is also a useful reminder of why "social feminism" has also been critiqued as "not feminist enough."

Because women are in practice the ones who provide the bulk of the housework and childcare, "making allowances" for their "prior" responsibilities is a concrete benefit that makes daily life more manageable for many women. Nonfeminists, already accustomed to the state's preference for male workers, tend to see the so-called privileges of "mommy politics" as unearned but accept their dependence on them as "natural." But East German feminists are acutely aware of the costs that women pay for such support. They affirm that there is an important practical difference between a policy designed to challenge a gender division of labor for both women and men and one that merely supports women in performing "their" dual role.

As East German feminists have pointed out, what East German socialist policies failed to do was to recognize any essential *positive* contributions of engaging in unpaid reproductive labor for the development of the *human* personality. Thus, women's "difference" continued to be defined as deficiency, and socialist theory failed to provide a theoretical rationale for why men should (and should want to) participate in doing reproductive labor or why men should also move into typically female jobs. As a consequence, socialist practice not only failed to challenge the gender division of labor but actually entrenched it more securely. Although recognizing society's need for reproductive labor, the GDR defined its provision as *women's* responsibility alone, cementing an instrumental and patriarchal understanding of women in its fundamental policies. As East German feminists reclaim an autonomous voice and criticize these arrangements, they demonstrate women's ability to articulate the positive values and perspectives that reproductive work can foster in *all* those who engage in it.

Notes

1. Anne Hampele, "Der unabhängige Frauenverband," in *Von der Illegalität ins Parlament*, ed. Helmut Müller-Enbergs, Marianne Schultz, and Jan Wielgohs (Berlin: Links-Druck Verlag, 1991), 221–82; Eva Schäfer, "Die fröhliche Revolution der Frauen," in *Wir wollen mehr als ein Vaterland: DDR-Frauen im Aufbruch*, ed. Gislinde Schwarz and Christine Zenner (Reinbek bei Hamburg: Rohwohlt Taschenbuch Verlag, 1990), 17–34; Cordula Kahlau, ed., *Aufbruch! Frauenbewegung in der DDR* (Munich: Frauenoffensive, 1990).
2. Barbara Einhorn, "Socialist Emancipation: The Women's Movement in the German Democratic

Repubic," in *Promissory Notes: Women in the Transition to Socialism*, ed. Sonia Kruks, Rayna Rapp, and Marilyn Young (New York: Monthly Review Press, 1989), 282–305; Virginia Penrose, "Vierzig Jahre SED-Politik: Ziele, Strategie, und Ergebnisse," *IFG: Frauenforschung* 8, no. 4 (1990): 60–77.

3. I use the terms "stage one" and "stage two" with reference to Betty Friedan's book, *The Second Stage* (New York: Simon & Schuster, 1981), which was one of the first calls in the United States for a feminist politics that would focus on the conditions supporting women in combining paid employment and motherhood. Among the more influential of the many recent books and articles that have picked up this theme are Sylvia Hewlett, *A Lesser Life: The Myth of Women's Liberation in America* (New York: Morrow, 1986); and Felice Schwartz, "Management Women and the New Facts of Life," *Harvard Business Review* 67 (January/February 1989): 65–76.

4. This is the official figure and is widely used and believed, and it is therefore significant. But it is not directly comparable with statistics on labor force participation in the West, because it includes those women on official childcare leave or in occupational training. More refined statistics are being developed but are not yet available. See Sabine Schenk, "Gleichstellungspolitik und geschlechtsspezifische Arbeitsteilung: Erwerbstätige Frauen in der DDR," in *Gleichstellungspolitik in der DDR und der BRD*, ed. Helga Voth and Johanna Kootz (Berlin: Zentrum interdisziplinäre Frauenforschung, Humboldt University, 1990), 45–60. Based on an Institut für angewandte Sozialwissenschaft (INFAS) sample survey, Fremerey and Kupierschmid estimate 86 percent of women aged sixteen to sixty were in the labor force in 1990—71 percent employed, 7 percent on educational or childcare leave, and 8 percent unemployed. See Ulrike Fremerey and Peter Kupierschmid, *Materialien zur Frauenpolitik: Frauen in den neuen Bundesländern im Prozeß der deutschen Einigung* (Bonn: Bundesministerium für Frauen und Jugend, 1991).

5. A good compendium of official statistics from the GDR is Gunnar Winkler, *Frauen report '90*, Ministerium für die Gleichstellung von Frauen und Mannern (Berlin: Verlag Die Wirtschaft, 1990). Statistics plus thoughtful analyses are available in Katrin Bastian, Evi Labsch, and Sylvia Müller, "Zur situation von Frauen als Arbeitskraft in der Geschichte der DDR," originally published in *Zaunreiterin* (Leipzig, 1990), reprinted in *Streit* 8, no. 2 (1990): 59–67; Hildegard Maria Nickel, "Geschlechtertrennung durch Arbeitsteilung: Berufs und Familienarbeit in der DDR," *Feministische Studien* 8 (May 1990): 10–19; Schenk.

6. Nickel, "Geschlechtertrennung durch Arbeitsteilung"; Eva Malek-Lewy, "Gleichstellung contra Patriarchat," in *Gleichstellungspolitik in der DDR und der BRD*, 14–44.

7. See the review of English-language critiques offered in Natalie Sokoloff, *Between Money and Love: The Dialectics of Women's Home and Market Work* (New York: Praeger, 1981); cf. Uta Röth, "Die klassenlose Gretchenfrage," in *DDR-Frauen im Aufbruch*, 132–44.

8. Penrose and Frederike Maier provide a history of these policies and their justifications. The relative success of both "stage one" and "stage two" can be measured by comparison with West German patterns: In the "old" Federal Republic of Germany, only 38 percent of university students are women, 35 percent of mothers of children under six are in the labor force, only 4 percent of children under age three are in childcare (but waiting lists are extensive), and fewer than 10 percent of engineering degrees go to women. In the GDR, in 1989, women were 51 percent of university students and 20 percent of engineering students and, apart from the approximately 10 percent of sixteen-to-thirty-five-year-olds in their "baby year," over 90 percent of women aged twenty to fifty were continuously employed. See Frederike Maier, "Geschlechterverhältnisse der DDR im Umbruch—Zur Bedeutung von Arbeitsmarkt und Sozialpolitik," *Zeitschrift für Sozialreform* 37 (November/December 1991): 648–62. See Hedwig Rudolph, Eileen Appelbaum, and Frederike Maier, "Beyond Socialism: The Ambivalence of Women's Perspectives in the United Germany," discussion paper, Wissenschaftszentrum Berlin, 1991.

9. Susanne Stolt, "Ursachen und Formen der geschlechtlichen Arbeitsteilung in der DDR" (Diplomarbeit: Universitat Hannover, 1990); Einhorn; Bettina Musall, "Viele dachten, die spinnen,'" *Die Spiegel*, 18 Mar. 1991, 68–84.

10. Irene Dölling, "Situation und Perspektiven von Frauenforschung in der DDR," *Bulletin*, no. 1 (1990), Zentrum interdisziplinäre Frauenforschung, Humboldt University, Berlin, 1–25; Hildegard Maria Nickel, "Frauen und soziale Risiken: Versuch einer Bilanz" (Paper presented at German Sociological Association Meeting, Frankfurt am Main, October 1990); Alice Schwarzer, "Interviews with Bärbel Bohley, Christina Schenk, and the editors of *Für Dich*," *Emma*, January 1990, 22–28; Birgit Gabriel, "Was ist aus den selbstbewußten DDR-Frauen

geworden?" (Presentation at Fourth Annual Women's Week, Würzburg, FRG, 1991).

11. Hildegard Maria Nickel, "Women in the German Democratic Republic and the New Federal States: Looking Backward and Forward," *German Politics & Society*, no. 24–25 [Winter 1992]: 34–52; see also Nickel, "Geschlechtertrennung durch Arbeitsteilung"; Schenk; Stolt; Irene Dölling, "Between Hope and Helplessness: Women in the GDR after the Turning Point," *Feminist Review*, no. 39 [Winter 1991]: 3–15.

12. Nickel, "Geschlechtertrennung durch Arbeitsteilung." For comparison, West German women employed full-time took home DM 1,745, or 68 percent of comparable men's wages. See Deutsches Institut für Wirtschaftsforschung, *Wochenbericht*, no. 19 (10 May 1990); and Schenk.

13. See Maier; Schenk; also Dölling, "Between Hope and Helplessness"; Nickel, "Geschlechtertrennung durch Arbeitsteilung."

14. See the reflections on problems and priorities in Röth; Gislinde Schwarz and Christine Zenner, "Nachbetrachtung," in *DDR-Frauen im Aufbruch*, 145–55; Ina Merkel, "Frauenpolitische Strategien in der DDR," in *Soziale Lage und Arbeit von Frauen in der DDR*, ed. Sabine Gensior, Frederike Maier, and Gabriele Winter (Paderborn: Arbeitskreis Sozialwissenschaftliche Arbeitsmarktforschung, 1990), 56–70.

15. Stolt; Einhorn; Penrose.

16. Gisela Ehrhardt, "Frauen und Karriere," in *DDR-Frauen im Aufbruch*, 120–31; Hanna Behrend, "Die Hypertrophie des Vergangenen: Aufbruch und Elend der DDR-Frauen," *Das Argument* 32 (November/December 1990): 859–64.

17. Sabine Berghahn and Andrea Fritzsche, "Bringt neues Recht mehr Frauenrecht?" in *Gleichstellungspolitik in der DDR und der BRD*, 75–124. Portions reprinted in *Frankfurter Rundschau* (15 Nov. 1990): 29–30; cf. Stolt, and Dölling, "Between Hope and Helplessness."

18. Nickel, "Frauen und soziale Risiken"; Röth; and Merkel.

19. Einhorn; Stolt.

20. Jutta Gysi, "Frauen in Partnerschaft und Familie," in *DDR-Frauen im Aufbruch*, 99–101; Margret Lünenburg, "Die harten Fakten," *Ypsilon* 1 (April 1991): 26.

21. Doris Hess et al., "Frauen in den neuen Bundesländern im Prozeß der deutschen Einigung," Final Project Report (Bad Godesberg: Institut für angewandte Sozialwissenschaft, 1992). These authors also report that most women do not see marriage as essential for childrearing: only 17 percent of women under twenty-five and 46 percent of women over forty-five agreed that children emotionally need married parents.

22. Röth; Musall.

23. Nickel, "Geschlechtertrennung durch Arbeitsteilung"; Dölling, "Between Hope and Helplessness"; Schenk; and Maier, 653.

24. Men's resentments are discussed in Annemarie Tröger, "Brief an eine französische Freundin: Die Intelligenz in der Wende—Gedanken zu den Veränderungen in der DDR" *Feministische Studien* 8 (May 1990): 113–22; and in Stolt, 55; Women's perceptions are well expressed in Gislinde Schwarz, "Abschied von der DDR," *Emma* 11 (October 1990): 26–30.

25. A content analysis of photographs and themes is offered in Irene Dölling, "Frauen und Männerbilder: Eine Analyse von Fotos in DDR-Zeitschriften," *Feministische Studien* 8 (May 1990): 35–49; cf. political debates discussed in Penrose.

26. Nickel, "Geschlechtertrennung durch Arbeitsteilung"; Barbara Bertram, "Berufs-wahl und berufliche Lebensentwürfe von Frauen in der DDR," in *Soziale Lage und Arbeit van Frauen in der DDR*, 16–25.

27. Gabriel; Merkel.

28. Nickel, "Frauen und soziale Risiken."

29. Ehrhardt; Bastian, Labisch, and Müller.

30. Ute Kretzschmar, "Gleichstellung statt Gleichberechtigung," in *DDR-Frauen im Aufbruch*, 66.

31. Such arguments reflect age-undifferentiated statistics as reported in Winkler, and are expressed, for example, in Nickel, "Frauen und soziale Risiken"; Kretzschmar; and Merkel. A comparison of the division of housework and childcare hours among young (sixteen to thirty-five year old) couples with children when wives have full-time jobs shows that wives did 7.28 hours and husbands 2.55 hours (or 26 percent) in the West; wives did 5.48 hours and husbands 2.94 hours (or 35 percent) in the East (Sibylle Meyer and Eva Schulze, "Wendezeit—Familienzeit: Veränderungen der Situation von Frauen und Familien in den neuen Bundesländern," IFG: *Frauenforschung* 10, no. 3 [1992]: 45–57], but this comparison is misleading as very few young mothers in the West hold full-time jobs and a much higher proportion of young mothers in the East are raising children without a partner. What it does indicate is that what was perceived as inadequate involvement in the East was nonetheless slightly higher than what was typical in the West.

32. See the accounts of politicization collected in Schwarz and Zenner; also the political program of the UFV in Ina Merkel et al., eds., *Ohne Frauen*

ist kein Staat zu machen (Hamburg: Argument Verlag, 1990).

33. Malek-Lewy; Ehrhardt.

34. Myra Marx Ferree and Frederick D. Miller, "Mobilization and Meaning: Some Social Psychological Contributions to the Resource Mobilization Perspective," *Sociological Inquiry* 55 (Winter 1985): 38–61.

35. Dorothea Böck, "'Ich schreibe, um herauszufinden, warum ich schreiben muß: Frauenliteratur in der DDR zwischen Selbsterfahrung und ästhetischem Experiment," *Feministische Studien* 8 (May 1990): 61–74.

36. Kretzschmar.

37. Personal accounts of such developing contacts and consciousness are provided in Irene Dölling, "Situation und Perspektiven von Frauenforschung in der DDR"; Hanna Behrend, "Women Catapulted into a Different Social Order: Women in East Germany," *Women's History Review* 1, no. 1 (1992): 143; Regine Othmer-Vetter and Annemarie Tröger, "Atemschwelle—Versuche, Richtung zu gewinnen: Diskussion mit Autorinnen des Heftes," *Feministische Studien* 8 (May 1990): 90–106.

38. Ursula Sillge, *Un-Sichtbare Frauen: Lesben und ihre Emanzipation in der DDR* (Berlin: LinksDruck Verlag, 1991). See also Henriette Wrege, "Neue Frauen hat die DDR," *Emma* 11 (January 1990): 20–22; Kahlau.

39. Alberto Melucci, "Getting Involved: Identity and Mobilization in Social Movements," in *From Structure to Action: Comparing Social Movement Research across Cultures*, ed. Bert Klandermans, Hanspeter Kriesi, and Sidney Tarrow (Greenwich, Conn.: JAI Press, 1988), 329–48.

40. Schwarz and Zenner, 13.

41. The text and names of the signatories are reprinted in *Emma* 11 (January 1990): 25. See the discussion of the process and effects of writing this call in Schwarz and Zenner.

42. Gislinde Schwarz, "Abschied van der DDR."

43. Kahlau, 146.

44. Gislinde Schwarz, "Aufbruch der Hexen," in *Aufbruch! Frauenbewegung in der DDR*, 8–24; see also Eva Schäfer, "Die frohliche Revolution der Frauen," in *DDR-Frauen im Aufbruch,* 17–34.

45. See Hampele. The role of the UFV in national political debate is particularly striking, as this is quite unlike feminist organization in West Germany, which has deliberately eschewed any national-level group or formal coalition. Organizationally, the UFV looks much like the American NOW in its early, more collectivist days.

46. Malek-Lewy.

47. Wrege; Schwarzer.

48. See Kahlau; Lisa DiCaprio, "East German Feminists: The Lila Manifesto," *Feminist Studies* 16 (Fall 1990): 621–34; Merkel et al.

49. Malek-Lewy; and Renate Bremmert-Hein, "Partnerschaft mit DDR-Gleichstellungs-beauftragten" (Berlin: Bezirksamt Neukölln, 1990), provides a good overview of the equality offices; Carolin Lorenz, "Ärmel krempeln und los," *Emma* 11 (August 1990): 46; and Kahlau focus on women's centers.

50. Kretzschmar.

51. Ibid.

52. Marina Beyer, "Wer liegt unten?" *Emma* 11 (September 1990): 13.

53. Merkel et al.

54. Schäfer.

55. Ulrike Helwerth, "Keine Zeit mehr für Neurosen," *Die Tageszeitung (taz)*, 19 Oct. 1990.

56. Dölling, "Between Hope and Helplessness."

57. Myra Marx Ferree, "Equality and Autonomy: Feminist Politics in the United States and West Germany," in *The Women's Movements of the United States and Western Europe*, ed. Mary Katzenstein and Carol McClurg Mueller (Philadelphia: Temple University Press, 1987), 172–95.

58. As of January 1993, a new combined law that would preserve the first trimester option of GDR law but tie it to mandatory counseling was awaiting review by the supreme court as to its constitutionality. See Jeremiah Riemer, "Reproduction and Reunification: The Politics of Abortion in United Germany," in *The New Germany in the New Europe*, ed. Michael Huelshoff and Andrei Markovits (Ann Arbor: University of Michigan Press, 1992), for a full discussion of the political debate that produced this compromise.

59. Frank Drieschner et al., "Wie die Zukunft aus dem Parlament verschwand," *Die Zeit*, 14 Dec. 1990, 9–12.

60. Dolling, "Between Hope and Helplessness"; Ulrike Helwerth, "Das verlorene Paradies der DDR-Feministinnen," *Die Tageszeitung (taz)*, 12 Mar. 1991.

61. Hanna Behrend, "UFV—ein Jahr danach: Ein Bericht vom II. Kongress in Leipzig," *Ypsilon* 5 (May 1991): 15.

62. Birgit Gabriel, "Transformation der patriarchalen Wissenschaft" (Paper delivered at the DDR Sociology Association Meeting, Leipzig, 24–26 May 1991); Christine Richter, "Frauen werden als erste auf der Straße stehen," *Berliner Zeitung* 123 (30 May 1991): 134. Ironically, feminists are also being ejected for having taken positions in the course of "the change" that formerly (and still officially) belonged to the Marxism/Leninism

Department. See the fuller discussion in Myra Marx Ferree and Brigitte Young, "Three Steps Back for Women: German Unification, Gender, and University 'Reform'" (Paper to be delivered at the Eastern Sociological Society Annual Meeting, Boston, April 1993).

63. Schwarz and Zenner, 152; Maier.
64. Only about one-half of all those who have lost their jobs show up in the official unemployment statistics. The other half are divided fairly evenly between those who have left the labor force (predominantly older workers) and those in make-work (ABM) and job-retraining programs. See Maier, 658.
65. Schenk.
66. Maier, 658. See also Elke Holst and Jürgen Schupp, "Frauenerwerbstätigkeit in den neuen and alten Bundeslandern—Befunde des Socio-ökonomischen Panels," Discussion paper, German Institute for Economic Research, Berlin, 1992.
67. Holst and Schupp, 7.
68. Uta Krautkrümer-Wagner, *Die Verstaatlichung der Frauenfrage: Gleichstellungsinstitutionen der Bundesländer—Möglichkeiten und Grenzen staatlicher Frauenpolitik* (Bielefeld: Kleine Verlag, 1989).
69. Maier.
70. Holst and Schupp, 4.
71. Deutsches Institut für Wirtschaftsforschung, *Wochenbericht*, no. 18 (30 Apr. 1992): 236.
72. Musall.
73. Kretzschmar, 62.
74. Holst and Schupp, 13. This compares with approximately 20 percent of women and 15 percent of men aged thirty-five to forty-nine who accord it this rank in a parallel survey in West Germany in 1989.
75. Fremerey and Kupierschmid.
76. In a sample survey in the former GDR conducted by INFAS in November 1990, 67 percent of women aged sixteen to sixty favored bringing men into typically women's jobs, and 61 percent favored bringing women into typically male jobs as aspects of achieving equal rights. See Hess et al., 43.
77. Gislinde Schwarz, "Abschied von der DDR," 30.
78. Holst and Schupp, 12.
79. Barbara Holland-Cunz, "Bemerkungen zur Lage der deutsch-deutschen Frauenbewegung," *links*, September 1990, 38.
80. Maier points out how the wage differential between women and men as well as overt hiring discrimination will increase by applying standard West German procedures in the East German situation.
81. An example of such a shift is Christina Klenner, "Wit wollen unser Recht auf Arbeit," in *Handbuch: Wegweiser für Frauen in den fünf neuen Bundesländern*, ed. Katrin Rohnstock (Berlin: BasisDruck, 1991), 200–203. See also Hanna Behrend, "Women Catapulted into a Different Social Order," 141–53.
82. For a review of this literature, see Hanspeter Kriesi, "The Interdependence of Structure and Action: Some Reflections on the State of the Art," in *From Structure to Action*, 349–68; Melucci.
83. Carol McClurg Mueller argues that among the most significant outcomes of any wave of movement mobilization are the resources it creates for future mobilizations; see "Collective Consciousness, Identity Transformation and the Rise of Women in Public Office in the United States," in *The Women's Movements of the United States and Western Europe*, 89–108.
84. Some important contributions to this debate include Merkel; Schwarz and Zenner; and Behrend, "Die Hypertrophie des Vergangenen."
85. See *Handbuch*.
86. See the discussion of the concept in Verta Taylor, "Social Movement Continuity: The Women's Movement in Abeyance," *American Sociological Review* 54 (October 1989): 761–75.
87. I treat this issue more fully in "Institutionalizing Equality: Feminist Politics and Equality Offices," *German Politics & Society*, no. 24–25 (Winter 1992): 53–66.
88. See discussions of need and interest-based politics in Anna Jonasdottir, "On the Concept of Interest, Women's Interests, and the Limitations of Interest Theory," in *The Political Interests of Gender*, ed. Kathleen Jones and Anna Jonasdottir (London: Sage Publications, 1988) , 33–65: and Nancy Fraser, "Struggle over Needs: Outline of a Socialist Feminist Theory of Late-Capitalist Political Culture," in *Women, the State, and Welfare*, ed. Linda Gordon (Madison: University of Wisconsin Press, 1990), 199–225.
89. Schwartz: Friedan.
90. See, for example, Elizabeth Schneider, "The Dialectic of Rights and Politics: Perspectives from the Women's Movement," in *Women, the State, and Welfare*, 226–49.

Work and Poverty

The readings in this section take up two major issues affecting women worldwide: the changing structure of work and the persistence of poverty, including debates over welfare reform. From 1945 to 1975, wages rose and poverty rates declined in the United States. Since the mid-eighties however, despite the fact that corporate profits have risen to a twenty-five year high and productivity growth is strong, wages are falling and the number of American families living in poverty has increased from 5.5 million in 1979 to 7.5 million in 1995. In the United States, beginning in the mid-1980s, the wage gap narrowed so that women now earn 70 cents for every dollar men earn. This change in part reflects shifting occupational patterns and a decline in gender segregation—more kinds of jobs are open to both men and women. Yet inequality persists, and gains in the past ten years are not shared equally among women: factors such as race, language, education, experience, skills and family obligations all make a difference in a woman's earning power.[1]

The first reading addresses women in the global workplace. Cynthia Enloe examines the effect of international trade policies on women's work, in particular the recently negotiated North American Free Trade Agreement (NAFTA) and the General Agreement on Tariffs and Trade (GATT). Enloe focuses on the sneaker industry, which has moved manufacturing jobs from North America to South Korea, Thailand, Indonesia, China, and most recently to Russia. She documents the successful organizing efforts of women in South Korea and the struggles of women workers in other countries and suggests new strategies for securing a living wage. She also questions how "feminine" qualities that are valued for women in the home may reinforce their subordination at work; for example, concerns about female respectability and women's continuing family responsibilities often make it more difficult for women workers to attend after-work organizing meetings. How might these attitudes about women, the family, and the role of work intersect to keep women dependent on employers or male family members? Enloe focuses us on the global stage, on the myriad connections among national economies and the influence of international politics on local events. It is no longer possible, says Enloe, to organize in national frameworks as capital has taken an international approach to labor.

The final articles return us to the United States context to consider a contemporary debate—progress of women in the workforce. Joan Acker considers how gender is produced in the apparently neutral processes employers use to describe and evaluate jobs, creating organizational hierarchies. Drawing on insights from scholars who argue that social structure and social processes are gendered, Acker's article focuses our attention on the assumptions that undergird the category of the worker to "puzzle out how gender provides the subtext for arrangements of subordination." Virginia Valian's article "Running in Place" focuses on a very different group of women—women in the corporate world and academia—women who appear to have "made it." She finds that inequality in wages, promotions and professional opportunities between professional men and women persists, despite the real gains made by women in the last thirty years. What accounts for the continuing inequality between men and women in the workforce?

Note

1. Statistics in this section are drawn from Susan Meyer and Christopher Jencks, "War on Poverty: No Apologies, Please," *New York Times*, November 9, 1995; Mimi Abromovitz, "Welfare and Women's Lives: Towards a Feminist Understanding of the Reform Debate," *Democratic Left* (May/June 1995): 5–8; Christopher Jencks and Kathryn Edin, "Do Poor Women Have a Right to Bear Children?" *The American Prospect* (Winter 1995): 43–52.

Suggestions for Further Reading

Agarwal, Bina, et al., eds. 1992. *Women's Work in the World Economy*. New York: New York University Press.

Ashfar, Haleh, and Bina Agarwal, eds. 1989. *Women, Poverty and Ideology in Asia: Contradictory Pressures, Uneasy Resolutions.* Basingstoke, U.K.: MacMillan.

Bakker, Isabella, ed. 1994. *The Strategic Silence: Gender and Economic Policy*. London: Zed Press.

Bello, Walden, Shea Cunningham and Bill Rau. 1994. *Dark Victory: The United States, Structural Adjustment, and Global Poverty*. London: Pluto.

Benerja, Lourdes, and Shelley Feldman. 1992. *Unequal Burden: Economic Crises, Persistent Poverty, and Women's Work*. Boulder, CO: Westview Press.

Buvinic, Mayra, and Sally W. Yudelman. 1989. *Women, Poverty and Progress in the Third World*. New York: Foreign Policy Association.

Casper, Lynne M., Sara S. McLanahan and Irwin Garfinkel. 1994. "The Gender-Poverty Gap: What We Can Learn from Other Countries," *American Sociological Review*, 59, 594–605.

Folbre, Nancy, Barbara Bergmann, Bina Agarwal and Maria Floro, eds. 1992. *Women's Work in the Global Economy*. New York: New York University Press.

Gilbert, Alan. 1994. "Third World Cities: Poverty, Employment, Gender Roles and the Environment During a Time of Restructuring," *Urban Studies*, 31, 605–633.

Goldberg, Gertrude S. and Eleanor Kremen, eds. 1990. *The Feminization of Poverty: Only in America?* New York: Praeger.

Hondagneu-sotelo, Pierrette. 1995. "Women and Children First: New Directions in Anti-Immigrant Politics," *Socialist Review*, 25, 169–190.

House-Midamba, B. and F.K. Ekechi, eds. 1995. *African Market Women and Economic Power: The Role of Women in African Economic Development.* Westport: Greenwood Publishing Group.

Jumani, Usha. 1991. *Dealing with Poverty: Self-Employment for Poor, Rural Women.* Newbury Park, CA: Sage Publications.

Leacock, Eleanor L. and Helen I. Safa, eds. 1986. *Women's Work: Development and the Division of Labor by Gender.* South Hadley, MA: Bergin and Garvey.

McClanahan, Sara S., Lynne M. Casper and Annemette Sorensen. 1992. *Women's Roles and Women's Poverty in Eight Industrialized Countries.* Madison, WI: University of Wisconsin-Madison, Institute for Research on Poverty.

Nash, June, and Maria Fernandez-Kelly, eds. 1983. *Women, Men, and the International Division of Labor.* Albany, NY: State University of New York Press.

Ramphele, Mamphela. 1989. "The Dynamics of Gender Politics in the Hostels of Cape Town: Another Legacy of the South African Migrant Labour Sytem," *Journal of Southern African Studies*, 15, 393–414.

Rowbotham, Sheila, and Swasti Mitter. 1994. *Dignity and Daily Bread: New Forms of Economic Organizing Among Poor Women in the Third World and the First.* London and New York: Routledge.

Snyder, Margaret. 1995. *Transforming Development: Women, Poverty, and Politics.* London: Intermediate Technology Publications.

Thomas, Susan L. 1994. *Women and Poverty.* New York: Garland Publishers.

Waring, Marilyn. 1988. *If Women Counted: A New Feminist Economics.* San Francisco: Harper and Row.

Wilkerson, Margaret B. and Jewell Handy Gresham. 1989. "Sexual Politics of Welfare: The Racialization of Poverty," *The Nation*, 24 (31), 126–132.

The Globetrotting Sneaker

Cynthia Enloe

Four years after the fall of the Berlin Wall marked the end of the Cold War, Reebok, one of the fastest growing companies in United States history, decided that the time had come to make its mark in Russia. Thus it was with considerable fanfare that Reebok's executives opened their first store in downtown Moscow in July 1993. A week after the grand opening, store managers described sales as well above expectations.

Reebok's opening in Moscow was the perfect post-Cold War scenario: commercial rivalry replacing military posturing: consumerist tastes homogenizing heretofore hostile peoples; capital and managerial expertise flowing freely across newly porous state borders. Russians suddenly had the "freedom" to spend money on U.S. cultural icons like athletic footwear, items priced above and beyond daily subsistence: at the end of 1993, the average Russian earned the equivalent of $40 a month. Shoes on display were in the $100 range. Almost 60 percent of single parents, most of whom were women, were living in poverty. Yet in Moscow and Kiev, shoe promoters had begun targeting children, persuading them to pressure their mothers to spend money on stylish, Western sneakers. And as far as strategy goes, athletic shoe giants have, you might say, a good track record. In the U.S. many inner-city boys who see basketball as a "ticket out of the ghetto" have become convinced that certain brand-name shoes will give them an edge.

But no matter where sneakers are bought or sold, the potency of their advertising imagery has made it easy to ignore this mundane fact: Shaquille O'Neal's Reeboks are stitched by someone; Michael Jordan's Nikes are stitched by someone; so are your roommate's, so are your grandmother's. Those someones are women, mostly Asian women who are supposed to believe that their "opportunity" to make sneakers for U.S. companies is a sign of their country's progress—just as a Russian woman's chance to spend two month's salary on a pair of shoes for her child allegedly symbolizes the new Russia

As the global economy expands, sneaker executives are looking to pay women workers less and less, even though the shoes that they produce are capturing an ever-growing share of the footwear market. By the end of 1993, sales in the U.S. alone had reached $11.6 billion. Nike, the largest supplier of athletic footwear in the world, posted a record $298 million profit for 1993—earnings that had nearly tripled in five years. And sneaker companies continue to refine their strategies for "global competitiveness"— hiring supposedly docile women to make their shoes, changing designs as quickly as we fickle customers change our tastes, and shifting factories from country to country as trade barriers rise and fall.

The logic of it all is really quite simple: yet trade agreements such as the North American Free Trade Agreement (NAFTA) and the General Agreement on Tariffs and Trade (GATT) are, of course, talked about in a jargon that alienates us, as if they were technical matters fit only for economists and diplomats. The bottom line is that all companies operating overseas depend on trade agreements made between their own governments and the regimes ruling the countries in which they want to make or sell their products. Korean, Indonesian, and other women workers around the world know this better than anyone. They are tackling trade politics because they have learned from hard experience that the trade deals their governments sign do little to improve the lives of workers. Guarantees of fair, healthy labor practices, of the rights to speak freely and to organize independently, will usually be left out of trade pacts—and women will suffer. The recent passage of both NAFTA and GATT ensures that a growing number of private companies will now be competing across borders without restriction. The result? Big business will step up efforts to pit working women in industrialized countries against much lower-paid working women in "developing" countries, perpetuating the misleading notion that they are inevitable rivals in the global market

All the "New World Order" really means to corporate giants like athletic shoemakers is that they now have the green light to accelerate long-standing industry practices. In the early 1980s, the field marshals commanding Reebok and Nike, which are both U.S.-based, decided to manufacture most of their sneakers in South Korea and Taiwan, hiring local women. L.A. Gear, Adidas, Fila, and Asics quickly followed their lead. In short time, the coastal city of Pusan, South Korea, became the "sneaker capital of the world." Between 1982 and 1989 the U.S. lost 58,500 footwear jobs to cities like Pusan, which attracted sneaker executives because its location facilitated international transport. More to the point, South Korea's military government had an interest in suppressing labor organizing, and it had a comfortable military alliance with the U.S. Korean women also seemed accepting of Confucian philosophy, which measured a woman's morality by her willingness to work hard for her family's well-being and to acquiesce to her father's and husband's dictates. With their sense of patriotic duty, Korean women seemed the ideal labor force for export-oriented factories.

U.S. and European sneaker company executives were also attracted by the ready supply of eager Korean male entrepreneurs with whom they could make profitable arrangements. This fact was central to Nike's strategy in particular. When they moved their production sites to Asia to lower labor costs, the executives of the Oregon-based

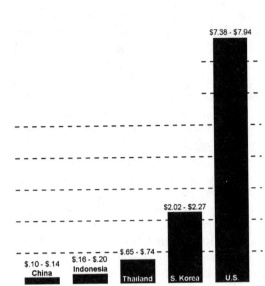

$7.38 - $7.94

$2.02 - $2.27

$.65 - $.74

$.10 - $.14
China

$.16 - $.20
Indonesia

Thailand

S. Korea

U.S.

Figures are estimates based on 1993 data from the International Textile, Garment, and Leather Workers Federation; International Labor Organization; and the U.S. Bureau of Labor Statistics.

Figure 1. Hourly wages in athletic footwear factories.

company decided to reduce their corporate responsibilities further. Instead of owning factories outright, a more efficient strategy would be to subcontract the manufacturing to wholly foreign-owned—in this case, South Korean—companies. Let them be responsible for workers' health and safety. Let them negotiate with newly emergent unions. Nike would retain control over those parts of sneaker production that gave its officials the greatest professional satisfaction and the ultimate word on the product: design and marketing. Although Nike was following in the footsteps of garment and textile manufacturers, it set the trend for the rest of the athletic footwear industry.

But at the same time, women workers were developing their own strategies. As the South Korean pro-democracy movement grew throughout the 1980s, increasing numbers of women rejected traditional notions of feminine duty. Women began organizing

in response to the dangerous working conditions, daily humiliations, and low pay built into their work. Such resistance was profoundly threatening to the government, given the fact that South Korea's emergence as an industrialized "tiger" had depended on women accepting their "role" in growing industries like sneaker manufacture. If women reimagined their lives as daughters, as wives, as workers, as citizens, it wouldn't just rattle their employers; it would shake the very foundation of the whole political system.

At the first sign of trouble, factory managers called in government riot police to break up employees' meetings. Troops sexually assaulted women workers, stripping, fondling, and raping them "as a control mechanism for suppressing women's engagement in the labor movement," reported Jeong-Lim Nam of Hyosung Women's University in Taegu. It didn't work. It didn't work because the feminist activists in groups like the Korean Women Workers Association (KWWA) helped women understand and deal with the assaults. The KWWA held consciousness-raising sessions in which notions of feminine duty and respectability were tackled along with wages and benefits. They organized independently of the male-led labor unions to ensure that their issues would be taken seriously, in labor negotiations and in the pro-democracy movement as a whole.

The result was that women were at meetings with management, making sure that in addition to issues like long hours and low pay, sexual assault at the hands of managers and health care were on the table. Their activism paid off: in addition to winning the right to organize women's unions, their earnings grew. In 1980, South Korean women in manufacturing jobs earned 45 percent of the wages of their male counterparts; by 1990, they were earning more than

Labor $1.66
(Total allocation for the 45 to
60 employees who work on
one pair of shoes)

Subcontractor's Profit $1.19

Nike Markup $22.95
(After paying subcontractor $14.65, Nike adds on $22.95 for
costs and profits, selling shoes to retailer for $37.80)

Retailer Markup $32.20
(Retailer adds on $32.20 for costs and profits,
selling shoes for $70)

Materials $9.18

Administration and Overhead $2.82

Source: Nike, Inc.

Figure 2. A $70 pair of Nike Pegasus: Where the money goes.

50 percent. Modest though it was, the pay increase was concrete progress, given that the gap between women's and men's manufacturing wages in Japan, Singapore, and Sri Lanka actually *widened* during the 1980s. Last but certainly not least, women's organizing was credited with playing a major role in toppling the country's military regime and forcing open elections in 1987.

Without that special kind of workplace control that only an authoritarian government could offer, sneaker executives knew that it was time to move. In Nike's case, its famous advertising slogan—"Just Do It"—proved truer to its corporate philosophy than its women's "empowerment" ad campaign, designed to rally women's athletic (and consumer) spirit. In response to South Korean women workers' newfound activist self-confidence, the sneaker company and its subcontractors began shutting down a number of their South Korean factories in the late 1980s and early 1990s. After bargaining with government officials in nearby China and Indonesia, many Nike subcontractors set up shop in those countries, while some went to Thailand. China's government remains nominally Communist: Indonesia's ruling generals are staunchly anti-Communist. But both are governed by authoritarian

regimes who share the belief that if women can be kept hard at work, low paid, and unorganized, they can serve as a magnet for foreign investors.

Where does all this leave South Korean women—or any woman who is threatened with a factory closure if she demands decent working conditions and a fair wage? They face the dilemma confronted by thousands of women from dozens of countries. The risk of job loss is especially acute in relatively mobile industries; it's easier for a sneaker, garment, or electronics manufacturer to pick up and move than it is for an automaker or a steel producer. In the case of South Korea, poor women had moved from rural villages into the cities searching for jobs to support not only themselves, but parents and siblings. The exodus of manufacturing jobs has forced more women into the growing "entertainment" industry. The kinds of bars and massage parlors offering sexual services that had mushroomed around U.S. military bases during the Cold War have been opening up across the country.

But the reality is that women throughout Asia are organizing, knowing full well the risks invoked. Theirs is a long-term view; they are taking direct aim at companies' nomadic advantage, by building links among workers in countries targeted for "development" by multinational corporations. Through sustained grassroots efforts, women are developing the skills and confidence that will make it increasingly difficult to keep their labor cheap. Many are looking to the United Nations conference on women in Beijing, China, this September, as a rare opportunity to expand their cross-border strategizing.

The Beijing conference will also provide an important opportunity to call world attention to the hypocrisy of the governments and corporations doing business in China. Numerous athletic shoe companies followed Nike in setting up manufacturing sites throughout the country. This included Reebok—a company claiming its share of responsibility for ridding the world of "injustice, poverty, and other ills that gnaw away at the social fabric," according to a statement of corporate principles.

Since 1988, Reebok has been giving out annual human rights awards to dissidents from around the world. But it wasn't until 1992 that the company adopted its own "human rights production standards"—after labor and advocates made it known that the quality of life in factories run by its subcontractors was just as dismal as that at most other athletic shoe suppliers in Asia. Reebok's code of conduct, for example, includes a pledge to "seek" those subcontractors who respect worker's rights to organize. The only problem is that independent trade unions are banned in China. Reebok has chosen to ignore that fact, even though Chinese dissidents have been the recipients of the company's own human rights award. As for working conditions, Reebok now says it sends its own inspectors to production sites a couple of times a year. But they have easily "missed" what subcontractors are trying to hide—like 400 young

women workers locked at night into an overcrowded dormitory near a Reebok-contracted factory in the town of Zhuhai, as reported last August in the *Asian Wall Street Journal Weekly.*

Nike's cofounder and CEO Philip Knight has said that he would like the world to think of Nike as "a company with a soul that recognizes the value of human beings." Nike, like Reebok, says it sends in inspectors from time to time to check up on work conditions at its factories: in Indonesia, those factories are run largely by South Korean subcontractors. But according to Donald Katz in a recent book on the company, Nike spokesman Dave Taylor told an in-house newsletter that the factories are "[the subcontractors'] business to run." For the most part, the company relies on regular reports from subcontractors regarding its "Memorandum of Understanding," which managers must sign, promising to impose "local government standards" for wages, working conditions, treatment of workers, and benefits.

In April, the minimum wage in the Indonesian capital of Jakarta will be $1.89 *a day*—among the highest in a country where the minimum wage varies by region. And managers are required to pay only 75 percent of the wage directly; the remainder can be withheld for "benefits." By now, Nike has a well-honed response to growing criticism of its low-cost labor strategy. Such wages should not be seen as exploitative, say Nike, but rather as the first rung on the ladder of economic opportunity that Nike has extended to workers with few options. Otherwise, they'd be out "harvesting coconut meat in the tropical sun," wrote Nike spokesman Dusty Kidd, in a letter to the *Utne Reader.* The all-is-relative response craftily shifts attention away from reality: Nike didn't move to Indonesia to help Indonesians; it moved to ensure that its profit margin continues to grow. And that is pretty much guaranteed in a country where "local standards" for wages rarely take a worker over the poverty line. A 1991 survey by the International Labor Organization (ILO) found that 88 percent of women working at the Jakarta minimum wage at the time—slightly less than a dollar a day—were malnourished.

A woman named Riyanti might have been among the workers surveyed by the ILO. Interviewed by the Boston *Globe* in 1991, she told the reporter who had asked about her long hours and low pay: "I'm happy working here. . . . I can make money and I can make friends." But in fact, the reporter discovered that Riyanti had already joined her coworkers in two strikes, the first to force one of Nike's Korean subcontractors to accept a new women's union and the second to compel managers to pay at least the minimum wage. That Riyanti appeared less than forthcoming about her activities isn't surprising. Many Indonesian factories have military men posted in their front offices who find no fault with managers who tape women's mouths shut to keep them from talking among themselves. They and their superiors have a political reach that extends far beyond the barracks. Indonesia has all the makings for a political explosion, especially since the gap between rich and poor is widening into a chasm. It is in this setting that the government has tried to crack down on any independent labor organizing—a policy that Nike has helped to implement. Referring to a recent strike in a Nike-contracted factory, Tony Nava, Nike representative in Indonesia, told the Chicago *Tribune* in November 1994 that the "troublemakers" had been fired. When asked about Nike policy on the issue, spokesman Keith Peters struck a conciliatory note: "If the government were to allow and encourage independent labor organizing, we would be happy to support it."

Indonesian workers' efforts to create unions independent of governmental control were a surprise to shoe companies. Although their moves from South Korea have been immensely profitable [see chart, page 551], they do not have the sort of immunity from activism that they had expected. In May 1993, the murder of a female labor activist outside Surabaya set off a storm of local and international protest. Even the U.S. State Department was forced to take note in its 1993 worldwide human rights report, describing a system similar to that which generated South Korea's boom 20 years earlier: severely restricted union organizing, security forces used to break up strikes, low wages for men, lower wages for women—complete with government rhetoric celebrating women's contribution to national development.

Yet when President Clinton visited Indonesia last November, he made only a token effort to address the country's human rights problem. Instead, he touted the benefits of free trade, sounding indeed more enlightened, more in tune with the spirit of the post-Cold War era than do those defenders of protectionist trading policies who coat their rhetoric with "America first" chauvinism. But "free trade" as actually being practiced today is hardly *free* for any workers—in the U.S. or abroad—who have to accept the Indonesian, Chinese, or Korean workplace model as the price of keeping their jobs.

The not-so-new plot of the international trade story has been "divide and rule." If women workers and their government in one country can see that a sneaker company will pick up and leave if their labor demands prove more costly than those in a neighbor country, then women workers will tend to see their neighbors not as regional sisters, but as competitors who can steal their precarious livelihoods. Playing women off against each other is, of course, old hat. Yet it is as essential to international trade politics as is the fine print in GATT.

But women workers allied through networks like the Hong Kong-based Committee for Asian Women are developing their own post-Cold War foreign policy, which means addressing women's needs: how to convince fathers and husbands that a woman going out to organizing meetings at night is not sexually promiscuous; how to develop workplace agendas that respond to family needs; how to work with male unionists who push women's demands to the bottom of their lists; how to build a global movement.

These women refuse to stand in awe of the corporate power of the Nike or Reebok or Adidas executive. Growing numbers of Asian women today have concluded that trade politics have to be understood by women on their own terms. They will be coming to Beijing this September ready to engage with women from other regions to link the politics of consumerism with the politics of manufacturing. If women in Russia and Eastern Europe can challenge Americanized consumerism, if Asian activists can solidify their alliances, and if U.S. women can join with them by taking on trade politics—the post-Cold War sneaker may be a less comfortable fit in the 1990s.

Notes

This article draws from the work of South Korean scholars Hyun Sook Kim, Seung-kyung Kim, Katharine Moon, Seungsook Moon, and Jeong-Lim Nam.

Running in Place

Virginia Valian

After thirty years on the fast track, women are still hobbled by the cumulative effects of sexual stereotyping–a bias that begins in infancy and persists even among the most enlightened employers.

In 1980, as part of a school economics project, a group of fifth and sixth graders bought six shares of stock in the Mohasco Corportaion, a carpet and furniture manufacturer then based in New York City. The fledgling investors later attended a Mohasco shareholders' meeting, where an eleven-year-old girl asked the company's president and chief executive officer: "What are you doing to improve the role of women in your company?"

"Learning very young, isn't she?" the CEO replied. "As a company we have promoted—that didn't come out quite like I intended—we have encouraged the expanded use of young ladies in various parts of our company. We have no officers who are young ladies, though we have them moving up the ranks. We have very brilliant young ladies in management roles, in the area of computer programming. We'll have a place for you in a few years."

Whatever one might think about the ingenuousness of the CEO's response, his company's subsequent record of promoting women to upper-management jobs cannot be examined. Mohasco suffered several financial setbacks in the 1980s and is now a privately held company. One can, however, look at the overall figures for corporations in the United States. In 1978, two years before the eleven-year-old asked her question, there were two women heading Fortune 1000 companies; in 1994 that number had not changed. In August 1996, sixteen years after the question, there were four.

From Virginia Valian, *Why So Slow? The Advancement of Women*, (Cambridge, MA: The MIT Press, 1997) excerpted as it appeared in *The Sciences*, January/February 1998.

Perhaps even more telling, a 1996 review of the 1,000 largest firms in the United States showed that only 1 percent of the top five jobs in those corporations—sixty posts out of 5,000—were filled by women.

The story is similar in academe. According to a major study published in 1996 by the National Science Foundation, 60 percent of the women in science and engineering in 1993 had tenure or tenure-track positions, compared with 77 percent of men. And women were overrepresented in non-tenure-track positions: 14 percent held those jobs, compared with 8 percent of men. (The remainder of each sex held jobs to which tenure does not apply; women were more likely to find themselves in that category as well.)

The women in the study also lagged behind in salary. The median income of women from all scientific disciplines combined—including mathematics, computer specialties, psychology, the social sciences, physics, chemistry, biology and engineering—was 78 percent of the men's: $48,400, compared with $61,500 for men. And within each of those fields, women earned less: from 93 percent of men's salaries in mechanical engineering to 76 percent in environmental science.

In virtually every profession I have examined—business, academe, medicine, law, sports—the picture looks the same: men earn more money and achieve higher status than women do. After more than three decades of struggles for gender equality, the progress of women continues to be slow and slight. Differences in education and experience sometimes explain part of the disparity in pay and rank, but gender always explains another, more subterranean, part.

From the first day women set foot on a career path, they are required to meet a higher standard.

At a restaurant in Manhattan near the end of the lunch hour I sit watching the manager's child, not quite two, toddling among the mostly empty tables. The child is wearing a jacket and pants of bright red, blue and yellow fabric. A baseball cap worn back-to-front partly cover's ear-length curly blond hair. Is the child a girl or a boy? The baseball cap and pants suggest a boy, but the har length suggests a girl. The toddler's adventurousness might signal a boy, but its looks are androgynous and I cannot make up my mind.

The first thing adults want to establish about a child—even a newborn—is its sex. But what does sex, which is largely independent of a baby's behavior, tell an adult about the child? The answer is that the label "girl" or "boy" gives the adult a starting point from which to interpret the child's behavior, even its physical features. The label allows the adult to categorize an attractive baby as pretty, if it is a girl, or handsome, if it is a boy. The label brings into play the adult's preexisting beliefs about differences between the sexes. Those beliefs—some conscious and some not—make up an intuitive concept or schema of gender.

In white, Western, middle-class society, the gender schema for men includes being independent, assertive and task-oriented. Men act. The gender schema for women is different; it includes being nurturant, expressive and concerned about others. Women take care of people and express emotions.

The social consensus about basic differences between males and females can be gleaned from the greeting cards people send to congratulate parents on a new baby. A 1993 study by the psychologist Judith S. Bridges of the University of Connecticut in Hartford found, as expected, no pink ones for boys and no blue ones for girls. Pictures of toys, rattles and mobiles appear more often on girls' cards, and balls, sports equipment and vehicles show up more often on boys' cards. Female babies are pictured sleeping or immobile more often than male babies are, whereas boys are shown more often in active play.

Decorative elements on the cards show gender biases, too. Frills, lace, ribbons, flowers and hearts are all used more for girls than for boys. Verbal descriptions of infants also differ; the term *sweet*, for instance, crops up far more often for girls than for boys. The most striking difference is that expressions of happiness or joy are found more often on cards for boys—64 percent of cards—than for girls—49 percent of cards. People expect parents to be happier about the birth of a boy than about the birth of a girl. Greeting cards thus project babies as already embodying gender schemas. One clas of babies is decorative; the other is physically active—and brings the greater joy.

Men and women carry around similar gender schemas for both sexes. In one study investigators asked college students to rate the behavior of a baby who had been videotaped crying. Some students were told that the baby was a boy and others that it was a girl. Regardless of their own gender, students described the baby labeled as male as angrier than the same infant labeled as female.

In another study parents were asked to rate their newborns on several different attributes when the babies were no more than twenty-four hours old. By objective measures, there were no differences in weight, height, color, muscle tone, reflex responses, heart rate or respiratory rate between the girls and the boys. Yet the parents of the baby boys saw their sons as bigger than the parents of daughters saw their baby girls. Furthermore, fathers of sons judged their babies to be better coordinated, more alert, stronger and hardier than did fathers of daughters. Knowing a child's sex skews perceptions.

But do such faulty concepts of gender have any real consequences? To answer that question, ask another one: Which baby seems better suited to an active and successful professional life—the baby who is better coordinated, more alert, hardier and stronger, or the one who is less coordinated, less alert, less hardy and weaker? Which baby is better suited for housework and child care? Just as it is unfair to picture one child as less capable than she is, it is also unfair to see the other as more capable than he is. From the first child too little will be expected; from the second too much.

As children grow up, they learn the gender schemas of their parents. Those schemas will affect their own performance as professionals, not to mention their expectations of other men and women, and their evaluations of other people's work. The most important consequence of those gender schemas for professional life is that men are consistently overrated and women are underrated. Whatever helps people focus on a man's gender gives him a small advantage, a plus mark. Whatever accentuates a women's gender results in a small loss for her, a minus mark.

That consequence emerges in sharp relief in the results of a 1991 survey of U.S. professionals working in international business. The economists Mary Lou Egan and Marc Bendick Jr. of Bendick & Egan Economic Consultants in Washington, D.C., analyzed the contributing factors in determining men's and women's salaries: number of graduate degrees, range of occupations pursued, number of years' experience, kinds of strategies used for career advancement, whether or not the person is designated "fast track," number of hours worked per week and the like. The investigators found that favorable marks on such factors typically helped both men and women make higher salaries, but they helped the women to a lesser extent; fourteen of the seventeen factors examined benefitted men more. The result is just what gender schemas would lead one to expect: women's achievements, qualifications and professional choices are worth less than men's are.

A bachelor's degree, for instance, contributed $28,000 to men's salaries but only $9,000 to women's. A degree from a high-prestige school contributed $11,500 to men's salaries but *subtracted* $2,400 from women's. Not holding back one's career for the benefit of a spouse's was worth $21,900 a year for men but only $1,700 a year for women. Being designated "fast track" added $10,900 for men but only $200 for women. Experience living outside the United States added $9,200 to men's salaries but, like high-prestige education, subtracted from women's—$7,700 a year. Similarly, deliberately choosing international work added $5,300 for men but subtracted $4,200 for women. Finally, speaking another language added $2,600 for men but took away $5,100 for women.

Egan and Bendick conjectured that the assets of speaking another language and having lived outside the United States are interpreted differently for men than for women. A man is seen as choosing to live aboard or learn a language not for fun but for the professional benefits such activities can bring. The choice signals a commitment to his career. In the gender schema for women, on the other hand, a woman goes abroad or learns a language simply for pleasure. Such a woman telegraphs indifference to her career.

Gender schemas are usually unarticulated. Their content may even be disavowed. Most men and women in the professions and academe explicitly, and sincerely, profess egalitarian beliefs. But consciuous beliefs and values do not fully control the workings of gender schemas. Egalitarian beliefs help, but they do not guarantee objective and fair evaluation and treatment of other people.

A true story about a science department at a prestigious university, circa 1990, illustrates how expectations that arise out of gender schemas can drag down a woman's career. A newly hired young woman Ph.D. has a conference with the chair of her department, a man, about the courses she will teach. She is eager to teach a large introductory lecture course. The chair refuses, saying the students will not accept a woman instructor in that role. The woman presses a bit, saying she thinks she can do it and would like to try. The chair does not want to take a chance, and he assigns her instead to a laboratory course. The woman is not happy with the substitution, because laboratory courses eat up time. As a young faculty member, she needs to spend as much time as possible developing her research and writing for publication, so that she will be able to earn promotion and tenure. And as circumstances have it, the competition for such promotion will be both direct and unfair. A male peer, also a new Ph.D., is assigned to the lecture course, and he will thereby have more time for research than she will.

The example captures the many different forces—particularly the gender expectations—that merge to put a woman on swampy ground. The chair thinks he is being objective about the students' preferences and is shielding an important course from risk. Nothing about the meeting causes him to think his decision might have been unfairly guided by gender schemas. The conference has also set a bad precedent. It has activated the chair's nonconscious views about women and tied them to the new faculty member. In the future he is likely to reactivate those views whenever he evaluates her. In a way, she has already failed, because he has already labeled her to himself as an unacceptable lecturer.

The glass ceiling—a popular term for subtle biases that keep women from reaching the top levels of organizations—is held up in part by gender schemas. But another force is also at work keeping the glass intact: the long-term buildup of small differences in the evaluation and treatment of men versus women.

A useful concept in sociology is the accumulation of advantage and disadvantage. It suggests that, like the interest on invested capital, advantages accrue, and that, like the interest on debt, disadvantages also pile up. Very small differences in treatment can, over time, give rise to large disparities in salary, promotion rates and prestige. It is unfair to neglect even minor instances of group-based bias, because they add up to major inequalities.

A computer model of promotion practices at a hypothetical company convincingly shows the powerful cumulative effects of even small-scale bias. In 1996 the psychologists Richard F. Martell of Columbia University in New York City, David M. Lane of Rice University in Houston, Texas, and Cynthia Emrich of the University of Otago in Dunedin, New Zealand, simulated a company with an eight-level hierarchy staffed at the bottom level by equal numbers of men and women. The model assumed that over time a certain percentage of employees would be promoted from one level to the next. It also assumed a minuscule bias in favor of promoting men, a bias accounting for only 1 percent of the variability in promotion. After many series of simulated promotions, the highest level in the hierarchy was 65 percent male.

Statistics on women's progress in the professions back up the idea that a series of small setbacks, such as not getting a good assignment, results in widening chasms in advancement. Women at each rank of academe, regardless of their subject, have lower average salaries than men do. Moreover, the inequalities are progressive: the disparity is smaller at the assistant professor level than at the full professor level.

In academe, as well as in business and law, the interaction between salary and rank can lead to fuzzy comparisons between men's and women's earnings. A more informative picture would compare peers. But if male full professors—like male law partners—are on average older than female full professors, they will have more experience and earn higher salaries. Comparisons within the upper ranks, therefore, can overestimate income disparities.

In junior ranks, however, comparing apparent peers can have the opposite effect: it can cause an underestimation of income disparities. Since male assistant professors are promoted at a faster rate than female assistant professors, the people in a lower rank will include not only young men and women but also older women who should have been promoted out of that rank. Data on the incomes of men and women who are the same number of years post-degree, or who have the same number of years' experience, regardless of rank, make the fairest comparisons.

The 1996 National Science Foundation study tabulated such data from 1993. It found that among the newest Ph.D.'s in science and engineering—those with degrees earned in 1991 or 1992—women scientists at universities and four-year colleges earned 99 percent of the median salary of their male counterparts. For more experienced women, though, the slope got icy. Women academics whose degrees were awarded between

1985 and 1990 earned 92 percent of men's salaries; women with degrees from between 1980 and 1982 earned 90 percent; and those with degrees from between 1970 and 1979 earned 89 percent. Thus the most recent female graduates start out on a roughly equal salary footing with their male counterparts, but are likely to lose that equality as early as three years after earning their Ph.D.'s

A different sample of male and female scientists, intended to represent those who show high achievement early in their careers, was followed from 1987 to 1990 by the sociologist Gerhard Sonnert and the physicist Gerald Holton, both of Harvard University. The participants had won postdoctoral fellowships from either the National Science Foundation or the National Research Council between 1952 and 1985. Because those national fellowships are prestigious, the men and women who earn them are roughly equal in education, experience and performance at the start of their academic careers. Nevertheless, except for biologists, women with such fellowships had less success climbing through the ranks than men did. For example, women who had earned their doctorates in the physical sciences, mathematics and engineering after 1978 languished almost a full rank behind their male peers; women in the social sciences were more than three-quarters of a rank behind.

The women in Sonnert and Holton's sample were somewhat less productive than the men, but even when productivity was considered, the women (again, except the biologists) held lower ranks than comparable men. Thus, even women who have a prestigious credential profit from it less than men do.

Why young female and male biologists fare equally well is not known. One possible explanation comes forom a 1995 study by Sonnert, in which senior biologists rated a small group of junior biologists on a four-point scale. Although not asked to do so, the senior biologists implicitly took quality, as well as quantity, of publications into account. Their ratings of the women were slightly higher than those of the men, a difference that vanished when citation rates were not considered. Taken together, the data suggest that biologists' assessments are more sensitive to quality than those of other scientists and that the difference helps women gain equal ground.

What is true for academe holds even more stongly in the corporate world. A 1990 *Fortune* magazine survey of 799 of the largest U.S. industrial and service companies showed that only nineteen women—less than one-half of 1 percent—were listed among the more than 4,000 highest-paid officers and directors. In business as in academe, women earn less than men (two of those nineteen women had cash compensation under $85,000 a year), are promoted more slowly and work in less prestigious institutions.

On the positive side, women's earnings have improved. In a 1996 survey of the twenty highest-paid women in U.S. corporations, the lowest total compensation was $833,350. But 615 men earned more than the twentieth woman on the list. And again, as in academe, to the extent that performance can be accurately measured, men and women appear to perform equally well. Independent of all other factors, gender appears to play a key role in people's ability to get ahead.

The inequality in status between men and women professionals will not go away by itself. It will not be smoothed by normal economic tides or by women's acquisition of more and better work skills. Excellent work skills are necessary for success, but they are not enough to guarantee equality.

So where do we go from here? Affirmative-action policies, legislation and court action remain important roads to change in the workplace. But the elusive nature of gender schemas demands more subtle remedies as well. The most important remedy is learning about gender schemes in the first place: how they develop, how they work, how they are maintained and how they skew hopes and expectations. With that knowledge, men and women can begin to find ways to neutralize them.

One successful long-term program was developed recently at the Johns Hopkins University School of Medicine in Baltimore, Maryland. At medical schools throughout the United States, women are underrepresented in the top professorial rank. After an internal report documented lower pay and slower rates of promotion for women faculty in the Johns Hopkins department of medicine, the (male) chair of the department appointed a committee to design procedures for improving women's status.

The committee members found that women were put up for promotion later than their male peers. The problem seemed to have many facets, ranging from the failure of evaluators to identify qualified women, to ignorance on the part of the women themselves of the criteria for promotion. The solution aimed to change all those facets. Each female faculty member (and later, each male faculty member) was evaluated annually annd given an explicit progress report. A monthly meeting was established to give women faculty concrete information about how to move through their professional careers and how to handle problems that might arise. Those meetings were needed in part because mentors of male junior faculty were more likely to pass along that advice informally than were mentors of female junior faculty.

Another change was to teach senior faculty how to act as mentors, in an effort to level unequal treatment of junior men and junior women. The committee members had learned, for instance, that mentors invited male junior faculty to chair conferences (and thereby receive public exposure) six times as often as they invited junior female faculty.

Within five years, the program became extremely successful. In 1990 there were only four women associate professors; by 1995 there were twenty-six. The improvement did not spring from changes in promotion criteria. What did change was women's knowledge of what was needed for promotion. In 1990 only 26 percent of the women reported that they were advised about the criteria, but in 1993, 46 percent reported being advised. It is likely that the knowledge of promotion requirements helps candidates mold their behavior accordingly. One must notice too, however, that slightly more than half the women still had not gotten the facts about how to climb through the ranks.

The Johns Hopkins program shows that institutions can, with major efforts, keep their female employees from getting stuck in the marshy bottoms of their professions. Yet the limits of the program also suggest the need for remedies that take more direct aim at gender schemas, such as those that would train evaluators in reasoning and judging.

Unless everyone—women and men alike—understands how gender schemas hobble women professionally, women will not get the positive evaluations their work merits. They will get less than their fair share—and their progress will continue to be painfully slow.

Hierarchies, Jobs, Bodies:
A Theory of Gendered Organizations

Joan Acker

Most of us spend most of our days in work organizations that are almost always dominated by men. The most powerful organizational positions are almost entirely occupied by men, with the exception of the occasional biological female who acts as a social man (Sorenson 1984). Power at the national and world level is located in all-male enclaves at the pinnacle of large state and economic organizations. These facts are not news, although sociologists paid no attention to them until feminism came along to point out the problematic nature of the obvious (Acker and Van Houten 1974; Moss Kanter 1975, 1977). Writers on organizations and organizational theory now include some considerations of women and gender (Clegg and Dunkerley 1980; Mills 1988; Morgan 1986), but their treatment is usually cursory, and male domination is, on the whole, not analyzed and not explained (Hearn and Parkin 1983).

Among feminist social scientists there are some outstanding contributions on women and organizations, such as the work of Moss Kanter (1977), Feldberg and Glenn (1979), MacKinnon (1979), and Ferguson (1984). In addition, there have been theoretical and empirical investigations of particular aspects of organizational structure and process (Izraeli 1983; Martin 1985), and women's situations have been studied using traditional organizational ideas (Dexter 1985; Wallace 1982). Moreover, the very rich literature, popular and scholarly, on women and work contains much material on work organizations. However, most of this new knowledge has not been brought together in a systematic feminist theory of organizations.

A systematic theory of gender and organizations is needed for a number of reasons. First, the gender segregation of work, including divisions between paid and unpaid work, is partly created through organizational practices. Second, and related to gender segregation, income and status inequality between women and men is also partly created in organizational processes; understanding these processes is necessary for understanding gender inequality. Third, organizations are one arena in which widely disseminated cultural images of gender are invented and reproduced. Knowledge of cultural production is important for understanding gender construction (Hearn and Parkin 1987). Fourth, some aspects of individual gender identity, perhaps particularly masculinity, are also products of organizational processes and pressures. Fifth, an important feminist project is to make large-scale organizations more democratic and more supportive of humane goals.

In this article, I begin by speculating about why feminist scholars have not debated organizational theory. I then look briefly at how those feminist scholars who have paid attention to organizations have conceptualized them. In the main part of the article, I examine organizations as gendered processes in which both gender and sexuality have been obscured through a gender-neutral, asexual discourse, and suggest some of the ways that gender, the body, and sexuality are part of the processes of control in work organizations. Finally, I point to some directions for feminist theory about this ubiquitous human invention.

Why So Little Feminist Debate on Organizations?

The early radical feminist critique of sexism denounced bureaucracy and hierarchy as male-created and male-dominated structures of control that oppress women. The easiest answer to the "why so little debate" question is that the link between masculinity and organizational power was so obvious that no debate was needed. However, experiences in the feminist movement suggest that the questions are not exhausted by recognizing male power.

Part of the feminist project was to create nonhierarchical, egalitarian organizations that would demonstrate the possibilities of nonpatriarchal ways of working (Gould 1979; Martin 1990). Although many feminist organizations survived, few retained this radical-democratic form (Martin 1990). Others succumbed to the same sorts of pressures that have undermined other utopian experiments with alternative work forms (Newman 1980), yet analyses of feminist efforts to create alternative organizations (Freeman 1975; Gould 1979) were not followed by debates about the feasibility of nonpatriarchal, nonhierarchical organization or the relationship of organizations and gender. Perhaps one of the reasons was that the reality was embarrassing; women failing to cooperate with each other, taking power and using it in oppressive ways, creating their own structures of status and reward were at odds with other images of women as nurturing and supportive.

Another reason for feminist theorists' scant attention to conceptualizing organizations probably lies in the nature of the concepts and models at hand. As Dorothy Smith (1979) has argued, the available discourses on organizations, the way that organizational sociology is defined as an area or domain "is grounded in the working worlds and relations of men, whose experience and interests arise in the course of and in relation to participation in the ruling apparatus of this society" (p. 148). Concepts developed to answer managerial questions, such as how to achieve organizational efficiency, were irrelevant to feminist questions, such as why women are always concentrated at the bottom of organizational structures.

Critical perspectives on organizations, with the notable exception of some of the studies of the labor process (Braverman 1974; Knights and Willmott 1985), although focusing on control, power, exploitation, and how these relations might be changed, have ignored women and have been insensitive to the implications of gender for their own goals. The active debate on work democracy, the area of organizational exploration closest to feminist concerns about oppressive structures, has been almost untouched by feminist insights (Rothschild 1987; Rothschild-Whitt, 1979). For example, Carole Pateman's influential book, *Participation and Democratic Theory* (1970), critical in shaping the discussions on democratic organization in the 1970s, did not consider women or gender. More recently, Pateman (1983a, 1983b, 1988) has examined the fundamental ideas of democracy from a feminist perspective, and other feminist political scientists have criticized theories of democracy (Eisenstein 1981), but on the whole, their work is isolated from the main discourse on work organization and democracy.

Empirical research on work democracy has also ignored women and gender. For example, in the 1980s, many male Swedish researchers saw little relation between questions of democracy and gender equality (Acker 1982), with a few exceptions (Fry 1986). Other examples are studies of Mondragon, a community in the Spanish Basque country, which is probably the most famous attempt at democratic ownership, control, and organization. Until Sally Hacker's feminist study (1987), researchers who went to Mondragon to see this model of work democracy failed to note the situation of women and asked no questions about gender. In sum, the absence of women and gender from theoretical and empirical studies about work democracy provided little material for feminist theorizing.

Another impediment to feminist theorizing is that the available discourses conceptualize organizations as gender neutral. Both traditional and critical approaches to organizations originate in the male, abstract intellectual domain (Smith 1988) and take as reality the world as seen from that standpoint. As a relational phenomenon, gender is difficult to see when only the masculine is present. Since men in organizations take their behavior and perspectives to represent the human, organizational structures and processes are theorized as gender neutral. When it is acknowledged that women and men are affected differently by organizations, it is argued that gendered attitudes and behavior are brought into (and contaminate) essentially gender-neutral structures. This view of organizations separates structures from the people in them.

Current theories of organization also ignore sexuality. Certainly, a gender-neutral structure is also asexual. If sexuality is a core component of the production of gender identity, gender images, and gender inequality, organizational theory that is blind to sexuality does not immediately offer avenues into the comprehension of gender domination (Hearn and Parkin 1983, 1987). Catharine MacKinnon's (1982) compelling argument that sexual domination of women is embedded within legal organizations has not to date become part of mainstream discussions. Rather, behaviors such as sexual harassment are viewed as deviations of gendered actors, not, as MacKinnon (1979) might argue, as components of organizational structure.

Feminist Analyses of Organizations

The treatment of women and gender most assimilated into the literature on organizations is Rosabeth Kanter's *Men and Women of the Corporation* (1977). Moss Kanter sets out to show that gender differences in organizational behavior are due to structure rather than to characteristics of women and men as individuals (1977, 291–92). She argues that the problems women have in large organizations are consequences of their structural placement, crowded in dead-end jobs at the bottom and exposed as tokens at the top. Gender enters the picture through organizational roles that "carry characteristic images of the kinds of people that should occupy them" (p. 250). Here, Moss Kanter recognizes the presence of gender in early models of organizations:

A "masculine ethic" of rationality and reason can be identified in the early image of managers. This "masculine ethic" elevates the traits assumed to belong to men with educational advantages to necessities for effective organizations: a tough-minded approach to problems; analytic abilities to abstract and plan; a capacity to set aside personal, emotional considerations in the interests of task accomplishment; a cognitive superiority in problem-solving and decision making. (1974, 43)

Identifying the central problem of seeming gender neutrality, Moss Kanter observes: "While organizations were being defined as sex-neutral machines, masculine principles were dominating their authority structures" (1977, 46).

In spite of these insights, organizational structure, not gender, is the focus of Moss Kanter's analysis. In posing the argument as structure *or* gender, Moss Kanter also implicitly posits gender as standing outside of structure, and she fails to follow up her own observations about masculinity and organizations (1977, 22). Moss Kanter's analysis of the effects of organizational position applies as well to men in low-status positions. Her analysis of the effect of numbers, or the situation of the "token" worker, applies also to men as minorities in women-predominant

organizations, but fails to account for gender differences in the situation of the token. In contrast to the token women, White men in women-dominated workplaces are likely to be positively evaluated and to be rapidly promoted to positions of greater authority. The specificity of male dominance is absent in Moss Kanter's argument, even though she presents a great deal of material that illuminates gender and male dominance.

Another approach, using Moss Kanter's insights but building on the theoretical work of Harmann (1976), is the argument that organizations have a dual structure, bureaucracy and patriarchy (Ressner 1987). Ressner argues that bureaucracy has its own dynamic, and gender enters through patriarchy, a more or less autonomous structure, that exists alongside the bureaucratic structure. The analysis of two hierarchies facilitates and clarifies the discussion of women's experiences of discrimination, exclusion, segregation, and low wages. However, this approach has all the problems of two systems theories of women's oppression (Young 1981; see also Acker 1988): the central theory of bureaucratic or organizational structure is unexamined, and patriarchy is added to allow the theorist to deal with women. Like Moss Kanter, Ressner's approach implicitly accepts the assumption of mainstream organizational theory that organizations are gender-neutral social phenomena.

Ferguson, in *The Feminist Case Against Bureaucracy* (1984), develops a radical feminist critique of bureaucracy as an organization of oppressive male power, arguing that it is both mystified and constructed through an abstract discourse on rationality, rules, and procedures. Thus, in contrast to the implicit arguments of Moss Kanter and Ressner, Ferguson views bureaucracy itself as a construction of male dominations. In response to this overwhelming organization of power, bureaucrats, workers, and clients are all "feminized," as they develop ways of managing their powerlessness that at the same time perpetuate their dependence. Ferguson argues further that feminist discourse, rooted in women's experiences of caring and nurturing outside bureaucracy's control, provides a ground for opposition to bureaucracy and for the development of alternative ways of organizing society.

However, there are problems with Ferguson's theoretical formulation. Her argument that feminization is a metaphor for bureaucratization not only uses a stereotype of femininity as oppressed, weak, and passive, but also, by equating the experience of male and female clients, women workers, and male bureaucrats, obscures the specificity of women's experiences and the connections between masculinity and power (Brown 1984; see also Martin 1987; Mitchell 1986; Ressner 1986). Ferguson builds on Foucault's (1979) analysis of power as widely diffused and constituted through discourse, and the problems in her analysis have their origin in Foucault, who also fails to place gender in his analysis of power. What results is a disembodied, and consequently gender-neutral, bureaucracy as the oppressor. That is, of course, not a new vision of bureaucracy, but it is one in which gender enters only as analogy, rather than as a complex component of processes of control and domination.

In sum, some of the best feminist attempts to theorize about gender and organizations have been trapped within the constraints of definitions of the theoretical domain that cast organizations as gender neutral and asexual. These theories take us only part of the way to understanding how deeply embedded gender is in organizations. There is ample empirical evidence: We know now that gender segregation is an amazingly persistent pattern and the gender

identity of jobs and occupations is repeatedly reproduced, often in new forms (Bielby and Baron 1987; Reskin and Roos 1987; Strober and Arnold 1987). The reconstruction of gender segregation is an integral part of the dynamic of technological and organizational change (Cockburn 1983, 1985; Hacker 1981). Individual men and particular groups of men do not always win in these processes, but masculinity always seems to symbolize self-respect for men at the bottom and power for men at the top, while confirming for both their gender's superiority. Theories that posit organization and bureaucracy as gender neutral cannot adequately account for this continual gendered structuring. We need different theoretical strategies that examine organizations as gendered processes in which sexuality also plays a part.

Organization as Gendered Processes

The idea that social structure and social processes are gendered has slowly emerged in diverse areas of feminist discourse. Feminists have elaborated gender as a concept to mean more than a socially constructed, binary identity and image. This turn to gender as an analytic category (Connell 1987; Harding 1986; Scott 1986) is an attempt to find new avenues into the dense and complicated problem of explaining the extraordinary persistence through history and across societies of the subordination of women. Scott, for example, defines gender as follows: "The core of the definition rests on an integral connection between two propositions; gender is a constituitive element of social relationships based on perceived differences between the sexes, and gender is a primary way of signifying relationships of power" (1986, 1067).

New approaches to the study of waged work, particularly studies of the labor process, see organizations as gendered, not as gender neutral (Cockburn 1985; Game and Pringle 1984; Knights and Willmott 1985; Phillips and Taylor 1986; Sorenson 1984) and conceptualize organizations as one of the locations of the inextricably intertwined production of both gender and class relations. Examining class and gender (Acker 1988), I have argued that class is constructed through gender and that class relations are always gendered. The structure of the labor market, relations in the workplace, the control of the work process, and the underlying wage relation are always affected by symbols of gender, processes of gender identity, and material inequalities between women and men. These processes are complexly related to and powerfully support the reproduction of the class structure. Here, I will focus on the interface of gender and organizations, assuming the simultaneous presence of class relations.

To say that an organization, or any other analytic unit, is gendered means that advantage and disadvantage, exploitation and control, action and emotion, meaning and identity, are patterned through and in terms of a distinction between male and female, masculine and feminine. Gender is not an addition to ongoing processes, conceived as gender neutral. Rather, it is an integral part of those processes, which cannot be properly understood without an analysis of gender (Connell 1987; West and Zimmerman 1987). Gendering occurs in at least five interacting processes (cf. Scott 1986) that, although analytically distinct, are, in practice, parts of the same reality.

First is the construction of divisions along lines of gender—divisions of labor, of allowed behaviors, of locations in physical space, of power, including the institutionalized means of maintaining the divisions in the structures of labor markets, the family, the state. Such divisions in work organiza-

tions are well documented (e.g., Moss Kanter 1977) as well as often obvious to casual observers. Although there are great variations in the patterns and extent of gender division, men are almost always in the highest positions of organizational power. Managers' decisions often initiate gender divisions (Cohn 1985), and organizational practices maintain them—although they also take on new forms with changes in technology and the labor process. For example, Cynthia Cockburn (1983, 1985) has shown how the introduction of new technology in a number of industries was accompanied by a reorganization, but not abolition, of the gendered division of labor that left the technology in men's control and maintained the definition of skilled work as men's work and unskilled work as women's work.

Second is the construction of symbols and images that explain, express, reinforce, or sometimes oppose those divisions. These have many sources or forms in language, ideology, popular and high culture, dress, the press, television. For example, as Moss Kanter (1975), among others, has noted, the image of the top manager or the business leader is an image of successful, forceful masculinity (see also Lipman-Blumen 1980). In Cockburn's studies, men workers' images of masculinity linked their gender with their technical skills; the possibility that women might also obtain such skills represented a threat to the masculinity.

The third set of processes that produce gendered social structures, including organizations, are interactions between women and men, women and women, men and men, including all those patterns that enact dominance and submission. For example, conversation analysis shows how gender differences in interruptions, turn taking, and setting the topic of discussion recreate gender inequality in the flow of ordinary talk (West and Zimmerman 1983). Although much of this research has used experimental groups, qualitative accounts of organizational life record the same phenomena: Men are the actors, women the emotional support (Hochschild 1983).

Fourth, these processes help to produce gendered components of individual identity, which may include consciousness of the existence of the other three aspects of gender, such as, in organizations, choice of appropriate work, language use, clothing, and presentation of self as a gendered member of an organization (Reskin and Roos 1987).

Finally, gender is implicated in the fundamental, ongoing processes of creating and conceptualizing social structures. Gender is obviously a basic constitutive element in family and kinship, but, less obviously, it helps to frame the underlying relations of other structures, including complex organizations. Gender is a constitutive element in organizational logic, or the underlying assumptions and practices that construct most contemporary work organizations (Clegg and Dunkerley 1980). Organizational logic appears to be gender neutral; gender-neutral theories of bureaucracy and organizations employ and give expression to this logic. However, underlying both academic theories and practical guides for managers is a gendered substructure that is reproduced daily in practical work activities and, somewhat less frequently, in the writings of organizational theorists (cf. Smith 1988)

Organizational logic has material forms in written work rules, labor contracts, managerial directives, and other documentary tools for running large organizations, including systems of job evaluation widely used in the comparable-worth strategy of feminists. Job evaluation is accomplished through the use and interpretation of documents that describe jobs and how they are to be evaluated. These documents contain symbolic indicators of structure; the ways that they are interpreted and talked about in the process of job evaluation reveals the underlying organizational logic. I base the following theoretical discussion on my observations of organizational logic in action in the job-evaluation component of a comparable worth project (Acker 1987, 1989, 1990).

Job evaluation is a management tool used in every industrial country, capitalist and socialist, to rationalize the organizational hierarchy and to help in setting equitable wages (International Labour Office 1986). Although there are many different systems of job evaluation, the underlying rationales are similar enough so that the observation of one system can provide a window into a common organizational mode of thinking and practice.

In job evaluation, the content of jobs is described and jobs are compared on criteria of knowledge, skill, complexity, effort, and working conditions. The particular system I observed was built incrementally over many years to reflect the assessment of managers about the job components for which they were willing to pay. Thus today this system can be taken as composed of residues of these judgments, which are a set of decision rules that, when followed, reproduce managerial values. But these rules are also the imagery out of which managers construct and reconstruct their organizations. The rules of job evaluation, which help to determine pay differences between jobs, are not simply a compilation of managers' values or sets of beliefs, but are the underlying logic or organization that provides at least part of the blueprint for its structure. Every time that job evaluation is used, that structure is created or reinforced.

Job evaluation evaluates jobs, not their incumbents. The job is the basic unit in a work organization's hierarchy, a description of a set of tasks, competencies, and responsibilities represented as a position on an organizational chart. A job is separate from people. It is an empty slot, a reification that must continually be reconstructed, for positions exist only as scraps of paper until people fill them. The rationale for evaluating jobs as devoid of actual workers reveals further the organizational logic—the intent is to assess the characteristics of the job, not of their incumbents who may vary in skill, industriousness, and commitment. Human beings are to be motivated, managed, and chosen to fit the job. The job exists as a thing apart.

Every job has a place in the hierarchy, another essential element in organizational logic. Hierarchies, like jobs, are devoid of actual workers and based on abstract differentiations. Hierarchy is taken for granted, only its particular form is at issue. Job evaluation is based on the assumption that workers in general see hierarchy as an acceptable principle, and the final test of the evaluation of any particular job is whether its place in the hierarchy looks reasonable. The ranking of jobs within an organization must make sense to managers, but it is also important that most workers accept the ranking as just if the system of evaluation is to contribute to orderly working relationships.

Organizational logic assumes a congruence between responsibility, job complexity, and hierarchical position. For example, at lower-level positions, the level of most jobs filled predominantly by women, must have equally low levels of complexity and responsibility. Complexity and responsibility are defined in terms of managerial and professional tasks. The child-care worker's responsibility for other human beings or the complexity facing the secretary who serves six different, temperamental bosses can only be minimally counted if the congruence between position level, responsibility, and complexity is to be preserved. In addition, the logic holds that two jobs at different hierarchical levels cannot be responsible for the same outcome; as a consequence, for example, tasks delegated to a secretary by a manager will not raise her hierarchical level because such tasks are still his responsibility, even though she has the practical responsibility to see that they are done. Levels of skill, complexity, and responsibility, all used in constructing hierarchy, are conceptualized as existing independently of any concrete worker.

In organizational logic, both jobs and hierachies are abstract categories that have no occupants, no human bodies, no gender. However, an abstract job can exist, can be transformed into a concrete instance, only if there is a worker. In organizational logic, filling the abstract job is a disembodied worker who exists only for the work. Such a hypothetical worker cannot have other imperatives of existence that impinge upon the job. At the very least, outside imperatives cannot be included within the definition of the job. Too many obligations outside the boundaries of the job would make a worker unsuited for the position. The closest the disembodied worker doing the abstract job comes to a real worker is the male worker whose life centers on his full-time, life-long job, while his wife or another woman takes care of his personal needs and his children. While the realities of life in industrial capitalism never allowed all men to live out this ideal, it was the goal for labor unions and the image of the worker in social and economic theory. The woman worker, assumed to have legitimate obligations other than those required by the job, did not fit with the abstract job.

The concept "a job" is thus implicitly a gendered concept, even though organizational logic presents it as gender neutral. "A job" already contains the gender-based division of labor and the separation between the public and the private sphere. The concept of "a job" assumes a particular gendered organization of domestic life and social production. It is an example of what Dorothy Smith has called "the gender subtext of the rational and impersonal" (1988, 4).

Hierarchies are gendered because they also are constructed on these underlying assumptions: Those who are committed to paid employment are "naturally" more suited to responsibility and authority; those who must divide their commitments are in the lower ranks. In addition, principles of hierarchy, as exemplified in most existing job-evaluation systems, have been derived from already existing gendered structures. The best-known systems were developed by management consultants working with managers to build methods of consistently evaluating jobs and rationalizing pay and job classifications. For example, all managers with similar levels of responsibility in the firm should have similar pay. Job-evaluation systems were intended to reflect the values of managers and to produce a believable ranking of jobs based on those values. Such rankings would not deviate substantially from rankings already in place that contain gender typing and gender segregation of jobs and the clustering of women workers in the lowest and the worst-paid jobs. The concrete value judgments that constitute conventional job evaluation are designed to replicate such structures (Acker 1989). Replication is achieved in many ways; for example, skills in managing money, more often found in men's than in women's jobs, frequently receive more points than skill in dealing with clients or human relations skills, more often found in women's than in men's jobs (Steinberg and Haignere 1987).

The gender-neutral status of "a job" and of the organizational theories of which it is a part depend upon the assumption that the worker is abstract, disembodied, although in actuality both the concept of "a job" and real workers are deeply gendered and "bodied." Carole Pateman (1986), in a discussion of women and political theory, similarly points out that the most fundamental abstraction in the concept of liberal individualism is "the abstraction of the 'individual' from the body. In order for the individual to appear in liberal theory as a universal figure, who represents anyone and everyone, the individual must be disembodied" (p. 8). If the individual were not abstracted from bodily attributes, it would be clear that the individual represents one sex and one gender, not a universal being. The political fiction of the universal "individual" or "citizen" fundamental to ideas of democracy and contract, excluded women, judging them lacking in the capacities necessary for participation in civil society. Although women now have the rights of citizens in democratic states, they still stand in an ambiguous relationship to the universal individual who is "constructed from a male body so that his identity is always masculine" (Pateman 1988, 223). The worker with "a job" is the same universal "individual" who in actual social reality is a man. The concept of a universal worker excludes and marginalizes women who cannot, almost by definition, achieve the qualities of a real worker because to do so is to become like a man.

Organization Control, Gender, and the Body

The abstract, bodiless worker, who occupies the abstract, gender-neutral job has no sexuality, no emotions, and does not procreate. The absence of sexuality, emotionality, and procreation in organizational logic and organizational theory is an additional element that both obscures and helps to reproduce the underlying gender relations.

New work on sexuality in organizations (Hearn and Parkin 1987), often indebted to Foucault (1979), suggests that this silence on sexuality may have historical roots in the development of large, all-male organizations that are the primary locations of societal power (Connell 1987). The history of modern organizations includes, among other processes, the suppression of sexuality in the interests of organization and the conceptual exclusion of the body as a concrete living whole (Burrell 1984, 1987; Hearn and Parkin 1987; Morgan 1986).

In a review of historical evidence on sexuality in early modern organizations, Burrell (1984, 98) suggests that "the suppression of sexuality is one of the first tasks the bureaucracy sets itself." Long before the emergence of the very large factory of the nineteenth century, other large organizations, such as armies and monasteries, which had allowed certain kinds of limited participation of women, were more and more excluding women and attempting to banish sexuality in the interests of control of members and the organization's activities (Burrell 1984, 1987; Hacker and Hacker 1987). Active sexuality was the enemy of orderly procedures, and excluding women from certain areas of activity may have been, at least in part, a way to control sexuality. As Burrell (1984) points out, the exclusion of women did not eliminate homosexuality, which has always been an element in the life of large all-male organizations, particularly if members spend all of their time in the organization. Insistence on heterosexuality or celibacy were ways to control homosexuality. But heterosexuality had to be practiced outside the organization, whether it was an army or a capitalist workplace. Thus the attempts to banish sexuality from the workplace were part of the wider process that differentiated the home, the location of legitimate sexual activity, from the place of capitalist production. The concept of the disembodied job symbolizes this separation of work and sexuality.

Similarly, there is no place within the disembodied job or the gender-neutral organization for other "bodied" processes, such as human reproduction (Rothman 1989) or the free expression of emotions (Hochschild 1983). Sexuality, procreation, and emotions all intrude upon and disrupt the ideal functioning of the organization, which tries to control such interferences. However, as argued above, the abstract worker is actually a man, and it is the man's body, its sexuality, minimal responsibility in procreation, and conventional control of emotions that pervades work and organizational processes. Women's bodies—female sexuality, their ability to procreate and their pregnancy, breast-feeding, and child care, menstruation, and mythic "emotionality"—are suspect, stigmatized, and used as grounds for control and exclusion.

The ranking of women's jobs is often justified on the basis of women's identification with childbearing and domestic life. They are devalued because women are assumed to be unable to conform to the demands of the abstract job. Gender segregation at work is also sometimes openly justified by the necessity to control sexuality, and women may be barred from types of work, such as skilled blue-collar work or top management, where most workers are men, on the grounds that potentially disruptive sexual liaisons should be avoided (Lorber 1984) On the other hand, the gendered definition of some jobs "includes sexualization of the woman worker as part of the job" (MacKinnon 1979, 18). These are often jobs that serve men, such as secretaries, or a largely male public (Hochschild 1983).

The maintenance of gendered hierarchy is achieved partly through such often-tacit controls based on arguments about women's reproduction, emotionality, and sexuality, helping to legitimate the organizational structures created through abstract, intellectualized techniques. More overt controls, such as sexual harassment, relegating childbearing women to lower-level mobility tracks, and penalizing (or rewarding) their emotion management also conform to and reinforce hierarchy. MacKinnon (1979), on the basis of an extensive analysis of legal cases, argues that the willingness to tolerate sexual harassment is often a condition of the job, both a consequence and a cause of gender hierarchy.

While women's bodies are ruled out of order, or sexualized and objectified, in work organizations, men's bodies are not. Indeed, male sexual imagery pervades organizational metaphors and language, helping to give form to work activities (see Hearn and Parkin 1987, for an extended discussion). For example, the military and the male world of sports are considered valuable training for organizational success and provide images for team-work, campaigns, and tough competition. The symbolic expression of male sexuality may be used as a means of control over male workers, too, allowed or even encouraged within the bounds of the work situation to create cohesion or alleviate stress (Collinson 1988; Hearn and Parkin 1987). Management approval of pornographic pictures in the locker room or support for all male work and play groups where casual talk is about sexual exploits or sports are examples. These symbolic expressions of male dominance also act as significant controls over women in work organizations because they are per se excluded from the informal bonding men produce with the "body talk" of sex and sports.

Symbolically, a certain kind of male heterosexual sexuality plays an important part in legitimating organizational power. Connell (1987) calls this hegemonic masculinity, emphasizing that it is formed around dominance over women and in opposition to other masculinities, although its exact content changes as historical conditions change. Currently, hegemonic masculinity is typified by the image of the strong, technically competent, authoritative leader who is sexually potent and attractive, has a family, and has his emotions under control. Images of male sexual function and patriarchal paternalism may also be embedded in notions of what the manager does when he leads his organization (Calas and Smircich 1989). Women's bodies cannot be adapted to hegemonic masculinity; to function at the top of male hierarchies requires that women render irrelevant everything that makes them women.

The image of the masculine organizational leader could be expanded, without altering its basic elements, to include other qualities also needed, such as flexibility and sensitivity to the capacities and needs of subordinates. Such qualities are not necessarily the symbolic monopoly of women. For example, the wise and experienced coach is empathetic and supportive to his individual players and flexibly leads his team against devious opposition tactics to victory.

The connections between organizational power and men's sexuality may be even more deeply embedded in organizational processes. Sally Hacker (1989) argues that eroticism and technology have common roots in human sensual pleasure and that for the engineer or the skilled worker, and probably for many other kinds of workers, there is a powerful erotic element in work processes. The pleasures of technology, Hacker continues, become harnessed to domination, and passion becomes directed toward power over nature, the machine, and other people, particularly women, in the work hierarchy. Hacker believes that men lose a great deal in this transformation of the erotic into domination, but they also win in other ways. For example, many men gain economically from the organizational gender hierarchy. As Crompton and Jones (1984) point out, men's career opportunities in white-collar work depend on the barriers that deny those opportunities to women. If the mass of female clerical workers were able to compete with men in such work, promotion probabilities for men would be drastically reduced.

Class relations as well as gender relations are reproduced in organizations. Critical, but nonfeminist, perspectives on work organizations argue that rational-technical systems for organizing work, such as job classification and evaluation systems and detailed specification of how work is to be done, are parts of pervasive systems of control that help to maintain class relations (Edwards 1979). The abstract "job," devoid of a human body, is a basic unit in such systems of control. The positing of a job as an abstract category, separate from the worker, is an essential move in creating jobs as mechanisms of compulsion and control over work processes. Rational-technical, ostensibly gender-neutral, control systems are built upon and conceal a gendered substructure (Smith 1988) in which men's bodies fill the abstract jobs. Use of such abstract systems continually reproduces the underlying gender assumptions and the subordinated or excluded place of women. Gender processes, including the manipulation and management of women's and men's sexuality, procreation, and emotion, are part of the control processes of organizations, maintaining not only gender stratification but

contributing also to maintaining class and, possibly, race and ethnic relations. Is the abstract worker white as well as male? Are white-male-dominated organizations also built on underlying assumptions about the proper place of people with different skin colors? Are racial differences produced by organizational practices as gender differences are?

Conclusion

Feminists wanting to theorize about organizations face a difficult task because of the deeply embedded gendering of both organizational processes and theory. Commonsense notions, such as jobs and positions, which constitute the units managers use in making organizations and some theorists use in making theory, are posited upon the prior exclusion of women. This underlying construction of a way of thinking is not simply an error, but part of processes of organization. This exclusion in turn creates fundamental inadequacies in theorizing about gender-neutral systems of positions to be filled. Creating more adequate theory may come only as organizations are transformed in ways that dissolve the concept of the abstract job and restore the absent female body.

Such a transformation would be radical in practice because it would probably require the end of organizations as they exist today, along with a redefinition of work and work relations. The rhythm and timing of work would be adapted to the rhythms of life outside of work. Caring work would be just as important and well rewarded as any other; having a baby or taking care of a sick mother would be as valued as making an automobile or designing computer software. Hierarchy would be abolished, and workers would run things themselves. Of course, women and men would share equally in different kinds of work. Perhaps there would be some communal or collective form of organization where work and intimate relations are closely related, children learn in places close to working adults, and workmates, lovers, and friends are all part of the same group. Utopian writers and experimenters have left us many possible models (Hacker 1989). But this brief listing begs many questions, perhaps the most important of which is how, given the present organization of economy and technology and the pervasive and powerful, impersonal, textually mediated relations of ruling (Smith 1988), so radical a change could come about.

Feminist research and theorizing, by continuing to puzzle out how gender provides the subtext for arrangements of subordination, can make some contributions to a future in which collective action to do what needs doing—producing goods, caring for people, disposing of the garbage—is organized so that dominance, control, and subordination, particularly the subordination of women, are eradicated, or at least minimized, in our organization life.

References

Acker, Joan. 1982. Introduction to women, work and economic democracy. *Economic and Industrial Democracy* 3(4):i-viii.

___. 1987. Sex bias in job evaluation: A comparable worth issue. In *Ingredients for women's employment policy,* edited by Christine Bose and Glenna Spitze. Albany: SUNY Press.

___. 1988. Class, gender and the relations of distribution. *Signs* 13:473–97.

___. 1989 *Doing comparable worth: Gender, class and pay equity.* Philadelphia: Temple University Press.

___. 1990. The Oregon case. In *State experience and comparable worth,* edited by Ronnie Steinberg, Philadelphia: Temple University Press.

Acker, Joan, and Donald Van Houten. 1974. Differential recruitment and control: The sex structuring or organizations. *Administrative Science Quarterly* 19:152–63.

Bielby, William T., and James N. Baron. 1987. Undoing discrimination: Job integrations and comparable worth. In *Ingredients for women's employment policy,* edited by Christine Bose and Glenna Spitze. Albany: SUNY Press.

Braveman, Harry. 1974. *Labor and monopoly capital.* New York: Montly Review Press.

Brown, Wendy. 1984. Challenging bureaucracy. *Women's Review of Books* 2(November):14–17.

Burrell, Gibson. 1984. Sex and organizational analysis. *Organization Studies* 5:97–118.

___. 1987. No accounting for sexuality. *Accounting, Organizations and Society* 12:89–101.

Calas, Marta B., and Linda Smircich. 1989. Voicing seduction to silence leadership. Paper presented at the Fourth International Conference on Organizational Symbolism and Corporate Culture in Fountainbleau, France.

Clegg, Stewart, and David Dunkerley. 1980. *Organization, class and control.* London: Routledge & Kegan Paul.

Cockburn, Cynthia. 1983. *Brothers: Male dominance and technological change.* London: Pluto Pres.

___. 1985. *Machinery of dominance.* Londo: Pluto Press.

Cohn, Samuel. 1985. *The process of occupational sextyping.* Philadelphia: Temple University Press.

Collinson, David L. 1988. Engineering humour: Maculinity, joking and conflict in shop-floor relations. *Organization Studies* 9:181–99.

Connell, R. W. 1987. *Gender and power.* Stanford, CA: Stanford University Press.

Crompton, Rosemary, and Gareth Jones. 1984. *White-collar proletariat: deskilling and gender in clerical work.* Philadelphia: Temple University Press.

Dexter, Carolyn R. 1985. Women and the exercise of power in organizations: From ascribed to achieved status. In *Women and work: An annual review,* Vol. 1, edited by Laurie Larwood, Ann H. Stromberg, and Barbara A. Gutek. Beverly Hills, CA: Sage.

Edwards, Richard. 1979. *Contested terrain.* New York: Basic Books.

Eisenstein, Zillah R. 1981. *The radical future of liberal feminism.* New York: Longman.

Feldberg, Roslyn, and Evelyn Nakano Glenn. 1979. Male and female: Job versus gender models in the sociology of work. *Social Problems* 26:524–38.

Ferguson, Kathy E. 1984 *The feminist case against bureaucracy.* Philadelphia: Temple University Press.

Foucault, Michel. 1979. *The history of sexuality,* Vol. 1. London: Allen Lane.

Freeman, Jo. 1975. *The politics of women's liberation.* New York: Longman.

Fry, John. 1986. *Toward a democratic rationality.* Aldershot: Gower.

Game, Ann and Rosemary Pringle. 1984. *Gender at work*. London: Pluto Press.

Gould, Meridith. 1979. When women create an organization: The ideological imperatives of feminism. In *The international yearbook of women's studies 1979*, edited by D. Dunkerley and G. Salaman. London: Routledge & Kegan Paul.

Hacker, Barton C., and Sally Hacker. 1987. Military institutions and the labor process: Non-economic sources of technological change, women's subordination, and the organization of work. *Technology and Culture* 28:743–75.

Hacker, Sally. 1981. The culture of engineering women: Women, workplace and machine. *Women's Studies International Quarterly* 4:341–54.

___. 1987. Women workers in the Mondragon system of industrial cooperatives. *Gender & Society* 1:358–79.

___. 1989. *Pleasure, power and technology*. Boston: Unwin Hyman.

Harding, Sandra. 1986. *The science question in feminism*. Ithaca, NY: Cornell University Press.

Hartmann, Heidi. 1976. Capitalism, patriarchy and job segregation by sex. *Signs* 1:137–70.

Hearn, Jeff, and P. Wendy Parkin. 1983. Gender and organizations: A selective review and critique of a neglected area. *Organization Studies* 4:219–42.

———. 1987. *Sex at work*. Brighton: Wheatsheaf.

Hochschild, Arlie R. 1983. *The managed heart: Commercialization of human feeling*. Berkeley: University of California Press.

International Labour Office. 1986. *Job evaluation*. Geneva: ILO.

Izraeli, Dafna N. 1983. Sex effects or structural effects? An empirical test of Kanter's theory of proportions. *Social Forces* 61:153–65.

Kanter, Rosabeth Moss. 1975. Women and the structure of organizations: Explorations in theory and behavior. In *Another voice*, edited by Rosabeth Kanter and Marci Millman. New York: Doubleday.

___. 1977. *Men and women of the corporation*. New York: Basic Books.

Knights, David, and Hugh Willmott. 1985. *Gender and the labour process*. Aldership: Gower.

Lipman-Blumen, Jean. 1980. Female leadership in formal organizations: Must the female leader go formal? In *Readings in managerial psychology*, edited by Harold J. Leavitt, Louis R. Pondy, and David M. Boje. Chicago: University of Chicago Press.

Lorber, Judith. 1984. Trust, loyalty, and the place of women in the organization of work. In *Women: A feminist perspective*, 3d ed., edited by Jo Freeman. Palo Alto, CA: Mayfield.

MacKinnon, Catharine A. 1979. *Sexual harassment of working women*. New Haven, CT: Yale University Press.

———. 1982. Feminism, Marxism, method and the state: An agenda for theory. *Signs* 7:515–44.

Martin, Patricia Yancey. 1985. Group sex composition in work organizations: A structural-normative view. In *Research in the sociology of organizations*, edited by S. A. Bacharach and R. Mitchell. Greenwich, CT: JAI.

___. 1987. A commentary on *The feminist case against bureaucracy*. *Women's Studies International Forum* 10:543–48.

___. 1990. Rethinking feminist organizations. *Gender & Society* 4:182–306.

Mills, Albert J. 1988. Organization, gender and culture. *Organization Studies* 9(3):351–69.

Mitchell, Diane. 1986. Review of Ferguson, *The feminist case against bureaucracy*. Unpublished manuscript.

Morgan, Gareth. 1986. *Images of organization*. Beverly Hills, CA: Sage.

Newman, Katherine. 1980. Incipient bureaucracy: The development of hierarchies in egalitarian organizations. In *Hierarchy and society*, edited by Gerald R. Britan and Ronald Cohen. Philadelphia: Institute for the Study of Human Issues.

Pateman, Carole. 1970. *Participation and democratic theory*. Cambridge: Cambridge University Press.

___. 1983a. Feminist critiques of the public private dichotomy. In *Public and private in social life*, edited by S. I. Benn and G. F. Gaus. Beckenham, Kent: Croom Helm.

___. 1983b. Feminism and democracy. In *Democratic theory and practice*, edited by Graeme Duncan. Cambridge: Cambridge University Press.

___. 1986. Introduction: The theoretical subversiveness of feminism. In *Feminist challenges*, edited by Carole Pateman and Elizabeth Gross. Winchester, MA: Allen & Unwin.

___. 1988. *The sexual contract*. Cambridge, MA: Polity.

Philips, Anne, and Barbara Taylor. 1986. Sex and skill. In *Waged work*, edited by Feminist Review. London: Virago.

Reskin, Barbara F., and Patricia Roos. 1987. Status hierarchies and sex segregation. In *Ingredients for women's employment policy*, edited by Christine Bose and Glenna Spitze. Albany: SUNY Press.

Ressner, Ulla. 1986. Review of K. Ferguson, *The feminist case against bureaucracy*. *Economic and Industrial Democracy* 7:130–34.

___. 1987. *The hidden hierarchy*. Aldershot: Gower.

Rothman, Barbara Katz. 1989. *Recreating motherhood: Ideology and technology in a patriarchal society*. New York: Norton.

Rothschild, Joyce. 1987. Do collectivist-democratic forms of organization presuppose feminism? Cooperative work structures and women's values. Paper presented at Annual Meetings, American Sociological Association, Chicago.

Rothschild-Whitt, Joyce. 1979. The collectivist organization. *American Sociological Review* 44:509–27.

Scott, Joan. 1986. Gender: A useful category of historical analysis. *American Historical Review* 91: 1053–75.

Smith, Dorothy E. 1979. A sociology for women. In *The prism of sex: Essays in the sociology of knowledge,* edited by Julia A. Sherman and Evelyn Torten Beck. Madison: University of Wisconsin Press.

___. 1988. *The everyday world as problematic.* Boston Northeastern University Press.

Sorenson, Bjorg Aase. 1984. The organizational woman and the Trojan horse effect. In *Patriarchy in a welfare society,* edited by Harriet Holter. Oslo: Universitetsforlaget.

Steinberg, Ronnie, and Lois Haignere. 1987. Equitable compensation. Methodological criteria for comparable worth. In *Ingredients for women's employment policy,* edited by Christine Bose and Glenna Spitze. Albany: SUNY Press.

Strober, Myra H., and Carolyn L. Arnold. 1987. Integrated circuits/segregated labor: Women in computer-related occupations and high-tech industries. In *Computer chips and paper clips: Technology and women's employment,* edited by H. Hartmann. Washington, DC: National Academy Press.

Wallace, Phyllis A., ed. 1982. *Women in the workplace.* Boston: Auburn House.

West, Candace, and Don H. Zimmerman. 1983. Small insults: A study of interruptions in conversations between unacquainted persons. In *Language, gender and society,* edited by B. Thorne, C. Kramerae, and N. Henley. Rowley, MA: Newbury House.

___. 1987. Doing gender. *Gender & Society* 1:125–51.

Young, Iris. 1981. Beyond the unhappy marriage: A critique of dual systems theory. In *Women and revolution,* edited by L. Sargent. Boston: South End Press.

Popular Culture

PART IX

The authors in this section investigate how new cultural forms, technologies and global entertainment industries transform feminist issues providing new challenges and possibilities for theory and activism. As aspects of popular culture, TV talk shows, films, hip hop music and computer games reach across national borders influencing ideas about gender, sexuality, race and national identity in diverse cultures. The "global village" is created in part by the almost instantaneous exchange of images and ideas made possible to those who have access to new technologies like the Internet. Feminist scholars, including Teresa de Lauretis, E. Ann Kaplan, and Tania Modleski were among the first to recognize the importance of understanding the power of these technologies, particularly film, to shape conceptions of gender and diversity. Currently, the field of popular culture studies ranges from scholars who analyze "the ways of life in which and by which most people in any society live" to those with more specific concerns about the technologies used to convey images and ideas, or in exploring how audiences receive, resist and reconfigure what they see and hear. The authors of the first essay investigate a new arena, the design and use of computer games to pose questions about the potential of technology to reconfigure existing cultural definitions of masculinity, femininity and race. The girls and boys they studied had different fantasies about technology. What do these desires suggest about existing genres of games? How might games for boys and girls allow children to express the contradictions inherent in current definitions of femininity and masculinity? The next two articles examine TV talk shows and their role in exporting American preoccupations with sexuality both to new audiences locally and globally. Debbie Einstein and Deborah Lynn Steinberg analyze a script about relationships from the *Oprah Winfrey Show* to determine how complex issues about gender and power fare in this genre. While admiring Oprah's goals for the show, to educate and empower viewers to challenge abuse, discrimination and prejudice, they ask whether the therapeutic self help model and a strong presumption of heterosexuality embedded in the script enable viewers to effectively confront relations of power and inequality. In "Publicity Traps" Josh Gamson looks at the recent, increased visibility of lesbian, gay, bisexual and transgender lives on

557

television talk shows. How does this visibility, frequently driven by money and ratings to focus on 'fringe' members of these communities, affect gay, bisexual, transgender politics and collective identity? The final articles look outside the United States. The recent explosion of interest in hip hop music among Japanese youth prompts author Nina Corneytz to reflect on racialism and national identity. If Japan's defeat in World War II and subsequent occupation by American forces "feminized" Japanese national identity, does hip hop, and the commodification and selling of black style, provide a way to re-imagine the nation as masculine, transforming the meaning of Japaneseness? Lila Abu-Lughod probes decisions by some female film and stage stars in Egypt to give up their careers and put on the *higab* and the positive reactions to their decision by women in rural districts. The *higab* is a new kind of head-covering, currently the most visible symbol of a self-consciously Muslim identity. Her analysis of this "new veiling" counters most Western observers who understand the actresses' actions as an uncritical embrace of fundamentalism to uncover the multiple, contested meanings of their actions in Egypt.

Suggestions for Further Reading

Barthes, Roland. 1970. *Mythologies.* Paris: Editions du Seuil.

De Grazia, Victoria. 1996. *The Sex of Things: Gender & Consumption in Historical Perspective.* Berkeley: University of California Press.

De Lauretis, Teresa. 1987. *Technologies of Gender: Essays on Theory, Film and Fiction.* Bloomington: Indiana University Press.

___ 1984. *Alice Doesn't: Feminism, Semiotics and Cinema.* Bloomington: Indiana University Press.

Dent, Gina, ed. 1992. *Black Popular Culture.* Seattle: Bay Press.

Ewen, Stuart H. 1999. *Consuming Images: The Politics of Style in Contemporary Culture.* New York: Basic Books.

Evans, Jessica, and Stuart Hall. 1999. *Visual Culture.* Thousand Oaks: Sage Publications.

Fiske, John. 1987. *Television Culture.* New York: Routledge.

Franco, Jean. 1989. *Plotting Women: Gender & Representation in Mexico.* New York: Columbia University Press.

Franklin, Sarah, Ceila Lury, and Jackie Stacey. 1991. *Off Centre: Feminism & Cultural Studies.* New York: HarperCollins.

Frith, Simon. 1981. *Sound Effects: Youth, Leisure and the Politics of Rock 'n' Roll.* New York: Pantheon Books.

Gibian, Peter, ed. 1997. *Mass Culture and Everyday Life.* New York: Routledge.

Grossberg, Lawrence. 1997. *Mediamaking: Mass Media in a Popular Culture.* Durham: Duke University Press.

Grossberg, Lawrence, Cary Nelson and Paula A. Treichler, eds. 1992. *Cultural Studies.* New York: Routledge.

Hebdige, Dick. 1988. *Hiding in the Light: On Images and Things.* New York: Routledge.

Horkeimer, Max, and Theodor W. Adorno. 1991. *Dialectic of Enlightenment.* New York: Continuum.

Kaplan, E. Ann. 1987. *Rocking Around the Clock: Music, Television, Postmodernism and Consumer Culture.* New York: Metheun.

___ 1992. *Motherhood and Representation: The Mother in Popular Culture and Melodrama.* New York: Routledge.

Levine, Lawrence. 1988. *Highbrow/Lowbrow: The Emergence of Cultural Hierarchy.* Cambridge: Harvard University Press.

Modleski, Tania. 1984. *Loving with a Vengeance: Mass Produced Fantasies for Women.* New York: Metheun.

Modleski, Tania, ed. 1986. *Studies in Entertainment. Critical Approaches to Mass Culture.* Bloomington: Indiana University Press.

Morley, David and, Kwan-Hsing Chen, eds. 1996. *Stuart Hall: Critical Dialogues in Cultural Studies.* New York: Routledge.

Penley, Constance, and Andrew Ross, eds. 1991. *Technoculture.* Minneapolis: University of Minnesota Press.

Radway, Janice A. 1984. *Reading the Romance: Women, Patriarchy and Popular Literature.* Chapel Hill: University of North Carolina Press.

Rose, Tricia. 1994. *Black Noise: Rap Music & Black Culture in Contemporary America.* Hanover: Wesleyan University Press.

Ross, Andrew. 1989. *No Respect: Intellectuals and Popular Culture.* New York: Routledge.

Varnedoe, Kirk and, Adam Gopnik. 1990. *High and Low: Modern Art and Popular Culture.* New York: Museum of Modern Art.

Williams, Patricia J. 1995. *The Rooster's Egg.* Cambridge: Harvard University Press.

Girl Games and Technological Desire

45

Cornelia Brunner
Dorothy Bennett
Margaret Honey

Gender and Technological Desire

During the past ten years, a research and design group at the Center for Children and Technology has spent time investigating issues of gender and diversity as they relate to the ways in which students, particularly girls, use and engage with technologies. Our approach to these issues has been both psychological and sociological: we have investigated the ways in which children and adults construct meanings in relation to different technological environments, and we have examined the social and cultural barriers that tend to affect the ways we engage with technologies. We have also experimented with designing technological environments that can engage diverse populations of learners—not just the white boys.

It has become clear to us over time that the problem of designing for gender and diversity is quite complicated, particularly with respect to technology. A variety of forces affect our understanding of gender and make it very hard for us to think our way out of more or less conventional understandings of "masculinity" and "femininity." They include such sociological issues as the fact that girls and students of color still opt out of advanced-level science and math courses at a greater rate than do Caucasian males. As a result, scientific, engineering, and technological fields that are responsible for technological design are still largely dominated by white men. They also include economic factors, such as the fact that successful interactive "edutainment" products, often linked to other commercially successful products such as

Cassell, Justine, and Henry, From *Barbie to Mortal Kombat: Gender and Computer Games,* 1998, published by MIT Press. Used with permission.

television series, are the ones to find shelf space in CompUSA and other large retail outfits. And they include psychological factors, such as the ways in which we as consumers have been strongly encouraged to collude in the kinds of narratives that the vast majority of interactive products offer, particularly in the gaming industry. In this paper we focus on the latter point: the *psychological paradox*, the question of how we address issues of concern to young women that are glaringly absent in technological design without colluding in stereotypical understandings of femininity.

One of our strategies in exploring the psychological complexities that surround technological design has been to start with ourselves. We noticed that the women in our office seemed to respond quite differently to the sight of boxes of high-tech equipment arriving in the office than most of our male colleagues. The men seemed magnetically drawn to the boxes, tearing them open, practically salivating at the sight of the shiny, new machines emerging from their styrofoam nest. Then there would be the sound of happily boastful speculation about the speed, the power, the number of bips per bump the machine could produce or consume, and how it compared to a range of other machines with whose model numbers everybody seemed intimately familiar. We women tended to stay back and watch this frenzy with some amusement and a strong dose of skepticism, best summarized in the polite request that they let us know when they had put the thing together and had figured out what it was good for. We knew that there was no difference in technical expertise to explain this difference in attitude. Several of the women were more technically sophisticated than some of the men who were spitting stats at the new machine, and these women would probably end up setting up the machine, figuring out how to make

good use of it—and then explaining it to the men.

As researchers and designers we decided to explore some of these casually observed differences in more depth. The Spencer Foundation funded a series of studies involving interviews with users of technology, from architects to NASA scientists, from filmmakers to programmers (Bennett 1993; Brunner, Hawkins, and Honey 1988; Brunner 1991; Hawkins, Brunner, Clements, Honey, and Moeller 1990; Honey, Moeller, Brunner et al., 1991; Honey 1994). All of these individuals were deeply engaged in computer-related activities, including programming, multimedia design and authoring, computer-assisted design, and engineering. We asked them about a wide range of topics, from their career paths and their mentoring experiences to their personal feelings about their work. We also selected a subsample of twenty-four respondents, balanced by gender and profession, and asked them to participate in a study of their technology fantasies.

In the fantasy study, we were interested in exploring women's and men's feelings about technology—the nonrational aspect of how we interpret technological objects. Assuming that people might be less self-conscious about sharing such fantasies with a computer than with a human interviewer, we made a software program that invited our respondents to spin fantasies directly into the computer. We made the program look fanciful rather than serious, hoping to invite respondents to censor themselves as little as possible. We posed the following question: "if you were writing a science fiction story in which the perfect instrument (a future version of your own) is described, what would it be like?" Our analysis of the adult fantasies focused on five major topics: 1) the role of technology in integrating people's home and work lives; and technology's relationship to 2) nature, 3) the human body, 4) the process of creation, and 5) the process of communication.

What emerged from this study were two distinct and highly gendered perspectives on technology. Across our sample, women fantasized about small, flexible objects that facilitate sharing ideas and staying in touch, that can be used anywhere and fulfill a number of quite different functions—something that can be a camera one minute, for instance, and a flute the next. For the women in our sample, technology is a fellow creature on the earth, a child of humanity, promising but problematic (because, like all good things, there can be too much of it), needing care and guidance to grow to its best potential within the balance of things surrounding it, within the social and natural network in which it lives. The women wrote stories about tools that allow us to integrate our personal and professional lives and to facilitate creativity and communication. The following is typical of the fantasies written by women:

> The "keyboard" would be the size of a medallion, formed into a beautiful piece of platinum sculptured jewelry, worn around one's neck. The medallion could be purchased in many shapes and sizes. The keyed input would operate all day-to-day necessities to communicate and transport people (including replacements for today's automobile). The fiber-optic network that linked operations would have no dangerous side effect or byproduct that harmed people or the environment.

In contrast, men's fantasies were about mind-melds and bionic implants that allow their owners to create whole cities with the blink of an eye, or to have instant access to the greatest minds in history, to check in and see, as they get dressed in the morning, what Ghandi might have thought about a problem they are facing in the office that day. In their stories technology frees us from the earth, from social problems, possibly from humanity itself. The men praised technology because it increases our command and control over nature and each other. It allows us to extend our instrumental power into god-like dimensions, to transcend the limitations of time, space, and our physical bodies. For the men technology is a magic wand (pun intended), and scenarios like the following were typical:

> A direct brain-to-machine link. Plug it into a socket in the back of your head and you can begin communications with it. All information from other users is available and all of the history of mankind is also available. By selecting any time period the computer can impress directly on the user's brain images and background information for that time. In essence a time-machine. The user would not be able to discern differences between dreams and reality and information placed there by the machine.

Table 1 illustrates how we chose to summarize some of the most striking differences in how men and women fantasized about technology (Bennett, Brunner, and Honey 1996).

During the past decade, we have also conducted similar studies investigating children's technology fantasies and have collected fantasy machines, mostly from elementary and middle school students. In an analysis of the fantasy tasks of forty-seven preadolescent boys and girls, we asked children to create a blueprint for a machine of their own creation. Boys tend to make vehicles that take them wherever they want to go instantaneously. Typically, these vehicles have elaborate model numbers. Figure 1 represents what boys tend to imagine. The New 1994 Mazing Hover Carr is further illustrated in Figure 2. This one has a "twin valve seven rotor 4 class booster rocket," hidden turbo jets—and a snack bar.

Table 1. Technology

Women fantasize about it as a **MEDIUM**	Men fantasize about it as a **PRODUCT**
Women see it as a **TOOL**	Men see it as a **WEAPON**
Women want to use it for **COMMUNICATION**	Men want to use it for **CONTROL**
Women are impressed with its potential for **CREATION**	Men are impressed with its potential for **POWER**
Women see it as **EXPRESSIVE**	Men see it as **INSTRUMENTAL**
Women ask it for **FLEXIBILITY**	Men ask it for **SPEED**
Women are concerned with its **EFFECTIVENESS**	Men are concerned with its **EFFICIENCY**
Women like its ability to facilitate **SHARING**	Men like its ability to grant them **AUTONOMY**
Women are concerned with **INTEGRATING** it into their personal lives	Men are intent on **CONSUMING** it
Women talk about wanting to **EXPLORE** worlds	Men talk about using it to **EXPLOIT** resources and potentialities
Women are **EMPOWERED** by it	Men want **TRANSCENDENCE**

Source: Brunner 1994.

Girls' fantasies about technology differed in nature from those of boys. The machines that girls typically invented tended to be human-like household helpers or improvements to existing technologies that aimed to solve real-life problems. They often highlighted functions rather than the features of their machines, and they were situated in context. Figure 3 shows an example of what girls typically imagine: instead of features, there are functions.

The Season Chore Doer (Figure 4) is a sophisticated, multifunctional device. It senses what is needed and provides just the right tool: a seeder in spring, an umbrella in summer, a rake in the fall, and a shovel in winter. It does not, however, eliminate the need for the chore itself. If this gadget had been designed by a boy, chances are it would not provide a rake to collect the leaves—it would probably pulverize them.

Implications for the Design of Girl Games

One way of summarizing the implications of our research for the development of new technologies is to say that women and girls are much more likely to be concerned with how new technologies can fit into the social and environmental surroundings, whereas men are much more likely to be preoccupied with doing things faster, more powerfully, and more efficiently regardless of social and environmental consequences. Women are also far less likely to push the technological envelope and tend to be willing to make do with available tools. Men, in contrast, tend to draw upon their technological imaginations to extend the capabilities of technologies and to attempt to "go where no man has ever gone before." What are the implications of these differences for girl-friendly electronic games?

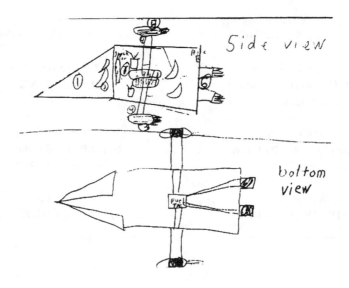

Figure 1

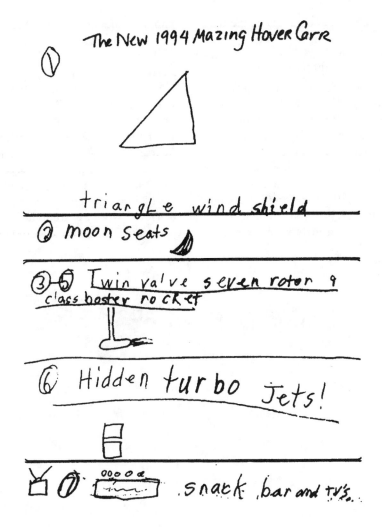

Figure 2

When thinking about the design of technological environments—particularly in relation to entertainment and educational products—it has been exceedingly difficult for us to imagine our way out of antithetical positions. The common approach in interactive design, or perhaps the path of least resistance, is to develop story lines that reinforce extreme notions of gender. The result is that "Mortal Kombat" becomes the archetypal video game for boys. In the girls' arena, programs like "McKenzie & Company" are beginning to emerge. This product presents scenarios that revolve around how to handle problems with boyfriends or would-be boyfriends, and how to dress and what kind of makeup to wear. These kinds of stories are not bad in and of themselves, but if they are the only available options, they run the danger of reinforcing stereotypic thinking about gender. Just as the fantasy life of boys who enjoy playing games like "Mortal Kombat" should not be curtailed by scenes of mindless violence. the social decision-making options in a game like "McKenzie & Company" are too simplistic to represent the kind of human problem-solving situations girls think about all the time. Products such as these enlarge an already gaping gender divide, making it harder for us to imagine approaches that do not privilege an either/or paradigm: Conquest or A Day at the Mall. We have to engage both boys and girls with electronic games that can incorporate multiple perspectives and varying themes.

To consider what our research means for designing a new genre of game that is not rigidly overdetermined, we first have to consider the function of games and play. One of the functions of playing games, as Henry Jenkins (this volume) notes, is to rehearse and explore what it means to have a gender. Games provide a safe place to explore issues of femininity and masculinity. Game playing can deliberately expand our sense of who we are. The appeal of role-playing games among both children and

SEASON CHORE DOER

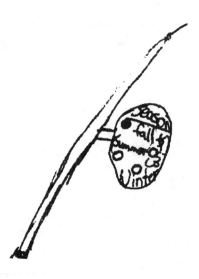

Figure 3

[handwritten margin note: Reinforces focus of dev'ing / compared research / ve'ac of play activity in adols girls' lives.]

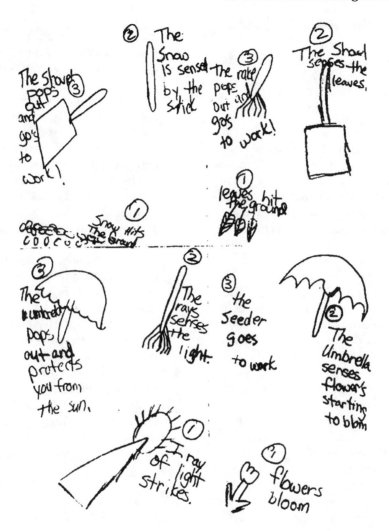

Figure 4

adults is testimony to this fact. The kinds of worlds represented in electronic games tend to be one dimensional. Typically these games appeal to boys. They are about conquest, winning, scoring points, assertion, and domination. The player becomes the active protagonist, whether the game is played from a first- or third-person perspective. The player is central, makes things happen, and determines the outcome. There usually are no other roles. There are few partner roles, few helper roles, few participant-observer roles. Making ourselves so big and so powerful that nobody can touch us is hardly preparation for the multiplicity of roles that people, particularly women, play in life. We need to make games that stretch the potential of different play paradigms.

Games have traditionally privileged:

✦ Victory over justice.
✦ Competition over collaboration.
✦ Speed over flexibility.
✦ Transcendence over empathy.
✦ Control over communication.
✦ Force over facilitation.

We need game environments that offer players options—where you can pick and choose from a range of personas, decide on varying strategies, and discover that different actions result in variable outcomes. We need a more complex relationship between actions taken and results obtained, and we need contexts that offer rich and varied opportunities for exploration.

Based on our research, and on a variety of experiments with designs that are deliberately open-ended (such as leaving choice in the hands of the user), we have conditional faith in the following generalizations about designing games for both boys and girls. It must be stressed, however, that these observations are speculative. We have never actually investigated the design features that make games more attractive to girls. We are merely applying the characteristics we have found to make for good electronic learning environments for girls to the domain of electronic games. What follows, then, is a nonprescriptive attempt to transform traditionally privileged design elements, and imagine alternative scenarios for play.

✦ *Technological sophistication.* The kinds of games that encourage flexibility in decision making require a more sophisticated technology than current games. Mitchel Resnick (Resnick 1991) learned years ago that girls wanted to build Lego Logo devices that could interact with each other. Instead of thinking about a single object that did one thing very well, designers had to pay attention to multiple objects that would interact with each other.

✦ *Winning and losing.* It probably matters more to girls what you win and what you lose than whether you win or lose. Girls are not that interested in conquering the world. Girls really prefer triumphs of a more personal sort. Many girls are seriously preoccupied with perfecting themselves, which is quite different from a more masculine desire to become stronger and more powerful, or with having total control over some part of the universe. This preoccupation with self-improvement and perfection is a tricky business, no simpler nor more beneficial than the masculine focus on power over others, except, perhaps, that the damage is more likely to be internal than external. It is, however, a rich ground for interesting stories and meaningful problems to solve.

✦ *Success and sacrifice.* Girls are interested in thinking about the issues that adult women must face these days, including how to juggle career and family, how to be successful at work while helping others, and how to stay part of the group. Girls want to figure out what the issues are and what sacrifices one may have to make. They want to anticipate and rehearse the complex dance that adult women, particularly those in nontraditional professions, must perform in order to make their lives work. This is good material for all kinds of adventure games.

✦ *The contradictions of femininity.* What constitutes femininity is open to question these days. For the young women we interviewed, femininity is linked to notions of social justice. Defining femininity is a live issue and a complicated one. Theories that absolve girls from the need to be feminine are of no help in the real world of their everyday lives. Things have not changed that much in junior high school, and popularity and traditional femininity still go together. Not much help is given to young women on how to rethink these issues. We believe that one function of role-playing games could be to help provide an imaginary space allowing girls to fool around with the notions of femininity that make sense to them, and offer rich, complex stories that raise questions about the consequences of the social prescriptions for femininity.

✦ *Persuasion versus conquest.* Women and girls tend to value persuasion, not conquest. Persuading is a more complex act than conquering. It is easy to simulate shooting somebody dead. It is harder to simulate persuading somebody—the interaction is more nuanced. Persuasion cuts both ways, of course. We have always wanted to make a game in which rumors create both havoc and opportunity. Instead of pulling out a sword when confronted with a complex situation, we want to let fly a rumor and have interesting things happen as a result of it—as in real life.

✦ *Humor.* Girls are very interested in humor. We think girls have less tolerance for humorlessness when it comes to games than boys do, because boys have something else that they can fool around with even in the absence of humor—weapons and victory. They still get to rack up points and shoot off weapons. The humor girls appreciate is based on character and situation rather than putdown. A certain level of sarcasm can be a lot of fun, but when the humor is based on pointing out people's shortcomings, it no longer appeals to girls as much.

✦ *Adventure.* What is adventure for girls? Rescue and romance are adventures. There is plenty of rescue and romance in current games, but the females in the story rarely get to experience that adventure directly. Girls do not just want to get rescued, they want to do the rescuing—without having to abandon femininity to do it. And they want to do more than come up with the right approach to get a guy to ask them out! Adventure means risk. In many games, the payoff is getting more strength, accumulating wealth or power, and figuring out what risks to take to achieve those gains. The kinds of risks that interest girls may have to do with defying conventions rather than gaining authority. Let us have some games about that—more romantic heroines striking out to make a place for themselves and their kind in a world that misunderstands or undervalues them.

✦ *Puzzles and obstacles.* Let us also have more games in which you play at outwitting your opponent rather than vanquishing the enemy. Many games have puzzles that occasionally are very clever and require real thought. They are, however, rarely integral to the story. There are exceptions, of course, including "Myst." The puzzle solving is fun, even when it is just an artificial obstacle to pursuing the story, but it might be a lot more entertaining to girls if the puzzles contributed to the story. Since girls are less motivated by winning than by following the flow of the story, such unintegrated puzzles can be frustrating and discouraging. Boys, on the other hand, often appreciate the opportunity to rack up more points.

✦ *Writing.* Girls are very interested in letter-writing and in other forms of communication across a variety of media.

They like to think about what to say and how to say it. Girls enjoy analyzing responses, mulling over phrasings, and testing alternatives. They like to illustrate their messages, comment on them, and compare and contrast them with other statements. Girls might be interested in games that focus on how things are communicated, not just on what is being said.

✦ *Design.* Girls like designing living spaces—not blueprints, but actual spaces. With VRML and VR technologies, it should be possible to see people move through a space you have designed, to report on how it feels, to look at it from their perspective, and to watch which kinds of interactions the design privileges and which are prohibited.

✦ *Being chosen.* The girls we interviewed often mentioned that they might like games about being chosen. But girls are not nearly as interested in thinking about how to seduce someone into choosing them as they are in the complexity that results once you have been chosen. Being chosen, as we all know, is a complicated thing. You lose some friends, you gain some things, stuff happens. Games that focus on dealing with that stuff might be extremely interesting to young women.

✦ *Mysteries.* Girls like mysteries because they have complex plots and intelligent action. There is something to think about and to talk over with friends. The kinds of action required to solve a mystery—keeping track of information, sifting through it, thinking it over, trying it again, looking at it from a different perspective—are the kinds of adult skills girls want to rehearse. It is what we like to do.

Some existing software, though not necessarily intended for girls, is designed in ways that seem compatible with the kind of feminine perspective on technology we have described here. Interactive comics, for instance, are an interesting new use of the electronic medium. The interactive features are a good fit with the way kids actually read comics, bringing each panel to life with sound and movies or animation. The comics provide a strong, linear narrative structure but utilize the nonlinear nature of the medium to offer a choice between multiple perspectives. The plot remains the same, the speech bubbles and the images inside the panels don't change, but the context and commentary in the descriptive labels changes, as does the accompanying information. This makes for a complex narrative of multiple voices, which lends itself beautifully to interactive storytelling. Unfortunately, this feature is not used in most of the interactive comics for children. These comics may include multimedia but they don't offer any conceptual interactivity. They are more like Living Books. Moreover the comics we have seen, such as "Reflux" by Inverse Ink, are interesting to look at and beautifully designed, but their content is strongly masculine. Nonetheless the genre makes a lot of sense for girls. Looking at a situation from multiple perspectives is a very attractive activity for girls.

Rather than leaving their mark on the world by conquering territory or even by amassing resources, girls might like to make a difference in a social situation, right an injustice, save a whale or two, or discover a cure for cancer. Some educational games allow for this kind of thinking, including the SimGames by Maxis and the Trail games by MECC. In the entertainment realm, there are some adult games, such as "Voyeur II" by Philips, that allow you to solve a mystery and thus prevent a murder rather than to avenge one. In "Voyeur II" you are a private eye, observing the shenanigans of a wealthy family in a fancy mansion through your fabulous binoculars. Sex, romance, and family tensions are the main elements of the plot, rather than war, violence, or world domination.

The themes matter, and so do the activities themselves. In "The 1st Degree" by Broderbund, a game for adults in which you are the district attorney (male, with a young, white, smart-alecky woman assistant who develops much of the context information), you have to make a case for first-degree murder. You interview witnesses in their surroundings to get an idea of the context in which they live. The point of the game is not to solve the mystery but to make the case, which requires figuring out people's motivations and relationships, rather than establishing facts. Witnesses from whom you have learned the truth will lie on the stand if you have not persuaded them to join you. The story is more about the underlying emotional realities than about the grisly deed. This makes sense to girls.

Games with an electronic doll-house "feel" seem to be attractive to girls. An example is "SimTown" by Maxis, an environmental problem-solving game that lets you customize your own character, find out how the population feels, and lift the roof off the houses to see what's going on inside. "Hollywood" by Viacom is another kind of electronic doll house. Here, you can make animated movies with a set of characters and settings. You can write dialogue, select actions for character animation, customize the characters by giving them personality traits, and then record and play the movie. "Imagination Express" by Edmark is another doll house with good backgrounds, plenty of characters and objects, and the ability to add a little animation as well as captions. This program makes constructing settings fun because the objects, people and things, have a good deal of intelligence built

into them. They twist and turn and place themselves appropriately behind, in front of, over or under things, and change size to maintain the illusion of depth.

Some of the new software coming out for girls, such as "Let's Talk About Me" by Simon & Schuster Interactive, are not exactly games. "Let's Talk About Me" is marketed as a handbook, and provides some activities girls might like. As for the other new electronic girls' games, some are good, some are not so good. The main differences are in the content rather than in the kind of activity they privilege. Most puzzles are still too unintegrated, and the choices are too few. The interactivity is still not conceptual enough. And we worry that the folks likely to have the money to develop complex activities may confuse content with marketing and end up reaffirming stereotypes. They may fail to realize that the desired forms of activity can be applied to a wide range of content girls are interested in, not just to catching a boyfriend. But at least somebody's finally working on the problem.

Our final thought is this. Boys can use games to escape into a fantasy world which allows them to prepare themselves for the requirements of adult masculinity. They can gird their digital loins with magical potencies and vanquish enemies with their limitless strength. They can also get killed, over and over, along the way, until they have achieved the degree of mastery that makes them champions. Then they can reach into the full storehouse of boy games and accept another challenge. The cultural prescriptions for masculinity are harsh and exacting. Few boys can feel secure about achieving a sufficient degree of masculinity. The pressure is relentless—and these games provide a fun, painless opportunity to boost their sense of masculinity and let off some steam.

The cultural prescriptions for femininity are equally stringent—and they are also internally contradictory. Girls are expected to be both frail and enduring, helpless and competent, fun loving and sensitive, emotional and available, needy and nurturing, vain and moral. <u>Girls need games in which they can rehearse and express the ambiguities and contradictions of femininity.</u> Navigating the shoals of femininity is the stuff girls think about. It is an endless conundrum: how to do the right thing when all the available options force you to choose against yourself, how to maintain a sense of pleasure and confidence in yourself when all the paths before you lead to danger; how to satisfy everybody without calling undue attention to yourself. Girls need games in which they can take their own side, act out, throw caution to the winds and watch what happens. They need games in which they survive, again and again, until they have achieved a state of grace that makes them happy. Then they need to reach into a growing storehouse of girl games and play another story. The pressure on girls is relentless, too. Becoming a woman is a tricky business. Girls could use some games that provide a fun, painless opportunity to bolster their sense of femininity and to stretch their wings.

References

Bennett, D. 1993. "Voices of Young Women in Engineering." Paper presented at the 10th International Conference on Technology in Education. Cambridge, MA: Massachusetts Institute of Technology.

Bennett, D., Brunner, C., and Honey, M. 1996. "Gender and Technology: Designing for Diversity." Paper written for the Regional Equity Forum on Math, Science and Technology Education. Cosponsored by EDC's WEEA Equity Resource Center, Northeastern University Comprehensive Resource Center for Minorities, TERC, and Mass Pep.

Brunner, C. 1991. "Gender and Distance Learning." In L. Roberts and V. Horner, eds., *The Annals of Political and Social Science.* Beverly Hills: Sage Press, 133–145.

Brunner C., Hawkins, J., and Honey, M. 1988. "Making Meaning: Technological Expertise and the Use of Metaphor." Paper presented at the American Educational Research Association, New Orleans.

Hawkins, J., Brunner, C., Clements, P., Honey, M., and Moeller, B. 1990. "Women and Technology: A New Basis for Understanding." Final report to the Spencer Foundation. New York: Center for Children and Technology, Bank Street College of Education.

Honey, M. 1994. "Maternal Voice in the Technological Universe." In D. Bassin, M. Honey, and M. Kaplan, eds., *Representations of Motherhood,* New Haven: Yale University Press.

Honey, M., Moeller, B., Brunner, C., Bennett, D. T., Clements, P., and Hawkins, J. 1991. "Girls and Design: Exploring the Question of Technological Imagination." Tech Rep. No. 17. New York: Bank Street College of Education, Center for Technology in Education.

Resnick, M. 1991. "Xylophones, Hamsters, and Fireworks: The Role of Diversity in Constructionist Activities." in I. Harel and S. Papert, eds., *Constructionism.* Norwood, MA: Ablex Publishing, 151–158.

46

All Het Up!:
Rescuing Heterosexuality on the *Oprah Winfrey Show*

Debbie Epstein
Deborah Lynn Steinberg

Keywords

feminist media studies; heterosexuality; sexuality; television; therapy; kinship

Introduction

The *Oprah Winfrey Show* is one of the United States' major cultural exports. It enjoys massive popularity in countless countries. Indeed, as Corinne Squire (1994) has pointed out, in one of the very few analytical discussions of the *Oprah Winfrey Show,* Oprah Winfrey has emerged as a significant cultural icon: one, we would suggest, who is on a scale comparable to that of Madonna; for example, both women have been subjected to an enormous amount of tabloid press attention and both have talked about and are embodiments of female celebrity writ large. However, while Madonna's life and cultural appeal have been minutely examined within a broad-ranging set of critical and feminist discourses (see, for example, hooks, 1992; Schwichtenberg, 1992), Oprah Winfrey seems to have generated a surprisingly small amount of attention from that quarter.

It appears that Madonna's version of "in your face" transgression has fed into and been fed by the current interest (if not "vogue") in the cultural study of sexuality.[1] Madonna not only presents herself as a sexual subject/object, but expressly proposes sexuality (graphic and confrontational) as a praxis of and towards artistic freedom, women's liberation and indeed, gay liberation. In this sense she can be seen to align herself with queer politics and even queer theory. hooks (1992) has critiqued Madonna's version of liberation and emancipatory praxis through sexuality as one which draws its substance from its "play" with the boundaries of white femininity counterposed against racialized/racist controlling myths of black (and we would add, lesbian and gay) sexualities. Oprah, on the other hand, does not present herself, and is not (usually) discussed,[2] in explicitly sexualized terms. However, if one examines her programmes, it is clear that her work raises many of the same significant issues as Madonna's work, including issues around gender and sexuality politics, around classism and racism and around feminism (among many other things). Moreover, while the terrain of the sexual *seems* to belong to Madonna, Oprah easily stakes an equal claim to this ground. Indeed, sexuality, its negotiation and mediation, is one of the core elements of the *Oprah Winfrey Show.*

In this regard, the show provides an interesting set of contradictions. On the one hand, it appears to challenge common-sense assumptions about relationships, specifically heterosexual relationships (for example, by consistently raising issues of sexual violence within a heterosexual context). Yet at the same time, Oprah's presentation often works to reinforce precisely the norms she seeks to challenge. Through a close analysis of a selection of programme clips from one particular programme among many about relationships, sexuality and families, this article will consider the ways in which the *Oprah Winfrey Show* both problematizes and yet normalizes the boundaries of heterosexuality. We shall discuss both the resolute exposure and exploration of what could be termed the casualties of normative (and compulsory) heterosexuality and, paradoxically, its recuperation as a "rational" ideal.

In exploring the ways in which this recuperation takes place, we shall begin with a brief consideration of the show on a broader scale. There are a number of discourses which shape it. We shall focus specifically on two: the discourse of therapy and that of kinship.[3] Our analysis of the sexual politics

of the *Oprah Winfrey Show* in these terms will focus on the programme, "How to Make Love Last" (18 January 1993). This programme is characteristic of the show both in the prominence it gives to therapeutic and kinship discourses and in the way it illustrates not only a presumption of universal heterosexuality but an active reinscription of heterosexuality as an idealized institution. Like so many other programmes, "How to Make Love Last" intends to highlight and deal with problems within heterosexual relationships as distressing but solvable (through the medium of therapeutic self-help). At another level, however, the programme also (unwittingly) reveals a different order of problems which, ironically, can only be reinforced by the mode of rescue proposed and staged. We have chosen to examine this programme, in part because of the prosaic character of problems experienced by each couple. That is to say, the programme "treats" the daily grind of unequal heterosexual relationships, rather than presenting overt or dramatic instances of abuse or violence. In this way, it represents one end of the continuum of problems which the show addresses in relationships between women and men. Indeed, as we shall see, within the programme itself connections are overtly as well as implicitly made (though not necessarily critically) between the "mundane" and the "extreme."

Our interest in exploring the sexual politics both of "How to Make Love Last" and of the *Oprah Winfrey Show* more generally is fuelled by the ways in which Oprah positions herself and her show within traditions of dissent drawn from feminism, the Civil Rights Movement and contemporary anti-racist struggle. Mellencamp (1992) and Squire (1994), for example, have commented on Oprah's women-centredness in both topic choice and personal manner; and Squire particularly locates Oprah within the general sphere of black feminism. Moreover, Oprah has consistently explained on the programme that it is her aim that the show be a source of education for personal empowerment and for challenging forms of abuse, discrimination and prejudice. For us, as feminist viewers, these dimensions of the programme are a central part of our investment in and enjoyment of it. They are also the source of some of our frustrations at those moments when or in those ways in which the format and framework of the programme work to undermine its anti-discriminatory possibilities. Our analysis of the ways in which these contradictions are illustrated in "How to Make Love Last," then, is forwarded against the backdrop of the radicalizing, anti-discriminatory potential we see and desire in the programme.

It is important to note that in examining dominant discourses which shape and are reproduced in the *Oprah Winfrey Show*, we are not suggesting that audiences necessarily receive the show in straightforward terms: indeed, the fact that we ourselves have been able to read against the grain of the show is evidence that this is not the case. However, we suggest that the presumption of heterosexuality, heterosexual kinship and discourses of therapy are strongly encoded into the *Oprah Winfrey Show* in ways which provide contradictory, but nevertheless preferred, readings. Neither have we used audience research for this particular article (although this is part of our much wider project about the show), since what interests us here are the ways in which the strong encodings of heterosexist and therapeutic discourses work within the text of the show itself. This article provides, then, a detailed deconstruction of the text of one *Oprah Winfrey Show* in relation to several specific but typical discourses in play within it.

The Fifty-Minute Hour

Therapy is one of the key dimensions of the *Oprah Winfrey Show*. It is manifested in the format of the programme and it provides a lens through which the programme's issues are understood. Characteristic of the programme are a number of therapeutic signifiers: for example, the ubiquitous "expert" (usually a psychologist with a Ph.D.); the mediating of a kind of group therapy encounter involving audience and guests under the direction of the "expert" and Oprah; and the staging of "therapy sessions" for guests (and sometimes for Oprah herself), which are witnessed by the audience (both studio and televisual).[4] The invited "expert" has, almost invariably, written a popular self-help book which is repeatedly plugged during the course of the programme and which is used to set the agenda both for the topic of the programme and for the way that topic is handled.

There is a certain appeal beyond the solely voyeuristic in the therapeutic format of the programme. First, it provides a space within which personal experience can be aired and validated. The importance of this should not be underestimated, particularly in the context of a programme aimed, as Oprah herself has frequently stated, at empowering people who generally do not have social power (for example, African-Americans and other "ethnic minorities" and women), at challenging discrimination and abuse through public education and at promoting a kind of encapsulated "democracy in action." Second, the *Oprah Winfrey Show*, along with the efforts of feminist activists, has been instrumental in making issues of violence and abuse by men against women and children publicly speakable. We recognize that making violence and abuse speakable cannot, by itself, solve the problems. Neither is the speakability of abuse unchallenged, as we can see from the recent publicity given to "false memory syndrome" (a notion which has infiltrated more than one of Oprah's shows). Finally, there is a relationship between the kind of testimony offered by Oprah's guests and the role which testifying has played in fuelling the organized pursuit of social justice in both the Civil Rights and Women's Liberation movements.

Despite this appeal, there are a number of tensions produced when a therapeutic discourse is used as a medium through which to understand personal and social issues. We would suggest that these tensions accrue to therapy as a framework in general as well as to the particular brand of therapy which is characteristic of the *Oprah Winfrey Show*. Elsewhere, we have explored problems with the discourse of therapy with respect to the show in more detail (see Epstein and Steinberg, 1995a, 1995b). It is beyond the scope of this article to reproduce these discussions. Nevertheless, it is important to outline some of the key issues raised by the therapy dimension of the *Oprah Winfrey Show* in order to contextualize our analysis of the negotiation of heterosexuality in the programme "How to Make Love Last."

The particular mode of therapy employed on the show is one which derives from the popular end of the self-help movement. This is typified in the "how to . . ." books which are often used to frame the programme. A common element of both self-help and therapy in general is that it tends to be very individualistic.[5] Problems are typically posed as individual pathologies subject to individual solutions. Moreover, within this context, the self and family are seen as the world and this has the effect of erasing both power relations and social context. As will be seen below, for example, issues around abuse are constructed as "negative patterns we repeat" rather than as indictments of unequal social relations. This kind of formula-

tion locates responsibility for suffering, and indeed for abuse, primarily, if not only, within the "victim" and sets up terms of enquiry which do not (and perhaps cannot) interrogate perpetrators.

A second and related assumption underpinning the therapy mode of the *Oprah Winfrey Show* is the notion that "we can help ourselves" (and, indeed, that *only* we can help ourselves). Thus, if we set up our own destructive patterns in order to repeat them, we can break these cycles by "working on ourselves." Again in this context, the emphasis is on personal healing rather than social change, on individual rather than collective action. Personal healing is clearly a key issue for "survivors"[6] of abuse and other kinds of damage. But a limited focus on the personal can beg the question of how personal healing can be possible *without* an analysis of the power relations and social contexts within which sexual, physical or emotional abuses take place. Furthermore, we would hold that even where "negative patterns" do not involve obvious forms of abuse, all relationships are implicated in and bespeak a range of social inequalities.

In this context there is an implication that the route to self-healing can he accomplished centrally, if not totally, through a set programme of therapeutic exercises or steps (whether twelve or not). The reliance on this kind of programmatic "therapy" is, inevitably, reductionist and mechanistic. To make a healing process programmatic, in itself implies that all problems can be dealt with in the same way. It mitigates against making necessary distinctions, for example, between different forms or levels of abuse and miscommunication and making necessary connections between the personal and the social/political. Moreover, it implicitly suggests that things can be "fixed" quickly, if not in a fifty-minute television programme, then in the space of a popular book, or, as Oprah wishfully suggests on "How to Make Love Last," seven hours of Harville and Helen Hendrix (the former being the invited expert) talking about their "conscious marriage" on video.

Kith and (un)kin(d)

Kinship work, that is, mediating the making, breaking and negotiating of familial and romantic relationships, is another staple of the *Oprah Winfrey Show*. As with therapy, kinship work is specifically staged. Countless programmes feature reunions of estranged family members, meetings of blood relations who have never met ("Fathers and the Sons they Never Knew," 31 October 1990; "Baby Selling," 26 May 1993), introductions of potential (heterosexual) partners (e.g. "Desperate Women meet Alaskan Men," 17 February 1989) and issues around sexual, romantic and family relationships (e.g. "Obnoxious Husbands," 11 January 1989, "Raising a Child with Family Values," 6 April 1993 (Part IV of the "Family Series")).

Therapy often provides the conceptual foundations for the evaluation of kinship relations. For example, there seems to be a general assumption that almost all family relationships are, in the language of the show itself, "dysfunctional" (until you work on yourself). It seems to us that when people on the programme say things like "I come from a dysfunctional family," what they are trying to describe is an experience of unhappiness, abuse and/or betrayal in relation to their own families. The term "dysfunction" clearly describes this unhappiness and simultaneously invokes the possibility of change. This, in our view, is an obvious reason for the currency which has been gained by the term "dysfunctional family" on and beyond the programme. Another reason may be the ways in which therapy has become a key part of American popular cul-

ture and indeed has provided a kind of lingua franca for discussing personal and emotional difficulties. It is interesting to consider how this particular dimension of the language of the *Oprah Winfrey Show* translates in a British context where therapy has not become embedded in popular common sense (or experience) to anything like the same extent. Yet, whatever particular participants in the programme might mean when they use it, to invoke the term "dysfunction" nevertheless also calls into play the specifically medicalized, pathological connotations of the word. Furthermore, "dysfunction" implies "function." Because of this, programme participants' investments in escaping their unhappiness become inextricably entwined with an investment in the fantasy of the "functional family," a notion which has historically been defined as the conventional, nuclear family.

Indeed, the discourse of kinship underpinning the *Oprah Winfrey Show* has particular racialized and class-specific dimensions. It is the white, middle-class family which is constructed as both the object of desire and project of therapy. In this context, a range of familial relationships are made Other. This is illustrated in programmes such as "Lesbian and Gay Baby Boom" (10 May 1993), in which Oprah places lesbian and gay parents in a defensive position by stating that "[t]he big question that a lot of people want to, ask, I know, is will their kids also grow up to be gay or will they be emotionally damaged?" (p. 2). Although the grammar of this sentence may suggest that the children will be emotionally damaged if they are *not* gay, the meaning of the sentence, in context, is clearly that being gay bespeaks emotional damage and that having a gay parent is, axiomatically, emotionally damaging to children. It is this accusation against which her lesbian and gay guests were required to defend themselves;

that is, much of the show was devoted to disproving the accusation. In addition, this programme clearly assumed a heterosexual audience; it was not lesbians and gays who constituted the "many people who want[ed] to know." The "Othering" process is also illustrated in the ways in which working-class parents often come in for audience abuse, being blamed for the oppressions and deprivations that they experience which may be damaging to their children. We would suggest that this process results from an underestimation of the power of common-sense discourses. Oprah frequently frames a programme by posing a question which she clearly wishes to have nullified, for example, "won't children be damaged by having gay parents?" Effectively, this means she is positioning her audience, herself and her guests inside the discourse. At the same time she lays the responsibility for the overthrow of the discourse at the feet of the very people who are disempowered, thus ironically locking the programme into the very common sense she is trying to challenge.

Furthermore, there is a racialization of Oprah's kinship work which takes place in a number of different ways. First, it is rare to see any but white/Anglo families presented as the ideal. (In the four months during which we taped every programme transmitted in the UK, there was not one occasion on which a family of colour was held out as a positive example.) Indeed, most of Oprah's guests are white (although the studio audience is normally mixed). Second, the configuration of the ideal family is itself exclusive. As shown in the programme "Raising a Child with Family Values" (6 April 1993), these values are implicitly linked with wealth, particular assumptions underpinning white middle-class culture and quite conventional heterosexual divisions of labour. Third, Oprah's invited experts are virtually all white, and where they have been black that has largely been in the context of programmes about racism. So, in effect, much of Oprah's work involves the mediation of white expertise and white kinship relations. The combination of expertise and selection of guests thus provides a white heterosexual and middle-class backdrop against which all kinship relations are to be measured.

So far then, we have noted that the *Oprah Winfrey Show* makes the link between kinship and work at two levels. First, there is the work, performed by Oprah and her invited experts, of mediating the relationships of guests and various audience members. Second, kinship is, in itself, posited *as* work, specifically (and ideally) as therapeutic work on oneself. As numerous feminists have argued, kinship work is generally done by women. Moreover, not only is it gendered (Chodorow, 1978, 1989; Rubin, 1975); it is also racialized and classed within a broader "heterosexual matrix." For example, the maintenance of white families has often been done by black women both under slavery and after its abolition (Collins, 1990; hooks, 1982). Furthermore, the modes of kinship work and conditions under which it takes place are class and culture specific (Anthias and Yuval-Davis, 1992; Barrett and Macintosh, 1982; Delphy, 1984). As we shall see on "How to Make Love Last," these dimensions of the politics of kinship work are reflected and reproduced on the *Oprah Winfrey Show*.

The therapeutic kinship, work which is done (and promoted) on the programme often takes the form of an attempt to retrieve what is seen as "dysfunctional" in order to make it desirable, ideal and in every way "functional." In other words, the underpinning framework is one which identifies much that is "wrong" in normative heterosexuality, but draws back from using this as a basis of critique of the institutions of heterosexuality. Rather, building on the therapy mode, the *Oprah Winfrey Show* locates these problems centrally in the individual and the work, on the self and, in the process, maintains the heterosexual family and heterosexual relationships as ideal.

In this context, the show could be said to provide a window on "the long grey stream of heterosexual misery" (Duncker, 1993: 142).[7] The programmes display a continuum of gendered abuse in relationships (from men who don't listen to women to those who are violent to their female partners and their children).[8] However, within the therapeutic/kinship framework of the show, a gendered analysis of power seems to be resolutely resisted. Thus, for example, while child abuse and domestic violence are regularly interrogated and condemned, they are not examined in relation to gendered social inequalities. This is typically manifested in the ways which female "survivors" of domestic violence are invariably subjected to interrogation by expert guests, Oprah and the audience while male perpetrators are taken for granted. In this context, women survivors are typically asked to defend themselves against the accusatory question "why didn't you leave him?," a question which implicitly constructs the woman as "passive" aggressor and as responsible for the commission of (male) violence against her. We have only viewed two occasions during scores of programme hours on this topic, in which a male perpetrator is asked to explain and defend *his* choice to injure and violate a (female) partner or a child (who has not injured him). Instead, as noted above, concerns are raised about "patterns *we* set up and repeat," about misunderstandings and miscommunications, all of which may be remedied by a combination of therapy and "rational" dialogue. Precisely because it does not con-

sider the issues of power and inequality, the currency of the notion of "patterns we repeat" makes comprehensible why women are interrogated for not leaving situations of domestic violence. Leaving could be construed both as "breaking the pattern" and as a "rational" response to the situation. Thus kinship is located not within a matrix of power relations, but rather within one of presumed equality where relationship problems derive only from unresolved and irrational patterns which we (sic) set up in childhood.

A Stitch In Time? Making Love Last

"How to Make Love Last" (broadcast in the UK as "Unsuccessful in Love") invites us, the audience, to observe the mediation of two heterosexual relationships which are "having problems": Cari and Dale are seeking a divorce and Jay and Madelene, a relatively "new" couple, are beginning to run into problems. In the expert seat is Harville Hendrix Ph.D., therapist and author of two self-help books: *Getting the Love you Want* and *Keeping the Love you Find* and, as Oprah informs us, "he also has this great new series of home videos for couples that [we are] going to be seeing . . . throughout this program" (p. 1).[9] The show stages each couple undertaking a potted therapy session following the format which we are given to understand is proposed in Harville's second book. Harville and Oprah put each couple through a series of paces on stage. It is made clear that these are intended to provide a model for us, the audience, to work on ourselves as a way of working on our relationships and ultimately to make love last, or failing that, to dissolve our relationships in a "rational" fashion.

Framing Heterosexuality

Oprah: OK. So you're smart and you're strong. And you're successful in every area of your life but love. What *is* it that keeps you from having a happy love life? This show today is going to help you unlock a lot of those fears, 'cause that's really what it is. And the beauty of this show is, is that it applies to everybody, whether you're married, whether you're divorced, whether you're single, whether you're looking, whether you're looking and single, looking to get rid of the man you already have, the woman you already have—everybody! (*Audience laughter*) (p. 1).

From the start, Oprah invokes a universal "you." This "you" in fact locates the programme squarely within a terrain of heterosexual kinship on at least two levels. First, Oprah's litany of "whethers" has some obvious omissions. While there are explicit referents for heterosexual partnering (e.g. "married," "divorced") such referents are lacking, for example, for lesbian and gay relationships. It could be argued that this omission is not deliberately exclusive.[10] And, indeed, "getting rid of the man you already have . . . etc." could conceivably refer to same-sex partners. However, we would suggest that such a reading would necessarily be against the grain of the flow of the list of relational possibilities which purportedly includes "everybody." We would suggest that Oprah's list assumes heterosexual guests, audience and a heterosexual issue, all of which are taken as universal.

Second, there seems to be a related assumption that people whose relationships *are* excluded from the list can (and should) nevertheless relate to and through the parameters of heterosexuality. Thus, for example, the lesbian or gay viewer is offered a straight subject position through which to understand her or his own relationships and to participate in the ostensible global vil-

lage of Oprah's educative democracy. In this context, what is offered at best is a kind of "liberal equivalence"[11] drawn between (rather conventional) straight relationships and nonstraight relationships. To draw this kind of equivalence, which is characteristic of the *Oprah Winfrey Show* more generally (and in relation to a range of issues), has the effect of erasing social context and material relations of social inequality. It denies that the character of sexual/intimate/familial/friendship relationships (amongst others) are shaped through the social positions of the people involved in them.[12] Furthermore, the presumption of heterosexuality set up in Oprah's opening speech is reinforced and further narrowed as we are introduced to Oprah's guests, the ubiquitous white professional expert and the two white couples whose visual presentations are clearly affluent as well as conventionally attractive.[13]

Framing Therapy

After opening the programme in this way, Oprah's introduction of her expert guest, Harville Hendrix, initiates an interchange which locates the programme firmly within the therapy discourse. Here, we see the key assumptions, discussed above, with respect to the therapeutic discourse of the programme more generally, exemplified in strikingly stark terms. Right from the start, Oprah tells us that Harville is going to help us "examine the patterns *we* set up in our childhood" (p. 1, our emphasis).

Oprah: . . . there are a lot of things that I like about this [Harville's work] is that there are a whole lot of cause and effects that you set up.
Harville: Yes.
Oprah: One that concerns me is if you were abused as a child, you may pick an abusive partner or be an abuser yourself.
Harville: Yes. That—that's always the case. Whatever happens in childhood,

whether its mild or intense, there is something that's going to replicate itself in adulthood in an intimate partnership. Because the early childhood experience where there's a wound has to be repaired. And it always has to be repaired in adulthood with somebody similar to your parents.

Oprah: Now, doesn't—can't you get over that, though? Because, see, I believe that—that all of my relationships in my 20s and early 30s were—were—I continued the abusive pattern that *I* set up in my childhood.

Harville: Yes.

Oprah: Stedman is not an abusive person. So I think I've gotten over that.

Harville: Yeah. And that's the clue, when you're saying that in the 20s and 30s, you began to work on some things in yourself (p. 2).

Here we see a painful example of the theory of the "cycle of abuse" and the way in which it shifts responsibility from the abuser to the abused. Indeed, it is excruciating to see Oprah talking about her experience of being abused as a child in terms of "the abusive pattern that *I* set up in my childhood." In other programmes Oprah has been clear that abuse is not the fault of the child and it seems likely that she would extend that to herself. It seems a testament to the seductiveness of the cycle of abuse theory that she could make such a reversal in this context. This shifting of responsibility is reinforced twice more. Not only are those who have been abused effectively held, within this formulation, to be responsible for the original abuse, but they are also held to be responsible for any repetition of these abusive dynamics in their adult relationships. Moreover, it seems as if they are seen as ultimately able to challenge these dynamics only by changing ("working on") themselves rather than, for example, calling upon abusers to change (or indeed calling upon the police).

This construction is all the more disquieting for its refusal to acknowledge or consider the gendered character of child abuse (particularly of child sexual abuse) and of abuse within adult relationships. At the very least, if we take into consideration the skewed gender profile of abusers and abused, to posit those who are abused as responsible for "setting up the patterns" implicitly posits girls/women as responsible for what is largely male perpetrated abuse. Thus the call to "work on ourselves" means, in effect, a call primarily for women to be the ones who change. As we shall see below, this responsibility is also located with the women (i.e. Cari and Madelene) in the particular relationships under scrutiny in this programme. Moreover, within this paradigm, there seems to be an extraordinary implication that men have no agency or responsibility in relationships.

A second point which emerges from this interchange is the mechanistic and unidimensional construction of cause and effect in the formulation of repeated patterns. It seems, from what Harville says, that the future life of the "wounded" child is pre-indeed, over-determined. This point is driven home through a subsequent exchange in which Oprah asks Harville to explain the outcome of a range of childhood "wounds" (e.g. having a jealous parent, a critical parent, a parent who abandons you and so on). Harville's response is to explain that all these patterns are invariably repeated by the child-as-adult. More specifically, he posits that:

Harville: You either pick 'em, provoke 'em or project on to them. But if you had—if you had a problem in childhood, you're going to pick somebody to help you redo it. If they don't, then you'll project on to them that they are. And if they aren't, you'll provoke them into doing it. Because we have to resolve that issue . . . . . . It's like—in an adult relationship, you'll either act like

the child that you did with your parents
or you'll behave like the parents behaved toward you as a child.
Oprah: Isn't that fascinating?
Harville: It's really fascinating and it's so
predictable (pp. 5-6).

In addition to the stark and mechanistic
determinism of this posited pattern, we see
here a case in point of the construction of
parents as world-entire for the child. Moreover, Harville seems to consider two parents
as a single entity. If this were not the case,
it would not be possible to choose *a* partner
like "your parents."

Rescuing Heterosexuality

What Harville is saying then, is that children are invariably wounded in and through
their relationships with their parents and
that they are then trapped into repeating
those wounding patterns in their adult relationships (and implicitly with their own
children). If this is true,[14] it could be construed that Harville is making a considerable indictment of normative heterosexual
paradigms of "the family." However, it is
clear in the context of the programme that
this is far from Harville's (or Oprah's) intention. This is demonstrated by the way
that, having defined "the problem" in these
terms, Harville then goes on (with Oprah) to
recuperate conventional modes of family
and marriage. This recuperation is achieved
in two ways. First, through the display of
Harville and Helen Hendrix as living the
ideal (or as Helen puts it "conscious") marriage. Here a short extract of Harville's
seven hours of instructive self-help video is
screened, showing Harville and Helen talking rather mawkishly about their relationship. Oprah shows us how we are meant to
respond to this spectacle when she comments:

Oprah: So that clip we just saw . . . that
was Harville and his wife. And I was

saying that is really—that's—I mean I
got a little goosebump looking at it because that's what marriage should feel
like. You should feel like you're—it
should be like unconditional love. You
should feel like you're totally supported
and loved just because of who you are
(p. 11).

The notion of "conscious marriage"
seems a rather odd, if not invidious proposition. At one level it seems to posit that the
problem with most marriages is that they are
in some basic way "irrational." There is also
a connotation here that they are "involuntary." A "conscious" marriage is constructed as an act of rational agency.
Together with Oprah's understanding of
this as a state of (implicitly egalitarian) "unconditional" love and acceptance, there is
the implication that *we* can determine the
fundamental character of our relationships
abstracted from the conditions in which
they occur, that we can, as male and female
individuals, for example, simply *choose* to
be equal. Indeed, this would posit that individual "consciousness" can supersede or
cancel out the social/legal/economic meanings of marriage as a contract historically
premised upon sexual/gender inequality. In
sum, the notion of "conscious" marriage
either presumes a gendered social equality
that does not exist and/or it promises that
individualized "consciousness" is a route to
interpersonal equality which, in itself, implicitly overrides *social* inequalities. We
are not suggesting that heterosexual couples
have no agency in their relationships. However, we would argue that all choices are
constrained by and through social conditions and the complex social positions of the
actors. In addition to the romanticization of
the very relationships which were earlier
problematized by Harville (and Oprah), a
second way that conventional heterosexuality is recuperated is through the notion of
self-help. The idea of self-help, as we noted

earlier in this article, is premised upon those therapies adopting programmatic approaches to individual change. Harville's books (and videos) are seen to provide a rational route to the realization of this ideal of heterosexual love. Underlying the process is the assumption of equality within heterosexual relationships and it is presumably necessary that both men and women undertake this work. However, as we shall see, the primary responsibility for the work of self-help is clearly laid at the feet of the women in the relationships shown on the programme.[15]

Setting the Women Up (1)

The next phase of the programme begins with Oprah introducing Dale and Cari Reporto who are about to get a divorce. As noted above, what will follow is that Dale and Cari will undertake a brief therapy session, mediated by Harville, for the dissolution of their marriage. It is therefore necessary for Oprah and Harville first to locate Dale and Cari's relationship problems within Harville's framework. Thus, Oprah's opening sentence to Dale and Cari is: "Did any of this sound familiar to you?" (p. 14). Cari responds by saying that she recognized the pattern of herself being critiqued by Dale, a pattern which she had experienced from her parents. Dale agrees:

> *Dale:* Yeah. Well, I know I'm very critical of her.
> *Oprah:* Uh huh.
> *Dale:* So that's exactly what you're talking about.
> *Oprah:* And you were criticised a lot as a child? (p. 15).

At this point, one might have expected Dale to answer Oprah's question ("And you were criticised a lot as a child?") since it was his comment that provoked it (and since within Harville's framework either/both being criticized and/or being a critic would be

the result of having critical parents). In other words, it would have been logical for the "you" in Oprah's question to have referred to Dale. Yet what actually happens is that it is Cari who responds by saying:

> *Cari:* In a lot of ways, it was for the betterment . . . (ibid.).

So, within the space of a moment, the emphasis on the problems of the *couple* shifted to an emphasis on Cari's problematic patterns; that is, the "you," as the object of enquiry, became female. In viewing the programme, we were initially perplexed about how the shift of attention from Dale to Cari as the object of the "you" had been accomplished. With the camera focused on Dale, what was immediately visible was that, following Oprah's question, he looked towards Cari to answer. What we were not clear about at first was whether he or whether Oprah had instituted the shift. It was only when we watched the video in slow motion that we were able to detect that Oprah, herself, had turned her gaze on Cari as she asked the question.

After being introduced in this way, there follows a "good-bye process." Harville explains the purpose of the exercise:

> *Harville:* The—the whole point is that you need—in preparation for marriage, you need to finish what you didn't finish or what's left over from another relationship. And this good-bye process is, in a sense, an essential ingredient in getting ready to go on to your next relationship or to go on with your life if you decide not to go on to another relationship, but to finish that (p. 18).

This suggests that although *a* marriage may have been negative and therefore in need of dissolution, the desirable outcome is the repetition of the pattern of getting married. This is despite Harville's disclaimer which, as one views the programme, clearly comes through as an afterthought. In other words, while marriage is understood at one level to be constituted out of negative patterns by the individuals involved in it, at another level the *institution* of marriage is seen as being a positive pattern and (re)marriage is set up again as an unquestioned object of desire. (Interestingly, Harville's view that one needs to resolve problems in one relationship before moving on to another one through a "good-bye process" excludes the very relationship, i.e. with the parents, which Harville identifies as the origin of all "problem patterns.")

The staged therapy that follows illustrates the implicit assumption that problematic patterns are located in the woman. The actual exercise consists of each partner in turn going through a set sequence of "saying good-bye," first to the "bad parts" of the marriage, then to the "good parts," then to the dream of what might have been and finally to the marriage as a whole. The other partner is asked to "mirror" back what has just been said (i.e. "if I'm hearing you right, you are saying good-bye to . . ."). In this process, there is an appearance and, indeed, an ostensible assumption of equality between the two partners. With Dale and Cari, this is visually reinforced by the way they are sitting: each faces the other (squared off) and in profile to the audience with Harville, facing front, between them. There are two particular interchanges in which the gender bias of the process becomes poignantly clear.

In the first exchange, Cari has just been asked to begin the "good-bye" to the "bad things" in the marriage.

> *Cari:* I'd like to say good-bye to being critiqued as often as I was. To always having to prove that I'm better than what you thought I was. And I'd like to say good-bye to some of the frugality that existed between us. And I'll be happy to say good-bye to the struggling with who I am on the one hand to make

you happy and on the other hand to make me happy.
> *Harville:* OK. So just—just briefly, can you paraphrase back the part—the bad part she's saying good-bye to in the relationship?
> *Dale:* Sure. As to the critiquing, she's right I . . .
> *Harville:* Yeah. And don't explain it. Just say, so I'm hearing you say—you're saying good-bye to the critiquing.
> *Dale:* Right.
> *Harville:* Just mirror it back and paraphrase it back.
> *Dale:* To the living up to my standards instead of yours and doing what I want you to do. And I really don't feel any of that's true.
> *Harville:* No. I don't want you to comment. *(audience laughter)* (pp. 18-19).

In a later exchange, Dale is "saying good-bye" to the "good stuff" about the marriage:

> *Harville:* OK. Now shift to the good stuff that won't ever be again with the end of this marriage.
> *Oprah: (whispering off camera)* Oh this is so sad.
> *Dale:* OK. The good stuff . . .
> *Harville:* Say good-bye to that.
> *Dale: (looking at Harville)* With a lot of fun, a lot of good conversations.
> *Harville:* And tell it to *her.*
> *Dale:* Your enthusiasm about everything you did from who you came in to [sic] work and who you talked to. And that I never really had to carry a conversation, that you could carry the whole conversation; that you're always smiling; you're always up. You were never depressed. That when you were depressed, it was over minor things like—oh, just nonsense things. I can't even think of them. And that we could go places and do things and I never had to be embarrassed of you or that you would never be, you know . . . (p. 25).

It is interesting to note that Dale finds it difficult both to listen to Cari and to address her. Not only does he need repeated reminders to paraphrase what Cari has said, he also often fails to talk *to* her when he is saying his good-byes. By contrast, Cari addresses Dale throughout and, when it comes to her turn to paraphrase, does so with great articulacy and accuracy.[16] This would suggest that what we are seeing here, ironically, *is* a pattern in the relationship, but one which is not commented upon by Harville, Oprah or, indeed, by Dale or Cari: that is, a pattern of relating in which the listening is mostly one way (i.e. Cari listens to Dale but not vice versa). We would argue that in a performance situation (such as appearing on television or in front of an audience) it is difficult to do that which you have not rehearsed. It seemed to us that the reason Cari was able to perform the exercise easily and Dale was not was because she was practiced in listening to and engaging with someone else and he was not. Indeed, this seems precisely what Dale means when he tells us that he "never had to really carry a conversation, that [Cari] could carry the whole conversation." Not only does this seem to be a pattern in Dale and Cari's particular relationship, it is well documented that active listening is gendered (see, for example, Cameron, 1985; Spender, 1980).

Second, it is striking that Dale describes, as one of the good things about the marriage, that Cari was depressed only over minor things which he was unable to remember. In the context of everything they had both said about the relationship, this appears to represent a trivialization of Cari's feelings. It seems likely that Cari's experiences of depression were not "trivial" to her (and indeed, it is likely that the experience of being married to someone who has difficulty listening to you and who criticizes you constantly would be profoundly depressing). It is also possible that Cari had been depressed over "serious things" (like being constantly critiqued/put down) and Dale did not register it. Cari's body language and facial expression (shown in reac-

tion shots) during this speech seemed to emanate considerable frustration and anger, suggesting that her experience was quite different from Dale's version of it. This seems to be another pattern of gendered inequality between Dale and Cari which escapes comment in the programme.

Finally, and most importantly, what is made clear here is that Dale's problem in the marriage concerns the sort of person Cari is. Cari's problem, on the other hand, is Dale's problem with her, as she indicates in her comment about "always having to prove that I'm better than what you thought I was." In other words, Cari is, in herself, the territory of dispute here. This is clear even when Dale is saying good-bye to the good parts of the marriage. The blatant arrogance of the statement that one of the good things was "never [having] to be embarrassed of [her]" is a clear indication that she was expected to live out his fantasies of what marriage should be and of what a wife should be. Her inevitable "failure" to do so is obviously the subject of his constant criticism of her. Moreover, it is reinforced throughout the rest of the exercise that Dale also has a problem with Cari having a life and relationships outside of her relationship with him. More specifically, Dale criticizes Cari for having friendships which, in his view she prioritizes over him, and indeed, he points out that even her son Drake claims more of Cari's attention than he does (though he superficially acknowledges that this is understandable).

Setting the Women Up (2)

The final segment of the programme involves what Harville terms "a process called changing our frustration into a positive communication—a behaviour change request" (p. 31) in relation to the second (recently formed) couple, Jay and Madelene. As with Dale and Cari, the segment begins with an identification of the couple's "problem" within Harville's therapeutic framework. The exercise then follows the same pattern as the good-bye exercise in two ways: first, what they are asked to do is programmatic in the same terms (i.e. involving the mirroring process); and second, the terrain of the problem is located in the woman.

> *Oprah:* Joining us are Jay and Madelene. They've been going out now for about a year, but they already have minor conflicts. She's shy and he's the life of the party. And how's that bringing about conflict, guys?
>
> *Madelene:* When we go out—before we go out, I usually ask him who will be there. And if there's anyone I know that will be there. And he gets mad at me that I ask him that. And I'm the type—well, he'll go to a party, he'll walk in. And he'll just—he won't know anyone, but he'll just talk to anyone. And I'm the type where I'll walk in, I'll talk to people, but it takes me a while to warm up.
>
> *Oprah:* And isn't that what attracted you to him?
>
> *Madelene:* Yes. *(audience laughter)*
>
> *Oprah:* So why is there now conflict?
>
> *Madelene:* He—'cause he gets mad at me.
>
> *Oprah:* For not being . . .
>
> *Madelene:* For—well, he gets mad at me when I ask him about—when I ask him questions, "well, who's going to be there?" (p. 28).

What we see here is that Madelene is describing a dynamic similar to the one between Dale and Cari; that is, as Madelene puts it, Jay has a problem with her shyness and Madelene has a problem with Jay's problem with her. The subject of the whole interchange was supposedly Madelene's frustration with Jay. However, this is quickly turned into an enquiry into Madelene herself when Oprah asks "isn't that what attracted you to him?", a question which is not at any time asked of Jay. Jay, by contrast, is never asked what attracted

him to Madelene. The shift of scrutiny is reinforced when Harville then explains:

> *Harville:* You always are attracted to somebody who has a strength you don't have. Then, when you get involved in the relationship, that strength becomes a problem to you and then you criticise them and ask them to give that strength away (p. 30).

Clearly, Harville's comment cannot be ascribed to Jay. It can only be Jay's ability to "get on with people," not Madelene's shyness, which is construed as the strength the other partner does not have. Nor, within these parameters can we know what "strength" (if any) Jay is attracted to in Madelene since only her "weakness" (shyness) is mentioned. We would argue, furthermore, that there is a mis-ascription here. Harville seems to he saying that Madelene is both attracted to (if not envious of) and critical of Jay's outgoing personality and ability to mix. However, it seems to us that while she is indeed attracted to his gregariousness, what angers her is his insensitivity to her feelings. Harville conflates extroversion and insensitivity—two quite different qualities. Furthermore, according to Harville's analysis, *Madelene* seems to have constructed (or projected) her own frustration with herself on to Jay. In other words, Madelene only *has* a problem because she *is* the problem. Jay, on the other hand, has a problem because Madelene is a problem.

Given this reversal, it is hardly surprising that the exercise which ensues becomes a parody of itself:

> *Harville:* Madelene is going to communicate a frustration to Jay.
>
> *Madelene:* Jay, it gets me really mad when we are going out that you jump down on me and say, "Why do you get that way?" I want to—it gets me mad that you know how I am but you yell at me for how I—I am.

Harville: So then, the next process is to mirror that back so you're sure you've got it, Jay. So, if I got it right . . .

Jay: If I got it right, I—I understand that I shouldn't be getting all over you for, you know, not being more aggressive or—or not being as loud as I am.

Harville: Did I get it?

Jay: Did I get that right?

Madelene: Yes.

Harville: OK. Now, we want you to change that frustration into what you would want instead, which if you had it, you wouldn't be frustrated. We call that "the desire hidden in the frustration."

Madelene: Jay, when we go out, I wish that when we're at a party or some where where I don't know a lot of people, that you would come up to me and put your arm around me and say "How're you doing?" (pp. 31-2).

At this point, it seems clear that what Madelene is asking for is for Jay to be aware of how she is feeling, to notice her when they are in company and, in fact, to be *with* her. It is significant that she describes her feeling about Jay's behaviour as anger ("it makes me mad") while Harville again misascribes to her a very different emotion. "Frustration" is defined as "having a sense of discouragement and dissatisfaction" *(Chambers Twentieth Century Dictionary)* which may indeed lead to anger but is not the same thing. In attributing to Madelene frustration rather than anger, Harville effectively trivializes what she actually says. It is also important to note that, while Harville seems to construct Madelene as "criticising Jay's strength," Jay, by contrast, seems to understand that Madelene is criticizing his insensitivity in expecting her to be "aggressive or— . . . as loud as [he is]." However, in the exchange which follows, Harville and Oprah, between them, subvert Jay's understanding by requiring from Madelene a mechanistic, behaviour modification type of demand. Harville says:

Harville: OK. Now I want you to refine it a little more. And say how many—usually we give a timeframe to it, which is the practice, the training period. Like for the next month, each time we're at a party, I'd like you to come up to me once or twice or three times or whatever . . .

This forces Madelene into the rather absurd position of saying:

Madelene: Jay, for the next month, I'd like—when we do go to a party, I'd like you to come up to me and introduce me to people and to . . .

Oprah: How—how many times?

Harville: Once—once or twice or three times?

Madelene: Three times.

Harville: Three times *(audience laughter)*. All right.

Jay: OK. If I—Madelene, if I got it right, you want me to, in the course of the next month, when we go to these parties, I'll come up to you at least three times and tell you that I'm thinking of you and that I know you're there. Do I have this right?

Madelene: You got it right.

Harville: OK. And now . . .

Oprah: Can I just stop you here and say— and make note of how important this is? The reason why this struck me—I don't know if it struck you guys, too, and you guys watching at home—is because so many times—like when she said that at first . . .

Harville: Yes.

Oprah: . . . Like, "I'd like you to come up to me at a party." You have in your own mind about how many times it would make you comfortable.

Harville: That's right.

Oprah: But he doesn't know what those times are unless you say it. But you assume that because you've now said, "I want you to come up to me at the party," that he knows how many times. That's why the how many times, although it sounded a little corny, really was really effective and essential (p. 33).

Once more, Jay seems, despite the mention of frequency, to understand the gist of what Madelene was really saying. But Harville and Oprah's insistence on putting a number on Madelene's request again makes light of what is a far from trivial problem. It misconstrues as quantitative a problem which is, in fact, qualitative. As with Dale and Cari, what seems at issue here is a pattern of male expectations of ideal wife/girlfriend imposed on his partner through critique of her person. The audience's laughter during this exchange seems to indicate an awareness of how inappropriate the quantification of the request is. This is perhaps why Oprah seems to feel impelled to justify it in order to re-place the audience *with* the flow of the programme. Furthermore, it is disquieting to note that the misconstruction of what Madelene wants places her in an invidious position. Although this is clearly not their intention, Oprah and Harville nevertheless set up conditions for the further disempowerment of Madelene within the relationship. If Jay and Madelene follow through with the exercise for the next month, Madelene will not get the kind of consideration she (quite reasonably) wants and yet Jay will have done exactly what he was supposed to do (to the number). In other words, she will have no come-back if she is still angry or unhappy; it will be even more *her* problem than it was before. Rather than a recipe for improved relations, as was intended, it seems to us that the couple have been given a recipe for disaster.

Recuperations

We are not trying to argue here that the ideas put forward by Harville and Oprah have nothing of value to offer. It makes sense to us to recognize that good relationships require work, that people carry their previous experiences with them and that these experiences affect how they behave in

the present. It is also clear that active listening is important and needs to be demonstrated in the course of dialogue, particularly where people are struggling with problems in their relationships. However, for both couples, we can see that the exercises they are asked to undertake are, at best, problematic and, at worst, damaging. Just how dubious they can be as ways of "solving" problems or "saying good-bye" can be seen if we apply them to situations involving violence and abuse. Imagine, for example, the good-bye process redeployed:

> *Her:* I'm saying good-bye to the times you came home drunk, to the beatings, to the rapes, to the terror you inflicted on me and the children. . . .
> *Harville:* Now say good-bye to the good stuff that won't ever be again.

Any attempt to rewrite either of these exercises, or indeed Harville's self-help approach as a whole, to apply to patterns of severe abuse would inevitably emerge, at the very least, as inappropriate. This is precisely because of the absence of a framework which could recognize inequality as a central problem in heterosexual relationships.[17]

As we have seen, "How to Make Love Last" is characterized by a repeated pattern of mis-ascription, misrecognition and misunderstanding. Power relations are understood only in terms of individual unresolved patterns from childhood; problems between couples are construed as the problems of the woman; problems within marriage are dissected without reference to the institutional character of marriage. In a similar vein, choice and responsibility are invoked in ways which assume equality of position between men and women but inequality of responsibility. Women are seen to be responsible both for the origin and solution of problems within heterosexual relationships. Indeed, women are effectively seen to *be* the problem and to be the site for and agent of remedial work. Moreover, heterosexuality is assumed to be a site of dysfunction and the "repetition of [women's] bad patterns" on the one hand, and yet on the other hand the universal ideal. Furthermore, because of the lack of a critical framework which considers power relations, it is possible at one and the same time both to invoke and to deny the continuities between "extreme" forms of abuse and "mundane" misunderstandings. Clearly, then, the model of self-help therapy underpinning the programme is not capable of resolving the issues raised within it precisely because it rules out the possibility of considering the social character of the relationships under scrutiny and the social positions of the actors involved. In this context, the exercise of "mirroring" back can be not only mechanical, but can also be a way of appearing to understand the other while in fact reinscribing (her) Otherness. All this is demonstrated forcibly in Oprah and Harville's final summary of the lessons of the programme:

> *Harville:* That's why marriages don't work. There's no commitment to mutual healing and mutual helping.
> *Oprah:* 'Cause that's what marriage is? A commitment to . . .
> *Harville:* That's what marriage is. Marriage—marriage is a structure for healing. And if you do meet each other's childhood needs, you'll have the marriage of your dreams. And if you don't, you'll have the marriage of your nightmares. And you can predict that (p. 38).

To posit marriage as "a structure for healing" seems, at best, wishful thinking and, at worst, activity deceitful. Surely it contradicts the evidence amply provided in this and many other *Oprah Winfrey Shows* that, far from being a structure for healing, marriage can be seen as a structure for "wounding" and for the disempowerment of women and children. Harville himself makes this

point, albeit not with the intention of critiquing the institution or framework of marriage in itself. Not only does this facile exchange contradict the predominant experience of marriage, but it also contradicts the historical meaning of the legal/economic/social contract of marriage which has served as a structure for ensuring patrilineal inheritance and for the inscription of women (and their children) as property. (Marriage has also served as a structure for the eugenic reproduction of particular social and cultural formations, i.e. "desirable" populations. This is reflected in rules or social conventions about who is allowed, disallowed or forced to marry whom.) In other words, it contradicts the history of marriage as an institution which has emerged from and reproduces a range of social inequalities.

Conclusions

As our analysis shows, the twin frameworks of therapy and presumed heterosexuality have all but ruled out the possibility for questions to be raised about power relationships and patterns of social inequality. It seems to us that it inevitably becomes a contradiction in terms to seek to challenge common sense and common forms of oppression through frameworks which mitigate against such questions. We would suggest that a very different picture of Dale, Cari, Jay and Madelene's situations would have emerged, given a framework which questions the social character of individual patterns in relationships, which interrogates gendered and other forms of inequality and which challenges expertise and dominant social institutions.

The close reading which we have given to this one programme reveals a significant disjuncture between Oprah's explicit goals for her show and the contradictory effects of its framework. Indeed, what we have seen is that the framework and format of the show can easily subvert the challenging educational objectives of the kind of socially responsible television which Oprah is aiming to produce and can disempower precisely those people whom she is aiming, through the show, to empower.

Notes

1. Of course, this article could be said to be part of that vogue.

2. A notable exception is the tabloid obsession with Oprah's body size and, to a somewhat lesser extent, her long-standing engagement to Stedman.

3. We use the term "kinship" in this article to describe both relationships between people in general and relatedness (or what is seen to count as being related to another person in familial terms).

4. It is beyond the scope of this article to consider this issue in depth. However, it is important to at least note that the presentation of therapeutic interactions as entertainment in itself constitutes a breach of the confidentiality which is considered to be axiomatic to any school of therapy or counselling.

5. Even within schools of psychoanalysis which attempt to locate the individual psyche within the social (e.g. R.D. Laing and existentialist approaches; Nancy Chodorow and other feminist approaches), there are none the less tensions between the overall propensity of treatment towards individualism and the attempt to theorize behaviours, emotions, experience, etc. in relation to the social.

6. Note, however, Kelly *et al.*'s (1994) argument that neither "victim" nor "survivor" are appropriate descriptors for people who have experienced sexual abuse.

7. Duncker uses this phrase to describe a central theme she sees in Margaret Atwood's fiction.

8. The *Oprah Winfrey Show* does also occasionally feature issues about women's abusive behaviour towards male partners or children. It is beyond the scope of this article to examine these programmes and the ways in which they challenge or reinforce feminist critiques of patriarchal power. In any case, they do not represent either the vast majority of shows or the more general picture of the ways abuse is gendered.

9. Unless otherwise indicated, all quotations have been drawn from the programme transcript produced by Burrelle's Transcription Services. However, where there were obvious mistakes in

the transcript, we have made the appropriate corrections.

10. This is, of course, a liberal humanist argument in its assumption of a universal subject and in its presumption of human equality abstracted from the material inequalities which actually pertain in any given situation or between any given subjects. Elsewhere (Epstein and Steinberg, in press), we have discussed the ways in which the *Oprah Winfrey Show* is characterized more generally by liberal politics.

11. We use the term "liberal equivalence" to describe the tendency to equate situations which involve unequal power relations as if they were equal. We see this as characteristic of liberal politics more generally and of the *Oprah Winfrey Show* specifically.

12. These kinds of relationships are typically, within liberal thought, understood as "private" and therefore, not political or beyond politics. It is an interesting dimension of the *Oprah Winfrey Show* that it both challenges the public/private distinction of liberal politics (for example, by putting relationships on a public stage) and at the same time reinscribes it by examining relationships in terms which effectively exclude a consideration of power relations.

13. For example, Cari was wearing an obviously expensive (possibly designer) suede outfit and Dale a suede jacket. All the guests looked as if they were very well-heeled indeed. This was reinforced in more subtle ways by their manners of self-presentation, the language they used to describe themselves and the activities they referred to in their day-to-day lives.

14. Although we would disagree with an individualized cycle of abuse approach and with Harville's particular version of it, it is nevertheless clear that many children, if not most, are indeed damaged by "family life."

15. This includes Harville and Helen's "ideal relationship." For example, in a subsequent extract from their video, it emerges that they have been in conflict about Helen's habitual lateness, but while Helen has had to learn to accept Harville's impatience with this, he has apparently not had to learn anything:

Helen: I mean, you know, he can pick up a paper. He's always complaining that he doesn't have time to read. And he could just flow with it. And I had to learn to first acknowledge that you were never going to flow with my being late.
Harville: Yeah.

Helen: Then second, really respect and honour it. And then—and now, I think it's rather charming that you—and dear.

Harville: That I won't flow with your being late (p. 27).

16. For example:

Dale: I want to say good-bye to feeling third and fourth choice . . .

Harville: And tell *her.*

Dale: . . . where our son came first, which was understandable. But her parents came second; her friends came third.

Harville: And say *your* friends. *Your* friends.

Dale: Your friends.

Harville: Your parents.

Dale: Your parents came third, and then me in every consideration and every way she . . .

Harville: You. You.

Dale: . . . handled all of our . . .

Harville: Say *you.*

Dale: You—in every way that you handled all of our—our friendships. It was always your friends. . . .

Cari: If I got it, you are saying good-bye to being third, fourth, and fifth. My putting our son, which was understandable, but my family and friends ahead of you. . . . And basically to sum it up, that I never, ever made you number one (pp. 24-5).

17. This is not to suggest that lesbian and gay relationships are not characterized by problems relating to a range of inequalities, or that sexist inequality is the only form of inequality inscribing compulsory heterosexuality. We are also well aware that heterosexual couples (and all couples) can actively struggle against sexist and other forms of inequality within their relationships. By "struggle" here, we are not arguing that individuals can simply opt for their relationships to be exempt from being shaped by social inequalities. What we are suggesting is that the personal is political and that relationships are therefore a site of personal/political struggle.

References

Anthias, F. and Yuval-Davis, N. with Cain, H. (1992) *Racialised Boundaries: Race, Nation, Gender, Colouring Class and the Anti-Racist Struggle* London: Routledge.

Barrett, M. and MacIntosh, M. (1982) *The Anti-Social Family* London: Verso.

Cameron, D. (1985) *Feminism and Linguistic Theory* London: Macmillan.

Chodorow, N. (1978) *The Reproduction of Mothering* Berkeley: University of California Press.

___. (1989) *Feminism and Psychoanalytic Theory* New Haven: Yale University Press.

Collins, P. H. (1990) *Black Feminist Thought: Knowledge, Consciousness and the Politics of Empowerment* London: Unwin Hyman.

Delphy, C. (1984) *Close to Home: A Materialist Analysis of Women's Oppression* London: Hutchinson.

Duncker, E. (1993) "Heterosexuality: fictional agendas" in Wilkinson and Kitzinger, editors.

Epstein, D. and Steinberg, D. L. (1995a) "12 steps to heterosexuality: common-sensibilities on the *Oprah Winfrey Show"* *Feminism and Psychology* Vol. 5, No. 2: 275-80.

___. (1995b) "Heterosensibilities on the *Oprah Winfrey Show"* in Purvis and Maynard, editors.

___. (in press) "Love's labours: playing it straight on the *Oprah Winfrey Show"* in Steinberg, Johnson and Epstein, editors.

___. (in preparation) "'American Dreamin': Discoursing Liberally on the *Oprah Winfrey Show."*

hooks, b. (1982) *Ain't I a Woman* London: Pluto.

___. (1992) *Black Looks: Race and Representation* London: Turnaround.

Kelly, L. (1986) *Surviving Sexual Abuse* London: Polity.

Kelly, L., Regan, S. and Burton, L. (1991) "Short summary of findings from an exploratory study of the prevalence of sexual abuse in a sample of 16-18 year olds." Mimeograph. Polytechnic (now University) of North London.

___. (1994) "The victim/survivor dichotomy: beyond an identity defined by violation." Paper given at the British Sociological Association Conference, University of Central Lancashire.

Mellencamp. P. (1992) *High Anxiety: Catastrophe, Scandal, Age and Comedy* Bloomington, Indiana: Indiana University Press.

Purvis, J. and Maynard, M. (1995) editors, *(Hetero)Sexual Politics* London: Taylor and Francis.

Reitter, R. (1975) editor, *Toward an Anthropology of Women* New York Monthly Review Press.

Rubin, G. (1975) "The traffic in women" in Reiter, editor.

Schwichtenberg, C. (1992) editor, *The Madonna Connection* Boulder: Westview Press.

Spender, D. (1980) *Man Made Language* London: Routledge.

Squire, C. (1994) "Empowering women? The *Oprah Winfrey Show" Feminism and Psychology: "Shifting Identities: Shifting Racisms," (Special Issue)* Vol. 4, No. 1: 63-79.

Steinberg, D. L., Epstein, D. and Johnson, R. (in press) editors, *Border Patrols: Policing the Boundaries of Heterosexuality* London: Cassell.

Wilkinson, S. and Kitzinger, C. (1993) editors, *Heterosexuality: A Feminism and Psychology Reader* London: Sage.

Publicity Traps:
Television Talk Shows and Lesbian, Gay, Bisexual, and Transgender Visibility

Joshua Gamson

Tolerance is the result not of enlightenment, but of boredom.

Quentin Crisp (1997 [1968]: 204)

On American television over the last year, one could watch a handsome doctor apologize to his boyfriend for hitting him *(Melrose Place),* a black gay city government professional placing bets with his female coworker on the sexual preferences of a cute male focus group participant *(Spin City),* and two chiseled soap-opera hunks discussing their upcoming cohabitation as a straight relative awkwardly offers his blessing *(All My Children).* Nothing out of the ordinary or stereotypical in the villains-or-victims sense; just good-looking, professional gay men who could be your next door neighbors. There are still some problems (none of the making out that the straight *Melrose* characters get to do all the time, always the bridesmaid and never the bride), but the 1990s have witnessed a storm of

"happen to be gay" television, culminating in the much-hyped coming-out of *Ellen's* central character and star.

By the conventions of much gay and lesbian media studies and advocacy, this is a dream come true. After all, since taking off with Vito Russo's ground-breaking *The Celluloid Closet* (1987), studies of the portrayals of gay men and lesbians in film and television have soundly demonstrated how homosexual lives have been subject to systematic exclusion and stereotyping as victims and villains; how "aspects of gay and lesbian identity, sexuality, and community that are not compatible or that too directly challenge the heterosexual regime are excluded" from mainstream television (Fejes and Petrich, 1993: 412; see also Gross, 1989); how television has produced "stereo-

Reprinted by permission of Sage Publications Ltd. from *Sexualities,* Vol. 1, 1, 1998 by Joshua Gamson.

typical conceptualizations of AIDS that vilify gays and legitimate homophobia" (Netzhammer and Shamp, 1994: 104); how even "positive" portrayals of lesbians "serve as mechanisms to perpetuate hetero/sexism" (Hantzis and Lehr, 1994: 118; see also Moritz, 1994). Now, having made the move from occasional soupy movie-of-the-week issue to soap and sitcom regulars, lesbians and gay men look more or less like everybody else on sitcoms and soaps: clean, with really good apartments. Their homosexuality is more or less incidental, not much more than a spicy character flip. This would seem to be progress.

The desire to be publicly recognized is especially powerful for marginalized groups, whose cultural visibility is often so minimal, or distant enough from the way people live their lives to render them unrecognizable even to themselves. The positive effects of visibility are quite plain: "Cultural visibility can prepare the ground for gay civil rights protection," as Rosemary Hennessy sums it up, and "affirmative images of lesbians and gays in the mainstream media . . . can be empowering for those of us who have lived most of our lives with no validation at all from the dominant culture" (Hennessy, 1994–95: 31–2). The desire to be recognized, affirmed, validated, and to lay the cultural groundwork for political change, in fact, are so strong they have tended to inhibit careful analysis of the dynamics of becoming visible. At a time when a major sitcom character and the lesbian playing her have come out amidst a coterie of gay and lesbian supporting characters, when a drag queen has her own talk show on VH-1, when big movie stars no longer see gay roles as career poison, and when one soap opera has had a transsexual storyline and another a gay talk-show-murder storyline, it is no longer enough to think in terms of invisibility and stereotyping. Cul-

tural visibility especially when it is taking place through commerce, is not a direct route to liberation, in fact, it can easily lead elsewhere.

Talk shows, which have been making nonconforming sex and gender lives public for a good two decades, are a great place to turn for complication. The dramatic new visibility in commercial television fiction, and the slower changes in commercial popular nonfiction media (Alwood, 1996) is only the spread of the logic and imagery of TV talk shows, which long ago incorporated lesbians, gay men, transgenders, and bisexuals into their daily dramas. What makes them interesting spots, moreover, is not only the high visibility of gay, lesbian, bisexual, and transgender people, but the (at least partial) *agency* of those people within the genre. Until very recently, lesbians and gay men had little input into our own representation. Almost without exception, the literature on homosexuality and the media has therefore treated the process of representation as a one-sided one. Larry Gross captures this approach very well:

> Representation in the mediated "reality" of our mass culture is in itself power; certainly it is the case that nonrepresentation maintains the powerless status of groups that do not possess significant material or political power bases. Those who are the bottom of the various hierarchies will be kept in their place in part through their relative invisibility; this is a form of symbolic annihilation. When groups or perspectives do attain visibility, the manner of that representation will itself reflect the biases and interests of those elites who define the public agenda. And those elites are mostly white, mostly middle-aged, mostly male, mostly middle- and upper-middle class, and (at least in public) entirely heterosexual. (Gross, 1994: 143)

On talk shows, however, bisexuals, lesbians, transgendered people, and gay men are actively invited to participate, to "play themselves" rather than be portrayed by others, to refute stereotypes rather than simply watch them on the screen. Talk shows mess up our thinking about the difficulties and delights of becoming visible—and, in a more general sense, about the political benefits and dilemmas of cultural representation. And as the dust settles, they can clear our thinking up.

Beginning with a brief introduction to the recent class-cultural history of U.S. daytime television talk, I want to point towards three related political difficulties that talk show visibility brings to the fore and exacerbates. First, drawing from interviews with talk show producers and guests, I suggest that the shows build on and make heavier a class division in gay, lesbian, bisexual, and transgender political organizing—a division tied to the political tension between the pursuit of either a queer difference or an acceptable sameness. Talk show producers, in part as a response to the organized control activities of activists, have turned to those with little connection to middle-class gay, transgender, bisexual, or lesbian organizing, with little interest or experience in the politics of representation, giving themselves freer reign as producers and infuriating many middle-class activists. The longstanding invisibility (both outside and within gay and lesbian communities) of gay, lesbian, bisexual, and transgender people of color, and of those from lower economic statuses, is cracked open by the talk shows; yet at the same time the shows, with their selection of nasty, rowdy, exhibitionist, not-great-to-look-at poor and working-class guests, encourage those interested in social acceptability to disown the visibility of some of their own. A predicament already present in the politics of sexual social change is brought to a head: as we make ourselves visible, do those among us with less status get to speak just as anyone else

(increasing the risk of further stigma as the price for democratic diversity) or do the more acceptable get the upper hand (reproducing class and racial hierarchies as the price for gaining legitimacy)? Any path to visibility must face this question.[1]

Second, drawing from content analysis of talk show transcripts and videos, I argue that the production of rowdy outrageousness draws out and intensifies animosities between the populations (gay men, lesbians, bisexuals, transgendered people) making up the larger movement. Tolerance of visible gayness, put simply, is bought largely through the further stigmatization of bisexuality and gender nonconformity. Talk shows are surely too money-oriented, capricious, and thin to do much deliberate ideological service, but both their loose liberal-therapeutic dogmas and their everyday pursuits—even, and perhaps especially, when they are fixated solely on the "personal"—lead them nonetheless to sharpen political lines of division.

Finally, drawing from focus group interviews with heterosexual talk show viewers, I argue that gay, lesbian, bisexual, and transgender visibility triggers deeper battles over the meaning and ownership of public space. Heterosexual liberal viewers tend to see talk shows as damaging, exploitative contributors to the ongoing victimization of sex and gender deviants. Sympathy for the "exploited," however, is often tempered by a sometimes subtle, sometimes brash animosity towards "trash"—those people who will display themselves outrageously, the bad, low-class queers. Thus, right up next to "leave them alone" is "leave me alone": get out of my face, stop flaunting it. Conservative talk show viewers tend to take this position to the extreme, understanding talk shows as part of a pro-gay publicity apparatus, one of many ways in which queer life is "shoved down their throats."[2]

Talk shows on sex and gender nonconformity are experienced, then, largely as funny pieces in the midst of serious culture wars; primarily through the class divisions to which they are beholden, they encourage viewers to separate "bad" gays from "good" ones, and to link the appearances of sexual nonconformists to inappropriate uses of public space. The various political battles that talk shows elicit, profit from, and amplify, all take a part in a more general war: over the lines between public and private, and over who benefits from changing or conserving current public-private divisions.[3] Talk shows open up these cultural battles not so much through the particular discussions they facilitate, not through anything specific that gets said, but through their simple encouragement of publicly visible sex and gender nonconformity. Symbolic political battles over sex and gender norms energize a bigger whirlwind, and are then sucked right into it. Through talk shows, class and sex and publicity and gender provocatively mix, offering more general lessons about the dilemmas of publicity.

Class, Queerness, and Public Visibility

At *Tempestt,* there was an 18-year-old girl sitting next to me who was outed by someone she went to school with, who was a loud, obnoxious, drag queen kid who had no place being on that show. The girl next to me was crying hysterically. Then we had one lesbian who was outed by her ex-husband who was, the only way I can describe her is a loud-mouthed woman from the boroughs who just used foul language at every opportunity I'm not sure that rehashing it on national television does us as gay people any good, does her any good emotionally, does him any good. It's an issue that should have been talked about in the privacy of a psychiatrist's or psychologist's office, not on national television, where someone was playing with the emotions to make money and make ratings. They made it into a circus, and there was no one rational to present gay people in a positive perspective on that show in the beginning, just a bunch of hysterical people screaming and yelling at each other, with Tempestt as a moderator— and a weak one at that. They did put me on after two segments, but all the listeners got for the most part were gay people who had horrible coming out experiences, who were manipulated by the producers and by Tempestt to put on a circus of a show, screaming and yelling and using four-letter words, behavior that is entirely inappropriate for adults in a public setting, with no voice of reason. When I finally did have the opportunity to speak, I think I tried to put some reason into a situation that was unreasonable. Unfortunately, a lot of the people on that show were what the press focuses on—stereotypical, you know, drag queens. The press already looks at us as freaks, and the more we play into that with these freak shows that they put on TV, the worse it is for our movement. The talk shows play into that. They play into all of the freakish, radical elements of our community. (Out Magazine publisher and *Tempestt* guest Harry Taylor)

The whole idea of sexual freedom and personal freedom is that no one else has to find it acceptable. It's your own business. And we shouldn't be concerned about what the image is. Intellectually I understand the anger of militant gays. If I lived in society and all of a sudden heterosexuality was taboo, and I had to live my whole life either not ever being with a woman or if I was with a woman making sure that no one ever found out, lying about it, having to, you know, marry a man and go through the motions of that, and sneak out to find a woman to satisfy me, boy would I be militant. I can understand a person being really, really pissed off about something as necessary and vital to a being as their sexuality. So I don't mind showing the outrageousness and the anger in all that. (Talk show host Jerry Springer)

Talk shows, in a general sense, stretch back to earlier public traditions emerging from different, and sometimes opposed, class cultures, and they still operate with the awkward tension between sensation and conversation growing from these roots. Propriety, of course, is not a middle-class property and working-class and underclass people certainly do not own irreverence and emotion, but the talk show genre is fashioned from particular cultural pieces historically associated with different classes: relatively sober, deliberative, "polite" middle-class forms of participating in and presenting public culture embodied in literary circles and the lyceum, for instance, and irreverent, wild, predominantly lower-class public leisures such as the carnival, the cabaret, the tabloid, and the 19th-century theater (see Gamson, 1998, Ch. 2; Munson, 1994; Shattuc, 1997).[4]

For their first 20 years, beginning with *Donahue* in the early 1970s, television talk shows were heavily weighted towards the middle-class, people-sitting-around-talking-about-issues model. But with the quick success of *Ricki Lake* in the mid-1990s—which targeted a younger, more mixed-race audience through the programming of rowdy, conflict-filled, interpersonal subjects and a studio audience made up primarily of young audiences—the balance tipped. *Ricki* and her imitators demonstrated the success of a combination of class voyeurism and class empowerment, inviting guests who were much less likely than *Donahue's* or *Oprah's* to be highly educated, organizationally affiliated, and middle-class, and audiences who were also more likely to be young, urban, working- or poverty-class people of color. Guests were less commonly recruited, moreover, through organizations, and more commonly through toll-free numbers flashed on the screen: the guests nominated themselves for TV appearances (see

Gamson, 1998; Grindstaff, 1997; Tuchman, 1974).

Having discovered the profitable appeal of younger, less educated, more boisterous guests, talk shows have come to feature calm, educated, older guests less and less; they simultaneously appropriate, exaggerate, and give expression to the straightforward, not-afraid-of-conflict emotionalism of some poverty-class and working-class cultures, providing imagery of gays, lesbians, transgenders, and bisexuals from all kinds of racial, cultural, and class backgrounds. At the same time, using the low-risk strategy of class voyeurism, many shows select guests from the bottom of the social barrel. Nearly anyone can feel superior watching people whose speech, dress, bodies, relationships and accents mark them as "trash."

Especially as the "outrageous" shows took off, and the class (and age) profile of the genre started to shift, middle-class activist guests found themselves and their political agendas edged out. The gay, lesbian, bisexual, and transgendered people who have slowly replaced them—often flamboyant, unaffiliated, untrained in political agendas, and of lower educational, economic, and social status—threaten the mainstreaming agenda of many in the gay movement. They can be loud-mouthed, foul-mouthed, freakish, radical, obnoxious, stereotypical, irrational, emotional: that is, great talk show guests. They emphasize, deliberately and not, a queer *difference* from the mainstream, and not a terribly appealing one, since on these talk shows it is conflated with "lower class," which is equated with various sorts of ugliness, which do not make the best case for tolerance, acceptance, freedom, and rights.

This dynamic brings to a head class divisions within gay, lesbian, bisexual, and transgender life. Legitimacy, in talk show land as elsewhere, is associated with symbols of social class (educated speech, calm manner, clean dress); uneducated speech, rambunctious manner, and show dress signify a dismissible lower status. If talk shows are now filled with "trashy" people (many of them people of color), and also with queers, sexual difference is easily conflated with class and racial inferiority; if "classy" white gay people have no monopoly on the conversation, sexual difference can no longer be legitimized by an association with higher educational, racial and class status. Those seeking mainstream legitimacy therefore avoid the stigma of rowdy, poor and working class, mixed-color shows, aligning with the polite, middle-class, predominantly white strand of talk shows. Television talk show visibility thus amplifies the class divisions of the populations on which the shows greedily feed.

Many middle-class activist guests, who had earlier had a virtual monopoly on the non-heterosexual talk show guest list, are trying to move towards the demonstration that gay people (or cross-dressers, or bisexuals, or transsexuals) are regular, civilized, unthreatening, reasonable, conforming folks—for good reason, since media images elsewhere have tipped so heavily in the other direction. Craig Dean, for instance, went on *Donahue* twice—the second time on a show that included a gay wedding:

> We were going up there to talk. And talk about issues, you know, and I knew the show was a freak show to begin with because of what they were doing. Not only was it a gay black couple, but it was a short black man—it was a freak show. And they wanted us to come on to lend legitimacy to what they were doing. They wanted to use us, you know, and I felt for the good of the gay rights movement, that we needed to be there to present something a little more palatable to the American public. . . . These guys came up, vrooom, they got mar-

ried. There was no humanization—and people reacted like, "You faggots, look at this shit you're putting in our face." As opposed to "We love each other and we're going to express our commitment to each other." Yeah, there's a really big difference, so I'm pissed at what happened. (Priest, 1995: 117)

Gay writer Eric Marcus intentionally dresses up as "sort of the boy next door, well-educated, well-groomed, polite, would never get angry at anyone, wouldn't hurt anyone, not a threat at all." By comparison to right-wing discredited psychologist Paul Cameron ("he's sitting there talking about fecal matter and all the semen that we ingest, and I'm sitting next to him in a blue shirt, nice crisp tie, my hair's combed properly, I'm very polite"), and even to activist-writer Michelangelo Signorile ("he came across as a nut case"), he looks "sane" and "normal." But increasingly, Marcus promotes his books and his "best possible case for gay people" in an environment in which the polite, well-educated, well-groomed image is an anomaly. While they still help sell his books, the talk shows have started to run counter to Marcus's political agenda. Marcus offers the example of a gay kid at the *Sally* show wearing a midriff t-shirt, elbow length gloves, pearls, a top hat, and makeup.

> If I were in charge, I would say, "Stay home." I think of those television talk shows as propaganda that can be used in a very productive way. Someone like that doesn't help further my political agenda. He's on there, I'm on there, so people do get to see that gay people come from all walks of life, but in that moment of the show he created quite an uproar, and the argumentativeness of the show increased because of this kid with the elbow length gloves and makeup. So the argument is lost because of what he looks like.

And so two political impulses battle it out through these appearances. We must behave appropriately in public, says one, and work through our ugly stuff in private, in a doctor's office maybe, the way classy people do. Shrink, shmink, says the other, let's go on TV. We are sick of being told what to do and where we can do it, and we're going to take our scary, inappropriate selves as public as we can go.

Ironically, it is in part because of the successes and increased savvy of movement activists in the talk show arena that many middle-class organizers now find themselves on the defensive. For one thing, from the point of view of talk shows, they have pretty much had their time. For another, they have trained themselves in the basics of using-the-talk-show-for-our-own-purposes, and their haggling and negotiating and caution makes them sometimes more trouble than they're worth. It is much easier simply to turn to guests with little agenda other than a few minutes of TV fame and an out-of-town trip. "I wish there was a pool of nice gay folks they called on to do these sorts of things," says Marcus, "but these shows thrive on combativeness, on arguments. They don't want reasonable guests, except as so-called experts."

The fact that not-nice, unreasonable people who get crazy are many shows' guests of choice has led some mainstream organizations to simply refuse to assist shows altogether. For the Renaissance Education Association, an organization which provides "education and support to the transgender community and the general public," talk shows had been an important tool for both visibility and outreach throughout the 1980s and early 1990s. By the time I spoke with members in 1996, they had decided to impose a moratorium on talk show appearances by their members, inspired partly by a moratorium call by the Executive Director of the Sexuality Information and Education Council of the US (SIECUS) (Hafner, 1995: 6, 16). Transsexual radio host Cheryl-Ann

Costa describes similar talk about talk shows in her own circles.

> Springer had a person who had a sex change, and they dragged his family on there. His two sons saying, "We ain't going to talk to him anymore." And his little 11-year-old daughter stands up in the audience, says, "I don't want to ever see him again." And Springer stands up with his last 5 minute little comment and says, "If you're thinking about having one of these things and you brought kids into the world, why don't you just keep your pants on until they're grown up and out of the house and then do what you're going to do." That was an outright attack on our community and we are desperately trying to dry up his supply of transgenders. They'll still find people. They're going to have to find an awful lot of rogue people, though, people that aren't connected, because anybody who's connected with anything, we're going to basically say, "This show is quarantined." We're going to shut him down as far as transsexuals are concerned.

Opting out, of course, is no guarantee of change. "You get people in our own community who are willing to say anything the producers want them to say in order to create that controversy," says a member of the Manhattan Gender Network, a transgender organization. "The problem is, those of us who don't want to have our brains picked on national television, we leave that to those people who will do whatever is necessary, who look to get on every talk show that they possibly can."

Talk shows, Marcus notes, "show us in all of our awful diversity": swearing Hispanic homosexuals, tongue-kissing mountain boys, borough broads, dysfunctional Ozark lesbians, guys in pearls and make-up, rogue transsexuals in giant pink hair, gay kids without media training. But many middle-class activists see little advantage to this diversity, which would only seem to increase the stigma they are trying to remove in the pursuit of civil rights. This is primarily a pragmatic position (we cannot afford these images right now), but one also often tinged with animosity (these people don't know how to behave in public), and the confidence that comes from having long felt entitled to call the shots (these people don't get it). Mainstreaming activists are rightly concerned that talk shows provide a distorted image of gay life—but then again, the image, although more socially acceptable, was no less distorted when it was only white, middle-class, gay movement movers and shakers. Lurking underneath the concern, encouraged by the class dynamics of TV talk, are hints of class, racial, and regional superiority. When gay was just *us,* things were going so well, people seem to want to say. Why did they have to go and give *those* people the microphone?

Talk shows certainly did not *create* the division between moderates with an eye towards assimilation, who want to demonstrate middle-class legitimacy and similarity to heterosexuals, and in-your-face radicals, who use the difference from heterosexuals to create space for themselves. This is a longstanding strategic dispute in sex and gender politics, as it is in most social movements. For a good long time, picking up extra steam in the last decade, civil-rights strategists favoring integration into the "normal" have met with resistance from others favoring a transgressive, confrontational "queer" politics which pushes at the boundaries of normality (D'Emilio, 1983; Gamson, 1995; Seidman, 1996; Vaid, 1995; Warner, 1993). Of course, it takes a somewhat different form here, since most of the antiassimilation imagery comes not from organized radical activists, but from unaffiliated individuals seizing the opportunity for televisual confirmation of their social significance. Talk shows, though, take the line between

"fringe" and "center"—a divider that, in my own eyes and the eyes of many others, is neither necessary nor productive for political organizing by sex and gender dissidents—and dig away at it, deepening it into an almost-unbridgeable chasm. (This comes not just from the strategies of outrageousness-selling shows, but also from those like *Oprah,* which create a "respectable" environment in which people from the wrong side of the tracks are excluded.) The structure of the talk show world intensifies the tension over who rightfully represents "gayness," making it nearly impossible for legitimacy-seeking activists *not* to close ranks, disrespecting and disowning their own.

This is no deliberate divide-and-conquer on the part of talk show producers. The opening up of the center-fringe, or sameness-difference, fault line is a result of the way producers make their money, and of the ambivalence built into the talk show genre (high/low class, polite/rude, rational/emotional). An array of "fringe" characters make it to talk TV because of how they play on screen, and because they are easy to recruit and easier to manipulate; they say and do things in public that others are not always willing to say and do. In a genre shot through with class cultural divisions, in a place where authentic class cultural expression is indistinguishable from its exaggerated displays, where "trash" is a synonym for "lower class," working class guests (and, through that weird American confusion of race and class, often guests of color as well) are placed directly against the comfortable calm of the middle-class mainstream; bisexual, gay, lesbian, and transgender guests who are not middle class are quite easily placed in the same trash basket. It is not too surprising that many middle-class activists and viewers, informed by a sense that political gains are at stake, are not too excited about joining them there.

Normality and Public Visibility

The talk show world rips open existing class divisions within transgender, bisexual, lesbian, and gay politics, but not only these: it also rips away at the tenuous alliance among these nonconforming populations, primarily by rewarding some populations with "acceptability" at the expense of others. Many mainstream gay activist guests and viewers express the worry not only that images of dysfunctional, angry and uneducated parts will be taken to represent the whole, but that disproportionate representation of "abnormal" parts will make it harder for all of us to become "normal." The freaks—especially the gender freaks—are giving us all a bad name.

Again, this is a pre-existing tension, and the attempt to ally all sorts of sex and gender dissidents under one flag—drag queens, passing transsexuals, guppies, lipstick lesbians, dykes, cross-dressers, queer kids, monogamous and non-monogamous bisexuals, and so on—is relatively new, complex and extremely hard-going (Vaid, 1995). Bisexuals and transgendered people, most notably, have waged difficult battles for recognition and inclusion in organizations and celebrations, and centrist gay men and lesbians argue, with some realpolitikal evidence on their side, that some battles (the Employment Non-Discrimination Act, for instance) are not currently winnable with bisexuals and transgenders on the list of claimants. The talk show world reinforces these divisions not only by using transgendered people as display objects and bisexuals as symbols of promiscuity, but also by offering homosexuals a tempting option: distance yourself from bisexuals and transgendered people, keep your sex and gender

practices conservative, and you will be rewarded with acceptance.

Take, for instance, the common "love triangle" structure into which many shows on bisexuality are structured. On a 1992 *Jane Whitney* show on bisexuality, while a white, bearded bisexual guest named Cole is attacking the myth of bisexuality as simultaneous relationships ("I don't have to be in a relationship with both a man and a woman"), a label appears under his image. "Cole," it reads, "Intimate with both men and women." The show, like many others on bisexuality is structured as a series of triangles: Cole is involved with Hector who doesn't appear) and with Laura (Latina, bisexual) who is involved with Marcia (African-American, lesbian); Jill is involved with both Woody and Rebecca, who has a long-term lover. ("No," says Whitney introducing them, "they're not involved with Laura. They're another bisexual triangle.") Not surprisingly, despite a variety of attempts by panelists to disaggregate bisexuality and non-monogamy, and to distinguish committed, honest non-monogamy from sex-crazed disloyalty, commitment and sexual monogamy become the focus of audience questions and attacks. "How do you decide," asks a young white guy with long, rock-star hair, "flip a coin?" to laughter and applause. "They're changing their preferences every day like they're changing their shirts," says an older white man, and soon a young blond man asks, "Why do you have to have sex with all of them?" to which a tie-wearing, buzz-cut man adds, "As a gay man, I think you're doing a disservice, you should be pursuing the one person and not all this free love." "Don't you believe in commitment?" a series of people ask in a variety of ways. Given the show's Marcia and Laura and Cole and Hector set-up, the answers, all of

them well articulated, get lost in the applause for monogamy (Unitel Video, 1992).

What is also lost, though, is any concern
with the "abnormality" of same-sex relationships, in place of an attack on non-monogamous relationships (equated on the
show with bisexual ones). Sexual loyalty,
whoever its subjects, is what's really being
protected here. In fact, audience members
and the host express sympathies and concern for the gay boyfriends and lesbian girlfriends of bisexuals, whose partners "can't
commit" (as when *Jane Whitney's* Marcia,
for example, the sole lesbian on the panel,
is encouraged to stop putting up with being
a "third wheel"). In these very common "triangle" shows, where bisexuality functions
primarily as a stand-in for promiscuity and
is therefore denigrated, monogamous sexuality gets the high ground, taking monogamous *homosexuality* along for the ride. In
this cultural set-up, from the point of view
of gay men or lesbians on the verge of mainstream acceptance and political gains, ally-
ing with bisexuals is indeed a risky
proposition.

The appearance of cross-dressing on gay-
themed shows, which can often lead to the
denigration of homosexuality, is a flashy
mirror of this process. The early 1990s series of shows on conventionally feminine
lesbians, for instance, used the term "lipstick lesbians" as something of a mind-
blower and stereotype-breaker, as Maury
Povich's introduction, spiked with the
straight-porn image of girly-girls going at
it, captures: "They are beautiful, they're
sexy, glamorous, and successful, so one
would assume that they have more men than
they can handle. But it's not the men they
want. Instead, these stunning beauties prefer other women" (cut to video of women's
bodies putting on lingerie and lipstick and
nail polish). "What about the women who
are butch and proud of it?" (cut to shots of

Dykes on Bikes and other butch lesbians in
a pride match).

There is much talk here about debunking
stereotypes, many questions about how one
can be simultaneously lesbian and conventionally feminine, a gratuitous male guest
named Tommy, who thinks he can "turn a
lesbian straight," and much manly-man rib-
bing. (Maury to four young guys in the front
row: "You're not interested anymore,
right?" Guy: "No, we've been interested
from the start." Maury: "Well, you know,
hot blood has no conscience, guys.") But it
is the presence of *Village Voice* writer
Donna Minkowitz, a broad-faced, short-
haired, witty and somewhat wired woman,
that galvanizes the audience. Wearing a red
blazer and men's pants and shoes, Minkowitz talks with an impish smile about being
attracted to "women in military uniforms,
women in LL Bean jackets, women who
look like they mean business." Over the
course of the show, Minkowitz is pelted
with insults. Her violation, it seems, is not
being lesbian, but being unconventionally
female. Povich asks Tommy, the apparent
expert on heterosexual male desire, whether
he thinks the two femme women on the
panel are attractive (yes), and then if he
thinks Donna is attractive (no). Big applause. Several times, the camera pans
Donna from toe to head, as if to punctuate
the point. Minkowitz explains herself well
("I'm not trying to embody a man, excuse
me, I'm trying to embody a butch lesbian
which is something I love, I'm not trying to
be a man, I'm trying to be Donna Minkowitz, in all my glory"), but there is not
much of a reception for her argument that
"sex roles are crazy, they're just a fiction."
Instead, she is told she's "a frustrated male,
you look like you want to be a man and were
born a woman, unfortunate, I guess," and
"you like to wear men's clothes, you like to
wear a jockstrap?" While her lesbianism is

generally unproblematic, or at least goes uncondemned, her gender nonconformity is penalized with vigor (Paramount Pictures, 1992). Indeed, a lesbian who is unmarked, unbutch, who obeys the norms of gender conformity, looks exciting, pretty, and normal by comparison. A public alliance between lesbians who "pass" ("stunning beauties") and those who do not ("frustrated males") is rendered more difficult to make; same-sex desire itself comes to seem unremarkable, but only if the coalition of women who "look like women" (hetero and homo) is favored over that of women who love women.

Even a 1992 *Donahue* show, in many ways a typical bigot-bashing political debate about an anti-gay referendum in Concord, California, manages to set "good," gender-confirming gays against "bad" gays in drag. Pastor Lloyd Mashore and his colleague square off against a young activist named Ken Stanley and another pastor; the anti-gay activists argue about special rights, the homosexual agenda, family values, picnics and Little League ball games, while the pro-gay activists talk about equal rights, pride, and love; Phil asks, as always, "What do you want to do with these gay people?" The audience takes this side and that one. But what tips the discussion is the presence of Gil Block, in his persona as Sadie, one of the Sisters of Perpetual Indulgence.

Gil as Sadie is dressed in full red, white, and blue drag, with red gloves, a big white wig, one dramatic eye with white stars over blue shadow and the other with red stripes over white shadow. Political theater, he claims, but once a male caller attacks Sadie, the audience lets loose a barrage of hostility. "Oh, get off the stage," another caller says to audience applause, "you're up there on the platform dressed like an idiot, and you expect to be taken seriously." ("Something should be done with them," she continues, "All they seem to do is cause problems. If we all got together and talked about it, maybe we could figure out what could be done with them. I really think they should all go back in the closet and make life peaceful again.") The two gay activists fighting discrimination are fine, says an audience member shortly thereafter, but Gil, who "is making a mockery of what they're trying to do, is just stupid." Gil tries to talk about being a patriotic American, but it doesn't really work. "I don't understand," says a young white man with a Philadelphia accent, "how dressing up like an oversized Captain America is going to help the gay cause." Laughter, applause. ("I think they should keep it to themselves," adds a young Southern white woman with hoop earrings. "I don't make a big point that I'm heterosexual.") A male caller finishes him off. "I'm 26 years old, I'm a gay white male, and I'm embarrassed by the man on the end there," he says. "People think I come home from work and put on a dress and swing from the chandeliers because of people like him" (Multimedia Entertainment, 1992). The young man captures the political division talk shows amplify and reinforce: between chandelier-swinging, cross-dressing flamboyants and suit-wearing, privacy-loving passers. The political affinities between them—their shared lack of civil rights protections, for example—are overshadowed by the colorful, provocative lines of gender convention so favored by talk shows.

Thus we reach one of the talk show's true political scandals. The scandal isn't so much that talk shows ambush people, or cynically use people's intimate lives to make a buck, or any of that utterly unsurprising and ugly activity. Nor is it even the fact of their drawing of lines that irks; after all, line-drawing is one of the things that culture is always about. The scandal is the *kinds* of lines they emphasize, setting apart potentially powerful sets of political and cultural partners, helping to cut the threads tying working-class lesbian to transsexual to drag queen to gay professional to butch lesbian to bisexual to rural gay kid. That's not of course something they do alone, but they are central to the process, partly because they help it along in such unintentional ways, such entertaining ways, and partly because they mix it, to great effect, with pleas for tolerance, enlightenment, and love. Those alliances are critical because we are engaged in a strange, complicated conflict, which talk shows embody but by no means exhaust: a fight over public space.

Sexual Nonconformity and the Public-Private Divide

> You know what? Nobody has any business in the bedrooms of any nation or in the closets. If you want to be gay, just be gay, like just be gay and shut up about it. *Donahue* audience member (Multimedia Entertainment, 1995a)

> I'm sick to death of the entertainment industry cramming homosexuality down our throats. It's disgusting and I'm fed up with it. *Donahue* caller (Multimedia Entertainment, 1992)

"No one's suggesting that you shouldn't be gay," host Jerry Springer tells an 18-year-old gay man in men's pants and sweater, painted nails and high heals, blatantly misrepresenting the sentiments of many in his audience. "If you're gay, you're gay, period. But why is it necessary to just let everybody know all the time?" Having recruited gay male guests on the basis of their effeminacy and cross-dressing—many of whom are treated to hoots and hollers from a ridiculing audience—Springer wonders aloud at the end of his show about "why gays so often seem to flaunt their sexuality, almost an exaggeration of their effeminateness." He understands it, he tells his viewers, since if you put yourself in the position of having your "sexuality constantly repressed or kept in the closet," you would see that "most of us would go crazy." Many gays, he says, are understandably angry, and unwilling to take it any more. "And they're coming out with a vengeance," he says, "suddenly a militancy polite society has never witnessed before" (Multimedia Entertainment, 1995b).

In the midst of the obvious hypocrisy and the moldy, ignorant equation of male homosexuality and effeminacy, Springer accidentally makes an excellent point: "polite society" is annoyed. His show scripts a backlash against gay visibility (and transgender and bisexual visibility, to a lesser degree) that is quite commonplace, exposing and participating in a culture war that is partly his own creation. "The homosexuals wouldn't have any problem at all if they would just keep it to themselves, and stop trying to act like they're special cause they're gay," says a caller to the *Donahue* show with Reverend Mashore facing off against Sister Sadie, as the camera catches smiling, applauding faces. "Why is there such a need to come out of the closet?" an audience member asks on another *Donahue,* this one on gay cops (Multimedia Entertainment, 1994). Indeed, the talk show structural emphasis on separating "appropriate" gay people (middle-class professionals, especially those who pass as heterosexual) from "inappropriate" (lower- and poverty-class people, especially those who do not pass) is powered by an overlapping tension that talk shows manifest: between their push, in alliance with gay people and others, to make "private" matters public, and the various people interested in keeping certain things, such as homosexuality, away from public view.[5] For many in "polite society," it seems, public declarations of lesbian, gay, transgender, or bisexual identity are inherently inappropriate, impolite, and nobody's business.

"I really don't have anything against your sexuality," a man tells John and Jerry, who had just kissed each other hello on a "gay and gorgeous" *Jenny Jones* show, for instance. "But the intimacy, the things that men and women that I think should be doing, stroking your hair—I see you guys holding hands and kissing. I'm sorry, but it really, it disgusts me" (Jenny Jones Show, 1995). Why do you have to flaunt it? audience members ask in various ways on TV talk shows. Why do you have to have parades, and why do you have to go on television announcing it to everybody? Talk shows, as prime purveyors of public visibility of sex and gender nonconformity, are terrific foci for the anxieties and hostilities that a queer presence evokes.

Daytime talk television, in fact, by publicizing the "private," widens yet another fault line in gay and lesbian politics. "Privacy" is already quite a vexed, complex political issue in sexual politics. On the one hand, lesbian and gay political and social life in the past quarter of a century has been built on making sexual identities public, arguing that ours is a political and social status; since everyone is implicated in oppressing us, in part by keeping us invisible and spreading lies about us, it is everybody's business that we are gay. What we do out of bed, not what we do in bed, is what is most relevant about us. Coming out in public, especially through major public institutions such as schools, the workplace, and communications media, is a way of asserting the public relevance of what others deem private—that is, demonstrating and demonstrating against a second class, stigmatized social status. (The more recent bisexual and transgender movements have followed this same model.) Talk shows, as

we have amply seen, are approached by activists in this light.

At the same time, guided by the logic of constitutional claims-making, gay and lesbian activists have long put forward an argument that retains traditional divisions between private and public, in order to pursue protection under the individual "right to privacy" (Mohr, 1988). The only difference between homo and hetero, they have said, is what we do in bed, and what we do in bed is nobody's business, and especially not the business of the government. Thus comments such as this one, from a 30-year-old Latina secretary, in the midst of a discussion of talk shows with a bunch of women: "I feel like it's none of my business. Whatever you do in your bedroom is no concern of mine, just like what I do in my bedroom is none of your business." This is about sex, sex belongs in private, and personal privacy is protected from public intrusion. (The political right, tellingly, has used the basic elements of this argument to great effect, arguing that homosexuality is indeed private, sexual behavior, and that sexual behavior is not the basis for either minority status or rights.) While the legal argument for privacy is certainly not incompatible with public visibility, talk shows seem to run against the rhetorical gist of privacy claims. Many heterosexual talk show participants and viewers seize hold of this conflict: you keep saying how your sexuality is none of my business, yet here you are again on television chatting and yelling and kissing and getting married and making fools of yourselves. If you want privacy, then keep it private.

Talk shows invite this perspective on themselves, largely because they seem to be the sorts of places where, to many viewers, all kinds of people are doing and saying things that are nobody else's business. Television itself, as Joshua Meyrowitz (1985, Chapter 6) has pointed out, messes with the public-private lines: it is a "public" space brought into the "privacy" of home. Daytime talk shows, given that they profit from the discussion of taboo subjects, are hotbeds of impropriety and the discussion of impropriety, more or less by definition; these public living rooms, moreover, sit noticeably in your own private one. The discussion and display of atypical sexualities and genders is often filtered through an ambivalence about just who is doing what now in public—and, more fundamentally, just to whom public space belongs. The first clue to this dynamic comes from the common "where do they find these people?" disdain expressed by all kinds of talk show viewers. Many of the viewers with whom I had discussions, even though they often watch the less genteel fare, take offense at the unseemliness of it all, disparaging guests who bring private talk out of the house, airing their dirty laundry in front of God and everybody when they should be down in their own basement washing it. "I can't believe they would air all this stuff on the air, I mean in front of a general public, so to speak," says Barbara, a 56-year-old non-working African-American woman in one of my heterosexual discussion groups. "It's so sleazy," Joni, a white woman a few years older, agrees. "Who needs to put that garbage in your head?" Every discussion includes this kind of statement (more often from older participants than younger). "I think it's getting a little, um, past risque to the point of really just obnoxious and distasteful," says Ed, a 54-year-old African-American human resources director in another group, for instance. "Distasteful. Distasteful," he repeats. "It's just very distasteful for people to get on national TV and just tell all of their business."

The divider between inappropriate and appropriate public talk is, moreover, as viewers' conversations capture, a marker of social statues; the aversion of middle-class viewers for "sensationalistic," "exploitative" programming expresses an aversion for the déclassé. "It's like middle class and lower class," Judi, a 32-year-old homemaker, explains simply, as discussion turns to the comparison of *Oprah's* audience with *Richard Bey's*. Joni responds by explaining why she prefers *Oprah:*

> On one show she did, she said, "Aren't these a very clean audience?" Because they all looked dressed, they all looked like nice, middle-class people. They didn't look trashy. Everybody looked so nice and clean. And it's true, she gets a better class of people. And if I have to watch something, I'd rather watch that. *Oprah* has an average American that knows that they don't spit in public, and they don't do certain things in public, and that's how they conduct themselves. Whether it's false or not, it's civilized. That's what we do in America.

It is not just spitting in public that we don't do. We don't *display our sexual selves in public*. Judith, a 55-year-old white teacher in another group, makes the connection between class, privacy, and sexuality quite explicit.

> I wouldn't watch all this garbage. Who's sleeping with who, what's going on with this couple because they were two women living together, or whatever. I can't better myself, I can't get more class to me, and I think class is very important. I think a lot of people have lost it. And this is all just—people are entitled to their private lives, It should be private. And anything that's put on display is just garbage. There's nothing wrong with having sexual topics on television. To put it on display is what's wrong. When it's private, you work with it, but when you put it on television live, it becomes dirt. If you're going to open it up, have a psychologist there, make it a very proper thing.

The public display of "private life," especially sexuality, is not something classy people do. It is improper. Watching it, one becomes dirtier, less classy. In the eyes of many middle-class talk show watchers, sexual impropriety is really just the most important and obvious version of unsavory uses of public space. It is not so much the *gayness* that is bothersome, it's the *publicness*.

So, for many viewers, an ambivalence about homosexuality maps quite effortlessly onto an ambivalence about the making-public of sexual status, which itself maps onto a more generalized resistance to changes in what they see as their own public territory: a queer presence easily becomes another example of people behaving improperly. Even though very few talk-show discussions of homosexuality are discussions of sexual practice, they are easily and commonly swept into the category of "inappropriate." As viewers invariably point out, for one thing, talk shows in recent years have tipped the balance towards sensationalized, exploitative treatments of sex and gender differences, going for the "sleazy," the "circus," the "extreme," and so on—so that homosexuality, bisexuality and gender-crossing appear largely in the pile marked "distasteful." Moreover, homosexuality and bisexuality are more often than not, even when they are not framed as purely sexual on a show, placed by viewers in the category of "sexual." While viewers often emphasize "tasteful" presentations of sex and gender nonconformists (a focus on individual experience, a respectful conversation), it is nonetheless a short step from the general grouchiness about what are seen as gauche, low-class uses of the public space of television to a specific animosity towards the public visibility of gay people. Talk shows make it especially easy for same-sex desire to slide quickly into the category of things that are not the business of polite, civilized, clean, nice people to hear about. They offer

occasions for middle-class social anxieties about changes in public space to come into sharper focus, by attaching to the unruly class cultures and unusual sexual beings who seem to populate the public space of talk shows.

For liberal viewers, this tends to be expressed as a concern for the damage done to decent gay folks by "fringe" gay guests, for instance, who might be taken to represent the whole. The problem with those talk show guests, they say, is that they do not know how to keep it quiet. But listen a bit more closely, and you begin to hear how the charge that people "flaunting it" on talk shows blends smoothly into a general resistance to gayness in public space. Judi, a 32-year-old white homemaker, has this to say, for instance:

> My girlfriend's sister is gay, and they're living their lives the way they want to. On TV, they're doing it for the gimmick, they want the attention, whereas my friends aren't like that at all. They don't flaunt it around. If they love each other, that's their problem. They don't sit there and advertise it all the time.

Rosanne, a 47-year-old white bookkeeper in another group, has a different starting point, but comes back to a similar punchline:

> I don't particularly even like to walk down the street and see a guy and a girl making out, so seeing two guys kiss or two girls kiss, it annoys me just as much to see a guy and a girl carrying on in the middle of the street. I think if everybody believes in what they want to believe in, and don't try to make a big issue out of it, like, "Oh, you have to let me do this because I'm a lesbian," or "You have to let me do this because I'm a gay," everybody just staying on their own road, whether it's a road of what some people call normal and some people call abnormal.

When she continues later, it becomes clear where talk show impropriety fits into

Roseanne's picture: keep anything but talking behind closed doors:

> Let's educate some people, let people become aware of what's going on, and try to do it in a subtle way that doesn't make everything seem like smut. And if they're doing it behind their private doors, that's their business. If they come out sitting next to each other and talking and everything else, that's fine. If they start lovey-dovey, to me, I don't think it's appropriate for anyone to act that way. Whatever you do in your own home, and everything else, that's fine.

For Bobby, a 24-year-old African-American interior decorator, it is not just "lovey-dovey" behavior that is the problem, but any public announcement of homosexuality:

> My understanding on a lot of gay shows is, like gay people have to force their sexuality on you. They want to let you know that they're gay so bad. They have to let you know. I don't have to let a person know that I'm a heterosexual male. I mean, I don't force it on people. We already have rights for men and rights for women. I don't see why it has to be gay rights and all that type of stuff. Why do they have to let people know that they're gay and this is what we do? I don't see why. I get annoyed with it, by them always forcing on you, and they have to be so flamboyant and so gay and so out there. Just keep it to yourself.

Ask liberal talk show watchers what they think about shows on gay people, and this is often what comes out of them, right alongside "live and let live": don't flaunt it, keep it to yourself, stay off my road.

Viewers with conservative views on homosexuality, who often tend to be more tuned in to the political aspects of homosexuality, demonstrate this connection most clearly: they tend to see talk shows as part of a damaging intrusion by the wrong people into public space. Vincent, a 63-year-old telephone company manager and the most vehement conservative on gay issues in a group of male conservatives, is very up-front about this. Over the course of the discussion, he argues against same-sex marriage ("if they do it for the homosexuals to get married, they're going to have to do the same damn thing for the Man-Boy Love Association"), the Supreme Court ("talking about how you can't restrict even porno on the Internet"), gay protests at the St. Patrick's Day Parade ("the homosexuals were promoting their lifestyle"), and a *New Yorker* cover of two male sailors kissing. "Why can't it be 'don't ask, don't tell?'" he asks. "They don't want to be satisfied with that today. It's not hatred against them, believe me when I say I have a feeling for them and what they're going through, but damn it, don't tell, keep it in the closet." Talk shows, for him and the other men in that discussion group ("it's sort of like social engineering," says Dave, a 45-year-old engineer), fit into a more general assault by gay people into what they see as their own public space. "Homosexuals are here to stay," Vincent says. "The talk shows only bring them to the forefront. They are here to stay, just like the pornographic shows, where you can go buy tapes and so forth and so on." In another hint of the way middle-class politeness plays into a condemnation of gay publicness, he offers the example of a homosexual glee club, whose members were "professional people, they're not running around the streets or anything like that."

> The talk show gave me the wrong picture of these people. I think if they want to promote themselves, they should have something like this choir I saw. They weren't hurting anybody, and they were pretty damn good singers. Have your own lifestyle. Have your own lifestyle. Have your own clubs, your own choirs. Don't stick your nose into St. Patrick's Day Parade. Don't stick your nose here and there. In many instances it's in your face, and I don't think it should be that way. These

people should have their own lifestyle. Don't ask, don't tell.

Unless you are singing, that is, please keep quiet, or at least keep it away from us. Stick to your own road.

A group of conservative women, talking about how topics become passé after a while, winds up quite close to Vincent's perspective. "It's like, if that's what they want to do, if that's how you want to live, live that way," says Lynn, a 34-year-old white saleswoman. "But it would have been better if they'd stayed in the closet and no one knew. Now it's like, we have to have these rights, gays have to have these rights." *They're pushing,* says Peggy, a 59-year-old non-working woman. "They're pushing too far," Lynn agrees, invoking the privacy argument. "It's not anybody else's business. If you want to be gay, you know, stay in your house with your partner and do what you have to do. But to have to like parade down the street and show everybody, I don't like that." I *don't either,* Peggy says. *They're flaunting it.* For these women, the visibility of sexual nonconformity on talk shows is continuous with a more general invasion of public space, a sort of tasteless greediness, by gays and lesbians, who parade down streets and now parade on television right into our homes.

The sense that talk shows are part of an invasion, that when they involve gay people they must be battled rather than watched, can be extraordinarily intense. In the midst of a long, heated argument in a male discussion group, Jim ("Rush Limbaugh is my main man"), a 55-year-old retired police officer, puts it as clearly as it can be put.

> I'm not anti-gay, I just don't want the gays invading my space. I tolerate them, but I don't want them coming in my face. I think the gays and lesbians, it was better when they were in the closet. Now they come out, and they're trying to force their views on us. More and more every day. Lesbians and gays, fine, they want to do their thing, fine, but don't get in my space. Because I have my beliefs, and I don't want them messing with my family, because my family's the way I raised my family. I'm a churchgoer, I'm a father, and I don't want to see this happen to my children, or my grandchildren. And I want them to stay where they are, and don't impose their views on everybody else. *I don't want my space invaded, very simply, and I'll fight to keep my space from being invaded. I don't want them in my house, period.* They're right in your face, all the time, and the shows don't help. The shows don't help. They have the people right out there, and they're flaunting it. The talk shows make it look like, oh, it's great, it's better than what you might have. I've always tolerated their lifestyle, I just don't want them to put it in my face, that's all, and when they do it on TV, they're putting it in your face.

Exploitation and propriety are of no concern here, but the elements left are shared with more liberal, gay-sympathetic viewers: *keep out of my face, keep out of my space.*

When sex and gender statuses become politicized—when the personal becomes political—as the feminist movement has dramatically demonstrated, they often meet with this kind of backlash. This makes good sense, since what under the old rules had seemed like a natural privilege (man public, woman domestic; heterosexual public, homosexual secret) is now claimed to be an exertion of power. The political battle becomes, in part, a battle over ownership of public space. Both talk shows and gay, lesbian, bisexual, and transgender movements (along with the feminist movement) have been aggressively moving previously private issues into the public sphere; television has, moreover, taken the newly public back into the privacy of home. That move, and all the anxieties about changes in the public sphere that congeal around it, make talk shows politically relevant despite the hollow twaddle of which they are so often composed.

Privacy and sexual supremacy, daytime talk and the previously private, talk shows and sex and gender movements—these relationships are undeniably tight. For those with an interest in protecting traditional divisions between public and private, TV talk shows featuring lesbians, gays, bisexuals, and transgenders thus look and feel like a double whammy. The shows want to make public space something entirely different, by giving it to people who have never before made much successful claim on it. Liberal heterosexual viewers worry about exploitation and propriety, beneath which seems to lurk a sense that they are losing control of public space; conservative viewers bring that anxiety to its extreme, watching those shows, when they can stand to, as though they are holding their fists in front of their faces, ready to fend off the onslaught. While lesbian and gay, bisexual, and transgender activists are waging their struggles for visibility, these viewers are waging their own battle with the television set. They are blocking their throats from the talk shows' fast and furious force-feeding of sex and gender deviance. They are wishing these people would just shut up, not quite understanding why they need to flaunt it in other people's faces, why they have to use television to stick queer noses were they don't belong.

Conclusion: Visibility and Collective Identity

We're assumed to consist entirely of extreme stereotypes: men ultraswishy and ultraviolet, Frankenstein thug-women with bolts on their necks, mustachio'd Dolly Parton wanna-bes, leather-men in boots and whips, ombudsmen of pederasty squiring their ombudsboys—all ridiculous, deranged, or criminal. And when we are *finally* allowed to rally and march, to lay our case before the cameras of the straight American public, what do we do? We call out of the woodwork as our ambassadors of bad will all the screamers, stompers, gender-benders, sadomasochists, and pederasts, and confirm America's worst fears and hates. You can call it gay liberation if you like: we say it's spinach, and we say to hell with it! (Kirk and Madsen, 1989: 144)

> What is a "positive" representation of a gay or lesbian character? Is it any image that avoids the harshest stereotypes? Is it a highly assimilated image that makes it impossible to "tell" whether someone is straight or gay? Is it an image that attributes transgressive gender roles to a gay character—an "effeminate" man or "masculine" woman—but does so from a "sympathetic" perspective? Is it simply any such "transgressive" image, available for a potentially empowering appropriation by lesbian or gay viewers, irrespective of the ways in which non-gay viewers might react? (Schacter, 1997: 727)

All told, talk shows make "good publicity" and "positive images" and "affirmation" hard concepts to hold. They offer a visibility that diversifies even as it amplifies internal class conflicts, that empowers even as it makes public alliances between various subpopulations more difficult, that carves out important new public spaces even as it plays up an association between public queerness and the decay of public decorum. Talk shows suggest that visibility cannot be strategized as either positive or negative, but must be seen as a series of political negotiations.

For instance, a glance at the emphasis on outrageousness that many talk shows have come to promote—the source of much complaining about negative imagery of lesbian, gay, transgender and bisexual people—makes it hard to hold onto the notion that talk show selection of "the fringes" is necessarily and always a bad thing. This kind of exoticizing imagery certainly makes social acceptability harder to gain by overemphasizing difference, often presented as frightening, pathological, pathetic, or silly; it is annoying and painful for pretty much everybody involved. But at the same time it can push out a space: an emphasis on difference, especially on a scary kind of difference, can keep those watching at a distance. Like the in-your-face radicalism of some recent "queer" organizing, a freaky otherness is useful, for some purposes. When people push away from you, or think of you as harmless and dismissible, they tend to leave you alone, and sometimes being left alone is exactly what is needed for independent political and cultural organizing. As one queer writer put it in the early 1990s, "If I tell them I am queer, they give me room. Politically, I can think of little better. I do not want to be one of them. They only need to give me room" (Chee, 1991: 15). The same might be said of the talk shows' money-driven interest in the more provocative edges of lesbian, bisexual, transgender, and gay populations: while they Other us, they also give us *room*. Of course, this is also exactly the problem many people have with them, since at least the appearance of normality seems necessary to winning political *rights*. It's a tension built into talk show visibility, and into the emergence of other marginalized people into commercial media recognition. As Jane Schacter (1997: 728) points out, what's "positive" or "negative" depends "in large part upon what underlying theory of equality has been adopted—one that prizes assimilation or transformation, sameness or difference." The same imagery that is damaging for some kinds of political work (assimilation into the mainstream) is effective for other kinds (the autonomous carving-out of political space). Both kinds of work are necessary. Talk shows, simply through their pursuit of

ratings, inadvertently amplify a political dilemma inherent in becoming visible, in which both exaggerating and playing down our collective eccentricity is vital.

Indeed, the same risk-averse logic of television that has led to the sensationalizing of sexual and gender nonconformity (the weirder it is, the less the risk of people changing channels) has made the sensations repeat and repeat (it worked before, or it works for others, so let's keep doing it). The shocking gets less and less preposterous as it is repeated; the selection of a population's stigmatized extremes may hem in the population as a whole, but the habitual selection of extremes may simply deaden the stigma. "It is not the simple statement of facts that ushers in freedom," Quentin Crisp (1997[1968]: 204) has suggested. "It is the constant repetition of them that has this liberating effect." Over time, the talk shows have managed to do for their audiences what no one else has: to make televised homosexuality and even transsexualism and bisexuality nearly dull. The "fringes," as they show up on TV every week, become run of the mill; they become like a desperate Madonna, whose simulated sex and outside-the-clothing lingerie drew yawns after not too long. Critics of talk shows here have a point: talk shows, through their continual exhibition of the most colorful side-show figures, "define deviance down."[6] From the perspective of those resisting a political and cultural system that labels them deviant, this is a good thing: the edges of normality push ever outward. Tolerance, Crisp informs us, is boredom's offspring.[7] Where exactly is the "positive" in all of this, and where the "negative"?

The difficulty goes much deeper than any talk show will ever go. Talk shows accentuate not only the tension between legitimacy-buying and diversity-promoting visibility but also central dilemmas of collective identity. A sense of collective identification—that this is us, that we are each other—is personally and politically critical: it is an anchor, offering the comforts and resources of family and, at least in this political system, a foundation from which to organize and wage political battles. Identity requires stable, recognizable social categories. It requires difference, knowing where you end and where others begin. It thus makes good sense to do as gay and lesbian movements, modeling themselves on civil rights movements, have done: to build a quasi-ethnicity with its own political and cultural institutions, festivals, and neighborhoods. Underwriting this strategy moreover, is typically the notion that gays and lesbians share the same sort of essential self, one with same-sex desires (D'Emilio, 1983; Epstein, 1987; Seidman, 1993). All of this solidifies the social categories of "gay" and "lesbian," clarifying who "we" are and are not, even as it also stabilizes the categories of "heterosexual man" and "heterosexual woman."

At the same time, though, it is exactly through the fixed, dichotomous categorization into apparently distinct species of gay and straight (and male and female) that anti-gay, anti-bisexual, and anti-transgender oppression is perpetuated. Even as the categories that mark us as different are necessary for claiming rights and benefits, making them unworkable provide its own protections; if there is no sure way to distinguish gay from straight, for instance, the basis for anti-gay legislation is arguably weakened. From this angle, *muddying* the categories rather than shoring them up, painting out their instability and fluidity along with their social roots, is the key to liberation. The political advantages of scrambling the code are always also in competition with those of keeping it clear, not only for people who want to retain their status on a sexual hierarchy, but also for

people resisting that hierarchy, who need a coherent sense of collective identity, a cohesive foundation from which to fight, for instance, for rights as gay people.

This tension between a politic that treats the homo-hetero divide as a given and goes about the business of equalizing the sides, and a politic that seeks to *attack the divide itself,* always present in contemporary gay and lesbian politics, has come to the fore most recently with the controversial emergence of "queer" movements in politics and academia. Queer theory and politics, as Michael Warner puts it, protests "not just the normal behavior of the social but the *idea* of normal behavior" (Warner, 1983: xxvii). Especially with the vocal challenge from transgendered and bisexual people—who do not so easily fit into the gay-straight and man-woman binary worldview—the question of the unity, stability, viability, and political utility of sexual identities has been called into question. The queer politics of "carnival, transgression, and parody," with its "anti-assimilationist" and "decentering" politics, has been met with heavy resistance from those rightly seeing it as a threat to civil rights strategies (Stein and Plummer, 1996: 134; see also Epstein, 1996; Gamson, 1995). The problem, of course, is that both the category-strippers and the category-defenders are right: fixed identity categories are both the basis for oppression and the basis for political power.

Talk shows create much of their sex-and-gender fare, especially when transgender and bisexual people are involved, on exactly this tension. Talk shows, even though they reinstate them, mess up those reassuring dichotomies. On talk shows, the categories stretch and contract, stretch and contract. Much talk show visibility, for one thing, is "queer," in the meaning of the term favored by academics, spotlighting "a proliferation of sexualities (bisexual, transvestite, pre-

and post-op transsexual, to name a few) and the compounding of outcast positions along racial, ethnic, and class, as well as sexual lines—none of which is acknowledged by the neat binary division between hetero- and homosexual" (Hennessy, 1994–95: 34).[8] The disruptions are fleeting, as audiences work hard to put the categories back together, but they are disturbances nonetheless.

For lesbian, gay, bisexual, and transgender collectives, in particular, these moments of diverse visibility are a crisis: both an opportunity to challenge the *cultural* logic of homo-hetero distinction, and a threat to the sense that "we" make the kind of sense we need, *politically,* to make. Talk shows, with their peculiar interest in the out-there and the in-between, bring out this queer dilemma. The ubiquity of people who do not quite fit the simple categories advances an important cultural agenda, by reminding viewers that the "neat binary division between hetero- and homosexual" is not as neat as all that, tarnishing the certainty of clear, natural differences between sexualities and genders. Even with all the attempts to defuse the identity threats housed by these sorts of disruptions, the sense that "normal" and "natural" are distinguishable from their opposites unravels in bits and pieces. Media visibility, talk shows tell us, is riddled with this difficulty—and the more diverse and democratic it gets, the more the dilemma comes alive.

The conditions of visibility, of course, are not of our own making. The tight rope on which bisexuals, transgenders, gays and lesbians balance as we emerge into visibility gets especially tangled in a time and place where the "public" into which we walk is a space in turmoil. Talk shows, which make their money primarily by publicizing personal issues, only make this anxiety easier to see. Sex and gender non-

conformists participate in, and detonate, an anxiety about the shifting boundaries between public and private—much as they have taken a place in other "moral panics," such as the 1950s equation of homosexuality and communism, where pervasive fears and anxieties attach to sexual "deviants" (see D'Emilio, 1983; Rubin, 1993 [1984]; Weeks, 1981). The very televised presence of gay, lesbian, bisexual and transgendered people makes public space, to many people, appear to be crawling with indecency. In an environment where public and private have blurred into new forms, gay, lesbian, bisexual, and transgender visibility comes to symbolize a breakdown in the meaning of publicness.

The charge of public indecency is, moreover, a call to get out: this is *my* space, it says, and you do not belong here. Becoming media-visible, especially if your social identity, is rooted in a status previously understood to belong to the realm of "private" life, calls the question on who owns public space. The issue of what can and cannot be spoken about and seen in public, which the televised collective coming out of the past 20 years evokes, is really the issue of who is and is not considered a legitimate member of "the public." This ongoing cultural war over public space and public participation is what makes talk shows—even when they are devoid of anything remotely political—socially relevant, and turns them into such zany, vibrant, coarse scenes. In part, they exist to isolate the socially challenging in a discredited space, offering the heady opportunity to be lords and ladies of a vapid kingdom, while the real powerhouses command the rest of the empire. In part, they exist to provide a concrete locale at which the question of just what public space can look like, and under just whose jurisdiction it falls, is kept alive for everybody to look at and toss around. Entering media space means joining this fight, and the other ones attached to it, with these questions and predicaments scribbled on your hand.

Notes

1. This question is especially critical in a period when one edge of the sword is increasingly cutting the path. With the recent "discovery" of gay and lesbian markets, it is primarily those with buying power who come to be seen and heard, even in the publications and programs produced by and for gay, lesbian, bisexual, and transgender people. "As the economic logic of national advertising begins to drive publications aimed at the lesbian and gay community," Fejes and Petrich claim (1993: 411), "the only voice being heard is that of an upper income, urban, de-sexed white male." "The increasing circulation of gay and lesbian images in consumer culture has the effect," Rosemary Hennessy (1994–5: 32) adds, "of consolidating an imaginary, class-specific gay subjectivity for both straight and gay audiences." As affluent, assimilated gays and lesbians are being marketed and marketed to, talk shows, with their restless class cultural mix, are a refreshing counterpoint.

2. This essay works from interview, transcript, video and focus-group data collected for a book-length study, *Freaks Talk Back: Tabloid Talk Shows and Sexual Nonconformity* (Gamson, 1998). Although only a small portion is discussed here, the data consist of the following: in-depth, semi-structured interviews with 20 talk show production staff and 44 talk show guests; quantitative and qualitative content analysis of the 160 available transcripts in which lesbian, gay, bisexual, and gender-crossing subjects made a significant appearance, for the years 1984–1986 and 1994–1995; interpretive analysis of about 100 hours of videos; 12 focus-group discussions with regular talk show viewers (a total of about 75 people), nine with heterosexually identified viewers in suburban New Jersey, three with lesbians and gay men in Manhattan (one group of lesbians, one of gay men, and one of mixed men and women), and one discussion with members of the Manhattan Gender Network, a transgender organization. The data cover experiences on just about every topic-driven daytime talk show that has had a life: *Beatrice Berry, Richard Bey, Danny Bonaduce, Carnie, Donahue, Gordon Elliott, Gabrielle, Mo Gaffney, Geraldo, Jenny Jones, Ricki Lake, Leeza, Marilu, Oprah, The Other Side, Charles Perez, Maury Povich, Susan Powter, Dennis Prager, Jane Pratt, Sally Jessy Raphael, Joan Rivers, Rolonda, Jerry*

Springer, Tempestt, Mark Walberg, Jane Whitney, and *Montel Williams.* Unless otherwise noted, quotations are from author interviews and focus groups.

3. Since my concern is much more how ordinary viewers make sense of "publicness," I do not take up the rich, Habermas-inspired theoretical discussions now taking place over the nature and meaning of the public sphere. For some of these, see Habermas, 1991; Calhoun, 1996; Weintraub and Kumar, 1996. On the relationship between talk shows and theories of the public sphere, see Carpignano et al., 1990; Livingstone and Lunt, 1994.

4. On the history of talk shows since the rise of electronic broadcasting, see also Rose, 1985; Heaton and Wilson, 1995, especially Chapter 1.

5. As Jeff Weintraub points out, there are quite a few overlapping meanings of the distinction between "public" and "private." Most generally, one verion contrasts "what is hidden or withdrawn" with "what is open, revealed, or accessible," and another version contrasts "what is individual, or pertains only to an individual" with "what is collective, or affects the interests of a collectivity of individuals" (Weintraub, 1996: 5). While on talk shows certainly both versions are being negotiated, the first seems primarily to be at play, and it is this hidden/revealed distinction that therefore informs my analysis most.

6. This phase was repeated by Willaim Bennett and Joseph Lieberman in their 1995 attacks on daytime television talk. See Empower America (1995). For related criticisms of talk shows, see Abt and Seesholtz, 1994; Chidley, 1996; Gabler, 1995; Heiton and Wilson, 1995; Kurtz, 1996.

7. Clearly, as I have indicated, there is more room in this genre than in others for the repetition of controversial, norm-breaking images and subjects. Homosexual, bisexual, and transgender subjects are still hardly uncontroversial in Hollywood film and television. But as the response to the coming-out of sitcom character Ellen Morgan and sitcom star Ellen Degeneres indicates, the repetition of these controversial images dulls their edge rather quickly: while audiences tuned in to watch the "coming out" *Ellen* in large numbers, and the usual suspects (Jerry Falwell, Donald Wildmon) decried the "promotion of homosexualtiy," there was so much commentary, amidst months of media hype for the event, that by the time Ellen and Ellen came out nobody was anywhere near shocked. Through repeated publicity, Ellen's shocking revelation became mundane.

8. This kind of proliferation and sexual indeterminacy is also taking shape in other media

arenas, some of which do very little to put the categories back together again. Discussing advertisements that take a "dual market approach," targeting homosexual and heterosexual markets simultaneously, for instance, Danae Clark (1993: 188, 195) points out that such ads often use models who "bear the signifiers of sexual ambiguity or androgynous style" and "employ representationl strategies that generally refer to gays and lesbians in anti-essentialist terms," depicting them as not inherently different from heterosexuals.

References

Abt, Vicki and Seesholtz, Mel (1994) "The Shameless World of Phil, Sally and Oprah: Television Talk Shows and the Deconstructing of Society," *Journal of Popular Culture* 195–215.

Alwood, Edward (1996) *Straight News: Gays, Lesbians, and the News Media*. New York: Columbia University Press.

Calhoun, Craig, ed. (1992) *Habermas and the Public Sphere*. Cambridge, MA: MIT Press.

Carpignano, Paolo, Andersen, Robin, Aronowitz, Stanley and DiFazio, William (1990) "Chatter in the Age of Electronic Reproduction: Talk Television and the 'Public Mind,'" *Social Text* 25: 33–55.

Chee, Alexander (1991) "A Queer Nationalism," *Out/Look* 11:15.

Chidley, Joe (1996) "Talking In the Trash," *McClean's* (19 Feb.): 50–3.

Clark, Danae (1993) "Commodity Lesbianism" in Henry Abelove, Michele Aina Barale and David Halperin (eds) *The Lesbian and Gay Studies Reader*, pp. 186–201. New York; Routledge.

Crisp, Quentin (1997 [1968]) *The Naked Civil Servant*. New York: Penguin.

D'Emilio, John (1983) *Sexual Politics, Sexual Communities: The Making of a Homosexual Minority in the United States*. Chicago, IL: University of Chicago Press.

Empower America (1995) "Press Conference," Washington, DC: Federal Document Clearing House, 26 October.

Epstein, Steven (1987) "Gay Politics, Ethnic Identity: The Limits of Social Constructionism," *Socialist Review* 17(3–4): 9–54.

Epstein, Steven (1996) "A Queer Encounter Sociology and the Study of Sexuality," in Steven Seidman (ed.) *Queer Theory/Sociology*, pp. 145–67. Cambridge, MA: Blackwell.

Fejes, Fred and Petrich, Kevin (1993) "Invisibility, Homophobia and Heterosexism: Lesbians, Gays and the Media," *Critical Studies in Mass Communication* (December); 396–422.

Gabler, Neal (1995) "Audience Stays Superior to the Exploitalk Shows," *Los Angeles Times* (19 March); M1.

Gamson, Joshua (1995) "Must Identity Movements Self-Destruct? A Queer Dilemma," *Social Problems* 42(3): 390–407.

Gamson, Joshua (1998) *Freaks Talk Back: Tabloid Talk Shows and Sexual Nonconformity*. Chicago, IL: University of Chicago Press.

Grindstaff, Laura (1997) "Producing Trash, Class, and the Money Shot: A Behind the Scenes Account of Daytime TV Talkshows," in James Lull and Stephen Hinerman (eds.) *Media Scandals*. London: Polity Press.

Gross, Larry (1989) "Out of the Mainstream; Sexual Minorities and the Mass Media," in Ellen Seiter (ed.) *Remote Control: Television, Audiences, and Cultural Power*, pp. 130–49. New York: Routledge.

Gross, Larry (1994) "What Is Wrong with This Picture? Lesbian Women and Gay Men on Television," in R. Jeffrey Ringer (ed.) *Queer Words, Queer Images: Communication and the Construction of Homosexuality*, pp. 143–56. New York: New York University Press.

Habermas, Jurgen (1991) *The Structural Transformation of the Public Sphere*. Cambridge: MIT Press.

Hafner, Debra W. (1995) "Talk Show Chaos," *Renaissance News & Views* (September): 6, 16.

Hantzis, Darlene M. and Lehr, Valerie (1994) "Whose Desire? Lesbian (Non)Sexuality and Television's Perpetuation of Hetero/Sexism," in R. Jeffrey Ringer (ed.) *Queer Words, Queer Images: Communication and the Construction of Homosexuality*, pp. 107–21. New York: New York University Press.

Heaton, Jeanne Albronda and Wilson, Nona Leigh (1995) *Tuning in Trouble: Talk TV's Destructive Impact on Mental Health*. San Francisco, CA: Jossey-Bass.

Hennessy, Rosemary (1994–95) "Queer Visibility in Commodity Culture." *Cultural Critique* (Winter): 31–75.

Jenny Jones Show (1995) "Jenny Jones" (*Gorgeous and Gay!* 21 March). Kirk, Marshall and Madsen, Hunter (1989) *After the Ball: How America Will Conquer Its Fear & Hatred of Gays in the 90s*. New York: Plume.

Kurtz, Howard (1996) *Hot Air: All Talk, All the Time*. New York: Times Books.

Livingstone, Sonia and Lunt, Peter (1994) *Talk on Television: Audience Participation and Public Debate*. London: Routledge.

Meyrowitz, Joshua (1985) *No Sense of Place: The Impact of Electronic Media on Social Behavior*. New York: Oxford University Press.

Mohr, Richard (1988). *Gays/Justice: A Study of Ethics, Society, and Law.* New York: Columbia University Press.

Moritz, Marguerite J. (1994) "Old Strategies for New Texts: How American Television is Creating and Treating Lesbian Characters," in R. Jeffrey Ringer (ed.) *Queer Words, Queer Images: Communication and the Construction of Homosexuality,* pp. 122–42. New York: New York University Press.

Multimedia Entertainment (1992) "Donahue" (*Concord Anti-Gay Referendum,* 13 February).

Multimedia Entertainment (1994) "Donahue" (*Gay Cops,* 9 June).

Multimedia Entertainment (1995a) "Donahue" (*What, They're Gay? Lipstick Lesbians and Gorgeous Gay Guys,* 12 September).

Multimedia Entertainment (1995b) "The Jerry Springer Show" (*Please Act Straight!,* 23 October).

Munson, Wayne (1994) *All Talk: The Talkshow in Media Culture.* Philadelphia, PA: Temple University Press.

Netzhammer, Emile C. and Shamp, Scott A. (1994) "Guilt by Association: Homosexuality and AIDS on Prime-time Television," in R. Jeffrey Ringer (ed.) *Queer Words, Queer Images: Communication and the Construction of Homosexuality,* pp. 98–106. New York: New York University Press.

Paramount Pictures (1992) "Maury Povich" (*Lipstick Lesbians,* 29 May).

Priest, Patricia J. (1995) *Intimacies: Talk Participants and Tell-All TV.* Cresskill, NJ: Hampton Press.

Rose, Brian G. (1985) "The Talk Show," in Brian G. Rose (ed.) *TV Genres: A Handbook and Reference Guide.* Westport, CT: Greenwood Press.

Rubin, Gayle (1993 [1984]) "Thinking Sex: Notes for a Radical Theory of the Politics of Sexuality," in Henry Abelove, Michele Aina Barale and David Halperin (eds.) *The Lesbian and Gay Studies Reader,* pp. 3–44. New York: Routledge.

Russo, Vito (1987) *The Celluloid Closet: Homosexuality in the Movies,* 2nd edn. New York: Harper & Row.

Schacter, Jane S. (1997) "Skepticism, Culture and the Gay Civil Rights Debate in Post-Civil-Rights Era," *Harvard Law Review* 110 (January): 684–731.

Seidman, Steven (1993) "Identity Politics in a 'Postmodern' Gay Culture: Some Historical and Conceptual Notes," in Michael Warner (ed.) *Fear of a Queer Planet.* Minneapolis: University of Minnesota Press.

Seidman, Steven (ed.) (1996) *Queer Theory/Sociology.* Cambridge MA: Blackwell.

Shattuc, Jane (1997) *The Talking Cure: TV Talk Shows and Women.* New York: Routledge.

Stein, Arlene and Plummer, Ken (1996) "I Can't Even Think Straight: 'Queer' Theory and the Missing Sexual Revolution in Sociology," in Steven Seidman (ed.) *Queer Theory/Sociology,* pp. 129–44. Cambridge, MA: Blackwell.

Tuchman, Gaye (1974) "Assembling a Network Talk Show," in Gaye Tuchman (ed.) *The TV Establishment: Programming for Power and Profit,* pp. 119–35. Englewood Cliffs, NJ: Prentice-Hall.

Unitel Video (1992) "Jane Whitney" (*Bisexuality,* 17 December).

Vaid, Urvashi (1995) *Virtual Equality: The Mainstreaming of Gay & Lesbian Liberation.* New York: Anchor Books.

Warner, Michael, ed. (1993) *Fear of a Queer Planet,* Minneapolis: University of Minnesota Press.

Weeks, Jeffrey (1981) *Sex, Politics, and Society: The Regulation of Sexuality Since 1800.* New York: Longman.

Weintraub, Jeffrey (1996) "The Theory and Politics of the Public/Private Distinction," in Jeffrey Weintraub and Krishan Kumar (eds.) *Public and Private in Thought and Practice: Perspectives on a Grand Dichotomy,* pp. 1–42. Chicago, IL: University of Chicago Press.

Weintraub, Jeffrey and Kumar, Krishan, eds. (1996) *Public and Private in Thought and Practice: Perspectives on a Grand Dichotomy,* Chicago, IL: University of Chicago Press.

48

Hip Hop and Racial Desire in Contemporary Japan

Nina Cornyetz

Flipping television channels late one insomniac night in Tokyo in the winter of 1990, I happened upon a Japanese dancing duo performing with darkened faces, singing, outfitted in the trendiest costumes: baseball caps with brims turned to the back, expensive sneakers, and baggy trousers. That same year, a friend who was visiting Japan entered a dance hall which to his surprise appeared to be peopled almost exclusively by black youths. Upon closer scrutiny he realized that the "black" young men were Asian: Japanese with darkened faces, some with dreadlocks and some with fades, performing hip hop dance steps and breaking to rap music.

The encounter of teenage and young adult Japanese men and women with rap music, hip hop style, and signs of blackness is a multifaceted reconfiguration of these variant signs, bound to global commodity exchange, Japanese racialism, and Japanese national identity. The contemporary pop-culture Japanese rendering of hip hop and rap consists of a fascination with the aural and visual styles (the sounds, movements, body languages and outfits) and an African American symbolic presence signaled by fetishizing black skin and hairstyles. This disposition of hip hop style requires *as its foundation* a separation of hip hop and rap from the specifics of American racialism, and a reconstruction bounded by Japanese racialism.

The phenomenon of nonblack youth dressing themselves in "black style" is not unique to Japan. In the United States, white teenagers have also adopted the clothing, mannerisms, hairdos, vernacular, and other markers of hip hop style. In Japan, special salons advertise their expertise in "dread-hair" *(doreddo hea),* a process which may cost dearly in time and money; in America, white girls may plait their hair in small braids.[1] What is strikingly different in Japan is that black skin is incorporated as an essential signifier of hip hop style. Japanese youth enamored of hip hop regularly darken their complexions with makeup, especially when they go out dancing.

Recent works by John Russell have mapped out a domain of Japanese representations of blacks which he holds to be directly imported from the West. But present-day Japanese "black face" is usually not determined by the American historical counterpart.[2] In the United States, the history of white entertainers in blackface has marked as racist the darkening of the skin in imitation of African Americans. The debacle of Ted Danson at the New York City Friars Club roast of comic Whoopi Goldberg in October 1993 affirmed that blackface remains a taboo in contemporary America.[3] The American version, a caricature, made use of certain coded images and props such as white gloves and exaggerated lips: American blackface did not seek realistic representations of African Americans.[4] Japanese black face, on the other hand, emulates hair and clothing styles (akin to the "white Negro" phenomenon in the United States) but also fetishizes skin color in an attempt to mask the Japanese self with a realistic black visage. Russell has argued convincingly that the new popularity of black style in Japan reproduces old stereotypes, yet I think that for some Japanese youth, reconfigurations of themselves in black images mark a processing of blackness qualitatively different from earlier representations and reveal a subject of racial and erotic desire.

That the blackening of the bodily self has become a desired index in Japan upsets conventional twentieth-century inferential symbolic homilies on black skin. While, as Tricia Rose has argued, hip hop originates within commodity-driven urban African American youth subculture (availing itself of already circulating recorded music, audio and video technology, and fashion), it also originates as a venue for black youths' subversive voice.[5] In America the massification of rap and hip hop style to access a broader, white market inevitably entails a partial elision of hip hop's subversive origins in the service of "sanitized" white narratives and further exploits the collusion with commodity culture.[6] In the Japanese reproduction, while many of the origins of hip hop and rap are erased, they are erased differently; most notably, they are not "whitened."

Although rap and hip hop have been successfully utilized by corporate advertisers throughout the world, each reproduction represents a hybrid of the dominant local culture and the imported African American subculture. Hip hop is globalized yet is ceaselessly remade regionally through its interaction with variant social, political, ideological, and other contexts. This decentering and unification of desire for goods and the capacity to acquire them are situated within the globalization of capital production in the contemporary period. Goods sold to a targeted region must *resonate* with an extant aesthetic and/or appeal on an imagistic level to a perceived need or desire. Marketing campaigns must redirect existing desire toward novelty commodities.

The dispensation of goods in late capitalism frequently employs an erotic subtext. Sex bolsters sales. Wolfgang Haug has argued that when commodities are divorced from utilitarian value, they compete on the level of illusion and appearance: an image is created and sold through the suggestion of erotic sensualism (or libidinal urge). Apparel, for example, is frequently sold by means of "a language of clothes conveying sexual feelings."[7] Haug's erotic subtext has particular relevance for Japanese hip hop style. In Japan, the sexual message encoded in hip hop style is directly identified with phallic empowerment for both men and women, a consequence of Japanese racial attitudes toward American blacks. Other co-present subtexts, such as rebellion against adult mainstream society, provide youth with, in Umberto Eco's words, a text for "semiotic guerrilla warfare" against the world of their parents.[8]

During the American occupation in the immediate postwar period, Japan was perspectively "feminized" and metaphorically raped as a result of its subordinate positioning. The writer Sakaguchi Ango (1906–55) envisioned a future Japan bereft of Japanese men, peopled by American men, Japanese women, and their mixed-blood children.[9] In Shinoda Masahiro's film *MacArthur's Children,* a central female character is raped upstairs at the very moment that the villagers are entertaining the occupation troops downstairs. The young boys from whose viewpoint the film is narrated speak in awe of the massive size of American (black and white) penises.[10] Against the assumedly superior American penis and phallus, Japanese men were materially and symbolically demasculinized. Prewar Japanese and American collusive productions of each other had already situated Japan within a binary system as a shadowed, unknowable, and mysterious other, persistently occupying the same polarity, and alterity, as the feminine.[11] In Japan, discourses mirroring European and American racialism have historically regarded dark skin as a sign of nature and physicality; in the postwar period, African American soldiers paradoxically *also* occupied the dominant position vis-à-vis a surrendered Japan.

Hip hop style, which is marked in Japan with black skin, is interwoven with the phallus as a signifier of a subtext of masculine, heterosexual *body* power. Young men seek to incorporate this power by remodeling themselves in hip hop style. For young women, hip hop style includes the acquisition of male African American lovers, bound to the same subtext of phallic empowerment, but transgressive of assumed (racially exclusive) Japanese male access to their sexual bodies and belittling of Japanese masculine identity. The doubled perception of threat and desire produced through the fetishization of blackness is a product of contemporary Japanese representations of self and mechanisms of othering, nuanced by reforming gender and power distribution.

For the older generation, "whiteness" was a signifier of American economic, ideological, and political putative superiority, against which murky Japanese "yellowness" was a sign of being below the standard. As the nation-state Japan is increasingly perceived to have surpassed American capitalist initiative, a somnambulant anti-Japanese sentiment has reawakened in America. In Japan, the younger generation has begun to challenge the monolithic myth of white supremacy. In the shadow of a reviving Japanese nationalism are other perceptions straining against the delineations of racialism bounded by the antipodal notions of black and white. Young Japanese reproducing themselves in black style signifies a potential transnational identity, supplementary to a previously introjected, Western imperialist black-white binary paradigm, revelatory of a desire and a propensity for racial identificatory slippage.

Hip Hop as Commodity

While rap and hip hop originated as expressions of young black resistance and represented attempts to "negotiate the experiences of marginalization, brutally truncated opportunity, and oppressions within the cultural imperatives of African-American and Caribbean history, identity, and community," they were also, as Rose has argued, always already indebted to commodity consumption.[12] Their formal attributes (rap as rhyming, not singing, to synthesized music and a beat box, over which previously recorded music is sampled and variously "deconstructed"; hip hop as a broader term inclusive of dance and dress style) were thus primed for crossover first into a mainstream (white) United States youth culture and subsequently into the global market.[13] Rap and hip hop were soon marshalled to the promotion of clothing, soft drinks, and other items appealing to young people. Corporations endeavoring to sell goods to the youthful consumer have remolded hip hop subculture into a form more palatable to a larger, lucrative market by retaining many of its formalist resistance-signifying codes but divesting it of the particularized defiance and subjective agency of urban African American youth.[14] Hip hop thus makes its appearance in Japan (and other global contexts) tethered to commodity circulation and prepared for recirculation in a form already partly sundered from African American resistance.

While employed as interpreter to one of Japan's top "idols" (pop stars) during a television-commercial shoot in New York City in 1990, I was surprised when she and her entourage asked to go to Brooklyn, a place, in my experience, usually met with disinterest by young visiting Japanese. I began to expound upon the history of Brooklyn's various communities, but she interrupted me to explain that they wanted to visit the Spike Lee shop to buy clothing and other memorabilia. They had no interest in his neighborhood, or in any other part of Brooklyn. The pop star did not want her attention diverted from the purchase of goods recreating a film version of a subculture (an invented and reflected version) to the material object of Brooklyn itself. She was apparently on the cutting edge of hip Japanese style: now Japanese bus tours make the trip to Brooklyn just to purchase T-shirts and movie paraphernalia at the Spike Lee store. Spike Lee himself promotes Japanese blue jeans in a Japanese advertisement.[15]

In spite of the subtexts informing Japan's embrace of hip hop style, such as phallic empowerment, erotic desire, and racial liminality, Japan's enthusiasm for African American style does not emanate from an internal, alternate discourse. Rather, it is introduced through mostly American images (MTV, movies, commercials), which are then reproduced by Japanese youth. In Japan, a contemporary focus on "surface," coinciding with a mature capitalist disengagement of style from content, facilitates extreme forms of disjunctive montage which reverberate with the formal aspects of hip hop's reconfigurations. For Japanese rap performers and audience alike, sampling (incorporating portions of previously recorded music and lyrics and then rearticulating them through the rapper's manipulations of the original) resonates with a contemporary taste for pastiche. Phrases in rhymed rap intonations may be interspersed with lines sung to Japanese pop melodies.

The pasting together of disparate surfaces is not new to Japan. Masao Miyoshi has described Edo-period (1600–1868) *gesaku* (prose fiction) as "engrossed in the thick texture of verbal surface, and thus . . . inhospitable to characterization and employment. . . . Its playful sophistication contains at least potential traits of postmodernity."[16] The *gesaku* and other genres that played with dispersal of meaning are indicative of previous narratives which share the current taste for pastiche, presently conjoined with the circulation of information, novelty, and commodities and with the appropriation of foreign subculture(s). According to the critic Karatani Kōjin, in the 1980s "Japan has become a highly developed information-consumption society, in which meaning is information and desire is the desire of the Other, because the 'subject' of the nineteenth-century West has never existed in Japan."[17]

The nonconstitution of the subject in Japan facilitates a type of "play" which, while it resembles the postmodern, structurally replicates an antecedent literary and artistic intertextuality reliant upon authorizing, factual sources extrinsic to the work of art. Television programs, newspaper and magazine articles, *and* the commodities sold side by side with, or within, them (both text and advertisement) have taken on the structural function of exterior, factual repositories to which the text(s) may refer for affirmation and authority. This authority reaffirms a myth of Japanese homogeneity through its implied unification of desire and, as Harry Harootunian has said, intimates that "everybody belongs to the 'middle stratum' despite all the differences which exist in fact."[18] Hip hop style, both art and item, may be utilized as a source of self-identificatory authorization.

A very popular fictional narrative *(shōsetsu)* written in 1980, *Natonaku, kurisutaru* (Somehow, crystal), which describes a two-week period in a young couple's life, comes complete with copious notes that explicate the hundreds of Western brand names and foreign words throughout.

The narrative incited the wrath of several academic scholars. Miyoshi's scathing criticism follows:

Nantonaku, kurisutaru . . . presents disembodied adolescent voices, or mildly erotic daydreams, whose only existential testimonies are store names, miscellaneous foreign words, and trade names that are carefully annotated in the book's 442 footnotes. Hardly gathered into sentences,

nouns—especially names like "Dior" and "Jaeger"—echo in the hollows of dead narrative possibilities. Presented in a succession of slick commercials, these names are meant to guide the reader in the glossy world of buying and consuming.[19]

The narrator guides the reader toward certain items in an assumption of absolute, communal commodity value. Hip hop as commodity targets youth and subverts the notion of Japanese homogeneity while it *also* fosters a youth subgroup communalism. Hip hop takes its place among countless Western imports, its entry into the marketplace smoothed by the antecedent movement erasing difference between high and low art and, by extension, between text and commercial. Globally, the conjoining of art (narrative, pictorial, and performative) and consumer products has become commonplace, but it has taken an extreme form in Japan. Marilyn Ivy notes that

CMs [television commercials] are tied together only by sheer seriality, and perhaps by their presentation of commodities (something which is, however, often subverted or elided in Japanese commercials). . . . In Japanese magazines as well, the distinction between text and commercial is often blurred; in fact, with their highly developed graphics, visuals, and advertising concepts, Japanese commercials often override program or text in interest.[20]

The Japanese pop star's desire for "authentic" hip hop goods has been stimulated by filmic and other representations of African American culture, and her capacity to purchase the goods and her very presence in the States are facilitated by the strong yen. The manner in which hip hop style is manufactured in Japan is bound to the focus of capital on consumption.

During the 1980s the power of the rising yen made New York City a popular location to film print and television commercials, soft news programs, and sitcoms. Japanese video and photographic crews, capturing the "New York scene" for the audience back home, were fixtures on Manhattan street corners. For a national hip hop dance contest aired on Japanese television, a production team and "talent" (performers) were sent to New York to obtain footage to complement and "internationalize" the program. The contest was broadcast on a Sunday-night program, Tensai Takeshi no genki ga deru terebi.[21] The opening act was a Japanese rap duo, L. L. Brothers. Contestants competed in groups affiliated with various high schools but called themselves by such names as Scrap and Trash, Slum G., and Imperial. The production team dispatched to New York traveled with L. L. Brothers and videotaped them performing in Manhattan. There was additional footage of street performances by African American New Yorkers. Studio commentators discussed the contest in segments intercut with location footage. The African American male dancers were asked to show off their footwear, and the Japanese titles identified the boots as wangan sensō būtsu (Desert Storm boots) and gave the price. The segment shot in the States thus functioned as both entertainment and advertisement of "authentic" (native) apparel. Further highlighting the complicity between advertisement and hip hop style, L. L. Brothers were featured in a magazine print (photo) shoot of the making of a television commercial.[22]

The overlap between journalistic, narrative, or other noncommercial text and advertisement is not limited to media that materially alternate between the two, such as magazines and television, but, as evidenced by Somehow, Crystal, has made the leap in Japan to popular fiction. Somehow, Crystal is art in the service of commodity aesthetics. In her "Somehow: The Postmodern as Atmosphere," Norma Field contends

that 80 percent of the notes designate Western things and people and that characters identify themselves through their consumption of these foreign brand-name goods: they are what they buy. Descriptions of the characters' erotic encounters and fantasies which intersect the listing of commodities serve to highlight the commingled "motifs of body, race, and commodity" set within an assumedly communal repository of knowledge.[23]

The commingling of commodity consumption and erotic fantasy in Japanese popular fiction (and subculture) results in advertisements that appeal directly to, in Ivy's words, "desire within the symbolic economy."[24] The scene is thus set for the conflation of hip hop performances, erotic and gendered subtexts, and an enticing display of hip hop goods. On the "Genki TV" special, an impromptu interview at Kennedy International Airport with a member of the winning dance group reveals his reason for going to New York: "To see, and steal, the fashion of black men of my age group."

Densely enmeshed with commodities, hip hop style is encoded with a braid of subtexts of symbolic desires and with questions of national and individual identity. Since the late 1980s the hippest Japanese youth have sought to reproduce themselves through an alternate yet communal identity, articulated through hip hop commodities: clothing, music, magazines, tanning lotions, hair preparations, and so forth. Rap self-expression consists of inscribing an individual name and associated difference to an extant, borrowed expression of another. Sampling commingles the rapper's own statements with an existing discourse and produces the voice of the individual both within and without his or her immediate subgroup.

One popular means of inscribing self-articulation within the shared repository of music, lyric, and beat is self-naming (similar to graffiti tagging; the name is usually a nickname, sometimes acquired, sometimes chosen). From the indeterminacy of the mix of self and other, the naming proclaims subjectivity. Likewise, in Japan, L. L. Brothers announce themselves, calling out in English, "L. L. Brothers, you can check it out!" For L. L. Brothers, even the name is conflated with their adopted African American style. "L. L." references the famous African American rapper, L. L. Cool J. The "Brothers" part of their name has two meanings: they are siblings, and the word brothers (*burāzazu*) is the hip term for "African American." Dance and rap groups in Japan frequently adopt a name that fosters stereotypical images of black America—Zoo, Slum G., Vibe Seduction—although there are instances of transidentity such as Yellow Monkey Crazy.[25] The Japanese rapper thus proclaims a hybrid self through his or her affixed foreign name representing African American urban culture. As evidenced by Yellow Monkey Crazy, the transidentified self appropriates American racialist stereotyping for an ambivalent self-identification. The Japanese self is integrated with its "coloredness," and thereby with blackness, while it simultaneously introjects the Western (white) imperialist gaze by which Japanese and blacks become "monkeys."[26] Naming, sampling, hip hop dress, turning hair into dreadlocks, and darkening the skin all function to produce an ambivalence in Japanese youths' embrace of African American style: individual and national identity (self-as-Japanese) and transidentity (self as allied with color) are proclaimed and erased.

Japanese hip hop employs an image of blackness while it sells goods to Japanese youth, and provides a context for a *difference* in self-identification. Akin to the narrative texts and television shows which become arenas for advertising brand names,

hip hop style (which is also dressing black) envelops the targeted consumer in an incited desire, simultaneously promising (illusory) satiation through identification with the created icon, or purchase of the commodity being sold.

Japanese youth have responded to the media images of African Americans by attempting to incorporate signs that re-create themselves in a black image; this image functions on some level to challenge mainstream adult sensibilities. Following Eric Lott's general analysis of blackface, while representations of African Americans in Japan reduce the other to spectacle, they also may represent the attempted incorporation of an image of the other and/or an expression of an unconscious erotic desire for the other.[27] Reconceptualized in consideration of Japanese female agentive solicitation of black male lovers, erotic desire is not repressed but flaunted. Hebdige has noted that in Britain, blacks can be seen as the ultimate symbol of the other within the dominant culture, and therefore aspects of black style can be sampled by the white subculture in defiance of dominant social mores, resulting in a semiotic dialogue.[28] To recast Hebdige's analysis within a formulation acknowledging a fundamental power imbalance as the cornerstone of the fetishization of blackness, hip hop style in Japan is not a dialogue between Japanese and African American youth but a plundering of an empowered body image. Most of the interaction between Japanese and African American youth is indirect (because there are still so few African Americans in Japan). Accordingly, the object of desire is generally encoded within and is limited to interaction with the variant signs.

At the end of the dance contest, the father of one of the contestants is called to the stage, where he proudly basks in his son's glory. In another scene, the young man who accepts the trophy for the winning team is so moved by the public acknowledgment that he weeps while thanking his audience. Rap and hip hop as anti-establishment, abrasive, defiant self-expression and insubordination by (primarily) African American youth are absent from this scenario. Instead, a transidentified Japanese youth reveals his vulnerable desire for affirmation not just from his peers but from his parents and the school officials, who are also present. The concert winners stand in the midst of acclaim, outfitted in the latest international style, purchased with the power of the yen and proudly worn as a symbol of modern Japanese consumption.

Phallic Empowerment: The Meaning of Blackness

In spite of the apparent case with which hip hop style has been commodified, the retention of a (represented) African American presence signals that the sign of blackness is an important subtext. The information encoded in the sign should be read in the context of how African Americans (not Japanese remodeling themselves in a black image) have been represented in modern Japan, as productive of the "meaning" of Japanese youth in hip hop style.

Racial othering in Japan, as elsewhere, is promoted, as David Goldberg has asserted regarding the general structure of racialist essentialism, as a mode of exclusion based on a perceived natural (physical, bodily) difference, which conceptually unifies both self and other in homogeneous groupings.[29] Japanese racialism has historically marked differences between Asians by positing a variety of discourses on physical (bodily) distinctions, which include the notion of "pure blood lineage" and the association of purity and acculturation with light skin, discourses which also mark inhabitants of the nation-state Japan as other. John Dower

writes in *War without Mercy* that "the Japanese themselves looked down on all the other 'colored' races. . . . They had esteemed 'whiteness' since ancient times."[30] Modern Japanese racial ideology is thus classical in what Etienne Balibar identifies as the anthropological universal of marking difference along the axis of humanity (culture) and animality (nature).[31]

As John Russell has shown, the dominant, pre-World War II images of Africans and African Americans that circulated in Japan were fettered by the binarism of black equals savage and white equals civilization. Such delineations buttressed the Japanese racial ideology that had represented darker Asians as inferior. Russell has argued convincingly that images of American blacks in Japan have frequently reproduced American racialist stereotypes, evidenced by the popularity of *The Story of Little Black Sambo*, and the modern yet still reductive portrayals of African Americans as "sexual objects, studs, fashion accessories and quintessential performers," imagistic changes that Russell dismisses as "more old wine in new bottles."[32]

While I concur with Russell's conclusion that the vast majority of "expanded roles" remain within set domains (musicians, athlete, stud), I think that for Japanese youth, African Americans as signs are encoded with additional, new significations: the images of African Americans are not the same old thing but something *different* (even if they are still also informed by antecedent discourses). For many young Japanese, admiration replaces former fear and distaste, as evidenced by the quote "I am mesmerized [akogareta] by black people."[33] *Akogareta*, "to yearn for, to be in awe of," has been affixed to things foreign in the past to mean "desired," but until very recently African Americans were definitely not considered part of desired America.

When working as a production coordinator for Japanese television and commercials ten years ago, I would be asked to find American extras to appear in various minor roles. *American* unequivocally meant "white." Black extras were reserved to illustrate criminal activities. Asian faces would not do, because Asian faces don't signify "America" within Japanese codes. Ten years ago, producers, "talent," and crew would whisper to me their fears of black people, known to them only through American media and filmic portrayals of African Americans holding guns to the heads of putatively normative, law-abiding whites. They would ask, "Why are black people so violent?" Ten years ago, the *akogareta* United States constructed by Japanese television advertisements was exclusively white. Today, a different yet still "desired America" is *also* signified by hip hop-styled African Americans. The reimaging of America to include ethnicity begins within America itself but is reconfigured to suit Japan's positioning, supplemental to a black-white binarism, revealing moments of slippage and indeterminacy, mirroring the concurrent, subtle repositionings of dominance between the two nations.

Twentieth-century Japanese national racial identity was contructed in the shadow of Western black-white binarism, into which Japan could not neatly configure itself. Japanese (and other Asians), who inhabited an in-between space of being neither white nor black, experienced a certain degree of identificatory irresolution.[34] Japanese racial identity frequently took on a relationalism: "colored" in comparison to whites, "pale" against blacks. For the writer Natsume Sōseki, catching a reflection of his own countenance while visiting London in 1900 was a lingering moment of racial shame and self-hatred. Sōseki described in a letter how he saw a midget with a strangely colored face approaching him while he was taking a walk near his boardinghouse, only to awaken to the shocked realization that the midget was his own reflection in a mirror. In her 1994 essay "Fearful Terrain: The Underground and the Continent in the Works of Natsume Sōseki," Katsuyo Motoyoshi writes:

> Frantz Fanon would have had no trouble understanding. . . . before the ironic, and perhaps uncomfortable laugh, before the shocking flash of recognition, who was that "midget" that Sōseki had seen? . . . the identity of the midget caught in Sōseki's glimpse cannot be understood if the reflective surface of the mirror is falsely equated with transparency. Here, the mirror stands for a specific intervention, that of the Western imperialist gaze which has been interiorized by Sōseki.[35]

In 1933, the writer Tanizaki Jun'ichiro noted that, although the Japanese had long esteemed whiteness, "this whiteness of ours differs from that of the white races": Japanese whiteness, he asserted, is clouded by irrepressible shadows, and therefore

> when one of us goes among a group of Westerners it is like a grimy stain on a sheet of white paper. . . . A sensitive white person could not but be upset by the shadow that even one or two colored persons cast over a social gathering. . . . [During the American Civil War] when persecution of Negroes was at its most intense, the hatred and scorn were directed not only at full-blooded Negroes. . . . [Even] those with the slightest taint of Negro blood . . . had to be ferreted out and made to suffer. . . . how profound is the relationship between shadows and the yellow race.[36]

Frequently Japanese situated themselves medially along the familiar evaluative axis of white supremacy-black inferiority, yet Sōseki's misrecognition of himself and Tanizaki's empathy for Western racialism illustrate how the Western imperialist gaze has also been introjected when beholding the self and has collapsed within extant discourses on colored others. As Japanese racialism renders blackness alongside the natural and the bestial (as do many racial systems), it accommodates a production of blackness commingled with "body-ness" and an uncontrolled, excessive sexual drive, differentiating the slightly tainted whiteness of the yellow race from the deeply polluted black race. Michael Dyson's commentary on black masculinity and sexuality in America is also true of Japanese racialism:

> Few images have counted more anxiety in the American sexual psyche than the black male embodiment of phallic prowess. A sordid range of stereotypes, jealousies and fears have been developed around black men wielding their sexuality in ways that are perceived as untoward, unruly, or uncontrolled.[37]

The widely disseminated stereotype of black men possessing mythic phallic power has its foundation in an association of black skin with a masculinized primal.[38] The protagonist of the contemporary author Shimada Masahiko's "Momotaro in a Capsule" collusively visualizes the black phallus as a symbol of supreme masculine prowess:

> From the time he was twelve, Kurushima idolized the brave beautiful phalluses of primitive sculpture. Phalluses like oversized nightsticks: heavy, gleaming, black, hard, glaring provocatively heavenward, brimming with a fearless laughter, as if they had a special connection with some omnipotent god. "Wish I had a cock like that." . . . Whenever Kurushima eyed his [own], he grew depressed. "My genitals were made for masturbation."[39]

To possess the black phallus is to wield the weapon that threatens white masculinity; a black phallus affixed to the Japanese body would invert the "feminization" imposed by the occupation troops. The psychoanalytic term *fetish* has been substantially broadened in academic discourses, increasingly detached from a corporeal materiality, and utilized, for example, to describe the psychic mechanisms that dominate perspectivist imaginings of (and appended anxieties over) sexual difference and colonial desire.[40] My use of *fetish* is meant to be inclusive of the establishment of a replacement object to stand in for the missing penis in protection of the index of male subjective identity, because not just the phallus as symbol but the penis itself is woven directly into the signification of blackness in the contemporary Japanese context. My usage is also inclusive of the broadened application of *fetish:* appropriate to the polysemic symbol of black skin in Japan today, inextricable from the variant historical texts of representations of African Americans in the modern period. One such text is the African American presence in occupied Okinawa.

American forces that occupied Japan in the immediate postwar period were soon centralized in Okinawa, creating a "colonized" site where black and white Americans became "others within."[41] It was a limited, specialized site, however, which did not infiltrate mainstream society. Interracial marriages and liaisons between soldiers and native women of Okinawa were common, but Okinawans themselves were (and are) excluded from the category of the (conceptualized) pure Japanese.[42] The Americans' sources of income were independent of the Japanese economy and offered no threat of monetary competition to dominant classes.[43] The Japanese Home Ministry organized local associations of prostitutes (poor women) in the exclusive service of the occupation troops in an attempt to maintain the "racial purity" of the dominant classes. In the aftermath of the war, Japan as nation was "feminized," deprived of self-governance, forced to surrender and capitulate to the Western other, upsetting the terms of power and masculinity.

Today, anxiety expressed over the black penis in Japanese magazines, on television shows, and in narrative texts is still often accompanied by an assessment of Japanese penises as inferior. In 1992, a young black man identified as Luke was an advice columnist for a popular magazine, *Video on Stage.* One Japanese youth wrote, "Luke, please listen to my problem. I am mesmerized by brothers like you, I go to tanning salons and I'm determined to do my very best at dance and fashion. But [my penis is] small."[44] His inadequate penis was, he complained, the reason why he had just been dumped. While Luke asserted that technique was more important than size, he concluded by assuring readers that his own penis was enormous. The prewar image of a bestial black man was reconstituted as a sex symbol, and the once threatening black phallus (and suppressed erotic curiosity) was re-imaged as overtly desirable, and commodified.

When Japanese male inferiority is thus centralized in the penis, and black men are equated with phallic power, the outfits imagistically bound to African American black youth promise to transform the wearer into a stud. The establishment of a fetishized object averts (or displaces) the threat (of emasculation, or feminization, or disempowerment). In Japan, black skin is both metonomy and metaphor, mimicry and menace, not as an appendix to the lacking other but as a reconfiguration of the lacking self in the empowered, masculinized image of the other.

Contemporaneous with the popularity of hip hop style among (mostly young) Japanese men has been a fad among young Japanese women to seek African American lovers. For these women the penis is the transcendental signifier of a now desired masculine prowess. While most of the African Americans in Japan for extended stays are affiliated with the military, jazz musicians who came to tour Japan in the postwar period have been followed in the contemporary period by other entertainers, including hip hop and rap artists.[45] A second letter to columnist Luke is from a Japanese teenage girl who confesses her desire to have sex with black men and asks advice on how to solicit them. It is not that the young woman is enamored of a particular black man, but rather that she wants to try sex with any black man. Blackness for this young woman is desired for its symbolic meaning. In *Banana Chips Love,* a popular television miniseries videotaped on location in New York City in 1991, a Japanese woman who has apparently mastered the art of living abroad in Manhattan peripherally establishes the program's internationalism by regularly appearing flanked by African American men.[46] She, the program intimates, is the epitome of sophistication and independence from Japanese tradition, and the black men on her arm(s) represent her subjective, erotic agency.

Recent newspaper and magazine articles report the new reluctance of young Japanese women to marry and the dilemma of their male counterparts, who are eager to settle down. In general, young Japanese women enjoy their greatest economic and experiential freedom before they marry.[47] Most live with their parents and work at office jobs, so that they have plenty of money for travel and shopping. Because their education is less directed toward career goals, women are freer to study liberal (and/or traditional) arts such as literature, music, and languages. Once married, the majority quit their jobs, become the head of their household, and dedicate themselves to child rearing, housework, and domestic needs. Babysitters and day-care centers are exceptions. When help is needed, women usually turn to their mothers, in-laws, or other (female) family members. Because Japanese men are required to spend long overtime hours at work and often commute well over an hour each way, it is logistically impossible for most of them to participate as fathers more than nominally.

Sexual and other relationships with non-Japanese offer these young women, and those Japanese men who have foreign partners, release from certain expectations: both partners are somewhat relieved of the burdens of cultural norms (although other racial and national expectations exist).[48] The young women usually do not expect relationships with non-Japanese men to become permanent or serious. Foreigners are curiosities, and much as Asian women have been eroticized in the male American imagination, so too have black men become symbolic of desirable erotic exoticism for Japanese women.

During my visits to Japan, from 1974 to the present, I have repeatedly been asked, in frank discussions with young Japanese women, about the mythic penis size, sexual appetite, and stamina of African American men. The object of these women's curious desire, the black penis, is symbolically present in black skin, with which Japanese male youths have conflated their selfhood. Conjoining the desire for the phallic power of blackness is the threat that Japanese phallic inferiority will displace the Japanese male from his position of power over Japanese women. Female rage lurks beneath the phenomenon: by choosing an African American lover, encoded with a text of phallic empowerment, and by rejecting the economic and social stability of a Japanese husband, the Japanese woman has availed herself of a passive-aggressive act of resistance.

A comic from a men's pornographic magazine illustrates the male anxiety awakened by Japanese women's choice of other lovers. Two young men at a bar are lamenting their miserable sex lives. One sobs that his girlfriend has been stolen by a "black alien"; the other commiserates that his girlfriend is having an affair with a married "entity X." Sighing over their virginity and the growing scarcity of available Japanese women, the two young men exchange glances and embrace, one saying, "gee, the more I look at you the cuter you get," the other replying, "My, you too." The final caption reads. "The anxiety over Japan's future continues."[49]

The choice of African American lovers by Japanese women emasculates Japanese men. In the cartoon, blackness functions as an icon of desired and omnipotent heterosexuality, against which Japanese men have become homosexualized—not by choice but simply by displacement from heterosexual practices. By taking on an African American sexual partner, the Japanese woman, who is socially, economically, politically, and otherwise subordinate to her male counterpart, liberates herself and threatens Japanese male heterosexual subjective agency, although she sidesteps the issue of Japanese male dominance. Removing Japanese men as lovers and husbands from their immediate, personal circumstances places women outside the Japanese norm and does not, in the short term at least, affect directly the systems of power distribution between the sexes in mainstream society.

The woman most famous in Japan for proclaiming her interest in African American men as erotic objects is the contemporary best-selling novelist Yamada Eimi. Yamada herself has an African American husband, and most of her texts are about Japanese women and their African American lovers. The power positioning between her characters inverts the prewar (im)balance of power between Japanese prostitute and black soldier; now black men service Japanese women. Yamada's first work, *Beddotaimu aizu* (Bedtime eyes [1987]), which won the Bungei prize, depicts the relationship between a black American soldier, "Spoon," and his Japanese lover, Kim. Kim describes a common economic arrangement between black American soldiers and their Japanese lovers: "The women . . . purchase and support the man as a *pet to be played with [kau]* however they pleased."[50] Many of Yamada's female protagonists flaunt their sexual and economic dominance over their black lovers, overturning the immediate postwar paradigm by which Japanese prostitutes serviced black soldiers. The bodily myth of black American masculinity that permeates Japanese representations is the iconic ideation that paves the way for such power inversions. The basis for Kim's attraction is Spoon's "bestiality," which affirms her "purity." As translated by Russell:

From his arm pits came a strange smell. A corrupt odor, but definitely not unpleasant. As if by being assaulted by a dirty thing, I am made aware I am a pure thing. That kind of smell. His smell gives me a sense of superiority. It makes me yearn like a bitch in heat driven by the smell of musk.[51]

In Yamada's *Haremu wārudo* (Harem world [1990]), protagonist Sayuri introduces her black lover, Stan, to her Japanese lover, Shinichi, who agonizes:

A black man—the so-called very incarnation of sexuality. He had heard that once a woman tasted that, she would never return to Japanese men. [Sayuri] had said that the size of his (Shinichi's) penis was not a problem, but if she knew how good that one [the black man's penis] was, then she surely would switch [to a black lover].[52]

The supreme mark of difference that inverts the conventional superior-inferior bi-narism (which would situate Japanese men in the empowered position) is the "perfect black phallus." The black phallus remains a transcendental signifier of power, which denigrates by its perfection the phalluses of white and Japanese men. Simultaneously, Yamada's heroines are empowered by manipulating this transcendental (black) phallus. Boasting of a tryst with another black man, Sayuri proclaims, "His dick is the best. . . . Do you think white people have dicks?"[53] Yamada's female protagonists devalue the Japanese penis with equal vigor while paying homage to the black penis. In *Bedtime Eyes,* Kim describes Spoon's penis:

His dick bore no resemblance to those reddish, nasty cocks that white men have; and it was also different from Japanese men's childlike, pathetic ones which were completely incapable of self-assertion unless they were stuck inside some helpless Japanese pussy.[54]

Hizamazuite ashi o oname (Kneel down and lick my feet [1988]) is the story of a dominatrix, Shinobu, who services (tortures) Japanese men, whom she refers to as jerks and slaves. Erotically detached from her work, Shinobu contemptuously claims that clients' penises "look like a bunch of wriggly vegetables out of some cartoon."[55] She delights in the (temporary) power reversal: "Show me another job where you can abuse men and have them thank you."[56] There is a startlingly vulgar and graphic description of needles being inserted into the penis of a pathetic (Japanese) client. Yamada's textual engagement of black male characters is thus indebted to their symbolic functions (as is the teenage girl's erotic interest), as threatening to Japanese phallocentrism and as indicative of female erotic agency. Her works also take their place within and reinforce the commodity aesthetic of African American men.

A student of mine reported that during a recent visit to Japan he noticed, and queried his Japanese companion about, the increasing numbers of young Japanese women seen arm in arm with black men. His companion responded that it was the latest fad: Japanese women sought black men because they looked good on one's arm, akin to the latest pocketbook or other fashion accessory. As accessory, African American lovers are reduced to reflections of Japanese symbolic desire. Alone in her bathroom, the female narrator of Yamada's "X-Rated Blanket" (1988) looks at herself in the mirror and sees the reflection of her own desire when she fantasizes about her lover George: "Twisted, I am wet; water floods high enough to wet my eyes. That's how I clearly recognize my own desire when I look in the mirror"—much as commodities reflect back the inner desire of the consumer, according to Haug.[57]

Just as advertisements arouse a libidinal desire that the acquisition of goods only inflames, sex with George, confesses Yamada's narrator, is always accompanied by more desire: "As the sensation of satiations fills me—the satisfaction of having at last become one—I savor an intense pleasure tinged already with the mingling of a new, ongoing hunger."[58] The consumption of her lover yields only temporary satisfaction because, like goods sold by image and not by use value, the symbolic desire targets an imagination, not a reality. The writer Shimada Masahiko cites Yamada's narratives as examples of easily accessible, circulated, and consumed prose: narrative in the service of the market economy.[59]

Abetting the wide range of racialist stereotypes, the borrowing of elements of style sundered from context is facilitated by the status of blacks as foreigners in Japan, rather than others within. Attitudes toward American blacks are not the direct outgrowth of tensions within mainstream society (although earlier discourses on racial

purity are). Japanese refabrications of elements of black youth culture are thus primarily limited to ones that operate on the level of signs originated elsewhere and split from their referents. Accordingly, there is an increased potential for reductive mythic images of African Americans. For both the young women seeking African American lovers and the young (primarily) men who dress themselves in hip hop style, blackness is frequently affixed to an antecedent erotic subtext that fetishizes black skin as symbolic of phallic empowerment.

National or Transnational: The Meaning of Japaneseness

Racial distinctions were efficacious for distinguishing Asians from blacks and from whites, yet they would not suffice for the clear-cut differentiation *between* Asians required by the building of the nation-state. In the modern period, Japan has identified itself as Asian in oppositional relationship to non-Asian nations, and as "Japan" to differentiate itself from other Asian nations. The perception of unity is established on the creation of a social discourse postulating multiple communal positions of subjectivity that are dependent upon the erasure of difference in the categories of race, ethnicity, language, culture, geography, and sexuality.

Japan relegated "culture" to a repository of Japaneseness, an ideology informed by the necessary internalization of technology, then the science of the other. "Culture" was construed as the essence of Japaneseness, common to all Japanese and unknowable to non-Japanese; a category of Japanese superiority to offset the self-perception of inferiority in science and technology. Tetsuo Najita has described the prewar Japanese discourse on "culture" as follows:

In general, "culture" . . . contained ideal "forms" that withstood the passage of time, including the corrosive forces of modernity and development. Culture, in this sense, was "anti-modern"; it was articulated self-consciously in this manner so as to distinguish internal truthfulness from the otherness [of the West] within.[60]

In the mobilization of the nation for World War II, in Najita's words, "a national cultural certitude" was employed to legitimize the theory of the Japanese people *(Nihonjinron),* which further subsumed the individual within a community of The Nation.

In the 1980s, numerous academics and journalists, in Japan and the States, commented on the resurgence of "Japanism," the assertion of the existence of a particular, historically transcendental Japanese racial group commonality or essence. Karatani has analyzed this resurgence as an outgrowth of the extreme "play" (dispersal of meaning) characterizing contemporary Japan, suggesting two alternative future scenarios: total absence of "meaning" or the reinvestment of word with "content." One "content" vying for dominance since the late 1980s has been ultranationalism.[61] This ultranationalism is laden, as it was in the prewar period, with Japanism.

Japanism *(Nihonjinron)* is evident in a statement by a studio commentator for the "Genki TV" dance contest: "Just like transistors, [hip hop] was originated elsewhere, but we the Japanese can imitate it and do it even better." For this commentator, *Nihonjinron* has once again begun to fill previously emptied signs with an absolute inferiority.

The reinscription of Japanism into social, ideological, and other discourses was accompanied by a consumption-based "ethnic boom" in the 1980s, during which ethnic commodities (outfits, foodstuffs, handicrafts, folk arts, and so on) associated with varied regions and peoples, including Southeast Asians, Koreans, and urban African Americans, flooded Japanese markets. The ethnic boom can be read variously: as the fine-tuning of self-identificatory categories through a "discovery" of and "familiarity" with others and/or as a multiculturalism resistant to valorizations of Japanese "uniqueness."

Undoubtedly, for many Japanese, the sense of their own Japanese identity (validating economic and political power over others within and without) is still so solid that the appearance or look or atmosphere of the other can be donned like a hat or coat and just as easily shed, leaving no mark or impact on the idea of self-as-Japanese. Japanese desire for blackness exposes an ambivalence while it reproduces nature-culture, animal-human binarisms. The experience of "playing black" does not necessarily alter this racialism. A Japanese *Video on Stage* columnist rambles through a discourse unified only by media images of blacks around the world: a brief reference to starvation in Somalia is followed by an explication of the English word *wicked,* after which Spike Lee's *Malcolm X* is (positively) reviewed.[62]

Such processing of the African American other lends itself to essentialist analysis. Karen Kelsky's critique of young Japanese women's affairs with Western men, "Intimate Ideologies: Transnational Theory and Japan's Yellow Cabs," blurs the distinctions between the Japanese processing of whiteness and blackness and thus is not attentive to the role of power informing the logic of a black-white antipodal paradigm and the resultant production of Japanese hybridity. Concluding that affairs between Japanese women and (all) Western men function purely as reaffirmations of the Japanese self, Kelsky asserts that

in nearly all cases the women viewed the gaijin [foreign] male as a brief fling, to be enjoyed before settling down to the serious work of marriage with a Japanese man. . . . she approaches him with clearly defined parameters marked by her sense of the gaijin as Other; he is irreconcilably alien from and antithetical to her own essence as "Japanese."[63]

As evidenced by the admission implicit in Kelsky's "nearly all cases," *some* Japanese women *do* remain with their lovers. It should be reiterated that Yamada Eimi, to whose work Kelsky refers repeatedly, *has* married an African American. While much of Yamada's work affirms racial difference, some of her heroines labor to erase distinction: "I realize that this body draped over mine is a completely different type of body. I move my hips, raise my voice, trying to transform his type into the same type as mine."[64] In *Harem World,* the narrative subject position is occupied by a female protagonist who is herself part African American.

Kelsky's essay focuses on Japanese female liaisons with Western men, but when these encounters are viewed within the wider context of the *ambivalent* othering by women such as Yamada, of hip hop style embraced by mostly male youth, and of the meaning of blackness as a signifier, the closure of her conclusion is compromised. Although the "Genki TV" commentator (who represents a "disengaged" audience, not a fan of hip hop or a hip hop stylist or rap performer) employs hip hop style as a means of othering to affirm his belief in Japanese uniqueness, is this also true for the youth in black face dancing to hip hop music? In its insistence on a (constructed) difference, signaled by the intentional sign of ethnic otherness, black skin, many youth situate themselves oppositionally against the myth of Japanese racial homogeneity. At the same time, difference is affirmed through the surety that outfits and skin darkening do not erase their own Japaneseness. As a young

magazine columnist put it, "Mesmerized by black people . . . I cannot turn black. Of course not."[65]

The selling of black style has the potential to unsettle discourses on Japanese racial purity. The "desanitization" of desired (*akogareta*) America to incorporate blackness and the positioning of blackness as a signifier connoting desire destabilize the familiar constructs of racially based evaluative systems. Remodeling the Japanese self in an African American image reproduces an indeterminacy and interlocation in Japanese racial self-identification. Reconfiguring blackness as desirable also provides greater possibilities for African American (bodily) presence in Japan, which generates interactive dialogue rather than unilateral plundering of image.

The very new popularity of black lovers among young Japanese women (not Okinawans but Tokyoites) constitutes a further site of resistance to Japanese myths of homogeneity: interracial coupling challenges Japanese male ownership of Japanese women and threatens to defile "pure" blood lineage (the essence of Japanese superiority). Although, as Kelsky claims, most of these young women neither marry their African American lovers nor birth babies of mixed heritage, some do (as has Yamada), and others will. If, and when, more of the liaisons sought by Japanese women with African American men progress beyond accessory to husband, their children will produce, of necessity, a site of resistance that will further challenge Japanese homogeneity by broadening the categories of heterogeneous voices within.

Notes

1. Japanese salons advertise expertise in African American hairstyles such as dreadlocks, high-tops, and fades. An advertisement in a popular magazine, *Video on Stage,* 1 November 1992, 87, claims, "We do 'club hair' including 'dread-hair'

[doreddo hea]." See Andrew Jones, "Black like Me," *Spin* 9, no. 1 (1 October 1993), 74–78, for a good description of the hip hop trend in Japan. See "Reviled for Their Love of Hip-Hop Style," *People Weekly*, 31 January 1994, 60–61, for reportage on white youth dressing themselves in "black" hip hop style. All translations from Japanese source materials are mine unless indicated otherwise.

2. John Russell, "Narratives of Denial: Racial Chauvinism and the Black Other in Japan," *Japan Quarterly* 38, no. 4 (October 1991), 416–28; "Race and Reflexivity: The Black Other in Contemporary Japanese Mass Culture." *Cultural Anthropology* 6, no. 1 (February 1991), 3–25. These two articles are pioneering discussions of modern Japanese discourses on blackness. To distinguish Japanese from American practice, I reconfigure the word *blackface* as two words, *black face,* when referring to the Japanese.

3. Typical samples of the media response to Danson's "performance" include "Whoopi, Ted, We Are Not Amused," *Los Angeles Times,* 13 October 1993; "Racial Jokes Spur Apology from Friars," *New York Times*, 10 October 1993; "What Are You Laughing At?" *San Francisco Chronicle,* 17 October 1993.

4. I am indebted to Eric Lott, "Love and Theft: The Racial Unconscious of Blackface Minstrelsy," *Representations* 39 (summer 1992), 23–49; and John G. Blair, "Blackface Minstrels: Cross-Cultural Perspective," *American Studies International* 28, no. 2 (October 1990), 52–65, for my understanding of the fetishization by American and English blackface minstrels. See Russell, "Narratives of Denial" and "Race and Reflexivity," for discussions of representations culled from American ones. Although such images still exist, most of the Japanese youth darkening their complexions in today's hip hop style do not imitate these exaggerated models.

5. Telephone conversation with Tricia Rose, 27 July 1994. See Tricia Rose, *Black Noise: Rap Music and Black Culture in Contemporary America* (Hanover, N.H.: Wesleyan University Press, 1994); "Orality and Technology: Rap Music and Afro-American Cultural Resistance," *Popular Music and Society* 13, no. 4 (winter 1989), 35. There is undoubtedly another side to the topic of Japanese reproductions of African American style, namely, African American agency. What role do black entertainers and athletes who make commercials for Japanese television and magazines, or who tour Japan, or who record music there, have in the present Japanese reordering of hip hop? How have African Americans in Japan processed the "black fad" there? What is the

relationship between contemporary African American productions of self and Japanese youth? Because this essay focuses on Japanese processing of blackness such questions are beyond its immediate scope, and my questions are posed hopefully pending ethnographic studies that might address the issue from the "other side."

6. Elizabeth Blair argues that rap has entered a stage characterized by the "sanitization" of hip hop subculture as it makes its appearance in mass culture. The process of sanitization includes a negation of hip hop's association with the (specific) conditions of being black in America, partly by placing whites with blacks as producers and consumers of rap. See Elizabeth Blair, "Commercialization of the Rap Music Youth Subculture," *Journal of Popular Culture* 27, no. 3 (winter 1993), 21–33, esp. 31–32. My reading also follows Hebdige's analysis of subculture in Britain. Hip hop, which originated as a challenge to the dominant (white) culture by a disenfranchised (black) class in America, was first incorporated by white youth subculture and then appropriated by capitalist production at large, mass produced and in the process defused of much of its subversive attributes. See Dick Hebdige, *Subculture: The Meaning of Style* (New York: Methuen, 1979). Rose also cites Hebdige in her discussion of rap's commercialization *(Black Noise,* 40–41).

7. Wolfgang Haug, *Critique of Commodity Aesthetics: Appearance, Sexuality, and Advertising in Capitalist Society,* trans. Robert Bock (Minneapolis: University of Minnesota Press, 1986), 56.

8. Quoted in Hebdige, *Subculture,* 105.

9. Sakaguchi Ango, *Sensō to hitori no onno* (The war and a woman), *Darakuron* (Essay on depravity), and *Tennō shōron* (Short essay on the emperor), in *Sakaguchi Ango zenshū* (Tokyo: Chikuma Bunko, 1990), 4:171–88; 14:511–22, 523–24. Japanese names are cited following the Japanese custom of placing the last name first, with no comma between last and first names. Japanese-American names follow the Western model.

10. Shinoda Masahiro, *MacArthur's Children* (English subtitled version distributed by Pacific Arts Video, Beverly Hills. Calif., 1985). The rape of the woman Komako becomes a metaphor for the rape of Japan as a nation by the American occupation. Komako is raped by her brother-in-law Tetsuo, whose assumption of the "right" to access her body after her husband is (erroneously) proclaimed a war casualty parallels the assumption of rights and privilege by Americans to the nation-state Japan.

11. Because the Western subject is putatively male and Japan has been conceived of as the other to this subject, Japan is in effect feminized. This postulate, to which the works of Marguerite Duas are a glaringly obvious exception, is reinforced by the erotic absence of the Japanese male in Western constructions.

12. Rose, *Black Noise*, 21; see chap. 2, "'All Aboard the Night Train': Flow, Layering, and Rupture in Postindustrial New York," 21–61. "Hip hop has always been articulated via commodities and engaged in the revision of meanings attached to them" (ibid , 41).

13. Rose, "Orality and Technology," 35; Elizabeth Blair, "Commercialization of the Rap Music Youth Subculture."

14. I identify African American subjective agency and community, expressed in lyric, gesture, and movement, and disdain for standard copyright and for notions of originality and ownership of both lyric and sound as resistant formalist codes of hip hop and rap which are reproduced by whites, Japanese, and others. The process of reproduction invests these codes with additional subtexts. For studies of resistance and African American hip hop and rap, see Rose, *Black Noise;* Elizabeth Blair, "Commercialization of the Rap Music Youth Subculture"; Ted Swedenburg, "Homies in the "Hood: Rap's Commodification of Insubordination," *New Formations* 18 (winter 1992), 53–66. Swedenburg argues that American rap reorders back into a "black" context "white" music (rock and roll, for example) from which black origins have been elided and samples old rhythm and blues in postitive acknowledgment of the origins of African American contemporary music. In Japan, rap and hip hop are severed from the specifics of American racialism, and (inevitably) from the reordering into a "black" context, and are frequently montaged with Japanese lyrics and rhythms. Japanese rap and hip hop are thereby usually divested of specific references to the economic, political, and other material and ideological contexts germane to being African American in the United States. There are occasional instances when Japanese rappers use rap as a vehicle for conscious political oppositional statements, reframed within the context of specific Japanese insubordination. See Jones, "Black like Me," for an interview with one such Japanese rapper.

15. See Jones, "Black like Me," for a description of this advertisement.

16. Masao Miyoshi, "Against the Native Grain: The Japanese Novel and the 'Postmodern' West," *South Atlantic Quarterly* 87, no. 3 (summer 1988),

532–33. Hereafter, this issue of *South Atlantic Quarterly* is referred to as *SAQ*.

17. Karatani Kōjin. "One Spirit, Two Nineteenth Centuries," *SAQ*, 627. In the Meiji period (1868–1912), Japanese writers attempted to validate "fiction," which in the premodern period was devalued as low art. Edward Fowler has argued that for the early-twentieth-century *shishōsetsu* (personal fiction), which became the primary modern Japanese fiction genre, the author's life and personal corpus became the "authority" (factual repository) which posterior works referenced in place of other historical validation (*The Rhetoric of Confession: Shishōsetsu in Early Twentieth Century Japanese Fiction* [Berkeley: University of California Press, 1988], 16–18). Karatani has argued that, by the Taishō period (1912–26), the *shishōsetsu* had already "overcome the modern" by its rejection of a "Western subject" (an interiorized thinking subject who reflects upon the world of objects). Although the *shishōsetsu* prototype diminished as a genre in the 1980s, fictional prose narratives became more, not less, resistant to the idea of subject and structure. This sort of play, which incorporates information consumption, is made possible by the nonconstitution of the subject in Japan. Conversely, the strong constitution of the subject in the Western tradition prevents the same degree of play in Western texts. See Karatani Kōjin, "Nihon seishin bunseki," *Hihyō kūkan* 4 (January 1992), 271–81. The critic Asada Akira concurs, in "Infantile Capitalism and Japan's Postmodernism: A Fairy Tale," *SAQ*, 629–34, attributing the contemporary Japanese passion for pastiche to the absence of "the subject" in Japan.

18. Harry Harootunian, "Visible Discourses/Invisible Ideologies," *SAQ*, 449.

19. Miyoshi, "Against the Native Grain," 539. The author of *Somehow, Crystal* is Tanaka Yasuo.

20. Marilyn Ivy, "Critical Texts, Mass Artifacts: The Consumption of Knowledge in Postmodern Japan," *SAQ*, 432–33.

21. "Tensai Takeshi no genki ga deru terebi," Nippon Television, Tokyo, 1990, videotape; hereafter referred to as "Genki TV."

22. *Video on Stage,* 61.

23. Norma Field, *"Somehow:* The Postmodern as Atmosphere," *SAQ*, 555, 557.

24. Ivy, "Critical Texts, Mass Artifacts," 436.

25. *Video on Stage,* 1–10, 69, 72.

26. For a discussion of American World War II racial discourses on Japan and the Japanese, see John Dower, *War without Mercy: Race and Power in the Pacific War* (New York: Pantheon, 1986).

27. Lott, "Love and Theft."

28. Hebdige, *Subculture,* 44–45.

29. David Goldberg, "The Social Formation of Racist Discourse," in *Anatomy of Racism,* ed. David Goldberg (Minneapolis: University of Minnesota Press 1990), 306.

30. Dower, *War without Mercy,* 12. The valuation of white complexions existed in the tenth century, when it was employed to distinguish the economically dominant, nonlaboring Heian aristocracy from the working classes. In the modern period, members of the outcaste group known as *burakumin,* Korean Japanese, Okinawans, the Ainu and other aborigines, children of mixed racial parentage, and, more recently, Southeast Asian and Chinese immigrants, fall into the category of "other within." For essays on discrimination in modern Japan, see Hirota Masaki, *Sabetsu no shosō* [Various aspects of discrimination] (Tokyo: Iwanami, 1990). On the burakumin, see George De Vos and H. Wagatsuma, eds., *Japan's Invisible Race* (Berkeley: University of California Press, 1967).

31. Etienne Balibar, "Paradoxes of Universality," in Goldberg, *Anatomy of Racism,* 290

32. See Russell, "Narratives of Denial," 5–7; "Race and Reflexivity," 19, 21. Most of the Africans and African Americans with whom prewar Japan had contact were the slaves and servants of European and American traders.

33. *Video on Stage,* 77.

34. While some Japanese clearly recirculated stereotypes, as argued by Russell in "Race and Reflexivity" and "Narratives of Denial," and thus appear identified with whites, others deplored American racism and allied themselves as people of color with African Americans, both prior to and immediately following World War II. See Dower, *War without Mercy.* For studies of Japanese and Okinawan racialism, see Michael Molasky, "Burned-Out Ruins and Barbed Wire Fences: The American Occupation in Japan and Okinawan Literature" (Ph.D. diss., University of Chicago, 1994); "Poetry of Protest from Okinawa: Arakawa Akira's 'The Colored Race'" (Unpublished manuscript, 1994).

35. Katsuyo Motoyoshi, "Fearful Terrain: The Underground and the Continent in the Works of Natsume Sōseki" (Paper presented at the workshop "The Politics of Exclusion in Modern Japanese Literature and Culture," Boston, 25 March 1994).

36. Tanizaki Jun'ichirō, *In Praise of Shadows,* trans. Thomas J. Harper and Edward Seidensticker (New Haven, Conn.: Leete's Island Books, 1977), 31–32.

37. Michael E. Dyson, *Reflecting Black: African-American Cultural Criticism* (Minneapolis: University of Minnesota Press, 1993), 169.

38. Frantz Fanon, "The Fact of Blackness," and Nancy Leys Stepan, "Race and Gender: The Role of Analogy in Science," in Goldberg, *Anatomy of Racism,* 109–26; 38–57.

39. Shimada Masahiko, "Momotaro in a Capsule," in *Monkey Brain Sushi,* trans. Terry Gallagher (Tokyo: Kōdansha, 1991), 113.

40. The basis for fetish can be read as anxiety related to sexual performance, identity, masculinity, and, by extension, power. The fetishized object transforms the threatening sexual lack into eroticized presence and allows for the circulation of desire. In Japan, as elsewhere, the black phallus becomes an index of eroticized power, alternately perceived as a threat or as an object of desire. As Griselda Pollack has argued in "Fathers of Modern Art, Mothers of Invention," *Differences* 4, no. 3 (fall 1992), 107–8, following John Ellis, Freud's "penis" (anatomy-bound material object), as explicated in "Fetishism" (1927), in *Collected Papers* (New York: Basic Books, 1959), 5:198–204, can be recontextualized within an expanded symbolic context: "Fetishism is not just a disavowal of a lack of penis; it is potentially also to be understood as a contorted form of masculine resistance to a whole system, the phallic structuring of sexual difference. . . . Fetishism can then be understood as a structure of substitution of signifiers determined in relation to the phallus/language/difference/power, which is not exclusively tied . . . to a sexual difference which is . . . a matter of masculine versus feminine." Homi Bhabha has further "detached" the penis from its corporeal context by reading the commingled perception of threat and the desire felt by the colonist when confronted with the native as imbued with the same psychic mechanisms that inform the construction of the fetish. For Bhabha, black skin becomes the sign of difference that engenders anxiety and the fabrication of discourses of likeness/presence and dissimilarity/lack (metaphor and metonymy). See Homi Bhabha, "The Other Question" and "Of Mimicry and Man," in *The Location of Culture* (New York: Routledge, 1994), 66–84; 85–92. Fetish has also been used to explicate the psychic mechanisms of commodity exchange. Karl Marx, "The Fetishism of the Commodity and Its Secret," in *Capital* (New York: Vintage, 1977), 1:163–77, paves the way for Haug's Marxist and psychoanalytic analysis of commodity exchange.

41. While Japan as a nation has not undergone colonization (and conversely has played the role of colonizer), the experience of the United States as

occupier in the immediate postwar period is partly analogous to colonization.

42. Okinawa was invaded by the Shimizu Clan from the Japanese islands in the seventeenth century and remained a Japanese colony until the Pacific War. After the war, Okinawa was under United States sovereignty until it was "returned" to Japan in 1972. See Molasky, "Burned-Out Ruins and Barbed Wire Fences," for Okinawan and Japanese literary processing of the occupation.

43. Dower, *War without Mercy,* 308.

44. *Video on Stage,* 76. The column, "Mr. Luke no mi no shita sōdan," rewrites the common idiomatic "discussions pertaining to one's circumstances *(mi no ue)*" with "discussions pertaining to the lower half of the body *(mi no shita)*."

45. The racialist structures of European and American societies determine in large measure the limited realms in which blacks excel; African Americans celebrated in American media comprise increasing percentages of Americans touring Japan, which reinforces the association of blacks with music and athletic achievement, to the exclusion of intellectual, political, and other arenas.

46. *Banana Chips Love,* Fuji Television, Tokyo 1992, videotape.

47. The brief explication here on sex and gender roles and the status of women in contemporary Japan cannot do justice to the topic. Nor should the reader assume a correlation between premodern or modern Western and Japanese gender politics and the class issues that inform these politics. In premodern Japan, neither upper- nor lower-class women were exclusively responsible for child care or cooking; they were primarily responsible for the management of "stem households" *(ie)*. The relegation of cooking and child care to women is a twentieth-century reformation. A few English-language sources for a general introduction to political, economic, social, literary, and other contemporary and historical positionings of women in Japan, to modern and premodern gender roles, to women's status, and to sexual politics include Gail Lee Bernstein, *Recreating Japanese Women, 1600–1945* (Berkeley: University of California Press, 1991); Ueno Chizuko, "The Position of Japanese Women Reconsidered," *Current Anthropology* 28 (1987), 575–84; Sharon Sievers, *Flowers in Salt: The Beginnings of Feminist Consciousness in Modern Japan* (Stanford, Calif.: Stanford University Press, 1983). More recent studies may be found in the English supplements to the *U.S.-Japan Women's Journal,* nos. 1–6 (1991–94). See especially Karen Kelsky, "Postcards from the Edge: The 'Office Ladies' of Tokyo," *U.S.-Japan Women's Journal, English Supplement* 6 (March 1994), 3–26, and

"Intimate Ideologies: Transnational Theory and Japan's Yellow Cabs," *Public Culture* 6 (1994), 465–78, for discussion of Japanese women's relationships with non-Japanese men, particularly relevant to this essay. The reader may also consult Kathleen Uno, "The Death of 'Good Wife, Wise Mother,'" and Sandra Buckley, "Altered States: The Body Politics of 'Being-Woman,'" both in *Postwar Japan as History,* ed. Andrew Gordon (Berkeley: University of California Press, 1993), 293–322; 347–72.

48. American men, for example, are expected to be more *yasashii* (indulgent, gentle).

49. *Goro* (February 1992), 173.

50. Yamada Eimi, *Beddotaimu aizu* (Tokyo: Kawade Shobō Shinsha, 1987), 112; my emphasis.

51. Quoted in Russell, "Narratives of Denial," 423. The original is in Yamada. *Beddotaimu aizu,* 13. Many of Yamada's female protagonists also labor to dissolve this difference and form a community aligned with black men through shared marks of bodily otherness. For a thorough discussion of the production of femaleness and blackness in Yamada's texts, see Nina Cornyetz, "Power and Gender in the Narratives of Yamada Eimi." In *Gender and Theory in Japanese Women's Writings,* ed. Paul Schalow and Janet Walker (forthcoming).

52. Yamada Eimi, *Haremu wārudo* (Tokyo: Kōdansha Bunko, 1990), 100; hereafter referred to as *Harem World.* The title is a "Japanized" pronunciation of (originally) English words, written as the phonetic syllabary for transliteration of non-Chinese foreign words. Transliteration of the title back into English renders two possibilities, *Harem World* and *Harlem World.* In Japanese the dual meaning is most likely intentional. In the afterword, Yamada claims to have been inspired by Spike Lee's film *She's Gotta Have It.*

53. Yamada, *Harem World,* 9.

54. Yamada, *Beddotaimu aizu,* 14.

55. Yamada Eimi, "Kneel Down and Lick My Feet," in Gallagher, *Monkey Brain Sushi,* 191. All quotes are from this excerpted translation. The original text is entitled *Hizamazuite ashi o oname* (Tokyo: Shinchōsha, 1988).

56. Yamada, "Kneel Down and Lick My Feet," 189.

57. Yamada Eimi, "X-Rated Blanket," in *Boku wa biito* (I am beat) (Tokyo: Kadokawa Shoten, 1988), 59; Haug, *Critique of Commodity Aesthetics,* 52. See also Yamada Eimi, "X-Rated Blanket," trans. Nina Cornyetz, in *New Japanese Voices* (New York: Atlantic Monthly, 1991), 50–54. Pagination references the Japanese-language text.

58. Yamada, "X-Rated Blanket," 14.

59. Inoue Hisashi, Takahashi Gen'ichirō, and Shimada Masahiko, "Soshite, ashita wa dō naru ka," in

"Kono issatsu de wakaru Shōwa no bungaku," *Shinchō* special issue (February 1989), 447–50.

60. Tetsuo Najita, "On Culture and Technology in Postmodern Japan," SAQ, 413. In the modernization process, "others within," who are conceptually excluded from "homogeneous" Japan, are summarily erased in Japanese self-representation. See also Naoki Sakai, "Modernity and Its Critique: The Problem of Universalism and Particularism," SAQ, 475–504.

61. Karatani, "One Spirit," 627. See also Harootunian, "Visible Discourses/Invisible Ideologies," and Najita, "Culture and Technology," on Japanism.

62. *Video on Stage,* 77.

63. Kelsky, "Intimate Ideologies," 473

64. Yamada, "X-Rated Blanket," 12.

65. *Video on Stage,* 77.

Movie Stars and Islamic Moralism in Egypt

Lila Abu-Lughod

In Egypt, local westernized elites are singled out as sources of corruption and moral decadence by Islamic groups deploying a populist rhetoric. An absence of faith is portrayed as the cause of this elite's immorality and greed, while the embracing of Islam is offered as the solution to the country's considerable social and economic problems. Despite the efforts such groups have made to provide social services, and especially medical clinics, for the poor who are not well served by overtaxed state institutions now under IMF and USAID pressure to privatize, they seem to have no serious programs for wealth redistribution, while at the same time they support capitalism and private property.[1] An important question that no one seems to have explored is why a political discourse in which morality displaces class as the central social problem is so appealing.

Instead of focusing on the social programs or philosophies of such groups, I want to explore this question by way of a close analysis of a sensationalized phenomenon: the decision by some female film and stage stars to give up their careers and take on the *higab*, the new kind of head-covering that is the most visible symbol of the growing popularity of a self-consciously Muslim identity in Egypt and elsewhere in the Muslim world. The complex reactions of rural and poor women toward these stars, I will argue, illuminate the dynamics of the Islamist appeal. Leila Ahmed has suggested, with some justification, that the dominance of the new veiling and the affiliation with Islamism it represents mark "a broad demographic change—a change that has democratized mainstream culture and mores," whereby the emergent middle classes, rather than the formerly culturally dominant upper and middle classes, define the norms.[2] I will argue, however, that the case of the media stars shows how the discourse of morality associated with the new veil works to produce a false sense of egalitarianism that distracts from the significant and ongoing problems of class inequality in Egypt.

Born Again Stars

On display during the first months of 1993 in the bookstores and street stalls of Cairo was a small but controversial book marking (and marketing) what it claimed was a major social phenomenon. On the front cover was a bold announcement that the book, published in 1991, was in its eighth printing; on the back cover, a quote from the widely popular conservative religious figure Sheikh Al-Sha'rawi, himself a media star because of his weekly television program: "After more than 20 actresses and radio personalities had adopted the veil *[hi-gab]* . . . war was declared on them . . . Those carrying the banner of this war are the 'sex stars' and 'merchants of lust.'"[3]

Entitled *Repentant Artists and the Sex Stars,* the book was coauthored by a man and a woman, 'Imad Nasif and Amal Kho-dayr. Yet only a photo of the man can be found on the title page: he is youthful, wearing a loud patterned shirt and sitting thoughtfully at a desk. One presumes that the coauthor is veiled and does not want to appear. Below the photo is a quotation, un-attributed, suggesting the authors' admiration for what they represent as the courage of these embattled "born again" stars: "The most honorable eagle is the one that flies against the wind and the powerful fish is the one who swims against the current . . . and truth is worth dying to achieve." On the following pages are the assertion of copyright protection (the book has no publisher and only lists the post office box and fax number of the authors) and a quote from the Koran about how God loves those who repent.

Intended to promote the so-called repentant actresses, this little book includes lengthy interviews with many of these famous actresses, belly dancers, and singers, stars of film and stage, who have given up their careers and have taken on the veil. The women tell their stories and present "confessions." The book also contains some interviews with their supportive husbands, an approving interview with Sheikh Al-Sha'rawi, and a brief section at the end in which prominent actresses still in the business tersely give their opinions on what their "repentant artist" sisters have done (usually stressing individuals' freedom of choice) and defend the value and religious correctness of acting and of "true art" (often in distinction from the commercial productions of the last fifteen years).

As the pitiful confession of Hala Al-Safy, a famous belly dancer, illustrates, the discourse of these repentant stars demonizes the world of performing and portrays their renunciation of it as a way of becoming closer to God. The authors state that she wrote, in her own hand, the following words for the book:

> I confess and acknowledge that I, Suhayr Hasan Abdeen and famous as the dancer Hala Al-Safy . . . left my life in the hands of the Devil to play with and to do what he wanted without my feeling the sins of what I did, until God willed and desired to remove me from this swamp . . . and I acknowledge and confess that the life that they call the life of art . . . is empty of art and I acknowledge that I lived this life. . . . Just as I acknowledge and confess that I regret . . . regret . . . regret every moment that I lived far from God in the world of night and art and parties. . . . I entrust God to accept my remorse and my repentance. (33)

The dramatic story told by Shams Al-Barudy, a movie star whose name, according to the authors, "was associated with se-duction roles" (49), repeats these themes. Some lengthy quotes give the full flavor of the "born again" narratives. Al-Barudy re-counts two experiences as transformative: reading a modern poem about veiling, and going to Mecca to perform the lesser pil-grimage ('umra):

> I was at home preparing sweets when my little daughter Nariman came in. She was happy carrying her schoolbag. She kissed me and I hugged her lovingly to my breast. She said, "Mom, Mom look at the present my teacher gave me for getting good grades." She was talking about a book of poetry. I kissed her and took the book from her. I skimmed through it and my eyes stopped at one poem that began this way: "Let them talk about my veil, I swear to God I don't care./ My religion has protected me with the veil and deemed me lawful./ Shyness will always be my makeup and modesty my capital."

And another verse in which the poet says:

> "They cheated her by saying she was beauti-ful, the beautiful are duped by praise." When I read these verses I had a strange feeling. I sat down wearily and found tears falling from my eyes. I repeated what I'd just read. I said to myself, modesty and bashfulness don't de-scribe me so I don't have any capital. At this moment I realized the secret behind the con-tinuous anxiety that had spoiled the happy moments of my life. Those who told me that I was an actress of great beauty had cheated me. Those who had put my picture on the covers of magazines and in their pages had duped me. It struck me in the heart and after that my life changed completely. I started hating acting and art. My pictures on the billboards dis-gusted me. I started thinking about everything . . . myself, my husband, my children, death. (50–1)

She then recounts that her father suggested they go to Mecca to perform the lesser pil-grimage. She was overwhelmed by the holy places and remorseful about her life. Her discourse here turns on the Devil, prefaced by the lament, "Oh, this damn Devil who steals the best years of our lives and we only recognize him after it is too late" (51). Then comes the description of the epiphany while in Mecca:

> At night I felt a constricting of my chest as if all the mountains in the world were on top of me. My father asked me why I couldn't sleep. I told him I wanted to go the Grand Mosque [Haram]. He was surprised but pleased that I had requested this. When we got to the sanc-tuary and I greeted it and began to circumam-bulate, my body began to tremble. I started sweating. My heart seemed to be jumping out of my chest and I felt at that moment as if there was a person inside trying to strangle me. Then he went out. Yes, the Devil went out and the pressure that was like all the mountains of the world weighing on my breast lifted. The worries were gone. And I found my tongue burst forth with prayers for my children and my husband and I began crying so hard that it was as if a volcano had burst and no one could stop it.
>
> As I reached the shrine of the Prophet Ibra-him, I stood up to pray and recited the opening verse of the Koran as if for the first time. I started recognizing its beauty and meaning as if God had graced me. I felt there was a new world around me. Yes I was reborn. I felt I was a bride and that the angels were walking in my wedding march. Everything around me brought me happiness. I felt I was a pure white bird who wanted to fly in the sky, singing and warbling, setting down on flowers and green branches. I felt the world around me had been created for me. I would no longer feel fatigue, anxiety, or misery. (52–3)

She then describes how her father came for her; when he took her by the hand, she felt like a small child, totally innocent. She prayed the dawn prayer among her Muslim sisters and from then on began wearing the veil (higab). She concludes her interview with the following words, again invoking the Devil:

I'll never go back to acting. I won't go back to the Devil who stole everything from me. I've tasted the sweetness of faith and closeness to God . . . just as I tasted the Devil's life. (58)

Immoral Lives

The first time I had heard about this new phenomenon was in the summer of 1987. Two adolescent girls in the Bedouin community in Egypt's Western Desert where I was doing research were entertaining themselves by flipping through a clandestine movie magazine. One was literate, the other had never been to school. The latter, who stared carefully at the grainy black and white photographs, stopped when she got to one. This actress, she pointed out approvingly, had given it all up and taken on the *higab*. By way of explanation she added, somewhat harshly, "She got cancer and they had to chop off her breasts." After a pause, to make sure I had understood, she said, "God had punished her for exposing them."

In this girl's reaction is a key to the complex attitudes ordinary women in Egypt have toward the world of media stars. She had conflated immoral lifestyles with an absence of religion, as if only religion guided women to live proper, respectable lives. God had punished the actress for her sins and, as a result, she had come to recognize the importance of religious faith. The girl could feel self-righteous and yet, there she was, poring over a magazine filled with news of the others who were still part of that fascinating world.

Although film and radio stars are among the most widely known and popular public figures in Egypt, the "repentant artists" demonization and religious renunciation of the world they represent is not so surprising. Nor is the widespread approval of these women's choices. But I think the roots of this acceptance are complex, confounded by

ordinary people's continuing and simultaneous infatuation with media stars.

The born-again discourse of performance as the work of the Devil carries weight, first, because it resonates with long-standing traditional views in the Muslim world that performers are disreputable. Women performers mixed with strange men and appeared in public when no other women did; they were also linked, justifiably or not, to "the oldest profession." More important, in the contemporary period media stars are criticized for their immoral life-styles and, in the lingo of the religious critics, for their involvement in the world of animal instinct, sexual desire, and temptation. My young Bedouin friend's interpretation of the film star's breast cancer as due to the wrath of God is indicative of a widespread recognition that media stars are the victims and perpetrators of what we call "sexploitation."

Women stars today are perceived as problematic for a host of related reasons, however. First, they are the most public of women and the most visibly independent of family control, violating some basic assumptions about gender in rural and many segments of urban Egypt. Many stars, especially dancers, use stage names, as the confession of Hala Al-Safy above illustrates, frequently with only a first name—Lucy, Shirihan, Yusra, or Sabrin, for example. This is a striking sign of their difference, and particularly their independence from family ties and genealogical definitions in a country where the father's name is always one's second name, and the grandfather's is often the surname.

Their denial of family responsibility, widely assumed to be part of a woman's self-definition, is also problematic. A recurring theme in the narratives of the reformed actresses, bolstered by the interviews with their husbands that accompany their stories, is how their careers had caused them to neglect their husbands and children. As Shams Al-Barudy notes, "I now live a happy life in the midst of my family, with my noble husband who stood by me and encouraged me and congratulated me on each step . . . and my three children"(56). Her husband, a former actor and movie director, explains, "I had long wished that Shams would retire from acting and live for her household" (60).

This husband is echoing a sentiment being widely disseminated in the press and other media, especially in the last two decades of increasing unemployment, that women's proper place is in the home with their families. Actresses and other show business personalities epitomize the challenge to that domestic model and are targeted in part because they are the most extreme and visible case of a widespread phenomenon: working women.

That the problem is also class related—the working women being criticized are privileged—is apparent in a short article by Anis Mansour, an establishment journalist, in the official government newspaper *Al-Ahram* in 1989. In alarmist language it lays out the links between careerist mothers and unhappy children, stressing actresses' special culpability as women who are wealthy enough to send their children to boarding schools. It was translated in *The Egyptian Gazette* as follows:

Obsessed with her career and the cut-throat competition with others to ascend the ladder of success, today's mother has not got enough time to look after her children and get to grips with their problems. Thus in her scramble for business success, the mother leaves behind her poor children for nannies and servants to bring up. Many film stars are characteristically interested in sending their children away to be brought up and receive their education. There is no doubt that this lifestyle takes its toll on the mental and psychological growth of these children who develop a devastating sense of powerlessness and even feel unwanted and isolated. . . . The whole issue boils down to the fact that unless the child gets enough parental care and protection he is bound to fall into the abyss of brothels, drug dens and deviation.[4]

Ultimately, the problem with stars is that they represent a nouveau riche westernized elite. Their sexual immorality is often associated with Western life-styles, but there is also a general impression that they are different from ordinary Egyptians. The women wear expensive, fashionable clothes, plenty of make up, and dramatic hairdos, perceived by Egyptians to be "Western." Moreover, many of the most famous actors and actresses are known to travel to Europe for film festivals and holidays.

The statements of a Cairene domestic who was especially immersed in and knowledgeable about the media world affirm this association of actors with the immorality, and even illegality, of the wealthy. Commenting on an actor in a rerun of a television serial, she said he had just died a few months previously. He was at a seaside resort, having a good time. He had an asthma attack but he probably died because he was snorting drugs and had a fatal overdose. She added that all the "artists" do drugs; they have lots of money and that is what they do with it. When I asked her how she knew this, she said it was reported in the newspapers, on radio, and on television. This particular actor had been arrested a few years earlier, his apartment raided, and drugs seized. But he was acquitted. When I expressed surprise that she said he had also been a prosecuting attorney, she tried to convince me that "all these people" are rich and run the country. By contrast, she concluded, it was only people like her (ordinary poor people) who were suffering these days, barely managing to cope with rising prices.

Entitlement and Distance

From these attitudes toward stars and the repentant stars' own denunciations of their former lives, one might expect that most women in Egypt are wholly disapproving of actresses and other media stars. And yet, my recent fieldwork in a village in Upper Egypt suggests that this is certainly not the case. The Bedouin girl who so self-righteously condemned the actress with cancer spoke with the confidence of someone who was part of a community that had maintained enough independence from the urban centers and from state institutions to retain a sense of pride about their different social and moral standards. She was part of a wealthy family that did not need to feel shame.[5]

In the Upper Egyptian village in which I have been working, however, most people were relatively poor. Many men were forced to migrate to the city or abroad to find work and people generally were aware of the disdain with which they were regarded by urban and wealthier Egyptians. They knew this from migrants but also because they were more involved in state institutions and more connected to mass media than the Awlad 'Ali Bedouin families I had known.[6] The younger generation especially could not manage the same pride, although most saw more dignity in their customs and community than other Egyptians granted.

The villagers spoke about media stars with a mix of entitlement and distance. They seemed to feel as if the stars were "theirs," somehow belonging to them as viewers as much as they belonged to anyone else in Egypt. All except the old men and women knew the names of stars who appeared on their television screens, volunteering their previous roles and often some tidbits about their off-screen lives in answer to my questions about television drama plots. Many

offered opinions about the popularity and success of various careers.

Yet no one would have considered the stars as like themselves. In this, stars resembled the films and television serials in which they acted, which villagers appreciated as having been broadcast for their pleasure but, as I describe in more detail elsewhere, perceived as depicting the lives of others who had different problems, followed different rules, and did not belong to the local moral community.[7]

The black-and-white televisions on which most villagers watch these stars sit in rooms of mud-brick houses whose walls are decorated with odd bits of gift wrap and newspaper, small posters of Egyptian soccer teams, and abstract hangings fashioned from the foil wrappers of a popular candy bar advertised on television. These are different from the rooms they see in the serials, where even village homes are depicted with decent furniture and identified by primitivist wall hangings showing village scenes, the kind of weavings popular only with tourists and affluent westernized Egyptians.

The village might be considered atypical. School teachers from the nearby town believed it was unusually liberal, the people kinder, more hospitable, and less attached to their traditions and customs (implied negative) than in other communities in Upper Egypt. It was certainly extraordinary in its enmeshment in the tourist industry. A Pharaonic temple was set in its midst and many men made some kind of living through work with the Antiquities Organization and foreign archaeological missions. One heard octogenarians reminiscing about the Met, others praising New York University, and yet others mentioning the work they had done for the Germans, the Poles, the Canadians, and the French. Even village women had seen foreigners close up; several middle-aged tourists had married young men in the village, buying them hotels or taxis. One American expatriate had built himself a house in the village and a number of folklorists had set up shop there, collecting funeral laments or simply using the village as a base while studying epic poets further south. When I arrived, a friend of these folklorists, I was asked their news and asked if I didn't know other foreigners and urban Egyptians people knew—a miscellany of filmmakers, journalists, architects, and others.

Despite their savvy about other worlds, some of it derived, as in other villages across Egypt, from watching television, these villagers were typical of other rural Egyptians in the problems they confronted. Trying to make ends meet with low wages and unemployment, many children, and insufficient land to be farmed, were not the problems dramatized in television serials or faced by movie stars. As in other agricultural areas, land was distributed unevenly; the largest landowner worked hundreds of *feddans* (approximately acres), while most of the families fortunate enough to own land counted it in *qirats* (1/24 of a *feddan)*. Some families were embarrassed to admit, when I found them picking through the stubble of a recently harvested wheat field, that they were grateful when kind landowners permitted them to glean the grains of wheat left behind.

Women lived in a different world from the film stars. They worked hard at household chores like baking bread and with the tasks associated with raising animals as large as water buffalo and sheep and as small as pigeons. When rented or owned fields were close by, the women cut the *barseem* (clover) for the animals and carried it home in large bundles on their heads or on donkeys their sons brought out to the fields. They worried about sons failing in school or getting daughters married. Some were fortu-

nate in their husbands; others put up with husbands who were unhappy and cruel or who had migrated to Cairo only to take second wives. Some had good in-laws, some did not. Some had brothers who were generous with them; others found themselves in disputes over inheritance.

And they certainly did not perceive the stars as part of their moral community. For village women, matters of reputation were crucial. Although relations between men and women seemed more relaxed than in the Bedouin community I had known, men and women greeting each other more readily and people who had known each other for a long time sitting and talking together, the men still sat perched on the benches while the women sat on the floor. In large extended households where everyone did watch television together, the women tended to be circumspect. All but the young generation of school-age women still wore heavy black dresses and head coverings when they went on formal visits or to the nearby town. Even around the village they were careful to wrap shawls around their heads and straighten out their black overdresses. Young women were delighted when they got water piped into their houses because they could avoid the public exposure of fetching water, since people were so ready to judge each other and talk about how women and girls behaved.

In contrast, the villagers displayed a kind of tolerance and suspension of moral judgment toward the media stars. This was striking in its difference from their critical evaluations of neighbors and kin. The story I heard from a mother of a married daughter shows the way discourses of morality are crucial in discrediting others. As in many patrilineal societies in which brothers are expected to share a household even after marriage, in-marrying wives are prone to conflict, their interests being at odds, especially regarding the division of the patrimony at the death of their father-in-law. To explain why a high wall had been built between the house of her daughter and her husband and his brother's family, this old woman, the wife of a wealthy landowner in another hamlet of the village, constructed it as a matter of moral difference between her daughter and the sister-in-law. *That* woman, she began, was from a village in which all the people are worthless. But the real difference could be seen in these women's teenage daughters. Her grandchild, she explained proudly, was like a cat. No one ever saw her. She would come out to say hello to you and then disappear. She never went out and wouldn't let even the best known and most harmless male family friends into the house if her mother was not home. The other woman's daughter, she went on, had gone across the river in a car to Luxor (the large town) alone with an old European man who had bought her things. He had fallen in love with the girl and moved into the house. She claimed that the young girl would go up to his room.

I happened to know this family she was disparaging and had been told by her daughter's vibrant and friendly rival about the old Norwegian man who had, she claimed, not been comfortable at his hotel and so they had given him a room in their house. He had been generous with them, she implied, because he pitied their circumstances. They ran a small restaurant in their front room that catered to budget tourists, the business they had started after her lame husband had been fired from his job as the cook for the German Archaeological Mission—because he drank, others told me. She had showed me the Norwegian's room, still kept for him, but the old man had never returned after the Gulf War.

Other women in the village, ones less directly involved, told the story somewhat differently. One woman told me that an old European had befriended the family and helped them out financially. She didn't know why he had done this but thought he must have had no family of his own. She explained that he had taken a liking to one of the girls, but she made it seem more innocent. She did disapprove strongly of the fact that he took the girl to Luxor to buy her things.

Whether they assumed the worst and loudly condemned the behavior, in order to side with a daughter against her sister-in-law in a dispute over their husbands' share of an inheritance as well as the disparities in standing (the other brother having taken over the disgraced brother's position with the German archaeologists), or whether they withheld final judgment, the moral standards were clear and the scrutiny of neighbors and kin considered absolutely appropriate.

Knowing the standards by which the villagers judged one another, I was always shocked by what people took for granted on television. For instance, no one blanched at the fact that the highly anticipated annual "quiz shows" (fawazir) of Ramadan, the holy month of fasting, involved sexy women wearing extravagant, often skin-tight costumes, dancing western-style and Arab numbers. In 1990, people were excited at the return of Nelly to the small screen. She was blonde, petite, and quite agile; she was reputed to be sixty years old. In 1993, her replacement Shirihan was watched with more ambivalence, everyone impressed with her total recovery from a serious back injury (treated abroad, they all stressed) suffered in a car accident under scandalous circumstances. Despite the whispers and the rumors about these circumstances, women and children in the village watched every evening. They had no idea what the riddles meant and even the references of her costumes (sometimes 1920s flappers, sometimes Caribbean, sometimes Arab) must have passed them by. Yet that was one of the things Ramadan was about.

A favorite Ramadan program in 1993 was "Without Talk," a kind of celebrity charades that pitted teams of stars against each other: men on one side, women on the other. When they are being themselves, out of costume and without lines, one can sense how fundamentally urban, sophisticated, and westernized the media stars are. Again, though, what I found surprising was how easily village children related to the program. Those with whom I watched it were so excited that they eventually started reproducing it in the field in front of their house, down to the competition between girls and boys. And when I remarked on the stars' clothing, many of the women in slacks or sporty culottes that were far from anything one would see on local women, some adolescent girls explained knowledgeably that this was the fashion. They knew, they said, because they'd seen city women who came as tourists.

It was touching to see young adolescents even seeking ways to sympathize with the plights of these stars. Some girls were anxious to tell me that Yusra, one of the most westernized and sophisticated film stars, had never married.[8] There was pathos in what they added: "She says she loves children and has photos of children on her walls."

The television and film industries, of course, have a strong interest in fostering viewers' attachment to the stars. They do so through television programs in which actors and actresses are interviewed about productions currently being filmed, compete in often silly games like relay races at the Pyramids, and invite viewers into their homes. There are programs showing highlights of new works, and magazines devoted

to the world of cinema and stage. Most recently, a new biweekly newspaper called "Stars" began publication. Only the adolescents and young men in the villages had access to the latter since they were literate and, for school or work, went into a town where such reading matter was sold. But everyone was exposed to the television promotions of these stars.

The pleasures village women and girls took in their access to the world of the stars was undeniable. They could not only tolerate the differences in these women's lifestyles, so far removed from their own, but were fascinated by them. I never sensed any envy of the stars, or fantasies about joining them, although one evening when left on their own with no interesting shows to watch, the children in one family had what they described to me as a party. The eldest daughter had played the role of broadcaster and each of her siblings took the name of a movie star. She interviewed them about such things as how many films they had made and about their marital lives. It was great fun, but make-believe. What one sensed was that viewers enjoyed being entertained by the stars, in their roles on- and off-screen, and in having a very different and glamorous world to know about, to discuss, and to include in their gossip.

What happens when these stars change, taking on the veil and renouncing that world, is that they are suddenly brought closer. They seem to step out of their screen worlds and enter into the same world these village women live in, a world where religion and morality are taken for granted as the foundation of social existence. This, I believe, provokes a certain satisfaction while lending moral weight to the women's ambivalence about the world of stars. For women who know they are peripheral and disadvantaged compared to the urban and the wealthy, the confirmation provided by these actresses enables them to more freely express, as did my young Bedouin friend, their self-righteous disapproval of the immorality of that world and to feel good about their own.

False Vindication

The "repentant" actresses have done what an increasing number of urban Egyptian women have done: adopted the new modest Islamic dress as part of what they conceive of as their religious awakening.[9] Because they are such well-known figures, their actions have been publicized and capitalized on by the Islamists to further legitimize the trend toward women's veiling and to support their call for women's return to the home.

Secularists and progressives, many of whom see feminist ideals as integral to their projects, are opposed to veiling as a sign of "backwardness." Whether they are westernized liberals of the cultural elite for whom women's emancipation has been of longstanding interest, advocated first by turn-of-the-century reformists and "modernizers—like the well-known figure, Qasim Amin, and upper-class women whose work we are only now discovering—or leftists carrying the banner of Nasser's policies of state feminism in the 1960s (stressing general employment and education), they see in veiling the loss of women's rights.[10]

Some feminist intellectuals and political activists, like television writer Fathiyya al-'Assal, who is also a leading member of the Egyptian leftist party *(hizb al-tagammu')*, suspiciously accuse these actresses of taking fat salaries from the Islamic groups for hosting study groups at which conservative religious authorities or unqualified women proselytize. Others concerned with women's issues, like the liberal writer Wafiyya Kheiry, express resentment when censors interfere with their productions. Noting that most of the censors for television are veiled women, Kheiry asks, "How can I accept a veiled woman dictating to me what can and cannot be said? If I am veiled, won't my thinking be veiled too?"

But such study groups have cropped up everywhere, and the decision to adopt the *higab*—while initially, in the late 1970s, mostly a form of political action by intelligent university women, usually the first in their families to be educated—has now spread down to working women of the lower middle classes and up to a few rebellious upper-class adolescents and movie stars. In rural areas, educated girls declare their difference from their uneducated kinswomen, without jeopardizing their respectability, by means of this form of dress.[11] Adopting the *higab* now has an extraordinary number of meanings and co-implications that need to be distinguished.

And yet, just as the Western press treats the phenomenon monolithically, as a simple sign of fundamentalism, so most women in Egypt (except the urban middle-class secularists described above and Coptic Christians, most of whom share the Western view) read the new veiling simply as a sign of piety and morality. When such women see prominent women known to have operated under very different rules from themselves—performing, traveling abroad, wearing Western fashions, living independent of family constraints, seemingly unconcerned with reputation and respectability—take on the veil, they interpret this as a renunciation of such foreign values and an embracing of the same morality and religious identity that they see as guiding their own lives.

The stars' choice to veil is taken as a vindication of the life patterns of these other women, who live in communities or come from classes that do not offer the other choices to women—the choices of wearing make up or high heels on an everyday basis, of having careers, or of going to glamorous parties. The women delude themselves into thinking that these stars are now women like themselves, sharing their moral values and thus other aspects of their situations. This is especially true for the younger women who, if they attend school, begin to take on the same *higab* they see their teachers wearing in communities that have become less lax about religious matters in the past decade.

When asked about how his wife had changed, the actress Shams Al-Barudy's husband was quoted in *Repentant Artists and the Sex Stars* as saying, "Shams has now become a wife who cares for her husband . . . and a mother who tends her children *and lives her life like any other wife* . . . she is a mother with a calling [to raise her children in a Muslim way]" (61, my emphasis).

Yet she is not like "any other wife"—especially a wife in rural Egypt. The home she gives up her career for is comfortable, with fancy furniture, shiny bathrooms, and plenty of servants. It is not mud-brick, with insufficient room for expansion when her sons marry, or requiring constant battle with flies because of the sheep and water buffalo housed within. Her closets are stocked with clothes, the old fashionable ones now replaced with "modest dress" that nevertheless is of high quality fabric and color coordinated. She does not have to wait for the religious feasts to get a piece of fabric to make a new dress. She probably has savings and a husband with a decent income, not a migrant laborer who has left her with five children to feed and fields to be worked, or an asthmatic husband who makes $35 per month working for the Antiquities Organization. She never walks back from the market carrying her purchases on her head, or is forced to squeeze into a crowded bus or climb into the back of a pickup truck fitted with narrow benches; she drives, or,

more likely, is driven around in an imported car. It is this which allows her the leisure to tend to her husband and to oversee the raising of her children, helping them with their homework, taking them for lessons or to the club for swimming, or delivering them to their friends' birthday parties.

Veiling and retiring from acting do not change her class position and its privilege. Nor do they affect the bourgeois ideas about domesticity informing her (not to mention her husband's) vision of herself as wife and mother, ideas very different from the ones guiding women in this village in Upper Egypt and elsewhere.[12]

To take on the *higab* is a very different thing from having always worn some sort of head covering, having always thought of yourself as religious and moral, or having never left the bounds of family control. Yet, in the new Islamic consciousness in Egypt, a discourse of morality serves to erase the distinctions between these experiences and to mask the persistent divisions of class and life-style. This gives poor and rural women the comforting illusion of equality with their Muslim sisters everywhere, something no other political discourse can offer.

Notes

1. The literature on the Islamic groups in Egypt is considerable. Some important sources are Ali E. Hillal Dessouki, ed., *Islamic Resurgence in the Arab World* (New York: Praeger, 1982); Saad Eddin Ibrahim, "Anatomy of Egypt's Militant Islamic Groups," *International Journal of Middle East Studies* 12 (1980): 423–53; Gilles Kepel, *The Prophet and Pharaoh: Muslim Extremism in Egypt* (London: El Saqi Books, 1985); Gudrun Kramer, "The Change of Paradigm: Political Pluralism in Contemporary Egypt," *Peuples méditerranéens* 41–2 (1987–88): 283–302; Barbara Stowasser, ed., *The Islamic Impulse* (Washington D.C.: Center for Contemporary Arab Studies, Georgetown University, 1987). Two more recent special issues on political Islam make *Middle Last Report* 179 (November–December 1992) and 183 (July–August 1993) especially useful.

2. Leila Ahmed, *Women and Gender in Islam* (New Haven, Conn.: Yale University Press, 1992), 225.

3. Barbara Stowasser's "Religious Ideology, Women and the Family: The Islamic Paradigm," in her *The Islamic Impulse,* op. cit., 262–96, gives a good sense of the views of Sheikh Al-Sha'rawi.

4. Anis Mansour, "Victims," *The Egyptian Gazette,* 6 November 1989, 3.

5. I have written extensively about the pride of this community and its sense of difference from the rest of Egypt. See, for example, Lila Abu-Lughod, *Veiled Sentiments: Honor and Poetry in a Bedouin Society* (Berkeley: University of California Press, 1986) and *Writing Women's Worlds: Bedouin Stories* (Berkeley: University of California Press, 1993).

6. For a rich analysis of the place of Sa'idis (Upper Egyptians) in the imaginaries of urban Egyptians, see Martina Rieker, "Marginality and Modernity: Figuring the Sa'idi Peasantry in the Egyptian Nation," (paper presented at the SSRC conference on "Questions of Modernity," Cairo, Egypt, May 1993).

7. See my forthcoming article, "The Objects of Soap Opera," in *Worlds Apart: Modernity Through the Prism of the Local,* ed. Daniel Miller (London: Routledge, 1995).

8. The news of her marriage in 1993 was the cover story on numerous Arabic magazines.

9. The phenomenon of "the new veiling" is extremely complex and interesting. Among those who have written insightfully on it, showing clearly how the religious motivation for it needs to be balanced by an understanding of how veiling contributes to greater freedom of movement in public, easier work relations in mixed sex settings, respectability in the eyes of neighbors and husbands, greater economy, and social conformity, are Leila Ahmed, *Women and Gender in Islam* (New Haven, Conn.: Yale University Press, 1992); Fadwa El Guindi, "Veiling Infitah with Muslim Ethic," *Social Problems* 28 (1981): 465–85; Mervat Hatem, "Economic and Political Libera(liza)tion in Egypt and the Demise of State Feminism," *International Journal of Middle Fast Studies* 24 (1992): 231–51; Valerie Hoffman-Ladd, "Polemics on the Modesty and Segregation of Women in Contemporary Egypt," *International Journal of Middle East Studies* 19 (1987): 23–50; and Arlene MacLeod, *Accommodating Protest* (New York: Columbia University Press, 1990). Elizabeth Fernea's documentary film, *A Veiled Revolution,* is especially good at revealing many meanings of the new modest dress.

10. I discuss these progressives and the issue of feminism in my unpublished paper, "The Woman Question in Egypt: Notes on a Dynamic of Postcolonial Cultural Politics." Good sources on feminism in Egypt include Leila Ahmed, op. cit.; Beth Baron, *The Women's Awakening in Egypt* (New Haven, Conn.: Yale University Press, 1994); and Margot Badran, *Feminists, Islam, and Nation* (Princeton, N. J.: Princeton University Press, 1995). For a discussion of Nasser's state feminism, see Mervat Hatem, op. cit.

11. See Abu-Lughod, *Writing Women's Worlds,* op. cit., chap. 5.

12. For a discussion of the difference between urban and Islamist notions about the roles of wives and mothers and those with which some rural women work, see my unpublished paper, "The Woman Question in Egypt: Notes on a Dynamic of Postcolonial Cultural Politics."

Ways of Making Change

PART X

In this final section, you will learn how women have organized to combat a number of different problems. The articles highlight the changes in feminist theories and organizing brought about by recognition of the differences among women produced by geopolitical location, race, ethnicity, class, and sexuality. Today, many feminists seek to build a movement that is not merely "inclusive" or "tolerant" of differences among women. Rather, they envision a movement of multiple, shifting alliances informed by considerations of race, class, sexuality, ethnicity, religion, and regional ties. The problems facing feminist activists and theorists call for models of thinking, writing and action that begin with the interconnections among multiple forms of oppression.

bell hooks sets the tone for this section by arguing that the goal of feminist activism should not be women's equality with men, but the eradication of the ideology of domination and subordination which permeates Western society. This would mean that not just sexism, but all forms of oppression—including racism, imperialism, class oppression, homophobia— would be acknowledged as feminist concerns. Srilatha Batliwala points out that both men and women stand to gain from such a change, both materially and psychologically, by gaining access to a better quality of life and a more expansive notion of masculinity and femininity. The remaining articles suggest some of the ways that women have tried, and are trying, to end oppression. Alice Echols revisits the women's liberation movement of the late sixties and early seventies to connect feminist politics to the wider world of sixties radicalism. Like new leftists and black radicals, activists in the women's liberation movement rejected liberalism and capitalism for a transformative politics that "was not about the subordination of self to some larger political cause; instead, it was the path to self-fulfilment." The idea that politics was rooted in identity proved powerful and problematic. What lessons can be gleaned from the politics and activism of women's liberation in confronting current challenges? What is the "New Politics of Sexuality"? Essayist June Jordan takes up the challenge of rethinking identity politics in a world where old certainties and divisions, straight vs. gay, black vs. white, are less than helpful in theorizing new categories of personhood and identity. Present-

651

ing bisexuality as a significant challenge to forms of either/or thinking that bolster inequality Jordan argues for complexity as the heart of any freedom struggle. How does Jordan's analysis compare to bell hooks' goals for feminist politics? Charlotte Bunch and Margaret Plattner describe contemporary efforts of women around the world to redefine discrimination and abuse against women as human rights violations which the state has a responsibility to end. The 1995 U.N. World Conference on Women in Beijing was one such recent effort. Conference participants drafted a "Platform for Action" which outlined ways for governments and the private sector to achieve equality, peace and development for women in twelve critical areas, including education, healthcare, employment, politics, and the media. Why is it important to acknowledge women's rights as human rights? Why do some nations, including the United States, resist ratifying and implementing United Nations' conventions governing women's rights?

Suggestions for Further Reading:

Agarwal, Bina. 1992. "The Gender and Environment Debate: Lessons from India," *Feminist Studies*, 18, 119–158.

Ashworth, Georgina. 1992. "The U.N. Women's Conference and International Linkages in the Women's Movement." In Peter Willets, ed. *Pressure Groups in the Global System*. London: Frances Pinter.

Basu, Amrita, ed. 1995. *The Challenge of Local Feminisms: Women's Movements in Global Perspectives*. Boulder, CO: Westview Press.

Bell, Judith Kjellberg. 1992. "Women, Environment and Urbanization in a Third World Context: A Guide to the Literature," *Women and Environments*, 13, 12–17.

Bhushan, Anjana and Minh Chau Nguyen. 1995. *Advancing Gender Equality: From Concept to Action*. Washington, DC: The World Bank.

Bisi, Ogunleve. 1993. "Local Initiative: Key to Women's Voice in Global Decision Making for a Healthy Environment in Africa," *Women and Environments*, 13, 15–17.

Bulbeck, Chilla. 1988. *One World Women's Movement*. London: Pluto Press.

Elshtain, Jean Bethke. 1995. "Exporting Feminism," *Journal of International Affairs*, 48, 541–558.

Kammen, Paula. 1991. *Feminist Fatale: Voices from the Twentysomething Generation Explore the Future of the Women's Movement*. New York: Donald I. Fine.

Macleod, Arlene Elowe. 1992. "Hegemonic Relations and Gender Resistance: The New Veiling as Accommodating Protest in Cairo," *Signs*, 17, 533–557.

Mies, Maria and Vandana Shiva. 1988. *Ecofeminism*. London: Zed Books.

Ogundipe-Leslie, Molara. 1994. *Re-Creating Ourselves: African Women and Critical Transformations*. Trenton, NJ: Africa World Press.

Omi, Miho. 1994. "On Women's Centers in Japan," *Social Justice*, 21, 155–160.

Orr, Catherine M. 1997. "Charting the Currents of the Third Wave," *Hypatia*, 12 (3), 29–45.

Feminism:
A Movement to End Sexist Oppression

bell hooks

A central problem within feminist discourse has been our inability to either arrive at a consensus of opinion about what feminism is or accept definition(s) that could serve as points of unification. Without agreed upon definition(s), we lack a sound foundation on which to construct theory or engage in overall meaningful praxis. Expressing her frustrations with the absence of clear definitions in a recent essay, "Towards A Revolutionary Ethics," Carmen Vasquez comments:

> We can't even agree on what a "Feminist" is, never mind what she would believe in and how she defines the principles that constitute honor among us. In key with the American capitalist obsession for individualism and anything goes so long as it gets you what you want. Feminism in American has come to mean anything you like, honey. There are as many definitions of Feminism as there are

feminists, some of my sisters say, with a chuckle. I don't think it's funny.

It is not funny. It indicates a growing disinterest in feminism as a radical political movement. It is a despairing gesture expressive of the belief that solidarity between women is not possible. It is a sign that the political naïveté which has traditionally characterized woman's lot in male-dominated culture abounds.

Most people in the United States think of feminism or the more commonly used term "women's lib" as a movement that aims to make women the social equals of men. This broad definition, popularized by the media and mainstream segments of the movement, raises problematic questions. Since men are not equals in white supremacist, capitalist, patriarchal class structure, which men do women want to be equal to? Do women share a common vision of what equality

From *Feminist Theory: From Margin to Center* by bell hooks. Copyright © 1984 by South End Press. Reprinted by permission of the publisher.

means? Implicit in this simplistic definition of women's liberation is a dismissal of race and class as factors that, in conjunction with sexism, determine the extent to which an individual will be discriminated against, exploited, or oppressed. Bourgeois white women interested in women's rights issues have been satisfied with simple definitions for obvious reasons. Rhetorically placing themselves in the same social category as oppressed women, they were not anxious to call attention to race and class privilege.

Women in lower class and poor groups, particularly those who are non-white, would not have defined women's liberation as women gaining social equality with men since they are continually reminded in their everyday lives that all women do not share a common social status. Concurrently, they know that many males in their social groups are exploited and oppressed. Knowing that men in their groups do not have social, political, and economic power, they would not deem it liberatory to share their social status. While they are aware that sexism enables men in their respective groups to have privileges denied them, they are more likely to see exaggerated expressions of male chauvinism among their peers as stemming from the male's sense of himself as powerless and ineffectual in relation to ruling male groups, rather than an expression of an overall privileged social status. From the very onset of the women's liberation movement, these women were suspicious of feminism precisely because they recognized the limitations inherent in its definition. They recognized the possibility that feminism defined as social equality with men might easily become a movement that would primarily affect the social standing of white women in middle and upper class groups while affecting only in a very marginal way the social status of working class and poor women.

Not all the women who were at the forefront of organized women's movement shaping definitions were content with making women's liberation synonymous with women gaining social equality with men. On the opening pages of *Woman Power: The Movement for Women's Liberation,* Cellestine Ware, a black woman active in the movement, wrote under the heading "Goals":

> Radical feminism is working for the eradication of domination and elitism in all human relationships. This would make self-determination the ultimate good and require the downfall of society as we know it today.

Individual radical feminists like Charlotte Bunch based their analyses on an informed understanding of the politics of domination and a recognition of the interconnections between various systems of domination even as they focused primarily on sexism. Their perspectives were not valued by those organizers and participants in women's movement who were more interested in social reforms. The anonymous authors of a pamphlet on feminist issues published in 1976, *Women and the New World,* make the point that many women active in women's liberation movement were far more comfortable with the notion of feminism as a reform that would help women attain social equality with men of their class than feminism defined as a radical movement that would eradicate domination and transform society:

> Whatever the organization, the location or the ethnic composition of the group, all the women's liberation organizations had one thing in common: they all came together based on a biological and sociological fact rather than on a body of ideas. Women came together in the women's liberation movement on the basis that we were women and all women are subject to male domination. We saw all women as being our allies and all men

as being the oppressor. We never questioned the extent to which American women accept the same materialistic and individualistic values as American men. We did not stop to think that American women are just as reluctant as American men to struggle for a new society based on new values of mutual respect, cooperation and social responsibility.

It is now evident that many women active in feminist movement were interested in reform as an end in itself, not as a stage in the progression towards revolutionary transformation. Even though Zillah Eisenstein can optimistically point to the potential radicalism of liberal women who work for social reform in *The Radical Future of Liberal Feminism,* the process by which this radicalism will surface is unclear. Eisenstein offers as an example of the radical implications of liberal feminist programs the demands made at the government-sponsored Houston conference on women's rights issues which took place in 1978:

> The Houston report demands as a human right a full voice and role for women in determining the destiny of our world, our nation, our families, and our individual lives. It specifically calls for (1) the elimination of violence in the home and the development of shelters for battered women, (2) support for women's business, (3) a solution to child abuse, (4) federally funded nonsexist child care, (5) a policy of full employment so that all women who wish and are able to work may do so, (6) the protection of homemakers so that marriage is a partnership, (7) an end to the sexist portrayal of women in the media, (8) establishment of reproductive freedom and the end to involuntary sterilization, (9) a remedy to the double discrimination against minority women, (10) a revision of criminal codes dealing with rape, (11) elimination of discrimination on the basis of sexual preference, (12) the establishment of nonsexist education, and (13) an examination of all welfare reform proposals for their specific impact on women.

The positive impact of liberal reforms on women's lives should not lead to the assumption that they eradicate systems of domination. Nowhere in these demands is there an emphasis on eradicating the politic of domination, yet it would need to be abolished if any of these demands were to be met. The lack of any emphasis on domination is consistent with the liberal feminist belief that women can achieve equality with men of their class without challenging and changing the cultural basis of group oppression. It is this belief that negates the likelihood that the potential radicalism of liberal feminism will ever be realized. Writing as early as 1967, Brazilian scholar Heleith Saffioti emphasized that bourgeois feminism has always been "fundamentally and unconsciously a feminism of the ruling class," that:

> Whatever revolutionary content there is in petty-bourgeois feminist praxis, it has been put there by the efforts of the middle strata, especially the less well off, to move up socially. To do this, however, they sought merely to expand the existing social structures, and never went so far as to challenge the status quo. Thus, while petty-bourgeois feminism may always have aimed at establishing social equality between the sexes, the consciousness it represented has remained utopian in its desire for and struggle to bring about a partial transformation of society; this it believed could be done without disturbing the foundations on which it rested . . . In this sense, petty-bourgeois feminism is not feminism at all; indeed it has helped to consolidate class society by giving camouflage to its internal contradictions . . .

Radical dimensions of liberal women's social protest will continue to serve as an ideological support system providing the necessary critical and analytical impetus for the maintenance of a liberalism that aims to grant women greater equality of opportunity within the present white supremacist capitalist, patriarchal state. Such liberal women's rights activism in its essence diminishes feminist struggle. Philosopher Mihailo Markovic discusses the limitations of liberalism in his essay, "Women's Liberation and Human Emancipation":

> Another basic characteristic of liberalism which constitutes a formidable obstacle to an oppressed social group's emancipation is its conception of human nature. If selfishness, aggressiveness, the drive to conquer and dominate, really are among defining human traits, as every liberal philosopher since Locke tries to convince us, the oppression in civil society—i.e. in the social sphere not regulated by the state—is a fact of life and the basic civil relationship between a man and a woman will always remain a battlefield. Woman, being less aggressive, is then either the less human of the two and doomed to subjugation, or else she must get more power-hungry herself and try to dominate man. Liberation for both is not feasible.

Although liberal perspectives on feminism include reforms that would have radical implications for society, these are the reforms which will be resisted precisely because they would set the stage for revolutionary transformation were they implemented. It is evident that society is more responsive to those "feminist" demands that are not threatening, that may even help maintain the status quo. Jeanne Gross gives an example of this co-optation of feminist strategy in her essay "Feminist Ethics from a Marxist Perspective," published in 1977:

> If we as women want change in all aspects of our lives, we must recognize that capitalism is uniquely capable of coopting piecemeal change . . . Capitalism is capable of taking our visionary changes and using them against us. For example, many married women, recognizing their oppression in the family, have divorced. They are thrown, with no preparation of protection, into the labor market. For many

women this has meant taking their places at the row of typewriters. Corporations are now recognizing the capacity for exploitation in divorced women. The turnover in such jobs is incredibly high. "If she complains, she can be replaced."

Particularly as regards work, many liberal feminist reforms simply reinforced capitalist, materialist values (illustrating the flexibility of capitalism) without truly liberating women economically.

Liberal women have not been alone in drawing upon the dynamism of feminism to further their interests. The great majority of women who have benefited in any way from feminist-generated social reforms do not want to be seen as advocates of feminism. Conferences on issues of relevance to women, that would never have been organized or funded had there not been a feminist movement, take place all over the United States and the participants do not want to be seen as advocates of feminism. They are either reluctant to make a public commitment to feminist movement or sneer at the term. Individual African-American, Native American Indian, Asian-American, and Hispanic American women find themselves isolated if they support feminist movement. Even women who may achieve fame and notoriety (as well as increased economic income) in response to attention given their work by large numbers of women who support feminism may deflect attention away from their engagement with feminist movement. They may even go so far as to create other terms that express their concern with women's issues so as to avoid using the term feminist. The creation of new terms that have no relationship to organized political activity tend to provide women who may already be reluctant to explore feminism with ready excuses to explain their reluctance to participate. This illustrates an uncritical acceptance of distorted definitions of feminism rather than a demand for redefinition. They may support specific issues while divorcing themselves from what they assume is feminist movement.

In a recent article in a San Francisco newspaper, "Sisters—Under the Skin," columnist Bob Greene commented on the aversion many women apparently have to the term feminism. Greene finds it curious that many women "who obviously believe in everything that proud feminists believe in dismiss the term 'feminist' as something unpleasant; something with which they do not wish to be associated." Even though such women often acknowledge that they have benefited from feminist-generated reform measures which have improved the social status of specific groups of women, they do not wish to be seen as participants in feminist movement:

> There is no getting around it. After all this time, the term "feminist" makes many bright, ambitious, intelligent women embarrassed and uncomfortable. They simply don't want to be associated with it.
>
> It's as if it has an unpleasant connotation that they want no connection with. Chances are if you were to present them with every mainstream feminist belief, they would go along with the beliefs to the letter—and even if they consider themselves feminists, they hasten to say no.

Many women are reluctant to advocate feminism because they are uncertain about the meaning of the term. Other women from exploited and oppressed ethnic groups dismiss the term because they do not wish to be perceived as supporting a racist movement; feminism is often equated with white women's rights effort. Large numbers of women see feminism as synonymous with lesbianism; their homophobia leads them to reject association with any group identified as pro-lesbian. Some women fear the word "feminism" because they shun identification with any political movement, especially one perceived as radical. Of course there are women who do not wish to be associated with women's rights movement in any form so they reject and oppose feminist movement. Most women are more familiar with negative perspectives on "women's lib" than the positive significations of feminism. It is this term's positive political significance and power that we must now struggle to recover and maintain

Currently feminism seems to be a term without any clear significance. The "anything goes" approach to the definition of the word has rendered it practically meaningless. What is meant by "anything goes" is usually that any woman who wants social equality with men regardless of her political perspective (she can be a conservative right-winger or a nationalist communist) can label herself feminist. Most attempts at defining feminism reflect the class nature of the movement. Definitions are usually liberal in origin and focus on the individual woman's right to freedom and self-determination. In Barbara Berg's *The Remembered Gate: Origins of American Feminism,* she defines feminism as a "broad movement embracing numerous phases of woman's emancipation." However, her emphasis is on women gaining greater individual freedom. Expanding on the above definition, Berg adds:

> It is the freedom to decide her own destiny; freedom from sex-determined role; freedom from society's oppressive restrictions; freedom to express her thoughts fully and to convert them freely into action. Feminism demands the acceptance of woman's right to individual conscience and judgment. It postulates that woman's essential worth stems from her common humanity and does not depend on the other relationships of her life.

This definition of feminism is almost apolitical in tone; yet it is the type of definition many liberal women find appealing. It evokes a very romantic notion of personal freedom which is more acceptable than a definition that emphasizes radical political action.

Many feminist radicals now know that neither a feminism that focuses on woman as an autonomous human being worthy of personal freedom nor one that focuses on the attainment of equality of opportunity with men can rid society of sexism and male domination. Feminism is a struggle to end sexist oppression. Therefore, it is necessarily a struggle to eradicate the ideology of domination that permeates Western culture on various levels as well as a commitment to reorganizing society so that the self-development of people can take precedence over imperialism, economic expansion; and material desires. Defined in this way, it is unlikely that women would join feminist movement simply because we are biologically the same. A commitment to feminism so defined would demand that each individual participant acquire a critical political consciousness based on ideas and beliefs.

All too often the slogan "the personal is political" (which was first used to stress that woman's everyday reality is informed and shaped by politics and is necessarily political) became a means of encouraging women to think that the experience of discrimination, exploitation, or oppression automatically corresponded with an understanding of the ideological and institutional apparatus shaping one's social status. As a consequence, many women who had not fully examined their situation never developed a sophisticated understanding of their political reality and its relationship to that of women as a collective group. They were encouraged to focus on giving voice to personal experience. Like revolutionaries working to change the lot of colonized people globally, it is necessary for feminist activists to stress that the ability to see and

describe one's own reality is a significant step in the long process of self-recovery; but it is only a beginning. When women internalized the idea that describing their own woe was synonymous with developing a critical political consciousness, the progress of feminist movement was stalled. Starting from such incomplete perspectives, it is not surprising that theories and strategies were developed that were collectively inadequate and misguided. To correct this inadequacy in past analysis, we must now encourage women to develop a keen, comprehensive understanding of women's political reality. Broader perspectives can only emerge as we examine both the personal that is political, the politics of society as a whole, and global revolutionary politics.

Feminism defined in political terms that stress collective as well as individual experience challenges women to enter a new domain—to leave behind the apolitical stance sexism decrees is our lot and develop political consciousness. Women know from our everyday lives that many of us rarely discuss politics. Even when women talked about sexist politics in the heyday of contemporary feminism, rather than allow this engagement with serious political matters to lead to complex, in-depth analysis of women's social status, we insisted that men were "the enemy," the cause of all our problems. As a consequence, we examined almost exclusively women's relationship to male supremacy and the ideology of sexism. The focus on "man as enemy" created, as Marlene Dixon emphasizes in her essay, "The Rise and Demise of Women's Liberation: A Class Analysis," a "politics of psychological oppression" which evoked world views which "pit individual against individual and mystify the social basis of exploitation." By repudiating the popular notion that the focus of feminist movement should be social equality of the sexes and emphasizing eradicating the cultural basis of group oppression, our own analysis would require an exploration of all aspects of women's political reality. This would mean that race and class oppression would be recognized as feminist issues with as much relevance as sexism.

When feminism is defined in such a way that it calls attention to the diversity of women's social and political reality, it centralizes the experiences of all women, especially the women whose social conditions have been least written about, studied, or changed by political movements. When we cease to focus on the simplistic stance "men are the enemy," we are compelled to examine systems of domination and our role in their maintenance and perpetuation. Lack of adequate definition made it easy for bourgeois women, whether liberal or radical in perspective, to maintain their dominance over the leadership of the movement and its direction. This hegemony continues to exist in most feminist organizations. Exploited and oppressed groups of women are usually encouraged by those in power to feel that their situation is hopeless, that they can do nothing to break the pattern of domination. Given such socialization, these women have often felt that our only response to white, bourgeois, hegemonic dominance of feminist movement is to trash, reject, or dismiss feminism. This reaction is in no way threatening to the women who wish to maintain control over the direction of feminist theory and praxis. They prefer us to be silent, passively accepting their ideas. They prefer us speaking against "them" rather than developing our own ideas about feminist movement.

Feminism is the struggle to end sexist oppression. Its aim is not to benefit solely any specific group of women, any particular race or class of women. It does not privilege women over men. It has the power to transform in a meaningful way all our lives. Most importantly, feminism is neither a lifestyle nor a ready-made identity or role one can step into. Diverting energy from feminist movement that aims to change society, many women concentrate on the development of a counter-culture, a woman-centered world wherein participants have little contact with men. Such attempts do not indicate a respect or concern for the vast majority of women who are unable to integrate their cultural expressions with the visions offered by alternative woman-centered communities. In *Beyond God the Father,* Mary Daly urged women to give up "the securities offered by the patriarchal system" and create new space that would be woman-centered. Responding to Daly, Jeanne Gross pointed to the contradictions that arise when the focus of feminist movement is on the construction of new space:

> Creating a "counterworld" places an incredible amount of pressure on the women who attempt to embark on such a project. The pressure comes from the belief that the only true resources for such an endeavor are ourselves. The past which is totally patriarchal is viewed as irredeemable.

> If we go about creating an alternative culture without remaining in dialogue with others (and the historical circumstances that give rise to their identity) we have no reality check for our goals. We run the very real risk that the dominant ideology of the culture is re-duplicated in the feminist movement through cultural imperialism.

Equating feminist struggle with living in a countercultural, woman-centered world erected barriers that closed the movement off from most women. Despite sexist discrimination, exploitation, or oppression, many women feel their lives as they live them are important and valuable. Naturally the suggestion that these lives could be simply left or abandoned for an alternative "feminist" lifestyle met with resistance. Feeling their life experiences devalued, deemed solely negative and worthless, many women responded by vehemently attacking feminism. By rejecting the notion of an alternative feminist "lifestyle" that can emerge only when women create a subculture (whether it is living space or even space like women's studies that at many campuses has become exclusive) and insisting that feminist struggle can begin wherever an individual woman is, we create a movement that focuses on our collective experience, a movement that is continually mass-based.

Over the past six years, many separatist-oriented communities have been formed by women so that the focus has shifted from the development of woman-centered space towards an emphasis on identity. Once woman-centered space exists, it can be maintained only if women remain convinced that it is the only place where they can be self-realized and free. After assuming a "feminist" identity, women often seek to live the "feminist" lifestyle. These women do not see that it undermines feminist movement to project the assumption that "feminist" is but another prepackaged role women can now select as they search for identity. The willingness to see feminism as a lifestyle choice rather than a political commitment reflects the class nature of the movement. It is not surprising that the vast majority of women who equate feminism with alternative lifestyle are from middle class backgrounds, unmarried, college-educated, often students who are without many of the social and economic responsibilities that working class and poor women who are laborers, parents, homemakers, and wives confront daily. Sometimes lesbians have sought to equate feminism with lifestyle but for significantly different reasons. Given the prejudice and discrimination against lesbian women in our society, alternative communities that are woman-centered are one means of creating positive, affirming environments. Despite positive reasons for developing woman-centered space, (which does not need to be equated with a "feminist" lifestyle) like pleasure, support, and resource-sharing, emphasis on creating a counter-culture has alienated women from feminist movement, for such space can be in churches, kitchens, etc.

Longing for community, connection, a sense of shared purpose, many women found support networks in feminist organizations. Satisfied in a personal way by new relationships generated in what was called a "safe," "supportive" context wherein discussion focused on feminist ideology, they did not question whether masses of women shared the same need for community. Certainly many black women as well as women from other ethnic groups do not feel an absence of community among women in their lives despite exploitation and oppression. The focus on feminism as a way to develop shared identity and community has little appeal to women who experience community, who seek ways to end exploitation and oppression in the context of their lives. While they may develop an interest in a feminist politic that works to eradicate sexist oppression, they will probably never feel as intense a need for a "feminist" identity and lifestyle.

Often emphasis on identity and lifestyle is appealing because it creates a false sense that one is engaged in praxis. However, praxis within any political movement that aims to have a radical transformative impact on society cannot be solely focused on creating spaces wherein would-be-radicals experience safety and support. Feminist movement to end sexist oppression actively engages participants in revolutionary struggle. Struggle is rarely safe or pleasurable.

Focusing on feminism as political commitment, we resist the emphasis on individual identity and lifestyle. (This should not be confused with the very real need to unite theory and practice.) Such resistance engages us in revolutionary praxis. The ethics of Western society informed by imperialism and capitalism are personal rather than social. They teach us that the individual good is more important then the collective good and consequently that individual change is of greater significance than collective change. This particular form of cultural imperialism has been reproduced in feminist movement in the form of individual women equating the fact that their lives have been changed in a meaningful way by feminism "as is" with a policy of no change need occur in the theory and praxis even if it has little or no impact on society as a whole, or on masses of women.

To emphasize that engagement with feminist struggle as political commitment we could avoid using the phrase "I am a feminist" (a linguistic structure designed to refer to some personal aspect of identity and self-definition) and could state "I advocate feminism." Because there has been undue emphasis placed on feminism as an identity or lifestyle, people usually resort to stereotyped perspectives on feminism. Deflecting attention away from stereotypes is necessary if we are to revise our strategy and direction. I have found that saying "I am a feminist" usually means I am plugged into preconceived notions of identity, role, or behavior. When I say "I advocate feminism" the response is usually "what is feminism?" A phrase like "I advocate" does not imply the kind of absolutism that is suggested by "I am." It does not engage us in the either/or dualistic thinking that is the central ideological component of all systems of domination in Western society. It implies that a choice has been made, that commitment to feminism is an act of will. It does not suggest that by committing oneself to feminism, the possibility of supporting other political movements is negated.

As a black woman interested in feminist movement, I am often asked whether being black is more important than being a woman; whether feminist struggle to end sexist oppression is more important than the struggle to end racism and vice versa. All such questions are rooted in competitive either/or thinking, the belief that the self is formed in opposition to an other. Therefore one is a feminist because you are not something else. Most people are socialized to think in terms of opposition rather than compatibility. Rather than see anti-racist work as totally compatible with working to end sexist oppression, they are often seen as two movements competing for first place. When asked "Are you a feminist?" it appears that an affirmative answer is translated to mean that one is concerned with no political issues other than feminism. When one is black, an affirmative response is likely to he heard as a devaluation of struggle to end racism. Given the fear of being misunderstood, it has been difficult for black women and women in exploited and oppressed ethnic groups to give expression to their interest in feminist concerns. They have been wary of saying "I am a feminist." The shift in expression from "I am a feminist" to "I advocate feminism" could serve as a useful strategy for eliminating the focus on identity and lifestyle. It could serve as a way women who are concerned about feminism as well as other political movements could express their support while avoiding linguistic structures that give primacy to one particular group. It would also encourage greater exploration in feminist theory.

The shift in definition away from notions of social equality towards an emphasis on ending sexist oppression leads to a shift in attitudes in regard to the development of theory. Given the class nature of feminist movement so far, as well as racial hierarchies, developing theory (the guiding set of beliefs and principles that become the basis for action) has been a task particularly subject to the hegemonic dominance of white academic women. This has led many women outside the privileged race/class group to see the focus on developing theory, even the very use of the term, as a concern that functions only to reinforce the power of the elite group. Such reactions reinforce the sexist/racist/classist notion that developing theory is the domain of the white intellectual. Privileged white women active in feminist movement, whether liberal or radical in perspective, encourage black women to contribute "experiential" work, personal life stories. Personal experiences are important to feminist movement but they cannot take the place of theory. Charlotte Bunch explains the special significance of theory in her essay, "Feminism and Education: Not By Degrees":

> Theory enables us to see immediate needs in terms of long-range goals and an overall perspective on the world. It thus gives us a framework for evaluating various strategies in both the long and the short run and for seeing the types of changes that they are likely to produce. Theory is not just a body of facts or a set of personal opinions. It involves explanations and hypotheses that are based on available knowledge and experience. It is also dependent on conjecture and insight about how to interpret those facts and experiences and their significance.

Since bourgeois white women had defined feminism in such a way as to make it appear that it had no real significance for black women, they could then conclude that black women need not contribute to developing theory. We were to provide the colorful life stories to document and validate the prevailing set of theoretical assumptions. Focus on social equality with men as a definition of feminism led to an emphasis on discrimination, male attitudes, and legalistic reforms. Feminism as a movement to end sexist oppression directs our attention to systems of domination and the inter-relatedness of sex, race, and class oppression. Therefore, it compels us to centralize the experiences and the social predicaments of women who bear the brunt of sexist oppression as a way to understand the collective social status of women in the United States. Defining feminism as a movement to end sexist oppression is crucial for the development of theory because it is a starting point indicating the direction of exploration and analysis.

The foundation of future feminist struggle must be solidly based on a recognition of the need to eradicate the underlying cultural basis and causes of sexism and other forms of group oppression. Without challenging and changing these philosophical structures, no feminist reforms will have a long range impact. Consequently, it is now necessary for advocates of feminism to collectively acknowledge that our struggle cannot be defined as a movement to gain social equality with men; that terms like "liberal feminist" and "bourgeois feminist" represent contradictions that must be resolved so that feminism will not be continually co-opted to serve the opportunistic ends of special interest groups.

Nothing Distant about It:
Women's Liberation and Sixties Radicalism

Alice Echols

On 7 September 1968 the sixties came to the Miss America Pageant when one hundred women's liberationists descended on Atlantic City to protest the pageant's promotion of physical attractiveness and charm as the primary measures of women's worth. Carrying signs that declared, "Miss America Is a Big Falsie," "Miss America Sells It," and "Up against the Wall, Miss America," they formed a picket line on the boardwalk, sang anti-Miss America songs in three-part harmony, and performed guerrilla theater. The activists crowned a live sheep Miss America and paraded it on the boardwalk to parody the way the contestants, and, by extension, all women, "are appraised and judged like animals at a county fair." They tried to convince women in the crowd that the tyranny of beauty was but one of the many ways that women's bodies were colonized. By announcing beforehand that they would not speak to male reporters (or to any man for that matter), they challenged the sexual division of labor that consigned women reporters to the "soft" stories and male reporters to the "hard" news stories. Newspaper editors who wanted to cover the protest were thus forced to pull their female reporters from the society pages to do so.[1]

The protesters set up a "Freedom Trash Can" and filled it with various "instruments of torture"—high-heeled shoes, bras, girdles, hair curlers, false eyelashes, typing books, and representative copies of *Cosmopolitan, Playboy,* and *Ladies' Home Journal.* They had wanted to burn the contents of the Freedom Trash Can but were prevented from doing so by a city ordinance that prohibited bonfires on the boardwalk. However, word had been leaked to the press that the protest would include a symbolic bra-burning, and, as a consequence, reporters were everywhere.[2] Although they burned no bras that day on the boardwalk, the image of the bra-burning, militant feminist remains part of our popular mythology about the women's liberation movement.

The activists also managed to make their presence felt inside the auditorium during that night's live broadcast of the pageant. Pageant officials must have known that they were in for a long night when early in the evening one protester sprayed Toni Home Permanent Spray (one of the pageant's sponsors) at the mayor's booth. She was charged with disorderly conduct and "emanating a noxious odor," an irony that women's liberationists understandably savored. The more spectacular action occurred later that night. As the outgoing Miss America read her farewell speech, four women unfurled a banner that read, "Women's Liberation," and all sixteen protesters shouted "Freedom for Women," and "No More Miss America" before security guards could eject them. The television audience heard the commotion and could see it register on Miss America's face as she stumbled through the remainder of her speech. But the program's producer prevented the cameramen from covering the cause of Miss America's consternation.[3] The television audience did not remain in the dark for long, because Monday's newspapers described the protest in some detail. As the first major demonstration of the fledgling women's liberation movement, it had been designed to make a big splash, and after Monday morning no one could doubt that it had.

In its wit, passion, and irreverence, not to mention its expansive formulation of politics (to include the politics of beauty, no less!), the Miss America protest resembled other sixties demonstrations. Just as women's liberationists used a sheep to make a statement about conventional femininity, so had the Yippies a week earlier lampooned

the political process by nominating a pig, Pegasus, for the presidency at the Democratic National Convention.[4] Although Atlantic City witnessed none of the violence that had occurred in Chicago, the protest generated plenty of hostility among the six hundred or so onlookers who gathered on the boardwalk. Judging from their response, this new thing, "women's liberation," was about as popular as the antiwar movement The protesters were jeered, harassed, and called "commies" and "man-haters." One man suggested that it "would be a lot more useful" if the protesters threw themselves, and not their bras, girdles, and makeup, into the trash can.[5]

Nothing—not even the verbal abuse they encountered on the boardwalk—could diminish the euphoria women's liberationists felt as they started to mobilize around their own, rather than other people's, oppression. Ann Snitow speaks for many when she recalls that in contrast to her involvement in the larger, male-dominated protest Movement,[6] where she had felt sort of "blank and peripheral," women's liberation was like "an ecstasy of discussion." Precisely because it was about one's own life, "there was," she claims, "nothing distant about it."[7] Robin Morgan has contended that the Miss America protest "announced our existence to the world."[8] That is only a slight exaggeration, for as a consequence of the protest, women's liberation achieved the status of a movement both to its participants and to the media; as such, the Miss America demonstration represents an important moment in the history of the sixties.[9]

Although the women's liberation movement began to take shape only toward the end of the decade, it was a paradigmatically sixties movement. It is not just that many early women's liberation activists had prior involvements in other sixties movements, although that was certainly true, as has been ably documented by Sara Evans.[10] And it is not just that, of all the sixties movements, the women's liberation movement alone carried on and extended into the 1970s that decade's political radicalism and rethinking of fundamental social organization, although that is true as well. Rather, it is also that the larger, male-dominated protest Movement, despite its considerable sexism, provided much of the intellectual foundation and cultural orientation for the women's liberation movement. Indeed, many of the broad themes of the women's liberation movement—especially its concern with revitalizing the democratic process and reformulating "politics" to include the personal—were refined and recast versions of ideas and approaches already present in the New Left and the black freedom movement.

Moreover, like other sixties radicals, women's liberationists were responding at least in part to particular features of the postwar landscape. For instance, both the New Left and the women's liberation movement can be understood as part of a gendered generational revolt against the ultradomesticity of that aberrant decade, the 1950s. The white radicals who participated in these movements were in flight from the nuclear family and the domesticated versions of masculinity and femininity that prevailed in postwar America. Sixties radicals, white and black, were also responding to the hegemonic position of liberalism and its promotion of government expansion both at home and abroad—the welfare/warfare state. Although sixties radicals came to define themselves in opposition to liberalism, their relation to liberalism was nonetheless complicated and ambivalent. They saw in big government not only a way of achieving greater economic and social justice, but also the possibility of an increasingly well managed society and an ever more remote government.

In this chapter I will attempt to evaluate some of the more important features of sixties radicalism by focusing on the specific example of the women's liberation movement. I am motivated by the problematic ways "the sixties" has come to be scripted in our culture. If conservative "slash and burn" accounts of the period indict sixties radicals for everything from crime and drug use to single motherhood, they at least heap guilt fairly equally on antiwar, black civil rights, and feminist activists alike. By contrast, progressive reconstructions, while considerably more positive in their assessments of the period, tend to present the sixties as if women were almost completely outside the world of radical politics. Although my accounting of the sixties is in some respects critical, I nonetheless believe that there was much in sixties radicalism that was original and hopeful, including its challenge to established authority and expertise, its commitment to refashioning democracy and "politics," and its interrogation of such naturalized categories as gender and race.

Women's discontent with their place in America in the sixties was, of course, produced by a broad range of causes. Crucial in reigniting feminist consciousness in the sixties was the unprecedented number of women (especially married white women) being drawn into the paid labor force, as the service sector of the economy expanded and rising consumer aspirations fueled the desire of many families for a second income.[11] As Alice Kessler-Harris has pointed out, "homes and cars, refrigerators and washing machines, telephones and multiple televisions required higher incomes." So did providing a college education for one's children. These new patterns of consumption were made possible in large part through the emergence of the two-income family as wives increasingly "sought to aid their husbands in the quest for the good life." By 1960, 30.5 percent of all wives worked for wages.[12] Women's growing participation in the labor force also reflected larger structural shifts in the U.S. economy. Sara Evans has argued that the "reestablishment of labor force segregation following World War II ironically reserved for women a large proportion of the new jobs created in the fifties due to the fact that the fastest growing sector of the economy was no longer industry but services."[13] Women's increasing labor force participation was facilitated as well by the growing number of women graduating from college and by the introduction of the birth control pill in 1960.

Despite the fact that women's "place" was increasingly in the paid workforce (or perhaps because of it), ideas about women's proper role in American society were quite conventional throughout the 1950s and the early 1960s, held there by a resurgent ideology of domesticity—what Betty Friedan called the "feminine mystique." But, as Jane De Hart-Mathews has observed, "the bad fit was there: the unfairness of unequal pay for the same work, the low value placed on jobs women performed, the double burden of housework and wage work."[4] By the mid-1960s at least some American women felt that the contradiction between the realities of paid work and higher education on the one hand and the still pervasive ideology of domesticity on the other had become irreconcilable.

Without the presence of other oppositional movements, however, the women's liberation movement may not have developed at all as an organized force for social change. It certainly would have developed along vastly different lines. The climate of protest encouraged women, even those not directly involved in the black movement and the New Left, to question conventional gender arrangements. Moreover, many of the women who helped form the women's liberation movement had been involved as well in the male-dominated Movement. If the larger Movement was typically indifferent, or worse, hostile to women's liberation, it was nonetheless through their experiences in that Movement that the young and predominantly white and middle-class women who initially formed the women's liberation movement became politicized. The relationship between women's liberation and the larger Movement was at its core paradoxical. If the Movement was a site of sexism, it also provided white women a space in which they could develop political skills and self-confidence, a space in which they could violate the injunction against female self-assertion.[15] Most important, it gave them no small part of the intellectual ammunition—the language and the ideas—with which to fight their own oppression.

Sixties radicals struggled to reformulate politics and power. Their struggle confounded many who lived through the sixties as well as those trying to make sense of the period some thirty years later. One of the most striking characteristics of sixties radicals was their ever-expanding opposition to liberalism. Radicals' theoretical disavowal of liberalism developed gradually and in large part in response to liberals' specific defaults—their failure to repudiate the segregationists at the 1964 Democratic National Convention, their lack of vigor in pressing for greater federal intervention in support of civil rights workers, and their readiness (with few exceptions) to support President Lyndon B. Johnson's escalation of the Vietnam War. But initially some radicals had argued that the Movement should acknowledge that liberalism was not monolithic but contained two discernible strands—"corporate" and "humanist" liberalism. For instance, in 1965 Carl Oglesby, an early leader of the Students for a Democratic Society (SDS), contrasted *corporate liberals,* whose identification with the system made them "illiberal liberals," with *humanist liberals,* who he hoped might yet see that "it is this movement with which their own best hopes are most in tune."[16]

By 1967 radicals were no longer making the distinction between humanist and corporate liberals that they once had. This represented an important political shift for early new leftists in particular who once had felt an affinity of sorts with liberalism.[17] Black radicals were the first to decisively reject liberalism, and their move had an enormous impact on white radicals. With the ascendancy of black power many black militants maintained that liberalism was intrinsically paternalistic, and that black liberation required that the struggle be free of white involvement. This was elaborated by white radicals, who soon developed the argument that authentic radicalism involved organizing around one's own oppression rather than becoming involved, as a "liberal" would, in someone else's struggle for freedom. For instance, in 1967 Gregory Calvert, another SDS leader, argued that the "student movement has to develop an image of its own revolution . . . instead of believing that you're a revolutionary because you're related to Fidel's struggle, Stokely's struggle, always someone else's struggle."[18] Black radicals were also the first to conclude that nothing short of revolution—certainly not Johnson's Great Society programs and a few pieces of civil rights legislation—could undo racism. As leftist journalist Andrew Kopkind remembered it, the rhetoric of revolution proved impossible for white new leftists to resist. "With black revolution raging in America and world revolution directed against America, it was hardly

possible for white radicals to think themselves anything less than revolutionaries."[19]

Radicals' repudiation of liberalism also grew out of their fear that liberalism could "co-opt" and thereby contain dissent. Thus, in 1965 when President Johnson concluded a nationally televised speech on civil rights by proclaiming, "And we *shall* overcome," radicals saw in this nothing more than a calculated move to appropriate Movement rhetoric in order to blunt protest. By contrast, more established civil rights leaders reportedly cheered the president on, believing that his declaration constituted a significant "affirmation of the movement."[20] Liberalism, then, was seen as both compromised and compromising. In this, young radicals were influenced by Herbert Marcuse, who emphasized the system's ability to reproduce itself through its recuperation of dissent.[21]

Just as radicals' critique of materialism developed in the context of relative economic abundance, so did their critique of liberalism develop at a time of liberalism's greatest political strength. The idea that conservativism might supplant liberalism at some point in the near future was simply unimaginable to them. (To be fair, this view was not entirely unreasonable given Johnson's trouncing of Barry Goldwater in the 1964 presidential election.)

This was just one of many things that distinguished new leftists from old leftists, who, having lived through McCarthyism, were far more concerned about the possibility of a conservative resurgence. For if sixties radicals grew worlds apart from liberals, they often found themselves in conflict with old leftists as well. In general, new leftists rejected the economism and virulent anticommunism of the noncommunist Old Left. In contrast to old leftists, whose target was "class-based economic oppression," new leftists (at least before 1969, when some new leftists did embrace dogmatic versions of Marxism) focused on "how late capitalist society creates mechanisms of psychological and cultural domination over *everyone*."[22] For young radicals the problem went beyond capitalism and included not only the alienation engendered by mass society, but also other systems of hierarchy based on race, gender, and age. Indeed, they were often more influenced by existentialists like Camus or social critics like C. Wright Mills and Herbert Marcuse, both of whom doubted the working class's potential for radical action, than by Marx or Lenin. For instance, SDS president Paul Potter contended that it would be "through the experience of the middle class and the anesthetic of bureaucracy and mass society that the vision and program of participatory democracy will come."[23] This rejection of what Mills dubbed the "labor metaphysic" had everything to do with the different circumstances radicals confronted in the sixties. As Arthur Miller observed, "The radical of the thirties came out of a system that had stopped and the important job was to organize new production relations which would start it up again. The sixties radical opened his eyes to a system pouring its junk over everybody, or nearly everybody, and the problem was to stop just that, to escape being overwhelmed by a mindless, goalless flood which marooned each individual on his little island of commodities."[24]

If sixties radicals initially rejected orthodox and economistic versions of Marxism, many did (especially over time) appropriate, expand, and recast Marxist categories in an effort to understand the experiences of oppressed and marginalized groups. Thus exponents of what was termed "new working-class theory" claimed that people with technical, clerical, and professional jobs should be seen as constituting a new sector of the working class, better educated than the traditional working class, but working class nonetheless. According to this view, students were not members of the privileged middle class, but rather "trainees" for the new working class. And many women's liberationists (even radical feminists who rejected Marxist theorizing about women's condition) often tried to use Marxist methodology to understand women's oppression. For example, Shulamith Firestone argued that just as the elimination of "economic classes" would require the revolt of the proletariat and their seizure of the means of production, so would the elimination of "sexual classes" require women's revolt and their "seizure of control of reproduction."[25]

If young radicals often assumed an arrogant stance toward those remnants of the Old Left that survived the 1950s, they were by the late 1960s unambiguously contemptuous of liberals. Women's liberationists shared new leftists' and black radicals' rejection of liberalism, and, as a consequence, they often went to great lengths to distinguish themselves from the liberal feminists of the National Organization for Women (NOW). (In fact, their disillusionment with liberalism was more thorough during the early stages of their movement building than had been the case for either new leftists or civil rights activists because they had lived through the earlier betrayals around the Vietnam War and civil rights. Moreover, male radicals' frequent denunciations of women's liberation as "bourgeois" encouraged women's liberationists to distance themselves from NOW.) NOW had been formed in 1966 to push the federal government to enforce the provisions of the 1964 Civil Rights Act outlawing sex discrimination—a paradigmatic liberal agenda focused on public access and the prohibition of employment discrimination. To women's liberation activists, NOWs integrationist, access-oriented approach ignored the racial and class inequities that were the very foundation of the "mainstream" that NOW was dedicated to integrating. In the introduction to the 1970 bestseller *Sisterhood Is Powerful,* Robin Morgan declared that "NOW is essentially an organization that wants reforms [in the] second-class citizenship of women—and this is where it differs drastically from the rest of the Women's Liberation Movement."[26] In *The Dialectic of Sex,* Shulamith Firestone described NOW's political stance as "untenable even in terms of immediate political gains" and deemed it "more a leftover of the old feminism rather than a model of the new."[27] Radical feminist Ti-Grace Atkinson went even further, characterizing many in NOW as only wanting "women to have the same opportunity to be oppressors, too."[28]

Women's liberationists also took issue with liberal feminists' formulation of women's problem as their exclusion from the public sphere. Younger activists argued instead that women's exclusion from public life was inextricable from their subordination in the family and would persist until this larger issue was addressed. For instance, Firestone claimed that the solution to women's oppression was not inclusion in the mainstream, but rather the eradication of the biological family, which was the "tapeworm of exploitation."[29]

Of course, younger activists' alienation from NOW was often more than matched by NOW members' disaffection from them. Many liberal feminists were appalled (at least initially) by women's liberationists' politicization of personal life. NOW founder Betty Friedan frequently railed against women's liberationists for waging a "bedroom war" that diverted women from the real struggle of integrating the public sphere.[30]

Women's liberationists believed that they had embarked on a much more ambitious project—the virtual remaking of the world—and that theirs was the real struggle.[31] Nothing short of radically transforming society was sufficient to deal with what they were discovering: that gender inequality was embedded in everyday life. In 1970 Shulamith Firestone observed that "sex-class is so deep as to be invisible."[32] The pervasiveness of gender inequality and gender's status as a naturalized category demonstrated to women's liberationists the inadequacy of NOWs legislative and judicial remedies and the necessity of thoroughgoing social transformation. Thus, whereas liberal feminists talked of ending sex discrimination, women's liberationists called for nothing less than the destruction of capitalism and patriarchy. As defined by feminists, patriarchy, in contrast to sex discrimination, defied reform. For example, Adrienne Rich contended, "Patriarchy is the power of the fathers: a familial-social, ideological, political system in which men—by force, direct pressure, or through ritual, tradition, law and language, customs, etiquette, education, and the division of labor, determine what part women shall or shall not play, and in which the female is subsumed under the male."[33]

Women's liberationists typically indicted capitalism as well. Ellen Willis, for instance, maintained that "the American system consists of two interdependent but distinct parts—the capitalist state, and the patriarchal family." Willis argued that capitalism succeeded in exploiting women as cheap labor and consumers "primarily by taking advantage of women's subordinate position in the family and our historical domination by man."[34]

Central to the revisionary project of the women's liberation movement was the desire to render gender meaningless, to explode it as a significant category. In the movement's view, both masculinity and femininity represented not timeless essences, but rather "patriarchal" constructs. (Of course, even as the movement sought to deconstruct gender, it was, paradoxically, as many have noted, trying to mobilize women precisely on the basis of their gender.)[35] This explains in part the significance abortion rights held for women's liberationists, who believed that until abortion was decriminalized, biology would remain women's destiny, thus foreclosing the possibility of women's self-determination.[36]

Indeed, the women's liberation movement made women's bodies the site of political contestation. The "colonized" status of women's bodies became the focus of much movement activism. The discourse of colonization originated in Third World national liberation movements but in an act of First World appropriation, was taken up by black radicals who claimed that African Americans constituted an "internal colony" in the United States. Radical women trying to persuade the larger Movement of the legitimacy of their cause soon followed suit by deploying the discourse to expose women's subordinate position in relation to men. This appropriation represented an important move and one characteristic of radicalism in the *late* 1960s, that is, the borrowing of conceptual frameworks and discourses from other movements to comprehend the situation of oppressed groups in the United States—with mixed results at best. In fact, women's liberationists challenged not only tyrannical beauty standards, but also violence against women, women's sexual alienation, the compulsory character of heterosexuality and its organization around male pleasure (inscribed in the privileging of the vaginal over clitoral orgasm), the health hazards associated with the birth control pill, the definition of contraception as women's responsibility, and, of course, women's lack of reproductive control. They

also challenged the sexual division of labor in the home, employment discrimination, and the absence of quality child care facilities. Finally, women's liberationists recognized the power of language to shape culture.

The totalism of their vision would have been difficult to translate into a concrete reform package, even had they been interested in doing so. But electoral politics and the legislative and judicial reforms that engaged the energies of liberal feminists did little to animate most women's liberationists. Like other sixties radicals, they were instead taken with the idea of developing forms that would prefigure the utopian community of the imagined future.[37] Anxious to avoid the "manipulated consent" that they believed characterized American politics, sixties radicals struggled to develop alternatives to hierarchy and centralized decision making.[38] They spoke often of creating "participatory democracy" in an effort to maximize individual participation and equalize power. Their attempts to build a "democracy of individual participation" often confounded outsiders, who found Movement meetings exhausting and tedious affairs.[39] But to those radicals who craved political engagement, "freedom" was, as one radical group enthused, "an endless meeting."[40] According to Gregory Calvert, participatory democracy appealed to the "deep anti-authoritarianism of the new generation in addition to offering them the immediate concretization of the values of openness, honesty, and community in human relationships."[41] Women's liberationists, still smarting from their firsthand discovery that the larger Movement's much-stated commitment to egalitarianism did not apply equally to all, often took extraordinary measures to try to ensure egalitarianism. They employed a variety of measures in an effort to equalize power, including consensus decision making, rotating chairs, and the sharing of both creative and routine movement work.

Fundamental to this "prefigurative politics," as sociologist Wini Breines terms it, was the commitment to develop counterinstitutions that would anticipate the desired society of the future.[42] Staughton Lynd, director of the Mississippi Freedom Schools and a prominent new leftist, likened sixties radicals to the Wobblies (labor radicals of the early twentieth century) in their commitment to building "the new society within the shell of the old."[43] According to two early SDSers, "What we are working for is far more than changes in the structure of society and its institutions or the people who are now making the decisions. . . . The stress should rather be on wrenching people out of the system both physically and spiritually."[44]

Radicals believed that alternative institutions would not only satisfy needs unmet by the present system, but also, perhaps, by dramatizing the failures of the system, radicalize those not served by it but currently outside the Movement. Tom Hayden proposed that radicals "build our own free institutions—community organizations, newspapers, coffeehouses—at points of strain within the system where human needs are denied. These institutions become centers of identity, points of contact, building blocks of a new society from which we confront the system more intensely."[45]

Among the earliest and best known of such efforts were the Mississippi Freedom Democratic Party and the accompanying Freedom Schools formed during Freedom Summer of 1964. In the aftermath of that summer's Democratic National Convention, Bob Moses [Parris] of the Student Nonviolent Coordinating Committee (SNCC) even suggested that the Movement abandon its efforts to integrate the Democratic Party and try instead to establish its own state government in Mississippi. And as early as 1966 SNCC's Atlanta Project called on blacks to "form our own institutions, credit unions, co-ops, political parties."[46] This came to be the preferred strategy as the sixties progressed and disillusionment with traditional politics grew. Rather than working from within the system, new leftists and black radicals instead formed alternative political parties, media, schools, universities, and assemblies of oppressed and unrepresented people.

Women's liberationists elaborated on this idea, creating an amazing panoply of counterinstitutions. In the years before the 1973 Supreme Court decision decriminalizing abortion, feminists established abortion referral services in most cities of any size. Women's liberationists in Chicago even operated an underground abortion clinic, "Jane," where they performed about one hundred abortions each week.[47] By the mid-1970s most big cities had a low-cost feminist health clinic, a rape crisis center, and a feminist bookstore. In Detroit, after "a long struggle to translate feminism into federalese," two women succeeded in convincing the National Credit Union Administration that feminism was a legitimate "field" from which to draw credit union members. Within three years of its founding in 1973, the Detroit credit union could claim assets of almost one million dollars. Feminists in other cities soon followed suit. Women's liberation activists in Washington, D.C., formed Olivia Records, the first women's record company, which by 1978 was supporting a paid staff of fourteen and producing four records a year.48 By the mid-1970s there existed in most cities of any size a politicized feminist counterculture, or a "women's community."

The popularity of alternative institutions was that at least in part they seemed to hold out the promise of political effectiveness without co-optation. Writing in 1969, Amiri Baraka (formerly LeRoi Jones), a black nationalist and accomplished poet, maintained, "But you must have the cultural revolution. . . . We cannot fight a war, an actual physical war with the forces of evil just because we are angry. We can begin to build. We must build black institutions . . . all based on a value system that is beneficial to black people."[49]

Jennifer Woodul, one of the founders of Olivia Records, argued that ventures like Olivia represented a move toward gaining "economic power" for women.[50] "We feel it's useless to advocate more and more 'political action' if some of it doesn't result in the permanent material improvement of the lives of women." Robin Morgan termed feminist counterinstitutions "concrete moves toward self-determination and power."[51] The situation, it turned out, was much more complicated. Women involved in nonprofit feminist institutions such as rape crisis centers and shelters for battered women found that their need for state or private funding sometimes militated against adherence to feminist principles.

Feminist businesses, by contrast, discovered that while they were rarely the objects of co-optation, the problem of recuperation remained. In many cases the founders of these institutions became the victims of their own success, as mainstream presses, recording companies, credit unions, and banks encroached on a market they had originally discovered and tapped.[52] For instance, by the end of the 1970s Olivia was forced to reduce its staff almost by half and to scuffle its collective structure.[53] Today k. d. lang, Tracy Chapman, Michelle Shocked, and Sinead O'Connor are among those androgynous women singers enjoying great commercial success, but on major labels. Although Olivia helped lay the groundwork

for their achievements, it finds its records, as Arlene Stein has observed, "languishing in the 'women's music' section in the rear [of the record store] if they're there at all."[54]

The move toward building counterinstitutions was part of a larger strategy to develop new societies "within the shell of the old," but this shift sometimes had unintended consequences. While feminist counterinstitutions were originally conceived as part of a culture of resistance, over time they often became more absorbed in sustaining themselves than in confronting male supremacy, especially as their services were duplicated by mainstream businesses. In the early years of the women's liberation movement this alternative feminist culture did provide the sort of "free space" women needed to confront sexism. But as it was further elaborated in the mid-1970s, it ironically often came to promote insularity instead—becoming, as Adrienne Rich has observed, "a place of emigration, an end in itself," where patriarchy was evaded rather than confronted.[55] In practice, feminist communities were small, self-contained subcultures that proved hard to penetrate, especially to newcomers unaccustomed to their norms and conventions. The shift in favor of alternative communities may have sometimes impeded efforts at outreach for the women's liberationists, new leftists, and black radicals who attempted it.

On a related issue, the larger protest Movement's great pessimism about reform—the tendency to interpret every success a defeat resulting in the Movement's further recuperation (what Robin Morgan called "futilitarianism")—may have encouraged a too-global rejection of reform among sixties radicals. For instance, some women's liberation groups actually opposed the Equal Rights Amendment (ERA) when NOW revived it. In September 1970 a New York-based group, The Feminists, denounced the ERA and advised feminists against "squandering invaluable time and energy on it."[56] A delegation of Washington, D.C., women's liberationists invited to appear before the senate subcommittee considering the ERA testified, "We are aware that the system will try to appease us with their [sic] paper offerings. We will not be appeased. Our demands can only be met by a total transformation of society which you cannot legislate, you cannot co-opt, you cannot *control*."[57] In *The Dialectic of Sex,* Firestone went so far as to dismiss child care centers as attempts to "buy women off" because they "ease the immediate pressure without asking why the pressure is on *women*."[58]

Similarly, many SDS leaders opposed the National Conference for New Politics (NCNP), an abortive attempt to form a national progressive organization oriented around electoral politics and to launch an antiwar presidential ticket headed by Martin Luther King, Jr., and Benjamin Spock. Immediately following NCNP's first and only convention, in 1967, the SDS paper *New Left Notes* published two front-page articles criticizing NCNP organizers. One writer contended that "people who recognize the political process as perverted will not seek change through the institutions that process has created."[59] The failure of sixties radicals to distinguish between reform and reformism meant that while they defined the issues, they often did little to develop policy initiatives around those issues.[60] Moreover, the preoccupation of women's liberationists with questions of internal democracy (fueled in part by their desire to succeed where the men had failed) sometimes had the effect of focusing attention away from the larger struggle in an effort to create the perfect movement. As feminist activist Frances Chapman points out, women's liberation was "like a generator that got things

going, cut out and left it to the larger reform engine which made a lot of mistakes."[61] In eschewing traditional politics rather than entering them skeptically, women's liberationists, like other sixties radicals, may have lost an opportunity to foster critical debate in the larger arena.

If young radicals eschewed the world of conventional politics, they nonetheless had a profound impact on it, especially by redefining what is understood as "political." Although the women's liberation movement popularized the slogan "the personal is political," the idea that there is a political dimension to personal life was first embraced by early SDSers who had encountered it in the writings of C. Wright Mills.[62] Rebelling against a social order whose public and private spheres were highly differentiated, new leftists called for a reintegration of the personal with the political. They reconceptualized apparently personal problems—specifically their alienation from a campus cultural milieu characterized by sororities and fraternities, husband and wife hunting, sports, and careerism, and the powerlessness they felt as college students without a voice in campus governance or curriculum—as political problems. Thus SDS's founding Port Huron Statement of 1962 suggested that for an American New Left to succeed, it would have to "give form to . . . feelings of helplessness and indifference, so that people may see the political, social, and economic sources of their private troubles and organize to change society."[63] Theirs was a far more expansive formulation of politics than what prevailed in the Old Left even among the more renegade remnants that had survived into the early sixties.[64] Power was conceptualized as relational and by no means reducible to electoral politics.

By expanding political discourse to include personal relations, new leftists unintentionally paved the way for women's liberationists to develop critiques of the family, marriage, and the construction of sexuality. (Of course, nonfeminist critiques of the family and sexual repressiveness were hardly in short supply in the 1950s and 1960s, as evidenced by *Rebel without a Cause, Catcher in the Rye,* and Paul Goodman's *Growing Up Absurd,* to mention but a few.) Women's liberationists developed an understanding of power's capillary-like nature, which in some respects anticipated those being formulated by Michel Foucault and other poststructuralists.[65] Power was conceptualized as occupying multiple sites and as lodging everywhere, even in those private places assumed to be the most removed from or impervious to politics—the home and, more particularly, the bedroom.

The belief of sixties radicals that the personal is political also suggested to them its converse—that the political is personal. Young radicals typically felt it was not enough to sign leaflets or participate in a march if one returned to the safety and comfort of a middle-class existence. Politics was supposed to unsettle life and its routines, even more, to transform life. For radicals the challenge was to discover, underneath all the layers of social conditioning, the "real" self unburdened by social expectations and conventions. Thus, SNCC leader Stokely Carmichael advanced the slogan, "Every Negro is a potential black man."[66] Shulamith Firestone and Anne Koedt argued that among the "most exciting things to come out of the women's movement so far is a new daring . . . to tear down old structures and assumptions and let real thought and feeling flow."[67] Life would not be comfortable, but who wanted comfort in the midst of so much deadening complacency? For a great many radicals, the individual became a site of political activism in the sixties. In the black freedom movement the task was very much to discover the black

inside the Negro, and in the women's liberation movement it was to unlearn niceness, to challenge the taboo against female self-assertion.[68]

Sixties radicalism proved compelling to many precisely because it promised to transform life. Politics was not about the subordination of self to some larger political cause; instead, it was the path to self-fulfillment. This ultimately was the power of sixties radicalism. As Stanley Aronowitz notes, sixties radicalism was in large measure about "infus[ing] life with a secular spiritual and moral content" and "fill[ing] the quotidian with personal meaning and purpose."[69] But "the personal is political" was one of those ideas whose rhetorical power seemed to sometimes work against or undermine its explication. It could encourage a solipsistic preoccupation with self-transformation. As new leftist Richard Flacks presciently observed in 1965, this kind of politics could lead to "a search for personally satisfying modes of life while abandoning the possibility of helping others to change theirs."[70] Thus the idea that "politics is how you live your life, not who you vote for" as Yippie leader Jerry Rubin put it, could and did lead to a subordination of politics to lifestyle.[71] If the idea led some to confuse personal liberation with political struggle, it led others to embrace an asceticism that sacrificed personal needs and desires to political imperatives. Some women's liberation activists followed this course, interpreting the idea that the personal is political to mean that one's personal life should conform to some abstract standard of political correctness. At first this tendency was mitigated by the founders' insistence that there were no personal solutions, only collective solutions, to women's oppression. Over time, however, one's self-presentation, marital status, and sexual preference frequently came to determine one's standing or ranking in the movement. The most notorious example of this involved the New York radical group.[72] The Feminists, who established a quota to limit the number of married women in the group. Policies such as these prompted Barbara Ehrenreich to question "a feminism which talks about universal sisterhood, but is horrified by women who wear spiked heels or call their friends 'girls.'"[73] At the same time, what was personally satisfying was sometimes upheld as politically correct. In the end, both the women's liberation movement and the larger protest Movement suffered, as the idea that the personal is political was often interpreted in such a way as to make questions of lifestyle absolutely central.

The social movements of the sixties signaled the beginning of what has come to be known as "identity politics," the idea that politics is rooted in identity.[74] Although some New Left groups by the late 1960s did come to endorse an orthodox Marxism whereby class was privileged, class was not the pivotal category for these new social movements.[75] (Even those New Left groups that reverted to the "labor metaphysic" lacked meaningful working-class participation.) Rather, race, ethnicity, gender, sexual preference, and youth were the salient categories for most sixties activists. In the women's liberation movement, what was termed "consciousness-raising" was the tool used to develop women's group identity.

As women's liberationists started to organize a movement, they confronted American women who identified unambiguously as women, but who typically had little of what Nancy Cott would call "we-ness," or "some level of identification with 'the group called women.'"[76] Moreover, both the pervasiveness of gender inequality and the cultural understanding of gender as a natural rather than a social construct made it difficult to cultivate a critical consciousness about gender even among women. To engender this sense of sisterhood or "we-ness," women's liberationists developed consciousness-raising, a practice involving "the political reinterpretation of personal life."[77] According to its principal architects, its purpose was to "awaken the latent consciousness that . . . all women have about our oppression." In talking about their personal experiences, it was argued, women would come to understand that what they had believed were personal problems were, in fact, "social problems that must become social issues and fought together rather than with personal solutions."[78]

Reportedly, New York women's liberationist Kathie Sarachild was the person who coined the term *consciousness-raising*. However, the technique originated in other social movements. As Sarachild wrote in 1973, those who promoted consciousness-raising "were applying to women and to ourselves as women's liberation organizers the practice a number of us had learned in the civil rights movement in the South in the early 1960s.[79] There they had seen that the sharing of personal problems, grievances, and aspirations—"telling it like it is"— could be a radicalizing experience. Moreover, for some women's liberationists consciousness-raising was a way to avoid the tendency of some members of the movement to try to fit women within existing (and often Marxist) theoretical paradigms. By circumventing the "experts" on women and going to women themselves, they would be able to not only construct a theory of women's oppression but formulate strategy as well. Thus women's liberationists struggled to find the commonalities in women's experiences in order to formulate generalizations about women's oppression.

Consciousness-raising was enormously successful in exposing the insidiousness of sexism and in engendering a sense of identity and solidarity among the largely white, middle-class women who participated in "c-r" groups. By the early 1970s even NOW, whose founder Betty Friedan had initially derided consciousness-raising as so much "navel-gazing," began sponsoring c-r groups.[80] But the effort to transcend the particular was both the strength and the weakness of consciousness-raising. If it encouraged women to locate the common denominators in their lives, it inhibited discussion of women's considerable differences. Despite the particularities of white, middle-class women's experiences, theirs became the basis for feminist theorizing about women's oppression. In a more general sense the identity politics informing consciousness-raising tended to privilege experience in certain problematic ways. It was too often assumed that there existed a kind of core experience, initially articulated as "women's experience." Black and white radicals (the latter in relation to youth) made a similar move as well. When Stokely Carmichael called on blacks to develop an "ideology which speaks to our blackness," he, like other black nationalists, suggested that there was somehow an essential and authentic "blackness."

With the assertion of difference within the women's movement in the 1980s, the notion that women constitute a unitary category has been problematized. As a consequence, women's experiences have become ever more discretely defined, as in "the black female experience," "the Jewish female experience," or "the Chicana lesbian experience." But, as Audre Lorde has argued, there remains a way in which, even with greater and greater specificity, the particular is never fully captured.[81] Instead, despite the pluralization of the subject within feminism, identities are often still imagined as monolithic. Finally, the very premise of

identity politics—that identity is the basis of politics—has sometimes shut down possibilities for communication, as identities are seen as necessarily either conferring or foreclosing critical consciousness. Kobena Mercer, a British film critic, has criticized the rhetorical strategies of "authenticity and authentication" that tend to characterize identity politics. He has observed, "if I preface a point by saying something like, 'as a black gay man, I feet marginalized by your discourse,' it makes a valid point but in such a way that preempts critical dialogue because such a response could be inferred as a criticism not of what I say but of what or who I am. The problem is replicated in the familiar cop-out clause, 'as a middle-class, white, heterosexual male, what can I say?'"[82]

The problem is that the mere assertion of identity becomes in a very real sense irrefutable. Identity is presented as not only stable and fixed, but also insurmountable. While identity politics gives the oppressed the moral authority to speak (perhaps a dubious ground from which to speak), it can, ironically, absolve those belonging to dominant groups from having to engage in a critical dialogue. In some sense, then, identity politics can unintentionally reinforce Otherness. Finally, as the antifeminist backlash and the emergence of the New Right should demonstrate, there is nothing inherently progressive about identity. It can be, and has been, mobilized for reactionary as well as for radical purposes.[83] For example, the participation of so many women in the anti-abortion movement reveals just how problematic the reduction of politics to identity can be.

Accounts of sixties radicalism usually cite its role in bringing about the dismantling of Jim Crow and disfranchisement, the withdrawal of U.S. troops from Vietnam, and greater gender equality. However, equally important, if less frequently noted, was its challenge to politics as usual. Sixties radicals succeeded both in reformulating politics, even mainstream politics, to include personal life, and in challenging the notion that elites alone have the wisdom and expertise to control the political process. For a moment, people who by virtue of their color, age, and gender were far from the sites of formal power became politically engaged, became agents of change.

Given the internal contradictions and shortcomings of sixties radicalism, the repressiveness of the federal government in the late 1960s and early 1970s, and changing economic conditions in the United States, it is not surprising that the movements built by radicals in the sixties either no longer exist or do so only in attenuated form. Activists in the women's liberation movement, however, helped bring about a fundamental realignment of gender roles in this country through outrageous protests, tough-minded polemics, and an "ecstasy of discussion." Indeed, those of us who came of age in the days before the resurgence of feminism know that the world today, while hardly a feminist utopia, is nonetheless a far different, and in many respects a far fairer, world than what we confronted in 1967.

Notes

1. See Carol Hanisch, "A Critique of the Miss America Protest," in *Notes from the Second Year: Women's Liberation,* ed. Shulamith Firestone and Anne Koedt (New York: Radical Feminism, 1970), 87; and Judith Duffet, "Atlantic City Is a Town with Class—They Raise Your Morals While They Judge Your Ass," *Voice of the Women's Liberation Movement* 1, no. 3 (October 1968). The protesters also criticized the pageant's narrow formulation of beauty, especially its racist equation of beauty with whiteness. They emphasized that in its forty-seven-year history, the pageant had never crowned a black woman Miss America. That weekend the first Black Miss America Pageant was held in Atlantic City.

2. See Lindsy Van Gelder, "Bra Burners Plan Protest," *New York Post,* 4 September 1968, which appeared three days before the protest. The *New York Times* article by Charlotte Curtis quoted Robin Morgan as having said about the mayor of Atlantic City, "He was worried about our burning things. He said the boardwalk had already been burned out once this year. We told him we wouldn't do anything dangerous—just a symbolic bra-burning." Curtis, "Miss America Pageant Is Picketed by 100 Women," *New York Times,* 8 September 1968.

3. See Jack Gould's column in the *New York Times,* 9 September 1968.

4. The Yippies were a small group of leftists who, in contrast to most of the Left, had enthusiastically embraced the growing counterculture. For a fascinating account of the 1968 convention, see David Farber, *Chicago '68* (Chicago: University of Chicago Press, 1988).

5. Curtis, "Miss America Pageant."

6. For the sake of convenience, I will use the term *Movement* to describe the overlapping protest movements of the sixties—the black freedom movement, the student movement, the antiwar movement, and the more self-consciously political New Left. I will refer to the women's liberation movement as the *movement*; here I use the lower case simply to avoid confusion.

7. Snitow, interview by author, New York, 14 June 1984. Here one can get a sense of the disjuncture in experiences between white and black women; presumably, black women had not felt the same sense of distance about their civil rights activism.

8. Robin Morgan, *Going Too Far: The Personal Chronicle of a Feminist* (New York: Random House, 1978), 62.

9. Yet virtually all the recently published books on the sixties either slight or ignore the protest. This omission is emblematic of a larger problem, the failure of authors to integrate women's liberation into their reconstruction of that period. Indeed, most of these books have replicated the position of women in the larger, male-dominated protest Movement—that is, the women's liberation movement is relegated to the margins of the narrative. Such marginalization has been exacerbated as well by the many feminist recollections of the sixties that demonize the Movement and present women's liberation as its antithesis. Sixties books that textually subordinate the women's liberation movement include James Miller, *Democracy Is in the Streets: From Port Huron to the Siege of Chicago* (New York: Simon and Schuster, 1987); Tom Hayden, *Reunion: A Memoir* (New York: Random House, 1988); Todd Gitlin, *The Sixties: Years of Hope, Days of Rage*

(New York: Bantam, 1987); and Nancy Zaroulis and Gerald Sullivan, *Who Spoke Up? American Protest against the War in Vietnam* (Garden City, NY: Doubleday, 1984). A notable exception is Stewart Burns, *Social Movements of the 1960's: Searching for Democracy* (Boston: Twayne, 1990).

10. Sara Evans, *Personal Politics: The Roots of Women's Liberation in the Civil Rights Movement and the New Left* (New York: Vintage Books, 1979).

11. Sara Evans has argued that in their attempt to combine work inside and outside the family, educated, middle-class, married white women of the 1950s were following the path pioneered by black women. See Evans, *Born for Liberty: A History of Women in America* (New York: Free Press, 1989), 253–54. As Jacqueline Jones and others have demonstrated, black women have a "long history of combining paid labor with domestic obligations." According to Jones, in 1950 one-third of all married black women were in the labor force, compared to one-quarter of all married women in the general population. One study cited by Jones "concluded that black mothers of school-aged children were more likely to work than their white counterparts, though part-time positions in the declining field of domestic service inhibited growth in their rates of labor force participation." Jones, *Labor of Love, Labor of Sorrow: Black Women, Work, and the Family, from Slavery to the Present* (New York. Vintage Books, 1986), 269.

12. Alice Kessler-Harris, *Out to Work: A History of Wage-Earning Women in the United States* (New York: Oxford University Press, 1982), 302.

13. Evans, *Born for Liberty*, 252.

14. Jane De Hart-Mathews, "The New Feminism and the Dynamics of Social Change," in *Women's America: Refocusing the Past*, 2d ed., ed. Linda Kerber and Jane De Hart-Mathews (New York: Oxford University Press, 1987), 445.

15. I think that this was an experience specific to white women. The problem of diffidence seems to have been, if not unique to white women, then especially acute for them. This is not to say that issues of gender were unimportant to black women activists in the sixties, but that gender seemed less primary and pressing an issue than race. However, much more research is needed in this area. It could be that the black women's noninvolvement in women's liberation had as much, if not more, to do with the movement's racism than any prioritizing of race.

16. Carl Oglesby, "Trapped in a System," reprinted as "Liberalism and the Corporate State," in *The New Radicals: A Report with Documents*, ed. Paul Jacobs and Saul Landau (New York: Vintage Books, 1966), 266. For a useful discussion of the New Left's relationship to liberalism, see Gitlin, *The Sixties*, 127–92.

17. See Howard Brick, "Inventing Post-Industrial Society: Liberal and Radical Social Theory in the 1960's" (paper delivered at the 1900 American Studies Association Conference). In September 1963 the electoral politics faction of SDS had even succeeded in getting the group to adopt the slogan "Part of the Way with LBJ." Johnson's official campaign slogan was "All the Way with LBJ." See Gitlin, *The Sixties*, 180.

18. Gregory Calvert, interview, *Movement* 3, no. 2 (1967): 6.

19. Andrew Kopkind, "Looking Backward: The Sixties and the Movement," *Ramparts* 11, no. 8 (February 1973): 32.

20. That evening seven million people watched Johnson's speech to Congress announcing voting rights legislation. According to C. T. Vivian, "a tear ran down" Martin Luther King's cheek as Johnson finished his speech. Juan Williams, *Eyes on the Prize: America's Civil Rights Years, 1954–65* (New York: Penguin, 1988), 278.

21. Elinor Langer discusses the ways Marcuse's notion of repressive tolerance was used by the Movement. See her wonderful essay, "Notes for Next Time," *Working Papers for a New Society* 1, no. 3 (fall 1973): 48–83.

22. Ellen Kay Trimberger, "Women in the Old and New Left: The Evolution of a Politics of Personal Life," *Feminist Studies* 5, no. 3 (fall 1979): 442.

23. Potter quoted from Miller, *Democracy Is in the Streets*, 196.

24. Miller quoted from Gitlin, *The Sixties*, 9. Although the broad outlines of Miller's argument are correct, some recent scholarship on 1930s radicalism suggests that it was considerably more varied and less narrowly economistic than has been previously acknowledged. For example, recent books by Paula Rabinowitz and Robin Kelley demonstrate that some radicals in this period understood the salience of such categories as gender and race. See Paula Rabinowitz, *Labor and Desire: Women's Revolutionary Fiction in Depression America* (Chapel Hill: University of North Carolina Press, 1991); Robin Kelley, *Hammer and Hoe: Alabama Communists during the Great Depression* (Chapel Hill: University of North Carolina Press, 1990).

25. Shulamith Firestone, *The Dialectic of Sex: The Case for Feminist Revolution*, rev. ed. (New York: Bantam Books, 1971), 10–11.

26. Robin Morgan, in *Sisterhood Is Powerful*, ed. Morgan (New York: Vintage Books, 1970), xxii.

27. Firestone, *The Dialectic of Sex,* 33. For a very useful history of women's rights activism (as opposed to women's liberation in the postwar years, see Cynthia Harrison, *On Account of Sex: The Politics of Women's Issues,* 1945–68 (Berkeley: University of California Press, 1988).

28. Ti-Grace Atkinson, *Amazon Odyssey* (New York: Link Books, 1974), 10. In contrast to other founders of early radical feminist groups, Atkinson came to radicalism through her involvement in the New York City chapter of NOW, admittedly the most radical of all NOW chapters. Atkinson made this remark in October 1968 after having failed badly in her attempt to radically democratize the New York chapter of NOW. Upon losing the vote she immediately resigned her position as the chapter's president and went on to establish The Feminists, a radical feminist group.

29. Firestone, *The Dialectic of Sex,* 12.

30. Betty Friedan, *It Changed My Life: Writings on the Women's Movement* (New York: Random House, 1976), 153. Friedan was antagonistic to radical feminism from the beginning and rarely missed an opportunity to denounce the man-hating and sex warfare that she claimed it advocated. Her declamations against "sexual politics' began at least as early as January 1969.

31. Due to limitations of space and the focus of this chapter, I do not discuss the many differences among women's liberationists, most crucially, the conflicts between "radical feminists" and "politicos" over the relationship between the women's liberation movement and the larger Movement and the role of capitalism in maintaining women's oppression. This is taken up at length in Alice Echols, *Daring to Be Bad: Radical Feminism in America, 1967–75* (Minneapolis: University of Minnesota Press, 1989).

32. Firestone, *The Dialectic of Sex,* 1. It is the opening line of her book.

33. Adrienne Rich quoted from Hester Eisenstein, *Contemporary Feminist Thought* (Boston: G. K. Hall, 1983), 5.

34. Ellen Willis, "Sequel: Letter to a Critic," in *Notes from the Second Year,* ed. Firestone and Koedt, 57.

35. See Ann Snitow, "Gender Diary," *Dissent,* spring 1989, 205–24; Carole Vance, "Social Construction Theory: Problems in the History of Sexuality," in *Homosexuality, Which Homosexuality?* ed. Anja van Kooten Niekark and Theo van der Maer (Amsterdam: An Dekken/Schorer, 1989).

36. Ellen Willis discusses the centrality of abortion to the women's liberation movement in the foreword to *Daring to Be Bad.* For the young, mostly white middle-class women who were attracted to women's liberation, the issue was forced reproduction. But for women of color, the issue was as often forced sterilization, and women's liberationists would tackle that issue as well.

37. Stanley Aronowitz, "When the New Left Was New," in *The Sixties without Apology,* ed. Sohnya Sayres, Anders Stephanson, Stanley Aronowitz, and Fredric Jameson (Minneapolis: University of Minnesota Press, 1984), 32.

38. C. Wright Mills quoted from Miller, *Democracy Is in the Streets,* 86.

39. The phrase is from SDSs founding statement, "The Port Huron Statement," which is reprinted in full as an appendix to Miller's book, *Democracy Is in the Streets,* 333. For instance, Irving Howe, an influential member of the Old Left who attended a couple of SDS meetings, called them "interminable and structureless sessions." Howe, "The Decade That Failed," *New York Times Magazine,* 19 September 1982, 78.

40. The statement appeared in a pamphlet produced by the Economic Research and Action Project of SDS. Miller quotes it in *Democracy Is in the Streets,* 215.

41. Gregory Calvert, "Participatory Democracy, Collective Leadership, and Political Responsibility," *New Left Notes,* 2, no. 45 (18 December 1967): 1.

42. See Breines's summary of prefigurative politics in *Community and Organization in the New Left, 1962–68* (New York: Praeger, 1982), 1–8.

43. Staughton Lynd, "The Movement: A New Beginning: *Liberation* 14, no. 2 (May 1969).

44. Pat Hansen and Ken McEldowney, "A Statement of Values," *New Left Notes,* 1, no. 42 (November 1966): 5.

45. Tom Hayden, "Democracy Is . . . in the Streets," *Rat* 1, no. 15 (23 August–5 September 1968): 5.

46. The Atlanta Project's position paper has been reprinted as "SNCC Speaks for Itself," in *The Sixties Papers: Documents of a Rebellious Decade,* ed. Judith Clavir Albert and Stewart Albert (New York: Praeger, 1984), 122. However, the title assigned it by the Alberts is misleading because at the time it was written in the spring of 1966, it did not reflect majority opinion in SNCC.

47. Rosalind Petchesky, *Abortion and Woman's Choice: The State, Sexuality, and Reproductive Freedom* (New York: Longman Press, 1984), 128.

48. Michelle Kort, "Sisterhood Is Profitable," *Mother Jones,* July 1983, 44.

49. Amiri Imanu Baraka, "A Black Value System," *Black Scholar,* November 1969.

50. Jennifer Woodul, "What's This about Feminist Businesses?" *off our backs* 6, no. 4 (June 1976): 24–26.

51. Robin Morgan, "Rights of Passage," *Ms.,* September 1975, 99.

52. For a fascinating case study of this as it relates to women's music, see Arlene Stein, "Androgyny Goes Pop," *Out/Look* 3, no. 3 (spring 1991): 26–33.

53. Kort, "Sisterhood Is Profitable," 44.

54. Stein, "Androgyny Goes Pop," 30.

55. Adrienne Rich, "Living the Revolution," *Women's Review of Books* 3, no. 12 (September 1986): 1, 3–4.

56. Quoted from Jane Mansbridge, *Why We Lost the ERA* (Chicago: University of Chicago Press, 1986), 266.

57. "Women's Liberation Testimony," *off our backs* 1, no. 5 (May 1970): 7.

58. Firestone, *The Dialectic of Sex,* 206.

59. Steve Halliwell, "Personal Liberation and Social Change," *New Left Notes,* 2, no. 30 (4 September 1967): 1; see also Rennie Davis and Staughton Lynd, "On NCNP," *New Left Notes* 2., no. 30. (4 September 1967): 1.

60. See Charlotte Bunch, "The Reform Tool Kit," *Quest* 1, no. 1 (summer 1974).

61. Frances Chapman, interview by author, New York, 30 May 1984. Here Chapman was speaking of the radical feminist wing of the women's liberation movement, but it applies as well to women's liberation activists.

62. For more on the prefigurative, personal politics of the sixties, see Breines, *Community and Organization in the New Left;* Miller, *Democracy Is in the Streets*; and Aronowitz, "When the New Left Was New."

63. Quoted from Miller, *Democracy Is in the Streets,* 374.

64. Although individual social critics such as C. Wright Mills influenced the thinking of new leftists, the noncommunist Left of the 1950s and early 1960s remained economistic and anticommunist. Indeed, the fact that the board of the League for Industrial Democracy—the parent organization of SDS in SDSs early years—ignored the values section of the Port Huron Statement suggests the disjuncture between old and new leftists. For another view stressing the continuities between the Old and the New Left, see Maurice Isserman, *If I Had a Hammer . . . The Death of the Old Left and the Birth of the New Left* (New York: Basic Books, 1987).

65. See Judith Newton, "Historicisms New and Old: 'Charles Dickens' Meets Marxism, Feminism, and West Coast Foucault," *Feminist Studies* 16, no. 3 (fall 1990): 464. In their assumption that power has a source and that it emanates from patriarchy, women's liberationists part company with

66. Carmichael quoted from Clayborne Carson, *In Struggle: SNCC and the Black Awakening of the 1960's* (Cambridge: Harvard University Press, 1981), 282.

67. Firestone and Koedt, "Editorial," in *Notes from the Second Year,* ed. Firestone and Koedt.

68. However, the reclamation of blackness was often articulated in a sexist fashion, as in Stokely Carmichael's 1968 declaration, "Every Negro is a potential black man." See Carmichael, "A Declaration of War," in *The New Left: A Documentary History,* ed. Teodori Massimo (Indianapolis: Bobbs-Merrill, 1969), 277.

69. Aronowitz, "When the New Left Was New," 18.

70. Richard Flacks, "Some Problems, Issues, Proposals," in *The New Radicals,* ed. Jacobs and Landau, 168. This was a working paper intended for the June 1965 convention of SDS.

71. Excerpts from Jerry Rubin's book, *Do It,* appeared in *Rat* 2, no. 26 (26 January–9 February 1970).

72. "The Feminists: A Political Organization to Annihilate Sex Roles," in *Notes from the Second Year,* ed. Firestone and Koedt, 117.

73. Ehrenreich quoted from Carol Ann Douglas, "Second Sex 30 Years Later," *off our backs* 9, no. 11 (December 1979): 26.

74. The term *identity politics* was, I think, first used by black and Chicana feminists. See Diana Fuss, *Essentially Speaking: Feminism, Nature, and Difference* (New York: Routledge, 1989), 99.

75. Jeffrey Weeks locates the origins of identity politics in the post-1968 political flux. He argues that "identity politics can be seen as part of the unfinished business of the 1960's, challenging traditionalist hierarchies of power and the old, all-encompassing social and political identities associated, for example, with class and occupation." Perhaps Weeks situates this in the post-1968 period, because class held greater significance for many British new leftists than it did for their American counterparts. Weeks, "Sexuality and (Post) Modernity" (unpublished paper).

76. Nancy Cott, *The Grounding of Modern Feminism* (New Haven: Yale University Press, 1987), 5.

77. Amy Kesselman, interview by author, New York, 2 May 1984.

78. "Me New York Consciousness Awakening Women's Liberation Group" (handout from the Lake Villa Conference, November 1968).

79. Kathie Sarachild, "Consciousness- Raising: A Radical Weapon," in *Feminist Revolution,* ed. Redstockings (New Paltz, NY. Redstockings, 1975), 132.

80. Betty Friedan, *It Changed My Life* (New York: Norton, 1985), 101.

81. Audre Lorde, *Zami: A New Spelling of My Name* (Freedom, CA: Crossing Press, 1982), 226.

82. Lorraine Kenney, "Traveling Theory: The Cultural Politics of Race and Representation: An Interview with Kobena Mercer," *Afterimage,* September 1990, 9.

83. Mercer makes this point as well in Kenney, "Traveling Theory," 9.

A New Politics of Sexuality

June Jordan

As a young worried mother, I remember turning to Dr. Benjamin Spock's *Common Sense Book of Baby and Child Care* just about as often as I'd pick up the telephone. He was God. I was ignorant but striving to be good: a good Mother. And so it was there, in that best-seller pocketbook of do's and don't's, that I came upon this doozie of a guideline: Do not wear miniskirts or other provocative clothing because that will upset your child, especially if your child happens to be a boy. If you give your offspring "cause" to think of you as a sexual being, he will, at the least, become disturbed; you will derail the equilibrium of his notions about your possible identity and meaning in the world.

It had never occurred to me that anyone, especially my son, might look upon me as an asexual being. I had never supposed that "asexual" was some kind of positive designation I should, so to speak, lust after. I was pretty surprised by Dr. Spock. However, I was also, by habit, a creature of obedience. For a couple of weeks I actually experimented with lusterless colors and dowdy tops and bottoms, self-consciously hoping thereby to prove myself as a lusterless and dowdy and, therefore, excellent female parent.

Years would have to pass before I could recognize the familiar, by then, absurdity of a man setting himself up as the expert on a subject that presupposed women as the primary objects for his patriarchal discourse on motherhood, no less! Years passed before I came to perceive the perversity of dominant power assumed by men, and the perversity of self-determining power ceded to men by women.

A lot of years went by before I understood the dynamics of what anyone could summarize as the Politics of Sexuality.

I believe the Politics of Sexuality is the most ancient and probably the most profound arena for human conflict. Increas-

---

From *Technical Difficulties* by June Jordan. Copyright © 1992 by June Jordan. Reprinted by permission.

ingly, it seems clear to me that deeper and more pervasive than any other oppression, than any other bitterly contested human domain, is the oppression of sexuality, the exploitation of the human domain of sexuality for power.

When I say sexuality, I mean gender: I mean male subjugation of human beings because they are female. When I say sexuality, I mean heterosexual institutionalization of rights and privileges denied to homosexual men and women. When I say sexuality I mean gay or lesbian contempt for bisexual modes of human relationship.

The Politics of Sexuality therefore subsumes all of the different ways in which some of us seek to dictate to others of us what we should do, what we should desire, what we should dream about, and how we should behave ourselves, generally. From China to Iran, from Nigeria to Czechoslovakia, from Chile to California, the politics of sexuality—enforced by traditions of state-sanctioned violence plus religion and the law—reduces to male domination of women, heterosexist tyranny, and, among those of us who are in any case deemed despicable or deviant by the powerful, we find intolerance for those who choose a different, a more complicated—for example, an interracial or bisexual—mode of rebellion and freedom.

We must move out from the shadows of our collective subjugation—as people of color/as women/as gay/as lesbian/as bisexual human beings.

I can voice my ideas without hesitation or fear because I am speaking, finally, about myself. I am Black and I am female and I am a mother and I am bisexual and I am a nationalist and I am an antinationalist. And I mean to be fully and freely all that I am!

Conversely, I do not accept that any white or Black or Chinese man—I do not accept that, for instance, Dr. Spock—should presume to tell me, or any other woman, how to mother a child. He has no right. He is not a mother. My child is not his child. And, likewise, I do not accept that anyone—any woman or any man who is not inextricably part of the subject he or she dares to address—should attempt to tell any of us, the objects of her or his presumptuous discourse, what we should do or what we should not do.

Recently, I have come upon gratuitous and appalling pseudoliberal pronouncements on sexuality. Too often, these utterances fall out of the mouths of men and women who first disclaim any sentiment remotely related to homophobia, but who then proceed to issue outrageous opinions like the following:

✦ That it is blasphemous to compare the oppression of gay, lesbian, or bisexual people to the oppression, say, of black people, or of the Palestinians.

✦ That the bottom line about gay or lesbian or bisexual identity is that you can conceal it whenever necessary and, so, therefore, why don't you do just that? Why don't you keep your deviant sexuality in the closet and let the rest of us—we who suffer oppression for reasons of our ineradicable and always visible components of our personhood such as race or gender—get on with our more necessary, our more beleaguered struggle to survive?

Well, number one: I believe I have worked as hard as I could, and then harder than that, on behalf of equality and justice—for African-Americans, for the Palestinian people, and for people of color everywhere.

And no, I do not believe it is blasphemous to compare oppressions of sexuality to oppressions of race and ethnicity: Freedom is indivisible or it is nothing at all besides sloganeering and temporary, short-sighted, and short-lived advancement for a few. Freedom is indivisible, and either we are working for freedom or you are working for the sake of your self-interests and I am working for mine.

If you can finally go to the bathroom wherever you find one, if you can finally order a cup of coffee and drink it wherever coffee is available, but you cannot follow your heart—you cannot respect the response of your own honest body in the world—then how much of what kind of freedom does any one of us possess?

Or, conversely, if your heart and your honest body can be controlled by the state, or controlled by community taboo, are you not then, and in that case, no more than a slave ruled by outside force?

What tyranny could exceed a tyranny that dictates to the human heart, and that attempts to dictate the public career of an honest human body?

Freedom is indivisible; the Politics of Sexuality is not some optional "special-interest" concern for serious, progressive folk.

And, on another level, let me assure you: if every single gay or lesbian or bisexual man or woman active on the Left of American politics decided to stay home, there would be *no* Left left.

One of the things I want to propose is that we act on that reality: that we insistently demand reciprocal respect and concern from those who cheerfully depend upon our brains and our energies for their, and our, effective impact on the political landscape.

Last spring, at Berkeley, some students asked me to speak at a rally against racism. And I did. There were four or five hundred people massed on Sproul Plaza, standing together against that evil. And, on the next day, on that same plaza, there was a rally for bisexual and gay and lesbian rights, and students asked me to speak at that rally. And

I did. There were fewer than seventy-five people stranded, pitiful, on that public space. And I said then what I say today: That was disgraceful! There should have been just one rally. One rally: freedom is indivisible.

As for the second, nefarious pronouncement on sexuality that now enjoys mass-media currency: the idiot notion of keeping yourself in the closet—that is very much the same thing as the suggestion that black folks and Asian-Americans and Mexican-Americans should assimilate and become as "white" as possible—in our walk/talk/music/food/values—or else. Or else? Or else we should, deservedly, perish.

Sure enough, we have plenty of exposure to white everything so why would we opt to remain our African/Asian/Mexican selves? The answer is that suicide is absolute, and if you think you will survive by hiding who you really are, you are sadly misled: there is no such thing as partial or intermittent suicide. You can only survive if you—who you really are—do survive.

Likewise, we who are not men and we who are not heterosexist—we, sure enough, have plenty of exposure to male-dominated/heterosexist this and that.

But a struggle to survive cannot lead to suicide: suicide is the opposite of survival. And so we must not conceal/assimilate/integrate into the would-be dominant culture and political system that despises us. Our survival requires that we alter our environment so that we can live and so that we can hold each other's hands and so that we can kiss each other on the streets, and in the daylight of our existence, without terror and without violent and sometimes fatal reactions from the busybodies of America.

Finally, I need to speak on bisexuality. I do believe that the analogy is interracial or multiracial identity. I do believe that the analogy for bisexuality is a multicultural, multi-ethnic, multiracial world view. Bi-sexuality follows from such a perspective and leads to it, as well.

Just as there are many men and women in the United States whose parents have given them more than one racial, more than one ethnic identity and cultural heritage to honor; and just as these men and women must deny no given part of themselves except at the risk of self-deception and the insanities that must issue from that; and just as these men and women embody the principle of equality among races and ethnic communities; and just as these men and women falter and anguish and choose and then falter again and then anguish and then choose yet again how they will honor the irreducible complexity of their God-given human being—even so, there are many men and women, especially young men and women, who seek to embrace the complexity of their total, always-changing social and political circumstance.

They seek to embrace our increasing global complexity on the basis of the heart and on the basis of an honest human body. Not according to ideology. Not according to group pressure. Not according to anybody's concept of "correct."

This is a New Politics of Sexuality. And even as I despair of identity politics—because identity is given and principles of justice/equality/freedom cut across given gender and given racial definitions of being, and because I will call you my brother, I will call you my sister, on the basis of what you *do* for justice, what you *do* for equality, what you *do* for freedom and *not* on the basis of who you are, even so I look with admiration and respect upon the new, bisexual politics of sexuality.

This emerging movement politicizes the so-called middle ground: Bisexuality invalidates either/or formulation, either/or analysis. Bisexuality means I am free and I am as likely to want and to love a woman as I am likely to want and to love a man, and what about that? Isn't that what freedom implies?

If you are free, you are not predictable and you are not controllable. To my mind, that is the keenly positive, politicizing significance of bisexual affirmation:

To insist upon complexity, to insist upon the validity of all of the components of social/sexual complexity, to insist upon the equal validity of all of the components of social/sexual complexity.

This seems to me a unifying, 1990s mandate for revolutionary Americans planning to make it into the twenty-first century on the basis of the heart, on the basis of an honest human body, consecrated to every struggle for justice, every struggle for equality, every struggle for freedom.

The Meaning of Women's Empowerment: New Concepts from Action[1]

53

Srilatha Batliwala

Since the mid-1980s, the term *empowerment* has become popular in the field of development, especially in reference to women. In grassroots programs and policy debates alike, *empowerment* has virtually replaced terms such as *welfare, upliftment, community participation,* and *poverty alleviation* to describe the goal of development and intervention. In spite of the prevalence of the term, however, many people are confused as to what the empowerment of women implies in social, economic, and political terms. How empowerment strategies differ from or relate to such earlier strategies as integrated rural development, women's development, community participation, conscientization, and awareness building is even less clear.

Nonetheless, many large-scale programs are being launched with the explicit objective of "empowering" the poor and "empowering" women. Empowerment is held to be a panacea for social ills: high population growth rates, environmental degradation, and the low status of women, among others.[2]

The attention given here to women's empowerment is based on the premise that it is an enabling condition for reproductive rights (Correa and Petchesky, this volume). This chapter attempts an operational definition of women's empowerment, and delineates the components and stages of empowerment strategies, on the basis of insights gained thorough a study of grassroots programs in South Asia. Undoubtedly, the nature and priorities of the women's empowerment process in South Asian countries are shaped by the historical, political, social, and economic conditions specific to that region. Still, there are sufficient commonalities with other regions—such as an extended period of colonial rule; highly

From *Population Policies Considered: Health Empowerment and Rights* by Gita Sen, Adirenne Germain, and Lincoln C. Chen, editors. Copyright © 1994 by Harvard Center for Population and Development Studies. Reprinted by permission.

stratified, male-dominated social structures; widespread poverty and vulnerable economies; and fairly rigid gender- and class-based divisions of labor—to render the definition and analytic framework for empowerment presented in this essay more widely relevant.

The Concept of Empowerment

The concept of women's empowerment appears to be the outcome of several important critiques and debates generated by the women's movement throughout the world, and particularly by Third World feminists. Its source can be traced to the interaction between feminism and the concept of "popular education" developed in Latin America in the 1970s (Walters 1991). The latter had its roots in Freire's theory of "conscientization," which totally ignored gender, but was also influenced by Gramscian thought, which stressed the need for participatory mechanisms in institutions and society in order to create a more equitable and nonexploitative system (Forgacs 1988; Freire 1973).

Gender subordination and the social construction of gender were a priori in feminist analysis and popular education. Feminist popular educators therefore evolved their own distinct approach, pushing beyond merely building awareness and toward organizing the poor to struggle actively for change. They defined their goals in the following terms:

. . . To unambiguously take the standpoint of women; [and] . . . demonstrate to women and men how gender is constructed socially, . . . and . . . can be changed . . . [to show] through the lived experience of the participants, how women and men are gendered through class, race, religion, culture, etc.; . . . to investigate collectively . . . how class, [caste], race and gender intersect . . . in order to deepen collec-

tive understanding about these relationships . . .

. . . To build collective and alternative visions for gender relations . . . and . . . deepen collective analysis of the context and the position of women . . . locally, nationally, regionally and globally, . . . To develop analytical tools . . . to evaluate the effects of certain development strategies for the promotion of women's strategic interests . . . [and develop strategies] to bring about change in their personal and organizational lives . . .

. . . To help women develop the skills to assert themselves . . . and to challenge oppressive behavior . . . to build a network of women and men nationally, [and internationally] . . . [and] . . . to help build democratic community and worker organizations and a strong civil society which can pressurize for change (Walters 1991).

Meanwhile, in the 1980s feminist critiques emerged of those development strategies and grassroots interventions that had failed to make significant progress toward improving the status of women. They attributed the failure mainly to the use of welfare, poverty alleviation, and managerial approaches, for example, that did not address the underlying structural factors that perpetuate the oppression and exploitation of poor women (Moser 1989). These approaches had made no distinction between the "condition" and the "position" of women (Young 1988). Young defined *condition* as the material state in which poor women live—low wages, poor nutrition, and lack of access to health care, education, and training. *Position* is the social and economic status of women as compared with that of men. Young argues that focusing on improving the daily conditions of women's existence curtailed women's awareness of, and readiness to act against, the less visible but powerful underlying structures of subordination and inequality.

Molyneux (1985) made a similar distinction between women's "practical" and "strategic" interests. While women's practical needs—food, health, water, fuel, child care, education, improved technology, and so forth—must be met, they cannot be an end in themselves. Organizing and mobilizing women to fulfill their long-term strategic interests is essential. This requires

> . . . analysis of women's subordination and . . . the formulation of an alternative, more satisfactory set of arrangements to those which exist . . . such as the abolition of the sexual division of labor, the alleviation of the burden of domestic labor and child care, the removal of institutionalized forms of discrimination, the establishment of political equality, freedom of choice over childbearing and . . . measures against male violence and control over women (Molyneux 1985).

It is from these roots that the notion of empowerment grew, and it came to be most clearly articulated in 1985 by DAWN[3] as the "empowerment approach" (Sen and Grown 1985). Empowerment, in this view, required transformation of structures of subordination through radical changes in law, property rights, and other institutions that reinforce and perpetuate male domination.

By the beginning of the 1990s, women's empowerment had come to replace most earlier terms in development jargon. Unfortunately, as it has become a buzzword, the sharpness of the perspective that gave rise to it has been diluted. Consequently, its implications for macro- and micro-level strategies need clarification. The key question is: How do different approaches to women's "condition," or practical needs, affect the possibility or nature of changes in women's "position," or strategic interests?

This question is most pertinent to the whole issue of women's reproductive rights. Many of the existing approaches to contraception and women's reproductive health, for example, focus entirely on improved technologies and delivery systems for birth control, safe delivery, prenatal and postnatal care, and termination of fertility. But none of these addresses the more fundamental questions of discrimination against girls and women in access to food and health care; male dominance in sexual relations; women's lack of control over their sexuality; the gender division of labor that renders women little more than beasts of burden in many cultures; or the denial by many societies of women's right to determine the number of children they want. These issues are all linked to women's "position," and are not necessarily affected by reduced birthrates or improvements in women's physical health. This is one of the dichotomies that an empowerment process must seek to address.

What Is Empowerment?

The most conspicuous feature of the term *empowerment* is that is contains the word *power*, which, to sidestep philosophical debate, may be broadly defined as control over material assets, intellectual resources, and ideology. The material assets over which control can be exercised may be physical, human, or financial, such as land, water, forests, people's bodies and labor, money, and access to money. Intellectual resources include knowledge, information, and ideas. Control over ideology signifies the ability to generate, propagate, sustain, and institutionalize specific sets of beliefs, values, attitudes, and behaviors—virtually determining how people perceive and function within given socioeconomic and political environments.[4]

Power thus accrues to those who control or are able to influence the distribution of material resources, knowledge, and the ideology that governs social relations in both public and private life. The extent of power held by particular individuals or groups corresponds to the number of kinds of resources they can control, and the extent to which they can shape prevailing ideologies, whether social, religious, or political. This control, in turn, confers the power of decision making.

In South Asia, women in general, and poor women in particular, are relatively powerless, with little or no control over resources and little decision-making power. Often, even the limited resources at their disposal—such as a little land, a nearby forest, and their own bodies, labor, and skills—are not within their control, and the decisions made by others affect their lives every day.

This does not mean that women are, or have always been, totally powerless; for centuries they have tried to exercise their power within the family (Nelson 1974; Stacey and Price 1981). They also have taken control of the resources to which society has allowed them access, and even *seized* control of resources when they could—the Chipko movement in northern India and the Green Belt movement in Kenya, for example (Misra 1978; Rodda 1991). They have always attempted, from their traditional position as workers, mothers, and wives, not only to influence their immediate environment, but also to expand their space. However, the prevailing patriarchal ideology, which promotes the values of submission, sacrifice, obedience, and silent suffering, often undermines even these attempts by women to assert themselves or demand some share of resources (Hawkesworth 1990; Schuler and Kadirgamar-Rajasingham 1992).

The process of challenging existing power relations, and of gaining greater control over the sources of power, may be termed *empowerment*. This broad definition is refined by feminist scholars and activists within the context of their own regions. For instance:

> The term empowerment refers to a range of activities from individual self-assertion to collective resistance, protest and mobilization that challenge basic power relations. For individuals and groups where class, caste, ethnicity and gender determine their access to resources and power, their empowerment begins when they not only recognize the systemic forces that oppress them, but act to change existing power relationships. Empowerment, therefore, is a process aimed at changing the nature and direction of systemic forces which marginalize women and other disadvantaged sections in a given context (Sharma 1991–1992).

Empowerment is thus both a process and the result of that process. Empowerment is manifested as a redistribution of power, whether between nations, classes, castes, races, genders, or individuals. The goals of women's empowerment are to challenge patriarchal ideology (male domination and women's subordination); to transform the structures and institutions that reinforce and perpetuate gender discrimination and social inequality (the family, caste, class, religion, educational processes and institutions, the media, health practices and systems, laws and civil codes, political processes, development models, and government institutions); and to enable poor women to gain access to, and control of, both material and informational resources. The process of empowerment must thus address all relevant structures and sources of power:

> Since the causes of women's inferior status and unequal gender relations are deeply rooted in history, religion, culture, in the psychology of the self, in laws and legal systems, and in political institutions and social attitudes, if the status and material conditions of women's lives is to change at all, the solutions must penetrate just as deeply (Schuler and Kadirgamar-Rajasingham 1992).

Theories that identify any one system or structure as the source of power—for instance, the assertion that economic structures are the basis of powerlessness and inequality—imply that improvement in one dimension would result in a redistribution of power. However, activists working in situations where women are economically strong know that equal status does not necessarily result. If anything, ample evidence exists that strengthening women's economic status, though positive in many ways, does not always reduce their other burdens or eradicate other forms of oppression; in fact, it often led to intensifying pressures (Brydon and Chant 1989; Gupte and Borkar 1987; Sen and Grown 1985). Similarly, it is evident that improvements in physical status and access to basic resources, like water, fuel, fodder, health care, and education, do not automatically lead to fundamental changes in women's position. If that were so, middle-class women, with higher education, well-paid jobs, and adequate nourishment and health care, would not continue to be victims of wife beating or bride burning.

There is widespread confusion and some degree of anxiety about whether women's empowerment leads to the disempowerment of men. It is obvious that poor men are almost as powerless as poor women in terms of access to and control over resources. This is exactly why most poor men tend to support women's empowerment processes that enable women to bring much-needed resources into their families and communities, or that challenge power structures that have oppressed and exploited the poor of both genders. Resistance, however, occurs when women compete with men for power in the public sphere, or when they question the power, rights, and privileges of men within the family—in other words, when women challenge patriarchal family relations

(Batliwala 1994). This is, in fact, a test of how far the empowerment process has reached into women's lives; as one activist put it, "the family is the last frontier of change in gender relations. . . . You know [empowerment] has occurred when it crosses the threshold of the home" (Kannabiran 1993).

The process of women's empowerment must challenge patriarchal relations, and thus inevitably leads to changes in men's traditional control over women, particularly over the women of their households. Men in communities where such changes have already occurred no longer have control over women's bodies, sexuality, or mobility; they cannot abdicate responsibility for housework and child care, nor physically abuse or violate women with impunity; they cannot (as is the case in South Asia at present) abandon or divorce their wives without providing maintenance, or commit bigamy or polygamy, or make unilateral decisions that affect the whole family. Clearly, then, women's empowerment does mean the loss of the privileged position that patriarchy allotted to men.

A point often missed, however, is that women's empowerment also liberates and empowers men, both in material and in psychological terms. First, women greatly strengthen the impact of political movements dominated by men—not just by their numbers, but by providing new energy, insights, leadership, and strategies. Second, as we saw earlier, the struggles of women's groups for access to material resources and knowledge directly benefit the men and children of their families and their communities, by opening the door to new ideas and a better quality of life. But most important are the psychological gains for men when women become equal partners. Men are freed from the roles of oppressor and exploiter, and from gender stereotyping, which limits the potential for self-expression and personal development in men as much as in women. Furthermore, experiences worldwide show that men discover an emotional satisfaction in sharing responsibility and decision making; they find that they have lost not merely traditional privileges, but also traditional burdens. As one South Asian NGO spokeswoman expressed it:

> Women's empowerment should lead to the liberation of men from false value systems and ideologies of oppression. It should lead to a situation where each one can become a whole being, regardless of gender and use their fullest potential to construct a more humane society for all (Akhtar 1992).

Process of Empowerment

In order to challenge their subordination, *women must first recognize the ideology that legitimizes male domination and understand how it perpetuates their oppression.* This recognition requires reversal of the values and attitudes, indeed the entire worldview, that most women have internalized since earliest childhood. Women have been led to participate in their own oppression through a complex web of religious sanctions, social and cultural taboos and superstitions, hierarchies among women in the family (see Adams and Castle in this volume), behavioral training, seclusion, veiling, curtailment of physical mobility, discrimination in food and other family resources, and control of their sexuality (including concepts like the "good" and "bad" woman). Most poor women have never been allowed to think for themselves or to make their own choices except in unusual circumstances, when a male decision maker has been absent or has abdicated his role. Because questioning is not allowed, the majority of women grow up believing that this is the just and "natural" order.

Hence, the demand for change does not usually begin spontaneously from the condition of subjugation. Rather, empowerment must be externally induced, by forces working with an altered consciousness and an awareness that the existing social order is *unjust* and *unnatural.* They seek to change other women's consciousness: altering their self-image and their beliefs about their rights and capabilities; creating awareness of how gender discrimination, like other socioeconomic and political factors, is one of the forces acting on them; challenging the sense of inferiority that has been imprinted on them since birth; and recognizing the true value of their labor and contributions to the family, society, and economy. Women must be convinced of their innate right to equality, dignity, and justice.

The external agents of change necessary for empowerment may take many forms. The anti arrack[3] agitation of 1992–1993 in Nellore District of Andhra Pradesh State in southern India, for instance, in which thousands of women participated, was triggered by a lesson in an adult literacy primer depicting the plight of a landless woman whose husband drank away his meager wages at the local liquor shop. The agitation has created a major political and economic crisis for the state government, which earns huge revenues through licensing of liquor outlets and excise duties on liquor (see Box 1; also, Anveshi 1993; Joseph 1993).

A key role of the external activist lies in giving women access to a new body of ideas and information that not only changes their consciousness and self-image, but also encourages action. This means a dynamic educational process. Historically, the poor in much of South Asia, and specially poor women, were beyond the pale of formal education, and so developed learning systems of their own. Valuable oral and practical traditions evolved to transfer empirical

Women's Mobilizing: Anti-Liquor Agitation by Indian Women

"Even a cow must be fed if you want milk. Otherwise it will kick you. We have kicked! We will do anything to stop saara [country liquor] sales here" (Villager, Totla Cheruvupalli, Andhra Pradesh).

The anti-liquor movement that began in the southern Indian state of Andhra Pradesh in 1992 is unusual among popular uprisings. Initiated and led entirely by poor rural women in a few villages of one district (Nellore), the movement spread rapidly throughout the state. It has no centralized leadership or base in any political party, but is led entirely by groups of women in each village. It has no unified strategy; rather, women use whatever tactics they find most appropriate. The movement has been enormously successful, even overcoming the state government's interest in revenues from taxes on arrack (a crude liquor).

The movement was triggered by the Akshara Deepam (Light of Literacy) campaign, launched by the government and several volunteer organizations in Nellore District. The campaign not only brought women literacy programs, but also raised their consciousness about their status and potential to act. One of the chapters in the literacy primer described the plight of a poor woman whose husband drank away his wages at the local liquor shop. Ignited by this story, which mirrored their own reality all too well, the women readers asked: How is it that liquor supplies arrive in a village at least twice a day, but there are always shortages of food in the government-controlled ration shops, kerosene for lighting, drinking water, medicines at the health center, learning materials for schoolchildren, and myriad other basic essentials?

A decade earlier, the party in power in the state launched the Varuna Vahini (Liquor Flood) policy, through which the state's liquor excise revenues increased from 1.5 billion rupees in 1981–82 to 6.4 billion rupees in 1991–1992. The state government's development outlay for 1991–1992 was 17 billion rupees. Many local employers and landlords pay part of men's wages in coupons that can be used at the local liquor shop, further boosting liquor sales—and ensuring that in most poor households, men's earnings fatten the liquor lobby and state government, while their families struggle for daily food and sur-

vival. Regular harassment and physical abuse by drunken men drives some women to suicide.

The anti-liquor movement began with a few women picketing liquor shops and forcing their closure. News spread through the village grapevine and the media, and soon the whole of Nellore District, then the entire state of Andhra Pradesh, was taken up in the cause. Women used a wide variety of tactics with substantial symbolic import: In one village, for example, the women cooked the daily meal, took it wrapped in leaves to the liquor shop, and demanded that the owner eat all their offerings. "You have been taking the food from our bellies all these years, so here, eat! Eat until it kills you, the way you have been killing us!" The terrified proprietor closed shop and ran, and has not reopened since.

With less arrack being consumed, there is more money for food and other essentials, less physical and emotional abuse of women, and far less violence in general. For the most part, men have reacted surprisingly passively to the whole movement, perhaps because women directed their outrage and attacks at the liquor suppliers, rather than at their men.

The greatest victory of the movement is that no politician or party has been able to derail it, nor has the state government been able to suppress it. It cannot, after all, be characterized as antigovernment or seditious, since it is upholding one of the directive principles of the Indian constitution. However, the state is trying to repress the movement in more devious ways. Officials have floated a rumor that if liquor sales are not resumed, the price of rice will be increased. Attempts are also afoot to sabotage the literacy program that gave rise to the movement. Further, since legal sales have been effectively stopped, liquor contractors and local officials are promoting underground sales by smuggling liquor into villages in milk cans and vegetable baskets.

Though women in the anti-liquor movement have not directly challenged the state, they have managed to weaken it by attacking the nexus between the state and the liquor lobby. Poor women have mobilized and struck a blow for themselves and their families.

Source: Joseph 1993.

knowledge and livelihood skills from generation to generation: about agriculture, plant and animal life, forest lore, weaving, dying, building craft, fishing, handicrafts, folk medicine, and a myriad of other subjects. This body of traditional knowledge and skills was, however, developed within specific ideological and social frameworks. Such knowledge and practices are often suffused with taboos, superstitions, and biases against women. For example, menstruating women are prohibited from touching books, and women and men of certain castes are forbidden to touch religious books.

Through empowerment, women gain access to new worlds of knowledge and can begin to make new, informed choices in both their personal and their public lives. However, such radical changes are not sustainable if limited to a few individual women, because traditional power structures will seek to isolate and ostracize them. Society is forced to change only when large numbers of women are mobilized to press for change. The empowerment process must organize women into collectives, breaking out from individual isolation and creating a united forum through which women can challenge their subordination. With the support of the collective and the activist agent, women can re-examine their lives critically, recognize the structures and sources of power and subordination, discover their strengths, and initiate action.

The process of empowerment is thus a spiral, changing consciousness, identifying areas to target for change, planning strategies, acting for change, and analyzing action and outcomes, which leads in turn to higher levels of consciousness and more finely honed and better executed strategies. The empowerment spiral affects everyone involved: the individual, the activist agent, the collective and the community. Thus, empowerment cannot be a top-down or one-way process.

Armed with a new consciousness and growing collective strength, women begin to assert their right to control resources (including their own bodies) and to participate equally in decisions within the family, community, and village. Their priorities may often be surprising, even baffling, to the outsider. In the aftermath of the 1991 Bangladesh cyclone, one of the first demands made by women in a badly affected area was the rebuilding of the schoolhouse and the providing of schoolbooks to their children; this was in stark contrast to the demands of the local men, who talked only about houses, seeds, poultry, and loans (Akhtar 1992). In another project in southern India, one of the first issues taken up by the emerging Mahila Sangha (women's collective) of one village was the demand for a separate *smashana* (cremation ground); being scheduled castes, they said, they were not allowed to use the upper-caste area. In both cases, external activists were surprised by the women's priorities, which were quite different from those issues the activists considered most pressing.

Traditionally, women have made choices—if, indeed, they can be called choices—only within tight social constraints. For example, a woman can pay a dowry and marry off her daughter, or run the risk that the daughter will remain unmarried and be a burden to the family; a woman can bear many children, especially sons, to prove her fertility, or face rejection by her husband and in-laws. Because of the acute poverty and overwhelming work burden of poor women, most activists face a recurring dilemma: Should they respond to women's immediate problems by setting up services that will meet their practical needs and alleviate their condition? Or should they take the longer route of raising consciousness about the underlying structural factors that cause the problems, and organize women to demand resources and services from the state? Or should they enable women to organize and manage their own services with resources from the state and themselves?

A New Understanding of Power

Empowerment should also generate new notions of power. Present-day notions of power have evolved in hierarchical, male-dominated societies and are based on divisive, destructive, and oppressive values. The point is not for women to take power and use it in the same exploitative and corrupt way. Rather, women's empowerment processes must evolve a new understanding of power, and experiment with ways of democratizing and sharing power—building new mechanisms for collective responsibility, decision making, and accountability.

Similarly, once women have gained control over resources, they should not use them in the same shortsighted and ecologically destructive manner as male-dominated capitalist societies. Women's empowerment will have to lead women—and the "new men"—to address global concerns and issues, including the environment; war, violence, and militarism; ethnic, linguistic, religious, or racial fanaticism; and population.

Such radical transformations in society obviously cannot be achieved through the struggles of village or neighborhood women's collectives. Just as individual challenges can be easily crushed, so can the struggles of small, local collectives of women be negated by far more powerful and entrenched socioeconomic and political forces. In the final analysis, to transform society, women's empowerment must become a political force, that is, an organized mass movement that challenges and trans-

forms existing power structures. Empowerment should ultimately lead to the formation of mass organizations of poor women, at the regional, national, and international levels. Only then can the poor women of the world hope to bring about the fulfillment of their practical and strategic needs, and change both the "condition" and the "position" of women. They can form strategic alliances with other organizations of the poor—such as trade unions, and farmers and tenant farmers groups—and thus involve men in the change process as well. Most important, these federations must remain wholly autonomous and maintain a suprapolitical stance to prevent the cooptation and dilution of the empowerment process by pervasive patriarchal forces. This does not mean that women leaders who emerge through grassroots empowerment cannot participate in political processes like elections; on the contrary, they can, and have done so. However, they should run as candidates of existing parties, not as representatives of autonomous women's federations. This way, the latter can play a vigilant role and call to account its own members if they betray women's aspirations and needs in their performance of other roles.[6]

In a study of selected South Asian NGOs (nongovernmental organizations) engaged in women's empowerment, I was able to gather and review project reports and other published and unpublished material, discuss the empowerment question with project leaders and field workers, and visit with field organizers. Three major approaches to women's empowerment were identifiable: integrated development programs, economic development, and consciousness-raising and organizing among women. These are not mutually exclusive categories, but they help to distinguish among the differing interpretations of the causes of women's powerlessness and, hence, among the different interventions thought to lead to empowerment.

The integrated development approach ascribes women's powerlessness to their greater poverty and lower access to health care, education, and survival resources. Strategies are focused on providing services and enhancing economic status; some NGOs also emphasize awareness building. This approach improves women's condition mainly by helping them meet their survival and livelihood needs.

The economic development approach places women's economic vulnerability at the center of their powerlessness, and posits that economic empowerment has a positive impact on other aspects of women's existence. Its strategies are built around strengthening women's position as workers and income earners by mobilizing, organizing or unionizing, and providing access to support services. Though this approach undoubtedly improves women's economic position *and* condition, it is not clear that this change necessarily empowers them in other dimensions of their lives.

The consciousness-raising and organizing approach is based on a more complex understanding of gender relations and women's status. This method ascribes powerlessness to the ideology and practice of patriarchy and socioeconomic inequality in *all* the systems and structures of society. Strategies focus more on organizing women to recognize and challenge both gender- and class-based discrimination in all aspects of their lives, in both the public and the private spheres. Women are mobilized to struggle for greater access to resources, rather than passively provided with schemes and services. This approach is successful in enabling women to address their position and strategic needs, but may not be as effective in meeting immediate needs. A more detailed

analysis of the goals, strategies, and dilemmas of each of these approaches is contained in box on next page.

Lessons for a Women's Empowerment Strategy

No one magic formula or fail-safe design exists for empowerment. Nonetheless, experience clearly shows that empowerment strategies must intervene at the level of women's "condition" while also transforming their "position," thus simultaneously addressing both practical and strategic needs. Within the conceptual framework developed in the first part of this chapter, several elements appear essential. They are designed to challenge patriarchal ideology, and to enable poor women to gain greater access to and control over both material and informational resources. Although these elements are set out below in a particular sequence, they may be reversed or interchanged, or several may be undertaken concurrently, depending on the context.

An organization concerned with bringing about women's empowerment must begin by locating the geopolitical region (urban or rural) in which it wants to work, and identifying the poorest and most oppressed women in that area. Activists then have to be selected and trained. Intensive preparatory training is critical; it must impart to activists an awareness of the structures and sources of power, especially gender, and it must equip them with skills needed to mobilize, while learning from, the women whose consciousness they plan to raise. In general, female activists are preferable, since they are in a better position to initiate the empowerment process with other women, notwithstanding differences in class, caste, or educational background.

In the field, the activists encourage women to set aside a separate time and space for themselves—as disempowered women

Empowerment: Three Approaches

Three experimental approaches to empowering women have been undertaken in South Asia: integrated development, economic empowerment, and consciousness-raising. While these approaches differ from each other in concept, most organizations working on the ground take a mix of approaches. Common to all three is the importance placed on group formation to build solidarity among women.

The *integrated development* approach views women's development as key to the advancement of family and community. It therefore provides a package of interventions to alleviate poverty, meet basic survival needs, reduce gender discrimination, and help women gain self-esteem. This approach proceeds either by forming women's collectives that engage in development activities and tackle social problems such as dowry, child marriage, and male alcoholism (Proshika in Bangladesh; RDRS in Rajasthan, India), or by employing an "entry point" strategy, using a specific activity, such as a literacy class or health program, to mobilize women into groups (Gonoshastya Kendra in Bangladesh, United Mission to Nepal, Redd Barna in Nepal).

The *economic empowerment* approach attributes women's subordination to lack of economic power. It focuses on improving women's control over material resources and strengthening women's economic security. Groups are formed using two methods: organizing women around savings and credit, income generation, or skill training activities

(Grameen Bank in Bangladesh, Program of Credit for Rural Women in Nepal); or by occupation or location (SEWA in India, Proshika). These groups may work in a range of areas, including savings and credit, training and skills development, new technologies or marketing, as well as provide such ancillary supports as child care, health services, literacy programs, and legal education and aid.

The *consciousness raising* approach asserts that women's empowerment requires awareness of the complex factors causing women's subordination. This approach organizes women into collectives that tackle the sources of subordination (ASTHA, Deccan Development Society, Mahila Samakhya, WOP in India; Nijera Kori in Bangladesh). Education is central and is defined as a process of learning that leads to a new consciousness, self-worth, societal and gender analysis, and access to skills and information. In this approach, the groups themselves determine their priorities. Women's knowledge of their own bodies and ability to control reproduction are also considered vital. The long-term goal is for the women's groups to be independent of the initiating NGO. This approach uses no particular service "entry point" and attempts to be open-ended and nondirective. It gives considerable emphasis to fielding "change agents," who are trained to catalyze women's thinking without determining the directions in which a particular group may go.

---

rather than as passive recipients of welfare or beneficiaries of programs—collectively to question their situation and develop critical thinking. These forums should enable women to evolve from an aggregate of individuals into a cohesive collective, wherein they can look at themselves and their environment in new ways, develop a positive self-image, recognize their strengths, and explode sexist misconceptions. The activists also help women collectively to claim access to new information and knowledge, and to begin to develop a critical understanding of the ideology of gender, the systems and institutions through which it is

perpetuated and reinforced, and the structures of power governing their lives. This is the process that expands women's awareness beyond their "condition" to their "position."

With a growing consciousness and collective strength, women's groups prioritize the problems they would like to tackle. They begin to confront oppressive practices and situations both inside and outside the home, and gradually to alter their own attitudes and behavior; this often includes changing their treatment of their girl children and asserting their reproductive and sexual rights. In the course of both individual and collective struggles for change, women also build their skills of collective decisionmaking, action, and accountability and they may forge new strategies and methods, such as forming alliances with other groups of exploited and oppressed people, or involving sympathetic men of their own communities. With the help of training and counsel provided by the NGO or activists working with them, they also acquire real skills—vocational and managerial know-how, literacy and arithmetic competence, basic data collection techniques for conducting their own surveys—that enhance their autonomy and power.

These women's collectives then begin to seek access to resources and public services independently, demanding accountability from service providers, lobbying for changes in laws and programs that are inaccessible or inappropriate, and negotiating with public institutions such as banks and government departments. Collectively they may also set up and manage alternative services and programs, such as their own child care centers, savings banks, or schools. Finally, village- or neighborhood-level women's collectives may form associations at the local, regional, national, and global levels, through which poor women can more effectively challenge higher-level power structures and further empower themselves for the well-being of society as a whole.

Conclusion

Grassroots experiments in empowerment have made considerable headway since the mid-1980s, but it is clear—at least in South Asia—that they have a long way to go. One obvious reason is the absence of a democratic environment. An empowerment process of the kind outlined here is impossible without democratic space for dissent, struggle, and change. Theocratic, military, or other kinds of authoritarian states, based on

ideologies of dominance and gender subordination, simply will not allow radical women's empowerment movements to survive. Perhaps for this reason, many approaches to empowerment in South Asia tend to avoid overtly political activities; activists provide women with opportunities and services, and encourage a certain level of awareness, but avoid more serious challenges to the dominant ideology or power structures.

A second, more pervasive, obstacle is a fragmented understanding of the concept and process of empowerment itself, with an accompanying lack of clarity about the nature of power, patriarchy, and gender. Male domination and gender discrimination tend to be oversimplified, equated with conspicuously oppressive practices like child marriage, dowry demands, wife beating, bigamy and polygamy, and denial of women's rights to equal food, employment, education, or physical mobility. The resultant approach focuses on women's practical rather than strategic needs. The organizing and consciousness-raising approach has come somewhat closer to a holistic strategy of empowerment, but still needs to solve many methodological problems before the complexities of the social construction of gender—and the ways in which family, class, caste, religion, and other factors perpetuating women's subordination—can be changed.

Notes

1. This chapter is based on the author's study of empowerment programs in three South Asian countries, entitled "Women's Empowerment in South Asia: Concepts and Practices" (forthcoming), sponsored by the Freedom from Hunger Campaign and Asia South Pacific Bureau of Adult Education).

2. This has come through clearly in my interactions in South Asia with nongovernmental organizations (NGOs), international aid agency representatives,

academics, women's activists, government bureaucrats, and others.

3. Development Alternatives with Women for a New Era, a South-driven network of feminist scholars and women's groups, formed in 1984 in Bangalore, India.

4. The promotion of religious obscurantism in India, with its accompanying redefinition of Hinduism, is a case in point. We in the subcontinent are experiencing the revival and spread of a whole ideology, which culminated in the destruction of the Babri Mosque on December 6, 1992.

5. Arrack is a form of country liquor.

6. In India, members of a peasant and landless women's federation in southern Maharashtra, and of an urban slum women's federation (with chapters in 10 major cities) have successfully contested and won elections to municipal and local government bodies with different party platforms. The federations thereafter exercised the right to monitor their performance vis-à-vis the agenda for women's advancement, thus continually pressuring the concerned political parties to take up such issues.

References

Akhtar, F. (UBINIG, an NGO engaged in empowerment of rural women, Dhaka). 1992. Personal communication.

Anveshi. 1993. *Reworking gender relations, redefining politics: Nellore village women against arrack.* Hyderabad.

Batliwala, S. 1994 (forthcoming). *Women's empowerment in South Asia: Concepts and practices.* New Delhi: Food and Agricultural Organization/Asia South Pacific Bureau of Adult Education (FAO/ASPBAE).

Brydon, L., and S. Chant. 1989. *Women in the Third World: Gender issues in rural and urban areas.* New Brunswick, N.J.: Rutgers University Press.

Forgacs, D. (ed.). 1988. *An Antonio Gramsci reader: Selected writings, 1916–1935.* New York: Schocken Books.

Freire, P. 1973. *Pedagogy of the oppressed.* New York: Seabury Press.

Gupte, M., and A. Borkar, 1987. *Women's work, maternity and access to health care: Socioeconomic study of villages in Pune District.* Bombay: Foundation for Research in Community Health.

Hawkesworth, M. E. 1990. *Beyond oppression: Feminist theory and political strategy.* New York: Continuum.

Joseph, A. 1993. Brewing trouble. *The Hindu,* March 7.

Kannabiran, K. (a feminist activist of ASMITA, a women's resource center in Hyderabad, India). 1993. Personal communication.

Misra, A. 1978. *Chipko movement: Uttarakhand women's bid to save forest wealth.* New Delhi: People's Action.

Molyneux, M. 1985. Mobilization without emancipation? Women's interests, the state, and revolution in Nicaragua. *Feminist Studies* 11:2.

Moser, C. 1989. Gender planning in the Third World: Meeting practical and strategic needs. *World Development* 17:1799–1825.

Nelson, C. 1974. Public and private and politics: Women in the Middle Eastern world. *American Ethnologist* 1(3):551–563.

Rodda, A. 1991. *Women and the environment.* London: Zed Books.

Schuler, M., and S. Kadirgamar-Rajasingham. 1992. *Legal literacy: A tool for women's empowerment.* New York: UNIFEM.

Sen, G., and C. Grown. 1985. *Development alternatives with women for a new era: Development crises and alternative visions.* London: Earthscan.

Sharma, K. 1991–1992. Grassroots organizations and women's empowerment: Some issues in the contemporary debate. *Samya Shakti* 6:28–43.

Stacey, M., and M. Price. 1981. *Women, power, and politics.* London and New York: Tavistock Publications.

Walters, S. 1991. Her words on his lips: Gender and popular education in South Africa. *ASPBAE Courier* 52:17.

Young, K. 1988. *Gender and development: A relational approach.* Oxford: Oxford University Press.

Bringing the Global Home

54

Charlotte Bunch

One of the most exciting world developments today is the emergence of feminism all over the globe. Women of almost every culture, color, and class are claiming feminism for themselves. Indigenous movements are developing that address the specific regional concerns of women's lives and that expand the definition of what feminism means and can do in the future.

This growth of feminism provides both the challenge and the opportunity for a truly global women's movement to emerge in the 1980s. But a global movement involves more than just the separate development of feminism in each region, as exciting and important as that is. Global feminism also requires that we learn from each other and develop a global perspective within each of our movements. It means expansion of our understandings of feminism and changes in our work, as we respond to the ideas and challenges of women with different perspectives. It means discovering what other perspectives and movements mean to our own local setting. Any struggle for change in the late-twentieth century must have a global consciousness since the world operates and controls our lives internationally already. The strength of feminism has been and still is in its decentralized grass-roots nature, but for that strength to be most effective, we must base our local and national actions on a world view that incorporates the global context of our lives. This is the challenge of bringing the global home.

A global feminist perspective on patriarchy worldwide also illustrates how issues are interconnected, not separate isolated phenomena competing for our attention. This involves connections among each aspect of women's oppression and of that subordination to the socioeconomic conditions of society, as well as between local problems and global realities.

To develop global feminism today is not a luxury—it requires going to the heart of the problems in our world and looking at nothing less than the threats to the very survival of the planet. We are standing on a precipice facing such possibilities as nuclear destruction, worldwide famine and depletion of our natural resources, industrial contamination, and death in many forms. These are the fruits of a world ruled by the patriarchal mode—of what I call the "dynamic of domination," in which profits and property have priority over people, and where fear and hatred of differences have prevented a celebration of and learning from our diversity.

Feminists are part of a world struggle that is taking place today over the direction that the future will take. Crucial choices are being made about the very possibilities for life in the twenty-first century—from macro-level decisions about control over resources and weapons to micro-level decisions about control over individual reproduction and sexuality. At this juncture in history, feminism is perhaps the most important force for change that can begin to reverse the dynamic of patriarchal domination by challenging and transforming the way in which humans look at ourselves in relation to each other and to the world.

Leadership Versus Control over Women

Global feminism is emerging as part of a process in which women everywhere are demonstrating a growing determination to be actors who participate in shaping society rather than to remain victims. Yet, as women's potential as a newly activated constituency is recognized, more groups are competing over who will lead—or, all too often, control—women's political energies.

Governments, political organizations, and political parties are seeing the usefulness of organizing our support for their politics. The patronizing attitude of male powers who view women as needing to be "directed" is reflected in manipulative expressions such as "mobilizing" women's votes or "harnessing" women's labor power. Still, many male-dominated groups are well organized and successful in offering a direction for women's energies and frustrations. If feminists do not provide leadership that can activate large numbers of women on our own behalf, we will find that women will be—as we so often are—separated by existing male-defined political divisions.

This situation has been clearly demonstrated throughout the United Nations Decade for Women. In 1975 at the UN International Women's Year Conference in Mexico City, most governments and the media generally treated the conference as a joke and/or as a perk for their wives or whichever women they owed a favor. A Plan of Action with measures to improve women's status was passed, but the process was not taken too seriously by male power structures.

By 1980, however, when the UN held its Mid-Decade Conference on Women in Copenhagen, the mood had changed. Not that governments were now profeminist—none of the existing patriarchal powers are feminist to any real extent, although some certainly treat women better than others. The difference in 1980 was that they no longer considered it amusing for women to talk together about politics. They saw it as potentially threatening. Therefore, governments sought to keep this second conference under tight control.

Most government officials and many UN bureaucrats see their political, economic, and social power, their jobs and their lifestyles, as dependent on maintaining the existing divisions in the world. They are not about to let a bunch of idealistic women get out of hand and shake up the way they rule. In the nongovernmental (NGO) events held simultaneously with the UN Conferences in Mexico and in Copenhagen, there were pockets of discussion and networking that brought women together across male political lines. While this was not powerful enough to change the UN conference, it did point the way toward such possibilities, which were realized further at the NGO Forum in Nairobi in 1985.[1]

If women are prepared—even determined—to get "out of hand," it is possible to come together across male divisions. To do this does not require, as some have suggested, that women avoid "politics" and "male issues," but that we redefine these from women's perspectives. Feminists must provide new ways of looking at political struggles. We must imagine other approaches in every area, including such difficult problems as the Arab-Jewish conflict, apartheid in South Africa, or the international debt that is crippling economies in Latin America.

If feminists are to provide leadership and political direction in the coming years, we must recognize and believe in the potential power of women and in the potential of feminism as a politics emerging from women's experiences. To challenge the dynamic of domination at all levels, from the home to the military, and to demand a world based more on cooperation than on conquest, would indeed be revolutionary. Patriarchal powers see feminism as a threat because they recognize just such a potential for women to organize outside of male control and value systems. They are committed to preventing that possibility and will use every opportunity to keep women divided. Unless we see this potential as clearly and organize around it, feminism will be limited

in its impact on the structures that control most women's lives.

To talk about how feminism can provide such leadership, I need to reassert the basic premise on which all of this rests: global feminism exists. Feminist activity and thought are happening all over the world. There is much diversity among us and no agreed-upon body of doctrine or central organization. Yet, there is a similarity in our approaches and in our fundamental questioning of society. While the particular forms that women's oppression takes in different settings vary and often pit some women against others, there is a commonality in the dynamic of domination by such women are subordinated to the demands, definitions, and desires of men.

You can see this commonality in the numerous feminist periodicals in the Third World, as well as in the West, that have emerged during this decade. These discuss a variety of issues from reproductive rights to female poverty, from legislation to sexuality, from violence against women to the violations of the military. You can see it also in the local, regional, and international gatherings that have been held among activists, academics, policy makers, health practitioners, social workers, and community leaders, from Sri Lanka to Switzerland to Senegal. A good illustration was the Second Feminist Encuentro (Meeting) for Latin America and the Caribbean, where over six hundred women gathered in Lima in 1983 to discuss patriarchy in the region in relation to a list of some nineteen proposed topics and still had to keep adding to the agenda. The vitality and breadth of feminism are also seen in the myriad of grass-roots projects, centers, demonstrations, celebrations, and meetings where women voice their demands for a greater say over their lives. Here, too, they take the time and space to plan together how to develop visions into reality.

A Global View of Feminism

The excitement and urgency of issues of global feminism were brought home to me at a Workshop on Feminist Ideology and Structures sponsored by the Asian and Pacific Centre for Women and Development in Bangkok in 1979. Women from each region presented what they were doing in relation to the themes of the UN Decade for Women. In doing this, we realized the importance of the international male-dominated media in influencing what we knew and thought about each other before we came to Bangkok.

We saw how the media has made the women's movement and feminism appear trivial, silly, selfish, naive, and/or crazy in the industrialized countries while practically denying its existence in the Third World. Western feminists have been portrayed as concerned only with burning bras, having sex, hating men, and/or getting to be head of General Motors. Such stereotypes ignore the work of most feminists and distort even the few activities the media do report. So, for example, basic political points that women have tried to communicate—about what it means to love ourselves in a woman-hating society—get twisted into a focus on "hating" men. Or those demonstrations that did discard high-heeled shoes, makeup, or bras, as symbolic of male control over women's self-definition and mobility, have been stripped of their political content.

Thus, women who feel that their priorities are survival issues of food or housing are led to think that Western feminists are not concerned with these matters. Similarly, media attempts to portray all feminists as a privileged elite within each country seek to isolate us from other women. The real strength of feminism can be seen best in the fact that more and more women come to embrace it in spite of the overwhelming effort that has gone into distorting it and trying to keep women away.

By acknowledging the power of the media's distortion of feminism at the Bangkok workshop, we were able to see the importance of defining it clearly for ourselves. Our definition brought together the right of every woman to equity, dignity, and freedom of choice through the power to control her own life and the removal of all forms of inequalities and oppression in society. We saw feminism as a world view that has an impact on all aspects of life, and affirmed the broad context of the assertion that the "personal is political." This is to say that the individual aspects of oppression and change are not separate from the need for political and institutional change.

Through our discussion, we were able agree on the use of this concept of feminism to describe women's struggles. While some had reservations about using the word "feminism," we chose not to allow media or government distortions to scare us away from it. As one Asian pointed out, if we shied away from the term, we would simply be attacked or ridiculed for other actions or words, since those who opposed us were against what we sought for women and the world and not really concerned with our language.

In Copenhagen at the 1980 NGO Forum, the conference newspaper came out with a quote-of-the-day from a Western feminist that read: "To talk feminism to a woman who has no water, no home, and no food is to talk nonsense." Many of us felt that the quote posed a crucial challenge to feminists. We passed out a leaflet, "What Is Feminism?," describing it as a perspective on the world that would address such issues, and we invited women to a special session on the topic. Over three hundred women from diverse regions gathered to debate what feminism really means to us and how that has been distorted by the media even within our own movements.

The second challenge we saw in the quote was that if it were true and feminists did not speak to such issues, then we would indeed be irrelevant to many women. We therefore discussed the importance of a feminist approach to development—one that both addresses how to make home, food, and water available to all and extends beyond equating "development" with industrialization. Terms like "developing nations" are suspect and patronizing. While we need to look at the real material needs of all people from a feminist perspective, we can hardly call any countries "developed." For this reason, while I find all labels that generalize about diverse parts of the world problematic, I use "Western" or "industrialized" and "Third World," rather than "developing" and "developed."

Recently at a meeting in New York, I saw another example of confusion about the meaning of feminism. Two women who had just engaged in civil disobedience against nuclear weapons were discussing feminism as the motivating force behind their actions, when a man jumped up impatiently objecting, "But I thought this meeting was about disarmament, not feminism." It was the equivalent of "to talk feminism in the face of nuclear destruction is to talk nonsense." Such attitudes portray feminism as a luxury of secondary concern and thus both dismiss female experience as unimportant and limit our politics. They fundamentally misconstrue feminism as about "women's issues" rather than as a political perspective on life.[2]

Seeing feminism as a transformational view is crucial to a global perspective. But to adopt a global outlook does not mean, as some feminists fear and male politicos often demand, that we abandon working on the "women's issues" that we fought to put on the political agenda. Nor does it imply setting aside our analysis of sexual politics. Rather it requires that we take what we have learned about sexual politics and use feminist theory to expose the connections between the "women's issues" and other world questions. In this way, we demonstrate our point that all issues are women's issues and need feminist analysis. For example, we must show how a society that tacitly sanctions male violence against women and children, whether incest and battery at home, rape on the streets, or sexual harassment on the job, is bound to produce people who are militaristic and believe in their right to dominate others on the basis of other differences such as skin color or nationality. Or we can point out how the heterosexist assumption that every "good" woman wants to and eventually will be supported by a man fuels the economic policies that have produced the feminization of poverty worldwide. This refusal to accept a woman who lives without a man as fully human thus allows policy makers to propose such ideas as keeping welfare payments or even job opportunities for single mothers limited since they "contribute to the destruction of the family."

The examples are endless. The task is not one of changing our issues but of expanding the frameworks from which we understand our work. It means taking what we have learned in working on "women's issues" and relating that to other areas, demanding that these not be seen as competing but as enabling us to bring about more profound change. To use the illustration above, to seek to end militarism without also ending the dynamic of domination embedded in male violence at home would be futile. And so, too, the reverse: we will never fully end male violence against individual women unless we also stop celebrating the organized violence of war as manly and appropriate behavior.

Making Connections

The interconnectedness of the economic and sexual exploitation of women with militarism and racism is well illustrated in the area of forced prostitution and female sexual slavery. It is impossible to work on one aspect of this issue without confronting the whole socioeconomic context of women's lives. For example, females in India who are forced into prostitution are often either sold by poverty-stricken families for whom a girl child is considered a liability, or they have sought to escape arranged marriages they find intolerable. In the United States, many girls led into forced prostitution are teenage runaways who were victims of sexual or physical abuse at home, and for whom there are no jobs, services, or safe places to live.

In parts of Southeast Asia, many women face the limited economic options of rural poverty; joining assembly lines that pay poorly, destroy eyesight, and often discard workers over thirty; or of entering the "entertainment industry." In Thailand and the Philippines, national economies dependent on prostitution resulted from U.S. military brothels during the Vietnam War. When that demand decreased, prostitution was channeled into sex tourism—the organized multimillion-dollar transnational business of systematically selling women's bodies as part of packaged tours, which feeds numerous middlemen and brings foreign capital into the country. In all these situations, the patriarchal beliefs that men have the right to women's bodies, and that "other" races or "lower" classes are subhuman, underlie the abuse women endure.

Feminists organizing against these practices must link their various aspects. Thus,

for example, women have simultaneously protested against sex tourism and militarism, created refuges for individual victims who escape, and sought to help women develop skills in order to gain more control over their lives. Japanese businesses pioneered the development of sex tourism. Feminists in Japan pioneered the opposition to this traffic. They work with Southeast Asian women to expose and shame the Japanese government and the businesses involved in an effort to cut down on the trade from their end.

On the international level, it is clear that female sexual slavery, forced prostitution, and violence against women operate across national boundaries and are political and human rights abuses of great magnitude. Yet, the male-defined human rights community by-and-large refuses to see any but the most narrowly defined cases of slavery or "political" torture as their domain. We must ask what is it when a woman faces death at the hands of her family to save its honor because she was raped? What is it when two young lesbians commit suicide together rather than be forced into unwanted marriages? What is it when a woman trafficked out of her country does not try to escape because she knows she will be returned by the police and beaten or deported? An understanding of sexual politics reveals all these and many more situations to be political human-rights violations deserving asylum, refugee status, and the help that other political victims are granted. As limited as human rights are in our world, we must demand at least that basic recognition for such women, while we seek to expand concern for human rights generally.

In these areas as well as others, feminists are creating new interpretations and approaches—to human rights, to development, to community and family, to conflict resolution, and so on. From local to global interaction, we must create alternative visions of how we can live in the world based on women's experiences and needs in the here-and-now.

Learning from Diversity

In sharing experiences and visions across national and cultural lines, feminists are inspired by what others are doing. But we are also confronted with the real differences among us. On the one hand, our diversity is our strength. It makes it possible for us to imagine more possibilities and to draw upon a wider range of women's experiences. On the other hand, differences can also divide us if we do not take seriously the variations on female oppression that women suffer according to race, class, ethnicity, religion, sexual preference, age, nationality, physical disability, and so on. These are not simply added onto the oppression of women by sex, but shape the forms by which we experience that subordination. Thus, we cannot simply add up the types of oppression that a woman suffers one-by-one as independent factors but must look at how they are interrelated.

If we take this approach, we should be more capable of breaking down the ways in which difference itself separates people. Patriarchal society is constructed on a model of domination by which each group is assigned a place in the hierarchy according to various differences, and then allocated power or privileges based on that position. In this way, difference becomes threatening because it involves winning or losing one's position/privileges. If we eliminated the assignment of power and privilege according to difference, we could perhaps begin to enjoy real choices of style and variations of culture as offering more creative possibilities in life.

The world has been torn apart by various male divisions and conflicts for thousands of years and we should not assume that women can overcome and solve in a short time what patriarchy has so intricately conceived. The oppressions, resentments, fears, and patterns of behavior that have developed due to racism, classism, nationalism and sexism, are very deep. We cannot just wish them away with our desire for women to transcend differences. Above all, we do not overcome differences by denying them or downplaying their effects on us—especially when the one denying is in the position of privilege.

A white woman can only legitimately talk about overcoming differences of race if she struggles to understand racism both as it affects their personally and as she affects it politically. A heterosexual can get beyond the divisions of sexual preference only by learning about the oppression of lesbians and by acknowledging the insights that come from that orientation. A U.S. American must understand the effects of colonialism before she can hope for unity with women beyond national boundaries. Too often the call to transcend differences has been a call to ignore them at the expense of the oppressed. This cannot be the route of global feminism. We can only hope to chart a path beyond male divisions by walking through them and taking seriously their detrimental effects on us as women. This examination of and effort to eliminate other aspects of oppression does not come before or after working on sexism—it is simultaneous.

A crucial part of this process is understanding that reality does not look the same from different people's perspectives. It is not surprising that one way that feminists have come to understand about differences has been through the love of a person from another culture or race. It takes persistence and motivation—which love often engenders—to get beyond one's ethnocentric assumptions and really learn about other perspectives. In this process and while seeking to eliminate oppression, we also discover new possibilities and insights that come from the experience and survival of other peoples.

In considering what diversity means for a global movement, one of the most difficult areas for feminists is culture. In general, we affirm cultural diversity and the variety it brings to our lives. Yet, almost all existing cultures today are male-dominated. We know the horrors male powers have wrought over the centuries in imposing one cultural standard over another. Popular opposition to such imposition has often included affirmation of traditional cultures. Certainly none of our cultures can claim to have the answers to women's liberation since we are oppressed in all of them.

We must face the fact that in some instances male powers are justifying the continuation or advocating the adoption of practices oppressive to women by labeling them "cultural" and/or "resistance to Western influence." Feminists must refuse to accept *any* forms of domination of women—whether in the name of tradition or in the name of modernization. This is just the same as refusing to accept racial discrimination in the name of "culture," whether in the South of the USA or in South Africa. Feminists are seeking new models for society that allow for diversity while not accepting the domination of any group. For this, women in each culture must sort out what is best from their own culture and what is oppressive. Through our contact with each other, we can then challenge ethnocentric biases and move beyond the unconscious cultural assumptions inherent in our thinking.

In taking into account and challenging the various forms of domination in the world, we do not necessarily accept existing male theories about or solutions to them.

We must always have a woman-identified approach—that is, one of seeking to identify with women's situations rather than accepting male definitions of reality. Such a process enables us to distinguish what is useful from male theories and to see where feminist approaches are being or need to be applied to issues such as race, class, and culture. Further, in a world so saturated with woman-hating, it is through woman-identification, which involves profoundly learning to love women and to listen for women's authentic perspectives, that we can make breakthroughs in these areas.

We confront a similar dilemma when examining nationalism. From a feminist perspective, I see nationalism as the ultimate expression of the patriarchal dynamic of domination—where groups battle for control over geographic territory, and justify violence and aggression in the name of national security. Therefore I prefer the term "global" to "international" because I see feminism as a movement among peoples beyond national boundaries and not among nation-states. Yet, nationalism has also symbolized the struggle of oppressed peoples against the control of other nations. And many attempts to go beyond nationalism have simply been supranational empire-building, such is the idea of turning Africans into "Frenchmen." Further, in the context of increasing global control over us all by transnational corporations, many see nationalism as a form of resistance. In seeking to be global, feminists must therefore find ways to transcend patriarchal nationalism without demanding sameness, and while still preserving means of identity and culture that are not based on domination.

Think Globally, Act Locally

A major obstacle that feminists face in seeking to be global is our lack of control over the resources necessary for maintaining greater contact worldwide. It takes time and money as well as energy and commitment to overcome the problems of distance, language, and culture. Feminists have little control over existing institutions with global networks, such as the media, churches, universities, and the state, but sometimes we must utilize such networks even as we try to set up our own.

Since feminists have limited resources for global travel and communication, it is vital that we learn how to be global in consciousness while taking action locally. For this, we must resist the tendency to separate "international" work into a specialized category of political activity that is often viewed as inaccessible to most women. This tendency reflects a hierarchical mode in which the "world level" is viewed as above the "local level." For those whose work focuses primarily on the global aspects of issues, the challenge is not to lose touch with the local arena on which any effective movement is based. For those whose work is focused locally, the challenge is to develop a global perspective that informs local work. For all of us, the central question is to understand how the issues of women all over the world are interrelated and to discern what that means specifically in each setting.

Global interaction is not something that we choose to do or not to do. It is something in which we are already participating. All we choose is whether to be aware of it or not, whether to try to understand it and how that affects our actions. For citizens of the U.S., we begin our global consciousness with awareness of the impact that our country's policies have on other people's daily lives. I learned in the antiwar movement that often the most useful thing that we can do for people elsewhere is to make changes in the U.S. and in how it exercises power in the world.

There are many well-known issues such as military aggression, foreign aid and trade policies, or the possibility of worldwide destruction through nuclear weapons or chemical contamination that we see as global. But there are numerous less obvious illustrations of global interrelatedness, from the present world economy where women are manipulated as an international cheap labor pool to the traffic in women's bodies for forced prostitution. Therefore, any attempt we make to deal with the needs of women in the U.S., such as employment, must examine the global context of the problem. In this instance, that means understanding how multinational corporations move their plants from country to country or state to state, exploiting female poverty and discouraging unionization by threatening to move again. We must use global strategies, such as that proposed by one group on the Texas-Mexico border advocating an international bill of rights for women workers as a way to organize together for basic standards for all. In a world where global forces affect us daily, it is neither possible nor conscionable to achieve a feminist utopia in one country alone.

Developing Global Consciousness

When women from different countries interact authentically, sharing our own experiences, while also recognizing that our work has cultural limits, we can learn from each other. As we listen to others' views, we see our ethnocentric biases more clearly and can discover ways to overcome these. For while feminism draws strength from its grounding in the concept of "the personal is political," this also has limitations. Each of our personal perceptions of women's needs and reality have been so shaped by the racism, anti-Semitism, classism, and so on, of our cultures that we cannot depend on our perceptions alone as the basis for analysis and action. We need to learn from other women's lives and views as well.

In discussing global connections with women in the U.S., I often find a tendency toward two extremes—arrogance or guilt. The arrogant stance implies that since this wave of feminism developed early in the U.S. and has been very active here, we are the "leaders" of the world movement and must show others what to do. On the opposite extreme are those who feel so apologetic about being U.S. citizens that they assume that women in other countries always know best and that we have nothing to offer except unquestioning support. Both of these attitudes are patronizing and unproductive and have little to do with real solidarity among women. Instead, we must strive for an openness and equality with other women in which we all learn and teach, as we seek common denominators in our work.

Specifically, this means that we should not negate what feminists here have achieved, but should offer our insights and experiences unapologetically, trusting that other women can discern what is useful to them. Even on issues that many consider taboo or touchy internationally, such as lesbianism, I have found that my personal openness and clarification of what this issue means to women in the U.S. have been accepted—and often even welcomed—when explained without defensiveness. What no woman anywhere wants concerning any issue is for someone else to tell her what it means in her context or what she must do about it in her country. Only through honest sharing can we learn from each other.

As feminism develops around the world, all of us can benefit enormously from the ideas, actions, and creativity that go with that expansion. It can also help us to make breakthroughs in each of our movements at home. This is not unlike what white women are learning from the growing movement of women of color in industrialized countries, which is creating new understandings of feminism. For as each group of women from varying backgrounds defines feminism and its significance for themselves and for the world, our understanding of feminism in all areas grows.

The development of feminism among diverse groups offers greater possibilities for all feminists even as we must respond to its challenges. First we must try to alter our individual behavior and change our movements internally where oppression occurs. But we should not assume that our task is only within the movement, or worse yet, that we can somehow become perfect nonoppressive beings through just talking about the "-isms." The test of our individual changes is in our actions. It can be seen in how we expand the feminist struggle against these oppressions more forcefully in the world, and in how we broaden our approach to feminism. Just as feminism does not mean adding women and stirring them into male theories and institutions without changing those, so, too, understanding global perspectives or the insights of women of color involves altering our approaches and not just adding in an issue or a person here and there.

At this point it seems useful to look at why it is so difficult for many women to think globally. Perhaps the most obvious reason is that most countries are nationalistic, and the information reported through mainstream media and schools is generally distorted by narrowly defined "national interest." What is taught in schools about the Third World is generally separated from the core content, and just as with the separate curriculum of women's history or black studies, this gives the impression that such material is not essential. Another problem stems from the fact that much of what is called "international" is only "North Atlantic"—that is, it only concerns Europe and North America, which contributes to the invisibility of the Third World. These problems can be countered by making ourselves better informed about the world by seeing it from perspectives other than our nation's mainstream.

Information alone, however, is not the issue. Many women feel overwhelmed by hearing about global problems because they do not think that they can do anything with the information. Feminists are often burdened with just trying to cope with "domestic issues" and survival. It is vital, therefore, that we develop a world view or framework for seeing the local-global connections in order that we can grow from this information rather than become numbed by it.

Certainly none of us can possibly hope to know everything in today's world, and global feminism does not mean that we must understand and act on all issues all the time. The point is not to exhaust ourselves trying to be superwomen. Rather, the challenge is to develop a global perspective from the information we do have and learn to apply that to whatever occurs. For this it may be helpful to focus on one particular country or issue and seek to understand that in some depth as part of expanding one's perspective. Once we see the world in greater depth and from various approaches in one area, it becomes easier to question our biases and look at issues differently in another. This is an ongoing process of learning, questioning, and changing that does not occur all in one moment.

I must reiterate here that a global perspective can be developed anywhere. Spending time in another country can be useful because it removes us from the usual context and assumptions of our lives. But this is not necessary to expand one's world view. For example, in most cities there is a diversity of racial and ethnic groups and communities of people who have left their countries for political or economic reasons or to study. We can learn much from them and by understanding diversity better at home.

There are also techniques that can expand one's perspectives, such as seeking to put ourselves, even if only temporarily, in the position of being "the other." For example, I have suggested that heterosexual women act as if they are lesbians for a week: go places only with women and tell important people in their lives, as a way of gaining clearer view on this issue. Similarly, one can learn from putting oneself in the position of being in the minority—a white at a predominantly black or Indian event, a person who speaks only English in a Spanish-speaking environment, and so on. While any technique has limitations and can become artificial, it can also be useful if one is genuine in trying to expose one's assumptions and grow in one's perception of the world.

A Matter of Perspective

Beyond techniques and information, the primary task remains one of attitude, approach, and perspective. The point is not that we necessarily change the focus of our work but that we make connections that help to bring its global aspects to consciousness—in our programs, our slogans, our publications, and our conversations with other women. It is when we try to make a hierarchy of issues, keeping them separate and denying the importance of some in order to address others, that we are all defeated.

To use a previous example, if I cannot develop an analysis and discuss openly the ways in which heterosexism supports the international feminization of poverty, without having some women's homophobia prevent them from utilizing this insight, or without having some lesbians fear that I have abandoned "their issue" by working more on global poverty, then work in both areas is diminished. I believe that the path to effective global feminist theory and action is not through denial of any issue or analysis but through listening, questioning, struggling, and seeking to make connections among them.

To work locally with a global perspective does require stretching feminism, not to abandon its insights but to shed its cultural biases, and thus to expand its capacity to reach all people. In this process, we risk what seems certain at home by taking it into the world and having it change through interaction with other realities and perceptions. It can be frightening. But if we have confidence in ourselves and in the feminist process, it can also be exciting. It can mean the growth of a more effective feminism with a greater ability to address the world and to bring change. If we fail to take these risks and ignore the global dimensions of our lives, we lose possibilities for individ-

ual growth and we doom feminism to a less effective role in the world struggle over the direction of the twenty-first century.

My visions of global feminism are grand, perhaps even grandiose. But the state of the world today demands that women become less modest and dream/plan/act/risk on a larger scale. At the same time, the realization of global visions can only be achieved through the everyday lives and action of women locally. It depends on women deciding to shape their own destiny, claiming their right to the world, and exercising their responsibility to make it in some way, large or small, a better place for all. As more women do this with a growing world perspective and sense of connection to others, we can say that feminism is meeting the challenge of bringing the global home.

Notes

1. See "Reflections on Global Feminism After Narobi," pp. 346-352.
2. See section on "transformational politics" in "Going Public with Our Vision," pp. 69-71.

55

The Status of Women Under International Human Rights Law and the 1995 U.N. World Conference on Women, Beijing, China

Margaret Plattner

Introduction

In 1888, the first International Council of Women was held in Washington, D.C. The delegates consisted mainly of educated, affluent women from the United States and Europe. The primary issue for these women in the late nineteenth century was gaining the right to vote.[1] Lack of property rights, inequitable inheritance laws, and limited parental rights were also of concern to the fledgling women's movement.[2]

One hundred seven years later, the women's movement has assumed a global dimension, inclusive of women from every socioeconomic and educational background. Yet similar issues of limited property rights and inheritance laws still challenged nations participating in the 1995 United Nations ("U.N.") Fourth World Conference on Women in Beijing, China.[3]

The problems facing women in 1995 were also more comprehensive and complex than the 1888 Council gathering. The world had changed from a singular, nationalistic perspective in the nineteenth century into a dynamic international political, social, and economic matrix of the twentieth century. Examples such as the girl-child sold into prostitution in Bankok, Thailand[4] and the bride burnings in the rural villages of India[5] are of international concern as human rights violations and no longer considered isolated, local problems. Legalistic mechanisms established by treaties and customary international law no longer tolerate such practices.[6]

However, many countries continue to have traditional, customary, and religious practices involving women that are in direct conflict with these standards and laws. As the Deputy Secretary of the United Nations, Ismat Kittani, stated in his opening speech

From *Kentucky Law Review*, 84, pp. 1249-1275. Copyright © 1995 by Kentucky Law Journal. Reprinted by permission.

at the Beijing Conference: "[T]he challenge is how to make [existing] laws take effect in the daily lives of women."[7] This is the challenge which faces the human rights of women, notwithstanding the fact that their rights are supposed to be inalienable, integral and indivisible parts of universal human rights.[8]

The 1995 U.N. World Conference on Women presented the world community with the opportunity to reaffirm, support, and strengthen women's rights as an integral part of the international human rights paradigm.[9] Furthermore, the Conference aimed to rekindle the momentum gained at previous U.N. women's conferences, to heighten awareness of recurring issues, and to focus on a coherent strategy to implement the Conference's objectives. As such, the status of women under international human rights law and the Beijing Conference Plan for Action are the focus of this Article.

I. Summary of International Law Treaties and Women's Rights

A. Historical Background

In order to better understand the international context of the Beijing Conference, "women's rights [as] human rights" requires a historical summary. First, the term "human rights" is a broad, interrelated term with various applications:

> [H]uman right are understood to represent individual and group demands for the shaping and sharing of power, wealth, enlightenment, and other cherished values in community process, most fundamentally the value of respect and its constituent elements of reciprocal tolerance and mutual forbearance. . . . [I]f a right is determined to be a human right it is quintessentially general or universal in character. . . .[10]

Second, human rights, by definition, encompass all aspects of women's issues. Whether the issue is education, economics, or government, equal rights with respect to opportunity and status is a fundamental component of a woman's liberty and dignity. By establishing an international code of behavior, through human rights treaties and conference documents, these efforts strengthen the world community's obligations toward women and enhance her own self-worth in society.[11]

Since the inception of the U.N. in 1945, the definition of human rights has been codified into law by international human rights treaties. In practice, however, international treaties occasionally play a subordinate role to the "realpolitik" and interests of a sovereign nation. As a result, governments circumvent international law and allow human rights abuses of certain individuals or groups to suit their own ends.[12]

Historically, the U.N. has rarely intervened in a country's internal affairs to enforce international human rights laws, because that body is legally obligated to recognize the self-determination of a sovereign nation.[13] Ultimately, protecting the rights of women becomes an internal matter subject to domestic laws. Legally binding international documents are, therefore, rendered ineffective unless a government actually enforces international human rights law, or implements national laws which prohibit gender discrimination. The Beijing Conference highlighted this legal dilemma.

The U.N. attempted to secure human rights for both men and women beginning with the Charter of the United Nations, signed in 1945. This document, which established the U.N., states in Article 1 that the United Nations is responsible for "promoting and encouraging respect for human rights and for fundamental freedoms for all without distinction as to race, *sex*, language, or religion."[14] The legislative body of the United Nations, the General Assembly, adopted the Universal Declaration of Human Rights in 1948.[15] Delegate Eleanor Roosevelt encouraged consideration of the rights of women and as a result, the preamble of that document states that "the peoples of the United Nations . . . reaffirm their faith in fundamental human rights . . . and in the equal rights of men and women."[16] These documents were the beginning of international recognition for the equal rights of women and their right to full participation in all areas of life. Unfortunately, there was no U.N. monitoring organization designed to enforce these human rights for quite some time.[17]

In 1966, the International Covenant on Economic, Social and Cultural Rights was signed.[18] However, as it repeatedly failed to receive the approval of a majority of member nations, it did not go into force until December, 1976.[19] This Covenant centered on the rights of self-determination for all peoples.[20] Under the terms of the Covenant, self-determination means that people should be able to determine their political status, and have the right to freely pursue their economic, social, and cultural development.[21] Article 2 emphasizes that the rights enunciated in the Covenant "will be exercised without discrimination of any kind as to race, colour, or *sex* . . ."[22] Article 3 provides that all states party to the Covenant undertake to ensure the equal rights of both men and women regarding the enjoyment of all economic, social, and cultural rights set forth in the Covenant.[23] Specifically, the rights enunciated in the Covenant include the following: to earn a living as one freely chooses;[24] to receive fair wages;[25] to work under reasonable conditions;[26] to protect one's family;[27] to be free from hunger,[28] the opportunity to receive an education;[29]

and to engage in a cultural life without punishment.[30] This last right recognizes the right of the individual to participate in the literary or artistic field without fear of governmental retribution.[31]

The International Covenant on Civil and Political Rights ("ICCPR"), entered into force in March, 1976, highlighted the civil and political rights of all men and women.[32] The ICCPR established that governments must allow for a competent judicial, administrative, or legislative authority when an individual seeks a redress of grievances;[33] that no one shall be subject to compulsory labor;[34] that an accused is considered innocent until proved guilty;[35] and that there exist the rights of religious freedom and freedom of association.[36]

The above Covenants specifically bind acceding or ratifying states to undertake and ensure that women and men are accorded equal rights status.[37] Furthermore each Covenant translates the principles of the Universal Declaration of Human Rights into a legally binding form.[38]

Between 1947 and 1962, the U.N. Commission on the Status of Women helped initiate the procedures which led to the enactment of these Covenants and Declarations.[39] In addition, the Commission was instrumental in organizing several conventions on women's issues, including Rights of Women,[40] the Convention on the Nationality of Married Women,[41] and the Convention on Consent, Minimum Age and Registration of Marriages.[42] The Commission believed that the major issue facing women was that of their marital status, and it sought to clearly define these practices and uphold the rights of women as individuals.[43]

B. The Convention on the Elimination of All Forms of Discrimination Against Women

Despite the fact that international instruments existed to legally protect women, there was not an internal U.N. legal framework to specifically monitor discrimination against women and to react to such practices.[44] The Convention on the Elimination of All Forms of Discrimination Against Women ("CEDAW") came about because the protection and promotion of women's rights was fragmentary, as the U.N. failed to deal with discrimination in a comprehensive and juridical way.[45] As a result, the Commission on Women was invited in the 1960s to prepare a draft declaration that would articulate specific international standards regarding discrimination against women. The Commission submitted a declaration, known as "The Declaration on Elimination of Discrimination Against Women," which was formally adopted by the General Assembly in November, 1967.[46] However, even this Declaration did not have the contractual force of a treaty.

In the 1970s, the women's movement was achieving more prominent international recognition. Gender discrimination became more apparent as the world community's consciousness was raised. While women comprised half of the world's population,[47] they were still marginally represented in both the public and private sectors.[48] Five years after the adoption by the U.N. General Assembly of the Declaration of the Elimination on Discrimination Against Women, the Commission on the Status of Women was most interested in a binding commitment that would have the legal force of a treaty. The instrument would be an international, comprehensive document, whose purpose was to eliminate discrimination against women. Moreover, such a document was necessary to help establish a *means* to enforce these ideas and to eliminate gender discrimination. This instrument became known as CEDAW.

CEDAW, adopted in 1979 by the U.N. General Assembly, requires those nation-states agreeing to implement it to take appropriate measures to eliminate discrimination against women in government, law, education, employment, health care, business, reproductivity, and family life.[49] States party to the agreement thus agree to initiate "all appropriate measures, including legislation, to ensure equality."[50] The Convention further established a committee of twenty-three nongovernmental experts to oversee compliance with the provisions of the Convention.[51] At least every four years, parties to the treaty are expected to submit a report indicating appropriate measures taken to carry out the spirit and the letter of the treaty.[52] Governments are also to report to this committee on the implementation of CEDAW provisions.[53] In essence, CEDAW codified international legal standards exclusively for women.

Presently, 139 Member-States have ratified CEDAW; the agreement came into force in 1981.[54] The United States was an active participant in drafting this treaty and signed it on July 17, 1980, under the Carter administration.[55] However, to date, the United States Senate has failed to fully ratify CEDAW. Under general treaty practices of international law, "ratification is usually the second step in a two-stage process" after signing it.[56] The signature of a state authenticates the text of the agreement, but national authorities must approve the treaty by some form of governmental mechanism to cement the ratification process.

In this country, CEDAW has not been ratified by the United States Senate due to certain provisions which are in question.

The United States Justice Department has stated in a Memorandum of Law that some provisions do not conform with current American laws.[57] Notwithstanding President Clinton's overall support of CEDAW, his administration has entered four reservations, three understandings, and two declarations to the treaty.[58]

The first reservation the United States government made is "the broad definition of discrimination against women [in the treaty] appears [to apply] to private organizations and areas of personal conduct not covered by United States law."[59] According to this interpretation, Articles 2, 3, and 5 of CEDAW require broad regulation of private conduct in order to eliminate discrimination.[60] The second reservation involves women's status in the military.[61] In the United States, women may only serve in certain combat roles, and are specifically prohibited from serving directly as infantry in ground warfare.[62] However, since CEDAW seeks to eliminate gender discrimination in every sphere, including the military, all combat positions would be made available to women.[63]

The third objection to CEDAW stems from the idea of "comparable worth." United States law requires equal pay for equal work in jobs that are substantially similar.[64] However, the United States government has refused to accept any obligation under CEDAW to enact legislation codifying the doctrine of "comparable worth," a subject of controversy in this country.[65]

The fourth objection to CEDAW involves Article 11(2)(b), which addresses the issue of paid maternity leave without fear of loss of employment, seniority, or social allowances. While the 1993 Family Leave Act permits women to take unpaid maternity or paternity leave for twelve weeks, it does not require paid parental leave by any employer.[66] Thus, the United States Senate has declined to ratify CEDAW for its unwanted effects on private employers, military operations, and businesses.

The Senate's advice and consent is also subject to three understandings, which may alter the provisions of CEDAW as enacted. First, the Senate will implement the CEDAW provisions as enumerated, only *to the extent* that such law is consistent with the U.S. Constitution.[67] Thus, under the Supremacy Clause,[68] CEDAW may not be inconsistent with the Constitution.

The Senate's second qualifying understanding involves CEDAW Articles 5, 7, 8, and 12, which grant equal protection to women in a variety of areas.[69] The United States government asserts that these Articles may restrict the rights to individual freedom of speech, expression, and association as provided in the First and Fourteenth Amendments to the United States Constitution.[70] It is put forth that free speech and equal protection guarantees would be denied to men if, for example, they were not allowed to run for political office due to a mandatory quota for women to hold certain elected positions. In response to that position, the government has a substantial interest in permitting benign discrimination in order to rectify the disproportionate percentage of males to females holding elected positions. However, it is doubtful that Congress will every accede that this interest is "substantial."[71]

Finally, Senator Jesse Helmes (R-North Carolina) has stated that the Convention shall not be construed as promoting abortion as a family planning method.[72] The issue of abortion is so extremely controversial in the United States, and it seems the Senate is hesitant to overtly embrace a program which specifically promotes reproductive choice, including abortion, on an international level.

What are the ramifications of the United States Government's reservations to CEDAW? This Convention permits ratification despite a member-state's reservations that they will not abide legally by all of the Convention's provisions.[73] As long as the reservations are not incompatible with the "object and purpose" of CEDAW, the reservations are not unacceptable.[74]

In this case, if the Convention accepts the reservations, the United States is not obligated to carry out the specific provisions of CEDAW to which the reservations apply. Nonetheless, the treaty does become binding on the United States despite their accepted reservations. If the reservations are found to be fundamentally inconsistent with the "object and purpose" of the Convention, then the United States may not become a state-party to CEDAW. Whether the Senate will do so remains to be determined. As of this writing, the Chairman of the Senate Foreign Relations Committee, Senator Jesse Helms, has held up a vote on CEDAW due to overall foreign policy differences with the Clinton administration.[75]

Advocates of CEDAW argue the paramount importance of this treaty. In a speech at the Beijing Conference, Ivanka Corti, Chairperson of CEDAW, stated:

CEDAW is the most comprehensive charter of women's human rights. . . . CEDAW brings together in a single Convention all the various instruments concerning the status of women. . . . Its legally binding and internationally accepted nature makes the Convention the basic, legal framework for a far-reaching strategy to protect and promote the fundamental rights of women and to eradicate de jure and de facto inequality and discrimination.[76]

In that same speech, Corti also recited compelling statistics as she highlighted the need for CEDAW. For example, women worldwide are paid thirty to forty percent less than men;[77] women represent a dispro-

portionate share of the unemployed in *every* age group and region in the world;[78] several multi-religious countries have separate laws for women, especially with respect to domestic relations;[79] inheritance rights are given more significant weight to male heirs than female heirs;[80] and women on average comprise 10.5% of legislators and 6.1% of decision makers at the ministerial level, though women make up fifty-six percent of the total population.[81] In response to such low statistics, some countries have adopted quota systems for women to ensure increased political participation in domestic legislative bodies.[82]

With the obvious lack of equality for women in most areas of life and government the need for aggressive change is apparent. One of CEDAW's goals is to restructure political systems to include greater numbers of women in positions of authority.[83] The United States has not yet joined the above countries in this effort. CEDAW would require more aggressive United States policies in support of women. This would include strengthening affirmative action programs to ensure that women have equal access to political and economic power centers.[84] However, the electoral process in this country is unlikely to be altered to accommodate greater representation of women in the Congress or at the state legislative level. Moreover, since affirmative action has received heavy criticism by opponents,[85] it is doubtful such programs would be strengthened unless there is a substantial governmental interest.

Another idea in restructuring political representation is "cumulative voting."[86] Cumulative voting is currently a practice used by corporations in selecting board members. This is a concept whereby a person may vote a number of times based on the number of candidates running for that same office. For example, if five candidates run for the same elective office, a voter in that district may vote five times. Five votes may be spread out to different candidates for the same office, or attributed all to the same candidate, Advocates of this voting procedure believe that minority representation would increase in time over the traditional "one person, one vote" method.[87] However, cumulative voting is an idea whose time has not yet come in American politics.

Finally, CEDAW has had a positive effect in other countries. Ratification has led to policy changes regarding the equality of women and men. For example, the constitutions of many countries now incorporate clauses providing equality of the sexes before the law. Furthermore, a number of parties to CEDAW have incorporated the principles of the Convention into their national laws. The Convention has even influenced litigation in the field of discrimination.

C. Post-CEDAW Developments

Documents involving women's issues subsequent to CEDAW's ratification include the Vienna Declaration and Programme of Action 2,[88] the Declaration on the Elimination of Violence Against Women,[89] and the Cairo Declaration on World Population.[90] The Vienna Declaration and Programme of Action 2 lists the human rights of women as a top priority for nations and the U.N. The Vienna Declaration supports the creation of a new mechanism whereby complaints relating to gender discrimination would be recorded, and involved the appointment of a special Rapporteur on violence against women. The Rapporteur reports information on violence against women to the U.N. Commission on Human Rights.[91] Finally, the Declaration states that violence against women, sexual harassment and exploitation, including cultural prejudice and international trafficking

of women, are incompatible with the dignity and the worth of the individual.[92] The Declaration on the Elimination of Violence Against Women placed the issue of violence in a human rights context.[93]

The Cairo Declaration, which addressed family planning issues, established that cultural norms and traditions should be respected.[94] This is in contrast to the Vienna Declaration, which focused on the theme of "universality" of women's issues. As mentioned previously, several countries have established cultural, religious practices and beliefs which conflict with the message of women's rights.[95]

The above mentioned Declarations, while not binding in force, substantially reinforce the goals of CEDAW and encourage governments to act swiftly to promote the rights of women in their respective societies. Those Declarations also conform with the principles and objectives of international human rights law.

In summary, international law establishes that "women's rights are human rights."[96] The challenge for the U.N. is to maintain pressure on its member-states who signed CEDAW to implement this instrument and other human rights documents affecting women. In order for treaties like CEDAW to have any real practical effect, countries must be held accountable to the agreements to which they have committed themselves. For those counties who remain uncommitted to the ideals of CEDAW, persuasion and incentives, and perhaps even censure, must be exercised by the U.N.

II. United Nations Conferences on Women

From Mexico City to Beijing, there have been four U.N. world conferences on women.[97] The purpose of U.N. sponsored women's conferences is to bring together diverse systems, cultures, and traditions and seek consensus on women's issues.[98] The Women's Conference documents are non-binding, yet serve a two-fold purpose: first, to reinforce human rights treaties protecting women; and second, to highlight new and unique concerns to women.

The first U.N. conference was held in 1975 during the International Women's Year in Mexico City. This time was deemed the "U.N. Decade for Women."[99] That particular conference adopted a Plan of Action that led to the declaration by the U.N. General Assembly of the "U.N. Decade for Women." That legislative body also demonstrated its commitment to women that year by adopting CEDAW.[100]

The second conference, held in 1980 in Copenhagen, Denmark, adopted a Program for Action for the second half of the U.N. Decade for Women. The emphasis was on education, employment, and health.[101] The third conference took place in Nairobi, Kenya, in 1985, where the members reviewed obstacles encountered by women world-wide, and measured progress on women's issues since the Mexico City conference.[102] The Nairobi Forward-Looking Strategies for the Advancement of Women to the Year 2000 were adopted by consensus at this conference. "The Strategies provided a framework for action at the national, regional, and international levels to promote empowerment of women and their enjoyment of human rights."[103]

In 1990, the Nairobi Forward-Looking Strategies were reviewed by the U.N. Commission on the Status of Women. The Commission indicated that the world community had to become more responsive and sensitive to women's issues.[104] However, the Commission also determined that there seemed to be some loss of momentum in the implementation of the Strategy's objectives.[105] One of the Beijing Conference's goals was to build momentum on the strate-gies set out by previous women's conferences.

While the Nairobi Forward-Looking Strategies are not legally binding, they provided important, factual support and conclusions for the *Platform for Action* ("PFA"), the foundation for the document adopted at the Beijing Conference. A second review of the strategies was conducted in 1994, and provided the following recommendations for Beijing: redirecting resources to low-income women; ensuring females have the same access to education as their male counterparts; enacting laws that guarantee women equal access to land, assets, and employment opportunities; and developing strategies to reduce poverty.[106]

III. The 1995 U.N. World Conference on Women in Beijing, China

A. The Platform for Action Recommendations; Twelve Areas of Concern

In September 1995, thousands of women from around the globe travelled to Beijing, China for the express purpose of empowering women and transforming their status quo in society. Additionally, participants assessed the progress of the women's movement from the 1985 Nairobi Forward-Looking Strategies, and sought to make the concerns of women a high priority on the international agenda. First Lady Hillary Rodham Clinton set the tone of the Conference by proclaiming in her speech to delegates that "women's rights are human rights.[107]

The blueprint adopted at the Beijing Conference, the PFA, offers strategic actions for governments, the international community, the private sector, and nongovernmental organizations to fulfill the conference's goals of equality, peace, and development. These goals are the foundation for the concept that human rights are also women's rights.

The draft PFA listed twelve areas of critical concern to women.[108] First, the issue of poverty more greatly afflicts a woman statistically than her male counterpart. For example, women constitute nearly seventy percent of the world's 1.2 to 1.3 billion poor.[109] A changing global economic climate, dislocation due to war, and persistent external debt problems are contributing factors that lead to poverty for both women and men.[110] However, women face the additional burdens of cultural prejudice, minimal participation in decision-making positions, and unequal inheritance and property laws. These additional obstacles increase the number of women who live in poverty and further prevent their escape from such an environment.

The PFA recommends an overall poverty reduction strategy: governments should perform an analysis on national policies and programs regarding women's issues; develop and implement policies to evenly distribute resources between women and men where such laws still promote inequitable inheritance laws; enhance women's access to credit from lending institutions; and provide job assistance programs to low-income women.[111]

The second area of concern involves education. Female children today receive an education in greater numbers than in previous years.[112] However, girls continue to be denied the quality of education that boys receive, particularly in the fields of science and technology.[113] Moreover, two-thirds of the world's illiterate are women, the majority from rural areas.[114] For example, the only public education in rural Ghana is for boys.[115] Additionally, school drop out rates are higher for girls than for boys.[116]

The PFA proposes that governments close the gender gap in primary and secondary education by the year 2005; reduce the female illiteracy rate, focusing particularly on girls from rural areas and in developing countries; and promote the sciences equally between girls and boys.[117]

The third area of concern is the health of women. Women's health is influenced by many factors, such as biological differences and social conditions. In general, impoverished conditions lead to more significant health problems for women and men.[118] Specifically, reproductive health problems for women in a poverty stricken environment remain statistically high, often leading to higher mortality rates.[119] For example, a half million women die each year due to pregnancy complications;[120] another 100,000 die from unsafe abortions.[121] Furthermore, lack of adequate nutrition, inadequate housing, and drinking water pose a threat to rural women's health.[123] These problems are also more significant in impoverished areas.

The PFA recommended that governments work in collaboration with the U.N. system, the medical community, research institutions, and nongovernmental organizations ("NGO"s) to design and implement gender-sensitive health programs; provide affordable primary health care; and promote research on women's health.[124]

Fourth, violence against women is a global problem. Women lack access to legal information about and protection from violence,[125] face inadequate laws to address violence,[126] and suffer laws that are not enforced.[127] The submission of women due to cultural patterns also contribute to violence against women.[128] Statistics demonstrate that a woman is physically abused every twelve seconds in the United States;[129] five women are burned every day in India over dowry disputes;[130] and a survey conducted in Papua, New Guinea has demonstrated that sixty-seven percent of women are found to be victims of domestic violence.[131]

Actions proposed by the PFA include developing educational programs which condemn violence against women and modify those cultural behaviors which place women in an inferior status.[132] The PFA also suggests that governments ratify and enforce bans on prostitution and trafficking of women and girls.[133]

The fifth PFA area deals with the fact that men and women often have different experiences during armed conflict. In many instances, women are the primary source for maintaining the family while men engage in warfare.[134] Women are also victims of torture and rape during armed conflict.[135] Women and their dependents constitute eighty percent of the world's twenty-three million refugees.[136]

The PFA proposes that governments consider ratifying treaties on the protection of women and children during armed conflict;[137] hasten the conversion of military resources into more peaceful uses;[138] condemn the systematic practice of rape and other degrading treatment as an instrument of war;[139] and provide safe havens for refugees.[140] As a practical realization, the paramount interests of a nation's leaders are to project power and defend during wartime. Human rights standards are generally overlooked while countries engage in acts of aggression. As such, the mistreatment of people continues unabated.

Sixth is the fact that women comprise a large segment of the global work force. In 1990, about 854 million women, approximately thirty-two percent of the world's labor force, were economically active.[141] Conversely, women are poorly represented in top-level managerial positions in proportion to their numbers in the work force.[142] Most female managers are concentrated in

lower level positions of management. For example, in the United States, only one in one hundred executives is a woman.[143] Furthermore, women in comparison to men make less money per year, and their contributions are undervalued.[144]

Actions proposed by the PFA include encouraging governments to enact legislation to guarantee the rights of women and men to equal pay for equal work;[145] adopt and implement laws against gender based discrimination in the work force;[146] promote women in business by strengthening their access to capital;[147] and devise mechanisms whereby women may gain greater access to high-level positions in management.[148] The PFA also encourages national and international lending institutions to support small-scale entrepreneurs and low-income women in order to achieve greater economic security.[149] The final document emphasizes that economic independence for women leads to creating a "safety net" and changing one's own realities.[150]

The seventh and eighth critical areas of concern include women in decision-making roles and the need to create national and international machineries to place women into higher positions of authority. Worldwide, women have made considerable advances in the political arena, particularly at the local level. As of 1994, ten women headed their national governments, an unprecedented number at the time.[151] Yet, statistics again indicate that women, who comprise half of the world's population, constitute only a small number at top decision-making levels, such as heads of state, diplomats, or policy makers. Current information also indicates that more than one hundred countries do not have any women in their legislatures, and only 6 of the 185 members of the U.N. have women representatives.[152] Negative stereotypes of women and cultural practices contribute to the limited number of women who represent their local, state, or national governments.[153] The PFA recommends that nations commit to gender balance in decision-making bodies.[154] This could be achieved by establishing quotas for minority representation.[155]

The ninth area of concern involves human rights for women. As previously stated, women often have rights guaranteed by law, but governments fail to insure that the laws are carried out.[156] Appropriate recourse mechanisms also require strengthening at the national and international levels. Furthermore, nations which have not ratified CEDAW subject women to less legal protection and a greater likelihood of experiencing political, social, and economic discrimination than those who have enacted it.

Actions recommended by the PFA include creating or strengthening national institutions to protect women's rights.[157] Governments are also encouraged to review national laws and repeal laws that discriminate against women,[158] and educate public officials about gender sensitivity.[159]

Tenth, the PFA is critical of how women are depicted in the mass media. Certain images of women reinforce negative stereotypes and reflect outdated views.[160] In Africa, Asia, and Latin America, positions for women in broadcasting average below twenty-five percent.[161] A ten country study conducted by the U.N. reveals that only 1.4% of television news items deal with women's issues; three quarters were presented by men.[162]

The PFA recommends that the media exercise greater gender sensitivity when presenting the news.[163] Private organizations need to create media watchdog groups, which would place pressure on the media to increase the number of women in the broadcasting field and management positions.[164]

The eleventh PFA concern places an emphasis on women's environment and development. Often, governmental policies do not take into account the impact of economic development on the environment and its link to daily lives.[165] Sustainable development of the environment is of considerable importance to people who live directly off the land.

To illustrate, women account for half of the food production in developing countries.[166] In India, women provide seventy-five percent of the labor for transplanting and weeding rice, sixty percent for harvesting, and thirty-three percent for threshing.[167] According to the U.N. Economic Commission for Africa, women perform up to three quarters of all agricultural work in addition to their domestic responsibilities.[168] The group most affected by the environment is rural and indigenous women, whose livelihood and daily subsistence depends directly on sustainable ecosystems.[169] Understanding the impact of poverty and the environment on urban women is also critical.

The PFA encourages governments to include women in all environmental decision-making concerning management of resources.[170] The PFA further supports increased research and education in the environment and its effect on women.[171]

Finally, the PFA is concerned about the fact that, in many countries, girls are discriminated against both socially and educationally. For example, boys receive greater encouragement than girls to pursue opportunities.[172] Cultural bias against a girl early in life is often reflected later where her impact may not be as significant as her male counterpart. The U.N. Department of Public Information statistics also indicate that more than two million girls undergo genital mutilation.[173] Trafficking young girls in prostitution is another problem, particularly amongst the poor.[174]

The PFA recommends that governments pass strict laws that require a minimum age for marriage;[175] protect the safety and security of girls from all forms of violence;[176] enact legislation that prohibits using girls as an economic commodity;[177] take appropriate legislative measures to protect girls from domestic abuse;[178] and eliminate discriminatory practices against girls in education.[179]

B. Challenged Areas in the Platform for Action

Controversy initially surrounded the comprehensive PFA as more than half of the original language was opposed by at least one of the 181 delegations attending the Beijing Conference.[180] However, the contentious build-up subsided as the tone of the Beijing Conference grew more collaborative than confrontational. As Filippino Patricia Licuanan, president of the final drafting committee for the Beijing declaration, noted: "The debates are not as shrill this time. People are very pragmatically trying to work out differences. The atmosphere is more friendly."[181] Any perceived controversial language in the draft declaration subsided at a record rate during the final negotiations amongst the delegations.

Several reasons were given for the mostly noncontentious atmosphere at the Conference. First, reproductive health and abortion were strongly debated at the Cairo Population Conference in 1994.[182] Therefore, much of the groundwork on this issue was paved for the Beijing Conference. For example, the final document adopted in Beijing evidenced a compromise between reproductive choice advocates and reproductive choice opponents. While women had the right to make their own decisions about child bearing,[183] the document also supported the family as the basic unit of society.[184] After much opposition in the area of abortion, the Vati-

can conceded and accepted such language.[185]

Moreover, American domestic politics was another reason for the overall agreeable, pragmatic atmosphere in Beijing. Hillary Rodham Clinton's speech to the Conference delegates, condemning China's one child policy and forced sterilization programs, played well to the Vatican and American conservatives at home. This tempered animosity between liberals and conservatives attending this Conference.[186]

The Vatican, represented by a woman for the first time,[187] made considerable efforts not to block the passage of the final document. For example, during negotiations over a paragraph dealing with human immunodeficiency virus ("HIV"), the paragraph called for the distribution of condoms to prevent the disease from being further transmitted. The Vatican initially objected to the reference to condoms because of its opposition to any artificial birth control and ordered that section to be bracketed.[188] Later, however, during the Conference, Vatican negotiator Sherry Ricquert agreed that the brackets be dropped.[189] Thus, the reference to the use of condoms remained. Politics may have persuaded the Vatican to drop the brackets. African countries, faced with a devastating AIDS epidemic, would certainly have fought the Holy See on this issue.

Finally, some controversy did arise over the reference to "sexual orientation," which was mentioned at least four times in the draft document.[190] Such references were bracketed due to opposition from conservative delegations, including the Vatican and Islamic countries. Lesbian organizations viewed the reference to "sexual orientation" as a formal recognition of one's right to control her sexuality, and lobbied strongly for the term to be included in the anti-discrimination section of the PFA.[191] Lesbian advocacy groups counted on the United States delegation to stand firmly behind their position.[192] Initially, the American delegation supported the reference to the "sexual orientation" as a protected right, reasoning that discriminatory practices against particular groups are reprehensible. Yet, that delegation acquiesced to the term "right to control sexuality" rather than "sexual orientation," so that there were not any obstacles to finalizing the document. Lesbian groups, although disappointed, accepted the reference to the "right to control sexuality" because this term implies that sexual orientation is to be a protected right.

The Fourth World Women's Conference concluded with more than sixty delegations commenting upon and more than half of the 181 delegations submitting formal reservations to sections on sexual and reproductive rights. In particular, many Islamic and several Latin American countries believed such rights did not conform to Islamic law.[193] Only ten countries said they would accept the entire final document.[194]

Ultimately, the final, adopted PFA reaffirmed the universality of human rights. Furthermore, the PFA recommended that governments develop implementation strategies from the final document by the end of 1996.[195] This will be a large task for more conservative countries who have yet to adopt many of the programs suggested.

C. NonGovernmental Organization Forum in Huairou, China

Prior to the Nongovernmental Organization ("NGO") Forum, which was to be held in conjunction with the Conference, the Chinese government decided that the forum would be held in a separate setting from Beijing. NGO Forum coordinators were unhappy with the selection of Huairou as a location because this site was ninety minutes from the Conference site. Fearing security problems and demonstrations against China's human rights record, that government wanted to eliminate any potentially embarrassing situation by separating a large number of women from one location.[196] Reportedly, the Chinese also blocked visa entries for some NGO participants as a way to measure control over the Forum.[197]

Huairou, a small resort town, was not prepared for the thousands of women who attended the Forum. Conditions were substandard compared to western standards.[198] Nevertheless, women worldwide attended to network, exchange information, and organize.

At the Conference, selected NGO members lobbied Conference delegates and influenced the final document. Although there was no formal interchange between the forum and the delegations to the government conference, the two events did influence one another.

At the grass roots level, NGOs play a vital role in fighting existing practices, laws, and customs which subjugate women. They represent the organizations outside of government which maintain pressure on governments and society at large to eliminate gender discrimination. The Beijing document acknowledged the importance of NGOs in advancing legislation to ensure the promotion of women in society.[199]

Conclusion

The question must be asked: Can a human rights document, such as that formulated in Beijing, make a difference in women's lives? The U.N. platform adopted in Beijing is not a legally binding document, but rather a guide for governments to implement. However, without the legal force of a treaty, implementation of a document's objectives is more difficult to achieve.

Moreover, questions arise as to whether the document's goals and strategies will be realized. This is based partially on the fact that previous women's conferences have not yielded the ambitious goals articulated in their respective documents. Yet change *has* occurred incrementally for women since the creation of the U.N., the promulgation of international human rights treaties, and U.N. sponsored women's conferences.

Perhaps treaties and Conference documents may be most useful in developing countries by discouraging practices, such as bride burnings, genital mutilation, and kidnapping; although carrying out change is often most difficult for those who live in traditional societies and under limited legal systems. International pressure, through the weight of international law, and the strengthening of grass roots movements, are methods of forcing change in societies where change is least likely to occur, or where women's rights are restricted.

Another real challenge for governments is the actual implementation and/or enforcement of international human rights treaties that protect women and ensure their equal status to men. For example, treaties and nonbinding human rights documents, which are in conformity with the purposes and principles of international law, are vital to women in instances where domestic laws will not suffice. Conversely, when both domestic law and international law prohibit gender discrimination, governments must be encouraged to carry out the spirit and the intent of either sphere of law which better protects women.

The Beijing document, focused and comprehensive in scope, has laid the fundamental groundwork for women into the early next century. Despite certain obstacles, such as inadequate laws or traditional social customs prejudiced against women, the U.N., NGOs, and state and regional governments must work hard to ensure that women have a strong voice in society. As Nobel Peace Prize winner and former Myanmar political prisoner, Aung San Suu Kyi, stated at the NGO Forum, "It is time to apply in the arena of the world the wisdom and experience women have gained."[200] Affirming Aung San Suu Kyi's words, United States Ambassador to the U.N. Madeleine Albright summarized in her speech to the Conference, that "it is time to unleash the full capacity for production, accomplishment, and the enrichment of life that is inherent in the women of the world."[201]

Finally, the history of women's conferences, like history itself, has a "ripple effect" whereby one idea provides the foundation for another idea. The women's conference in 1888 and the Beijing Conference are benchmarks in the women's movement, measuring where women have been and where they are going. In viewing the historical continuum, it is evident that women have made inroads toward achieving greater political, economic, and social prominence. However, much work needs to be done, and great efforts must continue despite the hardships. Women's conferences are one way to influence social policy in a rapidly changing world and to define the responsibility of government toward women.

Notes

1. Alma Lutz, *Created Equal: A Biography of Elizabeth Cady Stanton* 48 (photo, reprint 1974) (1940).
2. *Id.*
3. Rev. Lillian Valentin de Forrey, *Live From Beijing: Reselection and Learning Process Will Continue, Lancaster New Era*, (Pa.), Sept. 24, 1995, at G1.
4. Paula Story, *War on Child Prostitution, Seattle Times*, Nov. 23, 1994, at A12.
5. Basu Rekha, *Burning Brides: The Outrage Grows, Des Moines Reg.*, Oct. 9, 1995, at 1.
6. *See*, e.g., Convention on the Rights of the Child, Nov. 20, 1989, at 20, 28 I.L.M. 1448 (entered into force Sept. 2, 1990).

7. Li Xing, *U.N. Conference Opens, World Women*, Sept. 4, 1995, at 1.

8. World Conference on Human Rights: Vienna Declaration and Programme of Action, June 25, 1993, 32 I.L.M. 1661, 1667 [hereinafter Vienna Declaration and Programme of Action].

9. *Sending the World a Vital Message, Chi. Trib.*, Sept. 26, 1995, at 16.

10. Burns H. Weston et al., *International Law and World Order* 730 (2d ed. 1990).

11. *See, e.g.*, Convention on the Elimination of All Forms of Discrimination Against Women, Dec. 18, 1979, 19 I.L.M. 33 (entered into force Sept. 3, 1981) [hereinafter CEDAW] (noting that all people are born with equal dignity and rights).

12. *See A Clarion Call to End Nigeria's Misrule, Post-Standard* (New York), Dec. 13, 1995, at A9 (reporting the murder of a pro-democracy activist by the head of the Nigerian dictatorship).

13. *U.N. Charter* art. 2 ¶ 7.

14. *U.N. Charter* art. 1, ¶ 3 (emphasis added).

15. Universal Declaration of Human Rights, Dec. 10, 1948.

16. Universal Declaration of Human Rights, pmbl., Dec. 10, 1948.

17. This lack of monitoring and enforcement led to the Convention on the Elimination of All Forms of Discrimination Against Women ("CEDAW") beginning in the early 1960s. *See infra* notes 45–87 and accompanying text.

18. Center for the Study of Human Rights, Columbia University, *Twenty-five Human Rights Documents* 10 (1994).

19. *Id.*

20. International Covenant on Economic, Social and Cultural Rights, Dec. 16, 1966, art. 1, 999 U.N.T.S. 31, 6 I.L.M. 360 (entered into force Jan 3, 1976).

21. *Id.*

22. *Id.* art. 2.

23. *Id.* art. 3.

24. *Id.* art. 7.

25. *Id.*

26. *Id.*

27. *Id.*

28. *Id.* art. 11.

29. *Id.* art. 13.

30. *Id.* art. 15.

31. *Id.*

32. International Covenant on Civil and Political Rights, Dec. 16, 1966, 999 U.N.T.S. 171, 6 I.L.M. 368 (1967) (entered into force Mar. 23, 1976).

33. *Id.* art. 2.3(b).

34. *Id.* art. 8.3.

35. *Id.* art. 14.2.

36. *Id.* arts. 18, 22.

37. *Id.* art. 2.1.

38. *Id.; see supra* notes 15–17 and accompanying text.

39. *Progress Achieved in the Implementation of the Convention on the Elimination of All Forms of Discrimination against Women* (1995), *available at* gopher://gopher.undp.org:70/00/unconfs/women /off/a—7.en (hereinafter *Progress Achieved in Implementation of CEDAW*].

40. Convention on the Political Rights of Women, Mar. 31, 1953, 193 U.N.T.S. 135, *reprinted in* 2 *World Treaty Index* 704 (2d ed. 1983) (entered into force July 7, 1954).

41. Convention on the Nationality of Married Women, Jan. 9, 1947, 36 U.N.T.S. 145, *reprinted in* 2 *World Treaty Index* 704 (2d ed. 1983) (entered into force Aug. 3, 1949).

42. Convention on Consent, Minimum Age and Registration of Marriages, Dec. 10, 1962, 451 U.N.T.S. 269, *reprinted in* 3 *World Treaty Index* 1168–69 (2d ed. 1983) (entered into force Dec. 9, 1964).

43. *See supra* note 39 and accompanying text.

44. *See supra* note 17 and accompanying text.

45. Vienna Declaration and Programme of Action, *supra* note 8.

46. G.A. Res. 2263, U.N. GAOR, 22d Sess., Supp. No. 16, U.N. Doc. A1 6716 (1967).

47. *See, e.g., Statistical Abstract of the United States: 1995*, at 14 (115th ed. 1995) (in 1970, women accounted for 51.3% of the United States population).

48. *Id.* at 402 (in 1970, women accounted for 38.1% of the United States civilian work force).

49. *See generally* CEDAW, *supra* note 11.

50. *Id.* art. 3.

51. *Id.* art. 17.

52. *Id.* art. 18 ¶ 1.

53. *Id.*

54. CEDAW, *The United Nations and the Status of Women, available at* http://www.on.org/Conferences/ women/pubinfo/status/home.htm.

55. Id.

56. Thomas Burgenthal & Harold G. Maier, Public International Law 97 (1991).

57. Laurel Fletcher et al., *Human Rights Violations Against Women*, 15 Whittier L. Rev. 319, 334–35 (1994).

58. Michael J. Corbera, *The Women's Convention and the Equal Protection Clause*, 26 *St. Mary's L. J.* 755, 778 (1995).

59. Congressional Research Service report on file with author.

60. Corbera, *supra* note 58, at 778.

61. *Id.*

62. CEDAW, *supra* note 11, at art. 11.

63. *See* D'Ann Campbell, *Combating the Gender Gulf,* 2 *Temp. Pol. & Civ. Rts. L. Rev.* 63 (1992);

Lucinda J. Peach, *Women at War: The Ethics of Women in Combat*, 15 Hamline J. Pub. L. & Pol'y 199 (1994); Pamela R. Jones, Note, *Women in the Crossfire: Should the Court Allow It?*, 78 Cornell L. Rev. 252 (1993).

64. Equal Pay Act of 1963, 29 U.S.C. § 206 (1992).
65. Corbera, *supra* note 58, at 778.
66. Family and Medical Leave Act of 1993, 29 U.S.C. § 2612 (1995).
67. Corbera, *supra* note 58, at 777.
68. *U.S. Const.* art. VI, cl. 2
69. CEDAW requires that countries grant equal protection for women by eliminating cultural bias; that state-parties take all appropriate measures to eliminate discrimination against women in political and public life; that state-parties shall eliminate discrimination against women in the health care field, and provide access to health care services, including family planning.
70. *See* Sarah C. Zearfoss, Note, *The Convention for the Elimination of All Forms of Discrimination Against Women: Radical, Reasonable, or Reactionary?*, 12 Mich. J. Int'l L. 903, 905 (1991) (noting that adopting the Convention would require amending the Constitution to reach the private sector).
71. *See* Regents of the Univ. of Cal. v. Bakke, 438 U.S. 265 (1978).
72. Editorial, *Failure to Sign Treaty Embarrasses U.S.*, Oakland Tribune, Sept. 6, 1996, at A-14.
73. *Progress Achieved in Implementation of CEDAW*, *supra* note 39, at 61.
74. Burgenthal & Maier, *supra* note 56, at 99.
75. World Unite for Equality, *Seattle Post-Intelligencer*, Sept. 3, 1995, at E2.
76. Remarks by CEDAW Chair (Ivanka Corti) to CEDAW Committee, Sept. 1995, Beijing, China.
77. *Id.*
78. *Id.*
79. *Id.*
80. *Id.*
81. *Id.*
82. These quotas range from 20% to 50% These countries include Argentina, Austria, Belgium, Denmark, France, Germany, Greece, Iceland, Israel, Netherlands, Norway, Spain, Sweden, and Venezuela.
83. *See*, e.g., CEDAW, *supra* note 11, at arts. 3, 7.
84. *See, e.g., id.* at arts. 10, 11.
85. *E.g.*, Terry Eastland, *The Case Against Affirmative Action*, 34 Wm. & Mary L. Rev. 33, 35–38 (1992) (discussing problems with affirmative action).
86. *See, e.g.*, Lani Guinier, *No Two Seats: The Elusive Quest for Political Equality*, 77 Va. L. Rev. 1413,

1502–05 (1991) (discussing cumulative voting as a means of assuring minority representation).
87. *Id.* at 1502.
88. Vienna Declaration and Programme of Action, *supra* note 8.
89. Declaration on the Elimination of Violence Against Women, Feb. 23, 1994, 33 I.L.M. 1049.
90. The U.N. International Conference on Population and Development, Oct. 18, 1994, A/Conf.171/13, *available at* gopher://gopher.undp.org.to/oo/ungophers/popin/icpd/conference/offeng/poa [hereinafter Cairo Declaration]. At Cairo in 1994, women's health, empowerment, and reproductive rights were placed at the center of population-related development policies.
91. Vienna Declaration and Programme of Action, *supra* note 8.
92. *Id.* at 1668–19.
93. Declaration on the Elimination of Violence Against Women, *supra* note 89, at 1050.
94. See Cairo Declaration, *supra* note 90 and accompanying text.
95. *See supra* notes 4–7 and accompanying text.
96. *See supra* note 8 and accompanying text.
97. Sarah Prosser, *Beijing Conference Visit Bolsters Hoosier Woman's Commitment*, Indianapolis Star, Oct. 1, 1995, at J1.
98. Li Xing, *supra* note 7, at 1.
99. Alison Mayes, *Toast to Women in Film Explores Myths, Struggles: "But Men Are Completely Welcome,"* Calgary Herald, Feb. 1, 1995, at B6.
100. *See supra* notes 45 & 49 and accompanying text.
101. *Bureau of Public Affairs, United States Department of State, Focus on 4WCW, Background on U.N. Conferences and NGO Forums* (1995).
102. *Id.*
103. *Report on the Fourth Annual World Conference on Women, Annex II, Platform For Action* (1994), available at gopher://gopher.undp.org:70/11/unconfs/women/off/plateng [hereinafter *Platform for Action*].
104. *Id.*
105. *Id.*
106. *U.N. Department of Public Information, United Nations Summary on the Platform for Action: Critical Areas of Concern Pamphlet,* DPI/1578/Devl/Wom-95-16831-June1995-30M [hereinafter *Critical Areas of Concern*].
107. *See supra* note 9 and accompanying text.
108. *Platform for Action, supra* note 103, at 3.
109. *Critical Areas of Concern, supra* note 106, § 1.
110. *Id.*
111. *Platform for Action, supra* note 103.
112. *Id.* ¶¶ 70–71.
113. *Id.* ¶ 75.
114. *Critical Areas of Concern, supra* note 106, § 2.

115. This fact is based on the author's personal experience with Ghana.

116. *Critical Areas of Concern, supra* note 106, § 2.

117. *Platform for Action, supra* note 103, ¶, 80.

118. *Id.* ¶ 91.

119. *Id.* ¶ 94.

120. *Critical Areas of Concern, supra* note 106, § 3.

121. *Id.*

122. *Id.*

123. *Platform for Action, supra* note 103, ¶ 106.

124. *Physicians and Domestic Violence: Ethical Considerations* (Report from the American Medical Association's Council of Ethical and Judicial Affairs), 267 JAMA 3190 (1992) (battered women/domestic violence).

125. *See generally Domestic Violence, Not Just a Family Matter, 1995: Hearings Before the Subcomm. on Labor, Health and Human Services, Education and Related Agencies of the Senate Comm. on Appropriations* (1995) (prepared testimony of Donna Lawson, mother of homicide victim) (seeking funding for the Violence Against Women Act) [hereinafter Lawson].

126. *Id.*

127. *Photo Reveals Much More than a Woman, Buffalo News,* July 14, 1994, at C2. *But see* Lily Eng, *Study Challenges Views of Wife Beaters and Their Victims, Sacramento Bee,* Aug. 21, 1993, at A2.

128. *Ann Koize, Don't Reward Women Abusers, Cincinnati Enquirer,* Feb. 6, 1995, at A13 (citing World Watch estimates).

129. *Fourth U.N. Women's Conference, Guardian* (London), Aug. 28, 1995, at 11. *See also* William Claiborne, *Dowry Killings Show Social Stress in India, Wash. Post,* Sept. 22, 1984, at A1 (analyzing the bride burning phenomenon and its social causes).

130. Marcela Valente, *Human Rights—Women: Domestic Violence a Major Threat to Safety, Inter Press Service,* July 4, 1994, available in *Westlaw, Allnews* database.

131. *Platform for Action, supra* note 103, ¶ 124(k).

132. *Id.* 130(a).

133. *Id.* 133

134. Senthil Ratnasabapathy, *Women: Beijing Meet Urged to Take Action to Halt Rape in War, Inter Press Services,* Sept. 1, 1995, *available in Westlaw, Allnews* database.

135. *Budget for Overseas Refugee Assistance, FY 95: Hearings Before the Subcomms. on Foreign Operations, Export Financing, and Related Programs of the House Comm. on Appropriations* (1994) (testimony of Roger P. Winter, Director, United States Committee for Refugees).

136. *Platform for Action, supra* note 103, ¶, 144(a).

137. *Id.* 143(a).

138. *Id.* 145(c).

139. *Id.* 147(c).

140. *United Nations, 1994 World Survey on the Role of Women in Development* (1995) [hereinafter *1994 World Survey*].

141. Andrea Shalal-Esa, *"Glass Ceiling" Still in Place, Report Says, L.A. Daily News,* Aug. 12, 1992, at B1.

142. *1994 World Survey, supra* note 140.

143. *Wages, Education, Two-Career Families and Earnings Gaps, Marketing to Women,* Apr. 1, 1995.

144. *Platform for Action, supra* note 103, ¶ 165(a).

145. *Id.* 165(b).

146. *Id.* 166(a).

147. *Id.* 178(a)–(p) (outlining various specific measures to eliminate occupational segregation and all forms of employment discrimination).

148. *Id.* ¶, 167(c).

149. *Id.*

150. *U.N. Fourth World Conference on Women, Action for Equality, Development, and Peace, Fact Sheet 7, Politics and Decision-Making* (1995).

151. *Id.*

152. *Id.*

153. *Platform for Action, supra* note 103, 190(a).

154. *Id.*

155. *See generally* Lawson, *supra* note 125 (seeking funding for the Violence Against Women Act).

156. *Platform for Action, supra* note 103, ¶, 230(e).

157. *Id.* 232(d).

158. *Id.* 232(i).

159. *Women: Battle for Equality Must be Waged with Words and Images, Inter Press Service,* Nov. 9, 1993, *available in Westlaw, Allnews* database.

160. *Critical Areas of Concern, supra* note 106, § 10.

161. Melissa Fletcher Stoeltje, *Female Rights Spelled out in Blueprint, Houston Chron.,* Sept. 8, 1995, at 1.

162. *Platform for Action, supra* note 103, ¶ 235.

163. *Id.* ¶, 240.

164. *Id.* ¶ 246

165. *Women—Food: More Equality for Women Could Raise Food Production, Inter Press Service,* Aug. 10, 1995, *available in Westlaw, Allnews* database.

166. *United Nations Development Program, Human Development Report* (1995).

167. *U.N. Fourth World Conference on Women, Action for Equality, Development, and Peace, Fact Sheet 1, Poverty* (1995).

168. *Id.*

169. *Platform for Action supra* note 103, ¶¶ 253(a), 256(a).

170. *Id.* ¶ 256(f) (addressing the role of women, particularly rural and indigenous women, in managing the environment).

171. *Teachers Encouragement of Girls Doesn't Make the Grade, Study Says, Indianapolis Star,* May 14, 1994, at B3.

172. *Anti-Women Violence Condemned by All—But Tolerated Globally, Chi. Trib.,* Aug. 30, 1995, at 2.

173. *See, e.g.,* Molly Moore, *"Even if I Ran Away, Where Would I Go?" Third World Prostitutes: Entrapped by Fate in a Sordid Trade Series: Third World, Second Class: Women in the City, Wash. Post,* Feb. 16, 1993, at A25 (discussing Southeast Asian prostitution).

174. *Platform for Action, supra* note 103, 274(e).

175. *Id.* ¶ 283(d).

176. *Id.* ¶ 282(a) (referring to the employment of girls in the work force, not to prostitution).

177. *Id.* ¶ 283(b).

178. *Id.* ¶¶ 277(a), 279–280 (setting forth specific steps for governments and NGOs to take to eliminate discrimination in education).

179. Rone Tempest, *Fight Brewed Before Beijing Conference, But It Never Percolated; Women: Legwork on Controversial Issues at Cairo Gathering Paves Way for Pragmatic China Talks, L.A. Times,* Sept. 9, 1995, at 18.

180. *Id.*

181. *Id.*

182. *Report on the Fourth Annual World Conference on Women, Annex I, Beijing Declaration* at 17 (1995), *available at* gopher://gopher.undp.org:701/11/unconfs/off/plateng [hereinafter *Beijing Declaration*].

183. *Platform for Action, supra* note 103, ¶, 29.

184. Tempest, *supra* note 179.

185. *First Lady Denounces Abuse of Women Around the World, China Criticized: Her Forceful Speech Singles Out Beijing for Trying to Curb Free Discussion at the World Conference, Atlanta J. & Const.,* Sept. 6, 1995, at A3.

186. *Id.* Mary Ann Glendon, a noted Harvard law professor, was the delegate.

187. Bracketing language in a document usually indicates that a reference was controversial and opposed.

188. Tempest, *supra* note 179.

189. *Id.*

190. *Id.*

191. *Id.*

192. Tiffany Brown, *Agence France-Presse,* Sept. 14, 1995, *available in Westlaw, Allnews* database.

193. *The Fourth World Conference on Women, Closing Plenary Summary, available at* http://www.iisd.ca:80/linkages/4wcw.

194. *Platform for Action, supra* note 103, ¶ 297.

195. Sheila Tefft, *China Holds Fast to Isolating Thousands of Blunt Women: Some Concessions on NGO Forum During U.N. Women's Meeting This Fall, Christian Sci. Monitor,* June 16, 1995.

196. *Id.*

197. *Id.*

198. *Beijing Declaration, Supra* note 182, at 20.

299. Remarks to the Fourth World Conference on Women, Ambassador Madeleine K. Albright U.S. Permanent Representative to the United Nations, Sept 6, 1995, Beijing, China (quoting Aung San Suu Kyi).

200. *Id.*

Index